THE OXFORD HANDBOOK OF

CRIMINAL PROCESS

THE OXFORD HANDBOOK OF

CRIMINAL PROCESS

Edited by

DARRYL K. BROWN

JENIA I. TURNER

and

BETTINA WEISSER

OXFORD
UNIVERSITY PRESS

OXFORD
UNIVERSITY PRESS

Oxford University Press is a department of the University of Oxford. It furthers the University's objective of excellence in research, scholarship, and education by publishing worldwide. Oxford is a registered trade mark of Oxford University Press in the UK and certain other countries.

Published in the United States of America by Oxford University Press
198 Madison Avenue, New York, NY 10016, United States of America.

Library of Congress Cataloging-in-Publication Data
Names: Brown, Darryl K., editor. | Turner, Jenia I., editor. |
Weisser, Bettina, editor.
Title: The Oxford handbook of criminal process/Darryl K. Brown,
Jenia I. Turner, Bettina Weisser.
Description: New York: Oxford University Press, 2019. |
Includes bibliographical references and index.
Identifiers: LCCN 2018027958| ISBN 9780190659837 ((hardback): alk. paper) |
ISBN 9780190659844 ((paperback): alk. paper)
Subjects: LCSH: Criminal procedure. | Criminal law. | Criminal justice,
Administration of. | Criminal procedure—European Union countries.
Classification: LCC K5401 .B76 2019 | DDC 345/.05—dc23 LC record available at
https://lccn.loc.gov/2018027958

1 3 5 7 9 8 6 4 2

Printed by Sheridan Books, Inc., United States of America

Table of Contents

PART IV CRIMINAL PROSECUTION AND ITS ALTERNATIVES

PART V PREPARATION FOR ADJUDICATION

PART VI ADJUDICATION: TRIALS AND ALTERNATIVES

PART VII APPEALS AND POST-CONVICTION REVIEW

PART VIII PROCEDURE IN INTERNATIONAL TRIBUNALS

Notes on the Contributors

Lorena Bachmaier, Professor of Law, Universidad Complutense, Madrid

Martin Böse, Professor of Criminal Law, Criminal Procedure, International and European Criminal Law, Director of the Institute of Criminal Law, University of Bonn

Darryl K. Brown, O.M. Vicars Professor of Law and Barron F. Black Research Professor, University of Virginia School of Law

Michele Caianiello, Professor and Dean of the Department of Legal Studies, University of Bologna

Ed Cape, Emeritus Professor of Criminal Law and Practice, University of the West of England, Bristol

Meike M. de Boer, Former Trainee, Netherlands Institute for the Study of Crime and Law Enforcement

David Dixon, Professor of Law, University of New South Wales

Markus D. Dubber, Professor of Law and Director, Centre for Ethics, University of Toronto

Gary Edmond, Professor of Law at the University of New South Wales and Research Professor (fractional) at Northumbria University

Helen Fenwick, Professor of Law and Director of the Human Rights Centre, Durham University

Richard D. Friedman, Alene and Allan F. Smith Professor of Law, University of Michigan

Brandon Garrett, L. Neil Williams, Jr., Professor of Law, Duke University School of Law

Gwladys Gilliéron, Associate Professor in Criminal Law and Criminology, University of Zurich

Sabine Gless, Professor of Criminal Law and Criminal Procedure, University of Basel

Johanna Göhler, Research Associate, Institute for Foreign and International Criminal Law, University of Cologne

Elisabetta Grande, Professor of Comparative Law, Università degli Studi del Piemonte Orientale

Valerie P. Hans, Professor of Law, Cornell University

Rebecca K. Helm, Lecturer in Law, University of Exeter Law School

Jacqueline S. Hodgson, Professor of Law, University of Warwick

Tatjana Hörnle, Professor of Criminal Law, Legal Philosophy and Comparative Criminal Law, Humboldt University, Berlin

John Jackson, Professor of Comparative Criminal Law and Procedure, University of Nottingham, School of Law

Maria Kaiafa-Gbandi, Professor of Criminal Law, Director of the Research Institute for Transparency, Corruption and Financial Crime, Aristotle University of Thessaloniki

André Klip, Professor of Criminal Law, Criminal Procedure and the Transnational Aspects of Criminal Law, Maastricht University

Ho Hock Lai, Amaladass Professor of Criminal Justice, National University of Singapore

Katalin Ligeti, Professor of Law, University of Luxembourg

Richard L. Lippke, Professor, Department of Criminal Justice, Indiana University

Marijke Malsch, Senior Researcher, Netherlands Institute for the Study of Crime and Law Enforcement; Lecturer, VU University Amsterdam

Marie Manikis, Assistant Professor of Law, McGill University

Nicola McGarrity, Senior Lecturer and Director of the Terrorism Law Reform Project, University of New South Wales

Bernadette McSherry, Professor of Law and Foundation Director, Melbourne Social Equity Institute, University of Melbourne

Grischa Merkel, Professor of Law and Ethics, University of Basel

Valsamis Mitsilegas, Professor of European Criminal Law and Global Security and Deputy Dean for Global Engagement (Europe), Queen Mary University of London

Yu Mou, Lecturer in Criminal Law, SOAS, University of London

Neil Richards, Thomas & Karole Green Professor of Law and Director of the Institute for Policy in Medicine and Law, Washington University

Kent Roach, Professor of Law and Prichard Wilson Chair in Law and Public Policy, University of Toronto

Paul Roberts, Professor of Criminal Jurisprudence, University of Nottingham, School of Law

Jacqueline E. Ross, Prentice H. Marshall Professor of Law, University of Illinois College of Law

Helmut Satzger, Professor of Law, Director of the Chair of German, European and International Criminal Law and Criminal Procedure as well as Business Criminal Law, Ludwig-Maximilians-Universität, Munich

Carl-Friedrich Stuckenberg, Professor of German and International Criminal Law and Criminal Procedure, Comparative Criminal Law, and Criminal Law History, University of Bonn

Elisavet Symeonidou-Kastanidou, Professor of Criminal Law, Dean of the Faculty of Law, Aristotle University of Thessaloniki

Stephen C. Thaman, Professor of Law, Emeritus, Saint Louis University

Juliette Tricot, Centre de Droit Pénal et de Criminologie, University of Paris Nanterre

Jenia I. Turner, Amy Abboud Ware Centennial Professor in Criminal Law, Dedman School of Law, Southern Methodist University

Mary Vogel, Professor of Law, Chair in Criminal Law, University of Manchester

Joëlle Vuille, Senior Researcher, School of Criminal Justice, University of Lausanne

Michael Washington, Fellow, Washington University Institute for Policy in Medicine and Law

Thomas Weigend, Professor of Criminal Law (ret.), University of Cologne

Bettina Weisser, Professor of Criminal Law, Director of the Institute for Foreign and International Criminal Law, University of Cologne

Frank Zimmermann, Postdoctoral Research Fellow, Ludwig-Maximilians-Universität, Munich

PART I

FOUNDATIONS

CHAPTER 1

CRIMINAL PROCESS IN THE DUAL PENAL STATE

A Comparative-Historical Analysis

MARKUS D. DUBBER*

I. Introduction

This chapter is about a way of thinking about criminal process, with bits and pieces of criminal process making an appearance for illustrative purposes. Actually, it's about two ways of thinking about criminal process, from parallel perspectives that correspond to two modes of state governance, law and police, characteristic of the law state (*Rechtsstaat*) and the police state (*Polizeistaat*), respectively. Using comparative-historical analysis, this chapter locates the study of criminal process within the two-track project of critical analysis of penal power in the modern liberal state as penal law and penal police: the dual penal state. Illustrations include lay participation, plea bargaining, the legality principle, habeas corpus, and possession offenses, among others.

Comparative-historical analysis plays a key role in this conception of the study of criminal process, in both the construction and genealogy of the dual penal state framework and in its application to various aspects of criminal process across various jurisdictions. The scope of the inquiry into criminal process presented here is systemic, rather than jurisdiction-specific. The conception of the dual penal state, and the distinction between law and police as two modes of state governance more generally, is associated with the historical moment of the launch of the modern liberal legal-political project. The study of the criminal process considered here, therefore, is more specifically a study of the modern liberal criminal process, that is, the criminal process that is consistent

* Thanks to the Alexander-von-Humboldt Foundation, the Royal Society of Canada, and the Social Sciences and Humanities Research Council of Canada for financial support, and to Klaus Günther (Goethe-University Frankfurt/Excellence Cluster "Normative Orders") and Tatjana Hörnle (Humboldt-University Berlin) for their kind hospitality.

with the pursuit of the ideal of liberal law to which states that regard themselves—or wish to be regarded by others—as participants in the modern liberal legal-political project are committed.

The comparative analysis applied in this chapter, and in the conception of the study of criminal process it considers, therefore is instrumental in the sense that it facilitates the critical analysis of criminal process in a particular legal-political system, or project, that appears in various forms in a cluster of states, or jurisdictions. The point of the comparative analysis is not only to illuminate certain features of a given jurisdiction, or several jurisdictions, or to assess the extent to which jurisdictions have implemented their shared ideal of liberal law, but ultimately also to critically assess the defining ideal itself.

This comparative analysis, operating at a fairly high level of abstraction, will focus on the—literally—systemic features of various penal regimes, rather than on specific doctrines. It will also rely on familiar stand-ins for "common law" and "civil law" countries: the United States and Germany.[1] It doesn't proceed from the assumption that the distinction between common law and civil law countries is useful (never mind "real" in some sense) and therefore isn't concerned with deviations in a given jurisdiction from the supposed norm of one or the other. If a meaningful distinction should emerge between the responses by two sets of jurisdictions to the challenge of liberal law in general, and liberal penal law in particular, and this distinction tracks some version of the traditional distinction between "common law" and "civil law" countries, that would be interesting. But it would not affect dual penal state analysis one way or another.

The key feature of dual penal state analysis is the notion that the moment of the Enlightenment (however long and whenever it is thought to have occurred) did not simply mark the end of one mode of state governance—police—and the beginning of another—law. Rather than the *Rechtsstaat* replacing the *Polizeistaat*, both legal and policial aspects are taken to have persisted in state governance, and in state penal governance in particular, as modern manifestations of the age-old tension and interplay between autonomy and heteronomy, rooted in the beginnings of Western legal-political history in ancient Athens.

This means that the critical analysis of criminal process in light of the familiar commitments of the modern, autonomy-based, conception of liberal law is only one side, and one half, of the story. The other side is the parallel analysis of criminal process from the perspective not of law, but of police, as a continuing manifestation of the state's police power, and its penal power in particular. This policial analysis was no more rendered obsolete than the law state replaced the police state in one fell swoop. To regard the place of penal police in the modern dual penal state as an anachronistic remnant on the exceptional margins of a penal law state progressively perfected over the last two centuries (or more) is to fail to appreciate the significance of the relation and connection between law and police as constituent tensions.

The underlying tension, of autonomy and heteronomy, is familiar throughout the history of the Western legal-political project. The launch of the modern liberal project, however, exposed and sharpened it, by defining itself as the radical rejection of one of its modes

[1] For a doctrine-focused particularized comparative analysis of criminal law using the United States and Germany as representative "common law" and "civil law" jurisdictions, see Markus D. Dubber & Tatjana Hörnle, *Criminal Law: A Comparative Approach* (2014).

by the other, of police by law, and of the police state by the law state. Once the capacity for autonomy is universalized from an elite characteristic of householder-citizens to the distinctive feature of all persons, the tension can no longer be accommodated, or hidden, by distinguishing categorically between governor and governed, subject and object of government and between a sphere of heteronomy (the household, oikos, familia) and of autonomy (the city state, agora, forum). The police state could not survive the enlightenment because the enlightenment was defined in contradistinction to it. Penal police was impossible; it *could* not exist, because it was essentially incompatible with the law state. Dual penal state analysis, by contrast, insists on the persistence of the tension between autonomy and heteronomy and between law and police, and it rejects simplistic, self-serving yet ultimately self-defeating, tendencies to condemn the police power, including notably in the penal realm, to the dustbin of antiquarian historiography.

Insofar as the legitimacy of the modern liberal state is grounded in the autonomy of its constituent subject-objects as persons (rather than as householders, say), the critical analysis of the state's penal power goes to the heart of the paradox of liberal state power: the threat, imposition, and infliction of penal violence intentionally violates the autonomy of the very persons whose autonomy undergirds its legitimacy. (Punishment is prima facie crime.) If the state's penal power can be legitimated in terms of the Grundnorm of autonomy, then the legitimacy of the state's power in general appears possible. At the same time, if the state's penal power cannot be legitimated, then what's the point of legitimating other, less intrusive, kinds of state action?

The critical analysis of criminal process forms part of the critical analysis of the state's penal regime. That much is clear. Less clear is how important that part turns to be. The answer to this question will depend not only on how one defines "criminal process" and, therefore, what a critical analysis of "criminal process" would encompass but also, perhaps less obviously yet not unrelatedly, who is asking (or answering) the question.

We'll take up the question of the place of the critical analysis of criminal process in the critical analysis of the dual penal state in Sections II and III, focused on Germany and the United States, respectively. But first, in Section I, we'll start out with an overview of the analytic framework: the conception of a dual penal state based on the historically situated distinction between law and police as modern modes of state governance in general, and of state penal governance in particular.

II. Dual Penal State

Dual penal state analysis is one aspect of dual state analysis, which in turns illustrates critical analysis of law, a contextual interdisciplinary approach to legal studies. Underlying, and driving, these various scholarly enterprises is the distinction between law and police as modes of modern state governance.[2]

[2] See generally Markus D. Dubber, *The Dual Penal State: The Crisis of Criminal Law in Comparative-Historical Perspective* (2018); Markus D. Dubber, *The Police Power: Patriarchy and the Foundations of American Government* (2005).

Critical analysis of law, and dual penal state analysis as an application, attempts to overcome unproductive categorical distinctions between traditional (doctrinal, intradisciplinary) and "modern" (interdisciplinary), "common law," and "civil law" conceptions of legal studies in general, and criminal law in particular. Ultimately, critical analysis of law pragmatically pursues the aim of transforming legal scholarship into a communal, transnational enterprise of engaged scholarship, that marshals the collective competence of scholars trained in law to tackle the pressing issue of vigilantly observing and critiquing the exercise of state power—and state penal power—through law in a modern liberal democratic state.

Critical analysis of law subjects the exercise of state power through law to internal and external critique. Internal critique tests the comprehensiveness, coherence, and consistency of legal norms, much as traditional doctrinalism has done for decades (though more flexibly and contextually). External critique, more important and interesting, leaves the positivistic constraints of traditional doctrinalism behind and critiques state action in the name of law in light of normative commitments associated with the modern liberal conception of law.

Rather than treat these commitments as if they were handed down ready-made and fully formed by some deus ex machina or other, critical analysis of law regards them as historically and contextually situated. In particular, it views the modern conception of law and its attendant normative commitments as having arisen, or rather having been actively constructed, in contradistinction to an alternative mode of governance. State power as law was legitimate, just; state power as police was alegitimate, ajust. The absence of legal norms did not imply the absence of all norms. But policial norms did not affect the legitimacy or justice of state power through police; instead, they were framed as advisory maxims of prudence, wisdom, efficiency, rationality, addressed to sovereign state householders who might decide to allow their unlimited discretion to be guided by them. Violations of principles of law (or "legality") threatened the state's legitimacy; deviations from self-adopted and self-policed maxims of police did not, and could not, because the idea of a critique of the legitimacy of the sovereign state householder was inapposite.

The very notion of a critical analysis of state power was regarded, and presented, as novel. Since the seventeenth century, a police science had developed that generated an ever-broadening stream of analysis and advice on the ever-more complex tasks of governing the state household, ranging from Machiavelli's proto-policial ruminations on princely statecraft to the tomes and compendiums on "good police" produced by eighteenth-century *Polizeiwissenschaft* and "political oeconomy" in Germany and France (and, by Adam Smith and Patrick Colquhoun, in Scotland and London). But none of these texts concerned itself with questions of "legitimacy," whatever this would have meant. They were manuals on good governance, or rather good housekeeping, contributions to the long-standing genre of *oikonomia* and *Hausväterliteratur* on the grand, public scale of the state.[3]

[3] See generally Grant A. Nelsestuen, Oikonomia *as a Theory of Empire in the Political Thought of Xenophon and Aristotle*, 57 Greek, Roman, and Byzantine Stud. 74 (2017).

To appreciate the historical context, and the elements of continuity and disruption, of the construction, and appearance, of the modern notion of law, it helps to assume the perspective of the longue durée. Law and police, and law in contradistinction to police as an alternative mode of governance, is the modern manifestation of the basic distinction between autonomy and heteronomy, or self- and other-government. This is the continuity. The autonomy of modern law, however, is not the autonomy of the few (the householder/governor/subject) but the autonomy of all (persons as such). This is the disruption. With the discovery, or pronouncement (or invention[4]), of the autonomy of the person as such, with autonomy now serving as the universal characteristic (or, more precisely, the capacity) shared by all rather than the marker of distinction that categorically separated the few (householders) from the rest (household), the traditional accommodation between autonomy and heteronomy collapsed. Autonomy had turned from making government patently possible to making it facially illegitimate.

The modern concept of law, in this view, appears as the response to the Enlightenment's challenge of universal-personal autonomy in the political sphere. The legitimacy of modern state power through law turns on its compliance with the Grundnorm of autonomy; legitimate government is self-government, all the way down.

Just what this ideal means, and how one might go about implementing it is anything but obvious, of course. In fact, the history of the legal-political project in modern Western liberal democratic states can be seen as a history of the struggle to answer these questions. But this is only one, if common, way of telling the story. Regarding modern Western legal-political history as a series of progressive attempts to better implement the vision of liberal law, and autonomous government, risks viewing it through a narrow, Whiggish, lens that focuses on only one mode of state governance, law, as if the declaration that "Law is King" (Thomas Paine) swept away centuries, or millennia, of quasi-patriarchal governance on the household model. This view is Whiggish even if one rejects its crude and most familiarly suspect version, which sees constant progress toward liberal perfection. The exclusive focus on law is Whiggish, no matter in what version, insofar as it takes the launch of the modern legal-political project to mark the beginning of a shift from one analytic framework to another, from police to law, rather than the evolution of a two-track framework that reflects the persistence of the long-standing tension between autonomy and heteronomy, now modernized and sharpened to the point of facial illegitimacy in the tension between law and police. The modern liberal state is not defined by one mode of governance (law) with exceptions defined only as such; instead, the apparent exceptions in turn reflect an alternative mode of governance (police) that stands in uncomfortable tension with the "new" mode of governance (law) that is presented not only as dominant but as exclusive, as the (only) norm.

Dual penal state analysis, as the most urgent instance of dual state analysis, then, pursues a parallel analysis of state power from both perspectives, law and police. This means at least two things. First, each mode of governance, and its attendant mode of analysis, is

4 J.B. Schneewind, *The Invention of Autonomy: A History of Modern Moral Philosophy* (1998).

defined in terms of the other and, ultimately, in terms of the tension between autonomy and heteronomy. Law and police are not two concepts that "exist" independently of one another and might happen, occasionally, to overlap. They are inextricably linked, through the "modern" historical moment of their emergence (law state versus police state) and their longue durée grounding in the interplay between autonomy and heteronomy in classical Athens (agora versus oikos).

Second, dual penal state analysis always considers the possibility that an apparent exception to the norm of a supposedly exclusive (or merely dominant) mode of governance may in fact reflect another mode of governance altogether. Instead of continuously recording the inconsistency of a given state norm, practice, or institution with some legal "principle" or other, for instance, dual penal state analysis instead asks the preliminary question of whether that critique is simply inapposite because the state action in question is conceived as a matter of police, rather than as a matter of law. It is beside the point to note, again and again, that, say, criminal liability for possession flies in the face of fundamental principles of criminal law (actus reus, most obviously) if possession offenses perform a key role in a comprehensive penal police regime designed to permit state officials to exercise their essentially unlimited and unreviewable discretion to identify and incapacitate "offenders"—individuals or groups who give offense in the specific sense of disturbing the king's, or later on the public's, peace (in the lingo of English or American criminal law) or are "disturbers" (Störer) who "compromise public safety and order" (in the lingo of German "police law").[5]

It's important here to recognize that dual penal state analysis is just that, a critical analysis of the state's penal power as a whole from the perspectives of law and police. The entire penal regime is subject to this two-track analysis in all of its nooks and crannies, down to the level of specific doctrinal features (such as the crime of possession). Contrast this with an attempt to identify specific legal or policial aspects or elements that add up to a legal-policial checkerboard regime. While it is certainly possible, and in fact likely, that individual features of the penal regime may align more easily with one mode of penal governance than another (possession, again, provides an example), it is important not to lose sight of the fundamental nature of the tension between law and police. Identifying and then eliminating particular "policial remnants" within a penal law regime will not resolve the tension or eliminate police as a type of penal governmentality any more than announcing that the birth of the law state killed off the police state.

The persistence of policial governmentality and therefore of the fundamental tension between law and police as modes of governance has frequently been suppressed, or denied, rather than acknowledged and addressed. In Germany, and other European countries, the once sprawling and eventually all-encompassing field of police science vanished over the course of the nineteenth century. Rather than analyzing the operation of the state as an *oeconomic* household manifesting its police power, attention shifted to the study of the supposed legal limits of that awesome sovereign power in a brand new

[5] See Markus D. Dubber, *Policing Possession: The War on Crime and the End of Criminal Law*, 91 J. Crim. L. & Criminology 829 (2002).

legal discipline: administrative law (including, most explicitly, in Germany, the subdiscipline of "police law"). Police scientists turned into administrative law scholars, if not overnight, then from one tome to the next;[6] the legalization of police was achieved as soon as it was named, never mind that the new courts of administrative law, whether or not they were considered part of the administrative apparatus, could at best occasionally police the margins of the vast administrative regime of the modern state, which continued to grow in scope and complexity unconcerned with, if not aided by, the rebranding of the state from police state to law state. The administrative state continued to be defined by discretion through and through, with supposed law constraints coming in the shape of formal guidelines, rarely enforced and, if so, always with an eye toward retaining the essential discretion at the core of the administrative enterprise. In the end, it might appear that rather than law legalizing police, police policified law: administrative "law" did not place law-appropriate and legitimacy-based constraints on administrative police, but was integrated into it, and appropriated by it.

Across the Atlantic, there was no American police science; as a result, there was nothing to dismantle or rebrand. In fact, the notion of police power (if not police science) played an explicitly central role in the American federalist compromise. Defined by its indefinability, utterly discretionary and all-encompassing, it was the governmental manifestation of sovereignty. To be sovereign meant to have the power to police, the "power to govern men and things within the limits of its dominion."[7] To say that the states retained their sovereignty therefore was to say that they retained the power to police. At the same time, and for the same reason, the federal "government" did not, and could never, have that flexibly all-devouring *oeconomic* power that would have reduced the states to members of the national state household under the discretionary power of a national state householder, a presidential patriarch. Originary state sovereignty would have become delegated sovereignty, the limits of which drawn and then policed at the discretion of the national state householder (ultra vires).

And yet, while it served the federalist compromise (at least on paper, if not in fact, as the federal government soon went about knitting together an all-encompassing de facto police power from its various "enumerated" powers) to marvel at, and insist on, the limitless awesomeness of state sovereign power within the new federalist structure, this very feature of the police power also brought into stark relief its apparent incompatibility with the presumably even more awesome, though strictly limited, law power in a country where the Law is King.

This incompatibility, however, was merely apparent. For it turned out that the police power and the law power rested on radically different conceptions of the objects of state power, and their relation to its subjects. The incompatibility of law and police is, at bottom, the incompatibility of autonomy and heteronomy. Autonomy and heteronomy are incompatible only if the distinction between governor/subject and governed/object has

[6] Compare Ernst Freund, *The Police Power: Public Policy and Constitutional Rights* (1904) with Ernst Freund, *Cases on Administrative Law Selected from Decisions of English and American Courts* (1911).

[7] Slaughter-House Cases, 83 U.S. 36, 62 (1873).

been abandoned. If, however, there are objects of governance who lack the capacity for autonomy and therefore are regarded as mere objects, rather than also as potential subjects, of state power, the tension between autonomy and heteronomy can be managed as it had been for millennia, through the logic of the relationship between householder and household, between governor and governed, according to entirely discretionary prudential maxims of good governance.

The only question in this accommodation was where the distinction between subject and object should be drawn, who would end up on which side of the sovereign divide. Initially, women, children, slaves, and the poor fell on the object side of the divide, along with—for our purposes particularly interesting—criminal offenders. It has long been American blackletter law that the state's penal power is an instance of the police power. This meant, as we saw, that criminal law was—and remains—primarily a matter of state law, with federal law treated as a narrow specialized supplement (a fiction increasingly difficult to maintain as federal criminal law dramatically expanded). The power to punish was seen as intimately connected to the very idea of sovereignty; if a sovereign must have any power, it must be the power to punish those who give offense, by challenging his sovereignty or, since the Middle Ages, by breaking his (household) peace.

While the supposed "localness" (i.e., stateness) of the police power within the federalist arrangement got—and continues to get—the bulk of the attention, its intimate connection to the sovereignty of the householder, which reaches back through the Middle Ages to the beginnings of Western political history in classical Greece, captures its heteronomous governmentality, a mode of governance that connects the Athenian oikos to the Roman familia to the medieval mund to the early modern King's peace to the early modern state's "good police" (*gute Policey*) and eventually "public safety and order."

The criminal offender remains outside the scope of the modern legal-political project associated with the liberal ideal of law as the mode of state governance that rejects the radical distinction between governor and governed and instead turns on the radical identity of all persons as potential subject-objects of autonomous government. Criminal offenders personify the object of disciplinary power that threatens the subject's sovereignty. They are the paradigmatic object of police power and, as such, beyond the scope of law power. Their crime is a police offense: the status of being a threat to sovereign power, as opposed to the act of violating the autonomy of another person, say. Disciplining them, at the discretion of the householder-sovereign, reasserts the householder-sovereign's authority, and in this way reaffirms the radical distinction between governor and governed, householder and household. By contrast, in a liberal law-based conception of crime, the paradigmatic crime would be interpersonal, rather than antistatal, and punishment (rather than hierarchical discipline) would reassert the identity of victim and offender, and ultimately—through the construction of self-government and -punishment—also the identity of punisher and offender.

This isn't the place to lay out a detailed parallel account of penal law and penal police, or the results of a critical analysis of the penal state from the perspectives of law and police. Instead, let's move on to a two-track analysis of criminal process in the dual penal state in comparative-historical perspective, by focusing on Germany and the United States.

III. Germany

The first issue that a comparative analysis of dual penal state regimes should address is whether the comparators are relevantly similar. Insofar as dual penal state analysis draws on the liberal conception of law, it makes no sense to apply it to a state that doesn't regard—or represent—itself as participating in the modern legal-political project.

Germany is generally assumed to clearly fit this bill. This may be surprising, given Germany's more than checkered legal-political history, even if the Nazi period is presented as a radically anomalous episode after which the German penal regime resumed the pursuit of the ideal of liberal criminal law, or perhaps is regarded as a sort of prolonged stress test that, in the end, illustrated the principled steadfastness of German criminal law science, which survived the period (remarkably) unscathed, by and large.

There is much more to be said (and much more than has been said) on the place of the Nazi era in German criminal legal history—for instance, on the continuity between pre-1933 proposals implemented by the Nazis and Nazi reforms that remained in force post-1945. But, for present purposes, let's stick with how German criminal law tends be regarded in Germany (including among the German criminal law professoriate, i.e., the practitioners of German criminal law science) and in the many other countries—not only (or even primarily) in Europe, but also elsewhere (including, notably, in East Asia and much of Latin America)—that assign to it a certain model status.

In this view, foundational figures of German criminal law played a key role in recognizing and formulating the central challenge of state penal power in the modern law state, not only in Germany but for the liberal legal-project as a whole. According to this account, Kant is the single most important figure in what Schneewind called the invention of autonomy,[8] the central innovation of the Enlightenment and the centerpiece of "modern" moral and political philosophy. While Kant's own musings about the state's power to punish tend to receive less attention than one might expect (presumably because they might be considered radically inconsistent with the "modern" conception of state penal power their author is said to have inaugurated), one of his contemporary admirers, Paul Johann Anselm Feuerbach, is widely considered the "father" of modern German criminal law. It's at least unclear to what extent Feuerbach's views on criminal law[9] are faithful to Kant's views on the subject (whatever that would mean given Kant's either vaguely suggestive or specifically troubling remarks) or instead hew closer to those of Kant's consequentialist nemesis, Beccaria, whose pamphlet *Of Crimes and Punishments* (1764) so profoundly influenced thinking and writing on state punishment

[8] See Schneewind, *supra* note 4.

[9] Set out in early (philosophical and later jurisprudential) writings, an influential textbook that appeared in fourteen editions between 1801 and 1847, a Bavarian criminal code often cited as a model in Germany and elsewhere, and, eventually, in "narratives of remarkable criminal trials," based on his experience as a provincial Bavarian trial judge. See generally Gustav Radbruch, *Paul Johann Anselm Feuerbach: Ein Juristenleben* (1934); Paul Johann Anselm Feuerbach, *Textbook of the Common Penal Law in Force in Germany*, in *Foundational Texts in Modern Criminal Law* 373 (Markus D. Dubber ed., 2014).

that authors as otherwise violently opposed as Blackstone, Bentham, and Jefferson were content to simply cite, if not directly quote, Beccaria's definitive pronouncements as theoretical preambles to their own writings (which then again might differ radically not only from each other but also in their connection to Beccaria's general theory).[10]

Feuerbach, as a Kantian-Beccarian, is off to a bit of a rough start as father of German criminal law. Kant certainly considered Beccaria's views on punishment diametrically opposed to his own, and Beccaria and Kant ever since have been used as convenient stand-ins for the centuries-long fight between "consequentialist" and "retributivist" theories of punishment. Anyone who thought otherwise, then, and promulgated a Kantian-Beccarian account of criminal law would run the risk of being suspected of having failed to grasp the basic thrust of either view (or both) unless that person had a fairly involved story to tell that would account for their compatibility.

There is the additional problem that, taking Kant seriously, Beccaria is not only wrong, but wrong in the very sense that concerns us here: the conception of law grounded in the invention of autonomy as the distinctive characteristic of all persons as such. The problem with the utilitarian position, on this view, is precisely that it fails to regard the objects of punishment as persons endowed with the capacity for autonomy, but as slaves to their experience and anticipation of pain or pleasure who are properly governed through the threat and infliction of pain, as "a man who lifts his stick to a dog" (as Hegel put it a little later) or, as we might say, as a householder who disciplines a mere human household resource.

It turns out, however, that Beccaria and Kant did agree on one point: the classification of criminal offenders as slaves (of the state) and their punishment as enslavement.[11] "Consequentialist" or "retributivist," these two paragons of Enlightened penality saw nothing incompatible or troubling in regarding and treating the objects of state penal power as paragons of heteronomy. This may be more surprising in Kant's case, given his association with an autonomy-based conception of personhood, but in either case it raises disquieting questions about the very foundation of the modern liberal legal-penal project, across the supposedly fundamental consequentialist-retributive/Beccarian-Kantian divide.

It appears, then, that from the very start the supposedly all-inclusive, radically egalitarian Enlightenment project of state power through law in general, and through penal law in particular, countenanced a distinction so basic and ingrained as to have escaped critical reflection: the radical distinction between persons and offenders that tracks the boundary of the legal-political project. Fichte, unlike Hegel, enthusiastically pursued

[10] See Wolfgang Naucke, *Kant und die psychologische Zwangstheorie Feuerbachs* (1962).

[11] E.g., Cesare Beccaria, *On Crimes and Punishments* §§ 16, 30 (1764); Immanuel Kant, *Rechtslehre* A193-194/B222-224 (1790) (Wilhelm Weischedel ed., 1977) (1790); Arnd Koch, *Das Jahrhundert der Strafrechtskodifikation: Von Feuerbach zum Reichsstrafgesetzbuch*, 122 *ZStW* 741, 750–52 (2010); see also P.J.A. Feuerbach, *Entwurf des Gesetzbuchs über Verbrechen und Vergehen für das Königreich Bayern* arts. 12–14 (1810); see generally Dubber, *Dual Penal State*, supra note 2, at 141–53.

this exclusionary aspect of Kant's view, which generally does not figure in the orthodox narrative of a Kant-based evolution of modern criminal law.[12]

More important for our purposes, penal enslavement figures prominently in Feuerbach's work, particularly in his work on the Bavarian criminal code of 1813, hailed as the first modern German criminal code, if not the first modern criminal code, period. Only recently has German historiography begun to note this feature of Feuerbach's codification work, after decades of largely unadulterated adulation. Even the most casual reader of Feuerbach's draft could hardly miss Feuerbach's detailed descriptions of all aspects of the design and infliction of various brutal penal measures, including permanent "civil death" made real through solitary confinement, during which the penal slave wears "on both feet a long chain with a heavy iron ball." That Feuerbach is not alone in endorsing penal enslavement (or, in Thomas Jefferson's case, literally penal measures cribbed from medieval dooms in the original Anglo-Saxon) merely shifts focus from Feuerbach, the "father" of German criminal law and criminal codification, to the liberal legal-political project of state penal power itself.

But let's assume, for purposes of our quick comparative look at the dual penal state in Germany and the United States, that the challenge of liberal state penal power was indeed framed explicitly and comprehensively in Germany, starting with a potent combination of philosophical reflection and jurisprudential-doctrinal implementation associated with the work of Kant and Feuerbach (along with contributions by Hegel, if not Fichte) during the long turn of the nineteenth century. The discovery, or invention, of autonomy as the distinctive characteristic of personhood implied a fundamental critique not only of morality but also of politics. State power was legitimate only insofar as it was conceived of, and exercised through, law as the mode of governance that regarded the objects of government as persons capable of self-government, rather than as mere objects of quasi-patriarchal (even if benevolent) police power. Penal power posed the greatest challenge to the legitimacy of state power, and penal law both manifested and answered that challenge (still captured by Franz von Liszt's slogan a century later that "the criminal law is the magna charta of the criminal law").

To recognize, and to frame, the paradox of modern state penal power, however, is not the same as addressing it, never mind resolving it. We've already noted the surprising unwillingness to subject the founding texts of liberal penal state power to serious critical scrutiny. Beccaria and Kant each framed their—otherwise diametrically opposed—Enlightened conception of state punishment in a way that, with what now appears as a brazen sleight of hand, excluded key aspects of the penal regime from its legitimatory reach. To put it differently, Beccaria's and Kant's ideals of modern state penal power already contain the radical distinction among objects of penal power that marks the dual penal state.

[12] Cf. Günther Jakobs, *Bürgerstrafrecht und Feindstrafrecht*, 5 HRRS 88 (2004); *Zur Theorie des Feindstrafrechts*, in *Straftheorie und Strafgerechtigkeit* 167 (Henning Rosenau & Sanyun Kim eds., 2010) (English translation: *On the Theory of Enemy Criminal Law*, in *Foundational Texts in Modern Criminal Law* 415 (Markus D. Dubber ed., 2014)).

Meeting the challenge of legitimating penal power in a modern liberal state, however, requires not only scrutinizing the foundational texts that set out the challenge and point the way to its resolution. It also requires constantly testing existing penal norms, practices, and institutions against the relevant legitimatory norm. Whether this essential process of ongoing legitimacy scrutiny continues to this day in Germany is at least debatable. Since the nineteenth century, German legal scholarship has seen itself as being engaged in a self-consciously positivistic enterprise of "legal science." Since 1871, German criminal legal science revolves around the German criminal code, and pursues a comprehensive project of constructing a doctrinal system ostensibly based on, or at least constrained by, the code (which, however, is short, incomplete, and vague enough to leave considerable room for scientific maneuvering). A parallel, similarly positivistic, though far less ambitious, doctrinalist project concerns itself with the (considerably more detailed) 1878 German code of criminal procedure. In general, this vast multigenerational doctrinalist criminal law project is self-contained, with critical analysis confined to concerns about coherence, comprehensiveness, and consistency, rather than tackling fundamental questions of legitimacy. The state's power to punish, instead, is taken for granted and, for some time now, the challenge has been one of doctrinal refinement, rather than of continuous legitimacy scrutiny.

Lay participation, for instance, has long been considered at best pointless and at worst problematic because, while it might have acted as a check on state power in the nineteenth century, officials of the German law state (judges and prosecutors) have long been independent enough to no longer require such scrutiny. In fact, lay participants are regarded as injecting an element of irrationality and incompetence into an essentially rational and competent legal process run by state officials trained in German legal science. The independent jury was abandoned several decades ago; and even the lay participants in the remaining "mixed" courts are less appreciated than tolerated, largely because it is an open secret that their role in the criminal process is largely ceremonial (despite the startling fact that they have the power, and the numbers, to outvote professional judges, a power they never exercise).

If we again assume that German criminal law, thanks to Kant and Feuerbach (with a somewhat incongruous assist by Beccaria), saw and formulated the novel challenge of legitimacy posed by the very notion of the threat and use of penal violence by the state against its own autonomous constituents, the continued legitimation of the state's penal power has fallen into desuetude because the recognition and framing of a problem has been confused with its solution. The legitimation of state penal power in a modern liberal democratic state requires its continuous fundamental critique, not the complacent sense that the legitimacy question has been asked and answered as long as two centuries ago.

The legitimacy of state penal power can never be definitively settled in a modern liberal state grounded in the autonomy of its constituents. There is no such thing as a once-and-for-all systemic legitimation of state penal power. The design of the penal regime is, of course, crucial for the legitimation of the violence that is threatened and inflicted under it, but it is not sufficient. The actual interference with the autonomy of specific state constituents in every aspect, substantive and procedural, personal and institutional, of every case must be justified in terms of the legitimatory Grundnorm (autonomy).[13]

An internal conception of legal science that (ostensibly) limits itself to rearranging the doctrinal furniture on the assumption that legitimatory questions have been resolved, then and forever, may become indistinguishable from the statist project of police science that the launch of the law state rendered anachronistic and relabeled as "administrative law" (or "police law"). Legal scholarship that pursues legal science as positivistic doctrinalism, with a brief (again ostensibly) limited to the ever more correct rationalization of state norms (most important, but not limited to, the criminal code), functions as an organ of good governance whose collective advice may, or may not, find the ear of state officials, without the uncomfortable suggestion that the issue of legitimacy, rather than of more prudent administration, might be at stake. Criminal law scholarship thus conceived may amount to science (in some limited, technical sense), but it would not amount to legal science in the modern sense of law.

Finally, consider the German penal state from the perspective of the distinction between substantive and procedural criminal law. In German criminal law, substance has long been privileged over process. The bulk of legislative, jurisprudential, and scholarly attention has been devoted to the substantive norms of criminal law, and more specifically to the general principles of criminal liability (the general part of criminal law) that apply to all criminal offenses (which make up the so-called special part). Kant showed very little interest in procedural aspects of criminal law; the same goes for Feuerbach (and Hegel, Fichte, Köstlin, Binding, Liszt) and every other significant German criminal law scholar since. Except for occasional (political) moments of procedural excitement, notably around the adoption of the jury in the nineteenth century (initially under French occupation, which introduced the French jury to large swaths of Germany, and then, again, during the German "revolutions" of the mid-1800s), the debate has been about substantive criminal law, that is, about the discovery of penal norms, rather than their interpretation or implementation.

To simplify, with substantive norms regarded as essentially self-executing (and self-interpreting), the question of interpretation and implementation not surprisingly attracted little serious scientific interest. To the extent that the possibility of discretion—and therefore variance—in the execution of the scientifically derived (and therefore presumably correct) norms was acknowledged, it was regarded as an unpleasant nuisance that interfered with the proper application of authoritative norms. It therefore had to be eliminated. The rule of compulsory prosecution (*Legalitätsprinzip*) was designed to prohibit the use of discretion by members of the newly minted prosecutorial corps—which guaranteed both equal and faithful application of the applicable substantive norm, thus preventing pro-state favoritism and guaranteeing correct and complete implementation

[13] Cf. John Rawls, *Two Concepts of Rules*, 64 Phil. Rev. 3 (1955).

of state norms, at the same time.[14] Today, the rule of compulsory prosecution is balanced by a rule of discretionary non-prosecution (*Opportunitätsprinzip*): a rule that is conceptualized as carving out a narrow exception to the general non-discretionary rule. (Police officers, incidentally, are not subject to the rule of discretionary non-prosecution; they remain subject to the rule of compulsory prosecution, or rather investigation.)

Just as prosecutors may stand in the way of the correct application of rational norms, so may lay participants. The essentially ornamental lay members of German mixed courts are today often seen as amateurishly interfering with the rational and proper interpretation and implementation of penal norms according to the strict (three-step) analytic process determined by criminal legal science, and reviewed by appellate courts (and legal commentators).

The process of application and implementation, in sum, is seen as a problem, a source of errors in what ideally would be an immediate, automatic coming-to-life of the abstract norms of substantive criminal law. It raises exclusively issues of administration, of eliminating the gap between norm and imposition, between the general and the particular. Having invested such tremendous communal effort in generating a rational scientific system of criminal law, how frustrating it must be to see the fruits of this labor spoiled in police stations and courtrooms through the incorrect exercise of discretion by state officials (never mind laypeople). Best to eliminate this discretion altogether and view any remnant as a necessary evil that should be minimized to the extent possible.

This subordinate role of criminal process in the German penal state not only reflects a lack of appreciation of the need to justify the threat and certainly the imposition and infliction of penal violence on particular persons, rather than merely as a matter of abstract norms, at both the individual level and the institutional level (Rawls). It also, once again, reflects a policial, merely formal, conception of criminal process (consistent with the policial conception of "legal" science mentioned above). To regard criminal process as merely a possible (and perhaps even inevitable) source of error is to fail to see its key role in contributing to the legitimation of the exercise of penal (law) power. To regard the function of criminal process as merely the correct application of scientifically derived norms to correctly determined facts rather than as also (and crucially) the legitimation of this norm application in this particular case, that is, to put it in more familiar (and grandiose) term, to see the trial as merely finding truth rather than as also doing justice, is to adopt a view that is compatible with a policial conception of criminal process, not a legal one. To return to the example of lay participation: a policial conception of criminal process in administrative terms of non-erroneous implementation has no room for a jury (or meaningful lay participation of any kind), as the jury is merely a pointless source of error (of law or fact), rather than a procedural manifestation of the Grundnorm of autonomy, through vicarious judgment of fellow members of the relevant community, with actual self-judgment—confession—reduced to evidentiary significance, rather than being treated as a prerequisite (torture).

[14] See Peter Collin, *"Wächter der Gesetze" oder "Organ der Staatsregierung": Konzipierung, Einrichtung und Anleitung der Staatsanwaltschaft durch das preußische Justizministerium, von den Anfängen bis 1860* (2000).

IV. United States

The American story differs from the German one in several basic respects. The challenge of penal power in a modern liberal state was never recognized, or properly framed. And procedural criminal law received all of the attention, at the expense of substantive criminal law. In the end, both penal regimes can be seen as falling short of the awesome task of legitimating liberal penal power, but in radically different, even diametrically opposed, ways.

The "founding fathers" thoroughly scrutinized the institutional mechanics of governing, pondered the design of a federalist system of government, and gave much thought to any number of aspects of individuals' relation to "their" government and many other things besides. But they never subjected the state's most awesome power over its constituents to serious scrutiny in light of the fundamental principles of their new political order marked by democratic self-government, of the people, by the people, for the people (in Lincoln's words during America's second constitutional moment), where not the King, but the Law, is King (to quote Paine once more). The English conception of criminal law as the manifestation of the sovereign's discretionary and essentially unlimited power to protect *his* (the King's) peace, the most immediate manifestation of the state's power to police survived the revolution and its attendant communal reflection about all things government virtually unscathed. The King's peace was replaced by the peace of the Commonwealth of X, or of the State of Y, or the People of Z, or simply the "public," but the police logic of penal power remained, pitting the (now impersonal) sovereign against threats to its (rather than his or her) peace.

The closest thing to a Kant or a Feuerbach the United States produced during its foundational period was Thomas Jefferson, who was Kant and Feuerbach rolled into one, as both philosopher and implementer, both drafter of the Declaration of Independence and governor of Virginia (and, eventually, president of the United States). For our purposes most significant, Jefferson also was the drafter of the closest thing to a criminal code that the founding fathers produced, the 1779 "Bill for Proportioning Crimes and Punishments."[15] This bill belonged to a comprehensive project to "review" the laws of Virginia in light of the principles driving the revolution (and underlying the Declaration of Independence):

> our whole code must be reviewed, adapted to our republican form of government, and, now that we had no negatives of Councils, Governors & Kings to restrain us from doing right, that it should be corrected, in all it's parts, with a single eye to reason, & the good of those for whose government it was framed.

Forced to pick up the criminal law file because the committee member in charge of it had dropped out, Jefferson showed little interest in, and even less familiarity with, the

[15] See generally Markus D. Dubber, *"An Extraordinarily Beautiful Document": Jefferson's Bill for Proportioning Crimes and Punishments and the Challenge of Republican Punishment*, in *Modern Histories of Crime and Punishment* 115 (Markus D. Dubber & Lindsay Farmer eds., 2007).

subject. The result is a document so bizarrely brutal and haphazardly disjointed that Jefferson scholars have struggled to make sense of it as anything other than an opportunity for Jefferson to practice his penmanship, "an extraordinarily beautiful document"[16] drafted in the marginalia-heavy style of Jefferson's beloved Coke and filled with "extracts from the Anglo-Saxon laws, the sources of the Common Law," which he "wrote in their original, for [his] own satisfaction."[17]

In short, then, and obviously simplifying dramatically (but I don't think unfairly): whereas in Germany the challenge of penal power in the modern liberal law state, grounded in the Enlightenment invention of the capacity for autonomy of all persons as such, was recognized and framed, in the United States the state's penal power was simply taken for granted as an obvious incidence of sovereignty and, as an exercise of the quasi-patriarchal police power, remained outside the scope of the autonomy-based legal-political project launched by the founding revolutionary generation. As a result, in the United States, the legitimatory challenge of penal power in the modern liberal law state was never recognized, never mind framed. Rather than being regarded as central to the legitimation of state power in the new republic, the matter of penal power remained on a separate and well-worn track (even as other initial remainders were eventually, at least nominally, integrated into the general legal-political project: women, nonwhites, the poor). The second great foundational moment in American constitutional history (the Civil War and its aftermath), instead of challenging the exclusion of criminal offenders from the legal-political project, cemented it by explicitly excluding the use of penal power against them from the abolition of slavery and involuntary servitude (Thirteenth Amendment) and, as a prosaic matter of doctrine, classified prison inmates as "slaves of the state."

The civil rights era (and, arguably, the third constitutional moment) of the mid-twentieth century brought the recognition of various (procedural) constitutional protections as part of a push by the federal government, including the U.S. Supreme Court, against open official racism in the American South. As a consequence, blatant tools of oppression (such as the widespread vagrancy ordinances that, incidentally, were derived from medieval English public police provisions, notably the Statute of Laborers) gave way to more formally sophisticated and far more effective instruments of discretionary mass interference and incapacitation (such as the regime of possession offenses, which—unlike vagrancy—ranges from minor offenses to serious felonies punishable by life imprisonment without the possibility of parole). The result eventually—in combination with a vast and constitutionally unchecked expansion in the general scope and severity of substantive criminal norms ("overcriminalization") and sanctions ("overpenalization")—was the world's greatest project of mass incarceration, by a wide margin, and with devastating effects particularly on members of racial and ethnic minorities.

[16] Dumas Malone, 1 *Jefferson and His Time: Jefferson the Virginian* 269–70 (1948).

[17] *Letter to George Wythe, Nov. 1, 1778*, in 2 *The Writings of Thomas Jefferson 2 (1776–1781)*, at 203 n.1, 203 (Paul Leicester Ford ed. 1893).

The failure ever even to recognize and frame the challenge of penal power in a modern liberal state, not to mention the sheer enormity and ubiquity of penal violence in the United States, particularly during the past half century of the so-called war on crime, raises the question whether it makes sense to subject the American penal regime to critical analysis in light of the fundamental commitments associated with the modern liberal legal-political project.

A comparative analysis of German and American criminal law against a common systemic background, however, may prove useful nonetheless insofar as we accept that there is a general liberal American legal-political project (without pretending that the differences between American and, to stick with our example, German constitutional history are any less significant than those between English and German constitutional history), and that the question is not whether the United States can be seen as participating in a common liberal project but whether American criminal law in particular is regarded as forming part of that project. The latter question, however, would be internal to the general liberal project, regardless of the answer, and therefore would not preclude comparative analysis with other states participating in that project.

Let's assume, then, that a comparative-historical analysis of German and U.S. criminal law around the idea of the modern liberal state makes enough sense, on its face, to see where it might lead us. So far, we've seen that the German and U.S. penal projects differed from the outset. One recognized and framed the challenge of penal power in a liberal state; the other did not. One then fairly quickly considered the penal challenge addressed and solved, confusing the formulation of general norms with their implementation and the postulation of fundamental legal principles with the discovery of immutable scientific truths, and, in general, treating the legitimation of liberal state penal power as a one-time affair rather than a continuing process, at all levels and in all aspects of the penal process. The other had no such worries since, after all, it failed to see the new and urgent need to legitimate penal power in the new liberal state in the first place, given that criminal offenders remained outside the legal-political project, as mere objects of the state's police power.

The other, not unrelated, difference between German and U.S. penality that deserves attention concerns the relative significance each assigns to criminal process. As we've already seen, German penality is all substance, no process. American penality, by contrast, is all process, no substance.

Ideally, German penality would begin and end with the formulation of penal norms, thus eliminating the process of interpretation and implementation as a source of error as numerous, varied, and therefore ultimately unmanageable as the enormous number of officials charged with the task of norm imposition (and, eventually, infliction). Process plays no role in the legitimation of penal power; it is a necessary evil that threatens to compromise the rationality of a scientifically constructed system of penal norms, complete with a detailed instruction manual (the three-part analysis of criminal liability).

American penality, having failed to appreciate the novel legitimatory challenge of penal power in the New Republic of Law, showed no interest in generating new principles of criminal liability (the general part of substantive criminal law) or radically revising the conception of crime and its various manifestations (the special part), and instead adopted (and barely adapted) the premodern, English, radically heteronomous, monarchical, patriarchal conception of crime as violation of the sovereign's peace. At the same time, no one saw any need to rethink the procedural aspects of the penal regime; and so the English criminal process, too, was simply continued, as if the revolution had not happened, or rather had nothing whatsoever to do with any aspect, substantive or procedural, of the exercise of the state's most awesome power.

Still, while the federal constitution said nothing of consequence about substantive or procedural criminal law, the federal Bill of Rights included several provisions dealing with matters of criminal process. None of the procedural provisions, however, broke new ground; rather than reflect a fundamental reconception of the procedural aspect of the state penal regime, they enumerated long-familiar features of a criminal process long-familiar from centuries of patriarchal English penality. The list's very familiarity and deep English roots were thought to weigh heavily in its favor.

So, the process of American penality was no more the result of revolutionary revision than was its substance. But at least the process attracted enough attention among the founding generation to find its way into the new republic's formative texts. After all, the key revolutionary grievance of "taxation without representation" was itself framed in procedural terms. Taxation was not the problem; procedurally improper taxation was.

To say that the procedural features, or for that matter the substantive ones, of the not-so-new American penal regime were compatible with a radically heteronomous conception of patriarchal penality based on the idea of crime as offense against the sovereign's household peace and the sovereign-householder's unquestionably and intimately connected discretionary power to mete out penal discipline against anyone (or anything) that gives such offense, however, is not to say that these familiar norms, practices, and institutions could not be regarded from different perspectives in the light of the American revolution or, more generally, the launch of the liberal legal-political project. Consider, for instance, the complaint about taxation without representation. From a policial perspective, this grievance may well make sense in an essentially heteronomous regime that nonetheless, over the course of centuries, has evolved to include features or privileges, including "participation," that can be seen as placing some constraint on the still-awesome power of the sovereign-householder, if only in the form of privileges bestowed as a matter of grace, rather than as rights in the Enlightenment sense of universal characteristics of persons as such.

At the same time, however, the complaint about taxation without representation can be framed as a new insistence on compliance with the Grundnorm of legitimacy in the new liberal state: autonomy. From the perspective of law, rather than police, taxation was fine; taxation without representation was heteronomous, and therefore not only imprudent, but illegitimate.

Many of the long-familiar procedural "rights" enumerated in the federal Bill of Rights, along with other procedural features of modern penality (in the United States and elsewhere) can be subjected to a similar two-track analysis. The jury has been read both as an instrument of royal oppression, and as manifestation of local self-government;[18] the privilege of habeas corpus as a procedural tool of royal courts' interference with local courts' jurisdiction, and as the very incarnation of personal liberty;[19] the privilege against self-incrimination as a tool of royal courts' limitation of ecclesiastical jurisdiction, and as a safeguard of defendant autonomy;[20] the legality principle and the *ultima ratio* principle as discretionary police maxims, and as the rule of law incarnate;[21] even plea bargaining has been regarded both as a quintessential act of unlimited policial discretion and as a locus of autonomy through negotiation in an otherwise hierarchical process dominated by state officials.[22] Often, these contrasting conceptions of a given norm, practice, or institution are presented sequentially, with one portrayed as neatly taking the place of another; usually, this is a happy story, one that marks the transition from a heteronomous (or, in hindsight, policial) conception to an autonomous (or legal) one, thereby re-enacting the supposed paradigmatic transition from the police state to the law state. Dual penal state analysis instead remains alert to the possibility that the object of critical analysis retains both political and legal aspects, and in this way reflects the continuing underlying tension between police and law as modes of governance in the penal realm.

V. Conclusion: Criminal Process and Criminal Procedure

The most significant sense in which American penality has focused on process over substance (in contradistinction to German criminal law) is not in the enumeration of procedural, rather than substantive, features of the penal regime in the federal bill of rights. It is rather in the conception of the state penal system in its entirety as a process (rather than as a collection of substantive norms more or less correctly implemented), in the same sense that the study of "legal process" by the U.S. Legal Process School considered (or, in its occasional reincarnations still considers) the entire state as process. Criminal process (which we might distinguish from criminal procedure, as the study of the procedural aspect of the penal state) in this sense regards state penality from soup to nuts, including all the subject matters of the three traditional subdisciplines of criminal law

[18] See Markus D. Dubber, *The Schizophrenic Jury and Other Palladia of Liberty: A Critical Historical Analysis*, 3 Comp. Legal Hist. 306 (2016).

[19] Paul D. Halliday, *Habeas Corpus: From England to Empire* (2010).

[20] John H. Wigmore, *Nemo Tenetur Seipsum Prodere*, 5 Harv. L. Rev 71 (1891).

[21] Markus D. Dubber, *The Legality Principle in American and German Criminal Law: An Essay in Comparative Legal History*, in *From the Judge's Arbitrium to the Legality Principle: Legislation as a Source of Law in Criminal Trials* 365 (Georges Martyn et al. eds., 2013); Markus D. Dubber, Ultima Ratio *as Caveat Dominus: Legal Principles, Police Maxims, and the Critical Analysis of Law*, https://ssrn.com/abstract=2289479 (July 3, 2013).

[22] See Markus D. Dubber, *American Plea Bargains, German Lay Judges, and the Crisis of Criminal Procedure*, 49 Stan. L. Rev. 547 (1997).

(substantive criminal law: *Strafrecht*, procedural criminal law: *Strafprozeßrecht*, prison, or punishment execution, law: *Strafvollzugsrecht*).

This integrative approach, which ignores traditional doctrinal and institutional distinctions to capture the penal system as a whole (and therefore can subject it to critical analysis in all of its aspects, a crucial prerequisite for the legitimation of penal power in general, rather than of some slice of it or another), deserves a closer look insofar as it may accommodate a project of critical analysis of state penal power without prejudicing substance over process (Germany), or vice versa (United States). The criminal process approach produced three of the most significant texts in modern American criminal law: Herbert Wechsler's *Model Penal Code* (1962), Herbert Packer's *Two Models of the Criminal Process* (1964/1968), and Henry Hart's *The Aims of the Criminal Law* (1958). Of the three, Wechsler's is the most influential, Packer's the most similar to the dual penal state approach, and Hart's the shortest, as well as the most promising.

Wechsler's Model Penal Code[23] (MPC) was ostensibly about substantive criminal law (the American Law Institute having produced a forgettable model code of criminal procedure in 1930). As I've argued at length elsewhere, read as a criminal process document the MPC appears not as a model criminal code, but as a model code of treatment administration, which aims to assign the complex task of diagnosing and then prescribing and eventually administering the appropriate peno-correctional treatment for an offender's abnormal dangerousness to the appropriate official in the criminal process (from the judge's preliminary diagnosis to the warden and the parole board).[24] Not unlike contemporary German criminal law science, it regards all fundamental questions about the purpose of state punishment (or rather state peno-correctional *treatment*) as scientifically settled. That its version of scientific truth differs significantly from the German version is ironic; it's also beside the point.

That said, it is also true that the MPC's conception of crime/offense and punishment/treatment studiously avoids "philosophical" questions about the capacity for autonomy and instead adopts what we might call a thoroughly policial approach that, for the sake of (social) science, regards the central issue not as one of guilt or autonomous choice but as one of criminal dangerousness. It replaces atavistic punishment for wrongful conduct with "modern" treatment for sociopathy. The MPC designs a penal system that competently implements this treatmentist conception of state penality as peno-correctional treatment. It is uninterested in substance, because the substantive issue has been settled and only process (in the institutional sense of a system of implementation) remains. The Model Penal Code, then, is an exercise in police science dressed up as a criminal law codification project.

Wechsler, the Legal Process scholar in charge of the MPC project, recognized, however, that the code could not function properly as a system for the processing of criminal suspects from preliminary diagnosis through to indicated peno-correctional treatment if it amounted to nothing more than a collection of substantive norms (regarding the

[23] *Model Penal Code* (Am. Law Inst. Proposed Official Draft 1962).

[24] Markus D. Dubber, *The Model Penal Code, Legal Process, and the Alegitimacy of American Penality*, in *Foundational Texts in Modern Criminal Law* 239 (Markus D. Dubber ed., 2014).

general and special parts of criminal law). To be successful, the code needed to concern itself with questions of institutional design, including the identification and ordering of required tasks, their assignment to the appropriate state officials, and, finally, the delegation of the appropriate scope of discretion to each official and its guidance through the appropriately formulated norms (from broad flexible standards on one end to narrow and rigid rules on the other). These features of the criminal process were not grounded in concern about the legitimation of state penal power; they were designed to make a rational system run rationally, to advance the aim of the identification and elimination of penal objects diagnosed as indicating abnormal dangerousness. All features of the penal system, including substantive principles of criminal liability (mens rea, most notably) and offense definitions (possession, endangerment, inchoate offenses), as well as procedural and institutional aspects (preliminary judicial diagnosis of dangerousness, followed by expert diagnosis by psychiatrists and penologists, reviewed by prison officials) were designed with this goal in mind.

Packer's framework of two models of the criminal process likewise encompasses the entire penal system, including substantive and procedural features. The "due process" model (characterized by a firm commitment to mens rea, in the substantive realm, and the jury trial and the presumption of innocence, procedurally speaking) pursued justice; the "crime control" model (characterized by strict liability, plea bargaining, and the presumption of guilt) pursued efficiency. It is not difficult to see Packer's two models as a particular, post–World War II, American version of the distinction between penal police and penal law, one that proceeds from a happy consensus about the decency of state officials pursuing the public interest, with no inkling of the decades-long radically divisive and racialized war on crime that was to come. Packer first drew the distinction in 1964; the book version, hopefully entitled *The Limits of the Criminal Sanction*, appeared in 1968,[25] the same year that Richard Nixon called for a war of "the peace forces" against "the criminal forces in this country."

Hart's great article on "The Aims of Criminal Law"[26] is a Legal Process tour de force that regards the criminal process from the perspectives of its designers and participants, ranging from constitution-makers to legislators to police and prosecutors to courts to "correctional authorities" (though not the jury, the defendant, the defense attorney, or the victim). Unlike Wechsler in the MPC, Hart was not content to assume that the new social sciences (including criminology and penology) had produced the definitive scientific account of crime and its punishment, or rather "treatment," which stayed clear of vague and indeterminate concepts such as autonomy, voluntariness, the will, or guilt. By contrast, Hart did not treat the very idea of punishment as taboo and refused to replace references to punishment with the euphemism of "treatment"; instead, he declared sweepingly, and (to his mind) self-evidently, that "the function of law" and therefore also of *criminal* law, "is to enable [man] to realize his potentialities as a human

[25] Herbert L. Packer, *The Limits of the Criminal Sanction* (1968); Herbert L. Packer, *Two Models of the Criminal Process*, 113 U. Pa. L. Rev. 1. (1964).

[26] Henry M. Hart Jr., *The Aims of the Criminal Law*, 23 L. & Contemp. Probs. 401 (1958).

being through the forms and modes of social organization," and, in particular, the "personal capacity for responsible decision."[27]

Hart didn't produce an argument for these majestic assertions, in terms of the commitments of the modern liberal legal-political project in general, or of the American version of this project in particular, nor did he lay out a historical, or comparative, account of the foundation and evolution of this conception of law in general, and of criminal law in particular. But he did recognize the need to address these basic issues of law as a mode of governance, and of criminal law as one—and one uniquely significant—instance of that mode. At the same time, Hart took a systemic view of penality as criminal legal process, including all of its aspects regardless of their traditional classification as substantive or procedural, with an eye toward designing it to best serve "the aims of criminal law."

Viewed in this light, Hart's essay illustrates one way of moving beyond the distinction between the substance-centered German approach and the process-centered American approach to the analysis of state penal power through law. Only an integrative, systemic perspective on the state penal regime can hope to generate an account of its features and operation comprehensive enough to make possible the sort of deep, wide, and continuous critique of the exercise of state penal power against the legitimatory Grundnorm of law, autonomy, that a commitment to the modern liberal legal-political project would require.

References

Comparative Criminal Procedure (Jacqueline E. Ross & Stephen C. Thaman eds. 2016)

Markus D. Dubber, *The Police Power: Patriarchy and the Foundations of American Government* (2005)

Markus D. Dubber, *The Dual Penal State: The Crisis of Criminal Law in Comparative-Historical Perspective* (2018)

Markus D. Dubber & Tatjana Hörnle, *Criminal Law: A Comparative Approach* (2014)

Adhémar Esmein, *A History of Continental Criminal Procedure: With Special Reference to France* (1913)

Foundational Texts in Modern Criminal Law (Markus D. Dubber ed., 2014)

From the Judge's Arbitrium to the Legality Principle: Legislation as a Source of Law in Criminal Trials 365 (Georges Martyn, Anthony Musson & Heikki Pihlajamäki eds., 2013)

Paul D. Halliday, *Habeas Corpus: From England to Empire* (2010)

The Handbook of Comparative Criminal Law (Kevin Heller & Markus D. Dubber eds., 2010)

Henry M. Hart Jr., *The Aims of the Criminal Law*, 23 L. & Contemp. Probs. 401 (1958)

Douglas Hay, *Property, Authority and the Criminal Law*, in *Albion's Fatal Tree: Crime and Society in Eighteenth-Century England* 17 (Douglas Hay et al. eds., 1975)

Maximo Langer, *The Long Shadow of the Adversarial and Inquisitorial Categories*, in *The Oxford Handbook of Criminal Law* 887 (Markus D. Dubber & Tatjana Hörnle eds., 2014)

Herbert L. Packer, *Two Models of the Criminal Process*, 113 U. Pa. L. Rev. 1 (1964)

Symposium, *Lay Participation in Modern Law*, 3:2 Comp. Legal Hist. 224–324 (2016)

James Q. Whitman, *Harsh Justice: Criminal Punishment and the Widening Divide between America and Europe* (2005)

[27] *Id.* at 409, 440.

CHAPTER 2

FUNDAMENTAL VALUES OF CRIMINAL PROCEDURE

RICHARD L. LIPPKE

I. Introduction

THE aim of this chapter is to consider what fundamental values ought to inform criminal procedure. Put differently, the chapter steps back from the rules and procedures that exist in legal jurisdictions throughout the world and examines what we ideally should want from them. To some extent, the answer to this question might seem obvious—we very much want them to produce accurate outcomes, in the form of true convictions and the avoidance of false ones. Yet one suspects that what we want is more complex than accurate sorting, which, as anyone who has examined it already knows, is complex enough in its own right. The more complex thing we want likely will contain internal tensions, as it will be challenging to wrangle all of the fundamental values that ought to guide criminal procedure into a single, well-managed corral. Nothing I say in what follows should be taken as the last word on these matters. In fact, in closing the chapter, I consider whether there are other fundamental values of criminal procedure that my account sleights. I concede that there might be. My aim is to start a conversation, or continue one, that seems more often implicit than explicit in scholarship on criminal procedure.

The three fundamental values identified in this chapter are human dignity, truth, and fairness. The value of truth is parsed into two subsidiary values, integrity and rigor. It is easier to come up with a list of such values than to determine which of them are basic and which are derivative, to what extent they conflict or overlap, and how they are to be organized into a coherent scheme. My aim is the modest one of offering characterizations of them and illustrations of the ways in which they can be upheld or subverted by criminal justice practices. The illustrations I employ are drawn primarily from the United States, in the main because I know its system of criminal procedure best.

However, reference is also made to criminal procedure in other countries, including those in the civil law tradition.

It is natural to believe that criminal procedure begins with the investigation of crimes, or alleged crimes, except that efforts by the police to elicit crimes also fall under its purview.[1] A broad and diverse variety of legal requirements and ethical best practices guide the actions of criminal justice officials as they conduct investigations, arrest suspects, formally charge them with crimes, urge the courts to require postings of bail or institute pretrial detention, see to the adjudication of charges, assign sentences in cases of conviction, and participate in any post-conviction appeals. Criminal procedure ends when all post-conviction appeals are exhausted, though in some jurisdictions, new evidence might emerge after it appears that all appeals have been spent, evidence that the courts, or other official bodies, are tasked with evaluating.[2] Hence, just as the beginning of criminal procedure might be difficult to pinpoint, so is its cessation.

Importantly, the fundamental values identified in this chapter are abstract enough that they are unlikely to imply that there is a single best way to structure criminal procedure. There will instead be numerous ways to do so consistent with the values, as the diverse practices of criminal procedure in countries throughout the world suggest. Nonetheless, the values have enough determinacy to provide the basis for a critique of many existing practices.

II. Human Dignity

The first fundamental value is in some ways the easiest to identify and interpret, which is not to say that it poses no difficulties in interpretation.[3] It is the value of human dignity, according to which criminal justice officials of all kinds must conduct themselves in ways that are consistent with and supportive of the dignity of the persons against whom, as well as on behalf of whom, they act. The concept of "human dignity" is fraught. There is ongoing debate about what it means—in particular, whether it refers to some distinctive nonnatural property of humans or is simply another way of referring to certain natural

[1] As the debate about forms of proactive policing, and in particular what is known as "entrapment," illustrates. For an overview of that debate, see Maura F.J. Whelan, *Lead Us Not into (Unwarranted) Temptation: A Proposal to Replace the Entrapment Defense with a Reasonable Suspicion Requirement*, 133 U. Pa. L. Rev. 1193 (1985); Jonathan C. Carlson, *The Act Requirement and the Foundations of the Entrapment Defense*, 73 Va. L. Rev. 1011 (1987); and Gerald Dworkin, *The Serpent Beguiled Me and I Did Eat: Entrapment and the Creation of Crime*, 4 L. & Phil. 17 (1985).

[2] In England and Wales, a body known as The Criminal Cases Review Commission was set up to review apparent miscarriages of justice after all normal appeals have been exhausted. See Andrew Ashworth & Mike Redmayne, *The Criminal Process* 390 ff (4th ed. 2010).

[3] For illuminating discussion of some of the complexities of human dignity discourse in the context of judicial interpretation, see Christopher McCrudden, *Human Dignity and Judicial Interpretation of Human Rights*, 19 Eur. J. Int'l L. 655 (2008).

properties of humans, perhaps while exhorting us to respect those properties.[4] Though it is popular in some circles to dismiss Immanuel Kant's account of human dignity as being too focused on rationality, the core of that account, with its emphasis on the capacity of most adult human beings to reflect on their lives and attempt to shape them in accordance with that reflection, has rarely been improved upon.[5] Each of us is the subject of a life that typically matters, and matters significantly, to us. To respect and value our dignity is to act in ways that ensure that we can engage in self-shaping, subject to doing so in ways that allow others to do so.[6] It is relatively straightforward, from this account of reflective self-direction as the core of human dignity, to derive certain basic moral rights to which all persons are entitled. Such rights function to protect the prerequisites of reflective agency, in the forms of life, freedom from physical and psychological harm, liberty, privacy, and basic welfare.[7]

The dignity of individuals, with the basic moral rights it entails, normatively constrains the actions of all individuals, including those with responsibilities for investigating crimes, charging persons with them, and adjudicating the charges. One way to think about the way in which human dignity constrains the actions of criminal justice officials is in terms of its grounding presumptions against interfering with or infringing the basic moral rights of citizens. These presumptions, which can be rebutted, will vary in stringency, depending on the extent and ways in which official action intrudes upon individuals' basic rights.[8] For instance, stopping citizens and questioning them, which the police presumably must be able to do on occasion, constitute minimal and brief infringements on the rights of individuals. To justify them, and thus overcome the presumption that individuals ought to be able to exercise and enjoy their rights unfettered by official interference, the police should have to have (and be prepared to articulate and defend, in a court of law) something like "reasonable suspicion" of criminal activity on the part of those they stop. As measures more intrusive into the lives of the individuals they investigate are employed by the authorities, such as searches of suspects' homes, the burdens of justification on the authorities ought to rise. At the limit, before legal sanctions are imposed on individuals, state authorities should have to overcome the most stringent burden of proving their guilt beyond a reasonable doubt in a court of law. Short of that

[4] See, among others, Jeremy Waldron, *Dignity, Rank, and Rights* (2012); George Kateb, *Human Dignity* (2011); Michael Rosen, *Dignity: Its History and Meaning* (2012); Charles R. Beitz, *Human Dignity in the Theory of Human Rights: Nothing but a Phrase?*, 41 Phil. & Pub. Affairs 259 (2013).

[5] Immanuel Kant, *Groundwork of the Metaphysics of Morals* (Mary Gregor & Jens Timmerman trans., 2012), and *Critique of Practical Reason* (Mary J. Gregor trans., 1997).

[6] For a similar account of human dignity in the context of German constitutional law, see Edward J. Eberle, *Human Dignity, Privacy, and Personality in German and American Constitutional Law*, 1997 Utah L. Rev. 963.

[7] Here, I gloss over the debate about whether basic human rights are rights against interferences of various kinds by other individuals or state agents, or also include entitlements to basic welfare goods such as subsistence, education, and healthcare.

[8] I develop this account of rights as grounding progressively stronger presumptions against state agents interfering in the lives of suspects and accused persons in Richard L. Lippke, *Taming the Presumption of Innocence* (2016).

limit, if pretrial detention is used against persons charged with crimes, the presumption against interference with their basic rights should impose substantial burdens on criminal justice officials to justify such intrusive and enduring right-curtailment. Moreover, respect for the dignity of persons should require the authorities to provide material and symbolic conditions of pretrial detention that affirm their status as rational, self-directing beings whose lives matter and, just as important, have not yet been convicted of any crimes.[9] Thus, squalid and, degrading pretrial detention, marked by the absence of such things as proper sanitation, privacy, work, and visitation, should be seen as contrary to the dignity of suspects.

The dignity of suspects or of formally accused persons grounds numerous other constraints on their treatment by criminal justice officials. It rules out coercive interrogation techniques, or ones that rely on various forms of extended deprivation—of food, drink, sleep, or social interaction.[10] Abuses such as these will be less likely to occur if accused persons are provided access to defense attorneys. If the accused cannot afford them, then the state should see to it that competent and motivated attorneys are provided for them.[11] Defense attorneys also support their clients' dignity by ensuring that their sides of the story are presented to the authorities or the courts. Further, by insisting that police, prosecutor, and the courts abide by rules of full and fair due process, defense attorneys convey to their clients and to the world that their clients' reputations and liberty matter and cannot be taken from them without proper procedures being adhered to.

Non-trial charge adjudication can likewise comport poorly with the dignity of accused persons in some instances. Plea concessions, in the form of proffers by prosecutors (or judges) of reduced sentences or charges in exchange for guilty pleas or confessions, might be defended on the ground that they provide inducements that are not coercive. So long as accused persons will, if they refuse them and are convicted after trials, receive no worse than sentences proportional to the seriousness of their crimes, such concessions can be cast as providing accused persons with undeserved leniency.[12] Yet this defense of sentence and charge concessions is harder to make if sentences are systematically disproportionate to begin with and plea concessions serve only to bring them closer to proportionality.[13] Further, threats by prosecutors of added charges or trial penalties, aimed at accused persons who balk at admitting their guilt, seem undeniably coercive. If carried out, they can produce sentences that bear little relation to the seriousness of the

[9] *Id.* at 158–62.

[10] For discussion of dignity in the context of police interrogation, see Meghan J. Ryan, Miranda*'s Truth: The Importance of Adversarial Testing and Dignity in Confession Law*, 43 N. Ky. L. Rev. 413 (2016).

[11] The claim that indigent persons should be provided defense attorneys at state expense is more controversial than is sometimes acknowledged by legal scholars. For discussion, see Loren E. Lomasky, *Aid without Egalitarianism: Assisting Indigent Defendants*, in *From Social Justice to Criminal Justice* 84 (William Heffernan & John Kleinig eds., 2000), and Richard L. Lippke, *The Minimal State and Indigent Defense*, 35 Crim. Justice Ethics 1 (2016).

[12] See, e.g., Thomas W. Church Jr., *In Defense of "Bargain Justice,"* 13 L. & Soc'y Rev. 509 (1979).

[13] On the harshness of recent U.S. sentencing law, see Michael Tonry, *Sentencing in America, 1975–2025*, 42 Crime & Justice 141 (2013).

crimes committed by the accused; such vindictive add-ons exist to intimidate or punish exercise of the right to trial, in defiance of the dignity of the accused.[14]

The dignity of the accused is further undermined if state officials decline to reveal the nature and quality of the evidence against them. Yet there are jurisdictions in which accused persons enter guilty pleas in the absence of such knowledge. In the United States, for instance, the accused can seek discovery of the evidence against them, and by law prosecutors are supposed to comply with requests for its disclosure, although often only at trial rather than during plea negotiations.[15] However, the reality is that prosecutors often penalize accused persons whose attorneys make such requests by offering them poorer quality plea deals.[16] Outside the United States, disclosure of the evidence against accused persons is more often the norm, ensuring, as it does, that the accused (with the help of their attorneys) can make informed choices about what is surely an important decision in their lives.[17]

Finally, it is natural to see the vaunted right against self-incrimination as grounded in the value of human dignity. Much of the scholarly literature on the right against self-incrimination focuses on criminal trials and the question whether accused persons can be forced to testify on pain of being found in contempt of court if they refuse to do so.[18] There is also the question whether such refusals permissibly can be cited by prosecutors or judges as evidence of the guilt of the accused. Important as these issues are, state efforts to induce suspects and formally accused persons to incriminate themselves start well before trials occur, if they occur at all. Coercive or harsh police station interrogation techniques aim at getting suspects to admit their guilt.[19] Pretrial detention in squalid local jails can be seen as an indirect way of inducing the accused to accede to guilty pleas. Without question, menacing accused persons with substantial sentencing differentials should they insist on going to trial, especially when those differentials are born of threatened trial penalties or strategic over-charging, is a strategy aimed at compelling accused persons to admit their guilt. Arguably, all of these actions by government officials comport poorly with respecting the dignity of suspects and accused persons.

[14] See Richard L. Lippke, *The Ethics of Plea Bargaining* 43–49 (2011).

[15] See United States v. Ruiz, 536 U.S. 622, 628, 631 (2002) (holding that prosecutors can make plea bargains contingent on defendants waiving their right to disclosure of impeachment evidence against prosecution witnesses, and describing rights to exculpatory and impeachment evidence are "trial-related rights" that are "part of [the] basic 'fair trial' guarantee"); *id.* at 633–34 (Thomas, J., concurring) (disclosure rights are "not implicated at the plea stage").

[16] See Milton Heumann, *Plea Bargaining: The Experiences of Prosecutors, Judges, and Defense Attorneys* 69–70 (1978); *Ruiz*, 536 U.S. 622 (approving prosecutor tactic to make a favorable plea bargain contingent on defendant waiving some discovery rights). For other failures of "informed" consent in U.S. plea bargaining, see Jenia I. Turner, *Plea Bargaining across Borders* 40–41 (2009), and Darryl K. Brown, *Free Market Justice: How Democracy and Laissez Faire Undermine the Rule of Law* 107 (2016).

[17] Turner, *supra* note 16, at 40.

[18] For illuminating discussions, see David Dolinko, *Is There a Rationale for the Privilege against Self-Incrimination?*, 33 UCLA L. Rev. 1063 (1986), and John D. Jackson & Sarah J. Summers, *The Internationalisation of Criminal Evidence*, 241–84 (2012).

[19] Albert Alschuler, *A Peculiar Privilege in Historical Perspective*, in *The Privilege against Self-Incrimination: Its Origins and Development* (R.H. Helmholz et al. eds., 1997).

III. Truth

The claim that the dignity of persons establishes successive normative hurdles that criminal justice officials must surmount before they can justifiably inflict legal punishment on individuals points us in the direction of the second fundamental value of criminal procedure. The value of truth is more often trumpeted in civil law jurisdictions than common law ones.[20] Indeed, there is some tendency in common law jurisdictions, and especially in the United States, to cast criminal procedure as being primarily concerned with dispute resolution rather than with getting at the truth of the charges that officials have levied against individuals.[21] It might also seem that getting at the truth, as a fundamental value of criminal procedure, sets too lofty and abstract a goal—too lofty because we sometimes will not know whether we have achieved it, especially in complex criminal cases; too abstract because it might seem incapable of providing us with specific, practical guidance about how to structure investigatory and adjudicative processes.

However, if we take seriously the notion of honoring the dignity of persons, and especially of those charged with crimes, this would seem to require of us assiduous efforts to discern whether or not they have engaged in the criminal misconduct of which we suspect and have accused them.[22] Legal punishment condemns and imposes hard treatment on persons for public wrongs.[23] Acting in the public's name and on its behalf, legal officials thereby curtail some of the most basic moral rights of persons proven to be offenders. Legal punishment also damages individuals in ways that make it difficult for them to return to society and exercise their basic rights once their sentences have been served. If this is not a morally freighted enterprise, it is difficult to understand what would be. Moreover, the victims of crimes, when there are victims, likewise have significant stakes in having their interests vindicated by the criminal justice system.[24] Yet this will not occur if officials are incompetent, lazy, or cavalier about the outcomes of their work, or if they are more concerned to strike quick deals with the accused rather than achieve accurate outcomes in criminal cases. The truth about what happened to victims, just as the truth about what the accused have or have not done matters to them and all of us, or should.

Nevertheless, I have some sympathy for the notion that we should try to say, with greater specificity, how we should structure criminal procedure so that it will get at the

[20] See, e.g., Thomas Weigend, *Is the Criminal Process about Truth? A German Perspective*, 26 Harv. J.L. Pub. Pol'y 157 (2003); Mirjan R. Damaška, *Truth in Adjudication*, 49 Hastings L.J. 289 (1998); Elisabetta Grande, *Dances of Criminal Justice: Thoughts on Systematic Differences and the Search for the Truth*, in *Crime, Procedure and Evidence in Comparative and International Context: Essays in Honour of Professor Mirjan Damaška* (John Jackson, Máximo Langer & Peter Tiller eds., 2008).

[21] See Albert W. Alschuler, *The Changing Plea Bargaining Debate*, 69 Cal. L. Rev. 652 (1981).

[22] Though as Damaška, *supra* note 20, at 305 observes, there is a typically some asymmetry in the stringency of the criminal law's efforts to prove the guilt of the accused versus prove their innocence.

[23] On the criminal law as punishing "public wrongs," see R.A. Duff, Lindsay Farmer, Sandra Marshall & Victor Tadros, III, *The Trial on Trial: Towards a Normative Theory of the Criminal Trial* (2007).

[24] See, e.g., Jean Hampton, *A New Theory of Retribution*, in *Liability and Responsibility: Essays in Law and Morals* (R.G. Frey & C.W. Morris eds., 1991).

truth. I believe that it is useful to identify two subsidiary values in the service of truth. The first is integrity, according to which the various state agents tasked with arresting, investigating, and charging individuals with crimes, and seeing to the adjudication of charges, must respect and consistently abide by procedures that are reliable and evidence-driven. The second subsidiary value is rigor, according to which investigatory and adjudicatory processes must have checks and balances in place to ensure that the official decisions that advance individuals further into and through the criminal justice system are tested repeatedly, culminating, if need be, in trials at which the state must establish the guilt of the accused beyond a reasonable doubt. Let me elaborate these two values in turn.

1. Integrity

It is apparent that arrests, investigations, and prosecutions are subject to a wide variety of human errors and biases, ones that are often compounded by pressures on police, prosecutors, and the courts to efficiently process a high volume of cases.[25] Police and criminal investigators, in particular, must be trained and encouraged to avoid methods that are well known to produce errors. These include the use of coercive interrogation techniques, the manipulation of lineups for purposes of identifying possible perpetrators of criminal acts, and the threatening, co-optation, or coaching of witnesses. Worse than all of these, of course, is the planting of inculpatory evidence or the concealment of exculpatory evidence. Prosecutors also must be committed to an evidence-driven process, one that requires them to reveal exculpatory evidence to judges or the defense, and to avoid pressuring witnesses to alter or shade their testimony.[26] Prosecutors also should avoid the use of evidence that science has not validated or long history has shown to be dubious, or at least they should be judicious in drawing conclusions from such evidence or urging others to do so. Police and prosecutors also should be trained to recognize and resist their own biases—whether of racial, gender, or ethnic kinds—as well as to recognize and resist cognitive biases that push them toward hasty conclusions about those under their purview.[27]

It is tempting to believe that criminal procedure will be evidence-driven so long as criminal trials are appropriately structured. There must be a public airing of the charges and evidence against the accused, and the accused, aided by competent counsel, must have genuine opportunities to contest the state's case or put forward a defense. An impartial judge or jury that employs the reasonable doubt standard must then render a verdict. However, given the ubiquity of guilty pleas or confessions by the accused in

[25] See Keith A. Findlay & Michael S. Scott, *The Multiple Dimensions of Tunnel Vision in Criminal Cases*, 2006 Wis. L. Rev. 291 (2006).

[26] See Dan Simon, *The Limited Diagnosticity of Criminal Trials*, 64 Vand. L. Rev. 143 (2011).

[27] Findlay & Scott, *supra* note 25, at 307–22.

many legal systems, many cases never go to trial or have only perfunctory ones.[28] If such abbreviated adjudicative procedures are to be evidence-driven, prosecutors and judges must be denied the ability to pressure pleas or confessions with promises of substantial charge or sentencing concessions—or worse, threats of trial penalties if the accused insists on going to trial only to be subsequently convicted.[29] Simply put, the larger the potential sentencing differential between trial and non-trial adjudication, the less we will have assurance that it is the evidence, rather than the differential, that plays the crucial role in producing the outcomes of non-trial adjudication. The sentencing differential must be kept modest for this signally important reason.

Even criminal trials might not be as strongly or reliably evidence-driven as they should be. For instance, the evidence that juries in U.S. trials see is often "synthesized," meaning that it has been doctored or manipulated in a variety of ways by police, prosecutors and defense attorneys.[30] Eyewitnesses to crimes, or prosecution witnesses of other kinds, are often coached to appear more confident or consistent than they really are or were in their initial statements to the authorities. The process by which the police elicited "confessions" from suspects is rarely videotaped, and yet we have good reason to believe that many confessions are gained in ways that stain their credibility.[31] Defense attorneys also coach witnesses, of course. It might be hoped that coaching by both sides will more or less "even things out," but it is difficult to see how pervasive evidence manipulation will reliably enable jurors to arrive at sound judgments concerning the validity of the charges against the accused.[32] Importantly, jurors might not be aware of the extent to which the evidence with which they are presented has been doctored by advocates on both sides. In continental legal systems, by contrast, the judges who preside over trials receive full case dossiers in advance. This presumably enables them to ask probing questions of witnesses or the accused who testify. Judges in civil law countries might also be aware of the ways in which witnesses can be coached, and be prepared to ask the police hard questions about the conditions under which confessions were obtained.[33] Moreover, in some continental systems, even full confessions do not absolve the courts from inquiring into the other evidence against accused persons.[34]

[28] Even if plea bargaining, U.S. style, does not exist in many countries, plea concessions of various kinds do, as does reduced punishment for confessing. See Turner, *supra* note 16. See also Máximo Langer, *From Legal Transplants to Legal Translations: The Globalization of Plea Bargaining and the Americanization Thesis in Criminal Procedure*, 45 Harv. Int'l L.J. 1 (2004).

[29] On the distinction between rewards for pleading guilty and threats for failing to do so in the form of trial penalties, see Lippke, *supra* note 14, at 10–37.

[30] Simon, *supra* note 26, at 150–51.

[31] Findlay & Scott, *supra* note 25, at 334–41.

[32] See David Luban, *Lawyers and Justice: An Ethical Study* 68–74 (1988).

[33] Although witness coaching, or "proofing" as it is often termed, is prohibited in civil law countries. Nonetheless, judges armed with full case dossiers will be more capable of determining whether it has occurred. For more on civil law practices as opposed to U.S. practices in preparing witnesses, see Kai Ambos, *"Witness Proofing" before the ICC: Neither Legally Admissible nor Necessary*, in *The Emerging Practice of the International Criminal Court* 599 (Carsten Stahn & Göran Sluiter eds., 2009).

[34] Turner, *supra* note 16, at 74; Langer, *supra* note 28, at 11.

Jurors in common law systems, and particularly in the United States, are probably not helped with the difficult task of evaluating the evidence presented to them by the excesses of the adversary process.[35] The hope is that the adversary process will provide jurors with diverse and well-argued viewpoints on the evidence, ones that jurors will then have to sort through to arrive at conclusions about the state's success or failure at having satisfied the reasonable doubt standard. Yet it might be overly optimistic to believe that adversary efforts to (sometimes dishonestly or misleadingly) embellish the evidence in support of one side, while (sometimes dishonestly or misleadingly) discrediting the evidence in support of the other side will put citizen jurors in a position to figure out anything with a high degree of skill or confidence. The contrast between the adversary process in this regard and trials in civil law countries in which judges, armed with complete case dossiers in advance of the trial and concerned, ultimately, to get at the truth regarding the charges against accused persons, is stark. It is not that judges in civil law countries cannot or do not make mistakes or do not have axes to grind, so to speak. But defense attorneys and prosecutors in such systems, while they can suggest lines of inquiry to judges, are not permitted to try to intimidate or badger truthful witnesses, or trip up the accused who take the stand to testify, with little regard for the truthfulness of their testimony.[36]

To this point, I have emphasized the ways in which integrity requires us to devise investigatory and adjudicative processes that are driven by evidence that we have good reason to believe is accurate and reliable. Yet the value of integrity includes a vital attitudinal component.[37] Officials must not only employ reliable methods while gathering and evaluating evidence; they must be committed to doing so on a continuing basis. Thus, they must assiduously avoid corrupting or short-circuiting the process, even if this means tolerating its "inefficiency." To do so is, some would claim, part of what it means to abide by the "presumption of innocence" for individuals accused of crimes. The presumption is designed to regulate the attitudes and conduct of officials (and citizens more generally) during the course of the investigative and adjudicative process. Individuals arrested on suspicion of criminal conduct, charged with crimes, or awaiting disposition of their cases are to be presumed innocent so that officials, or the public, are not tempted to treat them as guilty and punish or ostracize them prematurely.[38]

Alternatively, it has been suggested that non-presumptions of material and probative guilt make more sense in the investigatory and adjudication phases.[39] After all, the presumption of innocence seems difficult to square with the many impositions on the

[35] Simon, *supra* note 26, at 184–89.

[36] See Richard S. Frase, *Comparative Criminal Justice as a Guide to American Law Reform: How Do the French Do It, How Can We Find Out, and Why Should We Care?*, 78 Cal. L. Rev. 545, 673 (1990).

[37] For an insightful consideration of "integrity" with regard to police investigation, witness preparation, plea negotiation, and related contexts, see *The Integrity of Criminal Process: From Theory into Practice* (Jill Hunter, Paul Roberts, Simon N.M. Young & David Dixon eds., 2016).

[38] See Thomas Weigend, *There Is Only One Presumption of Innocence*, 42 Netherlands J. Legal Phil. 193 (2013); R.A. Duff, *Who Must Presume Whom to Be Innocent of What?*, 42 Netherlands J. Legal Phil. 170 (2013).

[39] Lippke, *supra* note 8, at 129–54; Larry Laudan, *Truth, Error, and Criminal Law: An Essay in Legal Epistemology* (2006).

freedom of accused persons that are routinely tolerated. It also seems inconsistent with the real doubts about their innocence that may emerge well before any charges against them have been fully processed. What unites the standard position and this alternative is the critical importance of recognizing both the fallibility of criminal justice actors and the unpredictability of the process of investigating crimes and adjudicating charges. It is the premature rush to judgment about the material or probative guilt of the accused that, too often, produces mistakes that harm innocent, or perhaps partly innocent individuals.[40] The integrity of the process requires officials to be patient, to resist inclinations to "make the evidence fit" their initial (and sometimes premature) conclusions about the actual or provable guilt of the persons whom they have accused of crimes. It might be possible to capture everything that we want of these officials with an elaborate set of rules or procedures. But my sense is that even the best rules and procedures for gathering and compiling evidence will be undermined if officials are grudging in following them or cynical about doing so.

2. Rigor

It is widely accepted that the state must meet a high standard of proof in criminal cases before convictions of persons charged with crimes are warranted.[41] The dominant way of conceptualizing and justifying the commitment to the reasonable doubt standard is in terms of its enabling us to achieve an optimal distribution of the errors that criminal trials, and investigatory and adjudicative processes more generally, invariably produce.[42] This "error distribution" approach holds that we make trials stern tests of the government's evidence against the accused in order to minimize false convictions as we attempt to produce true ones. According to the venerable Blackstone ratio, we are to tolerate the acquittals of ten guilty persons to the false conviction of a single innocent one.[43] Though this degree of preference for acquitting the guilty to convicting the innocent is questioned by some who favor the error distribution account, the consequentialist logic of the approach is widely accepted by legal scholars. Still, one worrisome implication of such an approach is that it makes the exacting proof structure of criminal trials contingent on its role in producing whatever is believed to be the optimal distribution of errors. This means that, should assumptions about that optimal distribution change, so too might the grounds for insisting on the reasonable doubt standard or other safeguards for accused persons.[44]

[40] By "partly innocent" persons, I refer to individuals who, though they have committed crimes, have been overcharged by prosecutors.

[41] See Jackson & Summers, *supra* note 18, at 96.

[42] See Laudan, *supra* note 39, at 63–88. See also Erik Lillquist, *Recasting Reasonable Doubt: Decision Theory and the Virtues of Variability*, 36 U.C-Davis L. Rev. 85 (2002); Michael L. DeKay, *The Difference between Blackstone-Like Error Ratios and Probabilistic Standards of Proof*, 21 L. & Social Inquiry 95 (1996); John Kaplan, *Decision Theory and the Factfinding Process*, 20 Stan. L. Rev. 1065 (1968).

[43] 4 William Blackstone, *Commentaries on the Laws of England* 420 (1769; Beacon Press 1962).

[44] As vividly illustrated by Larry Laudan in *The Rules of Trial, Political Morality, and the Costs of Error: Or, Is Proof beyond a Reasonable Doubt Doing More Harm than Good?*, in *Oxford Studies in Philosophy of Law* 195 (Leslie Green & Brian Leiter eds., 2011).

On the alternative, rights-based approach sketched earlier in my discussion of the value of human dignity, the case for rigorously testing the government's evidence is grounded in an account of what taking the basic rights of persons seriously requires of state officials before they impose legal punishment on them.[45] Such an account holds that as the state increasingly intrudes upon the rights of persons during the investigatory and adjudicatory processes, it should have to surmount successively stronger evidentiary barriers designed to shield those rights from official depredation. At the limit, before it can curtail basic rights in profound and often enduring ways through the infliction of legal punishment, the state should have to provide powerful proof of the criminal misconduct of persons. On this account, the need for rigorous proof of the state's charges is not vulnerable to shifting views about what standard of proof will produce the best consequences. Instead, it is anchored in an understanding of what respect for the rights of persons morally requires of us.

Setting this debate about the ultimate grounds for the reasonable doubt standard to one side, it is important to note the other ways in which the value of rigor should inform criminal procedure. Again, many criminal cases are resolved without trials. Even on the assumption that some forms of non-trial adjudication can be (if sufficiently constrained) appropriate, rigor seems vital at both earlier and subsequent points in the criminal justice process. Accordingly, we should set up criminal investigatory and adjudicatory procedures so that the state power to arrest, investigate, charge, adjudicate charges, and sentence the convicted is subject to checks and balances of various kinds. Put differently, we should embrace "deliberate inefficiency" in the design of investigatory and adjudicatory processes. No single official or small group of them, no matter how wise or benevolent, should have the authority to arrest, investigate, adjudicate, and sentence offenders. The dangers to such consolidated power, in the forms of error, laziness, corruption, and malevolence, are well known. Yet it is not enough to spread such responsibilities across numerous officials; we must also encourage if not require them to check and, if necessary, challenge or overturn the work of other officials when they have grounds for believing that those officials have acted in error or bad faith.

At what junctures should such checking and rechecking occur? First, prosecutors should monitor and query the work of police, including scrutinizing the arrests they have made and the evidence they have gathered. Unfortunately, it is well known that prosecutors rely on the police to do much of the work of investigating crimes and are understandably reluctant to challenge the evidence and claims that the police bring forward. Comity sometimes takes precedence over integrity and rigor.[46] Also, there is considerable variation in the discretion that the police have to arrest persons and, more importantly, refer cases to prosecutors. In the United States, police discretion with regard to these matters is considerable.[47] In other countries, it is more limited, such that

[45] See Lippke, *supra* note 8, at 105–28. For a similar account, see Duff et al., *supra* note 23, at 89–90.

[46] Findlay & Scott, *supra* note 25, at 327–31. See also Randolph N. Jonakait, *The Ethical Prosecutor's Misconduct*, 23 Crim. L. Bull. 550 (1997); Daniel Medwed, *Emotionally Charged: The Prosecutorial Charging Decision and the Innocence Revolution*, 31 Cardozo L. Rev. 2187 (2010).

[47] Joseph Goldstein, *Police Discretion Not to Invoke the Criminal Process: Low Visibility Decisions in the Administration of Justice*, 69 Yale L.J. 543 (1960).

police lack the authority to not pursue charges against persons arrested on suspicion of criminal misconduct; only prosecutors can make those decisions.[48]

Judges should scrutinize the work of both police and prosecutors, to ensure that they have acted according to defensible procedures, and perhaps more broadly, "best practices" for gathering evidence and building cases against those accused of crimes. Indeed, even if the accused are prepared to admit their guilt in exchange for modest sentence concessions, ones that do not overwhelm the evidence in a given case, judges should be required to ensure that there is sufficient evidence to warrant translating their admissions of guilt into convictions.[49] In civil law countries, judges are required to be more vigilant in their scrutiny of confessions or tendered guilty pleas.[50] In the United States, party control over the evidence renders judges more in the way of passive bystanders in the plea process.[51]

Defense attorneys play a crucial role in promoting the rigor of criminal procedure, especially in common law systems in which judges are more passive. This is true whether defense attorneys are employees of the state, subsidized by the state, or privately employed. It is defense attorneys, more than the accused themselves, who can challenge evidence that is unreliable or insufficient, or who can complain if their clients are being pressured to admit guilt despite the scantiness of the state's evidence against them.[52] Also, as previously noted, defense attorneys can help to ensure that the accused are treated with dignity, rather than being deprived of more of their rights than is justified by the investigation and adjudication of charges.

Appellate review is a further layer of rigor, although what it consists of varies considerably across jurisdictions. Common law jurisdictions tend to limit review to the detection of legal errors and rights violations, whereas civil law systems lean toward more substantive re-evaluation of the verdicts rendered at trials, and sometimes permit the introduction of new evidence. These varying approaches to rigor are nonetheless consistent with providing those convicted of crimes some opportunity for further evaluation of the verdicts against them and the processes that produced them. However, in some jurisdictions, the higher courts have rendered appellate review something of a toothless tiger by adopting "harmless error" doctrines with regard to mistaken lower

[48] See Thomas Feltes, Uwe Marquardt & Stefan Schwarz, *Policing in Germany: Developments in the Last 20 Years*, in *Handbook on Policing in Central and Eastern Europe* (Gorazd Meško et al. eds., 2013).

[49] See Lippke, *supra* note 14, at 16–23.

[50] For an account of German judicial supervision of plea dispositions in cases in which the accused are prepared to confess, see Turner, *supra* note 16, at 114–17. For a more skeptical account of judicial supervision in such cases, see Abraham S. Goldstein & Martin Marcus, *The Myth of Judicial Supervision in Three "Inquisitorial" Systems: France, Italy, and Germany*, 87 Yale L.J. 240 (1977).

[51] The notion of "party control" over the evidence comes from Mirjan R. Damaška, *The Faces of Justice and State Authority: A Comparative Approach to the Legal Process* (1986). For the ways in which the abilities of prosecutors and defense attorneys to control the evidence the judge sees abets "fact bargaining" in the United States, see Nancy J. King, *Judicial Oversight of Negotiated Sentences in a World of Bargained Punishment*, 58 Stan. L. Rev. 593 (2005).

[52] See John B. Mitchell, *The Ethics of the Criminal Defense Attorney—New Answers to Old Questions*, 32 Stan. L. Rev. 293 (1980).

court rulings against the interests of the accused.[53] In the United States, convictions are also allowed to stand in spite of findings that the accused were inadequately represented by legal counsel, and this in spite of the well-known difficulties in determining whether the evidence against the accused would have been significantly different had a competent attorney been available to question it or block its introduction.[54]

Importantly, this checking and rechecking of the work of criminal justice officials by other officials, and perhaps also by the public, will be possible only if the grounds for decisions made by officials are, to the maximum extent feasible, transparent. Indeed, transparency might be trumpeted as a fundamental value of criminal procedure in its own right.[55] Here I treat it as subservient to the value of rigor. Officials throughout the system should be required and encouraged not only to act with integrity but to explain the grounds for their decisions. Doing so will enable others to evaluate those decisions and, if necessary, challenge or overturn them.

There is debate about the specific forms that the institutional commitment to rigor should take. In many of the civil law systems, the strong preference is for professionalized bureaucracies to handle the work of investigating and adjudicating criminal charges. Such bureaucracies provide education and training to officials and situate them in hierarchical organizations that continuously monitor and, if necessary, correct their work.[56] The public, as a further check on the workings of the criminal justice system, is kept at arm's length, since those workings tend to be conceived as matters involving expertise more than lay input.

In common law systems, at least some of the work of monitoring and checking the decisions of criminal justice officials is relegated to the public.[57] This is especially true in the United States, where key officials in the criminal justice system are elected. In common law jurisdictions, there is also the distinctive commitment to having juries populated by ordinary citizens. Some who defend jury trials cast them as a vital check on the power of the state to punish.[58] They do so in spite of the fact that citizen jurors are often untrained and inexperienced in deploying complex legal terms and rules, unaware of the extent to which the evidence they are presented with is "synthesized," and not required to provide reasons for their verdicts. The latter practice, in particular, appears to fly in the face of transparency; citizen juries are "black boxes" into which evidence is poured and from which verdicts emerge unexplained. It is possible to defend this practice as crucial to ensuring the independence of the jury's judgments from the control of other government

[53] Findlay & Scott, *supra* note 25, at 348–54. See also Brandon L. Garrett, *Innocence, Harmless Error, and Federal Wrongful Conviction Law*, 2005 Wis. L. Rev. 35 (2005); Harry T. Edwards, *To Err Is Human, But Not Always Harmless: Why Should Legal Error Be Tolerated?*, 70 NYU L. Rev. 1167 (1995).

[54] See Strickland v. Washington, 466 U.S. 669 (1984) For discussion of the limits of the ability of the courts to determine whether a more effective attorney would have produced a different outcome for the accused, see Stephanos Bibas, *The Psychology of Hindsight and After-the-Fact Review of Ineffective Assistance of Counsel*, 2004 Utah L. Rev. 1.

[55] See Stephanos Bibas, *Transparency and Participation in Criminal Procedure*, 81 NYU L. Rev. 911 (2006).

[56] See Damaška, *supra* note 51, at 18–23. [57] See Brown, *supra* note 16, at 25–60.

[58] For useful discussion of instrumentalist versus noninstrumentalist accounts of trials, see Duff et al., *supra* note 23, at 55–92. See also Albert W. Dzur, *Punishment, Participatory Democracy, and the Jury* (2012).

officials. Yet it is hard to see how general verdicts, so-called, are fully consistent with seeing to it that trials are rigorous and evidence-driven.[59]

Why separate integrity and rigor and insist on both? The answer to this question can be discerned by thinking about how employment of the reasonable doubt standard in determinations of guilt or its absence, though obviously crucial in the adjudicative process, will be useless if the authorities, up to that point, have fabricated, manipulated, or shaded evidence against the accused. Judges or juries tasked with rendering verdicts in criminal cases must work with the evidence provided to them. If that evidence has not been produced with integrity, then even the most stringent standard of proof will do little to shield the innocent, or partly innocent, from conviction. Even the more elaborate checks and balances of most criminal justice systems will be thwarted if some officials are determined to gain convictions dishonestly or without sufficient care. In short, rigor in the absence of integrity will be impotent to produce just adjudicative outcomes.

IV. Fairness

The third fundamental value is that of fairness. In light of the other values so far discussed, fairness might seem redundant. Surely, the other values already identified are necessary, and might be deemed sufficient, to ensure the fairness of criminal procedure. Yet the fairness to which I now draw attention has a distinctive and limited role. Suppose that the persons suspected of, arrested for, and charged with crimes are treated with dignity. Suppose also that the investigatory and adjudicative procedures to which they are subjected have integrity and rigor. What could possibly go wrong if all of these conditions are satisfied? To see the answer to this question, consider how persons are introduced into the system, and thereby become suspects, arrestees, or individuals formally accused of crimes. Police and prosecutors might routinely and systematically focus on some (apparently) non-law-abiding citizens while ignoring others who are equally or more (apparently) non-law-abiding. Historically, the tendency for the authorities to focus their attention on the apparent or real criminal misconduct of the poor, racial or ethnic minorities, or immigrants, while ignoring or not vigorously pursuing the apparent or real criminal misconduct of the wealthy, powerful, or ethnically or culturally dominant majority is deeply troublesome.

There are myriad reasons for this skewed focus. They range from overt prejudice to implicit bias to the ease with which socially marginal communities can be policed and their apparent malefactors arrested and prosecuted.[60] Police and prosecutors often are granted enormous discretion to carry out their difficult and complex tasks. The degree

[59] For discussion, see Richard L. Lippke, *The Case for Reasoned Criminal Trial Verdicts*, 22 Canadian J. L. & Jurisp. 313 (2009).

[60] See Michelle Alexander, *The New Jim Crow: Mass Incarceration in the Age of Colorblindness* (2010); Michael Tonry, *Malign Neglect: Race, Crime, and Punishment in America* (1996); William J. Stuntz, *Race, Class, and Drugs*, 98 Colum. L. Rev. 1795 (1998).

to which this discretion is monitored and limited by the courts, or by professional bureaucracies, varies considerably. In the United States, for instance, prosecutorial charging discretion is largely unfettered.[61] Chief prosecutors might exercise some oversight and control over the charging decisions of their subordinates, but whether and how far they do so varies and depends entirely on the inclinations of chief prosecutors. Judges rarely, if ever, second-guess prosecutorial charging decisions and the courts have made it difficult for accused persons who believe that those decisions have been made in biased fashion to legally contest them.[62] U.S. courts have also made pretextual police stops legal and turned a more or less blind eye to "stop and frisk" tactics that focus disproportionate police scrutiny on minority citizens.[63] Add into this mix the sorry state of the indigent defense system in the United States, along with the prodigious ability of prosecutors to manipulate the sentencing differential, and the path is cleared for quick and easy convictions of poor and minority members of society.

As critics of the U.S. system note, its "assembly line" approach is especially apparent in misdemeanor cases in which no one—not police, prosecutors, defense attorneys, or judges—have much interest in slowing the process or avoiding mistakes.[64] The unfortunate members of society who find themselves on the assembly line are often so demoralized by the apparent inevitability of its outcomes that they quickly accede to guilty pleas. As one scholar has noted, sometimes the only "evidence" against persons accused of misdemeanors is the fact that they have been arrested by the police.[65] There are costs to wider society in the perceived unfairness of a criminal justice system that picks on its most vulnerable members and subjects them to investigatory and adjudicative procedures that are not only cavalier about their actual guilt or innocence but ignore the equal or greater criminal misconduct of the privileged.[66] The alienation from the system that this sense of unfairness breeds will make it harder to police and prosecute legitimate crimes.

Hence, a third fundamental value, that of fairness, seems needed. It holds that state officials must strive to treat like citizens alike with respect to their apparent infidelity to the strictures of the criminal law. This value should inform the actions of police and criminal investigators, in the first instance. However, it should also shape the conduct of the prosecutors and judges who make decisions about whether to pursue or abjure charges, modify them, or seek alternatives to more standard forms of prosecution, such as restorative justice conferences, or specialty courts. The possibility that kinder or gentler case dispositions are afforded some offenders more often or quickly than other ones, based on factors such as race, gender, ethnicity, or class, should be something that is on

[61] See Angela J. Davis, *Arbitrary Justice: The Power of the American Prosecutor* (2007).

[62] See Alexander, *supra* note 60, at 114–19.

[63] *Id.* at 66–69. See also Jeffrey Fagan & Garth Davies, *Street Stops and Broken Windows: Terry, Race, and Disorder in New York City*, 28 Fordham Urb. L.J. 457 (2000).

[64] See Alexandra Natapoff, *Misdemeanors*, 85 S. Cal. L. Rev. 1313 (2012); Josh Bowers, *Punishing the Innocent*, 156 U. Pa. L. Rev. 1117 (2007).

[65] Natapoff, *supra* note 64, at 1344–45.

[66] See Jeffrey Fagan & Tracy L. Meares, *Punishment, Deterrence, and Social Control: The Paradox of Punishment in Minority Communities*, 6 Ohio St. J. Crim. L. 173 (2008). More generally, see Tom R. Tyler, *Why People Obey the Law* (1990).

every criminal justice official's radar. More than this, official records that detail the demographic characteristics of those arrested, charged, and convicted, as well as the grounds for decisions to continue or discontinue investigations and prosecutions, should be compiled and routinely made available to researchers, government officials, and other interested parties.[67] Again, transparency will enable vital checks and balances within the criminal justice system, and larger society, to operate more effectively—in this case, to ensure that all citizens are treated fairly.

In civil law systems, fair treatment of all citizens, at least by prosecutors, might seem more likely under long-standing principles of "mandatory prosecution."[68] Such principles are supposed to ensure that prosecutorial charging decisions are rendered according to the facts and the law, exclusive of other factors that might sway prosecutors one way or the other. However, the pressures of case-processing seem to have eroded these principles, especially with respect to less serious criminal offenses, and thus prosecutorial offers of reduced charges or sentences in exchange for admissions of guilt have emerged. Yet such practices inevitably give prosecutors more discretion, and what comes with that discretion—the possibility that it will be exercised unfairly.

V. Concluding Remarks

I have already indicated that the values herein identified might conflict. Evidence exclusion rules, premised on protecting the dignity of persons, in the form or their privacy or intimate relationships, might block the state's efforts to gather reliable evidence against those whom it suspects of crimes. Likewise, insisting on the transparency of the adjudicative process might seem to conflict with shielding the (merely) accused from public contempt or ignominy, with its damaging effects on the enjoyment of their basic rights.[69] These and other tensions between and among the values would need to be addressed in a fuller accounting of their roles in criminal procedure. Regrettably, these more ambitious tasks will have to be postponed to another occasion. As noted at the outset of this chapter, my aim has been the limited one of sparking a debate about the fundamental values that should inform and shape criminal procedure. I hope to have shown that there is some merit to this project. More than this, I hope to have shown that the fundamental values I have identified are cogent in their own right and useful in evaluating the complex of institutions, rules, and practices that collectively comprise criminal procedure.

[67] As noted in Davis, *supra* note 61, at 100–03, the Supreme Court in *United States v. Armstrong*, 517 U.S. 456 (1996), effectively shielded prosecutors from having to reveal the grounds for their charging decisions.

[68] See Shawn Boyne, *Is the Journey from the In-Box to the Out-Box a Straight Line? The Drive for Efficiency and the Prosecution of Low-Level Criminality in Germany*, in *The Prosecutor in Transnational Perspective* 37 (Erik Luna & Marianne Wade eds., 2012).

[69] For illuminating discussion of the many questions raised by the public identification of suspects and offenders, see James B. Jacobs, *The Eternal Criminal Record* (2015).

Instead of drawing this discussion to a tidy close, let me illustrate its complexities by briefly discussing two further candidates for inclusion on the list of fundamental values of criminal procedure. The first is what might be termed the "effectiveness" of criminal procedure. Surely some attention ought to be paid to the success or failure of criminal justice systems in arresting, charging, and seeing to the punishment of legal malefactors. In societies that appear to over-criminalize and overpunish the conduct of their citizens, it will seem dubious to urge more or better policing, swifter and more efficient prosecution, and timely sentencing by the courts. Yet it is possible to imagine institutions and practices of criminal procedure that are so encumbered by complex rules and procedures, or whose officials are so demoralized, lazy, or corrupt, that few crimes are ever fully investigated or processed. As a result, crime might go more or less unchecked in the social order. Perhaps we take the effectiveness of our police, prosecutors, and courts for granted. Yet we should not do so, and therefore effectiveness might be advanced as a fundamental value of criminal procedure.[70]

Though I concede that effectiveness is an important virtue of any system of criminal justice, my sense is that it is more secondary than fundamental. Granted, we very much want police, prosecutors, and the courts to perform their vital roles and to do so in effective fashion. Yet the undoubted value of that seems appropriately limited and constrained by the other, more fundamental values of dignity, truth, and fairness. Those values have priority, even if they should not be interpreted in ways that make the jobs of criminal justice officials unduly difficult. But the devil is in the details here, for it is apparent that tensions between effectiveness and these other, more fundamental values exist and merit further analysis.

The second candidate for inclusion in an account of the fundamental values of criminal procedure was alluded to in my discussion of the value of truth and its ancillary components, integrity and rigor. It is a value—call it the value of "expertise"—that highlights important differences between the common law and civil law traditions. According to it, the various decisions involved in arresting, charging, and prosecuting persons for crimes ought to be made by officials specifically educated and trained to make them. Those decisions also should be monitored and corrected by more senior officials tasked with ensuring that the decisions made by lower-level officials have been made in accordance with proper (and public) rules and procedures, ones designed to ensure integrity and rigor, and thus get at the truth of allegations against accused persons.

There is much in the value of expertise to recommend it. However, it is controversial in ways that the other fundamental values I have defended are not. Part of the controversy has to do with specifying how much education or training are needed and how formal these must be; part of it has to do with determining how much monitoring and correction by others, and what kinds of it, are necessary or advisable. Even the U.S. criminal justice system, which in some ways seems to value democratic participation more than expertise, does not wholly eschew the latter. Police officers and investigators receive

[70] See Herbert L. Packer, *The Limits of the Criminal Sanction* 158–63 (1968), where he discusses the underlying values of the "crime control" model.

formal training and are subject to supervision by superiors. They also are mentored more informally by experienced officers and investigators. Similar things are true of subordinate prosecutors, who are not elected but appointed by chief prosecutors and, one would hope, overseen by them. Still, it must be conceded that the degree and quality of supervision that subordinate prosecutors receive will vary. Also, their superiors might have been elected, or in some cases appointed, on mostly political grounds. Any monitoring and correction of the decisions made by criminal justice officials by the democratic electorate will be anathema to those in the civil law tradition; political considerations, they might maintain, should have no role to play in the decisions made by those who advance accused persons through the criminal justice process.[71]

Still, there are dangers in expertise-ruled systems. They might become insular or their workings so opaque as to undermine the sense among citizens that the system is operating in the public's interests. There is also room for debate about whether citizens in democratic societies should have no or very little role in the complex processes whereby suspicions by the authorities that individuals have committed crimes are transformed into criminal convictions and sentences, with their potentially devastating consequences for individuals.[72] It could be argued that the debate here ought to be about at what points and in what ways the public should have input into the workings of the criminal justice system, not about whether it should have input at all.

References

Mirjan R. Damaška, *Truth in Adjudication*, 49 Hastings L.J. 289 (1998)

R.A. Duff, Lindsay Farmer, Sandra Marshall & Victor Tadros, III *The Trial on Trial: Towards A Normative Theory of the Criminal Trial* (2007)

The Integrity of Criminal Process: From Theory into Practice (Jill Hunter, Paul Roberts, Simon N.M. Young & David Dixon eds., 2016)

Larry Laudan, *Truth, Error, and Criminal Law: An Essay in Legal Epistemology* (2006)

Richard L. Lippke, *Taming the Presumption of Innocence* (2016)

——, *The Ethics of Plea Bargaining* (2011)

Christopher McCrudden, *Human Dignity and Judicial Interpretation of Human Rights*, 19 Eur. J. Int'l L. 655 (2008)

Jeremy Waldron, *Dignity, Rank, and Rights* (2012)

[71] See Brown, *supra* note 16, at 25–59.

[72] See Dzur, *supra* note 58, at 125–48. See also Stephanos Bibas, *The Machinery of Criminal Justice* (2012).

CHAPTER 3

EMPIRICAL APPROACHES TO CRIMINAL PROCEDURE

JACQUELINE S. HODGSON AND YU MOU

I. Introduction

It is difficult to think of any area of law where empirical research can be more valuable in understanding its core than that of criminal justice, or more precisely, criminal procedure. As Meares suggests, empiricism's relevance to criminal procedure is almost banal.[1] In operationalizing the norms of criminal law and justice, criminal procedure defines the limits of state power in bringing offenders to justice, and it sets the conditions under which individual freedoms can be restricted or removed. In this way criminal justice is an important manifestation of state power and sovereignty and the values upheld by the state, or at least the government of the day. Understanding the nature and exercise of this power beyond the rhetorical claims of government has the potential to tell us something about the fundamental relationship between the state and the individual.

Empirical research is well placed to contribute to this understanding. Statistical information can provide crucial baseline data, demonstrating the dominant forms of case disposal, attrition rates within certain offense types, or the different case pathways and outcomes experienced by young offenders or those of color, for example. Qualitative studies are able to go beyond this and unpack legal actors' motivations as well as the institutional, economic, sociopolitical, and professional drivers and constraints they experience in carrying out their role. Observational methods in particular show us the "fine-grained institutional details" and the ways that processes and organizations function in practice—not only in the binary sense of what is within or outside

[1] Tracey L. Meares, *Three Objections to the Use of Empiricism in Criminal Law and Procedure—And Three Answers*, 517 U. Ill. L. Rev. 851, 852 (2002).

what is permitted by the law, but also in the vast expanse that lies between these two points, in the exercise of discretion.[2]

In addition to deepening our understanding of the practices of criminal justice, we might also consider why we need empirical evidence to understand criminal procedure at all. Why do we not assume that criminal justice practice conforms to the rhetoric of the law and simply trust state officials to do a good job in keeping us safe and punishing only those guilty individuals? By asking this question, we are suggesting that empirical researchers are inherently skeptical. This skepticism is important in a democratic society, given that criminal justice deals with the exercise of the coercive power of the state. Independent empirical accounts of practice can reveal unknown and unforeseen ways in which law operates, offering the perspectives of those operationalizing the criminal process as well as those who are its subjects. Such accounts provide a broader understanding of legal, occupational and political cultures, the ideologies of legal actors, and the impact of these features on the daily experiences of suspects, defendants, victims, witnesses, and those working within the criminal justice process. Empirical studies interrogate external factors such as compliance with human rights standards and pan-European legislative measures; domestic policies such as managerialism and austerity that demand faster, cheaper justice; and more overtly political drivers that govern and shape criminal justice in sometimes unarticulated ways. And perhaps most important, in mapping the exercise of state power, such studies can provide a form of accountability and a measure of legitimacy.

A chapter of this nature is necessarily selective. It would be impossible to do justice to the huge variety of empirical studies on criminal justice across different topics and jurisdictions. Instead, we have chosen three broad and recurring themes that capture something of the criminal justice system as a complex social institution—legal culture, discretion, and policy. In the first section, we explore criminal justice from a sociopolitical perspective, examining the place of legal and occupational cultures and their influence on criminal justice law and practice. The second section focuses on the studies that shed light on some routine criminal justice practices, particularly how criminal justice institutions, such as the police and the prosecution, exercise discretion, and factors that influence juries' decision-making. Finally, the last section investigates the relationship between law and policy, that is, how public policies (such as austerity) impact criminal justice practices, as well as how empirical research on law has facilitated evidence-based policy.

II. Legal Culture, Rhetoric, and Reality

By referring to criminal justice as a system, we do not mean to suggest that it is a well-orchestrated unit, comprised of interdependent official agencies working toward a clear

[2] Robert M. Lawless, *What Empirical Legal Scholars Do Best*, 87 Temple L. Rev. 711, 715 (2015).

and common goal. This conjured harmonious image is a long way from the realities of criminal justice, where multiple and sometimes competing aims are pursued by different participants, who may be in ignorance of one another, or in competition over the allocation of responsibility or funding. These contrasting aims influence the way in which those working in criminal justice agencies perceive their own role, and the development of professional cultures and ideologies in response to the challenges and constraints of practice.[3] Added to this, the decisions of federal-level and supreme courts, or the supranational layers of European Union (EU) criminal justice and the fair trial requirements of the European Convention on Human Rights (ECHR), place demands on national systems that are sometimes hard to incorporate.[4] Thus, decision-making, albeit undertaken by the individuals within criminal justice institutions, should be seen as part of a wider collectively defined enterprise.

This holistic perspective, as Keith Hawkins has argued, is the key to the comprehension of decision-making in the criminal process.[5] Hawkins suggests that the social context, which shapes the decision-making process, can be understood in three dimensional layers, namely *surround*, *field*, and *frame*. The *surround* is concerned with the social, political, and economic environment that influences all forms of individual and organizational decisions within the criminal justice system. This includes: public concerns over terrorist threats, potential riots, or other forms of antisocial behavior; financial constraints and a diminishing budget of public spending on criminal justice sectors; and the publication of crime statistics and their political implications. The idea of the *field* describes a more proximate legal decision-making context defined by political conceptions of the ends that are served by the law, by legal regulations that are designed to secure those ends, and by political perceptions of how those provisions ought to be used in order to further this objective. The term *frame* is concerned with a number of variables that form the subjective aspects of decision-making. It can refer to cognitive matters of the individual or illicit considerations such as the social class, ethnicity, or agenda of the accused.

1. Sociopolitical Culture

As we focus on *surround* for a moment, we see that a number of empirical studies suggest that the criminal process cannot be meaningfully understood apart from its sociopolitical culture. Here criminal procedure is not merely a branch of law; it is an

[3] Malcolm Davies et al., *Criminal Justice* 11 (2010).

[4] Jacqueline Hodgson, *EU Criminal Justice: Crime Control and Due Process within a Framework of Mutual Recognition*, 37 N.C.J. Int'l L. & Com. Reg. 307 (2011); Jacqueline Hodgson, *Safeguarding Suspects' Rights in EU Criminal Justice: A Comparative Perspective*, 14 New Crim. L. Rev. 611 (2011); *see also* Donald Dripps, *On Reach and Grasp in Criminal Procedure:* Crawford *in California*, 37 N.C.J. Int'l L. & Com. Reg. 349 (2011).

[5] Keith Hawkins, *Order, Rationality and Silence: Some Reflections on Criminal Justice Decision-Making*, in *Exercising Discretion: Decision-Making in the Criminal Justice System and Beyond* 187 (Loraine Gelsthorpe & Nicola Padfield eds., 2003).

integral part of a superstructure, which appreciates the "meaningful nature of the social world and the phenomena studied."[6] To understand how criminal justice functions, one must therefore consider a variety of social, economic, and political factors that serve as constraints and drivers of criminal justice in a particular context, studying how the wider social environment shapes the criminal process and its daily practices, and the impact that criminal justice has on society.

This broader sociopolitical context is often more apparent when looking comparatively at another legal system. A good example of this contextual approach is Mike McConville et al.'s empirical inquiry into criminal justice in China.[7] After immersion within that system for a significant period of time, the authors emphasize that Chinese criminal justice cannot simply be approached by relying on the "usual analytical grids," such as its promulgated laws, official documents, the roles of legal actors, or even public hearings, all of which have reached their limits in this particular instance. The authors conclude that the system can only be understood through knowing the specific sociopolitical context within which the criminal justice apparatus operates that "gives it its character, infuses it with particular values, determinants and performance indicators—which are necessarily largely systemic and non-individuated—and directs the conduct of those who run it on a daily basis."[8]

If we stay with China for a moment, we note that this finding is also reflected in Yu Mou's research of the Chinese prosecution service, conducted through extensive observations, case file analysis, and semi-structured interviews.[9] She suggests that the unique supervisory function of the Chinese prosecution service and its relationship with other criminal justice institutions (such as the police and the courts) should be set against China's specific political backdrop, which was influenced by the Soviet legal system. The behavior of prosecutors cannot be understood with reference only to the law. Institutional and political mandates inform all aspects of the prosecution function and better explain the nature and motivation of prosecutorial decision-making.

The significance of the social and political background to a criminal justice system can also be found in other comparative empirical studies. For instance, Ed Cape and Zaza Namoradze indicate that some Eastern European institutions are also influenced by the country's Soviet legacy, which in many ways hinders the effectiveness of criminal justice reforms and remains a continuing dominant force.[10] Stewart Field's observation of the *cour d'assises* suggests that French criminal courts' preoccupation with the defendant's character can be traced back to the French Revolution, which embedded the value of social cohesion.[11] Also in France, Jacqueline Hodgson's ethnography of investigation and prosecution explored the nature of judicial supervision as it operated in practice

[6] David Matza, *Becoming Deviant* 85 (1969).

[7] Mike McConville et al., *Criminal Justice in China: An Empirical Inquiry* (2011). [8] *Id.* at 450.

[9] Yu Mou, *Overseeing Criminal Justice: The Supervisory Role of the Public Prosecution Service in China*, 44 J.L. & Soc. 620 (2017).

[10] Ed Cape & Zaza Namoradze, *Effective Criminal Defense in Eastern Europe* 445–68 (2012).

[11] Stewart Field, *State, Citizen and Character in French Criminal Process*, 33 J.L. & Soc. 522 (2006).

and as understood by legal actors themselves.[12] She found that most of the supervision is carried out by the public prosecutor, who, although accountable to the Minister of Justice and working closely with the police, is understood as an independent judicial officer. Key to this understanding of the prosecutor's role is the strength and pervasiveness of the French Republican tradition, which sees prosecution accountability to the executive, and so to the people, not as an impediment, but a guarantee of independence.[13] Comparative studies in particular demonstrate that this broader politico-legal context is important in understanding the construction of the prosecution function within different processes of criminal justice.[14]

2. Occupational Culture

In addition to the wider political culture within which criminal justice operates and by which it is shaped, the working culture of legal actors often exerts a more immediate influence on how work is carried out. This can be expressed as ideas, values, or attitudes shared by the group; or a process by which "patterns learned and created in the mind" are embodied in communication and other interpersonal relationships; or in more concrete form as "artifacts" produced out of institutional creativity that is distinctive to the group.[15]

In this sense, culture constitutes the concept of the *field* that influences decisions relating to the criminal process, of which a dominant example is that of police subculture. Robert Reiner, for example, defines police culture as "complex ensembles of values, attitudes, symbols, rules, recipes, and practices."[16] The study of police culture was derived from early ethnographic studies inside the police, where researchers found that the way officers enforce the law is rarely guided by legal precepts, but rather some "informal occupational norms and values operating under the apparently rigid hierarchical structure of police organizations."[17]

Since then, police occupational culture has been researched extensively to understand the exercise of police discretion and the negative "working personality" that potentially

[12] Jacqueline Hodgson, *French Criminal Justice: A Comparative Account of the Investigation and Prosecution of Crime in France* (2005).

[13] The recent jurisprudence of the European Court of Human Rights (ECtHR) has, however, found the French public prosecutor not to be a judicial officer for the purpose of Article 5 ECHR. *See* Jacqueline Hodgson, *The French Prosecutor in Question*, 67 Wash. & Lee L. Rev. 1361 (2010).

[14] Jacqueline Hodgson, *The Democratic Accountability of Prosecutors in England and Wales and France: Independence, Discretion and Managerialism*, in *Prosecutors and Democracy: A Cross-National Study* (Máximo Langer & David Sklansky eds., 2017).

[15] Ben Bowling & Coretta Phillips, *Racism, Crime and Criminal Justice* 81 (2001).

[16] Robert Reiner, *The Politics of the Police* 118 (2010).

[17] Janet Chan, *Changing Police Culture*, 36 Brit. J. Criminology 109, 110 (1996). For early ethnographic studies, see Michael Banton, *The Policeman in the Community* (1964); Jerome Skolnick, *Justice without Trial* (1966); Maureen Cain, *Society and the Policeman's Role* (1973); William Westley, *Violence and the Police* (1970); Peter Manning, *Police Work: The Second Organization of Policing* (1977); Peter Manning, *The Encyclopedia of Police Science* (William Bailey ed., 1989); Simon Holdaway, *Inside British Police: A Force at Work* (1983).

subverts or obstructs external reforms affecting officers.[18] For example, Nigel Fielding approached police culture from a gendered perspective and argued that the aggressive, competitive, macho values perpetuated by so-called "canteen culture" contribute to miscarriages of justice and could lead to a crisis of police legitimacy.[19] Simon Holdaway's study of race within the police force suggests that the racialized rank-and-file occupational culture of officers is an outcome of a social process that constructs and sustains "race" in relation to the demands of the work they undertake.[20] In recent research on the recorded stop and search/account reform in the wake of the death of Stephen Lawrence,[21] Michael Shiner probed into the psychological defense mechanisms (such as denial, projection, splitting, and fantasies) employed by the police to ward off threats to their institutional ego. In examining the way that the police react to "the trauma of institutional racism," Shiner argues that police culture should be perceived as the collective minds of those involved, which are able to respond defensively to resist external forces, thereby blunting policing reform.[22] Presenting an alternative account, Peter Waddington reminds us that what the police discuss in the "remote recessive" canteen may not automatically be translated into their actions on the street.[23] The concept of "canteen culture" is in many ways merely a rhetoric that "gives meaning to experience and sustains occupational self-esteem";[24] hence it should not be seen simply as a taken-for-granted explanation accounting for all negative values, beliefs, and attitudes (such as macho, racist, and sexist) of the police.

3. Culture as Rhetoric

In addition to identifying factors that shape decision-making, socio-legal researchers also explore the significance of the gap between law's rhetoric and law's practice.

[18] Andrew Goldsmith, *Taking Police Culture Seriously: Police Discretion and the Limits of Law*, 1 Policing & Society: Int'l J. 91 (1990); Janet Chan, *Changing Police Culture*, 36 Brit. J. Criminology 109 (1996); Janet Chan, *Changing Police Culture: Policing in a Multicultural Society* (1997); Peter Waddington, *Police (Canteen) Sub-culture: An Appreciation*, 39 Brit. J. Criminology 287 (1999); Jan Terpstra & Dorian Schapp, *Police Culture, Stress Conditions and Working Styles*, 10 Eur. J. Criminology 57 (2013).

[19] Nigel Fielding, *Cop Canteen Culture*, in *Just Boys Doing Business* 46, 62–64 (Tim Newburn & Elizabeth A Stanko eds., 1994).

[20] Simon Holdaway, *Constructing and Sustaining "Race" within the Police Workforce*, 48 Brit. J. Sociology 18 (1997).

[21] The changed stop and search/account practice requires police officers to make a record of all stops and to provide a copy to the person who has been stopped. This is one of the seventy reform recommendations made by the judicial inquiry (Macpherson report) that looked into matters arising from the death of a black British teenager who was murdered in an unprovoked, racially motivated attack in London in 1993. The Macpherson report examined the flawed investigation conducted by the police and declared that the failure was caused by "a combination of professional incompetence, institutional racism and a failure of leadership by senior officers" Cluny MacPherson, *The Stephen Lawrence Inquiry: Report of an Inquiry* 46.1 (1999).

[22] Michael Shiner, *Post*-Lawrence *Policing in England and Wales*, 50 Brit. J. Criminology 935, 949 (2010).

[23] Peter Waddington, *Police (Canteen) Sub-culture: An Appreciation*, 39 Brit. J. Criminology 287, 297 (1999).

[24] *Id.* at 295.

Findings of malpractice or rule breaking are themselves problematic, but when situated within the wider framework of legal procedural protections and guarantees, they become more so. For example, poor quality custodial legal advice also has implications for the treatment of the accused later in the criminal process.[25] In contrast to unrepresented suspects who are understood to have been denied the advice and protection provided by a lawyer, appeals courts in the 1990s were unwilling to allow appellants who, on the face of it, received custodial legal advice, to challenge interrogation evidence. In fact, many of these suspects had not received anything that could meaningfully be termed "legal assistance," meaning that appellants were credited with a benefit that they had never received.[26]

This "culture as rhetoric" approach emphasizes the extent to which reality on the ground differs from the idealized legal culture inscribed within the text and the rhetoric of the law. Within French criminal justice, features central to inquisitorial systems, such as the ideology of judicial supervision, are generally considered to define its structures and procedures, providing different procedural guarantees to those found in more party-based adversarial procedure. Within this legal tradition, the judiciary is entrusted as the guardian of the public interest to safeguard the rights of the accused, requiring the defense to play a much smaller part than in the adversarial model. In contrast to the confirmation bias that has been observed in police investigations and miscarriages of justice in a variety of jurisdictions, the single, neutral judicial enquiry offers a model of non-partisan enquiry in which evidence exculpating, as well as incriminating, the suspect is investigated. However, Hodgson found that in practice, in most cases judicial supervision is understood to be provided by the public prosecutor (the *procureur*), rather than the more independent *juge d'instruction*. Furthermore, prosecutorial "supervision" is largely bureaucratic and retrospective, offering little more than a file-based review.

Andrew Sanders et al. have observed in relation to England and Wales that there is a gap between the rhetoric of the overall system (which claims to be due process), the legal rules (which reflect mixed values), and the reality (which is largely crime control).[27] For example, the law requires reasonable suspicion in the exercise of police powers, but Doreen McBarnet has observed that many police practices that might popularly be understood as deviant are in fact permitted within the text of the law, which allows for broad discretion. Furthermore, even where procedures are clearly established in statute, working rules and practices are used to circumvent these requirements.[28] For example, David Dixon et al. found that officers got around the statutory requirement of reasonable suspicion as a base for a stop and search by asking the person if the officer could search them.[29] If the person agreed, the police considered this a "consent" search rather

[25] Andrew Sanders et al., *Advice and Assistance at Police Stations and the 24-Hour Duty Solicitor Scheme* (1989); Mike McConville & Jacqueline Hodgson, *Custodial Legal Advice and the Right to Silence* (1993).

[26] Jacqueline Hodgson, *Tipping the Scales of Justice: The Suspect's Right to Legal Advice*, 1992 Crim. L. R. 854.

[27] Andrew Sanders et al., *Criminal Justice* 741 (2010).

[28] Doreen McBarnet, *Conviction: Law, the State and Construction of Justice* 4–5 (1981).

[29] David Dixon et al., *Safeguarding the Rights of Suspects in Police Custody*, 1 Policing & Soc'y: Int'l J. 115 (1990).

than a search carried out under the Police and Criminal Evidence Act 1984 (PACE) and so statutory safeguards were considered not to apply. The net result of legal rules regulating behavior or criminal procedure, therefore, can be to legitimate the reverse.

In China, McConville et al. observe that law reform resulted only in a change in the way that state officials *account for* their behaviors that, otherwise, remain largely unaffected.[30] Mou too found that despite the introduction of new due process safeguards in the Criminal Procedure Law in 2012, criminal justice continues to be dominated by the working rules of the legal apparatus, structured by the political mandate, the value of hierarchical structures and deference to authority, and a strong emphasis on retribution.[31] State officials who work under the new legal regime have made no changes in their routine practices and ideology. In this respect, it is not surprising that there exists an entrenched culture within the Chinese system, which ignores or violates the formal due process rules that are in many ways alien to it. This systemic transgression undermines the authority of the law, yet the law retains its power: it legitimates state practice and prevents the expression of critical judgment.

As with the various accounts of police culture, empirical researchers purporting to observe the same phenomena—the work and practices of criminal defense lawyers—do not always agree. McConville et al.'s wide-ranging study of the organization and practices of defense lawyers in forty-eight firms across England and Wales was criticized by Max Travers for presenting "a partial and one-sided account of the day-to-day activities of... criminal defense lawyers" built up by "a great deal of selection and omission" that "shows lawyers and clerks in a bad light."[32] In attacking McConville et al.'s analysis and research strategy, Travers used his own four-month ethnographic research in one law firm as an example, citing the importance of thick description of the context. In his research of "the work and talk" in the law firm, Travers proffered a glowing account of defense lawyers unreservedly devoted to their clients and satisfied clients who appreciated the standard of care they received.[33] However, in addition to the limited sample of a single firm, Lee Bridges et al. warn that by treating lawyers' perspectives unquestioningly, Travers's approach could easily "end up accepting at face value practitioners' own rationalizations for their (mal)practices."[34]

In the face of the oppositional images portrayed by the two studies, Daniel Newman's empirical enquiry was tasked to judge "which finding held good" by adopting an integrated methodology.[35] Although (a little like Travers) Newman's initial motivation was to support "the noble cause" that legal aid lawyers pursue, what he observed in the law

[30] McConville et al., *supra* note 7, at 425–74.

[31] Yu Mou, *Written Evidence and the Absence of Witnesses: The Inevitability of Conviction in Chinese Criminal Justice* 249–79, PhD thesis, University of Warwick 2015.

[32] Max Travers, *The Reality of Law: Work and Talk in a Firm of Criminal Lawyers* 370 (1997).

[33] Max Travers, *Preaching to the Converted? Improving the Persuasiveness of Criminal Justice Research*, 37 Brit. J. Criminology 359 (1997).

[34] Lee Bridges et al., *Can Critical Research Influence Policy? A Response to Max Travers*, 37 Brit. J. Criminology 378, 379 (1997).

[35] Daniel Newman, *Legal Aid Lawyers and the Quest for Justice* 27–30 (2013).

firms had strong resonance with McConville et al.'s conclusion.[36] In this updated study of the lawyer-client relationship, the professional standards of defense lawyers have not improved: they were observed to have treated their clients with disrespect, pushed them to plead guilty, and utilized their professional knowledge to control their clients. Newman illustrates the sharp discrepancy between how lawyers presented themselves when interviewed and the way they acted when observed. On the one hand, lawyers in interviews described themselves as dedicated professionals who fostered healthy relations with other legal actors for the benefit of the client; on the other, the participant observation revealed a rather different and depressing reality, "damning for this branch of the legal profession and tragic for the clients who depend on them."[37]

In this regard, the professional claims made by the lawyers in Newman's study can also be understood as rhetoric. Joan Leach suggests that rhetoric, as a conviction in the power of language, can shape the perception of the world and structure our way of thinking.[38] It is a pervasive way of communicating and interacting with people, which is constructed to justify a position as well as to attack any counterarguments. Thus, there are two functions of rhetoric: building up an idealized account (the "reification") and undermining of the reality discovered by others (the "ironizing").[39] Whereas empirical researchers should be wary of rhetoric that seeks to deflect from the truth, it is not meaningless and therefore does not warrant being dismissed. Rhetoric can express the law's claims and aspirations, and the ways that legal actors such as defense lawyers and public prosecutors believe themselves to be acting—protecting their client's interests or overseeing the police investigation to discover the truth. At the end of his book, Newman suggests that rhetoric somehow embodies the values that did and could exist and reflects the optimistic belief held by criminal defense lawyers.

III. Justice on the Ground and Discretionary Power

In outlining the broad setting of a cultural *surround* or organizational *field* that criminal justice activities take place, we have noted that one of the main achievements of empirical research has been to provide detailed accounts of how certain factors and considerations have influenced the way legal actors respond to legal and organizational mandates—the *frame* that decision-makers employ in deciding. This section highlights some of the empirical research on decision-making processes within the criminal justice system in England and Wales. We focus in particular on the exercise of discretion, a cornerstone

[36] *Id.* at 143–68. [37] *Id.* at 147–52 & abstract.

[38] Joan Leach, *Rhetorical Analysis*, in *Qualitative Researching with Text, Image and Sound: A Practical Handbook* 207 (Martin Bauer & George Gaskell eds., 2000).

[39] Jonathan Potter, *Representing Reality: Discourse, Rhetoric and Social Construction* 106–08 (1996); Newman, *supra* note 35, at 151.

of criminal justice that infuses all areas of practice and reveals something of the limits of the law as well as the broader exercise of power.

1. Police Discretion: Stop, Search, Charge

As already discussed, the disconnect between the official description of the way a certain process ought to work and how that process operates in practice is well recognized in empirical research. Institutions as large as the police and the Crown Prosecution Service (CPS), for instance, are inevitably subject to gaps between perception and reality, with their practices varying within units and at different organizational levels. It is also impossible to prescribe every action of police officers or prosecutors—the law necessarily allows them a broad degree of discretion in determining how to respond to each situation or case. One of the missions of empirical research is to make people aware of what exists in the gaps between theory and practice and in many instances, this will focus on how and why discretion is exercised in particular ways.[40] For example, in McConville et al.'s study of the construction of prosecution cases in England and Wales, the authors argue that the police, who dominate the evidence-gathering process, are accorded a high degree of autonomy to disregard competing accounts and construct the file of evidence toward conviction.[41] In mapping the way that prosecution cases develop from vague suspicions to carefully constructed edifices, their research demonstrates the ways in which rules and laws governing detention and interrogation can assist the police to create a suspect population. This understanding of case construction challenges Packer's Due Process/Crime Control dichotomy and undercuts the due process principles championed by PACE.[42] As McBarnet has argued in relation to the permissive nature of the legal text, their findings suggest that the rules that provide safeguards for the suspect can also serve crime control purposes: the enabling law is employed by the police to rationalize behavior undertaken for other reasons, and is rarely a consideration to regulate their behaviors.

In line with this pessimistic view of enabling law, the open-textured nature of the law and the latitude it offers are also exemplified in literature around the police power to stop and search. Empirical studies have suggested that ethnic minorities are selectively targeted by the police for discriminatory reasons.[43] Following the inquiry into the murder of the black teenager Stephen Lawrence, the Macpherson report found that the police

[40] Anthony Edwards, *The Value of Empirical Research in Criminal Justice*, 8 Crim. L. Rev. 533 (1997).

[41] Mike McConville et al., *The Case for the Prosecution*, ch. 5 (1991).

[42] Herbert Packer, *The Limits of the Criminal Sanction*, Part II (1968).

[43] These empirical studies include David Smith, 1 *Police and People in London: A Survey of Londoners* (1983); David Dixon et al., *Reality and Rules in the Construction and Regulation of Police Suspicion*, 17 Int'l J. Sociology L. 185 (1989); Clive Norris et al., *Black and Blue: An Analysis of the Influence of Race on Being Stopped by the Police*, 43 Brit. J. Sociology 207 (1992); Monica A Walker & Tony Jefferson, *Ethnic Minorities in the Criminal Justice System*, 1992 Crim. L. Rev. 83; Wesley Skogan, *The Police and the Public in England and Wales: A British Crime Survey Report* (1990); Wesley Skogan, *Contacts Between Police and Public: Findings from the 1992 British Crime Survey* (1994); Ben Bowling & Coretta Phillips, *Racism, Crime and Criminal Justice* (2001); Laurence Lustgarten, *The Future of Stop and Search*, 8 Crim. L. Rev. 603 (2002).

enjoyed only low levels of trust within ethnic minority communities, and stops and searches were clearly the "core conclusion of racist stereotyping."[44] The use of racial stereotyping, and poor relationships between the police and the black community in particular, is not new,[45] and recent studies point to continuing concerns in the use of stop-and-search powers, though researchers disagree as to how this should be measured: with reference to the residential population or those present in the area—the "availability" approach.[46]

The use of stereotyping in police stop and search is not limited to skin color. As Paul Quinton et al. suggest, even clothing and vehicle type can influence the exercise of police discretion.[47] In his ethnographic study, Satnam Choongh reports that the police have an entrenched prejudice against working class people, who are often seen as criminal-minded and dangerous. Parallel with McConville et al.'s research, he also argues that the law enables, rather than controls or constrains police discretion. In his account of police station procedures, police activities cannot be understood simply by reference to their responsibility to control and prevent crime—more importantly, they embody order and authority; suspects, who normally come from less privileged social backgrounds and ethnic origins, represent a threat to the orderly middle-class fabric and are in need of discipline by coercive power.[48]

Aside from illicit social considerations, police discretion is also influenced by other variables, especially the context in which the investigation takes place.[49] For example, Vicky Kemp found that the "offences brought to justice" (OBTJ) performance indicator plays a significant role in the police's decision-making process. The police performance indicator is part and parcel of a "command and control" style of managerial framework designed to ensure a commitment from the top down of the hierarchical organization. To meet the target, the majority of cases (including borderline criminal activities) are channeled to formal actions once they are reported to the police. In order to fulfill the required detection rate, the police target "easy hits" and minor offenses, failing to record crimes honestly, misusing cautions etc. to manipulate the figures. In attempting to reduce the number of cases dropped with no further action, the logic of response rate measures is to widen the net of criminalization to target easy wins, often at the expense of investigating more serious offenses.[50]

[44] MacPherson, *supra* note 21.

[45] *See* Leslie Scarman, *The Scarman Report: Report of an Inquiry* (1982).

[46] Marian FitzGerald & Rae Sibbitt, *Ethnic Monitoring in Police Forces* 64 (1997); HM Inspectoratrate of Constabulary, *Winning the Race: Embracing Diversity* 73(2000); MVA & Joel Miller, *Profiling Populations Available for Stops and Searches* 13–31 (2000); Joel Miller et al., *Measuring Stops and Searches: Lessons from U.K Home Office Research*, 4 Just. Res. & Pol'y 143 (2002); Philip Waddington et al., *In Proportion: Race, and Police Stop and Search*, 44 Brit. J. Criminology 889 (2004).

[47] Paul Quinton et al., *Police Stops, Decision-Making and Practice* vi (2000).

[48] Satnam Choongh, *Policing as Social Discipline* 44–106 (1997).

[49] Loraine Gelsthorpe & Nicola Padfield, *Exercising Discretion: Decision-Making in the Criminal Justice System and Beyond* ch. 1 (2003).

[50] Vicky Kemp, *PACE, Performance Targets and Legal Protections*, 4 Crim. L. Rev. 278 (2014).

It is interesting to see how empirical research has identified the same trends across quite different jurisdictions, with the same consequences. In France, this same process has occurred, as so-called "third way" alternatives to prosecution and trial are used to ensure that fewer cases are discontinued. The result in many areas is that prosecutors are focusing on minor offenses and devoting insufficient time and resources to more serious crime. This in turn has caused deterioration in prosecutor-police relations.[51] Officers resent the close scrutiny of their actions concerning relatively minor offenses, preferring the more light touch oversight that they enjoy in their relationship with the *juge d'instruction*.[52] Similarly in China, the police are found to have diverted a significant amount of resources into dealing with minor drug dealing and dangerous driving offenses in order to fulfill performance indicators, paying little attention to more serious and complex fraud offenses.[53]

2. Police Discretion: Enabling Suspects' Rights

Discretion is not confined to whether certain rules and procedures are conformed with; it is also about *how* the requirements are met in fulfilling the aims and purposes of criminal justice. It can be embodied in the police's attitude, for instance, which has an impact on the rights of the defense. When suspects are confused or uncertain whether to seek advice from legal counsel in police stations, the suggestion of the police (and especially of the custody officer, understood as the gatekeeper to the suspect's rights) might tip the balance.

Empirical research over the last three decades has identified that the police in a number of procedurally very different jurisdictions have resisted the introduction of a statutory right to custodial legal assistance in similar ways. Typically they may discourage the suspect from requesting a solicitor by telling him that he does not need one, by failing to mention that advice is free at the point of delivery,[54] or by persuading suspects who have sought legal advice to change their mind.[55]

The techniques used by the police to undermine suspects' access to legal rights can be imperceptible. For instance, defense lawyers could be barred from entering the police custody suite, creating an impression for suspects that requesting a lawyer would be time-consuming. This in turn might lead the suspect to give up the request, or to switch

[51] Hodgson, *supra* note 14; Jacqueline Hodgson & Laurène Soubise, *The Public Prosecutor in France*, in *Oxford Handbooks Online: Criminology and Criminal Justice* (2016).

[52] Hodgson, *supra* note 12, at 154–61, 185–89, 202–03.

[53] Yu Mou, *The Constructed Truth: The Making of Police Dossiers in China*, 26 Soc. & Leg. Stud. 69 (2017).

[54] Sanders et al., *supra* note 25; Dixon et al., *supra* note 29; Choongh, *supra* note 48; Hodgson, *supra* note 12; Ed Cape & Jacqueline Hodgson, *The Right of Access to a Lawyer at Police Stations: Making the European Union Directive Work in Practice*, New J. Eur. Crim. L. 450 (2014).

[55] These techniques have been observed in England and Wales, France, and the Netherlands. *See* Jodie Blackstock et al., *Inside Police Custody: An Empirical Account of Suspects' Rights in Four Jurisdictions* 274–75 (2014); Vicky Kemp, *Bridewell Legal Advice Study: Adopting a Whole-System Approach to Police Station Legal Advice* 18 (2013).

to less effective legal services, such as telephone contact. Similarly, whereas delays can be caused by a host of factors (such as the police investigation or charging process), police have constantly utilized the risk of delays to discourage suspects from having legal advice.[56] Here, it is not the wider legal culture that has been seen to determine police behavior (the *surround* or the *field*), but the more immediate threat (as the defense lawyer is understood to be) to the police mandate to investigate and gather evidence for the prosecution. In particular, the presence of the defense lawyer on police territory challenges the *frame* of police culture: the questioning of the suspect in order to obtain an admission. It is only when the defense lawyer's presence is seen to be compatible with the police task of interrogation (for example, when represented suspects regularly refrain from exercising their right to silence) that her role comes to be accepted.

In addition to managing suspects' access to defense lawyers, the police have substantial control over the disclosure of evidence. They have the option to decide the amount of evidence that they are willing to disclose to the suspect or the suspect's lawyer, either before or during the interview. This has resulted in varied legal practices, with some officers being more forthcoming with evidence and others tending to hold back information from the defense.[57] Divya Sukumar et al.'s observations of police station disclosure reveal that while police have generally satisfied the minimal requirement, evidence disclosure tactics (such as withholding information prior to the interview, exaggerating the strength of the evidence, use of evidence as an ambush) have frequently been used to pressure the suspect into making an admission of guilt.[58]

3. Prosecutorial Discretion

Criminal justice as a system is organized to allow decisions to be made serially. When a police case is handed on from the police to the prosecution, until (and even at) the point of case disposition, discretionary power is dispersed across criminal justice institutions and individuals.[59] Prosecutorial discretion, for instance, enables the prosecutor to "respond sensitively to the great diversity of factual situations and policy issues."[60] Although prosecutorial discretion is traditionally associated with the opportunity principle, which grants prosecutors a broad flexibility to take into account factors other than evidence in

[56] Sanders et al., *supra* note 25, at 23; Hodgson, *supra* note 12, at 192–93; Kemp, *supra* note 55, at 3.

[57] Vicky Kemp, *"No Time for a Solicitor": Implications for Delays on the Take-Up of Legal Advice*, 3 Crim. L. Rev. 184 (2013); Divya Sukumar et al., *Behind Closed Doors: Live Observations of Current Police Station Disclosure Practices and Lawyer-Client Consultations*, 12 Crim. L. Rev. 901 (2016); Divya Sukumar et al., *How the Timing of Police Evidence Disclosure Impacts Custodial Legal Advice*, 20 Int'l. J. Evid. & Proc. 200 (2016); Divya Sukumar et al., *Strategic Disclosure of Evidence: Perspectives from Psychology and Law*, 22 Psych. Pub. Pol'y & L. 306 (2016).

[58] Sukumar et al., *supra* note 57.

[59] Keith Hawkins, *Order, Rationality and Silence: Some Reflections on Criminal Justice Decision-Making, in Exercising Discretion: Decision-Making in the Criminal Justice System and Beyond* 8–9 (Loraine Gelsthorpe & Nicola Padfield eds., 2003).

[60] Andrew Ashworth, *The "Public Interest" Element in Prosecutions*, 9 Crim. L. Rev. 595 (1987).

making their decisions, it is also compatible with the principle of legality, provided that the decision is not arbitrary.

In England and Wales where the opportunity principle prevails, the decision to prosecute was historically part of the police function. This historical legacy has meant that the relatively recently created public prosecution service, the Crown Prosecution Service (CPS), remains subordinate to the power of the police in many respects. This relationship was presaged in Susan Moody and Jacqueline Tombs's empirical study of the Scottish procurator fiscal, which suggested that the prosecution service, even if it has a sphere of responsibility that is independent, is still largely dependent on the police who provide the information and determine the way in which it is presented.[61] This concern was further raised in Graham Mansfield and Jill Peay's research, which concluded that independence for the prosecutor may not be created simply by demarcating the role of investigators of crime and reallocating responsibility for the decision to prosecute.[62]

Issues concerning how the Crown Prosecutor exercises discretion are explored in the Home Office research conducted by Debbie Crisp and David Moxon. They found that although a good proportion of cases have effectively been filtered out of the system following the establishment of the CPS, some of the cases were dropped unnecessarily, because the police did not always respond to Crown Prosecutors' requests for further investigations.[63] With friction between the CPS and the police continuing to cause problems, the government proposed placing Crown Prosecutors in police stations in order to be on hand to provide pre-charge advice and to improve working relationships by fostering closer cooperation with the police. A pilot was conducted in twelve sites, but Adrian Hunt and John Baldwin's study of the scheme concluded that it was ineffective. Crown Prosecutors have no authority to direct the police to take their advice, and so making prosecutors available for pre-charge advice and consultation will "cater only for those officers perceptive enough to recognize a legal problem when they see one. This means that those officers in greatest need of advice are the ones least likely to benefit from what is on offer."[64]

The subsequent statutory charging scheme saw prosecutors located in police stations in England and Wales to advise on charges. It was hoped that this might improve relations and provide a more unified approach, but it was discontinued in favor of a centralized telephone system. Soubise's research suggests that co-location at the police station did not improve police-prosecutor relations. Crown Prosecutors told her in interviews that officers sometimes sought to pressure them into charging suspects: "The disadvantage [of being based at the police station] is basically the police can exercise pressure on you. You might have two or three officers . . . and they're sort of asking you questions and challenging your decisions there and then, which can be quite, I suppose, intimidating."[65]

[61] *See* Susan Moody & Jacqueline Tombs, *Prosecution in the Public Interest* 129–30 (1982).

[62] Graham Mansfield & Jill Peay, *The Director of Public Prosecutions: Principles and Practices for the Crown Prosecutor* 46–50 (1987).

[63] Debbie Crisp & David Moxon, *Case Screening by the Crown Prosecution Service: How and Why Cases Are Terminated* 28–29 (1994).

[64] Adrian Hunt & John Baldwin, *Prosecutors Advising in Police Stations*, 8 Crim. L. Rev. 521, 536 (1998).

[65] Laurène Soubise, *Prosecutorial Discretion and Accountability: A Comparative Study of France and England and Wales*, PhD thesis, University of Warwick 202 (2016).

Crown Prosecutors exercise considerable discretion when deciding whether a prosecution is justified on evidential grounds and in the public interest. The prosecution in England and Wales has long been criticized for not being robust enough to terminate those cases that do not have enough evidence to reach the threshold to stand jury trial. In the Crown Court study conducted by Michael Zander and Paul Henderson, judges and barristers suggested that weak prosecution cases account for 20 percent of all contested cases, but a number of them (4–8 percent) do end in conviction.[66] In exploring the reasons that led the CPS to continue these weak cases, John Baldwin pointed out that the CPS decision is overly dependent on police views (following the findings of McConville et al.), and the failure of these prosecution cases lies primarily in its reliance on a single, often vulnerable, witness, where there are unpredictable contingencies that cause collapse of prosecutions.[67] Strikingly, he found that many difficult cases where weaknesses were identified and consciously itemized still proceeded to trial. CPS lawyers relied on "instinct," "feeling," and "intuition," rather than required legal techniques, in conducting case reviews. When applying the evidential sufficiency test, Crown Prosecutors were unduly influenced by the gravity of the offense, thereby "clouding their judgments, pervading their thinking and approach, and inhibiting them in taking decisions to discontinue prosecutions."[68]

4. Discretion in the Jury Room

In contrast to the professional and legally regulated role played by police, prosecutors, and defense lawyers, the jury exists to provide a lay perspective. The judge provides legal direction, but ultimately, the jury determines the facts that in turn determine the guilt of the accused. With few rules on how jurors should evaluate evidence and determine the truth of witnesses, how do they arrive at their decision? As the least regulated and least visible form of decision-making in the criminal process (jurors provide no reasons for their verdict), juror behavior has long fascinated researchers. What happens when cases are tried by jury? Is this a fair and democratic process that ensures justice by injecting the experiences of ordinary citizens into adjudication on criminal guilt? Or is it an unregulated and unaccountable process that permits prejudice and discrimination into the justice process, without the possibility of challenge? Does lay decision-making temper the extremes of repeat player adversarial lawyers, or are jurors unable to resist the persuasive tactics of courtroom advocacy?

Despite legislation constraining empirical research conducted by using real jurors, there has been a large body of literature in common law countries (especially England and Wales, the United States, New Zealand, Canada, and Australia) devoted to different aspects of the jury undertaken by legal scholars, social scientists, and experimental

[66] Michael Zander & Paul Henderson, *Crown Court Study* 184–85 (1993).

[67] John Baldwin, *Understanding Judge Ordered and Directed Acquittals in the Crown Court*, 8 Crim. L. Rev. 536 (1997).

[68] *Id.* at 551.

psychologists,[69] many of them well captured in Penny Darbyshire et al.'s comprehensive literature summary.[70]

Early in the 1970s, Sarah McCabe and Robert Purves conducted arguably the best shadow jury experiment to date. The experiment was a replica of a real jury working process: the subjects were selected from the electoral register, watched court trials, deliberated and delivered verdicts just like actual juries.[71] A number of studies have also been dedicated to exploring the views of participants involved in the trial,[72] observing "simulated" or "mock" juries,[73] comparing jury verdicts with professional opinions,[74] and conducting questionnaires with actual jurors after the trial.[75]

More recent mock jury studies have diverged in their findings. Cheryl Thomas has explored the fairness of jury decision-making, using a "multi-method" approach, which encompasses a controlled simulation study, a large-scale analysis of all jury verdicts in Crown Courts in England and Wales between October 2006 and March 2008, and a post-trial survey of 668 jurors in sixty-two cases.[76] It examined some of the most critical factors that potentially influence the fairness of jury decision-making, including racial discrimination, consistency of jury verdicts, and jurors' comprehension of directions on the law. This research has dispelled some myths of jury trial, such that juries in certain areas do not convict and juries tend to acquit for certain offenses. The analysis suggests that jury trials are in fact very efficient, with less than 1 percent of juries being discharged and hung juries only occurring in 0.6 percent of the cases. Perhaps one of the more surprising findings of this study is that there are more convictions than acquittals in rape cases, which are even higher than other serious offenses, including attempted murder, manslaughter, and causing grievous bodily harm.[77]

Emily Finch and Vanessa Munro, and Louise Ellison and Vanessa Munro's research has focused on jury verdicts in rape trials and presents a less positive picture of juror behavior and motivation. The authors conducted a series of focus groups, trial reconstructions, and trial simulations to explore jurors' understanding and discussion of the critical issues in trials of rape cases, such as consent, complainant's intoxication status,

[69] Penny Darbyshire, *What Can We Learn from Published Jury Research? Findings for the Criminal Court Review*, 2001 Crim. L. Rev. 970.

[70] Penny Darbyshire et al., *What Can the England Legal System Learn from Jury Research Published up to 2001?* (2002).

[71] Sarah McCabe & Robert Purves, *The Shadow Jury at Work* 1–15 (1974).

[72] Mike McConville & John Baldwin, *Jury Trial* (1979).

[73] Geoffrey P. Kramer et al., *Pretrial Publicity, Judicial Remedies and Jury Bias*, 14 L. & Hum. Behav. 409 (1990); Larry Heuer & Steven Penrod, *Trial Complexity: A Field Investigation of Its Meaning and Its Effects*, 18 L. & Hum. Behav. 29 (1994); Amy L. Otto et al., *The Bias Impact of Pre-trial Publicity on Juror Judgements*, 18 L. & Hum. Behav. 453 (1994); David Rosenhan et al., *Notetaking Can Aid Juror Recall*, 18 L. & Hum. Behav. 53 (1994).

[74] Harry Kalven & Hans Zeisel, *The American Jury* (1966); Dennis J. Devine et al., *Strength of Evidence, Extraevidentiary Influence, and the Liberation Hypothesis: Data from the Field*, 33 L. & Hum. Behav. 136 (2009).

[75] Zander & Henderson, *supra* note 66.

[76] Cheryl Thomas, *Are Juries Fair?* (2010).

[77] Focusing on conviction rates takes no account, however, of the very high attrition rate in rape cases, from low reporting to failure to charge or prosecute.

public expectations regarding socio-sexual conduct, and the complainant's credibility in relation to her conduct during and post-assault.[78] In Ellison and Munro's recent study, 160 members of the public observed mini rape trial re-enactments, before then deliberating in jury groups. The authors found that juries, whether provided with written or oral directions, tended to fall back on their own personal views and experiences, rather than taking seriously the evidential burden to prove guilt beyond reasonable doubt. They also sought to understand how jurors might be affected by different modes of presenting evidence—live video links, screens, and prerecorded evidence.[79] Research suggests that victim witnesses find these measures helpful,[80] but the impact on jury decision-making had not been explored—in particular, the impact of disrupting the sequential narrative that jurors often find helpful in making sense of evidence. The research found that there was no clear and consistent response to different modes of evidence presentation in cases of adult female rape complainants. They were as likely to result in adverse prejudice to the victim as to the accused, leading the authors to conclude that their overall impact was not detrimental to the fairness of the trial.[81]

IV. Policy and Criminal Justice Reforms

Volkmar Gessner and John Thomas suggest that sociolegal research can be roughly categorized into two types: one evaluates the way law functions in a particular organizational, social, or political context; the other concerns policies, especially the intended or unintended consequences of law enforcement.[82] When it comes to criminal justice research, however, this distinction is very much blurred. Policy implementation has been an integrated part of the operation of the law enforcement agencies, and empirical

[78] Emily Finch & Vanessa Munro, *Breaking Boundaries? Sexual Consent in the Jury Room*, 26 Leg. Stud. 303 (2006); Emily Finch & Vanessa Munro, *Lifting the Veil: The Use of Focus Groups and Trials Simulations in Legal Research*, 35 J.L. & Soc. 30 (2008); Louise Ellison & Vanessa Munro, *Reacting to Rape: Exploring Mock Jurors' Assessments of Complainant Credibility*, 49 Brit. J. Criminology 202 (2009); Louise Ellison & Vanessa Munro, *Of "Normal Sex" and "Real Rape": Exploring the Use of Socio-sexual Scripts in (Mock) Jury Deliberation*, 18 Soc. & L. Stud. 291 (2009); Louise Ellison & Vanessa Munro, *Getting into (Not) Guilty: Examining Jurors' Deliberative Process in, and Beyond, the Context of a Mock Rape Trial*, 30 Leg. Stud. 74 (2010); Louise Ellison & Vanessa Munro, *A "Special" Delivery? Exploring the Impact of Screens, Live-Links and Video-Recorded Evidence on Mock Juror Deliberation in Rape Trials*, 23 Soc. & Leg. Stud. 3 (2014) [hereinafter *A "Special" Delivery?*].

[79] Louise Ellison & Vanessa Munro, *"Telling Tales": Exploring Narratives of Life and Law Within the (Mock) Jury Room*, 35 Leg. Stud. 201 (2015).

[80] Becky Hamlyn et al., *Are Special Measures Working? Evidence from Surveys of Vulnerable and Intimidated Witnesses* (Development and Statistics Directorate 2004); Mandy Burton et al., *Vulnerable and Intimidated Witnesses and the Adversarial Process in England and Wales*, 11 Int'l. J. Evid. & Proc. 1 (2007).

[81] Ellison & Munro, *A "Special" Delivery?*, *supra* note 78.

[82] Volkmar Gessner & John Thomas, *Socio-legal Research and Policy Studies: A Review of the Issues*, 10 L. & Pol'y 85 (1988).

researchers often cannot avoid considering the influence of policy when making sense of the way legal institutions function. Policy itself is a broad term and might be understood as a course of action proposed by the governing body of the state (public policy), which impacts on various aspects of the domain of criminal justice; but in less normative terms, it can also represent a system of more or less formalized principles adopted by criminal justice institutions (criminal justice policy) to guide decisions and pursue specified outcomes. Depending on the specific meaning that is implied, it can be a component part of the social *surround*, *field*, and *frame* that shapes criminal justice decision-making.

1. Austerity and Criminal Defense and Prosecution Practices in England and Wales

The consequences of government public sector austerity for the delivery of legal services and all aspects of the criminal justice process from policing through to prisons are examples of how public policies can direct criminal justice. Although an integral component of the right to a fair trial (Article 6 ECHR) and a necessary part of the proper functioning of adversarial procedure, the funding and provision of criminal defense services has been hard hit by government austerity. By 2014, the cost-cutting of public spending on criminal legal aid in England had accumulated to over £120 million, which, inevitably, has had a detrimental effect on defense rights of the accused.[83] For instance, Layla Skinns indicates that since the fee paid to visit the police station has been capped to include all costs incurred, duty lawyers are less willing physically to attend police interviews. As such, some suspects have to rely on telephone legal advice.[84] Alongside concerns around confidentiality, the absence of face-to-face contact undermines the lawyer's ability to establish the trust necessary for an effective lawyer-client relationship and so to assess and advise the suspect and begin to develop a defense strategy.[85] As already discussed, evidence disclosure by the police is also contingent on personal relationships, so it is unlikely that the lawyer will learn as much about the case without attending the police station in person. For these kinds of reasons, earlier research suggests that telephone advice can jeopardize the already vulnerable situation of the suspect by giving inappropriate advice.[86] It should be noted that telephone advice is not always the result of a lack of resources. Only one-eighth of suspects receiving custodial legal advice in Scotland between 2011 and 2013 were personally attended by a lawyer; the

[83] Asher Flynn & Jacqueline Hodgson, *Access to Justice and Legal Aid Cuts: A Mismatch of Concepts in the Contemporary Australian and British Legal Landscapes*, in *Access to Justice and Legal Aid: Comparative Perspectives on Unmet Legal Need* 1–2 (Asher Flynn & Jacqueline Hodgson eds., 2017).

[84] Layla Skinns, *"I'm a Detainee; Get Me Out of Here"—Predictors of Access to Custodial Legal Advice in Public and Private Police Custody Areas in England and Wales*, 49 Brit. J. Criminology 399 (2009).

[85] Blackstock et al., *supra* note 55.

[86] Mike McConville et al., *Standing Accused: The Organization and Practices of Criminal Defense Lawyers in Britain* 8–83 (1994).

majority were provided with telephone advice. Lawyers in Scotland have argued that within an evidential framework that requires corroboration, silence is always the best advice, and this could be done as effectively by telephone as in person.[87] Some, however, recognize that silence is a difficult position to maintain, and the lawyer's presence can assist suspects to resist persistent police questioning, especially if they have not been questioned by the police before.[88]

Furthermore, empirical studies have demonstrated the poor quality of criminal defense work that existed in the 1980s and 1990s, with unqualified and untrained clerks carrying out the bulk of case preparation, including attending clients in the office and at the police station.[89] Motivated by the greater profit that could be made from such wide-scale delegation, criminal defense solicitors failed to act in their client's interests. Since then, significant improvements have been made to professional training, practice, and regulation to address these deficiencies, and these reforms have been reinforced by a legal aid framework that tied public funding to the quality of defense services.

However, despite the improvements made in defense lawyer standards[90] and the often onerous nature of professional regulation, the sustained period of disinvestment in legal aid has made the reversion to poor practices almost inevitable. Within this chastened financial environment, lawyers have been found to adapt the service they are able to provide to "make ends meet," with discontinuous representation and diminished time devoted to individual cases.[91] The response in practice appears to be in accordance with Gwyn Bevan's supplier-induced demand thesis, which suggests that lawyers who simultaneously determine the cost of their work and secure a targeted income will inevitably abuse their position and conduct superfluous work in order to achieve monetary gains.[92] Just as Paul Fenn et al. observed in their research, lawyers sensitively adjusted their inputs according to the remuneration they received. The authors identified that when fixed standard fees were introduced that no longer cover the actual costs of defense work, defense lawyers switched to cost-control strategies, such as case-splitting and reduced time investment in case preparation and advocacy, to react to the constrained income.[93] In contrast, Lee Bridges et al. found solicitors working in the non-profit Public Defender Service, where salaries were fixed independently of case numbers or work carried out, perform generally better than private practice lawyers: public defenders were able to provide a more "holistic, client-centered service, and to adopt a more rigorous approach when representing their clients."[94]

[87] Blackstock et al., *supra* note 55, at 287–90. [88] *Id.* at 289.

[89] Sanders et al., *supra* note 25; McConville & Hodgson, *supra* note 25, at 21; McConville et al., *supra* note 86, at 83–86.

[90] Lee Bridge & Satnam Choongh, *Improving Police Station Legal Advice* 139–48 (1998).

[91] Newman, *supra* note 35, at 17–18.

[92] Gwyn Bevan, *Has There Been Supplier-Induced Demand for Legal Aid?*, 15 Civ. Just. Q. 98 (1996).

[93] Paul Fenn et al., *Standard Fees for Legal Aid: An Empirical Analysis of Incentives and Contracts*, 59 Oxf. Econ. Papers 662 (2007).

[94] Lee Bridges et al., *Evaluation of the Public Defender Service in England and Wales* 255 (2007).

The adoption of practices that seek to maximize efficiency, including the delegation of large portions of work, can also be seen in the working arrangements of the CPS, following the Optimum Business Model, introduced in 2008. Soubise describes how much of the case preparation is conducted by non-solicitors in a centralized and segmented system that sees files passed from one team to another, depending on the stage of the process the case has reached. Oversight by Crown Prosecutors is distant and no single lawyer retains case ownership, making difficult any discussion with defense counsel on disclosure or plea. Court work and trial preparation is also delegated to Associate Prosecutors—paralegals who have experience working in the CPS but who have received just two weeks of legal training. This work should be carried out under the supervision of Crown Prosecutors who alone are authorized to determine the charges to be brought. In practice, Laurène Soubise found that the pressure of the magistrates' court docket required Associate Prosecutors to make decisions independently (sometimes directly contradicting the Crown Prosecutor's written instructions), and only seek authorization retrospectively. This practice was tacitly acknowledged and the conclusion is that "[c]oncerns over flexibility and speed appear to overcome the need for accountability." More fundamentally, "[c]uts to legal aid and the increase in the number of unrepresented defendants mean that many magistrates' court hearings take place without qualified solicitors or barristers representing either party. This gives credibility to fears of 'de-lawyerization' of the magistrates' court and concerns for the quality of justice in summary proceedings."[95]

2. Promoting Best Defense Practices in the European Union

Internationally, empirical research is also a source of inspiration for constructive and effective programs and policies. In addition to empirical work that seeks to evaluate the success of criminal justice reforms, some studies take a forward-looking approach, providing accounts of practice to inform planned reform. A number of projects funded by the European Commission, for example, have been designed to bring together evidence of best practices as well as an understanding of what works and why. For empirical comparativists, this is a fascinating lens through which to study criminal justice—examining the practices of different criminal processes and the extent to which they are grounded in jurisdiction-specific cultures, and then identifying common strengths and weaknesses in their practical operation in order to shape and ensure the effectiveness of pan-European measures.

A variety of empirical research projects have been connected to specific EU Directives and to EU reform more broadly. Some are primarily desk-based accounts of law and practice, supplemented by interviews,[96] and others have new empirical data at the heart of the project.

[95] Soubise, *supra* note 65; Laurène Soubise, *Prosecuting in the Magistrates' Courts in a Time of Austerity*, Crim. L. Rev. (forthcoming 2018).

[96] Ed Cape et al. conducted a study of effective criminal defense in Europe (Belgium, England and Wales, Finland, France, Germany, Hungary, Italy, Poland, and Turkey) and Ed Cape and Zaza Namoradze

Spronken's study examined the information provided in writing to suspects in EU states, concerning their rights while in police custody immediately following arrest. Using questionnaires and interviews, the researchers gathered accounts of what information was provided and how this was done. Although required by law to provide basic information to suspects, the researchers found that this was done in a variety of ways, many of them wholly inappropriate and ineffective. A number of countries provided information in writing and several adopted the format of a Letter of Rights, but the language and format differed widely. Based on examples of best practices, they recommended the use of a clear and detailed template that ensured compliance with international norms such as the ECHR. The subsequent EU Directive on the right to information in criminal proceedings drew on these findings and included such an indicative Letter of Rights.[97]

Miet Vanderhallen et al.'s study of safeguards for young suspects during police interrogation also adopted a comparative European approach and focused specifically on best practices that might inform the proposed EU Directive.[98] Using focus group interviews of police, lawyers, and appropriate adults, as well as young suspects themselves, together with audio and video recordings of a sample of interrogations with juveniles, the study found that, despite common obligations under the ECHR, there were significant differences in the ways that young suspects were treated during the criminal investigation and in particular, in the safeguards provided during police interrogation. England and Wales and the Netherlands, for example, treat young suspects in the same way as adults, with the provision of some additional safeguards, such as the appropriate adult (a parent or other adult whose role is to facilitate communication and ensure that the young person understands the process). Poland and Belgium, on the other hand, adopt a more paternalistic approach, dealing with matters through the family courts. Although apparently less punitive, this approach was found to deny agency to those under investigation; under it, young suspects enjoy fewer rights, yet ultimately, can still have their liberty taken away. This and other findings from the research informed a set of guidelines designed "to contribute to shaping, defining and improving the well-being of juveniles who come into contact with juvenile punitive justice."[99]

Perhaps the most empirically rich of these recent comparative studies is that conducted across four jurisdictions by Jodie Blackstock et al. Researchers observed the detention and interrogation of suspects over a period of seventy-eight weeks, accompanying lawyers and being based in the police station for a number of weeks or months, thereby gaining both a police and defense perspective on the experience of custody.[100] The observation periods were followed by ninety-four semi-structured interviews with police and lawyers in all jurisdictions. Researchers were able to see firsthand how suspects were informed of their rights; were assessed and provided with an interpreter;

of Eastern Europe (Bulgaria, Georgia, Lithuania, Moldova and Ukraine). Ed Cape et al., *Effective Criminal Defense in Europe* (2010); Cape & Namoradze, *supra* note 10.

[97] Taru Spronken, *EU-Wide Letter of Rights in Criminal Proceedings: Towards Best Practice* (2010).

[98] The study examined the laws and practices in five EU states: Belgium, England and Wales, Italy, the Netherlands, and Poland. *Interrogation Young Suspects II: Procedural Safeguards from a Legal Perspective* (Miet Vanderhallen et al. eds., 2016).

[99] *Id.* at 385. [100] Blackstock et al., *supra* note 55.

how they were able to access legal advice and the quality of that advice; and how the police questioned suspects. While some practices reflected different frameworks of legal regulation—such as French lawyers being restricted to a thirty-minute client consultation and playing a passive role during the suspect's interrogation—other phenomena could be explained within a broader context of reform experience that was less about the specifics of the procedural roots of the jurisdiction and more about understanding the degree to which due process reforms had become embedded in a particular criminal process.

This offers valuable lessons for reformers. For example, Dutch police officers were resistant to the idea of lawyers advising suspects and being present in the interrogation room. They felt this new reform would undermine the effectiveness of the investigation and so took steps to discourage suspects from exercising their right to custodial legal advice. Hodgson found that French police responded in the same way in the 1990s when lawyers were first permitted to consult with suspects for thirty minutes prior to the police interrogation, but over time, came to accept this role and even found it to be useful in providing reassurance to detainees.[101] The same pattern was also observed in England and Wales in the 1980s following the statutory right to custodial legal advice provided by Section 58 of the Police and Criminal Evidence Act 1984 (PACE).[102]

These reforms occurred in different jurisdictions and in different decades, but the response of the police was the same. As discussed briefly above, believing that lawyers would interfere with and undermine the investigation, encourage the exercise of silence, provide false alibis to ensure suspects did not incriminate themselves, and generally behave in unhelpful or improper ways, officers across all jurisdictions engaged in strategies of rights avoidance designed to ensure that suspects were either unaware of the extent of their rights, or were disincentivized from exercising them. As a result, PACE Codes of Practice were altered to prohibit the police from discouraging suspects to exercise their rights, and EU legislation has also preempted some of these strategies.

V. Concluding Remarks

This brief overview has focused on a selection of empirical research that assists us in understanding criminal justice practices and the way decisions are made in a complex environment. Hence, it is far from a comprehensive account of the empirical studies, and many important works, regrettably, are not included due to limited space. It is well recognized that studying the legal rules alone can offer only limited insights into the way state power is exercised, and legal rules cannot effectively illustrate obscure concepts such as discretion. Therefore, empirical research is a useful tool in exploring these critical aspects of criminal justice.

[101] Hodgson, *supra* note 12, 135–39; Blackstock et al., *supra* note 55, at 298–300.

[102] Sanders et al., *supra* note 25.

Anthony Edwards argues that the public should not just be aware of what is supposed to happen, but is also entitled to know what actually happens.[103] Hence, conducting empirical research can be seen as a way of exercising the "right to know"—an engagement of the public and dissemination of knowledge by making specific criminal justice inquires. When embarking on empirical investigation, researchers face a range of challenges and a journey that is filled with uncertainties, risks, pitfalls, joys, and surprises. This choice, as Mandy Burton has commented, is an "uncomfortable necessity in that it involves practice and ethical choices which represent real challenges for the researcher."[104] Although we do not have the room to discuss the methodological issues that exist in collecting and analyzing the data, it is necessary to appreciate the obstacles that empirical researchers often confront—funding, resources, time, training, access to the field and research subjects, experience, cultural and language barriers, and often uncomfortable relationships—that constrain the success of the research.[105] Despite these challenges, the harvest outweighs the costs. There are also memorable stories behind every project, as many researchers have experienced and recalled.[106] In this regard, empirical research is not merely a productive process of acquiring knowledge, it is also a valuable experience that enriches our lives.

References

Jodie Blackstock et al., *Inside Police Custody: An Empirical Account of Suspects' Rights in Four Jurisdictions* (2014)

Janet Chan, *Changing Police Culture: Policing in a Multicultural Society* (1997)

Satnam Choongh, *Policing as Social Discipline* (1997)

Louise Ellison & Vanessa Munro, *"Telling Tales": Exploring Narratives of Life and Law within the (Mock) Jury Room*, 35 Leg. Stud. 201 (2015)

Loraine Gelsthorpe & Nicola Padfield, *Exercising Discretion: Decision-Making in the Criminal Justice System and Beyond* (2003)

Jacqueline Hodgson, *French Criminal Justice: A Comparative Account of the Investigation and Prosecution of Crime in France* (2005)

Jacqueline Hodgson, *Safeguarding Suspects' Rights in EU Criminal Justice: A Comparative Perspective*, 14 New Crim. L. Rev. 611 (2011)

Jacqueline Hodgson & Laurène Soubise, *The Public Prosecutor in France, in Oxford Handbooks Online: Criminology and Criminal Justice* (2016)

Adrian Hunt & John Baldwin, *Prosecutors Advising in Police Stations*, 8 Crim. L. Rev. 521 (1998)

Vicky Kemp, *Bridewell Legal Advice Study: Adopting a Whole-System Approach to Police Station Legal Advice* (2013)

[103] Edwards, *supra* note 40.

[104] Mandy Burton, *Doing Empirical Research: Exploring the Decision-Making of Magistrates and Juries*, in *Research Methods in Law* 81 (Dawn Watkins & Burton Mandy eds., 2013).

[105] Dame H. Genn et al., *Law in the Real World: Improving Our Understanding of How Law Works* 5–16 (2007).

[106] Simon Halliday & Patrick Schmidt, *Conducting Law and Society Research: Reflections on Methods and Practices* 277–82 (2009).

Mike McConville et al., *The Case for the Prosecution* (1991)
Mike McConville & Jacqueline Hodgson, *Custodial Legal Advice and the Right to Silence* (1993)
Mike McConville et al., *Standing Accused: The Organization and Practices of Criminal Defense Lawyers in Britain* (1994)
Mike McConville et al., *Criminal Justice in China: An Empirical Inquiry* (2011)
Yu Mou, *The Constructed Truth: The Making of Police Dossiers in China*, 26 Soc. & Leg. Stud. 69 (2017)
Yu Mou, *Overseeing Criminal Justice: The Supervisory Role of the Public Prosecution Service in China*, J. L. & Soc. (2017)
Daniel Newman, *Legal Aid Lawyers and the Quest for Justice* (2013)
Andrew Sanders et al., *Advice and Assistance at Police Stations and the 24-Hour Duty Solicitor Scheme* (1989)
Laurène Soubise, *Prosecutorial Discretion and Accountability: A Comparative Study of France and England and Wales*, PhD thesis, University of Warwick (2016)
Divya Sukumar et al., *Strategic Disclosure of Evidence: Perspectives from Psychology and Law*, 22 Psych. Pub. Pol'y & L. 306 (2016)
Max Travers, *The Reality of Law: Work and Talk in a Firm of Criminal Lawyers* (1997)
Michael Zander & Paul Henderson, *Crown Court Study* (1993)

CHAPTER 4

COMPARATIVE APPROACHES TO CRIMINAL PROCEDURE

Transplants, Translations, and Adversarial-Model Reforms in European Criminal Process

ELISABETTA GRANDE

I. Introduction

During the last few decades, European continental criminal procedures underwent extensive reforms, and in that process, the American adversary system often became the reference model for the overhaul. This chapter will discuss the idea of "Americanization/adversarialization" of European criminal procedures—that is, the possible convergence between American common law and European civil law criminal procedure systems toward a common adversary core structure—by examining the real impact of the transplanting of some American adversarial features into the non-adversary European soil. These include: pretrial investigations conducted by the police and the public prosecutor in lieu of the investigating judge typical of the civilian tradition; exclusionary rules; cross-examination; and jury trial. This chapter will argue that, short of diffusing American legal institutions in Europe and making the European criminal procedure systems more adversarial, the transfer has resulted instead in its opposite: that is, in the fortification of the civilian non-adversary structure and its tenets.

The analysis proposed in this chapter, which heavily builds upon some of my previous works,[1] will try to show how the imported adversarial legal arrangements were not

[1] Elisabetta Grande, *Dances of Criminal Justice: Thoughts on Systemic Differences and the Search for the Truth*, in *Crime, Procedure and Evidence in a Comparative and International Context—Essays in Honour of Professor Mirjan Damaška* 145 (John Jackson et al. eds., 2008); Elisabetta Grande, *Rumba Justice and*

simply reinterpreted according to the non-adversarial style of the recipient systems. They even worked to strengthen the most essential feature of a liberal non-adversary procedure, that is, the impartiality of a third-party official search for the truth. Thus the transplant did not result in making the two procedures converge; to the contrary, it had the paradoxical effect of widening—as far as the classical in-court procedure is concerned—the divergence between American common law and Continental European civil law criminal procedures.

One more transplant from the U.S. procedural system will be very briefly taken into consideration in the present chapter. It is plea bargaining, a feature that can hardly be reconciled with an adversarial character and with the search for the truth that the adversarial procedure (as much as the non-adversarial one, though according to different tenets) is aimed to bring about. Plea bargaining subverts the adversarial ideal of justice as much as the non-adversarial one. This is why, in my opinion, plea bargaining diffusion in continental European criminal procedure systems cannot be viewed as leading up to their "adversarialization," that is, as making them more adversarial. Nevertheless, the diffusion of plea bargaining poses a global risk that, in the name of speed and harmony, the search for the truth may too often be supplanted with the search for a deal, and that common law and civil law criminal procedures, while not converging on adversariness, could yet move further toward an overstretching negotiation procedure, which is increasingly pushing aside the "old-fashioned/anti-economical" non-adversary and adversary trial procedures.

II. Tango Justice v. Rumba Justice

In order to assess the impact of some classical American features upon Continental European systems, one needs to bring the difference between adversarial and non-adversarial models into sharper focus.[2] Following Professor Damaška, the two rival procedural models can be fruitfully organized around the contrast between features distinguishing a party-controlled contest, on the one hand, from an officially controlled inquiry, on the other.[3] The key difference between common law and Continental criminal

the Spanish Jury Trial, in *Handbook on Comparative Criminal Procedure* 365 (Jacqueline E. Ross & Stephen C. Thaman eds., 2016); Elisabetta Grande, *Legal Transplants and the Inoculation Effect: How American Criminal Procedure Has Affected Continental Europe*, 64 Am. J. Comp. Law 583 (2016).

[2] The analysis of the non-adversary/adversary or inquisitorial/accusatorial dichotomy has been at the core of the comparative criminal procedure studies and has been therefore extensively and deeply explored in a vast literature. For a quick reference, see Elisabetta Grande, *Comparative Criminal Justice*, in *The Cambridge Companion to Comparative Law* 191 (Mauro Bussani & Ugo Mattei eds., 2012).

[3] Mirjan R. Damaška, *Evidentiary Barriers to Conviction and Two Models of Criminal Procedure: A Comparative Study*, 121 U. Pa. L. Rev. 506 (1973); *see also* Mirjan R. Damaška, *Models of Criminal Procedure* 51 Zbornik PFZ (Collected Papers of Zagreb Law School) 477 (2001).

procedure, in his view, resides in the distinct roles that parties and judges play in the fact-finding process. In a common law model, two contestants shape the expression of their dispute and manage the presentation of the evidence. In a Continental model, fact-finding responsibilities are assigned to court officials.

These differences between the respective roles of parties and judges reflect contrasting approaches to the search for truth. Starting from the idea that a third party's search for the truth can be neutrally pursued, the non-adversary model maintains that the pursuit of justice requires judges to seek as close as possible the *objective* truth in adjudicating criminal liability. By way of contrast, the adversary system rests on the assumption that any third-party reconstruction of the facts is inevitably biased and nonobjective; thus, a truly non-partisan search for the truth is viewed as unachievable. The search for the truth in a legal process therefore needs to depart from ordinary cognitive practices and be pursued through a fair confrontation of two parties, each one promoting her side of the story in front of a passive adjudicator. The emerging truth, short of being *objective*, is the product of a contest between two interpretations of reality; it can be defined as an *interpretive* truth to point to its skepticism toward an objective reconstruction of reality.

The "relational" nature of the truth-discovering enterprise in an adversary system produces what I have elsewhere called a "tango" idea of justice. As in tango, where it takes two—and only two—to dance, in an adversarial conception, it takes two (yet in this case fighting against each other) to produce a reconstruction of reality that can be equated with truth. By contrast, the alternative notion of justice of the non-adversary system can be associated with the metaphor of a Cuban rumba dance. As in the dance, in "rumba justice," a variety of dancers perform together in a collective search for the *objective* truth. The dancers are: the defendant, her lawyer, the prosecutor, the victim, sometimes public complainants (i.e., private third parties unconnected to the offense who are allowed to participate provided they comply with a series of requirements, such as in Spain), or civil third-party defendants (i.e., persons that are liable for damages in lieu of the defendant should the latter be convicted and insolvent, such as in Italy or Spain), then the judges and the lay assessors or jurors.[4]

The two rival procedural models originated at the turn of the nineteenth century, when an influential liberal credo not only called for keeping the state at arm's length,[5] but also expressed a strong skepticism toward the "neutrality" of any third-party reconstruction of the facts—particularly if vested in government officials. In response to this critique, the common law tradition promoted the restructuring of the criminal process

[4] For a thorough explanation of the Cuban Rumba dancing metaphor, see Grande, *Dances of Criminal Justice*, *supra* note 1.

[5] This expression was used by Karl Llewellyn with regard to the adversary model, as opposed to a "parental" model, which Llewellyn used to describe the inquisitorial one. *See* Karl N. Llewellyn, *The Anthropology of Criminal Guilt*, in *Jurisprudence: Realism in Theory and Practice* 439, 444–50 (1962). For a further exploration of these models, see John Griffiths, *Ideology in Criminal Procedure or a Third "Model" of the Criminal Process*, 79 Yale L. J. 359 (1970).

as a dispute between two sides in front of a passive adjudicator.[6] By contrast, the civil law tradition reacted by transforming the third-party official reconstruction of the facts from a unilateral inquiry into a sort of collective enterprise.

Since it became clear that the more unilateral the inquiry, the higher the risk of undermining the truth-seeker's impartiality, over the course of the last two hundred years, Continental European criminal procedures provided more and more for the active participation of multiple actors in the third party's investigation into the truth—at both the pretrial and trial stages (therefore enhancing the *external* plurality of perspectives upon the official inquiry). They also provided for an increasing fragmentation of the official authority over the facts reconstruction, leading to a multiplication of perspectives within the decision-making process and therefore enhancing the *internal* plurality of perspectives upon the official inquiry.[7]

Multiplying *external* and *internal* perspectives on the third party's reconstruction of the facts authentically transformed Continental procedure from an official unilateral inquiry into a pluralist investigation. It therefore effectively increased the impartiality of the official in charge of the enquiry. That was the reply to the "neutrality problem" of a third-party search, which was raised critically by classic English liberalism. Thus the Continental world still considers neutrality attainable in the criminal process, the civil law tradition never replaced the search for an *objective* truth with a search for an *interpretive* truth, and officials, made as impartial as possible through their participation in a pluralist investigation, are still in charge of searching for it, as carefully as they can.

III. U.S. Criminal Procedure in Europe—Global Trend toward Adversary Justice?

This preliminary juxtaposition of the two kinds of criminal procedure models should allow us to intelligently interrogate the impact on Continental criminal procedures of the recent import from the American system of institutions such as a pretrial investigation conducted by the police and the public prosecutor (in lieu of the investigating magistrate classical of the civil law tradition), exclusionary rules, cross-examination, and the jury trial.

[6] On the impact of laissez-faire Lockean values on English institutional arrangements, see Mirjan R. Damaška, *Structure of Authority and Comparative Criminal Procedure*, 84 Yale L. J. 480, 532 & *passim* (1975); Mirjan R. Damaška, *The Faces of Justice and State Authority: A Comparative Approach to the Legal Process* (1986).

[7] For a detailed illustration of these questions, see Grande, *Legal Transplants*, *supra* note 1, at 592 ff.

1. Abolition of the Investigative Judge in Continental European Procedures

In the relatively recent past, Germany (in 1975),[8] Portugal (in 1987),[9] and Italy (in 1988)[10] abolished the examining magistrate or investigative judge as the central figure in charge of the pretrial investigation, entrusting such an activity to a prosecutor divested of any judicial role. This move could easily be interpreted as a step toward an "Americanization" and "adversarialization" of inquisitorial criminal procedure, since the investigative judge has always been considered a distinctive feature of the inquisitorial system[11] and the new "non-judicial" prosecutor seemed destined to acquire a more partisan stance.[12] Yet this interpretation proved to be highly misguided. Indeed, the replacement of the investigative judge with a "non-judicial" prosecutor in charge of the pretrial investigation did not mean the importation into Continental criminal procedure of tango justice or the party-centered contest with only limited state interference. It did not transform the Continental prosecutor into an adversary of the accused nor did it produce an alteration of her strong public nature. To the contrary, it fortified the rumba justice structure of the recipient systems.

To be sure, the Continental prosecutor in charge of the pretrial investigation in Germany, Italy, and Portugal, although now lacking judicial authority in her investigative activity, never became a party to the proceedings, but solidly maintained her non-partisan stance. This is the case in Germany and Portugal, where the prosecutor, as an impartial and objective investigator, collects the evidence for and against the defendant and participates in the proceedings with the aim to discover the truth and to obtain a just outcome.[13] It is also the case in Italy, which since 1988 has had the most "Americanized" of the Continental procedures. While the ambition of the reformers was to entrust the prosecutor with a partisan role, to define the Italian prosecutor as a party to the process would be highly misleading. The most one could say is that she occupies an ambiguous

[8] Erstes Gesetz zur Reform der Strafverfahrensrechts [1. StVRG] [First Criminal Procedure Reform Act], Dec. 9, 1974, Bundesgesetzblatt [BGB l] I (Ger.); *see also* Thomas Weigend, *Germany*, in *Criminal Procedure: A Worldwide Study* 243, 262 (Craig M. Bradley ed., 2d ed. 2007).

[9] Código de processo penal [C.p.p.] [Code of Criminal Procedure] art. 262 (Port.); *see also* Jorge de Figueiredo Dias & Maria João Antunes, *Portugal*, in *Criminal Procedure Systems in the European Community* 318 (Christine Van Den Wyngaert et al. eds., 1993).

[10] Codice di procedura penale [C.p.p.] [Code of Criminal Procedure] arts. 126ff. (It.); *see also* Elisabetta Grande, *Italian Criminal Justice: Borrowing and Resistance*, 48 Am. J. Comp. L. 227, 232 (2000); Giulio Illuminati, *The Accusatorial Process from the Italian Point of View*, 35 N.C. J. Int'l & Com. Reg. 297, 308 (2010); Luca Lupária, *Model Code or Broken Dream? The Italian Criminal Procedure in a Comparative Perspective*, in *The Italian Code of Criminal Procedure: Critical Essays and English Translation* 1 (M. Gialuz et al. eds., 2014).

[11] For a quick outline of the historical roots of this figure, see Mar Jimeno-Bulnes, *American Criminal Procedure in a European Context*, 21 Cardozo J. Int'l & Comp. L. 409, 424 (2013).

[12] *See* Gilberto Lozzi, *Lezioni di Procedura Penale* 114 (2012).

[13] On the German system, see Barbara Huber, *Criminal Procedure in Germany*, in *Criminal Procedure in Europe* 326 (Richard Vogler & Barbara Huber eds., 2008). On the Portuguese system, see De Figueredo Diaz & Joro Antunes, *supra* note 9, at 319.

position, working as a helper for the defense on many occasions.[14] Moreover, just like her German and Portuguese counterparts, the Italian prosecutor can and does move for acquittal of the defendant and can appeal a conviction.

In the United States, although the *public* prosecutor is addressed as "the government" or "the state" and was not resisted for centuries (in contrast to England, where it only emerged at the end of the twentieth century),[15] it does not bear the same strong association with the government as Continental European prosecutors do.[16] U.S. prosecutors are typically not lifelong career civil servants, hired according to technical qualifications and working in a bureaucratic and highly hierarchical agency.[17] The American chief prosecutor is generally a private lawyer and a politician, only temporarily in an official role. Being (often) elected at the state level or politically appointed at the federal one, she directly or indirectly represents the people, not merely the state administration. Vested in a democratic role, her prosecution (according to a liberal ideology) has a bottom-up as well as a top-down legitimization, and it is primarily the expression of the people's interest rather than that of the authoritarian bureaucratic state apparatus.[18]

By contrast, in Italy, Germany, and Portugal, the prosecutor has never loosened her solid association with the state apparatus, embedded as she is in a highly bureaucratic and hierarchical structure that gives her a strong character of state organ. The ideal severance between state bureaucratic administration and prosecutorial activity, which characterizes the arm's length adversarial model, did not occur in Continental Europe.

[14] For cases in which the Italian prosecutor can perform as a helper of the defense, see C.p.p. (It.) arts. 391bis(10), 368, 415bis(4); to some extent, art. 358; and until August 2017, art. 421 bis.

[15] On the English police acting as private prosecutors, see Douglas Hay & Francis Snyder, *Using the Criminal Law, 1750–1850: Policing, Private Prosecution, and the State*, in *Policing and Prosecution in Britain 1750–1850*, at 35, 43 (Douglas Hay & Francis Snyder eds., 1989) ("Although prosecutions were suits in the name of the Crown, they were viewed, in political ideology as well as in law, as adversarial proceedings between private individuals."); John H. Langbein, *The Origins of Public Prosecution at Common Law*, 17 Am. J. Legal Hist. 313, 441 (1973) ("When 'the police' prosecute, the correct analysis is that some individual has instituted proceedings, and the fact that this individual is a police officer does not alter the nature of the prosecution.") (quoting Richard M. Jackson, *The Machinery of Justice in England* 155 (6th ed. 1972)).

[16] *See* Joan E. Jacoby, *The American Prosecutor: A Search for Identity* ch. 1 (1980).

[17] For a comparative analysis of the prosecutor's power and functions, see John H. Langbein, *Controlling Prosecutorial Discretion in Germany*, 41 U. Chi. L. Rev. 439, 444 (1974). Even if outdated in some aspects, the article is still a landmark study on point. For a quite different approach, which emphasizes the similarities rather than the differences between the American prosecutor and her European counterparts, see David Alan Sklansky, *The Nature and Function of Prosecutorial Power*, 106 J. Crim. L. & Criminology 473 (2016).

[18] On the shortcomings of the American prosecutor's democratic accountability, see David Alan Sklansky, *Unpacking the Relationship Between Prosecutors and Democracy in the United States*, in *Prosecutors and Democracy: A Cross-National Study* 276 (Màximo Langer & David Alan Sklansky eds., 2017). On a different rationale for the historical reconstruction of the American salaried prosecutor's unique wide discretionary power to institute criminal proceedings as an instrument to accommodate the people's interests with that of the alien and distant government (especially at the federal level) "external to the community," see Nicholas R. Parrillo, *Against the Profit Motive: The Salary Revolution in American Government, 1780–1940*, at 258 (2013).

Instead, in the Continental European tradition, prosecutorial investigation rests firmly associated with an inquisitorial "parental" state.[19]

The sharp severance of the investigative and the judicial functions achieved by abolishing the investigative judge served instead the goal of improving the internal plurality of perspectives that can serve as the basis for solid and impartial judgments. It limited the prosecutor's role to the activity of gathering the evidence to be produced at trial, as opposed to the activity of taking the evidence that had been performed by the investigative judge. By eliminating the authoritative pretrial judicial evaluation of the evidence, the reform strengthened the autonomy of the trial judge in appraising the evidence. By multiplying the *internal* perspectives upon official facts reconstruction, it fortified the Continental rumba justice way, thus lengthening rather than shortening the distance from American tango justice.

2. U.S. Exclusionary Rules in Continental Europe

In the recent past, a number of European Continental countries adopted exclusionary rules modeled upon U.S. exclusionary rules. For example, Portugal, Italy, and Spain adopted the hearsay prohibition rule.[20] Italy and Germany introduced the so-called *Miranda* exclusionary rule, excluding statements of an accused who was not informed of her rights to remain silent in pretrial questioning.[21] Italy, Germany, and Spain (in different ways and in different terms) have also enacted inadmissibility rules against illegally obtained evidence, such as for instance evidence obtained by unlawful wiretapping.[22] In Spain and sometimes in Germany, the fruits of illegal searches are held inadmissible.[23]

[19] *Cf.* Llewelyn, *supra* note 5, at 444–50.

[20] The hearsay prohibition is banned in Portugal by C.p.p. art. 129 (Port.) and in Italy by C.p.p. art. 195 (It.). In Spain, hearsay testimony is allowed only formally since it is very much restricted in substance, with, indeed, the same results as in Italy, where in principle it is prohibited. *See* Fernando Gascón Inchausti & María Luisa Villamarín López, *Criminal Procedure in Spain*, in *Criminal Procedure in Europe* 541, 617–18 (Richard Vogler & Barbara Huber eds., 2008).

[21] C.p.p. art. 64 (3) and (3bis) (It.), as modified in 2001 (L.01/03/2001). On the *Miranda*-type exclusionary rule in Germany, see Sabine Gless, *Truth or Due Process? The Use of Illegally Gathered Evidence in the Criminal Trial—Germany*, in *German National Reports to the 18th International Congress of Comparative Law* 675, 700 (Jürgen Basedow et al. eds., 2010). For a wider comparative perspective, updated until 2000, see Stephen C. Thaman, Miranda *in Comparative Law*, 45 St. Louis U. L.J. 581 (2001).

[22] *See* C.p.p. art. 271 (It.). For Spain, see Article 11 (1) of Ley Orgánica del Poder Judicial [hereinafter 'LOPJ'], which relates not only to criminal procedure, but to all procedures ("evidence obtained either directly or indirectly in contravention of fundamentals rights and liberties will be with no effect") in connection with the fundamental right of the privacy of communications guaranteed by Article 18(3) of the Spanish Constitution. For Germany, see Huber, *supra* note 13, at 347 (noting that "evidence obtained by surveillance of telecommunication is inadmissible if the substantive precondition for surveillance (§ 100a) are not met [...] The lack of formal preconditions does not necessarily result in inadmissibility").

[23] For Spain, see LOPJ art. 11(1), in connection with the principle that the "home is inviolable" (Spanish Const. art.18.2). In Italy, despite the general provision of C.p.p. art. 191 (It.), which prescribes the inadmissibility of any evidence acquired in violation of the law, courts and academic commentators interpret it restrictively, and the fruits of unlawful searches and seizures are not excluded. In Germany,

Moreover, in exceptional cases of serious infringement of an individual's constitutional rights, even a type of "fruits of the poisonous tree" doctrine (according to which evidence that derives from illegal evidence is also illegal) has traveled to Germany.[24]

As the subsequent sections discuss, this import did not modify the basic tenets of the evidence law of the recipient systems and did not make them more adversarial. To the contrary, the Continental non-adversary context changed the structure of the imported American exclusionary rules according to its different needs, to the point that the imported arrangements not only lost their original adversarial character, but also strengthened the non-adversary way of searching for the truth.

a. *Adversarial Fairness: Rationale for Exclusionary Rules in the United States*

In the common law world, the law of evidence is the "child of the jury system."[25] Indeed, it is the need to take ex ante control over the rationality of an oracular and autonomous trier of fact—as the common law jury presents itself—that explains the shielding of jurors from evidence that could otherwise prejudice adjudication. In Damaška's words, it is the need "to shore up *ex ante* the legitimacy of inscrutable verdicts."[26]

Yet in the common law world, the law of evidence is also very much the "child of the adversary criminal procedure." In it the law of evidence plays the key role of establishing the rules that provide for a fair contest, allowing the system to be successful in its production of the *interpretive* truth. Indeed, American evidence law evens the playing field of the dispute by assuring the balancing of advantages between litigants in the proof-taking activity, thereby giving the parties equal opportunities to present their views of reality. In a battle between two parties, it would be unfair for the stronger party to benefit from an unlawfully obtained confession. Similarly, it would be unfair, and hence intolerable for the sake of the *interpretive* truth, for the prosecutor to gain an undue benefit from an illegal search or seizure or an illegal interception. Not giving one of the parties the opportunity to directly and vigorously examine the adverse and possibly intensively coached and briefed witness would likewise be unfairly preventing her from putting down the adversary. It would also be considered unfair to allow hearsay testimony, since the person whose utterance the hearsay witness reproduces cannot be tested by the opponent, "who is often justified in envisaging the out-of-court speaker as a hidden ally of his adversary—an ally who avoids courtroom challenge."[27] In all the above-mentioned instances, the contest would be prejudiced, just as the trial by mounted combat of medieval times would have been, if only one of the two combatants were provided with a horse and a sword.

courts regard evidence illegally seized as admissible, yet there is "a growing tendency toward rejecting evidence that was acquired in clear, conscious violation of a person's constitutional rights." Thomas Wiegend, *Should We Search for the Truth, and Who Should Do It?*, 36 N.C.J. Int'l L. & Com. Reg. 389, 401 n.57 (2011); *see also* Weigend, *supra* note 8, at 251 ff.

[24] Huber, *supra* note 13, at 348.

[25] James B. Thayer, *The Jury and Its Development*, 5 Harv. L. Rev. 249 (1892).

[26] Mirjan R. Damaška, *Evidence Law Adrift* 46 (1997). [27] *Id.* at 80.

Therefore, adversarial fairness underlies the process for seeking the truth in American evidence and procedure, and many exclusionary rules, such as the prohibition on hearsay, the privilege against self-incrimination (along with corroboration rules, compulsory process and cross-examination), and even rules for excluding illegally obtained evidence also seem designed to such an end.

The above discussion does not ignore, of course, that respecting adversarial fairness can bring about other desirable collateral effects, too. Sometimes deference to adversarial fairness results in a more accurate reconstruction of reality. At other times, exclusionary rules primarily designed to grant adversarial fairness have a different collateral outcome—a disciplinary effect on law enforcement authorities, who will hopefully be deterred from abusing their power against the rights of all citizens in the future.

Consistent with the tenets of an adversarial approach, exclusionary rules in the U.S. system are in general only conditionally applicable: they come to life only if the parties invoke them. Because the *assumption* is that litigants know what is best for them, and since no one else can establish better knowledge, no one, and especially not the distrusted state official, can impose his view on the parties. This is why, even if the judge has the theoretical power to suppress evidence on his own motion, he rarely does so, and anyway, he never has a *duty* to remedy a party's failure to object to inadmissible evidence.[28] The parties by and large draft their own script, and the accused is perceived as acting as a free individual, being able to freely make her strategic choice in shaping the evidentiary arrangements and therefore her own case.

b. *Protective Stance: Rationale for Exclusionary Rules in Continental Europe*

A different rationale than the one at play in the United States explains the very existence of exclusionary rules in Continental Europe. In civil law systems, exclusionary rules are primarily concerned with protecting the accuracy of official fact-finding. They ban evidence that is deemed to prevent the pursuit of the *objective* truth. Yet since officials today have to pursue their search for the truth more and more within the limits imposed by the respect of human dignity, they also have to guard the accused against the infringement of her fundamental human rights, even when that causes a deviation from the unveiling of the *objective* truth. In Continental Europe, therefore, it is not the adversarial fairness rationale that gives life to exclusionary rules. Rather, it is, first, the old goal to safeguard fact-finding accuracy, detectable in many inadmissibility rules meant to exclude evidence deemed to be unreliable. Examples are the rules that exclude anonymous

[28] Occasionally, a trial judge will have the discretion to act on her own motion. This is the case of the plain error doctrine, incorporated in Rule 103(e) of the Federal Rules of Evidence, according to which, even when a proper objection was not made, an appellate court *may in its discretion* notice a forfeited error and reject the result at trial whenever the committed error "seriously affects the fairness, integrity, or public reputation of judicial proceedings." Yet this represents an appellate court's discretionary power, and since "the adversary system, based on party responsibility, is deeply engrained in our jurisprudence, particularly in the field of evidence," the plain error doctrine is very rarely applied. *See* Michael H. Graham, *Evidence: A Problem, Lecture and Discussion Approach* 695–96 (3d ed. 2012).

documents or testimony based on word of mouth shared by the community,[29] the rule excluding hearsay testimony,[30] and to some extent the rule that excludes an accused's statement obtained in a way likely to modify the declarant's self-determination (via lie detectors, the administration of drugs, and so forth).[31] A more novel rationale is to protect the defendant from an otherwise too "dirty" and therefore unacceptable search for the substantive truth. This is particularly the case for exclusionary rules of recent adoption, such as the *Miranda*-type rule and the rules excluding illegally seized items or illegally obtained interception.

The "protective" rationale, as opposed to an adversarial one, explains why evidentiary regulation here, in contrast to what happens in the United States, is by and large the province of the judge and why it cannot in principle be displaced by unilateral waiver. In Continental European criminal procedure, the "imported" exclusionary rules lose their original adversarial rationale and acquire a different one consistent with the non-adversary context in which they now have to operate. In line with the different protective rationale, their observance remains mainly the responsibility of the court, since the parties, who can always raise the question of their inadmissibility, cannot in principle modify the evidence rules by waiving a relevant objection.[32] In those systems the judge, in the name of the search for an *objective* truth, but also in the name of protecting the defendant, keeps the power and *the duty* to raise statutory exclusionary rules ex officio. Even when, as is the case with the hearsay ban in Italy, the litigants can allow the production at trial of the hearsay witness by not vetoing it, the judge can ex officio act in their place by asking for the original declarant to take the stand.[33] Such rules, rather than working as the expression of the parties' freedom to draft their own script, act irrespectively of the parties' will.

In a non-adversary context, furthermore, where justice is associated with a neutral third-party search for an *objective* truth, rather than equated to "adversary fairness," it is essential to ensure that the evidentiary material is as complete as possible. The ensuing

[29] *See* C.p.p. art. 234 (3) (It.); C.p.p. art. 130 (Port.).

[30] On the intrinsic exclusionary rules rationale embedded in the Continental hearsay prohibition (i.e., "the insight that firsthand information is more reliable than information filtered through intermediary sources"), see Damaška, *supra* note 26, at 15 n.22 (quoting Mirjan Damaška, *Hearsay in Cinquecento Italy*, in *Studi In Onore Di Vittorio Denti* (Michele Taruffo ed., 1994)).

[31] *See, e.g., Strafprozessordnung* [German Code of Criminal Procedure, hereinafter 'StPO'] § 136a; C.p.p. arts. 64(2), 188 (It.).

[32] In Italy, in fact, their violation can (and has to) always be officially raised at any stage or level of the proceedings. C.p.p. art. 191(2) (It.). For a more extensive treatment, see Grande, *supra* note 10, at 248. For the Spanish system, see Gascón Inchausti &Villamarín López, *supra* note 20, at 614. Germany, however, seems to have quite recently deviated from this common attitude, at least in relation to some of its exclusionary rules (and without prejudice to StPO § 136a, which is always mandatorily applied by the court even if the accused consents to its admission). For the veto against the admission of the illegally gathered evidence by the person whose rights have been violated, advanced by German courts as a condition for some exclusionary rule to be enforced (*Widerspruchsloesung*), see Gless, *supra* note 21, at 686 (further noting the criticism this development has met in Germany). The basis of the German jurisprudence in that regard can be found in BGHSt 38, 214, at 225 (February 27, 1992) and those decisions following it. *See* Gless, *supra* note 21, at 686.

[33] C.p.p. art. 195(2) (It.).

desire to meet the adjudicator's investigative needs is therefore paramount. Accordingly, European civil law systems generally still permit the admission of hearsay evidence and out-of-court secretly gathered declarations of witnesses, whenever the original declarant is not available in court because of intervening death, mental illness, or some other reason that makes her previous declaration impossible to repeat.[34]

c. *The True Impact of the Adoption of Exclusionary Rules in Continental Europe*

In the Continental European context, the imported exclusionary rules have lost their original adversarial fairness rationale as well as their connection with an idea of individual freedom to shape evidentiary arrangements to suit each party's own tactical interests. Moreover, although maintaining the same name as their American counterparts, exclusionary rules operate in a very different manner in European systems. The inadmissible evidence is not excluded from the cognitive framework of the trier of fact; instead, it is eliminated from the written reasoning of the trier of fact. This represents a huge functional departure from the original model.[35] It seems therefore that the context of the receiving criminal justice systems ended up highly modifying, according to those systems' different needs, the original structure of the "imported" American exclusionary rules.

Yet the emergence of a pretrial stage devoted to the admission of evidence in the presence of all participants in the criminal process, as in Italy or Spain, did not remain without repercussions in Continental European systems.[36] In fact, a formal preliminary proceeding dedicated to motions to suppress evidence and separated from the proof-taking phase has increased the participation of *all* the various "dancers" of the Continental European criminal process with respect to the decision about the evidentiary material admitted at trial: an activity that beforehand was performed by the judge alone. Far from relegating the judge to the role of a mere umpire and from giving rise to a party-controlled dispute system, these evidentiary regulations allowed more room for the many dancers of the rumba justice in the preliminary crucial activity of questioning evidence admissibility. Thus, instead of leading Continental European criminal procedures toward the American model, the transplant ended up increasing the distance between them even more.

[34] *See* C.p.p. arts. 512, 195(3) (It.); StPO § 251 I, II; Ley de Enjuiciamiento Criminal [hereinafter LECrim] art. 730; *see also* Al-Khawaja and Tahery v. the United Kingdom, App. Nos. 26766/05 and 22228/06, Eur. Ct. H.R., December 15, 2011 (holding that the use at trial of untested hearsay testimony, when there is a good reason for the nonattendance of the witness, does not violate Article 6(3)(d) of the European Convention on Human Rights). This is so even in cases where the absent witness testimony is the sole or decisive basis for the conviction, provided that there are sufficient counterbalancing factors in place to ensure that the proceedings, when judged in their entirety, are fair.

[35] "Exclusion requires the [triers of fact] to delete the relevant information from their minds and to base their judgment on a fiction rather than on the facts known to them. Even if a judge is willing to obey the command of the law and to disregard excluded information, it is psychologically difficult for him to make a decision he knows to be unrelated to the 'real' facts of the case. [...] Exclusion of evidence thus just makes it more difficult for the court to *justify* a decision which may well have been influenced by the 'excluded' evidence." Weigend, *supra* note 8, at 254.

[36] C.p.p. arts. 493ff. (It.); LECrim art. 659.

3. Cross-Examination Travels

Direct and cross-examination as a witness questioning technique is no longer "a right unknown to systems of trial other than the common-law system."[37] Continental criminal procedures have recently introduced a cross-examination-based system to question witnesses and sometimes also experts and parties. In Spain, Portugal, and Italy, direct and cross-examination by representatives of the parties is now the unique method of questioning them.[38] Elsewhere, such as in Germany, it is only a subsidiary method of interrogation, since in principle the questioning of witnesses and defendants is still conducted by the presiding judge.[39] In France, parties' representatives have been provided with the (less empowering) opportunity to put questions directly to witnesses, defendants, and *parties civiles* with the permission of the presiding judge, after the court has questioned them.[40]

I argue that such a "revolutionary change of procedure," as one scholar has called it,[41] has not brought about an "adversarialization" of the European systems that experienced it.

a. *Cross-Examination in the United States*

Cross-examination in the American adversary process is the most dramatic and symbolic expression of the passivity of the judge in the fact-finding process. It is the emblem of a criminal process structured as a dispute between two sides—the prosecution and the defense—pursuing their opposing interests in front of an official, who—as a mere umpire—has virtually no involvement in the investigation of the actual facts.[42] It is therefore the best expression of adversary criminal procedure as an arm's-length model, assuring the individual of maximum freedom from the state.

Cross-examination as a style of witness questioning is the quintessence of the tango justice where two sides—and two sides only—participate in the fact-finding discovery process, opposing each other. In a party-controlled contest system, such as the American one, cross-examination represents the only effective questioning technique to test the reliability of a witness, who cannot but be strongly associated with one or the other party as her ally. Witness and expert witness are routinely coached in advance of the trial,

[37] Edmund M. Morgan, *Some Problems of Proof under the Anglo-American System of Litigation* 113 (1956).

[38] *See* LECrim. arts. 708 ff.; C.p.p. art. 348(4) (Port.); C.p.p. arts. 498–499, 503 (It.). In Italy, in the monocratic proceedings, however, the parties can waive their rights to cross-examine parties and witnesses. *See* C.p.p. (It.) art. 567(4).

[39] In Germany, StPO § 239(1) provides for direct and cross-examination of witnesses by the parties, but only upon a joint request by the prosecution and the defense. In this case, they question the witness while the judge is permitted only to pose additional questions.

[40] Code de procédure pénale [C. pr. pén.] [Code of Criminal Procedure] arts. 312, 442.1., 536.

[41] Richard Vogler, *Criminal Procedure in France*, in *Criminal Procedure in Europe* 171, *supra* note 13, at 216 (commenting on the French reform, which dates back to 2000).

[42] On the self-imposed passivity of American judges, even when by statute they are permitted to question witnesses, see Damaška, *supra* note 26, at 90; William T. Pizzi & Mariangela Montagna, *The Battle to Establish an Adversarial Trial System in Italy*, 25 Mich. J. Int'l L. 429 (2004).

being therefore highly suspect of false or distorted declaration until shaken off by a skilful cross-examination.

In a system where truth arises out of the opposing views of the parties, to prevent one of them from putting forward her own perspective in the highly effective way of cross-examination not only would be unfair, it would also preclude the very discovery of the *interpretive* truth. This is why the American law resists out-of-court written testimony, excludes a direct testimony, or even declares a mistrial if cross-examination cannot be completed.

Yet, of course, in an adversary system where parties shape their own case according to their own tactical needs, adversarial fairness can always be unilaterally renounced, with the result that the partisan testimony can go totally unchallenged, if the opponent so desires.

b. *Cross-Examination in Continental Europe*

When cross-examination landed in the European Continent, it was plunged into a procedure where the court holds a central position during the evidence-taking phase. Although there are different limits in various European countries, in their procedure the burden and the power of producing evidence is still at least in part the province of the court, which shares it with all the other actors in the process.[43] Consistent with the central role played by the court at trial, cross-examination landing in Continental European systems did not relegate the judge to the role of a mere umpire in the witness examination process. Nor did it convert witness questioning into a two-sided combat. It simply increased the role played by the different "rumba dancers" in the crucial activity of questioning the witnesses. The travel to Continental Europe has therefore profoundly modified cross-examination, transforming it into a sort of collective performance in search of an *objective* truth. The court, including lay judges or jurors (as is the case in Spain), most often intervenes on its own initiative in the questioning of the witnesses. Besides, more than two participants are involved in the cross-examination, given that more than two are the dancers of the rumba justice. Indeed, any of the following can participate in cross-examination: the prosecution and the defense, and, depending on the system, one or more of the following: the *partie civile* (which may include any person injured by the crime), the private prosecutor (a victim with different powers in the proceedings than the simple *partie civile*), the public complainant (also called popular

[43] On the stringent limits upon the Spanish trial court's power to produce evidence on its own initiative (mostly imposed by case law in interpreting LECrim art. 729 (2) that, as an exception to the principle of the exclusive party presentation of evidence at trial, allows the court to order evidence to be heard ex officio), see Gascón Inchausti &Villamarín López, *supra* note 20, at 613, 607, 561 & n.13, referring to the case law in point. On the reappropriation by the Italian trial court of a great power to introduce evidence ex officio, after the enactment of the new code of 1988 highly restricted it, see Grande, *supra* note 10, at 245–46, 250. In Germany, the court is in charge of discovering the truth, and therefore must examine all evidence relevant to the decision irrespective of whether one of the participants has asked for it. StPO § 244 II. Yet the parties may proffer their own evidence and may request the court to hear additional evidence suggested by the parties. StPO § 214 III, 220, 244, 245.

prosecutor; i.e., a private third party unconnected to the offense who is allowed to participate provided he or she complies with a series of requirements, such as in Spain), and any civil third-party defendants (i.e., persons that are liable for damages in lieu of the defendant should the latter be convicted and insolvent; they are allowed to participate in the proceedings in Italy and Spain). Thus, the possible intervention of one "dancer's" questioning in substitution for another nullifies any individual strategic choice to renounce the opportunity to cross-examine the opposing witness. This dramatically alters the fundamental character of cross-examination as an adversarial technique that allows each party to shape the expression of her own dispute.

In addition, unlike in the United States, in Continental European systems, cross-examination does not seem to be an indispensable instrument for challenging the credibility of a prima facie unreliable witness based on a concern about her association with one of the parties. The great involvement of impartial officials in the evidence gathering and in the fact-finding process, combined with a much less intense pretrial coaching than in the United States, reduces the risk of a one-sided distortion of information. Consequently, the need for an aggressive and destructive cross-examination *à l'americaine* to test the accuracy of the testimony is less compelling.[44]

Moreover, the lack of a strong partisan association between the witness and either of the parties, especially the one who is often the most powerful (the prosecutor), explains the usual (even if controversial) rule permitting courts to take into consideration a direct examination when cross-examination cannot be completed due to the sudden unavailability of the witness. It also explains (as already mentioned in the previous paragraph) the use of written out-of-court testimony exceptionally permitted by European Continental systems in order to satisfy the cognitive needs of the court in search of an *objective* truth. In non-adversary systems, the fact-finder has to provide a fully reasoned written judgment, which is subject to supervision by an appellate court. This prevents the fact-finder from overweighing the value of the evidence that the parties have not had the opportunity to confront. Thus, from a Continental perspective, the sacrifice of fairness (brought about by the use of a testimony that the parties have not confronted) does not necessarily preclude a just decision by the trial fact-finder.

In sum, introduced in Continental Europe, cross-examination as a style of questioning still works as an instrument to discredit an opposing witness, but the participation of multiple actors substantially modifies its strong adversarial character. As a means to obtain a more autonomous and direct involvement of a plurality of subjects in witness questioning, it improves the participatory fact-finding scheme and thereby the impartiality of the official third-party search for truth.

[44] For a deep analysis of these themes, see Damaška, *supra* note 26, at 79.

4. Jury Trial in Spain and the Collective Search for the Truth

In 1995, the Spanish Parliament passed legislation reviving trial by jury in certain criminal cases.[45] As I have argued more extensively elsewhere,[46] though it has often been celebrated as an Anglo-American import,[47] the jury trial operates quite differently in Spain than it does in the United States.

In the first place, the new jury system does not transform the Spanish criminal trial from a third-party search for the truth into a contest between two and only two parties in complete control of the fact-finding enterprise. Unlike in the United States, in Spain, the jury trial judge (the *magistrado-presidente*) is not merely an umpire of a forensic contest between the prosecutor and the defendant in a party-controlled process of developing the evidence, and the Spanish jury is not conceived as a passive adjudicator. Rather than a contest between two litigants shaping their own dispute according to their own interests in front of a passive adjudicator, the Spanish jury trial far more resembles a plural inquest in which many actors participate. These include the prosecutor (who can intervene in favor of the defendant, by asking for an acquittal),[48] the defendant, the victim (i.e., the private prosecutor), the public complainant (or popular prosecutor), any civil third-party defendants, the presiding judge, and the jurors (who also perform as active participants in the collective search for the truth). All assume an active and fluid role and share in the search for the substantive truth, and the roles are so fluid that even the private prosecutor can ask for the defendant's acquittal.

In the second place, unlike the U.S. jury, the Spanish jury does not symbolize complete independence from the government. The jury in U.S. trials is genuinely independent because of the exclusion of any judicial involvement in its deliberations. Moreover, its power to deliver a largely inscrutable general verdict, which is difficult to challenge on appeal from a conviction and impossible to challenge in case of acquittal, conveys the message that the jury is the champion of the individual against the state. Allowing the jury to render a truly final verdict of acquittal gives substance to the aspiration of the defendant to be free from government oppression, since no state official has the power

[45] Ley Orgánica del Tribunal del Jurado, B.O.E. n.122, May 22, 1995 (Spain), at http://dgraj.justicia.es/SecretariosJudiciales/docs/jurado.pdf. The crimes over which the jury court has jurisdiction are: homicide; threats; failure to comply with a legal duty to provide assistance; burglary; arson in forestland; and several crimes against the Public Administration, such as mishandling official documents, bribery, influence peddling, embezzlement of public funds, fraud, and illegal levies demanded by public officials; prohibited negotiations by public officials; and mistreatment of prisoners. For a detailed description of the Spanish jury and its history, see Stephen C. Thaman, *Spain Returns to Trial by Jury*, 21 Hastings Int'l & Comp. L. Rev. 241 (1998); *see also* Carmen Gleadow, *Spain's Return to Trial by Jury: Theoretical Foundations and Practical Results*, 2001–2002 St. Louis-Warsaw Transatlantic L.J. 57 (2001–2002); Carmen Gleadow, *History of Trial by Jury in the Spanish Legal System* (2000).

[46] Grande, *Rumba Justice, supra* note 1.

[47] *See, e.g.*, Gascón Inchausti &Villamarín López, *supra* note 20, at 628 ("A jury was introduced on the Anglo-American model.").

[48] For concrete cases of acquittal request put forward by the prosecutor, see Thaman, *supra* note 45, at 392–97.

to second-guess the jury's finding. The extreme version of this rationale is the jury's power of nullification: here, the peers make a final determination of acquittal even in the face of uncontroverted evidence proving the defendant guilty and even in defiance of clear judicial instruction.

By contrast, Spanish jurors do not enjoy the same level of autonomy and independence from state involvement in their decision-making. Spanish jurors vote on a list of factual propositions or questions, which are formulated in the verdict form by the judge, with the involvement of every other trial participant. Unlike the U.S. jury, yet consistent with a third-party quest for substantive truth and with the need to judicially check the third-party findings,[49] Spanish jurors also have to give reasons for their conclusions. When the reasons given by juries are determined to be inadequate, their verdicts are either returned to the jurors by the supervising magistrate-president[50] or reversed on appeal by the Regional Supreme Court.[51] This holds true even for verdicts of acquittal, thereby preventing jury nullification.

In sum, the introduction of the jury trial added a new actor in the participatory fact-finding process. By enhancing the plurality of perspectives over the factual inquiry, it provided for a more dynamic and pluralistic effort to make the third-party search for the truth more impartial.

IV. Plea Bargaining in Europe: Global Convergence toward a Different Rationale?

In order to assess the possible convergence between American and Continental European criminal procedure systems, the chapter will briefly address one more transplant from the United States to Europe—plea bargaining, or the consensual arrangement for avoiding

[49] This is done according to a vertical and internal check on the process, providing a plurality of perspectives within the decision-making process. The principle that in criminal proceedings conducted before professional judges, judgments have to be always reasoned and based on a rational evaluation of evidence to ensure an effective right to appeal, has been indeed established by the European Court of Human Rights in *Taxquet v. Belgium*. Taxquet v. Belgium GC, App. No. 926/05, Eur. Ct. H.R., Nov. 16, 2010, § 91; *see also* Stephen C. Thaman, *Should Criminal Juries Give Reasons for Their Verdicts?: The Spanish Experience and the Implications of the European Court of Human Rights Decision in* Taxquet v. Belgium, 86 Chi.-Kent. L. Rev. 613, 633 (2011). Moreover, European case law requires that in jury trials, verdicts be subjected to the requirement of "precise, unequivocal questions put to the jury by the judge, forming a framework on which the verdict is based or sufficiently offsetting the fact that no reasons are given for the jury's answers," in order for an appeal of the factual basis for a jury decision to be possible. *Taxquet*, GC, App. No. 926/05, § 92. As an application of *Taxquet*, see Lhermitte v. Belgium GC, App. N.34238/09, Eur. Ct.H.R., Nov. 29, 2016.

[50] Ley Orgánica del Tribunal del Jurado, *supra* note 45, art. 63(1)(d),(e).

[51] LECrim art. 846 bis(c)(a); Mar Jimeno-Bulnes, *Jury Selection and Jury Trial in Spain: Between Theory and Practice*, 86 Chi.-Kent L. Rev. 585, 601 (2011).

trial and punishing the defendant. Recognized as constitutionally valid in the United States since 1970,[52] plea bargaining worked in Germany for a long time in the shadow of the law and only very recently received legal recognition.[53] During the last few decades, moreover, plea bargaining has been introduced by statute in countries such as Italy,[54] France,[55] Spain,[56] Poland,[57] and Portugal.[58]

While differing considerably both from one another and from the U.S. model,[59] Continental European plea bargaining schemes share some essential traits. The outcome of criminal cases is not the result of a party contest or of an official inquiry. It is instead largely the product of an out-of-court negotiation, which involves the prosecutor, the defense lawyer, the court (to a different degree in different systems), and the defendant (too often only marginally). Contrary to what happens in court, players do not act for the sake of determining the defendant's guilt or innocence, but for the sake of agreeing upon the sentence or upon the charge (which then results in a reduced sentence) to be imposed on a surrendering defendant.

Given its party-centered structure, requiring only limited official involvement, plea bargaining, as a parties' consensual disposal of the case ratified by the judge, has often been considered a typical expression of the adversary system.[60] In other words, it has been regarded as an arrangement in tune with the tenets of a procedure that leaves with the parties the opportunity of shaping their dispute even to the point of ending it. Consequently, in the common law world, plea bargaining has not usually been regarded as an aberration from the regular process, as occurred when the practice was adopted in civil law systems. Here, plea bargaining immediately appeared to come into conflict with the tenets of the non-adversarial procedural style that gives to the court and not the parties the primary responsibility for case disposition and fact-finding.

Yet plea bargaining seems to depart from the logic of both the adversary and the non-adversary systems, subverting their common goals of ascertaining the facts and providing society with justice. When a plea bargain occurs, the search for the truth, no matter if pursued according to adversarial or non-adversarial tenets, is completely renounced for the sake of a different goal: the rapidity of the procedure. Under the constraint of efficiency, which is the new criterion for evaluating their performance, all *professional* players are incentivized to reach an out-of-court agreement that, irrespective of the

[52] Brady v. United States, 397 U.S. 742 (1970).

[53] Entwurf eines Gesetzes zur Regelung der Verständigung im Strafverfahren, Deutscher Bundestag: Drucksachen (2009).

[54] C.p.p. arts. 444 ff. (It.), introduced in 1989, as amended to expand the scope of plea bargaining in 2003.

[55] C. pr. pén. arts. 495–497, introduced in 2004.

[56] LECrim arts. 652, 688, 694, 787, 801, as amended in 2002.

[57] Kodeks postępowania karnego, arts. 335, 343, 387, introduced in 1998.

[58] C.p.p. arts. 344 (Port.), introduced in 1987 as amended to expand the scope of plea bargaining in 2008.

[59] *See* Máximo Langer, *From Legal Transplants to Legal Translations: The Globalization of Plea Bargaining and the Americanization Thesis in Criminal Procedure*, 45 Harv. Int'l L. J. 1 (2004); *World Plea Bargaining, Consensual Procedures and the Avoidance of the Full Criminal Trial* (Stephen C. Thaman ed., 2010); Regina Rauxloh, *Plea Bargaining in National and International Law: A Comparative Study* (2012).

[60] *See* Langer, *supra* note 59.

accuracy of the facts agreed upon, is the expression of their bargaining abilities and powers. It is therefore a setting at odds with the non-adversary process as much as with the adversary one. The opposing interests of the parties in presenting their side of the facts in front of a passive adjudicator, typical of the adversarial procedure, wane in search for a compromise. Plea bargaining emphasizes a cooperative posture among all participants, including the judge, whose fact-finding responsibilities are de facto null, unlike what happens in a non-adversarial procedure.[61] Even when the judge is given the power to refuse a deal struck by the other players in the name of preserving the principle of truth-finding (as happens in France,[62] Germany,[63] and Italy,[64] but also, albeit only nominally, in the United States[65]), she is urged to use it only exceptionally.[66] The pressure to avoid the trial for the sake of efficiency works hard also upon her, especially as her

[61] Indeed, the judge is not assigned the role of fact-finder, but that of a proactive (as in Germany or sometimes in the United States) or reactive (as in Italy, France, or Spain) notary of the deal struck by the parties. On the proactive role played by the German and the American judge, see Thomas Weigend, *The Decay of the Inquisitorial Ideal: Plea Bargaining Invades German Criminal Procedure*, in *Crime, Procedure and Evidence in a Comparative and International Context Essays in Honour of Professor Mirjan Damaška* 39 (John Jackson et al. eds., 2008); Yale Kamisar et al., *Basic Criminal Procedure: Cases, Comments and Questions* ch. 21.3(d) (14th ed. 2015). On the recent institutionalization of judicial involvement in plea bargaining in the United States, see the empirical study of Nancy J. King & Ronald F. Wright, *The Invisible Revolution in Plea Bargaining: Managerial Judging and Judicial Participation in Negotiations*, 95 Tex. L. Rev. 325 (2016). On a possible convergence of the American and the German plea bargaining procedures in terms of judicial involvement and defense discovery, see Jenia I. Turner, *Plea Bargaining and Disclosure in Germany and the United States: Comparative Lessons*, 57 Wm. & Mary L. Rev. 1549 (2016).

[62] According to a decision of the Conseil Constitutionel reinforced by a Ministry of Justice circular (CRIM 04-12 E8 of 02 September 2004), the French judge is responsible for verifying the guilt of the accused and the legal sufficiency of the charges. *See* Jacqueline Hodgson, *Guilty Pleas and the Changing Role of the Prosecutor in French Criminal Justice*, University of Warwick School of Law, Legal Studies Research Paper no. 2010-15, at 12; Jacqueline Hodgson, *Plea Bargaining: A Comparative Analysis*, in *International Encyclopedia of the Social and Behavioral Sciences* 226, 227–28 (J.D. Wright ed., 2d ed. 2015).

[63] Confirming a 2006 Federal High Court of Justice ruling, the new German Criminal Procedure Code Section (§ 257c) states that the deal can be accepted only if the court is convinced that the offense has been fully investigated and that there are grounds for believing that the admission of guilt is genuine.

[64] In Italy, according to C.p.p. (It.) art. 129, the judge is required to reject the deal and acquit the defendant only in the face of the defendant's obvious innocence or the violation of procedural requirements. Despite strong academic criticism, she is therefore not assigned the power to refuse a deal if the sentence agreed upon by the parties is not supported by the facts. While not questioning the content of plea agreements, the Italian judge tends instead to refuse a deal whenever she is not happy with the leniency of the sentence or the defendant does not pay damages to the victim.

[65] The accuracy determination of the plea (factual basis) is required in federal and many state jurisdictions. Yet the law does not specify how this determination should be made or the quantum of evidence required.

[66] Before § 257c was introduced in the German Criminal Procedure Code, many judges were ready to take an admission of guilt as the only basis for conviction, and it is highly doubtful that the new statute provision could change that. *See* Regina Rauxloh, *Formalisation of Plea Bargaining in Germany: Will the New Legislation Be Able to Square the Circle?*, 34 Fordham Int'l L.J. 296, 311 (2010–2011). In France, "[i]n practice, the procedure is designed for a speedy resolution and it seems unlikely that the judge would go beyond the agreement presented to the court." Hodgson, *Plea Bargaining: A Comparative Analysis*, *supra* note 62, at 228.

own professional capacity is more and more frequently measured by the speed of her case disposition.[67]

In sum, when plea bargaining occurs, both the public battle between adversaries and the official inquiry at trial (out of which the truth is assumed to be attained) are replaced by a largely out-of-court, informal, and private agreement among the actors. The contest or the multifaceted inquiry scenarios are transformed into a consensual setting, the dispute is appeased and dissolved, and the truth-finding goal is abandoned in favor of the system's efficiency. Therefore, the import of plea bargaining in European criminal procedure systems did not mean to make the latter more adversarial. Instead, it meant to introduce a new out-of-court procedure, neither adversarial nor non-adversarial in a Continental European sense, but consensual and alternative to both classical in-court procedures, where everybody wins except for any innocent defendant.[68]

V. Conclusion

In their transfer from the American system to Continental European ones, legal arrangements such as an investigation led by police or prosecutors in lieu of the examining magistrate, exclusionary rules, cross-examination of witnesses, and the jury trial, ended up highly modified by the new context, changing their original function and nature. They have lost their adversarial rationale and the features that in the U.S. model provide for a strong connection with the liberal idea of criminal procedure in adversarial terms. The introduction of these procedures into Continental European systems did not result in a rejection by the receiving systems of the very notion of officially controlled inquiry, nor did it help shield defendants against government activism by delegating all power and control over the process to the parties. Their transfer did not simply produce their "translation" into a non-adversarial style. Their introduction into Continental European criminal systems worked instead as a means of fortification of the most essential feature of a non-adversary procedure—its third-party official search for an *objective* truth. In line with previous Continental reforms aimed at coping with the "neutrality problem" of the third party, the imported features effectively made that search more pluralistic, participatory, and dynamic, and consequently more impartial. This helped protect the individual against a monopolistic, and therefore authoritarian, official search for the

[67] Moreover, as Nancy King and Ron Wright point out with regard to the U.S. system (and this is true in other systems as well), because technology makes judges' efficiency remarkably trackable, judges are more and more encouraged to secure pleas earlier in the process in order "not to be the low boy." King & Wright, *supra* note 61, at 362.

[68] The question of whether and how plea bargaining can hurt an innocent defendant is addressed by a vast literature in the United States and abroad. For a recent empirical study showing a possible percentage as high as 56 percent of innocent people pleading guilty, see Lucian E. Dervan & Vanessa A. Edkins, *The Innocent Defendant's Dilemma: An Innovative Empirical Study of Plea Bargaining's Innocence Problem*, 103 J. Crim. L. & Criminology 1 (2013).

truth, making the context of reception more liberal, though not more adversarial. In this sense, the transfer actually enhanced the implementation of a liberal idea of criminal procedure, yet not in an *adversarial* but in a *non-adversarial* logic. By strengthening the tenets of a rumba non-adversarial justice instead of creating adversarial tango justice, somehow unexpectedly, the journey of the American arrangements into the European context seems to have resulted in a distancing rather than a rapprochement of (American) common law and civil law criminal procedures styles.

Yet, notwithstanding the resistance of the in-court Continental European procedures to their Americanization, the global spread of a plea bargaining procedure largely of American origins has nowadays the potential to drive more and more common law as well as civil law systems toward a shared out-of-court procedural arrangement, neither adversarial nor non-adversarial in nature, nor based upon a justice motive, yet grounded upon the different rationale of efficiency. The main reason for the ubiquitous rise of plea bargaining seems to be the hypertrophic expansion of a substantive criminal law characterized by a preventive nature aimed at coping with the rise of a "risk society" in countries around the world.[69] The proliferation of danger crimes—that is, crimes punishing the causation of risks, not of harms—increases the length of investigation and trial and the uncertainty of trial outcomes. It is precisely the unpredictability of trial outcomes that makes pretrial agreements compelling for all the actors.[70] Since "prepressive" criminal law—that is, criminal law that is both preventive and repressive—appears universally on the rise,[71] informal settlements are increasingly overtaking in-court procedures. Plea bargaining, together with its replacement of the search for truth with the search for a deal, thus has the potential to become commonplace not only among common law systems, but also among civil law ones.[72]

References

Crime and Criminal Justice Systems in Europe and North America, 1995–2004 (Kauko Aromaa and Markku Heiskanen eds., 2008)

Criminal Procedure: A Worldwide Study (Craig M. Bradley ed., 2nd ed. 2007)

[69] *See* Ulrich Beck, *Risk Society: Toward a New Modernity* (1992).

[70] *See* Rauxloh, *supra* note 59.

[71] *See* Lucia Zedner, *Fixing the Future? The Pre-emptive Turn in Criminal Justice*, in *Regulating Deviance: The Redirection of Criminalisation and the Futures of Criminal Law* 35 (Bernadette McSherry et al. eds., 2009).

[72] For rates of guilty pleas and plea bargaining in the United States and England, see Mary Vogel, *Common Law Plea Bargaining*, in this volume. In Germany, for instance, in some regions, informal settlements can reach a percentage as high as 80 percent in certain areas of criminal law. Rauxloh, *supra* note 66, at 300; *see also* Thomas Weigend & Jenia Iontcheva Turner, *The Constitutionality of Negotiated Criminal Judgments in Germany*, 15 German L.J. 81, 82–83 (2014). In Spain, the rate of consensual disposal is around 60 percent. Hodgson, *Plea Bargaining: A Comparative Analysis, supra* note 62, at 228; Lorena Bachmaier & Antonio del Moral García, *Criminal Law in Spain* 226 (2010). In Italy and France, the percentage is definitely lower, around 30–40 percent and 15 percent, respectively. Hodgson, *Plea Bargaining: A Comparative Analysis, supra* note 62, at 226, 228.

Discretionary Criminal Justice in a Comparative Context (Michele Caianiello & Jacqueline S. Hodgson eds., 2015)

Mirjan R. Damaška, *The Faces of Justice and State Authority: A Comparative Approach to the Legal Process* (1986)

Mirjan R. Damaška, *Evidence Law Adrift* (1997)

Mirjan R. Damaška, *Truth in Adjudication*, 49 Hastings L. J. 289 (1998)

Harry R. Dammer & Jay S. Albanese, *Comparative Criminal Justice Systems* (5th ed. 2013)

European Criminal Procedures (Mireille Delmas-Marty & J.R. Spencer eds., 2002)

Criminal Justice Between Crime Control and Due Process: Convergence and Divergence in Criminal Procedure Systems (Albin Eser & Christiane Rabenstein eds., 2004)

Floyd Feeney & Joachim Herrmann, *One Case—Two Systems: A Comparative View of American and German Criminal Justice* (2005)

Richard S. Frase, *Comparative Criminal Justice as a Guide to American Law Reform: How Do the French Do It, How Can We Find Out, and Why Should We Care?*, 78 Cal. L. Rev. 539 (1990)

Richard S. Frase & Thomas Weigend, *German Criminal Justice as a Guide to American Law Reform: Similar Problems, Better Solutions?*, 18 B.C. Int'l & Comp. L. Rev. 317 (1995)

Elisabetta Grande, *Imitazione e diritto: Ipotesi sulla circolazione dei modelli* (2000)

Elisabetta Grande, *Italian Criminal Justice: Borrowing and Resistance*, 48 Am. J. Comp. L. 227 (2000)

Elisabetta Grande, *Comparative Criminal Justice*, in *The Cambridge Companion to Comparative Law* 189 (Mauro Bussani & Ugo Mattei eds., 2012)

Elisabetta Grande, *Rumba Justice and the Spanish Jury Trial*, in *Handbook on Comparative Criminal Procedure* 365 (Jacqueline E. Ross & Stephen C. Thaman eds, 2016)

Elisabetta Grande, *Legal Transplants and the Inoculation Effect: How American Criminal Procedure Has Affected Continental Europe*, 64 Am. J. Comp. L. 583 (2016)

Crime, Procedure and Evidence in a Comparative and International Context (John Jackson et al. eds., 2008)

John D. Jackson & Sarah J. Summers, *The Internationalisation of Criminal Evidence: Beyond the Common Law and Civil Law Traditions* (2012)

John H. Langbein, *Mixed Court and Jury Court: Could the Continental Alternative Fill the American Need?*, 1981 Am. B. Found. Res. J. 195

John H. Langbein, *The Origins of Adversary Criminal Trial* (2003)

John H. Langbein, *Torture and the Law of Proof: Europe and England in the Ancien Régime* (2006)

John H. Langbein et al., *History of the Common Law: The Development of Anglo-American Legal Institutions* (2009)

Prosecutors and Democracy. A Cross National Study (Máximo Langer & David A. Sklansky eds., 2017)

The Prosecutor in Transnational Perspective (Erik Luna & Marianne Wade eds., 2012)

Understanding Wrongful Conviction: The Protection of the Innocent Across Europe and America (Luca Lupária ed., 2015)

Gerhard O.W. Mueller & Fre Le Poole-Griffiths, *Comparative Criminal Procedure* (1969)

Regina Rauxloh, *Plea Bargaining in National and International Law: A Comparative Study* (2012)

Handbook on Comparative Criminal Procedure (Jacqueline E. Ross & Stephen C. Thaman eds., 2016)

Prosecutors and Politics: A Comparative Perspective (Michael Tonry ed., 2012)

Sarah J. Summers, *Fair Trials: The European Criminal Procedural Tradition and the European Court of Human Rights* (2007)

Richard J. Terrill, *World Criminal Justice Systems* (9th ed. 2016)
Stephen C. Thaman, *Comparative Criminal Law and Enforcement*, in *Encyclopedia of Crime and Justice* 207 (Joshua Dressler ed., 2nd ed. 2002)
Stephen C. Thaman, *Comparative Criminal Procedure: A Casebook Approach* (2nd ed. 2008)
World Plea Bargaining, Consensual Procedures and the Avoidance of the Full Criminal Trial (Stephen C. Thaman ed., 2010)
Jenia Iontcheva Turner, *Judicial Participation in Plea Negotiations: A Comparative View*, 54 Am. J. Comp. L. 199 (2006)
Jenia Iontcheva Turner, *Plea Bargaining and Disclosure in Germany and the United States: Comparative Lessons*, 57 William & Mary L. Rev. 1549 (2016)
Richard Vogler, *A World View of Criminal Justice* (2005)
Richard Vogler & Barbara Huber (eds.), *Criminal Procedure in Europe* (2008)
Thomas Weigend, *Prosecution: Comparative Aspects*, in *Encyclopedia of Crime and Justice* 1232 (Joshua Dressler ed., 2nd ed. 2002)
Thomas Weigend, *Criminal Procedure: Comparative Aspects*, in *Encyclopedia of Crime and Justice* 444 (Joshua Dressler ed., 2nd ed. 2002)
Thomas Weigend, *Criminal Law and Criminal Procedure*, in *Elgar Encyclopedia of Comparative Law* 214 (Jan M. Smits ed., 2006)
Thomas Weigend, *Should We Search for the Truth, and Who Should Do It?*, 36 N.C. J. Int'l L. & Com. Reg. 389 (2011)

CHAPTER 5

THE EUROPEAN CONVENTION ON HUMAN RIGHTS AND THE EUROPEAN COURT OF HUMAN RIGHTS AS GUARDIANS OF FAIR CRIMINAL PROCEEDINGS IN EUROPE

BETTINA WEISSER

I. Introduction

THE conclusion of the European Convention on Human Rights[1] in 1950 was a milestone in the evolvement of universal human rights standards on the European continent in the aftermath of World War II. The territorial scope of the Convention now covers forty-seven European member states. Hence, the Convention is binding in almost the whole of the European continent. Only the Vatican and Belarus remain non-parties to the Convention. Since the Convention is an international treaty, it is up to the treaty states to implement its human rights guarantees in national law. Some states have chosen to confer on ECHR provisions the status of constitutional rights at the national level (e.g., Austria); others acknowledge the Convention as an ordinary part of the national statutory law (e.g., Germany).

[1] European Convention on Human Rights, Nov. 4, 1950, 213 U.N.T.S. 221 [hereinafter ECHR].

The Convention defines a minimum standard of human rights for every person who is subject to acts of public authority in a contracting state. Article 34 provides a right to lodge a complaint with the European Court of Human Rights ("the Court") to every individual who claims a violation of human rights by state authorities—provided that the applicant has exhausted all judicial remedies at the domestic level (*subsidiarity principle*). Individuals lodging a complaint with the Court need not be nationals or inhabitants of the contracting state, since the guarantees of the Convention are applicable for every alleged violation of Conventional rights by contracting states' authorities.

Under Articles 44 and 46, the Court's judgments are binding on the respondent state only. Nevertheless, since the Court is the only institution competent to interpret the guarantees of the Convention, and since all treaty states have committed themselves to the Conventional guarantees, the case law of the Court serves as a benchmark of human rights guarantees for all treaty states.[2]

The preamble of the ECHR points to the rule of law as part of the European countries' common heritage. It is the legacy of the Enlightenment that the individual must never be deprived of his human dignity by the exercise of public authority. Therefore, defendants in criminal proceedings must always remain the subject—and not a mere object—of the criminal process.[3] This premise is the source of various safeguards, such as the right to a fair hearing (which encompasses a right to present one's case before the court as well as the right to remain silent) and the right to an effective defense. Since criminal procedures can bring about the most severe encroachments on the personal freedom of citizens, the guarantees of the ECHR are of paramount importance. The most prominent fundamental rights potentially implicated by a criminal process are ECHR Article 3 (prohibition of torture and inhuman treatment; *infra II. 1.*), Article 5 (right to liberty and security),[4] Article 6 (right to a fair trial), and Article 8 (right to respect for private and family life).[5] Protocol No. 7 to the ECHR[6] specifies further important procedural rights, including the right not to be tried or punished twice for the same offense (Article 4)[7] and the right to appeal (Article 2).[8]

The following analysis will concentrate on the specifically procedure-related guarantee of a fair trial and its various implications as they are laid down in Article 6 and shaped by the case law of the Court. The provision reads:

Article 6 ECHR: Right to a fair trial

1. In the determination of his civil rights and obligations or of any criminal charge against him, everyone is entitled to a fair and public hearing within a reasonable time by an independent and impartial tribunal established by law. Judgment

[2] *Compare* Omkar Sidhu, *The Concept of Equality of Arms in Criminal Proceedings under Article 6 of the European Convention on Human Rights* 61–62 (2017).

[3] *See id.* at 63; Stefan Trechsel, *Why Must Trials Be Fair?*, 31 Isr. L. Rev. 94, 100 (1997).

[4] *See* chapter 23 of this book.

[5] *See* chapters 8, 9, 15, 18, 31, and 37 of this book.

[6] E.T.S. No. 117.

[7] *See* chapters 21 and 22 of this book.

[8] *See* chapters 41 and 42 of this book.

shall be pronounced publicly but the press and public may be excluded from all or part of the trial in the interests of morals, public order or national security in a democratic society, where the interests of juveniles or the protection of the private life of the parties so require, or to the extent strictly necessary in the opinion of the court in special circumstances where publicity would prejudice the interests of justice.

2. Everyone charged with a criminal offence shall be presumed innocent until proved guilty according to law.
3. Everyone charged with a criminal offence has the following minimum rights:
   (a) to be informed promptly, in a language which he understands and in detail, of the nature and cause of the accusation against him;
   (b) to have adequate time and facilities for the preparation of his defense;
   (c) to defend himself in person or through legal assistance of his own choosing or, if he has not sufficient means to pay for legal assistance, to be given it free when the interests of justice so require;
   (d) to examine or have examined witnesses against him and to obtain the attendance and examination of witnesses on his behalf under the same conditions as witnesses against him;
   (e) to have the free assistance of an interpreter if he cannot understand or speak the language used in court.

The right to a fair trial has been invoked countless times before the Court. In 2016, the Court delivered 993 judgments and decided about 1,926 applications.[9] A quarter of the judgments concerned violations of Article 6; another 20 percent of the judgments concerned the prohibition of torture and inhuman treatment under Article 3.[10]

The Court's extensive case law on human rights safeguards in the criminal process has considerably affected the contracting states' judicial practice. Its influence on the shape of the criminal process has been significant, not only in national law enforcement but also in transnational and/or cooperative prosecution of cross-border crimes, mainly in the fields of organized crime or terrorism. Although the Convention does not aim to harmonize the procedural laws of the treaty states,[11] its procedural standards and the case law relating to it have to some extent affected the evolution of the contracting states' procedural laws. For example, the right to confront witnesses encompassed in Article 6 § 3(d) was not a familiar feature for inquisitorial procedural systems, since under such

[9] The discrepancy between the number of decided applications and delivered judgments is due to the fact that the Court joins applications if they raise similar questions. The combination of cases is meant to help overcome the Court's immense workload. *See* Public Relations Unit of the Eur. Ct. H.R., *The ECHR in Facts and Figures 2016*, at 6 (Mar. 2017), *available at* http://www.echr.coe.int/Documents/Facts_Figures_2016_ENG.pdf.

[10] *Id.*

[11] *See* Achour v. France, App. No. 67335/01, Eur. Ct. H.R. (Grand Chamber, hereinafter: [GC]), Mar. 29, 2006, § 51. All cited judgments are *available at* https://hudoc.echr.coe.int.

regime it is mainly for the court to call and question witnesses. In this regard, the Convention has paved the way for a typical feature of an adversarial procedure into Continental inquisitorial systems. Examples of the Convention's influence on several national procedural laws are discussed in chapters 8, 9, 15, 31, and 37 of this book, while this chapter focuses exclusively on the Council of Europe level.

II. The Scope of the Court's Judicial Authority over the Fairness of Criminal Proceedings

1. The Territorial Scope of the Right to a Fair Trial

Since the exercise of state authority is only legitimate on a state's own territory, the territorial scope of the Convention—and thereby the Court's judicial authority—is limited to acts that took place on the territory of contracting states. However, under exceptional circumstances, the guarantee of a fair trial can exert extraterritorial effects. Although in general, extradition or expulsion procedures do not belong within the concept of the "determination of a criminal charge" and therefore do not fall into the purview of Article 6, the Convention can limit a contracting state's ability to serve another country's request for extradition in order to avoid an imminent risk of a flagrant denial of justice. An extradition bears such risk of a flagrant denial of justice if it is requested by a state where capital punishment is still enforced,[12] for the death penalty is deemed an unacceptable violation of human rights and therefore completely abolished in treaty states. Second, an imminent risk that the applicant might face torture or other inhuman treatment prohibited under Article 3, or that evidence obtained by the use of torture might be admitted on trial in the third state, is also considered a risk of a flagrant denial of justice. Other situations amounting to a flagrant denial of justice arise in cases of convictions in absentia, detention without any chance of review, summary trials, or a systematic and deliberate denial of access to a lawyer.[13] Under such circumstances, Article 6 requires treaty states either to deny an extradition request or otherwise to ensure that violations of human rights in the third state will not occur (e.g., by subjecting the extradition to certain conditions).[14]

[12] Soering v. United Kingdom, App. No. 14038/88, Eur. Ct. H.R. [Plenary], July 7, 1989, § 113; Al Nashiri v. Poland, App. No. 28761/11, Eur. Ct. H.R., July 24, 2014, § 578.

[13] Othman v. United Kingdom, App. No. 8139/09, Eur. Ct. H.R., Jan. 17, 2012, § 259.

[14] *Id.* §§ 267, 285; *Al Nashiri v. Poland*, *supra* note 12, § 564.

2. The Temporal Scope of the Right to a Fair Trial

Fair trial rights are applicable throughout the entire criminal process, starting with the criminal investigation and ending with the final and non-appealable decision of the highest competent court.[15] After the decision has become res iudicata, Article 6 is no longer applicable. Hence, neither the convicted person's request for release or probation nor the call for a new trial is subject to the protection of Article 6.[16] The effect of Article 6 is then limited to the guarantee that the decision be implemented effectively. Thus, if the defendant has been acquitted, he must be released from custody immediately.[17]

As for the onset of Article 6, the Court has declared that "a 'criminal charge' exists from the moment that an individual is officially notified by the competent authority of an allegation that he has committed a criminal offence, or from the point at which his situation has been substantially affected by actions taken by the authorities as a result of a suspicion against him."[18] Article 6 is thus not limited to the official trial stage, but also applicable during the preliminary stage of an investigation. For example, in *Zaichenko v. Russia* the applicant had been stopped and questioned at a road check. Although he was not officially notified about the initiation of a criminal investigation, the Court held that the guarantees of Article 6 were already applicable and found a violation of Article 6 § 1 since the privilege against self-incrimination and the applicant's right to remain silent were ignored.[19]

3. "Overall Fairness" of Criminal Proceedings

The Convention aims to define a minimum standard of human rights for forty-seven differing procedural systems without any further aspiration to actively promote convergence among these systems. Therefore, it leaves a considerable "margin of appreciation"[20] for the treaty states when implementing the procedural safeguards into their national systems. Accordingly, the Court's jurisdiction is limited to the question as to whether domestic proceedings *as a whole* were fair under Article 6. It is not for the Court to answer whether the outcome of a domestic criminal procedure was lawful under the

[15] Bernadette Rainey, Elizabeth Wicks & Clare Ovey, *Jacobs, White & Ovey: The European Convention on Human Rights*, at 277 seq. (7th ed. 2017).

[16] *Id.* at 251.

[17] In Assanidze v. Georgia, App. No. 71503/01, Eur. Ct. H.R. [GC], Apr. 8, 2004, § 182–4, the Court found a violation of Article 6 § 1 E.C.H.R. since the applicant had remained imprisoned for three years after his acquittal.

[18] Eckle v. Germany, App. No. 8130/78, Eur. Ct. H.R., July 15, 1982, § 73; Ibrahim and Others v. United Kingdom, App. Nos. 50541/08 etc., Eur. Ct. H.R., Sept. 13, 2016, § 249; Simeonovi v. Bulgaria, App. No. 21980/04, Eur. Ct. H.R., May 12, 2017, § 110. *See also* John D. Jackson & Sarah Summers, *The Internationalisation of Criminal Evidence* 95–97 (2012).

[19] Zaichenko v. Russia, App. No. 39660/02, Eur. Ct. H.R., Feb. 18, 2010, § 36.

[20] Rainey, Wicks & Ovey, *supra* note 15, at 360 seq; Andrew Ashworth, Ben Emmerson & Alison Macdonald (eds.), *Human Rights and Criminal Justice*, paras. 2–115 to 2–137 (2d ed. 2007).

national law, let alone whether the domestic court's considerations about the facts and circumstances of a certain case were correct.[21] Furthermore, the Court is not competent to assess the evidence brought before a national court and, as a rule, the Court cannot decide about the admissibility of evidence in a trial.[22] In brief, the Strasbourg Court does not serve as a court of appeal for national jurisdictions. It is entirely up to the national judiciary to ensure the adherence of criminal proceedings to substantive as well as procedural laws within the national legal framework. According to this so-called "fourth instance doctrine," also known as the principle of subsidiarity, the Court's jurisdiction is limited to the assessment of the treaty states' adherence to the human rights guaranteed by the Convention.[23]

The Court's scrutiny of the fairness of criminal proceedings follows a "holistic approach" in many respects. First, the rationale of Article 6 implies an overall guarantee of fair criminal (and civil) proceedings in its section 1, whereas sections 2 and 3 spell out specific procedural rights for defendants charged with a criminal offense that are specific aspects of a fair trial under section 1 of Article 6.[24] Thus, a violation of specific rights listed in sections 2 and 3 can at the same time amount to a violation of the general guarantee in section 1. Since sections 2 and 3 of Article 6 only address some of the factors that can render a procedure unfair, this logic cannot be inverted—it cannot be presumed that the fairness of a process is already proven merely by compliance with sections 2 and 3 (see for example *infra* III.2.c). A second aspect of this holistic approach is that a collective examination of the rights listed in Article 6 sections 2 and 3[25] can lead to the judgment that several minor violations of different procedural safeguards taken together render the proceedings as a whole unfair.[26]

A third aspect of the holistic approach is that despite a violation of one of the procedural guarantees, the proceedings as a whole can still remain fair.[27] Depending on the circumstances of a case, the Court opens the assessment of the overall fairness of criminal

[21] Niculescu v. Romania, App. No. 25333/03, June 25, 2013, § 113; El Haski v. Belgium, App. No. 649/08, Eur. Ct. H.R., Sept. 25, 2012, §§ 81, 82; Leonard H. Leigh, *The Right to a Fair Trial and the European Convention on Human Rights*, in *The Right to a Fair Trial* 645, 646 (David Weissbrodt & Rüdiger Wolfrum eds., 1998).

[22] *See* Windisch v. Austria, App. No. 12489/86, Eur. Ct. H.R., Sept. 27, 1990, § 25; Allan v. United Kingdom, App. No. 48539/99, Eur. Ct. H.R., Nov. 5, 2002, § 42; Ramanauskas v. Lithuania, App. No. 74420/01, Eur. Ct. H.R. [GC], Feb. 5, 2008, § 52; Bátěk v. the Czech Republic, App. No. 54146/09, Eur. Ct. H.R., Jan. 12, 2017, § 37. *See also* Stefan Trechsel, *Human Rights in Criminal Proceedings* 324–25 (2006).

[23] Cornelis v. the Netherlands, App. No. 994/03, Eur. Ct. H.R. Dec. May 25, 2004, § 15; Rainey, Wicks & Ovey, *supra* note 15, at 275.

[24] Unterpertinger v. Austria, App. No. 9120/80, Eur. Ct. H.R., Nov. 24, 1986, § 29; *Niculescu v. Romania*, *supra* note 21, § 109.

[25] *See* Deweer v. Belgium, App. No. 6903/75, Eur. Ct. H.R., Feb. 27, 1980, § 56; Artico v. Italy, App. No. 6694/74, Eur. Ct. H.R., May 13, 1980, § 32; *Niculescu v. Romania*, *supra* note 21, § 109.

[26] Barberà, Messegué and Jabardo v. Spain, App. No. 10590/83, Dec. 6, 1988, § 89; *Unterpertinger v. Austria*, *supra* note 24, § 31, 33. *See also* William A. Schabas, *The European Convention on Human Rights* 287 (2015).

[27] *See infra* Section VI.2. (confrontation rights); see also Jackson & Summers, *supra* note 18, at 89.

proceedings up to countervailing considerations. This is mainly discussed in cases where the taking of evidence during the investigative stage violated certain procedural rights, such as if the accused was questioned without prior access to legal advice. Such procedural violations can be sufficiently remedied in a later procedural stage, thereby preserving the fairness of the proceedings as a whole. (In the example just noted, a new interrogation could be conducted with a defense lawyer present.) Second, the overall fairness of the criminal proceedings can be preserved if a balance can be struck among "the competing interests of the defence, the victim, and witnesses, and the public interest in the effective administration of defence rights."[28] This balancing mechanism is a means to retain the overall fairness of the proceedings as a whole. "[W]hen determining whether the proceedings as a whole have been fair the weight of the public interest in the investigation and punishment of the particular offence in issue may be taken into consideration and be weighed against the individual interest that the evidence against him be gathered lawfully."[29] But the balancing must not serve as a means to legitimize an irretrievable deprivation of procedural safeguards from the suspect: "However, public interest concerns cannot justify measures which extinguish the very essence of an applicant's defence rights."[30] This balancing mechanism is the Court's attempt to square public interests in an effective crime prosecution regime with accused person's rights to be treated fairly in criminal proceedings. However, since there are few crystal-clear cases of procedural rights breaches that render the proceedings irretrievably unfair, the main challenge is to determine the turning point from "barely fair" to "irretrievably unfair." The complexity of this evaluation is exacerbated by the vagueness of its main criterion: the fairness of criminal proceedings is not defined by any precise benchmark. Fairness consists of a "holistic" ensemble of various procedural safeguards the weight and significance of which can vary from case to case.[31] The following sketch of certain aspects of a fair trial will exemplify this further (see *infra* III.2., V, VI).

On the upside, the fact that the conventional guarantees leave ample room for interpretation allows for the Convention's character as a "living instrument": it is designed to preserve the substance of its guarantees even when they have to keep pace with new developments of procedural law. For instance, newly established plea bargaining procedures must—and can—be reconciled with conventional guarantees, although they can impose restrictions on defense rights.[32]

[28] Al-Khawaja and Tahery v. United Kingdom, App. Nos. 26766/05 and 22228/06, Eur. Ct. H.R. [GC], Dec. 15, 2011, § 146.

[29] Jalloh v. Germany, App. No. 54810/00, Eur. Ct. H.R., July 11, 2006, § 97.

[30] *Id.*

[31] In the given example the overall fairness would be preserved if the evidence taken during the first interrogation was not used at trial. Beyond that, it depends on a detailed examination of each case as to whether the fairness of the proceedings persists despite a restriction of defense rights.

[32] Natsvlishvili and Togonidze v. Georgia, App. No. 9043/05, Eur. Ct. H.R., Apr. 29, 2014, §§ 91–92: plea bargaining is not in principle incompatible with Article 6; see also *Deweer v. Belgium*, *supra* note 25, § 49; and chapters 32 and 33 of this book.

4. Legal Effects of the Court's Decisions

If the Court finds a human rights violation, the respondent state is bound to abide by the judgment pursuant to Article 46 section 1. The state must ensure that the violation of procedural rights cannot happen again. In some cases, this may lead to changes of the law; in other cases, a reopening of the case at hand will take place at the domestic level. Apart from the judicial finding of a human rights violation attributable to the respondent state, the Court can award the applicant just satisfaction under Article 41. The proper enforcement of judgments is supervised by the Committee of Ministers of the Council of Europe.[33]

III. The General Procedural Guarantees under Article 6 § 1

The ambit of the guarantees in section 1 of Article 6 extends to civil as well as criminal proceedings. Nevertheless, section 1 entails certain safeguards that embody constituent elements of a fair criminal procedure and therefore are not applicable to other procedures (e.g., the guarantee of equality of arms or the right to remain silent, see *infra* III.2.a–c, VI).

1. Independent and Impartial Tribunal

The independence and impartiality of the deciding body are indispensable prerequisites for the reliability of a judicial system—"what is at stake is the confidence which the courts must inspire in the public in a democratic society."[34] Independence and impartiality of the court are assessed along with several objective and subjective factors, none of which is necessarily decisive in a given case.[35] Objective factors are clearly defined procedures by which (lay and professional) judges are appointed and panels of judges are composed, as well as the security of judges during their previously defined term and the prohibition of inappropriate (hierarchical) links to institutions in another branch of government. Moreover, courts must be established by law; the Court has held, for example, that the U.S. military commissions set up specifically to try "certain non-citizens in the

[33] ECHR Article 46 § 2. The Committee of Ministers consists of the treaty states' Foreign Ministers, who are represented by national delegates.

[34] Piersack v. Belgium, App. No. 8692/79, Eur. Ct. H.R., Oct. 1, 1982, § 30; Coëme and Others v. Belgium, App. Nos. 32492/96 etc., Eur. Ct. H.R., June 22, 2000, §§ 98, 120–121.

[35] *Id.*; Elezi v. Germany, App. No. 26771/03, Eur. Ct. H.R., June 12, 2008, § 43.

war against terrorism" lacked this basis in law.[36] Finally, safeguards against outside pressures and the court's general appearance of independence are to be considered. Impartiality is generally defined as absence of prejudice or bias.[37] This is ascertained by a subjective assessment of the judges' unbiased personal conviction. It can be presumed as long as there is no proof of the contrary.[38]

2. Right to a Fair Hearing

Although sections 2 and 3 of Article 6 list a number of rights that aim specifically at the fairness of the proceedings in criminal cases, the adherence to these specific rights alone cannot guarantee the overall fairness of the proceedings. It is not possible to enumerate all aspects of the defendants' rights conclusively without any reference to the circumstances of the individual case at hand. Therefore, section 1 includes as an overarching principle the accused's right to a fair hearing, although an abstract definition of "fairness" does not exist. Instead, fairness is based on several principles that serve as general guidelines of a fair trial.

a. *Equality of Arms*

The principle of equality of arms requires that a fair balance of procedural rights is struck between the interests of the prosecution and the defense.[39] The court must ensure that the disputing parties enter the courtroom on the same footing and that they are afforded the same chance to present their cases convincingly before the court. One of the implications of this principle is reflected in Article 6 section 3(d), which explicitly stipulates the accused's right to call witnesses under the same conditions as the prosecution. This also shows that the defendant must not be degraded to a mere spectator in the court handling his case; he must be encouraged to play an active role in the process.[40] Equality of arms implies to some extent a right to an adversarial trial,[41] understood as a fair dispute between two parties presenting different cases to the court. To ensure equality of arms in this contest, a comparable level of information for both prosecution and defense is necessary. Linked to this is the need for full disclosure of all relevant evidence

[36] *Al Nashiri v. Poland*, *supra* note 12, § 567. The Court also stated an imminent risk of the use of torture evidence by the military commission (see *supra* II.1) and concluded that Poland's cooperation in delivering the applicant thereto violated Article 6 ECHR due to an imminent risk of a flagrant denial of justice.

[37] *Piersack v. Belgium*, *supra* note 34, § 30.

[38] Morice v. France, App. No. 29369/10, Eur. Ct. H.R., Apr. 23, 2015, § 74. For a general overview of the case law on impartiality and independence, see Sarah Summers, *Fair Trials* 99 (2007).

[39] *See* Jackson & Summers, *supra* note 18, at 83–85; Sidhu, *supra* note 2, at 113 seq.; Summers, *supra* note 38, at 104.

[40] *See* Sidhu, *supra* note 2, at 79.

[41] Rowe and Davis v. United Kingdom [GC], App. No. 28901/95, Eur. Ct. H.R., Feb. 16, 2000, § 60. *See also* Summers, *supra* note 38, at 110–12. *See also* chapters 37 and 38 of this book.

adduced before the court.[42] There are only a few exceptions to this principle. They are limited to cases where full disclosure would endanger a witness's physical or psychological health or an informant's or police officer's security, or where the disclosure would jeopardize an ongoing secret police investigation or operation. If it is legitimate to withhold some evidence, the court must ensure that other parts of the proceedings compensate for this curtailment of defense rights.[43]

b. *The Right to Remain Silent and the Privilege against Self-Incrimination*

The privilege against self-incrimination is one of the most important fundamental rights of suspects in criminal proceedings, although it is not addressed explicitly in Article 6 section 1.[44] The accused must not be forced to promote his own prosecution and conviction. He is in no way obligated to help the authorities prove the alleged offense(s)—*nemo tenetur se ipsum accusare*. Thus, the suspect has a right to remain silent; he need not give any statements or provide any evidence against himself.[45] The right to remain silent is applicable from the very first moment that a person is identified as a suspect. To ensure that the suspect can make use of his right to silence, he needs to be informed about this right by the authorities prior to the first interrogation.[46] The suspect's consent to being interrogated is only valid if it is based on the knowledge that he has the power to refuse the interrogation.

A difficult question arises if a court takes the accused's silence into account when assessing the likelihood of his having committed the alleged crime. The Court has stated that it contravenes the accused's right to silence if a conviction is based solely or mainly on the fact that the accused chose to remain silent. This might also entail a violation of his right to be presumed innocent under Article 6 section 2. The question as to whether a judgment is based to an undue extent on inferences from the defendant's silence can only be considered on a case-by-case basis. The proceedings remain fair if a conviction is based on a sufficient degree of corroborating evidence[47] and the court's inferences from the accused's silence were limited to "common-sense inferences" in "situations which clearly call for an explanation." Here, the defendant's silence "could be taken into account in assessing the persuasiveness of the evidence adduced... against him."[48]

[42] Reinhardt and Slimane Kaid v. France, App. Nos. 21/1997/805/1008 and 22/1997/806/1009, Eur. Ct. H.R., Mar. 31, 1998, §§ 105–107; Rowe and Davis v. United Kingdom [GC], App. No. 28901/95, Feb. 16, 2000, § 60. *See also* chapters 25, 26, and 31 of this book.

[43] Van Mechelen and Others v. the Netherlands, App. Nos. 21363/93 etc., Eur. Ct. H.R., Apr. 23, 1997, §§ 54, 58, 60.

[44] John Murray v. United Kingdom, App. No. 18731/91, Eur. Ct. H.R. [GC], Feb. 8, 1996, § 45. Trechsel, *supra* note 22, at 340, provides an overview of the guarantee's historical sources.

[45] General obligations to inform the authorities about the factual basis of tax liabilities or of minor motoring offenses (e.g., about the driver of a vehicle) do not touch upon the principle of *nemo tenetur*, as long as they are not linked to specific criminal liabilities.

[46] Brusco v. France, App. No. 1466/07, Eur. Ct. H.R., Oct. 14, 2010, § 54; Navone and Others v. Monaco, App. Nos. 62880/11 etc., Eur. Ct. H.R., Oct. 24, 2013, § 74.

[47] *John Murray v. United Kingdom*, *supra* note 44, §§ 47–8.

[48] *Id.* § 54; Condron v. United Kingdom, App. No. 35718/97, Eur. Ct. H.R., May 2, 2000, § 61.

The proceedings become unfair if inferences from the accused's silence have the effect of shifting the burden of proof from the authorities to the defendant. The Court came to this conclusion in *Telfner v. Austria*,[49] where the applicant was convicted of causing bodily harm by negligence in a car accident. He had confined his statement to the denial of being the driver of the car and had refused any further statements. His mother, the owner of the car, as well as his sister who also used it, refused to testify. The domestic court based the assumption that the accused had been involved in the accident on the fact that the car was mainly used by him. Since no corroborating evidence was offered, the Court concluded that the conviction was based on a shift of the burden of proof and therefore the trial was unfair.[50]

The general rationale of the privilege against self-incrimination is to ensure that the accused's will is respected.[51] Authorities therefore are not allowed to use coercive means to obtain a suspect's statement. The prohibition of coercive means is closely linked to the prohibition of torture or other inhuman or degrading treatment in Article 3 as the strongest means of coercion.[52] Here, the Court's case law is crystal clear: evidence obtained by torture is absolutely excluded and under no circumstances admissible at trial.[53] This is true not only for statements but also for other material evidence obtained by torture. If this rule is ignored, the proceedings are automatically deemed unfair.

By contrast, the use of evidence that was produced under ill treatment falling short of torture does not automatically render the proceedings unfair. The Court takes the view that unlike Article 3, Article 6 does not enshrine an absolute right.[54] Therefore, if the evidence obtained by ill treatment did not influence the outcome of the proceedings—neither the conviction nor the sentence—the overall fairness of the proceedings can still be preserved.[55]

With respect to the privilege against self-incrimination, statements have to be distinguished from other material evidence that exists independently from the suspect's will, such as "documents acquired pursuant to a warrant, breath, blood, urine, hair or voice samples and bodily tissue for the purpose of DNA testing."[56] Unlike oral statements, the production of these materials is considered not to fall into the purview of the privilege

[49] Telfner v. Austria, App. No. 33501/96, Eur. Ct. H.R., Mar. 20, 2001, § 18.

[50] For a more detailed assessment of the case law on adverse inferences from silence, see Andrew Ashworth, Ben Emmerson & Alison Macdonald, *supra* note 20, paras 15–101 to 15–114.

[51] *Jalloh v. Germany, supra* note 29, § 100–2; Pavlenko v. Russia, App. No. 42371/02, Eur. Ct. H.R., Apr. 1, 2010, § 100; Bykov v. Russia, App. No. 4378/02, Eur. Ct. H.R., Mar. 10, 2009, § 92; Saunders v. United Kingdom, App. No. 19187/91, Eur. Ct. H.R., Dec. 17, 1996, § 68.

[52] Article 3 ECHR ("No one shall be subjected to torture or to inhuman or degrading treatment or punishment.").

[53] *Jalloh v. Germany, supra* note 29, § 105; Gäfgen v. Germany, App. No. 22978/05, Eur. Ct. H.R. [GC], June 1, 2010, § 167.

[54] *Gäfgen v. Germany, supra* note 53, § 178.

[55] *Id.*; Alchagin v. Russia, App. No. 20212/05, Eur. Ct. H.R., Jan. 7, 2012, §§ 71–74; *El Haski v. Belgium, supra* note 21, § 85. For a critical assessment of the Court's case law, see Andrew Ashworth, *The Exclusion of Evidence Obtained by Violating a Fundamental Right: Pragmatism Before Principle in the Strasbourg Jurisprudence*, in *Criminal Evidence and Human Rights* 145, 154–60 (Paul Roberts & Jill Hunter eds., 2012).

[56] *Saunders v. United Kingdom, supra* note 51, § 69.

against self-incrimination that is meant to protect the suspect's will.[57] Regarding oral statements, on the other hand, the Court has opened the door to a balancing mechanism if coercive means were used to obtain them. In general, the right not to incriminate oneself requires that "the prosecution in a criminal case seeks to prove the case against the accused without resorting to evidence obtained through methods of coercion or oppression in defiance of the will of the accused."[58] However, as long as the procedure has not "extinguished the very essence of the privilege against self-incrimination," the Court may examine "the nature and degree of the compulsion, the existence of any relevant safeguards in the procedures and the use to which any material so obtained is put"[59] and conclude that the proceedings were still fair despite the use of a certain degree of coercive means—again, provided that sufficient corroborating evidence has been adduced.[60] Following its holistic approach, the Court has found, for example, that the use of evidence produced by the persistent questioning of a detained suspect by his cellmate who was an undercover police informant impinged on the suspect's right to silence and therefore turned the proceedings unfair.[61] On the other hand, the Court did not find a violation of Article 6 in *Bykov v. Russia*, where the applicant had not known that his supposed contract killer had turned to the police and wore a hidden radio-transmitting device when he tricked the applicant into incriminating statements asking him for his reward for the killing. The use of the evidence obtained from the covert operation did not turn the trial unfair because the Court found no unlawful coercion in merely tricking the suspect in a conversation.[62]

c. *Entrapment*

The Court has consistently held that it contravenes the rule of law if a law enforcement agency prosecutes criminal acts that were incited by its own members (or by private agents whose actions are imputable to them.)[63] The line between legitimate undercover investigations and unlawful police incitement is overstepped if the authorities do not confine themselves to a subsequent investigation of formerly committed crime but instead actively instigate an offense. In brief, "the police may act undercover but not incite."[64]

[57] *Jalloh v. Germany*, *supra* note 29, § 102; *Saunders v. United Kingdom*, *supra* note 51, § 69. *See also* Rainey, Wicks & Ovey, *supra* note 15, at 313 seq.

[58] *Jalloh v. Germany*, *supra* note 29, § 100; *Bykov v. Russia*, *supra* note 51, § 92; *Pavlenko v. Russia*, *supra* note 51, § 100; *Niculescu v. Romania*, *supra* note 21, § 111.

[59] *Id.*; see also *John Murray v. United Kingdom*, *supra* note 44, § 47. For an overview of the Court's case law, see O'Halloran and Francis v. United Kingdom, App. Nos. 15809/02 and 25624/02, Eur. Ct. H.R. [GC], June 29, 2007, §§ 45 seq.

[60] *Bykov v. Russia*, *supra* note 51, § 90; *Allan v. United Kingdom*, *supra* note 22, § 43; Khan v. United Kingdom, App. No. 35394/97, Eur. Ct. H.R., May 12, 2000, § 37.

[61] *Allan v. United Kingdom*, *supra* note 22.

[62] *Bykov v. Russia*, *supra* note 51, §§ 94 seq., 102.

[63] Sandu v. the Republic of Moldovia, App. No. 16463/08, Eur. Ct. H.R., Feb. 11, 2014, § 38.

[64] Teixeira de Castro v. Portugal, App. No. 25829/94, Eur. Ct. H.R., June 9, 1998, § 36-8; Khudobin v. Russia, App. No. 59696/00, Eur. Ct. H.R., Oct. 26, 2006, § 128; *Ramanauskas v. Lithuania*, *supra* note 22, § 54.

The Court determines entrapment by a substantive and a procedural test of incitement. The substantive test is based on the premise that the proceedings are unfair if the alleged crime would not have been committed without the influence exerted by persons whose actions are attributable to law enforcement authorities. This is indicated if the applicant does not have a previous criminal record, if he does not have any specific knowledge about the criminal "business" he engages in (for example, about prices paid for certain amounts of drugs),[65] or if he was pressured into the commission of an offense, for example, by an undercover agent simulating withdrawal symptoms to make the applicant provide illegal drugs. The procedural test evaluates whether the engagement of law enforcement agents followed relevant procedural guidelines and if some institutional or even judicial supervision was in place.[66] If the tests conclude that entrapment occurred, the defendant is deprived of a fair trial "right from the outset,"[67] and any evidence that was obtained through entrapment is inadmissible.[68]

If the defendant sufficiently substantiates that entrapment was used against him, the burden of proof shifts to law enforcement authorities to show the absence of unlawful entrapment.[69]

3. Public Hearing

Unlike the investigation of criminal incidents, which can be conducted secretly, trial hearings as well as the presentation of the court's decision must be held in public, in order to strengthen the public's confidence in the legitimate and effective administration of justice[70] and at the same time to safeguard the defendant's right to an effective defense. The principle of publicity also calls for the accused's presence in order to allow the court a proper determination of appropriate penal sanctions and to publicly express moral reprobation based on a convicted person's individual blame. The degree of individual blame can only be assessed if the defendant is present, because the assessment is based not only on a close scrutiny of the facts of a case but also on the defendant's personality and intellectual background. Since none of this is necessary in appeal proceedings that are limited to questions of law, a public hearing may not be required in appeal proceedings. Furthermore, the principle of publicity can be restricted due to certain individual or public interests, provided that the court has no alternative. Firstly, contravening security interests can require (parts of) the hearing to be held in camera—for example,

[65] *Id.* [66] *Ramanauskas v. Lithuania*, *supra* note 22, § 53.

[67] *Teixeira de Castro v. Portugal*, *supra* note 64, § 39; *Ramanauskas v. Lithuania*, *supra* note 22, §§ 53–73.

[68] *Teixeira de Castro v. Portugal*, *supra* note 64, § 36; *Khudobin v. Russia*, *supra* note 64, § 133; *Ramanauskas v. Lithuania*, *supra* note 22, § 60; Furcht v. Germany, App. No. 54648/09, Eur. Ct. H.R., Oct. 23, 2014, § 64; Lagutin and Others v. Russia, App. Nos. 6228/09 etc., Eur. Ct. H.R., Apr. 24, 2014, § 117.

[69] *Ramanauskas v. Lithuania*, *supra* note 22, § 70; *Lagutin and Others v. Russia*, *supra* note 68 § 94.

[70] Riepan v. Austria, App. No. 35115/97, Eur. Ct. H.R., Nov. 14, 2000, § 27; Diennet v. France, App. No. 18160/91, Eur. Ct. H.R., Sept. 26, 1995, § 33; see also Schabas, *supra* note 26, at 289.

if undercover agents must not be identified or if witnesses need to be protected against organized crime cartels. The same is true if juvenile victims need to be protected from secondary victimization. Finally, it can be in the interest of juvenile offenders that their trial be held in camera.

4. Hearing within Reasonable Time

Criminal proceedings need to take place in a timely manner in order to control negative repercussions on the accused's work and private life. The Court has issued numerous judgments concerning the defendant's right to a speedy trial.[71] The Court examines the appropriateness of a procedure's duration, from its very start with the initial charge until the judgment including the sentencing, in light of four factors:[72] the case's significance for the accused (detained defendants, for instance, deserve an expedited procedure) and the complexity of the case. A need for extended proceedings can arise due to the amount of proof to be evaluated or the complexity of the criminal incident itself, which is often the case in cross-border commission of crimes or large-scale organized crime ventures. If evidence can be obtained only with judicial assistance abroad, this may also cause a reasonable extension of the proceedings.[73] The conduct of the defendant and of the relevant authorities are also taken into account. Delay only amounts to a violation of procedural rights if it is attributable to the authorities. Accordingly, if a state claims that the duration of the proceedings could not be avoided due to an excessive workload of national courts, this will only be accepted for a certain amount of time, because it is the state's liability to provide an effective and accessible judicial system.[74] Apart from this, the Court examines whether the applicant confined himself to a reasonable use of his defense rights or made use of those rights with a view to unduly delay the proceedings (for example, by challenging the judge's impartiality on every occasion or by disclosing further evidence at the last possible moment). Finally, if the defendant fled during the proceedings, the caused delay cannot be attributed to the authorities.

If the Court concludes that the procedure's duration entailed a violation of the defendant's right to be tried in a timely manner, this does not by itself render the procedure unfair according to Article 6. The excessive duration of the proceedings can be compensated by a reduced sentence or the payment of financial compensations

[71] *See* Marc Henzelin & Héloise Rordorf, *When Does the Length of Criminal Proceedings Become Unreasonable According to the European Court of Human Rights?*, 5 N. J. Eur. Crim. L. 79 (2014) (in 2012, out of seventy-two ECtHR judgments that dealt with the length of proceedings, sixty-two judgments found that excessive duration violated Article 6 § 1 ECHR).

[72] Leading cases on excessive duration include Frydlender v. France, App. No. 30979/96, Eur. Ct. H.R. [GC], June 27, 2000, §§ 43, 45; Rumpf v. Germany, App. No. 46344/06, Eur. Ct. H.R., Sept. 2, 2010; Satakunnan Markkinapörssi Oy and Satamedia Oy v. Finland, App. No. 931/13, Eur. Ct. H.R., June 27, 2017, § 209; on redress, see Kaemena and Thöneböhn v. Germany, App. Nos. 45749/06 and 51115/06, Eur. Ct. H.R., Jan. 22, 2009, §§ 77–79.

[73] *See* Leigh, *supra* note 21, at 645, 651–63.

[74] Klein v. Germany, App. No. 33379/96, Eur. Ct. H.R., Oct. 26, 2000, § 43.

according to Article 13.[75] In extreme cases, the proceedings can be terminated to avoid a violation of Article 6 section 1.

IV. Article 6 Sections 2 and 3: Procedural Rights in Criminal Proceedings

The guarantees set out in Article 6 sections 2 and 3 are dedicated to criminal proceedings exclusively. In order to set their general ambit, the term "criminal charge" needs to be defined. In light of the diverging definitions in criminal procedure codes of the treaty jurisdictions—and to prevent the contracting states from circumventing the Convention and the Court's jurisdiction by declaring matters to be administrative or civil in nature when their real nature is criminal—the Court created an autonomous definition of the term "criminal charge" under European Human Rights Law. In 1976, the Court named three characteristic features of a criminal charge in its judgment in the *Engel* case (the so-called *Engel* criteria).[76] Most straightforwardly, a charge is clearly criminal if national law classifies the offense as criminal and stipulates its prosecution in a criminal procedure. However, if national law classifies an offense as a minor or a regulatory offense under administrative or disciplinary law, this is no more than a "starting point of formal and relative value."[77] Two further components need to be considered. First, the very nature of the offense is criminal if the provision is directed at the public in general and not at a specific group (as, for instance, certain health regulations for medical personnel at a hospital would be). Also, the severity of the maximum penalty that the offense carries, as well as the actual sentence imposed in the case at hand, are crucial factors. Second, if the punishment depends upon personal guilt and therefore carries a certain degree of moral reprobation, it is considered criminal. Finally, *Engel* stated that criminal sanctions are characterized by their punitive and deterrent purpose. None of these aspects is decisive by itself, but they form part of an overall assessment of the proceeding's effect on the defendant.[78] The Court's assessment can very well result in an application of the guarantees of Article 6 sections 2 and 3 despite an administrative or civil law approach of the national law.[79]

[75] *See* Corinna Ujkašević, *Die Kompensation von Verfahrensrechtsverstößen in der Rechtsprechung des Europäischen Gerichtshofs für Menschenrechte*, 2018, at 13 seq. and 61 seq.

[76] Engel and Others v. the Netherlands, App. Nos. 5100/71 etc., Eur. Ct. H.R., June 8, 1976, § 82.

[77] *Id.*

[78] *Id.* §§ 81–83; Bendenoun v. France, App. No. 12547/86, Eur. Ct. H.R., Feb. 24, 1994, § 47; Öztürk v. Germany, App. No. 8544/79, Eur. Ct. H.R., Feb. 21, 1984, §§ 53–54; *Deweer v. Belgium*, *supra* note 25, §§ 42–43.

[79] This is often true in cases of motoring or tax offenses. *See Bendenoun v. France*, *supra* note 78, § 47; Canady v. Slovakia (no. 2), App. No. 18268/03, Eur. Ct. H.R., Oct. 20, 2009, §§ 37, 42; Steininger v. Austria, App. No. 21539/07, Apr. 17, 2012, §§ 34–37.

V. Article 6 Section 2: The Presumption of Innocence

The suspect is to be presumed innocent until the prosecution proves otherwise.[80] The burden of proof for the accused's guilt is entirely on the authorities. Any doubts about the defendant's guilt work in favor of his position as an innocent citizen—*in dubio pro reo*.[81] The presumption of innocence is closely linked to the privilege against self-incrimination that ensures that the accused is in no way obliged to help dispel any of doubts about his guilt (see *supra* III.2.b).

The presumption of innocence extends to appeal proceedings even though the applicant was convicted in the first instance,[82] because the decision on the merits of the case becomes final only if the appeal proceedings confirm the first conviction's accuracy. This is also true if a case is reopened[83]—for instance after an ECtHR judgment that held the first trial was unfair under the Convention.

Since the judiciary is bound by the presumption of innocence, any infringement of this presumption on their part entails also a violation of the principle of impartiality under Article 6 (1).[84] Members of law enforcement authorities are free to inform the public about criminal proceedings if they are of public interest, but they must confine themselves to mere statements about the facts; no personal views about the likeliness of a conviction are allowed.[85]

VI. Article 6 Section 3: Specifically Listed Minimum Rights in Criminal Proceedings

The list of minimum rights laid down in section 3 is not exhaustive but is meant as an illustration of the components that ensure the fairness of a criminal procedure (see *supra* II.3).

[80] *See* Article 11 of the Universal Declaration of Human Rights (1948), United Nations General Assembly Resolution 217A.

[81] Telfner v. Austria, App. No. 33501/96, Mar. 20, 2001, § 15; Barberà, Messegué and Jabardo v. Spain, App. No. 10590/83, Eur. Ct. H.R., Dec. 6, 1988, § 77.

[82] Konstas v. Greece, App. No. 53466/07, Eur. Ct. H.R., May 24, 2011, § 36.

[83] *Dicle and Sadak v. Turkey*, App. No. 48621/07, Eur. Ct. H.R., June 16, 2015, §§ 57–58.

[84] Kyprianou v. Cyprus, App. No. 73797/01, Eur. Ct. H.R. [GC], Dec. 15, 2005, §§ 136–138.

[85] Allenet de Ribemont v. France, App. No. 15175/89, Eur. Ct. H.R., Feb. 10, 1995, § 36; Rushiti v. Austria, Eur. Ct. H.R., App. No. 28389/95, Mar. 21, 2000, § 31; Ismoilov and Others v. Russia, App. No. 2947/06, Eur. Ct. H.R., Apr. 24, 2008, § 161; Shuvalov v. Estonia, App. Nos. 39820/08 and 14942/09, Eur. Ct. H.R., May 29, 2012, § 75.

1. Prerequisites of an Effective Defense

An effective defense depends on full information about the allegations that are brought against the accused. Therefore, the prosecution is obliged to inform the accused about the alleged criminal actions ("cause") the charge refers to and about their legal classification ("nature").[86] This is to be done in time to allow the accused to properly prepare his defense strategy.[87] The information need not mention the evidence the charge is based upon.[88] Still, it must be detailed enough to enable the accused to fully understand the allegations against him and to prepare his defense effectively. This also requires that the information be delivered in a language the recipient can understand, or that a translation be provided. It need not necessarily be in writing, but in many cases, proper preparation of an effective defense will depend upon reliable written information about the charges at stake.[89] In case of mentally ill persons, the prosecution must ensure that persons taking care of the accused are informed properly.[90]

Besides, the accused has a right to an adequate "infrastructure" needed to concentrate on the preparation of his defense. If he is detained, the conditions thereof must allow him to concentrate on his defense strategy, to read and write,[91] and—most important—to have access to a defense counsel. This right—a fundamental feature of a fair trial[92]—is more specifically reflected in Article 6 section 3(c) and consists of three components: The defendant can either defend himself or he can choose a defense counsel. If he does not have sufficient means to retain a defense counsel at his own cost, he has a right to free assistance "if the interests of justice so require" (see *infra* VI.1).

The accused's right to defend himself implies his right to be present at the trial. This right can only be restricted if he disturbs the process by undue behavior or if for certain parts of the trial, he must be excluded due to overriding interests of others—for instance of victims who testify as witnesses for the prosecution (see *supra* III.3). The accused's right to be present is not limited to mere presence but entails a right to an "*effective participation*" including the right to call witnesses and to challenge evidence presented against him (see *infra* VI.2).

[86] Brozicek v. Italy, App. No. 10964/84, Eur. Ct. H.R. (Plenary), Dec. 19, 1989, § 42. This is also true if the legal classification of the alleged offense changes in the course of the proceedings, Mattoccia v. Italy, App. No. 23969/94, Eur. Ct. H.R., July 25, 2000, § 61.

[87] *See* Borisova v. Bulgaria, App. No. 56891/00, Eur. Ct. H.R., Dec. 21, 2006, §§ 43–45: it is insufficient if the accused is confronted only hours prior to the trial without assistance of a defense counsel.

[88] X. v. Belgium, App. No. 7628/76, Eur. Ct. H.R., May 9, 1977, § 1.

[89] The accused does not have a right to an exhaustive translation of all the case files. *See* X. v. Austria, App. No. 6185/73, May 29, 1975, Eur. Ct. H.R., Commission decision, § 2.

[90] Vaudelle v. France, App. No. 35683/97, Eur. Ct. H.R., Jan. 30, 2001, § 65.

[91] Mayzit v. Russia, App. No. 63378/00, Eur. Ct. H.R., Jan. 20, 2005, § 81; Moiseyev v. Russia, App. No. 62936/00, Eur. Ct. H.R., Oct. 9, 2008, § 221.

[92] Poitrimol v. France, App. No. 14032/88, Eur. Ct. H.R., Nov. 23, 1993, § 34; Salduz v. Turkey, App. No. 36391/02, Eur. Ct. H.R. [GC], Nov. 27, 2008, § 51; *Ibrahim and Others v. United Kingdom*, *supra* note 18, § 255.

Legal assistance should be offered from the very first moment a person is confronted with an allegation of criminal actions—usually from the first police interrogation[93]—until the final judgment. However, the accused is not afforded this right without limitation. Restrictions of the right of access to a lawyer are tolerated for compelling reasons.[94] In the case of *Ibrahim et al. v. United Kingdom*,[95] the Court found such compelling reasons because the arrested persons were suspected of having committed the bombing attacks on the London Underground in 2005 and the police feared an imminent risk of further attacks at the time of their first police interrogation. Therefore, they instituted a so-called "safety interview," denying the suspects prior access to a lawyer. Safety interviews are conducted in case of emergency if they seem appropriate to help avert harm to the public by preventing a future terrorist attack. The Court held that under these exceptional circumstances the proceedings as a whole remained fair despite the temporary denial of access to a defense counsel, because this was legitimized by the overriding interest of the security of the public.

If no compelling reasons exist for the denial of access to a lawyer, however, the burden of proof for the absence of a violation of Article 6 section 1 shifts to the respondent state. The government must then explain why the overall fairness of the trial was not irretrievably prejudiced by the temporary denial of access to a lawyer.[96] The Court lists numerous factors that can be considered in this assessment: whether the applicant was particularly vulnerable for reasons of age or mental capacity, whether there was a sufficient legal framework for the denial of access to a lawyer, whether the applicant was provided an opportunity to challenge the authenticity of the gained evidence, etc.[97] It is obvious that the Court grants the authorities a wide range of reasons to restrict an accused's access to a lawyer in case of perceived imminent terrorist threats. Although in its former decision in *Salduz v. Turkey*, the Court had stressed the importance of legal assistance from the first police interrogation,[98] the fairness test is now open to numerous considerations, and the outcome of the overall assessment naturally becomes less predictable. This of course poses a risk that domestic law enforcement authorities will feel less inclined to let a suspect's willingness to answer questions be affected by offered legal advice.[99]

[93] *Salduz v. Turkey*, *supra* note 92, §§ 54–55; Dayanan v. Turkey, App. No. 7377/03, Eur. Ct. H.R., Oct. 13, 2009, § 31; *Niculescu v. Romania*, *supra* note 21, § 112.

[94] *Salduz v. Turkey*, *supra* note 92, § 55; *Pavlenko v. Russia*, *supra* note 51, § 97; *Niculescu v. Romania*, *supra* note 21, § 112.

[95] *Ibrahim and Others v. United Kingdom*, *supra* note 18. For strong criticism, see Ryan Goss, *Out of Many, One? Strasbourg's Ibrahim Decision on Article 6*, 80 Mod. L. Rev. 1137, 1138 (2017).

[96] *Ibrahim and Others v. United Kingdom*, *supra* note 18, § 301.

[97] *Id.*, § 274.

[98] *Salduz v. Turkey*, *supra* note 92, § 55.

[99] For a general criticism, see Michele Caianello, *You Can't Always Counterbalance What You Want*, 25 Eur. J. Crime, Crim. L. & Crim. Just. 283, 292 (2017). On the *Salduz* and *Ibrahim* decisions, see Anneli Soo, *Divergence of European Union and Strasbourg Standards on Defence Rights in Criminal Proceedings?*, 25 Eur. J. Crime, Crim. L. & Crim. Just. 327, 333 (2017).

Some domestic criminal procedure laws (such as those in France, Germany, the Netherlands, and Poland) stipulated the exclusion of the defense counsel in case of the defendant's deliberate absence from the trial. The Court found that these regulations contravened the defendant's right to an active defense under Article 6 section 3(c). Accordingly, the Court held that while it is generally in line with the fair trial rights under the Convention to oblige the defendant to be present at the trial, it is not appropriate to entirely deprive him of a defense if he fails to comply with this obligation.[100]

The right to legal assistance includes the defendant's right to free and unrestricted access to his lawyer and the right to communicate with him confidentially.[101] This holds true even more if the defendant is in custody.[102]

Finally, the accused has a right to legal aid if fair administration of justice so requires. It is up to the domestic courts to decide whether this is the case. Aspects that are to be considered are the complexity of the case, the severity of the alleged offense(s), and the possible sentence(s) at stake. As a rule, if a prison sentence is at stake, the interests of justice require the assignment of a defense counsel.[103]

In general, the accused has a right to choose his defense counsel. Nevertheless, if particular circumstances require the defense counsel to have specific knowledge, the court can limit the accused's free choice accordingly.[104] The same is true for the defendant's right to represent himself. If the interests of justice require the assignment of a professional lawyer (for example, because of the complexity of the case), compulsory appointment of a lawyer is not prohibited under the Convention.[105]

Article 6 only protects against violations attributable to the state. Therefore, it does not fall into the court's responsibility to call the appointed lawyer to order—who of course is independent of the judiciary—in case of professional misconduct.[106] However, if a lawyer appointed for legal aid purposes fails entirely to provide any assistance, the accused's right to an effective defense—and thereby the fairness of the trial as a whole—can be undermined altogether. That again falls into the court's responsibility. Consequently, the court must intervene under such exceptional circumstances.[107]

[100] *Poitrimol v. France*, *supra* note 92, § 35 ("disproportionate"); Lala v. the Netherlands, App. No. 14861/89, Eur. Ct. H.R., Sept. 22, 1994, § 33; Pelladoah v. the Netherlands, App. No. 16737/90, Eur. Ct. H.R., Sept. 22, 1994, § 40; Neziraj v. Germany, App. No. 30804/07, Eur. Ct. H.R., Nov. 8, 2012, §§ 45, 51–67. Reacting to the ECtHR's decisions, the German legislature enacted a provision that allows an absent defendant to be represented by the present defense counsel under certain conditions.

[101] S. v. Switzerland, App. Nos. 12629/87, 13965/88, Eur. Ct. H.R., Nov. 28, 1991, § 48; Brennan v. United Kingdom, App. No. 39846/98, Eur. Ct. H.R., Oct. 16, 2001, § 58; Erdem v. Germany, App. No. 38321/97, Eur. Ct. H.R., July 5, 2001, §§ 61–70.

[102] Dayanan v. Turkey, App. No. 377/03, Eur. Ct. H.R., Oct. 13, 2009, § 31.

[103] Benham v. United Kingdom, App. No. 19380/92, Eur. Ct. H.R. [GC], June 10, 1996, § 61; Zdravko Stanev v. Bulgaria, App. No. 32238/04, Eur. Ct. H.R., Nov. 6, 2012, § 38.

[104] Croissant v. Germany, App. No. 13611/88, Eur. Ct. H.R., Sept. 25, 1992, § 29.

[105] *Id.*, § 27.

[106] Lagerblom v. Sweden, App. No. 26891/95, Eur. Ct. H.R., Jan. 14, 2003, § 56.

[107] *Artico v. Italy*, *supra* note 25, § 36; Daud v. Portugal, App. No. 22600/93, Eur. Ct. H.R., Apr. 21, 1998, §§ 38, 42 seq.

An effective defense further presupposes that the accused is provided with an interpreter at trial hearings if he cannot understand the language used in court. Article 6 section 3(e) stipulates that such interpretation is to be free of charge. This right is meant to support the defendant's ability to participate in the proceedings. Consequently, if the accused has sufficient language knowledge, he cannot claim a right to interpretation simply because he prefers another language—for example, the language of an ethnic minority he belongs to.[108] Furthermore, the right to free interpretation only applies for the defendant's communication with the court; it does not extend to his communication with his lawyer. Since it is the court's responsibility to ensure that the defendant can follow the trial, the court must control the reliability of the interpretation rendered in case of reasonable doubts concerning its quality.[109]

The costs of the interpretation are to be covered by the state; no subsequent charge of interpretation costs against the defendant is allowed.[110] If he stays away from the trial without an excuse, however, he could be charged for an interpreter who waited for him in court.[111]

2. Article 6 Section 3(d): The Right to Call and Confront Witnesses and to Examine Evidence Brought to Court

As noted above, the Court has consistently held that the taking of evidence and its use in court is exclusively a matter of the domestic law and not for the Court to examine (see *supra* I). Still, there are some minimum standards related to the taking and use of evidence that must be paid heed to in a fair trial. For example, the Court has stated that in cases where "crown" witnesses were offered certain advantages in exchange for their testimony, the domestic court must take the witness's personal interest into account when evaluating the credibility and conclusiveness of his statement.[112]

The most important provision concerning evidence is Article 6 section 3(d). First, the provision stipulates the accused's right to call witnesses "on his behalf" under the same conditions as the prosecution. Second, it entails the accused's right to examine or have examined witnesses against him. Both rights are perfect specifications of the principle of equality of arms (see *supra* III.2.a).[113]

[108] *Lagerblom v. Sweden, supra* note 106, § 62.

[109] Kamasinski v. Austria, App. No. 9783/82, Eur. Ct. H.R., Dec. 19, 1989, § 74; Hermi v. Italy, App. No. 18114/02, Eur. Ct. H.R. [GC], Oct. 18, 2006, § 70.

[110] Luedicke, Belkacem, Koç v. Germany, App. No. 6210/73 etc., Eur. Ct. H.R., Nov. 28, 1978, §§ 42 seq., 46.

[111] Fedele v. Germany, App. No. 11311/84, Eur. Ct. H.R. dec., Dec. 9, 1987, § 3.

[112] *See* Cornelis v. the Netherlands, App. No. 994/03, Eur. Ct. H.R. dec., May 25, 2004, § 15 seq. with further references.

[113] *See* Sidhu, *supra* note 2, at 120.

The Court defines the term "witness" "autonomously"[114] in the broadest possible way: a witness is any person whose statements are in fact taken into consideration by the court,[115] no matter whether the witness actually appears before the court or provides his statements otherwise.[116] The Convention's distinction between witnesses in favor or against the defendant is based on an adversarial conception of the criminal procedure. It is therefore not in line with the general principles of an inquisitorial process system, where the judge summons and (primarily) interrogates witnesses—hence all witnesses are in fact witnesses of the court. The question as to whether their statements favor the defendant or not can only be answered once the statement is evaluated. Notwithstanding the fact that inquisitorial systems do not distinguish witnesses in the way the Convention presumes, the guarantee is still applicable in the sense that every accused person is afforded the right to suggest witnesses to the court under the same conditions as the prosecution. This right does not imply that the court is obliged to call every witness named by the defendant, but the denial to call witnesses must be based on a reasonable and comprehensive reasoning.[117] The defendant on the other hand is obliged to give convincing reasons for the usefulness of witness statements.

Of paramount importance is the accused's right to challenge evidence pursuant to Article 6 section 3(d). Although the provision mentions only witnesses explicitly, the right to challenge evidence applies equally to all types of evidence, including statements of codefendants[118] as well as expert opinions.[119] Every piece of evidence the conviction is based upon must be produced in court with the defendant present and with the view to an "adversarial argument."[120] The right to question witnesses is not only indispensable for an active defense but also for an accurate determination of the truth, because the questioning can reveal inconsistencies in witnesses' submissions.[121] Hence, if the right to confront witnesses' statements is ignored, the reliability of the court's final decision can be jeopardized. Nevertheless, widely discussed are possible restrictions of this right in the interests of an effective prosecution or investigation, as well as in the interests of specifically vulnerable witnesses. The Court has consistently held that restrictions of the

[114] The term "autonomous definition" is meant to describe that the definition is not the result of a comparative analysis of the Member States' national definitions but that it is based on the European Convention on Human Rights and the case law of the ECtHR.

[115] Kostovski v. the Netherlands, App. No. 11454/85, Eur. Ct. H.R., Nov. 20, 1989, § 40; *Windisch v. Austria*, *supra* note 22, § 23; Lucà v. Italy, App. No. 33354/96, Eur. Ct. H.R., Feb. 27, 2001, § 41.

[116] Asch v. Austria, App. No. 12398/86, Eur. Ct. H.R., Apr. 26, 1991, § 25.

[117] Topić v. Croatia, App. No. 51355/10, Eur. Ct. H.R., Oct. 10, 2013, § 42; Polyakov v. Russia, App. No. 77018/01, Eur. Ct. H.R., Jan. 29, 2009, §§ 34–35.

[118] *Lucà v. Italy*, *supra* note 115, § 41.

[119] Mantovanelli v. France, App. No. 21479/93, Eur. Ct. H.R., Mar. 18, 1997, §§ 35–36.

[120] *Kostovski v. the Netherlands*, *supra* note 115, § 41; *Lucà v. Italy*, *supra* note 115, § 39; Khodorkovskiy and Lebedev v. Russia, App. Nos. 11082/06 and 13772/05, Eur. Ct. H.R., July 25, 2013, § 707; Poletan and Azirovik v. the former Republic of Macedonia, App. No. 26711/07 etc., Eur. Ct. H.R., May 12, 2016, § 81; *Bátěk v. the Czech Republic*, *supra* note 22, § 37; Štulíř v. the Czech Republic, App. No. 36705/12, Eur. Ct. H.R., Jan. 12, 2017, § 53. *See also* Jackson & Summers, *supra* note 18, at 86.

[121] *See* Mike Redmayne, *Confronting Confrontation*, in *Criminal Evidence and Human Rights* 283 (Paul Roberts & Jill Hunter eds., 2012).

accused's right to confront witnesses due to their absence at trial are conceivable if there is a "good reason"[122] to do so. Evidently a good reason is the sheer impossibility of hearing the witness personally in court, because he is deceased or too sick to personally attend the hearing. Shortcomings such as this are not attributable to the authorities.[123] If a witness is not easy to reach because he lives abroad or cannot be found, a good reason for his absence is only present if the court has made all reasonable efforts to get hold of him including a request for international legal assistance or a systematic search.[124] Another good reason for restrictions of the accused's right to confront witnesses can lie in the need to protect the witness's personal safety, for instance, if his life and freedom are imperiled in case he testifies personally in court. It can also be true for witnesses who are traumatized victims of sexual abuse crimes[125] and cannot be expected to testify with the defendant present. If a witness claims that he cannot testify because of fear, the Court accepts this as a good reason if the accused—or persons acting in his interest—threatened the witness. Apart from that, fear is only considered a good reason for the witness's absence if it is based on objective grounds.[126]

Difficult questions arise in the case of anonymous witnesses. Usually, the matter comes up in organized crime or terrorism cases in which investigations are conducted undercover. If such investigations lead to a trial, it can be crucial to conceal the identity of participating agents and to allow them to stay away from the trial. Therefore, the Court has accepted that under certain conditions, there are good reasons to use anonymous witnesses who are not present at the trial.

If there is a good reason for a witness not to testify in the presence of the accused, the court must employ the least severe restrictions on his right to confront the witness. Sometimes, the interrogation of the witness in another room with video transmission is possible, sometimes the accused can be offered the opportunity to pose questions and have them delivered by others.

If none of these measures is feasible, the absence of the witness brings about profound restrictions of the accused's right to confront witnesses. Therefore, the repercussions of these restrictions for the overall fairness of the proceedings need to be closely scrutinized. The Court follows a three-step examination concerning the overall fairness of the proceedings in such cases (the so-called "*Al-Khawaja* test").[127] If a restriction of confrontation rights is based on a good reason, the second step would be to evaluate whether the untested evidence was the sole or decisive evidence the finding of guilt was

[122] *Al-Khawaja and Tahery v. United Kingdom*, *supra* note 28 § 120; Gabrielyan v. Armenia, App. No. 8088/05, Eur. Ct. H.R., Apr. 10, 2012, §§ 78, 81–84; Rudnichenko v. Ukraine, App. No. 2775/07, Eur. Ct. H.R., July 11, 2013, § 104.

[123] *See* Gani v. Spain, App. No. 61800/08, Eur. Ct. H.R., Feb. 19, 2013, § 39: "... *impossibilium nulla obligatio est.*"

[124] *Bátěk and Others v. the Czech Republic*, *supra* note 22, § 38.

[125] Bocos Cuesta v. the Netherlands, App. No. 54789/00, Eur. Ct. H.R., Nov. 10, 2005, §§ 69 seq.

[126] *Al-Khawaja and Tahery v. United Kingdom*, *supra* note 28, §§ 122–125.

[127] *Al-Khawaja and Tahery v. United Kingdom*, *supra* note 28, § 119; Schatschaschwili v. Germany, App. No. 9154/10, Eur. Ct. H.R [GC], Dec. 15, 2015, § 107; *Štulíř v. the Czech Republic*, *supra* note 120, § 54; *Bátěk v. the Czech Republic*, *supra* note 22, § 38.

based upon ("sole-or-decisive rule").[128] The third step then would be an examination of the way in which the evidence was used and the weight that was given to it. The overall fairness of the proceedings can be preserved if restrictions of the defendant's right to challenge absent witnesses' credibility were sufficiently counterbalanced by strong procedural safeguards that appropriately compensated the "handicaps under which the defense labored".[129]

However, recently the Court has blurred the lines between the different steps of this test and at the same time watered down its criteria. On the one hand, the Court stated that the lack of a good reason does not automatically render the proceedings unfair because "it would not be correct . . . to apply this rule in an inflexible manner."[130] Instead, the fairness of the proceedings depends on the particular importance of the obtained evidence for the outcome of the process. The more important the evidence is, the more caution is needed in its assessment. Consequently, the need for counterbalancing factors depends on the weight of the untested evidence for the outcome of the proceedings.[131] No clear limits are defined. Even if untested evidence was of significant importance to the case, the unfairness of the proceedings is not inevitably established. The proceedings as a whole can still be fair if only the procedural safeguards compensating for the denial of confrontation rights were strong enough.[132] Such safeguards could consist of an extremely careful assessment of the untested statements, which due to this shortcoming, can only carry less weight. Moreover, the presentation of a sufficient degree of corroborating evidence is necessary.

In fact, the recent case law opens up each of the three steps of the *Al-Khawaja* test to considerations of the other steps and declares this to be a return to the "traditional way"[133] of determining the overall fairness of criminal proceedings. How it handles curtailments of the accused's confrontation rights is another manifestation of the Court's traditionally holistic approach to evaluating the proceeding's overall fairness. This approach not only favors the admissibility of evidence obtained in breach of conventional guarantees, it can also have the opposite effect. Even if untested evidence was not the sole or the decisive reason for the trial outcome, the proceedings can still be unfair if there was no good reason for a witness's absence.[134]

[128] Unterpertinger v. Austria, App. No. 9120/80, Eur. Ct. H.R., Nov. 24, 1986, § 33; *Van Mechelen and Others v. the Netherlands*, *supra* note 43, § 55; *Al-Khawaja and Tahery v. United Kingdom*, *supra* note 28, § 119; *Štulíř v. the Czech Republic*, *supra* note 120, § 54.

[129] *Al-Khawaja and Tahery v. United Kingdom*, *supra* note 28, § 147; *Schatschaschwili v. Germany*, *supra* note 127, § 107.

[130] *Al-Khawaja and Tahery v. United Kingdom*, *supra* note 28, § 146; *Schatschaschwili v. Germany*, *supra* note 127, § 113; *Bátěk v. the Czech Republic*, *supra* note 22, § 38; *Štulíř v. the Czech Republic*, *supra* note 120, § 54.

[131] *Schatschaschwili v. Germany*, *supra* note 127, § 116; *Štulíř v. the Czech Republic*, *supra* note 120, § 68.

[132] *Schatschaschwili v. Germany*, *supra* note 127, §§ 111–131; *Bátěk v. the Czech Republic*, *supra* note 22, § 38.

[133] *Al-Khawaja and Tahery v. United Kingdom*, *supra* note 28, § 146; *Schatschaschwili v. Germany*, *supra* note 127, § 112.

[134] *Rudnichenko v. Ukraine*, *supra* note 122, § 104.

In the end, the outcome of the Court's holistic fairness examination is not entirely foreseeable. Therefore, it is not surprising that the question of how the competing interests of the witness's interest in personal safety, the public's interest in effective law enforcement and crime prevention, and the accused's interest in an effective defense can be squared with each other, has generated ample case law[135] as well as extensive academic debate.[136] The core critique is that the Court's case law leads to uncertainties that might undermine the validity of the minimum standards set by the Convention.

VII. Conclusions

There is no doubt that the European Court of Human Rights' task is huge: the aim to provide precise minimum standards for fair criminal procedure in forty-seven states with significantly differing procedural systems is as noble as it is extremely difficult to achieve. Against this backdrop, the Court's resort to "softening mechanisms" as to give the states leeway to implement conventional guarantees (so-called margin of appreciation), or the Court's holistic approach in ascertaining the fairness of criminal proceedings, are manifestations of wise judicial self-restraint and respect for the domestic procedural systems. At the same time, the Court's readiness to accept the balancing of various factors in its case-by-case assessment of the overall fairness brings considerable risks for the project of creating reliable standards for fair trials. The criteria of the Court's holistic approach vary from case to case and comprise multiple disparate aspects. It remains unclear how exactly a balance can be struck between interests that have nothing in common and that serve diametrically opposed purposes. No specific hierarchy or even a certain benchmark is defined for the overall fairness-assessment. Due to the vagueness of this process, its outcome cannot easily be anticipated. Moreover, if among the factors to be considered are "the interests of the public and the victims, in seeing crime properly prosecuted,"[137] it seems conceivable that the more severe alleged crimes are, the more generous the Court will be in granting states leeway to diminish procedural rights.

Still, it would be unfair to dismiss the Court's fairness jurisprudence as inconclusive without considering the specific circumstances surrounding the Court's work. It is

[135] Compare the broad case law on the admissibility of anonymous statements on trial: *Kostovski v. the Netherlands, supra* note 115, §§ 35–45; *Windisch v. Austria, supra* note 22, §§ 27–32; Doorson v. the Netherlands, App. No. 20524/92, Eur. Ct. H.R., Mar. 26, 1996, §§ 69 seq.; Taal v. Estonia, App. No. 13249/02, Eur. Ct. H.R., Nov. 22, 2005, §§ 31 seq.; *Bátěk v. the Czech Republic, supra* note 22, §§ 36 seq.; *Štulíř v. the Czech Republic, supra* note 120, §§ 53 seq.

[136] Ryan Goss, *Criminal Fair Trial Rights* 124–39 (2016); Laura Hoyano, *What Is Balanced on the Scales of Justice?*, Crim. L. Rev. 4, 22 (2014); Redmayne, *supra* note 121, at 291; see also Mike Redmayne, *Hearsay and Human Rights: Al-Khawaja in the Grand Chamber*, 75 Mod. L. Rev. 865–93 (2012) (defending the Court's position).

[137] *Al-Khawaja and Tahery v. United Kingdom, supra* note 28, § 118; *Schatschaschwili v. Germany, supra* note 127, §§ 100–101; *Ibrahim and Others v. United Kingdom*, supra note 18, §§ 250–251; *Bátěk v. the Czech Republic, supra* note 22, § 36.

simply not possible to create detailed procedural black-letter rules that are applicable indiscriminately in varying procedural systems—nor does this lie within the Court's competence. Instead, the Court's mission is to defend an indispensable body of procedural guarantees that are at the core of a fair trial. In doing so, the Court cannot but decide on a case-by-case basis—naturally, the Court's approach can be nothing but casuistic.

The consequences for the Court's role as a guardian for fair criminal proceedings in the treaty states are twofold. Its task can only be fulfilled if an eye is kept on the states' willingness to accept Strasbourg judgments. The Court must certainly avoid frustrating the public's trust in a reliable law enforcement system by allowing suspected offenders to go unpunished due to procedural safeguards. If Strasbourg case law resulted in loss of public confidence on the national level, its acceptance and thereby its authority would be jeopardized.

Even more important is the second corollary of the Court's role: Treaty states should not lose sight of the fact that it is foremost their responsibility to ensure fair criminal proceedings at the national level and within their domestic procedural systems. Appeal to the Strasbourg Court is supposed to be a measure of last resort to secure some basic standards of the rule of law. In doing so, the Court does not shy away from taking a powerful stance if necessary (see *supra* I., II.1). Yet the Court should not be expected to solve everyday procedural problems such as the question of whether criminal proceedings are excessively long. Nor should the Court be expected to create hard-and-fast rules for the admissibility of dubiously obtained evidence. Instead, it is up to the treaty states to do their homework and thereby make complaints to the Strasbourg Court superfluous to the greatest extent possible. The Court, on the other hand, should be given enough room to resolve the major issues of overall fairness of criminal proceedings in the face of today's challenges. To name only one of them, a challenge ahead is the (further) validation of procedural standards in the pretrial stage. As abridged procedures that dispense with traditional trials gain more and more importance, so does the investigative stage of the criminal procedure. Yet if criminal proceedings are more and more reduced to pretrial proceedings, this calls for a reinterpretation of conventional guarantees. And it will be for the Court to ensure that Strasbourg jurisprudence lives up to the Convention's character as a "living instrument."

References

Ben Emmerson, Andrew Ashworth & Alison Macdonald (eds.), *Human Rights and Criminal Justice* (2nd ed. 2007)

Ryan Goss, *Criminal Fair Trial Rights* (2014)

Lara Hoyano, *What Is Balanced on the Scales of Justice? In Search of the Essence of the Right to a Fair Trial*, Crim. L. Rev. 4–29 (2014)

John D. Jackson & Sarah Summers, *The Internationalisation of Criminal Evidence* (2012)

Bernadette Rainey, Elizabeth Wicks & Clare Ovey, *Jacobs, White & Ovey, The European Convention on Human Rights* (7th ed. 2017)

William A. Schabas, *The European Convention on Human Rights* (2015)
Omkar Sidhu, *The Concept of Equality of Arms in Criminal Proceedings under Article 6 of the European Convention on Human Rights* (2017)
Sarah J. Summers, *Fair Trials* (2007)
Stefan Trechsel, *Human Rights in Criminal Proceedings* (2005)
Stefan Trechsel, *Why Must Trials Be Fair?*, 94 Isr. L. Rev. 31 (1997)

CHAPTER 6

THE EUROPEAN UNION AND THE RIGHTS OF INDIVIDUALS IN CRIMINAL PROCEEDINGS

VALSAMIS MITSILEGAS*

I. Introduction

The entry into force of the Lisbon Treaty[1] has enabled an unprecedented development in European Union criminal law: the adoption by the EU legislator of secondary legislation on human rights applicable in Europe's area of criminal justice. The legislation in question consists of a series of Directives introducing minimum standards on the rights of the individual in criminal proceedings. Legislating for human rights at the EU level in this context has been made a reality following the inclusion in the Lisbon Treaty of an express legal basis—Article 82(2) TFEU[2]—conferring on the Union express competence to adopt minimum standards on criminal procedure. This chapter will focus on analyzing the secondary legislation EU institutions have adopted under this legal basis in the field of procedural rights in criminal proceedings. The key elements of the main EU Directives in the field will be evaluated in view of their impact on the protection of fundamental rights and on the legal systems of EU Member States. The transformative potential of EU law on procedural rights when viewed within the broader constitutional and institutional context of the European Union will be highlighted.

* I would like to acknowledge the expert research assistance of Dr. Niovi Vavoula. The usual disclaimer applies.

[1] Treaty of Lisbon Amending the Treaty on European Union and the Treaty Establishing the European Community, Dec. 13, 2007, 2007 O.J. (C 306) 1.

[2] Consolidated Version of the Treaty on the Functioning of the E.U, Oct. 26, 2012, 2012 O.J. (C 326) 1.

II. The Content of EU Procedural Rights

At the time of writing, EU legislation in the field of procedural rights has reached a considerable degree of breadth and maturity. The adoption of focused and relatively modest pieces of legislation initially (such as Directives on interpretation and translation and on the right to information) has been followed by the adoption of Directives that apply to the heart of domestic criminal proceedings and that will have a significant impact—notwithstanding their framing as "minimum standards" instruments—on both the protection of fundamental rights at the national level and on the internal rules of domestic criminal justice systems. Directives on the rights to access to a lawyer and to legal aid and the Directive on the presumption of innocence constitute key examples in this regard. This section will flag the key elements of the Directives adopted thus far and will follow with a discussion on the feasibility of future legislation in the field of detention.

1. Interpretation and Translation

The Directive on the right to interpretation and translation[3] strengthens the visibility of these rights by translating into secondary EU law rights developed by the case law of the European Court of Human Rights (ECtHR) and at times extending the Strasbourg protection further.[4] With regard to the right to interpretation, the Directive places upon Member States a duty to ensure that suspected or accused persons who do not speak or understand the language of the criminal proceedings concerned are provided, without delay, with interpretation during criminal proceedings before investigative and judicial authorities, including during police questioning, all court hearings, and any necessary interim hearings.[5] Member States must ensure that, where necessary for the purpose of safeguarding the fairness of the proceedings, interpretation is available for communication between suspected or accused persons and their legal counsel in direct connection with any questioning or hearing during the proceedings or with the lodging of an appeal or other procedural applications.[6] Member States must ensure that a procedure or mechanism is in place to ascertain whether suspected or accused persons speak and understand the language of the criminal proceedings and whether they need the assistance of an interpreter,[7] and that, in accordance with procedures in national law,

[3] Directive 2010/64/EU of the European Parliament and of the Council on the right to interpretation and translation in criminal proceedings, 2010 O.J. (L 280) 1 [hereinafter Directive 2010/64/EU].

[4] For an analysis, see Sylvie Monjean-Decaudin, *L'Union Européenne Consacre le Droit à l'Assistance Linguistique dans les Procédures Pénales. Commentaire de la Directive Relative aux Droits à l'interprétation et à la traduction dans les procédures pénales*, 47 Revue Trimestrielle de Droit Européen 763–81 (2011).

[5] Directive 2010/64/EU, Art. 2(1). [6] *Id.* Art. 2(2).

[7] *Id.* Art. 2(4).

suspected or accused persons have the right to challenge a decision finding that there is no need for interpretation and, when interpretation has been provided, the possibility to complain that the quality of the interpretation is not sufficient to safeguard the fairness of the proceedings.[8] Advocate General Bot has interpreted Articles 1(2) and 2(1) of the Directive as allowing an individual who is the subject of a judicial decision in criminal matters and who does not know the language of the proceedings to launch an appeal in her own language, while the onus for ensuring the enjoyment of this right falls upon the competent national court.[9] With regard to the right to translation, the Directive places Member States under a duty to ensure that suspected or accused persons who do not understand the language of the criminal proceedings concerned are, within a reasonable period of time, provided with a written translation of all documents that are essential to ensure that they are able to exercise their right of defense and to safeguard the fairness of the proceedings.[10] Essential documents must include any decision depriving a person of his liberty, any charge or indictment, and any judgment.[11] The competent authorities must, in any given case, decide whether any other document is essential. Suspected or accused persons or their legal counsel may submit a reasoned request to that effect.[12] Exceptionally, an oral translation or oral summary of essential documents may be provided instead of a written translation on condition that such oral translation or oral summary does not prejudice the fairness of the proceedings.[13] Member States must ensure that, in accordance with procedures in national law, suspected or accused persons have the right to challenge a decision finding that there is no need for the translation of documents or passages thereof, and, when a translation has been provided, the possibility to complain that the quality of the translation is not sufficient to safeguard the fairness of the proceedings.[14]

2. Information

The Directive on the right to information[15] places Member States under an express duty[16] to ensure that suspects or accused persons are provided promptly with information concerning at least the following procedural rights, as they apply under national law, in order to allow for those rights to be exercised effectively: (1) the right of access to a lawyer, (2) any entitlement to free legal advice and the conditions for obtaining such advice, (3) the right to be informed of the accusation, (4) the right to interpretation and

[8] *Id.* Art. 2(5).

[9] Advocate General Bot, Opinion delivered on May 7, 2015, Case C-216/14, Covaci, § 81, *available at* https://curia.europa.eu.

[10] Directive 2010/64/EU, Art. 3(1). [11] *Id.* Art. 3(2). [12] *Id.* Art. 3(3).

[13] *Id.* Art. 3(7). [14] *Id.* Art. 3(5).

[15] Directive 2012/13/EU of the European Parliament and of the Council on the right to information in criminal proceedings, 2012 O.J. (L 142) 1 [hereinafter Directive 2012/13/EU].

[16] *Id.* preamble (18). The right to information about procedural rights, which is inferred from the case law of the European Court of Human Rights, should be explicitly established by this Directive.

translation, and (5) the right to remain silent.[17] Member States must ensure that the information is given orally or in writing, in simple and accessible language and taking into account any particular needs of vulnerable suspects or vulnerable accused persons.[18] A key component of the right to information is the provision of a Letter of Rights. Member States must ensure that suspects or accused persons who are arrested or detained are provided promptly with a written Letter of Rights. The Letter of Rights was one of the key innovations put forward by the Commission in its original proposal for a Framework Decision on procedural rights in 2004.[19] According to the Directive, suspects and accused persons must be given an opportunity to read the Letter of Rights and must be allowed to keep it in their possession throughout the time that they are deprived of liberty.[20] In addition to the information set out in Article 3 of the Directive (which sets out the procedural rights for which the right to information applies as a minimum), the Letter of Rights must also contain information about the following rights as they apply under national law: (1) the right of access to the materials of the case, (2) the right to have consular authorities and one person informed, (3) the right of access to urgent medical assistance, and (4) the maximum number of hours or days suspects or accused persons may be deprived of liberty before being brought before a judicial authority.[21] The Letter of Rights must also contain basic information about any possibility, under national law, of challenging the lawfulness of the arrest; obtaining a review of the detention; or making a request for provisional release.[22] The Letter of Rights must be drafted in simple and accessible language, with annex 1 to the Directive containing an indicative model Letter of Rights.[23] Member States must ensure that suspects or accused persons receive the Letter of Rights written in a language that they understand. Where a Letter of Rights is not available in the appropriate language, suspects or accused persons must be informed of their rights orally in a language that they understand. A Letter of Rights in a language that they understand must then be given to them without undue delay.[24] The duty of Member States to ensure the provision of a Letter of Rights extends also to European Arrest Warrant (hereinafter EAW) proceedings.[25]

The right of information of the applicable procedural rights is complemented by provision on the right to information about the accusation and the right of access to the materials of the case. The Directive thus reflects the case law of the ECtHR, which views the right to information in this context as inextricably linked with the defendant's right to an adversarial procedure.[26] As regards the right to information about the accusation, the Directive provides that Member States must ensure that suspects or accused persons are provided with information about the criminal act they are suspected or accused of having committed. That information must be provided promptly and in such detail as is necessary to safeguard the fairness of the proceedings and the effective exercise of the

[17] *Id.* Art. 3(1). [18] *Id.* Art. 3(2).

[19] Commission Proposal for a Council Framework Decision on certain procedural rights in criminal proceedings throughout the European Union, COM (2004) 328 final (April 28, 2004).

[20] Directive 2012/13/EU, Art. 4(1). [21] *Id.* Art. 4(2). [22] *Id.* Art. 4(3).

[23] *Id.* Art. 4(4). [24] *Id.* Art. 4(5). [25] *Id.* Art. 5.

[26] *Danayan v. Turkey*, App. No. 7377/03, Eur. Ct. H.R., October 13, 2009, §§ 35, 36.

rights of the defense.[27] Member States must ensure that suspects or accused persons who are arrested or detained are informed of the reasons for their arrest or detention, including the criminal act they are suspected or accused of having committed, and that, at the latest on submission of the merits of the accusation to a court, detailed information is provided on the accusation, including the nature and legal classification of the criminal offense, as well as the nature of participation by the accused person.[28] Member States must further ensure that suspects or accused persons are informed promptly of any changes in the information given where this is necessary to safeguard the fairness of the proceedings.[29] With regard to the right of access to the materials of the case, the Directive provides that this will be provided free of charge.[30] Where a person is arrested and detained at any stage of the criminal proceedings, Member States must ensure that documents related to the specific case in the possession of the competent authorities that are essential to challenging effectively, in accordance with national law, the lawfulness of the arrest or detention, are made available to arrested persons or to their lawyers.[31] Member States must ensure that access is granted at least to all material evidence in the possession of the competent authorities, whether for or against suspects or accused persons, to those persons or their lawyers in order to safeguard the fairness of the proceedings and to prepare the defense.[32] Access to these materials must be granted in due time to allow the effective exercise of the rights of the defense and at the latest upon submission of the merits of the accusation to the judgment of a court. Where further material evidence comes into the possession of the competent authorities, access must be granted to it in due time to allow for it to be considered.[33]

3. Access to a Lawyer

The right of access to a lawyer[34] is the cornerstone of procedural rights in criminal proceedings. It has been characterized as a "gateway" right, permitting the exercise of other rights and helping to make all these rights real and effective.[35] Negotiations on the Directive on access to a lawyer—which, as should be reminded, would have the modest aim of introducing merely minimum standards in the field under the legal basis of Article 82(2) TFEU—have proven to be complex. Negotiations focused on how best to achieve meaningful minimum standards without (as some Member States feared)

[27] Directive 2012/13/EU, Art. 6(1). [28] *Id.* Art. 6(2) and (3). [29] *Id.* Art. 6(4).
[30] *Id.* Art. 7(5). [31] *Id.* Art. 7(1). [32] *Id.* Art. 7(2). [33] *Id.* Art. 7(3).

[34] Directive 2013/48/EU of the European Parliament and of the Council on the right of access to a lawyer in criminal proceedings and in European arrest warrant proceedings, and on the right to have a third party informed upon deprivation of liberty and to communicate with third persons and with consular authorities while deprived of liberty, 2013 O.J. (L 294) 1 [hereinafter Directive 2013/48/EU].

[35] *See* Submission of Fair Trials International in Case *A.T. v. Luxembourg*, App. No. 30460/13, Eur. Ct. H.R., April 9, 2015, § 58; see also Debbie Sayers, *Protecting Fair Trial Rights in Criminal Cases in the European Union: Where Does the Roadmap Take Us?*, 14 Hum. Rts. L. Rev. 733, 748 (2014).

jeopardizing unduly national legal diversity in the field of criminal procedure.[36] The need to find compromises in order to reach agreement between the Council and the European Parliament in the post-Lisbon co-decision era has led to the adoption of a text accompanied by a lengthy Preamble consisting of no less than fifty-nine recitals.

The scope and content of the right to access to a lawyer is spelled out in Article 3 of the Directive. The opening paragraph states as a general rule that Member States must ensure that suspects and accused persons have the right of access to a lawyer in such time and in such a manner so as to allow the persons concerned to exercise their rights of defense practically and effectively.[37] This provision reflects the approach of the Strasbourg Court, according to which the lawyer must be able to provide effective and concrete assistance, and not an assistance that is merely abstract by the fact that she is present in the proceedings.[38] Suspects or accused persons must have access to a lawyer without undue delay. In any event, suspects or accused persons must have access to a lawyer from whichever of the following points in time is the earliest: (1) before they are questioned by the police or by another law enforcement or judicial authority, (2) upon the carrying out by investigating or other competent authorities of an investigative or other evidence-gathering act in accordance with point (c) of paragraph 3, (3) without undue delay after deprivation of liberty, or (4) where they have been summoned to appear before a court having jurisdiction in criminal matters, in due time before they appear before that court.[39]

The right of access to a lawyer is further articulated as entailing the following elements: (1) Member States must ensure that suspects or accused persons have the right to meet in private and communicate with the lawyer representing them, including prior to questioning by the police or by another law enforcement or judicial authority, (2) Member States must ensure that suspects or accused persons have the right for their lawyer to be present and participate effectively when questioned. Such participation must be in accordance with procedures under national law, provided that such procedures do not prejudice the effective exercise and essence of the right concerned. Where a lawyer participates during questioning, the fact that such participation has taken place must be noted using the recording procedure in accordance with the law of the Member State concerned. (3) Member States must ensure that suspects or accused persons must have, as a minimum, the right for their lawyer to attend the following investigative or evidence-gathering acts where those acts are provided for under national law and if the suspect or accused person is required or permitted to attend the act concerned, identity parades, confrontations, and reconstructions of the scene of a crime.[40] Member States must endeavor to make general information available to facilitate the obtaining of a lawyer by suspects or accused persons. Notwithstanding provisions of national law concerning the mandatory presence of a lawyer, Member States must make the necessary

[36] On the main issues arising in negotiations, see Steven Cras, *The Directive on the Right of Access to a Lawyer in Criminal Proceedings and in European Arrest Warrant Proceedings*, eucrim 32–44 (2014).

[37] Directive 2013/48/EU, art. 3(1).

[38] A.T. v. Luxembourg, App. no. 30460/13, Eur. Ct. H.R., Apr. 19, 2015, § 87.

[39] Directive 2013/48/EU, art. 3(2).

[40] *Id.* Art. 3(3).

arrangements to ensure that suspects or accused persons who are deprived of liberty are in a position to exercise effectively their right of access to a lawyer, unless they have waived that right in accordance with Article 9 of the Directive.[41] The Directive thus articulates in detail in EU secondary law the fundamental right of access to a lawyer as enshrined in Strasbourg case law, and in particular in the case of *Salduz*.[42] The Directive clarifies and strengthens the impact of *Salduz* on national law, by narrowing the national margin of appreciation in implementing the access to a lawyer obligations and in particular by expressly extending the application of the right of access to a lawyer in cases where no deprivation of liberty is involved.[43]

The challenges that even minimum harmonization of the right to access to a lawyer were perceived to pose for the integrity of national criminal justice systems and policies have led to the watering down of harmonization in four main respects: in limiting the reach of the application of the Directive by attempting to exclude minor offenses from its scope,[44] in introducing temporary derogations to rights,[45] in attempting to reach a compromise in the provision on confidentiality of communications between lawyers and defendants,[46] and in excluding from the scope of the present instrument provisions on legal aid, which as seen above are the subject of negotiations of a separate Directive under the Roadmap.[47] It is important to analyze here in detail the exceptions introduced by the Directive regarding minor offenses and temporary derogations. With regard to minor offenses, Article 2(4) states that without prejudice to the right to a fair trial, the Directive will only apply to the proceedings before a court having jurisdiction in criminal matters in respect of minor offenses where the law of a Member State provides for the imposition of a sanction by an authority other than a court having jurisdiction in criminal matters, and the imposition of such a sanction may be appealed or referred to such a court, or where deprivation of liberty cannot be imposed as a sanction. In any event, Article 2(4) continues by stating that the Directive will fully apply where the suspect or accused person is deprived of liberty, irrespective of the stage of the criminal proceedings. Moreover, the Preamble to the Directive confirms that the scope of application in respect of minor offenses should not affect the obligations of Member States under the ECHR.[48] Even with these important caveats, this provision may act as a limit to the effective application of the right to access to a lawyer in a significant number of cases. This exception, which also applies in the Directives on the right to translation and interpretation and the right to information,[49] sits however at odds with the case law of the ECtHR, and in particular the *Engel* jurisprudence according to which Article 6 ECHR is applicable in cases where there is a "criminal charge" against the effected

[41] *Id.* Art. 3(4). [42] Salduz v. Turkey, App. No. 36391/02, Eur. Ct. H.R., Nov. 27, 2008.

[43] *See* Directive 2013/48/EU, Art. 2(1); Cras, *supra* note 36. [44] Directive 2013/48/EU, Art. 2(4).

[45] *Id.* Arts. 3(5)–(6) and 5(3). [46] *Id.* Art. 4.

[47] According to Directive 2013/48/EU, art. 11, the Directive is without prejudice to national law in relation to legal aid, which must apply in accordance with the Charter of Fundamental Rights of the EU, 2000 O.J. (C 364) 1 [hereinafter CFREU], and the ECHR.

[48] Directive 2013/48/EU, recital 18.

[49] *See* Directive 2010/64/EU, art. 1(3); Directive 2012/13/EU, Art. 2(2).

individual.[50] This inconsistency with the protection afforded by the Strasbourg Court is even more evident when one reads recital 13 to the Directive, according to which "[w]ithout prejudice to the obligations of Member States under the E.C.H.R. to ensure the right to a fair trial, proceedings in relation to minor offending which take place within a prison and proceedings in relation to offences committed in a military context which are dealt with by a commanding officer should not be considered to be criminal proceedings for the purposes of the Directive." It is difficult to see how this blanket exclusion can apply without undermining the level of human rights protection provided by the ECHR.[51]

In a further extension of the scope of protection under EU law, the Directive on access to a lawyer extends the applicability of this right not only to the executing,[52] but also to the issuing Member State.[53] However, in a provision reflecting the case law of the Court of Justice of the EU on the requirement of speed regarding the operation of the EAW,[54] the Directive places the right to access to a lawyer in EAW situations under strict time limits: the right of a requested person to appoint a lawyer in the issuing Member State is without prejudice to the time limits set out in the European Arrest Warrant Framework Decision or the obligation of the executing judicial authority to decide, within those time limits and the conditions defined under that Framework Decision, whether the person is to be surrendered.[55]

4. Legal Aid

Directive 2016/1919/EU on legal aid for suspects and accused persons in criminal proceedings and for requested persons in EAW proceedings[56] is inextricably linked with the Directive on access to a lawyer. The purpose of Directive 2016/1919/EU is to ensure the effectiveness of the right to access to a lawyer, as detailed in Directive 2013/48/EU, by laying down minimum rules concerning the right to legal aid for suspects or accused persons in criminal proceedings who are deprived of liberty, and in certain other situations. —The Directive also ensures that legal aid is made available in EAW proceedings, upon the arrest of the requested person in the executing Member State. The scope of its application includes a right to ordinary legal aid—rather than a provisional one as was originally foreseen in the Commission proposal[57] at all stages of the criminal justice

[50] *See* Sayers, *supra* note 35, at 740.

[51] A number of temporary derogations have also been introduced by the Directive; see Directive 2013/48/EU, arts. 3(5) and (6), Art. 5(3).

[52] *Id.* Art. 10(1) [53] *Id.* Art. 10(4).

[54] Case C-168/13 PPU, Jeremy F., judgment of May 30, 2013, § 65, *available at* https://curia.europa.eu.

[55] Directive 2013/48/EU, Art. 10(6).

[56] Directive 2016/1919/EU of the European Parliament and of the Council on legal aid for suspects and accused persons in criminal proceedings and for requested persons in European arrest warrant proceedings, 2016 O.J. (L 297) 1 [hereinafter Directive 2016/1919/EU].

[57] For a discussion on how Member States shifted from provisional legal aid to general legal aid, see Steven Cras, *The Directive on the Right to Legal Aid in Criminal and EAW Proceedings*, eucrim 35, 39 (2017).

process. It includes a means test (to ascertain whether the person lacks sufficient resources to pay for legal assistance) and a merits test (to assess whether the provision of legal aid would be in the interests of justice in the light of the circumstances of the case), which may be used in order to determine whether a person is eligible for legal aid.

The personal scope of the Directive has been a controversial aspect in the negotiations. The Commission proposal envisaged the right to legal aid as applying to all suspects and accused persons who are deprived of liberty and who have the right of access to a lawyer, pursuant to Directive 2013/48/EU. However, a number of Member States disagreed with this approach and sought to reduce the scope of the Directive not only due to the financial implications,[58] but also owing to the view that legal aid should not be made available in relation to minor or less serious offenses.[59] This restrictive approach was in striking contrast with the quite ambitious agenda of the European Parliament in negotiations, whereby the Rapporteur took the view that the scope of the Directive should be aligned to the scope of Directive 2014/48/EU on access to a lawyer, namely to all suspects and accused persons irrespective of whether they were deprived of liberty or not.[60] In the end, it was agreed that although deprivation of liberty would remain as a necessary prerequisite for considering legal aid, two other circumstances were added. Therefore, according to Article 2(1), the Directive applies to suspects and accused persons in criminal proceedings who have a right of access to a lawyer and who are either (1) deprived of liberty, (2) required to be assisted by a lawyer in accordance with Union or national law (mandatory assistance), or (3) required or permitted to attend an investigative or evidence-gathering act, including (as a minimum) identity parades, confrontations, and reconstructions of the scene of a crime. Furthermore, the scope of the Directive includes persons who were not initially suspects or accused but became so in the course of questioning by the police or by another law enforcement authority.[61]

In terms of eligibility for legal aid, the basic rule replicates Article 47(3) CFREU and Article 6(3) ECHR. Article 4(1) of the Directive states that Member States must ensure that suspects and accused persons who lack sufficient resources to pay for the assistance of a lawyer have the right to legal aid when the interests of justice so require. In order to determine who is eligible for such legal aid, Article 4(2) envisages three possible options allowing discretion to Member States: a means test, a merits test, or both. Under the former, all relevant and objective factors, such as income, capital, and family situation, as well as the costs of the assistance of a lawyer and the standard of living in that Member State are to be taken into account. Therefore, as it has been correctly pointed out, if a person offers to prove his lack of sufficient resources and there are not clear indications to the contrary, it seems that the conditions relating to lack of sufficient resources is fulfilled.[62] Under the latter, Member States shall take into account the seriousness of the criminal offense, the complexity of the case, and the severity of the sanction at stake, in

[58] *See id.* at 37. [59] *Id.* at 36. [60] *Id.* at 37.

[61] Directive 2016/1919/EU, art. 2(3). But see the exceptions in Art. 4(4).

[62] Cras, *supra* note 57, at 40; see also *Pakelli v. Germany*, App. no. 8398/78, Eur. Ct. H.R., Apr. 25, 1983, § 34.

order to determine whether the interests of justice require legal aid to be granted. These criteria stem directly from the case law of the ECtHR in *Quaranta v. Switzerland*.[63] Given the ample space for Member States left by the merits test, Article 4(4) provides for a safety net—identical to that enclosed in the Directive on procedural safeguards of children,[64] where it is stated that in any event the merits shall be deemed to have been met (1) when a suspect or an accused person is brought before a competent court or judge in order to decide on detention at any stage of the proceedings within the scope of the Directive, and (2) during detention. Detention in this context has a limited meaning and is linked to pretrial procedure, attributed to the close link between the legal aid and the access-to-a-lawyer Directives. Moreover, since the detention has to be ordered by a court or a judge, police custody and other similar forms of deprivation of liberty are excluded from this notion.[65]

Furthermore, according to Article 4(5) of the Directive, legal aid must be granted in a timely manner ("without undue delay") and at the latest before questioning or before an investigative or evidence-gathering act is carried out. Legal aid must also be of adequate quality: Article 7 of the Directive requires Member States to take all necessary measures regarding funding to ensure that there is an effective legal aid system of an adequate quality and that legal aid services are of a quality adequate to safeguard the fairness of the proceedings. The Directive is thus an important benchmark to ensure effective protection of rights on the ground and the achievement of the full effectiveness of the right to access to a lawyer and to judicial protection more broadly. Key terms such as "without undue delay" or "adequate quality" are not defined in the text, but as will be seen below should be treated as autonomous concepts of EU law by the Court of Justice of the EU.

As for the extent of the right to legal aid in EAW proceedings, Article 5 of the Directive provides for double aid in both the issuing and the executing Member State, whereby the appointment of a lawyer in the issuing Member State is meant to assist the lawyer in the executing Member State by providing it with information and advice. Member States grudgingly accepted the insertion of provisions on double legal aid but subject to two conditions: only in relation to cases of EAW proceedings for the purpose of conducting a criminal prosecution, and only "in so far as such aid is necessary to ensure effective access to justice."[66] Therefore, Member States are granted considerable leeway in the implementation of the Directive; whilst there is no merits test—since this is met with the issuance of an EAW—Member States are allowed to introduce a means test.[67]

[63] Quaranta v. Switzerland, App. No. 12744/87, Eur. Ct. H.R., May 24, 1991, §§ 32–34; see also Cras, *supra* note 57, at 40.

[64] Directive (EU) 2016/800 of the European Parliament and of the Council on procedural safeguards for children who are suspects or accused persons in criminal proceedings, 2016 O.J. (L 132) 1. *See infra* Section II.5.

[65] Cras, *supra* note 57, at 41.

[66] Directive 2016/1919/EU, Art. 5(2).

[67] *Id.* Art. 5(3).

5. Procedural Rights of Children

The aim of the Directive on procedural safeguards for children who are suspects or accused persons in criminal proceedings[68] is to set out common minimum rules to ensure that suspected or accused children, who are subject to particular vulnerabilities, are able to understand and follow criminal proceedings so that their right of defense is safeguarded effectively. The main innovation of Directive 2016/800/EU involves the right of children to receive assistance by a lawyer without undue delay, unless such assistance is not proportionate in light of the circumstances of the case. Furthermore, child-specific rights to information, to an individual assessment,[69] to a medical examination, and to audio-visual recording of questioning are envisaged, as well as specific safeguards for children deprived of their liberty, in particular during pre- and post-trial detention.[70] Such measures are meant to facilitate the reintegration of children into society after being confronted within the criminal justice system.

The Directive applies to children—defined as persons below the age of eighteen[71]—who are suspects or accused persons in criminal proceedings or children who are requested persons.[72] Recital 12 states that Member States are "encouraged" to apply the Directive in cases of persons until the age of twenty-one, at least when these concern offenses that are committed by the same suspect or accused persons and that are jointly investigated and prosecuted as inextricably linked to criminal proceedings that were initiated against that person before the age of eighteen. In terms of its temporal application, the Directive applies until the final determination of the question of whether a person has committed a criminal offense, including where applicable, sentencing and the resolution of any appeal.[73] However, the sensitive question concerning the age of criminal liability is not covered by the Directive.

The right of information is encompassed in Article 4 and covers all rights prescribed in the Directive. Information about the existence of certain rights, such as the right of assistance by a lawyer, must take place promptly when children are made aware that they are suspects or accused. Other rights, such as the right to an individual assessment or medical examination, must be made known to the child at the earliest appropriate stage in the proceedings.[74] Given the needs of children, such information must be provided in a simple and accessible language.[75]

A groundbreaking provision of the Directive is Article 6 regards legal assistance. In comparison to the final text, the Commission proposal was quite ambitious and referred to mandatory access by a lawyer without exceptions,[76] but the Council distinguished

[68] Directive 2016/800/EU of the European Parliament and of the Council of 11 May 2016 on procedural safeguards for children who are suspects or accused persons in criminal proceedings, 2016 O.J. (L132) 1 [hereinafter Directive 2016/800/EU].

[69] *Id.* Art. 7. [70] *Id.* Art. 10. [71] *Id.* Art. 2(1) [72] *Id.* recital 10.

[73] *Id.* Art. 2. [74] *Id.* Art. 4(1)(b). [75] *Id.* Art. 4(2).

[76] Commission Proposal for a Directive of the European Parliament and of the Council on procedural safeguards for children suspected or accused in criminal proceedings, art. 6, COM (2013) 822 final (Nov. 27, 2013).

between the right to have access to a lawyer, which is exercised in accordance to Directive 2013/48/EU, and the right to be assisted by a lawyer, on the basis of the provisions of Directive 2016/800/EU. Consequently, the relationship between the two legal instruments is construed as follows; the existence of the right of access to a lawyer according to Directive 2013/48/EU is a prerequisite for assistance by a lawyer. Where the application of a provision of general nature would make it impossible for the child to be assisted by a lawyer under Directive 2016/800/EU, then that provision should be disapplied. At the same time, any derogation in that latter Directive should not affect the general right of access to a lawyer in accordance with the access-to-a-lawyer Directive.[77] As for the content of the right, mandatory legal assistance entitles children to be assisted "without undue delay" once they are made aware that they are suspects or accused persons.[78] Such assistance includes the right to meet in private and communicate with the lawyer representing them, including prior to questioning by the police or another law enforcement body; assistance when questioned; and assistance during certain investigative and evidence-gathering acts (identity parades, confrontations, and reconstructions of the crime scene).

6. Presumption of Innocence

Directive 2016/343/EU on the strengthening of certain aspects of the presumption of innocence and of the right to be present at the trial in criminal proceedings[79] was adopted on March 9, 2016. The approach taken by the EU legislator is rather broad, as the Directive encompasses two separate issues; presumption of innocence—linked to the right to remain silent and the right not to incriminate oneself—and the right to be present at one's trial. Furthermore, Member States will have to respect the following related obligations: before the final judgment, the authorities should abstain from giving the impression that suspects and accused persons are guilty when making public statements or by using measures of physical restraint or presenting them wearing prison clothes, at least where feasible. In addition, the burden of proof for establishing the guilt of suspects and accused persons is on the prosecution and any reasonable doubts as to guilt should benefit the accused. Moreover, Member States must ensure that suspects and accused persons have an effective remedy if their rights under this Directive are breached.[80]

As regards the scope *ratione personae* of the Directive, it is explicitly stated that it applies to natural persons only.[81] In terms of temporal applicability, as in the case of the rest legislative instruments in the field of procedural rights, the Directive applies at all

[77] Directive 2016/800/EU, recital 26. [78] *Id.* Art. 6(3).

[79] Directive 2016/343/EU of the European Parliament and of the Council on the strengthening of certain aspects of the presumption of innocence and of the right to be present at the trial in criminal proceedings, 2016 O.J. (L 65) 1 [hereinafter Directive 2016/343/EU].

[80] *Id.* Art. 10.

[81] *Id.* recital 12. For criticism of this approach, see Stijn Lamberigts, *The Directive on the Presumption of Innocence—A Missed Opportunity for Legal Persons?*, eucrim 36–42 (2016).

stages of the criminal proceedings, from the moment the persons concerned have been made aware—by official notification or otherwise—that they are suspected or accused of having committed a criminal offense until the decision on the final determination of whether that person has committed the criminal offenses concerned has become definitive.[82] Normally this involves decisions whereby an appeal is no longer possible and legal actions and remedies that are available only once a decision has become definitive, such as actions before the ECtHR are excluded from the scope of the Directive.[83]

Article 3 replicates Articles 6(2) ECHR and 48(1) CFREU by stating that suspected and accused persons should be presumed innocent until proven guilty according to law. Then, Article 4 involves the concrete action or inaction that should be taken by public authorities; public statements that refer to a person as guilty should not be made as long as that person has not been proven guilty. Another key provision is Article 6, which envisages that the burden of proof for establishing guilt is on the prosecution. A key problem in that respect involved the possibility of shifting this burden to the defense and if so, under which circumstances this shifting may take place. Such a possibility was included in the Commission proposal and was supported by the Council, but the European Parliament offered a series of concessions in order to remove these references from the final text. As a form of compromise between the institutions, the Directive instead makes references to the "use of presumptions of fact of law concerning the criminal liability of a suspect or accused person." Reflecting the ECtHR case law,[84] it is further explained that such presumptions should be confined within reasonable limits, taking into account the importance of what is at stake and maintaining the rights of the defense, and that the means employed should be reasonably proportionate to the legitimate aim pursued. Such presumptions should be rebuttable and in any event, should be used only where the rights of the defense are respected.[85] Article 6(2) further establishes that any doubt as to the guilt should be to the benefit of suspected or accused persons, including where the court assesses whether the person concerned should be acquitted. This provision may have significant implications on national criminal justice systems, particularly since the concept of doubt and its threshold is not defined in the Directive.

Article 7 of the Directive prescribes the right to remain silent and the right not to incriminate oneself. Both rights are not enshrined in the ECHR, but the ECtHR has attached them to Article 6 ECHR on the right to fair trial.[86] The Commission proposal enshrined these rights as absolute, but in the final text both rights have been qualified by the introduction of certain conditions and limits. As regards the right not to incriminate oneself, it is stated that competent authorities are not prevented from gathering evidence that may be lawfully obtained through the use of legal powers of compulsion and has existence independent of the will of suspected or accused persons.[87] Recital 29 explains that such evidence includes material acquired pursuant to a warrant, material

[82] *Id.* Art. 2. [83] *Id.* recital 12.

[84] Salabiaku v. France, App. No. 10519/83, Eur. Ct. H.R., Oct. 7, 1988, § 28.

[85] Directive 2016/343/EU, recital 22.

[86] Murray v. United Kingdom, App. No. 18731/91, Eur. Ct. H.R., Feb. 8, 1996.

[87] Directive 2016/343/EU, Art. 7(3).

in respect of which there is a legal obligation of retention and production upon request, breath, blood or urine samples and bodily tissue for the purpose of DNA testing. This reference to the use of compulsion reflects the ECtHR case law, particularly in the case of *Saunders*.[88] In addition, the exercise of either rights must not be used against the accused or considered as *evidence* that they have committed the criminal offense in question.[89]

The second part of Directive 2016/343/EU deals with the right to be present at the trial and the right to a new trial. The key issue addressed—but only to a certain extent—is the conditions under which Member States could proceed with a trial despite the absence of the suspect or accused person. The Directive begins by stating that Member States must ensure that suspects and accused persons have the right to be present at their trial.[90] However, it further allows Member States to provide that a trial that can result in a decision on the guilt or innocence of a suspect or accused person can be held in his or her absence, provided that the suspect or accused person has been informed, in due time, of the trial and of the consequences of nonappearance, or the suspect or accused person, having been informed of the trial, is represented by a mandated lawyer, who was appointed either by the suspect or accused person or by the Member State.[91] The Directive states that where Member States provide for the possibility of holding trials in the absence of suspects or accused persons but it is not possible to comply with the conditions laid down in the Directive because a suspect or accused person cannot be located despite reasonable efforts having been made, Member States may provide that a decision can nevertheless be taken and enforced. In that case, Member States must ensure that when suspects or accused persons are informed of the decision, in particular when they are apprehended, they are also informed of the possibility to challenge the decision and of the right to a new trial or to another legal remedy.[92]

III. Widening the Scope and Raising the Level of Protection of Procedural Rights

Although the Lisbon Treaty has conferred upon the EU the competence to legislate in the form of minimum rules, a careful reading of all Directives adopted thus far reveals that the scope and level of protection envisaged in EU law is considerable. With regard to the scope of application, it is important to note that, notwithstanding the link with mutual recognition that the legal basis to these instruments (Article 82(2) TFEU) entails, all adopted measures apply not only in cross-border cases involving the operation of the EAW system, but also in purely domestic cases.[93] This is an important

[88] Saunders v. United Kingdom, App. No. 19187/91, Eur. Ct. H.R., Dec. 17, 1996.

[89] Directive 2016/343/EU, Art. 7(5) and recital 28.

[90] Art. 8(1).

[91] Art. 8(2).

[92] Directive 2016/343/EU, Art. 8(4).

[93] Directive 2010/64/EU, Art. 1(1); Directive 2012/13/EU, Art. 1; Directive 2013/48/EU, Art. 1.

development as the implementation of the EU procedural rights measures in domestic law will have to cover all cases in the field of domestic criminal procedure that fall within the scope of the Directives. As *Caeiro* has noted, the Directives have created an autonomous, self-designed project for the protection of individual rights in criminal proceedings before the authorities of Member States.[94]

The EU Directives on procedural rights in criminal proceedings have translated, expanded and clarified rights enshrined in the ECHR—in particular in Articles 5 and 6—and in the CFREU, in particular in Articles 47 and 48.[95] The Directives themselves include provisions to address the key question of the relationship between general ECHR and CFREU human rights norms with the specific provisions of EU secondary law on procedural rights. As regards the ECHR, it has been acknowledged from the outset that its provisions constitute the starting point and the benchmark under which the legality and legitimacy of EU secondary legislation on procedural rights should be judged. The Preambles to the adopted EU Directives include extensive references to their relationship with the ECHR. In particular, the Preambles to a number of the Directives adopted earlier state that their provisions correspond to rights guaranteed by the ECHR and should be interpreted and implemented consistently with those rights, as interpreted in the relevant case-law of the ECtHR.[96] However, this wording leaves open the possibility of a higher level of protection for provisions that do not correspond to ECHR rights. Moreover, the possibility of offering a higher level of protection is further enshrined in the text of the Directives via the introduction of non-regression clauses. These affirm that nothing in the Directives must be construed as limiting or derogating from any of the rights and procedural safeguards that are ensured under the CFREU, the ECHR, or other relevant provisions of international law or the law of any Member State that provides a higher level of protection.[97] This is in particular the case in situations not explicitly dealt with by EU law.[98] The non-regression clauses confirm that the Court's case law in *Melloni* does not apply here:[99] national law that provides a high level of protection of procedural rights will apply, even if the level of protection is higher than that provided by EU (in any case minimum) standards. The *Melloni* principles of unity, primacy, and effectiveness of EU law take second place here, in particular as regards ensuring the operational effectiveness of the European Arrest Warrant system. As the Preamble to the access to a lawyer Directive 2013/48/EU states expressly, a higher level of protection by Member States should not constitute an obstacle to the mutual recognition

[94] Pedro Caeiro, *Introduction (or: Every Criminal Procedure Starts with a Bill of Rights)*, in *The European Union Agenda on Procedural Safeguards for Suspects or Accused Persons: The "Second Wave" and Its Predictable Impact on Portuguese Law* 13, 17 (Pedro Caeiro ed. 2015).

[95] The CFREU includes a general provision on the right to a fair trial (Article 47) and a specific provision guaranteeing respect for the rights of the defense of anyone who has been charged (Article 48(2)).

[96] *See* Directive 2010/64/EU, recital 33 (referring also to the CFREU and the interpretation by the Court of Justice of the EU); Directive 2012/13/EU, recital 42; Directive 2013/48/EU, recital 53.

[97] Directive 2010/64/EU, Art. 8; Directive 2012/13/EU, Art. 10; Directive 2013/48/EU, Art. 14; Directive 2016/1919/EU, Art. 11; Directive 2016/800/EU, Art. 23; Directive 2016/343/EU, Art. 13.

[98] Directive 2010/64/EU, recital 32; Directive 2012/13/EU, recital 40.

[99] Case C-399/11, Melloni, judgment of Feb. 26, 2013, *available at* https://curia.europa.eu/.

of judicial decisions that those minimum rules are designed to facilitate.[100] On the contrary, it is clear that a higher level of human rights protection would rather facilitate—and not hinder—mutual recognition.

IV. Ensuring the Enforcement and Effective Implementation of Rights in Member States

The EU Directives on the rights of the individual in criminal procedure will have a significantly positive impact on the protection of fundamental rights in domestic systems of criminal procedure. The Directives translate, clarify, and at times go beyond the standards enshrined by the ECHR and the ECtHR.[101] The standards established therein apply not only to cross-border, but also to domestic cases. And although the aim of the Directives has been to establish minimum standards, in essence they have introduced a series of binding norms that are designed to ensure the respect of human rights and that have been interpreted by the Court of Justice of the EU thus far from a teleological perspective aiming to ensure the full effectiveness, including the effective exercise, of these rights.[102] There are four main ways in which the Directives on procedural rights in criminal procedure will enhance the protection of fundamental rights in EU Member States. First of all, a number of key provisions conferring rights in the Directives have direct effect. This means that, in a system of decentralized enforcement of EU law, individuals can evoke and claim rights directly before their national courts if the EU Directives have not been implemented or have been inadequately implemented. Direct effect means in practice that a suspect or accused person can derive a number of key rights—such as the right to an interpreter or the right to access to a lawyer—directly from EU law if national legislation has not made appropriate provision in conformity with EU law. Second, this avenue of decentralized enforcement is coupled with the high level of centralized enforcement of EU criminal law that has been "normalized" after the entry into force of the Lisbon Treaty. The European Commission now has full powers to monitor the implementation of these Directives by Member States and has the power to introduce infringement proceedings before the Court of Justice of the EU when it considers that the Directives have not been implemented adequately. The scope of the Commission's monitoring exercises is broader than to check merely the provision of

[100] Directive 2013/48/EU, Preamble, recital 54.

[101] For instance, in an important move toward enhancing human rights protection, the Directive 2013/48/EU on the right to access to a lawyer clarifies and strengthens the impact of the Strasbourg ruling in the case of *Salduz, supra* note 42, on national law, by narrowing the national margin of appreciation in implementing the access-to-a-lawyer obligations and in particular by expressly extending the application of the right of access to a lawyer in cases where no deprivation of liberty is involved.

[102] Case C-216/14, Covaci, judgment of Oct. 15, 2015; Joined Cases C-124/16, Ianos Tranca, C-213/16, Tanja Reiter, and C-213/16, Ionel Opria, judgment of Mar. 22, 2017; see also Bot, *supra* note 9, §§ 32–33, 74.

national legislation adopted to implement specifically the EU Directives in question. The Commission is also entitled to monitor national criminal procedure systems more broadly to ensure that effective implementation has taken place, as well as to ensure that rights are applied in practice and not only in the books. Third, and lined to the point above, national criminal procedural law must be applied and interpreted in compliance and conformity with the Directives. The procedural standards set out in the Directives will have an impact on a wide range of acts under national criminal procedure.[103] Fourth, the implementation of the Directives must take place in compliance with the Charter of Fundamental Rights of the EU. The Charter will apply not only to national legislation that specifically implements the EU Directives on procedural rights, but also to all other elements of domestic criminal procedure that have a connection with EU law on procedural rights in criminal proceedings. In the case of *Fransson*,[104] the Court of Justice of the EU adopted a broad interpretation of the application of the Charter, including in cases where national legislation does not implement expressly or directly an EU criminal law instrument. Following *Fransson*, the Court of Justice of the EU ruled in *Siragusa*[105] that the concept of "implementing Union law," as referred to in Article 51 of the Charter, requires a certain degree of connection above and beyond the matters covered being closely related or one of those matters having an indirect impact on the other.[106] In the case of the Directives on procedural rights, there are a number of elements in domestic criminal procedures that, although not implementing specifically the Directives, meet this degree of connection required by the Court's case law and thus trigger the applicability of the Charter. This view is reinforced by the Court's finding in *Siragusa* that it is important to consider the objective of protecting fundamental rights in EU law, which is to ensure that those rights are not infringed in areas of EU activity, whether through action at the EU level or through the implementation of EU law by the Member States.[107]

V. Addressing Gaps in Protection Stemming from National Diversity—The Role of Autonomous Concepts

One of the key challenges in reaching agreement on EU standards on procedural rights in criminal proceedings has been to accommodate Member States' concerns with regard to the potentially adverse impact of EU law in the field of the diversity of national

[103] *See* Bot, *supra* note 9, §§ 105–106.

[104] Case C-617/10, Åklagaren v. Hans Åkerberg Fransson, Judgment of Feb. 26, 2013, available at https://curia.europa.eu/h.

[105] Case C-206/13, Siragusa, Judgment of Mar. 6, 2014, *available at* https://curia.europa.eu/.

[106] *Id.* § 24.

[107] *Id.* § 31.

criminal justice systems. Faced with the diversity of national criminal justice systems,[108] negotiations on the specific EU Directives on procedural rights after Lisbon have proven to be complex, notwithstanding the limited ambition to introduce minimum standards based on the ECHR and leaving via the introduction of non-regression clauses, Member States free to maintain or introduce higher standards of protection. The price of reaching agreement has been the adoption of a number of provisions (especially as regards the Directives on access to a lawyer, legal aid, and the presumption of innocence) that have been the outcome of comparative law exercises and of criminal policy compromises, with the Directives containing a number of exceptions and lengthy Preambular provisions. In spite of all these efforts, the existing EU Directives on procedural rights—even in their minimum standards form—will have a profound impact on national criminal justice systems. They will have an impact because, as Advocate General Bot has noted, the minimum standards character of EU law in the field does not mean that this is not equally binding as other standards of EU law—on the contrary, minimum standards must be interpreted broadly, to ensure the effectiveness of EU law in a field that is marked by considerable diversity between national legal systems.[109] Moreover, the Court of Justice of the EU will attempt to address the existence of national legal diversity in the field by developing autonomous concepts in the field of criminal procedure. The Court of Justice of the EU has developed autonomous concepts in order to ensure the uniform and independent interpretation of EU law, in cases where the latter does not refer expressly to national law as a tool for interpretation of the relevant EU law provisions. Autonomous concepts have been developed by the Court on the basis of a teleological and contextual interpretation, as well as on the basis of the need to ensure equality across the EU legal order.[110]

This approach is directly applicable to a number of provisions in EU criminal law, including the EU Directives on procedural rights in criminal proceedings. The need to agree on common EU minimum standards in the field while respecting national legal diversity has led to the inclusion, in all three Directives adopted thus far, of general and broad terminology that remains undefined in the EU instruments and that is not to be defined in accordance with national law. This choice renders the potential of the future development of autonomous concepts by the Court of Justice of the EU as a central mechanism to flesh out the meaning of these terms considerably. Key concepts that have the potential to be defined as autonomous concern both the determination of the scope and the applicability of the defense rights Directives, as well as the interpretation of the content of the rights granted. With regard to the *scope* of the Directives, it is noteworthy that the terms "suspect, "accused," and "criminal proceedings" are not defined in

[108] For an overview of different national systems of criminal procedure in the investigative context, see, for example, *Suspects in Europe: Procedural Rights at the Investigation Stage of the Criminal Process in the EU* (Ed Cape et al. eds., 2007).

[109] Bot, *supra* note 9, at §§ 32–33.

[110] Valsamis Mitsilegas, *Managing Legal Diversity in Europe's Area of Criminal Justice: The Role of Autonomous Concepts*, in *EU Criminal Justice and the Challenges of Legal Diversity. Towards A Socio-legal Approach to EU Criminal Policy* 125, 125–60 (Renaud Colson & Stewart Field eds., 2016).

the text. Treating these concepts as autonomous EU law concepts is key to ensuring the effectiveness of the measures and achieving equality and the key objective of establishing a level-playing field of protection across Europe. Autonomous concepts will also have an influence on the interpretation of further specific provisions on the applicability of the Directives. The Directives limit access to a lawyer[111] and to an interpreter[112] to proceedings before courts having jurisdiction in criminal matters. However, this limitation must be interpreted consistently with the ruling of the Court of Justice of the EU in *Balasz*,[113] where the Court adopted a broad definition of the concept of a "court having jurisdiction in criminal matters" as an autonomous concept of EU law. Notwithstanding detailed provisions in the Directives, aspects of the temporal scope of the Directive, including the precise time when rights become applicable or cease to become applicable, may be interpreted autonomously by the Court of Justice of the EU to create a level-playing field across the EU.

Autonomous concepts will also be a key in defining the *content* of the rights of suspects and accused persons. In the absence of a high level of legal certainty in a number of key Directive provisions where consensus has proven to be elusive in negotiations (see in particular the presumption-of-innocence Directive) the role of the Court of Justice of the EU in giving flesh to key rights will be crucial. Moreover, a number of provisions in the existing acquis on defense rights oblige Member States to ensure that rights are granted "promptly"[114] "without undue delay,"[115] "without delay,"[116] "in due time,"[117] or "within a reasonable period of time."[118] The Court will be called to interpret these concepts autonomously, as they are not defined further in the Directives nor are they defined by reference to national law. Treating these concepts as autonomous will give flesh to the rights enshrined in the Directives. The same will potentially occur in the Court defining other key concepts inherent in the content of the rights provided by EU law, including what constitutes access to "essential" documents for the purposes of the

[111] Art. 2(4) and Recitals 16 and 17 of Access to a lawyer Directive.

[112] Art. 1(3) of Directive on the right to translation and interpretation.

[113] Case C-60/12, Baláz, judgment of Nov. 14, 2013, *available at* https://curia.europa.eu/.

[114] Key rights in the right to information Directive 2012/13/EU including the right to information about rights (Article 3(1)), the right to information about the accusation and relevant changes in such information (Article 6 paragraphs (1) and (4) respectively), and the provision of the Letter of Rights (Article 4(1)).

[115] With regard to the Directive 2013/48/EU on access to a lawyer in particular, see the right to access to a lawyer (Article 3(2)), the right to communicate with third persons and with consular authorities (Articles 6(1) and 7(1) respectively), the obligation to inform persons deprived of liberty in the execution of a European Arrest Warrant that they have the right to appoint a lawyer in the issuing Member State (Article 10(4)); see also Legal Aid Directive 2016/1919/EU art. 4(5).

[116] The right to interpretation (Article 2(1)) of the Directive 2010/64/EU on the right to interpretation and translation).

[117] *See* Directive 2012/13/EU on the right to information on the right of access to the materials of the case (Article 7(3)).

[118] The right to translation (Article 3(1)) of the Directive 2010/64/EU on the right to interpretation and translation).

right to information[119] and right to translation,[120] what constitutes interpretation and translation "of sufficient quality to safeguard the fairness of the proceedings,"[121] what constitutes an "effective legal aid system of an adequate quality" and of "legal aid services of a quality adequate to safeguard the fairness of the proceedings,"[122] and what is the meaning of the right of access to a lawyer "in such time and in such a manner so as to allow the persons concerned to exercise their rights of defence practically and effectively."[123] The treatment of these concepts as autonomous will influence significantly criminal law and practice in EU Member States, in particular in view of the fact that the Directives apply not only to cross-border, but also to purely domestic cases. By superimposing a Union meaning of key domestic law concepts, autonomous concepts become a mechanism of enforcement of EU law that has significant impact on domestic criminal justice systems and legal cultures, in changing both perceptions and practice in national criminal justice systems.[124]

VI. Conclusion: The Transformative Effect of EU Legislation in the Field of Procedural Rights

The entry into force of the Treaty of Lisbon has led to a paradigm shift in the development of Europe's area of criminal justice under the principle of mutual recognition. The inclusion in the Treaty of an express legal basis conferring upon the Union legislators the power to adopt measures harmonizing criminal procedure has led to the European Union for the first time adopting secondary legislation on fundamental rights, taking the form of a series of Directives on the rights of suspects and accused persons in criminal proceedings. In this manner, the construction of Europe's area of criminal justice has moved from a paradigm privileging the interests of the state and of law enforcement under a system of quasi-automatic mutual recognition to a paradigm where the rights of

[119] According to Article 7(1) of the right to information Directive 2012/13/EU, Member States must ensure access to documents related to the specific case in the possession of the competent authorities that are essential to challenging effectively, in accordance with national law, the lawfulness of the arrest or detention.

[120] Article 3(1) of the Directive 2010/64/EU on the right to interpretation and translation grants a right to translation of essential documents.

[121] Articles 2(8) and 3(9) respectively of the Directive on the right to translation and interpretation.

[122] Article 7(1) of the legal aid Directive 2016/1919/EU.

[123] Article 3(1) of the Directive on access to a lawyer.

[124] On the concept of legal culture as one encompassing these elements, see David Nelken, *Using Legal Culture: Purposes and Problems*, in *Using Legal Culture* 1, 1–51 (David Nelken ed., 2012). On a view of legal culture as embracing the participants' experience, see Roger Cotterrell, *Comparative Law and Legal Culture*, in *The Oxford Handbook of Comparative Law* 709, 709–37 (Mathias Reimann & Reinhard Zimmermann eds., 2008).

individuals affected by such system are brought into the fore, protected and enforced in EU law. The Lisbon legal basis enables the adoption of Directives containing only minimum standards. However, the significance of these Directives for the protection of human rights in Europe's area of criminal justice should not be underestimated. Indeed, the EU Directives on procedural rights have the potential to have a transformative effect.[125] The Directives adopted thus far have a broad scope of application. Importantly, they go beyond the strict requirements of the Article 82(2) TFEU legal basis (which links harmonization in the field of criminal procedure with the effective operation of mutual recognition) in applying not only to cross-border, but also to purely domestic cases. In this manner, national criminal procedural law—to the extent that it implements the Directives—must be applied in conformity with EU law. This means that national rules of criminal procedure must be applied in conformity with EU secondary human rights law (the Directives on procedural safeguards) as well as with EU constitutional human rights law (the CFREU). The Court's case law on the applicability of the Charter indicates that the latter is applicable not only in cases where national law implements specifically EU law, but also to cases where national law has a connection with EU law. These findings are applicable to a wide range of national provisions on criminal procedure, which—in integrated national systems—are closely linked with the achievement of the objectives and the effective implementation of the EU Directives on procedural rights, which will in turn result in the effective exercise of these rights on the ground.

In addition to these avenues of protection, the normalization of large aspects of EU criminal law after Lisbon mean that secondary EU law on procedural rights enjoys the enhanced supranational enforcement mechanisms of EU law. At the level of decentralized enforcement, affected individuals can claim direct effect before national courts. At the level of centralized enforcement, the Commission now has full powers to monitor the effectiveness of the implementation of the procedural rights Directives in Member States and take action before the Court of Justice of the EU if such implementation is unsatisfactory. In view of the analysis above, the scope of the Commission's monitoring exercises is broader than to check merely the provision of national legislation adopted to implement specifically the EU Directives in question. The Commission is also entitled to monitor national criminal procedure systems more broadly to ensure that effective implementation has taken place, as well as to monitor compliance on the ground in addition to compliance on paper. Achieving effective implementation and enforcement of the Directives on procedural rights will be one of the key objectives in order to ensure that the individual emerges as the key focal point of Europe's area of criminal justice. EU harmonization and the enforcement of EU secondary fundamental rights law may be a challenge in view of the considerable diversity in national criminal procedure systems and standards. However, the very existence of EU law in the field triggers the intervention of EU institutions, and in particular the Court of Justice of the EU. It will be the task

[125] *See* Valsamis Mitsilegas, *Legislating for Human Rights after Lisbon: The Transformative Effect of EU Measures on Procedural Rights in Criminal Proceedings*, in *The European Union as an Area of Freedom, Security and Justice* (Maria Fletcher et al. eds., 2017).

of the Court to develop an effective level-playing field of fundamental rights protection across the European Union. The Court's case law on managing diversity (via the development of autonomous concepts in EU law), and ensuring the effective applicability of fundamental rights provides clear guiding principles in this context.

References

Steven Cras, *The Directive on the Right of Access to a Lawyer in Criminal Proceedings and in European Arrest Warrant Proceedings*, eucrim 32–44 (2014)

Steven Cras, *The Directive on the Right to Legal Aid in Criminal and EAW Proceedings*, eucrim 35–45 (2017)

Jacqueline Hodgson, *Criminal Procedure in Europe's Area of Freedom, Security and Justice: The Tights of the Suspect, in Research Handbook on EU Criminal Law* 168–188 (Valsamis Mitsilegas et al. eds., 2016)

Valsamis Mitsilegas, *Managing Legal Diversity in Europe's Area of Criminal Justice: The Role of Autonomous Concepts, in EU Criminal Justice and the Challenges of Legal Diversity. Towards a Socio-legal Approach to EU Criminal Policy* 125–60 (Renaud Colson & Stewart Field eds., 2016)

Valsamis Mitsilegas, *Legislating for Human Rights After Lisbon: The Transformative Effect of EU Measures on Procedural Rights in Criminal Proceedings*, in *The European Union as an Area of Freedom, Security and Justice* 2–17 (Maria Fletcher et al. eds., 2016)

Valsamis Mitsilegas, *EU Criminal Law After Lisbon: Rights, Trust and the Transformation of Justice in Europe* (2016)

PART II

PROCEDURAL ROLES

CHAPTER 7

THE PLACE OF THE PROSECUTOR IN COMMON LAW AND CIVIL LAW JURISDICTIONS

KATALIN LIGETI

I. Introduction

THE role of the prosecution is "key to understanding how a country's criminal justice system works,"[1] as it reflects fundamental choices regarding how crime should be tackled and how criminal law should be enforced. Traditionally, the existence of a divide between civil and common law prosecutorial traditions has been reported.[2] From the very origins of the common law tradition in England and Wales, "the enforcement of criminal law was largely a matter of private enterprise,"[3] with prosecution normally brought by private citizens, whereas the inquisitorial civil law tradition considered the state to be both the source and exclusive wielder of prosecutorial power.[4] All ancestors

[1] *See* Thomas Weigend, *A Judge by Another Name? Comparative Perspectives on the Role of the Public Prosecutor*, in *The Prosecutor in a Transnational Perspective* 377 (Erik Luna & Marianne L. Wade eds., 2012).

[2] *See* John R. Spencer, *Introduction*, in *European Criminal Procedures* 14 (Mireille Delmas-Marty & John R. Spencer eds., 2002); Candace McCoy, *Prosecution*, in *The Oxford Handbook of Crime and Criminal Justice* 667 (Michael Tonry ed., 2011); Mirjan Damaska, *Structures of Authority and Comparative Criminal Procedure*, 84 Yale L.J. 480 (1975).

[3] Spencer, *supra* note 2, at 13.

[4] For an account of the medieval origins of the public prosecutor under the French system and in the Church legal order, see Guillaume Leyte, *Les origines médiévales du ministère public*, in *Histoire du Parquet* 40 (Jean-Marie Carbasse ed., 2000). In addition, see Franco Cordero, *Procedura Penale* 187 (9th ed. 2012).

of the continental public prosecutor—*Inquisitores, promotores, gens du Roi, procureurs du Roi*—shared the public nature of their status.

The civil/common law divide, along with the differences it implied, is today of mainly historical importance. In general, shared developments and "hybridization" processes spanning the two traditions have gradually brought the workings of modern criminal justice systems closer together. The prosecutor has not escaped this trend.

This chapter will provide a comparative introduction to the public prosecutor in civil and common law systems, addressing four main points:

- the institutional positioning of the public prosecutor, particularly vis-à-vis the executive power;
- the role and the powers of the public prosecutor in regard to the pretrial phase;
- the discretion and the limits for the public prosecutor as to the decision on whether to prosecute a case;
- the increasing tendency to entrust the public prosecutor with quasi-judicial sanctioning powers in the context of out-of-court procedures ("prosecutorial adjudication").

Thereafter, the analysis will briefly examine the attempt of the EU legislature and some EU Member States to "supranationalize" the prosecutorial function through the establishment of the European Public Prosecutor's Office (EPPO)[5] in light of the four aspects outlined above.

II. Institutional Positioning of Investigative and Prosecutorial Powers

The institutional positioning of any public prosecutor is closely connected to the specific form of government adopted by a state. The centralized or federal structure of government, as well as different historical sensibilities and local concerns about the separation of powers, play an important role in this regard. Traditionally, these factors are reflected in two general distinctions regarding the public prosecutor: whether the office is attached to the executive power or to the judiciary, and whether it is organized in a centralized or decentralized structure.

[5] On October 12, 2017 the EU legislator adopted Council Regulation (E.U.) 2017/1939 implementing enhanced cooperation on the establishment of the European Public Prosecutor's Office (E.P.P.O.), 2017 O.J. (L 283) 1. For further details, see Section V, *infra*.

1. Prosecution Services and Executive Power: Hierarchy, Independence, and Accountability

Differently from judges, whose identification with the judiciary and independence from other powers are undisputed, the institutional positioning of the public prosecutor in the classical configuration of the *trias politica*[6] still varies considerably across the different legal orders. Given that these institutional choices express different sensibilities about the separation of powers and are often rooted in the specific national histories, an exhaustive systematization of the different solutions would prove extremely difficult. Nonetheless, three general approaches to the status of the public prosecutor may be sketched: (1) systems in which the public prosecutor is attached to the executive power, (2) systems in which the public prosecutor is formally embedded in the judiciary order and independent from the executive power, and (3) systems in which the prosecutor is considered as a sui generis actor exercising a judicial-executive function in a position of complete independence from those branches of government.

The first approach, based on a hierarchical relationship between the public prosecutor and the executive power, represents a typical (although not exclusive) feature of the Napoleonic tradition[7] and can still be retraced in several Continental systems such as Belgium, France, Germany, or the Netherlands. In principle, such a relationship implies the power for the government—normally the Minister of Justice—to issue orders or directives to the public prosecutor in regard to general aspects of prosecution policy or to individual cases.

In general terms, the power of the Minister to order or direct the action of the public prosecutor is considered as a necessary counterpart of his/her political accountability for the prosecutorial policy. At the same time, however, given the sensitive nature of criminal enforcement, it may be seen as a challenge to the objectivity of the exercise of the prosecutorial function. Nonetheless, from the perspective of supranational human rights institutions such as the Council of Europe, the public prosecutor's hierarchical subordination to the Minister is not deemed to conflict per se with the rule of law as long as adequate safeguards in relation to transparency and non-discrimination are provided.[8]

[6] Meaning the classical triad of executive, judiciary, and legislative power. The legislative power is not directly relevant in this context, although forms of general accountability of the public prosecutor toward the legislative power (parliament) do exist.

[7] The strong hierarchical dependence of the prosecutor under the Napoleonic tradition was historically counterbalanced by the independent status of the investigative judge (*juge d'instruction*).

[8] *See* Recommendation of the Committee of Ministers of the Council of Europe, Rec 2000 (19) on the Role of Public Prosecution in the Criminal Justice System, adopted on Oct. 6, 2000. In particular point 13(d) of the Recommendation states that:

> Where the government has the power to give instructions to prosecute a specific case, such instructions must carry with them adequate guarantees that transparency and equity are respected in accordance with national law, the government being under a duty, for example:—to seek prior written advice from either the competent public prosecutor or the body that is carrying out the public prosecution;—duly to explain its written instructions, especially when they deviate from the public prosecutor's advices and

The configuration of this hierarchical relationship[9] varies from one legal system to another, and a tendency in favor of limiting executive interference in individual cases seems to be emerging also in those jurisdictions marked by a strong Napoleonic imprint.

In France, for instance, while public prosecutors are formally considered magistrates (*magistrats*),[10] they have been historically subordinated to the Ministry of Justice, which holds the power to direct prosecution policy[11] and only recently lost the authority to issue instructions in individual cases.[12]

In the German system, the executive/judicial nature of prosecutorial function is debated;[13] prosecution offices nonetheless are hierarchically organized and are under the political responsibility of the Ministry of Justice (at the state or federal level), which has the authority to issue binding orders.[14] However, while general instructions by the Prosecutor General (*Generalstaatsanwälte*) and the Ministry of Justice are common, Ministry interference in individual cases is extremely rare.[15]

Hierarchical subordination of the public prosecutor to the Minister of Justice is present also in Belgium and the Netherlands. Those two systems represent clear examples of the recent trend toward limiting ministerial interference in day-to-day prosecutorial practice. Indeed, both adopted a similar solution to balance political accountability and prosecutorial objectivity by establishing intermediate bodies composed of prosecutors general—the *Collège des procureurs généraux* in Belgium[16] and the *College van*

to transmit them through the hierarchical channels;—to see to it that, before the trial, the advice and the instructions become part of the file so that the other parties may take cognisance of it and make comments.

[9] This hierarchical subordination to the executive ("external") is different and must be kept conceptually distinguished from the possible internal hierarchical organization of the prosecutorial function ("internal hierarchy"). As it will be shown in presenting the two following approaches, a prosecution service may be independent from the executive power and still maintain a hierarchical internal organization.

[10] The French system distinguishes in the judiciary (*magistrature*) between two categories of magistrates: the standing magistrates (the parquet, composed by prosecutors) and the sitting magistrates (investigative judges and trial judges). The prosecutors are hierarchically subordinated to the Minister of Justice, while judges are totally independent from executive control. *See* Jacqueline Hodgson, *A Comparative Account of the Investigation and Prosecution of Crime in France* 67 (2005).

[11] *See* Hodgson, *supra* note 11, at 67.

[12] Since 2013, the Minister of Justice can no longer issue instructions in individual cases; a reform passed in July of that year modified the provision of the Code of Criminal Procedure (Art. 30 para. 3) that previously allowed for such instructions. In this latter regard, see Jean Pradel, *Droit Pénal Comparé* 222 (4th ed. 2016) and Sara Sun Beale, *Prosecutorial Discretion in Three Systems: Balancing Conflicting Goals and Providing Mechanisms for Control, in Discretionary Criminal Justice in a Comparative Context* 40 (Michele Caianiello & Jacqueline Hodgson eds., 2015).

[13] The majority considers German public prosecutors to have a hybrid "judicial-executive" role. Werner Beulke, *Strafprozessrecht* 63 (13th ed. 2016) and Claus Roxin & Bernd Schünemann, *Strafverfahrensrecht, Ein Studienbuch* § 9 (29th ed. 2017).

[14] *See* Thomas Weigend, *The Prosecution Service in the German Administration of Criminal Justice*, in *Tasks and Powers of the Prosecution Services in the EU Member States* 212 (Peter J.P. Tak ed., 2004); Denis Salas, *Les Parquets sous influence*, in *Les Procureurs: entre vocation judiciaire et fonctions politiques* 162 (Philip Milburn et al. eds., 2010).

[15] In these terms, see Weigend, *supra* note 15, and Salas, *supra* note 15.

[16] Belgium introduced the *Collège des procureurs généraux* in 1997. In Belgium, the Minister of Justice is entitled to order the initiation of a prosecution in an individual case but not to stop an already running prosecution. *See* Dirk Van Daele, *The Belgian Prosecution Service, in* Tak, *supra* note 15, at 56; see also Salas, *supra* note 15, at 182.

procureurs-generaal in the Netherlands[17]—which specify prosecutorial policy and the directives of the Minister.

Outside the Napoleonic tradition, the two major common law jurisdictions, the United States and the United Kingdom, also tend to consider the prosecutorial function as an expression of the executive power, although they manifest a diversity of approaches. Whereas the prosecutorial function in the United States at the federal level is placed within the responsibility and control of the Department of Justice,[18] in England and Wales the Crown Prosecution Service (CPS) is considered a sui generis body that operates under the "superintendence" of the Attorney General but functionally independent from the government.[19]

The second and third approaches, on the other hand, assume a heightened degree of independence of the public prosecutor as a starting point for its institutional position within the legal system. Such approaches have been frequently endorsed by several civil law jurisdictions that emerged from dictatorships. Telling examples of the second approach include Italy[20] and Portugal,[21] whose constitutions formally qualify public prosecutors as magistrates enjoying a similar degree of independence vis-à-vis the government as judges.[22] Both systems opted for strong prosecutorial independence

[17] The *College van procureurs-generaal* was established in the Netherlands in 2002 as an "interface" between the executive and the judiciary and its role in determining prosecutorial policy is crucial, particularly with regard to the adoption of specific prosecutorial guidelines. The Ministry of Justice, on the other hand, is politically accountable for prosecution policy and retains a power of general or specific instruction. *See* Peter J.P. Tak, *The Dutch Prosecution Service, in* Tak, *supra* note 15, at 356; Salas, *supra* note 15, at 191.

[18] U.S. Attorneys are within the federal Department of Justice. The attorney general and the ninety-three U.S. Attorneys are appointed by the president with consent of the Senate. By contrast, in most states, the head prosecutor of each local jurisdiction (often called the district attorney) is elected locally and largely independent of the state attorney general. *See* Mirjan Damaska, *The Faces of Justice and State Authority: A Comparative Approach to the Legal Process* 223 (1986); Gwladys Gilliéron, *Public Prosecutors in the United States and Europe: A Comparative Analysis with Special Focus on Switzerland, France and Germany* 65, 314 (2013).

[19] In England and Wales the establishment of a prosecution service, the Crown Prosecution Service (CPS), occurred only in 1985 with the Prosecution of Offences Act. Originally, prosecution was brought by the victim and only after the establishment of professional police forces in 1829 was this task assigned to the police. The Director of Public Prosecutions, first established in 1879, on the other hand, had competence only in very limited cases. The CPS is competent to decide whether to prosecute, but without the power to direct the police during the investigations carried out beforehand. On the CPS, see Section III, *infra*.

[20] Under the Italian Constitution, Arts. 107 & 108 para 2, the public prosecutor (*pubblico ministero*) is considered part of the judiciary order (*magistratura*) together with the judge. This configuration of the status of the public prosecutor endorsed by the Italian Constitution in 1948 represented a reaction to the experience of the Fascist dictatorship. *See* Vladimiro Zagrebelsky, *Indipendenza del pubblico ministero ed obbligatorietà dell'azione penale, in Pubblico Ministero ed accusa penale* 12 (Giovanni Conso ed., 1979); Raphaele Parizot, *Au nom de l'indépendance, le ministère public en Italie, in Figures du Parquet* 113 (Christine Lazerges ed., 2006).

[21] *See* Portuguese Constitution Art. 219 para. 2; Pedro Salreu, *The Prosecution Service in Portugal*, in Tak, *supra* note 15, at 387; Salas, *supra* note 15, at 181.

[22] As mentioned, the "external independence," however, does not exclude the possibility of a hierarchical internal organization of the prosecution service, implying the subordination of the individual prosecutor to the directives or orders issued by a hierarchical superior (e.g., the Prosecutor General). In this regard, Italy and Portugal present two completely opposite approaches: the Italian system is indeed

as a reaction to earlier experiences of abuse of the prosecutorial function by the ruling parties.

In the same perspective, systems such as Hungary's have opted for "full independence" through a "sui generis" configuration of the prosecution service, so that it formally belongs neither to the executive branch nor to the judiciary.[23]

Under both these approaches, the independence of the public prosecutor is deemed essential to guarantee the objective exercise of the prosecutorial function. Nonetheless, in all those systems concerns persist regarding how to combine such independence with the coherence and democratic accountability of prosecutorial policy.[24]

2. Centralized or Decentralized Structure

The centralization or decentralization of prosecution services depends on the form of the state in each country. Federal systems such as the United States, Germany, and Belgium are normally more decentralized and employ separate prosecution offices for federal and state courts. Federal and state prosecution offices are generally independent of each other, with no hierarchical relationship between the two. Their jurisdiction and competencies can vary significantly between federal and state levels. In certain systems, such as Germany and Belgium,[25] the federal level deals with a limited number of offenses such as terrorism, espionage, treason, and crimes against humanity/war crimes; in others such as the United States, federal authority is considerably broader.

In contrast, states with a strong tradition of centralized administration, such as France, often employ unitary prosecution services that are hierarchically organized and territorially structured according to the different degrees of the judiciary, such as courts first instance, Court of Appeal, and the Court of Cassation.[26] A degree of autonomy is

characterized by a pronounced internal independence while the Portuguese is based on an internal hierarchical model.

[23] *See* László Miskolci, *The Hungarian Prosecution Service*, in Tak, *supra* note 15, at 258. The Hungarian Prosecutor General, who sits at the top of the prosecutorial hierarchy, is appointed and accountable to the Parliament. However, this form of accountability does not imply subordination to the Parliament, and excludes interference in individual cases.

[24] An interesting (although not absolute) correlation may be established between the strong independence of the public prosecutor and the limitation of his/her discretion under the legality principle; see Section IV, *infra*. In certain jurisdictions, indeed, the duty to prosecute is also perceived to counterbalance the prosecutor's lack of political accountability.

[25] The Belgian *Parquet Federal* was established in 2002, with authority limited to terrorism, crimes against the security of the state, international and war crimes, and organized crime. *See* Van Daele, *supra* note 17, at 57. However, the *Parquet Federal* exercises its competence only if it considers that it is "required by the good administration of justice." Code Judicaire, Art. 144ter § 1 (Belgium).

[26] In France, prosecutors are structured as district-level prosecutors (*procureur/parquet de la République près le Tribunal de grande instance*), appellate prosecutors (*procureur/parquet général de la République*), and prosecutors attached to the Court of Cassation (*procureur/parquet général près la Cour de Cassation*). Further centralization was introduced with the *Parquet National Financier* (PNF), a centralized prosecution service for economic and financial crimes in Paris with exclusive nationwide competence.

normally left to the territorial office, but within the context of a unitary structure. One also finds structural developments such as the *Juridictions Interrégionales Spécialisées* (JIRS), established in 2004 in France to handle organized crime and complex economic and financial crimes. JIRS offices have a multiregional jurisdiction and are an example of parallel specialization and centralization of investigative and prosecutorial functions.[27]

III. European Prosecutors in the Pretrial Phase: Between Autonomy and the Investigative Judge

In general, "pretrial procedure" runs from the start of the official investigation until the trial. There are significant differences in the structure of the pretrial procedure. In some states, pretrial procedure constitutes a single procedural phase that starts with the opening of the official investigation, includes preparation of the indictment and the filing of charges, and runs until the beginning of the trial. Other systems divide the pretrial procedure into two distinct phases: a preparatory phase referred to as *information*, and a formal judicial investigation called *instruction*.[28] *Information* and *instruction* have the same objective—both compile the dossier and gather evidence, but the rules applicable to each phase may differ. This section will address the role and powers of the public prosecutor during the pretrial stage in regard to the investigative activities that are conducted before trial.

In this stage, civil and common law traditions still take different approaches. In common law systems, investigative activities are ordinarily carried out by the police or other law enforcement authorities autonomously. The prosecutor steps in only at the end of the investigation to decide whether to bring the case to court. In England and Wales, most investigations are independently conducted by the police.[29] Police agencies are organized on a local basis; England and Wales currently have more than forty-three different police forces, in addition to various government departments and agencies that investigate specific offenses connected with their regulatory mandate, such as the Department of Health and Social Security, the Serious Fraud Office, Her Majesty's Revenue and Customs, and the Financial Services Authority.[30] It is important to highlight that until recent times, England and Wales (unlike the United States) did not have a prosecution service. It was only in 1985 that the Prosecution of Offences Act established the Crown Prosecution Service, which is headed by the Director of Public Prosecutions

[27] On the JIRS, see Pradel, *supra* note 13, at 219.

[28] This is the case for Belgium, Luxembourg, and France, which all derived the structure of their procedural codes from the French Napoleonic tradition.

[29] Weigend, *supra* note 1.

[30] Tricia Howse, *England—National Report*, in 1 *Toward a Prosecutor for the European Union* 136 (Katalin Ligeti ed., 2013).

and responsible for the prosecution of any offenses not assigned exclusively to another authority. Once police complete an investigation, the CPS decides whether to prosecute a case, but the CPS (see *infra*) has no power to direct police during the investigations.[31] In large-scale investigations, the CPS may be asked by the police for advice on possible lines of inquiry or evidential requirements, but even in these cases prosecutors cannot direct the police to perform specific acts.[32] In the United States, the story is similar in most state justice systems, where investigations are largely controlled by local police agencies. Federal prosecutors, however, actively lead many investigations and coordinate closely with federal law enforcement agencies.[33]

Civil law systems, on the other hand, tend to assign a judicial actor to lead investigations: the public prosecutor or, in some jurisdictions, the investigative judge (*juge d'instruction*).[34] On one end of the spectrum, several European civil law systems entrust the prosecutor with the power to manage the investigations and to direct the police: the prosecutor can order the police to take specific investigative measures, define the investigative strategy, and in some cases carry out investigative acts himself. The prosecutor is the central actor of the pretrial phase, although for some coercive measures (interception of telecommunications, certain types of searches, etc.) he needs the authorization of a pretrial judge, such as the *Ermittlungsrichter* in Germany.[35] It is important to highlight that rather than systematically supervising the investigation, in such systems pretrial judges are involved *ad acta*—upon request of the public prosecutor—for the authorization of a specific measure.

Whereas systems reformed after the 1970s, such as Germany and Italy, endorsed this approach, in other Continental systems the powers to direct investigations are not exclusive to the public prosecutor but shared with an investigative judge. That office was introduced for the first time in the French Napoleonic Code of 1808 and was subsequently

[31] Spencer, *supra* note 2, at 30; Howse, *supra* note 31.

[32] *See* Crown Prosecution Service, *Code for Crown Prosecutors* (January 2013), § 3.2, *available at* https://www.cps.gov.uk/publication/code-crown-prosecutors (England). Chris Lewis, *The Evolving Role of the English Crown Prosecution Service*, *in* Luna & Wade, *supra* note 1, at 224, observes that "[n]evertheless, the CPS does influence the investigation of cases in several ways, beginning with general guidelines in the Code for Crown Prosecutors." Indirect influence on the work of the police is indeed exerted through the assessment carried out by the CPS in the context of the charging decision.

[33] *See* Gilliéron, *supra* note 19, at 74; David A. Harris, *The Interaction and Relationship Between Prosecutors and Police Officers in the United States and How This Affects Police Reform Efforts*, *in* Wade & Luna, *supra* note 1, at 55.

[34] Thomas Weigend, *Prosecution: Comparative Aspects*, in 3 *Encyclopedia of Crime & Justice* 1235 (Joshua Dressler ed., 2d ed. 2002).

[35] *See* Thomas Weigend & Franz Salditt, *The Investigative Stage of the Criminal Process in Germany*, in *Suspects in Europe: Procedural Rights at the Investigative Stage of the Criminal Process in the European Union* 82 (Ed Cape et al. eds., 2007). The equivalent figure in Italy is the *Giudice per le indagini preliminari*. Before 1975, Germany had an investigative judge (the *Untersuchungsrichter*), but the position was abolished "because it was deemed to duplicate and inhibit the investigation." *Id.* Italy likewise had an investigative judge, the "*giudice istruttore*," but the office was abolished in the 1988 Code of Criminal Procedure.

endorsed by many of the Continental systems influenced by that codification.[36] The rationale behind its introduction was inspired by the inquisitorial ideal of the investigation as a search for the "material truth"—requiring an impartial investigator[37]—and intended to counterbalance the role of the *Procureur.* In contrast to Italian or German pretrial judges, the investigative judge not only authorizes investigative measures but co-conducts the investigation.

In France, the investigative judge conducts the *instruction*, a judicial investigation that is mandatory for serious crimes, optional for misdemeanors (*délits*),[38] and exceptional for petty offenses (*contraventions*).[39] When an *instruction* is opened,[40] the investigative judge can direct the police through so-called "rogatory letters" (*commissions rogatoires*). This gives the investigative judge a double, ambiguous nature of investigator and judge that has often been criticized. Indeed, revising the role of the investigative judge is currently being debated in several systems, including France.[41]

1. Specialized Law Enforcement Authorities and the Exercise of Investigative and Prosecutorial Functions

The specialization of investigative and prosecutorial functions represents a growing tendency in both common law and civil law systems. With regard to organized crime and certain specific forms of criminality requiring a higher degree of expertise or greater internal and international coordination, several European states have established specialized offices or authorities with exclusive competence *ratione materiae*. In some cases, those specialized offices are also entrusted with special investigative powers or with the authority to use special investigative techniques that would not be allowed—or (allowed only) subject to stricter requirements—in ordinary criminal proceedings. Examples are

[36] Belgium, Greece, Luxembourg, the Netherlands, and Spain are notable examples of systems retaining the role of the investigative judge. The abolished Italian Code of Criminal Procedure of 1930 foresaw too an extensive role for the investigative judge (*giudice istruttore*).

[37] The investigative judge is—at least on paper—formally obliged to investigate even-handedly (*à charge et à décharge*).

[38] The prosecutor, in these cases, will decide to ask for the opening of an instruction depending on the complexity of the case and the need to resort to certain investigative measures that can only be adopted by the investigative judge (such as telephone wiretaps).

[39] *See* Juliette Tricot, *France—National Report*, *in* Ligeti, *supra* note 31, at 228; *see also* Francesca Galli, *The Interception of Communication in France and Italy—What Relevance for the Development of English Law*, 20 Int'l J. Hum. Rts. 667 (2016).

[40] The *juge d'instruction* does not proceed ex officio: his/her jurisdiction is "activated" by a request from the public prosecutor (*réquisitoire introductif*), which determines the factual scope of the investigation.

[41] Notably, the investigative judge is no longer empowered to decide on the liberty of the suspect: since 2000, the decisions on preventive detention (*détention provisoire*), control measures (*contrôle judiciaire*), and certain searches and interceptions are within the competence of the *juge des libertés et de la detention*, a separate judge who does not directly investigate the case.

the Italian *Direzione Nazionale Antimafia e Antiterrorismo*, which investigates and prosecutes organized crime and terrorism offenses, and the recently established French *Parquet National Financier* (PNF), a specialized parquet headquartered in Paris and competent for financial and economic crimes across the entire national territory.[42] It is worth emphasizing that the tendency toward the specialization in specific areas of crime often seems intertwined with processes of centralization of the prosecutorial function: again, France provides an interesting example with the PNF and JIRS, which have authority across regions of the country for complex cases of organized crime.[43]

2. Private Prosecution

The final point in this section concerns the possibility and limits of private prosecution in civil law systems. As mentioned in the introduction, whereas private prosecution represented the very starting point of the common law system, the role of the victim in European civil law systems has been and remains generally more limited and subsidiary to the role of the public prosecutor.

In most civil-law-based justice systems, the victim is entrusted with the power to counteract the inactivity of the public prosecutor or to oppose a pretrial dismissal.[44] At trial the victim can also intervene as *partie civile* alongside the public prosecutor.[45] Autonomous power to investigate and launch a prosecution, however, is provided in only a handful of states according to the model of the "*actio popularis.*" Among European civil law countries, Spain provides the most remarkable example of this model: the possibility of launching a private prosecution is guaranteed in Article 125 of the Spanish Constitution to every citizen, association (including political parties), or administrative body of the state. The private citizen or association may trigger an investigation by the investigative judge, who remains competent to take relevant investigative actions. The private prosecutor, however, may conduct private investigations in parallel to the judicial one, within the limits of the law.[46]

[42] The *Parquet National Financier* was established in 2014.

[43] There are eight *Juridictions Interrégionales Spécialisées* in Paris, Lyon, Marseille, Lille, Rennes, Bordeaux, Nancy, and Fort-de-France. Before the establishment of the *Parquet National Financier* in 2014, the JIRS were also exclusively competent for complex economic and financial cases.

[44] In Italy, for instance, the victim can file an opposition against the prosecutor's request to dismiss a case. The opposition of the victim triggers a pretrial adversarial hearing before the pretrial judge to decide on the legitimacy of the request for dismissal.

[45] In France, the *Code de Procédure Pénale* Art. 418 et seq., enables the victim to intervene at the trial as a party (*partie civile*) and to claim reparation and compensation for the damages suffered.

[46] *See* Adán Nieto Martin, *Private Prosecution and the* European *Public Prosecutor's Office. Shaping the Power to Prosecute in* European *Criminal Law*, in 2 *The European Public Prosecutor's Office: Toward a Truly European Prosecution Service?* (Katalin Ligeti ed., forthcoming).

3. Coercive Measures and the Need for Judicial Authorization

During the pretrial stage, the most common investigative measures include questioning witnesses and suspects, searching premises and seizing items of evidence, intercepting communications, monitoring telecommunications traffic data, and—where deemed necessary—restricting the liberty of the suspect in pretrial detention. Certain investigative measures may interfere with the fundamental rights of the suspect and third parties (for instance, the right to privacy, to property, or personal liberty), although with different degrees of intensity. These measures are often referred to as "coercive measures," the most intrusive of which are normally subject to judicial authorization in order to ensure the legality and proportionality of their adoption. While the power to restrict the liberty of the accused is normally entrusted to a judge, authority for different investigative measures varies greatly among systems.

In certain cases, the public prosecutor may be able to order directly some coercive measures,[47] whereas others require a judge.[48] In countries where the investigative judge is still present, he or she usually oversees the most intrusive measures during the *instruction*.[49] In countries where the investigation is directed exclusively by the public prosecutor, such as Italy and Germany, a pretrial judge intervenes upon request of the public prosecutor and may authorize actions subject to statutory limits regarding the penalty threshold, threshold of suspicion, or necessity for the investigative measure. This authorization can be either ex ante (before the action) or *ex post* (after police or prosecutors carry out the measure). Ex post authorization is often reserved for emergency cases, where the execution of the measure (such as interception of telecommunications) cannot be delayed without irremediably compromising the possibility of gathering the evidence. In such cases, the public prosecutor or the police may be temporarily permitted to order or execute the measure subject to authorization subsequently obtained within a strict time limit. Where authorization ex post is not granted, this usually determines the non-admissibility of the elements of evidence gathered as a matter of emergency.

A peculiar case in this regard is the regime on the interception of telecommunications in England and Wales. Here, authorization of the measure required for police investigating the case is not granted by a judge but by the Secretary of State for Home Affairs. The English system represents a unicum in yet another respect: elements directly gathered through the interception of telecommunications (which are possible only in relation to

[47] As an example, in Italy, searches of premises can be ordered by the public prosecutor directly. *See Codice di procedura penale* (Code of Criminal Procedure) (It.) Art. 247.

[48] In France, searches of premises, normally, need to be authorized by the investigative judge in the course of the *instruction* or by the *juge des libertés et de la détention* during the *enquête préliminaire*. *See Code de Procédure Pénale* (Code of Criminal Procedure) (Fr.) Art. 76 paras. 3, 92.

[49] In France, however, since 2000, the task of authorizing certain searches and interception has been entrusted to a separate judge, the *juge des libertés et de la détention*.

serious crime) legally authorized by the Secretary of State cannot be used as evidence and are not admissible at trial under any circumstances.[50]

IV. Legality and Opportunity Principles across Common and Civil Law Traditions

1. Mandatory and Discretionary Prosecution: Justifications, Criticism, and Crossovers between Traditions

The third point of our comparative inquiry focuses on the decision of whether to prosecute a case after the investigation has concluded. Two approaches exist in this regard, represented by the legality principle (*Legalitätsprinzip* or *principe de légalité des poursuites*) and the opportunity principle (*Opportunitätsprinzip* or *principe de l'opportunité des poursuites*).

Under the legality principle, if there is sufficient evidence at the close of the investigation, the prosecutor is in principle duty-bound to press charges and cannot dismiss a case.[51] The legality principle is generally traced back to the French Revolution and to the distrust reformers harbored about the impartiality of public prosecutors during the Ancien Régime.[52] The legality principle is intended to guarantee the equality of citizens before the law by excluding any discretion for the prosecutor and thereby preventing favoritism or dismissals *pro amico*. On the other hand, the aim of prosecuting each and every offense underlying the legality principle might also be seen as a relic of the inquisitorial tradition and, in particular, of the metaphysical ideal developed under Canon Law that no crime should go unpunished ("*interest rei publicae ne maleficia remaneant impunita*").[53] The main criticisms of the legality principle focus on its capacity to overload criminal justice systems.[54]

[50] *See* Ed Cape & Jaqueline Hodgson, *The Investigative Stage of the Criminal Process in England and Wales*, in *Suspects in Europe: Procedural Rights at the Investigative Stage of the Criminal Process in the European Union* 68 (Ed Cape et al. eds., 2007); Howse, *supra* note 31.

[51] *See* Damaska, *supra* note 2, at 503.

[52] Weigend, *supra* note 35, at 1237; Pradel, *supra* note 13, at 434.

[53] The maxim is attributed to a decretal issued by Pope Innocent III (1161–1216) in 1203. It actually dated back to classic Roman law and entrenched the idea that "the failure to punish deviancy leads to moral and behavioural deterioration." *See* Richard M. Fraher, *The Theoretical Justification for the New Criminal Law of the High Middle Ages:* "Rei Publicae Interest, Ne Crimina Remaneant Impunita." *Articles by Maurer Faculty: Paper 1854*, U. Ill. L. Rev. 577, 579 (1984).

[54] Weigend, *supra* note 1, at 377 (highlighting that "it certainly would be illusionary to expect a practice of full enforcement today, after thousands of new criminal prohibitions have been created").

The opportunity principle, on the contrary, entrusts the prosecutor with the discretionary[55] choice of whether or not to prosecute a case.[56] More specifically, the opportunity principle allows the prosecutor to dismiss a case despite sufficient evidence to charge when, according to his/her discretionary assessment, a prosecution would not be in line with the public interest. Thus, the opportunity principle accepts that not all crimes may deserve prosecution, trial and, ultimately, punishment. By doing so, the opportunity principle provides prosecutors with leeway to determine the criminal enforcement policy of the day.

With regard to the endorsement of one principle or the other, the divide between the common law and civil law traditions has narrowed considerably. Common law jurisdictions have been based on and continue to rely on the opportunity principle,[57] but an increasing number of civil law jurisdictions have either endorsed the opportunity principle[58] or introduced exceptions to the legality principle in order to allow for a certain degree of prosecutorial discretion. Within Continental Europe, this gradual move toward the opportunity principle has been driven by efficiency concerns and the need in several states to cope with increasing caseloads in criminal courts.[59] The endorsement of the opportunity principle has also been promoted by the Committee of Ministers of the Council of Europe since the end of the 1980s as a means to rationalize, accelerate, and simplify the workings of criminal justice systems.[60]

Germany provides an excellent example of a civil law system based on the legality principle, which has introduced a significant number of exceptions, even if the general rule in the German Code of Criminal Procedure (*Strafprozessordnung* - StPO[61]) remains that there is the duty to bring the case to court where evidence is sufficient (Section 152

[55] McCoy, *supra* note 2, at 673 (recalling that Kenneth Culp Davis, *Discretionary Justice* (1969) defines discretion as "the capacity to choose between two or more equally permissible alternative courses of action").

[56] Weigend, *supra* note 35; Pradel, *supra* note 13, at 435; Mirjan Damaska, *The Reality of Prosecutorial Discretion: Comments on a German Monograph*, 29 Am. J. Comp. L. 120 (1981).

[57] *See* Lewis, *supra* note 33, at 215 (recalling, in regard to England and Wales, the words of Lord Shawcross from 1951: "It has never been the rule in this country—I hope it never will be—that suspected criminal offences must automatically be the subject of prosecution").

[58] In continental Europe, the systems endorsing the opportunity principle are Belgium, Denmark, France, Luxembourg, and the Netherlands. *See* Pradel, *supra* note 13, at 434.

[59] Weigend, *supra* note 1, at 383; Jörg-Martin Jehle, *The Function of Public Prosecution Within the Criminal Justice System*, in *Coping with Overloaded Criminal Justice Systems: The Rise of Prosecutorial Power Across Europe* 6 (Jörg-Martin Jehle & Marianne Wade eds., 2006); Marianne Wade, *The Power to Decide—Prosecutorial Control, Diversion and Punishment in European Criminal Justice Systems Today*, *in id.* at 28.

[60] The Recommendation R (87) 18 of the Committee of Ministers of the Council of Europe adopted on Sept. 17, 1987 and "concerning the simplification of criminal justice" stated under its point I.a.1 that: "the principle of discretionary prosecution should be introduced or its application extended wherever historical development and the constitution of member states allow; otherwise, measures having the same purpose should be devised."

[61] The original structure of the StPO dates back to 1877; the text has been modified several times.

and Section 170 StPO).[62] Starting from the 1960s, some elements of discretion and the statutory possibility to unconditionally dismiss cases involving less serious offenses (*Vergehen*, misdemeanors[63]) were introduced under Section 153 StPO.[64] The latter norm enables the prosecutor to dismiss the case without consequences if the guilt of the suspect is "of a minor nature"[65] and there is no public interest in the prosecution. Depending on the potential sanction provided for the misdemeanor,[66] a court's authorization may be required in order to dismiss the case. This approval, however, when required, "is almost invariably granted."[67] Over the years, other grounds have been introduced, allowing dismissal of cases concerning offenses committed abroad (Section 153c StPO), where political grounds exist (Section 153d StPO), or for reasons of prosecutorial efficiency (Section 154[68] and Section 154a StPO[69]). Although some other forms of dismissal

[62] *See* Thomas Weigend, *Germany—National Report, in* Ligeti, *supra* note 31, at 268; Gilliéron, *supra* note 19, at 269.

[63] The German Criminal Code (Strafgesetzbuch—StGB) (Ger.) classifies and distinguishes *Verbrechen* (felonies) and *Vergehen* (misdemeanors).

[64] Hans-Jörg Albrecht, *Criminal Prosecution: Developments, Trends and Open Questions in the Federal Republic of Germany*, 8 Eur. J. Crime Crim. L. & Crim. Just. 246 (2000), highlights how in the same period (1960s) "the phenomenon of mass crimes came up and with mass crimes serious capacity problems became visible."

[65] It is argued in literature that the lack of a definition of "guilt of a minor nature" or "public interest" affords the prosecutor wide discretion under § 153 StPO (Ger.). *See* Gilliéron, *supra* note 19, at 271.

[66] For misdemeanors punished *in abstracto* with a custodial sentence of less than one month's detention or less than five days for daily fines, there is no need to involve the court. *See* StGB §§ 38, 40 (Ger.).

[67] Weigend, *supra* note 63.

[68] § 154 StPO (Ger.) provides: "[Insignificant Secondary Penalties] (1) The public prosecution office may dispense with prosecuting an offense: 1. if the penalty or the measure of reform and prevention in which the prosecution might result is not particularly significant in addition to a penalty or measure of reform and prevention which has been imposed with binding effect upon the accused for another offense, or which he may expect for another offense, or 2. beyond that, if a judgment is not to be expected for such offense within a reasonable time, and if a penalty or measure of reform and prevention which was imposed with binding effect upon the accused, or which he may expect for another offense, appears sufficient to have an influence on the perpetrator and to defend the legal order. (2) If public charges have already been preferred, the court may, upon the application of the public prosecution office, provisionally terminate the proceedings at any stage. (3) If the proceedings were provisionally terminated on account of a penalty or measure of reform and prevention already imposed with binding effect for another offense, the proceedings may be resumed, unless barred by limitation in the meantime, if the penalty or measure of reform and prevention imposed with binding effect is subsequently not executed. (4) If the proceedings were provisionally terminated on account of a penalty or measure of reform and prevention which is to be expected for another offense, the proceedings may be resumed, unless barred by limitation in the meantime, within three months after the judgment imposed for the other offense has entered into force. (5) If the court has provisionally terminated the proceedings, a court order shall be required for their resumption." The English translation of the German StPO is *accessible at* https://www.gesetze-im-internet.de/englisch_stpo/.

[69] § 154a StPO (Ger.) provides: "[Limitation of Prosecution] (1) If individual severable parts of an offense or some of several violations of law committed as a result of the same offense are not particularly significant: 1. for the penalty or measure of reform and prevention to be expected, or 2. in addition to a penalty or measure of reform and prevention which has been imposed with binding effect upon the accused for another offense or which he may expect to be imposed for another offense, prosecution may be limited to the other parts of the offense or the other violations of law. Section 154 subsection (1), number 2, shall apply mutatis mutandis. The limitation shall be included in the records. (2) After the bill of

may entail conditions and instructions to be complied with by the suspect (Section 153a StPO), the other grounds mentioned are all unconditional. As such, some authors have observed that "taken together, these exceptions almost seem to swallow the rule" of mandatory prosecution.[70]

2. Prosecutorial Discretion: Criteria for Its Exercise and Control Mechanisms

Common law jurisdictions, as mentioned, traditionally relied on the opportunity principle. The exercise of discretion in choosing trial-worthy cases is an inherent feature of common law criminal justice systems. The need to ensure consistency in enforcement of the law and to avoid abuses, however, is present in those systems as well, and it is increasingly addressed through the adoption of criteria and guidelines to guide the discretion of the public prosecutor in the individual case.

In England and Wales, after the entry into force of the "statutory charging" scheme in 2005,[71] the CPS became the main—although not the exclusive[72]—"gatekeeper"[73] of the trial stage, responsible for deciding whether to prosecute a case investigated by the police. This decision is the result of a discretionary assessment and, for this purpose, the CPS adopted specific guiding principles and a two-stage test (the "Full Code Test"), all of which are contained in the *Code for Crown Prosecutors*.[74] The Full Code Test is composed of two stages: the evidential stage and the public interest stage. The evidentiary assessment, based on the threshold of "sufficient evidence to provide a realistic prospect of conviction,"[75] is preliminary to any further evaluation of the public interest and, if a case fails at this stage, the prosecutor must not proceed "no matter how serious or sensitive it [the case] may be."[76] The public interest stage, instead, entails an overall assessment of

indictment has been filed, the court, with the consent of the public prosecution office, may introduce this limitation at any stage of the proceedings. (3) At any stage of the proceedings the court may reintroduce into the proceedings those parts of the offense or violations of law which were not considered. An application by the public prosecution office for reintroduction shall be granted. If parts of an offense which were not considered are reintroduced, Section 265 subsection (4) shall apply *mutatis mutandis*."

70 Weigend, *supra* note 35, at 1238; *see also* Damaska, *supra* note 57, at 138.

71 The "Statutory Charging Scheme" was introduced by the Criminal Justice Act 2003.

72 Other law enforcement agencies and Government Departments (such as the Department of Health and Social Security-DHSS, the Serious Fraud Office-SFO, Her Majesty's Revenue and Customs-HMRC) have the power to investigate and prosecute certain specific offenses. *See* Howse, *supra* note 31, at 136.

73 *See* Lewis, *supra* note 33, at 221.

74 The *Code for Crown Prosecutors* is a public document issued by the Director of Public Prosecutions (the head of the CPS) and is intended to guide the CPS prosecutors in the charging decision. The latest edition of the Code (7th edition) was adopted in January 2013 and is available in several languages at https://www.cps.gov.uk/publications/code_for_crown_prosecutors/ (last visited Dec. 12, 2017).

75 According to the Code, to ascertain whether there is sufficient evidence the prosecutor must assess three essential aspects: the potential admissibility, the reliability (accuracy and integrity), and the credibility of the available evidence. *See Code for Crown Prosecutors*, *supra* note 75, § 4.6.

76 *See id.* § 4.4.

several factors to be weighed against one another: seriousness of the offense, level of culpability of the suspect, harm caused to the victim, the impact on the community, proportionality of the prosecution in terms of costs for the wider criminal justice system,[77] and efficiency. Beyond the *Code for Crown Prosecutors*, the CPS also issues additional "guidance" setting out the public interest factors in regard to specific offenses, such as the Guidance for Corporate Prosecutions,[78] the Guidelines for cases affecting the Media,[79] or immigration offenses.[80]

In the United States, it is acknowledged that public prosecutors "have extraordinarily wide discretion within a system that deliberately fragments prosecutorial authority."[81] However, direction and a certain degree of consistency, at least at the federal level,[82] is sought through the Principles of Federal Prosecution[83] contained in the *U.S. Attorneys' Manual*.[84] Following constitutional requirements, the Principles establish a preliminary—indispensable—requirement: the existence of probable cause.[85] If that requirement is fulfilled, then other grounds have to be assessed: the availability of sufficient admissible evidence to sustain a conviction and the presence of "a substantial federal interest." The factors for identifying a "substantial federal interest" are listed in an illustrative way and encompass a broad range of considerations, including "federal law enforcement priorities."[86] It is important to highlight that the Federal Principles are expressly qualified as internal guidelines and may not be relied upon by a party to litigation.[87] On the other hand, the decision to commence or decline prosecution is not amenable to review.[88]

[77] The Code specifies that the cost-factor cannot be the sole determining factor to assess the public interest.

[78] *Available at* http://www.cps.gov.uk/legal/a_to_c/corporate_prosecutions/ (last visited Dec. 12, 2017).

[79] *Available at* http://www.cps.gov.uk/legal/d_to_g/guidance_for_prosecutors_on_assessing_the_public_interest_in_cases_affecting_the_media_/ (last visited Dec. 12, 2017).

[80] *Available at* http://www.cps.gov.uk/legal/h_to_k/immigration/ (last visited Dec. 12, 2017).

[81] Beale, *supra* note 13, at 34; *see also* Ellen S. Podgor, *Prosecution Guidelines in the United States, in* Luna & Wade, *supra* note 1, at 9.

[82] At the state level, policy guidelines are adopted by state prosecutors' offices. However, each office enjoys a broad autonomy and, in most cases, such guidelines are not public.

[83] Dep't of Justice, *U.S. Attorneys' Manual* § 9-27.000 (last updated on 19th September 2018) (noting that the Principles of Federal Prosecution aim "to assure regularity without regimentation, and to prevent unwarranted disparity without sacrificing necessary flexibility"; at § 9-27.001).

[84] Gilliéron, *supra* note 19, at 79.

[85] *U.S. Attorneys' Manual*, *supra* note 84, § 9-27.200. In the U.S. system, "probable cause" represents a constitutional requirement for arrest and warrants and identifies a reasonable basis for believing that a crime may have been committed. The definition of probable cause is not provided by the U.S. Constitution, but has been elaborated, in a flexible way, by the U.S. Supreme Court in several judgments. *See, e.g.*, Brinegar v. United States, 338 U.S. 160 (1949); Illinois v. Gates, 462 U.S. 213 (1983).

[86] *See U.S. Attorneys' Manual*, *supra* note 84, § 9-27.230.

[87] *Id.* § 9-27.150.

[88] Gilliéron, *supra* note 19, at 78; Beale, *supra* note 13, at 34 (quoting United States v. Batchelder, 442 U.S. 114 (1979)); see also Bordenkircher v. Hayes, 434 U.S. 357 (1978); United States v. Nixon, 418 U.S. 683 (1974).

As mentioned above, some European civil law jurisdictions openly endorse the opportunity principle,[89] and they have also developed guidelines and criteria in order to contain and discipline discretion. In the Netherlands, for instance, prosecutorial priorities and (general or specific) instructions relating to the decision whether to prosecute a case are issued by the Board of Prosecutors General and are binding on individual prosecutors.[90]

3. Prosecutorial Discretion and Alternatives to Trial Proceedings

The last step of our analysis on the point of discretion addresses the increasing tendency—in both civil and common law traditions—to entrust the public prosecutor with quasi-judicial sanctioning powers in the context of out-of-court and simplified procedures. The trend toward what the literature has labeled "prosecutorial sentencing"[91] is also based on considerations of procedural economy (avoiding, to the maximum extent possible, a costly trial stage), but goes beyond the pure and simple pretrial dismissal examined in the previous paragraph. In this context, rather than taking a binary decision to prosecute or dismiss a case, prosecutors have at their disposal an array of intermediate alternatives that may entail the imposition upon the suspect of conditions to be fulfilled (such as participating in a mediation or rehabilitation program, performing community or non-profit service, donating a certain sum of money to a charity) or even, in certain cases, criminal sanctions (normally pecuniary). The procedural devices enabling "prosecutorial sentencing" are various and may differ greatly. Some of them may require the consent of the suspect or the involvement of a court (or, more often, of an investigative judge) ex ante or ex post. They can take the form of conditional dismissals, penal orders, transactions, plea bargaining, deferred or non-prosecution agreements.

All such forms of prosecutorial case termination share a common objective: avoiding a costly trial. In most cases, they are limited to misdemeanors or less serious crimes and may entail certain advantages for the suspect, such as the application of the minimum penalty or the exclusion of the collateral consequences of a conviction (professional disqualification, withdrawal of driving licenses, deportation of noncitizens, etc.). A relevant common feature, however, is represented by the limited form of judicial control

[89] For Belgium, France, the Netherlands, and Luxembourg, see, in particular, *Code d'Instruction Criminelle* (Code of Criminal Procedure) (Belg.) art 28-*quater*; *Code de Procédure Pénale* (Code of Criminal Procedure) (Fr.) Art. 40; *Wetboek van Strafvordering* (Code of Criminal Procedure) (Neth.) Art. 167 paras. 1–2; *Code de Procédure Pénale* (Code of Criminal Procedure) (Lux.) Art. 23.

[90] *See* Henk van de Bunt & Jean-Louis van Gelder, *The Dutch Prosecution Service*, 41 Crime & Just. 122 (2012). The Minister of Justice is also competent to issue specific instructions but "in practice, issuance of specific instructions and guidelines is exceedingly rare".

[91] *See* Weigend, *supra* note 1, at 386.

to which those procedural determinations are subject. When such control is allowed, either ex ante in the form of validation or ex post following a challenge or appeal from the suspect, the judge generally cannot conduct full review of the merits with the possibility of modifying the conditions or the penalty imposed or agreed between the parties, but can only validate or annul the procedural act. As such, the choice is to "take it or leave it,"[92] where "leaving" means sending the (often minor) case either back to the ordinary track or directly to trial.

This latter circumstance reinforces and to a certain extent transforms the role of the prosecutor into a hybrid actor, between a "quasi-judge" and a "crime regulator," whose central concern is the cost effectiveness of non-prosecution. The dynamics of prosecutorial sentencing, therefore, resemble the operation of an administrative system rather than the unfolding of a classic criminal proceeding.[93]

Relevant examples of procedural devices that enable "prosecutorial sentencing" include:

- the German conditional dismissal provided by Section 153a StPO, applicable only to misdemeanors and requiring the consent of the suspect and the approval of the court;[94]
- the Dutch transaction (*transactie*), an agreement whereby non-prosecution is secured in exchange, normally, for payment of a sum of money;[95]
- the French "*comparution sur reconnaissance préalable de culpabilité*" (CRPC), applicable in case of offenses punished with imprisonment of up to ten years and requiring both the consent of the suspect and the approval of the judge;[96]
- conditional cautions in England and Wales;[97]
- diversion programs, non-prosecution and deferred prosecution agreements in the U.S. system.[98]

[92] *See* Stephen Thaman, *The Penal Order: Prosecutorial Sentencing as a Model for Criminal Justice Reform?*, *in* Luna & Wade, *supra* note 1, at 161.

[93] These considerations have been debated in U.S. literature in regard to plea bargaining and the adversarial nature of the criminal justice system. *See, e.g.*, Gerard E. Lynch, *Our Administrative System of Criminal Justice*, 66 Fordham L. Rev. 2117 (1998).

[94] Albrecht, *supra* note 65, at 247.

[95] *See* Chrisje Brants, *Consensual, Abbreviated and Simplified Procedures in the Netherlands*, in *World Plea Bargaining* 202 (Stephen C. Thaman ed., 2010).

[96] *See* Jacqueline Hodgson, *Guilty Pleas and the Changing Role of the Prosecutor in French Criminal Justice*, *in* Luna & Wade, *supra* note 1, at 124.

[97] Cautions are warnings issued by the police as an alternative to prosecution. They may be simple or conditional. When the charging decision is under consideration by the CPS, the prosecutor can decide to decline to prosecute and instead ask the police to issue a simple or conditional caution. In this sense, see the *Code for Crown Prosecutors*, *supra* note 75, at §§ 7.1 and 7.2 and Lewis, *supra* note 33, at 228.

[98] *See* David M. Uhlmann, *Deferred Prosecution and Non-prosecution Agreements and the Erosion of Corporate Criminal Liability*, 75 Md. L. Rev. 1295 (2013); Bruce Zagaris, *Prosecutor and Judges as Corporate Monitors? The U.S. Experience*, in *Challenges in the Field of Economic and Financial Crime in Europe and the U.S.* 19 (Katalin Ligeti & Vanessa Franssen eds., 2017).

V. Supranational Challenges and Perspectives: The Establishment of the EPPO

In conclusion, a significant ongoing development in the context of European integration ought to be mentioned: the establishment of the European Public Prosecutor's Office,[99] a new supranational judicial body in charge of investigating and prosecuting before the national courts of the Member States offenses affecting the financial interests of the European Union (the so-called PIF offenses). The EPPO will begin operations from 2020 at the earliest and only in regard to the twenty EU Member States that joined the enhanced cooperation.[100] As the EPPO's supranational structure borrows from both common law and civil law traditions, it represents an important laboratory for comparative criminal procedure. An exhaustive critical analysis of the new Regulation is neither possible nor opportune in the context of this contribution.[101] Instead, this section will focus on how the four aspects previously analyzed (independence, centralization and decentralization, legality and opportunity of prosecution, and the alternatives to trial proceedings) have been translated to the supranational design of the EPPO.

Before addressing the details, it is important to recall that the EU as a supranational order is different from a classic national state and cannot be equated with a federal entity.[102] In the supranational environment, therefore, analyzing the EPPO's independence from the executive power may be less clear-cut than in either of those more familiar settings.[103] Furthermore, and additionally, it has to be considered that the establishment of the EPPO is both mandated and limited by the EU Treaties. While Article 86 of the Treaty on the Functioning of the European Union provides for the possibility of regulating "the conditions governing the performance of [the EPPO's] functions" and the "rules of procedure applicable to [the EPPO's] activities" (including those governing the admissibility of evidence), it does not empower the EU legislator to intervene and regulate the trial stage, which is expressly left to the national courts. Prosecutions by the EPPO, therefore, will be brought before national courts that will apply their national rules of

[99] Council Regulation 2017/1939/E.U. implementing the enhanced cooperation on the establishment of the Public Prosecutor's Office, 2017 O.J. (L 283) 1 [hereinafter E.P.P.O. Regulation].

[100] Austria, Belgium, Bulgaria, Croatia, Cyprus, Czech Republic, Estonia, Germany, Greece, Spain, Finland, France, Italy, Latvia, Lithuania, Luxembourg, Portugal, Romania, Slovenia, and Slovakia.

[101] For a more extensive analysis, see the contribution of Helmut Satzger & Frank Zimmermann, *Challenges of Trial Procedure Reform: Is European Union Legislation Part of the Solution or Part of the Problem?* in this volume.

[102] On the peculiar constitutional dimension of the EU Area of Freedom, Security and Justice, see Michiel Luchtman & John A.E. Vervaele, *European Agencies for Criminal Justice and Shared Enforcement (Eurojust and the European Public Prosecutor's Office)*, 10 Utrecht L. Rev. 132 (2014).

[103] On the issue of accountability within the EU Area of Freedom, Security and Justice, see Katalin Ligeti & Angelo Marletta, *EU Criminal Justice Actors: Accountability and Judicial Review vis-à-vis the EU Citizen*, 7 New J. Eur. Crim. L. 175 (2016).

procedure for the trial stage and their national substantive law (although the so-called "PIF offenses" are nowadays largely harmonized under EU law).[104] This circumstance is undoubtedly relevant to the analysis of the model of the EPPO since, historically, the physiognomy of the public prosecutor developed in accordance with the different configurations assigned by each domestic system to the trial stage.

1. Independence and Accountability

The independence of the EPPO has been a central theme ever since the idea of establishing a supranational prosecutor was coined. In the academic debate, in particular, clear support for an independent EPPO dates back to the *Corpus Juris* Project,[105] which expressly advocated an independent EPPO and stressed the need to exclude the risk of political interference. Accordingly, the EPPO Regulation states that the European Chief Prosecutor and all the members of the Office must act in the interest of the EU and must "neither seek nor take instructions from any person external to the E.P.P.O., any Member State of the European Union or any institution, body, office or agency of the Union in the performance of their duties."[106]

The rules for the appointment of the European Chief Prosecutor and of the European Prosecutors limit eligibility to active members of public prosecution services and of the judiciary and should, in principle, guarantee a sufficient degree of independence of the appointees.[107] Dismissal from the function is possible only if the Court of Justice—upon referral by the Commission, Council or the European Parliament—finds that the

[104] The definitions of the PIF offenses—and to a certain extent the penalties applicable—are now contained in Directive (E.U.) 2017/1371 on the fight against fraud to the Union's financial interests by means of criminal law, 2017 O.J. (L 198) 29. On the complex interplay between the E.P.P.O Regulation and the PIF Directive in determining the scope of material competence of the EPPO, see Katalin Ligeti & Anne Weyembergh, *The European Public Prosecutor's Office: Certain Constitutional Issues*, in *The European Public Prosecutor's Office: An Extended Arm or a Two-Headed Dragon?* 65 (Leendert Erkelens et al. eds., 2015). In critical terms, see also Rosaria Sicurella, *A Blunt Weapon for the E.P.P.O.? Taking the Edge off the Proposed P.I.F. Directive*, in *Shifting Perspectives on the European Public Prosecutor's Office* 121 (Willem Geelhoed et al. eds., 2018).

[105] *See* 1 *The Implementation of the* Corpus Juris *in the Member States* 314 (Mireille Delmas-Marty & John Vervaele eds., 2000). The *Corpus Juris* was an academic research project that gathered academics from several Member States and elaborated a set of rules (substantive and procedural) for the protection of EU financial interests and the establishment of a European Public Prosecutor. According to Art. 18, para 2 of the 2000 draft text of the *Corpus Juris*, the EPPO should have been independent from both national and Community (EU) institutions.

[106] *See* E.P.P.O. Regulation, *supra* note 100, Art. 6.

[107] Significantly, appointments are nonrenewable. *See* E.P.P.O. Regulation, *supra* note 100, Art. 14 para 1 and Art. 16 para 3. This should reduce the risk of the European Chief Prosecutor or the European prosecutors indulging in obliging or opportunistic attitudes in the hope of being reappointed. For a critique, considering the complex structure of the Regulation, see John A.E. Vervaele, *Criminal Investigation and Prosecutions by a European Public Prosecutor's Office in the EU: Di Meliora, in Vielfalt des Strafrechts im internationalen Kontext. Festschrift für Frank Höpfel zum 65. Geburstag* 673 (Robert Kert & Andrea Lehner eds., 2018).

European Chief Prosecutor or a European Prosecutor is no longer able to perform his or her duties or is guilty of serious misconduct. Accountability toward the European Parliament, the Council, and the Commission is stipulated, but only as to the general activities of the Office and cannot relate to individual cases. To this end, the EPPO will have a duty to submit a report each year on its activities to the three EU institutions and the European Chief Prosecutor will have to appear before the European Parliament.[108] The Office will also be under a duty to appear before national parliaments to give account of its general activities, if requested.[109]

2. Structure: Unity and Decentralization

Operating across the territory of several Member States (the twenty participant Member States, for the time being), the EPPO will be a "single office" organized on two levels: a central seat in Luxembourg and in the Member States. The central level will be composed of a European Chief Prosecutor, one European Prosecutor per Member State, a College gathering all the European Prosecutors and the European Chief Prosecutor, and several Permanent Chambers in charge of taking certain important operational decisions in individual cases. The decentralized level, represented by the European Delegated Prosecutors in the Member States, will be in charge of conducting investigations under the supervision of the central level.

To a certain extent, this model may recall the integrated model adopted for certain specialized investigation and prosecution services by some European civil law jurisdictions (e.g., the Italian *Direzione Nazionale Antimafia e Antiterrorismo*, which is organized as a central national office and twenty-six coordinated territorial offices, the *Direzioni Distrettuali Antimafia*). However, the EPPO will represent a sui generis structure, due to the heavy reliance of the regulation on the national law of the Member States. The powers assigned to the European Delegated Prosecutor in the individual Member State might potentially determine different configurations of the concrete "command chain."[110]

3. Power to Direct the Investigations and Authorization of Coercive Measures

As for the role of the EPPO in the pretrial stage, the peculiar nature of the new Office and the reliance on national law contained in the Regulation make it difficult to identify clear parallels with any of the different models described in this chapter. In principle,

[108] *See* E.P.P.O. Regulation, *supra* note 100, Art. 6. [109] *See id.* Art. 7, para. 2.

[110] On the "predictable dominant" role of national law in the concrete configuration of the EPPO "command chain," *see* Lothar Kuhl, *The European Public Prosecutor's Office—More Effective, Equivalent and Independent Criminal Prosecution against Fraud?*, eucrim 138 (2017/3).

the European Delegated Prosecutors in the Member States are responsible for the investigations and prosecutions on behalf of the EPPO.[111] Investigations, however, will be conducted through a complex set of interactions between the central office and the European Delegated Prosecutor(s) in the Member States, and, as mentioned, national law will play a relevant role in determining the scope and extent of the investigative powers that the new body will actually enjoy in a specific case.[112]

An interesting challenge will likely concern the relationship between the European Delegated Prosecutor and the national investigative judge (where this actor still exists) as regards the management of investigations. Only concrete practice will tell how the command chain and the cooperation patterns will develop from the central level of the EPPO to the national level of the investigation.

More specifically, the design of the investigative powers of the EPPO leaves room for several asymmetries and complexities. The regulation introduced only minimal harmonization of the EPPO's investigative powers: with regard to the authorization of coercive measures, the conditions and modalities for adopting such measures will be largely governed by national law.[113] The same limits are reflected in the context of cross-border investigations (investigations conducted by the office across the territory of two or more Member States) where the Regulation provides for a specific set of rules,[114] which, at least on paper, may turn out to be more complex and less convenient than the new system of mutual legal assistance based on mutual recognition (the European Investigation Order, or EIO[115]).

4. Legality, Opportunity, and Negotiated Pretrial Alternatives

When it comes to the legality and opportunity principles, the EPPO Regulation endorsed a compromise solution. More precisely, the European legislator has opted for a moderate version of the opportunity principle: The EPPO will indeed be able to dismiss a case unconditionally on the basis of specific grounds[116] and with the authorization of the Permanent Chamber. However, in order to accommodate the potential tensions

[111] *See* E.P.P.O. Regulation, *supra* note 100, Art. 13, para. 1.

[112] On the structure set under the E.P.P.O. Regulation, *see* Peter Csonka et al., *The Establishment of the European Public Prosecutor's Office*, eucrim 127 (2017/3). For an analysis of the possible alternative models to establish an EPPO, see Katalin Ligeti & Michele Simonato, *The European Public Prosecutor's Office: Toward a Truly European Prosecution Service?*, 4 New J. Eur. Crim. L. 7 (2013).

[113] *See* E.P.P.O. Regulation, *supra* note 100, Art. 30, paras. 1, 2, 5.

[114] *See id.* Art. 31.

[115] *See* Directive 2014/41/EU on the European Investigation Order in criminal matters, 2014 O.J. (L 130) 1. Significantly, the EU legislator seems to openly suggest to the future EPPO the possibility and opportunity to resort to the EIO in the context of cross-border investigations: *See* E.P.P.O. Regulation, *supra* note 100, Art. 31 para. 6. For an analysis of the possible inconsistencies between the E.P.P.O. Regulation and the EIO Directive, see András Csuri, *Towards an Inconsistent European Regime of Cross-Border Evidence: The E.P.P.O. and the European Investigation Order*, *in* Geelhoed et al., *supra* note 105, at 41.

[116] E.P.P.O. Regulation, *supra* note 100, Art. 39. The dismissal must be authorized by the Permanent Chamber on the basis of the criteria listed in the Regulation.

with Member States following the legality principle, the Permanent Chamber is prevented from dismissing a case when the European Delegated Prosecutor intends—or is obliged by its national law—to bring the case to court.[117]

The possibility of the EPPO resorting to negotiated alternatives to trial, such as plea bargaining, transactions, or conditional dismissals, was the object of lengthy discussions during the negotiations of the Regulation. The compromise solution in the final text endorses a permissive, if rather minimalist, approach: The EPPO can resort to any "simplified prosecution procedure aiming at the final disposal of a case on the basis of terms agreed with the suspect" according to the national law of the relevant Member State. In order to trigger this power, the Permanent Chamber must grant an express authorization to the European Delegated Prosecutor on the basis of a set of criteria enumerated in the Regulation.[118] In the abstract, the criteria indicated in the Regulation appear sufficiently flexible to grant the EPPO a certain margin of discretion. However, also on this point, the reliance on national law as to the form and conditions attached to those procedures (for instance, the magnitude of the benefits in terms of a "discount" on the possible penalty) will probably determine several asymmetries and, what is more, different "chances" for the defendant.

VI. Concluding Remarks

Although, historically, the role and powers of the public prosecutor have been viewed differently by civil law and common law traditions, these initial differences between the two models have become relative over time as the two traditions have extensively borrowed from each other. Beyond historical borrowing between the systems, further uniformity of the criminal procedural systems in Europe was prompted by the harmonizing effect of the case law of the ECtHR and of EU legislation. Nevertheless, the historical roots of a criminal process remain important in conceptualizing the prosecution in a given country as they help to understand the logic and procedural values that underpin national solutions.

Probably the biggest remaining differences between civil law and common law traditions concern the role of the prosecutor in the pretrial phase and the role of the victim. In common law systems today, investigative activities are still ordinarily carried out by the police or other law enforcement authorities autonomously. The prosecutor steps in only at the end of an investigation to decide whether to bring the case to court. Civil law systems, on the other hand, assign a judicial actor to lead investigations: the public

[117] *See* E.P.P.O. Regulation, *supra* note 100, Art. 36 para. 1.

[118] *Id.* Art. 40. The criteria for the authorization by the Permanent Chamber are: (1) the seriousness of the offense, based on in particular the damage caused; (2) the willingness of the suspected offender to repair the damage caused by the illegal conduct; (3) the compatibility of the procedure with the general objectives and basic principles of the E.P.P.O. Regulation. The application of the criteria will be further specified by the EPPO College that will have to adopt specific guidelines in this regard.

prosecutor or, in some jurisdictions, the investigative judge (*juge d'instruction*). As far as the role of the victim is concerned, as mentioned in the introduction, whereas private prosecution represented the very starting point of the common law system, the role of the victim in European civil law systems has been and remains generally more limited and subsidiary to the role of the public prosecutor.

In contrast to these differences, the above analysis demonstrated that strong cross-overs are traceable in three areas: namely in the practical shaping of the legality and opportunity principles, the discretion of the prosecutor to determine criminal enforcement policy, and the growth in importance of specialized prosecution services. Whereas the exercise of discretion in choosing trial-worthy cases is an inherent feature of common law criminal justice systems, efficiency concerns and the need in several states to cope with increasing caseloads in criminal courts have prompted many civil law countries to gradually move toward the opportunity principle. The proliferation of the opportunity principle is also confirmed at the supranational level where the European legislator has opted for a moderate version thereof for the prosecutions of the EPPO. This is remarkable, since the main objective of the EPPO is to ensure uniform and equivalent protection of the EU's financial interests in the Area of Freedom, Security, and Justice. This objective can arguably best be served by establishing a duty to prosecute and by limiting the EPPO's margin of appreciation to establishing the sufficiency of evidence. Nevertheless, due to pressure by the Member States in the Council, the compromise prevailed for allowing discretion.

In addition to extended discretion for the prosecutor to select trial-worthy cases, we are also witnessing a growing trend—in both civil and common law traditions—of entrusting the public prosecutor with quasi-judicial sanctioning powers in the context of out-of-court and simplified procedures. Although this tendency is clearly identifiable in all criminal justice systems, the various procedural devices enabling "prosecutorial sentencing" may differ greatly. Due to the limited extent of judicial control to which those procedural determinations are subject they raise fundamental concerns.

Finally, the specialization of investigative and prosecutorial functions is a growing trend in both common law and civil law systems. With regard to organized crime and certain specific forms of criminality requiring a higher degree of expertise or greater internal and international coordination, several European states have established specialized offices or authorities with exclusive competence *ratione materiae*. A marked example of this tendency at the European level is the EPPO, conceived from the beginning as a highly specialized prosecution service dealing exclusively with offenses against the financial interests of the European Union.[119]

[119] Even the most recent debate to extend the material scope of competence of the EPPO to terrorism maintains that logic. As indicated by the Letter of Intent accompanying President Juncker's State of the Union speech of September 13, 2017, the Commission will issue in September 2018 a Communication on a possible extension of the EPPO's competences—with a 2025 perspective—to cross-border terrorist crimes, on the basis of Article 86(4) of the Treaty.

References

Sara Sun Beale, *Prosecutorial Discretion in Three Systems: Balancing Conflicting Goals and Providing Mechanisms for Control*, in *Discretionary Criminal Justice in a Comparative Context* 27 (Michele Caianello & Jacqueline Hodgson eds., 2015)

Candace McCoy, *Prosecution*, in *The Oxford Handbook of Crime and Criminal Justice* 667 (Michael Tonry ed., 2011)

Mirjan Damaska, *Structures of Authority and Comparative Criminal Procedure*, 84 Yale L.J. 480 (1975)

The Implementation of the Corpus Juris *in the Member States* (Mireille Delmas-Marty & John Vervaele eds., 2000)

Gwladys Gilliéron, *Public Prosecutors in the United States and Europe. A Comparative Analysis with Special Focus on Switzerland, France and Germany* (2013)

Coping with Overloaded Criminal Justice Systems. The Rise of Prosecutorial Power Across Europe (Jörg-Martin Jehle & Marianne Wade eds., 2006)

Toward a Prosecutor for the European Union (Katalin Ligeti ed., 2013)

The Prosecutor in a Transnational Perspective (Erik Luna & Marianne L. Wade eds., 2012)

John R. Spencer, *Introduction, in European Criminal Procedures* 1 (Mireille Delmas-Marty & John R. Spencer eds., 2002)

Thomas Weigend, *Prosecution: Comparative Aspects*, in 3 *Encyclopedia of Crime & Justice* 1235 (Joshua Dressler ed., 2d ed. 2002)

CHAPTER 8

DEFENSE RIGHTS IN EUROPEAN LEGAL SYSTEMS UNDER THE INFLUENCE OF THE EUROPEAN COURT OF HUMAN RIGHTS

THOMAS WEIGEND

I. Introduction

When the Member States of the Council of Europe agreed, in 1950, on a Convention for the Protection of Human Rights and Fundamental Freedoms (ECHR), they considered "that the aim of the Council of Europe is the achievement of greater unity between its members and that one of the methods by which that aim is to be pursued is the maintenance and further realization of Human Rights and Fundamental Freedoms."[1] For that purpose, art. 19 ECHR established a permanent European Court of Human Rights (ECtHR) with the purpose of ensuring "the observance of the engagements undertaken" by the Member States. The ECtHR has since assumed a highly active role in interpreting the rights enshrined in the Convention and in adapting them to the changing circumstances, true to the idea that the Convention is a "living instrument".[2] The ECtHR is precluded, however, from compelling Member States to change their domestic laws so that

[1] European Convention on Human Rights (ECHR), Preamble, recital 3.

[2] *See* Tyrer v. United Kingdom, App. No. 5856/72, Eur. Ct. H.R., Apr. 25, 1978, § 31. For an analysis of the Court's use of this phrase, see George Letsas, *The ECHR as a Living Instrument: Its Meaning and Legitimacy*, in *Constituting Europe: The European Court of Human Rights in a National, European and Global Context* 106–41 (Andreas Follesdal, Brigitte Peters & Geir Ulfstein eds., 2013).

they comply with the Convention as interpreted by the Court. Member States' compliance has thus remained an ongoing challenge within the scheme of the ECHR.

This chapter will focus on a particular aspect of Member States' compliance with ECtHR case law, namely the rights of suspects and defendants under Article 6 ECHR. This focus is justified in that more than 40 percent of ECtHR judgments between 1959 and 2016 found violations of Article 6 ECHR, by far the largest group of violations if analyzed by article of the ECHR.[3] Moreover, Article 6 ECHR has posed a particular challenge for the European Court's effort at unifying human rights standards because the Member States of the Council of Europe have adopted conceptually different models of criminal procedure, commonly (though inaptly[4]) named "inquisitorial" and "adversarial." The regime of Article 6(3) ECHR with regard to the criminal process however, having been drafted by British lawyers,[5] is molded in the "adversarial" style.[6] For example, the rights to have adequate time and facilities "for the preparation of his defence" (art. 6(3) (b) ECHR) and to "examine" prosecution witnesses (art. 6(3)(d) ECHR) presuppose an active role of the defense—which is indispensable for the proper functioning of an adversarial trial but not strictly necessary in an inquisitorial process in which the judge is tasked with establishing the truth even if the defendant remains passive throughout the process.

There thus exists an inherent tension between the inquisitorial model's emphasis on the court's responsibility for finding the "truth" and the insistence on empowering the defense as a means of ensuring the fairness of the trial in Article 6(3) ECHR. The ECtHR has attempted to ease that tension by establishing notions such as "equality of arms" between prosecution and defense and the defendant's right to an adversarial trial (*contradictoire*)[7] as overarching principles of the criminal process under the ECHR.[8] But the question remains whether and to what extent Member States adhering to their inquisitorial heritage are willing to incorporate the "adversarial" features of the Strasbourg Court's concept of a fair trial.

Among the multitude of aspects of Article 6 ECHR, this chapter will concentrate on the right of a suspect to be informed about the accusation against him (art. 6(3)(a) ECHR), the right to legal assistance at the early stages of the criminal process (art. 6(3)(c) ECHR),

[3] *See* European Court of Human Rights, Overview 1959–2016, at 6, *available at* http://www.echr.coe.int/Documents/Overview_19592016_ENG.pdf. The percentage includes violations concerning the length of proceedings, which are not treated in this chapter.

[4] At least since the middle of the nineteenth century, the criminal process in the states on the European Continent has not been conducted as a unilateral "inquisition" by a judicial officer, as may have been the case in earlier centuries, but the public or private prosecutor as well as the defendant are recognized as parties with certain rights and obligations.

[5] *See* William A. Schabas, *The European Convention on Human Rights. A Commentary* 6–7 (2015).

[6] Hans Nijboer, *Common Law Tradition in Evidence Scholarship Observed from a Continental Perspective*, 41 Am. J. Comp. L. 299, 311 (1993); John D. Jackson & Sarah J. Summers, *The Internationalisation of Criminal Evidence* 81 (2012).

[7] For the importance of "adversariness" as an element of fair proceedings, see Daniela Demko, *"Menschenrecht auf Verteidigung" und Fairness des Strafverfahrens auf nationaler, europäischer und internationaler Ebene* 347–50 (2014).

[8] For a detailed account, see Jackson & Summers, *supra* note 6, at 83–85, 101–03.

the privilege against self-incrimination (incorporated in the right to a fair hearing, art. 6(1) ECHR), and the right to examine adverse witnesses (art. 6(3)(d) ECHR). The chapter will briefly outline the European Court's case law on these issues and will then look into how this jurisprudence has been received by the legislation and judge-made law in two Member States, namely France and Germany. Although this brief and selective sketch cannot claim to even come close to a comprehensive study of the adaptation of Member States' laws to the jurisprudence of the ECtHR, some conclusions can be drawn as to conditions that favor a positive impact of the Strasbourg Court on the practice of Member States.

II. Individual Rights under Article 6 ECHR

1. Right to Be Informed of the Accusation

a. *Case Law of the ECtHR*

Article 6(3)(a) ECHR guarantees everyone charged with a criminal offense the right "to be informed promptly, in a language which he understands and in detail, of the nature and cause of the accusation against him." In order to prepare a useful defense, a suspect needs to know what he is accused of; he must therefore be informed not only of the acts that he is alleged to have committed but also of the legal characterisation of those acts.[9] The relevant information must be given at such a time and in such a manner as to enable the suspect to build his defense strategy on it.[10] As a rule, the information about the accusation must therefore be provided as soon as investigatory proceedings have been instituted.[11]

Like other rights of suspects under Article 6(3) ECHR, the Convention ties the right to information to the fact that a person has been "charged" with a criminal offense. It is clear that "charging" is not synonymous with the filing of a written accusation with the trial court. Employing an autonomous definition, the ECtHR considers a person to be "charged" from the time that he "is made aware by the competent authorities that he is suspected or accused of having committed a criminal offense."[12] The information about

[9] Pelissier and Sassi v. France, App. No. 25444/94, Eur. Ct. H.R., Mar. 25, 1999, § 51.

[10] Mattoccia v. Italy, App. No. 23969/94, Eur. Ct. H.R., July 25, 2000, §§ 59, 60.

[11] The suspect's right to be informed about the accusation at an early stage of criminal proceedings should be distinguished from the defendant's right to learn about the prosecution evidence before trial. The latter right also is a prerequisite of a fair trial, but its timing needs to be balanced against possible countervailing interests in protecting the confidentiality of all or some evidence. *See, e.g.*, Fitt v. United Kingdom, App. No. 29777/96, Eur. Ct. H.R., Feb. 16, 2000, §§ 44, 45.

[12] Cf. Imbrioscia v. Switzerland, App. No. 13972/88, Eur. Ct. H.R., Nov. 24, 1993, § 36; John Murray v. United Kingdom, App. No. 18731/91, Eur. Ct. H.R., Feb. 8, 1996, § 62.

a suspicion need not be conveyed by a formal order or decree of inculpation; it is sufficient that an official act, such as an arrest warrant signed by a judge, indicates that a particular person is suspected of a crime and that an investigation is taking place.

b. *Application of the Right in Member States*

In 2012, the European Parliament and the Council of the EU addressed the topic in the Directive on the right to information in criminal proceedings,[13] issued on the basis of Article. 82(2) of the Treaty on the Functioning of the European Union. In parallel with the ECHR, the EU Directive links the right to information to the suspect's ability to prepare his defense and to the fairness of the proceedings.[14] Regarding the time when the information is to be given, the Directive specifies that a suspect's right to know about the accusation is triggered as soon as he is made aware by the competent authorities that he is suspected or accused of having committed a criminal offense.[15] At that point, he must be informed about the criminal act he is suspected of having committed "in such detail as is necessary to safeguard the fairness of the proceedings and the effective exercise of the rights of the defence."[16] At the latest when the accusation is submitted to the court, the authorities must inform the defendant on the nature and legal classification of the offense as well as the nature of his alleged participation, and grant him access to all material evidence in their possession.[17]

According to *French* law, the relevant information must be provided whenever a criminal investigation against a person is initiated. If a suspect is apprehended on the spot while committing a criminal offense, or with obvious traces of the offense (*flagrant crîme ou délit*), he may be interrogated on the relevant suspicion only after having been informed of the date and place of the offense as well as its legal qualification.[18] Another way of starting criminal proceedings against a person is to take him into provisional arrest (*garde à vue*) for up to forty-eight hours, based on the suspicion that he may have committed a criminal offense punishable by imprisonment.[19] The police officer in charge of *garde à vue* is obliged to immediately inform the person of the time and date of the alleged offense as well as its legal qualification.[20] The same information must be provided when the prosecutor initiates a preliminary investigation (*enquête préliminaire*)[21] and when an investigating judge (*juge d'instruction*) summons a person for an initial interrogation with a view toward starting a judicial pretrial investigation against that person. The judge must in the written summons and again orally at the beginning of the

[13] Directive 2012/13/EU of 22 May 2012 on the right to information in criminal proceedings, 2012 O.J. (L 142) 1 [hereinafter Directive 2012/13/EU of 22 May 2012].

[14] *Id.* Preamble recital 27.

[15] *Id.* art. 2(1). [16] *Id.* art. 6(1). [17] *Id.* arts. 6(3) and 7(2), (3).

[18] Art. 61-1(1°) French *Code de Procédure Pénale* [CPP] [Code of Criminal Procedure] (Fr.).

[19] Arts. 62-2, 63 (II) CPP (Fr.).

[20] Art. 63-1(1) (2°) CPP (Fr.). If the prosecutor determines that the legal qualification indicated by the police officer was not accurate, the suspect must subsequently be given the correct information; art. 63(I) CPP (Fr.).

[21] Art. 77 CCP (Fr.).

interrogation inform the suspect of the facts submitted to her for investigation by the prosecutor as well as the legal qualification of those facts.[22]

German law appears to be similar: A person under suspicion must at the beginning of his first interrogation be informed of what offense he is charged with and which provisions of the criminal law may be applicable.[23] This obligation applies to judges, prosecutors, and police officers, but police are not required to inform about the applicable legal provisions,[24] because they may not have sufficient legal expertise.[25] Moreover, any judicial warrant ordering the arrest of a suspect must contain a statement as to the time and place of the suspected offense, the applicable legal provisions, and the elements of the offense. As soon as the suspect has been arrested, he is given a copy of the judicial warrant.[26]

German law thus seems to be in compliance with international standards. Yet, there is no obligation for the prosecutor or the police to inform a suspect that a criminal investigation concerning him has been started. Section 163a(I) of the German Code of Criminal Procedure (Strafprozessordnung, *hereinafter* StPO) provides only that a suspect needs to be interrogated *before the end* of an investigation leading to an indictment. This means that the police and the prosecutor may defer a suspect's interrogation—and consequently, his information about the possible charges—until the very end of the investigation. This tactic seriously restricts the suspect's defense rights, which after all apply even during the investigation phase. Since Section 163a(I) StPO also provides that the suspect need not be interrogated if the proceedings are dismissed, the prosecutor and the police may conduct a lengthy investigation against a suspect and dismiss the case (for lack of evidence or for other reasons) without ever informing him of the investigation.[27] In that case, the suspect will never learn what he had been accused of.

This state of the law reflects the ancient inquisitorial system of the nineteenth century: the suspect is treated not as a party of the proceedings but as a mere object of a secret investigation.[28] In practice, German police and prosecutors seem to prefer an open style of investigating criminal offenses and do not as a rule attempt to keep the investigation concealed from the suspect for any extensive period. This may explain the fact that no case against Germany seems yet to have been brought before the ECtHR challenging the option of keeping the investigation concealed from the suspect as a violation of Article 6(3)(a) ECHR.

[22] Arts. 80-2(1), 116(1) CPP (Fr.).

[23] § 136(1) German *Strafprozessordnung* [StPO] [Code of Criminal Procedure] (Ger.).

[24] § 163a(4) StPO (Ger.).

[25] *See* Klaus Rogall, in *Systematischer Kommentar zur Strafprozessordnung* § 136 note 40 (Jürgen Wolter ed., 5th ed. 2016).

[26] §§ 114(2) 2nd sent., 114a StPO (Ger.).

[27] The prosecutor is required to inform the suspect of the dismissal of prosecution for lack of sufficient evidence only if the suspect had been interrogated or arrested, had specifically asked for a notice of dismissal, or if his particular interest in notification is "evident"; § 170(2) StPO (Ger.).

[28] For a critical assessment, see Ferdinand Gillmeister, *Rechtliches Gehör im Ermittlungsverfahren*, StrafverteidigerForum 114, 115 (1996).

The question whether German law violates Article 6(3)(a) ECHR depends on the definition of what it means to be "charged" with an offense. As has been pointed out above, "charging" presupposes, as a rule, an official communication to the suspect of the fact that he is under investigation. According to that definition, Article 6(3)(a) ECHR does not provide an effective protection against an investigation carried out in complete secrecy. This raises the question of whether Article 6(3) ECHR inherently conveys a *right to be charged*, so that the suspect would have to be informed in due course of the existence of a suspicion on the part of the police or prosecution.[29] Although the recognition of such a right would enhance the suspect's chance of promptly being informed of the accusation, it might raise difficult questions in practice. Since suspicion exists only in the mind of an observer, it would not be clear whose (personal) suspicion would trigger the obligation to inform the suspect. Moreover, since the facts and their assessment by police officers or prosecutors may change over time, it might be useful to require a certain strength or degree of suspicion. Finally, there may be legitimate grounds for not alerting a person to the fact that he is suspected of a crime, for example, the need to initially collect information without his knowledge or to prevent the suspect from putting pressure on witnesses. Given these considerations, a suspect's right to be informed of the charges should be tied to his legitimate interest in conducting an effective defense: he must be charged and provided the requisite information as soon as it is necessary for him to become active in his defense.[30]

2. Right to Counsel at the Initial Stage of the Investigation (Article 6(3)(c) ECHR)

a. *Case Law of the ECtHR*

According to Article 6(3)(c) ECHR, everyone charged with a criminal offense has the right to defend himself "through legal assistance of his own choosing." While the right to have the assistance of a lawyer at the criminal trial has never been in question, Member States had different rules as to the right to a lawyer in the initial stages of the criminal process, especially during or before police interrogations. In its landmark 2008 decision in *Salduz v. Turkey*, the ECtHR held that the right of a person "charged" (i.e., notified of the suspicion against him) to have access to a lawyer at the police station is a necessary element of a fair trial:

> (T)he Court finds that in order for the right to a fair trial to remain sufficiently "practical and effective", Article 6 § 1 requires that, as a rule, access to a lawyer should be provided as from the first interrogation of a suspect by the police, unless it is

[29] For an argument in favor of such a right, see Helmut Frister, *Der Anspruch des Beschuldigten auf Mitteilung der Beschuldigung aus Art. 6 Abs. 3 lit. a EMRK*, 18 Strafverteidiger 159, 160–61 (1998).

[30] Cf. Robert Esser, in *Die Strafprozessordnung und das Gerichtsverfassungsgesetz. Großkommentar* art. 6 EMRK note 548 (Ewald Löwe & Werner Rosenberg eds., 26th ed. 2012).

> demonstrated in the light of the particular circumstances of each case that there are compelling reasons to restrict this right. (...) The rights of the defence will in principle be irretrievably prejudiced when incriminating statements made during police interrogation without access to a lawyer are used for a conviction.[31]

Because the holding of *Salduz* was qualified in several ways,[32] the judgment left open a few issues of practical as well as theoretical importance. In subsequent cases, the ECtHR provided certain specifications: It is not sufficient that the suspect is permitted to talk with a lawyer before being interrogated, but the lawyer must be given the right to *attend* the interrogation;[33] the lawyer must moreover be afforded an opportunity to speak up in order to defend the suspect's rights.[34] Article 6(3)(c) ECHR further requires that the suspect be informed of his right to contact a lawyer before being questioned.[35] An express or tacit waiver of the right to counsel is generally acceptable, but the suspect's declaration in that regard requires prior information of his right to counsel; the waiver must be unequivocal and be attended by minimum safeguards commensurate to its importance.[36] The fact that a suspect, having been denied counsel, remained silent during police questioning does not prevent a finding that his rights under Article 6(3) ECHR had been violated; the assistance of a lawyer is not only necessary for protecting the suspect's right to silence, but counsel should also be in a position to actively secure fundamental aspects of the defense: "discussion of the case, organisation of the defence, collection of evidence favourable to the accused, preparation for questioning, support of an accused in distress and checking of the conditions of detention."[37]

The ECtHR also needed to resolve doubts concerning possible exceptions to the right to counsel at the police stage. In *Salduz*, the Court had noted that the right to contact a lawyer before the first police interrogation could be restricted for "compelling reasons," but also emphasized that any restriction must not unduly prejudice the rights of the accused.[38] In the 2016 case of *Ibrahim and Others v. United Kingdom*, which concerned

[31] Salduz v. Turkey, App. No. 36391/02, Eur. Ct. H.R., Nov. 27, 2008, § 55.

[32] The few operative sentences of the judgment are interspersed with qualifiers such as "as a rule," "in principle," "unless it is demonstrated in the light of the particular circumstances of each case that there are compelling reasons to restrict this right"; see *Salduz v. Turkey*, 36391/02, Eur. Ct. H.R., Nov. 27, 2008, § 55.

[33] *See, e.g.*, Brusco v. France, App. No. 1466/07, Eur. Ct. H.R., Oct.14, 2010, § 45; Sebalj v. Croatia, App. No. 4429/09, Eur. Ct. H.R., June 28, 2011, §§ 254–256; Yuriy Volkov v. Ukraine, App. No. 45872/06, Eur. Ct. H.R., Dec. 19, 2013, § 67.

[34] Aras v. Turkey No. 2, App. No. 15065/07, Eur. Ct. H.R., Nov. 18, 2014, § 40.

[35] Ibrahim and Others v. United Kingdom, App. No. 50541/08, Eur. Ct. H.R., Sept. 13, 2016, §§ 272–273; Simeonovi v. Bulgaria, App. No. 21980/04, Eur. Ct. H.R., May 12, 2017, § 119.

[36] Panovits v. Cyprus, App. No. 4268/04, Eur. Ct. H.R., Dec. 11, 2008, §§ 68, 72; Pishchalnikov v. Russia, App No. 7025/04, Eur. Ct. H.R., Sept. 24, 2009, § 77; Sakhnovskiy v. Russia, App. No. 21272/03, Eur. Ct. H.R., Nov. 2, 2010, § 90; Simeonovi v. Bulgaria, App. No. 21980/04, Eur. Ct. H.R., May 12, 2017, § 115.

[37] Dayanan v. Turkey, App. No. 7377/03, Eur. Ct. H.R., Oct. 13, 2009, § 32; A.T. v. Luxembourg, App. No. 30460/13, Eur. Ct. H.R., Apr. 9, 2015, § 64. For an assessment of the relevance of this statement, see John D. Jackson, *Cultural Barriers on the Road to Providing Suspects with Access to a Lawyer*, in *EU Criminal Justice and the Challenges of Diversity* 181, 194–95 (Renaud Colson & Stewart Field eds., 2016).

[38] Salduz v. Turkey, App. No. 36391/02, Eur. Ct. H.R., Nov. 27, 2008, § 55.

the interrogation, without legal assistance, of suspected terrorists for the alleged purpose of obviating continuing threats to public safety, the ECtHR explained that "restrictions on access to legal advice are permitted only in exceptional circumstances, must be of a temporary nature and must be based on an individual assessment of the particular circumstances of the case."[39] Domestic law must sufficiently circumscribe the scope and content of any restriction so as to guide operational decision-making by the police.[40] An urgent need to avert serious adverse consequences for life, liberty, or physical integrity qualifies as "compelling circumstances."[41] Yet, even where no compelling reasons for restricting access to legal advice were present, the trial as a whole may still have been "fair" if the restriction of access to legal advice did not prejudice the rights of the defense.[42]

As a rule, statements the suspect makes to the police in the absence of a lawyer must not be used as evidence against him, unless the suspect had validly waived his right to legal assistance.[43] Yet the ECtHR, in *Ibrahim and Others v. United Kingdom*, found that the right to counsel had been infringed, and still regarded the conviction of the defendants on the basis of their statements to the police (among other evidence) not to be unfair, taking into account the conduct of the proceedings as a whole.[44]

The *Salduz* court cited a variety of rationales for its decision, and it is not easy to decide which of these—unrelated—grounds the Court regarded as determinative. In fact, none of the mentioned rationales permits, by itself, a consistent explanation of the rule that a suspect may demand the advice and presence of a lawyer at his first (and any subsequent) police interview. If the emphasis is put on protecting the suspect against possible coercion, it is difficult to explain why the right to counsel is limited to interrogations and not extended to other possibly incriminating interactions, for example, identity parades or the extraction of body liquids.[45] Nor does this rationale explain the Court's view that the right to counsel under Article 6(3)(c) ECHR is violated even if the suspect does not make any statement to the police.[46] A more convincing explanation of *Salduz* and its progeny may lie in the insight that the "critical" phase in which the accused needs a lawyer most has moved forward from the trial to the police investigation, since

[39] Restrictions imposed by a systemic rule of domestic law have therefore been held to be inconsistent with the right to a fair trial; see Navone and Others v. Monaco, App. No. 62880/11, Eur. Ct. H.R., Oct. 24, 2013,§ 80; A.T. v. Luxembourg, App. No. 30460/13, Eur. Ct. H.R., Apr. 9, 2015, § 69.

[40] Ibrahim and Others v. United Kingdom, App. No. 50541/08, Eur. Ct. H.R., Sept. 13, 2016, § 258; Loboda v. Ukraine, App. No.8865/06, Eur. Ct. H.R., Nov. 17, 2016, § 33.

[41] Ibrahim and Others v. United Kingdom, App. No. 50541/08, Eur. Ct. H.R., Sept. 13, 2016, § 259.

[42] It is for the state to demonstrate the overall fairness in spite of the restriction of access to counsel; Ibrahim and Others v. United Kingdom, App. No.50541/08, Eur. Ct. H.R., Sept. 13, 2016, § 265; Loboda v. Ukraine, App. No.8865/06, Eur. Ct. H.R., Nov. 17, 2016, § 36.

[43] Panovits v. Cyprus, App. No.4268/04, Eur. Ct. H.R., Dec. 11, 2008, § 86.

[44] *See* the comprehensive analysis in Ibrahim and Others v. United Kingdom, App. No.50541/08, Eur. Ct. H.R., Sept. 13, 2016, §§ 280–294.

[45] John D. Jackson, *Responses to Salduz: Procedural Tradition, Change and the Need for Effective Defence*, 79 Modern L. Rev. 987, 1006–07 (2016).

[46] Dayanan v. Turkey, App. No.7377/03, Eur. Ct. H.R., Oct. 13, 2009, § 32; A.T. v. Luxembourg, App. No. 30460/13, Eur. Ct. H.R., Apr. 9, 2015, § 64.

evidence gathered at that early stage can easily be introduced at the trial and determine its outcome.[47]

b. *Application of the Right in Member States*

The European Union has responded to the European Court's *Salduz* judgment in 2013 by issuing a Directive on the right of access to a lawyer.[48]

Article 3(2) of the Directive fixes in detail the point in time at which the right to counsel attaches:

> Suspects or accused persons shall have access to a lawyer without undue delay. In any event, suspects or accused persons shall have access to a lawyer from whichever of the following points in time is the earliest: (a) before they are questioned by the police or by another law enforcement or judicial authority; (b) upon the carrying out by investigating or other competent authorities of an investigative or other evidence-gathering act in accordance with point (c) of paragraph 3[49] (...).

Article 3(3) of the Directive reflects the jurisprudence of the ECtHR with regard to the role of the lawyer at investigative acts:

> (a) Member States shall ensure that suspects or accused persons have the right to meet in private and communicate with the lawyer representing them, including prior to questioning by the police or by another law enforcement or judicial authority;
> (b) Member States shall ensure that suspects or accused persons have the right for their lawyer to be present and participate effectively when questioned. Such participation shall be in accordance with procedures under national law, provided that such procedures do not prejudice the effective exercise and essence of the right concerned. (...)

Concerning subparagraph (a) of art. 3 (3) of the Directive, the Strasbourg Court has never left any doubt of its view that an effective defense presupposes the possibility of confidential communication between the lawyer and his client.[50] Article 4 of the

[47] Cf. Yuriy Volkov v. Ukraine, App. No. 45872/06, Eur. Ct. H.R., Dec. 19, 2013, § 60; A.T. v. Luxembourg, App. No. 30460/13, Eur. Ct. H.R., Apr. 9, 2015, § 62.

[48] Directive 2013/48/EU of 22 October 2013 on the right of access to a lawyer in criminal proceedings and in European arrest warrant proceedings, and on the right to have a third party informed upon deprivation of liberty and to communicate with third persons and with consular authorities while deprived of liberty, 2013 O.J. (L 294) 1 [hereinafter Directive 2013/48/EU of 22 October 2013].

[49] Article 3(3)(c) of Directive 2013/48/EU of 22 October 2013 lists identity parades, confrontations, and reconstructions of the scene of a crime, thus extending the right to counsel to certain acts that imply a risk of (self-)incrimination even though no interrogation of the suspect takes place.

[50] *See, e.g.*, Brennan v. United Kingdom, App. No.39846/98, Eur. Ct. H.R., Oct. 16, 2001, § 58; Castravet v. Moldova, App. No. 23393/05, Eur. Ct. H.R., June 13, 2007, §§ 49–50. Jackson & Summers, *supra* note 6, at 291–92, point out, however, that the ECtHR will find a violation of fair trial only if the complainant can show that a denial of unsupervised communication with his lawyer negatively affected the effectiveness of his defense.

Directive re-enforces the protection of confidentiality between the suspect and his lawyer, albeit with certain reservations.[51]

Subsection (b) provides for an effective participation on the lawyer's part, which is a welcome step toward guaranteeing an active defense even at the first stage of the criminal process. However, the following sentence—inserted on the behest of the EU Council—more or less leaves the application of this principle to the discretion of Member States, whose national procedures are to prevail unless they "prejudice the effective exercise and essence" of the right to participation. The retreat from an earlier draft version, which had unambiguously afforded the lawyer the right to ask questions, request clarification, and make statements, has met with well-placed criticism.[52]

A further "escape clause" is contained in Article 3(6) of the Directive, which provides:

> In exceptional circumstances and only at the pre-trial stage, Member States may temporarily derogate from the application of the rights provided for in paragraph 3 to the extent justified in the light of the particular circumstances of the case, on the basis of one of the following compelling reasons:
>
> (a) where there is an urgent need to avert serious adverse consequences for the life, liberty or physical integrity of a person;
>
> (b) where immediate action by the investigating authorities is imperative to prevent substantial jeopardy to criminal proceedings.

Especially Article 3(6)(b) of the Directive, permitting Member States to temporarily block a suspect's access to counsel in order to prevent undefined "substantial jeopardy to criminal proceedings," although reminiscent of the ECtHR's language in *Ibrahim and Others v. UK*,[53] has the potential of affecting the very essence of the right to counsel.

In sum, it seems fair to say that the EU Directive on the right of access to a lawyer in criminal proceedings makes a halfhearted effort toward implementing *Salduz* and its progeny in the law of the EU Member States, leaving many critical decisions to their domestic legislation. Several Member States of the Council of Europe had, however, taken action even before the EU Directive was issued.[54]

[51] Directive 2013/48/EU of 22 October 2013, art. 4 provides: "Member States shall respect the confidentiality of communication between suspects or accused persons and their lawyer in the exercise of the right of access to a lawyer provided for under this Directive. Such communication shall include meetings, correspondence, telephone conversations and other forms of communication permitted under national law." The clause "permitted under national law" opens the door for restrictions based on national preferences. For criticism, see Ilias Anagnostopoulos, *The Right of Access to a Lawyer in Europe: A Long Road Ahead?* 4 Eur. Crim. L. Rev. 3, 15 (2014).

[52] Anagnostopoulos, *supra* note 51, at 11; Jackson, *supra* note 45, at 1012.

[53] *See* Ibrahim and Others v. United Kingdom, App. No. 50541/08, Eur. Ct. H.R., Sept. 13, 2016, §§ 262–265 (explaining that withholding access to counsel even without "compelling reasons" does not necessarily make proceedings unfair).

[54] For a comprehensive analysis of developments in several Member States (Belgium, Ireland, Netherlands, Scotland, and United Kingdom), see Dimitrios Giannoulopoulos, *Strasbourg Jurisprudence, Law Reform and Comparative Law: A Tale of the Right to Custodial Legal Assistance in Five Countries*, 16 Hum. Rts. L. Rev. 103 (2016) and Jackson, *supra* note 45, at 1012.

France has had a long tradition of *garde à vue*, the detention of persons that the police wishes to interview. During *garde à vue*—which may last, with prosecutorial approval, for up to forty-eight hours[55]—suspects were not permitted to have any contact with a lawyer.[56] This has been changed by a law passed in 2011 that amended the relevant provisions of the French Code of Criminal Procedure.[57]

The present state of French law largely reflects the case law of the ECtHR. Any person under suspicion of having committed a criminal offense punishable by imprisonment and interrogated on the spot by a police officer has the right to be assisted by a lawyer during the interrogation, and must be informed of that right.[58] If a person suspected of having committed an offense is taken into *garde à vue*[59] he must be informed that he has the right to be assisted by a lawyer.[60] If the suspect does not know the name of a suitable lawyer, he can ask the bailiff to find one for him.[61] The suspect may consult with the lawyer confidentially for thirty minutes during each twenty-four-hour-period of detention.[62] Since 2016, the suspect can demand that the lawyer be present during the interrogation. In that case, the questioning may, as a rule, start only two hours after the lawyer has been informed of the suspect's request for her assistance. If the lawyer arrives at the place of *garde à vue* more than two hours later and after questioning has started, the suspect may demand a break for consulting with counsel, and/or the lawyer may be present for the remainder of the interrogation.[63] If an immediate interrogation is necessary, the prosecutor may authorize questioning the suspect without counsel before two hours have elapsed.[64] Only in exceptional circumstances may the prosecutor or the judge of the investigation[65] permit, by written decree, an interrogation without the suspect having access to legal assistance; this is permissible if necessary for making it possible for police to obtain or retain evidence, or for obviating a serious and imminent risk to the life, health, or liberty of a person.[66] However, the *Article préliminaire* of the French

[55] Art. 63(2) CPP (Fr.).

[56] For descriptions of the pre-*Salduz* situation in France, see Jacqueline Hodgson, *Constructing the Pre-trial Role of the Defence in French Criminal Procedure*, 6 Int'l J. Evidence & Proof 1 (2002); Jacqueline Hodgson, *French Criminal Justice: A Comparative Account of the Investigation and Prosecution of Crime in France* 39 (2005).

[57] Loi no. 2011–392 du 14 April 2011 relative à la garde à vue. This law had been inspired by decisions of the French *Conseil constitutionnel* and the *Cour de cassation*, which had urged the legislature to adapt the *Code de procédure pénale* to the jurisprudence of the ECtHR; see Conseil constitutionnel, Décision n° 2010-14/22 QPC du 30 juillet 2010, nos. 28–29 (declaring unconstitutional the *garde à vue* without access to a lawyer); Cour de cassation, no. 10–17.049, 15 April 2011, Recueil Dalloz 2011, 1080.

[58] Art. 61-1(1)(5°) CPP (Fr.).

[59] The legal rules on access to lawyers applicable in the case of *garde à vue* also apply to other instances of prosecutorial investigation; see art. 77 CPP (Fr.).

[60] Art. 63-1(1) (3°) CPP (Fr.). [61] Art. 63-3-1(1) CPP (Fr.). [62] Art. 63-4(1)–(3) CPP (Fr.).

[63] Art. 63-4-2(1), (2) CPP (Fr.). [64] Art. 63-4-2 (3) CPP (Fr.).

[65] The prosecutor may defer access to counsel for twelve hours; the judge may do so for twenty-four hours; art. 63-4-2 (5) CPP (Fr.).

[66] Art. 63-4-2(4) CPP (Fr.). The second strand of the standards for allowing exceptions to the suspect's right to the assistance of counsel is in conformity with the ECtHR's judgment in *Ibrahim and Others v. United Kingdom*, App. No. 50541/08, Eur. Ct. H.R., Sept. 13, 2016, §§ 258–259. It is questionable, however, whether *Ibrahim* permits the broad exception in favor of obtaining evidence that is provided in art. 63-4-2(4) CPP (Fr.).

Code of Criminal Procedure provides that no one may be convicted of a non-petty criminal offense on the sole basis of statements he made without having had access to a lawyer.[67]

Contrary to French tradition, the present version of the Code of Criminal Procedure permits the lawyer to ask additional questions when the officer has finished his interrogation.[68] The lawyer's questions may be rejected, however, if they are found to be harmful to the orderly conduct of the investigation.[69] As long as the *garde à vue* lasts, the lawyer must not disclose any information about the interrogation to other persons.[70]

Germany has struggled less than France with granting suspects access to legal advice. The German Code of Criminal Procedure (*Strafprozessordnung*, StPO), which dates from 1877 (and has since been amended many times), affords suspects (*Beschuldigte*[71]) the right to use the services of a lawyer at any stage of the proceedings.[72] At the beginning of his first interrogation, a suspect must be advised of his right to consult with a defense lawyer even before the interrogation starts.[73] Since 2017, if the suspect indicates that he wishes to consult with a lawyer, he must be given information that makes it easier for him to establish contact with a lawyer, especially about existing emergency consultation services organized by the local bar.[74] If the suspect declares that he wishes to speak with a lawyer, the police must offer the suspect the opportunity to contact a lawyer and is prohibited from continuing with the interrogation.[75] The same applies if an attorney has informed the police that she is on her way to the police station.[76] The suspect may still waive his right to counsel;[77] but if the suspect, while waiting for the arrival of his lawyer, makes a single remark on a circumstance that is peripheral to the offense charged, that cannot be interpreted as a tacit waiver of the right to counsel.[78]

Until 2017, German law limited suspects arrested by police to *consulting* with a lawyer but did not grant counsel the right to *attend* the client's police interview.[79] This has been

[67] Article préliminaire (3), recital 7 CPP (Fr.).

[68] E contrario, this provision means that the lawyer is not entitled to interrupting the officer's interrogation by asking questions; cf. Giannoulopoulos, *supra* note 54, at 103, 118.

[69] Art. 63-4-3(2) CPP (Fr.) ("si celles-ci sont de nature à nuire au bon déroulement de l'enquête"). If questions have been rejected, the lawyer may include them in the written memorandum that he can submit to the prosecutor; art. 63-4-3(3) CPP) (Fr.).

[70] Art. 63-4-4 CPP (Fr.).

[71] German courts have interpreted the term *Beschuldigte* in a fashion very similar to the ECtHR's definition of a person "charged" with an offense; see Federal Court of Justice [*Bundesgerichtshof*, BGH] 1 StR 493/06, Nov. 29, 2006, 51 Entscheidungen des Bundesgerichtshofes in Strafsachen [BGHSt] 150.

[72] § 137(1) StPO (Ger.).

[73] § 136(1) StPO (Ger.). The obligation to inform the suspect of his right to consult with a lawyer extends to prosecutors as well as police officers; § 163a (4) StPO (Ger.).

[74] § 136(1), 3rd and 4th sent. StPO (Ger.).

[75] BGH, 4 StR 126/92, Oct. 29, 1992, 38 BGHSt 372, 373 nos. 5–6; BGH, 5 StR 341/05, Jan. 10 2006, no. 18.

[76] BGH, StB 4/08, 5/08, May 15, 2008, Neue Zeitschrift für Strafrecht 643 (2008).

[77] BGH, 5 StR 176/14, Oct. 20, 2014, no. 9, Neue Juristische Wochenschrift 722 (2014).

[78] BGH, 3 StR 435/12, June 27, 2013, nos. 12–19, 58 BGHSt 301.

[79] §§ 168c(5) and 163a(3) StPO (Ger.) provided that counsel had a right to be present whenever the suspect was interrogated by a judge or a prosecutor. § 163a(4) StPO (Ger.), which regulated police interrogations, did not refer to these provisions.

changed by an amendment to Section 163a (4) StPO, which now expressly affords the lawyer the right to be present during police interrogations of his client, thus bringing German law into conformity with the ECtHR's *Salduz* jurisprudence. There had never been any doubt that counsel, if he attends an interrogation of the suspect, may ask questions and make comments.[80] If the defendant has been denied the right to counsel, her statements made in absence of her lawyer must not be used as evidence over the defendant's objection.[81]

In sum, one can say that both French and German law have, although with a certain delay, amended their laws such that they reflect the jurisprudence of the ECtHR as well as the EU Directive on access to a lawyer.

3. Privilege against Self-Incrimination

a. *Case Law of the ECtHR*

The right of a suspect to refuse to provide information that can be used for convicting him ("privilege against self-incrimination") has not been explicitly incorporated in the European Convention on Human Rights.[82] Still, the ECtHR stated that "there can be no doubt that the right to remain silent under police questioning and the privilege against self-incrimination are generally recognised international standards which lie at the heart of the notion of a fair procedure under Article 6."[83] The ECtHR has however failed to provide a clear and convincing rationale for the privilege,[84] and has consequently vacillated with respect to its scope. On the one hand, the Court based the privilege against self-incrimination on the need to protect the suspect[85] against improper compulsion and to avoid "miscarriages of justice."[86] On the other hand, the Court indicated that the right is "closely linked to the presumption of innocence contained in art. 6 para. 2 of the Convention" in that it "presupposes that the prosecution in a criminal case seek to prove

[80] *See* Lutz Meyer-Goßner & Bertram Schmitt, *Strafprozessordnung. Kommentar* § 168c StPO note 1 (60th ed. 2017); Mark A. Zöller, in *Strafprozessordnung. Heidelberger Kommentar* § 168c note 3 (Björn Gercke et al. eds., 5th ed. 2012).

[81] BGH, 5 StR 576/94, Jan. 12, 1996 nos. 17–19, 42 BGHSt 15.

[82] *But see* Art. 14(3)(g) Int. Covenant on Civil and Political Rights ("In the determination of any criminal charge against him, everyone shall be entitled to the following minimum guarantees, in full equality: . . . (g) Not to be compelled to testify against himself or to confess guilt.").

[83] John Murray v. United Kingdom, App. No. 18731/91, Eur. Ct. H.R., Feb. 8, 1996, § 45. In the earlier judgment in *Funke v. France*, App. No. 10828/84, Eur. Ct. H.R., Feb. 25, 1993, § 44, the Court had assumed, without further explanation, that everyone charged with an offense has a right "to remain silent and not to contribute to incriminating himself".

[84] Mike Redmayne, *Rethinking the Privilege Against Self-Incrimination*, 27 Oxford J. Legal Stud. 209, 210 (2007).

[85] The ECtHR has consistently limited the privilege against self-incrimination to persons charged with a criminal offense; see Zaichenko v. Russia, App. No. 39660/02, Eur. Ct. H.R., Feb. 18, 2010, § 52.

[86] John Murray v. United Kingdom, App. No. 18731/91, Eur. Ct. H.R., Feb. 8, 1996, § 45.

their case against the accused without resort to evidence obtained through methods of coercion or oppression in defiance of the will of the accused."[87]

Since the privilege against self-incrimination is not listed among the specifically guaranteed defense rights in Article 6(3) ECHR, the Court submits the issue to its general approach toward establishing the overall fairness of the proceedings in accordance with Article 6(1) ECHR. This means that a person's interest in withholding incriminating information is subject to balancing against other important interests, including "the nature and degree of compulsion used to obtain the evidence; the weight of the public interest in the investigation and punishment of the offence in issue; the existence of any relevant safeguards in the procedure; and the use to which any material so obtained is put."[88] Proceedings are "absolutely" unfair only if a sanction imposed by the state on the suspect for remaining silent has "in effect destroyed the very essence of [the] privilege against self-incrimination and [the] right to remain silent".[89]

In addition to the uncertainty caused by the Court's predilection for "balancing" in the context of a fair trial analysis,[90] even issues concerning the scope of the privilege have not been resolved in a consistent fashion.[91] For example, some judgments seem to extend the right only to verbal statements,[92] others include the compelled production of documents,[93] and even the forced regurgitation of the contents of a person's stomach.[94] The question of what constitutes "compulsion" has likewise been given contradictory answers. Whereas the Court in *Heaney and McGuinness v. Ireland* held that the imposition of a criminal penalty for withholding certain (potentially self-incriminating) information violated the "very essence" of the privilege against self-incrimination,[95] it declared seven years later that the imposition of a criminal fine on a motorist for not disclosing the identity of the driver of a car registered under his name was compatible with Article 6(1) ECHR.[96] The Strasbourg Court has, moreover, given wide latitude to Member States (especially the United Kingdom) to employ indirect compulsion on suspects to respond to police questioning. The ECtHR has generally accepted the practice of English trial judges to alert the jury to the fact that the defendant made use of his right

[87] Saunders v. UK, App. No. 19187/91, Eur. Ct. H.R., Dec. 17, 1996, § 68. *See also* J.B. v. Switzerland, App. No. 31827/96, Eur. Ct. H.R., May 3, 2001, § 64; Panovits v. Cyprus, App. No. 4268/04, Eur. Ct. H.R., Dec. 11, 2008, § 65.

[88] Jalloh v. Germany, App. No. 54810/00, Eur. Ct. H.R., July 11, 2006, § 117; O'Halloran and Francis v. United Kingdom, App. Nos. 15809/02 and 25624/02, Eur. Ct. H.R., June 29, 2007, § 55.

[89] Heaney and McGuinness v. Ireland, App. No. 34720/97, Eur. Ct. H.R., Dec. 21, 2000, § 55.

[90] For criticism, see Andrew L-T Choo, *The Privilege Against Self-Incrimination and Criminal Justice* 115 (2014).

[91] For a helpful overview, see Frank Meyer, in *EMRK. Kommentar* Art. 6 notes 127–147 (Ulrich Karpenstein & Franz C. Mayer eds., 2012).

[92] Saunders v. United Kingdom, App. No. 19187/91, Eur. Ct. H.R., Dec. 17, 1996, § 69.

[93] Funke v. France, App. No. 10828/84, Eur. Ct. H.R., Feb. 25, 1993, § 44; J.B. v. Switzerland, App. No. 31827/96, Eur. Ct. H.R., May 3, 2001, § 71.

[94] Jalloh v. Germany, App. No. 54810/00, Eur. Ct. H.R., July 11, 2006, §§ 113–116.

[95] Heaney and McGuinness v. Ireland, App. No. 34720/97, Eur. Ct. H.R., Dec. 21, 2000, § 55.

[96] O'Halloran and Francis v. United Kingdom, App. Nos. 15809/02 and 25624/02, Eur. Ct. H.R., June 29, 2007, §§ 53, 57.

to silence when confronted with questions by the police early in the investigation.[97] In support of its deference, the ECtHR has argued that drawing inferences from the accused's silence "constitutes [...] a formalised system which aims at allowing common-sense implications to play an open role in the assessment of evidence."[98] While this practice may indeed reflect the existing mind processes of judges and jurors, the ECtHR by giving its seal of approval to it in fact permits "a penalty to be imposed by a criminal court on an accused because he relies upon a procedural right guaranteed by the Convention."[99]

The unsatisfactory state of the Court's jurisprudence may well have to do with the lack of a consistent rationale for the privilege against self-incrimination. This is, however, a general problem of the privilege, which haunts not only the ECtHR but national legislatures and theorists as well.[100] It is not clear whether a suspect (or indeed any other person) is to be protected from compulsion to incriminate himself because such compulsion would interfere with the integrity of the criminal process, with individual rights and/or the dignity of the person affected, or with the suspect's ability to mount an effective defense.[101]

b. *Application of the Right in Member States*

The European Union has in 2016 issued a Directive that covers, among other rights of suspects and accused persons, the right to remain silent and the right not to incriminate oneself.[102] The Directive reflects, by and large, the case law of the ECtHR and thus compels EU Member State to comply with the rules developed by the ECtHR. In consonance with the ECtHR, the Directive regards the right to remain silent as well as the privilege

[97] John Murray v. United Kingdom, App. No. 18731/91, Eur. Ct. H.R., Feb. 8, 1996, §§ 47–50; Beckles v. United Kingdom, App. No. 44652/98, Eur. Ct. H.R., Oct. 8, 2002, §§ 59–60; O'Donnell v. United Kingdom, App. No. 16667/10, Eur. Ct. H.R., April 7, 2015, §§ 49–51. While generally accepting the English practice, the Court formulated a few safeguards; in particular, the defendant's conviction must not be based exclusively on the fact that he remained silent when questioned by the police; *Beckles v. United Kingdom*, *supra*, § 58.

[98] John Murray v. United Kingdom, App. No. 18731/91, Eur. Ct. H.R., Feb. 8, 1996, § 54.

[99] John Murray v. United Kingdom, App. No. 18731/91, Eur. Ct. H.R., Feb. 8, 1996, Partly Dissenting Opinion of Judges Walsh, Makarczyk and Lohmus, § 3 (citing the opposite conclusion of the United States Supreme Court in Griffin v. California, 380 U.S. 609 (1965)). See also the critical analysis of Sarah J. Summers, *Fair Trials* 157–60 (2007); Jackson & Summers, *supra* note 6, at 263–64 (pointing out that drawing inferences from the defendant's silence is impermissible in many domestic and international jurisdictions).

[100] *See* John D. Jackson, *Re-conceptualizing the Right of Silence as an Effective Fair Trial Standard*, 58 Int'l Comp. L.Q. 835, 836 (2009).

[101] For discussion of various conflicting approaches, see Ian Dennis, *Instrumental Protection, Human Right or Functional Necessity*, 54 Cambridge L.J. 342 (1995); Redmayne, *supra* note 84, at 215–24; Jackson, *supra* note 100, at 842–46 (showing that ECtHR jurisprudence cannot be squared with any of the possible rationales of the privilege).

[102] Directive (EU) 2016/343 of the European Parliament and of the Council of 9 March 2016 on the strengthening of certain aspects of the presumption of innocence and of the right to be present at the trial in criminal proceedings, 2016 O.J. (L 65) 1 [hereinafter Directive (EU) 2016/343].

against self-incrimination[103] as "important aspects" of the presumption of innocence,[104] without explaining what the connection between the presumption and its "aspects" might be.

Concerning protected items, the Directive draws a line between words and objects that are products of the suspect's will on the one hand and items that have "an existence independent of the will of the suspects or accused persons" on the other.[105] By this quaint wording,[106] the authors meant to exclude from the scope of the privilege not only breath, blood, or urine samples and body tissue but also "material acquired pursuant to a warrant" and "material in respect of which there is a legal obligation of retention and production upon request."[107] The latter group, referring mainly to required business records, certainly does not exist "independent of the will" of the suspect or other person in charge, but seems not to be covered by the privilege against self-incrimination in several Member States.

The Directive also intends to follow the lead of the ECtHR with regard to the consequences of a suspect's reliance on his right to remain silent and to withhold active cooperation. The Directive emphasizes that the exercise of the right to remain silent shall not be used against suspects and "shall not be considered to be evidence that they have committed the criminal offence concerned."[108] However, the Directive expressly approves of the widespread practice of rewarding a defendant's active "cooperative behaviour" at the sentencing stage,[109] and with a nod toward English practice and ECtHR case law, Recital 28 of the Preamble provides that the prohibition of using the suspect's silence as evidence against him "should be without prejudice to national rules concerning the assessment of evidence by courts or judges, provided that the rights of the defence are respected." Finally, the critical question of whether suspects need to be *informed* of their right to remain silent before being interrogated is in effect left to the discretion of each Member State.[110]

France has, after long debate and procrastination, brought its law into conformity with the guidelines provided by the ECtHR jurisprudence and the EU Directive. Although the French Code of Criminal Procedure does not affirmatively grant persons suspected of crime a right to remain silent and to withhold incriminating information, this right is understood to follow from the presumption of innocence,[111] which is

[103] The Directive (EU) 2016/343 treats these two as separate "rights" without clarifying their relationship.

[104] Directive (EU) 2016/343, Preamble recitals 24 and 25.

[105] Directive (EU) 2016/343, art. 7(3).

[106] A similar description of the scope of the privilege can be found in *Saunders v. United Kingdom*, App. No. 19187/91, Eur. Ct. H.R., Dec. 17, 1996, § 69.

[107] Directive (EU) 2016/343, Preamble recital 29.

[108] Directive (EU) 2016/343, art. 7(5).

[109] Directive (EU) 2016/343, art. 7(4).

[110] Directive (EU) 2016/343, Preamble recitals 31 and 32 ("Member States should consider ensuring" that the relevant information is given). ECtHR case law is more affirmative in stating an obligation to inform suspects of their right to silence; see Zaichenko v. Russia, App. No. 39660/02, Eur. Ct. H.R., Feb. 18, 2010, § 53.

[111] *See* Conseil constitutionnel, Décision n° 2014–416 QPC du 26 septembre 2014, no. 15; Jean Pradel, *Procédure pénale* no. 468 (17th ed. 2013) (the prosecutor must be able to prove guilt without forcing the

guaranteed in the *Article préliminaire* of the Code of Criminal Procedure.[112] A person suspected of having committed a criminal offense must, at the beginning of any interrogation, be informed of the option of remaining silent, both if at liberty[113] and if taken into *garde à vue*.[114] In line with the jurisprudence of the ECtHR, French courts do not regard the "*droit de ne pas s'auto-incriminer*" as an obstacle to extracting breath and blood samples from a suspect.[115] Nor has the French *Cour de cassation* found a violation of the right to silence where the manager of a firm, after an accident of a worker, was requested to present the machinery used by the worker for an official report that was later made the basis of the manager's criminal prosecution.[116] If the defendant has remained silent, that fact is subject to the trial court's free evaluation of the evidence, but the judge may not use it as an indication of guilt.[117]

Even before the promulgation of EU Directive 2016/343, *German* law had gone beyond the requirements of European law in granting and protecting the privilege against self-incrimination. As in France, the principle that no one must be compelled to actively provide information or evidence that can lead to his criminal prosecution is not spelled out in any German statute,[118] but the right to silence is listed among the information that a suspect must be given at the beginning of any interrogation. According to Section 136(1) StPO, the suspect must be told that he is free, according to the law, to make a statement in response to the accusation or to remain silent.[119] Moreover, the German Constitutional Court has declared that the freedom from any compulsion to incriminate oneself is part of the principle of *Rechtsstaatlichkeit* (a state based on the rule of law) and linked to human dignity,[120] which is the supreme value of the German Constitution.[121] If the law compelled a person to disclose his criminally relevant misconduct, he would be faced with the dilemma of having either to incriminate himself or to expose himself to penalties for lack of disclosure; German doctrine regards this

suspect to collaborate); Bernard Bouloc, *Procédure pénale* no. 136 (25th ed. 2016); Frédéric Desportes & Laurence Lazerges-Cousquer, *Traité de procédure pénale*, no. 589 (4th ed. 2016).

[112] *See* Article Préliminaire CPP, sec. III: "Toute personne suspectée ou poursuivie est présumée innocente tant que sa culpabilité n'a pas été établie."

[113] Art. 61-1 (1) (4°) CPP (Fr.) (Information must be given of the right to make a statement, to answer questions, and to remain silent).

[114] Art. 63-1 (1) (3°) recital 7 CPP (Fr.). The same information must be given at other interrogations in the course of a prosecutorial investigation (art. 77 CPP), at the beginning of any interrogation by an investigating judge (art. 116 (4) CPP), and at the trial (art. 328 CPP) (Fr.).

[115] Desportes & Lazerges-Cousquer, *supra* note 111, at no. 590.

[116] Cour de cassation, Chambre criminelle, 07–80.031, 6 Nov. 2007.

[117] Pradel, *supra* note 111, at no. 852, 853; Desportes & Lazerges-Cousquer, *supra* note 111, at no. 632.

[118] However, Article 14(3)(g) International Covenant on Civil and Political rights is applicable law in Germany.

[119] If the suspect has not been informed of his right to silence, any statement he makes is inadmissible as evidence against him; BGH, 5 StR 190/91, Feb. 27, 1992, 38 BGHSt 214.

[120] Federal Constitutional Court (*Bundesverfassungsgericht*, BVerfG), 1 BvR 116/77, Jan. 13, 1981, 56 Entscheidungen des Bundesverfassungsgerichts 37, 41–43.

[121] *See* art. 1 (1) Basic Law [*Grundgesetz*, GG (Ger.)]: "The dignity of man is inviolable. All powers of the state are obliged to respect and protect it."

dilemma as a violation of the individual's right to freely develop his personality.[122] The law may demand the disclosure of potentially incriminating information, but such information provided is then inadmissible as evidence in a criminal trial of the declarant.[123]

According to German doctrine, the scope of the privilege against self-incrimination[124] extends beyond verbal statements, covering any activity that furnishes information or materials that can lead to the person's criminal prosecution. For example, suspects cannot be compelled to hand over papers and other materials to police investigators,[125] and even exhaling air into a breathalyzer is regarded as an "activity" that a suspect must not be compelled to undertake. Submitting to the taking of a blood sample, by contrast, has been held to be passive conduct, which is not privileged.[126]

German law does not limit the privilege to persons charged with a criminal offense. A witness may decline to reply to questions if his response would create the risk that he or one of his relatives is prosecuted for a criminal offense or an administrative infraction.[127] Witnesses must be informed of that right; if the information has not been given, their self-incriminating statements must not be used against them in a criminal trial.[128]

German law not only prohibits any direct compulsion to make self-incriminating statements, for example, by using force or threats or by imposing fines, but also prevents the court from using the suspect's silence as an indication of his guilt[129] or even as a factor in sentencing.[130] The same applies to the refusal of a witness to answer questions because his testimony would potentially incriminate a relative. For example, if the defendant's wife testifies as a witness but does not answer certain questions relating to the defendant's involvement in the crime charged, the fact of her partial silence must not be used as evidence of the defendant's guilt.[131]

In sum, France more or less follows the ECtHR's case law as reflected in EU Directive 2016/343. Germany regards the right not to provide self-incriminating information as an aspect of human dignity. German law therefore generously applies the privilege against self-incrimination in favor of suspects, defendants, and even witnesses.

[122] This right is protected in art. 2(1) GG (Ger.).

[123] *See* BVerfG, 2 BvR 467/08, Mar. 31, 2008; see also § 97 (1) *Insolvenzordnung* (insolvency law compelling the debtor to disclose even criminal acts relevant for his financial situation, but disclosed information cannot be used as evidence in the debtor's criminal trial).

[124] German writers often refer to the privilege by the Latin maxim *nemo tenetur se ipsum accusare* (no one shall be obliged to accuse himself).

[125] *See* Meyer-Goßner & Schmitt, *supra* note 80, at § 95 n.5.

[126] Werner Beulke, *Strafprozessrecht* n.241 (13th ed. 2016).

[127] § 55 (1) StPO (Ger.).

[128] Oberlandesgericht Celle, 32 Ss 101/01, Feb. 7 2001, Neue Zeitschrift für Strafrecht 386 (2002).

[129] BGH, 4 StR 171/74, Aug. 29, 1974, 25 BGHSt 365, 368; 5 StR 122/92, May 26, 1992, 38 BGHSt 302, 305; 3 StR 11/15, Sept. 17, 2015, Neue Zeitschrift für Strafrecht 59 (2016).

[130] Werner Theune, in *Strafgesetzbuch. Leipziger Kommentar*, Vol. 2, § 46 n.205 (Heinrich Wilhelm Laufhütte, Ruth Rissing-van Saan & Klaus Tiedemann eds., 12th ed. 2006).

[131] Cf. BGH, 5 StR 609/95, Nov. 28, 1995, Strafverteidiger 171 (1997).

4. Right to Confront Adverse Witnesses (Article 6(3)(d) ECHR)

Article 6 (3) (d) ECHR guarantees every person charged with a criminal offense inter alia the right to "examine or have examined witnesses against him." Of all the rights mentioned in Article 6 ECHR, this is probably the one that is most closely tied to the adversarial model of the criminal process; in an inquisitorial trial, it is difficult even to distinguish between witnesses "against" and "in favour" of the defendant. Until recently, the ECtHR has given the right to confront adverse witnesses an exceptionally broad reading, finding violations of this right (and often, as a consequence, denials of a fair trial) in a host of proceedings that were completely in line with the traditions of Continental criminal procedure. Perhaps more than any other procedural right, Article 6(3)(d) ECHR has led to a power struggle between the Strasbourg Court and domestic jurisdictions willing to defend their traditional ways of proceeding.

a. *Case Law of the ECtHR*

The ECtHR sees the rationale of the defendant's right to confront witnesses against him in considerations both of trial psychology and basic fairness:

> Experience shows that the reliability of evidence, including evidence which appears cogent and convincing, may look very different when subjected to a searching examination. (…) (T)he defendant must not be placed in the position where he is effectively deprived of a real chance of defending himself by being unable to challenge the case against him. (…) The Court's assessment of whether a criminal trial has been fair cannot depend solely on whether the evidence against the accused appears prima facie to be reliable, if there are no means of challenging that evidence once it is admitted.[132]

Based on the rationale of the confrontation right, the Strasbourg Court has determined that a "witness" in this context is any person whose statement is "in fact before the court and (…) taken into account by it".[133] The right to confrontation therefore extends to codefendants and experts as well as to persons whose information is brought before the trial court by a witness who relies on hearsay. The witness whom the defendant has a right to examine is thus not necessarily a person present at the trial.

As a general rule, all prosecution witnesses should give evidence at the trial so that they can be cross-examined by the defense, and the trial court must undertake all reasonable efforts to secure their attendance.[134] If the defendant did not have an

[132] Al-Khawaja and Tahery v. United Kingdom, App. Nos. 26766/05 and 22228/06, Eur. Ct. H.R., Dec. 15, 2011, § 142.

[133] Kostovski v. Netherlands, App. No. 11454/85, Eur. Ct. H.R., Nov. 20, 1989, § 40.

[134] Al-Khawaja and Tahery v. United Kingdom, App. Nos. 26766/05 and 22228/06, Eur. Ct. H.R., Dec. 15, 2011, § 120. Even where a witness cannot be located, the authorities must "actively search" for him and undertake everything reasonable in order to secure his presence at the trial; Lučić v. Croatia, App. No. 5699/11, Eur. Ct. H.R., Feb. 27, 2014, § 79.

opportunity to examine the witness before trial and no good reason can be cited for the witness's absence from the trial, this fact by itself may be sufficient reason to consider the proceedings unfair.[135] If the trial court made every reasonable effort to enable the defendant to confront the witness, but failed,[136] a prior statement of the witness adverse to the defendant may be introduced as evidence but must not be the sole or decisive evidence in support of the defendant's conviction.[137]

In its recent jurisprudence, the ECtHR has taken a more flexible approach, declaring that the rules on confrontation should not be used as "a blunt and indiscriminate instrument"; rather, the overall fairness of the proceedings needs to be examined, taking into account "the competing interests of the defence, the victim, and witnesses, and the public interest in the effective administration of justice."[138]

Although criminal proceedings as a whole can be fair even where the rules on confrontation were not scrupulously adhered to, the Strasbourg Court demands that there exist in such a case sufficient "counterbalancing factors, including the existence of strong procedural safeguards" to make up for any lack of an opportunity to examine an adverse witness.[139] What "counterbalancing factors" may be sufficient still needs to be determined. In *Schatschaschwili v. Germany*, the Court held, with a 9-8 majority, that the German court had not employed sufficient procedural safeguards when it assessed with great caution the reliability of a judge's hearsay testimony on the statements of two absent complaining witnesses[140] and supported the finding of guilt by several other pieces of evidence strongly implicating the defendant in the crime.[141] The return to an

[135] *See, e.g.*, Rachdad v. France, App. No. 71846/01, Eur. Ct. H.R., Nov.13, 2003, § 25; Bonev v. Bulgaria, App. No. 60018/00, Eur. Ct. H.R., June 8, 2006, § 44.

[136] For example, because the witness had disappeared or died, as in *Al-Khawaja and Tahery v. United Kingdom*, App. Nos. 26766/05 and 22228/06, Eur. Ct. H.R., Dec. 15, 2011.

[137] The Court used this formula for the first time in *Doorson v. Netherlands*, App. No. 20524/92, Eur. Ct. H.R., Mar. 26, 1996, § 76. For an extensive discussion of the "sole or decisive" test, see Al-Khawaja and Tahery v. United Kingdom, App. Nos. 26766/05 and 22228/06, Eur. Ct. H.R., Dec. 15, 2011, §§ 129–143. Jackson & Summers, *supra* note 6, at 88–90, have correctly pointed out that the "sole or decisive" test comports with the inquisitorial but not the adversarial style of proceeding; in the latter, the judge must conclusively determine which evidence is admissible before there is any question of whether it will be "decisive" for the verdict.

[138] Al-Khawaja and Tahery v. United Kingdom, App. Nos. 26766/05 and 22228/06, Eur. Ct. H.R., Dec. 15, 2011, § 146; *see also* Seton v. United Kingdom, App. No. 55287/10, Eur. Ct. H.R., Mar. 31, 2016, § 57. In *Kostecki v. Poland*, App. No. 14932/09, Eur. Ct. H.R., June 4, 2013, §§ 61–62, the Court consequently accepted the conviction of a defendant who had been unable to examine a prosecution witness but was able to challenge the testimony of two further witnesses present at his trial.

[139] Al-Khawaja and Tahery v. United Kingdom, App. Nos. 26766/05 and 22228/06, Eur. Ct. H.R., Dec. 15, 2011, § 147; *Seton v. United Kingdom*, App. No. 55287/10, Eur. Ct. H.R., Mar. 31, 2016, § 58 at (viii).

[140] The witnesses, two Lithuanian prostitutes, had returned to Lithuania after testifying before a German investigating judge, and could not be persuaded to return to Germany for testifying again at the trial.

[141] Schatschaschwili v. Germany, App. No. 9154/10, Eur. Ct. H.R., Dec.15, 2015, §§ 146–158. A similarly strict standard had been applied in *Hümmer v. Germany*, App. No. 26171/07, Eur. Ct. H.R., July 19, 2012, §§ 46–53.

open-ended balancing of interests[142] in cases where a prosecution witness could not be questioned by the defense has rendered ECtHR's case law less rigid, and at the same time less predictable.[143]

b. *Application of the Right in Member States*

The *French* Code of Criminal Procedure does not explicitly provide for a defense right to confront adverse witnesses. This right has nevertheless been recognized by French courts, which apply Article 6(3)(d) ECHR. directly. In terms of procedural theory, the confrontation right has been interpreted as a corollary of the *principe du contradictoire*[144] and the equality of arms between prosecution and defense.[145] French courts tend to exhibit greater tolerance than the ECtHR for practical difficulties in securing the presence of witnesses at the trial, for example, where the witness has been intimidated or traumatized.[146] In a whole series of cases, the ECtHR disapproved of this tendency and found violations of Article 6(3)(d) ECHR for lack of a sufficient effort of French courts to locate or subpoena prosecution witnesses for trial while using their prior statements to convict the defendant.[147]

Although the *German* Code of Criminal Procedure does not expressly provide for a confrontation right, German courts have generally acknowledged that right on the basis of Article 6(3)(d) ECHR. To a large extent, German courts are striving to follow the guidelines established by the ECtHR.

Practical problems have been created by the fact that German law affords witnesses the right not to incriminate themselves[148] and grants far-reaching testimonial privileges to the defendant's relatives.[149] The existence of these privileges sometimes precludes, for legal reasons, the defense examination of witnesses who make statements incriminating the defendant early in the proceedings but rely on their privilege to remain silent at the trial. For example, if a relative of the defendant had testified, in the course of the pretrial investigation, before an investigatory judge (*Ermittlungsrichter*)[150] and remains silent at the trial, the judge may relate at the trial, as a hearsay witness, what he had learned from

[142] *See* Seton v. United Kingdom, App. No. 55287/10, Eur. Ct. H.R., Mar. 31, 2016, §§ 59, 68.

[143] For criticism of this tendency, see Thomas Weigend, *Das Konfrontationsrecht des Angeklagten—wesentliches Element eines fairen Verfahrens oder Fremdkörper im deutschen Strafprozess?*, in *Gesamte Strafrechtswissenschaft in internationaler Dimension* 1145, 1155–56 (Mark A. Zöller et al. eds., 2013); Meyer-Goßner & Schmitt, *supra* note 80, at art. 6 MRK note 22g.

[144] Desportes & Lazerges-Cousquer, *supra* note 111, at no. 611.

[145] Serge Guinchard & Jacques Buisson, *Procédure pénale* no. 489 (10th ed. 2014).

[146] *See* Cour de cassation, Chambre criminelle, no. 88-81592, Jan. 12, 1989.

[147] Saidi v. France, App. No. 14647/89, Eur. Ct. H.R., Sept. 20, 1993, § 44; Rachdad v. France, App. No. 71846/01, Eur. Ct. H.R., Nov. 13, 2003, § 25; Mayali v. France, App. No. 69116/01, Eur. Ct. H.R., June 14, 2005, §§ 33–37; Vaturi v. France, App. No. 75699/01, Eur. Ct. H.R., Apr. 13, 2006, § 58; Zentar v. France, App. No. 17902/02, Eur. Ct. H.R., Apr. 13, 2006, §§ 29–31; Guilloury v. France, App. No. 62236/00, Eur. Ct. H.R., June 22, 2006, §§ 60–61.

[148] § 55 StPO (Ger.). [149] § 52 StPO (Ger.).

[150] According to § 162 StPO (Ger.), the prosecutor may request a judge to interrogate witnesses in the course of the pretrial investigation.

the defendant's relative when interrogating him.[151] In order to alleviate the confrontation problems in this situation, the German Federal Court of Justice decided that a lawyer has to be appointed for the suspect whenever a witness is to be interrogated by an investigative judge and there is a risk that the witness will not appear or not testify at the subsequent trial.[152] In 2017, the legislature amended the Code of Criminal Procedure, obliging the investigating judge to appoint a lawyer for the suspect whenever that appears necessary, in the light of the importance of the interrogation, for safeguarding the suspect's rights.[153]

German courts have, on the whole, been more generous than the ECtHR in accepting unconfronted testimony as evidence, which has in some instances led to conflicts with the Strasbourg Court. In its case law, the German Federal Court of Justice distinguished between situations in which state agents, through negligence or otherwise, were responsible for preventing the defendant from examining witnesses, and situations where the state is not to blame (e.g., because the witness died before trial).[154] In the former case, the trial court may use the (hearsay) evidence about the absent witness's earlier statement but must submit this evidence to a particularly strict scrutiny, which must be reflected in the written reasons of the judgment,[155] and must present significant additional evidence supporting a conviction.[156] The Federal Constitutional Court has endorsed this interpretation of the obligations under Article 6(3)(d) ECHR, denying any need to exclude evidence of an unconfronted witness's statement.[157] In a 2017 judgment, the Federal Court of Justice referred to what it regards as a "flexibilisation" of the ECtHR's jurisprudence in *Schatschaschwili v. Germany*[158] and suggested obiter that German courts should abandon the strict distinction between negligent and non-negligent state conduct in connection with confrontation rights; since unexamined witness statements should under all circumstances be subjected to close scrutiny, the question whether the state is to blame for the lack of an opportunity for examining the witness should not be determinative.[159] It may well be that future German case law follows this suggestion and, like the ECtHR, adopts a more flexible (and unpredictable) course toward evaluating evidence of unconfronted statements of witnesses absent from trial.

151 BGH, 1 StR 341/51, Jan. 15, 1952, 2 BGHSt 99. A situation of this kind came before the ECtHR in *Hümmer v. Germany*, App. No. 26171/07, Eur. Ct. H.R., July 19, 2012.

152 BGH, 1 StR 169/00, July 25, 2000, nos. 39, 40; 46 BGHSt 93. The lawyer has a right to take part in the judicial interrogation of the witness even if the defendant is excluded; § 168c(5) StPO (Ger.).

153 § 140(3), 4th sent. StPO (Ger.).

154 BGH, 1 StR 493/06, Nov 29, 2006, no. 19, 51 BGHSt 150. The Federal Court of Justice has based this distinction mainly on *Haas v. Germany*, App. No. 73047/01 (dec.), Eur. Ct. H.R., Nov. 17, 2005. From this judgment, the Federal Court of Justice drew the (inaccurate) conclusion that the lack of a possibility to confront the witness "must be accepted" by the defendant if the state was not to blame.

155 BGH, 1 StR 169/00, July 25, 2000, nos. 55, 65–68, 46 BGHSt 93.

156 BGH, 1 StR 493/06, Nov 29, 2006, nos. 21, 28, 51 BGHSt 150.

157 Bundesverfassungsgericht (Kammer), 2 BvR 1317/05, July 12, 2006, nos. 24–27, Neue Juristische Wochenschrift 204 (2007); 2 BvR 547/08, Oct. 8, 2009, nos. 13–15, 23–25, Neue Juristische Wochenschrift 925 (2010).

158 Schatschaschwili v. Germany, App. No. 9154/10, Eur. Ct. H.R., Dec. 15, 2015.

159 BGH, 3 StR 323/16, May 4, 2017, Strafverteidiger 776 (2017), nos. 26–30.

III. Conclusion

Our brief analysis has demonstrated that Article 6 ECHR and the Strasbourg Court's jurisprudence on various clauses of that article did have an impact on domestic laws, at least in the two jurisdictions studied here. That impact was even stronger when impulses from Strasbourg were taken up in Brussels, that is, EU Directives molded the ECtHR's interpretation of ECHR into concrete legislation. Perhaps the greatest Europe-wide success story in this regard concerns the right to have a lawyer present at the initial police interrogation—even states that had long resisted such "meddling" of defense lawyers changed their legislation and/or case law under the impression of a united front between the ECtHR and the EU Directive on the right to legal assistance.[160] In other areas, such as the right to confront adverse witnesses (Article 6(3)(d) ECHR), the Strasbourg Court has met with greater resistance, at least in some jurisdictions, and may have to back down from its initial attempt at establishing "bright lines" and imposing detailed evidentiary rules on Member States.

The reason for these differences in achieving compliance may not lie primarily in the old confrontation between adversarial and inquisitorial traditions. As John D. Jackson and Sarah J. Summers have shown, the ancient fault lines fail to explain some of the national reactions to the ECtHR's jurisprudence in sensitive areas.[161] In fact, the Strasbourg Court has to some extent managed to transcend the ancient dichotomy, developing from the words of the European Convention its own model of a criminal process based on rules of fairness and respect for human rights. A minimization of compulsion on the suspect, a right of all participants to be heard, equality of arms between prosecution and defense, and the opportunity for the defense to play an active part from the very beginning of the process[162] seem to be the key elements of this model,[163] which can be accommodated to both inquisitorial and adversarial environments.

Two preconditions appear to foster a successful implantation of this model in the legal context of the Member States of the Council of Europe: first, an avoidance on the part of the ECtHR of attempts to mini-manage each member state's procedural system, and second, a basic compatibility between member states' understanding of individual (especially defendants') procedural rights and those proclaimed by the ECtHR.

With regard to the first issue, the fate of the ECtHR's overcomplicated[164] and overbearing rules on the defendant's confrontation right (see II. 4., supra) demonstrates that

[160] Giannoulopoulos, *supra* note 54, at 112, 116–17; Jackson, *supra* note 45, at 1004 (2016).

[161] John D. Jackson, *Cultural Barriers on the Road to Providing Suspects with Access to a Lawyer*, in *EU Criminal Justice and the Challenges of Diversity* 181, 187, 195–96 (Renaud Colson & Stewart Field eds., 2016).

[162] On the defining relevance of this element in the modern "administrative" criminal process, see Jackson, *supra* note 37, at 196–97.

[163] For a similar analysis, see Jackson & Summers, *supra* note 6, at 101–04.

[164] It has correctly been pointed out that the clarity of rulings is an important prerequisite for achieving compliance; John D. Jackson & Sarah J. Summers, *Confrontation with Strasbourg: UK and Swiss Approaches to Criminal Evidence*, Crim. L. Rev. 114, 115 (2013).

it is preferable for the Court to not only pay lip service to the Member States' prerogative in designing their rules on procedure and evidence but to actually respect their different ways of balancing the legitimate interests involved. The ECtHR, rather than engaging in a power struggle with national tribunals, should be sensitive to national traditions and sensibilities, erring on the side of generosity rather than trying to force Member States into subordination. With respect to the need for Member States' willingness to embrace the values enshrined in the European Convention on Human Rights, the system of human rights protection will work best if Member States do not regard the ECtHR as a foreign entity imposing strange rules on them, but rather if they understand the rulings of the Court as interpreting the core aims of their own systems.[165]

References

Ilias Anagnostopoulos, *The Right of Access to a Lawyer in Europe: A Long Road Ahead?* 4 Eur. Crim. L. Rev. 3 (2014)

Dimitrios Giannoulopoulos, *Strasbourg Jurisprudence, Law Reform and Comparative Law: A Tale of the Right to Custodial Legal Assistance in Five Countries*, 16 Hum. Rts. L. Rev. 103 (2016)

Jacqueline Hodgson, *French Criminal Justice: A Comparative Account of the Investigation and Prosecution of Crime in France* (2005)

John D. Jackson & Sarah J. Summers: *The Internationalisation of Criminal Evidence* (2012)

John D. Jackson, *Cultural Barriers on the Road to Providing Suspects with Access to a Lawyer*, in *EU Criminal Justice and the Challenges of Diversity* (Renaud Colson & Stewart Field eds., 2016)

John D. Jackson: *Responses to* Salduz: *Procedural Tradition, Change and the Need for Effective Defence*, 79 Modern L. Rev. 987, 1004 (2016)

Mike Redmayne, *Rethinking the Privilege Against Self-Incrimination*, 27 Oxford J. Legal Studies 209 (2007)

Sarah J. Summers, *Fair Trials* (2007)

[165] Cf. Jackson, *supra* note 45, at 1005, 1014 (2016).

CHAPTER 9

DEFENSE RIGHTS, DUTIES, NORMS, AND PRACTICES IN COMMON LAW AND CIVIL LAW JURISDICTIONS

ED CAPE

I. Introduction

THE right to fair trial is regarded as an essential mark of a civilized society around the world. It is expressed, directly or indirectly, in all major international human rights instruments and many, if not most, national constitutions, and few if any governments would openly declare that it is anything other than a foundational principle of their justice systems. The Universal Declaration of Human Rights proclaims that "Everyone is entitled in full equality to a fair and public hearing… of any criminal charge against him" (Article 10) and this, in substance, is repeated in the International Covenant on Civil and Political Rights (ICCPR), the European Convention on Human Rights (ECHR), the Arab Charter on Human Rights (ArCHR), the African Charter on Human and Peoples' Rights (ACHPR), and the American Convention on Human Rights (ACHR). Most of these instruments expand on the right to fair trial in relation to criminal proceedings, articulating minimum rights that any person suspected or accused of a crime should possess: the presumption of innocence, the right to defend him- or herself, the right to be tried without undue delay and to have adequate time and facilities to prepare for trial, the right to legal assistance, the right to know the nature and substance of the accusation, the right to interpretation and translation, the right to examine witnesses, the privilege against self-incrimination, and the right to appeal.

These fair trial rights are, in principle, agreed and uncontroversial. Yet, as Sir Leon Radzinowicz observed, "[o]ften there are pious proclamations of goals to be pursued which are flagrantly contradicted by ugly realities."[1] Radzinowicz, writing in the 1990s, explained that fair trial objectives are "overshadowed by the impact of rising crime, by financial restrictions, and by the pressures to invest limited resources in attempts to alleviate other, more appealing social problems." While the rise in crime in the latter part of the twentieth century has not continued in all countries in the first two decades of the twenty-first century, his explanation remains broadly valid, but does not fully reflect the range of factors that inhibit the realization of defense rights in practice. While international efforts to further entrench fair trial principles in the criminal justice systems of jurisdictions across the world have continued, with the United Nations Principles and Guidelines on Access to Legal Aid in Criminal Justice Systems (adopted by the UN General Assembly in 2012) being one of the latest examples, in many countries fair trial rights fall well short of international standards. One important factor in this shortfall is the tension between procedural rights on the one hand, and efficiency and security on the other: a factor that is particularly significant at the investigative stage of the criminal process. Most criminal justice systems are, in practice, predicated on the assumption that the majority of people arrested and detained on suspicion of committing a criminal offense are guilty. The de facto function of the investigative stage, reflecting Herbert Packer's crime control model,[2] is to deliver an accused up to the courts with the determination of guilt having been assured; and with investigative skills and resources being in short supply in many countries, such assurance is often largely provided by a confession or admission extracted from the accused. Procedural rights that interfere with this process are regarded as inefficient, and as endangering public security by allowing the guilty to go free. While, historically at least, international, and domestic, standards regarding fair trial have focused on "the trial," for many accused either there is no trial, or the outcome of the trial is a foregone conclusion. Thus, it is important to recognize that there can be no fair trial if the process of trial, including the investigative stage, is not fair.

International fair trial norms are mediated through a range of factors that are relevant in any jurisdiction—laws, regulations, institutions, procedures, political and professional cultures, career trajectories, and resources. Underlying such factors are deep-seated attitudes regarding the relationship between the individual and the state. Unlike procedures for resolving civil disputes, criminal justice processes are deeply linked to notions of national identity and history. Despite the fact that criminal justice systems do change, and are capable of absorbing ideas from other jurisdictions,[3] they are often regarded as

[1] Leon Radzinowicz, *Penal Regressions*, 50 Cambridge L.J. 422, 428 (1991).

[2] Herbert Packer, *The Limits of the Criminal Sanction* (1968).

[3] John Jackson & Sarah Summers, *The Internationalisation of Criminal Evidence: Beyond the Common Law and Civil Law Traditions* (2012). A commonly cited example is the shift from an inquisitorial to an adversarial approach introduced by a new code of criminal procedure in Italy in 1989. *See EU Criminal Justice and the Challenges of Diversity: Legal Cultures in the Area of Freedom, Security and Justice* 11 (Renaud Colson & Stewart Field eds., 2016). As significant, if not more so, is a similar change in most,

reflecting something of the essence of a nation's character. This is evident in the major bifurcation between civil law jurisdictions that have an inquisitorial procedural tradition, and common law jurisdictions that are identified with the adversarial tradition.[4]

While there are major differences between the criminal procedures of countries that share a common tradition (or, at least, share a procedural approach that may be categorized as inquisitorial or adversarial), it is both possible and useful to sketch out the broad contours of the two major traditions. The adversarial approach embodies the notion that criminal procedure is informed and characterized by a contest between the individual and the state. If a citizen is accused by the state of having committed a criminal offense then it is for the state to prove it, without assistance from the accused, before an independent judicial tribunal. The tribunal has no investigative role, and must make its decision as to guilt or innocence on the basis, and only taking account, of evidence produced by the prosecution and, if they choose to adduce evidence, the accused. Only when guilt has been established will information relevant to sentence be considered. The role of the accused in this process is only to look out for themselves. Adversarialism reflects an individualistic philosophy, embodying deep skepticism about the ability (or, indeed, the legitimacy) of the state, and state functionaries, to act in a dispassionate and objective manner. Inquisitorialism, on the other hand, reflects a more collectivist relationship between the citizen and the state whereby the state is not only to be trusted to treat a subject fairly, but has an obligation both to preserving societal integrity and assisting a transgressor to reintegrate. Thus, a person suspected or accused of a crime is the subject of an investigation conducted by a judicial officer as part of a process directed at determining "the truth," and has a broad obligation to assist in that process. In judging guilt or innocence, the court will see, and can take account of, all relevant material collected during the investigation, and the principle function of the trial is to ensure that the material to be considered was lawfully and properly obtained. This being the case, there is no clear distinction between the trial and sentencing phases, and information relevant only to sentence is nevertheless available to the tribunal even before guilt has been established.

These descriptions are, of course, a caricature and do not necessarily reflect or explain the procedures and processes to be found in any particular jurisdiction. Moreover, those procedures and processes are subject to influences that may either increase the intensity of the procedural tradition or substantially challenge it. Two examples will

if not all, jurisdictions in Latin America over the first two decades of the twenty-first century. For an account of this transition in six of those countries, see Alberto Binder et al., *Effective Criminal Defence in Latin America* (2015).

[4] This chapter adopts the "traditional" approach to classifying the major criminal procedure traditions, but this is not uncontroversial. Damaska regarded the inquisitorial/adversarial dichotomy as unhelpful, unsupported by the evidence and placing too much emphasis on the trial stage of the criminal process. *See, e.g.*, Mirjan Damaska, *The Faces of Justice and State Authority* (1986), and for an appreciation of his work, see *Crime, Procedure and Evidence in a Comparative and International Context* (John Jackson et al. eds., 2008). Richard Vogler, *A World View of Criminal Justice* (2005), while accepting the contribution to comparative study made by Damaska, argues that it contains significant flaws, and developed a typology based on the more traditional approach, but adding a third dimension, the popular justice tradition.

suffice, illustrating the former and then the latter. Stewart Field has persuasively argued, in relation to France (which is closely associated with the origins of inquisitorialism), that "the trial is presented as part of a process of rehabilitating the accused as a citizen of the state."[5] In China (which can also be characterized as being inquisitorial, but mediated by the influence of both Confucian thought and authoritarian government), this is taken a step further: the notion of *familism* means that the accused is regarded as a subordinate member of a hierarchical "family" headed by the judge, and is under an obligation to "be *obedient* and *admit* his moral guilt."[6] In terms of challenges to the procedural traditions, a major influence in the current era is that of managerialism, embodying notions of efficiency and economy, although in some jurisdictions, such as the United States and England and Wales, it might be argued that such considerations long predate the political rise of managerialism. Thus, despite the characterization of the adversarial trial as being the epitome of the common law approach, the fact is that most defendants plead guilty, avoiding any form of adversarial process, and absolving the court of responsibility to consider the evidence and adjudicate upon guilt. In some jurisdictions, the pressure on defendants to cooperate in this process is substantial, with sentence-discount for guilty pleas and institutionalized plea bargaining resulting in even fewer trials. Those, and similar, mechanisms are increasingly to be found in jurisdictions with an inquisitorial tradition, where in practice investigations are normally conducted by the police with little or no judicial supervision.[7] As a result, one of the central tenets of inquisitorialism—judicial supervision of the investigative process—is increasingly diluted or completely absent.

While there is broad international agreement concerning defense rights and duties, whether and how they are translated into domestic laws and practices depends upon the procedural context within which they operate. That context encompasses a range of factors, including how, and the extent to which, they are regulated and translated into processes and procedures; the level of resources dedicated to those processes and procedures; and the professional roles and cultures of police officers, prosecutors, judges, and defense lawyers (and their relative status).[8] In the next section, the international norms regarding defense rights will be briefly set out. This will be followed by an examination of the "role" of the suspect and accused in common law and civil law systems. Using the European Union procedural rights program as an exemplar, the chapter will then examine the range of defense rights, at both the investigative and trial stages; how they may be articulated; and the challenges to implementation across both adversarial and inquisitorial jurisdictions. The chapter will conclude with consideration of the question of whether, in the context of different procedural traditions, and the significance of

[5] Stewart Field, *State, Citizen, and Character in French Criminal Process*, 33 J.L. & Society 522 (2006).

[6] Wei Wu, *Cultural Relativism and Universal Fair Interrogation Standards in Europe and China*, Maklu-Online, 30 (Sept. 14, 2012), *available at* http://www.maklu-online.eu/en/tijdschrift/gofs/2012/european-criminal-justice-and-policy/cultural-relativism-and-universal-fair-interrogati/.

[7] Fair Trials, *The Disappearing Trial: Towards a Rights-Based Approach to Trial Waiver Systems* (2017).

[8] Jacqueline Hodgson, *French Criminal Justice: A Comparative Account of the Investigation and Prosecution of Crime in France* (2005).

criminal justice processes in the development and confirmation of national identities, it is possible for normative standards to be meaningfully applied across jurisdictions.

II. Defense Rights and International Norms

As noted at the outset, the body of international human rights instruments establish and recognize a right to fair trial in criminal proceedings. However, without greater specification, this right would be open to such flexibility in interpretation as to render it almost meaningless. Therefore, most international instruments specify a range of procedural rights that may be regarded as constituent elements of the right to fair trial, although whether the absence of any particular element is to be treated as preventing a fair trial from taking place is a question that has taxed international tribunals without being conclusively resolved.[9]

The elements of the right to fair trial that are substantially reflected in international normative instruments are as follows:

- the right to liberty and security of the person, including the right not to be subjected to arbitrary arrest or detention, and for any such arrest or detention to be on such grounds and in accordance with such procedures as are established by law;
- the right of a person arrested or detained to be promptly informed of the reasons for his arrest or detention, and of any charges against him;
- the right of a person arrested or detained to be brought promptly before a judge or other judicial officer, to be entitled to trial within a reasonable time, and for detention pending trial not to be the norm;
- the right of an accused to defend herself in person, or through legal assistance of her own choosing;
- the right of a person charged with a criminal offense to be presumed innocent unless and until proven guilty according to law;
- the right to legal aid (i.e., legal assistance paid for by the state) if the accused cannot afford to pay for legal assistance, and it is in the interests of justice that he or she be represented;
- the right of an accused to be informed of the nature and cause of the accusation;
- the right of a person facing a criminal charge to adequate time and facilities for the preparation of his or her defense;

[9] For example, the European Court of Human Rights (ECtHR) developed an approach in a number of judgments that treated the denial of access to a lawyer as determinative of whether a fair trial had taken place. *See, e.g.*, Salduz v. Turkey [GC], App. No. 36391/02, Eur. Ct. H.R., Nov. 27, 2008. However, it appears to have resiled from that position, see Simeonovi v. Bulgaria [GC], App. No. 21980/04, Eur. Ct. H.R., May 12, 2017.

- the right of an accused to an interpreter if he or she does not understand the language of the court;
- the right of an accused to examine and have examined witnesses and to secure the attendance and examination of witnesses on his behalf on the same conditions as witnesses against him;
- the right to appeal.

The ICCPR, and some regional instruments, include the right of an accused not to be compelled to testify against him- or herself or to confess guilt, and while the ECHR does not include such a provision, the ECtHR has consistently held that the privilege against self-incrimination and the right to silence are "generally recognized international standards which lie at the heart of the notion of a fair procedure."[10] Missing from all of the international instruments, other than the Principles and Guidelines on the Right to a Fair Trial and Legal Assistance, issued by the African Commission on Human and Peoples' Rights (in respect of the right to a lawyer), and the UN Principles and Guidelines on Access to Legal Aid in Criminal Justice Systems, is a right of suspects and accused persons to be informed of their procedural rights.[11] This is a significant omission since, to state the obvious, a person who does not know of his rights cannot make a choice about whether to exercise them, and evidence from around the world suggests that criminal justice officials, particularly at the investigative stage, frequently seek to deny or undermine the procedural rights of suspects and accused persons.

Strictly, the first three rights set out above are not fair trial rights, and in international instruments are normally set out separately under the heading of the right to liberty and security. However, if fair trial is viewed in terms of a process (from initial suspicion through to trial, and appeal) rather than an event (that is, a court hearing at which guilt or innocence is determined), then those three sets of rights may legitimately be regarded as constituent elements of the right to fair trial. To support that contention, one need only note that in all jurisdictions, the majority of those who face trial will have been arrested and/or detained at some point, and that normally the primary evidence indicating guilt will have been collected during that period, often from the accused themselves. While in some inquisitorial jurisdictions evidence of police questioning of the suspect is not admissible, or (in principle, at least) not taken into account, at trial, in most jurisdictions of both traditions, the case file or dossier system (inquisitorial systems) and the right of the prosecution to adduce any relevant evidence (adversarial systems), mean that the court will know about, and is able to take account of, the response of the accused to police questioning. As the ECtHR has held, "[n]ational laws may attach

[10] Funke v. France, App. No. 10828/84, Eur. Ct. H.R., Feb. 25, 1993; confirmed in many subsequent decisions.

[11] Although there is some case law from the ECtHR and the Inter-American Court of Human Rights requiring the relevant authorities to ensure that suspects and accused person are made aware of their procedural rights. In addition, the UN Basic Principles on the Role of Lawyers (the "Havana Principles"), adopted by the 8th UN Congress on the Prevention of Crime and the Treatment of Offenders, Havana, Cuba, 27 August–7 September 1990, provide that persons arrested or detained must be informed of their right of access to a lawyer on arrest, detention, or charge (Principle 5).

consequences to the attitude of an accused at the initial stages of police interrogation which are decisive for the prospects of the defense in any subsequent criminal proceedings... the evidence obtained during this stage determines the framework in which the offense charged will be considered at the trial."[12] This raises the question of when fair trial rights arise, which, although relevant to many such rights, has been particularly problematic in respect of the right to legal assistance.

The right to legal assistance is generally framed in international instruments in terms of a right that applies where a person is required to face an accusation or has been charged with a criminal offense. The notion of criminal charge has a particular meaning in the context of adversarial systems, and marks the point at which, following an investigation, criminal proceedings commence. The term does not really make sense in the context of inquisitorial systems, in which the commencement of proceedings is a more fluid concept. In many adversarial jurisdictions, the rights dependent upon charge have been interpreted as applying only once a person suspected of a crime is charged with an offense (i.e., only after an investigation has been substantially completed and proceedings commenced). The same interpretation has, in effect, been drawn in inquisitorial jurisdictions, where the right has often been deferred until, at the earliest, the accused is first brought before a court or judicial officer. The justification for this has differed as between the two traditions. In inquisitorial systems, it is argued that the involvement of a lawyer at the investigative stage would interfere with the "truth-seeking" objectives of that stage of the process and that, in any event, the process is either conducted, or supervised, by a judicial officer, which obviates the need for legal assistance. In common law systems, such as that in England and Wales, the need for justification was obscured by the fiction that arrest and detention by the police was only for the purpose of bringing an accused before a court, and that any investigations carried out by the police were merely incidental to that objective.

However, despite these conceptual difficulties, over the past decade or so there has been a growing consensus that the right to legal assistance at the investigative stage is both mandated by the normative instruments, and vital not only to ensure fair trial but also to guard against abuse of other rights, especially the prohibition on torture. The UN Human Rights Committee has consistently held that failure to allow access to a lawyer during the initial period of detention, and during interrogation, amounts to a breach of the ICCPR, Article 14(3)(b) and (d).[13] The Statute of the International Criminal Court, and the Statute of the International Tribunal for the former Yugoslavia, both provide for a right to custodial legal advice, as does the case law of the ECtHR.[14] The UN Special Rapporteur on the Independence of Judges and Lawyers has stated that the presence

[12] *Salduz v. Turkey*, *supra* note 9, §§ 52, 53.

[13] *See, e.g.*, U.N. Human Rights Committee, *Gridin v. Russian Federation* (Communication No. 770/1997), U.N. Doc. CCPR/C/69/D/770/1997; U.N. Human Rights Committee, *Carranza Alegre v. Peru* (Communication 1126/2002), U.N. Doc. CCPR/C/85/D/1126/2002; U.N. Human Rights Committee, *Toshev v. Tajikistan*, (Communication No. 1499/2006), U.N. Doc. CCPR/C/101/D/1499/2006.

[14] *See, e.g.*, *Salduz v. Turkey*, *supra* note 9; Panovits v. Cyprus, App. No. 4268/04, Eur. Ct. H.R., Dec. 11, 2008; Mader v. Croatia, App. No. 56185/07, Eur. Ct. H.R., June 21, 2011; Sebalj v. Croatia, App. No. 4429/09, Eur. Ct. H.R., June 28, 2011.

of a lawyer during police interviews is a key safeguard against ill treatment, a view shared by the UN Special Rapporteur on Torture, and the European Committee for the Prevention of Torture and Inhuman and Degrading Treatment.[15] The UN Principles and Guidelines on Access to Legal Aid in Criminal Justice Systems, while not binding, provide that any person arrested or detained should have a right of access to a lawyer, underwritten by legal aid.

At the domestic level, some common law jurisdictions introduced or recognized a right of access to a lawyer at the investigative stage a number of decades ago. In 1966, the U.S. Supreme Court held that where the police intend to interrogate an arrested suspect, the police must inform her of her right to a lawyer before and during interrogation (a key aspect of the *Miranda* warning).[16] In England and Wales, a statutory right to custodial legal advice, again both before and during police interrogation, was introduced in 1986.[17] However, there has been, and continues to be, resistance to such a right at the levels of both policy and practice. While in England and Wales the right of access to a lawyer is almost absolute, and about half of suspects do secure access to a lawyer, in the United States the consensus is that while there is a great deal of variation between states, and as between federal and state cases, *Miranda* has largely had a "negligible effect" in practice.[18] In many European jurisdictions, both those with adversarial and inquisitorial procedural traditions, a right of access to a lawyer at the investigative stage was only introduced after the *Salduz* decision of the ECtHR in 2008, and in some the presence of a lawyer during interrogation is still restricted (for example, Ireland and, until recently, the Netherlands). In Latin America, while regional standards require that a suspect arrested and detained by the police is immediately entitled to access to a lawyer, in most countries this is generally not the case. In Mexico, Argentina, and Columbia, a right to custodial legal advice is provided for by law, but most suspects do not have access to a lawyer in practice. In Peru, the law does not provide for suspects to have a right of access to a lawyer during the first twenty-four hours of detention, and in Brazil the law does not provide for a right of access to a lawyer at the investigative stage. All of these countries have an inquisitorial tradition although, as noted earlier, they have undergone, or are undergoing, a significant shift toward adversarialism.[19] In China, the law provides that a suspect is entitled to appoint a lawyer only after he has been interrogated by an investigative agency for the first time or from the day on which compulsory measures are adopted against him.[20] Thus, suspects in China do not have a right of access to a lawyer during the initial period following arrest or detention by the police, and although a duty

[15] *See*, respectively, U.N. Special Rapporteur on Torture, Report to the U.N. Commission on Human Rights, E/CN.4/2003/68, 17 December 2002, and European Committee for the Prevention of Torture and Inhuman and Degrading Treatment or Punishment, CPT Standards, "Substantive" Sections of the CPTs General Report, CPT/Inf/E (2002) 1 - Rev. 2006, 2006.

[16] Miranda v. Arizona, 384 U.S. 436 (1966).

[17] By the Police and Criminal Evidence Act 1984, § 58.

[18] Richard Leo, *Police Interrogation and American Justice* 280 (2008).

[19] Binder et al., *supra* note 3.

[20] Michael McConville et al., *Criminal Justice in China: An Empirical Inquiry* 67 (2011).

lawyer scheme operates in all provinces, the lawyer's role is primarily to provide a suspect with information rather than advice and assistance.

Attempts at the international level to establish fair trial norms generally, and defense rights in particular, should not be regarded as mere "pious proclamations." They are often the result of considerable work, and commitment, by people and organizations dedicated to raising standards, and informed by experience of poorly functioning criminal justice systems. Implementation, however, is another matter. Generally, even where procedural rights are introduced in response to international norms, few governments acknowledge that source of inspiration. This is less true in Europe, where procedural rights have been introduced as a result of ECtHR decisions and/or EU legislation, although in respect of the former, the introduction of defense rights in some jurisdictions has been prompted by judicial decisions, leading reluctant governments to introduce the necessary reforms (for example, in France and Scotland). A prime example is the right of access to a lawyer at the investigative stage, resisted at the political level in many jurisdictions. Such resistance cannot be (fully) explained by the respective procedural traditions, since the development (or not) of the right is not necessarily aligned with either tradition. Nevertheless, in order to understand what those rights "mean" in any particular jurisdiction, it is necessary to understand the procedural context within which they are to operate. One important component of that context is the "role" of suspects and accused persons, which can only be understood by reference to the role of other key actors, the police, prosecutors, and the judiciary.[21]

III. The "Role" and Rights of Suspects and Accused in Inquisitorial and Adversarial Traditions

To consider the suspect or accused as having a "role" in criminal proceedings, in the sense of a function or responsibility, may appear to be an inappropriate enterprise. Suspects and accused persons are normally unwilling participants in a process that they did not choose to take part in. Yet procedural traditions, in effect, ascribe a role to them, and that role also has implications for the role of their legal representative, if they have one. The imputed role of the suspect and accused differs as between the two procedural traditions and also, to an extent, as between the investigative and the trial stages of the process.

As established earlier, the suspect or accused in the inquisitorial tradition is, in principle, the subject of a judicial enquiry aimed as discovering whether, and if so, by whom an offense has been committed. Her role is to assist in determining "the truth." During the early stages of the process, the suspect is required to submit herself to questioning.

[21] Jacqueline Hodgson, *Safeguarding Suspects Rights in Europe: A Comparative Perspective*, 14 New Crim. L. Rev. 611 (2011).

While a suspect may suggest lines of enquiry, she has no right to insist that particular enquiries be undertaken, or to conduct her own investigation. The trial is primarily based upon the material obtained during the investigation and conveyed to the court in the form of a case file or dossier, and the principle of free consideration of the evidence means that the judge can take account of any information contained in the case file or dossier that the judge regards as relevant. The conduct of the trial is directed by the judge, and while the accused may request that particular evidence or witnesses be subjected to scrutiny, the accused has no right to determine the course that the trial will take or to insist that any particular witness be called to give oral evidence. Any rights of the accused, and the legality of the process, are safeguarded by the fact that the trial is conducted by a judge, and in this context the role of the accused is limited and largely passive. While the accused's lawyer may actively represent the interests of his client, the judge is the "champion" of those interests, and the lawyer has only a subsidiary role.[22]

The accused in the adversarial tradition is a party to proceedings that are centered on the question of whether one party, the prosecution, can establish the guilt of the other party, the accused. The accused has a right to investigate the accusation, and a right to call any witness, or to adduce any evidence, that is relevant to the issues raised by the accusation. Examination and cross-examination is led by the parties, so the accused or their lawyer may examine the witnesses that they call to give evidence, and may cross-examine witnesses called by the prosecution or a codefendant. Compared to the inquisitorial approach, roles are reversed, so that the judge has only a subsidiary role in respect of the evidence: to determine whether any particular evidence is admissible, and a limited right (if any) to ask questions of witnesses. However, the adversarial tradition is focused on the trial, so that adversarial principles hardly inform the investigative stage. Prior to charge, the suspect is the subject of an investigation, and is treated as an informational resource of potential use to the prosecution. Such investigation is normally conducted by the police without prosecutorial or judicial supervision. The primary safeguard of procedural rights is the potential for exclusion of evidence: common law systems tend to have a highly developed approach to the admissibility of evidence at trial, so that prosecution evidence that has been unlawfully or unfairly obtained may be excluded from consideration by the court. While the suspect has a theoretical right to investigate the accusation, this is almost meaningless in circumstances where that person is under arrest or detention, and lacks relevant powers and resources.

Both the inquisitorial and adversarial approaches to the role of the suspect and accused raise questions concerning compatibility with international fair trial norms. Some can be relatively easily accommodated by both traditions. The right to liberty and security, to be informed of the reasons for arrest or detention, and to be brought promptly before a judicial officer do not challenge inquisitorial principles. In respect of the latter, prompt production is (in principle) facilitated by the fact that criminal investigations are essentially judicial enquiries. Nor do such rights challenge adversarial principles, provided that there is a mechanism for requiring the production of a

[22] *Id.* at 9.

detained suspect before a judge within a relatively short period of time following arrest or detention. Similarly, the right to interpretation and translation, the right to appeal, and the right to legal aid present no principled challenge to either tradition, although in the inquisitorial tradition the right to legal aid would reflect the more limited role of the defense lawyer.

However, a series of tensions exist in relation to other fair trial rights, which are manifest to a greater or lesser extent in both procedural traditions. In principle, the presumption of innocence should be easily accommodated by both. Whether an accused is the subject of an investigation, or a party to proceedings, neither tradition requires that the accused be treated as anything other than innocent until proven guilty. However, when the presumption is considered in the context of the concrete realities of the criminal process, the picture is not so clear. Both traditions allow for a suspect to be arrested and detained for the purposes of investigation, and for the suspect to be interrogated in conditions that, by their nature, are coercive. This constitutes an immediate challenge to the notion of the accused as a party to the proceedings and, even in the inquisitorial context, is inimical to the idea that a person is innocent unless and until proven guilty. The right to silence, which is closely associated with the presumption of innocence, is similarly challenging. From the inquisitorial perspective, a silent suspect or accused interferes with the objective of discovering "the truth." While the right to silence should be more easily accommodated in an adversarial context, as noted earlier, adversarial principles do not really apply during the investigative phase, and some jurisdictions, such as England and Wales, and Ireland, have undermined adversarial principles by allowing for adverse inferences to be drawn from "silence" at both the investigative and trial stages.

The question of whether an accused should be detained or released pending trial is one that, arguably, should transcend both traditions; since, in principle at least, it involves a risk assessment exercise counterposing the presumption of innocence and the right to liberty (which would indicate that an accused should be released) against risk to public security and the integrity of the investigation (which would favor detention). However, it presents particular difficulties in the context of the inquisitorial tradition since the decision regarding pretrial release or detention is potentially made by the same judicial officer who is conducting or supervising the investigation. For this reason, some inquisitorial jurisdictions, such as France, have created a specific judicial role, separate from the judicial officer responsible for the investigation, whose function is to make independent pretrial detention decisions.[23]

The right of an accused to defend himself, through legal representation if he so wishes, should not challenge the precepts of either tradition; although in practice, exercise of the right to a lawyer is problematic in jurisdictions from both traditions given the potential cost, the fact that most persons accused of crime are poor or relatively poor, and, in many jurisdictions, the dearth of lawyers willing, able, and competent to act in

[23] The overuse of pretrial detention is problematic globally, and is not necessarily associated with one procedural tradition rather than another. *See, e.g.*, Open Society Foundations, *Presumption of Guilt: The Global Overuse of Pretrial Detention* (2014).

criminal cases. However, challenges arise in relation to the role of the defense lawyer in general terms, and the involvement of lawyers at the investigative stage in particular. With regard to the former, the notion of an accused defending himself, or being defended by a lawyer, potentially has quite different meanings as between the two procedural traditions. This follows from the different roles ascribed to the accused. Thus, the right of defense can be accommodated in both traditions, but what that right means differs. However, the right to a lawyer at the investigative stage presents a challenge to inquisitorial principles, even more so if the right is understood to denote an active role for the lawyer. Since the purpose of the investigative process is to establish "the truth," the involvement of a lawyer may interfere with that objective; the lawyer intrudes between the suspects and their interrogator. Thus, even in those countries where the law provides for a right of access to a lawyer at the investigative stage, in many of them various impediments are placed in the way of suspects knowing about or seeking access to a lawyer, the right often does not extend to the lawyer's presence in interrogations, and even if this is permitted, limitations are placed on the role that the lawyer can play. Arguably, however, these features are not the function of a particular procedural tradition. As noted earlier, many common law jurisdictions have been slow to introduce a right to custodial legal advice, and some continue to restrict the lawyer's presence, and role, during interrogations,[24] whereas some inquisitorial jurisdictions have been able to accommodate such rights, at least in a formal sense, with relative ease.[25]

The international instruments referred to at the beginning of the chapter provide for a range of informational requirements; information about the reasons for arrest and detention, about any criminal charge, and the nature and cause of the accusation. In addition, an accused has a right to adequate time and facilities for preparation of her defense, and this implies that the accused should have timely access to, at least, the materials that will be presented to the court. As noted earlier, the first of these does not challenge either procedural tradition. The second, the right of an accused to be informed of charges against her, is problematic in terms of how it is to be interpreted since the notion of charge is familiar to adversarial systems but not to those with an inquisitorial tradition. International courts have had to interpret the meaning of "charge," but they do not necessarily define the term in the same way for all procedural rights, or in a way that reflects the meaning ascribed in adversarial jurisdictions. For example, the ECtHR has defined charge as being "the official notification given to an individual by the competent authority of an allegation that he has committed a criminal offence."[26] Thus "charge" as defined by the ECtHR is something that occurs prior to "charge" as understood from an adversarial perspective, and while this means that, at least from the moment of arrest, a

[24] For example, in Scotland, the right to custodial legal advice was not introduced until 2010, and in Ireland and Canada there is no legal right for a lawyer to be present in police interrogations.

[25] Many countries in Eastern Europe, all of which have an inquisitorial procedural tradition, introduced a right to custodial legal advice when they joined the EU, although there are significant impediments to exercise of the right in practice in most of them. *See* Ed Cape & Zaza Namoradze, *Effective Criminal Defence in Eastern Europe* (2012).

[26] First defined in this way in Eckle v. Germany, App. No. 8130/78, Eur. Ct. H.R., July 15, 1982.

person must be informed of the nature and cause of the accusation, the right of access to a lawyer (which is also defined in the ECHR as the right of a person who has been charged), does not necessarily arise at the same moment.[27] While it is generally agreed that access to case materials must be granted to the accused prior to trial, there is little agreement about precisely how much information, beyond the reason for arrest or detention and the nature and cause of the accusation, must be disclosed at the investigative stage. Furthermore, the approach to disclosing case materials prior to trial differs as between the two procedural traditions. In the inquisitorial tradition, the concept of the *dossier* or case file eases interpretation since, in principle (although often not in practice), the accused must be granted access to the whole file. In the adversarial tradition, however, while it is generally agreed that the accused must be granted access to the evidential materials that the prosecution intends to use at trial, there is less agreement about disclosure of materials gathered during the investigation that do not support the prosecution case and that they do not intend to use.

With regard to the calling and examination of witnesses, the common formulation is that the accused has the right to secure the attendance of witnesses and to examine them, or to have them examined, *on the same conditions as witnesses against him*. This does not provide for a right to call witnesses and to examine them, but rather that the accused has the same right in respect of witnesses in his favor as applies to witnesses against him. Thus, whether an accused does have a right to call witnesses, and does have a right to examine them, depends upon what rules apply in respect of other witnesses.

In adversarial systems, compliance is relatively straightforward. Witnesses are only heard at the trial,[28] each party has a right to call and examine witnesses, and each party has a right to cross-examine witnesses called by another party. However, in inquisitorial systems the issue is more complex. First, witnesses may be judicially examined during the pretrial stage, and even if not, statements made by them to the police will be included in the case file upon which the court may rely in determining guilt. Second, whether witnesses are called to give evidence at trial is a matter for the judge, and if the prosecution cannot insist that a particular witness be called, it follows from the normative formulation that the accused will not have such a right either. Third, there is the question of what the terms "examine" and "have examined" mean.[29] As a result, reconciling the normative rights with inquisitorial processes and, in turn, with fair trial rights more generally, has caused considerable difficulty for international courts called upon to interpret the rights in relation to the laws and procedures of particular jurisdictions. In respect of the first issue, having initially issued contradictory judgements as to whether it is permissible for a court to rely on a witness statement made to the police in circumstances where the accused had not had the opportunity to question the witness, the ECtHR has subsequently tended to consider the issue in the context of whether the

[27] *See, e.g.*, Zaichenko v. Russia, App. No. 39660/02, Eur. Ct. H.R., Feb. 18, 2010.

[28] In some jurisdictions, such as England and Wales, Scotland, and Australia, there are provisions enabling evidence to be prerecorded, but these are exceptions to the general rule and of limited application.

[29] *See generally*, Stefan Trechsel, *Human Rights in Criminal Proceedings* (2006).

evidence was the sole or decisive evidence leading to a conviction. With regard to the second issue, while in most inquisitorial jurisdictions the accused may apply to a judge to call a witness to give oral evidence, the decision whether to do so is for the judge, and the ECtHR has been willing to give the judge considerable latitude in making such decisions.[30] In respect of the examination of witnesses, many inquisitorial jurisdictions cling to the traditional view that it is for the judge to question witnesses, albeit that questions may be suggested by the accused. There are some signs of change, for example, in France and in some Latin American countries, but there is considerable cultural resistance.

The foregoing account of the role and rights of suspected and accused persons in the two major procedural traditions is inevitably superficial and approximate because, as noted earlier, the classification of jurisdictions as falling into one or the other of the traditions is itself imprecise, the detailed rules, processes and cultures differ considerably even within each category, and many jurisdictions are in the midst of change (which, as in Latin America, may explicitly be a change from one procedural form to another). However, a number of broad conclusions may be drawn at this stage. First, some procedural rights do not challenge the central tenets of either procedural tradition and, to the extent that their implementation is problematic in practice, results from more prosaic factors such as a lack of political will; an absence of appropriate legislation, regulation, and procedures; and a failure to approach rights from the perspective of those whose rights they are. A prime example concerns information about procedural rights, which in many jurisdictions is often not provided and, if it is, is frequently framed in language that is not designed to be understood by those to whom it is addressed.[31] Second, the conception of the accused in the inquisitorial tradition as the subject of a judicial investigation creates a predisposition toward treating the accused as a passive player, whose ability to actively participate in the trial process—by, for example, determining what evidence is relevant and directly subjecting evidence to scrutiny—is limited. Third, while the role of the accused and the process of trial differs considerably as between the two procedural traditions, this is less true at the investigative stage where, in both traditions, suspects may be subjected to interrogation under coercive conditions and with only a limited right to information regarding the offense of which they are suspected. Finally, the participatory rights contained in the international normative documents are primarily directed at the trial stage, and the guilty plea processes in adversarial systems (often accompanied by systemic incentives to plead guilty), the increasing use of similar procedures in many inquisitorial jurisdictions, and the growing popularity of out-of-court disposals in jurisdictions of both traditions, mean that such a focus is increasingly inappropriate, and ineffective, in ensuring a fair trial process.

[30] *See, e.g.*, Engel and Others v. Netherlands, App. Nos. 5100/71, 5101/71, 5102/71, 5354/72 and 5370/72, Eur. Ct. H.R., Nov. 23, 1976; Bricmont v. Belgium, App. No. 10857/84, Eur. Ct. H.R., July 7, 1989.

[31] Taru Spronken, *An EU-Wide Letter of Rights: Towards Best Practice* (2010); Fundamental Rights Agency (European Union Agency for Fundamental Rights), *Rights of Suspected and Accused Persons Across the EU: Translation, Interpretation and Information* (2016).

IV. Procedural Rights in the European Union

In 2009 the EU embarked on a program of reform to establish minimum standards regarding the procedural rights of suspected and accused persons across Member States.[32] The explicit rationale was to support and strengthen the actions taken by the EU regarding crime investigation and law enforcement by enhancing mutual trust, and thereby mutual cooperation between Member States, and also to reassure citizens that the EU will protect and guarantee their fair trial rights. It was argued that action by the EU was necessary because, while procedural rights are recognized in the ECHR, and have been developed by the ECtHR, for a range of reasons this is not sufficient to guarantee respect for procedural rights in practice in a rational and consistent manner across different jurisdictions. Under the program, the EU has adopted a number of Directives that must be given effect in the laws, regulations, and procedures of Member States, and that are subject to the jurisdiction of the Court of Justice of the European Union (CJEU). The significance of the role of the CJEU is that, unlike with the ECtHR, questions of compliance with the Directives can be referred to the court during criminal proceedings without domestic remedies having to be exhausted, and in some respects enforcement of its decisions is more effective.

The procedural rights program represents an ambitious experiment, involving the application of detailed procedural requirements across jurisdictions with different procedural traditions, at different stages of development, and with very different criminal justice histories and cultures; something that has not been attempted before on such a scale. Six Directives have been adopted, concerning: the right to interpretation and translation, the right to information, the right to a lawyer, the presumption of innocence and the right to be present at trial, special safeguards for children, and the right to legal aid.[33] The first three came into force in 2013, 2014, and 2016 respectively, and implementation of the remaining Directives is required to be completed by June 2019. It is too early to draw firm conclusions based on evidence about the progress of this experiment, although it is clear that some jurisdictions have struggled to introduce the necessary legislation, regulations, and procedures in respect of those Directives that are in force. However, it is possible to consider some of the challenges to implementation in different procedural contexts, many of which may also resonate in other parts of the world. For this purpose, the focus will be on the first three Directives.

The Directive on the right to interpretation and translation requires, essentially, that a suspect or accused must not be prevented from understanding his position or from effectively participating in the criminal process as a result of his inability to speak or

[32] Presidency of the Council of the E.U., Roadmap with a View to Fostering Protection of Suspected and Accused Persons in Criminal Proceedings, 1 July 2009, 11457/09 DROIPEN 53 COPEN 120.

[33] *See*, respectively, Directives 2010/64/EU, 2010 O.J. (L 280)1; 2012/13/EU, 2012 O.J. (L 142)1; 2013/48/EU, 2013 O.J. (L 294)1; 2016/343/EU, 2016 O.J. (L 65)1; 2016/800/EU, O.J. (L 132)1; 2016/1919/EU, O.J. (L 297)1.

understand the relevant language. Thus, any information given to a suspect or accused during the course of that process must be provided in a language that he can understand, anything he says or which is said in his presence must be interpreted (including interpretation of lawyer-client consultations), and documents that are essential to ensuring that he is able to exercise his right of defense and to safeguard the fairness of the proceedings must be translated. The cost of such interpretation and translation is to be borne by the state, which also has a responsibility to take measures to ensure quality. As noted earlier, none of this challenges either inquisitorial or adversarial principles. However, this does not mean that ensuring that these requirements are respected is unproblematic. Provisions of this kind require close attention to be paid to appropriate and workable procedures (e.g., for identifying the need for interpretation or translation, and the action to be taken where a need is identified), structures and mechanisms for delivering interpretation and translation of sufficient quality when and where it is needed, sufficient resources, and effective mechanisms for verifying that the requirements have been complied with and for remedying any significant default. Evidence suggests that most Member States have failed to devise adequate procedures and guidance for identifying need, and many have failed to ensure the availability of interpretation and translation of a sufficient quality. Significantly, some states expressly limit the provision of interpretation for lawyer/client communications or for certain procedures, do not pay sufficient regard to lawyer/client confidentiality and, contrary to the express requirement of the Directive, fail to guarantee the cost.[34]

The Directive on the right to information repeats the requirement in other international normative documents that a person who is arrested or detained must be informed of the reasons, and the nature and cause of the accusation, but in other respects either goes beyond international standards or specifies them in greater detail. It provides that a suspect or accused person must be given information about her procedural rights and, in the case of a person who is arrested or detained, that such information be provided in writing (a "Letter of Rights"). In both cases, the information must be provided in simple and accessible language. Detailed information on the accusation must be provided to the accused, at the latest on submission of the merits of the accusation to the court, by which time access to all material evidence must also be given. In addition, where a person is arrested or detained at any stage of the proceedings, she or her lawyer must be given access to documents that are essential to effectively challenging the lawfulness of the arrest or detention.

As with the right to interpretation and translation, the requirement that suspects and accused persons be provided with information about their procedural rights does not engage issues of principle by reference to the different procedural tradition. The problems in implementation tend to be related to the use of overly legalistic and complex language in Letters of Rights, failure to establish responsibility and procedures for providing information on procedural rights, and lack of effective verification mechanisms.[35] The obligation to provide detailed information on the accusation and

[34] Fundamental Rights Agency, *supra* note 31.

[35] *Id.*; Jodie Blackstock et al., *Inside Police Custody: An Empirical Account of Suspects Rights in Four Jurisdictions* (2014).

access to case materials does raise different considerations in jurisdictions with different procedural traditions, particularly resulting from the different approaches to the mechanisms by which the court is apprised of the evidence. This has consequences in terms of the way in which access may be provided. In some, although not all, inquisitorial jurisdictions in the EU the case file is available only for inspection by the accused or his or her lawyer, and copies of particular documents may only be taken at the expense of the accused; in adversarial jurisdictions, copies (at least of evidence that the prosecution intends to use at trial) tend to be provided, and provided free of charge. Furthermore, the tendency in inquisitorial jurisdictions is that it is for the accused to seek disclosure, whereas in adversarial jurisdictions a duty of disclosure rests on the prosecution irrespective of any request by the accused. However, otherwise, the same kinds of issues arise in jurisdictions from both traditions. In most, EU jurisdictions accused persons are not entitled to access to case materials until the end of the investigative stage; investigative authorities in both types of jurisdiction regard information as a strategic resource. The right of access by the accused to documents or materials that are relevant to the legality of arrest or detention varies considerably across jurisdictions, and such variation is not dependent upon procedural traditions.[36]

Of all the EU Directives, the Directive on the right of access to a lawyer presents some of the greatest challenges in terms of the respective procedural traditions: particularly the right of access at the investigative stage, and the role of the defense lawyer at both the investigative and the trial stages. In providing for a right of access to a lawyer at all stages of the criminal process, the Directive broadly reflects international norms, although it affords welcome clarity in that it explicitly states that the right of access applies during the investigative stage. Thus, it stipulates that the right of access to a lawyer must apply without undue delay after deprivation of liberty, and before and during questioning by the police or other law enforcement agency or judicial authority. In one respect, the Directive undermines the standard set by the ECtHR in that it provides for derogation in relation to procedures involving certain minor offenses, and (at the investigative stage) where access to a lawyer is inhibited by geographical remoteness. On the other hand, it specifies with greater clarity than the case law of the ECtHR the circumstances in which temporary derogation is permissible for "compelling reasons": defined as an urgent need to avert serious adverse consequences for life, liberty, or physical integrity of a person; or where immediate action is "imperative" to prevent substantial jeopardy to criminal proceedings. The provisions on waiver of the right to a lawyer reflect ECtHR case law, which provides that waiver must be knowing, voluntary, and unequivocal.[37]

The groundwork for compliance with the right of access to a lawyer for those arrested and detained by the police had already been laid by the ECtHR in its 2008 *Salduz* decision. As a result, most jurisdictions had introduced such a right before the Directive become operative although in some jurisdictions, as noted earlier, only after intervention by domestic courts. However, the right of access to a lawyer *during* interrogation

[36] *Id.* [37] *See, e.g.*, *Pishchalnikov v. Russia*, App. No. 7025/04, Eur. Ct. H.R., Sept. 24, 2009.

has been more problematic, and it has met resistance, and not only in inquisitorial jurisdictions. In the Netherlands (an inquisitorial jurisdiction), for example, the right was only provided for in legislation at a very late stage, and in Ireland (an adversarial jurisdiction) the Supreme Court has decided that no such right exists in domestic law.[38] However, the right of access to a lawyer at the investigative stage is also problematic in practice for a range of reasons, in addition to the question of affordability. Some states prioritize (supposed) investigative efficiency over the right to a lawyer, for example, by limiting the time that the police are required to wait for a lawyer to attend upon the suspect, or by limiting the time allowed for lawyer/client consultations. In many, if not most, EU jurisdictions the right of access to a lawyer is not supported by resources, institutions, structures, and procedures that enable impecunious suspects to routinely have access to a (competent) lawyer when they need one.[39]

The Directive does not explicitly define, or refer to, the role of the defense lawyer in general terms. However, it does provide that a lawyer who is present during an interrogation is entitled to "participate effectively," and must be able to attend evidence-gathering acts, such as identity parades and crime-scene reconstructions, if the suspect or accused is required or permitted to attend them. Beyond that, however, the role is not articulated. ECtHR case law suggests that one rationale for custodial legal advice is to protect the privilege against self-incrimination and the right to silence, and in one case the court held that the principle of the equality of arms requires that a suspect be afforded the complete range of interventions that are inherent to legal assistance; discussion of the case, investigation of the facts and search for favorable evidence, support of the suspect, and control of the conditions under which the suspect is detained.[40] Nevertheless, while in one adversarial jurisdiction (England and Wales) an active role is clearly articulated in a statutory code of practice, in some inquisitorial jurisdictions intervention by the lawyer during an interrogation is strictly limited (for example, in the Netherlands and France). However, this is not the case in all inquisitorial jurisdictions, and it is difficult, therefore, to sustain the argument that the form of the procedural tradition is the operative variable in restricting the role of the defense lawyer at the investigative stage.

V. Conclusions

A major assumption underlying both international fair trial norms and domestic approaches to criminal procedure, whether inquisitorial or adversarial, is that the criminal process is primarily directed at determining whether those persons identified as

[38] *The People v Doyle* [2017] IESC 1. Note that Ireland has not opted in to the EU Directive having, along with the UK and Denmark, negotiated special provisions regarding the applicability of this area of EU law.

[39] Which reflects the position in many, if not most jurisdictions around the world.

[40] Dayanan v. Turkey, App. No. 7377/03, Eur. Ct. H.R., Oct. 13, 2009; John Jackson, *Responses to Salduz: Procedural Tradition, Change and the Need for Effective Defence*, 79 Mod. L. Rev. 987 (2016).

possibly or probably guilty are guilty. On the basis of this assumption, the procedural rights of those suspected or accused of committing a criminal offense are focused on ensuring fair trial, and mechanisms for ensuring that a fair trial takes place are primarily located within that process. However, such a focus is not sufficient to ensure that suspects and accused are treated fairly, and have effective rights that are consistent with the principle that they are innocent unless and until proven guilty. For a range of reasons, a trial at which the putative facts are fairly presented and dispassionately judged will often not take place. Key "evidence" will frequently have been obtained from the accused under conditions that are coercive to a greater or lesser extent, and the court is routinely relieved of any obligation to judge the evidence as a result of guilty plea and similar mechanisms, or as a result of procedures designed to dispose of cases without a court hearing. In some jurisdictions, the criminal justice process is so dysfunctional that a trial may not take place until long after the relevant events—during which time the accused may have languished in pretrial detention, often in appalling conditions—or may not take place at all. And it is a mistake to assume that arrest and detention is necessarily for the purpose of investigation and placing the accused before a court. There are other reasons that the police arrest and detain people—bribe-taking, control of "risky" populations, or simply as a means of punishment.

When viewed from this perspective, it is clear that procedural rights need to apply from the earliest stages of the process, at the latest upon arrest or detention; that the process must be transparent and accountable; and that mechanisms be in place to ensure that rights are respected without reliance on a trial court to enforce them. In principle, the inquisitorial tradition is well equipped to ensure a fair process since it is based on the concept of a judicial inquiry. However, in most cases in most jurisdictions, judicial supervision is a myth—the majority of investigations are not conducted by a judge, prosecutors (although sometimes deemed to be judicial officers) are not sufficiently independent of the police or other investigating agency, and in some jurisdictions police officers are designated as (assistant) prosecutors, thereby undermining independence and objectivity. What of the adversarial approach? Adversarial principles are absent at the investigative stage, and while some jurisdictions have constructed mechanisms designed to regulate the police and to render the investigative stage transparent and accountable, most rely on trial mechanisms to guarantee that evidence is obtained fairly and lawfully and that procedural rights are respected. Such deficiencies are, to an extent, recognized by the EU procedural rights program, which applies rights to the investigative stage—and in particular the right of access to a lawyer—and which includes a number of mechanisms designed to ensure that they are respected and effective. The question is whether the supranational mechanisms—the European Commission and the CJEU—will be sufficiently robust to overcome political and cultural resistance in Member States.

The most significant divergence between the inquisitorial and adversarial traditions concerns the trial—the processes by which evidence is presented to and taken into account by the court, and the right of the accused to subject evidence to scrutiny and to introduce his or her own evidence. International norms largely avoid the tension inherent in such divergence. Although the accused has the right to a lawyer, and must be given adequate time and facilities to prepare his or her defense, the participatory rights to call and examine witnesses are expressed in comparative rather than absolute terms. This inevitably has implications for the role that the lawyer can play since it is heavily circumscribed by the procedural context. If the right to a fair trial is to have similar value across jurisdictions with different procedural traditions there must, at least, be an obligation of full disclosure by the prosecution in advance of trial, and an absolute right of the accused to fully interrogate that evidence and to produce evidence of his or her own. International norms do not currently go that far, but it is important to recognize that while procedural tradition is often used as a reason to limit or undermine procedural rights of the defense, this is frequently a pretext deployed to avoid granting rights to the accused for other reasons.

References

Alberto Binder, Ed Cape & Zaza Namoradze, *Effective Criminal Defence in Latin America* (Dejusticia, Bogota, 2015)

Ed Cape, Zaza Namoradze, Roger Smith & Taru Spronken, *Effective Criminal Defence in Europe* (Intersentia, 2010)

Ed Cape & Zaza Namoradze, *Effective Criminal Defence in Eastern Europe* (Soros Foundation—Moldova, 2012)

Fundamental Rights Agency (European Union Agency for Fundamental Rights), *Rights of Suspected and Accused Persons Across the EU: Translation, Interpretation and Information* (2016)

Jacqueline Hodgson, *Safeguarding Suspects' Rights in Europe: A Comparative Perspective*, 14 New. Crim. L. Rev. 611 (2011)

John Jackson, *Responses to* Salduz*: Procedural Tradition, Change and the Need for Effective Defence*, 79 Mod. L. Rev. 987 (2016)

John Jackson & Sarah Summers, *The Internationalisation of Criminal Evidence: Beyond the Common Law and Civil Law Traditions* (2012)

Richard Leo, *Police Interrogation and American Justice* (2008)

Sida Liu & Terrence Halliday, *Criminal Defense in China: The Politics of Lawyers at Work* (2016)

Stefan Trechsel, *Human Rights in Criminal Proceedings* (2006)

CHAPTER 10

PROCEDURAL ROLES

Professional Judges, Lay Judges, and Lay Jurors

REBECCA K. HELM AND VALERIE P. HANS

I. Introduction

MODERN criminal justice systems typically rely on one of three types of decision-making in criminal adjudication. First, many countries, most notably common law nations such as the United States and the United Kingdom, use juries composed of citizens drawn from the general population who deliberate independently to reach collective verdicts in criminal cases. Second, mixed courts or mixed tribunals, in which lay judges sit alongside professional judges to reach a collective verdict in criminal cases, are employed in many civil law countries including Germany, Italy, and Japan. Third, some jurisdictions, including South Africa and India, leave the decision-making process in criminal cases almost entirely in the hands of professional judges. The procedural roles of decision-makers, and the relationships between adjudicators and other actors in the criminal justice system, differ in these distinctive models.

Employing laypeople as jurors or lay judges in criminal adjudication is seen as an essential part of democracy in many jurisdictions.[1] Most countries in the world attach importance to the participation of members of the community in the administration of justice. Supporters see the jury as possessing a legitimacy akin to that of a democratic election. Jurors are able to draw on their own life experiences and viewpoints when making decisions, allowing trial decisions to reflect the community that a legal system is

[1] Marijke Malsch, *Democracy in the Courts: Lay Participation in European Criminal Justice Systems* (2009).

intended to serve. Juries can also act as a check on authority, by balancing the power that is given to state officials such as prosecutors and professional judges.[2]

However, there are also arguments for including professional judges in the decision-making process in the criminal justice system, either exclusively or in combination with laypeople.[3] Judges, by virtue of their advanced education, professional training, and experience in deciding cases, are expected to be more competent and to be evaluated as more competent by others.[4] This may mean they are more likely to be able to decide strictly in accordance with legal standards than jurors, who may reason in a less formal way.[5] Commentators maintain that trained professional judges are less likely than laypeople to be biased by emotion or pretrial publicity and better able to handle challenging and complex evidence.[6] Research has also suggested that professional judges may be more resistant than laypeople to certain cognitive biases, although they are equally susceptible to others.[7]

The history and legal traditions of a jurisdiction are key factors that help determine the model of criminal adjudication adopted by that jurisdiction. The modern criminal law jury dates back to ancient England, and many countries that were once part of the British Empire, including the United States, Australia, and New Zealand, inherited English common law legal procedures organized around the jury trial.[8] Following the French Revolution, France incorporated trial by jury into its civil law tradition, and Napoleon spread French civil law tradition including jury trials to the nations he conquered.[9] Although some colonial nations abandoned the jury after independence from Britain or France, others retained the jury as an important part of their legal systems.

In some political climates, the jury is viewed as less suitable as a decision-maker. For example, South Africa, which has a mixed legal system derived from civil law, common law, and indigenous law, abolished trial by jury in 1969, partly due to fears of racial prejudice among jury members, given South Africa's complex race relations.[10] Steven Colby raised a similar issue in asserting that a jury system was inadvisable for Israel.[11]

[2] Stephen C. Thaman, *Comparative Criminal Procedure: A Casebook Approach* (1st ed. 2002).

[3] Lawrence Baum, *The Puzzle of Judicial Behavior* (1998).

[4] Sanja Kutnjak Ivković, *An Inside View: Professional Judges' and Lay Judges' Support for Mixed Tribunals*, 25 Law & Pol'y 93, 108 (2003).

[5] *See* Rebecca K. Helm et al., *Unpacking Insanity Defense Standards: An Experimental Study of Rationality and Control Tests in Criminal Law*, 8 Eur. J. Psych. Applied to Legal Context 63 (2016).

[6] Toby S. Goldbach & Valerie P. Hans, *Juries, Lay Judges, and Trials*, in *The Encyclopedia of Criminology and Criminal Justice* 2716 (Gerben Bruinsma & David Weisburd eds., 2014).

[7] Chris Guthrie et al., *Blinking on the Bench: How Judges Decide Cases*, 93 Cornell L. Rev. 1 (2008) (examining decision-making in civil cases).

[8] John H. Langbein et al., *History of the Common Law: The Development of Anglo-American Legal Institutions* (2009); Valerie P. Hans, *Jury Systems Around the World*, 4 Ann. Rev. L. Soc. Sci. 275 (2008).

[9] Valerie P. Hans, *Trial by Jury: Story of a Legal Transplant*, 51(3) Law & Soc'y Rev. 471 (2017).

[10] South African Law Commission Issue Paper 6: Simplification of Criminal Procedure (1997), *at* http://www.justice.gov.za/salrc/ipapers/ip06_prj73_1997.pdf.

[11] Steven J. Colby, *A Jury for Israel?: Determining When a Lay Jury System Is Ideal in a Heterogeneous Country*, 47 Cornell Int'l L. J. 121 (2014).

Analyzing successful lay participation systems worldwide, he argued that "the vast majority of citizens should have a common national identity [and] the society must agree on a common set of laws to be employed."[12] He pointed to "deep divides among Israeli religious and ethnic groups,"[13] the lack of a common national identity, and the potential for discrimination against minorities, all of which, in his view, would pose serious problems for a jury system in Israel.[14]

Nonetheless, many multiethnic societies such as the United Kingdom and the United States successfully employ juries. Juries may add legitimacy to a multiethnic country's legal system, because juries are likely to better represent the range of racial and ethnic groups in the society, compared to judges who are typically drawn from a narrower and more elite slice of the community.

In countries that utilize all-citizen juries, the classic role of the jury is to decide whether a defendant is guilty or not guilty of a crime (although note that in some jurisdictions such as the United States jurors can also have a role in sentencing). Professional judges still play a prominent role as they preside over jury trials, rule on procedural and other legal issues, and provide legal instructions to guide the jury's decision-making.

Trial by jury is less established in the civil law tradition (although some civil law countries such as Spain and Austria do utilize all-citizen juries). In civil law systems, judges are more typically the decision-makers in criminal trials, sitting either alone or along with lay judges.[15] Where juries are utilized, there is more judicial control over jury decision-making, with jurors typically deciding on the answers to specific questions posed by judges rather than rendering general verdicts. Many civil law countries give the decision-making role exclusively to professional judges. Alternatively, in mixed decision-making tribunals, lay judges sit alongside professional judges to reach a collective verdict, and these decision-making bodies decide on both guilt and sentence.

This chapter describes the differing procedural roles of professional judges, lay judges, and lay jurors (Section II). We discuss the relationships between each actor and other participants in the criminal process, illustrating these points by using examples from specific jurisdictions within each of the three frameworks described above. We identify and discuss competing trends in the roles of each actor in systems across the world, documenting increased reliance on professional judges in some countries and introduction of new lay judge and jury systems in others (Section III). We evaluate the likely impact of these shifts by comparing patterns in judge versus jury decision-making (Section IV). We conclude by identifying reasons for global trends observed in the allocation of decision-making in criminal adjudication to particular actors. We recognize the desire for greater accountability in systems shifting toward more judicial control, and the attraction of democratizing decision-making in systems embracing trial by jury (Section V).

[12] *Id.* at 122. [13] *Id.* at 134. [14] *Id.* at 132–38.

[15] Stephen C. Thaman, *Should Juries Give Reasons for Their Verdicts?: The Spanish Experience and the Implications of the European Court of Human Rights Decision in* Taxquet v. Belgium, 86 Chi.-Kent L. Rev. 613 (2011).

II. The Roles of Jurors, Lay Judges, and Professional Judges

1. Jurors

Jurors are ordinary citizens who act as legal decision-makers in criminal trials. Early English juries were said to be "self-informing."[16] They were composed of landowning white men, who drew on their personal knowledge of legal disputes to resolve them. Over time, trial proceedings included increasing numbers of witnesses called by the parties, and jurors began to function more as evaluators of facts rather than generators of facts.[17] Today, in jury systems worldwide, individuals who are personally familiar with a case would most likely be excluded from the jury.[18]

In contemporary jury systems, the jury typically consists of a pre-specified number of jurors directly drawn at random from lists of eligible adults in a community. Jury size ranges from four to fifteen, depending on the jurisdiction and the type of case.[19] These jurors hear arguments from attorneys during a trial and are presented with evidence including witness testimony and exhibits. They then determine whether a defendant is guilty or not guilty of the criminal charges presented. In jury-focused systems, professional judges do not make factual determinations as to whether a defendant did or did not commit a crime; that is left to the jury.[20]

Instead, the professional judge oversees the trial. The trial judge instructs jurors on the law and on the jurors' task and makes legal rulings, such as the admissibility of proffered expert evidence or the voluntariness of a confession. If jurors determine that a defendant is guilty of a crime, the professional judge typically has the responsibility for sentencing the defendant. However, in some types of cases and in certain jurisdictions, juries are also given the task of jury sentencing. For instance, in the United States, in the federal and virtually all state systems, juries determine whether a defendant deserves the death penalty. Juries are tasked with sentencing in felony cases in a small number of states. In South Korea, an advisory jury decides on guilt independently under most circumstances, but then joins with the professional judges in a mixed decision-making body to assign a criminal sentence.[21]

Supporters of trial by jury note several significant benefits to the involvement of lay citizens in legal fact-finding. As noted above, jurors are drawn randomly from adults in

[16] Daniel Klerman, *Was the Jury Ever Self-Informing?*, 77 S. Calif. L. Rev. 123 (2003).

[17] Goldbach & Hans, *supra* note 6.

[18] Neil Vidmar & Valerie P. Hans, *American Juries: The Verdict* (2007).

[19] Neil Vidmar, *A Historical and Comparative Perspective on the Common Law Jury*, in *World Jury Systems* 1, 30 (Neil Vidmar ed., 2000). New Zealand allows four jurors in minor criminal cases whereas Scotland employs fifteen jurors. Jury sizes of six to twelve are most common. *Id.*

[20] Marijke Malsch, *Lay Adjudication around the World* (2014), *at* http://www.oxfordhandbooks.com/view/10.1093/oxfordhb/9780199935383.001.0001/oxfordhb-9780199935383-e-016.

[21] Valerie P. Hans, *Reflections on the Korean Jury Trial*, 14 J. Korean L. 81 (2014).

a population, incorporating citizens into the legal decision-making apparatus. This can provide a check on the power of the state and officials such as police officers and prosecutors, and can also ensure that the values of a society are reflected in its criminal justice system. This is done most effectively when jurors are representative of the population. Inadequate sampling of the population and uneven response rates to jury summonses can undermine jury representativeness.[22]

What is more, in some common law countries, including the United States, Canada, Australia, and New Zealand, lawyers can exercise a specified number of peremptory challenges of prospective jurors to remove them without providing a reason. Extensive research has confirmed that lawyers have taken advantage of the procedure to base their peremptory challenges on unacceptable factors such as race and gender.[23] In 1986, the U.S. Supreme Court ruled that a peremptory challenge in a criminal case may not be used to exclude jurors based solely on their race.[24] Subsequent decisions have expanded that principle, although critics question the efficacy of the rule by pointing to continuing patterns of apparent race-based peremptory challenges.[25] Despite these challenges, in many systems the representativeness of jurors is improving, in substantial measure because of technological advances and improved practices in the summoning process.[26]

There is also evidence that involving jurors in criminal adjudication improves civic engagement, by serving as an educational opportunity for jurors to learn about the law and the legal system, and by connecting jurors with each other and with the state in ways that are said to be inspiring, empowering, and habit-forming.[27] This is supported by research in the United States showing that acting as a juror causes previously infrequent voters to become more likely to vote in future elections,[28] and leads jurors to develop stronger faith in themselves, their government, and their fellow citizens.[29]

Opponents of jury-focused systems have pointed out weaknesses of jurors as legal fact-finders. For example, as evidence introduced in criminal trials becomes increasingly complex, jurors may struggle to understand evidence presented to them. Although it has been shown that jurors often appropriately weigh technical statistical evidence, research shows that jurors do face challenges when dealing with numbers, and that can lead to errors and inconsistencies.[30] In addition, there are concerns that jurors could be unduly influenced by pretrial publicity in the media, and extensive research confirms

[22] Ann M. Eisenberg, *Removal of Women and African-Americans in Jury Selection in South Carolina in Capital Cases, 1997–2012*, 9 Northeastern U. L.J. 299 (2017); Vidmar & Hans, *supra* note 18, at 76–81.

[23] Eisenberg, *supra* note 22.

[24] Batson v. Kentucky, 476 U.S. 79 (1986).

[25] Foster v. Chatman, 136 S. Ct. 1737 (2016); J.E.B. v. Alabama, 511 U.S. 127 (1994) (applying *Batson* to gender).

[26] Goldbach & Hans, *supra* note 6.

[27] John Gastil et al., *The Jury and Democracy: How Jury Deliberation Promotes Civil Engagement and Political Participation* 9 (2010).

[28] *Id.* at 26–51. [29] *Id.* at 129–153.

[30] Rebecca K. Helm et al., *Trial by Numbers*, 27 Cornell J.L. & Pub. Pol'y 107 (2017).

that pretrial news media can bias juror perceptions and judgments.[31] It would be a mistake, though, to think that problems of low numeracy and bias are limited to lay fact-finders. As we noted earlier, researchers have documented the fact that judges are susceptible to many of the same decision-making heuristics and biases that afflict juries.[32]

There is now a significant amount of research on the best trial procedures and practices that lawyers and judges may use to improve juror comprehension of evidence. For example, in the United States, the American Judicature Society's recommendations offer clear directions to ensure that the court and parties vigorously promote juror understanding of the facts and the law.[33] So-called "active jury" reforms include procedures such as allowing juror notetaking, juror questions to witnesses, and jury deliberation during the trial.[34] Another suggestion to improve juror comprehension of evidence is the use of "blue ribbon" juries. These are juries that are selected for their special qualities such as advanced education and training.[35] However, such juries are controversial since they are drawn from unrepresentative samples of the population.[36]

Although the jury's primary role is to make factual determinations, based on legal directions from a judge, about whether a defendant broke a specific law, juries are able to influence the legal system directly and indirectly. First, although they are legally required to follow the judge's instructions on the law, jurors deliberate in secret and in most cases need not explain the basis of their decision. These features of the classic jury system lead to the possibility of jury nullification. Jury nullification occurs when the defendant has been proven guilty beyond a reasonable doubt (the standard required for a guilty verdict), but the jury decides to find the defendant not guilty anyway.[37] This might happen when the jury believes that the law they are being asked to apply is unfair in general or unfair as applied to the particular defendant. Juries have an unlimited power to find a defendant not guilty even when this goes against the evidence, and an acquittal of a defendant by a jury generally cannot be appealed. Although jury nullification is rare, through this process, jurors can make sure that convictions under the law reflect public opinion, and signal to legislators that certain crimes have become too far

[31] *See, e.g.*, Geoffrey P. Kramer et al., *Pretrial Publicity, Judicial Remedies, and Jury Bias*, 14 L. & Hum. Behav. 409 (1990); James R. P. Ogloff & Neil Vidmar, *The Impact of Pretrial Publicity on Jurors: A Study to Compare the Relative Effects of Television and Print Media in a Child Sexual Abuse Case*, 18 L. & Hum. Behav. 507; Sarah M. Staggs & Kristen D. Landreville, *The Impact of Pretrial Publicity on "Eye for an Eye" Retributivist Support and Malicious Perceptions of Criminal Offenders*, 20 Mass. Comm. & Soc'y 116 (2017).

[32] Guthrie et al., *supra* note 7 (finding judges were susceptible to common heuristics and biases); Valerie P. Hans, *Judges, Juries, and Scientific Evidence*, 16 J. L. & Pol'y 19 (2007) (finding similarities in judge and mock juror responses to scientific evidence).

[33] American Bar Association, *Principles for Juries and Jury Trials* (2005).

[34] Valerie P. Hans, *U.S. Jury Reform: The Active Jury and the Adversarial Ideal*, 21 St. Louis U. Pub. L. Rev. 85, 90 (2002).

[35] Jordan M. Halle, *Avoiding Those Wearing Propeller Hats: The Use of Blue Ribbon Juries in Complex Patent Litigation*, 43 U. Balt. L. Rev. 435 (2014).

[36] James Oldham, *Trial by Jury: The Seventh Amendment and Anglo-American Special Juries* (2006).

[37] Darryl K. Brown, *Jury Nullification Within the Rule of Law*, 81 Minn L. Rev. 1149 (1996–1997); Paula L. Hannaford-Agor & Valerie P. Hans, *Nullification at Work? A Glimpse from the National Center for State Courts Study of Hung Juries*, 78 Chi.-Kent L. Rev. 1249 (2003).

removed from the values and sentiment of a community. This allows jurors to ensure that justice is done and to act as a check on the decisions of legislators and prosecutors.

Second, through their verdicts, jurors send signals to prosecutors and defense attorneys about the likely impact of going to trial, thus influencing decisions to proceed to trial, or to offer a plea bargain (an offer to the defendant of a reduced sentence or charge in exchange for pleading guilty rather than going to trial), or other settlement. For example, research suggests that when they do not have enough evidence to convict at trial, prosecutors offer substantial reductions in the sentence or charge in exchange for defendants pleading guilty.[38]

2. Lay Judges

Lay judges are citizens who are not expected to possess legal knowledge or training in legal decision-making. They typically participate in mixed tribunals (or mixed courts), in which they sit alongside professional judges to reach a collective verdict in criminal cases. These courts are typically employed in civil law countries, including European countries such as Germany, Austria, and Denmark, and former socialist countries such as Poland, Hungary, and the Czech Republic. Procedures for selecting lay judges depend on the jurisdiction. In many systems, including the German system, lay judges are short-term and are politically appointed to represent the court and become members of the court while they are in office. In other systems, such as the Italian system, lay judges are randomly drawn from lists of ordinary citizens, just as jurors are typically selected. They are not members of the court and are therefore more distinct from professional judges. One important variation of the mixed court is the expert assessor model.[39] In this system, expert laypeople such as teachers or doctors sit with professional judges and assist them in evaluating specific aspects of a case. Germany and Croatia require lay judges who hear juvenile cases to possess specialized skills, such as parenting experience or a degree in educational studies.[40]

These courts vary in terms of composition and the ratio of lay judges to professional judges. For example, in the German system there is a relatively low ratio of lay judges to professional judges (for example, a professional judge might hear cases with two lay judges), whereas in the Italian system there is a relatively high ratio of lay judges to professional judges (three lay assessors to one professional judge).[41] In Croatia, the number of judges and ratio of professional to lay judges varies according to the severity of the offense.[42]

[38] John H. Kramer & Jeffery T. Ulmer, *Downward Departures for Serious Violent Offenders: Local Court "Corrections" to Pennsylvania's Sentencing Guidelines*, 40 Criminology 897, 919 (2002).

[39] John D. Jackson & Nikolay P. Kovalev, *Lay Adjudication and Human Rights in Europe*, 13 Columbia J. Eur. L. 83 (2007).

[40] Sanja Kutnjak Ivković, *Exploring Lay Participation in Legal Decision-Making: Lessons from Mixed Tribunals*, 40 Cornell Int'l L. J. 429, 432 (2007).

[41] Jackson & Kovalev, *supra* note 39.

[42] Sanja Kutnjak Ivković, *Lay Participation in Criminal Trials: The Case of Croatia* (1999).

Mixed court systems can also differ in terms of which decisions are made by lay judges and professional judges. In many systems, lay judges decide all legal and factual issues, including guilt and sentencing determinations, alongside professional judges. But this is not the case in all systems. For example, in Japan, the professional judges have the authority to determine questions of law, while both lay and professional judges decide on the verdict and the sentence.[43]

Lay judges can also have a role in deciding cases without assistance from professional judges, particularly in less serious cases in lower courts. For example, in England and Wales, volunteer lay judges known as magistrates deal with minor offenses such as criminal damage, minor theft, and motoring offenses. Although magistrates are not required to have any legal qualifications, they undergo training prior to being appointed.

Utilizing lay judges in the criminal justice system can be said to have many of the advantages of involving jurors in a system, including introducing community values into a system and allowing citizens to participate in their legal system. In theory, utilizing both professional judges and lay judges means that professional judges have an opportunity to explain the law to lay judges, and lay judges have the opportunity to bring the fresh approach of an average citizen.[44] However, the expert assessor approach, in which lay jurors provide expert non-legal perspectives on their cases, draws on a unique slice of the community and hence is limited in representing the general population. This purposive selection of those with specialized skills can help in fact-finding, but makes the lay judges less representative of the population as a whole than those selected randomly from the general population. Systems in which lay judges or lay assessors are appointed rather than randomly selected, either to decide cases alone or to sit alongside professional judges, as in South Africa, are also apt to fall short in representing the range of public views.

In addition, when lay judges sit alongside professional judges, the influence of lay judges may be limited by the fact that the professional judges, by virtue of their knowledge and expertise, exert a strong influence within a mixed court. The chance to make meaningful contributions is constrained in some cases by procedural rules. For example, in some jurisdictions, lay judges are prohibited from reviewing the case dossier.[45] In some cases (for example, appellate cases in Sweden) lay judges are included in panels, but the majority vote is given to professional judges,[46] and in South Africa, professional judges have the discretion as to whether lay judges will participate in a particular trial.[47]

[43] Goldbach & Hans, *supra* note 6.

[44] Bolitha J. Laws, *Lay Assistance in Improving Judicial Administration*, 287 Annals Am. Acad. Pol. & Sci. 169 (1953).

[45] Valerie P. Hans & Claire M. Germain, *The French Jury at a Crossroads*, 86 Chi.-Kent L. Rev. 737 (2011).

[46] Christian Diesen, *Lay Judges in Sweden—A Short Introduction*, 72 Int'l Rev. Penal L. 313 (2001).

[47] Jeremy Seeking & Christina Murray, *Lay Assessors in South Africa's Magistrates' Courts* (1998).

3. Professional Judges

Legally trained professional judges have a role in all modern criminal justice systems. They can be appointed or elected to serve as judges. In many systems, political actors or legal professionals appoint professional judges. For example, in England and Wales, a Judicial Appointments Commission selects judges. However, other jurisdictions place more emphasis on popular control over the selection of judges and permit the election of judges. Different jurisdictions in the United States employ diverse methods of judicial selection. They may be appointed by elected leaders such as governors, presidents, or legislatures. In contrast, they may be elected to office through partisan election (in which judges run as candidates of particular political parties), nonpartisan election (in which judges run independently), or merit selection, in which a judge is appointed for an initial term of office and then is subject to a retention election. The federal system in the United States relies on appointment by the president with the approval of the U.S. Senate. In the state courts, 87 percent of state judges in thirty-nine of the fifty states face elections.[48]

The role of a professional judge will vary depending on the type of system employed by a jurisdiction. As described earlier, in jury-focused systems, a professional judge will typically oversee the jury trial, instructing jurors on the law and making judgments on matters of law, such as whether a particular piece of evidence is permitted. The extent to which judges intervene during a jury trial differs by jurisdiction. In the United States, the judge who oversees a trial is under no obligation to intervene on his or her own initiative, even when the judge recognizes a violation of the rules. Judges often do not intervene unless an objection is made by one of the parties.[49] In contrast, in England and Wales, judges play a more active role in controlling the trial process, and judges do not hesitate to interrupt lawyers regardless of whether an objection is made.[50] In addition, while judges in the United States instruct jurors only as to the burden of proof in a case and the specific law applicable in a case, English judges are obligated by law to provide the jury with a "correct but concise summary of the evidence and arguments presented by both parties, and a correct statement of the inferences which the jurors are entitled to draw from their particular conclusions about the primary facts."[51] The ability of English judges to comment on the case is controversial; critics worry that juries are overly influenced by judges' comments.[52]

In jury-focused systems where jurors make factual determinations, once the jury has reached a guilty verdict, the professional judge will typically decide on the

[48] Adam Skaggs, Brennan Center for Justice, *Buying Justice: The Impact of Citizens United on Judicial Elections* 2 (2010), *at* http://www.brennancenter.org/publication/buying-justiceimpact-citizens-united-judicial-elections#_edn9.

[49] Yue Ma, *Lay Participation in Criminal Trials: A Comparative Perspective*, 8 Int'l Crim. Just. Rev. 74, 79 (1998).

[50] *Id.* at 80. [51] *Id.* at 81.

[52] Sally Lloyd-Bostock & Cheryl Thomas, *The Continuing Decline of the English Jury*, in *World Jury Systems* 53, 84–85 (Neil Vidmar ed. 2000).

defendant's sentence. Some offenses, including petty crimes such as misdemeanors and infractions, are not eligible for jury trial, and are decided by judges. In other jurisdictions, defendants can choose to have their jury-eligible case heard by a judge rather than a jury. For example, in the United States, defendants can waive their constitutional right to a jury trial and have their guilt or innocence determined by a judge, although most U.S. jurisdictions require prosecutorial and judicial consent to the jury trial waiver.

In jury-focused systems, professional judges in appeals courts typically hear all appeals cases. In these cases, judges can overrule the decision of a jury in a lower court, but only where an important legal error was made in the trial court. In jury-focused common law systems, there are typically very strict limits on the ability of professional judges to review the factual determinations of juries. These limits have proved challenging for cases of actual innocence, in which convicted defendants argue that although there were no legal errors in their cases, the jury got the outcome wrong.[53] There is much greater latitude for review in civil law systems.

In mixed court systems, professional judges sit alongside lay judges to make decisions in criminal cases. Because the interactions and discussions are private, we do not know with certainty about the relative contributions of professional and lay judges. But as noted above, professional judges likely exert substantial influence in panels comprised of professional and lay judges. Professional judges also exclusively hear appeals cases in many mixed court jurisdictions. For example, in Croatia and China, only professional judges hear appeals.[54] However, in France, appeals to judgments from the *Cour d'assises*, the French mixed court of professional and lay judges, are heard by an appellate court that also combines lay and professional judges.[55]

In some jurisdictions, for example in India, Malaysia, and many African countries, professional judges decide legal and factual matters in all cases themselves without input from jurors or lay judges.[56] Systems that rely on professional judges for decision-making base this choice on the fact that judges have training and experience that make them better legal decision-makers. However, it is also important to note that research has confirmed that the decisions of professional judges can also be tainted by bias, ideology, or error.[57]

[53] Zachary Bend, Righting Wrongs via Judicial Federalism: State Supreme Courts and the Path to Overruling *Herrera v. Collins* (2015) (unpublished B.A. thesis, University of Delaware) (on file with author) (examining the law's treatment of innocence claims without accompanying claims of legal errors).

[54] Ivković, *supra* note 40 (describing Croatia); Liling Yue, *The Lay Assessor System in China*, 72 Int'l Rev. Penal L. 51 (2001) (describing China).

[55] Hans & Germain, *supra* note 45.

[56] Neil Vidmar, *Juries and Lay Assessors in the Commonwealth: A Contemporary Survey*, 13 Crim. L.F. 385, 397 (2002).

[57] *See, e.g.*, Guthrie et al., *supra* note 7.

III. Global Trends in Decision-Making in Criminal Adjudication

1. A Move toward Judicial Expertise and away from Citizen Participation in Criminal Adjudication

Sections I and II of this chapter showed differences in the typical procedures associated with systems that rely on professional judges, juries, lay judges, and mixed tribunals for their legal decision making. In Section III, we discuss recent shifts in legal systems both toward and away from reliance on lay participation. These trends are likely to have significant impact on criminal procedure.

Taking a global perspective, when it comes to relying on lay versus professional judges, one can observe two trends operating counter to each other. In some countries with long-standing jury systems, there is a marked decline in the use of lay citizen fact-finders. In contrast, other countries have introduced new systems of lay participation, requiring adoption of dramatically different criminal trial procedures. We take up each of these trends in turn.

In recent years, a number of jurisdictions with entrenched jury systems have modified or eliminated lay citizen participation in legal decision-making. Developments in both civil and common law jurisdictions have led to reductions in the proportion of cases decided by lay people. In addition, the European Court of Human Rights reached a major decision that appeared to challenge the use of untrained citizens as fact-finders in criminal cases.

2. Decline in the Use of Lay Participation in Civil Law Jurisdictions

Over the last century, there has been a gradual decline of the impact of laypeople in criminal matters, particularly in civil law jurisdictions, and the decline has intensified in recent decades. In the first part of the twentieth century, many Continental European countries, including France, Germany, and Italy, abolished the all-lay jury in favor of a mixed court of professional and lay decision-makers.[58] During the authoritarian Vichy regime, for cases heard in the *Cour d'assises*, which has jurisdiction over serious crimes, France replaced its twelve-person jury drawn from French citizens with a mixed court

[58] Ma, *supra* note 49, at 75.

of three professional and nine lay judges.[59] France fundamentally changed the institution, but retained the name "jury."

In the last decade, more civil law jurisdictions have moved away from lay participation. For example, prior to the Swiss Unification of Criminal Procedure Law, which was introduced in January 2011, each of the twenty-six jurisdictions in Switzerland had its own rules of criminal procedure. The Canton of Geneva was among the jurisdictions that provided for trial by jury. However, the jury system was effectively eliminated in Switzerland by the Unification of Criminal Procedure Law.

A reduction in lay participation has also occurred in Denmark. In 2005, Denmark was classified as having a "traditional" jury system, but reforms in 2006 converted the jury of twelve into a mixed court of either three professional judges and six lay jurors, who try cases as the court of first instance, or three professional judges and nine lay jurors, who hear cases on appeal.[60] Other countries in Europe have also debated whether to transfer from a jury system to a mixed court system. For example, a special commission in Belgium on the reform of the jury recommended the abolition of the jury system in 2004.[61] This proposal was not adopted and the Belgian jury remains the sole decider of guilt in criminal cases; however, following the European Court of Human Rights decision in *Taxquet v. Belgium* in 2009 (discussed below), Belgium adopted a requirement that juries give reasons for their verdicts.[62]

3. Decline in the Use of Lay Participation in Common Law Systems

Common law jurisdictions also reflect declining use of juries. Some of the pressure comes from the time and resources that are required to conduct a jury trial. Increases in sentencing length and mandatory minimum sentences have also elevated the power of the prosecutor in criminal cases and raised the incentives for defendants to plead guilty in exchange for prosecutors' reducing charges or recommending shorter criminal sentences. All these factors have proved to be potent forces creating a rise in guilty pleas as a means of disposing of criminal cases in many jurisdictions. For example, in the United States, plea bargaining is accepted as an essential and permanent component of the criminal justice system, since many practitioners (and the infrastructure of the criminal justice system) would find it challenging or even impossible to cope if all cases went to trial. This system encourages prosecutors to offer highly attractive plea offers in order to persuade defendants (likely including innocent defendants) to plead guilty rather than

[59] Hans & Germain, *supra* note 45. The mixed court was further reduced to a body of nine (three professional and six lay judges) in recent years.

[60] John D. Jackson & Nikolai P. Kovalev, *Lay Adjudication in Europe: The Rise and Fall of the Traditional Jury, Oñati Socio-Legal Series, at* http://opo.iisj.net/index.php/osls/article/viewFile/599/871 (last visited May 19, 2017).

[61] *Id.*

[62] *See* Thaman, *supra* note 15.

go to trial.[63] In 2015, 97.1 percent of federal cases that were resolved were settled through pleas, with only 2.9 percent adjudicated in bench or jury trials.[64] The result is a system where legal standards and ideals revolve around trial by jury, but where the majority of cases are not resolved this way in reality.[65]

In England and Wales, there has also been a decline in the use of juries. In the late 1990s, Lloyd-Bostock and Thomas observed that the English jury is vulnerable because the right to jury trial is not protected in the constitution. They noted that there had been a decline in the scope and powers of the English jury, and that jury trials were increasingly being seen as excessively expensive and time-consuming.[66]

Whole categories of cases in England and Wales have become ineligible for jury trial and have been shifted to Magistrates' Courts, where cases are decided by volunteer lay judges known as Justices of the Peace, or professional judges.[67] These include less serious offenses (known as summary offenses), which are generally not eligible for trial by jury, and intermediate offenses (known as either-way offenses), in which the defendant can elect to have his or her case heard in the Magistrates' Court rather than by a jury. (Having the case heard in the Magistrates' Court can have benefits since these courts do not have jurisdiction to impose severe sentences, although note that cases can be transferred to professional judges with greater sentencing powers where necessary.)

Today, many cases are heard in the Magistrates' Court rather than by a jury. In fact, the official website of the Courts and Tribunals Judiciary in England and Wales notes that "virtually all criminal cases start in a magistrates' court, and more than 90% will be completed there."[68]

In addition, Jackson and Kovalev observe that we are seeing for the first time in centuries the possibility of a professional trial usurping the role of the traditional jury in trials on indictment (trials involving serious offenses that have traditionally been heard by juries) in England and Wales.[69] The Criminal Justice Act of 2003 provides that a judge can continue a trial without a jury or order a new trial without a jury when he or she is satisfied that there is a real and present danger of jury tampering.[70] Although this has not been

[63] John H. Blume & Rebecca K. Helm, *The Unexonerated: Factually Innocent Defendants Who Plead Guilty*, 100 Cornell L. Rev. 157 (2014); Rebecca K. Helm et al., *Limitations on the Ability to Negotiate Justice*, 24 Psych. Crime & L. 915 (2018).

[64] United States Sentencing Commission, 2014 Sourcebook of Federal Sentencing Statistics, Fig. C (2014), *at* http://www.ussc.gov/research/2015-sourcebook/archive/sourcebook-2014; *see also* Blume & Helm, *supra* note 63.

[65] For a discussion of this phenomenon in the context of competency standards, see Rebecca K. Helm & Valerie F. Reyna, *Logical but Incompetent Plea Decisions: A New Approach to Plea Bargaining Grounded in Cognitive Theory*, Psych. Pub. Pol'y & L. (2017).

[66] Sally Lloyd-Bostock & Cheryl Thomas, *Decline of the "Little Parliament:" Juries and Jury Reform in England and Wales*, 62 L. & Contemp. Probs. 7 (1999).

[67] *Id.* at 53, 61–66.

[68] Courts and Tribunals Judiciary, *Magistrates Courts*), *available at* https://www.judiciary.gov.uk/you-and-the-judiciary/going-to-court/magistrates-court/ (last visited May 19, 2017).

[69] Jackson & Kovalev, *supra* note 60.

[70] Criminal Justice Act 2003 (England and Wales and Northern Ireland) § 44.

utilized much to date, it is symbolic of a move away from an emphasis on decision-making by laypeople and toward a more expedient alternative.

4. The Impact of *Taxquet v. Belgium*

A question that has recently been brought to the foreground of legal discourse is whether juries should have to give reasons for their verdicts.[71] Traditionally, requiring juries to give reasons for their verdicts has been seen as antidemocratic. Jurors freely evaluating the evidence under the general guidance of the judge are able to represent the community's voice without having to couch the justification for their decision in legal terms. However, whether juries should offer reasons for their verdicts was raised by the case of *Taxquet v. Belgium*, which was heard by the European Court of Human Rights (ECtHR). In Belgium's current jury system, three professional judges provide twelve laypeople with a list of questions to answer.

In the case of *Taxquet*, the defendant Taxquet was convicted of murder and attempted murder in Belgium and argued that his conviction violated Article 6(1) of the European Convention of Human Rights, because the jury's responses did not offer adequate reasons for its guilty verdict. The ECtHR held that although juries do not have to give reasons, the defendant must be able to understand the basis for the verdict. In this case, the ECtHR concluded that there had been insufficient safeguards in place in the proceedings for Taxquet to understand why he had been found guilty. Although the European Court of Human Rights asserted that its decision should not be interpreted as barring jury trials, scholars have persuasively argued that the insistence upon juries providing reasons undercuts the political power of the criminal jury.[72]

In sum, in recent decades a number of countries have taken steps to decrease reliance on lay citizens as decision-makers in their legal systems. The declines have occurred in both common law and civil law countries. Greater desires for accountability are reflected in legal decisions such as *Taxquet* and pose additional challenges for lay participation.

5. A Move toward Increasing Citizen Participation in Criminal Adjudication in Many Jurisdictions

In contrast to the substantial declines and pressures noted above in existing systems of lay participation, a remarkable countertrend has occurred in recent decades. A number of countries spanning the globe have introduced to their legal systems a lay participation component. Some have added mixed tribunals of professional and lay judges, whereas others have adopted new jury systems. These introductions have all occurred as part of

[71] Kayla Burd & Valerie P. Hans, *Reasoned Verdicts: Oversold?* 51 Cornell Int'l L.J. (forthcoming) (on file with authors).

[72] *See* Thaman, *supra* note 15.

democratizing political and social change, indicating that citizen participation in the legal system is seen as a potent symbol of democratic self-governance. The jury in particular appears to be emblematic of democracy around the globe.

This modern trend toward juries and lay judges began in Russia and other nations in the Soviet bloc during the time of glasnost and the breakup of the Soviet Union. Russia, which had a jury system in the nineteenth century and early twentieth century, until it was abolished by the Bolsheviks in 1917, reintroduced trial by jury in 1993 as part of a set of democratic and legal reforms.[73] Following the approach found in many civil law countries, the Russian jury was asked to answer specific questions about the facts, rather than providing only a general verdict. Although there was great excitement at the time of its introduction, it has proven to be a relatively weak democratic institution.[74] The procedural rules allowed trial judges to halt a jury trial at any time and return it to the prosecutor for additional investigation. This meant that if problems emerged in the prosecutor's case, the jury could be dismissed to prevent a not-guilty verdict. Russian jury trial convictions and acquittals were both able to be appealed. Thus the Russian jury is one with limited power. As for other former Soviet-bloc countries, trial by jury was included in a number of their constitutions, but their jury experiments remain at an early stage of development.[75]

Shortly after Russia introduced its jury system, Spain returned to trial by jury in 1995, sometime after the death of Franco.[76] Spanish scholars and legislators debated what form of jury trial was most appropriate for the country. There was heated debate over whether a mixed tribunal of lay and professional judges or a classic jury system met the constitutional guarantee of jury trial, and which was the best approach. Ultimately, Spain adopted a jury system. As with some other civil law countries, its jury procedure requires that the jury deliberates independently from the judge, but must deliver a reasoned verdict. At the conclusion of the evidence, the trial judge gives the jury a list of specific questions; the jury is to respond to the questions and provide written explanations of the reasons for their answer.

Researchers studying Spain's jury trials report that the requirement of reasoned verdicts has created problems. Judges have found it challenging to develop comprehensible questions for the jury that squarely address the legal issues. Especially in the early years, juries floundered in generating legally acceptable reasons, and the courts set aside their verdicts.[77] One remedy has emerged: The law-trained Clerk of the Court is allowed

[73] Nikolai Kovalev, *Criminal Justice Reform in Russia, Ukraine, and the Former Republics of the Soviet Union: Trial by Jury and Mixed Courts* (2010); Stephen C. Thaman, *The Nullification of the Russian Jury: Lessons for Jury-Inspired Reform in Eurasia and Beyond*, 40 Cornell Int'l L.J. 357 (2007).

[74] Thaman, *supra* note 73.

[75] Anna Valerie Dolidze & Valerie P. Hans, Jury Trial as Legal Translation: The Case of the Republic of Georgia, Paper presented at the annual meeting of the Law & Society Association, Boston, MA (May 30, 2013); Jackson & Kovalev, *supra* note 60.

[76] Mar Jimeno-Bulnes, *Jury Selection and Jury Trial in Spain: Between Theory and Practice*, 148 Studia Iuridica Auctoritate Universitatis Pecs Publicata 135 (2011); Stephen C. Thaman, *Spain Returns to Trial by Jury*, 21 Hastings Int'l & Comp. L. Rev. 241 (1998).

[77] Thaman, *supra* note 76, at 364–76.

to enter the jury room during the deliberation to offer assistance in the drafting of the jury's responses so that they are legally acceptable.[78] As with the secrecy in mixed courts, because the discussions between jurors and clerks are private, we do not know their content and the extent to which the clerk contributes to the jury's decision-making.

In Asia, both Japan and South Korea have introduced lay participation to their legal systems in efforts to promote better understanding and legitimacy among citizens. Their systems resemble those in other countries, but with some unique twists. Japan introduced a mixed tribunal system, influenced by models in France, Germany, and elsewhere, labeling their system *Saiban-in seido.* It includes three professional judges and six lay citizens, who together decide on both guilt and punishment. The tribunal hears serious criminal cases, including capital cases. Research on the new system shows that Japan's perennially high conviction rate of 99 percent has stayed the same. However, in line with arguments for lay participation, post-trial surveys show that the *Saiban-in* are very positive about their lay judge experiences and transparency of the legal system has increased.[79]

South Korea drew on traditional common law jury models and civil law mixed tribunals in designing its advisory jury system.[80] There are three judges, including the presiding judge, and eight jurors, who sit in a jury box during the trial. The jurors begin their deliberation independently. However, if they cannot reach unanimity, or if a majority of jurors request it, the presiding judge joins the deliberation to answer questions or give other guidance to the jury. The Korean jury's verdict is advisory; for constitutional reasons, the three judges consider the jury decision but make the binding decision on guilt. If the defendant is convicted, the jurors and judges together deliberate on the defendant's criminal punishment.

Finally, the world's newest jury systems are in Argentina.[81] Within the last decade or so, five Argentine provinces have passed jury bills. Here, too, a desire for greater democratic participation appeared to lead to the adoption of trial by jury. The drive to introduce lay participation crested in the 1990s when the Argentine legal system faced intense pressure over rising crime and personal insecurity, and activists searched for methods of improving the legal system's responsiveness.

In 2005, the province of Córdoba introduced a mixed court of three professional and eight laypeople (four men and four women).[82] With over a decade of experience, research confirms that the system appears stable and enjoys support from the citizens

[78] Mar Jimeno-Bulnes & Valerie P. Hans, *Legal Interpreter for the Jury: The Role of the Clerk of the Court in Spain*, Oñati Socio-Legal Series, https://papers.ssrn.com/sol3/papers.cfm?abstract_id=2784185 (last visited May 19, 2017).

[79] Valerie P. Hans, *What Difference Does a Jury Make?*, 3 Yonsei L. J. 36 (2012).

[80] Jae-Hyup Lee et al., *What's Happening in the Jury Room? Analyzing Shadow Jury Deliberations in Korea*, 13 J. Korean L. 41 (2013); Ryan Y. Park, *The Globalizing Jury Trial: Lessons and Insights from Korea*, 58 Am. J. Comp. L. 525 (2010).

[81] Valerie P. Hans, *Trial by Jury: Story of a Legal Transplant*, 51 L. & Soc'y Rev. 471 (2017).

[82] María Inés Bergoglio, *New Paths to Judicial Legitimacy: The Experience of Mixed Tribunals in Córdoba*, 14 Sw. J. L. & Trade in the Americas 319 (2008); María Inés Bergoglio, *Metropolitan and Town Juries: The Influence of Social Context on Lay Participation*, 86 Chi.-Kent L. Rev. 831 (2011).

who participate. Legislatures in four other provinces have now passed jury bills, but the bills call for the traditional common law jury rather than a mixed court. Juries now hear serious criminal cases in the provinces of Neuquén and Buenos Aires, with other provinces scheduled to begin their jury trial experiments in the coming years.

As these new systems of lay participation are introduced, legal actors, including judges, lawyers, and court officials, are challenged to develop new procedures to manage the many changes that flow from having lay legal and fact-finding. The challenges are especially acute in civil law systems such as Spain and Argentina. Instead of lawyers handing over bundles of written documents to a judge for the judge's later perusal, they must learn to present evidence and make arguments orally to fact-finders who often have no experience with the courts. Nonetheless, observers have noted that these challenges have required the courts to become much more transparent. Lawyers and judges must communicate the law and the evidence in a way that is accessible to lay fact-finders, and as a result, the court proceedings have also become more accessible to the public at large.

IV. Comparing the Decision-Making of Different Adjudicators

Seeing these global shifts, one has to wonder, what difference does it make for a nation to move from a jury-focused system to a mixed court approach or to a system that relies exclusively on professional judges? In this section, we review the available research comparing juries, lay judges, and professional judges.

There is extensive research literature on jury decision-making and the extent to which judges agree with jury verdicts.[83] A central research method used to examine jury verdicts is the judge-jury agreement approach, which to date has been employed primarily in the United States. Researchers ask judges who preside over jury trials to complete a questionnaire, asking the judge questions about the evidence and other aspects of the case and the jury's verdict. The judges are also asked to provide the verdict they would have reached had they been hearing the case in a bench trial. In some studies, questionnaires are also distributed to jurors, for comparison purposes. The studies are remarkably consistent: Trial judges agree with the substantial majority of verdicts reached by juries in cases over which they preside. Agreement rates vary from study to study, but between 75 percent to 80 percent of the time, these different decision-makers agree on the outcome. When they disagree, the judges tend to be more punitive, the juries more lenient toward the criminal defendant. Judges report their willingness to convict on evidence the jury sees as not meriting a criminal conviction. One project estimated that having a

[83] For a review, see Vidmar & Hans, *supra* note 18; *see also* Valerie P. Hans et al., *The Hung Jury: The* American Jury's *Insights and Contemporary Understanding*, 39 Crim. L. Bull. 33 (2003); Harry Kalven, Jr. & Hans Zeisel, *The American Jury* (1966).

judge rather than a jury decide the case would result in about a 10 percent increase in the likelihood of a conviction.[84]

Of course, the judge's decision is only hypothetical. But a recent analysis took advantage of the fact that the Korean advisory jury produces real advisory verdicts from juries and real binding verdicts from Korean judges.[85] The study compared jury decisions and judges' decisions over the first three years of the Korean advisory jury system. The agreement rate was very high: The jury and the judges agreed 90 percent of the time on the guilt of the accused. And when the judges disagreed with the jury, the jury was more likely to be lenient than the judges, just as in the U.S. judge-jury agreement studies. The higher agreement rate makes sense, considering the greater interaction that is permitted between the jury and the presiding judge in the Korean advisory jury system.

This body of work suggests that there will be modest differences in decision-making as a result of shifts from judge to jury or the reverse. We would expect that systems that move toward professional judges would see small increases in conviction rates, and the contrary would occur in systems that introduce new jury systems. If sentencing authority also shifted, we might also expect a small movement toward leniency.[86] This has been demonstrated in one context in the United States, where research examining the shift from jury to judge sentencing in death penalty cases in one U.S. state showed that the shift to judge sentencing significantly increased the number of death sentences.[87]

What about mixed courts, where professional and lay judges interact? Ivković examined research on mixed tribunals in a range of European and other countries that employ this method of lay participation.[88] She found that agreement rates between the professional and lay judges were very high. We noted earlier the possibility that professional judges would dominate mixed tribunals because of their greater background, knowledge, and familiarity with legal proceedings. The lay judges in the German system have been described as "puppets with strings in the hands of the professional judges."[89] Ivković's research confirmed that possibility, uncovering evidence that lay judges on mixed courts oftentimes speak with a muted voice. In mixed tribunal systems, legal professionals report that lay judges make only a minor contribution to the resolution of cases.[90] One study indicated that over 60 percent of professional judges did not believe that lay judges influenced verdicts, or believed that they influenced verdicts rarely, or even made them worse.[91] Research suggests that lay judges themselves have a more positive view

[84] Theodore Eisenberg et al., *Judge-Jury Agreement in Criminal Cases: A Partial Replication of Kalven and Zeisel's* The American Jury, 2 J. Emp. Legal Stud. 171 (2005).

[85] Sangjoon Kim et al., *Judge Jury Agreement in Criminal Cases: The First Three Years of the Korean Jury System*, 10 J. Emp. Legal Stud. 35 (2013).

[86] Hans, *supra* note 79.

[87] Valerie P. Hans et al., *The Death Penalty: Should the Judge or Jury Decide Who Dies?*, 12 J. Emp. Legal Stud. 70 (2015).

[88] Kutnjak Ivković, *supra* note 40, at 432.

[89] Arnd Koch, *CJA Mittermaier and the 19th Century Debate About Juries and Mixed Courts*, 72 Int'l Rev. Penal L. 347, 353 (2001).

[90] Kutnjak Ivković, *supra* note 40, at 432.

[91] *Id.* at 444.

about their performance and their influence on criminal trials, but still tend to feel that their contribution was not crucial to the outcome of a case.[92]

Even though the decision-making work suggests that lay and professional judges largely agree, and lay judges on mixed courts have only modest influence, it seems clear that substantial changes to criminal procedure are required when laypeople participate, and this has a salutary effect on the accessibility and transparency of the legal system.

V. Conclusion

As this chapter illustrates, the procedural roles of jurors, lay judges, and professional judges differ by jurisdiction. Traditionally, common law jurisdictions have utilized jurors as fact-finders in criminal cases with professional judges providing oversight and making legal judgments, while civil law systems have also involved professional judges in legal fact-finding. Although there is still a relationship between the history and legal traditions of a jurisdiction on the one hand and the choice of fact-finders in criminal adjudication on the other, recent years have seen some jurisdictions move toward increased lay participation in the criminal justice system and other jurisdictions move away from increased lay participation in the criminal justice system. Jurisdictions moving toward the all-citizen jury appear to have done so as part of democratizing political and social change, reflecting the important symbolic value served by juries and citizen participation in the legal system. These changes, especially changes from judge to jury, require significant changes to criminal procedure that on the whole make the trial process more comprehensible and more accessible to the general public.

Many of the jurisdictions moving away from traditional all-citizen jury systems appear to be doing so for practical rather than idealistic reasons. Jury trials can be time-consuming, unpredictable, and expensive. Both the defense and the prosecution may prefer to shorten the time, limit the cost, and know the outcome. Even if juries are restructured to minimize time and costs, jury trials still require resources such as the time of prosecutors, defense attorneys, and judges. Rising crime rates could produce incentives to offer enticing alternatives to jury trial in jury-focused jurisdictions.

These practicalities have led to the rise of plea bargaining in the United States and to many cases being dealt with by volunteer lay judges in England and Wales. However, other challenges to the traditional jury system stem from an increasing interest in accountability for legal decisions, an interest that has led to some jurisdictions requiring jurors to give reasons for their verdicts. While not inconsistent with a lay participation system, the requirement to give reasons challenges the traditional all-citizen jury model where jurors engage in the free evaluation of evidence. A final challenge is that some contemporary cases such as regulatory and white collar crimes can be extraordinarily complex.

[92] *Id.*

These cross-cutting global trends indicate some ambivalence about the reality, if not the ideal, of lay fact-finders in the criminal justice system. Legal procedures are required to adapt to lay participation to maintain the jury system given the evolution of logistical constraints and human rights considerations. Systems are evolving to ensure continued citizen participation at least in the most serious cases, and where defendants want their cases to be heard by a jury. However, the jury system, especially in its classic form, relies on a manageable number of criminal cases and is therefore dependent on the laws in place in a jurisdiction to ensure that the number of defendants opting for a jury trial does not become unmanageable. When this number does become unmanageable, jurisdictions are forced to deal with cases using plea deals or professional judges.

References

Theodore Eisenberg, et al., *Judge-Jury Agreement in Criminal Cases: A Partial Replication of Kalven and Zeisel's* The American Jury, 2 J. Emp. Legal Stud. 171 (2005)

John Gastil, et al., *The Jury and Democracy: How Jury Deliberation Promotes Civil Engagement and Political Participation* 9 (2010)

Chris Guthrie, et al., *Blinking on the Bench: How Judges Decide Cases,* 93 Cornell L. Rev. 1 (2008)

Valerie P. Hans, *Jury Systems Around the World,* 4 Ann. Rev. L. Soc. Sci. 275 (2008)

Sanja Kutnjak Ivković, *Exploring Lay Participation in Legal Decision-Making: Lessons from Mixed Tribunals,* 40 Cornell Int'l L. J. 429, 432 (2007)

John D. Jackson & Nikolai P. Kovalev, *Lay Adjudication in Europe: The Rise and Fall of the Traditional Jury, Oñati Socio-Legal Series,* http://opo.iisj.net/index.php/osls/article/viewFile/599/871 (last visited May 19, 2017)

Yue Ma, *Lay Participation in Criminal Trials: A Comparative Perspective,* 8 Int. Crim. Justice Rev. 74, 79 (1998)

Stephen C. Thaman, *Should Juries Give Reasons for Their Verdicts?: The Spanish Experience and the Implications of the European Court of Human Rights Decision in* Taxquet v. Belgium, 86 Chi.-Kent L. Rev. 613 (2011)

Neil Vidmar & Valerie P. Hans, *American Juries: The Verdict* (2007)

Neil Vidmar, *World Jury Systems* (2000)

CHAPTER 11

RIGHTS AND DUTIES OF EXPERTS

JOËLLE VUILLE*

I. Introduction

Fact-finders sometimes rely on experts to help them determine who committed a crime, how the offense was committed, or what the accused's mental condition was at the time of the offense. The use of expert evidence varies greatly in adversary and non-adversary criminal justice systems: adversary systems rely on experts who are hired, instructed, and paid by the parties, whereas non-adversary systems use mostly court-appointed experts.[1] The use of so-called partisan experts has been criticized on multiple grounds: it allows a party to shop for the expert most favorable to her case, it disadvantages defendants who do not have the financial means to retain the most prominent experts, and it leads to a polarization of expert opinions that can result in a distortion of the evidence. The use of court-appointed experts, on the other hand, has been celebrated as promoting the expert's independence and minimizing partisan bias.[2] But in both systems, the central difficulty resides in the fact that lay fact-finders must evaluate the

* The author wishes to thank the Swiss National Science Foundation for their financial support (grant PZ00P1_154955/1).

[1] Borrowing Damaška's terminology, we use the adjective adversary to describe the criminal justice systems found in the Anglo-Saxon world and the term "non-adversary" to describe the systems of the Continental European tradition. *See* Mirjan R. Damaška, *Evidentiary Barriers to Conviction and Two Models of Criminal Procedure: A Comparative Study*, 121 U. Pa. L. Rev. 506 (1973). It should be noted however that many continental European jurisdictions have now adopted traits typical of adversary jurisdictions, and many Europeans consider their system to be in fact mixed. *See* Craig M. Bradley, *The Convergence of the Continental and the Common Law Model of Criminal Procedure*, 7 Crim. L. Forum 471 (1996).

[2] G.L. Davis, *Court-Appointed Experts*, 5 Queensland U. of Tech. L. & Justice J. 89 (2005); John D.J. Havard, *Expert Scientific Evidence Under the Adversarial System: A Travesty of Justice?*, 32 J. Forensic Sci. Society 225 (1992); John R. Spencer, *Court Experts and Expert Witnesses: Have We a Lesson to Learn from the French?*, 45 Current Legal Probs., Part 2: Collected Papers 213 (1992).

reliability and probative weight of a type of evidence that can be highly complex, even though they lack any specialized knowledge in the matter.

This chapter aims to outline the rules governing the use of expert evidence in the non-adversary criminal justice systems most commonly found on the European continent. Limited reference will be made to adversary systems to highlight differences in conceptual approaches or everyday implementations. The discussion will seek to go beyond the theoretical considerations commonly found in comparative law literature, and to explore the real-world challenges faced by fact-finders and parties when expert evidence is adduced.

After defining the position and role of the expert in criminal investigations and trials (Section II), and describing the limits put on domestic legislators in that regard by the European Court of Human Rights (Section III), we will describe the process of hiring non-adversary experts and defining the questions put to them (Section IV). We will then discuss the duties that befall the expert (Section V), as well as the defendant's rights when expert evidence is brought against him (Section VI). In Section VII, we will see what the empirical literature says about the evaluation of expert evidence by jurors and professional judges, and then examine in Section VIII what sanctions can be imposed when an expert is grossly negligent or willfully misleads the court. Finally, we will briefly explore several issues that have arisen lately with regards to the use of expert evidence in criminal trials (Section IX).

II. Concepts and Definitions

An expert is brought into criminal proceedings because her specialized knowledge is necessary to help establish the facts of the case, whether it be the identity of the perpetrator, the manner in which he acted, or whether he was mentally responsible when he committed the offense.[3] An expert is called to evaluate *facts*, and is usually prohibited from opining as to questions of law (unless she is a legal expert called to explain, for example, what the law of a foreign state is). The expert gives her *opinion* as to the questions asked of her, and must be distinguished from the witness, who relates what he has seen, heard, or experienced regarding an event. Some systems, such as the German *Strafprozessordnung*, have an intermediary category between experts and witnesses, called *sachverständige Zeugen*—literally expert witnesses—that relates to persons who were not retained by a magistrate or a party to provide expert knowledge in the case but

[3] For a comparative perspective on the concepts and definitions surrounding the notion of expert evidence in the different Member States of the European Union, see The Law Society of England & Wales, *Safeguarding the Use of Expert Evidence in the European Union: Final Project Report* (2009), and its comparative matrix. *See also* John Hatchard et al., *Comparative Criminal Procedure* (B.I.I.C.L. 1996); Peter Alldridge, *Scientific Expertise and Comparative Criminal Procedure*, 3 Int'l J. Evid. & Proof 141 (1999); Robert F. Taylor, *A Comparative Study of Expert Testimony in France and the United States: Philosophical Underpinnings, History, Practice and Procedure*, 31 Tex. Int'l L.J. 181 (1996).

were nonetheless able to observe an event as a witness and interpret it thanks to their specialized knowledge. Such could be the case, for instance, of a medical doctor who happens to witness a traffic accident and sees and understands the manner in which the victim was injured.[4] It is important to underline that the expert's role is limited to *assisting* the fact-finder in establishing the facts of the case. In this respect, the fact-finder must be careful not to surrender her fact-finding responsibility to the expert, and the expert must not infringe on the fact-finder's area of competence by answering legal questions instead of purely factual ones.

In non-adversary criminal justice systems, a prosecutor or a judge (sometimes also the police) is competent to hire experts, either during the investigative stage of the procedure or later, once the case has been referred to a court. It is usually the magistrate's duty to evaluate whether an expert is needed in the case because the question to be answered exceeds the fact-finder's knowledge, or whether the matter can be left to the fact-finder to determine. However, expert evidence is sometimes mandated by law; in that case, the magistrate must appoint an expert and cannot rely on his own evaluation of the situation. Conversely, magistrates are usually not permitted to appoint an expert when the expert is not absolutely necessary, the fear being that the magistrate would then surrender his responsibility of establishing the facts to an outsider.

As to who can act as an expert in a criminal investigation or trial, domestic legal systems vary greatly. Some states adopt a liberal approach, where the magistrate can hire whomever she chooses. In France, on the contrary, a person can only act as an expert if he is registered on a list of experts administered by a court (*Cour de cassation* or *cour d'appel*). Some criminal justice systems adopt different approaches for different forensic subdisciplines. In Switzerland, for example, only a medical doctor with a specialized degree in forensic medicine can perform an autopsy.[5] If an instructing magistrate needs to secure the opinion of a handwriting expert, on the other hand, he is free to choose whomever he wants, and there are no lists of experts or registries to help him find the right person for the task. This example illustrates a problem that is pivotal to the whole system: the law needs to ensure that expert evidence of high quality is provided to the fact-finder, hence the accreditation and certifications schemes, but it also needs to be flexible enough to allow for the commissioning of people who have a type of highly specialized expertise whose need cannot be foreseen by the legislator, and who can thus not be incorporated in traditional vetting structures. When no official regulatory system exists, the magistrate is left to evaluate herself who possesses the required knowledge or skills to perform the expert's tasks, which can be problematic when the magistrate knows nothing about the matter involved.

In continental European systems, any field of specialized knowledge can usually be the topic of an expert report. Contrary to the situation in the United States, for example, admissibility of scientific evidence does not constitute a separate question from that of

[4] Michael Bohlander, *Principles of German Criminal Procedure* 147 (2012).

[5] Code de Procédure Pénale [CPP] art. 253 (Switzerland). *See* Thomas Hansjakob, *Kommentar Zur Schweizerischen Strafprozessordnung* 1450 (Schulthess 2014).

probative weight, the judge does not act as a gatekeeper, and the decision will not be made on the basis of a set of predetermined criteria. The approach is rather pragmatic: all evidence will be considered as long as it is not illegal and has not been improperly obtained, and its scientific reliability will be evaluated simultaneously with its probative weight in the context of the case at hand, given the costs and utilities of the possible verdicts.[6] For example, in a Swiss case in which a foreign woman was suspected of having used somebody else's visa to come to Switzerland and get married to a Swiss citizen whom she had met on the internet, an expert had been commissioned to do an anthropometric comparison of the picture on the visa and a picture of the defendant. The expert had reported to the investigating judge that the comparison supported the hypothesis that the defendant was not the person in the visa picture. The magistrate however felt that he did not understand the technique well enough to be able to evaluate its reliability, and said that, given the circumstances of the case, notably that the defendant was not a threat to public safety and that the husband-to-be wanted to marry her and live with her in Switzerland, he would probably disregard the expert report and abandon the charges.[7]

Finally, in the systems in which the expert is hired by a neutral magistrate and has the duty of informing the fact-finder in an unbiased manner, the expert can be recused by one of the parties if there is a fear that she could be partial. Typically, a person cannot act as an expert if she has a family or personal relationship with one of the parties or their counsel, if she is in business competition with one of the parties, if she treated the suspect as a patient previously, if she has expressed her opinion as to the case earlier, or if there is any other conflict of interest that can be established objectively. On the contrary, an expert can usually not be recused simply because she acted as an expert in the same case at an earlier instance, or because she acted as an expert in a previous case against the same defendant.

III. The Position of the Expert in the Proceedings according to the European Court of Human Rights

The status of the expert and her position and role on the proceedings has given rise to a rich case law by the European Court of Human Rights (ECtHR). It can be summarized as follows: the ECtHR accepts both court-appointed experts and partisan experts as modes of securing specialized knowledge in a criminal trial.[8] However, the principle of

[6] Christophe Champod & Joëlle Vuille, *Scientific Evidence in Europe—Admissibility, Evaluation and Equality of Arms*, 9 Int'l Commentary on Evidence 1 (2011).

[7] Interview with J17, Jan. 18, 2010 (on file with the author).

[8] C.B. v. Austria, App. No. 30465/06, Eur. Ct. H. R., Apr. 4, 2013, § 40.

equality of arms, which derives from the right to a fair trial guaranteed by Article 6 of the European Convention on Human Rights (ECHR), must be upheld at all times. This means that each party must have a reasonable opportunity to present its case in conditions that do not place it at a clear disadvantage vis-à-vis the other parties.[9] As a consequence, the fact that a partisan expert testifies at trial does not, in itself, constitute a breach of equality of arms. The ECtHR takes into account the position of the expert with regards to the parties, but also the role that the expert had in the proceedings, what her behavior was,[10] and what impact her report and/or testimony had on the fact-finder. However, the use of a court-appointed expert upholds the principle of equality of arms only if the expert's position in the proceedings is indeed neutral. If such is not the case,[11] the defense has a right to call a second expert to testify. In that latter case, the experts called for both parties must be given equivalent status.[12] Besides, if one party has objective reasons to suspect that the court-appointed expert might have been partial, he must be given the opportunity to have his own expert.[13] However, the mere fact that a court-appointed expert belongs to the same institute as the person who set in motion the proceedings does not render him or her partial.[14]

IV. Hiring the Expert and Determining the Expert Questions

Once the investigating magistrate has decided that an expert is needed, he will have to find the right person. Some systems allow the parties to give their opinion as to the person who should be hired, and what her mission should be with regards to the case at hand. Usually, a person can refuse to act as an expert in a criminal trial. There are exceptions, though. For instance, in Germany, people officially appointed as experts have a duty to accept if solicited to give expert evidence.[15]

[9] Stoimenov v. Macedonia, App. No. 17995/02, Eur. Ct. H.R., Apr. 5, 2007, § 41.

[10] G.B. v. France, App. No. 44069/98, Eur. Ct. H.R., Oct. 2, 2001.

[11] For example, in *Bönisch v. Austria*, App. No. 8658/79, Eur. Ct. H.R., May 6, 1985, a scientist working for the Vienna food authority had carried out an analysis to determine the content of smoked meat confiscated from the applicant. Finding that the meat contained illegal substances, the scientist had denounced the applicant to the local district attorney. On the basis of the report drawn by the scientist, an investigating magistrate decided to press charges against the applicant, and appointed the same scientist to inform him as to the content of the confiscated meat. During the proceedings, the court-appointed expert was put in a position that was privileged in comparison to the experts hired by the defense. The Court later convicted the applicant, basing its finding of guilt mainly on the expert's report. The ECtHR held that the expert, although appointed by a judge, could not be considered to be neutral under such circumstances.

[12] Bönisch v. Austria, App. No. 8658/79, Eur. Ct. H.R., May 6, 1985, § 32 f.

[13] Sara Lind Eggertsdóttir v. Iceland, App. No. 31930/04, Eur. Ct. H.R., July 5, 2007, § 52 f.

[14] Brandstetter v. Austria, App. Nos. 11170/84, 12876/87 and 13468/87, Eur. Ct. H.R., Aug. 28, 1991.

[15] Strafprozessordnung § 75 (Germany).

The magistrate then determines the questions to be asked of the expert, sometimes after consulting with the parties. It can be useful to have the expert help the magistrate define the questions that he will have to answer, because specialized knowledge is often required to define the questions in a manner that is not only relevant from a legal perspective but also answerable from a scientific point of view. Moreover, in the field of forensic science evidence, many scholars argue that the expert cannot perform her work properly if she is not informed of the *hypotheses* to be considered in the case, that is, the respective positions of the parties with regards to a given piece of evidence.[16] This is important, because failing to define properly the hypotheses to be taken into account will render the expert's conclusions useless at best, and misleading at worst. For example, until recently, DNA experts would often be commissioned with the implicit request to compare the profile of the trace found at the crime scene with the profile of the reference sample given by the suspect. The results would incriminate the defendant, and the matter would be considered to be settled. Only much later would the defense articulate the hypothesis that the defendant might be the source of the DNA, but for reasons independent from the commission of the crime. Such late explanations would often be brushed aside as a posteriori justifications for the evidence, and would not be evaluated seriously by the magistrate or the expert. This is not satisfactory anymore, because research has now clearly established that indirect transfers, contaminations, and other errors can lead to the implication of a person who is in fact innocent.[17] It follows that, in certain cases, multiple scenarios must be explored to explain why a DNA match seems to implicate the defendant. Of course, this necessity (from a scientific perspective) to consider different hypotheses while evaluating the evidence collides with the defendant's right to not incriminate himself. The defendant can choose to remain silent during the investigation and at trial, and not suggest any hypothesis to the expert to explain how the recovered trace evidence found its way on the crime scene. In such a case, the investigating magistrate must define the most reasonable hypothesis for the defense to be taken into account by the expert. And if she does not define the relevant hypotheses, the expert should take it upon himself to do it.

Once the expert questions have been defined, the expert receives the information necessary to carrying out his task. Domestic law determines to what information the expert can have access. In several European jurisdictions, the expert has access to the whole case file, and some experts can even attend police interviews and carry out their own investigations. In other jurisdictions, however, the magistrate only gives the expert the information necessary to the accomplishment of his mission, and the expert is not permitted to seek out further information.

[16] John Buckleton, et al., *Helping Formulate Propositions in Forensic DNA Analysis*, 54 Sci. & Justice 258 (2014).

[17] Georgina Meakin & Allan Jamieson, *DNA Transfer: Review and Implications for Casework*, 7 Forensic Science Int'l: Genetics 434 (2013). For a spectacular case of contamination recently in Germany (the so-called phantom of Heilbronn case), see Claudia Himmelreich, *Germany's Phantom Serial Killer: A DNA Blunder*, Time, Mar. 27, 2009. Available at: http://content.time.com/time/world/article/0,8599,1888126,00.html.

V. Duties of the Expert

An expert's duty is first and foremost to the fact-finder, whom she must inform to the best of her knowledge, in an objective and unbiased manner, about the matter that she was hired to evaluate. In some systems, the expert must take an oath. In other systems, no oath is taken, but the expert is made aware by the magistrate that she must testify truthfully and that she may be prosecuted if she falsifies the results of her examinations or if she lies in the course of her testimony.

Vis-à-vis the magistrate, the expert is normally free to decide how she should complete the task entrusted to her. However, in the disciplines where professional organizations exist, it is not uncommon for those organizations to adopt *standards or guidelines* that define how a certain examination or analysis should be carried out. For example, the European Network of Forensic Science Institutes (ENFSI) has several committees and expert working groups in each forensic discipline that adopt best practice manuals and guidelines that their members must follow when collecting evidence, conducting analyses, interpreting results, or reporting them to fact-finders.[18] Many professional organizations also have codes of ethics that their members must adhere to.[19]

Once the expert has carried out the analyses and interpretations necessary to answering the questions of interest, she will summarize her findings in a written report. Domestic law sometimes defines what elements the report must contain (substantively), and how it should be written (from a formal point of view). In that respect, the expert should be careful to express himself in a way that is clear and understandable for a person who has no knowledge of the field, and to explain any technical term that is used in the report. The expert must give her report in a timely manner, or alternatively, ask for an extension of the deadline given to her. Once the report has been filed, the expert must complete it or correct it if requested to do so by the magistrate. If the expert does not render the report within the decided deadline, the instructing magistrate may have the right to reduce or retain the payment due to the expert, or to dismiss her. In some jurisdictions, a failure to turn in the report in a timely manner could also lead to the expert being struck from the national registry of experts.[20] The expert will sometimes be asked to keep the results of his examinations confidential, either because the stage of the pretrial investigation requires it or because of the topic of inquiry.

It is often not necessary or practical to require that the expert provide, along with her report, all the working material on which she based her conclusions. However, questions can arise during the trial that can render necessary that such information be shared

[18] Guidelines and Best Practice Manuals are available on the ENFSI website, http://enfsi.eu/documents/.

[19] On ethics and the expert witness more generally, see Sheila Willis, *Forensic Science, Ethics and Criminal Justice*, in *Handbook of Forensic Science* 523 (J. Fraser & R. Williams eds., 2009); Joseph Sanders, *Expert Witness Ethics*, 76 Fordham L. Rev. 1539 (2007).

[20] *See, e.g.*, Code de Procédure Pénale [C.P.P.] art. 161 (Fr.).

with the court and/or the parties. That is why experts will usually be required to preserve all the material used for their examinations and to make them available to the court upon request. In the field of forensic science, this includes bench notes, the raw data produced during analysis, earlier drafts of the report, etc. For a psychiatrist or psychologist, this could include, for example, the notes taken during interviews, the video or audio recordings of conversations with the defendant or victim, or the drawings made by a child witness.

The principle of immediacy requires judges in many systems to hear the parties, witnesses, and experts in person, in court. It is thus not sufficient for the judge, during the hearing, to read aloud statements made earlier in the investigation by the expert. It follows that the expert has a duty to testify in court if required to do so by the judge. The rule is often relaxed in the case of routine analyses, however, such as blood-alcohol concentrations and straightforward DNA analyses, to avoid making such experts spend their days in court given the vary high number of cases in which their expertise is adduced. At the hearing, the expert will usually be questioned by the judge, although the prosecutor and attorneys can ask their own questions and comment on the statements made by the expert. Coaching the expert before she is heard in court is usually not permitted, as non-adversary courts value the spontaneity of testimonies (which is also evidenced by the fact that, contrary to the U.S. practice, witnesses and experts are encouraged to answer questions in a free narrative, instead of being limited to answering the questions put to them with yes or no).[21]

VI. The Defendant's Rights When Expert Evidence Is Adduced

As mentioned earlier, non-adversary criminal justice systems often grant the defense the right to be consulted regarding who will be appointed as an expert and what questions will be put to him. Besides, the ECtHR has derived from the right to a fair trial, under certain circumstances, a right to participate in the expert's examination. At a minimum, this means that the defense must have the right to read and comment on the expert's report before the authority reaches a verdict.[22] In certain cases, however, this is insufficient. When the question put to the expert is of a highly technical nature outside of the knowledge of the fact-finder, and when there is a risk that the fact-finder will be highly influenced by the expert's conclusions, the defense or her representative should

[21] For a fascinating illustration of the comparative attitudes and behaviors of American and French experts in a French trial, see Renee Lettow Lerner, *The Intersection of Two Systems: An American on Trial for an American Murder in the French Cour D'Assises*, U. Ill. L. Rev. 791 (2001). *See also* Bron McKillop, *Anatomy of a French Murder Case*, 45 Am. J. Compar. L. 527 (1997).

[22] Feldbrugge v. the Netherlands, App. No. 8562/79, Eur. Ct. H.R., May 25, 1986.

have a right to attend the examinations carried out by the expert, and be allowed to ask questions, make observations, and request further investigations.[23]

The defense must also have the opportunity to confront the expert.[24] In the realm of the ECHR, challenging expert evidence entails two distinct aspects: challenging the substance of the expert's testimony or report, and questioning the person who carried out the expert examination.[25] It is not necessary that the defense demonstrate why the questioning of the expert is relevant: if the prosecution relies on the expert to build its case, and if the court bases a guilty verdict on the expert's report and/or testimony, the defense has a right to direct confrontation. Moreover, even in an inquisitorial setting, the court must hear the expert at the trial stage if it is going to base its conviction mainly on the expert's report.[26] This holds even if the report does not contain any inconsistencies or irregularities: questioning the expert directly allows the court to investigate any potential conflicts of interests,[27] and it also allows the defense to bring to light any deficiencies in the material at the expert's disposal or flaws in the examinations carried out by the expert.[28]

If the defense is not satisfied with the conclusions reported by the court-appointed expert, they can under certain circumstances ask for a counter-expert to be commissioned by the instructing magistrate. If the magistrate accepts the request, the counter-expert becomes a second official expert, instructed and paid by the state, with a status that is equivalent to that of the first expert. If the first and second experts disagree, some systems provide for the appointment of a third expert to help the magistrate arbitrate between the two.

If the instructing magistrate refuses to appoint a counter-expert, the defense can hire a private expert, who will review the report filed by the court-appointed expert and advise the defense on further actions. The main obstacle in this situation is that the defense will have to pay for their private expert themselves, and many defendants cannot afford to do so, even with legal aid. Besides, the status of the defense expert can be less than that of the court-appointed expert in the proceedings, and in some systems fact-finders will give the private expert less weight than the court-appointed expert because of a suspicion that the expert is a "hired gun."[29]

It should be noted that when forensic science evidence is adduced, the position of the defense is not favorable for various reasons. First, the defense will usually not be present

[23] Mantovanelli v. France, App. No. 21497/93, Eur. Ct. H.R., Mar. 17, 1997, § 33 f.

[24] *See* Art. 6(3)(d) ECHR, which does not address explicitly the right to confront experts. However, according to case law, the concept of "witness" has an autonomous meaning under Article 6, and the right to confront experts is a component of the right to a fair trial. *See* Khodorkovskiy and Lebedev v. Russia, App. Nos. 11082/06 and 13772/05, Eur. Ct. H.R., July 25, 2013, § 711.

[25] Doorson v. the Netherlands, App. No. 20524/92, Eur. Ct. H.R., Mar. 26, 1996, §§ 81–82.

[26] *See*, mutatis mutandis, Unterpertinger v. Austria, App. No. 9120/80, Eur. Ct. H.R., Nov. 24, 1986, § 33.

[27] Duško Ivanoski v. Macedonia, App. No. 10718/05, Eur. Ct. H.R., Apr. 24, 2014, § 56.

[28] Khodorkovskiy and Lebedev v. Russia, App. Nos. 11082/06 and 13772/05, Eur. Ct. H.R., July 25, 2013, § 714.

[29] European Commission for the Efficiency of Justice (CEPEJ), Working Group on the Quality of Justice, *Study on the Role of Experts in Judicial Systems of the Council of Europe Member States* 17 (2014).

at the crime scene when the evidence is collected; unfortunately, any evidence that is not collected at this stage will be lost forever, which can seriously compromise the defense's ability to make their case effectively later in the investigation. Second, the defense does not have access to crime scene samples, and the authority will not always agree to release samples to allow for a retesting or re-examination of the evidence.[30] Third, it can be difficult for the defense to find an expert willing to work for them, because of a de jure or de facto monopoly of the state on certain experts, and because of a natural reluctance for many experts to go against colleagues. Fourth, even if a willing expert is found, she will often be a retired expert or an independent consultant who does not have access to the same type of facilities as the official experts, limiting the kind of examinations that she can carry out. Finally, as mentioned before, the private expert will oftentimes not have the same credibility, in the eyes of the authority, as the official expert. For these reasons, the right of the defense with regards to expert evidence has become a critical issue in recent years, especially as expert evidence becomes always more prominent in criminal cases.

VII. The Evaluation of Expert Evidence by the Fact-Finder

Whether the expert is court-appointed or hired by a party, the central difficulty in the use of expert evidence in criminal proceedings is that the fact-finder must evaluate the evidence critically even though she usually lacks the knowledge necessary to do so. In that regard, the relative advantage of court-appointed experts is that the fact-finder often does not need to arbitrate a battle of experts between specialists hired by the prosecution and specialists hired by the defense, who often present diverging opinions. Court-appointed experts are thus perceived as offering an important safeguard against inaccuracy in the evaluation of expert evidence by the fact-finder. This account must be nuanced however, for two reasons. First, even in non-adversary systems, the fact-finder can end up having to evaluate the opinions of multiple experts, that is, an expert and a private counter-expert hired by the defense, and sometimes even a private consultant hired by the *partie civile* in the systems that allow the victim to become a party to the criminal proceedings. In such a case, as we have seen earlier, the weight given to privately hired experts can be much lower than that given to court-appointed experts, but this amounts to a heuristic that has little to do with the actual quality of the various expert reports and can lead to inaccuracies in the establishment of the facts. Second, one study suggests that court-appointed experts could have an important drawback in that

[30] On the right to retest evidence, see, e.g., P.T.C. van Kampen, *Expert Evidence Compared, Rules and Practices, in the Dutch and American Criminal Justice System* 78 (Intersentia Rechtswetenschappen 1998).

the fact-finder invests them with a lot of trust or deference.[31] While it seems reasonable to trust or defer to an expert who has no incentive to be partisan, such an attitude can also lead the fact-finder to overlook the possibility that an expert made a mistake in her analyses and interpretations. Besides, even on a scientific matter, there can be divergent opinions; one court-appointed expert can explain to the fact-finder what those different opinions are, but there are no guarantees that she will.[32] In that respect, adversary systems that encourage skepticism towards expert claims could present an advantage.

Even when there is no battle of experts, how well lay fact-finders understand what experts report and how they interpret expert conclusions in the context of a given case has been a topic of speculation for a long time. The main fear is that the fact-finder will misinterpret the expert conclusions, give them too much or too little probative weight, or even base their evaluation on irrelevant factors. Empirical research suggests indeed that in certain circumstances, lay fact-finders will use cognitive heuristics to decide what weight should be given to an expert's conclusions, instead of basing their assessment on the quality of the evidence itself.[33] For example, some studies suggest that, when the content of the expert's discourse is complex, jurors use the expert's credentials and pay as proxies to evaluate the quality of the expert's conclusions.[34] Other studies suggest that the gender of the expert[35] or the intensity of the eye contact she gives the fact-finder[36] could have an impact on the evaluation of the expert's conclusions, via her perceived credibility.

Moreover, as expert conclusions in certain fields are increasingly presented in the form of probabilities, research has been conducted on how well fact-finders understand evidence presented in the form of statistics. It now seems clear that probabilistic evidence often leads to erroneous reasoning,[37] and that certain forms of probabilistic evidence are more misleading to jurors than others.[38] The majority of studies on how

[31] Joëlle Vuille, *Admissibility and Appraisal of Scientific Evidence in Continental Europe Criminal Justice Systems: Past, Present and Future*, 45 Austl. J. Forensic Sci. 389 (2013). This risk was also noted in the context of family law disputes by Anthony Champagne et al., *Are Court-Appointed Experts the Solution to the Problems of Expert Testimony?*, 84 Judicature 178 (2000).

[32] Ellen E. Deason, *Court-Appointed Expert Witnesses: Scientific Positivism Meets Bias and Deference*, 77 Or. L. Rev. 59 (1998).

[33] John Buckleton et al., *Helping Formulate Propositions in Forensic DNA Analysis*, 54 Sci. & Justice 2 (2014).

[34] Joel Cooper & Isaac M. Neuhaus, *The "Hired Gun" Effect: Assessing the Effect of Pay, Frequency of Testifying and Credentials on the Perception of Expert Testimony*, 24 L. & Human Behavior 149 (2000).

[35] Regina A. Schuller & Janice Cripps, *Expert Evidence Pertaining to Battered Women: The Impact of Gender of Expert and Timing of Testimony* 22 L. & Human Behavior 17 (1998).

[36] Tess M.S. Neal & Stanley L. Brodsky, *Expert Witness Credibility as a Function of Eye Contact Behavior and Gender*, 35 Crim. Justice & Behavior 1515 (2008).

[37] William C. Thompson & Edward L. Schumann, *Interpretation of Statistical Evidence in Criminal Trials*, 11 L. & Human Behavior 167 (1987); David H. Kaye & Jonathan J. Koehler, *Can Jurors Understand Probabilistic Evidence?*, 154 J. Royal Statistical Soc'y 75 (1991).

[38] Jonathan J. Koehler, *On Conveying the Probative Value of DNA Evidence: Frequencies, Likelihood Ratios, and Error Rates*, 67 U. Colo. L. Rev. 859 (1996). Kristy Martire et al., *On the Interpretation of Likelihood Ratios in Forensic Science Evidence: Presentation Formats and the Weak Evidence Effect*, 240 Forensic Sci. Int'l 61 (2014).

well fact-finders understand expert evidence has been carried out with jurors, however. Very little empirical work has explored the way professional judges evaluate such evidence. Yet, two independent studies carried out in Switzerland suggest that Swiss professional judges fall prey to many of the same cognitive traps as jurors.[39]

The studies on how well fact-finders understand expert evidence have led to numerous debates on how expert conclusions should be expressed to the fact-finder in order to improve their understanding and minimize the risk of suboptimal reasoning.[40] Guidelines have been issued by some professional organizations and are regularly being modified to adapt to new scientific developments and changing sensibilities in the relevant communities.[41] Some courts—mainly in the Anglo-Saxon world—have also occasionally chimed in, usually to express irritation as to the lack of transparency of certain expert conclusion formats.[42]

VIII. Sanctions in Case of Misconduct or Gross Negligence

If an expert breaches her expert duties as defined by her professional organization, the first consequence could be a disciplinary sanction from that organization. For example, a professor of pediatrics at the University of Leeds was struck from the British Medical Registry after his testimony in the *Sally Clark* case was deemed misleading by the General Medical Council.[43] Sally Clark had been prosecuted for murdering her two sons, who had died as infants two years apart.[44] Clark had said that she had found them dead in their crib, and the pathologists who examined the children were unable to give much information as to the cause and manner of death. The expert testified that, based on the fact that the probability of one cot death was 1 in 8,543, the probability of two cot deaths would be 1 in 73 million;[45] this, in turn, was later interpreted as a 1 in 73 million

[39] Mark D. Schweizer, *Kognitive Täuschung vor Gericht* (PhD Dissertation, Faculty of Law, Univ. Zurich, 2005); Joëlle Vuille, *Ce que la Justice Fait Dire à l'ADN (et que l'ADN ne dit pas vraiment): Étude Qualitative de l'évaluation de la Preuve par ADN dans le Système Judiciaire Pénal Suisse* (PhD Dissertation, Faculty of Law and Criminal Justice, Univ. Lausanne, 2011).

[40] On the communication of expert findings to fact-finders, see, e.g., Nicole M. Egli Anthonioz & Joëlle Vuille, *Communicating Scientific Findings in the Courtroom*, in *Oxford Bibliographies in Criminology* (2016).

[41] For an illustration (and critical discussion) of a series of reforms in the field of fingerprint comparison in the United States, see Simon Cole, *Individualization Is Dead, Long Live Individualization! Reforms of Reporting Practices for Fingerprint Analysis in the United States*, 13 L. Probability & Risk 117 (2013).

[42] *See, e.g.*, a footwear case in the UK, R v. T [2010] EWCA Crim 2439. For a fingerprint case in the United States, see United States v. Llera Plaza I, 179 F. Supp. 2d 492 (E.D. Pa. 2002); *reversed*, United States v. Llera Plaza II, 188 F. Supp.2d 549 (E.D. Pa. 2002).

[43] Nicole Martin, *GMC Strikes Off Meadow for "Abusing Position" in Cot Death Trial*, The Telegraph, July 16, 2005.

[44] R v. Clark [2000] EWCA Crim 54 (first appeal); R v. Clark [2003] EWCA Crim 1020 (second appeal).

[45] That is, 1 in 8,543 times 1 in 8,543.

chance that the children's death was accidental.[46] The Royal Statistical Society issued a statement[47] that denounced the expert's statistics as being invalid, because he had multiplied two probabilities that were not independent, which produced a total probability that was much smaller—hence more incriminating—than what was actually supported by the data.[48] Besides, implying that the number of 1 in 73 million represented the odds of Sally Clark being innocent was erroneous from a statistical point of view.[49] The doctor appealed the General Medical Council's decision, however, and it was reversed in 2006.[50]

Experts have occasionally been sued by people who were wrongfully convicted on the basis of their testimony. In Germany for instance, a court ordered an anthropologist to pay compensation to Donald Stellwag, after the latter was convicted and sentenced to eight years imprisonment for a bank robbery on the basis of the expert's testimony but was later exonerated.[51] In many European jurisdictions, an expert can thus be held civilly liable if she makes a grave mistake in her assessment of the evidence or intentionally misleads the fact-finder.[52] In the United States, experts have historically benefitted from immunity when they testified in a criminal case. The rule aimed at encouraging experts to participate in the proceedings and speak freely by shielding them from retaliation.[53] However, the protection seems to not be absolute anymore.[54]

We could not find any structured data on the frequency with which experts are sanctioned by their professional organization or sued by parties to a trial after giving erroneous or misleading testimony. Such cases seem to be rare, though.

IX. Current Issues in the Use of Expert Evidence in a Criminal Proceeding

The use of expert evidence in criminal trials raises the question of how the system can screen out evidence of bad quality to avoid mistakes in fact-finding. In the field of forensic

[46] R v. Clark [2003] EWCA Crim 1020, §§ 96–99.

[47] Royal Statistical Society, Press Release, Royal Statistical Society Concerned by Issues Raised in Sally Clark Case, Oct. 23, 2001.

[48] Cot deaths being linked to genetic and environmental factors, the chance of experience one cot death in a family that has already suffered from another cot death is higher than the probability of experiencing one cot death in the first place.

[49] Royal Statistical Society, *Letter from the President to the Lord Chancellor Regarding the Use of Statistical Evidence in Court Cases*, Jan. 23, 2002. For an explanation of the statistical fallacy, see I.W. Evett, *Avoiding the Transposed Conditional*, 35 Sci. & Justice 127 (1995).

[50] Joshua Rozenberg, *Sir Roy Meadow, the Flawed Witness, Wins GMC Appeal*, The Telegraph, Feb. 18, 2006.

[51] OLG Frankfurt 19. Zivilsenat, Aktenzeichen 19 U 8/07, Urteil vom 02.10.2007.

[52] CEPEJ, *Study on the Role of Experts*, *supra* note 29, at 12–13.

[53] Haskell M. Pitluck, *Legal Liability of an Expert Witness*, in *Bitemark Evidence: A Color Atlas and Text* (Robert B.J. Dorion ed., 2011).

[54] Randall K. Hanson, *Witness Immunity Under Attack: Disarming Hired Guns*, 31 Wake Forest L. Rev. 497 (1996).

science evidence especially, the courts have not been very effective in scrutinizing expert evidence and ensuring that it is accurate.[55] A number of wrongful convictions caused at least in part by erroneous or misleading scientific evidence have come to light in recent years, both in adversary[56] and non-adversary criminal justice systems.[57] Far from being isolated cases attributable to a few incompetent experts, it appears that there are systemic problems plaguing the field, notably a lack of empirical validation, an absence of standards, improper practices, and biased interpretations.[58] This situation was allowed to develop because of a general lack of regulation, and although regulatory initiatives have been taken in many jurisdictions in the last few years, they are still not comprehensive. One enduring problem is the inability of experts in most disciplines to provide the fact-finder with error rates for the techniques employed. Assessing the rate at which a forensic analysis or interpretation is mistaken is arguably difficult.[59] But it is also essential if one wants to assess accurately the probative weight of a given piece of evidence.[60] Efforts must be made in that respect in the future.

Cognitive biases on the part of experts have also been a topic of debate in the forensic science communities. Until the early 2000s, it was not uncommon to read that, as scientists, experts provided reports that were "objective" because they were based on hard data derived from the natural sciences. But in 2004, a fingerprint was found on a piece of explosive device retrieved from the Madrid train bombings, and Spanish authorities shared it with police forces around the world after they failed to find a match in the Spanish database. The FBI soon announced that they had identified the source of the print as Brandon Mayfield, an Oregon attorney. As the world would soon learn, that identification was mistaken (the print was later attributed to Ouhnane Daoud, an Algerian national). The mistake was caused in part by the fact that, after an initial mistake made by the first analyst, the latter asked his supervisor to check his conclusions,

[55] Darryl K. Brown, *The Decline of Defense Counsel and the Rise of Accuracy in Criminal Adjudication*, 93 Calif. L. Rev. 1585 (2005); Gary Edmond & Joëlle Vuille, *Comparing the Use of Forensic Science Evidence in Australia, Switzerland and the United States: Transcending the Adversarial/Non-adversarial Dichotomy*, 54 Jurimetrics 221 (2014).

[56] *See, e.g.*, Brandon L. Garrett & Peter J. Neufeld, *Invalid Forensic Science Testimony and Wrongful Convictions*, 95 Va. L. Rev. 1 (2009); Bibi Sangha et al., *Forensic Investigations and Miscarriages of Justice, The Rhetoric Meets the Reality* (Irwin Law Inc. 2010).

[57] Tim Slagman, Unschuldig in Haft—Wenn der Richter irrt, Die Welt, Jan. 21, 2013; Peter van Koppen, *Blundering Justice, The Schiedam Park Murder*, in *Serial Murder and the Psychology of Violent Crimes* 207 (R. Kocsis ed., 2008); Arno Heissmeyer, Fachmann für Fehlurteile, Focus, Aug. 6, 2001; Peter Holenstein, *Das Letzte Kapitel is Noch Offen*, Die Weltwoche, Oct. 21, 2006; Gisela Friederichsen, *Freispruch im Fall Harry Wörz, Triumph des Richters*, Spiegel Online, Oct. 22, 2009.

[58] National Research Council, *Strengthening Forensic Science in the United States: A Path Forward* (2009); President's Council of Advisors on Science and Technology, *Forensic Science in Criminal Courts: Ensuring Scientific Validity of Feature-Comparison Methods* (2016).

[59] National Research Council, Comm. on DNA Forensic Science, *The Evaluation of Forensic DNA Evidence* (1996).

[60] Jonathan J. Koehler, *Why DNA Likelihood Ratios Should Account for Error (Even When a National Research Council Report Says They Should Not)*, 37 Jurimetrics J. 425 (1997).

informing him that he had identified Mayfield as the source of the print. This led to a confirmation bias, an unconscious psychological phenomenon that leads the subject to search primarily for information that confirms his expectations and to interpret all ambiguous information as supporting those expectations.[61] After a decade of intense research, the existence of cognitive biases is now well-documented in many forensic fields and has led some scholars to suggest that experts be subjected to so-called blinding procedures that aim to shield analysts from contextual information about the case or the suspect at some stages of their examination.[62] Such procedures would be especially useful in adversary criminal justice systems, in which forensic practitioners work in close collaboration with the prosecuting authorities and as a consequence can in some cases come (unconsciously) to espouse their views. Other scholars have come out against such blinding procedures, arguing that analysts need some contextual information to be able to render conclusions that are useful to the fact-finder.[63]

Finally, the transnational use of expert evidence is bound to become an important issue in years to come. Many criminal prosecutions nowadays concern cases with an international component, because criminals cross borders, whether physically or virtually through the use of mobile phones and computers. It follows that investigating or prosecuting authorities increasingly in their own proceedings rely on evidence adduced abroad. Simultaneously, experts become increasingly specialized, to rationalize important investments in ever more costly infrastructures and complex technology. It follows that in some fields, there are only a handful of experts in Europe, and an investigating magistrate who needs such highly specialized knowledge would have no choice but to get it outside his own jurisdiction. However, the absence of standardization in the regulation of expert evidence across the different European states sometimes makes it difficult to use expert evidence adduced in one state in a prosecution and trial held in another state. The barriers are legal,[64] but also psychological and practical: in the absence of harmonization, it is difficult to know enough about a foreign expert to evaluate that expert's reports and testimony and to trust the accuracy of that evaluation. European states need to mutualize their forensic expertise and develop a structured system that would make foreign forensic expertise more legible for domestic fact-finders.

[61] Raymond S. Nickerson, *Confirmation Bias: A Ubiquitous Phenomenon in Many Guises*, 2 Rev. General Psych. 175 (1998).

[62] Michael J. Saks et al., *Context Effects in Forensic Science: A Review and Application of the Science of Science to Crime Laboratory Practice in the United States*, 43 Sci. & Justice 77 (2003); Dan E. Krane et al., *Sequential Unmasking: A Means of Minimizing Observer Effects in Forensic DNA Interpretation*, 53 J. Forensic Sci. 1006 (2008).

[63] Christophe Champod, *Research Focused Mainly on Bias Will Paralyse Forensic Science*, 54 Sci. & Justice 107 (2014).

[64] Sofie Depauw, *A European Evidence (Air)Space? Taking Cross-Border Legal Admissibility of Forensic Evidence to a Higher Level*, 6 Euro. Crim. L. Rev. 82 (2016).

X. Conclusion

Expert evidence plays an increasing role in criminal prosecution and adjudication, and there is a case to be made that, as the content of expert reports becomes ever more complex and difficult to understand for lay fact-finders, the expert will in effect usurp the role of the fact-finder with regard to the elements of fact that the expert was hired to evaluate. This is troubling on many grounds. First, there is a lack of regulatory mechanisms in many expert communities, with the consequence that the quality of expert evidence is uneven, and the fact-finder needs to scrutinize expert reports carefully. Second, the benefits of adversarialism are increasingly lost on the vast majority of defendants who have their case disposed of through expedited procedure. Who will counterbalance or challenge the expert's conclusions when the expert's report is not debated in the presence of all parties, and the expert is not heard? Finally, many non-adversary systems are slowly limiting the powers of the neutral investigating magistrate, and some have abolished the institution altogether, replacing the magistrate with prosecutors. It follows that experts are always more under the control of people who, even if the law tasks them with the pursuit of the truth, have an incentive to obtain a conviction. What will the impact be on the role of experts? The neutral court-appointed expert traditionally known in non-adversary criminal justice systems could slowly lose his independence and become a witness for the prosecution, on the model of his Anglo-American colleagues. There would then be a risk that the rights of the accused would not be realized when expert evidence is adduced, and that the right to a fair trial could become an empty shell. In the years to come, it will thus be critical to evaluate how criminal law reforms in a broad sense affect the use of expert evidence in non-adversary criminal justice systems, and how expert professional communities could be better integrated in the system to inform legal and judicial debates around the topic.

References

Peter Alldridge, *Scientific Expertise and Comparative Criminal Procedure*, 3 Int'l J. Evid. & Proof 141–64 (1999)

Christophe Champod & Joëlle Vuille, *Scientific Evidence in Europe—Admissibility, Evaluation and Equality of Arms*, 9(1) Int'l Commentary on Evidence 1–68 (2011)

European Commission for the Efficiency of Justice, Working Group on the Quality of Justice, *Study on the Role of Experts In Judicial Systems of the Council of Europe Member States* (2014)

J.D.J. Havard, *Expert Scientific Evidence Under the Adversarial System, A Travesty of Justice?*, 32(3) J. Forensic Sci. Soc'y 225 (1992)

Lirieka Meintjes-van der Walt, *Expert Evidence in the Criminal Justice Process—A Comparative Perspective* (Amsterdam: Rozenberg 2001)

Mike Redmayne, *Expert Evidence and Criminal Justice* (2001)

Michael J. Saks, *Expert Witness in Europe and the United States*, in *Adversarial versus Inquisitorial Justice* 235–44 (P. van Koppen & S. Penrod eds., 2003)

W.A. Schabas, *The European Convention on Human Rights: A Commentary* (2015)
John R. Spencer, *Court Experts and Expert Witnesses, Have We a Lesson to Learn from the French?*, 45 Current Legal Problems 213–36 (1992)
Law Society of England and Wales, *Safeguarding the Use of Expert Evidence in the European Union: Final Report* (2009)
Law Commission, *Expert Evidence in Criminal Proceedings in England and Wales* (Law Comm'n No. 325, 2011)
P.T.C. van Kampen, *Expert Evidence Compared, Rules and Practices in the Dutch and American Criminal Justice System* (Intersentia Rechtswetenschappen 1998)

CHAPTER 12

CONCEPTUALIZING THE VICTIM WITHIN CRIMINAL JUSTICE PROCESSES IN COMMON LAW TRADITION

MARIE MANIKIS*

I. Introduction

ALTHOUGH victims of crime in common law jurisdictions are not parties with standing in criminal proceedings, they are nevertheless central participants to the criminal justice process. Their role has continuously evolved across time and systems and impacts the role and interests of the other actors of the criminal justice process. The following chapter discusses the various philosophical foundations underpinning victim involvement in the criminal justice processes of common law jurisdictions by arguing that the public/private divide is frequently used to conceptualize victims' various roles.[1] It suggests that victims have at times been conceived as private entities with independent interests from those of the state, and at others as components of the public/state interest. Further, this piece offers a theoretical framework that enables a pluralistic view of victim

* The author is most grateful to the FRQSC and SSHRC for providing funds that contributed to the realization of this chapter.

[1] Understandings of the private/public divide vary depending on context. For instance, Tracy Higgins, *Reviving the Public/Private Distinction in Feminist Theorizing*, 75 Chicago-Kent L. Rev. 847 (2000) and Ruth Gavison, *Feminism and the Public/Private Distinction*, 45 Stan L. Rev. 1 (1992) discuss the divide in feminist theory. Derek McKee, *The Public/Private Distinction in* Roncarelli v. Duplessis, 55 McGill L.J. 461 (2010) challenges the distinction between state and civil society. In this chapter the private/public divide refers to the division between civil and criminal process (systemic), as well as private interests and public (state) interests.

participation. Finally, this piece suggests that the foundation and conception of victim involvement can affect the relationship among victims, prosecutors, and the defendant.

II. Conceiving and Defining the Victim in Criminal Justice Processes

Crime victims have always had a role in the criminal process, but it has taken different forms throughout history. Examining this role is particularly rich since it enables us to understand how victims have been used to reinforce but also challenge the public/private divide across time and jurisdictions.

In common law jurisdictions, rooted in liberal thought, crime is currently conceived as a public wrong—in other words, as harm to the state instead of an individual—giving rise to a public/private distinction. Prior to the thirteenth century, in early societies based on kinship ties and tribal organizations, the concept of public wrong did not exist. Crime was a tort and a private wrong instead of a matter of public concern beyond the interest of the families involved.[2] Thus, there were no centralized systems of criminal justice where the state protected the rights of victims and the accused.[3] Victims and their kin were expected to take care of wrongs by avenging and carrying out the blood feud.[4] These were gradually eliminated and replaced by an emerging system of tribunals that assessed injury and awarded compensation to the victim and his or her family. As feudalism developed in England, between 700 and 1066 A.D., lords and bishops began to replace kinship groups as recipients of compensation, as some forms of wrongs were considered violations against the fiefdom and morality.

During the King's Peace, wrongs began to take a public dimension, contributing to the public/private divide in the nature of crime. By the sixteenth and seventeenth centuries, the emergence of the nation-state and theories of sovereignty in modern political and legal thought crystallized a distinct public realm.[5] Within this conception, crime was considered a wrong against the monarch/state, and thus criminal proceedings were undertaken under his name. This private/public divide around the wrong however, did not immediately and consistently translate throughout the process. Victims were no longer the receptors of various remedies for harm, but remained for a great period of time the administrators of the criminal justice process as public representatives of the monarch. Indeed, they remained in charge of arrests, collecting evidence and prosecutions[6]—albeit

[2] Stephen Shafer, *Victimology: The Victim and His Criminal* (1977).

[3] Sir Henry Sumner Maine, *Ancient Law: Its Connection with the Early History of Society, and Its Relation to the Modern Ideas* (1861).

[4] Shafer, *supra* note 2; John Hagan, *Victims Before the Law: The Organizational Domination of Criminal Law* (1983).

[5] Morton J. Horwitz, *The History of the Public/Private Distinction*, 130 U. Pa. L. Rev. 1423 (1982).

[6] John H. Langbein, *The Criminal Trial Before the Lawyers*, 45 U. Chi. L. Rev. 263 (1978).

in the name of the sovereign. Hence it was "not only the privilege but the duty of the private citizen to preserve the King's Peace and bring offenders to justice."[7]

In the middle of the nineteenth century the public/private divide was reified to varying degrees across jurisdictions. In England since Henry VIII, numerous attempts were made to create a national system of public prosecutions, but it was only accomplished in 1879 with the Director of Public Prosecutions. The department was rather small and was only responsible for the most serious cases, which remained exceptional.[8] Although public prosecutions continued to expand in England and Wales, private prosecutions remained present and more available than in other common law jurisdictions. The expansion of public prosecutions lies in part on the Blackstonian model, which partly conceives crime as a wrong against the community: "public wrongs, or crimes and misdemeanours, are a breach and violation of the public rights and duties, due to the whole community, considered a community in [its] social aggregate capacity."[9] Yet, Blackstone also highlighted that "every public offense is also a private wrong."[10] Blackstone believed that victims' means of redress for their personal harms were primarily through private, civil remedies,[11] reiterating the public/private divide between systems.

In other common law jurisdictions, including Canada and the United States, the administration of justice was more rapidly professionalized through state agencies—namely police agencies and public prosecutors.[12] As part of this move, the victim's role became circumscribed. Across most common law jurisdictions, the role of individual victims became in great part an evidentiary one controlled by the state,[13] which focused on determining the victim's credibility and reliability as a witness and providing evidence about the crime. The actors of the criminal justice process—police, prosecutors, defense, and judges—decided when at the various stages of the criminal process victims would testify about the harm and factual events that occurred. The law regarded this person as a witness—advancing the public interest and public harm as defined by these actors rather than themselves.

[7] Peter Burns, *Private Prosecutions in Canada: The Law and a Proposal for Change*, 21 McGill L.J. 269, 271 (1975). *See also* Bernard Dickens, *Control of Prosecutions in the United Kingdom*, 22 Int'l & Comp. L.Q. 1, 2 (1973).

[8] Burns, *supra* note 7. [9] William Blackstone, 4 *Commentaries on the Laws of England* 5 (1857).

[10] *Id.* [11] *Id.* at 7.

[12] Burns, *supra* note 7. Private prosecutions remain and continue to be used in England. *See* Daniel Martin, *UK: The Rise of Private Prosecutions*, MONDAQ (Nov. 10, 2016), http://www.mondaq.com/x/541522/Crime/The+Rise+of+Private+Prosecutions. For guidance and examples of private prosecutions, see also The Crown Prosecution Service, *Private Prosecutions*, http://www.cps.gov.uk/legal/p_to_r/private_prosecutions/(last visited Apr. 3, 2017). American prosecutions are public professionalized bodies, which is not a result of the English common law heritage. *See* John L. Worrall, *Prosecution in America: A Historical and Comparative Account*, in *The Changing Role of the American Prosecutor* 3, 5–6 (John L. Worrall & M. Eliane Nugent-Borakove eds., 2008). In Canada, although private prosecutions are still on the books, in practice they are very rare and are generally taken over and pursued or stopped by public prosecutors. *See* Burns, *supra* note 7.

[13] Douglas Beloof, Paul Cassell & Steven Twist, *Victims in Criminal Procedure* 5–17 (3d ed. 2010); Juan Pablo Pérez-León Acevedo, *Victims' Rights, Human Rights and Criminal Justice: Reconceiving the Role of Third Parties*, 7 J. Int'l Crim. Just. 442, 442–43 (2009) (book review).

1. Toward an Individualized and Private Conception of the Victim

This public model of the criminal process has been challenged. Some began to question the public harm dimension as a foundational premise of the criminal justice process by highlighting that individual victims also suffer harm that needs to be recognized. Since there is also a private dimension to harm, private interests should also be recognized as separate from that of the states.[14] Although this vision questions the exclusively public character of criminal justice, and thus challenges the private/public divide between systems (civil versus criminal), it nevertheless reinforces the public/private divide within the criminal process by considering victims' interests as distinct from the public ones held by the state.

The victims' rights movement in the United States was particularly influential in challenging the exclusive public interest (as state) dimension of the criminal justice process by recognizing victims' individual and separate interests and harms within it. It conceived the victim as a separate actor of the process with independent interests from those of the state and the accused. The language of individual victims' rights was adopted and meant to be equal and balanced with defendants' individual rights in the criminal process.[15] The notion of "balance" supposed a possible clash between victims' rights and defendants' rights, criticized for failing to acknowledge that the justifications for victims' and defendants' rights may differ.[16]

This individual rights discourse in many ways also opposed the victim to the state/criminal justice agencies. Similar to the natural rights theories that were elaborated in the seventeenth century for the purpose of setting limits on state power to guarantee defendants' individual rights, this Lockean philosophy of "possessive individualism"[17] was transposed in the context of victims of crime. It defined victims as individual entities that not only suffered direct victimization in the hands of the accused, but also "secondary victimization" by the powerful state criminal justice system that can be harmful and often unresponsive to their needs.[18] Therapeutic jurisprudence as well as procedural

[14] Douglas Beloof, *The Third Wave of Crime Victims' Rights: Standing, Remedy, and Review*, 2 BYU L. Rev. 255 (2005); Danielle Levine, *Public Wrongs and Private Rights: Limiting the Victim's Role in a System of Public Prosecution*, 104 Nw. U. L. Rev. 335, 361 (2010); Paul Cassell & Steven Joffee, *The Crime Victim's Expanding Role in a System of Public Prosecution: A Response to the Critics of the Crime Victims' Rights Act*, 105 Nw. U. L. Rev. 164 (2011).

[15] *See* Beloof, *supra* note 14, at 294–96; Jonathan Doak, *Victims' Rights, Human Rights and Criminal Justice: Reconceiving the Role of Third Parties* 248 (2008).

[16] Ian Edwards, *An Ambiguous Participant: The Crime Victim and Criminal Justice Decision-Making*, 44 Brit. J. Criminology 967, 972 (2004).

[17] Crawford B. Macpherson, *The Political Theory of Possessive Individualism: Hobbes to Locke* 238 (2010); John Simmons, *The Lockean Theory of Rights* 397 (1992).

[18] Dean J. Kilpatrick & Randy K. Otto, *Constitutionally Guaranteed Participation in Criminal Proceedings for Victims: Potential Effects on Psychological Functioning*, 34 Wayne L. Rev. 7, 18–22 (1987). Examples of secondary victimization include situations where victims are left in the dark about the development and outcome of the process as well as situations where they have been excluded and their voice is not heard in the process.

justice theory were also invoked to bolster the argument that legal processes, including those that exclude victims, can affect litigants, so rules and their implementation must minimize adverse impacts on litigants and empower individuals.[19]

Sociolegal theorists and critical criminologists interested in realist perspectives have also contributed to reflection on the discriminatory and harmful ways that the state has defined victims. The "ideal victim" describes a structural inequality where certain victims possess attributes that are idealized by society and generate the most sympathy from the system. This concept enables us to understand and challenge the legal positivist definition of victims found in most legislation, which excludes some individuals from being recognized as worthy victims when their identities do not include idealized attributes.[20] These laws operate in ways that do not reflect that victims can have complex identities that are often interchangeable and interrelated with the accused's.[21]

The discourse arguing that victims' rights needed human rights protections against the state has been more notable in the United States, where the debate has focused on robust ways by which victims can claim their rights and obtain redress in case of breaches by state agencies. These rights are drafted as freedoms to choose to participate in the process and enable victims' voices to be heard in addition to the one offered by the state. Discussions about the constitutionalization of victims' rights by amending the federal and state constitutions has long been a movement in the United States, followed by discussions around the recognition of victim standing in criminal proceedings to uphold their individual rights and obtain remedies in cases of state violations.[22] This has reinforced the perception that victim protection and empowerment against state agencies need to be recognized as legally enforceable human rights. This language of rights developed in parallel to the discussion around accused's rights in the criminal justice process and has given rise to procedural changes that enable victims to raise issues independently from the state while being legally represented by counsel. This echoes reflections about individuals needing protection from the state and the idea that their interests may be different from public and state interests. While this approach to individual human rights that enables enforcement mechanisms against state action, supports a continued public/private distinction and liberal notion of

[19] Mary M. Giannini, *Measured Mercy Managing the Intersection of Executive Pardon Power and Victims' Rights with Procedural Justice Principles*, 13 Ohio St. J. Crim. L. 89 (2015); Edna Erez, *Integrating Restorative Justice Principles in Adversarial Proceedings through Victim Impact Statements*, in *Reconcilable Rights? Analysing the Tension Between Victims and Defendants* 81 (Ed Cape ed., 2004).

[20] Various legislation excludes individuals who may have committed the offensc. For instance, in Canada, the *Canadian Victims Bill of Rights* includes an exception to the definition of victims by highlighting that "an individual is not a victim in relation to the offence, or entitled to exercise a victim's rights under this Act, if the individual is charged with the offence, found guilty of the offence or found not criminally responsible on account of mental disorder or unfit to stand trial in respect to the offence." *See* Canadian Victims Bill of Rights, S.C., c. 13, s. 2 § 3 (2015) (Can.).

[21] Simon Singer, *Homogeneous Victim-Offender Populations: A Review and Some Research Implications*, 72 J. Crim. L. & Criminology 779 (1981); Terance Miethe & Robert Meier, *Crime and Its Social Context: Toward an Integrated Theory of Offenders, Victims, and Situations* (1994).

[22] Peggy Tobolowksy, *Constitutionalizing Crime Victim Rights*, 33 Crim. L. Bull. 395 (1997); Beloof, *supra* note 14.

criminal justice, it also simultaneously challenges the distinction by introducing an additional private party within an inherently public process.

Two types of rights have been developed in this respect, namely service and procedural rights.[23] "Service rights" have received broad recognition and aim to provide victims with better treatment and experience in the criminal justice system. They include rights to information/notification about important court dates and about the progress of their case, assistance for vulnerable victims, and state compensation schemes.[24] They are generally uncontroversial since they are viewed as compatible with the adversarial model and the independence of prosecutorial decision-making.[25] In England and Wales, service rights, including state compensations schemes and the right to information, are well developed.[26] Similarly, in the United States, notification rights exist for victims to be made aware of the different stages of the process, as well as decisions that relate to their case.[27]

Most proponents of the individualized rights approach have further argued that in addition to service rights, victims should also be offered greater participatory rights in criminal proceedings.[28] They argue that due to the risk of secondary victimization from exclusion and the independent interests that victims have, they should be afforded a voice in the process. Such rights are procedural rights and remain controversial within the adversarial context, since they provide victims with a more active role in the decision-making process—particularly when framed as separate from prosecutorial interests.[29] They include opportunities for victims to provide information and sometimes their opinions to criminal justice agencies and courts on key criminal justice decisions, including prosecution,[30] bail/custody, sentencing, parole release and license decisions, largely through "victim impact/personal" statements (VIS).[31] The forms of participation will be further discussed later in the chapter. Much American literature has articulated this

[23] Andrew Ashworth & Mike Redmayne, *The Criminal Process* (4th ed. 2010).

[24] *See, e.g.*, Andrew Sanders, *Victim Participation in an Exclusionary Criminal Justice System*, in *New Visions of Crime Victims* 197–222 (Carolyn Hoyle & Richard Young eds., 2002); Sandra Walklate, *Imagining the Victim of Crime* (2007); Rob Mawby, *Public Sector Services and the Victim in Crime*, in *Handbook of Victims and Victimology* (Sandra Walklate ed., 2007).

[25] *See, e.g.*, Dan Jones & Josie Brown, *The Relationship Between Victims and Prosecutors: Defending Victims' Rights? A CPS Response*, 3 Crim. L. Rev. 212 (2010).

[26] *See, e.g.*, Marie Manikis, *Rhetoric or Reality? Victims' Enforcement Mechanisms in England and Wales and the United States* (2014) (PhD dissertation, University of Oxford) (on file with the Faculty of Law, University of Oxford).

[27] *See, e.g.*, the right to notification in the Crime Victims' Rights Act, 18 U.S.C. § 3771(a)(2) (2004).

[28] Beloof, *supra* note 14. Parallels can be drawn between this view and the feminist literature that focus on the relationship between the distinction and assertions of power, choice, and the ability to access "private" rights. *See* Higgins, *supra* note 1.

[29] *See, e.g.*, A. Ashworth & M. Redmayne, *supra* note 23; Carolyn Hoyle, *The Role of the Victim in Criminal Justice in England*, 37 Crim. L. Rev. 490 (2014); Walklate, *supra* note 24.

[30] *See, e.g.*, the right to confer with the attorney for the government in the case in the Crime Victims' Rights Act 18 U.S.C. § 3771(a)(5) (2004).

[31] The victim impact and personal statement regime has been developed in several jurisdictions. For comparative perspectives on these schemes, *see* Julian Roberts & Marie Manikis, *Victim Personal Statements: A Review of Empirical Research* (Report for the Commissioner for Victims and Witnesses in England and Wales) (2011).

form of participation as a separate, often conflicting right from the state, which entitles victims to separate standing in criminal proceedings.[32] Examples can be found in several decisions where victims and prosecutors had separate interests and victims brought forward independent claims in front of courts.[33]

Criminal law scholars who reinforce the public/private divide between systems by reaffirming the public nature of the criminal justice process generally agree with improved services and treatment for individual victims by criminal justice agencies, but do not approve of a participatory role of victims in criminal proceedings.[34] They argue that the latter recognition would undermine the presumption of innocence and change the public adversarial nature of criminal proceedings between the state and the defendant. Since they consider victims as representative of private interests, they criticize their intrusion within a public system that is meant to advance public interests.

Challenging the public monopoly by the introduction of private interests has given rise to important discussions that were typically left within the remit of tort law. Legal scholars have debated which type of harms (direct or indirect; physical or psychological) should a person have suffered to be considered a "victim" to obtain participatory rights in criminal proceedings. These questions are particularly present in the United States, where victims have mainly represented individual interests that can often conflict with the public interest. For instance, the U.S. Supreme Court in *Paroline v. United States*[35] decided that only possessors of child pornography who have caused *proximate losses* to victims would be held accountable by paying restitution to victims for the impact of their conduct. This suggests that child pornography possessors will not be paying restitution for harm caused by others who have viewed the victim's image, which according to some could undermine the victim's status in those circumstances and her right to full reparation for all harms.[36]

Other debates around the proximity of harm[37] relate to the concept of secondary victims, or "ancillary harm." Roberts and Manikis have developed this conception of victims and examined legal developments in which family members of a murder victim were recognized as victims on the basis of the principle of proportionality at sentencing.[38]

[32] *See, e.g.*, Beloof, *supra* note 14; Cassell & Joffee, *supra* note 14.

[33] *In re* Dean, 527 F.3d 391 (5th Cir. 2008); *see also* United States v. BP Products North America Inc., 610 F. Supp. 2d 655 (S.D. Tex. 2009) in which the prosecutor representing the public interest decided it would not inform or allow victims to express their views in the context of a plea agreement. Also, in *Kenna v. U.S. Dist. Court*, 435 F.3d 1011, 1013 (9th Cir. 2006), the parties presented theirs during sentencing, while the victim was not allowed to present a victim impact statement. The victim challenged this decision and the 9th Circuit accepted the motion by making clear that victims also needed to be heard separately in the process.

[34] *See, e.g.*, Ashworth & Redmayne, *supra* note 23.

[35] Paroline v. United States, 134 S. Ct. 1710 (2014).

[36] Paul Cassell & James Marsh, *Full Restitution for Child Pornography Victims: The Supreme Court's* Paroline *Decision and the Need for a Congressional Response*, 13 Ohio St. J. Crim. L. 5 (2015).

[37] Darryl K. Brown, *Third-Party Interests in Criminal Law*, 80 Tex. L. Rev. 1383 (2002).

[38] Julian Roberts & Marie Manikis, *Victim Impact Statements at Sentencing: The Relevance of Ancillary Harm*, 15 Can. Crim. L. Rev. 1 (2010); Marie Manikis & Julian Roberts, *Recognizing Ancillary Harm at Sentencing: A Proportionate and Balanced Response*, 15 Can. Crim. L. Rev. 131 (2011).

Occasionally, "ancillary harm" has become a relevant factor at sentencing, and in some cases has also been considered an aggravating factor.[39] In response, some have argued that the concept of secondary victims should not be recognized because it would provide a platform for greater penalties and vengeance while diminishing the position on causation that rests on a contribution to harm at more than a de minimis level.[40] Others have defended this approach and provided additional American examples where ancillary harm and secondary victims were extended to include other types of victims and harms that are proximate to the ones suffered by the direct victim, including individuals with close familial, professional, or other ties to the victim.[41] In recent years, a third circle of victimization has also been recognized that considers the broader community as being exposed to the reporting of victimization.[42] Conceptually, this notion is closer to collective state harm, since it turns away from individuals and becomes closer to group pluralistic entities that form the state. Conceiving the victim as a private entity has introduced concepts typically addressed in tort law within the area of criminal justice.

2. Conceiving the Victim as Part of the Public Interest

Instead of framing victim interests as distinct, independent, and sometimes conflicting with those of the public state, this perspective conceives victims' interests as inherent components of the public interest. This conception upholds the public-private divide by reinforcing the public dimension of the criminal justice process, while simultaneously mudding it by referring to the public interest as aggregate individual or group interests. Within this conception, the victim takes on the role of an agent of the public interest, which can occur at various stages of the criminal justice process, including pretrial decisions. This conception of victim contribution is more aligned with the polity and decision-making than individuality in the criminal process. It also considers that more parties can contribute, often through the public prosecutor (but not always), including the victim, the defendant, and the community.[43]

[39] For instance, for submitting a victim impact statement, Canadian courts have adopted a wide definition of victims, which includes the immediate victim and her harm, but also family members who have suffered ancillary harm as a result of the criminal act against the principal victim. *See, e.g.*, R v. Johnny [2011] B.C.J. No. 487 (B.C. C.A.); R v. Cook (2009) 71 C.R. (6th) 369 (Que. C.A.).

[40] *See* Tim Quigley, *The Dangers of Victim Impact Statements: A Brief Reply to Roberts and Manikis*, 15 Can. Crim. L. Rev. 39 (2010); R v. Smithers [1978] 1 S.C.R. 506 (Can.); R v. Nette [2001] 3 S.C.R. 488 (Can.).

[41] *See* Paul Cassell & Edna Erez, *Victim Impact Statements and Ancillary Harm: The American Perspective*, 15 Can. Crim. L. Rev. 149 (2011); *e.g.*, United States v. Madoff, 09 Cr. 213(DC) (S.D.N.Y. 2009).

[42] This new form of victimization has also recently been recognized in Canadian law, where victim legislation has recognized community impact statements. The literature in the United States has also considered this third circle of victimization. *See, e.g.*, Katie Long, Note, *Community Input at Sentencing: Victim's Right or Victim's Revenge?*, 75 B.U. L. Rev. 187 (1995); Paul H. Robinson, *Should the Victims' Rights Movement Have Influence over Criminal Law Formulation and Adjudication?*, 33 McGeorge L. Rev. 749 (2002), which argues against individual VIS but in favor of community impact statements.

[43] This conception seems closer to Levine's view that victims' contribution is more aligned with the public model of prosecution. Levine, *supra* note 14, at 337. In England and Wales, the court in R v. Killick

The literature on the public interest and administrative discretion provides greater understanding of the underpinnings of this conception. Within this wider administrative field, scholars have increasingly looked at whether there is some role for democratic deliberation in ascribing content to the public interest in diverse areas. As highlighted by Feintuck, "in the emphasis it places on active citizen participation in deliberative processes, civil republicanism might seem to offer a legitimate and definite orientation for regulatory activity in the public interest, seeing regulation in effect as a 'surrogate deliberative process,' while simultaneously requiring the accountability of those who exercise such power."[44]

Feintuck's concept of public interest is rooted in equal citizenship within a democratic community.[45] This gives weight to citizenship values in the face of market forces, offering explicit justification for regulation in democratic, rather than exclusively economic, terms. It also aims to avoid the problems of majoritarianism associated with other theories of the public interest and thus extends beyond the mere aggregation of individual or group interests. According to Feintuck, this definition of the public interest is "a unitary theory that reflects the constant value of equality of citizenship within a democratic political community."[46]

According to this vision there needs to be a space to incorporate a specific set of non-commodity values into the process while ensuring that the citizen does not turn into a consumer. One of this concept's advantages is that it imposes on regulators a burden to show that they have taken a "hard look" at all relevant factors.[47] Applying the concept of public interest this way should assist in ensuring that regulation fulfills its potential as a locus of deliberation, and should encourage or require the courts to support and enforce that practice of deliberation. It is meant to serve accountability in a way that goes beyond a "Red Light" function of stopping excesses of power or jurisdiction and develops a "Green Light" function of encouraging and facilitating good administration.[48] The victim as an agent of the public interest in the context of various decisions would serve accountability and good administration.

Examples where victims are conceived as elements of the public interest exist throughout common law criminal justice history, particularly those that were rooted within the monarch's prerogative and thus included public dimensions. For instance, during the King's Peace citizens' arrest and private prosecutions were undertaken by private citizens in the name of the monarch. Hence the right and duty to arrest and prosecute were directly derived from the sovereign and the citizen acting in obedience to this royal command functioned as an arm of the state.[49] Today, existing mechanisms of

[2011] EWCA Crim 1608, at para. 48, highlighted that the prosecutor when making a decision in the public interest needs to take into account three main interests, those of the state, the defendant and the victim—suggesting that victims are an inherent component of the public interest.

[44] Mike Feintuck, "*The Public Interest" in Regulation* (2004). [45] *Id.*

[46] *Id.* at 253. [47] *Id.* at 254.

[48] Carol Harlow & Richard Rawlings, *Law and Administration* (2d ed. 1997).

[49] R v. Lerke, 25 DLR (4th) 403 (1986) (Alb. C.A.) analyzes historical sources suggesting that the citizen's power of arrest has remained and that "derived from the Sovereign it is the exercise of a state function" (para. 21).

citizens' arrest and private prosecutions are preserved in some common law jurisdictions[50] and continue to challenge the private/public divide. Indeed, although a victim or citizen can have a private interest in undertaking a citizen's arrest or private prosecution, the purpose and foundations of these mechanisms are mainly described as a public purpose embodied in maintaining the monarch's peace.[51]

Current policies also illustrate the strong public interest dimension that victims can encompass. In England and Wales, public prosecutors are increasingly obliged to take into account victims' interests and views during various decisions since they form part of the wider public interest.[52] Similarly, private prosecutors also need to consider the Full Code Test that applies to prosecutors, or risk seeing the prosecution stopped.[53] This test requires prosecutors to ensure that prosecutions are made in the public interest, which suggests that even private prosecutorial decisions encapsulate a very strong public dimension. Further, the House of Lords has highlighted the important public value of private prosecution, describing it as a "valuable constitutional safeguard against inertia or partiality on the part of the authority."[54] This objective suggests that when public prosecutors fail to respect their mandate by adequately representing the public interest, victims and private entities can remedy the situation. Private prosecutions are not meant to replace private civil actions, and both actions can take place in parallel for the same subject matter.

Additional mechanisms illustrating a conception of victims as part of the public interest in the criminal justice process enable victims to challenge and seek review of prosecutorial decisions. These decisions engage important public interest components by requiring the application of the same test prosecutors apply when deciding whether to prosecute. For example, in the *Janner* case, a decision was made by the Crown Prosecution Service not to prosecute Lord Janner over child sexual offense allegations because it would not be in the public interest due to his severe dementia. The victim requested an independent review under the Victims' Rights to Review Scheme (VRRS), and the DPP (Director of Public Prosecutions) concluded that it was in the public interest

[50] In England and Wales, this power is historically "preserved" by section 6(1) of the *Prosecution of Offences Act*, c. 23 (1985) (England & Wales), see Crown Prosecution Service, *supra* note 12. Private prosecutions should not only meet the evidential sufficiency stage, but also the public interest element to justify prosecutions. For the Canadian context, *see* Burns, *supra* note 7. Most American states have abolished private prosecutions. Reasons for this remain unclear, but in a system like the United States that favored a rigid private/public divide, it was noted that private prosecutions included too many private interests, giving rise to abuses. *See* Andrew Sideman, *The Outmoded Concept of Private Prosecution*, 25 Am. U. L. Rev. 754, 763 (1976).

[51] Similarly, the Alberta Court of Appeal in R v. Lerke, 25 DLR (4th) 403 (1986) (Alb. C.A.), noted that the citizen was acting as an agent of the state when exercising arrest powers under the Canadian Criminal Code. This argument can be extended to private prosecutions since they share historical roots and rationales.

[52] Examples include taking into account victims' views on whether a prosecution is required in the public interest (CPS Directorate, *Code for Crown Prosecutors* (CCP) § 4.18, (2010)), decisions on whether to accept guilty pleas (§ 10.3 CCP), and requests for compensation and ancillary orders (§ 15 CCP).

[53] *See* Crown Prosecution Service, *supra* note 12.

[54] *See* Gouriet v. Union of Post Office Workers [1978] AC 435 at 477, [1977] UKHL 5, [1977] 3 All E.R. 70.

to bring proceedings against Janner.[55] This decision suggests that victims have claims in partly defining the public interest in decisions not to prosecute, which in turn signals that they are inextricably part of the public interest.[56]

III. Typology of Victim Participation in Criminal Justice Processes

In addition to understanding some of the foundational premises and conceptions of the victim in criminal justice processes, it is also important to conceptualize the various meanings of victim participation in order to understand the role and space occupied by victims within some common law jurisdictions. There are various degrees and forms of victim participation that have changed through time and continue to evolve in different ways across various jurisdictions.

Several models of victim participation were developed throughout the years that enable a greater understanding of victim participation.[57] Edwards's contribution to this literature is of great importance. Arguing that service rights are not a form of participation since victims are considered passive in the process, his analysis primarily focuses on procedural rights that can be divided into various forms of participation.

Edwards suggests that there are two types of victim participation: dispositive (victim as decision-maker) and non-dispositive (victim can influence but not make decisions). Within these two categories, four corresponding forms of participation are described. First, within the *dispositive* type of participation, victims could *control* a particular decision; their participation and input is determinative. Victims are obliged to supply a preference, and the criminal justice actors have to follow it. In other words, the victim's views would veto any decision. Specific examples of this type of victim participation are not found within the common law, but can be found in some aspects of sharia law, where the victim supplies a determinative preference.[58] Edwards describes a criminal process in Pakistan in which relatives of victims of homicide and certain other offenses can choose among forgiveness, compensation claims (diyya), or imposition of the death penalty under the Holy Qur'an.[59] The *Qisas* and *Diyat* law made murder a private offense instead of a crime against society or the state, and thus its pursuit, prosecution, and punishment

[55] BBC, *CPS Grants Lord Janner Review*, BBC News, http://www.bbc.com/news/uk-32757978 (last visited Nov. 9, 2018). For analysis on this decision, see Marie Manikis, *Expanding Participation: Victims as Agents of Accountability in the Criminal Justice Process*, 1 Pub. L. 63 (2017).

[56] Although beyond the scope of this chapter, public interest is an elusive and vague concept. The *Janner* example seems to suggest that the public interest is represented by the state prosecutor, who as highlighted in this case is informed by several interests including those of victims.

[57] Edwards, *supra* note 16.

[58] Mahmoud Cherif Bassiouni, *Quesas Crimes*, in *The Islamic Criminal Justice System* 203–06 (Mahmoud Cherif Bassiouni ed., 1982).

[59] Yusuf Ali, *The Holy Qur'an* (1946) in Edwards, *supra* note 16.

is the responsibility of the victim's heirs and guardians.[60] This suggests a conception of victims as representing private interests.

Second, *non-dispositive* participation includes three specific forms of participation: *consultation, information-provision*, and *expression. Consultation* grants victims the option to provide their preferences and opinions about the appropriate policy to be formulated or decision to be taken, and criminal justice decision-makers have an obligation to seek them. However, this does not give victims a veto; their wishes will be weighed against other factors deemed useful in reaching a decision. This role of victims seems to align more with a private dimension where victims are personally invested in the endeavor. For instance, victims in the United States can provide in their victim impact statement (VIS) their opinions and recommendations about the sentence, a rarity for common law jurisdictions.[61] Generally, those statements have been limited to the description of harm, but in recent years, even Canada has opened up to victim sentencing recommendations or opinions with a court's approval.[62] However, since this latter example requires judicial approval and does not oblige criminal justice agencies to seek and consider victim preference prior to making their decision, it does not squarely fit within *consultation*. A recent development that would more readily include this type of participation is the possibility given to victims to consult with prosecutors before laying charges and deciding whether to prosecute.[63]

In an *information-provision* form of participation, criminal justice actors would be obliged to seek and consider victim information, which victims have an obligation to provide. This rests on the idea that victims have crucial information that the criminal process requires in order to render a complete and fair decision. Edwards highlights that this is the level at which victims, since the middle of the nineteenth century, have typically been involved, providing mere "evidentiary fodder"[64] when considered to be useful by the state. The victim's presence is dependent upon the decision-maker's *need* for this type of participation, and, when the need arises, the victim has no choice but to participate.

[60] Stephanie Palo, *A Charade of Change: Qisas and Diyat Ordinance Allows Honor Killings to Go Unpunished in Pakistan*, 15 U.C. Davis J. Int'l Law & Policy 15 (2008–2009).

[61] For instance, many U.S. states allow for sentencing recommendations. More recently the U.S. Supreme Court in *Bosse v. Oklahoma*, 137 S. Ct. 1, 580 U.S. __ (2016) held that victims are constitutionally barred from including opinions about the defendant and recommendations about his punishment in their VIS. In England and Wales, victims' opinions (or their relatives) as to the sentence are not relevant and the court is instructed not to pay attention to them. *See* Crown Prosecution Service, *Victim Personal Statements*, http://www.cps.gov.uk/legal/v_to_z/victim_personal_statements/(last visited Apr. 3, 2017).

[62] *See Criminal Code*, R.S.C., ch. C-46, § 722(4) (1985) (Can.); for further discussion on this aspect see Marie Manikis, *Victim Impact Statements at Sentencing: Towards a Clearer Understanding of Their Aims*, 65 U. Toronto L.J. 85 (2015).

[63] In the United States, many jurisdictions have recognized victims' right to consult with prosecutors before certain decisions. *See, e.g.*, Colo. Rev. Stat. § 24-4.1-303 (2001); Crime Victims' Rights Act, 18 U.S.C. § 3771(a)(5) (2004). Similarly, in Canada, the victim has the right to convey her views about decisions made by appropriate authorities including prosecutors. See Canadian Victims Bill of Rights, *supra* note 20, § 2, 14.

[64] Edwards, *supra* note 16, at 976.

This role would fit more with a conception of victims that forms part of the public interest since their involvement is primarily justifiable to advance public interests, conceived as those held by the state. Most models of victim impact statements are generally meant to provide information to decision-makers that they need to consider.[65] For these reasons, they would fit into this category of participation, but due to a more victim-witness-centric approach to evidence, victims generally have a choice to present the information contained in those statements even if they are considered evidence at sentencing.[66] The element of choice and their partial aim in providing restitution for victims, in some jurisdictions, would suggest that for some VIS models, victims are mainly conceived as private actors.

Finally, another form of victim participation is *expression*. Unlike the information-provision category, this form of participation involves the victim wanting to communicate feelings to the decision-maker.[67] The criminal justice process would need to provide this opportunity, and the victim can choose to participate. Arguably, since it primarily benefits victims and their personal interests, this fits more within a private conception. Examples of this type of participation can be found in jurisdictions that have accepted more expressive forms of victim impact statements. In some jurisdictions, including the United States and some Australian states, victims can deliver their statements through drawings, poems, music, videos, and other expressive means.[68] More recently, Canada has also recognized for the first time the possibility for victims to draw a picture or write a poem or letter to enable expression.[69]

It is worth noting that this framework predominantly focuses on participation in common law traditions. Developments in continental traditions are not encapsulated, such as the *partie civile* process in France, which enables victims to participate in the process by attaching a civil action for damages in criminal proceedings. The decision to file such action rests with victims, thus at first glance can be considered within the dispositive/control type of participation. However, contrary to that type, victims under the *partie civile* action decide whether they want to supply this preference or not. Adding types of victim participation to Edwards's model would enable a more comprehensive understanding of the varied roles victims have taken in different legal traditions.

More recently, an additional type of participation has been added as a complement to Edwards' model.[70] This type of victim participation conceives victims as *agents of accountability* and has been exemplified by various mechanisms, including private prosecutions, and complaints processes, as well as administrative and judicial review mechanisms. It presupposes that criminal justice agencies can make erroneous decisions and conduct

[65] *See, e.g., Criminal Code*, R.S.C., ch. C-46, § 722(1), which reads that decision-makers *must* take into account victim impact statements.

[66] In many common law jurisdictions the laws of evidence have changed to facilitate testimony, particularly when witnesses are also victims.

[67] Edwards, *supra* note 16, at 976.

[68] Manikis, *supra* note 62; Roberts & Manikis, *supra* note 31.

[69] *See Criminal Code*, R.S.C., ch. C-46, § 722(6).

[70] Manikis, *supra* note 55.

themselves contrary to their obligations, and victims are relevant parties to monitor these situations, bring forward claims of errors or violations, and achieve redress. In recent years, this form of participation has developed in England and Wales, the United States, and Canada, albeit in very different ways.

In England and Wales this form of participation exists in the procedural mechanisms available to victims to challenge decisions made by prosecutors to prosecute or not individuals. The rationales behind this form of victim participation rests on the basis that prosecutors can indeed make errors, and that victims (as well as citizens in some of those mechanisms) have an interest in those decisions. The victim's role within this jurisdiction seems to suggest they form part of the public interest as victims and prosecutors share similar interests in ensuring that prosecutions are correct and errors remedied. Various mechanisms of accountability are available. Victims can through the VRRS seek internal administrative review within the prosecution service of decisions not to prosecute,[71] as well as judicial review of both decisions to prosecute or not.[72] To seek review of these decisions, victims must challenge one or both of the criteria relied upon by the prosecution to decide whether to prosecute: (1) the presence of the required evidence for the alleged offense, or (2) the presence of public interest in prosecuting.[73] That victims can seek review of these decisions suggests that they are adequate assessors of the evidence as well as the public interest. Challenges to the first criterion are made through the collection of further evidence and expert testimony,[74] while the second criterion suggests that victims can have an important role in determining the public interest.[75] This seems to challenge the public and private divide by considering that the public interest also includes victims' interests, as explored below.

England and Wales remains one of the rare common law jurisdictions where victims and citizens can still launch private prosecutions without many limitations.[76] Although the mechanism of private prosecutions can be used independently of any errors made by prosecutors, it can also be a mechanism of accountability against faulty prosecutors

[71] The Crown Prosecution Service, *Victims' Right to Review Guidance*, http://www.cps.gov.uk/publications/docs/vrr_guidance_2016.pdf (revised July 2016). Contrary to judicial review, this internal review is only available to victims of crime and is more limited in scope than judicial review.

[72] In England and Wales victims have mainly been involved in judicial review of decisions not to prosecute, and have been successful in a number of cases, see R v. DPP Ex p. C [1995] 1 Cr. App. R. 136; R v. DPP Ex p. Manning [2001] Q.B. 330, [2000] 3 W.L.R. 463. Citizens also have this possibility to judicially review decisions.

[73] Crown Prosecution Service, *supra* note 71; The Crown Prosecution Service, *Reconsidering a Prosecution Decision*, http://www.cps.gov.uk/legal/p_to_r/reconsidering_a_prosecution_decision/#significant (last visited Apr. 3, 2017).

[74] *See, e.g.*, R v. DPP Ex p. C [1995] 1 Cr. App. R. 136, in which a judicial review of the decision not to prosecute was found in part because the prosecutor (DPP) failed to bring his mind to bear on the question whether the evidential sufficiency criteria were satisfied in relation to a more serious offense.

[75] *See, e.g.*, Manikis, *supra* note 55.

[76] *See Prosecution of Offenses Act*, *supra* note 50, § 6(1). This is very different to some common law jurisdictions such as Canada and Australia where the prosecution can be taken over by the public prosecutor in every case.

that may act partially by failing to prosecute certain crimes or over-prosecute others. Similarly, the *nebenklage* in Germany, which allows victims to participate as secondary prosecutors in the criminal process, also enables them to oversee the public prosecution, but by safeguarding their own personal interests (rather than the public interest). This mechanism also serves accountability, although arguably victims are conceived as private entities within this process rather than public ones, considering its primary aims and functions toward private interests.[77]

In the United States, discussions about accountability have long occupied the literature on victims' rights, particularly in relation to remedies for rights violations. The victims' literature has referred to a "third wave"[78] of victims' rights to describe a situation where criminal justice agencies ignore or willfully violate victims' rights or interests and the need for victims to be able to obtain redress for those violations. This form of accountability is meant to ensure that criminal justice agencies in breach account for their violations and provide redress to the victim. Proponents of this form of accountability have brought forward the different and often conflicting interests between victims, as private interests, and prosecutors, as public interest, and the need for victims to have a separate and independent voice in proceedings—preferably through legal counsel. Examples of such remedies have mainly been found in the federal jurisdiction under the *Crime Victims' Rights Act* and have recognized victim standing in criminal proceedings to assert their rights and launch mandamus actions in the appellate courts in the event that they fail to bring forward a successful claim at the lower court. Remedies for those violations include the recognition of restitution for victims,[79] possibilities to be heard in the criminal justice process—particularly at sentencing,[80] and being notified of the progress of their case.[81]

Accountability takes different shapes depending on the way the victim as an agent is conceptualized. The notion of accountability in England and Wales mainly rests on the idea that victims form part of the public interest, and thus prosecutorial decisions can be questioned under the public premise. Victims' role as agents of accountability enables greater systemic accountability for erroneous decisions that may be contrary to the public interest. In the United States and in Germany, accountability mainly rests on a conception of victims having private independent interests from the public interest and thus having separate claims toward them. This enables accountability for victims in the event that prosecutors have breached their obligations toward them or in situations where the interests of victims differ from those of prosecutors.

[77] Matthew Dyson, *Comparing Tort and Crime: Learning from Across and Within Legal Systems* (2015).

[78] Beloof, *supra* note 14.

[79] For example, in *United States v. Monzel*, 641 F.3d 528 (D.C. Cir. 2011), the victim sought restitution before the courts.

[80] Kenna v. U.S. Dist. Court, 435 F.3d 1011, 1013 (9th Cir. 2006).

[81] *In re* Dean, 527 F.3d 391 (5th Cir. 2008); United States v. BP Prods. N. Am. Inc., 610 F. Supp. 2d 655 (S.D. Tex. 2009).

IV. The Relationship between Victims and the Actors of Criminal Justice Processes: A Challenge to Victims as Agents of Punitivity?

In his seminal work on victims' rights, Kent Roach expanded Herbert Packer's models of criminal justice[82] by adding victims' rights to the existing models of crime control and due process.[83] This framework enables a greater understanding of the way that the criminal justice process has evolved to include victim participation. It suggests that initiatives related to victims can be divided into two different categories: the punitive model of victims' rights, which serves crime control interests, and the non-punitive model rooted in restorative justice initiatives. The punitive model stresses the innocence of victims, their victimization by the adversarial model, and the guilt of offenders, while defending the criminal sanction from due process challenges by the accused. The restorative justice model values a transformation of the existing criminal justice process that focuses on a system that restores relationships damaged by crimes and brings constituencies together to make them whole through mutual understanding, accountability, forgiveness, and compassion.

The following section explores the nuanced relationships that exist between victims and other actors of the criminal justice process, suggesting that depending on how victims are conceived in the process, their relationship and interests with law enforcement and defendants can differ. It argues that while victim participation in the criminal process can sometimes advance crime control and punitivity,[84] it can also advance non-punitive and due process interests within the criminal justice process, including accountability, without resorting to restorative justice.

1. The Relationship between Victims and Law Enforcement (Police And Prosecutors) in Criminal Justice Processes

Do victims participate in the process via law enforcement or should their interests be presented independently, if at all? Are they necessarily agents of punitivity when they operate within the criminal justice process? The answer to these complex questions will depend on the ways victims are conceived and their relationship vis-à-vis law enforcing actors in the criminal process. A model describing victims as agents of individual rights conceives victims as independent from systemic interests. The American model of victims'

[82] Herbert Packer, *Two Models of the Criminal Process*, 113 U. Pa. L. Rev. 1 (1964).

[83] Kent Roach, *Four Models of the Criminal Process*, 89 J. Crim. L. & Criminology 671 (1999).

[84] *Id.*

rights exemplifies this conception of victims within its processes. Indeed, the President's Task Force for Victims of Crime,[85] one of the first governmental initiatives that relates to victims' rights in the United States, suggested that victims' rights are essential to enable and facilitate prosecutions, but also recognized that victims' interests can sometimes conflict with prosecutorial interests. This model is predominantly based on victims having distinct and at times conflicting interests with state agencies that cause secondary victimization to victims and that often fail to respect victims' individual rights.[86] This conflict has been seen in several instances, including in cases where a prosecutor asks for a different amount in restitution than the one requested by the victim,[87] where victims have not been consulted during prosecutorial decisions,[88] or when prosecutors failed to allow victims to present victim impact statements at sentencing.[89]

It is also possible that victims' interests align with those of the state and law enforcement. In addition to the conflicting interests discussed above, a strong language of complementarity and alignment has at times been used in the American context to discuss the relationship between victims and law enforcement in the criminal justice process. For instance, in situations where victims participate as prosecutorial witnesses in the process, it is often the case that they share similar interests in ensuring testimonial credibility and reliability.[90] Again, depending on the conception of victim participation, views may differ.

Where victims are part of the public interest, there is much less of a conflicting framing between the interests of victims and those of the state. It is generally understood that the interests of victims in the criminal justice process align with those of law enforcement since they are meant to form an inherent part of the public interest. Within this approach, decision-makers that are part of law enforcement should have an interest in hearing victims' information and views at various stages of proceedings because of the public interest they are meant to represent. Although they usually align, disagreement between victims and law enforcement can occur. Possible conflicts can be understood in two ways. First, although victims form part of the public interest, they are not its exclusive component and therefore other elements may explain a different decision that is reached by decision-makers, who themselves also form parts of the public interest. As stated earlier, this conception of victims challenges the private/public divide since the

[85] *See, e.g.*, *President's Task Force on Victims of Crime* (1982), https://ojp.gov/ovc/publications/presdntstskforcrprt/87299.pdf (last visited Oct. 20, 2017).

[86] *See, e.g.*, Beloof, *supra* note 14, at 294–96.

[87] For instance, in *United States v. Monzel*, 641 F.3d 528 (D.C. Cir. 2011), the victim challenged the restitution amount on a petition for mandamus through her attorney, while the prosecution did not take on this challenge.

[88] For instance, in *United States v. Heaton*, 458 F. Supp. 2d 1271 (D. Utah 2006), the district court provided robust redress for the prosecutor's failure to consult with the victim. These different interests can also be seen in *In re Dean*, 527 F.3d 391 (5th Cir. 2008) and *United States v. BP Products N. Am. Inc.*, 610 F. Supp. 2d 655 (S.D. Tex. 2009).

[89] Kenna v. U.S. Dist. Court, 435 F.3d 1011, 1013 (9th Cir. 2006).

[90] Douglas Beloof, *Weighing Crime Victims' Interests in Judicially Crafted Criminal Procedure*, 56 Cath. U. L. Rev. 1135, 1150 (2007).

public interest can be understood as an aggregation of private interests. Second, it may be that the victim's contribution advances the public interest, but that public entities that are meant to make a decision that respects the public interest have failed to respect their mandate. In this sense, a different view to the state's would suggest that the victim would act as an agent of accountability toward decisions that may not be in the public interest. In these situations, victim participation would be relevant to the advancement of the public interest. An example of this was discussed earlier when referring to private prosecutions as a useful safeguard against inertia or partiality on the part of the public prosecutor. It can also be found in cases of judicial review (or internal administrative review) of decisions related to prosecution, including the way the *Janner* case was articulated above.[91]

2. The Relationship between Victims and the Defendant in Criminal Justice Processes: Challenging Victims as Agents of Punitivity

The literature on victim participation in the criminal justice process has often framed the interests of victims in opposition to those of the accused. Indeed, the rhetoric of balancing the interests of the accused with those of victim reinforces as a zero-sum game that exists within criminal processes. Similarly, Roach has highlighted this dichotomy by suggesting that victim participation in the criminal justice process amounts to greater punitivity.[92] Although tensions may exist in some situations, it is worth bearing in mind that victim involvement—whether conceived as independent from state interests, or as an inherent part of the public interest—can also align with those of defendants. This situation challenges the ways victims have been conceived as agents of punitivity when operating within the criminal justice process.

Several elements support this claim. First, empirical studies show that victims are not inherently punitive or vengeful, and that they do not seek harsh sentences. Victim responses across common law jurisdictions about their participation at sentencing reveal consistent trends about not wanting to influence the punitivity of sentences, but rather to be heard and express themselves to the authorities and the offender about the effect that the crime has had on them.[93] Second, in many respects, victims and defendants have similar due process interests, including the reduction of errors that could potentially lead to wrongful convictions.[94] It is the ways that laws and policies are drafted, shaped, and implemented by the system that mainly enable victim participation in situations where victims favor crime control and punitivity. An example of this can be found within the VRRS in England and Wales, discussed previously, where this internal administrative mechanism to seek review of prosecutorial decisions is only available for decisions not to prosecute. This limited right to review assumes that victims would only

[91] See an analysis of the *Janner* case in Manikis, *supra* note 55.

[92] Roach, *supra* note 83.

[93] Roberts & Manikis, *supra* note 31.

[94] Seri Irazola, Erin Williamson, Jeri Stricker & Emily Niedzwiecki, *Study of Victim Experiences of Wrongful Conviction* (U.S. Dep't of Justice, 2013).

participate in the process in instances where they would want to challenge a decision to not prosecute by promoting prosecution. Reality is more nuanced, and victims may want to challenge decisions to prosecute in situations where they may think a prosecution is not in the public or the defendant's interest.[95] As argued in the literature, a mechanism that promotes accountability would not only allow for internal review of decisions not to prosecute, but also for reviews of decisions to prosecute.[96] This expanded review would align with the conception that at times victims as part of the public interest may also share similar interests with the accused.

The mechanism of private prosecutions also encourages and advances punitivity and crime control. As a way to counter this and enable all victims to participate in the process, jurisdictions that retain private prosecutions may also want to adopt review mechanisms for victims to seek review of prosecutorial decisions to prosecute.

Finally, other mechanisms of victim participation in the criminal justice process such as victim impact statements can also serve the crime control/punitive model depending on their aims and limitations. For instance, in some jurisdictions, appellate courts have only allowed for information contained in victim impact statements to be considered as aggravating factors at sentencing, and not mitigating ones, which arguably advances punitivity.[97] Victims generally submit these statements at sentencing not to serve crime control aims and punitivity, but to be heard and express their harm to the system and the offender. In some contexts, the victim's involvement within victim impact statements has served as a mitigating factor[98] or as a message to the system/offender,[99] which challenges the punitive role attributed to victims in the criminal justice process and suggest that victims can also advance non-punitive and due process aims.

V. Conclusion

Victims have contributed to the criminal justice system within common law traditions albeit in different ways and at various degrees. The ways that victims have been conceived as either private, public, or both to varying degrees, has had important repercussions on

[95] *See, e.g.*, R v. Charbonneau (1990) 500-35-000381-908 (Super. Ct. of Quebec) (Can.) in which a complainant in Canada thought it would be best not to prosecute since it would affect the accused's therapy.

[96] Manikis, *supra* note 55.

[97] See discussion of Canadian appellate courts in Manikis, *supra* note 62.

[98] *See, e.g.*, Annette van der Merwe & Ann Skelton, *Victims' Mitigating Views in Sentencing Decisions: A Comparative Analysis*, 35 Oxford J. Legal Stud. 355 (2015); Trina Gordin & Stanley Brodsky, *The Influence of Victim Impact Statements on Sentencing in Capital Cases*, 7 J. Forensic Psychol. Pract. 45 (2007) that suggests that although VIS in capital proceedings did not necessarily have substantial effect on the acceptance of aggravation or mitigation issues, participants were more likely to be lenient in sentencing in the presence of the VIS when there were mitigating circumstances such as mental health issues, or sexual abuse as a child.

[99] Manikis, *supra* note 62, in which some Canadian appellate courts have noted the exclusively expressive aims of VIS, rather than tools in favor of punitivity.

their participative role and relationships with the various criminal justice actors. These conceptions of victims have also contributed to the private-public divide of the criminal justice process, while simultaneously offering various ways of questioning those rigid divisions. Criminal justice scholars as well as policymakers can certainly benefit from the theoretical models discussed in this chapter to further understand the complex evolving roles that victims have been playing in common law tradition. By relying on different conceptions of victims, this piece challenges in part the prevalent view that victims are generally inherent agents of punitivity within the criminal justice process, and only a role outside of criminal proceedings would enable victims to advance non-punitive objectives. Finally, although most of the analysis in this chapter relates to common law systems, expanding its focus across different legal traditions would deepen and enrich our understanding of this actor's role and impact across traditions.

References

Douglas Beloof, Paul Cassell & Steven Twist, *Victims in Criminal Procedure* 5–17 (3d ed. 2010)

Jonathan Doak, *Victims' Rights, Human Rights and Criminal Justice: Reconceiving the Role of Third Parties* 248 (2008)

Sandra Walklate, *Imagining the Victim of Crime* (2007)

Ian Edwards, *An Ambiguous Participant: The Crime Victim and Criminal Justice Decision-Making*, 44 Brit. J. Criminology 967, 972 (2004)

Marie Manikis, *Expanding Participation: Victims as Agents of Accountability in the Criminal Justice Process*, 1 Pub. L. 63 (2017)

Reconcilable Rights? Analysing the Tension Between Victims and Defendants (Ed Cape ed., 2004)

New Visions of Crime Victims 197–222 (Carolyn Hoyle & Richard Young eds., 2002)

Terance Miethe & Robert Meier, *Crime and Its Social Context: Toward an Integrated Theory of Offenders, Victims, and Situations* (1994)

CHAPTER 13

VICTIM RIGHTS IN CIVIL LAW JURISDICTIONS

JOHANNA GÖHLER

I. Introduction

In many civil law jurisdictions, victims of crime nowadays enjoy multiple and diverse rights during criminal proceedings and can embrace different procedural roles. Generally, they are conceived as material, yet not mandatory participants to a state-run criminal justice process. As such, their rights and interests can considerably impact the roles, interests, and duties of other actors in the system as well as the larger structure of the process itself.

This chapter first delineates the different types of victim rights that exist in civil law criminal justice processes. Given the many varied national systems, the analysis seeks to trace rough lines of common development rather than details of specific jurisdictions. Due to its harmonizing effect, supranationally applicable EU law on victim rights provides an ideal starting point for this endeavor. Additionally, the analysis draws on examples from domestic jurisdictions. Further, this chapter depicts the recently revived debate on a victim's entitlement to public criminal prosecution and punishment. Based on these findings, the victim's role in criminal proceedings and its repercussions on the other actors therein is evaluated. Finally, the chapter briefly highlights a lately proposed alternative to achieve justice for victims in parallel to the criminal process.

II. Rights during Criminal Proceedings

The victim's role in criminal proceedings has continuously evolved across time. In early Germanic times, victims themselves, together with their kin, were in charge of avenging violations of their interests.[1] Only when the concept of a state monopoly of force

[1] On the historic development, see Thomas Weigend, *Deliktsopfer und Strafverfahren* 24 seq. (1989); Petra Velten, *Systematischer Kommentar zur Strafprozessordnung, Band VIII* Vor. §§ 374-406h sec. 56 seq. (Jürgen Wolter ed., 4th ed. 2013).

emerged in political and legal theory and crime began to be conceived as a violation of the public order, criminal prosecution became the exclusive right and duty of the state, to be executed on behalf and in the interest of society.[2] This development toward a public criminal justice system slowly marginalized the victim's role in avenging crime. Through the establishment of the inquisitorial process in the sixteenth century, the victim completely lost power over investigation and prosecution.[3] Instead, these tasks were assigned to a judge as a representative of the public. Reforms of the inquisitorial process leading to its current accusatorial version in the eighteenth and nineteenth centuries did not considerably alter this situation. Although, for example, the German Code of Criminal Procedure of 1877 codified numerous rights for victims, their influence on the state-run criminal process remained marginal in practice and underdeveloped in theory. In fact, for the next century, in many European civil law jurisdictions, the victim's appearance in criminal processes was largely reduced to that of an informant and witness. In accordance with the principle of the separation of criminal and civil liability, victims had to pursue their own interests primarily in civil proceedings. It was only in the 1970s that victim rights experienced a newfound and lasting prominence in scholarship, politics, and consequently legislative reforms. Diverse social movements began to jointly protest against the marginalization of the victim, calling the victim the "forgotten man" in the criminal justice process. In response, national legislatures undertook multiple reforms to strengthen the victim's position in criminal proceedings. Around that time, the UN and the Council of Europe also started to promote victim rights in criminal proceedings.[4]

In the new millennium, the European Union joined these reformers and has since then considerably influenced the law on victim rights of many civil law jurisdictions in Europe. The EU has the power to adopt directives establishing minimum standards on the rights of crime victims, which the Member States have to transpose into their domestic law.[5] The first EU legal instrument on victim rights took effect in 2002: the Council Framework Decision 2001/220/JHA on the standing of victims in criminal proceedings.[6] This law primarily focused on information, protection, and support of victims, and entailed only a few rules on procedural rights. In 2012, the EU passed a second, more elaborate victim rights instrument: the Directive 2012/29/EU establishing minimum standards on the rights, support and protection of victims of crime.[7] This directive seeks to satisfy victims' needs comprehensively. To this end, it strengthens their rights to information, support, protection, and participation in criminal proceedings.

[2] Weigend, *supra* note 1, at 27. [3] *Id.* at 83 seq.

[4] Particularly influential were G.A. Res. 40/34, U.N. Doc. A/RES/40/34 (Nov. 29, 1985); Council of Europe, Recommendation of the Comm. of Ministers No. R.(85)11 (June 28, 1985); Council of Europe, Recommendation of the Comm. of Ministers No. R.(87)21 (Sept. 17, 1987), replaced by Recommendation Rec(2006)8 (June 14, 2006).

[5] The EU's power is regulated in Consolidated Version of the Treaty on the Functioning of the E.U. Art. 82(2), Oct. 26, 2012, 2012 O.J. (C326)01 [TFEU]. The Member States' obligation to transpose EU directives into national law derives from TFEU Art. 288(3) and Consolidated Version of the Treaty on E.U. Art. 4(3), Oct. 26, 2012, 2012 O.J. (C326)01.

[6] 2001 O.J. (L82)1. [7] 2012 O.J. (L315)57.

Through these reforms, victim rights have gained a growing impact on the roles of other actors in and the structure of the criminal process. Directive 2012/29/EU defines law that is, due to the transposition requirement, common to many European civil law jurisdictions. Therefore, the following analysis draws on this regime to illustrate the current consensus regarding victim rights in civil law criminal processes. Additionally, domestic criminal procedural rules are highlighted wherever appropriate to delineate further rights and remaining differences.

1. Information and Support

Information rights for victims can be divided into two categories. First, victims have a right to be informed about all rights and services that they are entitled to in the context of a crime and how they can realize these rights.[8] This information is essential for the empowerment of victims and the activation of their substantive rights. The second category concerns information about the criminal process. In this respect, Directive 2012/29/EU grants victims the right to be notified about certain aspects of the criminal proceedings, such as time and place of the trial, the nature of the charges, and the final judgment including its reasoning.[9] Additionally, victims have a right to interpretation and translation.[10] Many domestic jurisdictions further permit victims to attend the entire process, even nonpublic hearings and before they have testified as a witness.[11] Moreover, some national laws allow victims or their attorneys to inspect the court files, partly under the condition that the victim proves a legitimate interest in accessing the files.[12] These information rights illustrate that the law recognizes the victim's interests in criminal proceedings as different from those of the general public and concedes the victim a distinct position in criminal proceedings.

Whereas information rights of the first category are undisputed, some information rights regarding the criminal process are controversial. In particular, the right to inspect the files remains the subject of debate. Some scholars argue that knowledge of the files enabled the victim to design her/his witness testimony in order to tactically pursue private interests.[13] Consequently, the roles of a witness and a party to the proceedings could be blurred, the goal of determining the truth impaired, and defense rights unfairly impeded. Courts try to mitigate these apprehensions by considering a potential bias of the victim's testimony when they evaluate the evidence—according to the opponents, with inadequate success.[14]

[8] Directive 2012/29/EU, Art. 4. [9] *Id.* Art. 6. [10] *Id.* Art. 7.

[11] *See, e.g.*, Strafprozessordnung [StPO] [Code of Criminal Procedure], § 66(1)Nr.7 (Austria); trestní řád [Code of Criminal Procedure], § 43(1) (Czech).

[12] *E.g.*, StPO, § 68 (Austria); trestní řád, §§ 43(1), 65 (Czech); Strafprozessordnung [StPO] [Code of Criminal Procedure], § 406e (Ger.).

[13] *E.g.*, Bernd Schünemann, *Protection of Children and Other Vulnerable Victims Against Secondary Victimisation: Making It Easier to Testify in Court*, ERA Forum 387, 389 (2009).

[14] Bernd Schünemann, *Zur Stellung des Opfers im System der Strafrechtspflege*, Neue Zeitschrift für Strafrecht 193, 199 (1986).

With regard to support, Directive 2012/29/EU guarantees free access to confidential victim support services. They have to provide information, advice, and emotional and practical assistance independent from and outside of criminal proceedings.[15] Some national jurisdictions additionally offer distinct support measures within criminal proceedings. Under German law, for example, victims can avail themselves of psychological and emotional support from a trained social worker.[16] The social worker, obliged to neutrality, may accompany the victim during the entire trial, but must not engage in legal counseling or investigation.[17] The primary purpose is to meliorate the victim's experience during criminal proceedings and mitigate secondary victimization.[18] Furthermore, some domestic laws grant victims a right to legal representation.[19] A legal counsel can strengthen the victim's position in the process, notably opposite the accused. Therefore, scholars have criticized the fact that victim's legal representation could affect the equality of arms to the detriment of the defendant, especially if the latter is not legally represented.[20] Victim counsels, however, typically do not receive any autonomous procedural rights. Hence, they can merely support victims in exercising their existing procedural role without transforming it. The significance of the regulation of victim's legal representation therefore mostly consists in the distribution of costs: frequently, victims of certain crimes can have an attorney appointed by the court free of charge or at least obtain legal aid.[21]

2. Protection

Frequently, victims are required to participate in the criminal proceedings, in particular to testify as a witness. The obligation to appear before court, confront the defendant, and speak about the crime can invade the victim's privacy, traumatize the victim, and provoke reprisals by the defendant. Furthermore, a discourse founded on psychological studies and procedural justice theories suggests that an exclusionary criminal justice process can result in so-called secondary victimization of the victim.[22] The European Convention on Human Rights (ECHR), the Charter of Fundamental Rights of the EU (CFREU), and many national constitutions, however, protect the victim's interests in privacy, bodily integrity, life, liberty, and security. Therefore, it is uniformly recognized that states are under a positive obligation to safeguard victims by managing criminal proceedings in such a way that those interests are not unjustifiably imperiled and

[15] Directive 2012/29/EU, Art. 8, 9, recital 40. [16] StPO, § 406g (Ger.).

[17] StPO, § 406g (Ger.); Gesetz über die psychosoziale Prozessbegleitung [Code on Psychosocial Attendancy], BGBl. I-2015, 2529, § 2(2).

[18] Deutscher Bundestag: Drucksachen und Protokolle [BT] 18/6906, at 16, 26.

[19] StPO, § 406f (Ger.); Wetboek van Strafvordering [Sv] [Code of Criminal Procedure], § 51c (Dutch).

[20] Hans-Joachim Kurth & Bettina Weißer, *Heidelberger Kommentar Strafprozessordnung* § 397a sec. 2 (Björn Gercke et al. eds., 5th ed. 2012).

[21] Cf. Directive 2012/29/EU, Art. 13.

[22] Jim Parsons & Tiffany Bergin, *The Impact of Criminal Justice Involvement on Victims' Mental Health*, 23 J. Traumatic Stress 182 (2010).

secondary victimization is prevented or mitigated to the extent possible.[23] Hence, victim protection is largely framed in terms of human rights law.

Directive 2012/29/EU contains extensive rules on protection measures for victims. Some of them are of a practical nature. For example, court facilities have to be designed as to allow victims to avoid meeting the defendant unless the criminal process requires otherwise.[24] The majority of the provisions, though, establish measures to protect the victim during interrogations in the course of criminal investigations and proceedings. For instance, interviews with the victim have to be conducted without unjustified delay, their number should be kept to a minimum, and victims can be accompanied by an attorney.[25] Particularly vulnerable victims, such as children, are guaranteed additional concessions designed to alleviate potential impacts of testifying in court.[26] These include the use of communication technology, limitations on questions regarding the victim's private life, and the exclusion of the public. Whereas the directive reserves these measures for victims, many domestic criminal procedural codes provide them for vulnerable witnesses in general. Since vulnerable victims who assume the role of a witness can be classified as a subcategory of vulnerable witnesses, the latter approach appears more comprehensive and appropriate.

Whereas the obligation to protect victims and the different protection measures have come to be widely acknowledged among scholars and legislatures alike, the focus of attention has recently shifted to the distribution of these measures. The need for protection differs among victims. Therefore, Directive 2012/29/EU introduced a mechanism to individually assess the particular vulnerability of each victim during criminal proceedings and adapt the application of protection measures accordingly.[27] The assessment shall be conducted in a formalized manner as early as possible during criminal investigations and shall take into account the victim's personal characteristics including her/his relationship to the offender and type/nature and circumstances of the crime. Scholars have almost unanimously criticized this mechanism, for different reasons. From the victim's perspective, the assessment can restrict the victim's right to self-determination since victims can only object to the application of a specific measure, but not the assessment itself.[28] Furthermore, it has been argued that the assessment forced victims to revive memories of the crime and thus rather amplified than reduced secondary victimization.[29] From the defendant's perspective, the assessment has been accused of requiring investigations parallel to the criminal proceedings and thus impairing defense rights and impeding procedural fairness.[30] This criticism rests upon the fact that during the early stages of criminal proceedings, it has yet to be clarified whether the person asserting

[23] Doorson v. Netherlands, App. No. 20524/92, Eur. Ct. H.R., June 26, 1996, § 70.

[24] Directive 2012/29/EU, Art. 19. [25] *Id.* Art. 20. [26] *Id.* Art. 23, 24.

[27] *Id.* Art. 22. [28] *Id.* Art. 22(6).

[29] Stefanie Bock, *Das europäische Opferrechtspaket: zwischen substantiellem Fortschritt und blindem Aktionismus*, Zeitschrift für Internationale Strafrechtsdogmatik 201, 209 (2013).

[30] Conseil des barreaux européens, *Response to the European Commission Proposal for a Directive establishing Minimum Standards on Rights, Support and Protection of Victims of Crime* 11 (Oct. 2011), goo.gl/ETrXGr.

to have been victimized is in fact a crime victim, and who has committed this crime under what kind of circumstances. Thus, at the time of the assessment, many of the decisive factors are still undetermined. Directive 2012/29/EU, though, implies that the assessment is to be based on the victim's statement without any further investigations. Therefore, the concerns regarding parallel investigations miss the precarious point. However, if prosecutors and judges are required to adhere to the alleged victim's statement whenever they assess the victim's vulnerability or apply a certain protection measure in accordance with a previous assessment, the presumption of innocence can be impaired and the prosecutor/judge might be prejudiced during the following proceedings. Finally, the assessment has been opposed as practically infeasible.[31] Thus, while the intention to protect victims against secondary victimization in an individualized manner is beyond reproach, the current assessment mechanism does not appear ideal to achieve this goal. Future research should aim at exploring more suitable options to reconcile the different interests involved.

3. Participation

a. *Challenges to Participatory Rights*

Procedural rights allowing the victim to actively participate and influence decision-making in criminal proceedings have been and remain the most contentious among victim rights in civil law jurisdictions. The primary reason arises from criminal law and state theory. Since the beginning of the thirteenth century, crime has become conceived as a violation of the public order concerning society as a whole, instead of as harm to an individual.[32] The *ius puniendi* has become reserved to the state. As the owner of the monopoly of force, the state has the exclusive right and duty to prosecute crime and inflict punishment in the name of society. The individual harm suffered by the victim is traditionally dealt with in private law. This theoretical framework hampers an influential role of victims in proceedings that are designed to resolve a conflict between the public/state and the offender. Essentially, the legal-philosophical and normative foundation of participatory rights for victims is in tension with the theory that underpins the concept of crime and the purpose of criminal proceedings.

Furthermore, participatory rights have been opposed because of the victim's uncertain status during criminal proceedings. Before the final verdict is rendered, from a legal perspective, it is yet uncertain whether the person asserting to have been victimized is in fact a victim of crime. The criminal process might still conclude that the person is not a crime victim, not a victim of the accused standing trial, or not a victim of the counts for which the accused stands trial. Therefore, strictly speaking, criminal proceedings involve an alleged victim and an alleged perpetrator. As a consequence, some scholars

[31] Marc Groenhuijsen, *The Development of International Policy in Relation to Victims of Crime*, 20 Int'l Rev. Victimology 31, 37 (2014).

[32] *Supra* note 2.

argue that it would violate the presumption of innocence of the accused and undermine the guarantee of a fair trial if an unofficial presumption of victimhood was applied and the alleged victim was granted participatory rights.[33] This criticism has raised awareness for a more accurate terminology that emphasizes the tentativeness of the victim status during criminal proceedings. The Austrian Parliament, for example, has included a provision in the Austrian Code of Criminal Procedure that stresses that the procedural rights are conferred on persons who *could have been* aggrieved by a crime.[34] In other jurisdictions, scholars promote the use of comparable accurate terminology, with limited success.[35] Most national laws instead call and treat a person who claims to have been victimized as a de facto victim of crime for the purpose of criminal proceedings.[36] Regrettably, this holds true also for the terminology used to define victims in Directive 2012/29/EU, Article 2(1). Apart from the concerns about terminology, the criticism did not obstruct the implementation of procedural rights for (alleged) victims. From the majority perspective that victims merit at least some procedural rights in criminal proceedings, this is to be appreciated. If one wanted to ensure that procedural rights were exclusively conferred to real victims, one would need to clearly distinguish them from other alleged victims before the final verdict. This would be practically infeasible, and under due process standards impossible. Furthermore, statistically, it is rare that a person deliberately falsely pretends to be a crime victim.[37]

Finally, participatory rights face due process concerns. In this respect, some scholars argue that granting procedural powers to victims would infringe the defendant's fair trial right and result in a zero-sum game.[38] For instance, victims would mostly use their powers to support the prosecution, thereby unbalancing the equality of arms to the detriment of the defense. Moreover, victim influence would facilitate the intrusion of private views and spurious interests into public decision-making and, contrary to the principle of equality before the law, would cause disparity in prosecution and punishment in similar cases depending on the resilience or punitiveness of the victim.[39] Finally, it is suspected that the victim's subjective and sometimes distorted view could undermine the objectivity of criminal proceedings. The empirical data on the effect of victim participation on criminal trials is ambivalent. A contested recent study on the impact of the participation of victims as auxiliary prosecutors in German criminal trials suggests that victim participation prolongs the process and results in more convictions and overall

[33] On this criticism André Klip, *On Victim's Rights and Its Impact on the Rights of the Accused*, 23 Eur. J. Crime, Crim. L. & Crim. Just. 177, 186 seq. (2015).

[34] StPO, § 65 no.1a (Austria).

[35] Felix Bommer, *Offensive Verletztenrechte im Strafprozess* 258 seq. (2006); Klip, *supra* note 33; Schünemann, *supra* note 14, at 197 seq. For a different perspective, see Marion Brienen & Ernestine Hoegen, *Victims of Crime in 22 European Criminal Justice Systems* 30, 285 seq. (2000).

[36] E.g., Strafprozessordnung [StPO] [Code of Criminal Procedure], Art. 115(1) (Switz.).

[37] Anat Horovitz & Thomas Weigend, *Human Dignity and Victims' Rights in the German and Israeli Criminal Process*, 44 Isr. L. Rev. 263, 270 (2011).

[38] Schünemann, *supra* note 14, at 198.

[39] Cf. Julio Pérez Gil, *Private Interests Seeking Punishment: Prosecution Brought by Private Individuals and Groups in Spain*, 25 L. & Pol'y 151, 166 (2003).

harsher sentences.[40] Victim surveys, to the contrary, almost unanimously indicate that victims mostly do not desire harsh sentences but are more interested in support measures.[41] Hence, it would be wrong to consider victims as inherent agents of punitiveness in criminal proceedings. Yet surveys on victim needs do not immediately reveal anything about the actual effects that different kinds of victim participation might have on the process.

b. *Rationales Underpinning Participatory Rights*

Despite these apprehensions, victims have long had participatory rights in many civil law criminal processes, and since the 1970s these rights have even been strengthened in many jurisdictions. The rationales underpinning these rights are diverse and partly controversial. Some participatory rights are supposed to empower victims to seek compensation by the defendant; others shall facilitate protection and support. Occasionally, victims are employed as agents of accountability who control state actors, such as when they help to ensure the public prosecutor's impartiality. The oldest, yet most controversial rationale remains the pursuit of private vengeance, that is, the desire to see and contribute to the prosecution and punishment of the perpetrator. Closely related to this ancient motive, yet formulated in a less archaic manner, is an argument that has been proposed comparatively recently and has gained a growing number of advocates, primarily in the German-language literature on criminal procedure and penal theory. Essentially, it is postulated that victims seek the public recognition that a wrong, and not bad luck, has happened to them.[42] The goals of sentencing, therefore, it is argued, need to be extended to include satisfying this individual interest in reassurance. On these premises, some scholars justify participatory rights for victims in criminal proceedings with the argument that they were necessary to enable victims to pursue their interest in reassurance qua conviction/sentencing.[43] The participatory rights entailed in Directive 2012/29/EU appear to be inspired by a similar rationale. The directive aims at facilitating victim participation in criminal proceedings in order to provide victims with effective access to justice.[44] The need for access to justice, in turn, is described as the victim's wish to see justice done (distributive justice) and to be confident about how it is achieved.[45] The conception of victim participation as a means to provide distributive justice implies the conviction that participatory rights are supposed to serve the pursuit of an individual interest in the outcome of the criminal process, that is, in the conviction and punishment of the offender.

[40] Stephan Barton & Christian Flotho, *Opferanwälte im Strafverfahren* 238 seq. (2010); critical Heinz Schöch, *Opferschutz im Strafverfahren*, in *Täter, Taten, Opfer* 217, 224 (Dieter Dölling & Jörg-Martin Jehle eds., 2013).

[41] *E.g.*, Michael Baurmann & Wolfram Schädler, *Das Opfer nach der Straftat—seine Erwartungen und Perspektiven* 121 (1990).

[42] *Infra* Section III.1.

[43] Bommer, *supra* note 35, at 257 seq.; Dieter Dölling, *Täter, Opfer und Verfassung*, in *Verfassungsvoraussetzungen* 77, 83 (Michael Anderheiden et al. eds., 2013).

[44] Directive 2012/29/EU, Art. 1(1), recital 9.

[45] Commission Impact Assessment, at 12, SEC(2011) 580 final (May 18, 2011).

Several participatory rights granted to victims combine various justifications. For many, it is indeed controversial which purpose they are meant to serve. Some of these rationales, such as protection and support, do not interfere with the traditional theoretical perceptions of a crime as public wrong, an objective state-run criminal process, and prosecution and punishment in the public interest. Others, though, such as the pursuit of private vengeance, can create tensions in this respect. Finally, the purpose that underpins a certain procedural right has repercussions on the victim's role in and her/his relationship to other actors in the criminal justice system.

c. *Varieties of Participatory Rights*

RIGHT TO BE HEARD

Directive 2012/29/EU, Article 10 establishes the right of every victim to be heard during criminal proceedings and to provide evidence. The goal of this provision is to ensure that all victims—independent from their potential appearance as a witness—have an opportunity to provide information, views, and evidence during every stage of criminal proceedings. The relevant authorities are required to listen to and consider the victim's report during their decision-making.[46] Hence, the victim is given a real chance to influence the process. The provision does not guarantee victims an opportunity to personally appear and orally plead in open court, however. Instead, it suffices if they can make statements in writing.[47] A construction of the text of Article 10 together with contextual and teleological considerations suggests that the right to be heard is meant to serve three goals.[48] First, it should permit victims to contribute to the fact-finding process in order to pursue their private interests in the outcome of the criminal process and thus receive distributive justice. Second, the right should create procedural justice for victims, that is, make them feel confident about the final verdict and how it is achieved. Finally, the possibility to share their experiences should help victims to come to terms with the ordeal of the crime. The latter two purposes parallel the expressive function of so-called victim impact statements (VIS). VIS were first developed in common law countries, beginning in the 1980s, primarily in order to give victims a voice in criminal proceedings and remedy the absence of formal rights for them in common law.[49] Later, this development also initiated debates in civil law jurisdictions. The Netherlands introduced VIS in 2004,[50] whereas Germany considered adopting VIS in 2010 but eventually refrained from doing so. The German legislature, against the opinion of some scholars, took the view that VIS would be incompatible with structural principles and objectives of the reformed inquisitorial process as well as with constitutional

[46] Case C-404/07, Katz, 2008 E.C.R. I-07607, at para. 50.

[47] Directive 2012/29/EU, recital 41. [48] Cf. *id.* Art. 1(1), recital 9; Commission, *supra* note 45.

[49] Jo-Anne Wemmers, *Victim Policy Transfer: Learning from Each Other*, 11 Eur. J. Crim. Pol. Res. 121, 124 (2005). In some jurisdictions, VIS also serve to provide information for sentencing, Carolyn Hoyle, *Victims, the Criminal Process, and Restorative Justice*, in *The Oxford Handbook of Criminology* 398, 412 seq. (Mike Maguire et al. eds., 5th ed. 2012).

[50] Sv, §§ 51e, 302 (Dutch).

safeguards for the defendant.[51] Given the latest development on the EU level, however, it remains to be seen whether more civil law jurisdictions will follow the Dutch example and replicate this instrument. The European Commission, at least, recommends doing so for the transposition of Directive 2012/29/EU.[52]

RIGHT TO BECOME A CIVIL PARTY

Victims who have incurred damages as a result of a criminal offense are often granted the opportunity to become a civil party to a public prosecution in order to pursue civil damages from the offender during criminal proceedings. The system of a *partie civile* originated in Napoleonic France,[53] but today many civil law jurisdictions, including, Italy, the Netherlands, Austria, Poland, and Germany, provide for similar mechanisms.[54] Practically though, their use is more popular in Romanic countries than, for example, in Germany where the so-called adhesion procedure is rarely invoked.[55]

Essentially, the civil party system means that the victim's civil damages claim is attached to the criminal process and the criminal court is asked to rule simultaneously on the criminal and civil liability of the accused. As a civil party, victims enjoy a formal position and procedural rights in the criminal process that allow them to pursue their interest in obtaining compensation from the offender. To this end, civil parties are often given access to the case files, may choose to be legally represented at trial, apply to the court to collect or consider certain evidence, question witnesses and defendants, present arguments, and appeal the final judgment on grounds related to their civil interest.[56] In Belgium and France, the *partie civile* may also institute the prosecution.[57] Yet, although the victim thus becomes a party to the criminal proceedings, the public prosecutor remains in charge of the prosecution; the victim does not become a second prosecutor or exercises the state's *ius puniendi*.[58]

Hence, the civil party system primarily seeks to realize the victim's interest in obtaining monetary compensation from the offender, and not to satisfy private interests in

[51] Große Strafrechtskommission des deutschen Richterbundes, Gutachten zum Thema: Stärkung der Rechte des Opfers auf Gehör im Strafverfahren 58, 79 seq. (2010).

[52] Commission, DG Justice Guidance Document related to the transposition and implementation of Directive 2012/29/EU, at 29 (Dec. 2013).

[53] Wemmers, *supra* note 49, at 125.

[54] Codice di procedura penale [C.p.p.] [Code of Criminal Procedure], Art. 74 (It.); Sv, § 51f (Dutch); StPO, § 67 (Austria); Kodeks postępowania karnego [K.p.k.] [Code of Criminal Procedure], Art. 62 (Pol.); StPO, § 403 (Ger.).

[55] Thomas Weigend, *Internationale Entwicklungen bei der Stellung des Verletzten im Strafverfahren*, in *Ambivalenzen der Opferzuwendung des Strafrechts* 29, 35 (Stephan Barton & Ralf Kölbel eds., 2012).

[56] On rights of the *Adhäsionskläger* in German law, see Anna Zabeck, *Karlsruher Kommentar zur Strafprozessordnung* § 404 para. 9 seq. (Rolf Hannich ed., 7th ed. 2013); on the *Privatbeteiligter* in Austrian law StPO, Art. 67(6)(7) (Austria); generally Wemmers, *supra* note 49, at 125.

[57] *Infra* Section III.2.

[58] Jean Pradel, *France*, in *Criminal Procedure Systems in the European Community* 105, 116 (Christine van den Wyngaert ed., 1993).

vengeance.[59] It provides victims with the benefit of a fast and convenient means to acquire compensation while avoiding the burden of proof, additional effort, and expenses of a separate civil trial. However, the system has also been criticized from the victim's perspective with the argument that it forced victims to put a price tag on the (psychological) impact of the crime in order to receive a voice in criminal proceedings.[60] Further, compared to the mechanism of compensation orders, the civil party system has been opposed as burdensome for victims.[61] Compensation orders originate in common law countries where courts can sentence the perpetrator to pay compensation to the victim and states enforce the order. In the civil party system, instead, victims must participate in the criminal process to receive a verdict on their compensation claim, and must enforce it themselves. Some scholars therefore promote the adoption of compensation orders in civil law jurisdictions.[62] Finally, the civil party system has been questioned from a fair trial perspective as blurring the victim's procedural roles as biased claimant and neutral witness and prolonging the criminal process.[63]

Directive 2012/29/EU leaves much leeway on this issue. While Article 16(1) endorses opportunities for victims to obtain a decision on compensation by the offender in the course of criminal proceedings, Member States remain free to regulate that such decisions are made in other legal proceedings. Further, the EU treats adhesion procedures and compensation orders as equally suitable means to permit victims to attain a decision on compensation during criminal proceedings.[64]

RIGHT TO BECOME AN AUXILIARY PROSECUTOR

Another option for victims to formally participate in criminal proceedings is to assume the role of an auxiliary prosecutor. This option is less prevalent among civil law jurisdictions than the civil party system. It is available, for example, in Poland and Germany.[65] Whereas under Polish law, every person injured by an indictable offense can participate in the judicial proceedings as *oskarżyciel posiłkowy*,[66] German law

[59] Note, though, that the French *partie civile* is viewed to have a dual nature as compensatory and retributive, allowing the pursuit of compensatory and/or punitive purposes, Mathieu Jacquelin, *Victims Participation in French Criminal Proceedings: Current Status and Future Perspectives in View of Directive 2012/29/EU*, in *Victims and Criminal Justice* 83, 88 (Luca Lupária ed., 2015).

[60] Wemmers, *supra* note 49, at 125.

[61] John R. Spencer, *The Victim and the Prosecutor*, in *Hearing the Victim: Adversarial Justice, Crime Victims and the State* 141, 156 (Anthony Bottoms & Julian Roberts eds., 2010); Weigend, *supra* note 55, at 37.

[62] E.g., Weigend, *supra* note 55, at 37.

[63] *Id.* at 36.

[64] Commission, *supra* note 52, at 37.

[65] In Spain, every citizen can bring an *acusación popular* to prosecute *delito público*, Ley de Enjuiciamiento Criminal [LEC] [Code of Criminal Procedure], Art. 270 (Spain). The *acusador popular* has a prosecutorial position similar to the auxiliary prosecutor. Yet, since the possibility is available to every citizen, it is not a particular victim right, even though a victim as *acusador particular* receives some concessions. For details see Gil, *supra* note 39, at 151 seq. Under Czech law, victims generally enjoy quite elaborate procedural rights independent from any specific status, Zdeněk Karabec et al., *Criminal Justice System in the Czech Republic* 58 (2011); trestní řád, §§ 43(1), 215(1), 216(2) (Czech).

[66] K.p.k., Art. 53 (Pol.).

restricts the right to join as *Nebenkläger* to victims of certain, mostly severe offenses.[67] In Portugal, victims possess a similar right; they can request the status of an *assistente* who cooperates with the public prosecutor.[68] Directive 2012/29/EU does not provide for anything comparable.

Auxiliary prosecution gives victims comprehensive powers to influence criminal proceedings. As auxiliary prosecutor under German and Polish law, victims may attend the trial, inspect the case files, file evidentiary motions, question witnesses and defendants, challenge judges, make objections and requests, participate in the closing speeches, and appeal against decisions not to proceed and on limited grounds against the final verdict.[69] Further, they can seek the assistance of an attorney and apply for legal aid.[70] However, under German law, the monopoly to charge and to control the criminal process remain with the public prosecutor. The auxiliary prosecutor can merely join existing criminal proceedings as accessory private participant; she/he may not charge the defendant herself/himself or dispose of the subject matter of the proceedings. In Poland, victims may either join an action lodged by a public prosecutor, or if the public prosecutor decides to drop the charges, they may continue the prosecution themselves as a subsidiary auxiliary prosecutor.[71]

Whereas it is undisputed that the victim's right to become a civil party serves compensatory interests, the rationale underpinning the auxiliary prosecution is far from uncontested. Indeed, in Germany, the purpose, and even the legitimacy of this institution is one of the most contentious topics of victim rights law. The German legislature declared in its latest reform that its primary purpose was to protect particularly vulnerable victims.[72] A growing, yet controversial opinion, instead, refers to the victim's desire for vengeance: The auxiliary prosecution aimed to permit victims to pursue their interests in seeing the offender punished.[73] Yet another position dismisses particularly victim-centered rationales and instead identifies the control of a public prosecutor as a main purpose of the auxiliary prosecution.[74] This controversy exemplifies the difficulty in establishing a theoretically sound foundation for a victim's prosecutorial role in a public criminal process. In particular, the rationale to meet the victim's desire for vengeance

[67] StPO, § 395 (Ger.).

[68] Código de Processo Penal [CPP] [Code of Criminal Procedure], Art. 68 (Port.).

[69] StPO, §§ 397, 400 (Ger.); K.p.k., Art. 367(1), 370(1), 406(1) (Pol.); on German law Susanne Walther, *Victims' Rights: Procedural and Constitutional Principles for Victim Participation in Germany*, in *Therapeutic Jurisprudence and Victim Participation in Justice* 97, 104 seq. (Edna Erez et al. eds., 2011). On the rights of the *assistente* in Portugal CPP, Art. 69 (Port.).

[70] StPO, §§ 397(2), 397a (Ger.); for Poland Cezary Kulesza, *Directive 2012/29/EU of 25 October 2012 Establishing Minimum Standards on the Rights, Support and Protection of Victims of Crime*, in *Improving Protection of Victims' Rights: Access to Legal Aid* 139, 153 seq. (Paweł Wiliński & Piotr Karlik eds., 2014).

[71] K.p.k., Art. 54(2), 55 (Pol.); Kulesza, *supra* note 70, at 144, 155.

[72] Deutscher Bundestag: Drucksachen und Protokolle [BT] 16/12098, 9, 29. Scholars refute this theory as incompatible with the current normative structure, e.g., Thomas Weigend, *Das Opfer als Prozesspartei?*, in *Verbrechen, Strafe, Resozialisierung* 955, 957 seq. (Dieter Dölling et al. eds., 2010).

[73] Cf. Walther, *supra* note 69.

[74] Klaus Schroth, Die *Rechte des Opfers im Strafprozess* § 256 (2d ed. 2011).

has been refuted as irreconcilable with the concept of a neutral, state-run criminal justice system operating in the public interest.[75]

Independent from its purpose, the auxiliary prosecution is also contested because of its potential repercussions on the structure of the process. German scholars fear that it has unbalanced the distribution of power within the trial to the detriment of the defense and has enabled victims to exploit their prosecutorial powers to manipulate their witness testimonies and obstruct the truth-finding.[76] Similar concerns were raised in Poland where it is claimed that the auxiliary prosecution might impede proceedings and result in barratry.[77] Empirical research seems to support these suspicions; findings suggest that criminal proceedings conducted with an auxiliary prosecutor on average take longer, are more conflict-laden, and result in harsher sentences.[78]

RIGHT TO PRIVATE PROSECUTION

Finally, in many though not all civil law jurisdictions, the victim can appear as a private prosecutor.[79] Hence, the victim has the right to decide whether to bring charges against a defendant and represent the prosecution during regular criminal proceedings. Private prosecution is usually limited to certain less serious offenses, such as libel and defamation. As private prosecutors, victims are not bound to impartiality but may act for their own interests. However, private prosecutors do not have a private right to inflict punishment, but rather represent the state's *ius puniendi*.[80]

The existence of a right to private prosecution may astonish given the fact that the civil law tradition generally regards criminal prosecution as a state duty exercised by a public servant. Consequently, purpose and legitimacy of private prosecutions are highly controversial.[81] Frequently, they are interpreted as a device to relieve the public burden to prosecute misdemeanors and to decriminalize certain offenses because, in reality, victims rarely use their right to private prosecution.[82] Others purport that private prosecutions served to protect victims against intrusive public prosecutions or to gratify the victim's desire for vengeance.[83] Sporadically, private prosecutions are also interpreted as a safety valve against a public prosecutor's inactivity/arbitrariness or as a means to

[75] Weigend, *supra* note 72, at 959.

[76] Kurth, *supra* note 20, at § 395 sec. 11 seq.; Schünemann, *supra* note 14, at 197.

[77] Krzysztof Stefanowicz, *The Victim of Crime in Polish Criminal Law*, 21 Cap. U. L. Rev. 83, 88 (1992).

[78] Barton, *supra* note 40.

[79] *See, e.g.*, StPO, § 374 (Ger.); LEC, Art. 104, 270 (Spain); StPO, Art. 71 (Austria); K.p.k., Art. 59 (Pol.). For an overview see Jamil Ddamulira Mujuzi, *Participation in the Criminal Justice System in the European Union through Private Prosecutions: Issues Emerging from the Jurisprudence of the European Court of Human Rights*, 24 Eur. J. Crime, Crim. L. & Crim. Just. 107, 114 seq. (2016).

[80] Gil, *supra* note 39, at 154; Heinz Zipf, *Strafantrag, Privatklage und staatlicher Strafanspruch*, Goltdammer's Archiv für Strafrecht 234, 237 seq. (1969).

[81] *E.g.*, critical Gil, *supra* note 39, at 161 seq.; positive Mujuzi, *supra* note 79, at 130 seq.

[82] Statistisches Bundesamt, *Rechtspflegestatistik Fachserie 10 Reihe 2.3 Strafgerichte* 24 (2016), *available at* goo.gl/RKEiyZ, provides data on its use in Germany.

[83] Lutz Meyer-Goßner & Bertram Schmitt, *Strafprozessordnung* Einleitung sec. 90 (59th ed. 2016).

strengthen democracy.[84] At least in Germany, however, opponents promoting the abolition of private prosecutions hold the majority.[85] They reject the institution for normative as well as victim-related reasons. Normatively, it is criticized as a relic of ancient times incompatible with foundational principles of an objective public criminal justice system committed to guaranteeing a fair trial; arguments in its favor do not outweigh the structural frictions caused by permitting private prosecution. Moreover, decriminalization is better achieved by reforming substantive criminal law than by allowing victims to leave certain offenses unenforced. From the victim's perspective, private prosecutions are considered burdensome. The victim must invest time and money, carry the burden of proof without having the public prosecutor's investigatory powers, and often face the risk of a counterclaim by the defendant.[86] Overall, it is argued, victims would be better off if the state prosecuted. The same reluctance can be observed on the EU level. While Directive 2012/29/EU is silent on private prosecutions, the European Commission expressly discourages from adopting this institution, arguing that it constitutes an additional burden on the victim.[87]

III. Right to Criminal Prosecution (and Punishment)

1. Normative and Theoretical Foundation

While neither national constitutions nor penal codes explicitly entitle victims to have "their" perpetrator prosecuted and punished, a heated discourse is recently emerging about a right of crime victims to criminal prosecution (and punishment) of the offender.[88]

The debate partly originates in the jurisprudence of the European Court of Human Rights (ECtHR). The ECHR does not as such entail a right to require criminal proceedings to be instituted against third parties.[89] Neither does its Article 6(1) on a right to a fair trial confer any independent entitlement on crime victims to have third parties prosecuted or sentenced for a criminal offense.[90] Yet, in its case law, the ECtHR has developed the doctrine of the state's positive obligation to conduct effective investigations

[84] Council of Europe, Recommendation of the Comm. of Ministers Rec(2000)19 (Oct. 6, 2000), sec. 34; Mujuzi, *supra* note 79, at 108; (critical) Gil, *supra* note 39, at 161 seq.

[85] The opposite seems true, e.g., in Spain, Gil, *supra* note 39, at 166.

[86] Stefanowicz, *supra* note 77, at 86 seq.; Weigend, *supra* note 1, at 480.

[87] Commission, *supra* note 52, at 31.

[88] On this debate Johanna Göhler, *To Continue or Not*, 6 New J. Eur. Crim. L. 102, 113 seq. (2015).

[89] Šilih v. Slovenien, App. No. 71463/01, Eur. Ct. H.R., Apr. 4, 2009, § 194.

[90] Perez v. France, App. No. 47287/99, Eur. Ct. H.R., Feb. 12, 2004, § 70 seq.; Case C-507/10, X, 2011 E.C.R. I-14241 sec. 43. The fair trial guarantee only applies to victims with regard to matters affecting their "civil rights and obligations." Hence, only when a state's legal system allows the pursuit of a civil damages claim within the criminal trial can victims invoke the right to a fair trial concerning criminal proceedings.

of certain serious human rights violations committed by private individuals.[91] The Court derives this obligation from the respective substantive Convention right read in conjunction with the state's general duty under ECHR Article 1 to protect the rights defined in the Convention. Based on this duty to protect, a person who arguably claims to have been victimized can request the state to conduct a criminal investigation capable of identifying and punishing those responsible.[92] Founded on this jurisprudence, scholars argue that under the ECHR crime victims have a right against the state to effective criminal prosecution of the perpetrator.[93] Some national courts have followed this interpretation.[94] The doctrine of a victim's right to prosecution has remained controversial, however.[95] Opponents rebut the underlying doctrinal reasoning with the argument that the protection of Convention rights qua criminal prosecution was necessarily future-oriented and could only shield potential crime victims, that is, society at large, against the occurrence of future crimes. This counterargument becomes particularly graphic in the case of capital offenses. Further, the jurisprudential context suggests that the Court rather intended to establish an objective state duty to maintain an effective criminal justice system serving the public interest in the prevention of crime, rather than to create a subjective entitlement of the individual victim to criminal prosecution.[96] Finally, it should be noted that the ECtHR has restricted this case law to allegedly severe violations of Articles 2, 3, 5 and 8 of the Convention.

Another strain of the debate on a victim's right to punishment evolved from a theory developed by the German intellectual Jan Philipp Reemtsma. After he had been a victim of kidnapping, he proposed that in order to come to terms with the experience of the crime, victims desired the official reassurance that a wrong, rather than bad luck, had occurred to them.[97] Only the punishment of the offender could achieve this reassurance by reaffirming the victim that she/he was not responsible for what had happened nor had experienced bad luck, but that she/he had suffered from the criminal action of another person. Based rather on philosophy than on a firm legal reasoning, Reemtsma advocates that because this reassurance was necessary to prevent the persistence of moral damages suffered by the victim, the victim had a right against the state to punishment of the offender. This purported victim's need for reassurance is commonly referred to as

[91] Instead of many McKerr v. United Kingdom, App. No. 28883/95, Eur. Ct. H.R., May 4, 2001, § 111 seq.; Alastair Mowbray, *Duties of Investigation Under the European Convention on Human Rights*, 51 Int'l Comp. L Q. 437 (2002).

[92] *McKerr v. United Kingdom*, *supra* note 91, § 113.

[93] *E.g.*, Albin Dearing, *Das Recht des Opfers auf ein Strafverfahren und die Strafpflicht des Staates nach der EMRK*, in *Opferrechte in Österreich* 81, 82 (Id. & Marianne Löschnig-Gspandl eds., 2004).

[94] Bundesverfassungsgericht-Kammer [German Constitutional Court-Chamber], Feb. 4, 2010, 2 BvR 2307/06, sec. 19.

[95] See Göhler, *supra* note 88, at 113 seq.

[96] Klaus Ferdinand Gärditz, *Anmerkung*, 70 Juristenzeitung 896, 899 (2015).

[97] Jan Philipp Reemtsma, *Das Recht des Opfers auf die Bestrafung des Täters—als Problem* (1999). On his work in English, see Cornelius Prittwitz, *The Resurrection of the Victim in Penal Theory*, 3 Buff. Crim. L. Rev. 109, 121 seq. (1999–2000); Jesús-María Silva Sánchez, *Doctrines Regarding "The Fight Against Impunity" and "The Perpetrator to Be Punished"* 28 Pace L. Rev. 865, 880 seq. (2007–2008).

"interest in satisfaction" (*Genugtuungsinteresse*). Over time, multiple scholars have taken this purported victim's need as a starting point to develop full-blown theories on a crime victim's right to prosecution and punishment. Concepts include differently nuanced theories based on constitutional law,[98] as well as arguments originating in penal theory,[99] state theory,[100] sociology of law,[101] and legal history.[102]

The European Union does not explicitly express a view on this debate, but features of Directive 2012/29/EU convey the impression that it recognizes the prominent victim's interest in satisfaction. Scholars propagating a victim's right to prosecution and punishment remain the minority in civil law jurisdictions, however. The majority in scholarship, legislatures, and judicature accept the traditional model of a criminal justice system that respects and protects the victim, but operates in the public interest and on behalf of society. Reasons for this appear twofold. First, all given theories on the existence of a victim's right to prosecution/punishment can be somehow refuted as not entirely conclusive or as inconsistent with other arguably noble and essential legal principles. Second, a victim's legal right against the state to prosecution/punishment would have significant repercussions on the victim's role in criminal proceedings and the criminal process itself. It would transform the structure of criminal prosecution from bipolar to triangular and create a competition between the victim and the accused with regard to discretionary decisions and the scope of procedural principles. Moreover, a right to punishment would at least partly transform the *ius puniendi* of the state into a responsibility of the latter toward the victim. Under these premises, the goal of a rational, equal, and non-arbitrary prosecution of crimes according to societal interests could be difficult to maintain. Hitherto, these consequences have been insufficiently analyzed. Future research should focus on scrutinizing potential solutions in order to reconcile the victim's interest in the official recognition of the wrong with the interests of the defendant and society.

2. Right to a Review of a Decision Not to Prosecute

The debate on a victim's right to prosecution has also had repercussions on the control of prosecutorial dismissal decisions. For the first time on the EU level, Directive 2012/29/EU, Article 11, prescribes that victims must have a right to a review of a decision not to prosecute. The review applies to decisions taken by prosecutors, investigative judges,

[98] Tatjana Hörnle, *Anmerkung*, 70 Juristenzeitung 893, 895 seq. (2015); Thomas Weigend, *"Die Strafe für das Opfer"?—Zur Renaissance des Genugtuungsgedanken im Straf- und Strafverfahrensrecht*, Rechtswissenschaft 39 seq. (2010).

[99] Prittwitz, *supra* note 97; Lyane Sautner, *Opferinteressen und Strafrechtstheorien* 267 seq. (2008); Silva Sánchez, *supra* note 97.

[100] Cf. Dionysios Spinellis, *Victims of Crime and the Criminal Process*, 31 Isr. L. Rev. 337, 338 (1997); Hörnle, *supra* note 98.

[101] Wilfried Holz, *Justizgewähranspruch des Verbrechensopfers* (2007).

[102] Tatjana Hörnle, *Die Rolle des Opfers in der Straftheorie und im materiellen Strafrecht*, 61 Juristenzeitung 950, 956 (2006).

and law enforcement authorities, but not to judicial decisions, and must be conducted by an impartial body, but not necessarily by a court.[103] Whereas the directive does not explicitly regulate the consequences of a review, the principle of effectiveness of EU law requires that a victim's review request must be capable of inducing a prosecution.

Many domestic civil law jurisdictions have long had some legal remedy against public prosecutors' decisions not to prosecute: predominantly, either the possibility to bring a (subsidiary) private prosecution or to initiate proceedings to review prosecutorial dismissal decisions.[104] The latter option is more prevalent and considered more victim-friendly. The review procedures differ, however, with regard to the victim's role therein. In one model, applied in German law, the victim's request is compulsory for initiating the review.[105] Another model makes the review technically independent from the victim's initiative: If a prosecutor intends to drop a case under Italian law, she/he always has to lodge a request for dismissal with the pretrial judge.[106] The victim can get involved, though, by objecting to the prosecutorial dismissal request with a reasoned complaint.[107] Such complaints often significantly influence the judicial decision by instructing the court why prosecution should be continued.[108] A third model allows victims to seek a review, but does not make the review dependent on them. Instead, every person who has reported an offense, including the victim, may lodge an appeal against a decision to close the case.[109] Finally, some jurisdictions, such as France and Belgium, provide for a review mechanism that is tied to their *partie civile* institution. There, victims may institute criminal proceedings by filing a complaint with a request for compensation for damages caused by the offense, even when the public authority declined to investigate or prosecute.[110] By initiating the action before the *judge d'instruction*, the victim sets in motion not only the civil action, but also the public proceedings.[111]

These different designs demonstrate that the purpose of the review mechanisms has not traditionally been to enforce a victim's right to prosecution, but to scrutinize the

[103] Directive 2012/29/EU, recital 43.

[104] On the distribution of these models in Europe: E.U. Agency for Fundamental Rights, http://fra.europa.eu/en/publications-and-resources/data-and-maps/comparative-data/victims-support-services/prosecution (last visited July 12, 2017).

[105] StPO, § 172 (Ger.).

[106] Codice di procedurale penale [C.p.p.] [Code of Criminal Procedure], Art. 408(1) (Ital.). Guido Todaro, *The Italian System for the Protection of Victims of Crime: Analysis and Prospects*, in *Victims and Criminal Justice*, *supra* note 59, at 109.

[107] C.c.p., Art. 410(1) (Ital.). Todaro, *supra* note 106.

[108] Ante Novokmet, *The Right of a Victim to a Review of a Decision Not to Prosecute as Set Out in Art. 11 of Directive 2012/29/EU and an Assessment of Its Transposition in Germany, Italy, France and Croatia*, 12 Utrecht L. Rev. 86, 97 seq. (2016).

[109] E.g., Code de procédure pénale [C. Pr. Pén.] [Code of Criminal Procedure], Art. 40–3 (French); Jacquelin, *supra* note 59, at 93.

[110] For France: C. Pr. Pén., Art. 1(2), 85 (French); Novokmet, *supra* note 109, at 99 seq. For Belgium: Christine van den Wyngaert, *Belgium*, in *Criminal Procedure Systems in the European Community*, *supra* note 58, at 1, 17 seq.

[111] Pradel, *supra* note 58, at 115.

public prosecutor's compliance with her/his public duties.[112] Where legal standing to initiate a review had been granted particularly to victims, this was because victims were expected to be the most interested in the prosecution and thus motivated to contribute to the control of the public prosecutor. Hence, victims were employed to advance the public interest in the prosecution of criminal offenses.[113] The evolving debate on a victim's right to prosecution, however, has also impacted the interpretation of means to control prosecutorial dismissal decisions. In some jurisdictions, such as Germany, several scholars argue that the victim's exclusive legal standing evidenced that the law indeed recognized a victim's right to prosecution. In others, the recognition of the victim's interest in criminal prosecution has provoked the introduction of review systems as a means to allow victims to pursue this interest. Directive 2012/29/EU designs the review of prosecutorial dismissal decisions as a procedure specifically for crime victims, arguably in order to enable victims to express and pursue their desire for satisfaction.

IV. Conceiving the Victim's Role in Criminal Proceedings

Time has long passed that victims had been the "forgotten men" in civil law criminal procedures. Despite the differences in type and number of rights accorded to victims across European civil law jurisdictions, nowadays, victims are widely conceived as central participants to the criminal process with their own rights and abilities to influence the proceedings. This is also reflected in EU law. The framing of the EU's power to approximate victim rights in Article 82 TFEU bespeaks the conviction that victims merit a role in criminal proceedings. Further, although Directive 2012/29/EU does not prescribe a specific formal role for victims such as that of a party to the proceedings,[114] its provisions imply that victims are to be recognized as genuine participants to the criminal process with certain procedural rights and a legitimate interest in the outcome of the proceedings. Whereas the EU generally confers the same rights on all victims, many domestic jurisdictions additionally reserve a specifically conditioned, more elaborate procedural role for some victims, such as that of an auxiliary prosecutor under German law. Notwithstanding this difference, victim rights law generally perceives victims as presumptively interested in the criminal prosecution and punishment of the offender. Only very rarely does the victim's role include rights to veto a public prosecution or support the defense.[115]

[112] On this rationale in the context of a European public prosecutor's office Göhler, *supra* note 88, at 115 seq. On the objective to instigate such an authority Johanna Göhler, *European Criminal Justice Integration 5.0: Towards a European Public Prosecutor's Office*, 40 Yale J. Int'l L. 193 seq. (2015).

[113] Novokmet, *supra* note 109, at 87.

[114] Directive 2012/29/EU, recital 9.

[115] The legal requirement of a victim's compulsory criminal complaint, existing, e.g., in Czech, French, and German law, forms a rare exception. It makes the public prosecution of certain, mostly less serious offenses dependent on the victim's criminal complaint, and thus grants victims an indirect power to hinder public prosecution.

Despite the recognition of the victim as a material participant along with the defendant, prosecutor, and judge, the victim is not conceived as a necessary actor in the criminal process. In many criminal proceedings, no victim participates. This is obvious when the relevant crime has no individual victim. However, it is also possible that victims choose not to exercise any of their rights. As a consequence of criminal law's primary concern with the individual responsibility of the accused/perpetrator, the exercise of victim rights is deemed voluntary. Furthermore, although reforms of the victim's role have been frequently couched in the terminology of victim "rights," the extent to which these developments have in fact created rights in a legal sense is debatable. That is to say that Directive 2012/29/EU as well as most domestic jurisdictions still lack any effective mechanism for victims to enforce their "rights" and obtain redress when criminal justice agencies willfully ignore/violate them.

Victim rights can affect the roles and interests of other actors in the criminal process in various ways. Rights to information, support, and protection require some logistical effort of the authorities and so oppose the victim to state actors, namely prosecutors and occasionally courts, which bear the corresponding duties. By committing resources of criminal justice agencies, they also affect public interests. Moreover, victim rights can impact the position of the defendant. Note, however, that polemic theories of an unavoidable zero-sum game are unfounded. In other words, multiple victim rights do not conflict with the defendant's position; several procedural interests of victims and defendants actually converge. Protection measures for victims, though, can interfere with the defendant's ability to effectively defend herself/himself and occasionally with the court's duty to detect the truth, especially when those measures restrict evidence.[116] Similar concerns exist for victim's participatory rights, which can result in a prosecutorial advantage, thereby unbalancing the criminal process to the detriment of the defense. The main aim of a criminal process, however, is to investigate the behavior of the accused and, if the allegations made against her/him are found proven, to convict and appropriately punish the offender. The liberties at stake in a criminal process for defendants, therefore, rank among the highest. Consequently, the majority in scholarship views victims' concerns in the process as important, but assigns them second place. The ECtHR and the Court of Justice of the EU share this view. Both hold that protection measures for victims are only legitimate if they are strictly necessary to preserve the victim's fundamental rights and do not restrict the defense to an extent that is incompatible with the right to a fair trial.[117] These standards are also reflected in Directive 2012/29/EU. It subjects protection measures for victims to the caveat that the measures must not prejudice the prerogatives of the defense, hence presuming that defendant's rights eventually prevail over the victim's interests. Clear criteria for balancing these interests in practice, however, are rarely identified. Directive 2012/29/EU equally shifts this delicate challenge onto domestic decision-makers. A promising approach would relate to the assumption of innocence.

[116] Schünemann, *supra* note 13, at 394; Todaro, *supra* note 106, at 111.

[117] Jasper v. United Kingdom, App. No. 27052/95, Eur. Ct. H.R., Feb. 16, 2000, § 52; Case C-105/03, Pupino, 2005 E.C.R. I-5285 sec. 59 seq.

Finally, despite the consensus that victims deserve attention in criminal proceedings, the uncertainty as to the theoretical foundation of victim involvement in the criminal process remains. In particular, participatory rights that permit victims to pursue private (retributive) interests in the outcome of the proceedings—however understandable they may appear—are considered difficult to reconcile with two central tenets of traditional criminal justice and penal theory: first, that crime is conceived as an offense against the state, not the individual victim; and second that the purposes of criminal proceedings focus on the relationship between the offender and the public. Hence, contrary to occasional belief,[118] normatively, it is not necessarily less challenging to integrate a victim's participatory rights into the civil law environment than into the common law tradition. Legal reforms have commonly neglected this challenge. Recently, however, a tendency has emerged to redefine the nature of crime as consisting of a wrong against society as well as against the individual victim.[119] This approach would dissolve the traditional notion of public harm as the exclusive foundational premise of crime, criminal law, and the criminal justice process and, if applied stringently, would transform the procedural structure. While this conception could provide a theoretically more stringent basis to explain an elaborate role for victims in the criminal process, future research still has to analyze its potential consequences for the criminal process as such and the roles of other actors therein.

V. Parallel Justice for Victims

Traditionally, academia and policymakers have predominantly turned to the criminal justice system as a means to assist victims. Recently, though, this approach has been challenged by the proposal to additionally establish a parallel system for crime victims that is detached from the criminal process and exclusively focuses on meeting their needs.[120] Two main reasons appear to motivate this proposal. First, the theoretical foundation of victim involvement in the current model of criminal process has remained contested and eventually unresolved. Second, and foremost, it is argued that contrary to common beliefs, the criminal justice setting is unsuitable to effectively meet the victims' desires.[121] The criminal process has been created and designed to determine the defendant's criminal liability and punishment; therefore, it centralizes the defendant and her/his rights. Consequently, the nature and normative structure of criminal proceedings preclude attending full recognition to the interests of victims and often result

[118] Jonathan Doak, *Victims' Rights in Criminal Trials: Prospects for Participation*, 32 J. L. & Soc'y 294, 313 seq. (2005); Andrew Sanders, *Victim Participation in an Exclusionary Criminal Justice System*, in *New Visions of Crime Victims* 97, 108 (Carolyn Hoyle & Richard Young eds., 2002).

[119] *See, e.g.*, Directive 2012/29/EU, recital 9.

[120] Foundational Susan Herman, *Parallel Justice for Victims of Crime* (2010).

[121] *Id.* at 29 seq.

in unresponsiveness to their needs. Moreover, the exclusive focus on the criminal justice system neglects multiple victims, that is, the great majority whose cases never go to trial.

The concept of parallel justice for victims originated in the United States, but it has given rise to analogous debates in civil law jurisdictions. In particular, some German scholars were inspired by the idea and suggested similar mechanisms, which have even been the subject of parliamentary debates.[122] Whereas the parallel justice concept has already been implemented in some U.S. communities,[123] the debate has hitherto remained theoretical in Germany. In fact, the relevant research is in its infancy. The proposals still need to be refined, most importantly but not only with regard to safeguarding the defendant against detrimental side effects in the criminal justice system. Nevertheless, the general objective of installing an additional, independent, victim-centered system that seeks justice for every victim and satisfies their purported moral desire for public recognition and societal solidarity appears promising. It would amount to a paradigm shift that could potentially be able to reconcile the interests of defendants, victims, and society while avoiding the fractions and deficiencies that victim involvement frequently faces in the conventional criminal justice system. Yet, future research still needs to further develop and articulate this vision.

VI. Conclusion

Victim rights have become firmly established as an integral component of civil law criminal procedures, not least due to the influence of the ECtHR and the European Union. Today, scholars and policymakers on both the domestic and the EU level agree that victims merit core rights to information, support, protection, and reparation. Current debates tend to focus on the more contentious topic of participatory rights. While diverse participatory rights for victims exist in civil law proceedings, commentators remain divided as to the precise conception of victim participation, the extent of the victim's influence on the criminal process, and the objectives that victims may legitimately advance therein. New perceptions of the victim's active role in the process as well as the evolving debate on a victim's entitlement to prosecution increasingly challenge the long-established concept of crime and the conventional separation between criminal and civil liability. Finally, expanding future research on the recent proposals for an additional system of parallel justice for victims could deepen our understanding of the

[122] Margarete Gräfin von Galen, *"Parallel Justice" für Opfer von Straftaten—ein Verfahren mit "Opfervermutung" außerhalb des Strafrechts*, Strafverteidiger 171 (2013); Christian Pfeiffer, *Parallel Justice—warum brauchen wir eine Stärkung des Opfers in der Gesellschaft?*, in *Mehr Prävention—weniger Opfer* 179, 192 seq. (Erich Marks & Wiebke Steffen eds., 2014); Heinz Schöch, *"Parallel Justice" für Kriminalitätsopfer in Deutschland*, in *Kriminologie ist Gesellschaftswissenschaft* 565 seq. (Dirk Baier & Thomas Mößle eds., 2014).

[123] *E.g.*, in Burlington, Vermont, http://pjburlington.org/home.htm (last visited July 12, 2017).

victim's role in and its repercussions on traditional criminal proceedings, as well as analyze and specify what the criminal process can realistically offer to victims.

References

Marion Eleonora Ingeborg Brienen & Ernestine Henriette Hoegen, *Victims of Crime in 22 European Criminal Justice Systems: The Implementation of Recommendation (85) 11 of the Council of Europe on the Position of the Victim in the Framework of Criminal Law and Procedure* (2000)

European Commission, DG Justice Guidance Document related to the transposition and implementation of Directive 2012/29/EU of the European Parliament and of the Council of 25 October 2012 establishing minimum standards on the rights, support and protection of victims of crime, and replacing Council Framework Decision 2001/220/JHA, December 2013

Albin Dearing, *Das Recht des Opfers auf ein Strafverfahren und die Strafpflicht des Staates nach der EMRK*, in *Opferrechte in Österreich* 81 (Albin Dearing & Marianne Löschnig-Gspandl eds., 2004)

Julio Pérez Gil, *Private Interests Seeking Punishment: Prosecution Brought by Private Individuals and Groups in Spain*, 25 Law & Policy 151 (2003)

Johanna Göhler, *To Continue or Not—Who Shall Be in Control of the European Public Prosecutor's Dismissal Decisions?*, 6 New J. European Criminal L. 102 (2015)

Susan Herman, *Parallel Justice for Victims of Crime* (2010)

André Klip, *On Victim's Rights and Its Impact on the Rights of the Accused*, 23 European J. Crime, Crim. L. & Crim. Justice 177 (2015)

Luca Lupária, ed., *Victims and Criminal Justice: European Standards and National Good Practice* (2015)

Antony Pemberton & Marc S. Groenhujisen, *Developing Victim's Rights Within the European Union: Past, Present and Future*, in *Victimology and Human Security: New Horizons* 535 (Hidemichi Morosawa et al. eds., 2009)

Cornelius Prittwitz, *The Resurrection of the Victim in Penal Theory*, 3 Buff. Crim. L. Rev. 109 (1999–2000)

PART III

SURVEILLANCE AND INVESTIGATION

CHAPTER 14

BETRAYAL BY BOSSES

Undercover Policing and the Problem of "Upstream Defection" by Rogue Principals

JACQUELINE E. ROSS*

I. Introduction

WHEN former DEA undercover agent Michael Levine published *Deep Cover*, he subtitled it, *The Inside Story of How DEA Infighting, Incompetence and Subterfuge Lost Us the Biggest Battle of the Drug War.*[1] He presents his tale as the story of how top DEA officials went "rogue" and sabotaged his undercover operation (code-named Operation Trifecta), just as Levine was on the verge of implicating top government officials and military officers from three Latin American countries in a conspiracy to import Bolivian cocaine into the United States. Levine claimed that DEA supervisors deliberately ignored his numerous requests to tape-record calls to the high-level officials protecting the drug operation in Bolivia, Panama, and Mexico, in order to avoid embarrassing disclosures about the failure of the DEA's drug eradication program (Operation Snowcap) in Bolivia. He claims that DEA supervisors were aware of the severity of the corruption problem in Bolivia and that "the Bolivian cocaine traffickers were warned three days before every recon [reconnaissance] flight and that every cocaine seizure that [DEA operation] Snowcap did was 'a gift, to keep us happy.'" In order to keep this tacit arrangement with Bolivian authorities intact, Levine claims, DEA supervisors eventually sabotaged Operation Trifecta.

* I am very grateful to Amitai Aviram, Dhammika Dharmapala, and David Hyman for illuminating discussions of the issues explored in this chapter.

[1] Michael Levine, *Deep Cover: The Inside Story of How DEA Infighting and Incompetence and Subterfuge Lost Us the Biggest Battle of the Drug War* (1990).

Levine's claim of betrayal by his command hierarchy is not an isolated complaint. In interviews and memoirs, former undercover agents circle back to their disillusionment with immediate supervisors or distant management. A recurring theme in even the most triumphant accounts of undercover operations is that of undercover agents' bitterness about the command hierarchy's disloyalty either to themselves, as subordinates, or to the mission the agents thought they shared with their agency.

This is not the familiar problem of the rogue agent, which one might term the problem of downstream defection or the "agency problem": it is that of the rogue principal, and of upstream defection, which one might call the "principal problem."

The difficulty a government has in constraining its representatives is well known as the "agency problem." Scholars have long worried about how the sovereign can ensure the allegiance of its representatives, and about how the state can prevent its agents from going astray. In contrast with the recognized problem of downstream defection by those entrusted with carrying out an assignment, scholars have rarely addressed or even identified the reciprocal problem, which we call "upstream defection" by middle and upper management from those under their command.

Memoirs of undercover agents, along with interviews with undercover agents, reveal a common theme: complaints by undercover agents that they were betrayed by the very people responsible for their safety and for the integrity and success of their undercover investigations. To the extent that these principals compromise the mission with which they've been entrusted, their misconduct might be considered simply a variant of the agency problem. What makes such betrayals different from the typical problem of downstream defection by those entrusted with a mission is the impact of such betrayals—whether real or perceived—on officials lower down in the hierarchy, including undercover agents, who remain loyal to their mission but must find ways to accommodate themselves to what they view as the upstream defection by those higher up in the chain of command on whom they depend for support, success, and validation of their achievements.

What I term "the principal problem" is of course not unique to undercover operations, or even to policing. Similar complaints are a staple of memoirs by those who spent their careers in the military, in intelligence agencies, or, indeed, in any large bureaucracy, though it has rarely been recognized or studied as an upstream counterpart to the more familiar downstream abuse of delegated authority by a rogue agent on a "frolic and detour."[2]

However, undercover operations have a number of features that make upstream defection a serious concern. Identifying these features may not only help regulators anticipate and mitigate the problem for undercover investigations, it may also illuminate factors that may aggravate or reduce such pathologies in other organizational contexts. Focusing more broadly on what accounts for undercover agents' *experience*

[2] *But see* Zohar Goshen & Richard Squire, *Principal Costs: A New Theory for Corporate Law and Governance*, 117 Colum. L. Rev. 767 (2017), which notes a similar problem in the realm of corporate law and governance, terming it the problem of "principal costs," as distinguished from "agency costs."

of betrayal may also assist in distinguishing real upstream defection, as an analytical matter, from *perceived* upstream defection that can be ascribed to differences in institutional commitments and outlook between supervisors and ground-level personnel. Once the differences between real and apparent defection are distinguished from each other in theory, further empirical research can shed light on the further evidentiary question of how to distinguish real abuses from perceived betrayals.

As I will argue later in the chapter, problems of upstream defection are more severe for long-term deep cover operations than for briefer buy-bust operations. Because the United States has, in the twentieth century, been a pioneer of deep cover operations, many European legal systems designed their own undercover policing systems with an eye to problems that arose in the American experience with long-term undercover investigations. While upstream defection can occur in any policing system, both Germany and France have designed their undercover policing systems so as to protect undercover agents from certain types of abuses and institutional pathologies. Their efforts should be examined as part of any discussion of what policing systems can do to mitigate the risk of upstream defection.

The data concerning this phenomenon are drawn from memoirs by American undercover agents (as there are many fewer such memoirs in Europe) and from hundreds of semi-structured open-ended interviews the author conducted with former undercover agents and supervisors of undercover agents in the United States, Germany, and France, between 2001 and 2017. The interviews were designed to elicit information from interview subjects about the legal, institutional, and practical constraints that guided their tactical choices in the field, with an eye to identifying those factors that mattered most to them in the design and execution of undercover operations. Concerns about the incentives and behavior of supervisors and investigators emerged as a recurring theme in memoirs of undercover agents and interviews with former undercover agents along with supervisors, who echoed some of the undercover agents' own concerns in explaining why both France and Germany have made the regulatory choice to separate undercover units from investigative divisions. By contrast, American law enforcement agencies fold undercover personnel into investigative teams.

Section II of this chapter identifies the different forms that "upstream defection" can take in the context of undercover operations. Section III explores some of the features of undercover operations that bring undercover agents into conflict with investigative teams and supervisors and that can make undercover agents vulnerable to upstream defection, either real or imagined. Section IV differentiates the risks of betrayal facing undercover agents from those facing informants. Section V examines the differences between real and perceived "betrayals" and the analytical and evidentiary difficulties of distinguishing between them. Finally, Section VI explores some of the regulatory devices by which French and German law enforcement agencies seek to reduce the differences in outlook between undercover agents and other members of the law enforcement team, in order to mitigate the conflicts that can produce both real and perceived forms of defection within the chain of command.

II. What Kinds of "Betrayal" Do Undercover Agents Experience?

1. Jealousies, Credit Claiming, and Cornering the Market on Rewards

Many upstream defections reflect supervisors' jealousies—and sometimes their misunderstandings—of the task environments in which undercover agents operate. Undercover agents don't have to share the grunt work of ordinary officers, don't have to come in early in the morning, and don't have to abide by the constraints of standardized working shifts. Many regular officers resent the undercover agents' special "privileges," or what they view as a flashy lifestyle and freedom from the demands of a regular schedule and caseload. Accordingly, supervisors may become alienated from undercover agents even when undercover agents remain loyal both to the organization and to the mission.

Joseph Pistone's memoirs (with Charles Brandt) described his own experience with a supervisor who had little regard for undercover work. "The SAC (Special Agent in Charge) of the southern field office to which I belonged did not like undercover operations or undercover agents. He believed all undercover agents were slackers because they didn't come in to the office; they didn't sign in and sign out."[3]

Pistone's relationship with his supervisor grew tenser during the years Pistone spent assisting prosecutors in preparing for trial in the cases built on his undercover work. Once Pistone became a witness, "the S.O.B. SAC [Special Agent in Charge] vigorously campaigned to assert his dominion and control over me—even though I was actually working for various prosecutors and field offices around the country at the same time."[4] While he was preparing for trial in a Mafia case, for example, the supervisor assigned him to a wiretap, requiring him "to sit in a van with headphones on listening in on a wiretap regarding an investigation into alleged corruption at a large Texas prison."[5] Angry that "the FBI was already too inflexible to accommodate the job I did... and [that] it would only get worse for me... when I got a book deal," Pistone resigned, though he agreed to continue to testify for no pay, which he did from 1986 until 1992, when he returned to the Bureau.[6]

Another undercover agent recalled how a supervisor's suspicion of undercover work jeopardized a case. "The supervisor was jealous of undercover agents," the former FBI agent recalled. "He thinks we're partying and driving corvettes on Bureau time.... The supervisor said 'undercover work isn't real agent work. It doesn't count.'"[7] While the agent was working undercover on a complex long-term arms and drug smuggling investigation, the supervisor assigned him to time-consuming office tasks, such as going through evidence that had been taken from raids and was no longer needed for a case, in

[3] Joseph D. Pistone & Charles Brandt, *Donnie Brasco: Unfinished Business* 153 (2008).

[4] *Id.* at 154. [5] *Id.* at 157. [6] *Id.* at 159.

[7] Author's interview in New Jersey with former FBI agent.

order to return it to its original owners. "He wanted me to inventory it and dispose of it while I was undercover."[8] On the pretext that the agent's undercover work was interfering with his availability for routine assignments of this sort, the supervisor reassigned him from the case in the middle of negotiations for controlled deliveries of contraband, casting the continued viability of the operation into doubt. In order to assist his replacement in acquiring the trust of the targets, the undercover agent had to continue having meetings with his former targets without knowledge of the supervisor; simply disappearing would have created suspicion and endangered the other undercover agent.

Jealousies about the special "privileges" of undercover agents reinforced tensions with investigators as well as supervisors. "The agents on the case were resentful that I was getting a paid a per diem while getting my salary," an undercover agent reported. "I got a thousand dollars cash per diem once a month, and the case agent always made a comment about it. He resented it and pretended I was making a nice cushy living on it. But everything I owned was in another town, I couldn't talk to my friends, and I was using someone else's sheets and towels."[9]

At the same time, many of the sources of stress for undercover agents are invisible to all but those closest to them. Strains on agents included the unpredictable demands on their time, the danger, the difficulty of maintaining family relationships, and, in the United States, the unglamorous time spent writing reports, transmitting and transcribing recordings, preparing to testify, and subjecting themselves to cross-examination. As former undercover agents Joe Pistone and Terry Hake reported in their memoirs,[10] their role as trial witnesses lasted for years after the undercover operations had ended and continued after they left the Bureau. Pistone had to return to the FBI years later, as an instructor at Quantico, in order to qualify for the pension that he had forfeited when he resigned. Much like special forces units within the military, long-term undercover agents can find that their atypical assignments stall their advancement within the agency, in comparison with peers who pursue a more conventional career path.

Undercover agents frequently complained that jealous supervisors took credit for their work. When an international narcotics and arms smuggling operation resulted in eighty-seven arrests, a former agent reported, the same supervisors who "for a long time dragged their feet before allowing them to pursue the case" later won the FBI's Director award for their work on the case. "When the FBI held its Asian Organized Crime Conference in Hawaii to discuss the... case not long after it was over," neither of the undercover agents was invited to attend. Instead, "the two supervisors who had fought so hard from the beginning to keep [the agents] from pursuing the case at all went instead and took all the credit while sunning themselves on the beaches of Hawaii."[11] Fifteen participants in the investigation won awards from the FBI hierarchy, which included almost everyone involved in the investigation—except for the two undercover agents.[12]

[8] *Id.* [9] Author's interview in Chicago with FBI agent.

[10] Pistone & Brandt, *supra* note 3, at 402; Terry Hake, *Operation Greylord: The True Story of an Untrained Undercover Agent and America's Biggest Corruption Bust* 275 (2015).

[11] Book proposal of former FBI undercover agent.

[12] Author's interview in New Jersey of former FBI agent undercover agent.

Credit claiming may be an interpersonal betrayal but does not necessarily violate the operational or agency mission. However, premature reassignments out of jealousy or as part of an effort to steal credit for the success of the operation can certainly jeopardize the operational goals. These types of upstream defection violate the informal norms of reciprocity that make ground-level actors willing to take risks for the organization.

Supervisors could often "cash in" on the institutional rewards for successful operations well before undercover agents could stake their own claims. An undercover agent who worked on a long-term deep cover operation recalled that, because he had to testify, his involvement in the investigation far outlasted that of the case agent, supervisor, and other investigators. As a result, "the others all got to go where they wanted, such as Bern, Switzerland. I was a good soldier, but when it came time for me to ask [not to be transferred from his home city] everyone was gone and could no longer help me. The guy who had fixed that [for the others] had retired."[13] None of the supervisors or case agents had given any thought to what the undercover agent would do after his own assignment ended, and after they had obtained their preferred postings, as a reward for their success with the operation, their replacements in the command hierarchy felt no obligation to respect the undercover agent's own preferences or to reward him for an assignment in which they had not themselves been involved. Feeling "abandoned" by the command hierarchy, the undercover agent resigned.

2. Missed Opportunities

Other forms of upstream defection—real or perceived—stem from missed investigative opportunities. A former undercover agent complained that the FBI pulled him out of his long-term deep cover role inside a New York Mafia family just as he was on the verge of being "made" (i.e., inducted) by the Cosa Nostra. He was bitter about what he viewed as the premature end of the undercover investigation, believing that his position as a mole would have allowed him to learn of new alliances his bosses were forging with crime families in other cities and would have enabled him to vouch for other undercover agents who could have infiltrated offshoots of the criminal organization all over the United States.[14] His supervisors, however, worried about the diminishing marginal returns on continuing an already successful investigation.

Undercover agents also learn facts that may be inconvenient to their supervisors. In his memoirs, Jack Garcia reports that he wanted to continue his undercover work to fill in gaps and correct errors in the chart that the FBI had already compiled. In his view, this information was not welcome to his supervisors, who were invested in the accuracy of the chart and did not want to see it questioned.[15]

[13] Author's interview in Chicago of former FBI undercover agent.

[14] Author's interview in New York of former NYPD undercover agent.

[15] Joaquin "Jack" Garcia & Michael Levin, *Making Jack Falcone: An Undercover FBI Agent Takes Down a Mafia Family* 314 (2009).

Transnational cooperation on undercover operation sometimes compounded undercover agents' frustration with missed opportunities. An American undercover agent investigating the theft of more than a dozen works of art from a famous American art museum felt betrayed by his French law enforcement partners who, as he saw it, privileged the undercover buy-bust purchase of a single prestigious work of art stolen from a French private residence over a longer-running undercover operation that might have allowed the American investigators to trace and recover at least some of the masterpieces stolen from the American museum.[16]

3. Knowing Too Much—The Outsider's Perspective

Undercover work may put undercover agents on a collision course with their own department or other law enforcement agencies because such assignments provide undercover agents with an unusual *outside* perspective on the operations of their own law enforcement agency. Undercover work can reveal to operatives the way their agency is experienced by suspects or other members of the public.

For example, Italian undercover agents who investigated the extortion of construction crews by organized crime reported being put in the unwelcome position of exposing official corruption when they were shaken down for "street tax" payments by local mayors.[17] And American undercover agents frequently reported in interviews that their undercover role inadvertently made them privy to many forms of official misconduct by other police officers, even when their operation was aimed at other targets and other violations.[18]

Such discoveries could put supervisors in the unwelcome position of either deflecting their investigative priorities in directions that they had few institutional incentives to pursue or turning a blind eye to the abuse of power and position by official authorities, in order to protect an ongoing undercover operation of other offenses. Either choice could put them at odds with undercover agents and could be perceived as a form of upstream defection.

4. Knowing Too Much—The Insider's Perspective

Undercover work also provides agents with an insider's view of how their own command hierarchies really operate and what supervisors and team members care about as institutional actors. And what undercover agents find out about their own organization is sometimes more disconcerting to them than what they find out about their targets. Law enforcement agencies that investigate criminal activities such as prostitution, narcotics

[16] Author's interview in Philadelphia of former FBI undercover agent. This constituted a form of upstream defection to the extent that the American undercover agent was under the supervision of French authorities during the key phase of the operation, which took place in France.

[17] Author's interview in Rome of Italian undercover agent of the Direzione Nazionale Antimafia.

[18] Author's interviews in the United States with former undercover agents who infiltrated outlaw motorcycle gangs on the East and West Coasts of the United States.

trafficking, or other manifestations of organized crime may work out informal accommodations with the command hierarchies of criminal organizations, on the view that such deeply entrenched organizations can at best be managed and kept in check rather than rooted out completely.

In his memoirs, Michael Levine fumes at the tacit arrangements by which the DEA was able to obtain cooperation from corrupt Bolivian government officials who permitted the Americans to make limited seizures of cocaine in exchange for leaving the bulk of the cartel's operations undisturbed. These unacknowledged accommodations enabled the DEA to portray ongoing enforcement operations as a success. In Levine's view, the DEA had staked its continued survival as an agency and its access to future financing on staged seizures of token amounts of cocaine. Levine also believed that this symbiotic relationship with drug trafficking cartels allowed the CIA to preserve its relationships with Bolivian, Panamanian, and Mexican authorities who were assisting the CIA in training the Nicaraguan Contras to fight the Sandinistas.

The more Levine succeeded in climbing up the Bolivian supply chain and identifying Bolivian leaders and their Panamanian and Mexican facilitators, the more his undercover operation threatened to disturb these mutually beneficial arrangements, and the more resistance he encountered from his supervisors, who could neither acknowledge their grounds for opposing the progress of Levine's undercover operation nor allow it to succeed. Upstream defection—or the appearance of such defection to the undercover operatives—was thus the result of an overly successful undercover operation that threatened to expose or undermine the symbiotic relationship between enforcers and their targets.

Likewise, FBI agents who exposed the offer by a high-level foreign general to sell them a nuclear submarine reported finding themselves divested of the case by supervisors ceding jurisdiction to the CIA, which preferred to recruit the target as an asset instead of prosecuting him for an offense that could complicate the U.S. government's relationship with the target's government.[19]

Inside knowledge of organizational decision-making can expose undercover agents to retaliation when it leads them to become whistle-blowers. For example, Michael Levine's inside access to the investigation and behind-the-scenes wrangling of DEA and Customs and Border Protection allowed him to function as a whistle-blower even while working within the system, by disguising his exposé as compliance with the official mandate to report all allegations of DEA corruption. "I had to find a way of putting everything that had happened down on paper, on some kind of official report, and do it in such a way that the suits would not realize I was forcing them to investigate and *expose* themselves."[20] The report took the form of a memo reporting the informant's allegations of DEA corruption, though Levine himself did not believe the claims were substantiated. "I was doing an undercover job on the suits," he claimed,[21] knowing that the Office of Professional Responsibility would have no choice but to follow up on his claims. This

[19] Author's interview in New Jersey of former FBI undercover agent.

[20] Levine, *supra* note 1, at 227.

[21] *Id.* at 228.

would give him the opportunity he sought to describe the ways in which his supervisors had sabotaged the investigation.

Retaliation for whistle-blowing aside, inside knowledge of illegal tactics makes undercover agents vulnerable to efforts by supervisors to co-opt them into participating in illegal or ill-advised operations. Special Agent John Dodson's account of Operation Fast and Furious discloses efforts by his supervisors to co-opt him into participating in the investigative practices that he attempted to challenge.[22] In conducting the operation, ATF agents investigating straw purchases of firearms for Mexican cartels instructed hesitant gun dealers to go through with weapons sales to suspected straw purchasers, without intervening afterward to stop the straw purchasers from trafficking the weapons to Mexico. After Dodson challenged the investigators' decision not to intervene with arrests and seizures, his supervisors had him pose as a straw purchaser and then relinquish the weapons to a suspected trafficker. To avoid becoming complicit in providing the guns to the Mexican drug cartels, Dodson put in place a surveillance team that was supposed to arrest the target as soon as Dodson handed off the weapons he had purchased for him. After handing off the weapons, however, Dodson found that his surveillance team had been reassigned before they could arrest the buyer. This had the effect of involving Dodson in the same gun-walking practices that he was trying to stop.

But undercover agents are not only well positioned to learn of operational decisions that may be embarrassing to policymakers: their exposed role in the investigation, and the sometimes dramatic price that they and others may pay when decision-makers back off an investigation for political reasons, can exacerbate their sense of betrayal. Working undercover years before Operation Trifecta, Levine claims in his memoirs, he paid nine million dollars to a high-level Bolivian drug lord, only to see the defendant "almost immediately released from custody by the Miami U.S. Attorney's office, without the case being presented to the grand jury."[23] Once back in Bolivia, the defendant (or his associates) put a contract out for the undercover agent's murder. When Levine attempted to press for further investigation, he claims, "evidence began to 'mysteriously' disappear and pressure was exerted against me to "back off."[24]

After their return to Bolivia, Levine claimed, the defendant and his associates led a coup, torturing and killing the anticorruption faction of the police that had facilitated Levine's sting operation, with the result that "the Bolivian government [came] under the complete control of the [defendants'] organization," turning Bolivia into "the principal supplier of cocaine base to the then fledgling Colombian cartels, thereby making themselves the main suppliers of cocaine to the United States. And it could never have been done without the tacit help of DEA and the active, covert help of the CIA."[25]

At the same time, their training makes undercover agents adept at documenting real or perceived instances of upstream defection. Like other undercover agents, Levine came to compare the risks of betrayal he faced investigating targets with the betrayals he faced from supervisors, deciding that "*[T]his time* I was going to treat them as if they

[22] John Dodson, *The Unarmed Truth: My Fight to Blow the Whistle and Expose Fast and Furious* (2013).
[23] Levine, *supra* note 1, at 103. [24] *Id.* [25] *Id.* at 104.

were just as much an enemy as any drug dealer."[26] Precisely because they were drawn to comparisons between their target environment and their home bureaucracy, undercover agents could easily turn against their own supervisors the tactics that they had honed for use against drug dealers. "My years with DEA had made me the perfect undercover weapon. I knew how to put on a flawless acting performance and at the same time gather and document information, evidence, and statements with the efficiency of a human vacuum.... I found myself turning those talents against the people who were supposed to be my partners and protectors—and doing it with a vengeance."[27]

III. What Features of Undercover Operations Contribute to the Risk of Upstream Defection?

1. Secrecy and the Scapegoating Temptation

Secrecy is one risk factor for upstream betrayal. Few people other than an undercover agent's supervisor will be likely to know much about what the agent did to deserve or forfeit recognition. This makes credit claiming easier. "Stealing valor," as such abuses are known in the military, is more likely when supervisors can monopolize information about who did what in an investigation, benefiting from a bureaucratic bottleneck that isolates undercover agents from other institutional actors. Organizations may have difficulties managing low-visibility employees with a great deal of discretion when these are highly dependent on a limited number of intermediaries. Supervisors who function as go-betweens can easily derive short-term return for themselves by appropriating credit and rewards for the less visible field agents' performance.

Isolation puts undercover agents at the mercy of those who run such operation—whether supervisors or investigators—with little recourse when institutional relationships go awry. A female undercover agent reported hearing unfounded rumors about her romantic life while she was undercover and having no way of challenging the rumors, which falsely linked her to the case agent. "It was hard that my contact agent [handler] had heard these rumors too," she recalled, and the gossip undermined the trust between them. "I couldn't really say much about how I was doing to the contact agent, because he was close to the case agents."[28] The rumors also damaged her credibility with the informant, who became increasingly difficult to control.

Creating the impression that an undercover agent botched an investigation can sometimes be convenient for investigators and supervisors as a way of concealing embarrassing missteps or bureaucratic infighting on their part, either amongst themselves or with other agencies or prosecutors. A former undercover ATF agent reported that, in the

[26] *Id.* at 106. [27] *Id.* at 125. [28] *Id.*

aftermath of his undercover infiltration of a motorcycle gang, investigators and prosecutors had a falling out over the ATF's failure to disclose their follow-up investigation of suspects from the primary investigation. Prosecutors faced the wrath of the judge when it came out that information about the defendant had not been disclosed before trial, and the prosecutors and ATF agents blamed each other. According to the undercover agent:

> The Department of Justice did a review [and concluded that the prosecutors] cannot take this case into the courtroom now that they've called each other liars. So charges were dismissed and plea deals were cut. Defense attorneys started speculating that the undercover agents were corrupt. ATF and DOJ never corrected, that theory of the defense. This empowered the defendants to threaten me, and the ATF didn't investigate the threats. My house burned down and the ATF then tried to frame me as a suspect. Their theory was that I was so mad at the ATF that I did [it] to embarrass the ATF or to create a publicity stunt for my book. Their own investigators didn't back up this theory.[29]

An independent inquiry of the Inspector General concluded that the ATF had failed to provide the agent and his family with the resources to conceal their identity, had "needlessly and inappropriately" endangered the agent and his family, and had failed to follow up on reports from informants that the motorcycle gang had put a contract out on the undercover agent's life.[30] The agent later brought suit against the ATF in the Court of Claims, alleging that "Supervisors at ATF have subjected and are subjecting [him] to unheard-of malicious reprisals including... refusal to investigate the arson of his home and naming [him] as a suspect."[31]

2. A Significant Gulf between Law on the Books and Law in Practice

Undercover agents are also vulnerable to betrayal because they operate within the gulf between formally permitted "simulation" of crime and informally tolerated participation in criminal activity, which means that supervisors who know the tactics that agents actually use can always threaten to expose undercover agents to criminal liability simply by enforcing the law on the books. Undercover agents run the risk of criminal prosecution if revelations about their tactics embarrass their agencies.

This is the risk that former German undercover agent Koriath[32] faced when he published his so-called confessions about the "crimes" he committed undercover, in

[29] Author's West Coast interview with former ATF agent.

[30] OIG Report on Allegations by Bureau of Alcohol, Tobacco, Firearms and Explosives Special Agent, September 22, 2008.

[31] *Hells Angels Infiltrator Says U.S. Failed to Protect Him from Threats*, *Courthouse News*, Mar. 3, 2009, *at* http://www.courthousenews.com/hells-angels-infiltrator-says-u-s-failed-to-protect-him-from-threats/; Dennis Wagner, *Agent: ATF Tried to Link Him to Arson*, Arizona Republic, Jan. 9, 2009, *at* http://archive.azcentral.com/arizonarepublic/local/articles/2009/01/09/20090109atf0109.html.

[32] Gerold Koriath, *Straftaten bei verdeckten Ermittlungen: Ein Geständnis*, Kriminalistik 1992, 370.

an effort to expose the hypocrisy of the public debate in Germany about whether undercover agents should be permitted to engage in criminal activity as part of their undercover role. Institutional conflicts can arise simply from the shared awareness of all players that both undercover agents and supervisors can expose the hypocrisies of all members of the undercover team.

3. Different Incentive Structures

Performance measures may also create very different incentive structures for undercover agents, investigators, and supervisors, sowing the seeds of conflict over personnel decisions. During Joseph Pistone's undercover assignment, he reported, "I wasn't producing any stats for [his supervisor.] I counted as an agent, but I was not producing any arrests or convictions.... In fact, I was watering down and weakening the SAC's [supervisor's] statistics when the inspectors came by to evaluate his office."[33] When his long-term undercover work finally yielded arrests, none of them were credited to his own field office, since the targeted Mafia family had no ties to the city in which the field office was located. "Meanwhile, the Bureau had made no allowance for this supervisor because a long-term undercover operation like this had never been done before.... [T]here was no provision for me to be listed at Headquarters—not even on paper—because I wasn't a supervisor. So I had to stay on that field office's rolls."[34]

As a result of conflicting performance measures, undercover agents were often frustrated with the short time-horizons and limited investigative aims of supervisors who were more interested in producing an arrest and a prosecutable case of some sort rather than pursuing the leads generated by undercover operations. An undercover agent who worked for an organized crime task force recalled working for a supervisor who wanted to end an investigation that had produced evidence that jockeys were fixing races, drugging their horses, and bribing investigators to switch the horses' urine samples. "The chief said it was time to end the case and said, 'now find out who's supplying our informant with drugs and charge that guy.' Instead of taking the case further, he wanted to shut down the one racetrack we already had evidence on, which was already making no money. We could have learned about similar things that were going on in racecourses all around the country."[35]

Undercover agents need not worry only about supervisors. They may be subject to sabotage by informant handlers who viewed undercover agents as competitors who might interfere with the way they run an informant. A former undercover agent recalled that:

> [O]ur informant had a handler who was jealous because the source was getting along better with the undercover agents in the case than with him [the handler.] The handler told the Special Agent in Charge that the undercover agents are planning to go into the counterfeit cigarette business with the source. And as a result of this allegation,

[33] Pistone & Brandt, *supra* note 3, at 154. [34] *Id.*

[35] Author's interview in New York of former NYPD undercover detective.

> none of us [undercover agents] could testify at the trial of the two defendants who went to trial. The source was subpoenaed to testify in camera before the judge and was asked about the allegation, and he denied being in the counterfeit cigarette business and vouched for the undercover agents.[36]

As a result, the handler himself was subpoenaed to testify about the allegations he had made about the undercover agents, and the agent quit in order to avoid having to testify. "The defendant pled out to a really good deal, and no-one pressed the matter with [the handler] who quit two years short of retirement."[37]

4. Divergent Levels of Specialization and Expertise

Supervisors of investigative units may have little experience with undercover operations, putting them on a collision course with the needs of undercover agents. The problem, as a former agent saw it, was that "undercover work can be interfered with by local supervisors who want to transfer the agent out. We should be able to run without interference by supervisors [who were not themselves involved with the undercover operation.] You can have a supervisor directing an undercover agent when the supervisor has no experience [with] organized crime or undercover work, and the supervisor treats the undercover agents as fungible, all purpose" resources. In his view, "the FBI should make [the agents] directly answerable to [headquarters] and let [headquarters] run the undercover personnel without interference."[38]

Being supervised by agents who know little about undercover operations is one risk factor for undercover agents; being highly specialized oneself is another. Long-term deployments require investment in a knowledge base that is not easily transferred to other assignments. Undercover agents may build a capital or skills and useful connections, but their social capital may be in the criminal world rather than in their own organization. The undercover agent is objectively networked in two worlds, but most of his social capital is in the target environment. The foothold he has gained in the criminal world may be of limited value to him once the investigation closes. And his continuing value to the organization may likewise not be evident to supervisors, once the investigation is over and the social capital he holds in the criminal world has expired. Undercover agents know this, which is why they sometimes want to stay undercover as long as possible and to develop their social sway in the targeted organization, even at the expense of their organizational capital within their law enforcement agency, whose supervisors may perceive only diminishing marginal returns from prolonging the operation. Some law enforcement agencies might prefer investing in fungible, multi-use employees, who can work in a variety of law enforcement domains, while the specialized skills of undercover agents create what may not readily be perceived as long-term organizational capital, or may create one that is difficult to situate within the organization or use effectively.

36 Author's Interview of former FBI agent in New Jersey. 37 *Id.* 38 *Id.*

5. Undercover Agents as Bellwethers of Internal Corruption

Undercover agents are also made vulnerable to upstream defection by the likelihood that they would be the first to suffer the consequences of corruption in their own ranks. Worse, their supervisors might not find it convenient either to expose corruption or to take account of it in the design of operations. A former Special Agent for what was then the U.S. Customs Service, who sometimes worked undercover himself and who supervised many undercover operations, reported in his memoirs that the security of undercover operations was being compromised by the organization's merger with the U.S. Border Patrol, which he considered "[o]ne of the most corrupt law-enforcement agencies in existence," but which had acquired the authority, as a result of the merger, "to tell us what we could and could not do in the enforcement of laws."[39] Efforts to warn supervisors were futile:

> We told the new SAC that we had documented cases where we had supplied our information to the BP while trying to work alongside them, and that during the course of doing so the cases and investigations were compromised. We even told him that we had a stable of informants in Mexico telling us that certain corrupt BP agents were blowing our enforcement operations and investigations into the drug lords... None of this convinced the SAC, his deputy SACs, or the other REMFs in D.C. headquarters that it would be impossible for us to work securely and safely with the BP.... how would we ever be able to conduct an international criminal conspiracy investigation when the drug lords had BP agents on the payroll—the same BP guys who could get our operational plans and informant information?[40]

The supervisors did not disbelieve the agents' claims, according to the former Customs agent, but "these guys were telling us that a certain amount of corruption in the Border Patrol was acceptable, and that I would ignore it and order my ICE agents to work with the BP agents even if they knew they were corrupt.... [We] stood our ground. We knew at the time what it would cost us in the end: our jobs."[41] As a result of his open criticism of these directives, the agent claimed, he was eventually transferred and forced to retire.

6. Malleability of Operational Goals and Performance Indicators

Both disagreements about where to take the investigation and upstream (or downstream) defection are further exacerbated by the malleability of undercover investigations—what Manning describes as the almost unlimited potential for extending narcotics investigations, for example, by recruiting defendants as cooperators and using them

[39] Lee Morgan, II, *The Reaper's Line: Life and Death on the Mexican Border* 515 (2006).
[40] *Id.* [41] *Id.* at 516.

against new targets, who can themselves be turned.[42] Undercover operations can easily be expanded or contracted. They can also be instrumentalized for different institutional or investigative purposes, or at least re-oriented in mid-operation. Undercover investigations make it relatively easy for means to be reconfigured into ends, as when investigators decide to make an immediate arrest after what was initially meant to be a test buy of contraband.

The convenient ambiguity of operational goals also allows investigators to turn ends into means, as when investigators agree to dismiss charges against a defendant they have just arrested during a sting operation, after the defendant agrees to cooperate against others. What started as an investigation of syndicates that import bulk quantities of untaxed cigarettes eventually turned into an investigation of counterfeit supernotes that were peddled by the same targets, only to yield to an investigation of arms smuggling when the provider of supernotes boasted of his access to sophisticated siege artillery and even a nuclear submarine.[43]

Changes in direction can bring additional intelligence and law enforcement agencies into ongoing investigations, increasing the risk that one of the newcomers may hijack the investigation for its own institutional ends, as when the CIA eventually ended the undercover arms investigation that had started with untaxed cigarettes by recruiting the high-level military target as an asset. The legitimacy of that reconfiguration will depend on whether these reflect or deflect from policy choices made by the leadership. Defections that do occur will be unlikely to draw censure when the indicia of success themselves are malleable, as Levine bitterly noted in decrying DEA efforts to portray the buy-bust of low-level targets and the premature end of a promising undercover investigation as a success in the war against drugs.

7. Autonomy and Self-Sacrifice as Risk Factors

The relative autonomy undercover agents enjoy in their assignments and the significant degree of self-sacrifice required are powerful centrifugal forces in the relationship between undercover agents and their command hierarchy.

In particular, the sense of disillusionment voiced by many former deep cover agents resonates with the insight of Dorothy Leonard-Barton, a scholar of management strategy in the private sector, that corporate employees who are entrusted with wide discretion and are expected to be entrepreneurial on behalf of their organization often experience a betrayal by their organization. Leonard-Barton argued that individuals who are entrusted with a significant degree of autonomy in acting on behalf of their organization frequently "construe their empowerment as a psychological contract with the corporation, and yet the boundaries of their responsibility and freedom are not always clear. Because they undertake heroic tasks for the corporation, they expect rewards, recognition, and

[42] Peter Manning, *The Narc's Game* 134–36 (2004).
[43] Author's interview in New York of former FBI agent.

freedom to act."[44] If employees "exceed the boundaries of personal freedom that the corporation can tolerate, or their project is technically successful but fails in other ways, or their ideas are rejected, or their self-sacrifice results in too little recognition, they experience the contract as abrogated and often leave the company—sometimes with a deep sense of betrayal."[45]

Undercover agents who experience a sense of personal risk and great personal investment in their assignments may also expect a degree of freedom from interference in their decisions. To the extent the organization imposes restrictions that strain these expectations, agents may experience a failure of reciprocity. Leonard-Barton notes that "empowerment as a value and practice greatly aids in projects, until it conflicts with the greater corporate good. Because development requires enormous initiative and yet great discipline in fulfilling corporate missions, the management challenge is to channel empowered individual energy towards corporate aims—without destroying creativity or losing good people."

Autonomy made undercover agents unpredictable for their organizations and hence not fully trusted. For example, undercover agents whom the ATF viewed as "loose cannons" in interviews with the press found themselves facing what they viewed as retaliation for not presenting the "right" public face on behalf of the agency. Speaking of a fellow agent who had infiltrated the Mongols motorcycle club, another former undercover agent for the ATF stated, "the agency took away his guns, moved him away from his family, tried to drive him off the job. He just didn't fit the image" the ATF wanted to project.[46] It is an indication of the rift between long-term undercover agents and ATF management that, according to former and present agents, neither of the agency's two most experienced undercover agents has been invited to teach at the agency's undercover school, where, a former ATF agents report, "the cadre of volunteers has dwindled, as potential undercover agents are driven off."[47] Ironically, both agents have been hired to teach at the undercover schools of other federal agencies.

8. Competing Task Environments and the Institutionally Ambiguous Role of Undercover Agents

When two organizations with conflicting normative commitments compete for control over the agent's time, the home organization may question the loyalties of the undercover agent. The home organization may come to see undercover agents as liminal figures who belong to neither world completely because they pass freely between them; this may in turn reduce supervisors' loyalty to undercover agents and make supervisors more willing to take advantage of them by appropriating organizational recognition and rewards.

[44] Dorothy Leonard-Barton, *Core Capabilities and Core Rigidities: A Paradox in Managing New Product Development*, 13 Strategic Mgmt. J. 111, 119 (1992).

[45] *Id.*

[46] Author's West Coast interview with former ATF undercover agent.

[47] Author's West Coast interview of former ATF undercover agent.

This suggests that one risk factor for upstream defection may be the institutionally ambiguous position undercover agents inhabit as members of two competing task environments: that of their home agency and that of their targets. This means they may be simultaneously embedded in multiple conflicting forms of social coordination. Within law enforcement agencies, undercover agents are subject to the chain of command and the demands of obedience and accountability. At the same time, their dealings with targets may be governed by market norms, contractual obligations, norms of reciprocity, or parallel hierarchical expectations, if they have infiltrated a criminal organization as a recipient and giver of orders.

When expectations arising from these parallel forms of social coordination conflict, supervisors may be less attentive than undercover agents to the expectations of the agents' criminal associates. In interviews, an undercover agent complained that bureaucratic delays in approval for undercover buys delayed his meetings with counterfeiters and arms dealers and aroused the suspicions of his targets. In his memoirs, former undercover DEA agent Michael Levine reported that the command hierarchy had insisted on using a particular government-approved hotel for meetings with his Panamanian associates, despite his repeated warnings that the targets knew this to be the favored hotel of the DEA and that the choice of hotel would jeopardize the entire operation. In his second set of memoirs, Joseph Pistone noted dryly that his privileged position inside a Mafia crime family obligated him to participate in truck hijackings and then to conceal these activities from his supervisors, even though these actions were necessary to protect his cover.[48]

For undercover agents' supervisors, the agents' compliance with the norms of their target environments calls into question their continued compliance with the norms and expectations of their law enforcement agencies. Whether supervisors' actions were motivated by jealousy, distrust, or simply a failure to appreciate the consequences of bringing their agents into conflict with their target organizations' expectations, supervisory demands that undermined the viability of the undercover agent in his undercover role had the effect of reasserting the claims of the command hierarchy over the parallel conflicting expectations of the target environment—and undercover agents sometimes experienced this as a betrayal.

The parallel worlds undercover agents inhabit lead them to perceive similarities between the risks of betrayal they face in each. Indeed, one might compare the instabilities of the market for illegal commodities and of their distribution networks with the instabilities of investigative networks. They create similar opportunities and incentives for defection, similar concerns about losing control of one's customer base, similar fears of being cut out by suppliers, and similar incentives to preempt defections in situations in which higher- and lower-level actors can anticipate reciprocal risks of defection by each other.

Front-line officials' traditional distrust of rear echelon decision-makers compounds the complaints by those who inhabit two worlds that the organizational dynamics of the "good guys" are not much fairer to them than those of their target environment. Former

[48] Pistone & Brandt, *supra* note 3, at 34.

Border Patrol agent Lee Morgan, who worked both as a case agent in undercover operations and as an undercover agent, echoed complaints voiced by a number of undercover agents in comparing the risk of betrayal by their command hierarchy with the perils low-level drug dealers faced from their home organizations. "I'd have to say that border agents and mules have a good deal in common. They both work for REMFs who sit hundreds or even thousands of miles away and dictate policy without having any idea of what it's like to be in the real rodeo.... I've got more respect for these desert-humping ball-busting mules than I could ever have for the REMFs in D.C."[49]

Conflicts of interest between parallel systems of social coordination were multiplied when undercover agents were part of a task force or took part in transnational undercover operations. Command hierarchies can be expected to be more solicitous of field operatives who are part of their own agency—or *purely* part of their own agency—than those who are subject to conflicting demands from cooperating agencies.

IV. Upstream Defection and Informants

Understanding undercover agents' position in parallel systems of social coordination helps explain why the problem of upstream defection is not the same for informants and undercover agents. Law enforcement relationships with informants are often governed by contractual obligations rather than by norms of hierarchy or reciprocity (as distinct from mutual self-interest). Informants are not part of the law enforcement hierarchy, and their interactions with law enforcement are driven by self-interest. If law enforcement agents fail to pay them, or fail to honor promises of leniency, work permits, or the like, the defaulting "principal" violates market norms or breaches a contract (such as a plea agreement, as in the United States, or written promise of confidentiality, as in Germany, or informal understandings, as in most other places).

However, such norm violations are different from the upstream defections experienced by undercover agents. Informants and their police handlers are not embedded in the same bureaucratic hierarchy or the same system of shared professional values, nor do they share an investigative mission or guiding professional ethos. If a police officer sells out his informant, this is surely a betrayal, but he does not betray a subordinate member of his own profession or the mission that supposedly unites them, as the interest each serves may be very different, and as the betrayal itself may further the law enforcement mission (as when an officer reveals his informant's identity in order to call him as a witness). By contrast, upstream defection reported by undercover agents may violate both the hierarchical norms that govern law enforcement officers' relationships with each other and the shared mission of the agents.

[49] Morgan, *supra* note 39, at 283.

The distinction between obligations that law enforcement agencies owe to informants and those they owe to undercover agents helps explain why cooperating law enforcement agencies from different countries did not consider it satisfactory to treat foreign undercover agents as informants, as France and Italy used to do. France and Italy now afford foreign undercover agents and their domestic undercover agents the same legal status and protections, provided foreign undercover agents operate in-country with the French or Italian agency's knowledge and permission. Recognizing (foreign) undercover agents as law enforcement officers rather than as informants implicitly acknowledges institutional obligations toward foreign undercover agents as members of a coordinate system of authority with which a law enforcement agency maintains a continuing collaborative relationship. Both sides view these obligations as a more powerful bond than an ad hoc exchange such as a market transaction (such as payment for information) or a contractual arrangement with an individual in his private capacity (such as a plea agreement exchanging leniency for cooperation).

Yet undercover agents and informants can be jeopardized by the same concessions to political expediency. In his memoirs, Lee Morgan, a former special agent of the U.S. Customs Service, spoke scathingly of the so-called Brownsville agreement, which then-attorney general Janet Reno signed with the Mexican attorney general in 1988, and of the agreement's devastating impact on cross-border undercover operations. The agreement was an American concession to Mexico, in the wake of an unauthorized undercover operation on Mexican soil. Under the terms of the agreement, the U.S. attorney general obligated all law enforcement agencies under her command to provide Mexican authorities with advance notice of any cross-border enforcement activities, including undercover operations, involving narcotics trafficking, money laundering, and related offenses. The agreement obligated law enforcement agencies to reveal their informants' alphanumerical identity codes, along with the dates and locations of all operational activities in Mexico and "a synopsis of the informants' past and proposed future undercover dope buys from the specifically named traffickers."[50]

Until the agreement was signed, Morgan claimed, "[w]e had inside information on stash houses, how much drugs were being smuggled, the kind of drugs, the smuggling routes, the drivers' and mules' identities," and much more.[51] After the agreements, however, "the Mexicans wouldn't have to hunt our informants anymore. They were being served up on a silver platter." Morgan claimed this resulted in the murder of numerous Mexican informants and jeopardized all undercover agents and other personnel involved in cross-border investigations. Eventually, Morgan reported, many Customs officials simply stopped providing Mexican authorities with the disclosures required by the agreement. In his view, the agreement was a betrayal of all ground-level personnel involved in undercover operations, including investigators, undercover agents, and informants.[52]

[50] *Id.* at 427. [51] *Id.* at 428–29. [52] *Id.* at 425–34.

V. Upstream Defection: Real or Perceived?

Were these actions by the command hierarchy really forms of upstream defection? Determining whether this is really the best way to characterize the misalignment between agents and principals presents both analytical and evidentiary challenges.

In a hierarchical organization, upstream defection could be perceived either as the betrayal of the shared operational or agency mission, on the one hand, or of undercover agents themselves, on the other. In the latter case, perceived "relational betrayals" of undercover agents themselves could take such forms as reassignments, sanctions, or credit claiming; but what the undercover agent perceives as a "betrayal" of the supervisor's or handler's obligations to the undercover agent could, from the perspective of the supervisor, be an effort to improve operational oversight or allocate resources efficiently, just as a decision not to pursue an investigative opportunity could represent a cost-benefit decision, or a rational calculus about trade-offs between institutional goals, or a judgment about the damage that anticorruption efforts against foreign governments might do to institutional relationships and political alliances.

It is also possible that individual investigators and supervisors could act out of envy or animus, could usurp credit due to others, or could compromise the agency mission out of self-serving motives that could not be defended if they were known to higher-level decision-makers in the same agency. Upstream defection is thus a theoretical option, though the evidentiary problems of distinguishing between decisions that serve a competing vision of the agency's mission and those that might qualify as a form of upstream defection are as thorny as the challenge of distinguishing the defensible exercise of discretion by undercover agents from rogue activity.

In the case of agent Michael Levine, for example, his use of undercover tactics against his own supervisors might have seemed a form of downstream defection to his supervisors, whose own actions could also be viewed as a form of upstream betrayal both of the undercover agents in the case and of the agency mission.

A supervisor's decision to end an undercover assignment earlier than an undercover agent might like can thus be viewed in two ways. For undercover agents, much of their human capital is invested in case-specific relationships and intelligence. In interviews, undercover agents stressed the rewards of craft in learning how to win their targets' trust incrementally and in gathering information about an organization's membership and activities, which can be more time-consuming than their supervisors and the investigators would like. By comparison with undercover agents, investigators might prefer quick results and may focus more on the career rewards for making a quick arrest and moving on to the next case, viewing the benefits of prolonging the investigation to gather more intelligence as purely speculative, while more steeply discounting the marginal returns on expanding the investigation to encompass more targets and a greater range of offenses.

Case agents, in particular, must worry about the manpower costs of physical and electronic surveillance, which is often used as an auxiliary device to monitor targets' reactions to undercover agents or to conduct counter-surveillance of meeting sites. Case agents must also worry about the cost of backstopping the agents' cover or of fronting money for undercover purchases that do not yield an immediate arrest and therefore do not promise recovery of the buy money.

The investigative team may also focus on the risks to third parties of allowing targets to continue their illegal activity while postponing their arrest. They may also worry about the evidentiary and logistical challenges of continuing an investigation of mounting complexity. These will loom larger for case agents in charge of an investigation as a whole than for undercover agents, who see only their part of it, so that differences of opinion about how long to continue an investigation and how to design it may not involve defection by either side but may simply reflect the divergent vantage points from which each of them views the investigation.

At the same time, undercover agents, investigators, and supervisors may think differently about the opportunity costs of ending or continuing an undercover investigation. The memoirs of Jack Garcia, Joe Pistone, and Bob Wittman focused on the potential effect of the operation on the target environment and the potential for dismantling a given criminal network. Supervisors, both in their recounting and in interviews, had to translate that impact into institutional performance measures, such as volume of seizures, arrests, indictments, and potential embarrassing disclosures about the agency and its methods, not to mention the relevant time horizons for promotions or election cycles. They also compared the payoff from any given undercover operation with the potential payoffs of others that they could fund and staff with the same resources.

Undercover agents in turn may be concerned with their continued viability as undercover agents, which may be greatest in the investigative domain in which they have already invested so heavily, particularly since any subsequent testimony may "burn" them for future undercover assignments. Case agents and supervisors are diversified across a range of cases and may wish to avoid allowing any individual investigation (or undercover agent) to spin out of control, if undercover agents prove too difficult to control, generate too much work for support staff, and make too many demands on the organization's resources. Undercover operations may expose too much corruption or destabilize relationships with other agencies or government institutions. Investigators and supervisors may assign less value to gains that may not be visible or may not come to fruition during their tenure, so that undercover agents and supervisors may balance short-term and long-term objectives very differently from each other. Thus the decision to terminate an undercover operation can act as a salutary check on an undercover agent's desire to recoup the sunk costs of his investment in a case—just as such a decision can, in some circumstances, be a self-serving brake on an otherwise promising investigation.

The evidentiary difficulties of distinguishing real from apparent betrayals can thus be considerable. An undercover agent who had succeeded in infiltrating one of the five families of New York City objected to being pulled from his assignment just as he was on the verge of being "made" as a full member of the crime family. From the undercover agent's perspective, continuation of the investigation would have provided them with an unparalleled opportunity to complete the Bureau's diagram of the organization and to unsettle the organization by demonstrating its vulnerability to infiltration.[53]

From the perspective of supervisors, however, continuation of the undercover investigation would have been too dangerous for the undercover agent. The organization was on the verge of a power struggle with a rival organization, and leaving him in place would have exposed him to heightened risks of retaliation if the organization learned that he had been "made," since the organization might then have been willing to apply the retributive norms specific to full members of the organization, instead of the norms that ordinarily restrained the organization from assassinating federal agents.

In part, this difference of opinion reflected differences between what supervisors valued, in contrast to what undercover agents themselves considered important. The supervisors were focused on the opportunity cost of continuing the investigation, while the undercover agent himself focused only on the potential returns on his own investment in the undercover operation. The FBI as an organization also focused on the symbolic cost—that is, the unseemliness—of allowing one of its own to become a fully made member of the organization. As a former supervisor put it, "You can have your own wife pose as a prostitute, but why would you want to do that?"[54]

VI. How Legal Systems Deal with Misalignment among Undercover Agents, Investigators, and Supervisors: Examples from Germany and France

To some extent, American law enforcement agencies understand that undercover agents' perspectives may come to diverge from those of their home institutions. The FBI even seeks to warn agents about this and to recruit agents who are sufficiently committed to take that risk. An undercover agent for the FBI recalled that during training, former undercover agents would be brought in to warn them that "you should not do this [work undercover], because you will be hung out to dry. No-one will understand you. Your job will be brutal on your family."[55]

And if agents in some law enforcement agencies faced incomprehension or suspicion from supervisors who viewed undercover agents as prima donnas who shirked gruntwork or routine assignments, DEA undercover agents were less likely to encounter this kind of prejudice, since all DEA agents are required to work undercover during their

[53] Author's interview in New York of former NYPD undercover agent.

[54] Author's interview in New Jersey of former FBI supervisor of undercover operations.

[55] Author's interview in Chicago of FBI undercover agent.

probationary period. Undercover work in the DEA therefore tends to be treated less as a specialized calling than as a rite of passage for all DEA agents, who are in turn expected to acquire experience in a number of other investigative tactics as well, including wiretaps, money laundering operations, and the running and supervision of complex investigations. On the other hand, a former DEA supervisor recalled, "some minority DEA agents got pigeonholed as undercover agents and were always being sent to work undercover. We had some lawsuits against us for that. These agents couldn't work their own cases because they were always undercover in someone else's case."[56]

But conflict among undercover agents, investigators, and supervisors exists not only in the United States, but also in other countries that run long-term deep cover operations. A number of German supervisors discussed concerns about investigators who endanger undercover agents by pushing them to broach the topic of crime too quickly with their targets. In one of the Eastern states from the former German Democratic Republic, covert units encountered particular resistance in the popular press, and the police used primarily Western police as undercover agents. A supervisor from the undercover unit of one such state recalled that "it is possible for an undercover agent to become a handler for undercover agents later on, but so far all our undercover agents have left our service on bad terms, because there were problems with their undercover performance."[57] The happiest undercover agents interviewed turned out to be those who anticipated leaving their assignments to go into retirement, as they did not face the difficulties of reintegrating into a highly structured police routine.

Undercover agents are institutionally vulnerable in France as well. A French supervisor reported that "there are not enough undercover agents for them to have their own union, and undercover agents won't tell the police union what they do. It's not a specialty that can attract the interest of unions. For the union, an undercover agent is just another kind of specialist" within the police. The French supervisor viewed union protections as unnecessary "because undercover agents are already protected by not having to testify."[58]

However, both Germany and France have developed ways of dealing with the risks of defection—either downstream or upstream—that are such a recurrent theme in the memoirs and recollections of American undercover agents, and of long-term deep cover agents in particular. France, in contrast to Germany, simply avoids long-term deployments altogether; a supervisor indicated that he considered long-term assignments too risky both for the agency and the agent, and too stressful and damaging psychologically.[59]

France has also reduced the length of police officers' career deployments as undercover agents by shrinking the outer limits from a maximum of twenty years, to fifteen, and then to five, according to interviews with successive supervisors of undercover agents over a ten-year period.[60] A supervisor cautioned that "an undercover agent

[56] Author's interview in Chicago with a DEA supervisor of undercover operations, who was also a former undercover agent.

[57] Author's interview with a former undercover agent of a *Landeskriminalamt* in one of the new states from the former GDR.

[58] Author's interview in Paris of a French supervisor of undercover operations.

[59] *Id.* [60] *Id.*

wouldn't spend all his career doing undercover work. There are lifetime changes. One has kids, for example. They won't do undercover work forever and will do something different afterwards."[61]

Nonetheless, renewable four-month terms of deployment allow for medium-term deployments that can pose similar hazards on a smaller scale. And Germany, like the United States, employs specialized deep cover agents for long-term deployments; these agents may remain undercover, in various capacities, for up to ten or more years, though some states prefer to limit their careers to shorter terms.[62]

But both Germany and France have developed an institutional response to at least one source of conflict between undercover agents and other law enforcement personnel, namely, the difference in outlook between undercover agents and investigators, including case agents and other members of the law enforcement team. Both Germany and France run all undercover operations out of a separate covert policing unit that acts as a service provider to investigative units. In this way, agents' supervisors, as well as their handlers, can act as buffers between undercover agents and investigators. German supervisors and agents explained that this arrangement insulates undercover agents from the pressure for quick results, while French supervisors emphasized the avoidance of interagency rivalry through centralization.

The result of these reforms was an institutional barrier between investigators and undercover agents—one that ensured that supervisors and undercover agents could put the safety of undercover agents first, before the investigative goals of the case agents and their team. This also means that undercover agents won't be supervised by agents who have little experience with undercover operations, or who don't consider it "real" police work.

German and French covert units also seek to improve trust between undercover agents and supervisors by redeploying former undercover agents as supervisors and by professionalizing the career paths of the control officers who serve as the handlers of undercover agents, and as members of the undercover team, it is the job of these handlers to put the safety and well-being of the undercover agent ahead of the investigation's evidentiary goals or other bureaucratic concerns of the investigators' command hierarchy.[63] Some French and German handlers and supervisors, moreover, had themselves been undercover agents before assuming their new duties, giving them a better understanding of what undercover agents experience.[64]

The proliferation of specialized support staff, logistical personnel, surveillance agents, handlers, and supervisors makes it easier to create a supportive environment for former undercover agents within the police: one that makes use of their accumulated expertise and experience.

[61] *Id.*

[62] Author's interviews in fifteen of the sixteen German states with supervisors of undercover operations.

[63] Author's interviews in fifteen of the sixteen German states with supervisors of undercover operations.

[64] Author's interviews with supervisors of undercover operations in Germany and France.

Separating this ecology of actors from the investigative team reduces some of the institutional isolation that can put undercover agents at odds with and sometimes at the mercy of investigators and supervisors who have very different institutional incentives. Nonetheless, there can be no simple solutions for the moral hazards and differences in outlook that inhere in the pyramidal structure of the chain of command and in the tendency of undercover tactics to expose decision-making dynamics that a bureaucracy does not wish to acknowledge publicly. A first step toward addressing such concerns, however, is to recognize that the problem of defection is a two-directional phenomenon and that institutional design must protect agents from their bureaucracies no less than it protects bureaucracies from their agents.

References

John Dodson, *The Unarmed Truth: My Fight to Blow the Whistle and Expose Fast and Furious* (2013)

Joaquin "Jack" Garcia & Michael Levin, *Making Jack Falcone: An Undercover FBI Agent Takes Down a Mafia Family* (2009)

Terry Hake, *Operation Greylord: The True Story of an Untrained Undercover Agent and America's Biggest Corruption Bust* (2015)

Michael Levine, *Deep Cover: The Inside Story of How DEA Infighting and Incompetence and Subterfuge Lost Us the Biggest Battle of the Drug War* (1990)

Peter Manning, *The Narc's Game* (2004)

Gary T. Marx, *Undercover: Police Surveillance in America* (1988)

Undercover: Police Surveillance in Comparative Perspective (Gary T. Marx & Cyrille Fijnaut eds., 1995)

Lee Morgan, II, *The Reaper's Line: Life and Death on the Mexican Border* (2006)

Joseph D. Pistone & Charles Brandt, *Donnie Brasco: Unfinished Business* (2008)

Jacqueline E. Ross, *Undercover Policing and the Shifting Terms of Scholarly Debate: The United States and Europe in Counterpoint*, 4 Ann. Rev. L. & Soc. Sci. 17.1 (2008)

CHAPTER 15

INTERVIEWS OF SUSPECTS OF CRIME

Law and Practice in European Countries

MARIJKE MALSCH AND MEIKE M. DE BOER

I. Introduction

AFTER a crime has been committed, a suspect may be apprehended and brought to the police station. The police then start interrogating this person. Various types of interrogation techniques may be applied. Many suspects begin by denying the crime, and the aim of the police is then to obtain more information about the crime to make sure they have apprehended the right person. Other types of evidence are collected as well, and other persons are interviewed, such as witnesses and experts.

Depending on the other evidence that is available at the start of the interrogation, the police's belief regarding the suspect's guilt may vary from serious doubt to (almost) complete certainty. In many cases, however, the police are convinced that they have the right person and so may start from the assumption that their task is to get the suspect to admit to the crime.

Various countries around the world have witnessed cases where a wrong person was convicted for a crime, but was later acquitted. In most cases, it was DNA evidence that eventually pointed to the real perpetrator. In the United States, the so-called Innocence Project investigated a number of such cases and helped exonerate over two hundred prisoners.[1] England and Wales also witnessed miscarriages of justice in, among others, the Guildford Four, the Birmingham Six, and the Maguire Seven cases, and this led them to reform their interrogation practices. The Netherlands had at least five cases where a

[1] Innocence Project, *at* http://www.innocenceproject.org; *see also* Brandon L. Garrett, *Judging Innocence*, 108 Colum. L. Rev. 55, 142 (2008).

wrongful conviction took place,[2] of which the Schiedam Park Murder led to a serious evaluation and several recommendations for future criminal investigations.[3] In other European countries, wrongful convictions were reported as well.[4] This chapter attempts to examine the extent to which wrongful convictions have led to reform of interrogations in these countries.

Several factors associated with wrongful convictions have been identified. Among them are the factors of police misconduct and false confessions.[5] Attention was drawn to the suggestibility of persons with disabilities or mental retardation, and to adolescents, who in general are more susceptible to suggestion, and who may hold a naive belief that one's actual innocence will eventually prevail.[6] These individuals appear to be overrepresented in false confession cases. The reasons may be that they wish to please the investigator, they are inclined to say yes to all questions asked, and they easily waive their rights, including the right to legal assistance.[7]

Empirical findings of the past decade thus show that wrongful convictions do occur in practice and that there may be an association with the ways police officers interrogate suspects about their involvement in a crime, possibly leading to a false confession. In this chapter, we discuss the regulations of a number of European countries that govern the way police officers interrogate suspects of crime, and we examine how such interrogations are conducted in practice.

Later in this chapter, we use the word "interview" instead of "interrogation" when dealing with the situation where police officers question a suspect about his or her involvement in a crime. The reason for this is that the term "interview" has a more friendly and non-inquisitorial connotation than "interrogation." The term "interview" corresponds more closely to the way suspects are approached in most European countries when compared to the way this is done in the United States, where the term "interrogation" is more common.

We differentiate among models, interview methods, and interview techniques. We use the term "model" when referring to the procedure of the interview or interrogation from the start to the end. "Interview methods" are methods for questioning suspects and witnesses that find their basis in research and insights into how interviewing takes place in practice and the effects of various techniques. "Interview techniques" are defined as individual tricks or tactics that can be used and combined throughout the interview, of which the aim generally is to obtain a confession.[8]

[2] *See* Chrisje Brants, *Tunnel Vision, Belief Perseverance and Bias Confirmation: Only Human?*, in *Wrongful Convictions and Miscarriages of Justice* 161, 193 (C. Ronald Huff & Martin Killias eds., 2013).

[3] Frits Posthumus, *Evaluatieonderzoek in de Schiedammer Parkmoord* (2005); *see also* Peter J. van Koppen, *Blundering Justice: The Schiedam Park Murder*, in *Serial Murder and the Psychology of Violent Crimes* 207, 228 (Richard N. Kocsis ed., 2008).

[4] *See* C. Ronald Huff & Martin Killias, *Wrongful Convictions and Miscarriages of Justice* (2013).

[5] Michael K. Saks & Jonathan J. Koehler, *The Coming Paradigm Shift in Forensic Identification*, 309 Sci. 892, 895 (2005).

[6] Saul M. Kassin et al., *Police-Induced Confession: Risk Factors and Recommendations*, 34 L. & Hum. Behav. 3, 38 (2010).

[7] *Id.*

[8] Other authors may make different distinctions or use other definitions.

This chapter goes into the regulations and the interview practices of the following countries: Germany, France, Italy, Switzerland, Belgium, and the Netherlands. Information has been collected through literature analysis, desktop research, and interviews of experts via email and in person.[9] England and Wales are left out of the analysis, because another chapter in this book deals with these countries.[10]

This chapter does not cover all European countries, and not all countries are treated equally extensively in the chapter. The reason is the difficulty the authors encountered in obtaining information for some countries. Nevertheless, the information collected gives an interesting and comprehensive image of how police interview suspects of crime in the various countries, and how police interviews are regulated by law and other types of regulations.

The next section gives an overview of the many interview methods that are used by the police. It also discusses the risk that some techniques might generate a false confession. The subsequent section deals with the regulations and actual practice of suspect interviews in the different countries under review. In the concluding section, the various lines are drawn together. We attempt to give an overview as well as a characterization of the various types of regulations and interview techniques, and to draw conclusions.

We deal only summarily with rules and practices regarding the *Salduz* obligation to admit defense attorneys at the suspect interview and the extent to which practice complies with this obligation.[11] We also do not pay specific attention to other rights that suspects have when being interviewed or the rules and the practice regarding the recording of police interviews.

II. Interview Methods

In this section, we present various interview methods and techniques that may be used by the police when interviewing a suspect. We begin by explaining the differences between two main categories of questioning. The first category consists of methods that

[9] In total, eight police officers/experts were interviewed from four countries. Where we use information from the interviews, we will make this clear. The respondents were found through our personal and professional networks. More information about the respondents will be provided with their responses. The interviews were conducted by both authors and were mostly carried out face to face, at a location of the respondent's choice. The interviews were not recorded, and the respondents are kept anonymous. In the interviews in the Netherlands, a second research assistant was present to take digital notes. Naturally, the respondents are not representative of the populations they come from. Their answers, however, are helpful and illustrative of what was found in the literature and of how interviews are being conducted in practice. As appears from the interviews, practice may differ from the theory.

[10] David Dixon, *Interrogation Law and Practice in Common Law Jurisdictions*, in this volume.

[11] Salduz v. Turkey, App. No. 36391/02, Eur. Ct. H.R., Nov. 27, 2008.

use tricks to coerce the suspect into a confession. We will discuss this category by presenting the most famous example of the method: the Reid Technique, which was developed in the United States. The second category is based on building rapport and optimizing the communication between suspect and interviewer. The most famous example is the PEACE Model, which originates from England and Wales. After describing these two categories, we discuss individual techniques.

1. Obtaining a Confession: The Reid Technique

The purpose of the Reid Technique is to force a confession out of the suspect.[12] When police officers form the idea that a suspect is guilty, which in many cases is decided on the basis of his nonverbal behaviors,[13] they start the interrogation phase using *The Reid Nine Steps of Interrogation* (see Table 1).[14] Each step is seen as essential for the successful outcome of the interrogation—to get a confession. According to the Reid Technique, suspects are best interrogated in a space that isolates and discomforts the suspect.[15] Therefore, the interrogation room should be furnished as minimally as possible.

Table 1 The Reid Nine Steps of Interrogation[16]

Step	Description
1	Accusation; suspect is confronted with (false) evidence.
2	Use of minimization and maximization techniques.
3	Interrogator blocks denials, thereby avoiding lies.
4	Interrogator counters the arguments of the suspect's innocence.
5	Interrogator gets the suspect's attention by coming closer, touching him, and saying his name.
6	Suspect will feel defeated. Interrogator encourages him to talk about his motive and tries to make him feel remorse.
7	Interrogator wants an explanation for the crime.
8	Suspect elaborates his admission of guilt into a full confession.
9	A written statement is produced.

[12] Fred Inbau et al., *Criminal Interrogation and Confessions*, at viii (4th ed. 2001).

[13] Several studies have shown that professionals, just like laymen, are not able to detect lies from nonverbal behavior; assessors consistently perform around chance level. For an overview, see Aldert Vrij, *Why Professionals Fail to Catch Liars and How They Can Improve*, 9 Legal & Criminological Psychol. 159, 182 (2004). Assessors who have received the training on nonverbal lie detection that is part of the Reid Technique even appear to perform worse than assessors who were not trained. *See* Saul M. Kassin & Christina T. Fong, *"I'm Innocent!" Effects of Training on Judgments of Truth and Deception in the Interrogation Room*, 23 L. & Hum. Behav. 499, 516 (1999).

[14] Joseph P. Buckley, *The Reid Technique of Interviewing and Interrogation* 26 (2007).

[15] Inbau et al., *supra* note 12, at 46.

[16] *See* Buckley, *supra* note 14, at 185–310.

The most common characteristics of coercive interrogation methods such as the Reid Technique are: (1) isolation of the suspect, (2) confrontation and maximization, and (3) minimizing the crime.[17]

2. Finding the Truth: The PEACE Model

The PEACE Model was adopted by the police in England and Wales in 1992, after the discovery of a number of wrongful convictions.[18] There are three main ideas behind the PEACE Model. First, the interview with the suspect is about finding the truth and not primarily about obtaining a confession. Second, the police officer must not enter the interview with a preconception of guilt. Third, during the interview, the detective is expected to abide by certain decency standards.[19] The PEACE Model has been introduced in several countries besides England and Wales, including Australia, New Zealand, Iceland, Canada, and Norway.[20]

The PEACE Model consists of five phases, which are summarized in Table 2.

During the third phase, which is focused on finding the truth, detectives can use two different styles of interviewing: conversation management or cognitive interviewing, which will both be explained later in this chapter.[21] For interviews with witnesses, which also follow the PEACE Model, conversation management is advised when the witness is resistant, while cognitive interviewing is advised when the witness is cooperative.[22]

Table 2 Phases of the PEACE Model[23]

Phase	Label	Goal
P	Preparation & Planning	Increasing the quality of the interview.
E	Engage & Explain	Building rapport with the suspect.
A	Account	Finding out the truth, as accurate and complete as possible.
C	Closure	Verify everything is clear.
E	Evaluation	Improve interview performance; determine next steps in the investigation.

[17] Saul M. Kassin, *On the Psychology of False Confessions: Does Innocence Put Innocents at Risk?*, 60 Am. Psychologist 215, 228 (2005).

[18] Colin Clarke et al., *Interviewing Suspects of Crime: The Impact of PEACE Training, Supervision and the Presence of a Legal Advisor*, 8 J. Investigative Psychol. & Offender Profiling 149, 162 (2011).

[19] Tom Williamson, *Towards Greater Professionalism: Minimizing Miscarriages of Justice*, in *Investigative Interviewing: Rights, Research and Regulation* 147, 166 (Tom Williamson ed., 2006).

[20] Roel Boon et al., *Van verhoor naar forensisch interview. Naar een effectieve interviewstandaard voor de politie*, 78 Tijdschrift voor de Politie 20, 25 (2016).

[21] *Id.*

[22] Coral Dando et al., *The Cognitive Interview: Inexperienced Police Officers' Perceptions of Their Witness/Victim Interviewing Practices*, 13 Legal & Criminological Psychol. 59, 70 (2008).

[23] David W. Walsh & Rebecca Milne, *Keeping the PEACE? A Study of Investigative Interviewing Practices in the Public Sector*, 13 Legal & Criminological Psychol. 39, 57 (2008).

The Reid Technique and the PEACE Model have very different starting points and make use of different sub-methods and sub-techniques. The Reid Technique seems exclusively focused on obtaining a confession, and the use of tricks is allowed to induce a confession. The investigative interview, according to the PEACE Model, focuses on fact-finding and a decent treatment of the suspect, and it refrains from using tricks. It is not clear which of these methods actually leads to more admissions of guilt, and which parts of these confessions are correct or false, because systematic comparative research is not available.

3. Other Interview Techniques

The two models explained previously in this chapter each consist of several sub-methods. We will pay attention to them later. There may be a slight overlap between techniques and methods presented below.

a. *Techniques Associated with False Confessions*

Physical Violence includes beating, kicking, or even torture; prolonged incommunicado confinement; and deprivations of sleep or food.[24] These techniques have, in general, been forbidden by international treaties and conventions, such as the European Convention on Human Rights (ECHR) (Article 3) and the United Nations Convention against Torture, as well as in the national legislation in the countries that are parties to these treaties.

Psychological Coercion relies on manipulation, trickery, and deceit.[25] These techniques may be forbidden by international treaties, such as the ECHR (Article 3), and by national legislation in the countries that are parties to these conventions.[26]

Maximization involves a cluster of tactics designed to convey the interrogator's belief that the suspect is guilty and that all denials will fail. Such tactics include making an accusation, overriding objections, and citing evidence, real or manufactured.[27]

Minimization is the opposite of maximization and is primarily used with emotional suspects.[28] This method is designed to provide the suspect with moral justifications and excuses for having committed the crime. The interrogator offers sympathy and understanding. He or she normalizes and minimizes the crime by saying that everyone would have done the same in this situation. The tactic may suggest that a more lenient punishment can thus be expected, or even that the suspect is allowed to go home after he confesses.[29]

[24] Kassin et al., *supra* note 6, at 38. [25] *Id.* [26] *Id.*

[27] Fadia M. Narchet et al., *Modeling the Influence of Investigator Bias on the Elicitation of True and False Confessions*, 35 L. & Hum. Behav. 452, 465 (2011); Barry C. Feld, *Real Interrogation: What Actually Happens When Cops Question Kids*, 47 L. & Soc'y Rev. 1, 35 (2013).

[28] Buckley, *supra* note 14. [29] *Id.*

Presentation of False Evidence bears serious risks for inducing false statements.[30] U.S. police officers sometimes try to overcome a suspect's denials by presenting non-existing evidence of his or her guilt (e.g., a fingerprint, blood, or hair sample, or eyewitness identification).[31] This might lead to a false belief in one's own guilt, the belief that denials are useless, or to changes in the suspect's memory, which could all lead to a false confession.[32]

Imagination Techniques are techniques through which the police make the suspect imagine how the crime was committed. Research has shown that such techniques cause "imagination inflation": even when hypothetical events are imagined very briefly, these techniques can plant false memories.[33] In an evaluation of the police interrogations in the Dutch wrongful conviction in the Schiedam Park Murder, it was concluded that the police should not use imagination techniques in interrogations, since they may lead to false confessions.[34]

Hypnosis is a technique that can be used to help the suspect retrieve memories of the crime she supposedly committed. The validity of such memories is very low and the false memories they may induce pose a considerable risk for false confessions.[35]

Suggestive Questioning is a technique that is difficult to avoid. Suggestive questioning may be done consciously or, probably more often, unconsciously. As soon as the style of posing open questions is abandoned and more closed questions are asked, the risk of suggestive questioning emerges. Especially with vulnerable persons, such questioning styles may lead to more and easier admissions, which could include false convictions.[36]

The technique *Conversation Management*, which will be explained later, distinguishes between inappropriate assertion, inappropriate listening, and inappropriate content of the assertions.[37] Inappropriate assertion consists of behavior such as disruptive or excessive talk from the interviewer, and it shuts down the suspect. It includes counterproductive questioning, for example, asking leading, closed, or multiple questions.[38] Inappropriate listening consists of making assumptions about the answer before it has been given, being selective in the attention given to the answers, and lack of concentration. Finally, inappropriate content of the assertions shows insufficient knowledge of the case and ignorance of understanding the invalidity of the evidence.[39]

[30] Melissa B. Russano et al., *Investigating True and False Confessions Within a Novel Experimental Paradigm*, 16 Psychol. Sci. 481, 486 (2005).

[31] Kassin et al., *supra* note 6, at 38.

[32] Peter J. van Koppen, *De Schiedammer Parkmoord: Een Rechtspsychologische Constructie* 66 (2003).

[33] Maryanne Garry & Devon L. Polaschek, *Imagination and Memory*, 9 Current Directions Psychol. Sci. 6, 10 (2000).

[34] Posthumus, *supra* note 3, at 116.

[35] Saul M. Kassin & Katherine L. Kiechel, *The Social Psychology of False Confessions: Compliance, Internationalization, and Confabulation*, 7 Psychol. Sci. 125, 128 (1996).

[36] Lorana Bartels, *Police Interviews with Vulnerable Adult Suspects*, Criminal Research Council, Australian Government, Research in Practice, Report No. 21, at 2 (2011).

[37] Eric Shepherd, *Resistance in Interviews: The Contribution of Police Perceptions and Behaviour*, 18 Issues in Criminological & Legal Psychol. 5, 12 (1993).

[38] *Id.* at 8. [39] *Id.*

Bad Cop/Good Cop Technique (Mutt and Jeff Technique). This is a famous technique whereby one of the investigators plays an authoritative role, and the other is more empathetic toward the suspect.[40] The aim of this technique is to let the suspect, out of fear of the authoritative police officer, confess the crime to the friendly officer, who is—incorrectly—believed to act in the best interests of the suspect.[41]

Finally, we would like to draw attention to *Pre-interrogation Interviews*, used in the United States as part of, among others, the Reid Technique. These interviews create the risk of false confessions. The tendency for investigators to make false-positive errors of guilt during pre-interrogation interviews leads to a presumption of guilt in the actual interrogation phase. Investigators with such a presumption of guilt ask more guilt-presumptive questions, use more techniques, and exert more pressure to get a confession.[42]

b. *Techniques Developed to Prevent False Confessions*

The *Cognitive Interview* is a technique that was developed when it became clear that hypnosis may cause invalid memories. It is being suggested as one of the two possible interview styles in the "account" phase of the PEACE method.[43] This method is used in both witness and suspect interviews, and is based on principles that are generally accepted in the scientific literature on memory. The main characteristics of the cognitive interview are that the interviewee has to remember the context of the event and use different retrieval routes to search for the memory.[44] The interview consists of five phases, which are meant to encourage the suspect to express himself. The general idea of the cognitive interview is to first let the suspect speak freely and then slowly ask more and more detailed questions. It can be considered as a general guideline that asks for a lot of flexibility from the police officer.[45]

The other interview style that is recommended in the PEACE Model is *Conversation Management*.[46] This method was originally developed in the field of communication science, and it is directed at coping with resistance.[47] The two basic principles of conversation management are to talk as equals and to commit to cooperative talk.[48] A plan, or roadmap, of the conversation is made, which is communicated to the suspect.[49] The police officer should pay attention to the suspect's pace and allow silences during the talk. This will give the officer time to think and monitor the behavior of the suspect.[50] Additionally, responsive listening techniques are used.[51]

[40] Paul Ponsaers et al., *De ondervraging. Analyse van een politietechniek* 54–55 (2001).

[41] *Id.* [42] Kassin, *supra* note 16, at 228.

[43] Walsh & Milne, *supra* note 23, at 57.

[44] Ronald P. Fisher et al., *Field Test of the Cognitive Interview: Enhancing the Recollection of Actual Victims and Witnesses of Crime*, 74 J. Applied Psychol. 722, 727 (1989).

[45] Nathalie Dongois, *L'erreur judiciaire en matière pénale: Regards croisés sur ses contours et ses causes potentielles* 67–68 (2014).

[46] Walsh & Milne, *supra* note 23, at 57. [47] Shepherd, *supra* note 37, at 5, 12.

[48] Eric Shepherd, *Ethical Interviewing*, 18 Issues in Criminological & Legal Psychol. 46 (1993).

[49] Shepherd, *supra* note 37, at 12. [50] *Id.* [51] *Id.*

Tactical Method of Reasoning (TMR) is a military methodology with five overarching principles that are recommended for a criminal investigation. It was developed in Canada by psychologist Michèl St-Yves and has found its way to several French-speaking European countries. The recommendations can be used to effectively manage the strategy of an interrogation. The five principles are: (1) Maintaining objectivity, (2) Building a relationship, (3) Adopting active listening, (4) Being professional, and (5) Knowing how to conclude.[52]

An *Overview of Police Strategies* used in criminal cases in England and Wales and Northern Ireland, compiled by Leahy-Harland and Bull, outlines a number of strategies and tactics that may help in gaining detailed responses from interviewees. The effective ones all come down to open information-seeking questions.[53] The strategies of *presentation of evidence, challenge*, and *rapport/empathy* appeared to be the most common strategies employed in the sample. The frequency of challenges increased as the interviews progressed. The techniques of rapport/empathy appeared to be associated with suspects admitting the offense. The strategy of *describing trauma on the part of the victim* was associated with a decreased likelihood of suspects admitting an offense.[54]

III. European Law

1. European Convention of Human Rights (ECHR)

All countries described in this chapter are members of the Council of Europe, which means that they have to abide by the European Convention of Human Rights (ECHR).[55] The most relevant rules on suspect interrogation can be deduced from Article 6 of the ECHR, which states that suspects have the right to a fair trial. The ECHR describes human rights that are considered minimal but fundamental, leaving room for each Member State to further specify these rights in its national law.[56] The ECHR therefore only provides a few necessary conditions for an interrogation to be regarded as fair:

- the suspect has the privilege against self-incrimination and the right to remain silent;
- the burden of proof lies with the prosecution, which means that the suspect does not have to prove his or her innocence;

[52] M. St-Yves & J. Landry, *Psychology of Investigative Interviewing: From Research to Practice* (2004), in *International Developments and Practices in Investigative Interviewing and Interrogation: Volume 2: Suspects* 132 (David Walsh et al. eds., 2016).

[53] Samantha Leahy-Harland & Ray Bull, *Police Strategies and Suspect Responses in Real-Life Serious Crime Interviews*, 3 J. Police & Crim. Psychol. 1, 14 (2016).

[54] *Id.*

[55] The Convention for the Protection of Human Rights and Fundamental Freedoms, Nov. 4, 1950, 213 U.N.T.S. 221.

[56] Geert Corstens & Matthias J. Borgers, *Het Nederlands Strafprocesrecht* 27 (7th ed. 2011).

- evidence, including statements from the suspect, is obtained in a way that does not decrease its validity and reliability; and
- the suspect receives practical and effective (free) legal assistance from the time of his or her first police interrogation.

Concerning the right to legal assistance, the European Court of Human Rights has held that suspects have the right to a lawyer during police custody.[57] The reason legal assistance is considered so important is that it is a safeguard protecting the privilege against self-incrimination and protecting the suspect against ill treatment. The Court stipulated that "as a rule, access to a lawyer should be provided as from the first interrogation of a suspect by the police."[58] It furthermore ruled that "[t]he rights of the defense will in principle be irretrievably prejudiced when incriminating statements made during police interrogation without access to a lawyer are used for a conviction."[59] Such statements should thus be excluded from consideration by the court, which may lead to an acquittal.

2. European Union (EU)

Additionally, except for Switzerland, the countries we discuss are members of the European Union. The EU has issued a number of directives that elaborate on the rights formulated by the ECHR. First, the EU has created a directive on the right of access to a lawyer, which states that an effective defense means that the lawyer can ask questions, request clarifications, and make statements during the interview.[60] Second, the EU issued a directive on strengthening the presumption of innocence, in line with the case law of the European Court of Human Rights.[61] Finally, the EU made a directive on the questioning of minors as suspects, stating that their interrogations must be recorded audio-visually or, under exceptional circumstances, verbally transcribed.[62] The formulation of the questions asked must also take into account the age or maturity of the child.[63] In order to see whether there are any additional national rules that apply to suspect interviews in Europe, we have to look at the rules and practices of individual countries.

[57] Condron v. United Kingdom, App. No. 35718/97, Eur. Ct. H.R., May 2, 2000; John Murray v. United Kingdom, App. No. 18731/91, Eur. Ct. H.R., Feb. 8, 1996; Salduz v. Turkey, App. No. 36391/02, Eur. Ct. H.R., Nov. 27, 2008.

[58] Salduz v. Turkey, App. No. 36391/02, Eur. Ct. H.R., Nov. 27, 2008, § 55.

[59] *Id.*

[60] Directive on the right of access to a lawyer in criminal proceedings and in European arrest warrant proceedings, and on the right to have a third party informed upon deprivation of liberty and to communicate with third persons and with consular authorities while deprived of liberty, 2013/48/EU (Commentary Point 25).

[61] Directive on the strengthening of certain aspects of the presumption of innocence and of the right to be present at the trial in criminal proceedings, 2016/343/EU (Article 9).

[62] Directive on procedural safeguards for children who are suspects or accused persons in criminal proceedings 2016/800/EU.

[63] *Id.*

IV. Interview Methods and Regulations in European Countries

In this section, we will discuss interview methods and the relevant regulations of a number of European countries.

1. Germany

The German Code of Criminal Procedure, in Article 136a, lists a number of prohibited means and methods of interrogation. It provides that:

(1) The freedom of suspects to make decisions and to manifest their will shall not be impaired by ill treatment, induced fatigue, physical interference, administration of drugs, torment, deception, or hypnosis. Coercion may be applied only as far as this is permitted by criminal law. Threatening the suspect with measures not permitted under its provision of holding out the prospect of an advantage not envisaged by statute shall be prohibited.
(2) Measures that impair the memory of suspects or their ability to understand shall not be permitted.
(3) The prohibitions under subsection 1 and 2 shall apply irrespective of the suspect's consent. Statements obtained in breach of this prohibition shall not be used, even if the suspect consents to their use.[64]

Volbert and Baker further explain what is allowed and disallowed within the legal framework. The boundaries between permitted and prohibited interview methods are not always clear. Providing incorrect facts is not allowed, but posing trick questions is permitted. There are relatively few requirements on the manner in which police interviews should be conducted. Such an interview should follow an information-gathering approach rather than an accusatory approach.[65]

The PEACE Model is generally followed in training programs for the police. The literature recommends eliciting a free narrative, which is then followed by asking more specific questions.[66] Published guidelines on police interviews consistently recommend a strategy in which open-ended questions are asked of the suspect. However, there is less consensus regarding the treatment of suspects who are not willing to make a statement or who deny the alleged crime. In practice, police officers often call for techniques to motivate uncooperative suspects to make a statement or even a confession.

[64] Renate Volbert & Bianca Baker, *Investigative Interviewing of Suspects in Germany: Defining What Not To Do, in International Developments and Practices in Investigative Interviewing and Interrogation, supra* note 52, at 138, 140.
[65] *Id.* at 140. [66] *Id.* at 141.

Police interviews in Germany do not seem to be carefully monitored. Suspects in Germany have the right to assistance of a lawyer in all stages of the proceedings.[67] According to Weihmann, this implies that lawyers are allowed to be present during the suspect's interview.[68] This would, however, only be allowed for suspects who are questioned by a judge or prosecutor,[69] and not for suspects questioned by the police. Regarding this aspect of the right to a fair trial, Germany does not seem to meet the requirements of the Council of Europe and the European Union.[70] Furthermore, interviews can be recorded only in cases where there is mutual agreement on audio-visual recording,[71] which shows that recording is not the norm.

2. France

According to French law, a police officer is responsible for his choice of interview methods and for his acts of investigation.[72] However, all suspects must be treated under conditions that respect human dignity.[73] Based on information collected in the United Kingdom, North America, and Canada, the *Gendarmerie Nationale* (the national police force) developed a general procedure for interviewing suspects (*Processus Général de Recueil des Entretiens, Auditions et Interrogatoires*, or ProGREAI).[74] The ProGREAI method is an understanding-based procedure that makes use of active listening.[75] It incorporates the five steps of the PEACE Model and the five recommendations of the Tactical Method of Reasoning (both explained in Section II) and translates them into three steps: *Preparation, Interview*, and *Assessment*.[76]

During the *Preparation*, an interview strategy is determined, and the interrogator must know all facts and validations of the investigation, while eliminating assumptions. Potentially distracting elements, such as a telephone, are removed from the interrogation room.[77]

During the *Interview*, three phases can be distinguished. First, in a non-accusatory phase, the suspect is allowed to tell his version of the story without being interrupted. The second phase is the offensive phase, in which the interrogator asks for more details, based on what the suspect said earlier. During this phase, the aim is to gather information, regardless of its truth. The following phase of the interview is the accusatory phase, in which the interrogator implies that she believes that the suspect was involved in the crime. She asks "trap questions," which are meant to discomfort the suspect and generate doubt. With the trap questions, the interrogator insinuates that

[67] Strafprozessordnung [StPO] [Code of Criminal Procedure] art. 137.

[68] Robert Weihmann, *Handbuch Kriminalistik* 18 (2017).

[69] StPO art. 168c. [70] *Id.* [71] *Id.*

[72] Samuel Demarchi & Laurent Delhalle, *Interviewing Suspects in France*, in *International Developments and Practices in Investigative Interviewing and Interrogation, supra* note 52, at 131.

[73] *Code de Procédure Pénal* [C. Pr. Pén.] [Criminal Procedure Code] art. 63–5.

[74] Demarchi & Delhalle, *supra* note 72, at 134. [75] *Id.* at 135.

[76] *Id.* at 134. [77] *Id.*

there might be evidence against the suspect. The accusatory phase ends with a confrontation, in which the interrogator explicitly says that she thinks that the suspect committed the crime. The suspect gets the chance to respond to this by providing an alternative story. The interrogator also offers possible motives for the crime, to which the suspect can respond with a clarification. The aim of the confrontation is to generate discomfort in the suspect and bring the truth out of him.[78]

During the *Assessment* Phase, new information is considered in light of the known elements of the case, and its relevance and credibility are assessed. Additionally, the successes and failures of the interrogation in gathering information are evaluated. The interrogator must also perform a self-evaluation.[79]

Since each police officer remains responsible for the techniques he or she applies,[80] it is not known how suspects are interviewed in practice and to what extent police officers comply with the rules. Insight into French police interviews methods was provided by our respondent from the Gendarmerie.[81] According to the respondent, suspects who are held in custody in France are interrogated quite intensely. The custody, or *garde à vue*, lasts twenty-four hours with a possible extension of another twenty-four hours. During this time, the suspect will be interrogated until he confesses, or until the forty-eight hours are over. The interrogations are only interrupted for sleeping, smoking, drinking, and eating. The respondent would always start an interrogation with the idea that the suspect is the offender, because it could be expected that the suspect is not interrogated without reason. According to our respondent, it is easier to decrease this idea of guilt during the interrogation than to start with the idea that the suspect is innocent and then increase suspicion. If the suspect is not the offender, he can state that to the interrogators, and he can then be excluded as a suspect. The respondent says that although a bit mixed, the interview method used in France is closer to the Reid Technique than to the PEACE method. She describes a number of techniques that she uses or advises, which would lead to a confession of the suspect. We will deal with them briefly.

- During the night, the suspect has the right to sleep, but officers regularly walk in on him. While the officers pretend to perform medical tests to check whether the suspect is still alive, the actual reason for walking in on the suspect is to wake him up as often as possible, ensuring that he is in a bad physical state the next day. The officers are careful not to do this so often that the lawyer will complain afterward.

[78] *Id.* at 134–35. [79] *Id.* at 135. [80] *Id.* at 131.

[81] Our respondent works at the Gendarmerie and leads a team that advises interrogators during problematic interrogations, in which there is no other evidence available. She and her team also take the role as interrogator in these cases. She has a background in criminology, psychology, and law. The respondent was approached when the author attended a private lecture at a Dutch university. The interview took place in an office at this university and was carried out in English. We do not wish to imply that the practices described by our respondent are representative of all French police interviews.

- Another technique to make the suspect uncomfortable is to interrogate him in a "hard" room.[82] This means the chairs are hard and uncomfortable, there are no pictures on the wall, no sunlight can come in, and there is nothing to indicate any time or day. The aim of the "hard" room is to increase fear in the suspect, which is believed to lead to a confession.
- Interrogators often talk a lot about the bad food quality in French jails and keep talking about food until the suspect gets very hungry. Then, they promise the suspect a nice lunch instead of the jail food. During this lunch, the officers will keep talking to the suspect about topics that are unrelated to the crime, to make him talk and build up trust. While suspect interrogations of serious crimes are audio-visually recorded, these conversations at lunchtime are not considered part of the interrogation and are thus not videotaped.[83]
- The Gendarmerie often makes use of their so-called *forensics for dummies* technique. The interrogators teach the suspect about forensic techniques, to make him aware of the traces that can be found. During these explanations, they emphasize and exaggerate the forensic possibilities that would be available. This increases the forensic awareness of the suspect and can make him uncertain about possible traces he left.

Although the ProGREAI method is, in theory, based on the PEACE Model, police interviews in France may in practice often bear strong resemblances to the Reid Technique. There are several legal safeguards, however. To protect suspects in France from ill treatment, they have the right to have their lawyer present during the interview.[84] The role of the lawyer can be described as passive, which means that lawyers are limited in the extent to which they can contradict the officials.[85] A second way in which French police interviews are monitored is by audio-visual recording, which is standard in all serious crimes.[86] It is not fully clear how effective these legal safeguards are in practice, however.

3. Italy

In 1988, a new *Codice de Procedura Penale* (Code of Criminal Procedure) came into force in Italy. This new code is based on an adversarial model and was inspired by the Anglo-American system. It introduced a new set of rules regarding suspect

[82] A similar technique is used during the Reid Technique, in which it is advised to discomfort the suspect, for example, by means of isolating the suspect, and using certain furniture.

[83] In *Titarenko v. Ukraine*, App. No. 31720/02, Eur. Ct. H.R., Sept. 20, 2012, § 87, the ECtHR held that: "Any conversation between a detained criminal suspect and the police must be treated as formal contact and cannot be characterized as 'informal questioning.'" *See also* Kassin, *supra* note 16, at 228.

[84] *Code de Procédure Pénal* [C. Pr. Pén.] [Criminal Procedure Code] art. 63–4.

[85] Dimitrios Giannoulopoulos, *Custodial Legal Assistance and Notification of the Right to Silence in France: Legal Cosmopolitanism and Local Resistance*, 24 Crim. L.F. 291, 329 (2013).

[86] C. Pr. Pén. art. 63–1.

interrogations, but a number of aspects of the inquisitorial tradition still exert some influence on the procedures.[87]

Italian procedural law states that suspects, when questioned, must be free of all undue influence, both psychological and physical. Neither the police nor the prosecutor may use any methods or techniques that may influence the suspect's right to self-determination, or alter his or her memory or capability to evaluate facts. This right cannot be waived by the suspect under any circumstances, even if he or she so wishes.[88] As a consequence of this rule, police officers cannot lie to the suspect by, for example, letting him or her believe that they have certain evidence against him or her. Police officers are not allowed to use lie detectors, hypnosis, or any other method to force the suspect to remember what occurred.[89]

In Italy, there are no procedures or guidelines regarding the best way to conduct interviews. Zappalà et al. note that there seems to be a standard interview used by the majority of police officers, but that this is not supported by empirical findings.[90] According to our two respondents from the *carabinieri*,[91] one of them working at the national police force in Italy, regular police officers do not receive training in suspect interrogation. Therefore, everything they do during interrogations is learned from their more experienced colleagues.

The lack of official training in empirically validated interview techniques leads many police officers and public prosecutors to have a naive idea of the psychological mechanisms that work during an interview. There is a belief that nonverbal behaviors are a reliable indication of lying.[92] This was confirmed by our respondents, who said that they do not use any specific interrogation methods, but rather carefully observe the behavior of the suspect to see whether he is telling the truth or not. This, too, they learn from older colleagues. According to Zappalà et al., the good cop/bad cop technique is rather commonplace during suspect interviews. Police officers do not frequently make use of open-ended questions. The most common technique consists of prolonging the duration of the interrogation, which is expected to eventually lead the suspect to confess. Police officers basically ignore, or grossly underestimate, the phenomenon of false confessions.[93]

Our respondents partly confirm the findings of Zappalà et al. and partly contradict them. They say that with all the guarantees that now exist for the suspect, such as the right to silence and the presence of a lawyer at the police interview, it is practically impossible that a false confession would be brought about by the manner of questioning by the police.

[87] Angelo Zappalà et al., *Criminal Interrogation in Italy: Legal Procedures and Practices, in International Developments and Practices in Investigative Interviewing and Interrogation*, *supra* note 52, at 148.

[88] C. Pr. Pén. art. 64. [89] *Id.* [90] Zappalà et al., *supra* note 87, at 148.

[91] While visiting family in Italy, the second author met an Italian police officer from the *carabinieri*. Since he only spoke Italian, he invited his English-speaking colleague to the interview, who brought his Dutch wife. The interview took place in an old school, which is now a meeting place for the older generation of a small town in the northern part of Italy. The interview was carried out in English, Italian, and Dutch.

[92] Zappalà et al., *supra* note 87, at 148. [93] *Id.*

According to the respondents, the prosecutor and the police are, by definition, convinced of the suspect's guilt; otherwise the prosecutor would not have decided to start investigations against him or her. Still, they do not see how this could harm the suspect, since the entire Italian law is grounded on the protection of the rights of the accused. According to the respondents, Italian suspects are protected by the presence of a lawyer, and by a verbatim transcription of the interview. Additionally, the prosecutor or judge can decide that the interview is to be recorded audio-visually.

Zappalà et al. suggest that, in order to improve the quality of criminal interrogations, it is necessary to disseminate among public prosecutors and police officers the findings of the empirical research into what interview techniques work effectively.[94]

4. Switzerland

In 2011, a new Swiss Code of Criminal Procedure came into force, which is to be applied in all Swiss cantons. This new law not only has an impact on interview practices, but also on the training of police officers.[95] All investigators receive initial training with respect to interviewing suspects at the Police Academy. The protocol that can be used during interviews consists of:

(1) Preparation (and planning) of the interrogation;
(2) Legal aspects;
(3) Rapport building and communication/gathering information;
(4) Disclosure of evidence;
(5) Exploration of the fears and resistance of the suspect;
(6) Authentication of confession (if needed); and
(7) Closure of the interview.

Police officers also receive training on appropriate ways of questioning suspects, such as using open-ended questions and listening without interruption. Police officers are made aware of the risks, such as the contamination of the account by suggestive and leading questions. They are informed on precautions to be taken with people who are intellectually or psychologically vulnerable, in order to prevent false confessions.[96]

While there may be more, four types of suspect interviews are commonly used in Switzerland.[97] First, the *interrogatoire de justification* aims to exclude a suspect as the perpetrator of the alleged crime. It is used when, after a first interview, the police believe that the suspect did not commit the crime, but still have a couple of questions left before they can dismiss the suspect. In this type of interview, questions are asked very directly.[98]

[94] *Id.*

[95] Julie Courvoisier et al., *Investigative Interviewing of Suspects in Switzerland*, in *International Developments and Practices in Investigative Interviewing and Interrogation*, *supra* note 52, at 215, 215.

[96] *Id.* at 223. [97] Dongois, *supra* note 45. [98] *Id.* at 66.

The second type of interview is the *interrogatoire d'aveu*, which can be translated as the "admission interrogation." This style is adopted when the police believe that the suspect is guilty. During the admission interrogation, the police officer presents the incriminating evidence and facts to the suspect. In this type of interview, the police officer presents the suspect's guilt as a fact and does not show uncertainty regarding his belief in the suspect's guilt. The officer wants to understand why the suspect committed the crime and invites the suspect to explain his motivations. If the suspect does so, he indirectly admits his guilt. This style should only be used when the police are absolutely convinced of the guilt of the suspect, based on other evidence. If this is not the case, the interview might lead to a false confession, since it is very suggestive and leading.[99]

Another interview style that can be adopted when the police think that the suspect is guilty is the *interrogation d'enferrement*, which can be translated as "enclosure interrogation." It is used on suspects who are described as stubborn or recalcitrant and who are not likely to confess. In an enclosure interrogation, the police officer acts very passively and disinterested, giving the suspect the feeling that he has a lot of freedom. This makes the suspect feel very powerful. He will get the impression that the interview will have no consequences. Meanwhile, the police officer carefully writes down everything that the suspect says. Since the suspect is talking without being offered a framework, he might start to lie or contradict himself. The police officer will then point out the inconsistencies, inaccuracies, and obvious lies. In the absence of a confession, such factors may be sufficient to convince a judge that the suspect committed the crime.[100]

The final interview style that is used is the cognitive interview described earlier or, in French, *l'entrevue cognitive*. It is mostly used for witnesses, and it aims to obtain a statement that is as comprehensive and detailed as possible.[101] It is also used on suspects, and according to our respondent from Switzerland,[102] the cognitive interview, taught by psychologist Michèl St-Yves from Canada, is the recommended technique in the education of police officers.[103]

Suspects in Switzerland are entitled to a lawyer at any stage of the proceeding.[104] What is characteristic for Switzerland is that the suspect does not only have the right to remain silent:[105] he has an explicit right to be heard.[106] Suspect interviews are recorded in writing and can additionally be recorded audio-visually.[107] All recordings must be complete and correct.[108] Decisive statements must be recorded verbatim.[109]

99 *Id.* at 66–67. 100 *Id.* at 67. 101 *Id.* at 67–70.

102 We found our respondent from Switzerland through a former Swiss colleague. This respondent also appeared in the literature on the Swiss law system and the potential vulnerabilities in inquisitorial law systems. She was approached by email to elaborate on the information we found in the literature. She was not aware of the actual interview practices in Switzerland.

103 Recall that the ideas of Michèl St-Yves were also incorporated in the ProGREAI method, which is used in France.

104 *Code de Procédure Pénal* [C. Pr. Pén.] [Criminal Procedure Code] art. 129. 105 *Id.* art. 158.

106 *Id.* art. 3-2-c.; *see also* Martin Killias, *Wrongful Convictions in Switzerland: The Experience of a Continental Law Country, in* Huff & Killias, *supra* note 2, at 139, 155.

107 C. Pr. Pén. art. 76–4. 108 *Id.* art. 76–3. 109 *Id.* art. 78–3.

5. Belgium

For a long time, specific legislation on police interviewing was limited in Belgium. In 1998, a legislative reform with regard to interviewing victims, witnesses, and suspects was introduced by the so-called Franchimont law. New rules concerning the start of the interview (the "caution") were implemented.[110]

During the same period of time, the Board of Prosecutors-General approved the "Basic Interview Technique." This method is oriented toward an information-gathering interview style with an emphasis on "interview" instead of "interrogation." The technique is similar to the PEACE Model. It provides for a framework for interviewing and solely focuses on general techniques, such as basic communication skills and neutral confrontations (for example, to introduce evidence or to point out discrepancies in the statement). This might be the reason why, during training, various other techniques that are more related to obtaining a confession are promoted.

In a 2001 survey, Ponsaers et al. found that 28 percent of police officers mention that they frequently refer to evidence that actually is uncertain, and 9 percent refer to evidence that is not permitted (such as false evidence).[111] Of all interviewers that participated in the survey, 37 percent said that they display their conviction of guilt toward the suspect on a frequent basis.[112]

Suspects in Belgium can have a lawyer present during the police interview. In 2016, the role of the lawyer was extended in the law *Salduz Bis* and in the Criminal Procedural Code.[113] Before this extension, lawyers could only interfere when the police officers engaged in unlawful conduct. In the revised law, lawyers can also ask for clarification. The law lists three goals of the presence of the lawyer. She has to supervise: (1) that her client's right against self-incrimination and right to silence are respected, (2) that the police officers do not use coercion or unauthorized pressure, and (3) that the police officers notify the suspect of his rights.[114] Audio-visual recording of police interviews is not standard.[115]

In conclusion, Belgium has moved toward an evidence-based approach of police interviewing, inspired by English practices and research results. However, various techniques coming from more accusatorial interview styles still seem to be in use, suggesting that practitioners, academics, and instructors are not working in unison. Vanderhallen et al. observe that, in contrast to some other countries, Belgium has not yet been confronted with miscarriages of justice. In other countries, the discovery of such cases prompted fundamental reforms of the criminal investigation process as a

[110] Miet Vanderhallen et al., *Interviewing Suspects in Belgium*, in *International Developments and Practices in Investigative Interviewing and Interrogation*, *supra* note 52, at 85, 85.

[111] Paul Ponsaers et al., *supra* note 40; *see also* Vanderhallen et al., *supra* note 110, at 85, 93, 94.

[112] Vanderhallen et al., *supra* note 110, at 94.

[113] *Salduz bis: een uitdagende uitbreiding van de rechten van verdachten*, Desdalex, Dec. 13, 2016, *at* http://legalnews.be/straf-en-strafprocesrecht/salduz-bis-een-uitdagende-uitbreiding-van-de-rechten-van-verdachten-desdalex.

[114] Wetboek van Strafvordering [WSv] [Criminal Procedure Code] art. 47 bis § 6-7 a-c.

[115] Statutory Provision on Audio-Visual Interviews; Interviewing with Video Recordings art. 112 ter § 2.

whole and of suspect interview techniques in particular.[116] But because Belgium has not yet had to deal with the public outcry following the discovery of wrongful convictions, the country has not reformed and streamlined its interrogation techniques, and therefore still uses a variety of interrogation techniques, including accusatory and information-gathering tactics.[117]

6. The Netherlands

Dutch law contains only one explicit requirement for interviewing suspects. Article 29, Section 1 of the Code of Criminal Procedure states that interviewers must refrain from actions that may lead to suspect statements that are not voluntarily made.[118] The suspect is not obliged to answer questions, and this must be made clear to him prior to the interview (the "caution").[119] In addition to these legal regulations, the Prosecutions Office has issued a number of guidelines on interviewing vulnerable suspects and witnesses, which provide for certain safeguards and protection measures.

In the aftermath of the Schiedam Park Murder, a famous miscarriage of justice in the Netherlands, a number of criminal investigation methods were amended, including those for interviewing suspects.[120] Several new guidelines were issued related to training, preparation for interviews, coaching, and (de-)briefing the interviewers. Since 2006, every police region is obliged to have a protocol to ensure compliance with these new guidelines.[121]

Dutch suspect interviews consist of various stages, including the initial contact, the person-oriented interview, and the case-oriented interview. The so-called *Standaard Verhoorstrategie* (Standard Questioning Strategy) is generally advised for suspect interviews and is taught at the Police Academy. The fundamental ideas behind the Standard Questioning Strategy are: decreasing the resistance against telling the truth, building up pressure to let the suspect talk by confronting him or her with contradictory elements in the statement, offering rewards for certain behaviors, and encirclement (*omsingeling*).[122] Encirclement means that any possible alternative explanation for investigative leads is ruled out so that only an incriminating reading of the evidence remains. When a suspect adjusts his statement, he is rewarded instead of reproached for not having told the truth earlier. The aim of this approach is to encourage him to adjust his denials.[123]

[116] Vanderhallen et al., *supra* note 110, at 96. [117] *Id.* at 96.

[118] Wetboek van Strafvordering [Sv] [Criminal Procedure Code] art. 29 § 1.

[119] *Id.* art. 29 § 2.

[120] Martijn van Beek & Jos Hoekendijk, *The Investigative Interviewing of Suspects in the Netherlands*, in *International Developments and Practices in Investigative Interviewing and Interrogation*, *supra* note 52, at 157, 157.

[121] Programma versterking opsporing en vervolging, Den Haag (2005).

[122] Adri van Amelsvoort et al., *Handleiding verhoor* 447 (6th ed. 2015).

[123] Personal communication with officials from the Dutch Police Academy.

The main difference between the Standard Questioning Strategy and the Reid Technique is that the Dutch strategy disapproves of the use of tricks, such as deceit and promises.[124] According to Verhoeven and Stevens, the Standard Questioning Strategy bears resemblances to both an interview and an interrogation.[125] Our respondent, who professionally reviews police interviews as a legal psychologist,[126] said that he would characterize the Standard Questioning Strategy as being close to the Reid Technique. He feels that it provides too much freedom to the interviewer and leaves too much room for interpretation by individual police officers.

Van Beek and Hoekendijk observe that it is not clear whether and to what extent the Standard Questioning Strategy is used in the actual practice of suspect interviews. Methods applied may vary, and even trained investigators might still conduct interviews unsatisfactorily.[127] According to our respondent from the Dutch Police Academy,[128] the Standard Questioning Strategy should in principle be used in all suspect interviews. According to this respondent, the strategy is all about building up internal pressure in the suspect by confronting him with irregularities and contradictions in his story. All external pressure from the interviewer would be undesirable in this strategy. The legal psychologist interviewed, however, remarks that, while examining interviews, he observes many tactics that can be viewed as pressure. He witnesses a lot of exaggeration and even lying about the evidence in the interviews he examines. Occasionally the officers would even discuss the suspect's religion with him, which is not permitted according to the manual of police interviewing.[129]

After the *Salduz* decisions, the Dutch Supreme Court has ruled that all suspects must have a lawyer present during police interviews, unless they explicitly waive this right.[130] Defense lawyers are allowed to ask questions before and after, but not during the interview. During the interview, lawyers can make clear to the police officers that the suspect did not understand the question, complain when police officers use unauthorized pressure, or indicate when the suspect's condition asks for an immediate ending of the interview.[131] A guideline stipulates audio and video recording of interviews with victims, witnesses, and suspects in certain situations. The police mandatorily have to audio record suspect interviews: (1) if the victim has died, (2) if a conviction

[124] Willem-Jan Verhoeven & Lonneke Stevens, *The Lawyer in the Dutch Interrogation Room: Influence on Police and Suspect*, 9 J. Investigative Psychol. & Offender Profiling 69, 92 (2012).

[125] *Id.*

[126] This respondent works as a legal psychologist at a Dutch law faculty. He is a professional acquaintance of the authors and was approached because he regularly examines and reports on police interviews. The interview was carried out in Dutch at VU University in Amsterdam.

[127] Verhoeven & Stevens, *supra* note 124, at 92.

[128] Our respondent from the Dutch Police Academy teaches police officers in interviewing suspects and witnesses. He was approached by email and asked to cooperate with our study. The interview took place at an office at the Police Academy in Apeldoorn.

[129] Van Amelsvoort et al., *supra* note 122, at 340.

[130] HR 22 December 2015 (Dutch Supreme Court), ECLI:NL:HR:2015:3608.

[131] Politie, *Het Verhoor, Raad voor Rechtsbijstand* (2016), *at* http://www.rvr.org/binaries/content/assets/rvrorg/nieuws/raadsman-bij-politieverhoor/20160211-qa-rvr_nova.pdf.

could lead to twelve or more years of imprisonment, (3) in case of grievous bodily harm, (4) if the interrogation is about a sex crime that could lead to eight or more years of imprisonment, or (5) in case of sexual abuse in a dependency relationship.[132]

V. Analysis

In theory, the interview methods used in the European countries studied in this chapter bear more similarities to the PEACE Model than to the Reid Technique. Several countries explicitly grounded their (new) policies on the PEACE Model and used the developments in England and Wales as an example for their own country. Other countries were inspired by similar developments in Canada. In some of the investigated countries, such as the Netherlands, miscarriages of justice were the reason to change the rules on suspect interviewing and to invest in better training of police officers.[133] These wrongful convictions generated a lot of attention and led to a wider awareness of the fact that coercive interrogation techniques can produce false confessions. Attention to the risks of a false confession seems to be lacking more often in countries such as Belgium, which have *not* been confronted with such wrongful convictions and the subsequent public outcry.

In most countries under review, however, the rules on suspect interviewing do not appear to be very detailed. It is often not clear what falls within or outside the spectrum of a permissible suspect interview. Where there are clear guidelines on suspect interviews, such as in Germany, it is often unclear to what extent the police follow these guidelines in practice. From our interviews with professionals, we can cautiously conclude that the situation in practice may deviate from the legal norms and may sometimes show more similarities to the techniques that are disapproved of in the literature, including the Reid Technique tricks and tactics. However, systematic empirical studies of suspect interviews and of compliance to the norms are still lacking in all countries under review. Our interviews present a rather worrisome picture, especially for French and Dutch interviews. It should, however, be borne in mind that the interviewees are by no means representative of the groups of professionals they come from.

[132] Aanwijzing auditief en audiovisueel registreren van verhoren van aangevers, getuigen en verdachten, *at* http://wetten.overheid.nl/BWBR0032552/2013-01-01.

[133] Similar developments were noted for Norway. After a number of miscarriages of justice in the 1990s, the Norwegian police service introduced a national program for investigative interviewing, heavily influenced by the British process. Confession-based interrogation techniques were identified, warned against publicly, and replaced with conversation management and strategic use of evidence. Denmark also experienced several miscarriages of justice. This has, however, not generated a lot of attention from the media or the general public with regard to how the police conduct their interviews, and the police themselves have not yet been forced to make changes in their interview concept. *See* Ivar A. Fahsing et al., *Investigative Interviewing of Suspects in Scandinavia*, in *International Developments and Practices in Investigative Interviewing and Interrogation*, *supra* note 52, at 180, 181, 184.

Video and audio taping of police interviews would be helpful for monitoring compliance with the norms as set out by the European Convention of Human Rights and national regulations. In a growing number of countries, interviews with suspects are now mandatorily recorded, which offers such monitoring opportunities. Since lawyers are increasingly present during suspect interviews as a consequence of the case law of the European Court of Human Rights, their supervising role in this respect could be enhanced as well.

Both types of monitoring methods (recording of interviews and an enhanced role of defense lawyers in supervising rule compliance) could also be used by legal and criminal justice scholars for investigating suspect interviews in legal practice. Scholars could examine audio-visual records of police interviews, and they could make use of the experiences of lawyers collected while attending police interviews. Since practice may deviate from norms and regulations, and in view of the risks of false confessions related to some interrogation techniques, there is a strong need for expanding these opportunities for empirical research.

References

Lorana Bartels, *Police Interviews with Vulnerable Adult Suspects*, Criminal Research Council, Australian Government, Research in Practice, Report No. 21 (2011)

Roel Boon et al., *Van verhoor naar forensisch interview. Naar een effectieve interviewstandaard voor de politie*, 78 Tijdschrift voor de Politie 20 (2016)

Joseph P. Buckley, *The Reid Technique of Interviewing and Interrogation* (2007)

Colin Clarke et al., *Interviewing Suspects of Crime: The Impact of PEACE Training, Supervision and the Presence of a Legal Advisor*, 8 J. Investigative Psychol. & Offender Profiling 149 (2011)

Coral Dando et al., *The Cognitive Interview: Inexperienced Police Officers' Perceptions of Their Witness/Victim Interviewing Practices*, 13 Legal & Criminological Psychol. 59 (2008)

Nathalie Dongois, *L'erreur judiciaire en matière pénale: Regards croisés sur ses contours et ses causes potentielles* (2014)

Ronald P. Fisher et al., *Field Test of the Cognitive Interview: Enhancing the Recollection of Actual Victims and Witnesses of Crime*, 74 J. Applied Psychol. 722 (1989)

Brandon L. Garrett, *Judging Innocence*, 108 Colum. L. Rev. 55 (2008)

Maryanne Garry & Devon L. Polaschek, *Imagination and Memory*, 9 Current Directions Psychol. Sci. 6 (2000)

Dimitrios Giannoulopoulos, *Custodial Legal Assistance and Notification of the Right to Silence in France: Legal Cosmopolitanism and Local Resistance*, 24 Crim. L.F. 291 (2013)

C. Ronald Huff & Martin Killias, *Wrongful Convictions and Miscarriages of Justice* (2013)

Fred Inbau et al., *Criminal Interrogation and Confessions* (4th ed. 2001)

Saul M. Kassin, *On the Psychology of False Confessions: Does Innocence Put Innocents at Risk?*, 60 Am. Psychologist 215 (2005)

Saul M. Kassin et al., *Police-Induced Confession: Risk Factors and Recommendations*, 34 L. & Hum. Behav. 3 (2010)

Saul M. Kassin & Christina T. Fong, *"I'm Innocent!" Effects of Training on Judgments of Truth and Deception in the Interrogation Room*, 23 L. & Hum. Behav. 499 (1999)

Saul M. Kassin & Katherine L. Kiechel, *The Social Psychology of False Confessions: Compliance, Internationalization, and Confabulation*, 7 Psychol. Sci. 125 (1996)
Samantha Leahy-Harland & Ray Bull, *Police Strategies and Suspect Responses in Real-Life Serious Crime Interviews*, 3 J. Police & Crim. Psychol. 1 (2016)
Fadia M. Narchet et al., *Modeling the Influence of Investigator Bias on the Elicitation of True and False Confessions*, 35 L. & Hum. Behav. 452 (2011)
Paul Ponsaers et al., *De ondervraging. Analyse van een politietechniek* (2001)
Frits Posthumus, *Evaluatieonderzoek in de Schiedammer Parkmoord* (2005)
Melissa B. Russano et al., *Investigating True and False Confessions Within a Novel Experimental Paradigm*, 16 Psychol. Sci. 481 (2005)
Michael K. Saks & Jonathan J. Koehler, *The Coming Paradigm Shift in Forensic Identification*, 309 Sci. 892 (2005)
Eric Shepherd, *Ethical Interviewing*, 18 Issues in Criminological & Legal Psychol. 46 (1993)
Eric Shepherd, *Resistance in Interviews: The Contribution of Police Perceptions and Behaviour*, 18 Issues in Criminological & Legal Psychol. 5 (1993)
Adri van Amelsvoort et al., *Handleiding verhoor* (6th ed. 2015)
Peter J. van Koppen, *Blundering Justice: The Schiedam Park Murder*, in *Serial Murder and the Psychology of Violent Crimes* 207 (Richard N. Kocsis ed., 2008)
Peter J. van Koppen, *De Schiedammer Parkmoord: Een Rechtspsychologische Constructie* (2003)
Willem-Jan Verhoeven & Lonneke Stevens, *The Lawyer in the Dutch Interrogation Room: Influence on Police and Suspect*, 9 J. Investigative Psychol. & Offender Profiling 69 (2012)
Aldert Vrij, *Why Professionals Fail to Catch Liars and How They Can Improve*, 9 Legal & Criminological Psychol. 159 (2004)
International Developments and Practices in Investigative Interviewing and Interrogation: Volume 2: Suspects (David Walsh et al. eds., 2016)
David W. Walsh & Rebecca Milne, *Keeping the PEACE? A Study of Investigative Interviewing Practices in the Public Sector*, 13 Legal & Criminological Psychol. 39 (2008)
Robert Weihmann, *Handbuch Kriminalistik* (2017)
Tom Williamson, *Towards Greater Professionalism: Minimizing Miscarriages of Justice*, in *Investigative Interviewing: Rights, Research and Regulation* 147 (Tom Williamson ed., 2006)

CHAPTER 16

INTERROGATION LAW AND PRACTICE IN COMMON LAW JURISDICTIONS

DAVID DIXON

I. Interrogation Myths

According to popular understanding (and, all too often, professional claims), typical police interrogations have the following characteristics:

> Suspects resist questioning and interviews are tense, difficult encounters in which police dominate interaction. Their role is essentially a search for truth. Eventually, as a result of skillful police techniques (including the detection of deception from body language), they will find it, as suspects crack and shift from denial to full confession. Such confessions are reliable: innocent people would not confess to something they have not done unless they are unusually vulnerable through youth or disability. Restriction of police interrogation by legal regulation allows the guilty to escape justice. Audio-visual recording provides a simple answer to any concerns about interrogation.

The research literature suggests that such standard beliefs about interrogations are misleading. If police interrogation is to be properly understood, a series of myths has to be confronted.

This chapter seeks to dispel these myths by examining two central, related themes. First, interrogation law and practice are located in the broader fields of criminal process and investigative activity, allowing cross reference to other chapters in this Handbook. This connection tends to be understated in the psychological research literature that dominates the interrogation field. The discussion will suggest that interrogation practice in common law jurisdictions has been shaped by its criminal process context, which includes: the role of police in investigating and prosecuting crime; the preeminence of the guilty plea; criminal law's requirement that particular, provable mental states be included as elements of many offences; responses by criminal justice authorities to failures, problems, and embarrassments; and shifting priorities, values, and purposes of criminal process in changing political circumstances.

A key lesson of criminal justice scholarship is the need to focus on routine processes and everyday bureaucracy. While the headline cases are, of course, important, they should not distract attention from most suspects' experience of interrogation law and practice.[1] In commonplace criminal process, police questioning is less about dramatic interrogation than the dull slog of statement-taking. As one uniformed officer's quizzical response to my inquiry about "interrogation" indicated, some police may well not even think that their mundane processing of suspects constitutes anything as significant as interrogation. Nonetheless, the same patterns of construction and coercion discussed later on in the chapter can occur in both low and high policing.

Second, this chapter emphasizes the interactive, dialectical relationship between interrogation law and practice, focusing on commonalities and contrasts among common law jurisdictions. By the final third of the twentieth century, a model of investigative law and practice had become established, which was broadly shared across these jurisdictions. Police arrested suspects and took them to police stations where they were questioned before being passed on to other actors in the process—guards, prosecutors, judges. This familiar picture was the product of patterns of state formation in the nineteenth century. Police professionalized, developing sections specializing in crime control and investigation (in which skill in interrogating and success in producing confessions were highly valued). Meanwhile, magistrates withdrew from involvement in investigations to more judicial and administrative functions.

Only in retrospect does this process look natural and inevitable. An example makes clear that this was not so. In the interwar period in England, the legality of questioning detained suspects *at all* was moot. In 1929, a Royal Commission recommended "a rigid instruction to the Police that no questioning of a person in custody, about any crime or offence with which he is or may be charged, should be permitted."[2] How different contemporary policing would be if that recommendation had been implemented.

In similar societies with other legal traditions, civil law developed differently (as Malsch and de Boer show in chapter 15 of this volume). Meanwhile, an increasing divergence between law and practice in the United States and in other common law jurisdictions emerged toward the end of the twentieth century. Currently, interrogation practice is in a state of flux, with significant changes underway internationally.

[1] Yale Kamisar, *Equal Justice in the Gatehouses and Mansions of American Criminal Procedure*, in *Criminal Justice in Our Time* 3–95 (A.E. Dick Howard ed., 1965); Doreen McBarnet, *Conviction* (1981).

[2] *Report of the Royal Commission on Police Powers and Procedure*, Cmd. 3297 para. 169 (Home Office 1929). For the context, see David Dixon, *Law in Policing: Legal Regulation and Police Practices* 130–34 (1997).

II. Researching and Understanding Interrogation

The literature on interrogation law and practice falls into several general categories:

- Legal discussion of interrogation is dominated by the vast body of U.S. law review articles analyzing constitutional law issues. As regards legal analysis, Leo's complaint from two decades ago still rings true: "virtually all scholarship on American police interrogation is relegated to doctrinal analysis."[3]
- Official inquiries: while sometimes these have buried issues in stereotypical style, some—notably Royal Commission reports in England and Senate committee reports in the United States—have been important in giving authority to informed and critical accounts of state practices.[4]
- Sociolegal, sociological, criminological fieldwork: research commissioned by official inquiries into criminal justice in England and Wales provided a major boost to knowledge about interrogation, ensuring both funding for researchers and access to police organizations. Sociolegal scholars were able to provide accounts, overlapping with work by psychologists, of police interrogation in the context of broader projects on criminal investigation and the treatment of suspects. A particular focus was the politically charged issue of the right to silence.[5] Elsewhere, empirical work on interrogation has been less common. Significant exceptions are work on audio-visual recording of interrogation in Australia[6] and, most important, Richard Leo's *Police Interrogation and American Justice*[7] (and his continuing stream of high-quality journal articles and book chapters). Leo's work is vital, but limited by its focus on opportunity samples of serious cases.[8] There have also been some valuable studies focusing on the interrogation of young people.[9]
- In science, psychology dominates. There is now very extensive expertise in psychological research, particularly experimental work. Much has been done to increase our understanding of why suspects confess, sometimes to crimes they did not

[3] Richard A. Leo, *Miranda's Revenge: Police Interrogation as a Confidence Game*, 30 L. & Soc'y Rev. 259, 262 (1996).

[4] *E.g.*, *Report of the Royal Commission on Criminal Procedure* (H.M.S.O. 1981); Senate Select Comm. on Intelligence, *The Senate Intelligence Committee Report on Torture* (2014).

[5] For overviews, see Mandy Burton et al., *Sanders & Young's Criminal Justice* (2017); Dixon, *supra* note 2, at 228–66.

[6] David Dixon, *Interrogating Images* (2007).

[7] Richard Leo, *Police Interrogation and American Justice* (2009).

[8] *See* David Dixon, *Questioning Suspects*, 26 J. Contemp. Crim. Just. 426, 426–40 (2010).

[9] Barry C. Feld, *Kids, Cops and Confessions* (2013); Hayley M.D. Cleary, *Police Interviewing and Interrogation of Juvenile Suspects*, 38 L. & Human Behav. 271, 271–82 (2014).

commit.[10] Such work has significantly contributed to campaigns surrounding miscarriages of justice. In recent years, considerable resources have been put into psychological research sponsored by the High-Value Detainee Interrogation Group (see Section VIII.3). However, psychologists tend to underestimate the significance of the criminal process context and to focus on serious and dramatic rather than everyday cases.

- Training manuals: the most well known and influential is Inbau and Reid's *Criminal Interrogation and Confessions*.[11] It has had great impact across common law and other jurisdictions, whether through the text, training courses based on it, or derivatives, such as the publication of extracts from or work inspired by Inbau and Reid's work.[12] More recently, their critics have also published manuals and texts on investigative interviewing.[13]
- Investigative journalism and non-governmental organizations (NGOs): community activists and investigative journalists have done much to expose problems in interrogation, notably in miscarriage of justice cases.[14] The contribution of the Innocence Project in uncovering miscarriages of justice is legendary. Other NGOs, such as Human Rights Watch, are often the only source of information on some jurisdictions.
- Film: it might be thought trivial to include fictional, on-screen representations. Unfortunately, fiction and reality have become an unlikely duo in this field. There has been a circular process in which fictions have both reflected and influenced interrogation practice. A few examples: *The Bill* publicized the reforms to English policing in the 1990s; *NYPD Blue* used Inbau and Reid as source material; and *Lie to Me* has given a generation of officers inappropriate confidence in their ability to detect deception. More disconcertingly, the use of torture was legitimized by *24* and by movies such as *Man on Fire*, *Taken*, and, notoriously, *Zero Dark Thirty*. More recently, the first movie to feature the new "investigative interrogation," *Patriots (sic) Day*, has appeared.

Cumulatively, this material requires reconsideration of the myths outlined at the beginning. As Feld suggests, "Most of what appellate judges, criminologists, legal scholars, and the public think we know about interrogation derives from aberrational cases of

[10] Saul M. Kassin et al., *Police-Induced Confessions*, 34 L. & Human Behav., 3, 3–38 (2010); Christian A. Meissner et al. *Improving the Effectiveness of Suspect Interrogations*, 11 Ann. Rev. L. & Soc. Sci., 211, 211–33 (2015).

[11] Fred E. Inbau et al., *Criminal Interrogation and Confessions* (5th ed. 2011).

[12] J. Pete Blair, *What Do We Know About Interrogation in the United States?*, 20 J. Police & Crim. Psychol. 44, 44–57 (2005). On Inbau & Reid's impact on Continental Europe, see Marijke Malsch & Meike M. de Boer, *Interviews of Suspects of Crime: Law and Practice in European Countries, this volume*, chapter 15.

[13] *E.g.*, Eric Shepherd & Andy Griffiths, *Investigative Interviewing* (2d ed. 2013).

[14] Some notable examples: Sarah Burns, *The Central Park Five* (2012); Colleen Egan, *Murderer No More* (2010); Satish Sekar, *Fitted In: The Cardiff Three and the Lynette White Inquiry* (1997); Estelle Blackburn, *Broken Lives* (2005).

egregious abuses, false confessions and wrongful convictions, or television drama programs, 'reality' shows, and movies that misleadingly depict how police question suspects."[15] The conclusion will summarize a very different account of interrogation law and practice.

The very uneven coverage of common law jurisdictions in the literature must be acknowledged. While there is plenty on England and Wales and the United States, and some on Canada, Australia, and New Zealand, there is no relevant academic research tradition in others. India, the most populous common law jurisdiction, is represented only in highly critical reports by NGOs.[16]

III. Why Interrogate?

This section will discuss the purposes, uses, and functions of interrogation.

Evidence: Although there has been some research on the significance of confessional evidence in producing convictions, asking whether a confession was *necessary* in order to obtain a conviction can be misleading. Confessions can provide a shortcut to a conviction potentially obtainable by other means. The need to collect witness statements and physical evidence becomes less pressing if a confession is obtained. It can also be part of a routine bureaucratic practice of case construction. A denial that can be shown to be a lie may be even more useful to a prosecutor than an incomplete or vague admission.

Guilty pleas: There is a direct connection between confessions and a defining characteristic of common law jurisdictions—their reliance on guilty pleas rather than contested trials. If suspects confess, they are likely to plead guilty. Both confessions and guilty pleas are often made in expectation of reduced charges and preferential treatment, despite prohibitions on the offering of inducements to confess. Furthermore, investigators can improve detection statistics by getting suspects to accept responsibility for offenses that they may or may not have committed that will be "taken into consideration" or written off without an effect on sentence.

Truth-finding: Asking what interrogation is for may seem unnecessary: Isn't interrogation obviously about getting a suspect to tell the truth? When police officers are asked to explain their purpose in questioning suspects, they typically refer to the process as "a search for the truth." However, this explanation's simplicity and apparent indisputability are misleading.

First, it is almost trite to say that any account involves selection and construction. Memory works by selection and construction: it does not simply replay. Even a

[15] Feld, *supra* note 9, at 3.

[16] *E.g.*, Human Rights Watch, *Bound by Brotherhood: India's Failure to End Killings in Police Custody* (2016); Asian Centre for Human Rights, *Torture in India* (2010). There are also several professional guides, such as Uday Kumar, *Questioning and Interrogation: An Art of Establishing the Truth* (2013).

full, freely given confession is not an unmediated view of reality or "truth." All describing and accounting for action involves active interpretive work. Incidents are reconstructed as stories, in which legal definitions and requirements provide cues, plots, and character development. More than one account may be available: an adversary system of justice deals in contested versions of reality, not in absolute truths.

In police questioning, suspects' accounts are guided and molded in various ways. These include benign but inevitable direction and more potentially problematic interventions by investigators in the selection and construction process, ranging from excessive use of closed questions (which prompt simple yes or no answers) to the use of legal closure questions (whose apparent purpose is "to invite the suspect to provide information but in reality force information into a legally significant category in the hope that the suspect will 'adopt' it... so that it now 'fits' into an appropriate legal category"[17]) to comprehensive interrogation strategies in which suspects are eased to confession by being offered accounts of their (alleged) actions minimizing their moral (although not legal) responsibility.

Second, "searching for the truth" has too often been the gloss on a method of interrogation consisting of the interrogator seeking the suspect's confirmation of (confession to) an account of events (a truth) to which the interrogator is already committed. As the discussion of miscarriages of justice will show, well-known psychological and social processes have repeatedly caused problems in criminal process.

Legalization: Police questioning of suspects involves a very particular form of account construction, "legalization," which involves the interviewer organizing and framing the suspect's account according to legal criteria.[18] Normally, this involves mundane processes of translating material into a form appropriate for use downstream in the process, although malevolent manipulation has too often been evident in miscarriage cases.

An arrest becomes a legal matter in tangible and recognizable, standard form as an offense file is opened, information is entered and interpreted, previous documents (e.g., relating to earlier interrogations) are included or cross-referenced, and revisions and additions are subsequently made. Chatterton demonstrated the importance of "paperwork" in policing: the time spent creating prosecution files "produces the cases which enable the police organisation to interface with the courts and other organisations. Events, incidents and encounters are shaped, ordered and transformed through this paperwork into recognisable, typical cases."[19] Far from being residual or "marginal practices, mastery of paperwork and the ability to manipulate the 'paper reality' are core police skills.... The ability of the police to create a convincing paper record is a necessary part of successful case construction. Cases against

[17] Michael McConville et al., *The Case for the Prosecution* 70 (1991).

[18] Dixon, *supra* note 2, at 270–74.

[19] M.R. Chatterton, *Managing Paperwork*, in *Police Research* 110 (Mollie Weatheritt ed., 1989).

individuals... are cases made out on paper, subject to assessment on paper and, for the most part, decided upon paper."[20] The rules of substantive and procedural law provide the language and framework of the accounts that must be given of suspects' action and police reaction. Most detective work is not detection, but the transformation of an incident into a case and an individual into a defendant by the collection, categorization, and presentation of evidence. The creation of a record of interrogation—whether on paper or electronically for subsequent transcription—is a vital part of this process of "legalizing" accounts.

Most importantly, suspects have to be led to speak an account of their actions satisfying legal requirements of mens rea, so that, for example, reference is made to deliberate stealing, rather than simply to taking, or to acting recklessly, rather than accidentally. In preparing a file for prosecutors, police investigators have to cover the "points to prove" for the particular offense. So, for example, a suspect who had admitted to assaulting a homicide victim was asked:

Q ... when I asked you why you killed Nikki you said you didn't mean to kill her is that right?

A Yes.

Q Well, George, you hit Nikki with a brick across the head... on a number of occasions and you stabbed Nikki in the body, a number of times, when you did those actions, did you mean to kill her?

A No.

Q Well I put it to you that you must have done, George... That to me shows a clear intention on your part to kill her at that stage.[21]

A confession to murder is not just "I killed her" but acknowledgment of the required elements of actus reus (striking, stabbing) and mens rea (intending to kill). The monosyllabic responses in this exchange are significant. The suspect will often be invited to agree with the investigator's statement: "you intended to sell the drugs found in your car: do you agree?" Many police interviews are long sequences of closed "Do you agree?" questions that have to be understood as pretrial work.[22] The legal (re)construction is of course not a neutral process: as the police construct the case in their terms, so the suspect's version of reality may be marginalized, all too often producing suspects and defendants who are passive.

The social roles of interrogations and confession: While this chapter's focus is on the legal (and political) aspects of interrogation and confession, understanding their social role is also necessary, not least because this explains why they are symbolically as well as

[20] McConville et al., *supra* note 17, at 98 (quoting Goffman). This assessment is dated only by its reference to paper rather than e-files.

[21] From the transcript of Northumbria Police questioning George Heron, see David Dixon, *Integrity, Interrogation and Criminal Injustice*, in *The Integrity of Criminal Process* 75–97 (Jill Hunter et al. eds., 2016).

[22] Dixon, *supra* note 6, at 166–72.

instrumentally significant in criminal justice. Most obviously, the practice of confession has moral and religious dimensions that feed into social expectations and lay valuations of "owning up" and "getting it off your chest." Japanese police speak of using interrogation as the first stage in the process of rehabilitating the criminal.[23] The problematic nature of the assumption that the suspect is guilty and the potential for miscarriages of justice should be obvious.

Interrogation may also be about punishment, particularly at extremes involving coercive interrogation and torture.[24] More mundanely, it can be about social discipline: bringing a person to a police station and subjecting him or her to the process of detention and interrogation can be about the imposition and validation of power over individuals and communities.[25]

IV. Beyond the Police

While this chapter focuses on interrogation by police officers, the significance of interrogation by other state agents and private parties operating at the edges of criminal process or beyond should also be noted. On one hand, many state agencies (such as tax and welfare investigators) question suspects, relying on skills and training that originated in policing. Supervision and scrutiny of their activities and practices are scant compared to the attention given to police interrogation.[26] On the other hand, there is the role of security agencies of various types (including private contractors) that are involved in the interrogation of terrorist suspects and detainees. In recent years, the gap between security and police has reduced, disappearing at higher levels (not always in quite the way one might expect). There is a significant interplay of influence, as each sector has affected the other.

A crucial difference between security and police investigators is that the former may not expect or even be seeking a confession in antiterrorist and other preemptive operations. Rather, they may be seeking information as a basis for actionable intelligence, indicating a shift of paradigm from criminal justice to control process. In the criminal justice paradigm, police question a suspect between arrest and charge in order to obtain evidence about specific offenses allegedly committed by the suspect that may later be admissible in court. In the control process paradigm, the focus of interrogation is not (or not only) on the suspect's past actions but on what he or she knows about potential future action by others. If an interrogator does not anticipate the requirements for successful presentation, examination, and admission to evidence of interrogation in court,

[23] Taeko Wachi et al., *Japanese Suspect Interviews, Confessions and Related Factors*, 31 J. Police & Crim. Psychol. 217, 217–27 (2016).

[24] Charles Weisselberg, *Against Innocence*, in *The Integrity of Criminal Process* 354 (Hunter et al. eds., 2016).

[25] Satnam Choongh, *Policing as Social Discipline* (1997).

[26] For a rare study, see David W. Walsh & Rebecca Milne, *Keeping the PEACE?*, 13 Legal & Criminological Psychol. 39 (2008).

problems arise when attempts are made to cross paradigms. In several common law jurisdictions, authorities have faced significant problems when trying to use for evidential purposes material that had been collected for intelligence purposes.[27]

The admissibility of material obtained by violence is obviously problematic in the criminal justice paradigm. More complex issues are raised by confessions or admissions obtained during lengthy detention. In criminal justice, interrogation is normally confined to the period between arrest and charge. The permissible active investigative period is usually limited to a few hours, and even anti-terrorism laws allow only a few days. However, security detention may be much longer, even potentially infinite. As will be noted later on in the chapter, there has been a spillover of interrogation methods from criminal justice to security and back, as security officials appreciate the benefits of rapport-based methods. The problem is that rapport is most unlikely to be established with terrorist suspects in the short periods allowed under standard criminal justice regimes. As Gelles et al. suggest, "A rapport-building (or relationship-based) approach will yield the best results in an interview/interrogation that occurs over days/weeks/months."[28] Yet this runs counter to one of the basic principles of modern criminal justice regimes, which were constructed on an understanding that extended detention *in itself* could make confessions unreliable because people would say anything (even at long-term cost) to win a short-term reprieve from investigative detention.

If interrogation is intended to produce confessions and admissions that are acceptable to a criminal justice paradigm, lengthy pre-charge detention is unacceptable because it undermines the voluntariness that is a precondition of evidential admissibility. If interrogation is primarily intended to produce information and actionable intelligence rather than admissible evidence, then the concerns of criminal justice will not be paramount. But what happens when the lengthy interrogation for intelligence is over? If use of the regular criminal process is impossible, the options are permanent detention, release under administrative control orders limiting movements and contact, or the creation of an ersatz criminal justice, dressing up a militaristic control process with some trappings of legality. These are, of course, the questions that the United States has been grappling with in resolving the fate of detainees at Guantánamo Bay.[29]

It is worth adding a note on the purpose of torture and coercive interrogation. For centuries, critics have pointed out that torture produces unreliable confessions. However, torture may be intended not to produce reliable information immediately, but as part of a long-term strategy to deplete the detainee's personality, leaving him or her

[27] David Dixon, *From Criminal Justice to Control Process*, in *Handbook of Psychology of Investigative Interviewing* 91–106 (Ray Bull et al. eds., 2009); A and Others v. Secretary of State for the Home Department [2005] UKHL 71; United States v. Khalid Sheikh Mohammed, Walid Muhammad Salih Mubarak Bin 'Attash, Ramzi Bin Al Shibh, Ali Abdul-Aziz Ali & Mustafa Ahmed Adam Al Hawsawi (Guantánamo Bay Military Commission, ongoing; trial is expected to begin when pretrial hearings conclude . . . in 2021).

[28] Michael G. Gelles et al., *Al-Qaeda-Related Subjects*, in *Investigative Interviewing* 31 (Tom Williamson ed., 2006).

[29] Lou Dubose, *Trial Without End in Guantánamo*, Washington Spectator (Apr. 7, 2016), https://washingtonspectator.org/ksm-guantanamo-war-terror/.

open to a new dependent relationship with captors who may then be able to obtain reliable information. Despite all the debate about the need to use torture in "ticking-bomb" cases, its more significant "potential" may be elsewhere. The use of torture as part of or preliminary to long-term detention and interrogation raises very substantial issues of human rights and morality. It does not, however, raise legal issues: torture is unreservedly illegal under international law.

V. Judges and Rules

This section is concerned with the impact and significance of differing judicial and regulatory modes of attempting to control interrogation practice. While the United States relies primarily on ex post facto judicial rulings to oversee police investigative practice, jurisdictions such as England and Australia have attempted to regulate ex ante by developing legislative and other regulatory controls. In the United States, courts have developed an elaborate constitutional law jurisprudence. *Miranda v. Arizona*[30] has been endlessly dissected and analyzed in a huge library of cases, reports, and academic papers. Elsewhere, judges have developed concepts in the common law, while in Britain and Canada, judges have also increasingly used human rights standards from international conventions and domestic human rights instruments.

Judges have potentially potent, but essentially defensive, powers with which to regulate police interrogation. Of particular relevance here is judicial control over admissibility of confessions and admissions. Courts can insist that a confession should be obtained by methods meeting standards such as systemic integrity, voluntariness, reliability, lack of oppression, and fairness. Such standards vary across jurisdictions. For example, English and Australian courts have been much stricter than their U.S. counterparts in disapproving of deception by interrogators: standard U.S. practices such as lying to a suspect that incriminating physical evidence has been found should lead to exclusion by Anglo-Australian judges of a subsequent confession.[31] Another area of notable contrasts is the treatment of vulnerable suspects, such as young people, people with an intellectual or developmental disability, and those suffering from a mental illness.[32]

In addition, judges can indirectly influence police evidence-gathering practices. As noted above, when courts demand that the prosecution prove beyond reasonable doubt that a defendant intended an act, police are strongly encouraged to obtain a confession, providing a direct way of establishing intention. There was a significant (but, as yet, inadequately traced) relationship between the trend in areas of substantive criminal law

[30] Miranda v. Arizona, 384 U.S. 436 (1966).

[31] Dixon, *supra* note 21, at 91; Jill Hunter et al., *The Trial* (2015); Paul Roberts & Adrian Zuckerman, *Criminal Evidence* (2d ed. 2010).

[32] Burton et al., *supra* note 5; Leo, *supra* note 7.

toward requiring proof of subjective intention and police use of interrogation in order to obtain confessions.[33]

There are a number of intrinsic limitations stemming from the nature of the judicial function and the actual (rather than the rhetorical) position of judges in the criminal process. Judicial power focuses on the regulation of court proceedings. A court can regulate how its processes are used and judges can rule on material brought before them, but the criminal process is constructed around avoidance of court proceedings. If Anglo-American criminal justice has a defining characteristic, it is that the great majority of investigations end in guilty pleas, which are administratively processed rather than judicially tested.[34] There are multiple pressures on suspects and defendants to confess and plead guilty, and consequences for not doing so promptly. Equally, interrogators and prosecutors are constrained in their dealings with suspects by the need to ensure admissibility of confessions.

Second, courts cannot ensure the implementation of changes that they recommend or rule as necessary. The dominance of executive-controlled legislatures in contemporary states makes most judges take a realistically modest view of what they can achieve. For example, in a crucial decision by Australia's High Court, Justices Mason and Brennan refused to interpret the common law so as to provide authority for police to detain suspects for questioning, arguing that it was the legislature's responsibility to deal with such matters both as a matter of constitutional principle and because it "is able—as the courts are not—to prescribe some safeguards which might ameliorate the risk of unconscionable pressure being applied to persons under interrogation."[35]

As a mode of positive, prospective regulation, judicial control is confined by the vagaries of the case law process. Judges have to wait for a case to come before them. In criminal processes characterized by heavy reliance on guilty pleas and financial as well as legal barriers to appeals, an appropriate vehicle for an attempt at judicial regulation of interrogation may not come along. When it does, any judicial interest in regulating police may be tempered by the prospect of acquitting or allowing an appeal by someone they think is factually guilty. This familiar dilemma can be recognized by anyone other than ostrich-like legal formalists. Despite the persistent complaints from some police officers and many conservative media commentators about judicial liberalism and "softness to criminals," the historical record tells a rather different story.[36] Fine rhetoric about the liberty of the suspect has been mirrored by reluctance to engage in active regulation of custodial interrogation and disapproval of defense lawyers who criticize police. Even at the highest level, courts balance justice in the specific case, the general public interest, and the broader regulatory implications of the issues raised. There have also been serious

[33] Nicola Lacey, *In Search of Criminal Responsibility* (2016).

[34] George Fisher, *Plea Bargaining's Triumph* (2003); Michael McConville & Luke March, *Factory Farming and State-Induced Pleas*, in *The Integrity of Criminal Process* 99–116 (Jill Hunter et al. eds., 2016); Albert W. Alschuler, *A Nearly Perfect System for Convicting the Innocent* (Pub. L. and Legal Theory Working Papers, 2017), http://chicagounbound.uchicago.edu/public_law_and_legal_theory/602 (last viewed Apr. 10, 2017).

[35] *Williams v R.* (1986) 385 A.L.R. 398, 400 (Austl.).

[36] Dixon, *supra* note 2, at 126–227.

problems of deficient communication and understanding on both sides: a striking characteristic of judicial decisions on police interrogation, at least until the closing decades of the twentieth century, was the evident lack of basic knowledge about how the processes of arrest, detention, questioning, charge, and bail really worked. If judges were ignorant about policing, then police were also often ignorant about judicial decisions. The way in which court decisions are—or are not—communicated to operational officers deserves much more attention than it has received.

All too often, the result is frustrating for officers seeking clear regulatory guidance on interrogation. A legalistic slice through issues that are complex and interrelated is often unsatisfying for those whose concerns go beyond the individual case. Particularly problematic in regard to interrogation is the court's practice of giving police broad, vague instructions on what they *should not* do, rather than specific guidance on what they *should* do. Take the key issue of defining "oppression," the category of behavior that will render confessional evidence inadmissible under common law. Characteristically, when facing problems of definition, courts say that words should be given their ordinary meaning, and turn to the dictionary. Doing so is unlikely to be much help to an officer planning to interrogate a difficult suspect. In a much-quoted ruling in *Heron*, Judge Mitchell said that police questioning can be "persistent, searching and robust."[37] But an officer seeking guidance on what this means will be disappointed: "Where the line is to be drawn between proper and robust persistence and oppressive interrogation can only be identified in general terms." The interview must be considered as a whole: "occasional transgressions will not necessarily convert an otherwise properly conducted interrogation into an unfair one, let alone an oppressive one." The "age and character" of the suspect will also be relevant. What might lead a court to determine that "the admission of the evidence would have such an adverse effect on the fairness of the proceedings that the court ought not to admit it" is even harder to predict.[38]

What impact judicial regulation has had on police practice and effectiveness has been the subject of much controversy in the United States. The most convincing interpretation of the extensive research evidence is that heroic Supreme Court cases such as *Mapp*, *Miranda*, and *Escobedo* did not significantly reduce police ability to investigate crime, with officers soon finding ways to minimize the impact of those decisions.[39] However, they did have substantial indirect effects, hastening shifts in police training, supervision, and general professionalism. Leo argues that

> *Miranda* has had profound impact in at least four different ways: first, *Miranda* has exercised a civilizing influence on police interrogation behavior, and in so doing has professionalized police practices; second, [it] has transformed the culture and discourse of police detecting; third, [it] has increased popular awareness of

[37] Leeds Crown Court, 1 November 1993, unreported.

[38] *Id.*; *see* Dixon, *supra* note 21, at 80–84.

[39] Richard A. Leo, *The Impact of Miranda Revisited*, 86 J. Crim. L. & Criminology 621 (1996); *see also The Miranda Debate* (Richard A. Leo & George C. Thomas eds., 1998); George C. Thomas & Richard A. Leo, *Confessions of Guilt: From Torture to* Miranda *and Beyond* (2012); Albert W. Alschuler, Miranda*'s Fourfold Failure*, 97 B.U. L. Rev. 849 (2017).

> constitutional rights; and fourth, [it] has inspired police to develop more specialized, more sophisticated and seemingly more effective interrogation techniques.[40]

This experience suggests broader lessons about potential judicial contributions to regulation of interrogation. Judicial control tends to be distanced, unwieldy, non-responsive. If judges want their decisions to have more positive impact, they have to know more about the world they seek to regulate and to express their judgments more clearly and more positively, and with more emphasis on policy and less on the individual case. (Appeal courts, particularly at more senior levels, are obviously more able to do this than are trial judges.) They should be aware of the need to communicate decisions and to participate in processes that review their impact. Attention should be paid to indirect as well as direct effects.

In 1984, England and Wales took a different regulatory course, introducing a structure of statutory and other rules that provided a new framework of police powers. Crucially for present purposes, the Police and Criminal Evidence Act 1984 (PACE) regulated the context in which interrogation takes place—the arrest, detention, and treatment in custody of suspects.[41] Broadly similar legislation was subsequently introduced in Australia[42] and New Zealand.[43]

Regulatory measures should not be considered in isolation from each other. Judicial regulation will be affected by other pressures, particularly the structure of rules provided for the detention and interrogation of suspects, which are considered in the next section. It is appropriate to point out here that there was a significant shift in judges' approach to the regulation of interrogation following the introduction of PACE in England and Wales. Clearer statements of what was expected contributed here. But a change in rules is unlikely to be enough in itself: in both Britain and New South Wales, Australia, new legislation provided the tools, but it was disclosures of police malpractice that impelled judges into a more critical and active regulation of interrogation.

VI. The Impact of Miscarriages of Justice

Coerced confessions, miscarriages of justice, wrongful convictions, and failed prosecutions have driven change in interrogation law and practice in the UK, playing a major role in some of the most prominent and notorious cases. This was not just because people such as the Birmingham Six were finally shown to be innocent, but also because the perpetrators of some of England's worst crimes have never been brought to justice. This is a vital point: the state fails when it convicts the innocent not just by inflicting injustice on them, but

[40] Leo, *supra* note 39, at 668. [41] Burton et al., *supra* note 5.

[42] Francine Feld et al., *Criminal Procedure in Australia* (2014).

[43] Jeremy Finn & Don Mathias, *Criminal Procedure in New Zealand* (2d ed. 2015).

also because the wrongful conviction usually means that the guilty escape justice: it is a matter of crime control and public safety, not "just" due process and suspects' rights.

The typical causes of miscarriages of justice involving interrogation and false confessions in the twentieth century became familiar. Investigators were under pressure from their superiors, the media, and the public to solve the crime. The culture and organization of the police department—valuing independent, charismatic detectives—encouraged sole action. Investigators (and prosecutors) became committed to an account of the crime too early, thereafter developing tunnel vision and selecting material that confirmed the case theory and ignored or neglected other possibilities. Suspects' accounts were contaminated by police leaking information about their alleged crime to them. Interrogators thought they were much more skilled at their job than they were. Investigators then found what they expected to find, in textbook expressions of confirmation bias.[44]

All of these problems are well known, and all have remedies that should be relatively simple matters of training and organization. Investigators have to recognize and avoid the temptations to back hunches slavishly, to sideline inconsistent evidence, to push evidence into supporting hunches, to ignore alternative hypotheses. In addition to training individuals, the police organization must make itself resistant to tunnel vision by institutionalizing review and sharing authority. Police managers in England have tried to spread responsibility from the senior investigating officer to a team in which, it is hoped, case theories will be more critically assessed. Similarly, the product of an important interview will be reviewed by more than one person. Indeed, the interrogation itself may be conducted not by an officer previously involved in the investigation, but by a specialist in interrogating suspects. While other methods may help to limit the impact of case theories during an interrogation, such organizational change can have an early impact, preventing inevitable, possibly productive hunches from degenerating into inaccurate, misleading case theories.[45]

This is not to say that false confessions are the major reason for documented miscarriages: the Innocence Project reports a rate of around 25 percent,[46] while in the Exonerations Project's collection of 1,900 cases, 56 percent involve perjury or false accusation, 51 percent official misconduct, 30 percent mistaken witness identification, and only 12 percent false confessions.[47]

These probably understate false confessions for two reasons. First, innocence and exoneration cases largely rely on DNA evidence, and so sexual offenses in which DNA evidence is particularly significant are overstated: confessions, true or false, may be less likely in such cases. When the Exoneration Project narrowed the focus to miscarriages in homicide cases, the rate of false confessions rose to 21 percent. Second, false confessions may be more common in everyday, less serious cases than is usually assumed. Gross, the

[44] Leo, *supra* note 7, at 263–66; Keith A. Findley & Michael S. Scott, *The Multiple Dimensions of Tunnel Vision in Criminal Cases*, 2006 Wis. L. Rev. 291 (2006); Dan Simon, *In Doubt* 22–25 (2012).

[45] Michael Innes, *Investigating Murder* (2003).

[46] *See* False Confessions or Admissions, https://www.innocenceproject.org/causes/false-confessions-admissions/ (last viewed Apr. 10, 2017); Brandon L. Garrett, *Convicting the Innocent* (2011).

[47] Samuel R. Gross, *What We Think, What We Know and What We Think We Know About False Convictions*, 14 Ohio St. J. Crim. L. 753 (2017).

leading enumerator of exonerations, suggests that "the most common cause of false convictions, by far, is the prospect of prolonged pre-trial detention of innocent defendants who are unable to post bail in comparatively low-level prosecutions."[48] They do so because those "charged with misdemeanors and light felonies may face months, even years in jail waiting for trial, but get weeks or days—or no time at all—if they plead guilty."[49] False confessions and guilty pleas of this kind must be understood from a perspective that is only irrational to those fortunate to live different lives. The point is captured by Cohen:

> It was less trouble to Brian to plead guilty and get it over and done with, even if it meant admitting to something which subjectively, he felt he hadn't done. The alternative meant the trouble of dealing with lawyers, of being on remand, and possibly having to report to the local police station, above all the trouble of having the case hanging over his head, for a few weeks or even months. In addition, . . . if he was seen by the police to be making trouble for them in court, contesting the case, making counter allegations, then he would be, in his own words "a marked man", the Law would get its own back by getting him sent down for something else later on, and that might mean more and bigger trouble. Even if the case was contested he might not win, and then he would get an even stiffer sentence as a charge against the court's time. And then all the aggravation would have been for nothing. Brian was not interested in abstract principles of justice, but in minimizing the interruption to his real life. Such logics therefore incorporate the defendant's perceptions of the police perceptions of his situation with remarkable accuracy.[50]

Confessions (true, false, or a bit of each) have to be understood as constituent parts of the guilty plea process.

A chastening lesson is that the authorities may have higher priorities than rectifying miscarriages of justice. When apparently thinking that doing so would undermine the reputational integrity of the justice process, some have demonstrated an unfortunately pragmatic approach, preferring to turn a blind eye to police misconduct rather than to admit to systemic failure.[51] This may help to explain the slow pace of reform in the United States, despite evidence that false confessions have sent innocent people to death row.

VII. Electronic Recording as a Panacea

In the United States, calls for video recording have become ubiquitous in the literature on responses to miscarriages of justice. Increasing numbers of jurisdictions require video recording in some form.[52] There are similar trends elsewhere: video recording

[48] *Id.* at 777. [49] *Id.* at 26.

[50] P. Cohen, *The Great Chinese Takeaway Massacre*, unpublished, *quoted in* David Brown et al., *Criminal Laws* (1990).

[51] Dixon, *supra* note 21, 93–97.

[52] Some recording is required in twenty states and the District of Columbia. *See* Richard A. Leo, *Police Interrogations and Suspect Confessions*, Univ. of San Francisco Law Research Paper No. 2017-06 (2017).

is being promoted as the way to counter police torture in India.[53] It is attractive as an apparently objective technology, another in the long line including lie detectors, CCTV, DNA analysis, facial-recognition systems, body cameras, shotspotters, and license plate readers. Often police have initially been wary about or opposed to electronic recording, but become strong advocates for it when they gain experience of its use. All too often, audio-visual recording is regarded as a panacea, a reform that will right all ills by itself. American commentators would do well to pay more attention to other jurisdictions that have extensive experience of electronic recording. England and Wales has used audio recording since the late 1980s, while Australia has done so since the early 1990s. Extensive empirical research has been carried out in these jurisdictions, which should be taken into account by anyone considering electronic recording.[54]

Such research shows that recording can be valuable and effective in improving investigative performance. However, it also demonstrates that if relied upon excessively or inappropriately, electronic recording can be counterproductive. There are two key issues: the regulatory context of recording and its potential encouragement of problematic attempts at detection of deception.

First, recording requires much more than the provision of some technology in police stations. Useful and effective electronic recording must be part of effectively and comprehensively regulated treatment of suspects, including clear separation between the roles of custody officers and investigators during the detention and investigation of suspects. Crucially, regulation must ensure comprehensive recording of a suspect's treatment during detention (and, as body-worn technology improves, from the beginning of contact between police and a suspect outside the station[55]). If, as is common in the United States, in-station electronic recording is required only of the final, often rehearsed, confession, it is counterproductive in giving a gloss of authenticity to confessions that are little more reliable than those not recorded. Useful video recording has to show how the suspect came to make a confession, not merely its utterance. If this is not done, problems in interrogation practice are hidden.

The security of the audio-visual record must be assured. This has not been as great a problem as some expected: technology can deter or detect adulteration. Complete loss of records (e.g., the CIA's destruction of film recording waterboarding and other torture[56]) is less possible in a digital age. Of more everyday significance, what is recorded must be regulated: cameras must capture the image both of suspect and the investigators, not, as is too often the case, only or principally the suspect. Such regulation is possible: the records of how England and Wales reformed their process of custodial interrogation and how Australian jurisdiction introduced audio-visual recording provide useful experience of

[53] Asian Human Rights Commission, *India: Police Modernisation in Kerala, a Model for Asia* (Apr. 10, 2017, 9.15 PM), http://www.humanrights.asia/news/ahrc-news/AHRC-STM-017-2017.

[54] Dixon, *supra* note 6.

[55] Christopher Slobogin, *Manipulation of Suspects and Unrecorded Questioning*, 97 B.U. L. Rev. 1157 (2017).

[56] Senate Select Committee on Intelligence, *supra* note 4, at 332–33.

what and what not to do. However, it is not simple or easy, especially in a balkanized criminal justice process such as that in the United States.

A second potential problem is that video recording encourages its audience to interpret images by reading the "body language" of the suspect. Feeding off cultural beliefs in the power and meaning of images that are encouraged by schlock psychology, people—police, lawyers, jurors, judges—too often make assumptions about their ability to assess credibility and guilt by reading "body language." Reliable psychological research is unequivocal in rejecting this: such evaluations are as often wrong as they are right. Rejecting the widespread reliance on reading body language in the United States, leading researchers have moved on to study how deception may be detectable not from a twitching eyebrow but from discrepancies and contradictions in what suspects say.[57]

VIII. Policy and Training

Learning how to question suspects was long regarded as a matter of absorbing a craft skill, one to be acquired by watching and learning from senior colleagues. An Australian police inspector advised young officers in the following terms:

> Most outstanding interrogators will be able to help you with certain advice, but rarely are they able to define themselves just what makes them so successful in this field. It is an ability developed over the years, coupled with experience of all types of criminals, which enables them to sum up the suspect and ask the right questions at the appropriate time.[58]

This was not a skill that all could acquire equally well: Innes found that "at the heart of police notions of 'the good detective' was the sense that certain individuals had a particular flair for the work. The most valuable skills were held to be those developed through natural instinct and experience."[59] The policing craft has now been supplemented by a variety of training programs.

In a world characterized by policy transfer and globalization, it is unusual to find as sharp a contrast as that amongst leading common law jurisdictions on how suspects should be questioned. While the United States has long been dominated by persuasive and psychologically coercive confession-focused interrogation exemplified by the "Reid Technique," since the 1990s, England and Wales has emphasized the information-gathering priority of questioning through "investigative interviewing." Jurisdictions in

[57] Aldert Vrij et al., *Deception Traits in Psychological Interviewing*, 28 J. Police & Crim. Psychol. 115, 115–26 (2013).

[58] William D. Crowley, *The Interrogation of Suspects*, in *The Australian Criminal Justice System* 419–20 (Duncan Chappell & Paul Wilson eds., 1972).

[59] Innes, *supra* note 45, at 9.

Canada[60] and Australia[61] have been influenced by both. This section will comment on these contrasting styles and on a recent adaptation of investigative interviewing, "intelligence interrogation." Each developed in response to problems: the Reid Technique was produced as an alternative to physically coercive questioning, investigative interviewing to miscarriages of justice and failed prosecutions, and intelligence interrogation to controversies surrounding post 9/11 mistreatment of terrorist suspects. As this section will show, investigative interviewing is now strongly in the ascendant. While policy transfers usually travel from the United States to Europe, in this case, the direction is reversed.

1. The Reid Technique

Training in questioning suspects developed in the United States in response to the interwar challenge to the use of violence in questioning suspects, the "third degree." Notably and most influentially, the Reid Technique was developed as an alternative to such physical coercion, one that relied on lay psychology and professional experience. According to Leo, "virtually all modern American interrogation is a variation of the Reid method."[62] As well as being widely used in the United States, police and other agencies around the world have been trained in its use. The Reid Technique is a commercial product, offered by Reid & Associates, a Chicago-based firm. The commercial nature of the product is vital to understanding the way in which the brand has been maintained, including strong attacks on critics.

The purpose of the Reid Technique is to ease suspects toward confession once investigators have become convinced of their guilt. This is done by methods such as accusing, suggesting possible accounts and explanations of the offense to suspects, avoiding denials, minimizing culpability, and misrepresenting evidence.

While critics point to the lack of research basis for the Reid Technique, there is no doubt that it does lead suspects to confess. The problem is that the accuracy of these confessions is not assured. Despite Reid & Associate's attempts to refute this, the connection between persuasive and psychologically manipulative interrogation and wrongful convictions is now widely recognized[63] and has led to the development of the alternatives discussed in subsequent subsections. Because this critique is so well known, it will not be dwelt on here. Rather, it is appropriate to highlight other problems in the Reid Technique. Wrongful conviction is not the only problem in the U.S. criminal process.[64]

[60] Brent Snook et al., *Interviewing Suspects in Canada*, in *International Developments and Practices in Investigative Interviewing and Interrogation: Volume 2: Suspects* 229 (David Walsh et al. eds., 2016).

[61] Dixon, *supra* note 6, at 174–218; Brian Ord et al., *Investigative Interviewing Explained* (4th ed. 2014).

[62] Leo, *supra* note 52, at 12.

[63] Kassin et al., *supra* note 10.

[64] Weisselberg, *supra* note 24.

A perplexing characteristic of the Reid Technique is its surprising indifference to "the truth" of any suspect's confession. Having already decided in preliminary interview or other investigation that a particular suspect committed the crime under investigation, the interrogator's primary objective is to ease the suspect into confessing by suggesting an account of what might have happened that the suspect is able to accept and adopt. The recommended tactic is to minimize the suspect's culpability or in some other way "normalize" that person's offending, almost irrespective of what was actually done, through "theme development," wherein the interrogator presents "a 'moral excuse' for the suspect's commission of the offense or minimizing the moral implications of the conduct."[65] Some themes, it advises, "may offer a 'crutch' for the suspect as he moves towards a confession"[66] by "presenting reasons and excuses that will serve to psychologically (not legally) justify the suspect's behavior":

> Additionally, the interrogator minimizes the moral seriousness of the suspect's criminal behavior. Blame is shifted from the suspect to some other person or set of circumstances that prompted him to commit the crime... It is highly recommended that the interrogator be prepared to present at least five reasons and excuses to the suspect as to why he committed the crime and at least five additional ways to minimize the suspect's criminal behavior.[67]

While this approach may well produce confessions, it does so at a serious cost to fundamental principles—the commitments that the integrity of the criminal process is paramount, that criminals should get their just deserts for what they have done, and that victims' interests should be taken seriously. These problems are particularly apparent in sexual assault investigations. Reid & Associates provide a long list of "rape themes" for interrogators to deploy, most of which explicitly shift blame to the victim. Investigators are advised, for example, to "[b]lame the victim's style of dress for leading the suspect on" or "[b]lame the victim's actions... such as... rejecting the suspect's advances."[68] While such victim-blaming has been roundly condemned and rejected in modern criminal justice, Reid & Associates *train* interrogators to blame victims.

A clear distinction must be drawn here between the inevitable selection involved in constructing any account and the deliberate elicitation of an untrue account. As noted above, investigators distinguish between relevant and irrelevant information by selecting from a world of facts those that make sense in building an emergent account. What is not acceptable is that suspects should be brought to confess to crimes that they did not commit (even if they did do something else). Although it is not always possible to access full truth, a criminal justice system built on integrity would surely seek to minimize the gap between what actually happened and what the process records. Whilst it might be naive and idealistic to expect justice systems reliant on negotiated confessions, charges, and guilty pleas to take truth-finding so seriously, a criminal process committed to integrity should embrace that as its goal.

[65] Inbau et al., *supra* note 11, at 202. [66] *Id.*

[67] Louis C. Senese, *Anatomy of Interrogation Themes* 28–29 (2009). [68] *Id.* at 219–20.

2. PEACE and Investigative Interviewing

Investigative interviewing, usually associated with the acronym PEACE,[69] was developed in the 1990s in response to the problem of miscarriages of justice and failed prosecutions in England and Wales. These failures were attributed to investigative weakness, including the use of practices drawn from the Reid Technique. The critique of interrogation practice had a strong interdisciplinary and inter-professional character: researchers from sociology, law, criminology, and psychology collaborated in research programs with police officers, some of them notably impressive academic-practitioners. They built and developed PEACE as a method applicable to various types of criminal investigation. The use of PEACE has spread, and variants are now widely used in Europe as well as Australia and New Zealand. Its recommendation as the basis for worldwide standards on interrogation by the UN Special Rapporteur on Torture in 2016 is likely to spread its influence further.[70]

At its heart is a simple, but crucial shift of emphasis: rather than setting out to gain a confession that confirms a case theory to which the officer is firmly committed, the interrogating officer is encouraged to elicit the suspect's account and then to check its authenticity by questioning and by testing it against other evidence. Rapport-building replaces confrontation as the method, whereas information replaces confession as the goal. While officers may not in practice structure their interrogations according to the cognitive methodology of PEACE, more important is the fact that many officers are now trained to replace inefficient and/or coercive techniques with an approach incorporating basic elements of effective interviewing in any context, such as asking clear, open questions; listening to what the suspect has to say; responding appropriately; and treating the suspect decently. Crucially, new role models for the young officer become available: the tradition of arresting on hunches, interrogating, and giving weak cases a run has been challenged by according status to officers who investigate and collect evidence carefully, find ways of working within the rules, interrogate skillfully, and get convictions that are not overturned on appeal.[71]

PEACE was provided as a way of interrogating that would both withstand judicial scrutiny and produce results. Rather than imposing rules backed by threat of sanction—the classic command/control mode—PEACE provides a way of doing the job. The challenge was to provide an alternative to established working practices that were connected to cultural norms and values and beliefs—the imperative of obtaining confessions, the working style of the detective, the expectation that suspects will crack under coercive, persuasive questioning. The toehold that PEACE could exploit was the evidence that traditional practices were inefficient, leading to the conviction of the

[69] An acronym for Prepare, Engage, Account, Close, Evaluate. *See* Colin Clarke & Rebecca Milne, *Interviewing Suspects in England and Wales*, in *International Developments and Practices in Investigative Interviewing and Interrogation: Volume 2: Suspects* 101–18 (David Walsh et al. eds., 2016).

[70] Juan E. Mendez (Special Rapporteur on Torture), *Interim Report on Torture and Other Cruel, Inhuman or Degrading Treatment or Punishment*, U.N. Doc. A/71/298 (Aug. 5, 2016).

[71] Dixon, *supra* note 2, at 164–66.

innocent and the evasion of justice by the truly guilty. This provided an opportunity for a new approach to interrogation to become the standard way of working, making the crucial transition from externally imposed standard to working norm and self-regulation.[72]

3. Intelligence Interrogation and HIG

A significant feature of the reaction against the documented failures of torture and other coercive interrogation in the years following 9/11 as U.S. agencies and their allies fought the "war on terror" has been the promotion of PEACE-style interrogation. A now standard part of critiques of torture and related techniques is that other methods are more effective, even in questioning those allegedly involved in terrorism. In particular, it is argued that interviewers with appropriate language skills, cultural knowledge, and training can build rapport with suspects and thereby produce results.[73]

This critique led to the development of "intelligence interrogation." The High-Value Detainee Interrogation Group ("HIG") was set up in 2009 with President Obama's mandate to develop effective, lawful alternatives to torture and coercion.[74] The high point to date is its statement of "Interrogation best practices," published in 2016.[75] HIG is used specifically for interrogation designed to get actionable intelligence from detainees held under antiterrorist powers. However, a significant effort has been made to spread its lessons to regular law enforcement departments across the United States. Typically, the flow from military to criminal justice has been of hardware, militarizing civil law enforcement. Paradoxically, here we see noncoercive methods being spread from the security sector to civil police. After all, if a method is shown to work in interrogating terrorist suspects, it is reasonable to expect that it will work in those being investigated for lesser crimes. Despite the acknowledged differences, this is realistic because rather than treating terrorist detainees as a group requiring extreme measures, "intelligence interrogation" is founded on the belief that basic principles of investigative interviewing are applicable.

HIG's work grew out of *Educing Information*, a notable essay-collection on intelligence interrogation provided by a group advising "senior intelligence community leaders on emerging scientific and technical issues."[76] A key message was that lack of research constrained the development of good policy. The response has been a substantial investment in interrogation psychological research: the HIG has funded "world-renowned Ph.D.-level

[72] Clarke & Milne, *supra* note 69.

[73] Gelles et al., *supra* note 28; John Pearse, *The Investigation of Terrorist Offences in the United Kingdom*, in *Handbook of Psychology of Investigative Interviewing* (Ray Bull et al. eds., 2009).

[74] High-Value Detainee Interrogation Group ("HIG"), https://www.fbi.gov/about/leadership-and-structure/national-security-branch/high-value-detainee-interrogation-group (last visited Apr. 10, 2017); *see also* Rupert Stone, *Beyond Torture*, Newsweek, June 9, 2015, http://www.newsweek.com/2015/06/19/beyond-torture-new-science-interrogating-terrorists-340944.html.

[75] *See* High-Value Detainee Interrogation Group, *Interrogation Best Practices Report*, https://www.fbi.gov/file-repository/hig-report-august-2016.pdf/view (last visited Apr. 10, 2017).

[76] Intelligence Science Board, *Educing Information* (National Defence Intelligence College 2006).

scientists known for their expertise in interrogations and other related fields. To date, the H.I.G. has funded more than 100 interrogation research projects."[77] This has been primarily psychological research: the interdisciplinary style of research that led to PEACE has been less influential.

4. Takeover or Confluence?

A recent survey claimed that "a paradigm shift is underway across the globe, from the traditional interrogation model, with an emphasis on persuading suspects to confess, to the investigative interviewing model emphasizing a search for the truth and the collection of accurate and reliable information from interviewees."[78] In the United States, there have been two notable developments. First, the HIG claimed a major victory when the Los Angeles Police Department stated its intention to adopt investigative interviewing methods.[79] Second, a major commercial provider of interrogation training, Wicklander-Zulawski, very publicly announced that it was abandoning the Reid Technique and adopting investigative interviewing.[80] The influence of such big players is likely to be considerable: in turn, the change in the United States will encourage change in other jurisdictions in both the common and civil law worlds. As Malsch and de Boer show in chapter 15, investigative interviewing is already influential in continental Europe. The influence of Western approaches to criminal process is growing in East Asia, notably China, Japan, Taiwan, and South Korea. Missionaries going to the East find that their policy seeds grow in unexpected ways in very different conditions and that assumptions of the inevitable progress of liberal-democratic ideas are disappointed. In China, a garbled legislative version of PACE-like criminal procedure perversely coincided with a crack-down on defense lawyers who dared to represent dissidents.[81] Meanwhile, in Japan, sophisticated proponents of the Western approach face a familiar problem of opposition from those adhering to a distinctive, traditional approach.[82]

It would be naïve to think that these changes will come easily anywhere. Entrenched social, economic, and market interests will continue to seek to protect what have become

[77] HIG, *supra* note 74.

[78] Alison Redlich et al., *Introduction*, in *International Developments and Practices in Investigative Interviewing and Interrogation: Volume 2: Suspects* 1–2 (David Walsh et al. eds., 2016). This collection includes useful summaries of the situation in various common law jurisdictions including Canada, the United States, England and Wales, and New Zealand. Coverage of Australia, given its leading role in audio-visual recording, is surprisingly thin. There is nothing on the Asian subcontinent or Africa, which both include major common law jurisdictions.

[79] Robert Kolker, *Nothing but the Truth*, The Marshall Project (May 24, 2016), https://www.themarshallproject.org/2016/05/24/nothing-but-the-truth#.D7clnOPFy.

[80] W-Z Press Release, *Wicklander-Zulawski Discontinues Reid Method Instruction After More than 30 Years* (Mar. 6, 2017), https://www.w-z.com/portfolio/press-release.

[81] Sida Liu & Terence C. Halliday, *Criminal Defence in China* (2016); Marvin Zalman & Yuning Wu, *The Interrogation of Criminal Suspects in China*, in *International Developments and Practices in Investigative Interviewing and Interrogation: Volume 2: Suspects* 7 (David Walsh et al. eds., 2016).

[82] Wachi et al., *supra* note 23.

traditional interrogation methods. Cultural change in police departments will come slowly. There are already attempts to compromise, combining investigative interviewing and the Reid Technique.[83]

IX. Conclusion: Revisiting the Myths

This chapter opened with a summary of myths about police interrogation. The research literature indicates that reality is very different. In the world of everyday criminal process, most interrogations are mundane rather than tense, and suspects cooperate or, less often, deny allegations, whatever police do. Few suspects shift from denial to confession. In the past, many police have not interviewed well, but officers can be trained to be more efficient if they set aside coercive, persuasive tactics. Even though suspects are confined on police territory, everyday interviews are often more socially balanced than is usually assumed. Questioning serves a number of purposes, which cannot be reduced to a search for truth. Body language is not a reliable guide to detection of deception. While young suspects and those suffering from a disability are particularly vulnerable, inaccurate confessions are also made by suspects of all kinds. Far from harming police efficiency, good legal regulation increases it, maintaining confession and conviction rates and reducing wrongful convictions. Such regulation should include audio-visual recording as just one of a combination of managerial and legal controls over investigation and detention.

Finally, there are reasons for unfashionable optimism about the future of interrogation law and practice. Some collaboration between police and academics in this field has been exemplary. If police officers are shown how to improve their practices (rather than simply told what not to do) their response is often positive. They are most likely to respond in this way if they are convinced that changing their practices will not only serve the interests of legality, but will also make them more efficient. Or, to put it more bluntly, if they understand that traditional modes of questioning suspects have led not just to the wrong people being convicted, but also to the trully guilty being left free to carry out other crimes.

References

John Baldwin, *Police Interview Techniques: Establishing Truth or Proof?*, 33 British J. Criminology 325 (1993)

David Dixon, *Law in Policing: Legal Regulation and Police Practices* (1997)

David Dixon, *Interrogating Images: Audio-Visually Recorded Police Questioning of Suspects* (2007)

Gisli H. Gudjonsson, *The Psychology of Interrogations and Confessions* (2003)

Fred E. Inbau et al., *Criminal Interrogation and Confessions* (5th ed. 2011)

[83] Slobogin, *supra* note 55.

Martin Innes, *Investigating Murder* (2003)
Police Interrogations and False Confessions (G.D. Lassiter and C.A. Meissner, eds. 2010)
Richard A. Leo, *Police Interrogation and American Justice* (2009)
The Miranda Debate (Richard A. Leo & George C. Thomas, eds. 1998)
Christian A. Meissner et al., *Interview and Interrogation Methods and Their Effects on True and False Confessions* (2012)
Christian A. Meissner et al. *Improving the Effectiveness of Suspect Interrogations*, 11 Ann. Rev. L. & Soc. Sci., 211 (2015)
Senate Select Comm. on Intelligence, *The Senate Intelligence Committee Report on Torture* (2014)
Eric Shepherd & Andy Griffiths, *Investigative Interviewing* (2d ed. 2013)
George C. Thomas & Richard A. Leo, *Confessions of Guilt: From Torture to Miranda and Beyond* (2012)
Investigative Interviewing (Tom Williamson ed., 2006)

CHAPTER 17

DIGITAL CIVIL LIBERTIES AND THE TRANSLATION PROBLEM

MICHAEL WASHINGTON
AND NEIL RICHARDS

I. Introduction

LEGAL rules must always confront the problem of change. Law seeks to establish settled legal rules to apply in the future, but this goal is inevitably and constantly frustrated by the fact that human societies are not stable. Social and technological changes of one sort or another are a constant. In recent years, the enormous changes wrought by digital technologies—computers, the internet, mobile and "smart" phones and the Internet of Things—have had a particularly disruptive effect on legal rules. While it is commonplace to observe that the law has failed to keep up with our rapid pace of technological change, this problem shows no signs of abating, particularly as new waves of digital technologies—robotics and automation, genomics and "personalized" medicine, deep learning and advanced artificial intelligence—appear on the horizon. These new technologies promise tremendous improvements in the quality of human life, while also threatening ubiquitous surveillance, the end of work, the end of the middle class, and a widening gulf between rich and poor.[1]

Criminal procedure rules, which regulate the line between individual rights and police power, have particularly struggled to adapt to this new world of deepening personal

[1] *E.g.*, Neil Richards & Jonathan H. King, *Big Data and the Future for Privacy*, in *Handbook on Digital Transformations* (2016); Yuval Noah Harari, *The Meaning of Life in a World Without Work*, *The Guardian*, May 8, 2017, https://www.theguardian.com/technology/2017/may/08/virtual-reality-religion-robots-sapiens-book; Yuval Noah Harari, *Are We About to Witness the Most Unequal Societies in History?*, *The Guardian*, May 24, 2017, https://www.theguardian.com/inequality/2017/may/24/are-we-about-to-witness-the-most-unequal-societies-in-history-yuval-noah-harari.

information collection. Courts have long worked to adapt constitutional rules to new technological and social contexts, but emerging technologies may present the most daunting challenges yet. In a very real sense, the future of our civil liberties will be determined by how well we translate them into digital formats.

As Lawrence Lessig noted over two decades ago, when the Web was still a novelty, the Digital Revolution squarely presents the problem of *translation* for constitutional rules. It requires courts to answer the question how (or if) we will translate our hard-won protections of civil liberties into the digital environment.[2] In a broad sense, this challenge has been one of the basic stories of Fourth Amendment law since the emergence of the telephone in the late nineteenth century. Yet particularly since the emergency of the internet, the translation problem has proven particularly vexing. Nearly a century after it was recognized by Louis Brandeis in the case of *Olmstead v. United States* (1928), the question of how to provide fundamental constitutional protections to even the humble telephone remains only partially answered.[3] Translating ancient principles and doctrines to emerging technologies such as the cloud, location tracking, and encryption has proven so difficult as to threaten civil liberties themselves. One way or another, our response to this challenge will become our generation's defining legacy of civil liberties. It will determine whether we are remembered as fondly as the civil liberties activists of the 1960s, or as infamously as the protagonists of the Red Scares of the 1920s and 1950s. More fundamentally, it will determine whether our hard-won civil liberties endure, or whether they fail to survive the digital transformation and become remembered (if they are remembered at all) as an accident of history.[4]

This article explores the contours of the translation problem through four case studies. Each follows a similar pattern. In each case, there is a constitutional rule regulating government access to personal information (for example, the content of communications or location tracking), but allowing it under circumstances considered appropriate. However, each rule was also crafted in the context of its time, in which social and technological assumptions served to place substantial limits on government access in practice. And in each case, technology and social norms have changed to allow substantially greater government access. The question then becomes what to do, now that the technological and social norms on which the rule rested have been disrupted to the extent that the government access is now much greater in practice than may have been foreseeable when the regulation on that access was created in the first place.

Our argument proceeds in four parts. The first section focuses on the origins of the translation problem and the trouble with telephonic communications. Subsequent

[2] Lawrence Lessig, *Fidelity in Translation*, 71 Tex. L. Rev. 1165 (1993); *see also* Lawrence Lessig, *Code and Other Laws of Cyberspace* (2000) (applying this argument to the digital environment).

[3] Consider, for example, the Supreme Court's grant of certiorari during the drafting of this chapter in *United States v. Carpenter*, 819 F.3d 880 (2016) (presenting the issue of whether a warrant is required to obtain months of cell-site location data from a mobile phone).

[4] *Cf.* Jacob Kastrenakes, *Google's Chief Internet Evangelist Says "Privacy May Actually Be an Anomaly," The Verge*, Nov. 20, 2013, https://www.theverge.com/2013/11/20/5125922/vint-cerf-google-internet-evangelist-says-privacy-may-be-anomaly.

sections explore the four case studies. The second section examines how GPS and other location-tracking technologies have stretched the law to its doctrinal limits. The third section considers the translation problem in the contexts of smartphones and the cloud. The fourth section discusses how a single doctrine of judicial interpretation, the third-party doctrine, has threatened civil liberties around the globe.

II. The Translation Problem

What we are calling "the translation problem" is one of the perennial problems in law. Arguably, the translation problem is law's fundamental problem—how do you interpret language written in general terms for one set of problems as society changes? Fundamentally, the translation problem is a question of interpretation, meaning, and legal legitimacy. The meaning of a writing arises from the words of which it is composed and the context in which those words were written.[5] All aspects of a writing's context—syntactical, cultural, historical, legal—necessarily affect the way an author chooses to convey their meaning.[6] Because meaning depends upon context, a change in context will affect a change in meaning.[7] This is particularly true with normative texts, such as constitutional amendments, which must be applied in a context necessarily different from the contexts in which they were written. Simply put, sometimes fidelity to meaning and purpose requires something different than a mechanical application of language divorced from context. Lessig explains this point succinctly:

> If a diplomat is ordered to "be polite" while in Iraq (where belching after eating signals approval) and belches loudly at the end of her meal, it would not be [faithful] to her order to belch loudly at the end of her next meal with the British Monarch, even though (in an importantly impolite sense) she would have done the *same thing* as before. Change here—bowing rather than belching—is fidelity. We all know that this diplomat must *do something different* in Britain if she is to *do the same thing* as in Iraq.[8]

To cope with a change in meaning, the *meaning* of the original application must be made equivalent, or translated, into the current context.[9] Protecting civil liberties thus requires something more than a rote application of language divorced from social and technological context. At least, it must mean more than that if we are concerned with preserving the substance and principle of constitutional guarantees rather than maintaining just their form.

5 Lessig, *supra* note 2, at 1177–78.

6 *See, e.g.*, James Boyd White, *Justice as Translation: An Essay in Cultural and Legal Criticism* 34 (1990).

7 *See* Neil Richards, *The Third-Party Doctrine and the Future of the Cloud*, 94 Wash. U.L. Rev. 1441 (2017).

8 Lessig, *supra* note 2, at 1170–71.

9 *Id.* at 1185.

Sometimes, then, literal words must give way to purpose, at least if we care about purpose. Lessig explains that the Eighth Amendment, for example, prohibits the imposition of cruel and unusual punishments.[10] However, applying that protection in the present as it had applied in the past would require one to find that flogging, a common punishment at the time the Eighth Amendment was written, is neither cruel nor unusual.[11] Similarly, the First Amendment talks in terms of "speech" and "press," but the Supreme Court has wisely interpreted it to bar the government's ability to censor or restrict access to expression on the internet.[12]

If we want to explore the contours of the translation problem surrounding the Fourth Amendment, we must understand not just its text but the context in which that text was drafted. The Amendment's text proscribes unreasonable searches and seizures and requires the government to obtain a warrant supported by probable cause, an oath, and sufficient particularity.[13] But these words, like so many others in the law, embody principles that arose from historical practice. As demonstrated persuasively and exhaustively by William Cuddihy, the right against unreasonable searches and seizures was established to restrain the government from infringing the rights of the people.[14] The rejection of unreasonable searches thus emerged from a long history of "popular opposition to the surveillance and divulgement" caused by unreasonable searches in England, the colonies, and in the aftermath of the American Revolution.[15]

Since its inception, Fourth Amendment jurisprudence has had to contend with changes in technological and social context. As communications technology progressed from physical letters to electronic communications, the protections of the Fourth Amendment have been translated in kind. Perhaps the classic instance of the translation problem is presented by the Supreme Court's decisions in *Olmstead* and *Katz*, in which the Court had to contend with the Fourth Amendment status of the contents of telephone calls. In *Olmstead*, the Court interpreted the Fourth Amendment in a narrow, strict fashion, one that failed to properly translate the principles of the Fourth Amendment to modern conditions of communications technology.[16] It took almost forty years for the Supreme Court to correct this error in the case of *Katz*, in which it laid the blueprint for the modern Fourth Amendment and announced the now-governing "reasonable expectations of privacy" test.[17]

[10] U.S. Const. amend. VIII.

[11] Lessig, *supra* note 2, at 1187 (discussing Justice Scalia's failure to reconcile this discrepancy in his writings on originalism).

[12] *E.g.*, ACLU v. Reno, 521 U.S. 844 (1997); Packingham v. North Carolina, 137 S. Ct. 1730 (2017).

[13] U.S. Const. amend. IV ("The right of the people to be secure in their persons, houses, papers, and effects, against unreasonable searches and seizures, shall not be violated, and no Warrants shall issue, but upon probable cause, supported by Oath or affirmation, and particularly describing the place to be searched, and the persons or things to be seized.").

[14] William J. Cuddihy, *The Fourth Amendment: Origins and Original Meaning: 1602–1791*, at 727 (2009).

[15] *Id.* at 766.

[16] Olmstead v. United States, 277 U.S. 438 (1928).

[17] Katz v. United States, 389 U.S. 247 (1967).

The Fourth Amendment's close association with communications systems dates back to the colonial period, in which the British post office was an important part of the Crown's intelligence services.[18] The Post Office of the United States was first established in 1775 and later became an enumerated power of the federal government granted by the Constitution.[19] Although privacy in the postal system was desired during this period,[20] public opinion did not consider privacy in the mails on par with privacy in the home until the middle of the nineteenth century.[21] In the landmark case of Ex parte *Jackson* (1878), the Court held that the Fourth Amendment required the government to obtain a warrant before opening a sealed letter or parcel, even though letters were given to U.S. government postal carriers for delivery and usually protected against reading with nothing stronger than paper and glue, wax, or string.[22]

The rise of the public's desire for privacy in the postal system was paralleled by the reception to the invention of the telegraph in 1844.[23] Telegraph companies were responsive to the public's desire for communications privacy and lobbied the government to extend the privacy protections enjoyed by letters in the postal system to telegrams.[24] However, these efforts were unsuccessful, and the Supreme Court never ruled on the issue. Without legislative or judicial protection, the existing legal structures could not appropriately account for the realities of electronic communications. Unlike physical letters, telegrams were administered by private third parties and could be intercepted by wiretapping or by obtaining physical copies of them.

The development of electronic communications continued with the invention of the telephone in the 1870s. The telephone networks developed relatively quickly, and the technology evolved from a tool for business to a household service.[25] The lack of meaningful privacy protections for electronic communications came to a head in 1928 when the Court decided *Olmstead v. United States*.[26] Olmstead was the leader of a large-scale bootlegging operation in the Pacific Northwest during the Prohibition era.[27] The size

[18] Kenneth Ellis, *The Post Office in the Eighteenth Century: A Study in Administrative History*, at viii (1958); Anuj C. Desai, *Wiretapping Before the Wires: The Post Office and the Birth of Communications Privacy*, 60 Stan. L. Rev. 553, 559–63 (2007).

[19] U.S. Postal Service, Postal History, https://about.usps.com/who-we-are/postal-history/welcome.htm (last visited Oct. 14, 2017); U.S. Const. art. I, § 8, cl. 7.

[20] Neil M. Richards & Daniel J. Solove, *Privacy's Other Path: Recovering the Law of Confidentiality*, 96 Geo. L.J. 123, 141 (2007).

[21] David Seipp, Note, *The Right to Privacy in Nineteenth Century America*, 94 Harv. L. Rev. 1892, 1899 (1981).

[22] *Ex parte* Jackson, 96 U.S. 727 (1878).

[23] Ithiel de Sola Pool, *Technologies of Freedom* 25 (1983).

[24] Whitfield Diffie & Susan Landau, *Privacy on the Line: The Politics of Wiretapping and Encryption* 146–47 (updated and expanded ed. 2007).

[25] Richard R. John, *Network Nation: Inventing American Telecommunications* 383–85 (2010). While electricity took forty-six years to be used by a quarter of the American population, the telephone took only thirty-five years to reach the same level of use. Rita McGrath, *The Pace of Technology Adoption Is Speeding Up*, Harv. Bus. Rev., Nov. 25, 2013, https://hbr.org/2013/11/the-pace-of-technology-adoption-is-speeding-up.

[26] Olmstead v. United States, 277 U.S. 438 (1928).

[27] Neil Richards, *Intellectual Privacy: Rethinking Civil Liberties in the Digital Age* 139–40 (2015).

and complexity of his criminal enterprise required his home, offices, and manufacturing facilities to be connected by private telephone lines.[28] A long-term law enforcement investigation into his operations resulted in his arrest and conviction for violations of the National Prohibition Act.[29] Most of the evidence used to convict Olmstead was obtained through the warrantless wiretapping of the phone lines used to manage his bootlegging empire.[30] On appeal from the Ninth Circuit, the Supreme Court rejected Olmstead's argument that the warrantless wiretapping of his phones violated the Fourth and Fifth Amendments.[31]

Chief Justice Taft, writing for the Court, held that the government's warrantless wiretapping was not a search under the Fourth Amendment because the wiretap did not require government agents to trespass upon Olmstead's house, papers, or effects.[32] In reaching this holding, Taft expressly chose not to translate the protections of the Fourth Amendment into the modern context. In his view, the Fourth Amendment protected only "what was deemed an unreasonable search and seizure when it was adopted."[33] Under this view, then, the Fourth Amendment protected only against government trespass on persons, houses, papers, and effects, categories that the Court strictly construed. According to the chief justice, law enforcement merely listened to the conversations traveling through the wires and conversations are not among the material objects listed in the Amendment's text.[34] Indeed, Taft rejected any reading of the Fourth Amendment that would provide protection beyond the enumerated objects "or so to apply the words search and seizure as to forbid hearing or sight."[35] In his view, any protection against government wiretapping had to come from Congress rather than broad judicial readings of constitutional principle.[36]

Today, of course, *Olmstead* is better remembered for Justice Brandeis's celebrated dissenting opinion. Brandeis argued that a failure to translate the protections of the Fourth Amendment to the modern context of electronic communications risked eliminating its protections entirely. Brandeis began his analysis by noting the translation problem, one he pointed out that the Court had grappled with since at least the case of *McCulloch v. Maryland*.[37] Recognizing this problem, the Court, he argued, had consistently applied civil liberties protections "over objects of which the fathers could not have dreamed"[38] because the clauses of the Constitution "must have a . . . capacity of adaptation to a changing world." This led Brandeis to address several hallmarks of translation: that normative rules are prone to changes in meaning,[39] that changes in context create changes in meaning,[40] that time and technology can change context,[41] that

[28] *Olmstead*, 277 U.S. at 456. [29] *Id.* at 455–57. [30] *Id.* at 457. [31] *Id.* at 455.
[32] *Id.* at 463. [33] *Id.* at 465 (quoting Carroll v. United States, 267 U.S. 132, 149 (1925)).
[34] *Id.* at 463, 465. [35] *Id.* at 465. [36] *Id.* at 465–66. [37] 17 U.S. 316 (1819).
[38] *Olmstead*, 277 U.S. at 472 (Brandeis, J., dissenting). [39] *Id.*
[40] *Id.* ("[G]eneral limitations on the powers of government . . . do not forbid the United States or the states from meeting modern conditions by regulations which 'a century ago, or even half a century ago, probably would have been rejected as arbitrary and oppressive.'") (quoting Village of Euclid v. Ambler Realty Co., 272 U.S. 365, 373 (1926)).
[41] *Id.* at 472–73.

rigid application of the protections of the past to the present context can be destructive of meaning,[42] and that the preservation of meaning requires translation to account for modern contexts.[43]

Applying that framework to the Fourth Amendment, Brandeis argued that the Amendment should not be conditioned merely upon a trespass to property, but upon a broader principle of the protection of privacy in pursuit of both individuality and political freedom.[44] This was the case because its purpose was to protect citizens against "specific abuses of power."[45] He also recognized that the Fourth Amendment was intended to be a broad protection, focusing on the invasion of privacy regardless of how that invasion was achieved.[46] Finally, he warned that violations of the Fourth Amendment would become normalized in the public's mind if the judiciary failed to preserve those broad protections through what we are calling the process of translation.[47]

Most important, Brandeis addressed with a remarkable prescience the unique threats posed to privacy by electronic technologies. After establishing that the only invasions possible at the time the Fourth Amendment was written were physical,[48] Brandeis addressed the telephone. Unlike the interception of physical letters, he warned that wiretapping had the potential to expose every conversation between the target of the investigation and every other person that the target may call and vice versa.[49] This trespass-less surveillance capability, he argued, made writs and general warrants into "puny instruments of tyranny and oppression" in comparison.[50] Aware of this potential shown by electronic technology, Brandeis appears to have contemplated the invention of something like the internet and cloud computing, explaining that "[w]ays may some day be developed by which the government, without removing papers from secret drawers, can produce them in court, and by which it will be enabled to expose to a jury the most intimate occurrences of the home."[51]

Six years after *Olmstead*, Congress followed Justice Taft's invitation when it passed the Communications Act of 1934. This statute criminalized wiretapping by private parties and prohibited the government from introducing evidence in court that was obtained as a product of warrantless wiretapping.[52] Unfortunately, the Communications Act of 1934 proved to be only marginally effective at preventing warrantless wiretapping and similar abuses. The FBI's warrantless wiretapping of Martin Luther King Jr.,[53] for example, came at a time when the telephone was becoming ubiquitous in American

[42] *Id.* at 473 ("Under any other rule a Constitution would indeed be as easy of application as it would be deficient in efficacy and power."); *see also id.* at 476.

[43] *Id.* at 476–77. [44] *Id.* at 478. [45] *Id.* at 472.

[46] *Id.* at 478 ("They conferred, as against the government, the right to be let alone—the most comprehensive of rights and the right most valued by civilized men. To protect, that right, every unjustifiable intrusion by the government upon the privacy of the individual, whatever the means employed, must be deemed a violation . . . ").

[47] *Id.* at 485. [48] *Id.* at 473. [49] *Id.* at 475–76.

[50] *Id.* at 476. [51] *Id.* at 474.

[52] Daniel J. Solove & Paul Schwartz, *Information Privacy Law* 273–74 (5th ed. 2015); Daniel J. Solove, *Reconstructing Electronic Surveillance Law*, 72 Geo. Wash. L. Rev. 1264, 1273 (2004).

[53] David J. Garrow, *The FBI and Martin Luther King, Jr.* 117–18, 148–50 (Penguin Books 1984) (1981).

homes and helped to shape the emerging social norm of confidentiality in telephone conversations. In a somewhat ironic twist, the failure of the Communications Act of 1934 to account for the progress of technology was paralleled by a series of Warren Court Fourth Amendment cases that gradually undermined *Olmstead*'s strict holding. In *Lopez v. United States*,[54] for example, the Court narrowly upheld a conviction based upon a conversation recorded through the secret use of a "pocket wire recorder."[55] The concurring and dissenting opinions sharply criticized the majority for finding that the secret recording of the conversation did not violate the Fourth Amendment merely because "the device was not planted by means of an unlawful physical invasion of petitioner's premises under circumstances which would violate the Fourth Amendment."[56] The concurring opinion of Chief Justice Warren also signaled a shift away from *Olmstead* by issuing repeated warnings about the danger that electronic devices pose to civil liberties.[57]

Four years after *Lopez*, the Court reversed *Olmstead* and rejected its property-based view of the Fourth Amendment in *Katz v. United States*.[58] The facts of *Katz* are simple: The government placed a listening device on the outside of a public phone that Katz used to operate an illegal gambling business, and it didn't get a warrant.[59] In finding the government's actions to be unconstitutional, Justice Stewart, writing for the Court, held that "the Fourth Amendment protects people, not places."[60] Rejecting the parties' focus on whether the phone booth was a constitutionally protected area, the Court emphasized that Fourth Amendment protections are more properly found where one exhibits the intent to preserve privacy in a way that conforms to social norms.[61] "To read the Constitution more narrowly," wrote Justice Stewart, "is to ignore the vital role that the public telephone has come to play in private communication."[62] The Court's holding in *Katz* can be viewed as resolving the translation problem raised in *Olmstead*; by abandoning its property-based view, the Court accounted for the contextual gap created by the proliferation of telephones and the public's evolving views on privacy.

The *Katz* decision is better known today, however, for Justice Harlan's concurrence, in which he articulated the now standard "reasonable expectation of privacy" test.[63] This approach conditions Fourth Amendment protections on both an actual, subjective expectation of privacy, and "one that society is prepared to recognize as 'reasonable.'"[64] By requiring judges to consider society's expectations of privacy in the present, the rule also requires a contextual analysis of the same factors that defined the Fourth Amendment at the time of writing. For example, just as the Americans of the late 1780s were more concerned with the invasion of their privacy than with the type of warrant

[54] 373 U.S. 427 (1963). [55] *Id.* at 430.

[56] *Id.* at 439; *see also id.* at 449 (Brennan, J., dissenting) ("If a person communicates his secret thoughts verbally to another, that is no license for the police to record the words.").

[57] *Id.* at 441 (Warren, C.J., concurring) ("[T]he fantastic advances in the field of electronic communication constitute a great danger to the privacy of the individual; that indiscriminate use of such devices in law enforcement raises grave constitutional questions.").

[58] 389 U.S. 347 (1967). [59] *Id.* at 348. [60] *Id.* at 351. [61] *Id.* at 351–52.

[62] *Id.* at 352. [63] *Id.* at 361 (Harlan, J., concurring). [64] *Id.*

authorizing that invasion, the *Katz* test helps to ensure that the concerns of modern Americans remain relevant.

In the decades since *Katz*, the rate of technological advancement and diversification has only increased. The most obvious example of this change is Moore's Law, which accurately predicted that the computational power of digital technology will double roughly every eighteen months for many decades.[65] Powered by the exponential expansion of computing power, other digital technologies have arisen and proliferated across the globe at an ever-increasing rate.[66] Similarly, technologies such as the internet, personal computer, and cell phone have facilitated an astonishing accumulation and exchange of data—global internet traffic is set to double from 1 sextillion bytes per year in 2016 to 2 sextillion bytes in 2019.[67] Unsurprisingly, federal and state courts have struggled to translate the Fourth Amendment to account for these new technologies.[68]

III. LOCATION

The translation problem is complicated by the ability of digital technologies to generate new types of information that could never have been conceived of in the eighteenth century. This section examines a new type of information, location information, and how courts have struggled to navigate the translation problem when location information is involved. Accurate, real-time location information can be generated by a variety of electronic devices such as radio transponders, cell towers, and GPS receivers. Beyond providing an accurate description of one's location, these devices implicitly reveal the associations of the people they track—ranging from which friends, family, and doctors are visited, to the length of time the subject attends religious services, and everything in-between. In the early 1980s, the Supreme Court tangentially addressed the location issue in the *Knotts*[69] and *Karo*[70] cases, which held that the warrantless use of a radio transponder to track a criminal suspect violated the Fourth Amendment when the suspect was in the privacy of his home,[71] but not when the suspect was in public.[72]

The radio transponders at issue in the *Knotts* and *Karo* cases had little practical impact on society outside the contexts of law enforcement or scientific research. The limited footprint of location information expanded dramatically, however, with the introduction of satellite-based location information provided by the United States' Global Positioning

[65] *See* Gordon E. Moore, *Cramming More Components onto Integrated Circuits*, *Electronics*, Apr. 19, 1965, at 114–17.

[66] *See, e.g.*, Drew Silver, *Chart of the Week: The Ever-Accelerating Rate of Technology Adoption*, Pew Research Center, Mar. 14, 2014, http://www.pewresearch.org/fact-tank/2014/03/14/chart-of-the-week-the-ever-accelerating-rate-of-technology-adoption/; McGrath, *supra* note 25.

[67] Stephanie Pappas, *How Big Is the Internet, Really?*, *Live Science*, Mar. 18, 2016, https://www.livescience.com/54094-how-big-is-the-internet.html.

[68] *See* Richards, *supra* note 7, at 1464–65 (collecting cases).

[69] United States v. Knotts, 460 U.S. 276 (1983).

[70] United States v. Karo, 468 U.S. 705 (1984).

[71] *Karo*, 468 U.S. at 713–15.

[72] *Knotts*, 460 U.S. at 285.

System (GPS). First made available to civilians in the same year *Karo* was decided,[73] GPS allowed anyone to precisely determine her location anywhere on the globe within just a few meters.[74] Now a standard feature in smartphones, GPS tracking is practically universal in American society. According to a 2017 report by Pew Research, 77 percent of American adults and 92 percent of eighteen-to-twenty-nine-year-old adults own a smartphone.[75] Even though the substantial majority of adults are carrying devices that record a precise account of their physical movements, one survey nonetheless discovered that 50 percent of American adults consider the details of their physical location to be "very sensitive." Indeed, Americans consider location information to be the fifth most sensitive type of information behind only their social security numbers, medical history, and the content of their phone calls and email messages.[76]

The Supreme Court returned to the translation problem posed by location information in *United States v. Jones*.[77] The *Jones* case arose from an FBI investigation into suspected drug smuggling.[78] FBI agents obtained a warrant to place a GPS tracking device on Jones's vehicle but failed to execute the warrant before it expired.[79] Over the following four-week period, agents tracked the vehicle and recorded more than 2,000 pages of data from the device.[80] Jones was later arrested on drug trafficking charges and sentenced to life imprisonment.[81] At trial, the court denied Jones's motion to suppress the tracking data on the grounds that persons traveling on public roads enjoy no reasonable expectation of privacy in their movements.[82] On appeal, the D.C. Circuit reversed Jones's conviction and the Supreme Court granted the government's petition for certiorari.[83]

The translative difficulty faced by the Court in *Olmstead* and *Katz* played out again in *Jones*. While all nine justices agreed that the government violated Jones's Fourth Amendment rights, they disagreed on the appropriate translation of Fourth Amendment protections. Writing for the majority of five justices, Justice Scalia focused exclusively on how the Fourth Amendment applied at the time it was adopted. Justice Sotomayor, concurring, wrote separately to echo the majority's concern for original context but also warned that the modern context of location surveillance imperiled Fourth Amendment protections. Finally, Justice Alito, concurring in the judgment on behalf of the remaining four justices, sharply criticized the majority for straining the Fourth Amendment's language beyond its meaning.

[73] Mark Sullivan, *A Brief History of GPS*, *PCWorld*, Aug. 9, 2012, http://www.pcworld.com/article/2000276/a-brief-history-of-gps.html.

[74] GPS.gov, http://www.gps.gov/systems/gps/performance/accuracy/ (discussing the accuracy of GPS in the average cell phone).

[75] Pew Research Center, Mobile Fact Sheet, http://www.pewinternet.org/fact-sheet/mobile/ (last visited July 12, 2017).

[76] Mary Madden, *Americans Consider Certain Kinds of Data to Be More Sensitive than Others*, Pew Research Center, Nov. 12, 2014, http://www.pewinternet.org/2014/11/12/americans-consider-certain-kinds-of-data-to-be-more-sensitive-than-others/.

[77] 565 U.S. 400 (2012). [78] *Id.* at 402. [79] *Id.* at 402–03.

[80] *Id.* at 403. [81] *Id.* at 404.

[82] United States v. Jones, 451 F. Supp. 2d 71, 88 (D.D.C. 2006) (quoting United States v. Knotts, 460 U.S. 276, 281 (1983)).

[83] United States v. Jones, 565 U.S. 400, 404 (2012).

In Justice Scalia's view, the issue was whether the government's act of placing the GPS tracker on Jones's car was a search within the meaning of the Fourth Amendment.[84] The history of Fourth Amendment jurisprudence, he explained, "embod[ied] a particular concern for government trespass...."[85] Seeking to preserve this property-based conception, Justice Scalia ruled narrowly that the government's trespass was an unconstitutional search.[86] Although he acknowledged that the *Katz* line of cases expanded the Fourth Amendment inquiry beyond its property-based context, he rejected the idea that *Katz* foreclosed a property-based approach.[87] Taking this reasoning one step further, he found that the presence of a trespass in this case obviated the need to engage in a *Katz* analysis of Jones's reasonable expectations of privacy.[88]

Scalia's opinion in *Jones* bears a striking resemblance to Chief Justice Taft's opinion in *Olmstead*. Both justices defined the text of the Fourth Amendment strictly in terms of physical property, and drew analogies to trespass, focusing on the physical in spite of the intangible technologies at issue.[89]

Justice Sotomayor provided the necessary fifth vote to turn Scalia's opinion into a majority, but also concurred separately in what is clearly the most interesting opinion in the case. It is also the opinion that offers—in sharp contrast to the majority's narrow trespass theory—the broadest theory of Fourth Amendment protection, and the one most focused on ensuring fidelity in translation of the Fourth Amendment to new contexts. Sotomayor agreed with the majority that it must ensure that the "irreducible minimum" of Fourth Amendment protection was preserved.[90] However, Justice Sotomayor was willing to go much further than the majority.[91] In her view, the majority opinion failed to adapt Fourth Amendment protections to the clear threat posed by modern digital surveillance of location, including technologies that might not constitute even a technical trespass.[92]

Critical to Justice Sotomayor's approach was her recognition that GPS surveillance not only threatens fundamental civil liberties, but also threatens to do so in a way that evades traditional checks on excessive government policing. As she put it concisely:

> GPS monitoring generates a precise, comprehensive record of a person's public movements that reflects a wealth of detail about her familial, political, professional, religious, and sexual associations. The Government can store such records and efficiently mine them for information years into the future. And because GPS monitoring is cheap in comparison to conventional surveillance techniques and, by design, proceeds surreptitiously, it evades the ordinary checks that constrain abusive law enforcement practices: "limited police resources and community hostility."[93]

[84] *Id.* at 404–05. [85] *Id.* at 406. [86] *Id.* at 404–05.

[87] *Id.* at 407–08. [88] *Id.* at 404–05.

[89] Olmstead v. United States, 277 U.S. 438, 465 (1928); *Jones*, 565 U.S. at 404.

[90] *Id.* at 414 (Sotomayor, J., concurring). For a discussion on why narrow holdings play an important role in the preservation of meaning, see Lessig, *supra* note 2, at 1213.

[91] *Jones*, 565 U.S. at 416 (Sotomayor, J., concurring). [92] *Id.* at 414–15.

[93] *Id.* at 414–16.

This is an important point, and one that narrow textualist interpretations of constitutional doctrine can elide. If the goal of constitutional interpretation is to ensure that the principle embodied in the text remains vital (and admittedly, this might be a controversial assumption to some), then in the process of translation, it is important to take into account the contexts in which legal rules operate. Justice Sotomayor observes persuasively that in a physical world, policing that is legal but excessive is limited by both financial and democratic constraints. Suppose, for example, that the police wished to monitor the movements of dozens of people as they traveled around in public. In the absence of digital surveillance technology, that would require scores if not hundreds of paid officers or informants, which could prove to be prohibitively expensive. These agents, in turn, would likely provoke substantial opposition from the general public, which could lead to either costly resistance or democratic restraint. Sotomayor's point is that this costly physical surveillance could be replicated with dozens of inexpensive, discreetly placed GPS transponders. The relative cheapness of this technology would substantially reduce the cost constraint, and its secrecy would reduce the hostility constraint, on the grounds that people cannot get annoyed about things they know nothing about.

Sotomayor also described how allowing the government to collect sensitive location information threatens expressive freedoms:

> Awareness that the government may be watching chills associational and expressive freedoms. And the Government's unrestrained power to assemble data that reveal private aspects of identity is subject to abuse. The net result is that GPS monitoring—by making available at a relatively low cost such a substantial quantum of intimate information about any person whom the Government, in its unfettered discretion, chooses to track—may "alter the relationship between citizens and government in a way that is inimical to democratic society."[94]

In so doing, Justice Sotomayor echoed academic work on the values that privacy, and particularly intellectual privacy, serve—the importance of protecting spaces for intellectual activities, democratic deliberation, or just play—that are the foundation of a free society, and that can be threatened by government surveillance or interference.[95]

Finally, Justice Sotomayor touched upon an important aspect of the translation problem that often goes unnoticed by modern jurists. The failure to account for these non-trespassory surveillance techniques, she warned, is to permit them to shape the public's expectations of privacy and, in turn, the scope of the Fourth Amendment through the *Katz* test.[96] Although she acknowledged that this recursive effect threatens privacy

[94] *Id.* at 416 (quoting United States v. Cuevas-Perez, 640 F.3d 272, 285 (7th Cir. 2011) (Flaum, J., concurring)).

[95] Richards, *supra* note 27; Neil M. Richards, *The Dangers of Surveillance*, 126 Harv. L. Rev. 1934 (2013); Julie E. Cohen, *What Privacy Is For*, 126 Harv. L. Rev. 1904 (2013); Paul M. Schwartz, *Privacy and Democracy in Cyberspace*, 52 Vand. L. Rev. 1609, 1656–58 (1999); *see also* Julie E. Cohen, *Examined Lives: Informational Privacy and the Subject as Object*, 52 Stan. L. Rev. 1373, 1424–25 (2000).

[96] *Jones*, 565 U.S. at 415 (Sotomayor, J., concurring).

protections, she still agreed with the majority, at least implicitly, that the facts of *Jones* did not require the Court to decide whether nontrespassory location surveillance is unconstitutional.[97]

Justice Sotomayor's comment on the recursive nature of the *Katz* test was criticized by Justice Alito for failing to heed its own warning. Unlike other areas of law that progress more slowly, the rapid pace of technological development may foreclose the issue before the Court has cause to consider it. *Katz*, he wrote,

> rests on the assumption that this hypothetical reasonable person has a well-developed and stable set of privacy expectations. But technology can change those expectations. Dramatic technological change may lead to periods in which popular expectations are in flux and may ultimately produce significant changes in popular attitudes. New technology may provide increased convenience or security at the expense of privacy, and many people may find the tradeoff worthwhile. And even if the public does not welcome the diminution of privacy that new technology entails, they may eventually reconcile themselves to this development as inevitable.[98]

The ubiquity of GPS receivers in smartphones, despite the public's privacy concerns, is just one example of how social norms could be negatively influenced by digital technology.[99]

The thrust of Justice Alito's opinion sharply criticized the majority for failing to arrive at a self-consistent translation of the Fourth Amendment's protections.[100] In his view, the majority's conclusion was:

> dependent on the questionable proposition that [placing the tracking device on Jones' vehicle and recording the location information] cannot be separated for purposes of Fourth Amendment analysis. If these two procedures are analyzed separately, it is not at all clear from the Court's opinion why either should be regarded as a search. It is clear that the attachment of the GPS device was not itself a search; if the device had not functioned or if the officers had not used it, no information would have been obtained. And the Court does not contend that the use of the device constituted a search either. On the contrary, the Court accepts the holding in [*Knotts*], that the use of a surreptitiously planted electronic device to monitor a vehicle's movements on public roads did not amount to a search.[101]

Chastising Justice Scalia's focus on the "18th-century" theory of trespass, Alito found the proper issue to be the twenty-first-century threat of prolonged location tracking.[102]

[97] In an article relying on survey evidence, Lior Strahilevitz and Matthew Kugler contest this claim as an empirical matter. *See* Lior Strahilevitz & Matthew Kugler, *The Myth of Fourth Amendment Circularity*, 84 U. Chi. L. Rev. 1747 (2017).

[98] *Jones*, 565 U.S. at 427 (Alito, J., concurring).

[99] For another perspective on how consumers might unwillingly come to accept a decreased level of privacy, see Chris Oakes, *"E911" Turns Cell Phones into Tracking Devices*, *Wired*, Jan. 6, 1998, https://www.wired.com/1998/01/e911-turns-cell-phones-into-tracking-devices/.

[100] *Id.* at 419. [101] *Id.* at 420. [102] *Id.* at 424.

He criticized the Court for essentially ignoring Fourth Amendment case law from the previous fifty years in applying the iconic *Katz* "reasonable expectation of privacy" test.[103] In contrast, Justice Alito would have held that the government's long-term monitoring of Jones's location simply constituted an unreasonable search in violation of the Fourth Amendment.[104]

Importantly, Alito's opinion highlights the dynamic nature of the translation problem. The idea here is not that courts must adapt to the presence of *a* change in technology or *the* change it causes in society. Rather, Justice Alito's relation of the Court's disagreement in *Olmstead* to the Court's disagreement in *Jones* shows that the translation problem exists at a higher level of abstraction. The problem that courts must adapt to is technological *change itself*. This is the continuous, inexorable change inherent in the interaction between the development of technology and its use in society, against which constitutional principle embodied in text must either be adapted or else wither into irrelevance.

IV. Smartphones and the Cloud

A crucial part of the translation problem posed by the modern smartphone stems from how it enables common tasks and social functions to be performed in new and frequently unprecedented ways. As we briefly discussed in the last section, although the iPhone has barely existed for a decade, over 77 percent of American adults own a smartphone, with 95 percent of adults owning a cell phone of some kind.[105] Although smartphones are still used for voice calls, they are of course much more than that. Smartphones are in fact general purpose computers capable of being programmed for a variety of tasks, as the vast generative proliferation "apps" or "applications" for these small general purpose computers reveals.[106] Equipped with high-capacity flash storage, smartphones can carry thousands if not millions of emails, text messages, contacts, photos, videos, or any other type of digitized information. With the ability to connect to the internet, smartphones are used in nearly every aspect of personal life. According to one survey conducted in 2014, 62 percent of smartphone owners had used their phone to find information about a health condition, while 57 percent had used their phones for online banking.[107] Some of this information is contained on the phone but some of it may actually be in the "cloud"—physically stored somewhere else in the world but accessible through the

[103] *Id.* at 421–24. [104] *Id.* at 430–31. [105] Pew, *supra* note 75.

[106] James Grimmelmann, & Paul Ohm, *Dr. Generative, Or: How I Learned to Stop Worrying and Love the iPhone*, 69 Md. L. Rev. 910, 920–24 (2010) (describing the "generative" app ecosystem). Voice and video calls are the third most common feature used on smartphones behind internet use and text messaging. Pew Research Center, *U.S. Smartphone Use in 2015*, at 8, Apr. 1, 2015, http://www.pewinternet.org/files/2015/03/PI_Smartphones_0401151.pdf. "Generativity" is, of course, a term popularized by Jonathan Zittrain. *See* Jonathan Zittrain, *The Future of the Internet—And How To Stop It* (2008).

[107] *Id.* at 5.

internet. Even those Americans who own older cellphones still carry with them a contact list, call record, photos, and text messages, among other types of information.

The smartphone and its role in society are far afield from the originating context of the Fourth Amendment. In the 1700s, and indeed at any time until the invention of digital technology, it would have been essentially impossible for one person to carry all of the things that could be contained by a smartphone today. Without third parties such as modern corporations or banks, this information would generally be kept in the home. Indeed, the smartphone is so alien to the originating context of the Fourth Amendment that it threatens to undo whole categories of protections. As demonstrated in *Riley v. California*, by combining so many features in such a small package, cloud-linked smartphones put tremendous stress on existing doctrine.[108]

Riley is really two consolidated cases with similar facts. In each case, defendants were stopped by police officers and their persons were searched incident to a valid arrest.[109] The arresting officers seized cell phones from defendants: an older "flip phone" in one case and a modern smartphone in the other.[110] Officers searched the contents of defendants' cell phones without first obtaining a warrant and retrieved information (primarily contacts and incriminating photographs) that was later used to prosecute the defendants for crimes unrelated to their initial arrests.[111] At trial, both defendants moved to suppress the evidence gained from the search of their cell phones and the Supreme Court granted certiorari to decide the issue.[112]

All nine justices agreed that the Fourth Amendment protects the contents of a cell phone from warrantless search, even when possessed by a validly arrested suspect.[113] Unlike the majority's reasoning in *Jones*, the *Riley* Court did not look to the Fourth Amendment's application in the past to enforce that application in the present. Rather, Chief Justice Roberts's opinion for the Court eschewed property-based theories in favor of translating the *degree* of protection guaranteed by the Fourth Amendment into the modern context. Embracing the reasoning of Justices Sotomayor and Alito in *Jones*, the chief justice focused on the capabilities of digital technologies and their relationships to civil liberties.

The chief justice began his opinion by recalling that reasonableness is the fundamental touchstone of Fourth Amendment analysis.[114] The concept embraces the "search incident to arrest" doctrine, a well-settled exception to the Fourth Amendment's warrant requirement,[115] which permits law enforcement to search a validly arrested person and

[108] Riley v. California, 134 S. Ct. 2473 (2014). [109] *Id.* at 2480–82. [110] *Id.*

[111] *Id.* [112] *Id.*

[113] Justice Alito wrote separately, agreeing with the warrant requirement but disagreeing as to the source of the search incident to arrest doctrine and suggesting that the legislature is the appropriate body to address these privacy concerns. *Id.* 2495–98 (Alito, J., concurring in part and concurring in the judgement).

[114] *Id.* at 2482 (maj. op.).

[115] *Id.* Warrantless searches are "per se unreasonable" in the absence of "specifically established and well-delineated exceptions." Katz v. United States, 389 U.S. 347, 357 (1967).

certain property in his possession.[116] A trio of pre-*Riley* Supreme Court cases—*Chimel*, *Gant*, and *Robinson*—define that doctrine's contours and limits.

In *Chimel*, a valid arrest led officers to search the entirety of a three-bedroom home and its contents.[117] In assessing the reasonableness of a search incident to arrest, the Court found that the warrantless search of the entire premises was invalid, but that it was reasonable for an arresting officer to search the arrestee for weapons that might be used against the officer or to assist in an escape.[118] Similarly, the Court found it reasonable for the arresting officer to search the arrestee's person to prevent the destruction or concealment of evidence.[119] In *Robinson*, the Court applied the *Chimel* analysis to a search that led to the discovery of narcotics hidden in a cigarette packet on the arrestee's person.[120] The Court held that this search was reasonable without additional justification because the arrest was lawful.[121] However, this rule was subsequently limited to reach only that personal property "immediately associated with the person of the arrestee."[122]

Finally, in *Gant*, the Court limited the search incident to arrest doctrine in cases involving searches of vehicles.[123] There, the Court held that, except in certain narrowly defined circumstances, *Chimel* did not allow officers to search a vehicle after the arrestee has been secured and can no longer access the vehicle's interior.[124]

In *Riley*, Chief Justice Roberts addressed the question of whether allowing law enforcement to search the contents of cell phones incident to arrest would unmoor the doctrine from *Chimel*'s safety and evidentiary justifications.[125] The government, of course, had a strong argument on the doctrine: *Robinson* permitted the search of small containers found on an arrestee for evidence, and a mobile phone is a container that is approximately the same size as Robinson's cigarette packet. Yet the Court dismissed this analogy as facile, and in so doing demonstrated a commitment to fidelity in translation of Fourth Amendment civil liberties.

When viewed against those liberties, privacy foremost among them, the chief justice quickly dispensed with *Robinson's* categorical rule for physical containers.[126] The balance struck by the *Robinson* rule for physical objects and evidence, he concluded, was simply unpersuasive in the context of digital information.[127] The information stored on a cell phone could not pose a risk to the safety of officers or the integrity of evidence.[128] Although an arrestee's reasonable expectations of privacy are diminished, the privacy interests attendant on the modern cell phone were found to be simply too great.[129]

[116] *Riley*, 134 S. Ct. at 2482. [117] Chimel v. California, 395 U.S. 752, 753–54 (1969).

[118] *Id.* at 762–63. [119] *Id.*

[120] United States v. Robinson, 414 U.S. 218, 223 (1973). [121] *Id.* at 236.

[122] *Riley*, 134 S. Ct. at 2484 (quoting United States v. Chadwick, 433 U.S. 1, 15 (1991)). For example, a "200-pound, locked footlocker could not be searched incident to arrest." *Id.*

[123] Arizona v. Gant, 556 U.S. 322 (2009). [124] *Id.* at 335.

[125] *Riley*, 134 S. Ct. at 2485. [126] *Id.* at 2484–85. [127] *Id.* [128] *Id.*

[129] *Id.* at 2485. In response to government concerns about wiping data or the remote detonation of explosives the Court found that law enforcement could rely on the exigent circumstances exception. *Id.* at 2486–88, 2494.

In reaching his decision, Chief Justice Roberts recognized that a faithful translation of the Fourth Amendment would require a change in the way those protections would apply in the modern era. The *Robinson* rule, he explained, contemplates an invasion of the arrestee's privacy that is inherently limited by the physical nature of the objects subject to search.[130] While a handful of business cards or photos of loved ones might be stuffed into a wallet, a basic "flip phone" might easily store a thousand (or more) of such contacts or photos.[131] Addressing the storage capacity of modern smartphones, the chief justice explained that:

> Most people cannot lug around every piece of mail they have received for the past several months, every picture they have taken, or every book or article they have read—nor would they have any reason to attempt to do so. And if they did, they would have to drag behind them a trunk of the sort held to require a search warrant.[132]

Citing Justice Sotomayor's concurrence in *Jones*, the chief justice also discussed the qualitative differences between physical objects and the kind of information stored on cell phones.[133] Cell phones, he said, are in reality "minicomputers" that combine the functions of "cameras, video players, rolodexes, calendars, tape recorders, libraries, albums, televisions, maps, [and] newspapers."[134] Moreover, the internet and GPS technology standard on every smartphone may reveal an individual's most private interests or a precise record of that person's physical movements.[135] Beyond a concern for the sensitive nature of this information, Chief Justice Roberts also seemed to incorporate Justice Sotomayor's concerns about the recursive interplay between the *Katz* rule and society's ever-evolving relationship with technology. The cell phone's rapid adoption and pervasive presence were recurring themes in his analysis. To underscore the point, the chief justice went so far as to note that "[a]ccording to one poll, nearly three-quarters of smart phone users report being within five feet of their phones most of the time, with 12 percent admitting that they even use their phones in the shower."[136]

Roberts's opinion in *Riley* also addressed the dynamic relationship among technology, society, and civil liberties. In *Jones*, Justice Scalia's opinion for the Court was not concerned with how applying textual Fourth Amendment protections of the eighteenth century would impact privacy rights in the modern era. In *Riley*, however, the chief justice brought attention to the risks inherent in applying the Fourth Amendment protections of even the previous decades.[137] He recognized that the cell phone technology at issue in *Riley* would have been "nearly inconceivable" when *Chimel* and *Robinson* were decided in the late 1960s and early 1970s.[138] Moreover, he acknowledged that the quantity of personal information collected by law enforcement from arrestees a mere ten years prior was not comparable to that which could be collected from cell phones today.[139] "[I]t is no exaggeration," he wrote, "to say that many of the more than 90 percent of American adults who own a cell phone keep on their person a digital record of nearly

[130] *Id.* at 2489. [131] *Id.* [132] *Id.* [133] *Id.* at 2490.
[134] *Id.* at 2489. [135] *Id.* at 2490. [136] *Id.* [137] *Id.* at 2490.
[138] *Id.* at 2484. [139] *Id.*

every aspect of their lives..."[140] It was not lost on the Court that this dynamic trend would only increase in the future.[141]

Finally, the Court rejected the government's attempts to extend the search incident to arrest doctrine with arguments strikingly similar to the majority opinion in *Jones*. Declining to extend the exception to cell phones on the theory that they are merely physical containers, the Court was sensitive to the complicating issue of cloud computing.[142] The ability of cell phones to access data stored elsewhere, even distributed around the globe, "is yet another reason that the privacy interests here dwarf those in *Robinson*."[143] Similarly, the government suggested at oral argument that law enforcement should be able to obtain information from a cell phone that could have been obtained from its "pre-digital counterpart."[144] Chief Justice Roberts rejected this argument as well, finding it "implausible that [Riley] would have strolled around with video tapes, photo albums, and an address book all crammed into his pockets."[145]

The *Riley* case shows the Court's increasing familiarity with the translation problem and its willingness to protect digital civil liberties through translation. By looking to the degree of protection provided by the Fourth Amendment and the search incident to arrest doctrine when they were created, Chief Justice Roberts was able to preserve that protection through the process of translation. Keeping to the framework outlined by Justices Sotomayor and Alito in *Jones*, Chief Justice Roberts focused his analysis on the public's relationship with cellphones, the threats to privacy posed by ubiquitous cellphone use, the dynamic nature of that threat, and its potential to shape the public opinion. Translating the search incident to arrest doctrine and the Fourth Amendment at the same time also shows the Court's willingness to engage in the complexities of a nested translation problem.

Understanding the history of the Court's translative practice is key to understanding how it will address similar topics in the future. The strong signals sent by the Court in *Jones* became strong practice in *Riley*. In each of these cases, the Court also signaled its awareness that digital civil liberties were threatened by a legal theory known as the third-party doctrine. In the next section, we explore the contours of the translation problem in the context of the third-party doctrine and how the Roberts Court might tackle the issue in light of *Jones* and *Riley*.

V. The Third-Party Doctrine

The third-party doctrine, which holds that there is no reasonable expectation of privacy in information given to third parties,[146] was developed in the 1970s. When this reasoning is applied to the digital era, it threatens to exclude the substantial majority of

[140] *Id.* at 2490. [141] *Id.* at 2489. [142] *Id.* at 2491.
[143] *Id.* [144] *Id.* at 2493. [145] *Id.*
[146] *See generally* Neil M. Richards, *The Third-Party Doctrine and the Future of the Cloud*, 94 Wash. U. L. Rev. (forthcoming 2017).

Americans' information from the protection of the Fourth Amendment. In this section, we explore how the third-party doctrine developed in the predigital era, and its impact on privacy today. Finally, we explore how the Roberts Court is likely to translate the third-party doctrine in light of its decisions in *Jones* and *Riley*.

The third-party doctrine is derived from the so-called "misplaced trust" rule. According to this rule, one who confesses to a crime assumes the risk that his confidant might betray him to the police. The pre-*Katz* case of *Hoffa v. United States* applied this rule to oral communications.[147] In that case, defendant Hoffa unknowingly divulged to a police informant his plan to bribe the jury of another criminal case in which he was a defendant.[148] In upholding Hoffa's conviction, the Supreme Court found that the informant was lawfully present at the hotel where the conversation took place and that Hoffa's mistake was trusting that the informant would not betray him to law enforcement.[149]

A few years after *Katz*, the Court heard *United States v. White*, a similar case that added the wrinkle of electronic technology to *Hoffa*'s fact pattern.[150] There, the informant speaking with defendant White was wearing a "wire," or radio transmitter, that recorded their conversation.[151] According to the Court, the use of the wire did not create a need for a warrant, since the recording merely created a "more accurate" version of the conversation than the informant's memory.[152]

In the 1970s, the *Miller*[153] and *Smith*[154] cases established the third-party doctrine as it is known today by extending the misplaced trust rule to include certain kinds of customer records held by banks and telephone companies. The first case, *Miller*, involved a law enforcement investigation into an illegal distillery.[155] Based on an informant's tip, agents subpoenaed Miller's bank for "all records of accounts."[156] These documents were turned over to police and resulted in Miller's arrest and conviction.[157] The Supreme Court upheld Miller's conviction, finding that "there was no intrusion into any area in which [Miller] had a protected Fourth Amendment interest," for three reasons.[158] First, the Court found that the documents were not "within a protected zone of privacy" because they were copies of Miller's checks and deposit slips and were therefore not Miller's property but the bank's.[159] Second, the Court found that the depositor did not have a privacy interest in the original documents because they were "not confidential communications" and had been "voluntarily conveyed to the banks and exposed to their employees in the ordinary course of business."[160] Finally, citing *White*, the Court held that "[t]he depositor takes the risk, in revealing his affairs to another, that the information will be conveyed by that person to the Government."[161]

The expansive rule created in *Miller*, initially set apart from "confidential communication," expanded directly into the context of telecommunications in *Smith v. Maryland*.[162] In *Smith*, the Supreme Court held that warrantless seizure of the numbers dialed into a

147 385 U.S. 293 (1966). 148 *Id.* at 296. 149 *Id.* at 302. 150 401 U.S. 745 (1971).
151 *Id.* at 746–47. 152 *Id.* at 752–53. 153 United States v. Miller, 425 U.S. 435 (1976).
154 Smith v. Maryland, 442 U.S. 735 (1979). 155 *Miller*, 425 U.S. at 436.
156 *Id.* at 437. 157 *Id.* at 438. 158 *Id.* at 440. 159 *Id.* at 440–41.
160 *Id.* at 442. 161 *Id.* at 443. 162 442 U.S. 735 (1979).

telephone did not run afoul of the Fourth Amendment.[163] The case began when defendant Smith had been reported to police for robbing Patricia McDonough and harassing her with phone calls.[164] Without obtaining a warrant, the police installed a pen register device at the telephone company to record which phone numbers Smith dialed from his home.[165] The pen register soon recorded McDonough's number being dialed from Smith's phone and this evidence was used to help secure Smith's conviction at trial.[166] In upholding the conviction, the Supreme Court found that the Fourth Amendment had not been violated because Smith did not suffer an invasion of his property and because the pen register did not record the "contents" of his calls, which would have been protected by *Katz*.[167]

Applying *Katz*, the Court held that there is no reasonable expectation of privacy in the numbers dialed into a telephone, writing, "we doubt that people in general entertain any actual expectation of privacy in the numbers they dial. All telephone users realize that they must 'convey' phone numbers to the telephone company, since it is through the telephone company switching equipment that their calls are completed."[168] Citing the misplaced trust cases, the Court then found that any subjective expectation of privacy Smith held was unreasonable because "a person has no legitimate expectation of privacy in information he voluntarily turns over to third parties."[169]

The idea that the dialed numbers lacked content was criticized by Justice Stewart, who "doubt[ed] there are any who would be happy to have broadcast to the world a list of the... numbers they have called. This is not because such a list might in some sense be incriminating, but because it easily could reveal the identities of the persons and the places called, and thus reveal the most intimate details of a person's life."[170]

Much like Justice Brandeis's concerns in *Olmstead*, Justice Stewart's concerns would prove to be quite accurate. In the wake of the attacks of September 11, the National Security Agency (NSA) began the bulk collection of internet and telephone metadata through its warrantless dragnet surveillance program.[171] When that program was revealed by Edward Snowden in 2013, the government defended the legality of the surveillance by relying on *Smith* and the third-party doctrine.[172] A declassified opinion of the Foreign Intelligence Surveillance (FISA) court shows that the orders authorizing

[163] *Id.* at 742. [164] *Id.* at 737. [165] *Id.* [166] *Id.*

[167] *Id.* at 741. The distinction between contents and other information extends back to Ex parte *Jackson*, 96 U.S. 727, 732–33.

[168] *Smith*, 442 U.S. at 742. [169] *Id.* at 743. [170] *Id.* at 748 (Stewart, J., dissenting).

[171] Plaintiffs' Fed. Rule of Evidence Section 1006 Summary of Voluminous Evidence Filed in Support of their Motion for Partial Summary Judgement and Opposition to the Gov't Defendant's Cross-motion at 29–30, Jewel v. NSA, 965 F. Supp. 2d 1090 (N.D. Cal. 2013) (No. 08-CV-4373-JSW), 2012 WL 12355730.

[172] Glenn Greenwald, *NSA Collecting Phone Records of Millions of Verizon Customers Daily*, *Guardian*, June 6, 2013, https://www.theguardian.com/world/2013/jun/06/nsa-phone-records-verizon-court-order; Administration White Paper: Bulk Collection of Telephone Metadata Under Section 215 of the USA PATRIOT Act 19–20 (2013) [hereinafter White Paper], *available at* https://www.eff.org/document/administration-white-paper-section-215-patriot-act.

the bulk collection of metadata relied on similar justifications.[173] In reviewing one such authorization, the FISA court held that "where one individual does not have a Fourth Amendment interest, grouping together a large number of similarly situated individuals cannot result in a Fourth Amendment interest springing into existence. . . ."[174]

In the government's opinion, "if any Fourth Amendment privacy interests were implicated by collection of telephony metadata . . . it would be minimal."[175] However, the argument that metadata is less sensitive than "content" is entirely unpersuasive, even to the NSA. According to the NSA's former general counsel "[m]etadata absolutely tells you everything about a person's life . . . if you have enough metadata you don't really need content."[176] Indeed, even Steven Sachs, the Maryland attorney general who argued the state's case in *Smith*, disagrees with this justification. In an interview with *WIRED* magazine a few years ago, Sachs explained that *Smith* "was a routine robbery case. The circumstances are radically different today. There wasn't anything remotely [like] a massive surveillance of citizens' phone calls or communications. . . . [I]n my personal view, [it] is a bridge too far. It certainly wasn't contemplated by those involved in *Smith*."[177]

More concretely, a 2016 study conducted by researchers at Stanford University found that cell phone metadata could reveal highly detailed and sensitive information about the average citizen.[178] Analyzing only the numbers, times, and lengths of communications, researchers were able to determine a wealth of information about the participants, including their identities, details of chronic health conditions, romantic and platonic relationships, religious affiliations, drug use habits, and the ownership of firearms.[179] Indeed, the study found that metadata was so accurate that it could provide "Facebook-quality relationship inferences."[180] This study clearly shows that the third-party doctrine poses an existential threat to the Fourth Amendment in the digital age.

The danger posed by the third-party doctrine has not gone unnoticed by the Roberts Court. In *Jones*, Justice Sotomayor recognized the threat and expressly called for the third-party doctrine to be revisited.[181] Sotomayor found the idea that an individual has no expectation of privacy in information voluntarily disclosed to third parties to be "ill-suited to the digital age" given the wealth of information that must be given to third parties in the course of everyday life. Truly, mere participation in modern life requires one to communicate over the internet. Modern society also requires vast amounts of personal information to be stored with or sent through third parties—from banking and medical records to internet history, cell site location information, educational

[173] *In re* Application of the Federal Bureau of Investigation for an Order Requiring the Production of Tangible Things from [Redacted], No. BR 13-109 (FISA Ct. Aug. 29, 2013), *available at* https://www.wired.com/images_blogs/threatlevel/2013/09/br13-09-primary-order.pdf.

[174] *Id.* at 9.

[175] White Paper, *supra* note 172, at 21.

[176] Alan Rusbridger, *The Snowden Leaks and the Public*, *N.Y. Rev. Books*, Nov. 21, 2013.

[177] David Kravetz, *How a Purse Snatching Led to the Legal Justification for NSA Domestic Spying*, *Wired*, Oct. 2, 2013, https://www.wired.com/2013/10/nsa-smith-purse-snatching/.

[178] Jonathan Mayer et al., *Evaluating the Privacy Properties of Telephone Metadata*, 113 (20) Proc. of the Nat'l Acad. of Sci. of the U.S. 5536 (2016), http://www.pnas.org/content/113/20/5536.full#fn-13.

[179] *Id.*

[180] *Id.*

[181] United States v. Jones, 565 U.S. 400, 417–18 (2012) (Sotomayor, J., concurring).

records, purchase history, cloud storage, and more. Given the progress of technological development and adoption, this argument will only gain weight over time.

Citing to the dissenting opinions in *Smith*, Justice Sotomayor rejected the claim that privacy requires secrecy.[182] Going further, she warned that unfettered surveillance "evades the ordinary checks that constrain abusive law enforcement practices[:] limited police resources and community hostility."[183] Without reform, Justice Sotomayor argued that unchecked surveillance risked "alter[ing] the relationship between citizen and government in a way that is inimical to democratic society."[184]

In *Riley*, Chief Justice Roberts did not directly address the third-party doctrine but did signal a shift away from its reasoning.[185] For example, Roberts rejected the argument that information that could have been obtained in nondigital form should be obtainable in digital form. "[T]he fact that a search in the pre-digital era could have turned up a photograph or two in a wallet," he wrote "does not justify a search of thousands of photos in a digital gallery. The fact that someone could have tucked a paper bank statement in a pocket does not justify a search of every bank statement from the last five years."[186] This argument is in some tension with the FISA court's reasoning that drew no distinction between the search and seizure of one instance of one American's metadata and the search and seizure of all Americans' metadata.[187]

The chief justice also rejected the government's position at oral argument in *Riley* that law enforcement could develop methods of searching the data stored on a cell phone while avoiding data stored on the cloud.[188] If the third-party doctrine actually reached that information, then there should have been no objection to its being searched. The lack of dissent on this issue suggests that a majority of justices would interpret the third-party doctrine as being significantly narrower than the government has claimed.

Although the Court appears ready to translate the third-party doctrine to account for digital technology, it is unclear what that translation might look like. The scope of Fourth Amendment protection at the time of its drafting and ratification covered the vast majority of a person's information. And there were few third parties at which personal information was stored. Similarly, the colonial and post-revolutionary focus on the privacy of correspondence shows that privacy was not conditioned upon absolute secrecy.[189] Today, everyday life requires substantial amounts of information to be stored with third parties of all kinds despite the fact that Americans consider much of that information to be of the most sensitive kind. Under these circumstances, translating the third-party doctrine's hard-line rule is unlikely to yield a satisfactory balance from the government's perspective.

[182] *Id.* at 418.

[183] *Id.* at 416 (quoting Illinois v. Lidster, 540 U.S. 419, 426 (2004)) (quotation marks omitted).

[184] *Id.* (quoting United States v. Cuevas-Perez, 640 F.3d 272, 285 (7th Cir. 2011) (Flaum, J., concurring)).

[185] Riley v. California, 134 S. Ct. 2473 (2014).

[186] *Id.* at 2493.

[187] *In re* Application of the Federal Bureau of Investigation for an Order Requiring the Production of Tangible Things from [Redacted], No. BR 13-109, at 9 (FISA Ct. Aug. 29, 2013), *available at* https://www.wired.com/images_blogs/threatlevel/2013/09/br13-09-primary-order.pdf.

[188] *Riley*, 134 S. Ct. at 2493.

[189] *See* Richards & Solove, *supra* note 20, at 123.

In *Riley*, for example, Justice Alito criticized the Court's holding for "lead[ing] to anomalies," but admitted that he could "not see a workable alternative."[190] Creating a more nuanced rule for the technology at issue, he argued, would take "many cases and many years" to craft, and could not account for the technological and social change that took place in the meantime.[191] As noted by Chief Justice Roberts, the cost of privacy may fall on the government in the form of the warrant requirement.[192]

VI. Translation in the European Union

The translation problem will arise in any legal system where the text of a law was written in a context different than the one in which it is applied. In the United States, the problem of translating the Fourth Amendment to account for technological change is made difficult by the age of its text, the structure of the constitutional system, and the interpretative practices of U.S. judges, particularly the commitment to originalism. Even in systems such as the European Union, in which the language of its civil liberties is substantially newer and in which a more liberal style of interpretation is used, technological change has caused substantial social disruption, which will in turn inevitably create problems of translation.

As we have seen, the scope of Fourth Amendment protection was comprehensive in the late 1780s, but even its well-worded standard could not account for more than two hundred years of technological change. Like virtually all of the rights guaranteed by the U.S. Constitution, the Fourth Amendment is enforceable against the government but not against private actors. Structurally, these rights exist independently from one another, are subject to few qualifications, and are notoriously difficult to amend.

American civil liberties are also difficult to change by interpretation. Judges are reluctant to curtail civil liberties or to qualify them when compared against other rights or interests. For example, freedom of speech is a constitutional right in the United States, but there is no fundamental constitutional right of privacy or data protection enforceable against private actors. Thus, when the First Amendment right of free speech conflicts with harm caused by the disclosure of private facts, American courts do not seek to strike a "balance" between the two as coequal rights. Rather, the court will "measure" the competing interest "against a fixed constitutional yardstick, with any verdicts that do not measure up thrown out as unconstitutional."[193] The difficulty of changing civil liberties through interpretation is compounded by judicial commitments to originalism, which are shared to a greater or lesser extent across the political spectrum, though they

[190] *Riley*, 134 S. Ct. at 2497 (Alito, J., concurring). [191] *Id.* [192] *Id.* at 2493 (maj. op.).

[193] Kirsty Hughes & Neil M. Richards, *The Atlantic Divide on Privacy and Free Speech*, in *Comparative Defamation and Privacy Law* 7 (Andrew T. Kenyon ed., 2015).

are more common and likely to be stricter among judges who identify as judicial minimalists or conservatives.

One source of privacy protection in European law is the European Convention on Human Rights (ECHR).[194] Unlike the American constitutional system, the ECHR entered into force in the 1950s and provides Europeans with fundamental rights enforceable against the government and against private actors. Also unlike the American system, each of the fundamental rights provided by the ECHR must be balanced equally against other competing rights and interests.[195] The ECHR was followed by the Charter of Fundamental Rights of the European Union (the "Charter"), a largely similar treaty adopted in 2009 as a source of fundamental rights in the EU.[196]

To balance the rights provided by the ECHR and the Charter, European judges use a flexible method of interpretation often referred to as "dynamic."[197] When balancing the ECHR Article 8 right to privacy[198] against the Article 10 right to freedom of expression,[199] for example, the European Court of Human Rights deploys a multifactor test.[200] However, Article 8's relative youth and the dynamic nature of its interpretation has not insulated it from the translation problem. By the 1980s, the progress of computer technology forced the Council of Europe to adopt resolutions protecting Europeans' personal data and fundamental rights.[201]

In 1995, the newly formed European Union adopted the Data Protection Directive (the "Directive") in an effort to bolster the fundamental rights established in the ECHR and to regulate the processing of personal data.[202] To fulfill this purpose, the Directive provides individuals with rights enforceable against entities that control the processing of the individual's personal data ("Controllers").[203] For example, Article 12 provides individuals with the right to access data about themselves held by Controllers, while Article 14 provides individuals with the right to enjoin Controllers from processing their personal data.[204]

Although the Directive has certainly been successful as a legal instrument protecting the fundamental right of privacy, the mass adoption of personal computing and the advent of the internet undermined the strength of its language. The Directive was

[194] Convention for the Protection of Human Rights and Fundamental Freedoms, Nov. 4, 1950, 213 UNTS 221, in force Sept. 3, 1953, art. 8 [hereinafter ECHR].

[195] *Id.*

[196] Charter of Fundamental Rights of the European Union, Oct. 26, 2012, O.J. 2012 (C 326)391 [hereinafter Charter].

[197] *See, e.g.*, Société Colas Est and Others v. France, App. No. 37971/97, Eur. Ct. H.R., Apr. 16, 2002, at 41 (2002).

[198] ECHR, *supra* note 194.

[199] *Id.* at art. 10.

[200] Hughes & Richards, *supra* note 193, at 12.

[201] Convention for the Protection of Individuals with Regard to Automatic Processing of Personal Data, Jan. 28, 1981, E.T.S. No. 108, pmbl. [hereinafter Convention 108].

[202] *Id.*; Directive 95/46/EC of the European Parliament and of the Council of 24 October 1995 on the Protection of Individuals with Regard to the Processing of Personal Data and on the Free Movement of Such Data, 1995 O.J. (L 281) 31, at rec. 1–11 [hereinafter DPD].

[203] *Id.* at art. 12–15.

[204] DPD, *supra* note 202, at art. 12, 14.

written at a time when information about individuals was often stored in analog form and became more difficult to find over time. In the digital age, however, information uploaded to the internet is easily located through search engines such as Google, and can rarely be removed. The permanence of and ease of access to information on the internet precipitated the European Court of Justice's (ECJ) landmark opinion *Google Spain SL v. AEPD and Mario Costeja González*.[205]

In 2010, Mr. Costeja Gonzalez lodged a complaint with the Spanish data protection authority, Agencia Española de Protección de Datos (AEPD), regarding a 1998 newspaper article announcing the forced sale of a property he once owned.[206] The complaint sought to force the newspaper to delete the article from the internet and to prevent that information from being discoverable on Google's search engine.[207] AEPD denied the complaint against the newspaper but upheld the complaint against Google on the theory that search engines are Controllers subject to Articles 12 and 14 of the Directive. The issue, known as the right to be forgotten, was referred to the ECJ, the final arbiter of EU law, including the Directive and the Charter.

Quickly finding search engines to be "Controllers" within the meaning of the Directive,[208] the court addressed the right to be forgotten. Finding for AEPD, the ECJ translated the Directive to provide the degree of protection guaranteed by Articles 7 (respect for private and family life) and 8 (protection of personal data) of the Charter.[209] In the ECJ's view, the Article 7 and 8 fundamental rights are, "as a rule," greater than a search engine's economic interest in listing the data or in the general public's right to information.[210]

Although the examples of the translation problem explored earlier in this chapter arose in the legal system of the United States, the *Google Spain* case reveals that this problem can arise in other legal systems as well. Notice how this case also has all of the hallmarks of a classic translation problem that we noted at the outset of our analysis. We had first a fundamental rule regulating access to personal information (in this case, embodied in the Directive). This rule was of course crafted in the context of its time, in this case, the days of the very early internet, long before search engines, social media, or ubiquitous smartphones throughout European society. Like other cases, social and technological norms have changed to allow substantially greater access to information, in this case, long-archived notices in newspapers. The question confronting the ECJ became what to do, now that the technological and social norms on which the rule rested have been disrupted to the extent that the access to information was now much greater in practice than may have been foreseeable when the regulation on that access was created in the first place.[211]

[205] Google Spain SL, Google Inc. v. Agencia Española de Protección de Datos, Mario Costeja Gonzalez, C-131/12 (2014).

[206] *Id.* at 6. [207] *Id.* [208] *Id.* at 10.

[209] *Id.* at 19. [210] *Id.* at 20.

[211] There is one salient difference between the American cases and *Google Spain*, which is that the American cases have all involved government access, while the *Google Spain* involved public access by private actors as well as the government. But since European fundamental rights are broader than rights

In the *Google Spain* case, the ECJ translated the general guarantees of the Directive into a form of the "right to be forgotten" (or at least delisted by a search engine) in certain circumstances. This was the case even though neither the Charter nor the Directive expressed such a right in their texts; the implicit right to be forgotten, the ECJ suggested, was necessary to effectuate (we would say "translate") those rights into the new technological context of a highly searchable internet. Whether this is a faithful or effective translation of those rights is, of course, an interpretive question, but it is interesting to note that the right to be forgotten will not remain limited to search engines for long. In May 2018, the Directive was superseded by the substantially stronger General Data Protection Regulation (GDPR).[212] Unlike the Directive, the GDPR codifies the right to be forgotten and expands its application to any Controller of personal data.[213] And the translative process will no doubt continue under the GDPR.

VII. Conclusion

In his opinion in *Olmstead*, Justice Brandeis eloquently expressed what we have called the translation problem:

> Time works changes, brings into existence new conditions and purposes. Therefore, a principle, to be vital, must be capable of wider application than the mischief which gave it birth. This is peculiarly true of constitutions. They are not ephemeral enactments, designed to meet passing occasions. They are, to use the words of Chief Justice Marshall, "designed to approach immortality as nearly as human institutions can approach it." The future is their care, and provision for events of good and bad tendencies of which no prophecy can be made. In the application of a constitution, therefore, our contemplation cannot be only of what has been, but of what may be. Under any other rule, a constitution would indeed be as easy of application as it would be deficient in efficacy and power. Its general principles would have little value, and be converted by precedent into impotent and lifeless formulas. Rights declared in words might be lost in reality.[214]

Almost a century after he drafted those dissenting words, as the information revolution washes over our society and its legal system in earnest, Brandeis's prophesy (for lack of a

protected under the U.S. Constitution and extend to private actors (or put another way, the government's failure to protect fundamental rights against deprivation by private actors), we do not consider this difference to be significant to the larger claim we are making about the pervasiveness of the translation problem, particularly in the context of digital technologies.

[212] Regulation (EU) 2016/679 of the European Parliament and of the Council of 27 April 2016 on the Protection of Natural Persons with Regard to the Processing of Personal Data and on the Free Movement of Such Data, and Repealing Directive 95/26/EC (General Data Protection Regulation), 2016 O.J. (L119) 1.

[213] *Id.* at art. 17.

[214] Olmstead v. United States, 277 U.S. 438, 472–73 (1928) (Brandeis, J., dissenting).

better word) is more vital than ever. The assumptions on which many of our legal doctrines have rested—assumptions of tangibility, of physicality, and of limited surveillance resources—have been increasingly undermined by the information technologies that permit police surveillance in ways that have never before been imaginable, much less possible. This is a particular problem for Fourth Amendment law, but it is also a general problem. The challenge for our legal system will be whether the principles of constitutional criminal procedure endure by becoming translated to new contexts, or whether they remain rooted in and limited by the problems of the past. At stake is nothing less than whether our constitutional rules remain faithful to the principles that animated them, or whether they become little more than parchment barriers to government encroachments upon those principles.

References

William J. Cuddihy, *The Fourth Amendment: Origins and Original Meaning: 1602–1791* (2009)

Whitfield Diffie & Susan Landau, *Privacy on the Line: The Politics of Wiretapping and Encryption* (updated and expanded ed. 2007)

Kirsty Hughes & Neil M. Richards, *The Atlantic Divide on Privacy and Free Speech*, in *Comparative Defamation and Privacy Law* 7 (Andrew T. Kenyon ed., 2015)

Lawrence Lessig, *Fidelity in Translation*, 71 Tex. L. Rev. 1165 (1993)

James Boyd White, *Justice as Translation: An Essay in Cultural and Legal Criticism* (1990)

CHAPTER 18

PROSECUTION-LED INVESTIGATIONS AND MEASURES OF PROCEDURAL COERCION IN THE FIELD OF CORRUPTION

MARIA KAIAFA-GBANDI

I. Introduction

Corruption has been historically associated with bureaucratic structures of authority and government. Although a comprehensive approach to corruption would necessarily have to take into account deeper structural deficiencies affecting social reality, one cannot overlook that corruption is closely associated with financial crime.[1] Indeed, those who engage in an unbridled effort to maximize wealth by illicit means often resort to the bribery primarily of state officials to achieve their goal, thereby nurturing corruption. Besides, financial globalization as well as the emergence of cross-border organized crime have led to the internationalization of corruption.[2] Adding to the picture, various international organizations aptly associate the impact of corruption with contemporary problems[3] including poverty, migration, environmental degradation, and especially the

[1] Joachim Vogel, *Wirtschaftskorruption und Strafrecht—Ein Beitrag zu Regelungsmodellen im Wirtschaftsstrafrecht*, in *Festschrift für Weber Urlich* 395 (Bernd Heinrich & Eric Hilgendorf eds., 2004).

[2] *See* the critical appraisal of Thomas Weigend, *Internationale Korruptionsbekämpfung—Lösung ohne Problem?*, in *Festschrift für Jakobs Günther*, 757–58 (Michael Pawlik & Rainer Zaczyk eds., 2007).

[3] Transparency International, https://www.transparency.org/what-is-corruption#costs-of-corruption.

debasement of democracy and the rule of law; this is why those same organizations insist on measures by national jurisdictions, ranging from adopting new criminal offenses to implementing novel procedural measures.

In the context of criminal procedure, tactics such as undercover investigations or freezing and seizing criminal assets enhance national procedural systems and appear to be leading to their steadily progressing transmutation into essentially preventive mechanisms.[4] Whether such development is adequately balanced against the requirements of a fair trial—and more broadly against the central values that should govern a procedural system—is one of the main questions to be discussed in this chapter. The question becomes even more pressing if one takes into account that the scope of special procedural measures originally designed to tackle corruption more effectively is constantly being expanded to include forms of crime unrelated to either corruption or organized crime.

This chapter will focus on the prosecution-led investigative stage of corruption crimes. This procedural stage is particularly important due, first, to the presence of international legal instruments concerning repression of corruption through criminal law, which bring this procedural stage particularly to the fore, and second, to the inherent difficulties in unveiling and proving the facts in this area of crime owing to the complicity of all those involved, which ensures maximum secrecy and motivates the adoption of "new generation" investigative powers.

The problem to be addressed is how to adequately integrate in national procedure systems the measures envisaged in the international treaties on corruption within the investigative phase of a *fair* criminal trial.

Accordingly, the chapter begins by presenting in Section II the institutional framework surrounding the international legal instruments against corruption, in order to identify the basic parameters of investigation and prosecution in this field. Following a brief discussion in Section III of the purpose and principles underlying pretrial proceedings in light of fair trial guarantees, the focus shall then shift in Section IV to prosecution-led special investigative measures against corruption and the challenges in adhering to a fair trial, suggesting an array of pertinent safeguards. In Section V, the chapter discusses the freezing of criminal proceeds, a crucial coercive measure aimed at supplementing the investigations in the field of corruption, highlighting its adverse impact to fair trial guarantees, and proposing certain improvements. The chapter concludes by advocating for the introduction of an international—or at least an EU—framework of special procedural rights and principles to act as safeguards against the particularly onerous investigative and coercive authority employed during criminal proceedings concerning crimes of corruption, as well as other serious offenses; the proposal is premised on the idea that ensuring fundamental rights is a necessary step toward the convergence of different criminal procedural systems.

[4] Sabine Ottow, *Grundrechtseingriffe im Ermittlungsverfahren und nach dem Polizeirecht: Die Einwirkungen des europäischen Rechts auf das deutsche Strafverfahren* 100–01 (2004).

II. The Institutional Framework Underlying International Legal Instruments on Corruption: Parameters of Investigation and Prosecution

A proper starting point to provide a complete picture concerning the prosecution and investigation of corruption offenses beyond national procedural systems would be the international instruments on the repression of corruption through criminal law.[5] These can be examined in turn, starting with conventions of interest to the broader international community, followed by legal instruments adopted by the supranational organization of the EU. The EU avails itself of particularly strong means to bind its Member States to its adopted initiatives, including, but not limited to, those in the field of criminal procedure.[6]

1. The OECD Convention on Combating Bribery of Foreign Public Officials in International Business Transactions

The first international instrument preceding every other in this field is the OECD Convention on combating bribery of foreign public officials in international business transactions, signed in 1997.[7] That Convention is rather limited in scope, confining itself to the bribery of foreign public officials in international business transactions. In terms of procedural provisions, it mandates that:

- the investigation and prosecution of the bribery of a foreign public official shall not be influenced by considerations of national economic interest, the potential effect upon relations with another State or the identity of the natural or legal persons involved (Article 5);
- any statute of limitations applicable to the offense of bribery of a foreign public official shall allow an adequate period of time for the investigation and prosecution of this offense (Article 6);
- mutual legal assistance between State parties shall be prompt and effective, facilitated through: (i) the confinement of dual criminality to those cases where the offense

[5] For a survey, see Indira Carr, *Corruption, Legal Solutions and Limits of Law*, 3 Int'l J. Law Context 227, 238 (2007); Ioannis Androulakis, *Die Globalisierung der Korruptionsbekämpfung* 219 (2006).

[6] For a discussion of the EU's power to bind its Member States to specific policies in the field of criminal law, see Helmut Satzger, *International and European Criminal Law* 60 et seq. & 117 et seq. (2012).

[7] Mark Pieth, Lucinda Low & Peter Cullen, *The OECD Convention on Bribery: A Commentary* (2007).

for which the assistance is sought is within the scope of the convention, and (ii) the exclusion of banking secrecy from the grounds of refusal to provide mutual assistance (Article 9);
- States should carry out either extradition or prosecution, to the extent that their own nationals may not be extradited under national law (Article 10).
- The Convention also mandates the classification of bribery of a foreign official as a predicate offense to money laundering, irrespective of the place where the bribery occurred, as far as the bribery of a public official of the State party to the convention is also a predicate offense of money laundering (Article 7). Although this latter provision is not procedural in nature, it is crucial for the application of the Convention's procedural rules.

One discerns three central axes underlying the procedural rules established by the OECD Convention:

(i) promoting *the principle of legality* in investigation and prosecution;
(ii) facilitating *mutual legal assistance*, which is self-evident considering the nature of the offenses covered by the Convention; still, this particular goal is pursued by rather "traditional" means (such as extradition or the loosening of the dual criminality requirement), save for the attempt to lift banking secrecy;
(iii) rendering the bribery of a foreign public official a predicate offense for the purpose of applying domestic money laundering legislation on the same terms with the bribery of a given State's own public officials, with a view to availing oneself of the broad array of procedural measures designed for money laundering.

2. The Council of Europe Criminal Law Convention on Corruption

The Council of Europe 1999 Criminal Law Convention on Corruption also contains procedural provisions that, albeit limited in scope, are of particular significance in the field of investigation, especially in terms of searches.[8]

This particular Convention lays particular emphasis on:

(i) ensuring *cooperation* with and between national authorities and public officials to provide, upon request, *all necessary information* to those entrusted with investigating and prosecuting corruption offenses (Article 21), as well as to provide *effective and appropriate protection* to those who cooperate with the investigating or prosecuting authorities and to witnesses (Article 22);

[8] OECD, *A Glossary of International Standards in Criminal Law* 13 (2008).

(ii) amending national procedural systems so as to introduce *special investigative measures* to facilitate the *gathering of evidence*, to *identify, trace, freeze, and seize instrumentalities and proceeds of corruption*, and to lift bank secrecy to the effect of permitting competent authorities to gain access to bank, financial, or commercial records (Article 23); and

(iii) promoting *international judicial cooperation* (Articles 25 et seq.).

3. The United Nations Convention against Corruption

The most comprehensive instrument in terms of its procedural provisions against corruption is the United Nations Convention against Corruption[9] adopted in October 2003, shortly after the UN Convention against Transnational Organized Crime.

The UN Convention requires, inter alia, the following:

- an appropriate balance between any immunities or jurisdictional privileges accorded to public officials and the possibility of effectively investigating, prosecuting, and adjudicating offenses within the purview of the Convention (Article 30 para. 2);
- the exercise of any discretionary legal powers under domestic law relating to prosecution so as to maximize the effectiveness of law enforcement measures in respect of those offenses and with due regard to the need to deter their commission (Article 30 para. 3);
- measures on freezing, seizure, and confiscation of criminal proceeds and the property or equipment used to commit the pertinent offenses (Article 31), which shall also extend to proceeds transformed or converted into other property, intermingled with property acquired from legitimate sources, as well as to income derived from criminal proceeds;
- protection of witnesses, experts, victims (Article 32) and reporting persons (Article 33), as well as measures to encourage the cooperation with law enforcement authorities, including penalty mitigation or even immunity for persons offering substantial cooperation in the investigation or prosecution of an offense (Article 37);
- provisions enhancing cooperation not only between national authorities (Article 38), but also between national authorities and the private sector, in particular financial institutions (Article 39), as well as overcoming obstacles that may arise out of the application of bank secrecy statutes (Article 40);
- international cooperation to address corruption, including measures to ensure extradition (Article 44), the transfer of criminal proceedings with a view to "concentrating the prosecution" (Article 47), as well as mutual legal assistance

[9] Lucinda Low, *The United Nations Convention Against Corruption: The Globalization of Anti-corruption Standards*, available at: https://www.steptoe.com/assets/attachments/2599.pdf.

(Article 46), entailing, on the one hand, that the identification, freezing, and tracing of the proceeds of crime shall take place in accordance with the provisions of the Convention itself (rather than domestic law), and, on the other, that bank secrecy shall not be invoked as grounds for refusal;

- provisions concerning joint investigations (Article 49), especially special investigative techniques (controlled delivery, electronic surveillance, undercover operations) as well as the admissibility in court of evidence derived therefrom (Article 50); and last but not least,
- asset recovery (Articles 51 et seq.), which is declared as a fundamental principle of the Convention, requiring State parties to afford to one another the widest measure of cooperation and assistance possible in this regard.

It becomes evident that the UN Convention places particular emphasis on enhancing investigation and prosecution of acts of corruption. This goal is pursued by means of provisions that can be classified in four categories: (1) *encouraging the cooperation* of private individuals (accused persons included) with law enforcement authorities, including measures to protect witnesses, experts, and reporting persons; (2) *supplementing investigations with covert techniques*, and ensuring that their findings shall be admissible as evidence at trial; (3) *identifying and tracing the proceeds and instrumentalities of crime*, which would include their seizure with a view to facilitating subsequent confiscation; and (4) *promoting international cooperation*, which also entails an emphasis on identifying and freezing the proceeds of crime. One of the Convention's main axes is asset recovery, which is also of particular relevance to the investigation stage (Article 54 para. 2, Articles 55 et seq.), at least to the extent it is associated with confiscation (as opposed to measures entailing the direct recovery of property through civil action under Article 53). It is also of note that the Convention includes provisions reinforcing *the principle of legality of prosecution*, to the extent that it calls for an appropriate balance between any immunities or jurisdictional privileges accorded to public officials and the state capacity to effectively investigate, prosecute, and adjudicate offenses within the purview of the Convention. Likewise it calls for the exercise of any discretionary powers under domestic law relating to prosecution so as to maximize the effectiveness of law enforcement measures, with due regard to the need for deterrence.

4. The European Union Framework

Last but not least, the special institutional framework established by the European Union to address corruption by means of criminal law[10] consists of (1) the 1997 Convention against corruption involving officials of the European Communities or officials of Member States of the European Union (Council Act of 26 May 1997); (2) the Protocol to the Convention on the protection of the European Communities' financial

[10] *See* Maria Kaiafa-Gbandi, *Punishing Corruption in the Public and the Private Sector: Key Issues on Current EU Policy and Rule-of-Law Challenges*, in *Research Handbook on EU Criminal Law*, 376 (Valsamis Mitsilegas, Maria Bergström & Theodore Konstadinides eds., 2016).

interests on penalizing acts of corruption that damage or are likely to damage the financial interests of the European Communities (Council Act of 27 September 1996)[11]; and (3) the Framework Decision 2003/568/JHA of 22 July 2003 on combating corruption in the private sector.

The 1997 EU Convention is the only instrument among these that encompasses procedural provisions. These specifically concern cooperation of Member States in the investigation and prosecution of pertinent offenses; the concentration of the prosecution (Article 9) in a single Member State (to the extent possible); the affirmation of a State's obligation to exercise its own jurisdiction in the event of non-extradition of its nationals to other Member States (Article 8); and the transnational recognition of the *ne bis in idem* principle (Article 10).

It should be pointed out that these legal instruments, including the Convention, date back to an erstwhile European institutional regime that allowed the European Union a much more confined space of authority with respect to criminal law. In the post-Lisbon era, however, the EU has done much to promote judicial cooperation between its Member States. Such efforts have gone beyond the initial stage (expressed in the European arrest warrant) to advancing judicial cooperation on the basis of the principle of mutual recognition of judicial decisions and orders. This is evidenced, inter alia, through Directive 2014/41/EU on the European Investigation Order. Member States of the EU also have been called to harmonize their national laws on the freezing and confiscation of instrumentalities and proceeds of crime by virtue of Directive 2014/42/EU. One may conclude, then, that, despite "poor appearances," the EU retains the most powerful procedural tools to address corruption. One example is the European Investigation Order, which enables officials to obtain information on banking and other financial records of a natural or legal person subject to criminal proceedings in another Member State (Articles 26 and 27). The European Investigation Order also enables officials of States other than the forum State to conduct special investigative acts,[12] while the freezing and confiscation of the instrumentalities and proceeds of crime is addressed by virtue of a "harmonized" set of provisions based on minimum rules adopted on an EU level.

5. General Observations Arising Out of an Overview of the International Instruments against Corruption

The broader picture emerging from these international legal instruments on the investigation and prosecution of corruption is delineated by the following crucial features:

[11] This Protocol, along with the PIF-Convention, will be replaced by the Directive 2017/1371/EU on the fight against fraud to the EU's financial interests by means of criminal law on July 6, 2019.

[12] 2014/41/EU art. 28 (monitoring of banking or other financial operations; controlled deliveries), art. 29 (covert investigations), art. 30 (interception of telecommunications with the technical assistance by another Member State).

In terms of the *general principles* underlying the prosecution of the pertinent offenses, the various international conventions indicate a clear albeit reserved preference for *the principle of legality*. This is shown, first, in the desired balance between privileges and immunities against effective prosecution, and second in the confinement of prosecutorial discretion (where such discretion exists) to considerations pertaining to criminal deterrence. On the other hand, those same international legal instruments aim to guarantee adequate time for the investigation and prosecution of the offenses by, among other things, requiring the introduction of special provisions for statutory limitations. Both these features indicate a strong desire *to maximize the efficiency of criminal repression*, a goal openly declared by the UN Convention, which emphasizes the need to achieve a degree of deterrence against corruption.

Turning to the particular subject matters regulated by these international legal instruments, one discerns a tendency *to support the investigation* of the pertinent offenses. The main axes are:

- *sustaining the flow of information* via the cooperation of *private individuals as well as the accused persons themselves*, whose cooperation shall be considered as grounds of protection or as a mitigating factor, as the case may be;
- *supplementing investigations with special investigative powers* aimed at addressing the inherent probative difficulties associated with corruption offenses; these investigative acts pose serious constraints to citizens' freedoms, and are normally designed to address serious forms of crime such as organized crime and terrorism;
- enabling the *tracking and freezing of the proceeds of crime* with a view to facilitating confiscation; this goal is pursued not only by classifying the pertinent offenses as predicated offenses for the purpose of money laundering, but also through ensuring the cooperation of the banking sector and the lifting of banking secrecy; these measures are designed so as to apply the so-called "follow the money" principle, which has become a cornerstone of the fight against financial crime and corruption, in an effort to convey the message that "crime doesn't pay";
- last but not least, promoting *international cooperation*, not only within the EU but also on a broader international level, especially through enabling the flow of information concerning banking and other financial activities, as well as extradition, and the concentration of criminal prosecution within one jurisdiction to the extent possible. It is true, of course, that achieving judicial cooperation and concentrating criminal prosecution to one Member State is more readily attainable in the EU context.

These features indicate that, with respect to prosecuting corruption, the international community is steadily oriented toward *"new generation" investigative measures*.[13]

[13] Cf. Hans-Urllich Paeffgen, *Vernachrichtendienstlichung des Strafprozesses* 647 (GA 2003); Claus Roxin & Bernd Schünemann, *Strafverfahrensrecht* 288–89 (28th ed. 2014).

These measures are generally characterized by the cooperation with, or even the tasking of, private individuals (even the suspect himself), as well as by initiating a covert process that monitors or even actively involves the suspect unbeknownst to him. The aim of these investigative powers is not simply to expose the offense, but to track and confiscate any illicit proceeds. Moreover, given that corruption is closely linked with financial crime, and that the latter very often occurs across borders, these "new generation" investigative measures are supplemented by an *active reinforcement of (international) judicial cooperation* aimed at concentrating the prosecution in one State. Such cooperation is further reinforced in the EU context by the principle of mutual recognition, especially considering the possibility of police infiltration by agents of a Member State other than the one conducting the investigation, as well as by the existence of common minimum standards that enable the seizure and confiscation of the proceeds of crime in all Member States.

The pertinent international legal instruments prioritize *effectiveness*, without due regard to the rights of those involved in criminal processes. One response, at least in the EU context, is that the *ne bis in idem* principle could function as a counterweight to the problems posed by judicial cooperation by precluding a second prosecution of the same offense after a final judgment has been delivered in a given Member State.[14] Nonetheless, until the EU comes up with a streamlined process to assign the prosecution to a single Member State (in the event of conflicts of jurisdiction) based on a set of binding criteria, and unless the suspect/accused is given the right to appeal such resolution of jurisdictional conflicts, there can be no fair concentration of the prosecution in a single State.[15] In contrast, what seems to prevail in the EU now is the "first come first served" approach, under which the State that arrives at a final judgment first is the one triggering the application of the *ne bis in idem* principle. At the same time, the possibility of "forum shopping" cannot be excluded, especially on the part of prosecutorial authorities in the context of their cooperation with Eurojust, causing further concern for due process rights.

On the other hand, one might argue that it is up to Member States to ensure respect for due process rights upon the incorporation of international conventions into their domestic law. Besides, there are widely accepted international conventions concerning the protection of fundamental rights, including procedural rights aimed at keeping repression by means of criminal law under control. These conventions might be regarded as offsetting the invasive enforcement measures. This is all the more true of the EU's institutional framework, including the (now binding) Charter of Fundamental Rights, as well as certain rules derived from the EU's secondary legislation, incorporating a minimum (binding) level of protection of the rights of the suspect/accused. Still, this level of protection is hardly adequate. Indeed, the general recognition of procedural

[14] Martin Böse, *Ne Bis in Idem*, in 2 *Conflicts of Jurisdiction in Criminal Matters in the European Union: Rights, Principles and Model Rules* 129 (Martin Böse, Frank Meyer & Anne Schneider eds., 2014).

[15] Maria Kaiafa-Gbandi, *Jurisdictional Conflicts in Criminal Matters and Their Settlement Within EU's Supranational Settings*, 7 Euro. Crim. L. Rev. 38 (2017).

rights, such as the right to a fair trial or the presumption of innocence in the ICCPR, the ECHR, and the Charter of Fundamental Rights, falls short of a satisfactory level of guaranteeing due process.[16] Besides, the existing safeguards derived from the EU's secondary legislation do not specifically address or affect "new generation" investigative measures, which are the object of this discussion.[17]

It therefore becomes imperative to explore, in the dynamic legal environment of the EU, whether it is possible to attain a mandatory level of protection of citizens' due process rights against "new generation" *investigative* and repressive measures, especially against the central axes thereof, that is, the special investigative measures and those permitting the state to *freeze and confiscate* the proceeds of corruption offenses. This discussion must evoke the following principles.

III. The Purpose and Principles of Pretrial Proceedings in the Context of a Fair Trial

Criminal procedure sets the limits on state criminal law enforcement authority over citizens allegedly engaged in criminal activity.[18] That is why it is considered the Charter of Free People or the Individual's Magna Carta.[19] Hence, any attempt to place criminal procedure in a broader international context should not conceal an element that defines its very core, namely the position it reflects regarding the dilemma of whether to protect society from crime or protect the defendant. European jurisprudential culture has adopted a firm stance concerning this dilemma: the protection *of established fundamental rights* of the individual sets a clear *limit* on state power to repress wrongdoing through penal law.[20]

On the other hand, it should be recalled that the pretrial stage poses a conundrum to all procedural systems. During that stage, divergent interests of both the state and individuals must be balanced. Despite differences between various procedural systems, one might perceive—at least in theory—an apparent direction as to the *purpose* of pretrial proceedings, which is to investigate the facts of the case in light of the *presumption of innocence*.[21] In practice, things often progress differently, reducing the process into a one-sided effort to prove the defendant's guilt. Hence, it is imperative to ensure a status

[16] *See infra* Section IV. [17] *See infra* Section IV.

[18] For a comparative approach to different criminal procedural systems, see Tatjana Hörnle, *Unterschiede zwischen Strafverfahrensordnungen und ihre kulturellen Hintergründe, Zeitschrift für die gesamte Strafrechtswissenschaft* 834 (2005).

[19] *See* Claus Roxin, *Strafverfahrensrecht* § 1, Rn 2 (25th ed. 1998).

[20] Cf. Hans-Heinrich Kühne, *Strafprozessrecht: Eine systematische Darstellung des deutschen und europäischen Strafverfahrensrechts*, 1–2 (9th ed. 2015).

[21] *See id.* at 232 et seq.

that renders the accused capable of defending her position throughout the pretrial stage by bestowing *rights of defense*, and asserting the *principle of fair trial*.[22]

The most sensitive issue at the pretrial stage relates to *onerous investigative measures* that seriously infringe fundamental rights.[23] It is precisely due to this risk that in both the ICCPR and the ECHR, *the citizen is never to be used as an object*. These are measures taken against individuals presumed to be innocent and should thus stop short of punitive purposes; they should merely enable the criminal process.[24] In addition, the fact that they infringe fundamental rights necessitates that they be consistent with the *principle of proportionality*, as well as that they respect *the nemo tenetur se ispum accusare principle*, and the *rights to silence* and *to an effective defense*. Last but not least, the more invasive these measures are, the more vital it is to reserve *judicial review* in relation to them.[25]

On the other hand, statistically speaking, a significant portion of cases in all jurisdictions never actually make it to court following the pretrial stage.[26] This raises concerns about an equally significant number of potentially innocent citizens whose rights are jeopardized during investigative processes,[27] especially in light of a clear shift from crime control toward crime prevention ("preventive crime repression"), deeply influenced by the international and EU criminal policy. A pattern thus emerges where the invasion of fundamental rights takes place under much weaker safeguards.[28]

IV. Prosecution-Led Special Investigative Measures against Corruption and the Challenge of Adhering to Fair Trial Requirements

Special investigative tactics in the field of corruption (and beyond) are undoubtedly liable to severely infringe on fundamental individual rights. Freezing bank accounts, extensive telecommunication surveillance, and evidence gathering through undercover infiltration on the basis of alleged or presumed culpability for a criminal offense all pose threats to fundamental individual rights.

22 *Id.* at 233–35. Cf. Thomas Weigend, *Einführung*, in Thomas Weigend, Susanne Walther & Barbara Grunewald, *Strafverteidigung vor neuen Herausforderungen* 16, 21 (2008).

23 Ursula Nelles, *Grundrechte und Ermittlungsverfahren*, 18 Neue Kriminalpolitik 68, 70 et seq. (2006)

24 *See* Kühne, *supra* note 20, at 261.

25 *See id.* at 263 et seq.

26 With respect to organized crime, see *Münchener Kommentar StGB*, Bd. 2, § 129a, Rn 4.

27 *See, e.g.*, the recent effort to reform the investigation stage in the German procedural system and the continuing criticism emphasizing the rights of suspects and accused persons; Reinhold Schlothauer, *Reform des Ermittlungsverfahrens*, Strafverteidiger 613, 616 (2016).

28 Nelles, *supra* note 23, at 68.

On the other hand, the current state of affairs with regard to pretrial investigations in various jurisdictions is disquieting. Certain penal systems, such as Germany's, face the criticism that the defendant must undergo investigation without having enough possibilities of defense, even though subsequent processes are decisively shaped by the outcome of pretrial investigations.[29]

Procedural systems in Europe vary widely in terms of the organs that monitor the pretrial stage and decide about its product.[30] A case in point is French law, where the participation of the investigating judge at the pretrial stage constitutes a crucial feature shaping subsequent processes. Under common law, the investigation is traditionally assigned to the police.[31]

It is obvious that these differences are deeply rooted in each individual legal order and are partly—albeit crucially—determined by political motivation as well as by cultural factors. It would therefore not be prudent to seek the introduction of structural modifications to individual systems with respect to pretrial arrangements. However, the unsettling developments in a number of jurisdictions with regard to investigatory practices at the pretrial stage make it imperative to seek *the reinforcement of defendants' rights* as well as *a corresponding check over the infringement of fundamental rights of citizens during the investigation*. Such orientation appears to be sustained by the current international legal framework, which tends to influence domestic legal orders toward an enhanced protection of individual rights irrespective of the particular procedural system in a given jurisdiction.[32]

The international legal instruments endeavoring to afford these kind of safeguards include the ICCPR and the ECHR as well as new directives of the EU on the protection of certain procedural rights of suspects and defendants. Nonetheless, even the ECHR, which has helped develop a relatively extensive framework of guarantees (at least compared to the ICCPR) through the case law of the European Court of Human Rights, fails to afford an adequate level of protection of fundamental rights during the pretrial investigative stage. It is well known that, with the exception of measures consisting in deprivation of liberty (Article 5 §§ 2–4), the Convention does not recognize *special* guarantees over investigative measures that adversely affect fundamental rights. Procedural "safety valves" are only "activated" via the case law of the ECtHR, which requires the

[29] Cf. Richard Soyer & Stefan Schumann, *Verteidigungsrechte im Vorverfahren*, Strafverteidiger 495, 496 (2012).

[30] *See also* Bernd Schünemann, *Zur Reform des strafprozessualen Ermittlungverfahrens in Europa: Kontradiktorische Ausbalancierung statt Partizipation*, in *Gedächtnisschrift für Th. Vogel* 81, 91–92 (2004).

[31] *See* Kühne, *supra* note 20, at 720–21, 742–45, Thomas Weigend, *Unverzichtbares im Strafverfahrensrecht*, 113 Zeitschrift für die Gesamte Strafrechtswissenschaft 284–85 (2001).

[32] For a comparison of the criminal procedural systems of France, Germany, and the UK with particular regard to the pretrial phase, see Pierre Hauck, *Judicial Decisions in the Pre-Trial Phase of Criminal Proceedings in France, Germany and England* 33–35, 41–44, 64–67 (2008). For a broader comparison of criminal procedural systems, see John Jackson, *The Effect of Human Rights on Criminal Evidentiary Processes: Towards Convergence, Divergence or Realignment?*, 68 Mod. L. Rev. 737, 764 (2005); Thomas Weigend, *Should We Search for the Truth, and Who Should Do It?*, 36 N.C. J. Int'l L. 404–05 (2011).

invocation of a sound legal basis as grounds for infringing on a fundamental right, as well as necessity to offset such infringement (see, e.g., Article 8 § 2), thereby introducing an *abstract* clause of proportionality.[33]

This is clearly evidenced in the Court's case law concerning undercover investigations, one of the most intrusive methods often employed against corruption offenses.[34] The Court calls attention to the fact that, while the rise in organized crime requires that appropriate measures be taken, the right to a fair trial (Article 6 ECHR), from which the requirement of the proper administration of justice is to be inferred, nevertheless applies to all types of crime, from the most straightforward to the most complex.[35] At the same time, the Court underlines the need to delimit the conditions for implementing covert investigative methods, so that they are not reduced to police entrapment.[36] This is why the introduction of *procedural* safeguards for the conduct of undercover investigations is regarded as crucial.[37] On a *substantive* level, the Court requires *an essentially passive character of the police operation*, in order to draw a clear line separating lawful police action and police entrapment.[38] It also seeks to ensure that *national courts* (either *proprio motu* or upon the defendant's request) look into the possibility of police entrapment in a manner consistent with the right to a fair hearing.[39] In at least one instance, however (which concerned "luring" the suspect into confessing while being recorded by the authorities), the ECtHR faced the issue of evaluating police entrapment in light of the principle of non-self-incrimination and the right to silence. It found no breach of the right to a fair trial. Specifically, it was found that national courts only marginally relied on the evidence thus produced, while the defendant

[33] *See* Robert Esser, *Mindeststandards einer Europäischen Strafprozessordnung unter Berücksichtigung der Rechtsprechung des Europäischen Gerichtshofs für Menschenrechte*, Strafverteidiger Forum 337–38 (2003).

[34] *See, e.g.*, Ramanauskas v. Lithuania, App. No. 74420/01, Eur. Ct. H.R., Feb. 5, 2008.

[35] *See, e.g.*, Bannikova v. Russia, App. No. 18757/06, Eur. Ct. H.R., Nov. 4, 2010, §§ 33 f.; Ramanauskas v. Lithuania, App. No. 74420/01, Eur. Ct. H.R., Feb. 5, 2008, §§ 49 ff.; cf. Khudobin v. Russia, App. No. 59696/00, Eur. Ct. H.R., Oct. 26, 2006, § 128; Teixeira de Castro v. Portugal, App. No. 25829/94, Eur. Ct. H.R., June 9, 1998, § 36.

[36] *See* Bannikova v. Russia, App. No. 18757/06, Eur. Ct. H.R., Nov. 4, 2010, § 35; Ali v. Romania, App. No. 20307/02, Eur. Ct. H.R., Nov. 9, 2010, § 99; Ramanauskas v. Lithuania, App. No. 74420/01, Eur. Ct. H.R., Feb. 5, 2008, § 93.

[37] For instance, a formal authorization and supervision by a judge or prosecutor would be required. *See* Bannikova v. Russia, App. No. 18757/06, Eur. Ct. H.R., Nov. 4, 2010, §§ 48 ff.; Ramanauskas v. Lithuania, App. No. 74420/01, Eur. Ct. H.R., Feb. 5, 2008, § 53.

[38] Bannikova v. Russia, App. No. 18757/06, Eur. Ct. H.R., Nov. 4, 2010, § 37; *Ramanauskas v. Lithuania*, App. No. 74420/01, Eur. Ct. H.R., Feb. 5, 2008, § 55; Malininas v. Lithuania, App. No. 10071/04, Eur. Ct. H.R., July 1, 2008, § 35; Ali v. Romania, App. No. 20307/02, Eur. Ct. H.R., Nov. 9, 2010, § 99; Bulfinsky v. Romania, App. No. 28823/04, Eur. Ct. H.R., June 1, 2010, § 41; Gorgievski v. Macedonia, App. No. 18002/02, Eur. Ct. H.R., July 16, 2009, § 49.

[39] Bannikova v. Russia, App. No. 18757/06, Eur. Ct. H.R., Nov. 4, 2010, §§ 51 ff.; Ali v. Romania, App. No. 20307/02, Eur. Ct. H.R., Nov. 9, 2010, §§ 101 ff.; Bulfinsky v. Romania, App. No. 28823/04, Eur. Ct. H.R., June 1, 2010, §§ 43 ff.; Constantin and Stoian v. Romania, App. No. 23782/06 and 46629/06, Eur. Ct. H.R., Sept. 29, 2009, §§ 57 ff.

had been afforded ample procedural means to question the use and reliability of the evidence.[40] Still, there was strong dissent in the Court's Grand Chamber, expressed by one particular judge in the following words: "the right to remain silent would be truly 'theoretical and illusory' if it were accepted that the police had the right to 'make a suspect talk' by using a cover recording of a conversation with an informer assigned the task of entrapping the suspect."[41] It follows that, in the event of a police infiltration that is tantamount to a covert suspect interrogation (carried out via the targeted questioning of the unsuspecting individual after gaining his trust), the rights to non-self-incrimination and silence, as well as the right to a fair trial, must be regarded as violated. This type of investigation exceeds the passive character that should at all times remain the essential corollary of a fair trial.[42]

Still, it is evident that, even based on the case law of the ECtHR, neither *sufficient indications of guilt* nor a proviso for preventive—or at least subsequent—*judicial review* is required as a condition for the undertaking of onerous investigative measures. The sole protection afforded is only triggered after the investigative measures have been implemented. Such protection falls short of ensuring application of the principle (sensu stricto) of proportionality,[43] which would normally be required for the application of such measures. Rather, it is confined to determining whether this particular investigative technique has violated the right to a fair trial, viewing the entire process as a whole.

The legal instruments of the EU concerning procedural rights do not provide the necessary safeguards in the field of corruption either. Aside from instruments that are plainly unrelated to investigative techniques,[44] no such provisions are traced in pertinent instruments such as Directive 2012/13/EU on the right to information (which could have introduced an obligation to inform suspects/defendants of their rights in the event of special investigative measures), or Directive 2016/343/EU on the presumption of innocence, which provides for the right to remain silent and not to incriminate oneself yet stops short of setting boundaries on undercover investigative techniques in light of ECtHR case law. On the other hand, Directive 2013/48/EU, on the right of access to a lawyer, ensures the confidentiality of communication with one's lawyer (Article 4), so that surveillance operations do not infringe on this right. Based on Article 3 of the Directive, however, access to a lawyer is not granted during secret investigative acts, not even in the form of the appointment of an attorney absent the suspect's knowledge. Instead, that provision only recognizes this right

[40] Bykov v. Russia, App. No. 4378/02, Eur. Ct. H.R., Mar. 10, 2009, §§ 99 ff.

[41] *Id.* (Judge Costa, dissenting, ¶ 8).

[42] Maria Kaiafa-Gbandi, *The Recent Jurisprudence of the ECtHR on Police Infiltration and the Right to a Fair Trial*, Poiniki Dikaiosyni 66–67 (2011) [in Greek].

[43] *See* Esser, *supra* note 33.

[44] 2010/64/EU on the right to interpretation and translation, 2016/800/EU on procedural safeguards for children.

upon the carrying out by competent authorities of a non-secret investigative or evidence-gathering act.[45]

The aforementioned institutional framework is inadequate to reconcile such serious infringements of fundamental rights with the demands of a fair trial. Therefore, an improvement is called for, at least with respect to measures of procedural constraint and investigative measures of a more invasive character, such as the waiving of confidentiality, collection and processing of personal data, audio-visual surveillance of spaces, freezing of bank accounts, controlled deliveries, undercover investigations, use of police informants, etc.,[46] all of which are extensively used during the investigation of corruption offenses. These adjustments should be undertaken on an *international* or a *European* level. This could take place by virtue of a protocol attached to the international conventions on corruption, as well as to all other conventions mandating the introduction of similar (i.e., secret) "new generation" investigative measures, or even by virtue of an additional protocol to human rights conventions, which would encompass procedural rights in criminal processes. In the particular context of the EU, the necessary adjustments might take the form of a pertinent directive.[47] Whatever their precise form, these adjustments should entail the following:[48]

(1) *specify the extent to which the presumption of innocence* applies at this stage, that is, clarify that even special investigative measures aim at securing the process and are allowed only inasmuch as the prosecuting authorities are able to establish that they are absolutely necessary;
(2) insist on *sufficient indications of guilt* in addition to the self-evident requirement of the existence of a sound *legal basis*;
(3) require that such measures *abide by subsidiarity*, that is, are only permitted if the case cannot otherwise be investigated or it would otherwise be especially difficult to carry out investigations;
(4) require that these measures adhere to *the principle of proportionality* in terms of *the preservation of the procedure*, the *significance of the punishable act*, and the *indications of guilt*;
(5) introduce *preemptive* or, in exceptional cases, *immediately subsequent judicial review*;

[45] 2013/48/EU, art. 3 ¶ 3(c).

[46] *See also* Hans-Heinrich Kühne, *Grundrechte in einem grenzenlosen europäischen Strafrecht*, in *Europäischer Grundrechtsschutz* 60, 65 (Karl Kreuzer, Dieter Scheunig & Urlich Sieber eds., 1998).

[47] For the development of transnational undercover investigations especially by technical means, their importance and the need for legality safeguards and other pertinent limitations see Dominik Brodowski, *Verdeckte technische Überwachungsmaßnahmen im Polizei- und Strafverfahrensrecht*, 365 et seq., 598 (2016).

[48] Cf. Maria Kaiafa-Gbandi, *Harmonization of Criminal Procedure on the Basis of Common Principles: The EU's Challenge for a Rule-of-Law Transnational Crime Control*, in Cyrille Fijnaut & Jannemieke Ouwerkerk, *The Future of Police and Judicial Cooperation in the European Union* 381 (2010).

(6) set *clear boundaries* so that special investigative measures do not encroach upon professional privileges such as the attorney-client or physician-client privilege, and investigative acts such as police infiltration do not become tantamount to a covert suspect interrogation;
(7) make clear that special investigative measures are of *limited (and short) duration*, which should only be extended in exceptional cases upon justification;
(8) *prohibit the use of evidence* obtained via special investigative acts *for purposes other than those for which the acts were originally authorized*;[49] and
(9) *strictly prohibit the use of information obtained through the violation of the aforementioned rules.*

With particular regard to undercover operations by police agents or individuals acting on their behalf that are especially intrusive in nature, the necessary adjustments should additionally require:[50] (1) appointment of an *attorney* tasked with exercising the defendant's rights (absent his knowledge); (2i) supervision *by a competent judge* of such investigative acts; (3) imposition of clear limits on police agents or private individuals acting at their behest, who may only *facilitate the suspect to act upon his own decision to commit a criminal offense*; and (4) the *keeping of records* via audio- or video-recordings unless using such means is absolutely impossible.

Ensuring these conditions on an international or at least European level is crucial, since it might offer a common basis for protecting fundamental rights at the pretrial stage in fields such as corruption or organized crime, where particularly invasive investigative measures have become the norm.

However, two key concerns ought to be addressed in order to arrive at a solution: first, in common law jurisdictions, the investigation is typically carried out autonomously by the police, while investigative measures associated even with severe breaches of individual rights do not require authorization by a judicial authority. Instead, these systems employ other legal means to ensure the legality of the particular activities, which normally emerge *after* the conclusion of the pretrial stage.[51] Be that as it may, there are many who call for judicial oversight of police investigations, especially in view of numerous miscarriages of justice attributed to the poor quality of evidence gathered by law

[49] One might allow for very few exceptions, such as to corroborate an offense, to place a suspect under arrest, or to help prosecute members of a criminal organization other than one targeted by the initial undercover investigation.

[50] *See Financial Crime and Corruption in the Public Sector* 394–99 (Maria Kaiafa-Gbandi ed., 2015).

[51] For a comparison of various criminal procedural systems with particular regard to the pretrial phase, see Hauck, *supra* note 32; Sabine Gless, *Functions and Constitution of the Court at Pre-Trial and Trial Stage*, in *Strafjustiz im Spannungsfeld von Effizienz und Fairness—Criminal Justice Between Crime Control and Due Process* 344 (Albin Eser & Christiane Rabenstein eds., 2004).

enforcement authorities.[52] Thus, one might hope for a reorientation in the direction advocated above, at least with respect to onerous investigative measures.[53]

Designating the general conditions for the adoption of highly invasive investigative measures on an international or at least European level, as described previously, constitute an essential prerequisite to safeguarding citizens' liberties. Indeed, this would not only reinforce guarantees such as *equality of arms*, the *presumption of innocence*, the *nemo tenetur se ipsum accusare* principle, the *right to silence*, and the right *to an effective defense*, but would also strengthen transnational crime control itself. This is because, under these circumstances, it would be easier for states to accept evidence gathered in another state in the context of judicial cooperation.

The second, more pressing concern, is to *practically ensure* judicial oversight as a counterweight to the violation of fundamental rights occurring during the pretrial phase. It has aptly been remarked that the proviso in favor of judicial oversight often ends up being devoid of any actual meaning,[54] even in those legal orders where it actually applies.[55]

This must change. The best—albeit hard to implement—solution would be a streamlined mechanism in which *a specialized judge shall be exclusively authorized, by virtue of a set of special provisions, to review investigative measures as well as other measures of procedural constraint that are particularly invasive to fundamental rights.*[56] Additionally, offenses related to corruption and organized crime should be recognized as exceptions, provided that both terms are properly delimited. Currently they are defined too broadly, for instance in the definition of "organized crime" used in the pertinent EU framework decision.[57]

Judicial review over highly invasive investigative measures would ensure the application of basic procedural principles already enshrined, in general terms, in the international conventions protecting fundamental rights. These measures pose particular challenges, especially in the context of transnational crime control, which is pursued in the field of corruption in the face of divergences among national jurisdictions. That is an additional reason the regulation of these measures should be placed at the center of attempts to improve the investigative part of the pretrial phase. In addition, this would be an important step toward implementing a set of common international or at least European procedural principles in criminal matters. Corruption and organized crime,

[52] *See* Sabine Gless, "... *dass überall dem Gesetz ein Genüge geschehe"—Justizielle Einbindung und Kontrolle des strafrechtlichen Ermittlungsverfahrens*, Deutsche Richterzeitung 368–69 (2000); Kühne, *supra* note 20, at 720–21.

[53] *See* Hauck, *supra* note 32, at 65–66.

[54] Nelles, *supra* note 23, at 70–71.

[55] *See* Sabine Ottow, *Grundrechtseingriffe im Ermittlungsverfahren und nach dem Polizeirecht* 79–80 (2014).

[56] See also a proposal made by Schünemann, *supra* note 30, at 92.

[57] Maria Kaiafa-Gbandi, *Towards a New Approach of Organized Crime in the EU-New Challenges for Human Rights*, 14/2007 Zeitschrift für Internationale Strafrechtsdogmatik 537 (2007).

as well as other fields of cross-border crime, offer fertile ground for such a convergence, on the premise that the efficiency of crime deterrence cannot justify the unbridled violation of the rights and liberties of those involved in the criminal process.

V. Prosecution-Led Investigations of Corruption Offenses and Freezing/Confiscating Proceeds of Crime: An Important Tool and Its Impact on Fair Trial Rights

The recovery of criminal assets, like special investigative acts, is a crucial tool in addressing corruption[58] in accordance with international conventions and EU legal instruments.[59] Recovering assets requires not only the cooperation of banks with law enforcement authorities coupled with the lifting of banking secrecy (and the cooperation among states in combating crime), but also *the expansion of the object* of confiscation to include criminal proceeds not directly derived from the prosecuted offense (extended confiscation). Extended confiscation and its corollary, freezing an individual's assets during the investigation, is necessary given that "traditional" confiscation entails probative difficulties, including the requirement to establish a nexus between the particular criminal offense and the confiscated assets. These difficulties are widely regarded as obstacles to achieving recovery of criminal proceeds, especially in organized crime cases.[60] This is why the introduction of extended confiscation invariably involves abolishing the need to establish a nexus, as well as slackening procedural safeguards on the collection of evidence in the criminal process (e.g., reversing the burden or lowering the standard of proof).[61]

With respect to investigations of corruption offenses, asset recovery is an explicitly declared goal at least in the UN Convention against corruption. The most serious

[58] Indira Carr, *Recovering the Proceeds of Corruption: UNCAC and Anti-money Laundering Standards*, 2 J. Bus. L. 170 (2011); Mark Pieth, *Recovering Stolen Assets—A New Issue*, in *Recovering Stolen Assets*, 3–18 (Mark Pieth ed., 2008).

[59] On the confiscation of the proceeds of crime, see also The Council of Europe Convention on Laundering, Search, Seizure and Confiscation of the Proceeds from Crime (no. 141, Strasbourg 1990), as well as the Council of Europe Convention on Laundering, Search, Seizure and Confiscation of the Proceeds from Crime and on Financing of Terrorism (no. 198, Warsaw 2005).

[60] Johan Boucht, *Extended Confiscation and the Proposed Directive on Freezing and Confiscation of Criminal Proceeds in the EU: On Striking a Balance Between Efficiency, Fairness and Legal Certainty*, 21 Euro. J. Crime, Crim. L. & Crim. Justice 127, 128–29 (2013). Cf. Radha Ivory, *Corruption, Asset Recovery, and the Protection of Property in Public International Law: The Human Rights of Bad Guys* 55–57, 299–301 (2014). *See* Peter Alldridge, *The Limits of Confiscation*, 11 Crim. L. Rev. 829 (2011).

[61] International practice also includes concepts such as the so-called non-conviction-based confiscation; see Jon-Petter Rui & Urlich Sieber, *Non-conviction-based Confiscation in Europe* 245 et seq. (2015).

challenges here are associated with the *freezing* of the assets of those involved in the criminal process, which amounts to a grave impairment of their ability to conduct their affairs during the investigation and the ensuing criminal proceedings.[62] This is a fortiori the case in relation to assets that do not derive from the offense subject to investigation. It is true, of course, that, unlike lifting banking secrecy or tracing assets, the freezing of assets is not per se an investigative act. Nonetheless, it is a measure aimed at possible confiscation of assets and is therefore structurally connected with the investigation. This *measure of criminal constraint* purports to enable confiscation and is therefore an essential tool for concluding criminal proceedings.[63] Due to the importance attached to this measure in investigations of corruption offenses, it is crucial to delineate its defining attributes. Since the present discussion is not focused on national legal orders, the analysis will take place within the framework of international legal instruments.

The international conventions on corruption call upon state parties to enable the freezing of criminal proceeds and mandate judicial assistance to that end, but they do not contain itemized provisions or safeguards that would allow a complete appraisal of the particular features of this measure. The same is true of the UN Convention against transnational organized crime, which also requires states to freeze proceeds. The only international legal instrument that contains particular provisions, and thereby permits an assessment going beyond the idiosyncrasies of national jurisdictions, is Directive 2014/42/EU on the freezing and confiscation of instrumentalities and proceeds of crime in the European Union.[64] These provisions establish minimum rules for the dual purpose of harmonizing state laws on freezing and confiscating criminal proceeds and to facilitate the mutual recognition of judicial decisions among Member States under the auspices of the EU.

The preamble of this directive highlights the importance of freezing (and subsequently confiscating) criminal proceeds to "neutralize" them, as a means to effectively combat organized crime. Yet so-called extended confiscation (Article 5) is not confined to organized crime. Instead, the directive provides that extended confiscation involves either the whole or part of property belonging to a person convicted of a criminal offense and that is liable to give rise, directly or indirectly, to economic benefit. This requires that a court, on the specific facts and circumstances of the case in light of available evidence,[65] is satisfied that the property in question is derived from criminal conduct. Specifically, Article 5(2) of the directive provides for extended confiscation not only for participation in a criminal organization, but also for other offenses, including active and passive bribery in the private and public sectors (and other enumerated offenses), as well as for

[62] On the seriousness of the measure of freezing assets in the context of blacklisting terrorists, see Melissa van den Broek, Monique Hazelhorst & Wouter de Zanger, *Asset Freezing: Smart Sanction or Criminal Charge?*, 27 Merkourios 18, 27 (2010).

[63] Kühne, *supra* note 20, at 326.

[64] Michael Fernandez-Bertier, *The Confiscation and Recovery of Criminal Property: A European Union State of the Art*, 17 ERA Forum 323 (2016).

[65] Relevant indications would include, for instance, an assessment that the value of the property is disproportionate to the lawful income of the convicted person.

any criminal offense punishable by a custodial sentence of a maximum of at least four years. Thus, extended confiscation covers a broad array of offenses, including but not limited to corruption-related ones. Besides, extended confiscation necessarily entails a corresponding extension of freezing assets during the investigation, especially given the lack of an explicit exception to the pertinent provisions.

Indeed, the application of the provision concerning freezing (Article 7) is not tied to any additional prerequisite, and it extends to property in the possession of a third party. On the other hand, Article 8 of the directive provides for certain safeguards, according to which persons shall have the right to an effective remedy and a fair trial to uphold their rights (para. 1), the freezing order shall be communicated to the affected person as soon as possible after its execution (para. 2), and the person whose property is affected shall be entitled to challenge the freezing order before a court of law (para. 4) and to seek immediate return of the property that is not subsequently confiscated (para. 5). That noted, there remain obvious gaps in the measures of procedural constraint adopted during the investigation, especially in light of rule-of-law principles.

Setting aside the controversial issue whether extended confiscation (as envisaged in Article 5 of the directive) complies with the principle of guilt and the presumption of innocence,[66] one should note the following concerns about freezing criminal assets. Just like extended confiscation, freezing is not confined to serious offenses, even though it entails the risk of targeting "innocent" property.[67] Indeed, the array of offenses punishable with a maximum of at least four years is not limited to corruption in the public or private sector. Even where this is the case, however, the threshold is low enough to cover relatively minor offenses, posing serious issues with respect to the principle of proportionality.[68] In addition, the provisions on extended confiscation and freezing are not confined to offenses capable of producing considerable profit, as would be required by the principle of proportionality, nor do they presuppose the commission of a previous similar act capable of producing considerable profit. Moreover, there is no upper limit to property subject to freezing.[69] Disregard of the principle of proportionality is further evidenced

[66] See a critical appraisal in Maria Kaiafa-Gbandi, *Einziehung von Erträgen aus Straftaten in der Europäischen Union: Der Kommissionsvorschlag von 2012 und die neuen Herausforderungen für den Rechtsstaat*, in *Festschrift für Helmut Fuchs* 214 (Susanne Reindl-Krauskopf et al., eds., 2014); cf. art. 4 ¶ 2.

[67] *See* Boucht, *supra* note 60, at 129, 136–37, 139, 143, 145, 156, 160–61.

[68] *See id.* at 136–37 & 142 et seq. Although the ECtHR has questioned the nature of extended confiscation as concealed punishment (Phillips v. United Kingdom, App. No. 41087/98, Eur. Ct. H.R., July 5, 2001, §§ 34, 42 ff.; Van Offeren v. the Netherlands, App. No. 19581/04, Eur. Ct. H.R., July 5, 2005, § 2; Arcuri v. Italy, App. No. 52024/99, Eur. Ct. H.R., July 5, 2001, § 2; Raimondo v. Italy, App. No. 12954/87, Eur. Ct. H.R., 1994, §§ 28 ff., one should note that, aside from its punitive character, it also serves a deterrent purpose, just like criminal penalties. Thus, the need to respect the principle of proportionality should be taken for granted, even if extended confiscation were deemed to be a security measure. The same respect for proportionality is called for in the application of measures of procedural constraint, as in the case of freezing assets prior to applying extended confiscation.

[69] See the proposal in *A Comprehensive Model for Combating Financial Crime and Corruption in the Public Sector*, in *Financial Crime and Corruption in the Public Sector* 352–53 (Maria Kaiafa-Gbandi ed., 2015).

by the absence of a requirement to show that the property subject to "extended freezing" derives from criminal conduct, even a minor corruption offense. This is coupled with the lower standard of proof (Article 5 para. 1 of the directive) for extended confiscation, which is permitted if the court is *satisfied* that the property in question is derived from criminal conduct—although there is no definition of "criminal conduct," nor is there a temporal restriction that would limit the ability of the court to look far in the past for such conduct. It becomes clear that, whenever a person's assets exceed his income, extended freezing will likely become the norm. Besides, the list of safeguards does not include any exceptions to freezing, for instance in cases where the pertinent "criminal conduct" is not prosecutable due to a prior final acquittal of the person, or in other situations evoking the *ne bis in idem* principle.[70] There are not even exemptions for assets absolutely necessary to cover the person's daily needs or attorney fees, so that the individual may effectively exercise the right to legal redress. The absence of a requirement for reasoned decisions on freezing is also striking; that requirement is confined to confiscation (para. 6). Even the duration of freezing (as long as it is necessary to preserve the property with a view to possible subsequent confiscation) is clearly oriented toward unbridled effectiveness, without even the possibility of periodic review. That priority is further reinforced by the directive's minimum rules for mutual recognition of judicial decisions and orders issued by Member States, absent any of the aforementioned institutional guarantees. The only recourse available is for Member States to invoke a general fundamental rights ground of refusal, as upheld in the judgment of the ECJ in *Aranyosi and Căldăraru*.[71] Furthermore, even though the directive expressly alludes to the immediate return of the property that is not subsequently confiscated, one would expect a provision concerning reparations to those unjustly deprived of their property via extended freezing. Therefore, although the directive nominally calls upon Member States to provide a "fair trial" concerning the freezing and subsequent confiscation of assets, it stops short of requiring the conditions necessary for such fair trial. One cannot help but wonder what use is a provision concerning an effective remedy, absent a requirement of proportionality in freezing and confiscating assets. Without sufficient indications concerning the origin of the proceeds or the recognition of an exemption to at least allow the person to cover attorney fees (which is a necessary condition for legal redress), there can indeed be no fair trial.

It can safely be concluded, then, that the existing international rules concerning measures of procedural constraint in the field of corruption are far from serving, as they should, fundamental procedural principles or rights guaranteeing a fair trial, such as the principle of proportionality, the right to an effective defense, or the presumption of innocence. It is thus imperative to include these principles and rights in international instruments in tandem with measures aiming at enhancing efficiency in addressing corruption. In the "new generation" measures of procedural constraint systematically

[70] *But see* EU Commission Proposal, COM(2012) 85 final, art. 4 ¶ 2.

[71] Case C-404/15, ECLI:EU:C:2016:198 (Apr. 5, 2016).

employed against corruption, including the freezing of criminal proceeds with a view to subsequent confiscation, it is imperative to apply the same solutions with respect to special investigative acts. This becomes all the more evident considering the conflicting case law of the ECtHR, particularly with regard to extended confiscation. While some decisions regard extended confiscation as a form of concealed punishment or a criminal charge,[72] other decisions do not classify it as such,[73] which means confiscation (and, a fortiori, the preceding freezing of assets) is not subject to the ECHR's safeguards.[74]

VI. Conclusion

The adoption of harsh criminal law provisions, more often than not employed as a means to combat corruption or achieve political benefits, does not necessarily improve the effectiveness of criminal law. Instead, what is required to address corruption is an emphasis on prevention through education programs, the political rejection of blind obedience to the dictates of globalized economy, and the endorsement of societal values that do not revolve around the pursuit of material benefits. Appreciating the limits of the criminal law in its ability to deter corruption would help define the permissible scope of its provisions, as well as the safeguards that should accompany measures of procedural constraint. With particular regard to the initiatives adopted on the international level, especially in the supranational EU context, it is imperative that a balance be restored between an ever-expanding effectiveness of criminal repression and the guarantees afforded to protect individual rights. That balance has been disturbed by policies advanced on an international and EU level, which is precisely why its restoration should begin on an international initiative. The international community—and the EU in particular, which aims to create a common area of freedom, security, and justice—ought to recognize that there can be no fair trial based on outdated guarantees at a time when "new generation" investigative acts and measures of criminal constraint tend to thwart equality of arms. It would therefore be crucial to put together a set of specialized procedural rights and principles, including those outlined previously in the chapter in relation to particularly invasive measures of procedural constraint employed in the field of corruption and serious cross-border crime in general. If the international community can find common ground in measures increasing the effectiveness of criminal repression, then surely it can do so in adopting the accompanying safeguards. Reinforcing these

[72] Welch v. United Kingdom, App. No. 17440/90, Eur. Ct. H.R., Feb. 9, 1995, §§ 31 ff.

[73] Phillips v. United Kingdom, App. No. 41087/98 Eur. Ct. H.R., July 5, 2001, §§ 34, 42 f.; Van Offeren v. the Netherlands, App. No. 19581/04, Eur. Ct. H.R., July 5, 2005, § 2; Arcuri v. Italy, App. No. 52024/99, Eur. Ct. H.R., July 5, 2001, § 2, Raimondo v. Italy, App. No. 12954/87 Eur. Ct. H.R., Feb. 22, 1994, §§ 28 ff.

[74] For the issues arising during asset recovery see Radha Ivory, *Corruption, Asset Recovery and the Protection of Property in Public International Law* 140, 300–01 (2014).

safeguards has become necessary since the enhancement of effectiveness has rendered the traditional core of fundamental rights inadequate. Besides, the international protection of individual rights has had a largely positive impact on various procedural systems, which has led to their gradual convergence. The contemporary challenge is to keep up the pace, especially in those areas where the protection of individual rights is most required, such as prosecution-led investigations of corruption offenses, characterized by the adoption of particularly invasive measures against citizens who should be treated as innocent until proven guilty.

References

Peter Alldridge, *The Limits of Confiscation*, 11 Crim. L. Rev. 827 (2011)

Peter Alldridge, *Money Laundering Law: Forfeiture, Confiscation, Civil Recovery, Criminal Laundering and Taxation of the Proceeds of Crime* (2003)

Ioannis Androulakis, *Die Globalisierung der Korruptionsbakämpfung: Eine Untersuchung zur Entstehung, zum Inhalt und zu den Auswirkungen des internationalen Korruptionsstrafrechts unter Berücksichtigung der sozialökonomischen Hintergründe* (2007)

Johan Boucht, *Extended Confiscation and the Proposed Directive on Freezing and Confiscation of Criminal Proceeds in the EU: On Striking a Balance between Efficiency, Fairness and Legal Certainty*, 21 Euro. J. Crime, Crim. L. & Crim. Justice 127 (2013)

Melissa van den Broek, Monique Hazelhorst & Wouter de Zanger, *Asset Freezing: Smart Sanction or Criminal Charge?*, 27 Merkourios 18 (2010)

Indira Carr, *Recovering the Proceeds of Corruption: UNCAC and Anti-money Laundering Standards*, 2 J. Bus. L. 170 (2011)

Robert Esser, *Mindeststandards einer Europäischen Strafprozessordnung unter Berücksichtigung der Rechtsprechung des Europäischen Gerichtshofs für Menschenrechte*, Strafverteidiger Forum 335 (2003)

Michael Fernandez-Bertier, *The Confiscation and Recovery of Criminal Property: A European Union State of the Art*, 17 ERA Forum 323 (2016)

Sabine Gless, *Functions and Constitution of the Court at Pre-Trial and Trial Stage*, in *Strafjustiz im Spannungsfeld von Effizienz und Fairness*, 344 (Albin Eser & Christiane Rabenstein eds., 2004)

Pierre Hauck, *Judicial Decisions in the Pre-Trial Phase of Criminal Proceedings in France, Germany and England—A Comparative Analysis Responding to the Law of the International Criminal Court* (2008)

Radha Ivory, *Corruption, Asset Recovery, and the Protection of Property in Public International Law, The Human Rights of Bad Guys* (2014)

John Jackson, *The Effect of Human Rights on Criminal Evidentiary Processes: Towards Convergence, Divergence or Realignment?*, 68 Mod. L. Rev. 737 (2005)

Maria Kaiafa-Gbandi, *Harmonization of Criminal Procedure on the Basis of Common Principles: The EU's Challenge for a Rule-of-Law Transnational Crime Control*, in *The Future of Police and Judicial Cooperation in the European Union* 357 et seq. (Cyrille Fijnaut & Jannemieke Ouwerkerk eds., 2010)

Maria Kaiafa-Gbandi, *Punishing Corruption in the Public and Private Sector: Key Issues on Current EU Policy and Rule-of-Law Challenges*, in *Research Handbook on EU Criminal Law* 376 et seq. (Valsamis, Mitsilegas, Maria Bergström & Theodore Konstadinides eds., 2016)

Maria Kaiafa-Gbandi ed., *Financial Crime and Corruption in the Public Sector*, Vol. I (2014), Vol. III (2015) [in Greek]

Hans-Heinrich Kühne, *Strafprozessrecht: Eine Systematische Darstellung des deutschen und europäischen Strafverfahrensrechts* (9th ed. 2015)

Ursula Nelles, *Grundrechte und Ermittlungsverfahren*, Neue Kriminalpolitik 68 et seq (2006)

Mark Pieth, *Recovering Stolen Assets* (2008)

Jon Petter Rui & Urlich Sieber, eds., *Non-conviction-based Confiscation in Europe, Possibilities and Limitations on Rules Enabling Confiscation Without a Criminal Conviction* (2015)

PART IV

CRIMINAL PROSECUTION AND ITS ALTERNATIVES

CHAPTER 19

INTERNATIONAL CORPORATE PROSECUTIONS

BRANDON GARRETT

I. Introduction

One of the most remarkable stories in criminal law is the recent rise of corporate prosecutions across the world. In the past, even in countries that permitted corporations to be prosecuted for crimes, such prosecutions were not a common practice and any fines were minimal. In the last fifteen years, though, in the United States, the largest corporate prosecutions in the world have been brought, often involving international crimes by multinational companies. Billion dollar corporate penalties are now a regular occurrence. Multinational prosecutions have also involved cooperation by prosecutors across countries and parallel prosecutions of the same corporation for crimes committed in different countries.

Over the past decade and a half, federal prosecutors in the United States have adopted an approach in which settlement negotiations with companies are resolved, sometimes through a plea agreement, but in the largest cases, with agreements entered largely out of court and without judicial oversight. These agreements, called deferred and non-prosecution agreements, have added new flexibility but also some additional uncertainty to the practice of corporate prosecutions. This U.S. approach has impacted countries that have sought to emulate it or adopted approaches seeking to improve upon it. In this chapter, I discuss how this new U.S. approach has altered the international corporate prosecution landscape.

First, I discuss how traditionally, in most countries, corporate or entity-based criminal liability is limited and unavailable for many types of crimes. However, in recent years, this has changed. More countries have expanded corporate criminal liability, including in response to treaties such as the OECD (Organisation for Economic Co-operation and

Development) and the Lisbon Treaty, which encouraged EU members to adopt criminal sanctions to legal persons. An additional driver of these changes has been a response to enforcement approaches in the United States. Second, I discuss how when many countries do adopt criminal liability for entities, they do so for specific crimes. Indeed, although in the United States there is a general and broad federal respondeat superior standard, corporate criminal enforcement patterns vary quite a bit depending on the area. Settlements in foreign bribery cases look very different than settlements in pharmaceutical cases, and in some areas, as in antitrust, the entire enforcement approach is distinct.

The general approach relying on more informal settlements with corporations has also spread, making corporate prosecutors possible, perhaps, in countries that had been reluctant to bring criminal cases against corporations. In some criminal practice areas, such as foreign bribery prosecutions, almost all cases brought in the United States and around the world have been resolved through settlements. Both enforcers and corporations may seek to settle cases, since criminal convictions may implicate debarment or suspension of companies from government contracts or programs. In turn, more countries have considered adopting a U.S.-style corporate settlement program. In foreign bribery cases, that is already the case, not just in the United States, but in other countries, including Canada, Costa Rica, Denmark, Germany, Greece, Italy, Japan, the Netherlands, Nigeria, Norway, and Switzerland, in which corporate bribery cases have been resolved through settlements.[1] The UK has introduced a deferred prosecution agreement program modeled on that in the United States Law commissions and legislators in Australia,[2] Canada,[3] and Ireland[4] have considered adopting such approaches. In France, new bribery legislation adopted a modified settlement approach. The OECD Working Group on Bribery has raised detailed questions concerning out-of-court settlements.

If corporate cases are to be settled, due to their informality, flexibility, or reduced collateral consequences, a series of practical questions then arise. What should the substance of the terms of corporate prosecution agreements contain? How should fines be assessed? How should compliance be measured and evaluated? How should compliance or governance be improved through the use of such agreements? To what degree should collateral consequences be considered? To what degree should companies be rewarded for self-reporting or for cooperation in investigation of individual employees or officers? How long should the agreements be? What should the consequences be for a

[1] World Bank/Star, *Left Out of The Bargain: Settlements in Foreign Bribery Cases and Implications for Asset Recovery* 17–32 (2014), at http://star.worldbank.org/star/sites/star/files/9781464800863.pdf.

[2] Parliament of Australia, *An Inquiry into the Measures Concerning the Activities of Australian Corporations, Entities, Organisations, Individuals, Government and Related Parties with Respect to Foreign Bribery* (2016) (44th Parliament), at http://www.aph.gov.au/Parliamentary_Business/Committees/Senate/Economics/Foreign_Bribery/Terms_of_Reference (last visited Sept. 16, 2018).

[3] Institute for Research on Public Policy, *Finding the Right Balance: Policies to Combat White-Collar Crime in Canada and Maintain Integrity of Public Procurement* (Mar. 2016).

[4] Law Reform Commission, *Issues Paper on Regulatory Enforcement and Corporate Offences*, Jan. 27, 2016, (Ir.), at http://www.lawreform.ie/news/issues-paper-on-regulatory-enforcement-and-corporate-offences-.607.html.

breach, and who should decide whether there is a breach? Who should supervise the implementation of a corporate prosecution agreement? To what degree can victims be involved and compensated? What credit should be given for enforcement and penalties in other jurisdictions? Each of these questions raises important and challenging issues. Each has been the subject of real disagreement in the United States' experience with corporate prosecutions in recent years. To discuss corporate criminal liability, and not whether the corporation should cooperate in the prosecution of individual officers and employees, and to what degree those individual prosecutions should be prioritized, leaves out the central goal of criminal law: to hold wrongdoers accountable. The differences among enforcers regarding how to best answer those questions help to illustrate the challenges of holding corporations adequately accountable.

This chapter begins by discussing: (1) varying standards for corporate criminal liability, then (2) underlying corporate crimes and how standards and enforcement approaches may vary depending on the type of crime, (3) settlement approaches towards corporate criminal cases, (4) criticisms of corporate crime settlement approaches, and (5) international approaches and cooperation in corporate crime cases. There are no definitive answers to the question whether to adopt one approach or another toward corporate criminal liability. Corporate crimes can be incredibly costly and serious, but hopefully the experimentation with enforcement approaches will continue to produce increased enforcement and stronger deterrents against corporate crime across the globe.

II. Standards for Corporate Criminal Liability

Few foreign countries have anything like the broad standard for corporate criminal liability that the United States has long had in federal courts in any specific area of criminal liability, much less as a general standard for corporate criminal liability. Corporate criminal liability has long existed in the United Kingdom, the United States, and the Netherlands. Other common law countries such as Australia, Canada, and New Zealand also have some form of corporate criminal liability, but in most the concept remains quite narrow. However, civil law countries in Europe, Latin America, and elsewhere long had no corporate criminal liability except in limited areas, such as in antitrust or environmental crimes.[5]

Many countries viewed it conceptually problematic to hold an artificial entity liable for criminal acts of agents. For example, Germany has long lacked corporate criminal liability; instead, it may apply enhanced civil administrative penalties if a corporation

[5] For an excellent and detailed overview, see Mark Pieth & Radha Ivory, *Emergence and Convergence: Corporate Criminal Liability Principles in Overview*, in *Corporate Criminal Liability* (Mark Pieth & Radha Ivory, eds., 2011).

violates a criminal provision.[6] In the past two decades, more European countries have enacted corporate criminal statutes, partially in response to principles from the European Union and Council of Europe that Member States adopt some form of corporate criminal accountability. Another chapter in this volume discusses those changes.[7] France was the first European country to introduce corporate criminal liability, in 1994 (expanded to all offenses in 2005),[8] with Brazil introducing it in 1998, Belgium in 1999,[9] Italy in 2001,[10] and Spain in 2010.[11] Countries in Asia including China, India, Japan, and Korea, the Middle East, including Israel, Qatar, and the United Arab Emirates, and in Africa including South Africa, have also adopted corporate criminal liability.

The United States adopts the broadest standard for corporate criminal liability. State prosecutors targeted corporations for crimes, particularly the common law crime of nuisance, in the nineteenth century.[12] By the twentieth century, federal prosecutors began to pursue charges more often, particularly after the Supreme Court affirmed a respondeat superior standard for corporate criminal liability in 1909.[13] The respondeat superior standard used in federal courts in the United States permits a corporation to be prosecuted for the actions of an agent within the scope of employment. The crime committed by the employee must have been for the benefit of the corporation or organization, but they may have also benefited or even primarily benefited the employee. It does not have to be a high-level employee or officer. The company may have had policies counseling against such conduct or instructed its employees not do engage in such conduct, but the company is nevertheless strictly liable. That federal standard in the United States is the broadest in use in the world. However, that standard has been moderated in practice by charging guidelines used by the U.S. Department of Justice (DOJ) as well as by sentencing guidelines for organizations, which I will discuss further in sections to follow.[14]

Most countries that adopt some version of corporate criminal liability have begun to do so cautiously. Countries adopt corporate criminal liability either for certain specific crimes, or they limit corporate criminal liability under more general laws to conduct

[6] Article 30 of the Ordnungswidrigkeitsgesetz (OWiG), or the Administrative Offenses Act; for a description of the use of this provision in bribery cases in Germany, see OECD, *Phase 3 Report on Implementing the OECD Anti-Bribery Convention in Germany* 33 (2011), at http://www.oecd.org/germany/Germanyphase3reportEN.pdf.

[7] *See* Juliette Tricot, chapter 20 of this volume.

[8] 31 December 2005 (Law No 2004–204 of 9 March 2004) (Fr.).

[9] Law of 4 May 1999.

[10] *Decreto Legistativo no.* 231 of 2001 [hereinafter Law 231].

[11] Clifford Chance, *Corporate Liability in Europe* (Jan. 2012), at https://www.cliffordchance.com/content/dam/cliffordchance/PDFs/Corporate_Liability_in_Europe.pdf.

[12] Edward B. Diskant, *Comparative Criminal Liability: Exploring the Uniquely American Doctrine Through Comparative Criminal Procedure*, 118 Yale L.J. 126, 134–35 (2008).

[13] N.Y. Cent. & Hudson River R.R. v. United States, 212 U.S. 481, 491–95 (1909) (approving corporate criminal liability under a respondeat superior standard).

[14] U.S. Attorneys' Manual, § 9–28.000, *Principles of Federal Prosecution of Business Organizations* (revised in Nov. 2015), at http://www.justice.gov/usam/usam-9-28000-principles-federal- prosecution-business-organizations.

involving specific crimes or "leading persons" such as high-level officers.[15] Indeed, within the United States, many states do not use the federal respondeat superior standard, but instead the Model Penal Code requirement that conduct by an employee be permitted or tolerated by management.[16] In France, for example, the corporation may be convicted only if employees acted through express power of attorney or delegation of power to employees; however, more recent cases have expanded the concept of delegation to include negligent supervision or compliance.[17]

In the United Kingdom, an "identification approach" had long been followed. Corporations have long been held criminally liable in the UK.[18] A corporation is liable if senior officers acted as the "directing mind" in committing crimes. Although its courts had rejected respondeat superior liability,[19] the UK has adopted a respondeat superior approach in more recent legislation. The Corporate Manslaughter and Homicide Act of 2007 adopted respondeat superior for entities when gross negligence causes a person's death.[20] The UK Bribery Act of 2010 similarly permits strict liability for organizations that fail to prevent bribery.[21] Thus, the standards for corporate criminal liability have broadened and moved more toward a strict standard along the lines of the federal standard in the United States.

In Australia, most states follow the identification approach from the UK. However, as in the UK, legislation has broadened corporate criminal liability in recent years. The federal Criminal Code Act of 1995 adopts respondeat superior liability.[22] Further, if the crime requires only negligence, then the corporation can be held liable "as a whole" by "aggregating the conduct" of employees, agents, or officers.[23] Corporate culture can be considered when deciding whether a corporation should be held accountable for an offense requiring a showing of knowledge, recklessness, or intent. The corporation may also be liable for negligence based on corporate culture, including policies, practices, compliance, or training, or evidence the company tolerated or supported commission of such a crime.[24] For crimes with higher levels of intent required, a high-level agent must carry out or authorize the crime, or a company can be liable based on a corporate culture that "directed, encouraged, tolerated, or led to non-compliance."[25]

Canadian courts follow the same identification standard as in the UK, although they may look lower down in the corporation to identify the relevant "directing mind." A new law in Canada makes it a crime for a company to engage in gross negligence as well as negligent supervision that leads to harm to workers or the public. For crimes that require a higher mental state, prosecutors must show that higher-level officers had that intent.[26]

[15] Sara Sun Beale & Adam G. Safwat, *What Developments in Western Europe Tell Us About American Critiques of Corporate Criminal Liability*, 8 Buff. Crim. L. Rev. 110 (2004); Luca Enriques, *Bad Apples, Bad Oranges: A Comment from Old Europe on Post-Enron Corporate Governance Reforms*, 38 Wake Forest L. Rev. 911 (2003).

[16] MPC § 2.07. [17] Chance, *supra* note 11, at 11.

[18] Regina v. Birmingham & Gloucester Railway, 114 Eng. Rep. 492 (Q.B. 1842).

[19] *See, e.g.*, Tesco Supermarkets v. Natrass, [1972] A.C. 153 (H.L.) (appeal taken from Q.B.).

[20] Corporate Manslaughter and Homicide Act, 2007, c. 19, § 1 (Eng.).

[21] The Bribery Act 2010 (c.23). [22] Criminal Code Act, 1995, § 12.2 (Austl.)

[23] *Id.* § 12.4(2). [24] *Id.* § 12 (2). [25] *Id.* § 12.3(2)(c)–(d).

[26] Canada Crim. Code, R.S.C., ch. C-46, § 217.1 (2009).

A useful overview of corporate criminal liability standards in a range of countries can be found in a Fall 2016 OECD Stocktaking Report, which surveyed the corporate criminal liability standards of its member countries.[27] The OECD found that at least thirty-eight countries (93 percent of OECD members) can hold legal persons liable "when a person with the highest level of managerial authority commits the offence." At least thirty-one countries (76 percent) also hold an organization liable if a person with managerial authority directs or authorizes the criminal acts. At least twenty-nine countries hold companies liable if an officer or other manager fails to prevent the offence "through a failure to supervise . . . or . . . a failure to implement adequate controls." Still other countries adopt corporate criminal liability but permit, as a defense, a corporation to avoid criminal liability if it shows that it exercised due diligence. For example, Belgium, Italy, Poland, and Spain have such affirmative defenses.[28] There has been discussion among academics about whether such a defense would be useful in other countries, including the United States. One concern is whether a company at which crimes were committed could easily show that its compliance was adequate. A separate practical concern is that corporations tend not to want to litigate corporate crimes, and compliance may already informally affect settlement negotiations.

III. Underlying Corporate Crimes

In the United States, a variety of crimes are commonly charged as against corporations, including antitrust, environmental crimes, foreign bribery, fraud, money laundering offenses, securities fraud, and others. Some of these crimes, such as the federal ones of wire fraud and mail fraud, are incredibly broad. Different approaches to various crimes characterize how prosecutors respond to corporate criminal liability.

One of the most distinct and successful approaches is the U.S. Department of Justice's Antitrust Division's Leniency Program. That approach strongly incentivizes firms to be the first to report cartel behavior, relying on the inherent instability of price-fixing cartels among competitors.[29] Many countries have adopted similar approaches toward price-fixing cartel enforcement, and parallel civil litigation is now common. There has been a "convergence in leniency programs," with dozens of countries adopting programs modelled on the U.S. Antitrust Division approach.[30] In turn, this has made it "more attractive for companies to simultaneously seek and obtain amnesty in the United States, Europe, Canada and other jurisdictions."[31] Converging approaches, cooperation in

[27] OECD, *The Liability of Legal Persons for Foreign Bribery: A Stocktaking Report* (2016), at http://www.oecd.org/corruption/anti-bribery/Liability-Legal-Persons-Foreign-Bribery-Stocktaking.pdf.

[28] Chance, *supra* note 11, at 2.

[29] Antitrust Division, Leniency Program, at http://www.justice.gov/atr/leniency-program.

[30] Gary R. Spratling & D. Jarrett Arp, *The International Leniency Revolution* 8–9 (2003), at http://www.gibsondunn.com/publications/pages/TheInternationalLeniencyRevolution.aspx.

[31] J. Anthony Chavez, *More Aggressive Action to Curb International Cartels*, 1739 Practising L. Inst. Corp. 807, 813–16, 839 (2009).

investigations, and a priority on antitrust enforcement in countries such as the United States has encouraged more enforcement around the world.

Other groups of federal prosecutors in the United States have adopted their own distinct approaches. The U.S. Department of Justice's Tax Division adopted a programmatic amnesty program for Swiss banks facilitating tax evasion in the United States, with a structured set of settlement options designed to incentivize self-reporting, cooperation, and disclosure of names of taxpayers.

U.S. environmental crime enforcement is also distinct. The Environment and Natural Resources Division at the DOJ does not normally use deferred and non-prosecution agreements. Civil enforcers bring tens of thousands of civil actions each year, but they refer few cases to criminal prosecutors. When criminal cases are brought, plea agreements with criminal convictions are the norm. In the area of vessel pollution, the International Convention for the Prevention of Pollution from Ships has played an important role, leading to the enactment of the Act to Prevent Pollution from Ships (APPS) and to increased U.S. enforcement in recent years.[32] The cases are often brought to the attention of the Coast Guard due to a whistle-blower program rewarding seamen who report illegal oily discharges to them; the reward may consist in as much as half of the criminal fine, and the fines in these cases are sometimes in the millions of dollars.[33]

The Fraud Section has adopted a detailed pilot program for Foreign Corrupt Practices Act (FCPA) cases involving foreign bribery, with very detailed rules for what degree of leniency corporations may receive depending on their self-reporting and cooperation, as well as the conduct. The Fraud Section notes that the United States "is not going at this alone," and has been adopting "an international approach" by working collaboratively with law enforcement "around the globe." Recent cases depending on international cooperation included FCPA prosecutions of Acher Daniels Midland, Alcoa, Alstom, Dallas Airmotive, Hewlett-Packard, IAP, Marubeni, Parker Drilling, PetroTiger, Total, and Vimpelcome.[34]

As described, in some of these specific areas, countries that otherwise do not have corporate criminal liability have adopted corporate criminal liability statutes. In the area of foreign bribery, more countries now have specific legislation for corporate criminal liability. While the OECD does not require that member states adopt corporate criminal liability if their legal system does not currently have it, the OECD Anti-Bribery Convention and the UN Convention Against Corruption have encouraged enactment of anticorruption legislation generally.[35] As described, France adopted new corporate

[32] The Act to Prevent Pollution from Ships, 33 U.S.C. §§ 1901–15 (2006); see International Convention for the Prevention of Pollution from Ships, Nov. 2, 1973, 12 I.L.M. 1319, *amended by* Protocol, Feb. 17, 1978, 17 I.L.M. 546 (also known as MARPOL); see also H.R. Rep. No. 96–1224, at 1–2 (1980).

[33] 33 U.S.C. § 51908(b) (2006) ("An amount equal to not more than 1/2 of such penalties may be paid by the Secretary, or the Administrator as provided for in this chapter, to the person giving information leading to the assessment of such penalties.").

[34] U.S. Dep't of Justice, Fraud Section, *Foreign Corrupt Practices Act Enforcement Plan and Guidance*, 1–2 (Apr. 5, 2016), at https://www.justice.gov/criminal-fraud/file/838416/download.

[35] OECD Convention on Combating Bribery of Foreign Public Officials in International Business Transactions, Dec. 17, 1997, 31 I.L.M. 1 (1998) (OECD Anti-Bribery Convention); United Nations Convention against Corruption, Oct. 31, 2003, 2349 U.N.T.S 41 (UNCAC).

criminal provisions as part of its comprehensive anticorruption legislation. Ukraine also recently adopted corporate criminal liability as part of anticorruption legislation.[36] In Brazil, environmental offenses had been the only type of corporate criminal liability, with the Environmental Crimes Law enacted in 1998.[37] Criminal procedure rules, however, were not adapted to corporations, and criminal prosecutions for environmental crimes in Brazil remained rare.[38]

IV. Negotiated Corporate Settlements

In the United States, corporate prosecutions have exploded in size.[39] That is, more corporations are not being prosecuted by federal prosecutors, but the size of the penalties in the largest cases that have been exponentially increased. Multibillion dollar fines are now an annual occurrence. Many were quite high-profile prosecutions; well over half were public corporations, and many were Fortune 500 and Global 500 companies.[40]

In the 1990s, if corporations were prosecuted in the United States, they were typically convicted and sentenced by a judge. Today, far more of the truly important corporate prosecutions do not result in a conviction but rather are resolved by alternatives called deferred prosecution agreements. A deferred prosecution is filed with the court and consists in an agreement to toll the Speedy Trial Act deadlines and to keep the case inactive on the judge's docket until a time period for the defendant to comply is completed. Then the case is dismissed. Such agreements had been often used as an alternative to an indictment and conviction for first-time offenders or juveniles, but it was a new idea to use them in serious corporate cases. A *non*-prosecution agreement is a variant that is completely out of court; it is never filed with a judge. Rather, in it prosecutors agree that they will not file a case if the corporation complies with the terms of the agreement.

The adoption of the U.S. Sentencing Guidelines Chapter designed specifically for organizations, in 1991, heralded an increase in corporate criminal fines. Those Guidelines included provisions to reduce fines for corporations with effective ethics and compliance

[36] *See* Thomas Firestone & Yuliya Kuchma, *Ukraine Enacts Sweeping New Anti-corruption Legislation*, FCPA Blog, July 30, 2013, at http://www.fcpablog.com/blog/2013/7/30/ukraine-enacts-sweeping-new-anti-corruption-legislation.html.

[37] Environmental Criminal Law, 9.605/1998 (Braz.).

[38] Carlos Ayres, *Corporate Criminal Liability in the United States and Brazil: A Brief Comparative Analysis*, FCPAméricas Blog, Oct. 17, 2016, at http://fcpamericas.com/english/brazil/corporate-criminal-liability-united-states-brazil-comparative- analysis-2/.

[39] Brandon L. Garrett, *Too Big to Jail: How Prosecutors Compromise with Corporations* fig. A.2, 294 (2014) (describing an increase in average corporate fines over the past two decades, from less than $2,000,000 in average fines per year before 2000, to over $15,000,000 in average corporate fines by 2010).

[40] *Id.* at 62 (noting that 31 percent of corporations were either a Fortune or Global 500 firm the year they settled their prosecutions).

programs, and they also based fines on the size of a company and the involvement of top-level officials. Thus, although the federal respondeat superior standard is broad, these Guidelines attempted to set out a more nuanced approach toward punishing corporations criminally. Under the federal Alternative Fines Act, a company can also be ordered to pay up to twice the "gross gain or loss" from the offense; the provision is not frequently used, however.[41]

In 1999, under then-deputy attorney general Eric Holder, the DOJ issued its first memo providing a set of guidelines to advise federal prosecutors on how to bring corporate prosecutions.[42] At that time, however, prosecutors had only used a few deferred prosecutions with corporations. The idea was still novel. The deferred prosecution approach took off after a 2003 revision to the DOJ guidelines that added "Principles" for the prosecution of organizations in the *U.S. Attorneys' Manual* used by federal prosecutors.[43] The DOJ has revised the guidelines several more times, including in Fall 2015 to emphasize the importance of investigating individual wrongdoing in corporate cases. The new guidelines now contain a section announcing the new "focus on individual wrongdoers," including from the earliest stages in a corporate criminal investigation.[44] The revised principles also emphasize that cooperation credit will only be given to a company that identifies responsible individuals: "In order for a company to receive any consideration for cooperation under this section, the company must identify all individuals involved in or responsible for the misconduct at issue, regardless of their position, status or seniority."[45] Prosecutors weigh as a separate factor self-reporting by firms in the form of a "timely and voluntary disclosure."[46] The principles also add a section on coordinating parallel proceedings, to encourage cooperation between prosecutors and those pursuing civil, regulatory, and administrative actions.[47]

However, the guidelines largely maintain a flexible approach, encouraging consideration of a broad set of factors when deciding whether to pursue an indictment or conviction, or alternatively, a deferred or non-prosecution agreement. Those factors include: (1) the nature and seriousness of the offense; (2) the pervasiveness of wrongdoing within the corporation; (3) the company's history of similar conduct, including civil and criminal actions; (4) the corporation's willingness to cooperate in investigation of its agents; (5) the corporate compliance program; (6) timely and voluntary disclosure of wrongdoing; (7) any remedial actions, such as firing wrongdoers and cooperating with government agencies; (8) the collateral consequences that a prosecution would cause, including to shareholders; (9) the issue of whether it would be sufficient to impose civil or regulatory

[41] 18 U.S.C. § 3571(c)(3) (2016).

[42] Memorandum from Eric Holder, Deputy Att'y Gen., U.S. Dep't of Justice, to Component Heads and United States Attorneys, Bringing Criminal Charges Against Corporations (June 16, 1999).

[43] Memorandum from Deputy Att'y Gen. Larry D. Thompson, U.S. Dep't of Justice, to Heads of Dep't Components & U.S. Attorneys, Principles of Federal Prosecution of Business Organizations (Jan. 20, 2003) (the "Thompson Memo").

[44] U.S. Attorneys' Manual, § 9-28.210 (2015). [45] *Id.* § 9-28.700. [46] *Id.* § 9-28.900.

[47] *Id.* § 1-12.000.

remedies; and (10) the adequacy of prosecutions of individuals.[48] Those factors are "illustrative" and not an exclusive or "exhaustive" list, and "no single factor will be dispositive." Thus, prosecutors retain substantial discretion to weigh these various considerations in any given case.

Despite that flexibility, common approaches can be observed when reading the terms of these agreements. Deferred prosecution agreements are commonly quite complex, as are the goals of these corporate prosecution agreements. The agreements can include criminal fines, as well as other penalties such as restitution to victims, civil forfeiture, payments to regulators, and community service payments. They can specify compliance terms, including creation of new positions to supervise compliance, changes to governance, new auditing systems, and retention of independent monitors to supervise compliance. The DOJ's guidelines note prosecutors should try to assess whether the compliance program is just a "paper program," and should consider "whether the corporation has provided for a staff sufficient to audit, document, analyze, and utilize the results of the corporation's compliance efforts."[49] The DOJ has also made new efforts to conduct detailed review of such compliance provisions. These agreements typically last from two to three years.

I have examined the terms of these U.S. deferred and non-prosecution agreements with corporations in some details. About one-quarter require the retention of monitors to supervise compliance, but most do not. The fines are often not all that they could be. I collected a set of federal deferred and non-prosecution agreements beginning in 2001.[50] I was surprised to learn that in almost half of the deferred and non-prosecution agreements with companies entered from 2001 to 2012, no criminal fine was imposed.[51] I also found that for public companies prosecuted from 2001 to 2012, total payments made to prosecutors averaged just 0.09 percent of market capitalization.[52] From 2001 to 2014, prosecutors entered 306 deferred and non-prosecution agreements with companies. Among those, only 34 percent or 103 companies had officers or employees prosecuted, with 408 total individuals prosecuted. Few of those individuals were higher-up officers or executives.

U.S. prosecutors have also targeted financial institutions far more than ever before. In recent cases, they have not used deferred prosecution agreements but rather secured guilty pleas from banks.[53] The principles do say that "prosecutors should generally seek a plea to an appropriate offense," and also that "generally" this should be a plea to the "most serious, readily provable offense charged."[54] While the guidelines regarding

[48] *Id.* §§ 9–28.000–9–28.100, 9–28.300. [49] *Id.* § 9–28.800.

[50] I have maintained for some time the most complete data available on such federal deferred and non-prosecution agreements with corporations. *See* Brandon L. Garrett & Jon Ashley, Corporate Prosecution Registry, University of Virginia School of Law, (last updated Oct. 19, 2017), at http://lib.law.virginia.edu/Garrett/corporate-prosecution-registry/index.html.

[51] Garrett, *supra* note 39, at 69.

[52] *Id.* at 150 (noting that few deferred or non-prosecution agreements from 2001 to 2012 included a guidelines calculation (only thirty of them), and only three of those noted fines at the top of the applicable range).

[53] Brandon L. Garrett, *The Rise of Bank Prosecutions*, 126 Yale L.J. Forum 33 (2016).

[54] U.S. Attorneys' Manual, § 9–28.1500 (2015).

organizational prosecutions in the United States do not state with any specificity when a conviction is appropriate versus a deferred prosecution agreement, prosecutors have been more willing to seek convictions, including in high profile cases, than in the past decade, when many of the most significant corporate prosecutions were resolved out of court. In the past year, a new approach, borrowed from FCPA cases, has rewarded substantial cooperation and self-reporting by companies with declinations. U.S. enforcement may be moving in a more lenient direction under the new Administration.

1. Canada

In Canada, corporations may plead guilty, under a plea bargaining system in which the judge may accept or reject the plea and the judge ultimately imposes the sentence. The plea agreements are not made public, but the accompanying statements of facts are public.[55] In addition to any penalty, a 15 percent surcharge is added toward provincial victim restitution funds.[56] The approach does not permit the type of informal corporate settlements that are now common in the United States. However, in May 2018, Canada introduced deferred prosecution agreements in corporate prosecutions, calling them remediation agreements, and regulating their use in legislation with detailed criteria that prosecutors must consider.

2. United Kingdom

In the United Kingdom, corporations have long been criminally liable. Corporations have often settled criminal cases through guilty pleas. In such cases, the corporation admits guilt and receives a conviction. In addition, corporations may enter a Civil Recovery Order, in which a payment is made but there is no civil judgment.[57] The United Kingdom adopted deferred prosecution agreements with corporations by statute in the Crime and Courts Act of 2013.[58] One event prompting the legislation was the concern raised by the judge in the *Innospec* case, involving foreign bribery charges resolved in a 2010 settlement between the Serious Fraud Office, as well as prosecutors in the United States The judge called argued that in any criminal settlement process, "it is for the court to decide on the sentence and to explain that to the public."[59] The high

[55] OECD, *Phase 3 Report on Implementing the OECD Anti-Bribery Convention in Canada* (2011), 20, 22, at https://www.oecd.org/canada/Canadaphase3reportEN.pdf.

[56] *See* Dep't of Justice (Canada), *Provisions of Interest to Victims of Crime*, at http://canada.justice.gc.ca/eng/cj-jp/victims-victimes/code.html.

[57] World Bank/Star, *supra* note 1, at 26–27.

[58] Crime and Courts Act of 2013 (U.K.), at http://www.legislation.gov.uk/ukpga/2013/22/schedule/17/enacted.

[59] *See* R v. Innospec Ltd. [2010] Crim. L.R. 665 Crown Ct. (Southwark) ¶ 46, at http://www.banksr.co.uk/images/Other%20Documents/Crown%20Court%20decisions/R%20v%20Innospec.pdf.

court judge ruled prosecutors had unconstitutionally reached a sentencing arrangement with the company and that "no such arrangements should be made again."[60]

The 2013 legislation permits such corporate settlements, but only with judicial oversight and approval. A detailed code of practice for prosecutors was published by the Crown Prosecution Service and Serious Fraud Office accompanying the legislation, and emphasizing the importance of the public interest in whether to offer a deferred prosecution agreement.[61] The prosecutor must obtain a declaration from a judge that the deferred prosecution agreement is "likely to be in the interests of justice" and that the terms are "fair, reasonable, and proportionate."[62] Once the agreement is negotiated, the terms are presented to the Crown Court for approval, and the judge can review the substance of the agreement and decide whether the agreement is "fair, reasonable, and proportionate."[63] In addition, any failure to comply with a deferred prosecution agreement has consequences set out and a judge will adjudicate any possible breach. The first deferred prosecution agreement in the UK, with Standard Bank, was approved by the judge, noting, in contrast to the situation in *Innospec*, that the court was permitted to make a "detailed analysis" of the circumstances of the offense and the financial penalty imposed and that "there is no question of the parties having reached a private compromise without appropriate independent judicial consideration of the public interest."[64]

3. France

In France, while corporate criminal liability existed, a statutory scheme that permits judicially approved settlements with corporations in foreign bribery cases was recently enacted in Fall 2016. This Sapin II legislation calls for regulation of corporate compliance programs, the creation of a new French anti-bribery agency to issue such regulations, as well as the adoption of specific provisions regarding judicial review and approval of deferred prosecution agreements in criminal cases.[65] The French lawmakers explicitly rejected the proposal to adopt a U.S.-style model in which deferred prosecution agreements with corporations could be entered largely out of court. Instead, the Sapin II legislation adopts a model more along the lines of the UK approach in which judicial review is required, but also with more involvement and regulation by an administrative agency overseeing anticorruption efforts.

[60] *Id.* ¶ 45.

[61] Crown Prosecution Service and Serious Fraud Office, *Deferred Prosecution Agreements Code of Practice* (2014), at https://www.cps.gov.uk/publications/directors_guidance/dpa_cop.pdf.

[62] U.K. Crime and Courts Act 2013, §45 and sched. 17(7).

[63] *Id.* at sched. 17(8)(1).

[64] Serious Fraud Office v Standard Bank Plc: Deferred Prosecution Agreement (Case No: U20150854), English High Court, Queen's Bench Division (Leveson P), 30 November 2015, at https://www.judiciary.gov.uk/wp-content/uploads/2015/11/sfo-v-standard-bank_Final_1.pdf.

[65] White & Case, *Update on Sapin II Law*, Jan. 10, 2017, at https://www.whitecase.com/publications/alert/update-sapin-ii-law.

4. Additional Out-of-Court Settlement Approaches

Other countries have long used more informal settlement mechanisms in corporate crime cases. The Netherlands permits out of court settlements with corporations under Article 74 of the Dutch Criminal Code and a Directive on Large and Special Transactions.[66] Several foreign bribery cases have been resolved through such settlements. For example, in 2016, Openbaar Ministerie entered such a settlement with Russian telecom company Vimpelcom, which simultaneously settled with the U.S. Department of Justice, and with almost $400 million paid to Dutch and U.S. authorities.[67] In Norway, corporate prosecutions are also often settled out of court. In Norway, the mechanism is a penalty notice in which the prosecutor sets out the fine to be imposed.[68] Økokrim, the Norwegian authority that handles economic and environmental crimes, frequently uses penalty notices in corporate cases.[69] Økokrim explained to the OECD in 2011 that "economic crime trials are usually very lengthy and a much bigger burden on law enforcement resources . . . furthermore, representatives of companies sometimes also prefer a swifter conclusion to a case to minimise the reputational risks to their corporation."[70]

In Italy, corporations may settle criminal matters under the *patteggiamento* system, which resembles a plea bargain, and is overseen by judges.[71] If a company enters a *patteggiamento*, the entity may obtain a one-third reduction in the penalty, avoid making an admission of guilt, avoid debarment or other regulatory sanctions, and benefit from a possible "extinction" of the sentence after five years. The OECD has criticized the lack of information made public in cases in which companies settle charges using a *patteggiamento*.[72]

Other countries use informal mechanisms to resolve corporate charges. Switzerland uses a summary punishment order, typically used for misdemeanor offenses, and a mechanism called "Reparation" after which charges are dropped if the defendant provides compensation.[73] In foreign bribery cases, including regarding Alstom and a subsidiary

[66] Debevoise & Plimpton LLP, *Small Country, Big Punch: The Netherlands Anti-bribery Prosecution of SBM Offshore*, Dec. 2014, at http://www.lexology.com/library/detail.aspx?g=1ef21f00-f4af-4e39-a0f6-2b309dd9bb6f.

[67] Openbaar Ministrie, *Vimpelcom Pays Close to 400 Million Dollars to the Netherlands for Bribery in Uzbekistan*, Feb. 18, 2016 (Neth.), at https://www.om.nl/algemeen/english/@93227/vimpelcom-pays-close/.

[68] Frode Elgesem, *The Corruption Enforcement View from Norway*, TheBriberyAct.com, Dec. 20, 2014, at http://thebriberyact.com/2014/12/12/the-corruption-enforcement-view-from-norway-by-frode-elgesem/.

[69] OECD Working Group on Bribery, *Phase 3 Report on Implementing the OECD Anti-Bribery Convention in Norway*, June 2011, at http://www.oecd.org/daf/anti-bribery/anti-briberyconvention/Norwayphase3reportEN.pdf.

[70] *Id.* ¶ 64.

[71] OECD Working Group on Bribery, *Phase 3 Report on Implementing the OECD Anti-Bribery Convention in Italy*, Dec. 2011, at http://www.oecd.org/daf/anti-bribery/anti-briberyconvention/Italyphase3reportEN.pdf.

[72] OECD Working Group on Bribery, *Italy: Follow-up to the Phase 3 Report and Recommendations*, May 2014, at http://www.oecd.org/daf/anti-bribery/ItalyP3WrittenFollowUpReportEN.pdf.

[73] Schweizerische Strafprozessordnung (StPO) arts. 352, 358 (2007) (Switz.).

of Siemens, Reparation was used to settle cases.[74] Greece has settled foreign bribery cases against corporations using parliamentary decree.[75] In Brazil, the Federal Public Ministry has entered leniency agreements with corporations, most prominently, with Odebrecht regarding the national Operation Car Wash scandal; questions remain whether other government agencies will honor the settlement.[76]

V. Concerns with Corporate Prosecution Settlement Approaches

While the settlement-oriented approach toward corporate prosecutors has provided prosecutors with a great deal of flexibility, concerns have been raised with that approach in the United States and internationally. As discussed, countries such as the UK and France have adopted settlement regimes that involve more judicial supervision to alleviate concerns with such settlements, while preserving some of the flexibility that they provide. A series of functional considerations should be considered when deciding whether and how to pursue corporate prosecutions.

Transparency has been one concern raised regarding corporate settlements. Full trial or full criminal process can produce a public record concerning the crimes committed, full notification to victims, and a public trial or at least a public sentencing. Corporate defendants, of course, seek to avoid negative publicity in reaching a settlement with the authorities. One benefit corporate defendants may receive is the ability to not fully admit guilt (in the United States, that is done in civil cases, but an admission of guilt is routine in criminal settlements). Some settlements do report the amounts of fines paid and some description of the facts, but often not based on a complete record or a detailed statement of facts. A separate concern has been with the amount of the fines themselves and how they are calculated. The DOJ has stated that punishment and deterrence can be accomplished by "substantial fines."[77] What amount is appropriate, though, may be difficult to assess. The harm to victims may be difficult to calculate, and the profit to a corporation may be hard to measure if a financial scheme was not fully carried out. Legislation was proposed in the U.S. Senate, although not enacted, to require greater transparency in corporate fines.[78] Organizational sentencing guidelines in the United

[74] *See* Alstom Network Schweiz AG, Summary Punishment Order: Article 352 Swiss Code of Criminal Procedure, Case No. EAII.04.0325-LEN (Nov. 22 2011), available at https://star.worldbank.org/corruption-cases/; see also OECD Working Group on Bribery, *Phase 3 Report on Implementing the Anti-Bribery Convention in Switzerland*, Dec. 2011, at http://www.oecd.org/daf/anti-bribery/anti-briberyconvention/Switzerlandphase3reportEN.pdf.

[75] World Bank/Star, *supra* note 1, at 131–33.

[76] Maira Magro, *Odebrecht Fears "Government Disloyalty" in Leniency Agreements*, Valor Int'l, Mar. 13, 2017.

[77] U.S. Attorneys' Manual, § 9–28.1500 (2015).

[78] Danielle Douglas, *Senate Bill Targets Corporations That Deduct Settlement Payouts*, Wash. Post, Nov. 6, 2013 (describing proposed Government Settlement Transparency and Reform Act).

States set out detailed criteria for corporate fines, but they have been criticized and they are often not used in cases that settle through deferred or non-prosecution agreements.[79]

An additional concern has been with the structural or compliance terms of agreements. Without judicial review, prosecutors may be less able than judges or regulators to independently assess whether corporations are complying fully with the non-financial terms of the agreements. The DOJ has retained a compliance counsel to focus on reviewing and improving the compliance terms of corporate agreements.[80] Recently, the DOJ has issued guidance on the subject of corporate compliance, which is another improvement. In the past, many agreements had stated that a company should adopt best practices or a compliance program, but without specifying how it should do so or whether or how compliance efforts should be assessed.[81]

A separate concern has been that when prosecutors settle with corporations, while they may impose fines and compliance reforms, they may fail to prosecute or otherwise deter executives or other individual culprits. I have found, for example, that in only about a third of deferred and non-prosecution agreements, are any individuals prosecuted, and very few of those that are prosecuted are higher-up officers or executives.[82] Securing the cooperation of the corporation in investigations of individuals should be a central goal of corporate criminal liability, but in the past, that goal was not emphasized in the United States. The more recent changes to the prosecution guidelines, in the Fall 2015 Yates Memo, may have placed more focus on individual accountability, but it is too early to tell whether that additional guidance will be effective.

Judicial supervision may be limited for settlements. A separate concern has been that the public interest may be neglected without independent judicial review, or that prosecutorial discretion may be too great. The General Accountability Office criticized the DOJ in the United States for lack of criteria for deciding whether a company receives a deferred or non-prosecution agreement.[83] In 2013, federal judge Richard J. Leon rejected a deferred prosecution agreement with a company for foreign bribery, "looking at the DPA in its totality" and noting that not only were "no individuals . . . being prosecuted for their conduct at issue here" but also "a number of the employees who were directly involved in the transactions are being allowed to remain with the company."[84] However, the D.C. Circuit Court of Appeals rejected that ruling and held that the judge exceeded his discretion.[85] In another case, Judge Emmet Sullivan suggested that certain factors could provide "useful guideposts" when evaluating whether a deferred prosecution agreement

[79] *See, e.g.*, Jennifer Arlen, *The Failure of the Organizational Sentencing Guidelines*, 66 Miami L. Rev. 231 (2012). For an overview, see Garrett, *supra* note 39, at ch. 6.

[80] Press Release, Dep't of Justice, *New Compliance Counsel Expert Retained by the DOJ Fraud Section*, Nov. 3, 2015, at http://www.justice.gov/criminal-fraud/file/790236/download.

[81] Garrett, *supra* note 39, at ch.2.

[82] Jed S. Rakoff, *The Financial Crisis: Why Have No High-Level Executives Been Prosecuted?*, N.Y. Rev. Books, Jan. 9 2014; Brandon L. Garrett, *The Corporate Criminal as Scapegoat*, 101 Va. L. Rev. 1789 (2015).

[83] Gov't Accountability Office, *Preliminary Observations on the DOJ's Use and Oversight of Deferred Prosecution and Non-prosecution Agreements* 41 (June 25, 2009).

[84] United States v. Fokker Services B.V., Docket No. 1:14-cr-00121 (D.D.C. Jun 04, 2014).

[85] United States v. Fokker Servs., B.V., 818 F.3d 733, 742 (D.C. Cir. 2016).

with a company is truly "designed to secure a defendant's reformation," or whether the terms are "so vague and minimal as to render them a sham."[86] In contrast, in countries in which judges may review and decide whether charges are appropriately brought against a defendant, and judges decide upon the sentence ultimately imposed, prosecutors cannot exercise nearly as much discretion when negotiating with corporations.[87]

Countries have very different systems of criminal procedure, and those procedural rules may impact the desirability of settlement regimes and of corporate criminal liability itself. For example, in the United States, corporations may decide to waive attorney-client privilege on behalf of employees, giving them a great deal of leverage in negotiations and also making the cooperation of the corporation extremely important in order to access evidence during investigations.[88] In countries in which evidentiary privileges are narrower, corporate investigations might be more feasible without that corporate cooperation. In contrast, in countries in which employees are not typically at-will and labor protections are stronger, it may be far more difficult for a corporation to encourage or pressure employees or officers to cooperate with law enforcement. Civil law alternatives may be important as well. If a country has adequate resources for civil corporate investigations and sufficient penalties are available, civil enforcement may effectively substitute for criminal enforcement against corporations.

Prosecutorial power is extremely broad in the United States. Prosecutors have broad discretion to charge and to negotiate sentences through plea bargains and other types of agreements with defendants. That broad authority makes relatively more informal negotiated settlement regimes far more practicable in the United States than in countries in which judicial review would be presumed and out-of-court negotiations frowned upon or deemed unauthorized by law or unconstitutional. Prosecutors in the United States also have strong resources, the ability to bring complex cases to trial, and broad jurisdiction due to the role of trade with the United States, the role that the U.S. dollar plays in international finance, and the U.S.-based stock exchanges, over a wide range of international corporations. Multinational criminal cases can be readily brought in U.S. courts. The same is not true of the courts in many countries. That gives U.S. prosecutors an especially prominent role in corporate regulation generally, and in corporate criminal liability in particular.

Settlements also have some important advantages. They can permit more efficient use of law enforcement resources, particularly in highly complex cases. Settlements can avoid firms suffering collateral consequences of a conviction such as debarment or suspension from government contracting or participation in a regulated industry. In the United States as well as in the European Union, for example, bribery convictions can

[86] United States v. Saena Tech Corp., Memorandum Opinion 45 (D.D.C. Oct. 21, 2015).

[87] Jenia Iontcheva Turner, *Judicial Participation in Plea Negotiations: A Comparative View*, 54 Am. J. Comp. L. 199, 215 (2006).

[88] *See* Upjohn Co. v. United States, 449 U.S. 383 (1981).

result in debarment.[89] Fines may be reduced to encourage cooperation in investigations of other companies and individuals. Fines may also be reduced to reflect parallel settlements in other countries. Negative publicity may be reduced for the company. What balance is appropriate between the advantages of more informal and flexible settlements and the advantages of more formal and rule-governed judicial resolutions is a difficult moral and policy question. It is far from clear that any country has the right balance.

VI. International Cooperation

International organizations have played a role in corporate prosecutions and in promoting corporate accountability norms. For example, the United Nations and the World Bank have done so in foreign bribery cases.[90] The OECD has played an important role in antitrust and foreign bribery work. The OECD Anti-Bribery Convention has established binding legal standards on member nations, and as the first such international law regime, it has had a great deal of influence. In addition, the OECD has promoted best practices, made recommendations, and evaluated member countries in reviews and reports. In addition, the OECD has provided advice to countries to combat tax crimes.

Parallel and collaborative prosecutions are also increasingly common. For example, in the Siemens case, the DOJ and the Securities and Exchange Commission (SEC) in the United States collaborated with the Munich Public Prosecutor's Office and German authorities, including based on mutual legal assistance provisions of the OECD Convention. The plea bargain by Siemens included $800 million in fines paid to the DOJ and SEC and $800 million in fines paid to the Munich Public Prosecutor's Office.[91] The agreement also included two corporate monitors, one U.S. Independent Counsel, and a German corporate monitor, Dr. Theo Waigel, a former German Minister of Finance. The employees prosecuted in the case were convicted by Munich prosecutors; individuals were indicted in the United States. but none so far successfully extradited.[92] The Fraud Section at DOJ has emphasized the role that international cooperation plays in foreign bribery cases generally, which are international crimes. The Antitrust Division similarly

[89] For the EU, see Article 57 of Directive 2014/24/EU (effective Apr. 2016), at http://eur-lex.europa.eu/search.html?qid=1512597425986&text=32014L0024&scope=EURLEX&type=quick&lang=en; see also Article 45 of Council Directive 2004/18/EC (in effect until 2016); Public Contracts Regulations 2015, S.I. 2015/102, pt. II (U.K. implementation of Directive 2014/24/EU).

[90] WorldBank/Star, *supra* note 1 at 44.

[91] Press Release, Dep't of Justice, *Siemens AG and Three Subsidiaries Plead Guilty to Foreign Corrupt Practices Act Violations and Agree to Pay $450 Million in Combined Criminal Fines*, Dec. 15, 2008, at http://www.usdoj.gov/opa/pr/2008/December/08-crm-1105.html.

[92] *Ex-Siemens Execs Found Guilty in Bribery Case*, Reuters, Apr. 20, 2010, at Factiva, Doc. No. LBA0000020100420e64k00114.

has emphasized joint investigations and mutual assistance agreements in its cartel enforcement, and it has worked with the International Competition Network and the OECD to promote cooperation.[93]

VII. Conclusion

Corporate criminal enforcement has increased in frequency and in the size of monetary sanctions over the past decade. More countries have successfully prosecuted corporations, particularly in areas such as antitrust and foreign bribery. Most of the prosecutions and settlements have been brought in countries that are major financial centers, with the bulk being brought in the United States, but also in the United Kingdom, France, Germany, and increasingly in certain developing countries. The tools to resolve these corporate prosecutions become steadily more varied, using civil, criminal, and hybrid mechanisms. Parallel enforcement is far more common, with cooperation between enforcement agencies. As countries consider whether to adopt new tools to combat corporate crime, they should pay attention to both the successes of new approaches and to concerns raised regarding whether they serve the public interest. In the past, the common approach was to use corporate criminal enforcement sparingly and in limited form. As corporate crimes have grown in scale and in social harm, enhancing corporate liability for such crimes is a sensible idea. Tailoring enforcement to ensure both individual and corporate-level accountability, to ensure transparency and adequate incentives for cooperation and remediation, and to deter and prevent future crimes: that is the challenge going forward. The new international dialogue concerning corporate criminal liability will hopefully contribute to new experimentation and improved approaches toward corporate crime.

References

Sara Sun Beale & Adam G. Safwat, *What Developments in Western Europe Tell Us About American Critiques of Corporate Criminal Liability*, 8 Buff. Crim. L. Rev. 110 (2004)

Edward B. Diskant, *Comparative Criminal Liability: Exploring the Uniquely American Doctrine Through Comparative Criminal Procedure*, 118 Yale L. J. 126 (2008)

Brandon L. Garrett, *Too Big to Jail: How Prosecutors Compromise with Corporations* (2014)

Brandon L. Garrett, *Globalized Corporate Prosecutions*, 97 Va. L. Rev. 1775 (2011)

OECD, *The Liability of Legal Persons for Foreign Bribery: A Stocktaking Report* (2016)

Mark Pieth & Radha Ivory, *Emergence and Convergence: Corporate Criminal Liability Principles in Overview*, in *Corporate Criminal Liability* (Mark Pieth & Radha Ivory eds., 2011)

[93] Gary R. Spratling & D. Jarrett Arp, *The International Leniency Revolution* 8–9 (2003), at http://www.gibsondunn.com/fstore/documents/pubs/Spratling-Arp%20ABA2003_Paper.pdf.

CHAPTER 20

SPECIAL PROCEDURES FOR WHITE-COLLAR AND CORPORATE WRONGDOING

A European Perspective

JULIETTE TRICOT

I. Introduction

The prosecution and punishment of white-collar crime and corporate wrongdoing appear to share a feature common to most legal orders: they are rarely subject to the ordinary criminal procedure, but are handled instead via specialized procedures. This specialization, this separate treatment, has contributed to the founding of the criminological category of white-collar crime.[1] Although debated since its inception,[2] this category tends to aim at, without limiting itself to, offenses[3] that have a corporation as their framework, tool, or vehicle.[4] This study will focus principally on the procedures applicable to illicit corporate behavior, that is, to offenses committed by or within a corporation.[5]

[1] Edwin Hardin Sutherland, *The Problem of White Collar Crime*, in *White Collar Crime: The Uncut Version* 3–10 (1983).

[2] Samuel W. Buell, *"White Collar" Crime*, in *Oxford Handbook of Criminal Law* 837–61 (Martin Dubber & Tatjana Hörnle eds., 2014).

[3] Following Buell, id., the category can be identified with the following offenses: business fraud, fraud in government, fraud against government, and harm to public health and environment.

[4] "Some are necessarily related to the corporation: they can be committed only in the context of a corporation"; others "have only a sporadic relation to the corporation." In this case, they can be committed not only within or by the corporation, but also outside of any relationship with a corporation. *See* Geneviève Giudicelli-Delage, *Droit pénal des affaires* 13 (3d ed. 2006).

[5] As Celia Wells wrote in *Containing Corporate Crime: Civil or Criminal Controls*, in *European Developments in Corporate Criminal Liability* 13, 14 (James Gobert & Ana-Marie Pascal eds., 2011)

Paradoxically, the particular fate reserved for these offenders,[6] although it highlights a selective operation of the criminal justice system,[7] has not led to the adoption of measures to reintegrate them into the general (ordinary) system, nor to normalizing treatment of this kind of delinquency. Instead it is accompanied by a consolidation and deepening of this special treatment.[8] That is, the development of a special form of penal law focusing on business and targeting corporations (and natural persons involved, executives especially) has promoted a technical and instrumental conception of law enforcement generally—penal, civil, and administrative. It has led to an ancillary conception of criminal law enforcement in particular. Each is placed at the service of objectives to secure and guide the economy as well as to regulate markets rather than protect values. Special substantive and procedural rules have been devised for the business sector and its actors—professionals, insiders,[9] and firms.

With respect to substantive rules, their formal features now distinguish them from other penal and punitive standards, even at the risk of distancing them from the traditional principles and guarantees of criminal law.[10] Regarding procedural rules, the acknowledgment of the specific issues raised by corporate crime[11] has promoted two major trends. The first is the consensus that these specific problems posed by white-collar crime must be treated by equally specific procedural responses. The challenge is to overcome two sets of problems: those associated with the *detection* of clandestine behaviors, which are often very sophisticated and complex, and those linked to their *prosecution*, given the difficulty of proving either the required intent or that the conduct of some actors can be imputed to others. Another problem is the imbalance in resources:

("The corporation is for white-collar criminals 'what the gun or knife is for the common criminal.'"), quoting Stanton Wheeler & Mitchell Rothman, *The Organization as Weapon in White-Collar Crime*, 80 Mich. L. Rev. 1403–26 (1982).

[6] *See* Nicolas Fischer & Arnaud Spire, *L'Etat face aux illégalismes*, 87 Politix 7, 10 (2009/3): "Sutherland's contribution is that he not only casts light on the very low visibility of crime by the dominant but also shows that when it is penalized, it benefits from procedures different from those foreseen for the criminal justice system, as for example, settlements, arbitration, or administrative or civil penalties."

[7] Michel Foucault, *Discipline and Punish: The Birth of Prison* (1977); Anthony Amicelle, *Differential Management of Economic and Financial Illegalisms: Anti-money Laundering and "Tax Issues,"* 10 Champs Pénal/Penal Field (2013), *available at* https://champpenal.revues.org/8895#.

[8] *See* Anthony Amicelle, *Deux attitudes face au monde: la criminologie à l'épreuve des illégalismes financiers*, 94-95-96 Culture & Conflits 65, 68 (2014/2) ("Regulatory instruments, intended to produce equal treatment by generalizing the visibility of economic and financial illegalisms, succeeded one another at the irregular pace of political priorities and crisis contexts. However, in concrete, they show a process of conversion and adaptation of differentiation between illegalisms that (re)produce an inequality of treatment, according to the situations and the categories of the people concerned." (author's translation). *See also* the work of Pierre Lascoumes, who pointed out how "business crime" was very early differentiated from "ordinary crime" by the types of social response that it provoked, emphasizing in particular its true privilege, namely the plurality of legal frameworks likely to be applied to it. Pierre Lascoumes, *Les affaires ou l'art de l'ombre: les délinquances économiques et financières et leur contrôle* (1986); Pierre Lascoumes, *L'illégalisme, outil d'analyse*, 3 Sociétés & Représentations 79 (1996).

[9] Giudicelli-Delage, *supra* note 4.

[10] Buell, *supra* note 2.

[11] John Braithwaite & Gilbert Geis, *On Theory and Action for Corporate Crime Control*, 28 Crime & Delinq. 292, 314 (1984).

those deployed by white-collar or corporate offenders often vastly exceed those available to prosecuting authorities. The second trend is a consensus that the criminal justice system—compared to other law enforcement mechanisms—is not necessarily the best or even an adequate system[12] to tackle white-collar or corporate wrongdoing. Criminal justice must therefore be avoided or adapted. In any case, it is not viewed as the *only* appropriate system, so recourse to other law enforcement mechanisms must be envisioned as a replacement, alternative, or supplement to it. As a result, the procedural responses to corporate crime in Europe today appear to be characterized by combinations of a wide array of mechanisms with various natures and forms, ranging from criminal law enforcement to punitive administrative or civil law enforcement mechanisms.[13]

In the search for an ideal option between public and private enforcement—or among civil, administrative, and criminal procedures—the choice of one form over another has been replaced by the search for an ideal mix of various forms, whether integrated progressively, successively, or cumulatively. In this context, the question becomes determining the right features of each option and how to best link them in light of the nature of their targets (natural or legal persons)[14] and/or the enforcement objectives (neutralization, retribution, or remediation).

Thus, it may be assumed that the "supply" of law enforcement mechanisms available in a given legal system may be among the elements that determine how the power to prosecute is exercised. This is the case when a single authority can choose between several types of proceedings or more broadly among several responses to illicit conduct. In this respect, the possibility of compromise is obviously a key element in all prosecution policies. But it is also true where other authorities are vested with concurrent enforcement powers and may have de jure or de facto priority over criminal justice authorities to intervene against illicit behavior.

For this reason, although it is common to stress the rising power of prosecutors[15] at the expense of judges, an analysis of what might be called the supply of law enforcement measures details the boundaries, conditions, and reality of this rising power in the field of business crime. In particular, this kind of analysis observes not only the role played by the competing public institutional actors that control, wholly or in part, inputs into the criminal justice system, but also the growing influence of the defendants themselves[16] in the course of criminal or other enforcement proceedings.

[12] For a comparison in this regard between the U.S. and European approaches (with references mainly to the German system), see Edward B. Diskant, *Comparative Corporate Criminal Liability: Exploring the Uniquely American Doctrine Through Comparative Criminal Procedure*, 118 Yale L.J. 126 (2008).

[13] Nicholas Lord & Michael Levi, *Determining the Adequate Enforcement of White-Collar and Corporate Crimes in Europe*, in *The Routledge Handbook of White-Collar and Corporate Criminal Law in Europe* 39, 56 (Judith van Erp et al. eds., 2015).

[14] On this essential dimension, see David M. Uhlmann, *The Pendulum Swings: Reconsidering Corporate Criminal Prosecution*, 49 U.C. Davis L. Rev. 1235–83 (2016).

[15] In this sense, see Buell, *supra* note 2, at 846–47 (highlighting that where an offense can be punished criminally, sanctioned civilly, or both, "the mix [is] often determined not so much by legal doctrine as by prosecutor and enforce discretion").

[16] And among them, corporations at the expense of the natural persons, or at least of some of them.

For this purpose, it first is essential to return to the variety of the procedures applicable to corporate crime. Assessing the abundance of these procedures in a legal system offers the opportunity to take into account and reflect on the fact that this diversity is indicative of the transformation of the state's law enforcement power, broadly understood.[17] This metamorphosis is the result of various forms of expansion and redistribution of public powers as the meaning of State intervention evolves.[18] Accordingly, by carefully examining these underlying transformations and classifying the special procedures developed for corporate crime alongside ordinary penal procedures, it is possible to grasp the philosophy (or philosophies) behind them.

The comparison of these special procedures applicable to white-collar and corporate wrongdoing with standard criminal prosecutions also enables us to better understand the meaning and scope of their use instead of or as a complement to criminal prosecution. It is then necessary to identify the shared characteristics that distinguish these special procedures from standard criminal procedures. This task is facilitated by the influential harmonization of the "two Europes"—the European Union and the Council of Europe—in these areas and, more broadly, by the internationalization of economic and financial law.

Finally, to complete the analysis, attention should be paid to the relationships of these special procedures with the criminal justice system, and in particular to the use of criminal prosecutions in order to identify the effects—desired and induced—that the operation (and mere existence) of these special procedures exert on the criminal justice system.

Accordingly, Section II offers a classification of the diverse procedures applicable to white-collar and corporate wrongdoing, and of the factors that promote the development of one type over another. Section III identifies the essential, common characteristics of these procedures in order to clarify what (still) distinguishes them from criminal procedures and "ordinary" criminal prosecutions. Finally, Section IV determines the impact that these procedures are likely to have on the criminal justice system, particularly on prosecutorial powers.

II. The Variety of Special Procedures

Compared with other types of crime, referred to here as "classic" or "ordinary" crime, white-collar and particularly corporate crimes are a fertile ground for specialized procedures. These procedures can either lie outside the criminal system (and function concurrently with it or not) or be criminal proceedings especially adapted to deal with

[17] Fischer & Spire, *supra* note 6.

[18] Daniel Ohana, *Regulatory Offenses and Administrative Sanctions: Between Criminal and Administrative Law*, in *Oxford Handbook of Criminal Law* 1064, 1086 (Martin Dubber & Tatjana Hörnle eds., 2014).

this type of crime. Thus, diversification simultaneously takes place both inside and outside the criminal justice system.[19]

In continental Europe, a portion of the history of this diversity outside the criminal justice system dates back to the development, alongside the penal law, of an administrative penal law,[20] bearing in mind that the (relative) preference for an administrative alternative (broadly understood)[21] was also revived by the building of the European Union.

Indeed, beyond this lengthy history, several factors have contributed to the increased role of administrative enforcement, through expansion of its field of intervention and transformation of its uses. On the one hand, it is necessary to take into account the impact of changes in state intervention as the state has been transformed.[22] Those changes produced an apparent paradox. "Seeking to promote a logic of regulation based on negotiation and persuasion, the public authorities nonetheless little by little endowed independent administrative authorities with broad powers of sanction; the consequence has been a redeployment but also a reinforcement of administrative enforcement."[23] On the other hand, and not unrelated, one must also consider the influence and constraints imposed by the European Union and the international setting.[24]

It is important to understand the reasons for the development of this procedural variety. One approach is to classify them according to the sectors concerned (and their characteristic features), the enforcement philosophy that drives them, and the forces or constraints that promote recourse to one type rather than another. It is possible to distinguish three main types of procedures that, although they have appeared successively over history, have never replaced one another but instead served as additions to create more varied and extensive types of enforcement.

First, there are procedures derived from sovereign powers. A typical example are the police powers of tax or customs authorities. Closely linked to the history of each state, these procedures more than others reflect national particularities and traditions.

Second, more recent procedures evolved based on regulatory powers for which the European Union has shown a clear preference. It has thus substantially influenced their development, as illustrated in the emblematic areas of competition law and of the financial markets.

[19] *Infra* Section III.

[20] Traces of this history can be observed in the national reports drafted on the occasion of the conference of the International Association of Penal Law at the end of the 1980s, see *The Legal and Practical Problems Posed by the Difference Between Criminal Law and Administrative Penal Law (Stockholm, June 15–17, 1987)*, 59 Revue Internationale de Droit Pénal (1988). On the important discussion that enlivened German doctrine and radiated well beyond Germany's borders, see Ohana, *supra* note 18; for France, see also Mireille Delmas-Marty & Catherine Teitgen Colly, *Punir sans juger* (1992).

[21] Administrative enforcement will be understood broadly, including all forms of enforcement implemented not only by government departments, but also by an authority or public agency independent of the government.

[22] Ohana, *supra* note 18.

[23] Delmas-Marty & Teitgen Colly, *supra* note 20, at 7.

[24] *See infra* Section II.3, the example of anticompetitive practices and the example of anticorruption policies.

Finally, there are the procedures based on powers of co-regulation, which confer an essential role on private self-regulatory systems. These developed rapidly, although later in Europe than elsewhere, due to an international movement by the companies themselves. Corruption is one of the most significant areas covered by this type.[25]

1. Special Procedures and Sovereign Powers: The Example of Tax Crime

As illustrated by comparative analyses conducted by the OECD (Organisation for Economic Co-operation and Development),[26] but also more indirectly and less systematically by some cases brought before the two European supranational courts,[27] tax authorities, generally attached to the Ministry of the Economy or Finance, have investigatory and sanctioning powers comparable (or even superior) to that of judicial authorities and, in many cases, are likely to compete (or take place simultaneously) with them. As Advocate-General Cruz Villalón indicated in his conclusions in the *Åkerberg Fransson* case, "the imposition of both administrative and criminal penalties in respect of the same offence is a widespread practice in the Member States, especially in fields such as taxation.... However, the way in which penalties are accumulated varies enormously between legal systems and displays special features which are specific to each Member State."[28] It should be noted that the tax procedures developed alongside criminal enforcement are not themselves specific to corporate or white-collar crime. Nonetheless, business offenders are heavily represented in such cases, and special measures are generally arranged for them.[29]

In these historic sectors of tax collection and criminal law enforcement, the strength of these government departments reflects the construction of the state as a sovereign endowed with the powers necessary to protect essential attributes such as its finances. But other, more modern state capacities may also be noted. One is environmental protection, which had its source in the control (and thus regulation) of territory and property, before it took on the meaning and the scope it has today. In most EU Member States, enforcement is largely the prerogative of administrative authorities or agencies.[30] In the environmental law area, EU law has served first as a driver of administrative

[25] *See, e.g., Preventing Corporate Corruption* (Stefano Manacorda, Francesco Centonze & Gabrio Forti eds., 2014).

[26] Organization for Economic Co-operation and Development, *Tax Administration in OECD and Selected Non-OECD Countries: Comparative Information Series (2006)* (Feb. 2007), *available at* goo.gl/iGPM3P.

[27] The European Court of Justice of the E.U. and the Eur. Ct. H.R. of the Council of Europe.

[28] Case C-617/10, Åklagaren/Hans Åkerberg Fransson, conclusions presented June 12, 2012, by the Advocat General, Pedro Cruz Villalón, § 70.

[29] Alexis Spire & Katia Weidenfeld, *L'impunité fiscale* (2015).

[30] *Droit pénal des affaires en Europe* 467 (Geneviève Giudicelli-Delage ed., 2006).

enforcement. But, since its acquisition of the necessary competence,[31] EU law has also driven criminal law enforcement, despite the potential risk that Member States might be exposed to contradictory requirements vis-à-vis the *non bis in idem* principle,[32] as it will be seen below.[33]

The link with sovereignty here is very strong. Special procedures are expressions of sovereign power. Because of their subject matter—control of public finances and of the land—they are closely linked to the constitution of the state itself. This association with state sovereignty probably explains, for example, the initial reliance in France on administrative enforcement.[34] The penal (i.e., judicial) pathway came only later, as a supplement to administrative enforcement. Accordingly, the initial rationale is not that of competing proceedings (with administrative proceedings as an alternative to criminal prosecution) but reinforcement, in which supplemental criminal enforcement may be successive or cumulative. Nonetheless, in practice, triggering criminal enforcement depends largely on the actions of non-criminal authorities. As will be shown later in the chapter, this "organized dependence" of prosecuting authorities on administrative authorities is not exclusive to the tax domain, although it is more pronounced here than elsewhere. Hence, while the legal techniques may vary, the phenomenon is constant: in many areas of business regulation, criminal prosecution depends, in law or in fact, on the administrative authorities.[35]

The close association with state sovereignty also explains the persistence of the very close relation with the executive branch. The responsibility to prosecute and punish lies with ministerial services or their extension rather than independent authorities. This is doubtless one of the principal features by which the first type of special procedure (observed in the tax field) differs from the second, which characterizes in particular the area of competition.

2. Special Procedures and Regulatory Powers: The Example of Anticompetitive Practices

This second type of special procedure is distinguished from the preceding one by its purpose. Its concern is less preservation of sovereign powers than protection of market rules, of which the state has progressively become the guardian. The state thus exercises its coercive powers for regulatory purposes. Within the EU, European integration has

[31] First by the European Court of Justice (Case C-176/03, Commission v. Council, 2005 E.C.R. I-7879 *affirmed*); this decision led to the adoption of Directive 2008/99/EC of the European Parliament and of the Council of 19 November, 2008, on the protection of the environment through criminal law, 2008 O.J. (L 328)28, related to environmental protection by penal codes, and then, formally, by the Treaty of Lisbon (Art. 83 § 2 of the Treaty on the Functioning of the E.U., Oct. 26, 2012, 2012 O.J. (C326)01).

[32] *I.e.*, the "right not to be tried or punished twice in criminal proceedings for the same criminal offence," enshrined in Article 50 of the Charter of Fundamental Rights of the European Union.

[33] *Infra* Section III.

[34] Michel Foucault, *Théorie et institutions pénales* (Cours au Collège de France 1971–1972) (2015).

[35] *Droit pénal des affaires* 128 (Mireille Delmas-Marty & Geneviève Giudicelli-Delage eds., 2000).

greatly nourished this shift at the national level from the classic liberal state to the welfare state and now toward the regulatory state. In view of the EU founders' decision not to endow the European Communities with criminal law competence, the European project has relied from its origin on the development of a non-criminal and ad hoc punitive law enforcement system with a fairly administrative profile,[36] which some have described as a "control by sanction" model.[37] This law enforcement system was constructed on the basis of the Commission's direct sanctioning power with respect to misconduct affecting competition, especially the prohibition of cartels or trusts.[38] It tends to serve as a model for the Member States' policies about anticompetitive practices, particularly since the turning point marked by the enactment of regulation 1/2003.[39] According to a Commission communication published in 2014[40] and the recent Commission proposal for a Directive in March 2017,[41] this trend is destined not only to intensify but to extend beyond the area of competition, as the financial sector seems to show.

What are then the specific features of this enforcement model as they relate to the prosecution of illicit behavior? First of all, this model rests on the preference for public rather than private enforcement mechanisms[42] assigned to a regulatory authority with no criminal jurisdiction but that is vested with coercive powers to conduct investigations and, where appropriate, punish misconduct. In reality, this ad hoc enforcement system is characterized simultaneously by its close proximity to criminal law and procedure (from which it borrows some mechanisms and guarantees) and its very great distance from them. Relative to unilateral, compulsory, retributive (punitive) criminal law enforcement, this model favors an enforcement mechanism that is of administrative rather than criminal inspiration, participatory (as illustrated especially by the European[43] and national[44] leniency programs), negotiated (reflecting the importance of

[36] It has strong affinities with the national systems of administrative enforcement, whether they are streamlined, as in Germany or in Italy, or split up as in France, see Weigend, *The Legal and Practical Problems Posed by the Difference Between Criminal Law and Administrative Penal Law*, 59 Revue Internationale de Droit Pénal 67 (1988).

[37] Giudicelli-Delage, *supra* note 30, at 359.

[38] *Handbook on European Competition Law, Enforcement and Procedure* (Ioannis Lianos & Damien Geradin eds., 2013).

[39] Council Regulation (EC) No 1/2003 of December 16, 2002 on the implementation of the rules on competition laid down in Articles 81 and 82 of the Treaty, 2003 O.J. (L1)1; Wouter Wils, *Principles of European Antitrust Enforcement* (2005).

[40] Communication from the E.U. Commission, *Ten Years of Antitrust Enforcement Under Regulation 1/2003: Achievements and Future Perspectives* (COM(2014) 453, July 9, 2014).

[41] *See Proposal for a Directive of the European Parliament and the Council to Empower the Competition Authorities of the Member States to Be More Effective Enforcers and to Ensure the Proper Functioning of the Internal Market* (COM(2017) 142, Mar. 22, 2017).

[42] Although these are certainly not absent from the system.

[43] *See* the ECN (European Competition Network) Model Leniency Programme adopted in 2006 and revised in 2012 to ensure that potential leniency applicants are not discouraged from applying as a result of the discrepancies between the existing leniency programs within the ECN; all versions are *available at* http://ec.europa.eu/competition/ecn/documents.html.

[44] *See* List of National Competition Authorities that operate a Leniency Program (updated on November 22, 2012) provided by the ECN website, *available at* http://ec.europa.eu/competition/ecn/leniency_programme_nca.pdf.

the European[45] and national mechanisms of commitment[46] and settlement[47]), and more restorative or corrective of a broken economic or financial balance than of a troubled social order. The aim is to shape a law enforcement model adapted to markets that is rapid, specialized, professionalized, expert, and efficient. These needs are assumed to be met more effectively by specialized and independent agencies than by the criminal courts. The procedures through which they operate, the objectives they pursue, and the types of proceedings available to them are indexed to these requirements. This is apparent from the primary role of cooperation at the early stage when misbehavior is identified (leniency programs) until the decision phase (settlement proceedings or commitment decisions). The preference for ad hoc non-criminal law enforcement with administrative characteristics can be attributed "to the fact that these mechanisms reduce judicial overload and enable the administrative authority with the required expertise to control the fact-finding process, and flexibly tailor the penalty to serve its public policy objectives."[48]

The Commission's 2014 communication,[49] which takes stock of ten years of implementation of Regulation 1/2003 and prepares to extend it further, makes clear key elements of the institutional and procedural context of this enforcement system. Three points summarize the priorities for the years to come: (1) "further guarantee the independence of NCAs [National Competition Authorities] in the exercise of their tasks and that they have sufficient resources," (2) "ensure that NCAs have a complete set of effective investigative and decision-making powers at their disposal," and (3) "ensure that powers to impose effective and proportionate fines and well-designed leniency programs are in place in all Member States and consider measures to avoid disincentives for corporate leniency applicants." These three points underline the importance of independence as a crucial feature from the organic, institutional, and procedural perspectives. The aim is to set up a structure for mediation between professionals and public authorities. It also involves—insofar as national traditions allow—freeing the decisions of the regulators from the hierarchical power of the administration, while remaining within the state organization. Independence makes it possible to insist on the need for specialized, impartial entities that are also sufficiently autonomous to be able to conduct their own investigations, determine their own priorities, and especially set their own prosecution policies.

This model is designed solely for corporations ("undertakings" in the wording of EU law). In principle, however, nothing prevents its application to natural persons at the national level. Depending on the legal order, the latter may be handled by the enforcement mechanism applicable to corporations or by another—sometimes

[45] *See* the European Commission website on Competition, *available at* http://ec.europa.eu/competition/cartels/overview/index_en.html.

[46] About commitment decisions, see Article 9 of Council Regulation 1/2003, *supra* note 39; for settlements, see European Commission, *Communication from the Commission—Amendments to the Commission Notice on the Conduct of Settlement Procedures in View of the Adoption of Decisions Pursuant to Article 7 and Article 23 of Council Regulation (EC) No 1/2003 in Cartel Cases*, 2015 O.J. (C 256)2.

[47] *See* European Commission, *supra* note 45 (Competition policy).

[48] Ohana, *supra* note 18, at 1074.

[49] *See* E.U. Commission Communication, *supra* note 40.

criminal—law enforcement mechanism. The details of this connection are obviously crucial, as discussed below.

As pointed out above, this model has expanded beyond antitrust law to another market sector: financial markets. There too, since the end of the 1990s,[50] European integration has encouraged the development of specialized, independent national securities authorities with the power to investigate, prosecute, and impose sanctions.[51] But in contrast to the competition area, the EU since 2014 has reintroduced penal sanctions into the mix for this sector; regulations apparently recommend a combination of both criminal and non-criminal sanctions and proceedings.[52] In addition, this framework applies to anyone, professionals or not, natural persons or legal entities. It thereby confirms the extendibility of the model, *rationae materiae* and *rationae personae*. But this model is also capable of transformation, as illustrated by the third type of special procedure, which is examined next and which can be considered a variant or extension of that model.

3. Special Procedures and Co-regulation Powers: The Example of Anticorruption Policies

The example of anticorruption policies shows the existence of a third type of special procedures that differs from the two aforementioned types as to one key point. Under the special procedures examined in Sections II.1 and II.2, the state retains control over prosecution and sanctions. The enforcement power is reconfigured, but it remains the power of the State. This reconfiguration benefits administrative penal law rather than strictly penal law, and the dependence of the judicial authorities works in favor of administrative or independent authorities. What differs in this third model is the form of dependence—one that seems to benefit the potential wrongdoers.

Procedural mechanisms in which the offender becomes an active participant in the procedure have been adopted widely. As indicated in Section II.2, cooperation of the persons prosecuted is already a focal point in leniency, negotiation, and commitment

[50] Numerous directives were adopted in the securities sector between 1979 and 1993 (including Council directive 89/592/EEC of 13 November, 1989, coordinating regulations on insider dealing, 1989 O.J. (L 334)30), but it is especially since the adoption in 1999 of the FSAP (Financial Services Action Plan, COM/99/0232 final) that European instruments have almost all required the establishment of an administrative authority with investigatory powers.

[51] According to the Committee of European Securities Regulators' (CESR) *Report on CESR Members' Powers Under The Market Abuse Directive and Its Implementing Measures* 20 (June 2007, 07-380): In relation to administrative measures and sanctions, nearly all authorities are empowered to take appropriate measures or impose sanctions. Around three-quarters of authorities can do so directly and the remaining quarter of authorities can do so in conjunction with a judicial authority (in this case, these are civil rather than administrative sanctions). *See* more recently, ESMA, *Actual Use of Sanctioning Powers under MAD* (Apr. 26, 2012, ESMA/2012/270).

[52] *See* Regulation (E.U.) No 596/2014 of the European Parliament and of the Council of April 16, 2014 on market abuse (market abuse regulation, MAR), 2014 O.J. (L173)1, and Directive 2014/57/EU of the European Parliament and of the Council of 16 April 2014 on criminal sanctions for market abuse (market abuse directive, MAD), 2014 O.J. (L173)179.

decisions. The next step is to enlist them alongside (or even in place of) the public authorities (administrative or judicial, with or without criminal enforcement powers) to detect offenses, investigate indications of misconduct, correct and penalize where appropriate, and report all of this to the authorities who determine the measures to be taken. At this stage, the offender can also weigh in on the decision about the procedural track to be followed: about the decision whether to initiate proceedings and, if so, which type. Such "power" tends to be conferred exclusively on legal persons and therefore excludes natural persons.[53] These "transfers" of powers through a delegation of the functions ordinarily assumed by the criminal or regulatory authorities (detection, investigation, punishment) are a new form by which the state exercises its controlling powers via the mechanisms of co-regulation, or what can be called constrained and controlled self-regulation. Indeed, the development of these procedural mechanisms relies on the increasing role of compliance programs (internal self-regulation to prevent and correct misconduct) for law enforcement purposes.[54]

The spread throughout Europe[55] of corporate liability, whether of a penal or an administrative nature, has played an important role in this development and has been accompanied by the widespread use of compliance tools, sometimes as a component of the penalty,[56] or a ground for exemption, or as an imputation criterion.[57] But the impact of compliance programs (before or after the liability is incurred) is not only substantive. This effect extends results in new procedures specific for corporations, the characteristics of which can be summarized as "continental" versions or adaptations of the U.S. model of deferred and non-prosecution agreements[58] (DPA and NPA).[59]

As mentioned previously, this third type of procedure has developed in Europe partly within the framework of civil and administrative procedures, especially for market sectors and particularly in competition law. For this reason, this co-regulation model can thus be considered an extension of the procedures examined in Section II.2). But it is

[53] *See, e.g.*, the procedure, considered as the French DPA, recently introduced with the "Sapin 2" Law (on transparency, the fight against corruption, and the modernization of the economy) of 16 December 2016, in a new section 41-1-2 of the Criminal Procedure Code. It consists of an agreement between a prosecutor and a corporation suspected of certain offenses (bribery, tax fraud, and money laundering) whereby the company acknowledges the facts without admitting guilt and commits to implementing a compliance program under the monitoring of the French Anti-corruption Agency.

[54] *Compliance Programs for the Prevention of Economic Crimes: An Empirical Survey of German Companies* (Ulrich Sieber & Marc Engelhart eds., 2014); *El derecho penal en la era de compliance* (Luis Arroyo & Adan Nieto Martín eds., 2013).

[55] Geneviève Giudicelli-Delage, *Le champ personnel et matériel*, in *Corporate Criminal Liability and Compliance Programs* (First Colloquium) 3 (Antonio Fiorella & Alfonso Maria Stile eds., 2012).

[56] *See, e.g.*, Code Pénal § 131-39-2 (France).

[57] *Corporate Criminal Liability and Compliance Programs (Vol. II: Towards a Common Model in the European Union)* (Antonio Fiorella ed., 2012); Manacorda, Centonze & Forti, *supra* note 25.

[58] Which can be described summarily as agreements reached between a prosecutor and an organization that could be prosecuted. The agreement allows the prosecution to be suspended for a specified period of time (and if the procedure is conclusive not to initiate it) provided the organization meets certain conditions (amongst the main ones: full cooperation, payment of a fine, implementation of a compliance program under independent monitoring).

[59] Margot Sève & Michel Perez, *International Financial and White Collar Crime, Corporate Malfeasance and Compliance*, Revue Trimestrielle de Droit Financier 41 (2016).

rapidly expanding far beyond this initial framework. As anticorruption policies illustrate, self-regulation or co-regulation approaches, which are encouraged by a powerful international movement, have been integrated into criminal justice systems and extended beyond the market sectors. The monitoring mechanism for the OECD anticorruption convention illustrates the frequent recourse to out-of-court settlements[60] that more or less escape judicial review. Some national legal systems contain such procedures,[61] which can be extended to companies and may be preferred to ordinary criminal proceedings for reasons of efficacy and economy.[62] Recourse to them can also result from the adoption of ad hoc procedures inspired by U.S. DPAs and NPAs, as in the United Kingdom and France.[63]

These procedures in our third category tend to share three common characteristics.[64] First, they have the advantage of protecting the corporation from the risk of exclusion from national and international public procurement. This must be stressed, for it induces a change in paradigm since proof or recognition of guilt is no longer a prerequisite for the use of coercive powers. The authorities are relieved of the burden to prove the offenders' guilt, and offenders do not have to admit guilt. Second, transparency about the precise contents of the agreement is often low. Finally, their third common feature is the ambiguous fate of the natural persons involved: sometimes scapegoats are punished, and sometimes parties turn out to be irreproachable.

This classification, which could be more detailed and more complete, nonetheless provides keys to understanding the use of specialized procedures to deal with white-collar and corporate crime. It is therefore helpful to complete it by identifying the distinctive characteristics that these special procedures share.

III. The Distinctive Characteristics of Special Procedures

This section does not attempt to describe each type of procedure; even if possible, that would be of limited interest in this context. The aim instead is to identify and analyze the features that distinguish special procedures from ordinary criminal proceedings. European requirements that the protection of fundamental rights apply to these two types

[60] *Negotiated Settlement for Corruption Offences* (Abiola Makinwa ed., 2015).

[61] *See, e.g.*, Sr § 74 (Dutch Criminal Code), whereby prosecutors can enter into out-of-court settlements to resolve charges against companies, the Italian *patteggiamento* system, or the French mechanism of appearance upon prior admission of guilt, Code Pr. Pén. § 495-7 (French Criminal Procedure Code) (allows a reduction of penalty, overseen by a judge).

[62] *Id.*

[63] Michel Perez & Alizee Dill, *The Rise of the American Deferred Prosecution Agreement ("DPA") and Its European Avatars*, Revue Trimestrielle de Droit Financier 43 (2016).

[64] *See* Corruption Watch, *Out of Court, Out of Mind—Do Deferred Prosecution Agreements and Corporate Settlements Deter Overseas Corruption?* (Mar. 2016), *available at* https://www.cw-uk.org/.

of procedures have brought national systems closer together and helped to harmonize different punitive enforcement procedures within each national system around guarantees applicable to "criminal charges."[65] Nonetheless, distinctions continue to mark these special procedures, which seems to explain their continued attraction for both public authorities and corporations despite their rapprochement to ordinary criminal proceedings. Yet the following describes (1) how confusion of powers prevails over the separation of powers in these procedures (which affects the judge's role), (2) how the search to restore the equilibrium disrupted by misconduct prevails over condemnation and punishment and thus guides enforcement in a direction that is principally prospective rather than retrospective, and (3) why balance of power is a key issue.

1. Confusion versus Separation of Powers

The first characteristic common to these procedures is the exclusion of judges. Whether the investigation and decisions to prosecute (and where appropriate, punish) are assigned to the criminal justice system or to regulators, the designated authority is never a court. It is sometimes an independent agency or administrative authority, more or less associated with the executive power. Other times, it may be the office of public prosecution, also more or less strongly (depending on the legal system) responsible to the executive power. Accordingly, the exclusion of the judge takes place in a whole range of cases to the benefit of either the executive power or of a new type of bureaucracy functionally independent of the executive—although judges may later intervene to resolve disputes or validate the decision of the deciding authority.

Moreover, this transfer of coercive and punitive power also concentrates powers. That is, the powers to prescribe, judge, and execute tend to be in the same hands. This is particularly true for independent public authorities who have normative, investigatory, prosecutorial, and sanctioning powers.[66] They are thus called upon to monitor compliance with the norms they adopt, and to directly impose sanctions for clear misconduct.

The public prosecutor was transformed long ago into a sort of quasi-judge by the array of alternatives to prosecution and new types of prosecution. Neither national nor European-level judges have succeeded in controlling this movement. Alternatives to traditional prosecution are used most extensively for business crime: procedural measures

[65] Within the meaning of Article 6 of the European Convention on Human Rights. Indeed, the European Court of Human Rights has extended the scope of the guarantees applicable to criminal proceedings (namely the right to a fair trial and its corollaries (Article 6 of the European Convention on Human Rights), applying these guarantees to disciplinary, administrative, tax, customs, financial, and competition law proceedings where the criteria outlined in Engel and Others v. the Netherlands, App. No. 5100/71 a.o., Eur. Ct. H.R., June 8, 1976, § 82 f. are met, that is, the classification in domestic law, the nature of the offense, and the severity of the penalty that the person concerned risks incurring.

[66] Nonetheless, under pressure from the ECtHR, these functions tend to be exercised by different organs within the regulatory authority or agency.

initially conceived for petty crime have been extended to it while ad hoc measures specially designed for economic and financial criminals have developed.

2. Restore versus Punish

The second shared characteristic of these procedures relates to their objectives, which largely justify the transfer and concentration of powers mentioned above. The objective is less to punish (to sanction and seek retribution for blameworthy past behavior) than to quickly restore the equilibrium disrupted by a company's action or harmful inaction. Whereas restorative approaches for the treatment of petty crime sometimes seem hyperpunitive (and thus counterproductive), applied to corporate wrongdoing they appear perfectly adapted to the idea of correcting imbalances or restoring order by guiding corporate behavior to prevent initial or repetitive dysfunction.[67]

More broadly, these procedures pursue different objectives from those of standard criminal proceedings because they are borrowing their tools, and sometimes their philosophy, from regulatory models that function according to a distinct logic. In this framework, special procedures are not autonomous, stand-alone actions, as they can be in a criminal proceeding where they are intended to intervene as an exception. They are instead an ordinary component inherent in ongoing regulation.[68]

The fact that the sectors to which these procedures apply are sometimes highly technical or require extensive expertise also contributes to the justification for removing from them the punitive purpose and moral condemnation of criminal proceedings.[69]

Nonetheless, as seen earlier in this chapter, procedures for white-collar crime and especially for corporations are expanding well beyond technical sectors. They operate systemically, for example in the areas of taxation, environment, and corruption. One could hypothesize that these procedures were developed precisely to avoid the judgments of guilt or fault. This is what legitimizes ousting the judge and the front-line intervention of regulators or prosecutors with extensive coercive powers.

It is then possible to couple this hypothesis with another and assume that these procedures are evidence of what one might call in psychoanalytic (Freudian) terms the "return of the repressed" of the impossible guilt of collective entities. As it is well known, the impossibility of conceiving of the guilt of a nonhuman entity is why the adage *societas delinquere no potest* remained an obstacle to corporate criminal liability in continental Europe for so long and why it remains an insuperable constitutional barrier in some legal systems.[70] This impossibility of reproach or criminal blame is supposed to forbid

[67] Darryl K. Brown, *The Problematic and Faintly Promising Dynamics of Corporate Crime Enforcement*, 1 Ohio State J. Crim. L. 521, 523 (2004).

[68] *Regulation, Supervision, Compliance* (Marie-Anne Frison-Roche ed., 2017).

[69] Also in this sense, see Wells, *supra* note 5, at 17: "Regulation (...) is distinguished from criminal law (...) in two ways: it targets those engaged in specialised activities and its underlying purpose is said to be different in that regulation is concerned to mould or encourage behaviour rather than to condemn it."

[70] This is particularly the case in Germany or Italy, two countries that envisage the liability of legal persons only of an administrative or civil nature, excluding any criminal liability (sensu stricto).

both the imputation of criminal guilt and a retributive sanction. These special procedures, which allow (often severe) sanctions, have as their essential advantage that they do not require these elements. On the contrary, the misconduct suffices to trigger implementation of coercive powers for the purpose of constraining offenders through behavioral measures (such as compliance programs) or financial penalties that, while substantial, are oriented less toward the past than the present and future.

Everyone seems to win. Public authorities economize resources and obtain a relatively rapid outcome that appears to correspond to their regulatory objectives. The company escapes in part (or suffers more briefly) damage to its reputation and exclusion from public procurement. More precisely, everyone wins unless the "disappearance of the judge" represents also the disappearance of the public, including victims of the illicit conduct. Moreover, the exclusion of the judge is accompanied by keeping some facts obscured: not everything is brought to light. What may be happening is that again only what is visible on the surface—only the "artificial" forms of business crime—are dealt with; the rest are either ignored or treated as a less serious, less blameworthy "paper" crime.

3. Bilateralism versus Unilateralism

Finally, the third characteristic of these procedures, an extension of the first two, is that they tend to represent a face-to-face relationship between the prosecuting authority and the corporation. This feature presents two issues or risks.

The first is due to the shifts from a trial—a regulated legal interaction—to alternative procedures that resemble a balance of power between the two sides instead. One of the arguments advanced to promote these procedures in which negotiation and cooperation occupy a central role are the inadequate resources available to the public authorities compared to corporations' vastly greater resources. Accordingly, these procedures involve transferring to the corporation the costs (financial, human, and material) of the procedure and more broadly of enforcement. This changes the corporation's role. Corporations become the public authorities' partner in enforcement. It is not certain, however, that what is thus gained in terms of efficiency is not outweighed by losses in efficacy and control. More precisely, the relation between the results obtained and the resources used (efficiency) may well improve, while the relation between the results and the objectives sought (efficacy) deteriorates, as does the state's control over the process.

The unilateralism that characterizes criminal justice and ordinary criminal proceedings gives way to bilateral mechanisms in which the impartial third party—the judge—and the public both disappear, replaced by an inner sanctum where the response not only tends to become more bureaucratized but also more privatized.[71] This is the

[71] For a modern perspective on this old question, see Mireille Delmas-Marty, *Etat de droit, Etat de surveillance, surveillance sans Etat?* in *Le Code de la sécurité intérieure, artisan d'un nouvel ordre ou semeur de désordre ?* (Marc Touillier ed., 2017).

second issue. It corresponds with what some authors have termed "horizontal legality" ("mobilized" law), that, alongside abstract and vertical legality (legislative law), results from adjustments negotiated by the private actors to make their objectives coincide with the rules.[72] Research into white-collar crime has shown that, as Sam Buell stressed,[73] what makes procedures against white-collar criminals distinctive is that the discussion concentrates more on the law than on the facts. Going further, one can wonder whether this possibility for white-collar criminals (especially large corporations)—"for whom wealth is linked to the law, . . . to the possibility of making and unmaking, imposing and circumventing the law"[74]—is not now integrated into the strategies and dynamics of enforcement. Accordingly, it can be argued that settlements now allow corporations not only to debate the definitions of what is forbidden and to adjust the border between legal and illegal, but further (and potentially much more profitably) to change the very course of procedure for a prosecution. While the temptation of a purely self-managed response to the offense is generally rejected, it must be acknowledged that these practices increase the privatization of legal norms and their enforcement. After all, heads of firms, directly concerned as potential defendants, are transformed into de facto legislators, police officers, and judges. Yet this transformation disregards the most basic principles of separation of powers[75] and runs the risk "of passing from a supplementary ethics (intended to fill gaps in the law) toward an alternative ethics (intended to replace the law)."[76]

IV. The Impact of Special Procedures

Finally, the impact or function of these special procedures, established outside or within the criminal justice system, must be considered. The first question is thus whether the goal is (1) for these procedures to compete with the criminal justice system by promoting alternatives that are not strictly criminal, or (2) to displace ordinary criminal prosecutions with alternative prosecution forms. In either case, a third question remains whether this will effectively lead the actors toward more responsible conduct.

1. Alternatives to Prosecution

The idea of alternatives to prosecution can have several meanings. First, the alternatives might be narrowly understood to mean a binary choice between criminal and non-criminal proceedings. That is, they would be mutually exclusive options. In this case, non-criminal proceedings will be alternatives *to* criminal prosecution.

[72] Pierre Lascoumes, *Elites irrégulières: Essai sur la délinquance d'affaires* (1997).
[73] Buell, *supra* note 2.
[74] Michel Foucault, *La société punitive* (Cours au Collège de France 1972–1973) (2013).
[75] Delmas-Marty & Giudicelli-Delage, eds., *supra* note 35, at 31. [76] *Id.*

The issue of their differential protection of fundamental rights has been partially overcome as non-criminal procedures have progressively been required to provide criminal procedure guarantees.[77] Nonetheless, this issue has hardly been resolved, especially when intelligence-gathering tools of national security agencies, rather than domestic law enforcement agencies, are used to monitor undesirable behavior. Indeed, intelligence agencies' surveillance tactics and data gathering are part of "more radical bypass mechanisms [that] can function as true alternatives to criminal prosecution."[78] Yet, the use of such surveillance as an alternative to ordinary criminal investigation powers is a recent trend that seems to be developing in Europe. In France, for example, domestic surveillance has been deployed in the framework (or on the pretext) of the fight against terrorism.[79] Although in principle this surveillance pursues intelligence rather than evidence, the findings may pave the way for criminal prosecution. Moreover, the specialized procedures examined here share features with intelligence investigations, especially "in their capacity to subject targets to state surveillance and sometimes to sanctions, without resort to the criminal process."[80]

Another issue is also crucial: knowing who controls the interplay of these procedures. It may be the legislator, who determines, a priori, the procedural route to be followed by distinguishing different procedural regimes according to the legal characterization of the illicit conduct. Accordingly, while regulatory misconduct handled through administrative procedures conducted by a nonjudicial, non-criminal authority, criminal offenses will fall within the ordinary criminal procedure. This division is seen, for example, in the tax sector and cases of market abuse. Nonetheless, it can be criticized for resulting in parallel or consecutive proceedings, especially when the regulator, judge, or both blur the boundary between regulatory misconduct and criminal offenses. This situation risks violations of the *non bis in idem* principle, which can be used to challenge some proceedings. It is not always easy, however, to determine whether the principle applies in light of recent case law from the European Court of Human Rights or certain constitutional courts, which tolerate the coexistence of "complementary" procedures[81] or procedures that present a "sufficiently close connection in substance and in time."[82] When the *non bis in idem* principle is applicable, control of the alternatives may be entrusted to enforcement authorities (criminal or not) to maintain a dual-track enforcement system, as EU instruments sometimes encourage. Decisions about which procedure to follow occur on a case-by-case basis, either by coordination among the relevant authorities or by granting power to initiate the various alternatives to a single authority. Problems of separation, confusion, and transfer of powers that were examined in the preceding section reappear here.

[77] *See* Engel and Others v. the Netherlands, *supra* note 65 (ECtHR decision).

[78] Jacqueline E. Ross & Stephen C. Thaman, *Introduction*, in *Comparative Criminal Procedure* 27 (Jacqueline E. Ross & Stephen C. Thaman eds., 2016).

[79] Delmas-Marty, *supra* note 71.

[80] Ross & Thaman, *supra* note 78, at 30.

[81] As upheld by the French constitutional council for tax matters: Decision n° 2016–546 QPC dated June 24, 2016.

[82] According to the very controversial decision of the Eur. Ct. H.R. (GC): A and B v. Norway, App. No. 24130/11 and App. No. 29758/11, Nov. 15, 2016.

2. Alternative Types of Prosecutions

A broader conception of "alternative" is also possible; it can describe a range of options available to the penal authorities beyond the binary choice between initiating prosecution or dropping the case. In this conception, the alternatives are *between* types of criminal prosecutions.

By underlining the gap that separates these particular forms of prosecution (or non-prosecution) from ordinary criminal prosecutions, this broader approach allows one to gauge the extent to which the unique nature of procedures applied to corporations results from the nature of the prosecuting authority rather than from the type of procedure applied.

The influence of the special procedures is not limited to forms of competition or instrumentalization, as the first, narrower conception of the word alternative might let us think. Certainly, the non-criminal procedures can result in the marginalization of criminal prosecutions, especially when, as is often the case, the non-criminal prosecuting authority also has negotiation (i.e., settlement) powers. Because non-criminal authorities often act more rapidly than the criminal authorities and because their procedures offer more discretion, less opprobrium, and have a reasonable (financial or structural) cost, corporations prefer proceedings under the jurisdiction of these authorities. Moreover, these authorities benefit from the effect of these proceedings of precluding, in law or in fact, other procedures, including criminal ones. Similarly, the linking of civil and administrative to criminal proceedings can also be instrumentalized by government officials, who can use the criminal threat as an instrument more of regulatory strategy than of enforcement.[83] Accordingly, the regulator not only can filter criminal prosecutions, when it has the power to prosecute or to transfer the case to the criminal authorities, it can also choose to use criminal prosecution strategically to implement its own regulatory policy by, for example, transferring to criminal justice authorities only cases of repeat offenders, those with whom cooperation is impossible, or cases intended to serve as examples for general deterrence. "The criminal sanction is used, not [or no longer] only to punish, but to modify the balance of power relationships."[84]

But the influence exerted on the criminal justice system can be still more profound when it is criminal prosecutions that are themselves progressively transformed. On the one hand, unsurprisingly, the same diversification of procedural mechanisms observed outside of criminal proceedings can also be seen in the procedural tools within the criminal justice system. The "possibility for business illegalisms to be tied to different normative systems has the practical effect of hindering the application of the most coercive modalities, namely the choice of criminal prosecution, whether at the beginning of the case or in the course of its treatment."[85]

[83] *See* Weigend, *supra* note 36, at 189.
[84] Delmas-Marty & Giudicelli-Delage, *supra* note 35, at 29.
[85] Amicelle, *supra* note 8, at 78.

On the other hand, while the development of the alternatives *to* and *between* criminal prosecution for petty crimes led in practice to an extension of the "criminal net"—that is, the scope of criminal law[86]—in the context of corporate crime it tends instead toward mutation of criminal procedure, due to increasingly blurred differentiation between non-criminal and criminal prosecution. Not only are the boundaries ever more porous, but bridges between them are also multiplying. Paradoxically, this last development is promoted by the constraints resulting from protection of fundamental rights.

The requirements of foreseeability and proportionality nonetheless seem to call for a clearer differentiation of which procedures apply to a single sector. But as the market abuse field, for example, illustrates, the *non bis in idem* principle favored development of coordination rather than separation and differentiation between the distinct prosecutorial authorities. That increased discretion for these authorities, whose range of choices has grown considerably.

Moreover, the regulatory philosophy and tools of this ad hoc punitive enforcement system, which developed in both the sovereign and regulated sectors examined above, are progressively penetrating the field of strictly criminal enforcement. In doing so, the porosity of these procedures expresses and consolidates yet another loss of differentiation between regulation and criminal procedures over the course of reciprocal rapprochements and borrowings.

As noted previously, the guarantees and principles of criminal law first influenced the civil and administrative procedures that were progressively albeit partially subjected to them. But subsequently, the procedural tools developed in these non-criminal enforcement frameworks made their way into criminal proceedings to the point that "the lines between regulatory and criminal procedures are becoming more tangled and blurred."[87]

The question then arises what to think about such a development. One may wonder, in particular, whom it actually benefits. Is it really to the benefit of the prosecution authorities, which improve their efficacy and efficiency? Or is it to the advantage of the offenders, who benefit from mechanisms that appear severe but are actually painless or even provide escape routes from consequences? It may then be inevitable to ask who—companies or individuals—truly comes out best. And it remains to be seen whether justice is winning or losing.

3. Alternative to Justice?

Celia Wells already asked this question when she suggested that we:

> look... at the implications of using regulatory mechanisms in the criminal law sphere, and... focus more specifically on the corporate defendant. This is a (possibly subtle) variation on a familiar theme that crimes of the powerful tend to be downplayed or

[86] Michel Foucault, *Alternatives to Prison: Dissemination or Decline of Social Control?* 26 Theory, Culture & Soc'y 12, 24 (2009).

[87] Wells, *supra* note 5, at 17.

> marginalized. Whereas it has been argued that their wrongdoing is either differently labelled or selectively enforced, the argument here is that it is being *differentially enforced*. The rhetoric is of clampdown and control but the method is more benign. Or at least that is the question.[88]

It is indeed a question of method that this evolution of criminal procedure raises. Some have hypothesized that the emphasis placed on the procedure and especially on alternatives to the criminal trial is a response to, or rather a circumvention of, the problems raised by corporate criminal liability,[89] which are apparent during costly trials with uncertain outcomes. These procedural tools may thus serve to avoid facing the obstacles presented by substantive criminal law, mainly the proof of guilt and of participation in the offense, but also the distribution of liability between the collective entity and individual directors or managers. This effect has been described for the U.S. system; it also appears relevant to Continental Europe, where criminal prosecutions of corporate crime encounter similar problems even though the rules of imputation are not the same.

This evolution also appeals to putative offenders as a chance to escape a criminal trial and the reputational damage that accompanies it regardless of the ultimate, often delayed outcome. But the procedural method is decisive there as well, depending on whether its benefits flow more to individuals (or at least to some of them) or to the corporations; some may serve as cover or scapegoat for others. This is all the more true if a procedure presupposes the opacity of negotiations and the allegedly voluntary waiver of fundamental rights without proper control by a judge. In the end, the same two eternal challenges remain: to ensure fair and effective enforcement.

References

Anthony Amicelle, *Differential Management of Economic and Financial Illegalisms: Anti-money Laundering and "Tax Issues"* 10 Penal Field (2013), *available at* https://champpenal.revues.org/8895#ftn2

Martin Dubber & Tatjana Hörnle, eds., *Oxford Handbook of Criminal Law* (2014)

Geneviève Giudicelli-Delage, ed., *Droit pénal des affaires en Europe* (2006)

James Gobert &Ana-Marie Pascal, eds., *European Developments in Corporate Criminal Liability* (2011)

Abiola Makinwa (ed.), *Negotiated Settlement for Corruption Offences. A European Perspective* (2015)

Jacqueline E. Ross & Stephen C. Thaman (eds.), *Comparative Criminal Procedure* (2016)

Judith van Erp et al., eds., *The Routledge Handbook of White-Collar and Corporate Criminal Law in Europe* (2015)

88 *Id.* (emphasis in original).

89 Diskant, *supra* note 12, at 131.

CHAPTER 21

DOUBLE JEOPARDY AND *NE BIS IN IDEM* IN COMMON LAW AND CIVIL LAW JURISDICTIONS

CARL-FRIEDRICH STUCKENBERG

I. Introduction

TODAY, it is a universally accepted legal principle that "a man ought not to be tried twice for the same thing,"[1] or more precisely, that a person may only once be prosecuted, adjudicated, punished for, or acquitted of one and the same crime. However, the scope and the details of the implementation of this guarantee against the abuse of the power to prosecute vary greatly in national legal orders.[2] This article tries to analyze the main issues and to chart the principal commonalities and divergences found in the civil law and common law traditions.

The finality of court decisions and the concomitant prohibition of relitigating the same issue between the same parties belong to the most essential concepts of procedural law and can be found, from ancient times on, presumably in every advanced jurisdiction and in almost every type of judicial procedure whether its subject is civil or criminal, administrative, tax law etc. But it is only the finality of criminal court decisions that has evolved from a rather technical rule into a prominent political symbol since the Enlightenment era when criminal law was identified as an instrument of oppression that poses a constant threat to individual liberty. Consequently, this rather basic rule of procedural law has been recast as a fundamental freedom of constitutional rank in many

[1] R. v. Junior Bayode (JB) [2013] EWCA Crim 356 [15].

[2] For a comparative overview, see José Luis de la Cuesta, *Concurrent National and International Criminal Jurisdiction and the Principle "ne bis in idem"*, 73 Int'l Rev. Penal L. 707, 708–15 (2002); see also the country reports in that volume.

nations from the late eighteenth century on and acquired the status of a universal human right in the twentieth century. Closer inspection will show, however, that rhetoric and reality are not always easily reconciled, and that the devil's in the detail.

1. Taxonomy

In common law jurisdictions, the usual shorthand for the prohibition of repeated prosecutions for the same offense is "double jeopardy" after the Fifth Amendment to the United States Constitution ("nor shall any person be subject for the same offence to be twice put in jeopardy of life or limb"[3]), which resembles a famous passage from Blackstone.[4] In England and many Commonwealth jurisdictions, some of the so-called special pleas in bar first described in the sixteenth century[5] are still in use: The plea of "*autrefois acquit*" (former acquittal) and of "*autrefois convict*" (former conviction). Civil law jurisdictions commonly speak of "*ne bis in idem*" or "*non bis in idem*," which are condensations of Latin phrases such as "*bis de eadem re ne sit actio*"[6]. There is a number of similar expressions such as "*nemo debet bis puniri pro uno delicto*," "*nemo debet bis vexari*," familiar to both legal traditions.

The prohibition of repeated prosecutions is a legal consequence of the universal principle that court decisions eventually become final and conclusive. This concept of finality is known under the Roman law term "*res judicata*" (*chose jugée, cosa juzgada, cosa giudicata, Rechtskraft*) and has several aspects: In a formal sense (*force de la chose jugée, cosa juzgada formal, cosa giudicata formale, formelle Rechtskraft*), res judicata means that the decision cannot be attacked any longer by ordinary remedies such as appeal so that it becomes inalterable and binding on the parties. Many legal orders know extraordinary remedies (called e.g., revision, *révision, revisión, revisione, Wiederaufnahme, Restitution*) that can destroy the binding force of res judicata and then allow resumption of the original procedure. In a substantive sense (*autorité de la chose jugée, cosa juzgada material, cosa giudicata sostanziale, materielle Rechtskraft*), the final decision has a negative effect as it represents a bar to any new procedure regarding the same cause or matter (*exceptio rei judicatae*) because otherwise the finality of the first decision would be pointless.

[3] U.S. Const. amend. V.

[4] 4 William Blackstone, *Commentaries on the Laws of England* 329 (1769) ("First, the plea of *autrefoits acquit*, or a former acquittal, is grounded on this universal maxim of the common law of England, that no man is to be brought into jeopardy of his life, more than once, for the same offence.").

[5] First by William Staunford, *Les Plées del Coron* 105–08 (1557); later by Edward Coke, *The Third Part of the Institutes of the Laws of England* 212–14 (Clarke & Sons eds., 1817) (1642); William Hawkins, *A Treatise of the Pleas of the Crown*, book 2, ch. 35, at 368–79 (1721); 2 Matthew Hale, *History of the Pleas of the Crown* 240–41 (1736); Blackstone, *supra* note 4, at 329–32.

[6] For the rhetorical origin of the phrase, see Detlef Liebs, *Die Herkunft der "Regel" bis de eadem re ne sit actio*, 84 Zeitschrift der Savigny-Stiftung für Rechtgeschichte. Romanistische Abteilung 104, 124 (1967).

A corollary to the concept of substantive res judicata, which prohibits two or more successive trials, is the concept termed lis pendens (or *exceptio litis pendentis, litispendance, litispendencia, Rechtshängigkeit*), which prohibits two or more parallel trials.

It is a different question whether, in order to avoid inconsistent judgments, a final judgment has a binding effect on other procedures where only some of the same facts are relevant. The corresponding doctrinal concepts are known as "collateral estoppel," "issue estoppel," "issue preclusion" or *Bindungswirkung*.

The doctrines of res judicata and lis pendens prohibit subsequent and simultaneous procedures that have the same ("*idem*") object (*Prozessgegenstand*) as the first procedure. In both civil and common law jurisdictions, the object of a criminal procedure is fixed by an accusatory instrument that accuses a defendant of having committed one or more offenses by an alleged course of conduct and is filed either by a state agent or, less often nowadays, a private party. What the "object of a criminal procedure" exactly is will be discussed below (Section II.1.a).

The scope of *res judicata* usually depends on the scope of the jurisdiction (the German term is *Kognitionsbefugnis*) of the trial court, especially if and to what extent it has the authority to alter the legal characterization (*nomen iuris*) of the charge (see Section II.1.b). The practice of judicial re-characterization of the facts is widely accepted in civil law jurisdictions and sometimes[7] called *iura novit curia*.

2. Rationales

a. *Supporting Rationales*

The prohibition of multiple criminal procedures is often treated as axiomatic and self-evident so that little care is taken to adduce reasons for it. When rationales are put forward, they are more or less the same everywhere.[8] A frequently cited justification is the increased risk of wrongful conviction in a retrial,[9] because "the first trial for the same substantial crime, would be only a dangerous rehearsal to a second or a third, which must be fatal to the prisoner."[10] It is also said that the prosecution would enjoy an unfair tactical advantage when it knows the defense case in a retrial. This is presented as an empirical claim, which, however, appears unpersuasive because there is no empirical support for it or any known method to verify it.[11]

[7] Mainly in the context of international criminal law where legal cultures clash over this issue. "*Iura novit curia*" usually means that legal provisions need not be pleaded nor proven because the court is supposed to know the law.

[8] *Cf.* de la Cuesta, *supra* note 2, at 710; Law Commission, *Double Jeopardy (Consultation Paper No. 156)*, §§ 4.4–4.11 (1999) (U.K.); The Law Reform Commission of Hong Kong, *Report, Double Jeopardy*, §§ 2.4–2.13 (2012); David S. Rudstein, *Double Jeopardy: A Reference Guide to the United States Constitution* 37–43 (2004).

[9] *E.g.*, Martin L. Friedland, *Double Jeopardy* 4 (1969).

[10] R. v. James Foy, Vern. & Scriv. 540, 594 (1788), per Lord Earlsfort.

[11] *See* Paul Roberts, *Double Jeopardy Law Reform: A Criminal Justice Commentary*, 65 Mod. L. Rev. 393, 397–405 (2002).

The same is true for the alleged need to encourage efficient investigations. The assumption is that, if retrials can be easily had, investigating officials might work less diligently as they would if they had no "second bite at the cherry." Again, this is an unproven and barely provable empirical claim that appears plausible to some[12] and not to others.[13] In addition, the concern that retrials provide an incentive for sloppiness could be addressed by precautions, for instance, that a retrial cannot be based on evidence that could have been introduced before.[14]

The most general rationale is the one underlying the doctrine of res judicata, namely the need for finality. There are practical procedural reasons that a trial must come to an end sometime instead of being continued or reopened indefinitely. After some time, all relevant pieces of evidence have been presented, and all relevant legal arguments have been exchanged so that dragging on will not improve the accuracy of the court's decision; on the contrary, evidence often deteriorates over time, memories of witnesses fade, documents are lost, etc. There are also psychological reasons that the parties involved want to put "a line under emotive and contentious events, so that life can move on."[15] Finally, there is an institutional interest that legal relationships are not left in doubt too long but that legal certainty (*Rechtssicherheit*) and peace under the law (*Rechtsfriede*) are restored. Legal certainty can be considered as an element of "formal justice" (*formelle Gerechtigkeit*) in Max Weber's sense,[16] stressing the stability and predictability of the law. Finality is also a precondition of rehabilitation, saves resources, and avoids conflicting judgments. However, the need for finality may be countervailed by aspects of substantive justice.

A related argument points to the mental distress of the defendant, if he or she is subjected to the embarrassment of a trial for a second time (this is captured by the Latin phrase *nemo debet bis vexari*). Anxiety and distress are not confined to the defendant but may equally affect his or her family, and also witnesses on both sides, including the alleged victim.[17] While it is certainly true that no citizen should be exposed to unnecessary and unreasonable suffering, this is a fairly general consideration—in fact, it is only an instance of a general rule against disproportionate state action—and open to the objection that in some situations, inflicting this distress may be justified, for instance to correct a serious miscarriage of justice.[18]

Apart from this "psychological dimension of finality,"[19] there is another, arguably more convincing, political dimension that explains the character as a fundamental right or "one of the strong bulwarks of liberty."[20] The double jeopardy rule strikes a balance between the interests of the state and the individual when it allows the state only a single

[12] *E.g.*, Law Commission, *supra* note 8, § 4.11; Law Commission, *Report 70, Acquittal Following Perversion of the Course of Justice*, § 16 (N.Z.) (2001).

[13] Scottish Law Commission, *Discussion Paper on Double Jeopardy, No. 141*, § 2.23 (2009).

[14] Law Reform Commission of Hong Kong, *supra* note 8, § 2.13.

[15] Law Commission, *supra* note 8, § 4.8.

[16] *Cf.* Max Weber, *Wirtschaft und Gesellschaft* [*Economy and Society*] 468–513 (5th ed. 1972).

[17] Law Commission, *supra* note 8, § 4.7.

[18] Roberts, *supra* note 11, at 405–06.

[19] *Id.* at 405.

[20] Commonwealth v. Olds, 15 Ky. (5 Littell) 137, 139 (1824), per Mills, J.

attempt to conduct a criminal process with regard to the same crime, and this for several reasons: the historically oldest reason and the one most often recited in Anglo-American jurisprudence as well as in European writings of the early nineteenth century[21] is to shield the individual against government oppression by way of repeated criminal prosecutions:

> Every person acquainted with the history of governments, must know, that state trials have been employed as a formidable engine in the hands of a dominant administration. [...] To prevent this mischief, the ancient common law, as well as magna charta itself, provided, that one acquittal or conviction should satisfy the law; [...] To perpetuate this wise rule, so favorably and necessary to the liberty of the citizen, in a government like ours, so frequently subject to changes in popular feeling and sentiment, was the design of introducing into our Constitution the clause in question.[22]
>
> [...] the Double Jeopardy Clause stands as a constitutional barrier against possible tyranny by the overzealous prosecutor.[23]

Second, even if oppression is not at issue—sceptics argue that this aspect has become obsolete in modern criminal procedure[24]—in light of the overwhelming power and resources of the state,[25] one attempt to punish a citizen should normally be sufficient without endangering the effective administration of justice. Indeed, it seems that in the huge majority of cases, no need is felt to resume the procedure. Third, since human justice is imperfect, there is no such thing as a flawless criminal procedure, so there are always errors that could be corrected[26] in a second proceeding. But this is regularly neither worth the time and money of the state nor does it justify the harassment of the defendant. It is a political decision how this balance is exactly struck, if the prohibition of double jeopardy is absolute or if and how many exceptions are admitted in favor of or against the defendant. This balance has been recalibrated in a number of Commonwealth jurisdictions in the past twenty years (*infra* Section I.3.) to accommodate countervailing interests that are set out next.

b. *Conflicting Rationales*

If it is the aim of the criminal process to discover the "real" truth of whether the defendant has committed a punishable offense, then the procedure must be reopened

[21] *See, e.g.*, 2 Julius Graf von Soden, *Geist der peinlichen Gesetzgebung Teutschlands* § 681, at 310–11 (2d ed. 1792); for the German development see Giesbert Schwarplies, *Die rechtsgeschichtliche Entwicklung des Grundsatzes "ne bis in idem" im Strafprozeß* 64–97 (1970).

[22] *Olds*, *supra* note 20.

[23] Ashe v. Swenson, 397 U.S. 436, 456 (1970) (Brennan, J., concurring).

[24] Note, *Double Jeopardy and the Multiple-Count Indictment*, 57 Yale L.J. 132, 133 (1947); see also William H. Comley, *Former Jeopardy*, 35 Yale L.J. 674 (1926) ("ridiculous anachronism").

[25] *Cf.* the famous quote to Justice Black in Green v. United States, 355 U.S. 184, 188–89 (1957).

[26] *See* Albert Friedrich Berner, *Non bis in idem*, 3 Goltdammer's Archiv für Strafrecht 472, 475, 477 (1855); The Ampthill Peerage, [1977] A.C. 547, 569 (H.L.) (Lord Wilberforce).

anytime when subsequent better insight reveals that the final judgment was wrong. Civil lawyers usually speak of "material" or "substantive truth" (*vérité matérielle, verdad material, verità sostanziale, materielle Wahrheit*) in contrast to "formal" or "procedural truth" (*vérité formelle, verdad judicial, verità processuale, formelle Wahrheit*); the latter is defined as the fact-finding result of any fair and lawful proceedings made permanent by the principle of finality (*res judicata pro veritate accipitur*[27]). The discovery of the "real" truth is often regarded as the precondition of a just judgment, so it is said that the principle of "substantive justice" (*materielle Gerechtigkeit*), which commands that everybody receive his due, demands the search for the "whole" truth. Hence, the principle of finality as an emanation of formal justice enters into conflict with the principle of substantive truth as an emanation of substantive justice. This conflict cannot be resolved without curtailing one principle or the other: If truth is paramount, then there is no room for finality—during the heyday of the Continental European inquisitorial procedure (sixteenth to early nineteenth century) that was oriented toward the truth and the punishment of every crime (*ne delicta maneant impunita*), there were many ways to resume a procedure in order to convict the defendant, and influential writers thought that res judicata could not apply to inquisitorial criminal trials at all.[28] If finality is paramount, then the "real" truth must, at least partially, take second place.

Most legal orders opt for some form of compromise: In a first step, the truthfulness of the final decision can be enhanced by allowing appeals in fact and in law against a judgment of first instance. In a second step, even a final judgment may be quashed when the first proceedings were seriously flawed (*propter falsa*) or when relevant new evidence (*propter nova*) is discovered (see Section II.4).

3. Historical Origins

Historical accounts of the double jeopardy rule as a guarantee of individual liberty sometimes, in particular in the common law area, have a hagiographic touch, since courts and writers are tempted to assume that the revered rule must also have a long and venerable pedigree, dating back to the Bible,[29] the Codex of Hammurabi, or at least

[27] Dig. 50.17.207.

[28] *See, e.g.*, the leading authority of seventeenth century German criminal law, Benedikt Carpzov, *Practica nova Imperialis Saxonica rerum criminalium*, quaestio 125 no. 8 (1635), and in the early nineteen century Carl Joseph Anton Mittermaier, *Handbuch des peinlichen Processes* 578–79 (1812). Mittermaier later changed his mind, 2 *Das deutsche Strafverfahren in der Fortbildung durch Gerichts-Gebrauch und Partikular-Gesetzbücher* 379 (1st ed. 1827). For an overview, see Julius Wilhelm Planck, *Die Mehrheit der Rechtsstreitigkeiten im Prozeßrecht* 270–77 (1844).

[29] Nahum 1:9 ("What do ye imagine against the Lord? he will make an utter end; affliction shall not rise up the second time."). The interpretation "non judicabit Deus bis in idipsum" by Saint Jerome is more than questionable; see George C. Thomas III, *Double Jeopardy: The History, the Law* 72 (1998); R.H. Helmholz, *The Spirit of Classical Canon Law* 287–88 (1996); Peter Landau, *Ursprünge und Entwicklung des Verbotes doppelter Strafverfolgung wegen desselben Verbrechens in der Geschichte des kanonischen Rechts*, 56 Zeitschrift der Savigny-Stiftung für Rechtsgeschichte. Kanonistische Abteilung 124, 141 (1970).

Magna Charta,[30] implying that "it simply always existed"[31] or "is as old as the common law."[32] Those accounts are, if not outright false—neither an explicit nor an implicit double jeopardy provision can be found in the Codex Hammurabi,[33] in Magna Charta,[34] or in the English Bill of Rights[35]—at least problematic for being ahistorical. Fundamental rights aimed at the protection of individual liberty against state power are a modern notion that was alien to the legal thought of the Middle Ages and earlier times.[36] Looking to history for guidance in deciding contemporary problems may have very limited value.[37]

All that can be safely said is that there existed a few rather narrow procedural rules, versions of res judicata, against repeated civil and criminal actions brought by private parties in ancient Greek and Roman law.[38] The Roman rules were adopted and expanded in Canon law[39] and thus well known in medieval Continental Europe,[40] for example, in the thirteenth century *Siete Partidas*,[41] as well as in England.[42] The practical impact of these rules, fraught with exceptions and qualifications, was presumably very limited due to the type of criminal procedure and the general societal context of premodern times.[43] When, for example, from the fourteenth century on, in England every felony was punishable by death, the plea of *autrefois convict* could apply only to cases where the defendant had successfully pleaded his benefit of clergy; in the early times of the common law when the criminal procedure had strong inquisitorial characteristics[44] and when acquittals were "extremely rare,"[45] a successful plea of *autrefois acquit* was presumably rare, too. The Continental European inquisitorial procedure of the fourteenth to early nineteenth centuries accepted *ne bis in idem* only when the innocence of the defendant was positively proven, and almost completely disregarded it in every other situation so that trials could be resumed indefinitely.[46]

30 E.g., *Olds*, *supra* note 20.

31 Stout v. State *ex rel.* Caldwell, 78 P. 207, 219 (Okla. 1913).

32 Friedland, *supra* note 9, at 5.

33 Rudstein, *supra* note 8, at 1.

34 Jay A. Sigler, *Double Jeopardy* 4 (1969).

35 Charles L. Cantrell, *Double Jeopardy and Multiple Punishment: An Historical and Constitutional Analysis*, 24 S. Tex. L.J. 735, 768 (1983).

36 Jill Hunter, *The Development of the Rule Against Double Jeopardy*, 5 J. Legal Hist. 3–15 (1984); Helmholz, *supra* note 29, at 305–08.

37 Helmholz, *supra* note 29, at 309–10.

38 *Cf.* Demosthenes, *Speech Against Leptines*, XX:147, in *Orations I–XVII, XX* (J.V. Vince trans., 1998); see also Liebs, *supra* note 7, at 121–22. For Roman law, see Dig. 48.2.7.2; Code Just. 9.2.9.pr.; *Pauli Sententiae*, lib I. tit. 6, 1 ("De his criminibus, de quibus quis absolutus est, ab eo, qui accusavit, refricari accusatio non potest"); Planck, *supra* note 28, at 24–64; Landau, *supra* note 29, at 124–38.

39 *See* Helmholz, *supra* note 29, at 286–308; Landau, *supra* note 29, at 135–52; the resulting rule is X 5.1.6.

40 *See* Landau, *supra* note 29; Liebs, *supra* note 6; Berner, *supra* note 26; August Wilhelm Heffter, Non bis in idem 6–13 (1873); Helmholz, *supra* note 29, at 286–89.

41 *Las Siete Partidas del sabio Rey don Alfonso IX*, Partida VII, tit. I, ley 12 (1256–1263) (Gregorio López ed., 1559).

42 *See* Friedland, *supra* note 9, at 5–15; Sigler, *supra* note 34, at 4–21; Thomas, *supra* note 29, at 74–84; Hunter, *supra* note 36.

43 *See* Hunter, *supra* note 36, at 4–14.

44 *Cf.* Cantrell, *supra* note 35, at 755.

45 Max Radin, *Anglo-American Legal History* 228–29 (1936); see also 9 W.S. Holdsworth, *A History of English Law* 228–29 (1926).

46 *Supra* note 30.

The modern career of the old res judicata rule began, as mentioned, with the advent of the Enlightenment era and modern political philosophy, when it was reconceptualized as a guarantee of individual liberty and emphatically proclaimed, for example, in the American Bill of Rights of 1791,[47] the revolutionary French constitution of 1791,[48] and in Napoleon's *Code d'instruction criminelle* of 1808.[49] From then on, the principle was included in many modern codes, constitutions, and finally, in contemporary human rights treaties.

This success story suffered a setback from a recent trend in common law countries to introduce exceptions to the rule and allow retrials after acquittals, in particular, when "new and compelling evidence" is found.[50] The reforms react to incidents of public outrage caused by the broad application of the double jeopardy rule, for example, by upholding wrongful acquittals in child murder cases even when the defendant later confessed.[51] These exceptions have been very rarely used so far.[52]

4. Legal Status

Although not included in the Universal Declaration of Human Rights of 1948, the prohibition of double jeopardy or *ne bis in idem* is firmly embedded in international human rights law today. On the universal level, it is contained in Article 14(7) of the International Covenant on Civil and Political Rights[53] which has been ratified by 172 states. The principle is also guaranteed in several regional human rights instruments such as the

[47] *Supra* note 3. For the history of double jeopardy in America, see Sigler, *supra* note 34, at 27–34; Cantrell, *supra* note 35, at 760–68; Rudstein, *supra* note 8, at 11–29.

[48] French Constitution of 3 September 1791, title III, chapter V, art. 9, cl. 7 ("Tout homme acquitté par un juré legal, ne peut plus être repris ni accusé à raison du même fait.").

[49] Code d'instruction criminelle of 17 November 1808, art. 246 and 360 ("Toute personne acquittée légalement ne peut être reprise ni accusée à raison du même fait.").

[50] *See* Criminal Justice Act 2003 (England and Wales); Double Jeopardy Act 2011 (Scotland); Criminal Procedure Act 2010 (Ireland); Crimes Amendment (No 2) Act 2008 (New Zealand); in Australia: Crimes (Appeal and Review) Amendment (Double Jeopardy) Act 2006, New South Wales; Criminal Code (Double Jeopardy) Amendment Act 2007, Queensland; Criminal Law Consolidation (Double Jeopardy) Amendment Act 2008, South Australia; Criminal Procedure Amendment (Double Jeopardy and Other Matters) Act 2011, Victoria; Criminal Appeals Amendment (Double jeopardy) Act 2012, Western Australia; Criminal Code Amendment Act 2008, Tasmania. For an analysis, see Law Reform Commission of Hong Kong, *supra* note 8, at 43–123.

[51] *See, e.g.*, http://www.autrefoisacquit.info/index.html (last visited Nov. 2, 2018); http://www.double-jeopardyreform.org/ (last visited Nov. 2, 2018).

[52] *See* Marilyn McMahon, *Retrials of Persons Acquitted of Indictable Offences in England and Australia: Exceptions to the Rule Against Double Jeopardy*, 38 Crim. L.J. 159, 173–84 (2014).

[53] "No one shall be liable to be tried or punished again for an offence for which he has already been finally convicted or acquitted in accordance with the law and penal procedure of each country"; International Covenant on Civil and Political Rights, 16 Dec. 1966, 999 U.N.T.S. 171 and 1057 U.N.T.S. 407, *entered into force* 23 Mar. 1976 [the provisions of Article 41 (Human Rights Committee) entered into force 28 Mar. 1979].

American Convention on Human Rights (art. 8(4)[54]), and the Arab Charter on Human Rights (art. 19(1)[55]). In contrast, the African Charter on Human and People's Rights and the European Convention of Human Rights do not embrace the *ne bis in idem* principle, but in the latter case this lacuna has been filled by Article 4 of the Additional Protocol no. 7.[56] The maxim was accepted as an unwritten rule of European Union law[57] and is now enshrined in Article 50 of the Charter of Fundamental Rights of the European Union,[58] which is largely identical with Article 4 of the Additional Protocol. The only transnational *ne bis in idem* prohibition is contained in Article 54 of the Convention Implementing the Schengen Agreement of 14 June 1985,[59] which promotes transborder cooperation in criminal matters within the European Union.[60] Finally, the maxim is included in most of the statutes of international criminal tribunals.[61]

On the national level, the maxim is enshrined in more than fifty constitutions, for example, in Canada, Germany, India, Japan, New Zealand, Peru, Russia, South Africa, and the United States,[62] and is often part of the statutory law[63] or, in particular in common law jurisdictions, is recognized by the courts. Human rights norms and constitutional provisions are typically rather general, so that the relevant details are left either to

[54] "An accused person acquitted by a non-appealable judgment shall not be subjected to a new trial for the same cause"; American Convention on Human Rights, 22 Nov. 1969, 9 I.L.M. 673 (1970), *entered into force* 18 July 1978.

[55] "No one may be tried twice for the same offence"; Arab Charter on Human Rights, 22 May 2004, translation at 12 Int'l Hum. Rts. Rep. 893 (2005), *entered into force* 15 March 2008.

[56] "(1) No one shall be liable to be tried or punished again in criminal proceedings under the jurisdiction of the same State for an offence for which he has already been finally acquitted or convicted in accordance with the law and penal procedure of that State. (2) The provision of the preceding paragraph shall not prevent the reopening of the case in accordance with the law and penal procedure of the State concerned, if there is evidence of new or newly discovered facts or if there has been a fundamental defect in the previous proceedings, which could affect the outcome of the case"; Protocol No. 7 to the Convention for the Protection of Human Rights and Fundamental Freedoms, 22 Nov. 1984, E.T.S. no. 117, *entered into force* 1 November 1988.

[57] *See* Explanations Relating to the Charter of Fundamental Rights, 2007 O.J. C 303/7, 31.

[58] "No one shall be liable to be tried or punished again in criminal proceedings for an offence for which he or she has already been finally acquitted or convicted within the Union in accordance with the law"; Charter of the Fundamental Rights of the European Union, O.J. C 83/389, 30.03.2010.

[59] "A person whose trial has been finally disposed of in one Contracting Party may not be prosecuted in another Contracting Party for the same acts provided that, if a penalty has been imposed, it has been enforced, is actually in the process of being enforced or can no longer be enforced under the laws of the sentencing Contracting Party"; Convention implementing the Schengen Agreement of 14 June 1985 between the Governments of the States of the Benelux Economic Union, the Federal Republic of Germany and the French Republic on the gradual abolition of checks at their common borders, O.J. L 239/19, 19.06.1990.

[60] *See* Chapter 27 in this volume.

[61] *See* Chapter 27 in this volume and Helen Brady, Matteo Costi, Håkan Friman, Fabricio Guariglia & Carl-Friedrich Stuckenberg, *Charges*, in *International Criminal Procedure* 436–46 (Göran Sluiter et al. eds., 2013).

[62] *See* M. Cherif Bassiouni, *Human Rights in the Context of Criminal Justice: Identifying International Procedural Protections and Equivalent Protections in National Constitutions*, 3 Duke J. Comp. & Int'l L. 235, 288–89 (1993); de la Cuesta, *supra* note 2, at 709.

[63] *See* the country reports, *supra* note 2.

statute law or to the courts. Where the maxim lacks constitutional status (as in England, Scotland, Ireland, Australia, and Hong Kong), exceptions can be enacted with relative ease, while proposals to curtail the constitutional guarantee, for example in Germany[64] or the United States[65], proved difficult or hopeless.

II. *Ne Bis in Idem*: Structure and Scope

Proclaiming a general maxim prohibiting repeated prosecutions is one thing; making it work in practice is quite another. The formulations of the double jeopardy/*ne bis in idem*-maxim in international instruments and constitutions seem clear enough on the surface but underneath it, one will quite often find a complicated and even troublesome body of law that, at worst, can render the hallowed "bulwark of liberty" utterly ineffective.

The precise contours of the *ne-bis-in-idem* prohibition in a particular legal order are determined by the definitions of its ingredients, which may be termed the "*idem,*" the "*semel,*" and the "*bis.*" The *idem* serves to identify the "object of the trial," its cause or matter; its definition poses the greatest difficulty and is a prime source of confusion. The other prerequisite is that the defendant must have been in jeopardy already once (*semel*) which can be understood in several ways. The *bis* refers to the legal consequence and describes the prohibited categories of state action.

1. *Quid Est "Idem"*–What Is the "Same Thing"?

a. *Possible Approaches*

The choice of criteria for the identity of two procedures is crucial to the scope and effectiveness of the prohibition. If the *idem* is defined in a narrow way, so that identity of procedures is difficult to establish, then the double jeopardy prohibition will less often apply than in the hypothesis of a more broadly defined *idem*. A comparative survey confirms that there are two ideal types of approaches and many shades in-between. All approaches require the identity of the defendant and the identity of at least those facts that constitute the criminal offense charged.

The first ideal type describes the *idem* in purely factual terms ("*idem factum*") as the same historical event or occurrence, without regard to the legal qualification of these facts. The prohibition then bars any subsequent prosecution of the same defendant for "les mêmes faits" [the same facts], the "same act or omission," "same conduct," "same transaction," or the "same criminal episode" etc. irrespective of its legal significance.

[64] A bill allowing an exception for new DNA evidence failed in 2009.

[65] *Cf.* Richard Lippke, *Modifying Double Jeopardy*, 15 New Crim. L. Rev. 511, 514 (2012); U.S. Department of Justice, *Report of the Attorney-General, Double Jeopardy and Government Appeals of Acquittals, Truth in Criminal Justice Series, Report No. 6* (1987).

Example 1: D fires a pistol and is convicted of the misdemeanor of illegal use of firearms in a residential area. Police find out later that by this same shot he intentionally killed his neighbor. A strict *idem factum* approach bars a subsequent murder charge because it is based on the same set of facts. Most civil law countries,[66] but only a few common law jurisdictions,[67] and the Model Penal Code (with exceptions, *cf.* §§ 1.07(2), 1.09(1)(c)) employ an *idem factum* approach.

The opposite ideal type requires identity in fact *and* in law, that is, the same set of facts and the charge of the "same offense" (*idem crimen*); a variant appears in procedural garb as the "same evidence" requirement.[68] The *idem crimen* approach, modeled after civil res judicata (same cause of action), is the older one and was adopted by Roman law, Canon law, and the nineteenth century French jurisprudence, and is still prevalent in common law jurisdictions and Russia. Intricate problems arise in multiple-victim scenarios where *idem crimen* approaches tend to allow successive prosecutions in relation to each victim,[69] and in cases where the same conduct violates several provisions, a situation known in the civil law as *concursus idealis*; for example, a person paying a bill with a forged check may commit fraud and forgery. A strict *idem crimen* approach that equates "same offense" with "same provision of the criminal law" or "same statute" would allow parallel or subsequent prosecutions for each nominally distinct offense. Example 2: A conviction of negligent homicide would not bar a subsequent prosecution for murder based on the same facts.[70] However, wider understandings of "same offense" including lesser offenses as well as aggravated forms or extending to "effectively" or "substantially" identical provisions are not uncommon, but typically spawn considerable confusion.[71]

If formalistic "same offense" criteria are rejected as too narrow and purely factual approaches as excessively broad, this may lead to intermediate approaches, favored, for example, by the Netherlands,[72] which are content with a *similar* legal qualification, so that provisions that protect the same or a similar legal interest are regarded as identical

[66] *See* Brady et al., *supra* note 61, at 475–76.

[67] A few American states, see Rebecca A. Delfino, *Prohibition on Successive Prosecutions for the Same Offense—In Search of the "Goldilocks Zone": The California Approach to a National Conundrum*, 54 Am. Crim. L. Rev. 423, 433–39, 470–71 (2017).

[68] *Cf.* the American "*Blockburger* test" in Blockburger v. United States, 284 U.S. 299, 301 (1932) (two offenses are not identical when each requires proof of a fact that the other does not); see Delfino, *supra* note 67, at 427–31.

[69] *E.g.*, Ciucci v. Illinois, 356 U.S. 571 (1958). One evening, Ciucci killed his wife and three children. At the first trial for the wife's death he was convicted of murder and sentenced to twenty years' imprisonment. Dissatisfied with the sentence, the prosecutor sought a second trial for the death of one of the children, where the same evidence was introduced. Ciucci was sentenced to forty-five years' imprisonment. In a third trial for the murder of another child, Ciucci was finally sentenced to death. Since Illinois law treated each of the murders as a separate crime, the U.S. Supreme Court upheld the convictions. An *idem factum* or "same transaction" test would have yielded a different result, see the dissenting opinion.

[70] As in the French *Laurent* case, Cour de cassation [Cass. crim.], May 19, 1983, Bull. crim., No. 149.

[71] *See, e.g.*, American Law Institute, *Administration of the Criminal Law, Official Draft with Commentaries, Subject Covered: Double Jeopardy* 10 (1935); for English law, see John Sprack, *A Practical Approach to Criminal Procedure* § 17.46 (15th ed. 2015).

[72] André Klip & Harmen van der Wilt, *The Netherlands—Non Bis in Idem*, 73 Int'l Rev. Penal L. 1091, 1095, 1106–07 (2002).

for double jeopardy purposes. This would allow a new prosecution in Example 1 but not in Example 2. Some states employ a mixed system;[73] in others the criteria remain controversial.[74]

Idem factum approaches usually offer better protection against repeated trials than the narrower *idem crimen* approach and have for this reason been adopted by the Inter-American Convention on Human Rights,[75] the European Court of Human Rights,[76] and the Court of Justice of the European Union.[77] However, *idem crimen* approaches can be supplemented by other doctrines such as abuse of process (*infra* Section III) to reach a fair result. On the other hand, factual approaches typically encounter massive problems in determining the "sameness" of two incidents because there are no natural boundaries to a "criminal episode," "event" or the like. Additional criteria such as identity of the act or omission, of time and place, of defendant's intent and objective[78] are often helpful but not determinative in all cases. Formulas such as "identical facts or facts which are substantially the same,"[79] "a set of facts which are inextricably linked together in time, in space and by their subject-matter,"[80] or "the entire conduct of the defendant which, according to the views of real life, forms a unity with the historical event described in the accusatory instrument,"[81] merely restate the problem but fail to solve it. This is why everyday crime situations such as a drunk driver transporting drugs in a car pose major problems: May the drug offense be prosecuted after a previous fine for drunk driving or not?[82]

Approaches requiring the identity of the legal provisions such as the *Blockburger* test[83] are the easiest to apply but have the disadvantage that they "virtually annul the guarantee,"[84] whereas wider criteria such as "essentially the same offense" or "offenses protecting the same or a similar legal interest" soon run into a number of difficulties. Apparently, there is an inverse correlation between effectiveness of the protection and determinacy of the criteria.

b. *Interrelations with the Structure of Criminal Litigation*

The criteria for the "sameness" of two proceedings cannot be determined in isolation. The prohibition of "double jeopardy" is necessarily shaped by the nature of the "first

[73] In France, *idem factum* applies only to assize courts and *idem crimen* elsewhere, *see* Laurent Desessard, *France—Les compétences criminelles concurrentes nationales et internationales et le principe ne bis in idem*, 73 Int'l Rev. Penal L. 913, 915 (2002).

[74] *See, e.g.*, Ivan Bele & Vid Jakulin, *Slovenia—Ne Bis in Idem*, 73 Int'l Rev. Penal L. 1071, 1075–76 (2002).

[75] *See* I/A Court H.R., Loayza-Tamayo v. Peru, Judgment of September 7, 1997, Series C, No. 33, paras. 66, 77.

[76] Zolotukhin v. Russia [GC], App. No. 14939/03, Eur. Ct. H.R., Feb. 10, 2009, §§ 291, 320, overruling previous inconsistent decisions.

[77] Case C-436/04, *Van Esbroeck*, [2006] I E.C.R. 2333, 2363–66.

[78] *Cf.* Irene Gärtner, *Austria: Concurrent National and International Criminal Jurisdiction and the Principle "Ne Bis in Idem,"* 73 Int'l Rev. Penal L. 787, 788 (2002).

[79] *Zolotukhin*, *supra* note 76, at 320, 322.

[80] *Van Esbroeck*, *supra* note 77, at 2364–66.

[81] *E.g.*, RGSt 51, 127, 128 (Germany).

[82] *Cf.* the cases discussed by Delfino, *supra* note 67, at 447.

[83] *Supra* note 68.

[84] *Ashe*, *supra* note 23, at 451 (Brennan, J., concurring).

jeopardy," which ultimately boils down to the question of which crimes the defendant could have been convicted at the first trial. In other words, the scope of the bar of subsequent prosecutions usually mirrors the scope of the previous court's ability to adjudicate (*Kognitionsbefugnis*).

The nature of the "first jeopardy" varies significantly among national legal orders and depends on a host of technicalities such as rules of pleading and some basic principles. The underlying structural question is simple: Who decides of which crimes a court is entitled to convict or acquit? This question has a factual and a legal component.

In almost all modern criminal justice systems, an accusatory instrument fixes the facts that are submitted to the court's adjudication. But what about new facts discovered at trial? If a witness testifies or the accused confesses that he stole not only three but rather ten cars, used a weapon, and hit another person? Can these new facts be adjudicated in the same trial, for example, because they still are inextricably linked to the facts contained in the indictment? What if these facts are discovered after the trial when the first judgment has become res judicata? All jurisdictions have to decide whether only facts known to the prosecutor or the court belong to the *idem* so that subsequently discovered facts—not to be confused with subsequently discovered evidence concerning the same event—would justify a new prosecution or not. One might also ask which facts or evidence a diligent prosecutor or a diligent inquisitorial court could have dealt with at the first trial. What about those facts that neither prosecutor nor court could have known at the first trial because they did not exist, such as the subsequent death of a wounded person? Many jurisdictions do not extend res judicata and the double jeopardy prohibition to subsequent events because the first court could not decide on them[85], but some (Germany) do[86] if the later event belongs to the same historical episode.

The legal component concerns, apart from general legal obstacles to the exercise of the court's jurisdiction, mainly the question of which legal provisions are at issue at the trial. In accusatorial systems, the prosecutor draws up an accusatory instrument with counts that fix the legal qualification of the alleged behavior. In principle, the court takes a passive role and can only answer in the affirmative or in the negative, that is, whether the defendant is guilty of the offense charged, obviously modeled after a jury trial. There is a little flexibility, since a conviction may also be entered for a lesser included offense, but not much more. If the prosecutor is not sure whether the court will share her legal opinion, she might include alternative or cumulative charges that cover the same facts under different legal headings. During the trial, charges may also be amended or new counts inserted. With this type of trial, a narrow *idem crimen* approach to double jeopardy seems appropriate because the "first jeopardy" is equally narrowly tailored. On the contrary, a wide *idem factum* approach seems unwarranted if, for example, the defendant

[85] *E.g.*, R. v. Morris (1867) L.R. 1 C.C.R. 90; R. v. Thomas, [1950] 1 K.B. 26, 29, 31 (C.C.A.): a conviction of wounding before victim's death is no bar to subsequent indictment for murder; Diaz v. United States, 223 U.S. 442, 448–49 (1912).

[86] *Cf.* BGHSt 6, 92, 95; Carl-Friedrich Stuckenberg, *§ 264 StPO* in 6(2) Löwe & Rosenberg, *Die Strafprozeßordnung und das Gerichtsverfassungsgesetz* (Volker Erb et al. eds., 26th ed. 2013); § 264 StPO margin no. 16, 29.

was charged with theft and the court could not convict him of robbery although sufficient evidence surfaced at trial, then it makes no sense to bar a subsequent prosecution for robbery. Here, other techniques are necessary to avoid harassment by multiple trials. If the prosecutor enjoys wide discretion on what to prosecute, one possibility is to allow or to require the joinder of all charges based on the same facts.[87] This can be achieved indirectly by disallowing successive prosecutions for the event because they are deemed abusive (*infra* Section III.). In systems where courts lack the authority to alter the legal qualification of the facts, an *idem factum* approach to double jeopardy makes sense only if a fairly comprehensive legal evaluation of the facts is secured by other means, such as, for example, compulsory joinder of counts.

In modern inquisitorial systems—which mostly represent some form of mixed accusatorial-inquisitorial procedure—the legal qualification given in the accusatory instrument is merely provisional and does not bind the court, which is not only free to but often obliged to requalify the facts ("*iura novit curia*") if the evidence produced at trial so requires. This active investigating role of the court is the defining element of an inquisitorial procedure. The defendant must of course be notified and given sufficient opportunity to adapt his defense strategy. In systems that embrace the legality principle, not only the prosecutor but also the court may be obliged to make a comprehensive legal evaluation of all discoverable facts, that is, convict on all offenses that are proven. Here, an *idem factum* approach to *ne bis in idem* is warranted because at the first trial, the defendant was in jeopardy of being convicted of all conceivable crimes supported by the facts described in the accusatory instrument.

The procedural question of which offenses a court is entitled to convict on is linked to a further issue, namely the admissibility of cumulative charges, cumulative convictions, and sentencing for multiple offenses. In some jurisdictions such as the United States, the double jeopardy prohibition is also thought to forbid multiple punishments in a single prosecution[88] unless this is authorized by the legislature[89] while it was never so understood in England.[90] In civil law jurisdictions, this is regarded as a distinct question belonging to substantive criminal law known as *concursus delictorum* or *Konkurrenzlehre*, a set of doctrines that determine whether several offenses are applicable to the same facts and, if so, what this means for sentencing.

2. *Quid Est "Semel"*—When Does Jeopardy Attach?

A second criminal procedure is only prohibited if there has been a first one in the same cause. What constitutes a first procedure that implicates the double jeopardy prohibition? Paradigmatically, the double jeopardy protection is triggered by final judgments

[87] *Cf. Ashe*, *supra* note 23, at 454–55 (Brennan, J., concurring).

[88] *Ex parte* Lange, 85 U.S. (18 Wall.) 163, 173 (1873); North Carolina v. Pearce, 395 U.S. 711, 717 (1969); for an overview and the resulting problems, see Delfino, *supra* note 67, at 426–29.

[89] *Cf.* Whalen v. United States, 445 U.S. 684, 691–92 (1980).

[90] *Thomas*, *supra* note 85, at 31.

on the merits issued by criminal courts, that is, convictions or acquittals that have acquired the force of res judicata.

Typically, human rights and national provisions on *ne bis in idem* bar only multiple proceedings within the same state. Transnational situations and the relation to international criminal tribunals pose special problems, which are analyzed in Chapter 27 of this volume. Most federal states do not distinguish between domestic judgments, one notable exception[91] being the United States, where, according to the "dual sovereignty doctrine," a state prosecution does not bar a federal prosecution and vice versa;[92] although prosecutorial policies usually discourage successive trials.[93] Native American tribes are considered separate sovereigns as well.[94]

Decisions of civil courts, administrative authorities or courts, and disciplinary authorities, even if they are accorded the force of res judicata, usually do not bar a subsequent criminal prosecution for the same cause.[95] Yet, the distinction between criminal and civil or administrative proceedings can become dubious when substantial sanctions are pronounced.[96] The European Court of Human Rights employs an autonomous notion of "criminal charge" that can encompass administrative sanctions.[97]

Legal orders differ whether only final criminal court decisions trigger the prohibition. Whereas English law insists on a final verdict, in American federal law, "jeopardy attaches" already when a jury is empaneled and sworn, or, in a bench trial, when the judge begins to receive evidence,[98] because a second trial may be unfair to the defendant even if the first trial was not completed,[99] unless there was a manifest necessity to discontinue the trial.[100] Civil law jurisdictions usually accord the full protection only after a judgment has become res judicata.

What about other forms of final disposal of a case? Many jurisdictions know several forms to dispose of a case, ranging from refusals to prosecute for lack of evidence or dismissing a case because of triviality, refusals to commit a case to trial (no case to answer,

[91] The situation is less clear in Canada; see Law Reform Commission of Canada, *Working Paper 63, Double Jeopardy, Pleas and Verdicts*, at 19 (1991). In Australia, multiple prosecutions are expressly prohibited in Australian Crime Commission Act 2002, § 35A(1), and on the state level by § 39 of the identical Australian Crime Commission (State Provisions) Acts.

[92] United States v. Lanza, 260 U.S. 377, 382 (1922); Abbate v. United States, 359 U.S. 187, 188–96 (1959).

[93] *E.g.*, United States Attorney's Manual, § 9-2.031 (Oct. 2015) ("*Petite* policy"). A variety of corresponding rules exist on the state level.

[94] United States v. Lara, 541 U.S. 193, 199–210 (2004).

[95] *E.g.*, T. Vander Beken, G. Vermeulen & T. Ongena, *Belgium: Concurrent National and International Criminal Jurisdiction and the Principle "Ne Bis in Idem,"* 73 Int'l Rev. Penal L. 811, 812–13 (2002); Hudson v. United States, 522 U.S. 93, 98–105 (1997).

[96] *Cf.* United States v. Halper, 490 U.S. 435, 440–52 (1989): excessive civil penalty regarded as second punishment, but see *Hudson*, *supra* note 95.

[97] Gradinger v. Austria, App. No. 15963/90, Eur. Ct. H.R., Oct. 23, 1995, §§ 10, 15: A drunk motorist caused an accident that led to the death of a cyclist. The criminal conviction of causing death by negligence bars a subsequent administrative "sentence order" for drunk driving.

[98] United States v. Martin Linen Supply Co., 430 U.S. 564, 569 (1977); *compare* Model Penal Code, § 1.08(4) (Am. Law Inst., Proposed Official Draft 1962): after the first witness is sworn.

[99] Arizona v. Washington, 434 U.S. 497, 503–05 (1978).

[100] *Cf.* Wade v. Hunter, 336 U.S. 684, 688–91 (1949).

décision de non-lieu, etc.) to decisions in summary proceedings that impose a penalty (e.g., penal orders) or alternatives to punishments. Disposals of the case that impose a sanction or some sanction-equivalent may carry at least a reduced form of finality, so that a new prosecution may be brought only for a more serious offense.[101] Decisions of the public prosecutor not to prosecute are often not considered final and therefore have no *ne-bis-in-idem* effect although national views vary.[102]

In contemporary criminal justice systems, there are mostly one or two levels of appeal courts, so that the question arises whether double jeopardy is implicated when a higher court sets aside a trial judgment for error of fact or law and orders a new trial. Possible answers are that if the defendant appeals his conviction, he thereby waives his protection against repeated trials, or that it is in the interests of justice to correct mistakes by way of appeal and retrial, or that a retrial is not "an act of governmental oppression of the sort against which the double jeopardy clause was intended to protect."[103] By contrast, civil law jurisdictions adhere to a "continuing jeopardy" theory[104] that regards the entire proceedings as one until res judicata is reached, including the exhaustion of all ordinary remedies, even if they, in rare cases, may lead to multiple retrials.

3. *Quid Est "Bis"*—What Is Prohibited?

Several options exist on how to define the *bis*, that is, what exactly is forbidden after completion of the first proceedings. It may be that only a second verdict is barred or alternatively, that new court proceedings or new criminal investigations are barred altogether. Older formulations of the maxim are sometimes elliptic and not very precise while newer phrasings tend to be longer but more accurate, stating for example, that no one shall be "tried or punished again in criminal proceedings . . . for an offence for which he has already been finally acquitted or convicted."[105] This comprehensive understanding is common today: no (second) punishment after conviction, no (first) punishment after acquittal, in short, no further criminal proceedings of any type. If court proceedings are prohibited, it seems logical that police or prosecutorial investigations are, too,[106] unless they serve to determine if and to what extent a new prosecution is barred or to evaluate the possibilities of reopening the case.[107]

[101] *E.g.*, Gärtner, *supra* note 78, at 790–91; Wolfgang Schomburg, *Germany: Concurrent National and International Criminal Jurisdiction and the Principle "Ne Bis in Idem,"* 73 Int'l Rev. Penal L. 941, 943–45 (2002); Desessard, *supra* note 73, at 916.

[102] *E.g.*, Vander Beken et al., *supra* note 95, at 813.

[103] United States v. Scott, 437 U.S. 82, 91 (1978).

[104] Developed by Justice Holmes in the context of the appealability of acquittals, Kepner v. United States, 195 U.S. 100, 134 (1904).

[105] *Supra* note 58.

[106] *E.g.*, Toshihiro Kawaide, *Concurrent National and International Criminal Jurisdiction and the Principle "Ne Bis in Idem" in Japan*, 73 Int'l Rev. Penal L. 1031, 1032 (2002).

[107] *Cf.* Gärtner, *supra* note 78, at 791.

It is a peculiarity of most common law jurisdictions to regard acquittals by a trial court as final so that government appeals (at least for error of fact) are not allowed. This rule, which has an ideological root in the nullification power of the jury, has constitutional status in the United States because "the public interest in the finality of judgments is so strong that a defendant may not be retried even though 'the acquittal was based upon an egregiously erroneous foundation.' "[108]

Civil law jurisdictions do not share this view and quite naturally allow prosecution appeals of acquittals as an ordinary remedy because the accuracy of the judgment is given more weight. The asymmetrical privilege of acquittals has been criticized in common law countries as well,[109] and, as mentioned, was eroded in the first decades of the twenty-first century in England and several Commonwealth states.[110]

National views also differ on whether to allow administrative or disciplinary sanctions after criminal sanctions, which are often regarded as admissible because they serve different objectives.[111] According to the jurisprudence of the European Court of Human Rights, administrative and disciplinary sanctions may count as criminal and be barred while parallel proceedings are acceptable if they are "sufficiently closely connected in substance and time";[112] measures of a preventive nature do not fall under the prohibition.[113] Civil actions for example, for damages or even punitive damages are usually not precluded, *cf.* the O.J. Simpson case where three civil suits followed an acquittal.

If a subsequent prosecution is not for exactly the same cause but for partially identical facts, the question arises whether the res judicata of a previous acquittal or conviction has a binding effect on the later proceedings, also known as "issue preclusion," "issue estoppel," or "collateral estoppel," in the sense "that when an issue of ultimate fact has once been determined by a valid and final judgment, that issue cannot again be litigated between the same parties in any future lawsuit."[114] This kind of preclusion could avoid inconsistent decisions, and, more important, cancel out some of the ill effects of a narrow *idem crimen* approach, because an acquittal not only bars a subsequent prosecution of the "same offense" but also a subsequent prosecution for a different offense where "the second prosecution requires the relitigation of factual issues already resolved by the first"[115] as in the American case *Ashe v. Swenson*.[116]

[108] Arizona v. Washington, 434 U.S. 497, 503 (1978).

[109] *Supra* note 67. [110] *Supra* note 53.

[111] *See* Human Rights Committee, General Comment No. 32, § 57 (Ninetieth Session 2007), UN Doc. C.C.P.R./C/GC/32: Art. 14(7) ICCPR does not apply to disciplinary measures that do not amount to a sanction for a criminal offense.

[112] A and B v. Norway [GC], App. No. 24130/11 and 29758/11, Eur. Ct. H.R., Nov. 15, 2016, §§ 117–34.

[113] *Cf.* Storbråten v. Norway, App. No. 12277/04, Eur. Ct. H.R., Feb. 1, 2007; Haarvig v. Norway, App. No. 11187/05, Eur. Ct. H.R., Dec. 11, 2007.

[114] *Ashe, supra* note 23, at 443. [115] Brown v. Ohio, 432 U.S. 161, 166 n.6 (1977).

[116] *See Ashe, supra* note 23. In *Ashe*, three or four masked men broke into a home and robbed each of six poker players. Ashe was charged with having robbed one of the poker players but was acquitted "due to insufficient evidence." Six weeks later, Ashe was brought to trial again for the robbery of another participant in the poker game and convicted. The U.S. Supreme Court held that collateral estoppel is a part of the Fifth Amendment's guarantee against double jeopardy, which forbids the second trial.

However, the doctrine is not easy to apply and of very limited effect[117] because everything depends on which issues of ultimate fact have already been resolved, and jury verdicts have no reasons. English courts do not recognize issue estoppel in criminal law[118] although the prosecution in a second trial is normally estopped from challenging the correctness of a prior acquittal.[119] In a case such as *Ashe*, a civil law jurisdiction with an *idem factum* approach would have barred the second prosecution quite simply because the same historical event was at issue.

4. Exceptions

Although the scope of the *idem* is the most decisive factor, the effectiveness of the double jeopardy protection also depends on the existence of exceptions to res judicata that allow the reopening of the proceedings. Suppose the defendant is convicted of theft and it turns out later that he used a loaded weapon to get the booty. A narrow *idem crimen* approach may allow another prosecution for robbery while an *idem factum* approach does not. However, a number of jurisdictions allow exceptions to res judicata to the detriment of the defendant when new evidence (*nova*) has been discovered, so that a trial for robbery might be possible here. The difference is that exceptions to res judicata are usually subject to very restrictive conditions.

The European Convention on Human Rights Additional Protocol expressly allows the reopening of proceedings,[120] if new evidence is discovered or fundamental procedural defects exist which could have affected the outcome, while Article 14(7) of the ICCPR is silent on the issue but interpreted as not to prohibit the resumption of a criminal trial "justified by exceptional circumstances" such as the discovery of new evidence.[121]

The most common grounds for revision are, in civil law parlance, *falsa* and *nova*: Either the underlying procedure is later discovered to have been blatantly unlawful and the result is affected by this, for example, if the judge, jury, or witnesses were bribed, perjury committed, documents forged etc., or new facts have occurred (victim dies) or new evidence has been discovered (e.g., DNA tests, defendant's confession) that are highly likely to change the outcome. An asymmetry favoring the defendant is also quite common, so that in many legal orders wrongful convictions are easier to overturn than wrongful acquittals, which in some states may not be reconsidered at all. Today, it can no longer be said that privileging acquittals from resumption is a hallmark of common law countries because quite a number of civil law countries proscribe reopening

[117] *See* Rice v. Com., 703 S.E.2d 254, 257–58 (Va. Ct. App. 2011); Susan R. Klein & Katherine P. Chiarello, *Successive Prosecutions and Compound Criminal Statutes: A Functional Test*, 77 Tex. L. Rev. 333, 377–81 (1998); Rudstein, *supra* note 8, at 126–32.

[118] D.P.P. v. Humphrys [1977] A.C. 1, 21, 40–48, 56 (H.L.); for Australia, New Zealand, and Ireland, see Paul A. McDermott, *Res Judicata and Double Jeopardy* §§ 28.12–28.22 (1998); for Canada, see R. v. Mahalingan [2008] 3 S.C.R. 316.

[119] Sambasivam v. Public Prosecutor, Federation of Malaya, [1950] A.C. 458 (P.C.); but see R. v. Z [2002] 2 A.C. 483, 502–05 (H.L.).

[120] *Supra* note 58.

[121] *See* Human Rights Committee, *supra* note 111, § 56.

a case against the defendant *propter nova* while many common law countries have recently introduced appeals against "tainted acquittals"[122] or for "new and compelling evidence."[123] For further details, see Chapters 47 and 48 in this volume.

III. Alternative Approaches/ Functional Equivalents

The protection against multiple prosecutions for the same criminal occurrence can also be effectuated by other legal tools rather than a traditional double jeopardy rule. While English law favors a narrow understanding of *idem crimen*,[124] it has also accepted a principle against the succession of different charges, originally in ascending order,[125] based on the same facts. Today, this principle forms part of a broad doctrine against "abuse of process,"[126] which covers a variety of situations and is understood as the inherent discretionary power of the court[127] to (indefinitely) stay proceedings if, for instance, this is necessary to protect the integrity of the criminal justice system.[128] Where the narrow application of the *autrefois* pleas would "result in unfairness or injustice to a defendant amounting to oppression, the remedy lies in the power of the court to stay the proceedings."[129] The doctrine of "abuse of process" also exists, with some variations, in other Commonwealth countries.[130]

References

José Luis de la Cuesta, *Concurrent National and International Criminal Jurisdiction and the Principle "ne bis in idem"*, 73 Int'l Rev. Penal L. 707 (2002)
Martin L. Friedland, *Double Jeopardy* (1969)
Jill Hunter, *The Development of the Rule Against Double Jeopardy*, 5 J. Legal Hist. 3 (1984)
Paul A. McDermott, *Res Judicata and Double Jeopardy* (1999)
David S. Rudstein, *Double Jeopardy: A Reference Guide to the United States Constitution* (2004)
Jay A. Sigler, *Double Jeopardy: The Development of a Legal and Social Policy* (1969)
George C. Thomas III, *Double Jeopardy: The History, the Law* (1998)

122 *E.g.*, the English Criminal Procedure and Investigations Act 1996, §§ 54–57.

123 *E.g.*, the English Criminal Justice Act 2003, §§ 75–97.

124 While the speeches in Connelly v. D.P.P. [1964] A.C. 1254 (H.L.) leave some doubts as to the scope of the *autrefois* pleas, a narrow reading is now confirmed in *Junior Bayode*, *supra* note 1, at 17; R. v. J (JF) [2013] EWCA Crim 569; [2014] Q.B. 561, 566–72 (C.A.).

125 R. v. Elrington (1861) 121 Eng. Rep. 870 (K.B.); 1 B. & S. 688; R. v. Beedie, [1997] EWCA Crim 714; [1998] Q.B. 356, 361–66.

126 *See* Colin Wells, *Abuse of Process* (3d ed. 2017); Peter Hungerford-Welch, *Abuse of Process: Does It Really Protect the Suspect's Rights?*, Crim. L. Rev. 3, 9–10 (2017).

127 *Connelly*, *supra* note 124, at 1301–02, 1347–53, 1359–60; *J (JF)*, *supra* note 124.

128 *Cf.* R. v. Crawley [2014] EWCA Crim 1028 [17]; (2014) 2 Cr. App. Rep. 16.

129 *J (JF)*, *supra* note 124, at 572.

130 *See* Wells, *supra* note 126, § 1.38–§ 1.59.

CHAPTER 22

JURISDICTION AND TRANSNATIONAL *NE BIS IN IDEM* IN PROSECUTION OF TRANSNATIONAL CRIMES

ANDRÉ KLIP

I. Introduction

This chapter deals with the various jurisdictional principles that states have developed to apply their criminal law over human conduct. The concept of jurisdiction will be defined, as the various legal families in the world may apply the same terminology for different concepts. The following distinctions will be made: jurisdiction to prescribe, to adjudicate, and to enforce. These divisions also relate to the question of whether jurisdiction must be regarded as a rule of procedure or as an element of the crime. Criminal justice systems have different views on this, which do not correspond to the classical common law/civil law distinction.

Until some decades ago, there used to be a clear link with the choices states made on jurisdiction and their ideas on extradition of nationals. Common law states had jurisdiction over offenders on their territory and saw no difficulty in extraditing their own nationals for crimes committed abroad, whereas civil law jurisdictions prohibited the extradition of nationals because they could prosecute nationals for crimes committed outside the country. Although this more nationalistic or protectionist approach may no longer be generally valid, states still regard criminal jurisdiction as an exclusive competence, inherent to state sovereignty. Since the 1980s, both common and civil law states have expanded their extraterritorial jurisdiction on a large scale. States tend to forget that they have expanded extraterritorial jurisdiction to such an extent that concurrent jurisdiction and conflicts of jurisdiction have become a serious problem. While common law and civil law ideas on jurisdiction have converged to a large extent, some differences remain and neither system has been able to deal with the consequences of overlapping jurisdiction.

On the international plane, several disputes have emerged. Unsurprisingly, universal jurisdiction has led to serious problems between the state on which territory the offense was committed and the state whose national is being prosecuted or investigated. However, more frequently, disputes have arisen concerning two states both claiming that the offense occurred on their territory. These cases may not be as high profile as those relating to universal jurisdiction, but they raise more difficult questions, as the legitimatizing claim under international law is strong. One of the consequences of extraterritorial or multiterritorial jurisdiction is that more than one state may use the jurisdiction, as a result of which an accused may be prosecuted and convicted twice for the same crime. I will deal with the questions that arise here: When is a case finally disposed of? What is *idem*? On the basis of what is that assessed? What is a second prosecution? What should be done when a criminal prosecution is in one state and a non-criminal response is in another? Is there a common notion of what amounts to an *idem*? The question is what a recognition of *ne bis* means for state authorities.

II. Criminal Jurisdiction and International Law

Two approaches can be distinguished under international law in dealing with criminal jurisdiction. The first is that states may make use of their jurisdiction and extend it, as long as there is no explicit prohibitive rule precluding that. The second is that states may not exert jurisdiction, unless there is a permissive rule.[1] The first approach has been adopted by the Permanent Court of International Justice in the 1927 *Lotus* case. However, many states and some doctrinal sources prefer the second. In practice, it is difficult to identify which approach is leading. It seems that in an opportunistic way states may switch from one to another, depending on their position. If a state wishes to exert jurisdiction, it may opt for the first approach, as long as there is no prohibition. If a state wishes to prevent the use of extraterritorial jurisdiction by another state, it will refer to the absence of a clearly permissive rule.

1. The *Lotus* Case

The *Lotus* case is the first case in which an international court had to determine under which circumstances a state could use jurisdiction outside its own territory.[2]

[1] Cedric Ryngaert, *Jurisdiction in International Law* 21 (2008).

[2] SS Lotus (France v. Turkey), 1927 P.C.I.J. (ser. A) No. 10 (Sept. 7).

On August 2, 1926, on the high sea, a French ship, the *Lotus*, collided with a Turkish ship, the *Boz-Kourt*, resulting in the death of eight Turkish seamen. The Turkish authorities decided to prosecute the French lieutenant they regarded as responsible for the incident.[3] France opposed the prosecution and stated that it was contrary to international law. The two states subsequently brought the case to the Permanent Court of International Justice in The Hague.[4]

The Court needed to answer the question whether principles of international law precluded the application of Turkish criminal law to the conduct of French lieutenant Demons on the high sea.[5] The Court distinguished between two modalities of jurisdiction: the *jurisdiction to prescribe*, and the *jurisdiction to enforce*. Concerning *jurisdiction to enforce* the Court held:

> the first and foremost restriction imposed by international law upon a State is that—failing the existence of a permissive rule to the contrary—it may not exercise its power in any form in the territory of another State. In this sense jurisdiction is certainly territorial; it cannot be exercised by a State outside its territory except by virtue of a permissive rule derived from international custom or from a convention.[6]

However, the Court also held that *jurisdiction to prescribe* may be used extraterritorially:

> It does not, however, follow that international law prohibits a State from exercising jurisdiction in its own territory, in respect of any case which relates to acts which have taken place abroad, and in which it cannot rely on some permissive rule of international law. Such a view would only be tenable if international law contained a general prohibition to States to extend the application of their laws and the jurisdiction of their courts to persons, property and acts outside their territory, and if, as an exception to this general prohibition, it allowed States to do so in certain specific cases. But this is certainly not the case under international law as it stands at present. Far from laying down a general prohibition to the effect that States may not extend the application of their laws and the jurisdiction of their courts to persons, property and acts outside their territory, it leaves them in this respect a wide measure of discretion, which is only limited in certain cases by prohibitive rules; as regards other cases, every State remains free to adopt the principles which it regards as best and most suitable.[7]

The Court found justification for this in the fact that the international legal order consists of independent states.[8] It deducted two consequences from this. On the one hand states cannot enforce outside their territory respect for their legislation, because they would then act in violation of the principle of sovereign equality of states.[9] Jurisdiction,

[3] SS Lotus (France v. Turkey), 1927 P.C.I.J. (ser. A) No. 10, at 10–11 (Sept. 7).
[4] SS Lotus (France v. Turkey), 1927 P.C.I.J. (ser. A) No. 10, at 11–12 (Sept. 7).
[5] SS Lotus (France v. Turkey), 1927 P.C.I.J. (ser. A) No. 10, at 15 (Sept. 7).
[6] SS Lotus (France v. Turkey), 1927 P.C.I.J. (ser. A) No. 10, at 18–19 (Sept. 7).
[7] SS Lotus (France v. Turkey), 1927 P.C.I.J. (ser. A) No. 10, at 19 (Sept. 7).
[8] SS Lotus (France v. Turkey), 1927 P.C.I.J. (ser. A) No. 10, at 18 (Sept. 7).
[9] Ryngaert, *supra* note 1, at 23.

in the meaning of *jurisdiction to enforce*, is in that sense purely territorial. On the other hand, states may justify applying rules to individuals, possessions, and acts outside their territory, because "[r]estrictions upon the independence of States cannot…be presumed."[10] Jurisdiction, in the sense of *jurisdiction to prescribe*, can therefore be extraterritorial. The Court concluded that "[t]he territoriality of criminal law, therefore, is not an absolute principle of international law and by no means coincides with territorial sovereignty."[11]

2. International Customary Law

The findings of the Court in the *Lotus* case have been rejected in doctrine several times. The view is that international custom leads to no other conclusion than that vesting extraterritorial jurisdiction requires explicit permission.[12] This approach strengthens the primacy of territorial jurisdiction. The use of extraterritorial jurisdiction is, in this approach, not a consequence of territorial jurisdiction, but an exception to the main rule. Both principles refer to the sovereignty of states to support their view: "The former view, however, takes the perspective of the prescribing State, emphasizing its absolute sovereign right of unilaterally exercising jurisdiction, whereas the latter view takes the perspective of the State feeling the adverse effects of the jurisdictional assertions of the prescribing State, a view emphasizing notions of reciprocity that are necessary for any viable concept of sovereignty."[13]

3. The *Yerodia* Case

Seventy-five years after *Lotus*, the International Court of Justice was confronted with a new criminal jurisdiction issue in the *Yerodia* case.[14] A Belgian investigating magistrate had issued an arrest warrant against Abdulaye Yerodia Ndombasi at the time that he was Minister of Foreign Affairs of the Democratic Republic of Congo (DRC).[15] Yerodia was accused of war crimes and crimes against humanity committed against the Tutsis during

[10] SS Lotus (France v. Turkey), 1927 P.C.I.J. (ser. A) No. 10, at 18 (Sept. 7).

[11] SS Lotus (France v. Turkey), 1927 P.C.I.J. (ser. A) No. 10, at 20 (Sept. 7).

[12] Ryngaert, *supra* note 1, at 27. [13] *Id.* at 29.

[14] Arrest Warrant of 11 April 2000 (Democratic Republic of the Congo v. Belgium), 2002 I.C.J. 3 (Feb. 14). David Turns, *Arrest Warrant of 11 April 2000 (Democratic Republic of the Congo v. Belgium): The International Court of Justice's Failure to Take a Stand on Universal Jurisdiction*, 3 Melb. J. Int'l L. 383 (2002); Marc Henzelin, *La Compétence Pénale Universelle: Une Question non Résolue par l'Arrêt Yerodia*, 106 Revue générale de droit international public 820 (2002).

[15] Arrest Warrant of 11 April 2000 (Democratic Republic of the Congo v. Belgium), 2002 I.C.J. 3, 9 (Feb. 14).

an internal conflict in the DRC in 1998.[16] Belgium claimed jurisdiction on the basis of the 1993 Genocide-act, providing universal jurisdiction over these international crimes.[17]

Although the application of extraterritorial jurisdiction was at the heart of the *Yerodia* case, the Court decided not to deal with it.[18] The explanation of that lies in the fact that Congo initially stated that universal jurisdiction was in violation of international law and that an incumbent Minister of Foreign Affairs is immune under international law.[19] However, in its final pleadings the DRC dropped the question of jurisdiction.[20] Although the Court may not decide *non ultra petita*, it stated that it "nonetheless cannot preclude the Court from addressing certain legal points in its reasoning."[21] The Court interpreted the Congolese request as an invitation to debate on immunities.[22] Nevertheless, several judges expressed their views on universal jurisdiction and extra-territorial jurisdiction in general in *separate* and *dissenting opinions*.[23] Three of the opinions deserve closer attention.

In his separate opinion, the president of the Court, Judge Guillaume, made a historic analysis of the application of extraterritorial jurisdiction and noted that "[o]rdinarily, States are without jurisdiction over crimes committed abroad as between foreigners".[24] He accepted only one exception, piracy, that was recognized under customary law. In addition, Judge Guillaume held that universal jurisdiction in absentia had not been recognized in international conventions.[25] In essence, he confuses *jurisdiction to prescribe* and *jurisdiction to enforce*. Finally, he stated that the assessment of the Permanent Court of International Justice in the *Lotus* case was not convincing and that the principle of territoriality had become stronger since the adoption of the Charter of the United

[16] Ernst Hirsch Ballin, *Yerodia: Rechtsmacht, immuniteit en vervolgingsbeleid*, 51 Ars Aequi 741 (2002); Turns, *supra* note 14, at 384.

[17] *See further* Jan Wouters & Hendrik Vandekerckhove, *The Rise and Fall of Universal Jurisdiction for International Crimes in Belgium, Interactions Between Legislation and Case Law*, in *Liber Amicorum Chris Van den Wyngaert* 625–46 (Steven Dewulf (red.) la [CVDW], 2017).

[18] *See* Antonio Cassese, *When May Senior State Officials Be Tried for International Crimes? Some Comments on the* Congo v. Belgium *Case*, 13 Eur. J. Int'l L. 855–56 (2002); Mark Summers, *The International Court of Justice's Decision in* Congo v. Belgium: *How Has It Affected the Development of a Principle of Universal Jurisdiction That Would Obligate all States to Prosecute War Criminals?*, 21 B.U. Int'l L.J. 68 (2003); Turns, *supra* note 14, at 386.

[19] Arrest Warrant of 11 April 2000 (Democratic Republic of the Congo v. Belgium), 2002 I.C.J. 3, 10 (Feb. 14).

[20] Arrest Warrant of 11 April 2000 (Democratic Republic of the Congo v. Belgium), 2002 I.C.J. 3, 11 (Feb. 14).

[21] Arrest Warrant of 11 April 2000 (Democratic Republic of the Congo v. Belgium), 2002 I.C.J. 3, 19 (Feb. 14).

[22] Arrest Warrant of 11 April 2000 (Democratic Republic of the Congo v. Belgium), 2002 I.C.J. 3, 19 (Feb. 14). On immunities Helmut Kreicker, *Völkerrechtliche Exemtionen, Grundlagen und Grenzen völkerrechtlichen Immunitäten und ihre Wirkungen im Strafrecht* Band 1 & 2 (2007).

[23] See further Cassese, *supra* note 23, at 855–58; Henzelin, *supra* note 14, at 831–32 and 837–43; Hirsch Ballin, *supra* note 16, at 743–47; Summers, *supra* note 18, at 92–96; Turns, *supra* note 14, at 388–395.

[24] Arrest Warrant of 11 April 2000 (Democratic Republic of the Congo v. Belgium), 2002 I.C.J. 3, 37 (Feb. 14).

[25] Arrest Warrant of 11 April 2000 (Democratic Republic of the Congo v. Belgium), 2002 I.C.J. 3, 40 (Feb. 14).

Nations.[26] He regarded applications of extraterritorial jurisdiction in treaties as exceptions of territoriality:

> States primarily exercise their criminal jurisdiction on their own territory. In classic international law, they normally have jurisdiction in respect of an offence committed abroad only if the offender, or at least the victim, is of their nationality, or if the crime threatens their internal or external security. Additionally, they may exercise jurisdiction in cases of piracy and in the situations of subsidiary universal jurisdiction provided for by various conventions if the offender is present on their territory. But apart from these cases, international law does not accept universal jurisdiction; still less does it accept universal jurisdiction in *absentia*.[27]

In their joint separate opinion Judges Higgins, Kooijmans, and Buergenthal approached things entirely differently. First, they stated that the Court had to answer the question whether Belgium was allowed to use universal jurisdiction.[28] Second, they stated, unlike Judge Guillaume, that:

> [t]hat there is no established practice in which States exercise universal jurisdiction, properly so called, is undeniable (. . .) This does not indicate, however, that such exercise would be unlawful (. . .) In short, national legislation and case law—that is, State practice—is neutral as to exercise of universal jurisdiction.[29]

In addition, they held that the starting point in the *Lotus* case was comparable to "the high water mark of laissez-faire in international relations, and an era that has been significantly overtaken by other tendencies".[30] Third, the minority judges discussed the legality of universal jurisdiction in absentia. They argued that the presence of the accused is not a precondition for a state to make use of universal jurisdiction. They repeated a major rule of the *Lotus* case:

> [t]he only prohibitive rule (. . .) is that criminal jurisdiction should not be exercised, without permission, within the territory of another State. The Belgian arrest warrant envisaged the arrest of Mr. Yerodia in Belgium, or the possibility of his arrest in third States at the discretion of the States concerned. This would in principle seem to violate no existing prohibiting rule of international law.[31]

[26] Arrest Warrant of 11 April 2000 (Democratic Republic of the Congo v. Belgium), 2002 I.C.J. 3, 43 (Feb. 14).

[27] Arrest Warrant of 11 April 2000 (Democratic Republic of the Congo v. Belgium), 2002 I.C.J. 3, 43–44 (Feb. 14).

[28] Arrest Warrant of 11 April 2000 (Democratic Republic of the Congo v. Belgium), 2002 I.C.J. 3, 68 (Feb. 14).

[29] Arrest Warrant of 11 April 2000 (Democratic Republic of the Congo v. Belgium), 2002 I.C.J. 3, 76 (Feb. 14).

[30] Arrest Warrant of 11 April 2000 (Democratic Republic of the Congo v. Belgium), 2002 I.C.J. 3, 78 (Feb. 14).

[31] Arrest Warrant of 11 April 2000 (Democratic Republic of the Congo v. Belgium), 2002 I.C.J. 3, 79 and 80 (Feb. 14).

Subsequently, the minority concluded that states may exert pure universal jurisdiction, as long as they would respect the rules of international law, such as the immunities that exist under international law.[32] Christine van den Wyngaert, the Belgian ad hoc-judge, wrote a dissenting opinion. She held that a distinction must be made between *jurisdiction to prescribe* and *jurisdiction to enforce*. Exactly this distinction would allow the conclusion that the issuance of an arrest warrant against Yerodia would not violate rules of jurisdiction.[33] Concerning in absentia she argued that neither in international treaties nor in custom could a prohibition be found, and that the requirement of the presence of the accused on the territory of the state, as it can be found in various national legislation, was "not necessarily the expression of an *opinio juris* to the effect that this is a requirement under international law."[34] In the words of van den Wyngaert the Belgian legislation:

> giving effect to the principle of universal jurisdiction regarding war crimes and crimes against humanity, is not contrary to international law. International law does not prohibit States from asserting prescriptive jurisdiction of this kind. On the contrary, international law permits and even encourages States to assert this form of jurisdiction in order to ensure that suspects of war crimes and crimes against humanity do not find safe havens.[35]

Subsequently, van den Wyngaert discussed the issuance of an arrest warrant and stated that Belgium had not violated international law because it was never executed.[36] According to Judge van den Wyngaert issuing an arrest warrant falls within the *jurisdiction to prescribe*. The circulation of an arrest warrant among other states is something else and comes within the remit of *jurisdiction to enforce*.

III. State Practice on Jurisdictional Principles

Only very few cases of overlapping jurisdiction reach international tribunals, and it seems that states often do not pay attention to the case law of international courts. What states do in terms of jurisdiction is rather unilateral. They determine on the basis of their national law the exact formulation of the jurisdictional principle and to which offense it

[32] Arrest Warrant of 11 April 2000 (Democratic Republic of the Congo v. Belgium), 2002 I.C.J. 3, 80–81 (Feb. 14).

[33] Arrest Warrant of 11 April 2000 (Democratic Republic of the Congo v. Belgium), 2002 I.C.J. 3, 168 (Feb. 14).

[34] Arrest Warrant of 11 April 2000 (Democratic Republic of the Congo v. Belgium), 2002 I.C.J. 3, 171 (Feb. 14).

[35] Arrest Warrant of 11 April 2000 (Democratic Republic of the Congo v. Belgium), 2002 I.C.J. 3, 176–177 (Feb. 14).

[36] Arrest Warrant of 11 April 2000 (Democratic Republic of the Congo v. Belgium), 2002 I.C.J. 3, 178 (Feb. 14).

may apply. It is interesting to see that common law states and civil law states may use different techniques to do so. Civil law states have generally codified a general part of criminal law, in which jurisdictional principles often have found a place. In the absence of a general part, common law states have developed a practice by which they formulate the jurisdictional principle when legislating or deciding on a specific offense.

Jurisdiction can be defined as the power of the legislature to apply the law to certain forms of conduct. The relevant link to apply criminal law to conduct may relate to the place in which the conduct occurs. It may also relate to the person who performs the conduct, or against whom certain behavior took place. When discussing the jurisdictional principles in Subsections 1 through 10 , jurisdiction is often referred to via examples from widely ratified conventions. While conventional provisions can be regarded as legitimizing a jurisdictional claim as well as an obligation under international law, the absence of a convention does not preclude a state from extending its jurisdiction on the basis of national criminal law. Most states in the world require an explicit provision in national law as a basis for jurisdiction and cannot directly rely on a binding convention. States have developed the following principles of jurisdiction:

1. Territorial Jurisdiction

All criminal justice systems worldwide take *territorial jurisdiction* as the starting point of their criminal jurisdiction.[37] This means that crimes committed on the territory of a state fall within its jurisdiction by definition. This starting point has been called undisputed and undisputable. It is undisputed under international law and can be regarded as the ultimate expression of state sovereignty. To illustrate this, it is referred to in Article 5 of the Montreal Convention for the Suppression of Unlawful Acts against the Safety of Civil Aviation: "Each Contracting State shall take such measures as may be necessary to establish its jurisdiction over the offences in the following cases: (a) when the offence is committed in the territory of that State."[38] Thus, the principle requires a *nexus* with its territory, as determined by national law. International law generally leaves the method of determining the *locus delicti* (the place where the crime has been committed) to national law. However, there are a few exceptions. Occasionally, legal acts stipulate an extension upon the basis of the means by which the offense is committed. Jurisdiction includes "situations where the offence is committed by means of a computer system accessed from its territory, whether or not the computer system is on its territory."[39] In principle, the question of what amounts to their territory, or to their territorial waters, is

[37] *See* for a comparative overview Martin Böse, Frank Meyer & Anne Schneider (eds.), *Conflicts of Jurisdiction in Criminal Matters in the European Union, Volume I: National Reports and Comparative Analysis* 411–63 (2013).

[38] Convention concluded in Montreal, Sept. 23, 1971, U.N.T.S. 14118.

[39] Directive 2011/92/EU of the European Parliament and of the Council of 13 December 2011 on combating the sexual abuse and sexual exploitation of children and child pornography, 2011 O.J. (L 335) 1, art. 17, par. 3 [hereinafter Directive 2011/92/EU].

determined by states themselves. However, some conventions, predominantly the United Nations Convention on the Law of the Sea, have codified several rules.[40]

2. The Protective Principle

With this principle, which could be regarded as an interpretation of the effect theory of the *locus delicti* of the territorial principle, the relevant link for jurisdiction over the conduct committed abroad consists of the protection of the interests of the state. Its use relates to the idea that, otherwise, the enforcement of national law could not be dealt with effectively. Likewise, Article 7(2)(b) of the 1999 UN International Convention for the Suppression of the Financing of Terrorism applies the protective principle: "The offence was directed towards or resulted in the carrying out of an offence referred to in article 2, paragraph 1, subparagraph (a) or (b), against a State or government facility of that State abroad, including diplomatic or consular premises of that State."

3. The Flag Principle

The flag principle establishes jurisdiction over crimes committed on board a ship or aircraft that flies the flag of that state. One could consider this also as an extension of the territoriality principle, or, as the old, but still valid comparison deriving from common law, goes: ships are floating islands! Article 5 (b) of the Montreal Convention for the Suppression of Unlawful Acts against the Safety of Civil Aviation also provides this: "when the offence is committed against or on board an aircraft registered in that State." The nationality of a vessel or aircraft is determined under international law based on its registration in a specific state. There is no dual nationality for aircraft and vessels. International law further allows for innocent passage in the territorial waters of a Member State. There is very little practice on this principle.

4. The Active Nationality Principle

Active nationality is a jurisdictional principle that has found a place in many legal instruments. An example is found in Article 4 of the Convention against Torture and other Cruel, Inhuman or Degrading Treatment or Punishment: "Each State Party shall take such measures as may be necessary to establish its jurisdiction over the offences referred to in article 4 (...) (b) When the alleged offender is a national of that State."[41] The term "active nationality" (also called "active personality") means that a state has jurisdiction over crimes committed by its nationals. As a national of a state applying this

[40] Convention concluded in Montego Bay, Dec. 10, 1982, U.N.T.S. 31363.

[41] Convention concluded in New York, Dec. 10, 1984, U.N.T.S. 24841.

principle, wherever you go, your criminal code goes with you. Depending on whether national law provides corporate criminal responsibility, a criminal justice system may also allow for extraterritorial jurisdiction over nationals and legal persons established in its territory.

Originally, the principle had two justifications. The national was reminded of the fact that when he was abroad he also had to obey national criminal law (loyalty obligation/Treuepflicht). The other justification was found in extradition law. To prevent extradition of nationals to foreign jurisdictions it was necessary to arrange their prosecution at home. Whereas the first justification has almost completely disappeared, the second is also on the decline. Many states have abolished the (constitutional) impediment to the extradition of nationals.

There are two different modalities of the active nationality principle. Generally speaking, though somewhat surprisingly when compared to national criminal justice systems, the active personality or nationality principle has not been made conditional on the criminalization of the conduct in the locus state. However, there are also states that, inspired by the legality principle, make jurisdiction conditional to the conduct also being criminalized under the law of the place of commission.

A special category of perpetrators are those who obtained nationality after the fact. Again it is the national system that determines whether this allowed or not. A case in point here is that of Yvonne Ntacyobatabara. She was a Rwandese national who applied for asylum in the Netherlands after the genocide in Rwanda in 1994. In 2004 she obtained Dutch nationality. Shortly after having obtained that nationality, investigations started concerning her participation in the genocide in Rwanda on the basis of active nationality, and the criminal proceedings that followed led to a conviction.[42]

5. *Aut Dedere, Aut Judicare*

The *aut dedere, aut judicare* principle may often be found in legal instruments.[43] An example is taken from the formulation of Article 5, paragraph 2 of the Montreal Convention for the Suppression of Unlawful Acts against the Safety of Civil Aviation: "Each Contracting State shall likewise take such measures as may be necessary to establish its jurisdiction over the offences (. . .) in the case where the alleged offender is present in its territory and it does not extradite him." This obligation also has its origins in international criminal law. It imposes the obligation on the state that receives a request for extradition to choose between two options: either to extradite (*aut dedere*) the

[42] After the conviction had become irrevocable, the Dutch nationality was withdrawn on the ground that she committed a very serious offense. A request for review has been rejected by the Supreme Court of The Netherlands on May 12, 2015; see Netherlands' law reports/Nederlandse Jurisprudentie 2016/38, with case note by Klip. This decision raises the question how legitimate this rather temporary nationality link with the accused was.

[43] *See* M. Cherif Bassiouni & Edward M. Wise, *Aut Dedere Aut Judicare, The Duty to Extradite or Prosecute in International Law* (1995).

requested person, or to try (*aut judicare*) him. The possibility of opting for the latter presumes anterior jurisdiction over the crime. The obligation to prosecute an accused after a request for extradition has been rejected is based on the rule coined by Grotius (Hugo de Groot). A state will either extradite or try. There are numerous international conventions providing this obligation. The rationale relates to the idea that application of grounds for refusal may not lead to impunity. It is disputed whether the obligation to try is only triggered after an extradition request has been rejected or whether a state may prosecute without such a request.

6. The Passive Nationality Principle

With the passive nationality principle, the jurisdiction of a state is based on the fact that a national of that state has become a victim of a crime elsewhere in the world. An example is found in Article 5 of the Convention against Torture and Other Cruel, Inhuman or Degrading Treatment or Punishment: "Each State Party shall take such measures as may be necessary to establish its jurisdiction over the offences (...) (c) When the victim is a national of that State if that State considers it appropriate." The principle is not generally accepted and almost completely absent in common law jurisdictions. In civil law states, it is quite popular in states that have inherited their criminal law from Spain and France. Western and Northern European states often do not apply it. The justification lies in the will to protect nationals against the dangers elsewhere in the world and to be independent of a genuine justice system elsewhere. However, given the fact that in general there is no access to the crime scene, the principle has difficulties in living up to its protective function. There is not much state practice. As a consequence of that, there is also little knowledge about what exactly amounts to being a crime "committed against a national." This may at first sight look easier than it actually is. In the context of offenses with a high number of victims, such as the attack on the World Trade Center in New York on September 11, 2001, it raises the question whether the state of nationality of only one of the more than 3,000 victims has thereby obtained jurisdiction over the crime as a whole, or only in relation to the single victim of its nationality. In addition, cases based on passive nationality have a tendency to be very sensitive to the state where the offense was committed. This is even more the case when the nationality state suspects that the authorities of the locus state might be involved in (covering up) the crime.[44]

7. The Active Domicile Principle

The principle of *habitual residence*, also referred to as the *domicile principle* establishes jurisdiction over extraterritorial offenses of non-nationals who are domiciled, or have

[44] *See* Certain Questions of Mutual Assistance in Criminal Matters (Djibouti v. France), Judgment, 2008 I.C.J. 177 (June 4).

their habitual residence in the state. The justification for this principle is similar to the one for nationals. There is not a lot of practice on it yet. In the EU, the first appearance related to offenses typically committed by migrants living between two different cultures: circumcision.[45]

Even more rare is the *passive domicile principle*. It can also be found in EU legislation.[46]

8. The Principle of Universal Jurisdiction

Universal jurisdiction denotes the application of national criminal law to criminal conduct regardless of where or by whom a crime may have been committed. This principle may be applied concerning offenses that are so serious that they deserve to be combatted on a universal scale. It is applied in relation to international crimes, such as genocide, crimes against humanity, war crimes, and torture. Before the rise of modern international criminal law, it was generally accepted to apply universality to piracy.

Two forms may be distinguished: the unlimited or unconditional universal jurisdiction and the conditional application of universality. This unconditional exertion of jurisdiction does not require further conditions to be fulfilled. The second form does apply additional (post-offense) conditions that will relate to strengthening the legitimacy of the claim under international law. Many states apply presence of the accused on their territory as such a conditional universality. Other apply elements of the protective principle by requiring that the offense be committed against a state interest or against an aircraft registered under their flag, or the hijacked aircraft landed on their territory. Occasionally, there is a double criminality requirement.

In general, states are very reluctant in applying universality. An example of a relatively recent practice was the prosecution of pirates who were caught off the coast of Somalia by European marines. Initially, some European states, such as Germany and the Netherlands, brought them to Europe and adjudicated them. However, later on, agreements were concluded with countries in the region, as the European states were unable to deport the pirates after having served their sentence. The prosecution was transferred to Kenya, the Seychelles, and other states.[47]

[45] Directive 2011/92/EU, art. 17, par. 2 (c). *See also* art. 31, para. 1 (e) of the 2005 Council of Europe Convention on Action against Trafficking in Human Beings: "by one of its nationals or by a stateless person who has his or her habitual residence in its territory, if the offence is punishable under criminal law where it was committed or if the offence is committed outside the territorial jurisdiction of any State."

[46] Directive 2011/92/EU, art. 17, para. 2 (a).

[47] The EU concluded agreements with these states. Exchange of Letters between the European Union and the Republic of Seychelles on the conditions and modalities for the transfer of suspected pirates and armed robbers from EUNAVFOR to the Republic of Seychelles and for their treatment after such transfer, 2009 O.J. (L 315) 37; Exchange of Letters between the European Union and the Government of Kenya on the conditions and modalities for the transfer of persons suspected of having committed acts of piracy and detained by the European Union-led naval force (EUNAVFOR), and seized property in the possession of EUNAVFOR, from EUNAVFOR to Kenya and for their treatment after such transfer, 2009 O.J. (L 79) 49.

The most prominent condition that states apply is the condition of presence of the accused. This may be inspired by a relevant treaty. An example of that is Article 7, paragraph 1 of the Convention against Torture and Other Cruel, Inhuman or Degrading Treatment or Punishment: "The State Party in the territory under whose jurisdiction a person alleged to have committed any offence (...) is found shall (...), if it does not extradite him, submit the case to its competent authorities for the purpose of prosecution." This provision on the genuine link for universal jurisdiction based on the presence of the accused on the territory was heavily debated in the case of Pinochet visiting the Netherlands. Former junta leader general Pinochet was in Amsterdam on May 27–28, 1994. After a complaint was filed against him by Chilean refugees the police started an investigation, after he had left the country. The Amsterdam Court of Appeal held that the Netherlands had jurisdiction because of his presence, but that bringing a case was no longer opportune given his departure.[48] The Committee Against Torture held the Netherlands accountable and asked it to state reasons for not starting an investigation.[49]

The problem in practice with this condition of presence is that it amounts to de facto non-prosecution. As long as there is no presence of the accused, there will be no competence to conduct an investigation, as most legal systems in the world only allow the use of state powers to investigate when there is jurisdiction to prosecute. In the clear absence of jurisdiction, because the accused is not present on the territory, the authorities cannot collect evidence and will not be able to make any decision once the accused arrives.

9. The Principle of Complementary Jurisdiction/ Secondary Jurisdiction

Complementary jurisdiction denotes that a state may apply its own jurisdiction when another state having territorial jurisdiction cannot or does not use its own jurisdiction.[50] A state willing to apply jurisdiction may replace a locus or situation state that is unable or unwilling. Considerations of a fair administration of justice may be indicative to have a state not related to the offense doing the case.

[48] *See* Hof Amsterdam 4 januari 1995, rekest 578/94. The incident was debated widely in Dutch legal literature: M. Kamminga & M. Tijssen, *Pinochet, Nederland en het Verdrag tegen Foltering*, 20 NJCM-Bulletin 986–995 (1995); A.H. Klip, *Strafrechtelijke reactie op ernstige schendingen van mensenrechten in het buitenland*, in: *Er is meer, Opstellen over mensenrechten in internationaal en nationaal perspectief* 97–106 (C.H. Brants, C.Kelk & M. Moerings eds., 1996); C. Ingelse, H. van der Wilt & De zaak Pinochet, *Over universele jurisdictie en Hollandse benepenheid*, 71 Nederlands Juristenblad 280–285 (1996); A.H. Klip, *Komt er een eind aan de nationale strafvervolging van internationale misdrijven?*, in Iets Bijzonders, *Liber Amicorum aangeboden aan Mischa Wladimiroff ter gelegenheid van zijn 30-jarig jubileum als advocaat*, 266–69 (P van Russen Groen, D. Schreuders & C. Waling eds., 2002).

[49] *See* Summary Record of the Public Part of the 211th Meeting, Committee Against Torture, CAT/C/Sr.211, 1 May 1995, para. 28.

[50] A prominent example of this under international criminal law is the complementarity principle set out in Article 17 of the Statute of the International Criminal Court. U.N. Doc. A/CONF.183/9.

10. Justifications for States to Vest Extraterritorial Jurisdiction

On the basis of comparative research, several indicators for and against vesting jurisdiction over crimes committed outside the country can be distinguished.[51]

Indicators stimulating creating extraterritorial jurisdiction:

- the gravity of the offense
- preventing impunity
- state does not want to become a safe haven
- the particular modality of the crime
- the victim is a national or resident
- the perpetrator is a national or resident
- a treaty obliges to do so
- preventing that no state may have jurisdiction
- it concerns crimes of an universal interest
- the offenses are a hot item in the media
- perpetrator will be tried in his own country
- victim can attend trial in his own country
- victim cannot expect prosecution in the state where the offense was committed
- mobility of the objects of the crime
- mass victims and their multinationality

Indicators against extraterritorial jurisdiction:

- other states are competent
- collection of evidence is difficult
- own link is weak
- potential conflicts of jurisdiction
- not a serious offense
- other state may regard it as an interference with internal affairs
- stay outside sensitive disputes
- claim of the other state is a natural claim: it is not your case
- the treaty does not oblige it
- in absentia proceedings are not wanted
- after trial it is impossible to deport the accused/convicted
- damaging to economic interests
- passive nationality is an expression of distrust
- investigations are expensive and labor intensive

Of all jurisdictional principles it can be identified that they require a certain link or interest of the offense with the state claiming extraterritorial jurisdiction. The exception

[51] *See* André Klip & Anne-Sophie Massa, *Communicerende grondslagen voor extraterritoriale rechtsmacht* (2010), *available at* http://www.wodc.nl/onderzoeksdatabase/vestiging-rechtsmacht.aspx?cp=44&cs=6802.

to this is the principle of universal jurisdiction. The necessary links provided under national law are (albeit in combination with other links):

perpetrator-related;
request-related;
victim-related;
offense-related;
related to the presence of the accused.

IV. Prevention of Conflicts of Jurisdiction and Solution Mechanisms

States have a tendency to try to prevent a situation where conduct may not fall under the jurisdiction of any state, and have thus increasingly extended the scope of application of their criminal law.[52] While there is little evidence of cases in which states wanted to claim jurisdiction in practice, but were unable as a result of lacking jurisdiction, most states have widened their jurisdiction over the years. They intended to solve the potential problem that arises if there is not a single state able to apply its criminal law to certain conduct, and produced many situations of overlapping jurisdiction as a side effect. Additionally, the cross-border nature of the offense as such has increased multiple jurisdiction. As a consequence of the practice of widening the extraterritorial application of criminal law, in theory numerous positive conflicts exist by definition. Various questions can be raised as a result of it. Should this be prevented? Is this problematic? Does this lead to real problems in practice, or is it in essence an academic problem?[53] States have done much more to create conflicts of jurisdiction than to solve them. However, Article 82 of the Treaty on the Functioning of the European Union is the first legal instrument recognizing the need to prevent and solve conflicts of jurisdiction. To follow up on that, the European Law Institute adopted a proposal for a legislative instrument

[52] I will not use the commonly used term "negative conflict of jurisdiction," which I consider to be a confusing and wrong name tag to the situation. There is no conflict at all when there is no state that has jurisdiction over certain conduct. In the absence of applicable penal law there is not even a criminal offense. And in cases that there is no prosecution by a state having jurisdiction, another state may be upset about the inertia or decision not to prosecute. However, a state may have its reasons not to take action, as it may relate to prosecutorial discretion. States applying mandatory prosecution have difficulties in accepting that another state may knowingly decide not to do anything.

[53] In a comparative study commissioned by the Netherlands' Ministry of Justice, Klip and Massa conclude that there are hardly any prosecutions for crimes with a *locus delicti* outside a state's territory. *See* André Klip & Anne-Sophie Massa, *Communicerende grondslagen voor extraterritoriale rechtsmacht* (2010), *available at* http://www.wodc.nl/onderzoeksdatabase/vestiging-rechtsmacht.aspx?cp=44&cs=6802.

in 2017.[54] It aims at creating a breakthrough by recognizing that multiple jurisdiction is a common problem that requires common action and cannot be solved by unilateral means.

1. Transfer of Proceedings

By transferring the proceedings, a state transfers its right to prosecute to another state. The latter subsequently has the exclusive right to deal with the case. It may convict, acquit, or dismiss the case. Whatever it does, the transferring state must recognize the decision. The 1972 European Convention on Transfer of Proceedings of the Council of Europe is still the only multilateral convention on this form of international cooperation.[55] Article 2 provides for the constitutive transfer of proceedings: a state not having jurisdiction receives it from a state that does have jurisdiction. Article 3 governs the situation in which two states are both competent and the arrangement comes down to regulating concurrent jurisdiction. While paying attention to the interest of the states that have jurisdiction, as well as to the accused, victims, and witnesses, the Convention provides for a consultation procedure in cases of plurality of criminal proceedings (Articles 30–34). The Convention further provides for *ne bis in idem* protection, as well as a rather broad recognition of foreign decisions after transfer.

With the adoption of *Framework Decision 2009/948 on Conflicts of Jurisdiction*, a first but hesitant attempt toward a more general approach has been taken. This Framework Decision seeks to prevent parallel proceedings in two or more EU Member States with regard to the same offense committed by the same accused. It also aims to prevent a waste of the time and resources of competent authorities. It thus serves both the human rights of the accused, as well as the efficiency of law enforcement. On the other hand, the Framework Decision demonstrates some reluctance among EU Member States. It does not require anything more than consultation. Member States remain free to continue criminal proceedings for any criminal offense that falls under their jurisdiction.

2. An Extraordinary Case of Criminal Jurisdiction: The Downing of Flight MH17

A very prominent application of the principle of passive nationality is the case of the downing of Flight MH17 on July 17, 2014. On that day, Malaysia Airlines flight MH17 from Amsterdam to Kuala Lumpur was downed over Donetsk, Ukraine. All 298 people on board, passengers and crew died as a result of the plane being hit by a Buk air missile. As the majority of the victims (198 people) had Dutch nationality, the Dutch authorities

[54] Instrument on the Prevention and Settlement of Conflicts of Exercise of Jurisdiction in Criminal Law, *available at* http://www.europeanlawinstitute.eu/projects-publications/completed-projects/criminal-jurisdiction/.

[55] As of Dec. 11 2017, ratified by twenty-five states.

took the lead in establishing a *joint investigation team* to investigate the matter. An attempt in the Security Council to establish an international criminal tribunal was vetoed by Russia.[56] The Netherlands considered doing the criminal prosecution all on its own, but this was rejected because its own jurisdiction was limited to crimes committed against Dutch nationals.[57] This would mean that it would be unable to prosecute perpetrators for the crime committed against other victims, non-Dutch. The Netherlands therefore needed to receive jurisdiction from a state that had a better jurisdictional position. This was undoubtedly Ukraine as the locus state. Almost three years after the tragic incident, the Netherlands and Ukraine concluded an agreement by which Ukraine transferred its jurisdiction to the Netherlands.[58] The agreement can be characterized as an innovation in the world of international cooperation in criminal matters.[59] While it gives the Netherlands full jurisdiction to try the case before its criminal courts (Article 6), an accused present in the territory of Ukraine who cannot be extradited may stand trial in the Netherlands via a videolink (Article 8). After the trial, the execution of a sentence may be transferred from the Netherlands to Ukraine (Article 11).

V. Extraterritorial Jurisdiction and Legality

When states apply their criminal law to individuals not on their territory, the principle of legality gives rise to concern. Depending on the type of the offense, the question must be raised whether the perpetrator was able to know the forbidden norm. In other words, we must analyze what the legality principle requires in this setting. When applying the territoriality principle, states may argue that those who commit an offense on their territory must know the applicable legislation. However, with the wide interpretation of the territoriality principle, and even more with the other extraterritorial principles, perpetrators may commit crimes elsewhere without being present in the territory. This raises the question whether a perpetrator must be able to know that his conduct may

[56] *See* Security Council S/2015/562 of July 29, 2015 and its Annex Statute of the International Criminal Tribunal for Malaysia Airlines Flight MH17 (ICTMH17).

[57] Passive nationality had been introduced only the same month as the event took place. Article 5 of the Penal Code of the Netherlands [Wetboek van Strafrecht] provides effective July 1, 2014, jurisdiction over offenses under Dutch law punishable with imprisonment of eight years and more, against a Dutch national or a Dutch aircraft committed outside the Netherlands on condition that the conduct has been criminalized in the state where it has been committed.

[58] *See* Agreement between the Kingdom of the Netherlands and Ukraine on International Legal Cooperation regarding Crimes connected with the Downing of Malaysia Airlines Flight MH17 on 17 July 2014, Treaty Series of the Kingdom of the Netherlands 2017, 102.

[59] Agreement between the Government of the Kingdom of the Netherlands and the Government of the United Kingdom of Great Britain and Northern Ireland concerning a Scottish trial in the Netherlands, Treaty Series of the Kingdom of the Netherlands 1998, 237. *See further* André Klip & Mark Mackarel, The *Lockerbie Trial, a Scottish Court in the Netherlands*, 70 Int'l Rev. Penal L. 777–818 (1999).

affect criminal law elsewhere. States are inclined to accept that there is jurisdiction when the perpetrator wishes to reach that state.

The situation that is of concern to us relates to a perpetrator engaging in conduct abroad that falls within the jurisdiction of another state. It is relevant to make a distinction here, depending on whether the perpetrator aims at creating effects in the territorial state. At first sight, it seems to be logical to regard it foreseeable for the perpetrator engaged in the attack of a specific banking system intended to create results in a specific state. A similar approach can be taken in respect to content-related offenses targeted at a specific individual. With insults and hate speech targeted at a specific individual, there is an expectation that it causes effects there. However, this is different with regard to individual victims triggering jurisdiction in situations in which the perpetrator may be unaware of their identity or domicile.[60] In addition to the question deriving from the principle of legality, also the concept of the natural judge raises new questions. In many states, an accused is entitled to a specific judge, provided under national law, the natural judge. But who is that in cases in which there is more than one potential natural judge in different states?[61]

VI. Limitations to Jurisdiction

Whereas states are generally quite eager to extend their jurisdiction, also forms of limiting jurisdiction exist. Two main phenomena must be mentioned. The first is the general rule under international law that the premises of the representative missions of foreign states, such as embassies and consulates, are inviolable and that diplomats are also immune to being subjected to the jurisdiction of the host state. The 1963 Vienna Convention on Diplomatic Relations protects the interests of the sending state.[62] Article 22 of the convention stipulates that the premises shall be inviolable. This does not mean that the host state does not have jurisdiction, but means that it may not use it. A prominent example of this were the shots fired from the Libyan embassy in London in 1984 into a protesting crowd. British police officer Yvonne Joyce Fletcher was fatally shot. Following the shooting, the embassy was surrounded by armed police for eleven days. The British government eventually resolved the incident by allowing the embassy staff to leave the embassy and then expelling them from the country. The United Kingdom then ended all diplomatic relations with Libya.[63]

[60] This important topic has only recently received attention. *See* Catarina Abegão Alves, *O erro sobre a validade especial da lei penal* (AAFDL Editora, 2017).

[61] Mónica A. Antonini, *Aplicación extraterritorial de la ley penal y derechos humanos. Un Nuevo Sistema de reconocimiento e integración de órdenes para la regulación de casos penales extranjeros como garantía de derechos* 304–318 (2014).

[62] *See also* Luke T. Lee, *Vienna Convention on Consular Relations* (A.W. Sijthoff-Leyden publ., 1966).

[63] *See* https://en.wikipedia.org/wiki/Murder_of_Yvonne_Fletcher.

A second common practice of limiting jurisdiction is found in the agreements that states may conclude on the position of their armed forces abroad. A prominent example of these conventions is the 1951 Agreement between the Parties of the North Atlantic Treaty Organisation on the Status of Their Forces. Article VII stipulates the rules of criminal jurisdiction by giving a right of primacy to exercise jurisdiction to the authorities of the sending state. The territorial or receiving state may only exercise its jurisdiction in cases in which the sending state waives its right of primacy.[64]

1. Parallel Proceedings, Double Jeopardy, and *Ne Bis in Idem*

In principle, the question of whether a state has the right to prosecute is decided on the basis of its own national law, in particular its provisions on jurisdiction. The various bases of jurisdiction have already been discussed before. The primary focus is on the loss of the right to prosecute, notably as a result of the application of the *ne bis in idem* principle, which prohibits a second prosecution if the accused has already been tried for the same facts by another state. Very few international conventions stipulate anything on the matter. Human rights treaties often apply a double jeopardy provision, but that is limited to a second prosecution in the same jurisdiction.[65] Again, Europe stands out on this topic, as Article 54 of the Convention Implementing the Schengen Agreement (CISA) provides for a transnational recognition of *ne bis*/double jeopardy protection.

Some states regard the question of whether the state or the prosecution has the right or jurisdiction to prosecute as a preliminary issue and thus as an item of a formal character. Other states may regard the right to prosecute as something relating to whether criminal conduct has occurred, and is thus related to issues of substantive criminal law. The consequences of such a division are visible in the procedural decision that follows a finding that the prosecution no longer has the right to prosecute. States adopting the formal approach will take the decision that the case is inadmissible, that there is a finding of non-lieu, or that there is no case to answer. For these states, there is no assessment of the merits of the case. On the other hand, states that categorize the right to prosecute as an issue under substantive law will simply acquit. The principle of mutual recognition, as stipulated both in *ne bis in idem* rules and in the forms of international cooperation, may have an indirect effect of determining priority in cases of multiple jurisdiction. Article 54 of CISA functions upon the basis of a "first come, first served" principle.[66] The Member State that was the first to conclude criminal proceedings prevents all

[64] *See further* Serge Lazareff, *Status of Military Forces under Current International Law* (1971).

[65] *See* Art. 14, para. 7 of the International Covenant on Civil and Political Rights: "No one shall be liable to be tried or punished again for an offence for which he has already been finally convicted or acquitted in accordance with the law and penal procedure of each country."

[66] This is regarded as undesirable in doctrine. *See* Michiel Luchtman, *Choice of Forum in Cooperation Against EU Financial Crime. Freedom, Security and Justice and the Protection of Specific EU-Interests* (2013).

other Member States from exercising their jurisdiction. This arbitrariness justified the European Law Institute to present a model to allocate jurisdiction within the EU exclusively to a single state.[67]

2. Extraterritorial Law Enforcement

Extraterritorial enforcement is meant to describe the situations in which states will send their law enforcements agents to the territory of another state to investigate or make arrests. Although there is quite some practice, very little has been codified. Exceptions are both the Council of Europe and the EU that have, to a limited extent, created possibilities for law enforcement officials to operate on the territory of another (Member) State. Both organizations have followed the same underlying principles, based upon international law. The rules on extraterritorial operations are relatively simple and transparent. There is a general prohibition against operating in the territory of another state, as it is regarded as a violation of sovereignty when law enforcement officials enter the territory of another state.

However, there are two exceptions that remain fully in keeping with these sovereignty concerns. First, states may grant a general permission for certain operations and stipulate this in an agreement. Second, in the absence of a permanent international legal basis that governs the matter, states may grant ad hoc permission. In the past, these powers were provided in emergency situations. The hot pursuit and cross-border surveillance under Articles 40 and 41 of *CISA* are examples of this. Foreign officials may act and cross the border, because the local authorities are not there (yet). These provisions filled any penal enforcement lacunae, up until the moment in which the local authorities could take over.

A new generation of extraterritorial investigations, which does not relate to emergency situations but was instead developed to deal with specific cross-border crimes, has emerged. The controlled delivery, covert investigation, and joint investigation teams (Articles 12–14 EU Mutual Assistance Convention) are clear examples. These investigative techniques are tailored to the type of crime for which it is most likely that offenses have been committed in more than one state, and where there is a common interest to investigate. The foreign officials function under the supervision of the local authorities.

The foregoing demonstrates that states try to make use of the investigative powers they may have under their own legal system for investigations on their territory. As is the case with substantive criminal law jurisdiction, we see that states are inclined to locate things within their territory. This is reflected in attitudes according to which states do not ask for mutual assistance if it is uncertain where the data is held and in situations where they demonstrate that they are not really interested in knowing where information is.

[67] *See* Instrument on the Prevention and Settlement of Conflicts of Exercise of Jurisdiction in Criminal Law, *available at* http://www.europeanlawinstitute.eu/projects-publications/completed-projects/criminal-jurisdiction/. Last visited 15 September 2018.

States have also expanded their investigations to the publicly accessible Web, and it seems that the line is drawn where coercive methods of investigation are used or evidence is needed.

All of this may be different when investigating in cyberspace. A first observation is that this is not paralleled with a similar development with the physical presence of law enforcement officers in another country. This is logical to the extent that the infringement upon sovereignty is certainly less. One may even question whether there is an infringement of the sovereignty of another state if law enforcement agencies search the publicly available World Wide Web. Why would the sovereignty of a state that is unable to apply its legislation to a certain situation be infringed only because another state wishes to do something? What is state sovereignty in the context of the cyberworld?

The rules that are stipulated in this regard are rationalizations of sovereignty, following the patterns of physical presence. However, the question must be raised whether this makes sense. Which state is involved when the Web is browsed? This may change from moment to moment. States may not even know when they have sovereignty over something. At this moment, states have not even taken the initiative to make an attempt to regulate the matter, as a consequence of which investigations in cyberspace are more or less conducted in a Wild West scenario.

VII. Concluding Notions on Jurisdiction

By making use of jurisdiction outside their own territory, states wish to protect certain interests. Whereas jurisdiction within the borders is regarded as self-evident, this is not the case for applying jurisdiction outside the borders. This essentially relates to the concept of sovereignty of states under international law. Without needing any justification, a state will vest and exert jurisdiction on its own territory. Doing the same abroad requires a justification under international law.

In essence two intertwined factors are relevant in the determination of extraterritorial jurisdiction, and these are applied by all states: a link with the offense, and the gravity of the offense. Although all states use the same technique, they may give different weight to one or the other. If the link with the offense is very strong (such as territory), a state will apply jurisdiction over each tiny little offense. If the link is absent, a state may only apply jurisdiction in case of outrageous crimes, such as with genocide. All jurisdictional principles can be regarded as an expression of the link that a state has with the offense. That is the strongest with territory and the weakest with universality. In case of the latter, one could even say the link is absent.[68] Between these two extremes, the other jurisdictional

[68] *See* Pedro Caeiro, *Fundamento, conteúdo e limites da jurisdição penal do estado: o caso português* 210 (Diss. Coimbra, 2007).

principles have found a place. The conditional universal jurisdiction makes clear that the link is not self-evident and that the use of this jurisdiction requires an additional justifying ground. For active personality, the link of a state with its nationals is reasonable, but it is logical that jurisdiction is not unlimited and that it is subject to limitations as to the seriousness of the offense. It is a matter of criminal policy of a state how to balance or rank the different jurisdictional principles.[69] It is also a political choice which offenses are serious enough to qualify for application of one of the jurisdictional principles. For all states the challenge lies in finding the balance between two communicating factors.

References

Mónica A. Antonini, *Aplicación extraterritorial de la ley penal y derechos humanos. Un Nuevo Sistema de reconocimiento e integración de órdenes para la regulación de casos penales extranjeros como garantía de derechos* (2014)

Ernst Hirsch Ballin, *Yerodia: Rechtsmacht, immuniteit en vervolgingsbeleid*, 51 Ars Aequi 741 seq. (2002)

M. Cherif Bassiouni & Edward M. Wise, Aut Dedere Aut Judicare. *The Duty to Extradite or Prosecute in International Law* (1995)

Martin Böse, Frank Meyer & Anne Schneider (eds.), *Conflicts of Jurisdiction in Criminal Matters in the European Union, Volume I: National Reports and Comparative Analysis* (2013)

Antonio Cassese, *When May Senior State Officials Be Tried for International Crimes? Some Comments on the* Congo v. Belgium *Case*, 13 Eur. J. Int'l L. 855 seq. (2002)

Marc Henzelin, *La Compétence Pénale Universelle: Une Question non Résolue par l'Arrêt Yerodia*, 106 Revue générale de droit international public 820 seq. (2002)

Helmut Kreicker, *Völkerrechtliche Exemtionen: Grundlagen und Grenzen völkerrechtlicher Immunitäten und ihre Wirkungen im Strafrecht*, Band 1 & 2 (2007)

Cedric Ryngaert, *Jurisdiction in International Law* (2008)

[69] *See*, for instance, *Extraterritorial Criminal Jurisdiction*, Report of European Committee on Crime Problems, Council of Europe Strasbourg 1990.

CHAPTER 23

DETENTION BEFORE TRIAL AND CIVIL DETENTION OF DANGEROUS INDIVIDUALS

GRISCHA MERKEL

I. Pretrial Detention

1. Introduction

To guarantee the effective administration of justice and prosecution of offenses, the executive authorities in European countries have established a variety of pretrial security measures. Because it interferes with the right to freedom, detention is the most severe pretrial measure. If detention is imposed upon an innocent person, the days spent in custody cannot be restored. Detention may have serious negative effects on the arrestee's reputation, employment, and family. Furthermore, because it is enforced solely by the prosecution and is not based on a judicial decision, pretrial detention is especially prone to abuse.

In some countries, such as the United States, the number of pretrial detainees is high. According to the second edition of the World Pre-trial/Remand Imprisonment List of 2014,[1] there are 150 pretrial detainees for every 100,000 people in the United States, which is a higher percentage than in Russia (80 per 100,000) and most African and Asian states. In some European countries, including Greece, Malta, and the British territory of Gibraltar, pretrial detention is on the rise, but the number of pretrial detainees is

[1] Roy Walmsley, *The World Pre-trial/Remand Imprisonment List* (2d ed. 2014).

still less than 50 for every 100,000 people in the country. The Scandinavian countries, as well as Denmark, Germany, Austria, the United Kingdom, and Ireland, show low pretrial detention rates of less than 30 pretrial detainees for every 100,000 people.

Since public safety is one of the main factors to be considered in determining whether pretrial detention is warranted, acts of terrorism have influenced the handling of pretrial measures in recent years. The final section of this chapter (4 c) therefore provides a closer look at three different ways legal procedures can be affected by charges of terrorism. However, for a better understanding of the legal aspects applied in the context of pretrial detention in Europe, statutory law will be introduced (in Section 2) followed by an in-depth discussion of the decisions of the European Court (in Sections 3 and 4).

2. Legal Framework

a. *The European Convention on Human Rights*

All Member States of the European Union, as well as other countries such as Switzerland, Norway, Turkey, and the United Kingdom, have agreed to the legal principles of the European Convention for the Protection of Human Rights and Fundamental Freedoms or, in short, the European Convention on Human Rights (hereafter ECHR or the Convention), and to their interpretations by the European Court of Human Rights (ECtHR).[2]

Article 5 of the Convention, the central law on deprivation of liberty, limits the states' powers to specific lawful interventions. As the ECtHR points out, the "key purpose" of Article 5 of the Convention "is to prevent arbitrary or unjustified deprivations of liberty."[3] Article 5, section 1, sub-paragraph (c), governing pretrial arrest and detention, reads as follows:

> Everyone has the right to liberty and security of person. No one shall be deprived of his liberty save in the following cases and in accordance with a procedure prescribed by law: (...) the lawful arrest or detention of a person effected for the purpose of bringing him before the competent legal authority on reasonable suspicion of having committed an offense or when it is reasonably considered necessary to prevent his committing an offense or fleeing after having done so; (...).

The law further states:

> Everyone arrested or detained in accordance with the provisions of paragraph 1 (c) of this article shall be brought promptly before a judge or other officer authorised by law to exercise judicial power and shall be entitled to trial within a reasonable time or to release pending trial. Release may be conditioned by guarantees to appear for trial.[4]

[2] Treaty on European Union Art. 6 § 3.

[3] McKay v. United Kingdom [GC], App. No. 543/03, Eur. Ct. H.R., Oct. 3, 2006, § 30.

[4] European Convention on Human Rights, Art. 5, § 3, Nov. 4, 1950.

According to the ECtHR, Article 5, section 3 intends to "secure the rule of law by requiring a judicial control of the interference of the executive."[5] These regulations are complemented by general requirements in case of a deprivation of liberty. Article 5, sections 2, 4, and 5 of the Convention guarantee the right of the arrestee to be promptly informed, in a language she understands, about the reason for the arrest and charge(s) against her. She is also entitled to a prompt verification by a court of the lawfulness of the arrest. If the arrest is unlawful, she shall be released and may seek compensation if her human rights were violated.

Also, Article 5, section 1, sub-paragraph (c) of the Convention governs the pretrial detention of a minor (under the age of eighteen) "for the purpose of bringing him before the competent legal authority."[6] This applies only within observation periods, especially when medical and psychiatric reports need to be prepared.[7] Article 5, section 1, sub-paragraph (e) of the Convention governs the detention of adult suspects during medical observation periods in psychiatric housing.

All Member States have the opportunity to make reservations.[8] However, only a few reservations have been made concerning Article 5 of the Convention. Spain, for example, reserves its deviating rights concerning disciplinary rules in the armed forces, as does France, Moldova, Ukraine, and Portugal.[9] In countries without corresponding reservations, the "strict arrest" of soldiers, meaning being locked in cells day and night and excluded from normal duties, constitutes a deprivation of liberty.[10]

b. *International Regulations*

The International Covenant on Civil and Political Rights (ICCPR) also provides some binding regulations concerning pretrial detention worldwide and therefore influences the law of the European countries. Although not discussed here in detail, the general principles and reservations shall shortly be introduced: According to Article 9, section 3 of the ICCPR, "[i]t shall not be the general rule that persons awaiting trial shall be detained in custody, but release may be subject to guarantees to appear for trial, at any other stage of the judicial proceedings, and, should occasion arise, for execution of the judgement." Article 10, Section 1 of the ICCPR adds, "All persons deprived of their liberty shall be treated with humanity and with respect for the inherent dignity of the human person." And, Article 10, section 2, sub-paragraph (a) further specifies that "[a]ccused persons shall, save in exceptional circumstances, be segregated

[5] Ikincisoy v. Turkey, App. No. 26144/95, Eur. Ct. H.R., Dec. 15, 2004, § 100.

[6] *See* European Convention on Human Rights, Art. 5, §1(d).

[7] *See* X. v. Switzerland, App. No. 8500/79, Eur. Ct. H.R., Dec. 14, 1979, § 247.

[8] *See* European Convention on Human Rights, Art. 57.

[9] Reservations and Declarations for Treaty No.005—Convention for the Protection of Human Rights and Fundamental Freedoms, Council of Europe, https://www.coe.int/en/web/conventions/full-list/-/conventions/treaty/005/declarations?p_auth=9PU6I5wZ (last visited July 11, 2017).

[10] Engel and Others v. The Netherlands, App. Nos. 5100/71, 5101/71, 5102/71, 5354/72, 5370/72, Eur. Ct. H.R., June 8, 1976, § 63.

from convicted persons and shall be subject to separate treatment appropriate to their status as unconvicted persons."

For juvenile proceedings, the United Nations has provided basic and detailed regulations, such as The Beijing Rules[11] and the United Nations Rules for the Protection of Juveniles Deprived of Their Liberty.[12] Also, Article 10, section 2, sub-paragraph (b) of the ICCPR states, "Accused juvenile persons shall be separated from adults and brought as speedily as possible for adjudication."

Again, only a few reservations of European countries have been made. However, France rejects the enforcement of the rules pertaining to the disciplinary regime in the armed forces, and Belgium wants to provide the opportunity for accused persons, by their request, to take part with convicted persons in certain communal activities. With respect to Article 10 of the ICCPR, the Netherlands subscribes "to the principle set out in paragraph 1 of this article, but it takes the view that ideas about the treatment of prisoners are so liable to change that it does not wish to be bound by the obligations set out in paragraph 2 . . . of this article."[13] Regarding juvenile proceedings, some countries such as Belgium, Iceland, Norway, Sweden, the United Kingdom, Luxemburg, and Finland reserve for themselves a more flexible arrangement for the reason that some juveniles are treated and protected because they are minors, whereas others are considered adults in the eyes of the law.

3. Deprivation of Liberty and Prevention of Committing an Offense

According to the European Convention on Human Rights, a pretrial detention can either be based on reasonable suspicion of that person having committed an offense or "when it is reasonably considered necessary to prevent his committing an offense or fleeing after having done so."[14] Before discussing in detail pretrial detention based on reasonable suspicion of the commission of a crime, we should take a closer look at two major decisions made by the ECtHR concerning the question of which actions can be considered a deprivation of liberty, and under what circumstances the detention can be justified to prevent a person from committing a crime.

[11] G.A. Res. 40/33, United Nations Standard Minimum Rules for the Administration of Juvenile Justice (The Beijing Rules) (Nov. 29, 1985), http://www.ohchr.org/Documents/ProfessionalInterest/beijingrules.pdf.

[12] G.A. Res. 45/113, United Nations Rules for the Protection of Juveniles Deprived of Their Liberty (Dec. 14, 1990), http://www.ohchr.org/EN/ProfessionalInterest/Pages/JuvenilesDeprivedOfLiberty.aspx.

[13] International Covenant on Civil and Political Rights, Declarations and Reservations, Dec. 16, 1966, 999 U.N.T.S. 171.

[14] *See* European Convention on Human Rights, Art. 5, § 1(c).

a. *Deprivation of Liberty—Case of* Austin and Others v. The United Kingdom *(2012)*

On May 1, 2001, a group of demonstrators and passersby at Oxford Circus in the United Kingdom were contained ("kettled") by hundreds of riot police officers in order to maintain security and order and to protect the public. The group of approximately 3,000 people were kettled for six to seven hours in a relatively small area with no access to food, water, toilet facilities, or chairs. "Refusal to comply with [the officers'] instructions and restrictions was punishable by a prison sentence and could lead to arrest."[15]

To decide whether this technique of coercion falls within the scope of Article 5, section 1, the ECtHR refers to a statement the Court had made in previous rulings that the motive (e.g., the security of the public) is not relevant to the question of whether liberty is deprived, but it may be relevant to the question of whether a deprivation of liberty is justified.[16] The same is true of the requirement "to protect, treat or care in some way for the person taken into confinement" without her valid consent.[17] In *Austin and Others*, the Court noted, "The difference between deprivation of and restriction upon liberty is one of degree or intensity, and not of nature or substance."[18]

Despite these clear statements, the Court seems to take a step backward by pointing out that the context in which the action takes place can be significant to the inquiry of whether a deprivation of liberty has occurred. Referring to common situations, such as the unpleasant situation of being stuck on the motorway for hours because of police action following an accident, or crowd controlling at a football match, the Court concludes that these common actions cannot be considered a deprivation of liberty.[19] However, while the restriction in the case of unavoidable police action on a motorway after an accident is justified by legally recognized necessity (the imminent danger to drivers and passengers), crowd controlling at a football match is only lawful when single members of the crowd pose a threat to others or join a hostile crowd, and the measure itself is necessary and proportionate.

Given these distinctions, it seems remarkable that in *Austin and Others*, the Grand Chamber saw no reason to differentiate between the one applicant who was a demonstrator, and the three other applicants who were passersby.[20] As pointed out by the three dissenting judges, whereas one who takes active part in a non-peaceful demonstration (like in a fan crowd) must be aware that he or she will be subjected to police measures, others, just by coincidence passing by, should expect only to be kept away from a dangerous scene, not to have their liberty deprived.[21]

Since no explanation (besides effectiveness of the police operation) was given by the authorities for the fact that there was no way for peaceful protestants and passersby to

[15] Austin and Others v. United Kingdom, App. Nos. 39692/09, 40713/09 and 41008/09, Eur. Ct. H.R., Mar. 15, 2012, §§ 10–14 and Joint Dissenting Opinion of Judges Tulkens, Spielmann and Garlicki, § 14.

[16] *Id.* § 58. [17] *Id.* [18] *Id.* § 57. [19] *Id.* §§ 59, 65. [20] *Id.* § 63.

[21] *See id.* Joint Dissenting Opinion of Judges Tulkens, Spielmann and Garlicki, § 11.

exit the containment, no life or limb threatening circumstances were established,[22] and the duration of containment and the "herding" of applicants seemed unnecessary, the opinion of the dissenting judges that this was an unjustified deprivation of liberty for the peaceful demonstrators and passersby is arguably correct.

Additionally, the dissenting judges stress a weak point in the majority's argument regarding the containing technique. As the dissent points out, the "normality" of the containing technique, usually motivated by public-order considerations, misleads the majority to the rather naïve conclusion that these techniques usually cannot, on their own, be a deprivation of liberty. Such an approach leaves "the way open for carte blanche."[23] Therefore, regardless of whether a police measure is "normal," to be lawful within the meaning of Article 5, section 1, sub-paragraph (c) of the Convention, it ought to be a proportionate prevention of an imminent threat or danger, and should only be applied on the responsible or dangerous person (if not with consent).

b. *Prevention of Committing an Offense—Case of* Ostendorf v. Germany *(2013)*

In *Ostendorf v. Germany*, the applicant was arrested in 2004 as a leader of a hooligan group suspected of conspiring to use violence at soccer matches. In a pub in Frankfurt, the police observed the applicant meeting a member of a rival hooligan group, presumably to make arrangements for a fight. After his group left the pub to join a football match, the police found the applicant in a ladies' toilet in the pub. He was arrested and released approximately four hours later, one hour after the soccer match had ended.[24]

In earlier decisions, the Court had pointed out that sub-paragraph (c) can only be applied if a concrete and specific offense can be prevented, not where individuals pose a general threat of committing crimes.[25] However, this was not the problem in *Ostendorf*.

Pursuant to Article 5, section 1, sub-paragraph (c) of the Convention, the object of detention is the criminal process. Therefore, the alternative set forth in this sub-paragraph—"or when it is reasonably considered necessary to prevent his committing an offense or fleeing after having done so"—"only governs pre-trial detention and not custody for preventive purposes without the person concerned being suspected of having already committed a criminal offense."[26] The Court points out that "[a] detention under sub-paragraph (c) of article 5 § 1 may be ordered, in particular, against a person having carried out punishable preparatory acts to an offense in order to prevent his committing that latter offense."[27] Preventive police custody to protect the public from offenses may, however, be justified under sub-paragraph (b), which governs "the lawful arrest or detention of a person for non-compliance with the lawful order of a court or in order to secure the fulfilment of any obligation prescribed by law."[28]

[22] *Id.* § 8, 10. [23] *Id.* § 7.

[24] Ostendorf v. Germany, App. No. 15598/08, Eur. Ct. H.R., Mar. 7, 2013, §§ 10–12.

[25] *See* Guzzardi v. Italy, App. No. 7367/76, Eur. Ct. H.R., Nov. 6, 1980, § 102; M. v. Germany, App. No. 19359/04, Eur. Ct. H.R., Dec. 17, 2009, § 89.

[26] *Ostendorf v. Germany*, *supra* note 24, § 82 et seq. [27] *Id.* § 86.

[28] *Id.* §§ 89, 90 et seq.

In earlier decisions, the ECtHR has considered it "evident" that a deprivation of liberty can only be justified in the sense of sub-paragraph (c) when the arrest has the purpose of bringing the concerned before a competent legal authority.[29] In subsequent decisions, the Court has developed the opinion that "paragraph 1 (c) forms a whole with paragraph 3" to stress that the wording "competent legal authority" referred to in sub-paragraph (c) "is a synonym, of abbreviated form, for 'judge or other officer authorised by law to exercise judicial power.' "[30] It follows, as affirmed in *Jėčius v. Lithuania*, that deprivation of liberty within the meaning of Article 5, section 1, sub-paragraph (c) can only be justified "in the context of criminal proceedings."[31] Whereas in *Jėčius v. Lithuania*, the applicant was suspected of murder (although not charged with murder and was detained for over a month with no ongoing investigation), in the Case of *Ostendorf v. Germany* the applicant was detained only for preventative reasons.

The inherent subtle change in the interpretation of the law from the necessity of judicial control to the imperative of a criminal process was brought forward in the concurring opinion of Judges Lemmens and Jäderblim. Both judges were absolutely convinced that any detention based on sub-paragraph (c) must be reviewed by an independent judge. However, an interpretation of sub-paragraph (b) that justifies detention to keep a person from committing crimes in general—especially on the basis of pure presumption that these crimes might occur—is too wide in their opinion.[32]

Regarding the wording of sub-paragraph (c) "when it is reasonably considered necessary to prevent his committing an offense or fleeing after having done so," the first clause is clearly not saying "to prevent his committing *another* offense." Plus, with respect to the second clause—"fleeing after having done so"—*expressis verbis* requires a committed offense, which suggests that the first clause does not. The explanation of the Court that the first clause means to prevent only offenses after the carrying out of punishable preparatory acts is also not convincing. Whenever punishable preparatory acts have been carried out, the detention is justified because there is a reasonable suspicion of an offense having been committed (the punishable preparatory act). Hence, it would be more reasonable that sub-paragraph (c) also applies when either no offense or punishable preparatory acts have successfully been carried out yet but the person concerned is about to do so, or when it needs further investigation whether the preparatory action falls within the scope of criminal law. Finally, if deprivation of liberty according to sub-paragraph (b) "in order to secure the fulfilment of any obligation prescribed by law" applies in general to prevent a person from committing a crime, then this could surely lead to a wide application without the restrictions Article 5, section 3 of the Convention

[29] Lawless v. Ireland (No. 3), App. No. 332/57, Eur. Ct. H.R., July 1, 1961, § 14; see also Engel and Others v. The Netherlands, App. Nos. 5100/71, 5101/71, 5102/71, 5354/72, 5370/72, Eur. Ct. H.R., June 8, 1976, § 69.

[30] Schiesser v. Switzerland, App. No. 7710/76, Eur. Ct. H.R., Dec. 4, 1979, § 29; also, see de Jong, Baljet and van den Brink v. The Netherlands, App. Nos. 8805/79, 8806/79 and 9242/81, Eur. Ct. H.R., May 22, 1984, § 44; Ciulla v. Italy, App. No. 11152/84, Eur. Ct. H.R., Feb. 22, 1989, § 38.

[31] Jėčius v. Lithuania, App. No. 34578/97, Eur. Ct. H.R., July 31, 2000, § 50.

[32] *Ostendorf v. Germany*, supra note 24, Concurring Opinion, § 4.

provides. Therefore, if deprivation of liberty to prevent a person from committing a crime shall be lawful at all, the application of sub-paragraph (c) would be preferable to sub-paragraph (b).

4. Deprivation of Liberty on Reasonable Suspicion of Having Committed an Offense

The allegedly committed offense in question must be specific and concrete. Sub-paragraph (c) justifies neither "general prevention directed against an individual or a category of individuals who present a danger on account of their continuing propensity to crime,"[33] nor the prevention of any concrete crime, as long as the preparatory acts are not punishable themselves (see Section 3 b). The term "offense" covers all criminal offenses. However, to avoid circumvention of the law, determining whether an offense is of criminal origin cannot be decided by the aim of the national law only. More weight is given to factors such as punitive elements in the procedure (which may also be embodied in coercive measures) and the severity of the penalty.[34]

A reasonable suspicion is a *conditio sine qua non* for the initial arrest and pretrial custody. The reasonable grounds of the suspicion always depend on the specific circumstances of the case and the level of procedural proceeding.[35] They must be compelling to justify a conviction, and of a rather high level of certainty to bring a charge against the arrested. At the time of the first arrest, however, no certainty on an equivalent level is required.[36] Yet, to be reasonable, the suspicion must presuppose "the existence of facts or information which would satisfy an objective observer that the person concerned may have committed the offense."[37]

Nevertheless, Article 5, section 1, sub-paragraph (c) of the Convention also covers police arrest to confirm or dispel the suspicion grounding the arrest, even if the purpose of bringing the person concerned before the competent legal authority cannot be achieved. Hence, whenever sufficient evidence cannot be obtained during the custody, or a charge turns out to be not reasonable for other reasons, the deprivation of liberty may still be justified under sub-paragraph (c).[38] This "provisional confinement" is usually regulated separately from the order of arrest (detention on remand) by a judicial authority.[39]

[33] M. v. Germany, App. No. 19359/04, Eur. Ct. H.R., Dec. 17, 2009, § 89; see also *infra* Section II 4 b.

[34] Benham v. United Kingdom, App. No. 19380/92, Eur. Ct. H.R., June 10, 1996, § 56.

[35] Kudla v. Poland, App. no. 30210/96, Eur. Ct. H.R., Oct. 26, 2000, §§ 110 ff.

[36] O'Hara v. United Kingdom, App. No. 37555/97, Eur. Ct. H.R., Oct. 16, 2001, § 36.

[37] Fox, Campbell and Hartley v. United Kingdom, App. Nos. 12244/86, 12245/86 and 12383/86, Eur. Ct. H.R., Aug. 30, 1990, §§ 31 ff.

[38] *See* Brogan and Others v. United Kingdom, App. Nos. 11209/84, 11234/84, 11266/84 and 11386/85, Eur. Ct. H.R., Nov. 29, 1988, §§ 52–54.

[39] *See, e.g.*, Strafprozessordnung [StPO] [German Code of Criminal Procedure], §§ 112, 127.

a. *The Principle of Proportionality, and the Continuation of Detention*

According to the principle of proportionality, pretrial detention is reasonable only if the grounds are relevant and sufficient.[40] Grounds that contradict the presumption of innocence are of no relevance. Therefore, if the suspect denies the facts of suspicion, there is no relevant ground for his detention.

To be proportionate, the deprivation of liberty must be necessary to ensure the presence of the concerned at the trial and detention must be the only way to achieve that aim. Hence, whenever other, less stringent measures are sufficient for that purpose, detention is not proportionate.[41] According to the principle of presumption of innocence,[42] every detention, even on grounds of criminal suspicion, is to be regarded as an exception before the accused is convicted by a judgment of guilt. The interests of the public and the interests of the still-innocent suspect must be balanced carefully. "The presumption is in favour of release," the ECtHR stresses.[43] Remaining at liberty is therefore the rule, and anticipated punishment is unjustified in any case.

Article 5, section 3 of the Convention plays a prominent role with respect to maintaining a detention. Although it governs pretrial detention from the initial arrest until conviction or the verdict of not guilty, two judicial situations must be separated with respect to the principle of proportionality.[44] First, pursuant to Article 5, section 3 of the Convention, the initial arrest of a person by the states' authorities requiring a reasonable suspicion that the person committed an offense needs to be reviewed "promptly" by an independent judicial authority with the power to order release. Second, the remand detention also requires judicial review to determine the suspicion is still reasonable.

However, legitimate grounds will lose their relevance as time progresses.[45] The particular judicial responsibility must therefore display a flexibility of consideration, or "special diligence," as the ECtHR puts it. Regarding the ongoing detention in the light of the presumption of innocence, the right of the arrested to be released becomes more powerful as time lapses. Therefore, the reasons for detention, which were strong enough to justify the detention in the first place, cease to a point where the detention cannot be upheld anymore, although there may still be strong evidence that the arrested committed a crime.[46]

In *Kemmache v. France*,[47] the applicant's detention of nearly two years and nine months was based on four reasons that were generally accepted to be relevant by the Court: (1) the seriousness of the offenses and the severity of the sentence risked, (2) the

[40] Ladent v. Poland, App. No. 11036/03, Eur. Ct. H.R., Mar. 18, 2008, § 55.

[41] Ambruszkiewicz v. Poland, App. No. 38797/03, Eur. Ct. H.R., May 4, 2006, § 31.

[42] European Convention on Human Rights, Art. 6, § 2.

[43] McKay v. United Kingdom [GC], App. No. 543/03, Eur. Ct. H.R., Oct. 3, 2006, § 41.

[44] *Id.* § 31.

[45] Kudla v. Poland, App. No. 30210/96, Eur. Ct. H.R., Oct. 26, 2000, § 111; McKay v. United Kingdom [GC], App. No. 543/03, Eur. Ct. H.R., Oct. 3, 2006, § 45.

[46] *Id.* § 111; see also *McKay, supra* note 45, §§ 31 et seq.

[47] Kemmache v. France (No. 1 and 2), App. Nos. 12325/86 and 14992/89, Eur. Ct. H.R., Nov. 27, 1991.

requirements of public order, (3) the need to prevent pressure being brought to bear on the witnesses and the co-accused, and (4) the necessity of preventing the applicant from absconding.[48] Despite being regarded as relevant factors, the Court insisted on reasonable facts, confirming the reasons for detention. In particular, the ground of disturbance of public order can only be a relevant factor in exceptional cases and only if the threat to public order if the applicant were released remains and is based on facts.[49] However, even the seriousness of the offense that justifies pretrial detention in many European countries (e.g., Spain, Greece, Hungary, and Romania)[50] becomes less relevant as time lapses.[51] The same holds for the risk of absconding.[52] The risk of recurrent infringement has been discussed in *Trazaska v. Poland*.[53] However, since the domestic authorities had not expressly referred to this ground in any of their decisions, it did not seem plausible to the ECtHR that it had been a constituent factor for detention.[54]

Pursuant to Article 5, section 3 of the Convention, the detainee "shall be entitled to trial within a reasonable time or to release pending trial." This must not be understood as giving the judicial authorities a choice of either granting the detainee provisional release or bringing him to trial. Since the aim of the provision is to release the accused as soon as reasonable detention ceases, though provisional release can be subject to guarantees, detention beyond that point violates the law.[55]

b. *Alternatives in Case of Suspension of Detention*

The Fair Trials Organization lists a variety of alternatives to detention utilized by European countries. Especially in Ireland, and England and Wales, "the judges have wide discretion to craft conditions, which may include for example residence conditions, medical treatment and driving bans."[56] Travel bans and other geographic limitations such as house arrest (with or without electronic monitoring) are often accompanied by guarantees such as bail bonds. However, electronic monitoring and house arrest are rather new forms of alternative detention. Therefore, they are not widely used in Lithuania, Romania, Greece, and the Czech Republic, and have not been introduced in Poland. In Italy, as the Fair Trials Organization points out, these alternatives are considered forms of pretrial detention rather than alternatives to detention. The released may also be set under judicial or police supervision.

Problems occur if countries either do not regulate the consideration of alternatives at all (Romania), or link them to the primary judicial finding of pretrial detention, so suspension of detention is regarded as an exception and not vice versa (the Netherlands). "Rather, the judge should be required to first consider whether any alternative could

[48] *Id.* § 48. [49] *Id.* § 52.

[50] Fair Trials, *A Measure of Last Resort? The Practice of Pre-trial Detention Decision-Making in the EU* 18, https://www.fairtrials.org/wp-content/uploads/A-Measure-of-Last-Resort-Full-Version.pdf.

[51] *Kemmache*, *supra* note 47 § 50.

[52] Kudla v. Poland, App. No. 30210/96, Eur. Ct. H.R., Oct. 26, 2000, § 114.

[53] Trazaska v. Poland, App. No. 25792/94, Eur. Ct. H.R., July 11, 2000.

[54] *Id.* § 66. [55] Neumeister v. Austria, App. No. 1936/63, Eur. Ct. H.R., June 27, 1968, § 4.

[56] Fair Trials, *supra* note 50.

address the risk identified to the investigation, only moving on to consider detention if all available alternatives would be insufficient to secure it."[57]

Also, the Fair Trials Organization discovered judges making poorly reasoned decisions, detaining suspects unnecessarily. "Judicial reasoning was often vague and formulaic, and failed to engage sufficiently with practical alternatives to pre-trial detention that can protect the investigation, limit the possibility of reoffending and ensure defendants' presence at trial."[58] In addition, translation services for foreign suspects is poor in Italy and completely lacking in Greece, so detainees may not even be aware of their rights.[59]

c. *The Influence of Terrorism*

Since 9/11, and the subsequent invasion of Iraq and Afghanistan, Islamic terrorism has become a general threat to European countries, and new regulations have been put in place with the aim to protect the public. Yet, long before 9/11, terrorist groups such as the former Provisional Irish Republican Army (IRA), the former Euskadi Ta Askatasuna (ETA), and the Partiya Karkerên Kurdistanê (PKK) had posed a threat to the United Kingdom (IRA), Turkey (PKK), and Spain (ETA), respectively. Therefore, the ECtHR had already developed a routine in handling terrorist cases before the new Islamic terrorism came about. Although the Court regards terrorism as being a life-threatening danger, and prioritizes the safety of confidential information essential to combatting the threat, this does not serve as a carte blanche to undermine the principles of the ECHR and the Convention supervisory institutions.[60]

Regarding the handling of terrorism, at least three major conflicts with respect to pretrial detention occur. First, a broad interpretation of the term "terrorist" as well as a criminal law that targets behavior way ahead of the actual terrorist act, such as preparatory actions,[61] can lead to misuse of the provision of pretrial detention. In Turkey, for example, the definition of terrorism covers "propaganda against the unity of the nation and the territorial integrity of the State"[62] which can easily lead to a suppression of the right to freedom of expression (article 10 of the Convention), especially when the "essential role of the press in ensuring the proper functioning of political democracy" is involved.[63] In this context, a supposed "fight against terrorism" may even be a pretense to eliminate critical press or disagreeing representatives of other parties before important votes or elections take place.

Second, pre-trial detention requires a reasonable suspicion of the arrested having committed a crime (for details, see Section 4). Yet, in *O'Hara v. United Kingdom*, the

[57] *Id.* [58] *Id.* at 1. [59] *Id.* at 15.

[60] Murray v. United Kingdom [GC], App. Bo. 14310/88, Eur. Ct. H.R., Oct. 28, 1994, § 58; Ikincisoy v. Turkey, App. No. 26144/95, Eur. Ct. H.R., Dec. 15, 2004, § 102; Brogan and Others v. United Kingdom, App. Nos. 11209/84, 11234/84, 11266/84 and 11386/85, Eur. Ct. H.R., Nov. 29, 1988, § 61 et seq.; Klass and Others v. Germany, App. No. 5029/71, Eur. Ct. H.R., Sept. 6, 1978 (concerning restrictions on the secrecy of the mail, post, and telecommunications).

[61] For details as to the definition of terrorist offenses, see the European Union Council Framework Decision 2002/475/JHA of 13 June 2002 on combatting terrorism, arts. 1–4, 2002 O.J. (L 190) 1–20.

[62] Terörle Mücadele Kanunu [Law on Fight Against Terrorism of Turkey], no. 3713.

[63] *See* Case of Çamyar and Berktaş v. Turkey, App. No. 41959/02, Eur. Ct. H.R., Feb. 15, 2011, § 37.

ECtHR recognizes the particular problems terrorist crime poses, especially that information is regarded confidential and usually cannot be disclosed to the arrested, and sometimes not even to a judicial court without jeopardizing the informant. Still, the Court insists, "that the exigencies of dealing with terrorist crime cannot justify stretching the notion of 'reasonableness' to the point where the safeguard secured by article 5 § 1 (c) is impaired." For this, the authorities "have to furnish at least some facts or information capable of satisfying the Court that the arrested person was reasonably suspected of having committed the alleged offense."[64]

Third, pretrial detention provides both the police and prosecutors with the opportunity to gain further information from and about the suspect. This is highly appealing especially in terrorism cases since suspects may possess information about backers, structures, or the planning of a terrorist act. To gain extensive information, however, the time for questioning the suspect before charge must be as long as possible. Therefore, the motivation to bring the suspect "promptly before a judge or other officer authorised by law to exercise judicial power" is rather low, especially when no reasonable suspicion can be found.

In *Brogan and Others v. The United Kingdom*,[65] the applicants, all living in Northern Ireland, had been arrested by the police under the Prevention of Terrorism Act 1984. They were kept in custody for periods ranging from four days to almost seven days. During this time, they were questioned about specific terroristic attacks and their suspected membership in the IRA or the National Liberation Army, another proscribed terrorist organization.

The Court held that even a detention of four days without seeing a judge would be an "unacceptably wide interpretation of the plain meaning of the word 'promptly.'"[66] As the Court pointed out in *Kurt v. Turkey*, "Prompt judicial intervention may lead to the detection and prevention of life-threatening measures or serious ill-treatment which violate the fundamental guarantees contained in articles 2 and 3 of the Convention."[67] However, being kept in custody for less than three days without being charged or without seeing a judge does not amount to a violation of Article 5, section 3 of the Convention.[68] The ECtHR therefore finds no violation of Article 5, section 3 of the Convention if the detainee is quickly released after the three days.[69] In contrast, being kept in custody for eleven days without judicial review is not appropriate even when there is a connection between the behavior of the arrested and a terrorist threat.[70] After all, in the eyes of the Court, the "scope for flexibility in interpreting and applying the notion of promptness is very limited."[71]

Nevertheless, European countries such as France, Spain, and Ireland legitimize pre-charge detention of suspected terrorists for five days or longer. In the United Kingdom, the acceptable period of detention of a terrorist suspect without charge had even been

[64] O'Hara v. United Kingdom, App. No. 37555/97, Eur. Ct. H.R., Oct. 16, 2001, § 35.

[65] Brogan and Others v. United Kingdom, App. Nos. 11209/84, 11234/84, 11266/84 and 11386/85, Eur. Ct. H.R., Nov. 29, 1988.

[66] *Id.* § 62. [67] Kurt v. Turkey, App. No. 24276/94, Eur. Ct. H.R., May 25, 1998, § 123.

[68] Ikincisoy v. Turkey, App. No. 26144/95, Eur. Ct. H.R., Dec. 15, 2004, § 103.

[69] *Id.* § 103. [70] *Id.* §§ 104 *et seq.* [71] *Brogan and Others*, supra note 65, § 62.

extended to twenty-eight days with the enforcement of the Terrorism Act 2006. This period was reduced to a maximum of fourteen days by the Protection of Freedoms Act 2012, amending the Terrorism Act. However, it must be noted that this length of detention still contradicts basic human rights if done without any reasonable grounds. In the case of immigration detention, foreign nationals can even be detained for an indefinite period of time. Despite the rather overlapping legislation of the UK, according to the Fair Trials Organization, the prosecutors and judges of England and Wales seem to be a beneficial corrective in respecting the principle of detention as a last resort.[72]

II. Civil Detention of Dangerous Individuals

1. Introduction

Some individuals are considered to pose a threat to the public or to themselves not primarily because of criminal conduct. Even without any legal responsibility of the concerned for the threat they pose, a deprivation of liberty in accordance with a procedure prescribed by national law can still be lawful. According to Article 5, section 1, sub-paragraph (e) of the Convention, this applies to persons of unsound mind, alcoholics or drug addicts, vagrants, and people with infectious diseases. To avoid arbitrariness, the concerned persons may initiate proceedings to obtain a judicial decision on the lawfulness of the detention, and the decision to continue the detention or to release the concerned has to follow speedily.[73]

Obviously, not only medical, but also social reasons legitimize the deprivation of liberty on the legal basis of Article 5, section 1, sub-paragraph (e) of the Convention. However, both instances must be evaluated very carefully. First, medical and especially social reasons for detention already include an anticipation of proportionality that is dependent on and varies with contemporary social attitudes. For example, the detention of "vagrants" in Europe, historically defined as traveling people with no home and no civil rights, was due to public resentments and prejudice concerning their honesty and criminality because of their poor economic situation. In addition, general discrimination, especially of ethnic groups such as the Roma, was widespread in Europe. At the time of the introduction of the Convention in 1953, these resentments were still present, but decreased in the following decades (see also Section 6). A similar situation can be found with respect to the term "unsound mind" that cannot be given a "definitive interpretation." According to the ECtHR, "[I]t is a term whose meaning is continually evolving as research in psychiatry progresses, an increasing flexibility in treatment is developing

[72] Fair Trials, *supra* note 50.

[73] *See* European Convention on Human Rights, Art. 5, § 4.

and society's attitude to mental illness changes, in particular so that a greater understanding of the problems of mental patients is becoming more wide-spread."[74]

This brings us to the second reason to apply Article 5, section 1, sub-paragraph (e) of the Convention with caution: detention for medical or social reasons must not lead to discrimination restricted under Article 14 of the Convention. If a person injures people or damages property, it is unlikely that the deprivation of liberty is based on discriminating reasons only. However, the detention of persons causing social disturbance by acting oddly in public, for example, shameless or offensive behavior, always includes an element of discrimination. Although the ECtHR narrows the interpretation of the term "unsound mind" (see Section 4), and points out that it "cannot be taken as permitting the detention of a person simply because his views or behaviour deviate from the norms prevailing in a particular society,"[75] the Court still recognizes the national authorities "as having a certain discretion since it is in the first place for the national authorities to evaluate the evidence adduced before them in a particular case."[76] Thus, since history teaches us that it is only a short step to declaring awkward behavior the outcome of an unsound mind, uncertainty remains.

Third, conflicts may also occur with respect to Article 8, section 1 of the Convention, the right to respect family and private life. Especially, in cases of danger to oneself, although not exclusively in these cases, it must be carefully evaluated whether the concerned has a right to behave the way he does. Again, one may easily be declared mentally ill (e.g., depressive or psychotic) when hurting or trying to kill oneself, and often this diagnosis is correct. However, even suicide falls within the scope of Article 8, section 1 of the Convention, when the concerned "is capable of freely reaching a decision on this question and acting in consequence."[77] Still, there is a high risk that moral or political resentments concerning self-offending or odd behavior could be enforced by denying peoples' mental capabilities to justify their compulsory hospitalization.

In light of this rather high risk of misuse of Article 5, section 1, sub-paragraph (e) of the Convention, on the one hand, and of the severity of the intervention (compulsory confinement for a potentially infinite period of time) on the other, it does not seem reasonable that in cases of odd or self-offending behavior the detention is not reviewed by a judge automatically, analogous to Article 5, section 3 of the Convention. Since the detention of persons of unsound mind, alcoholics, or drug addicts affects vulnerable people, who may not have the ability to initiate a legal procedure, the same judicial control should also be applied in these cases, or the detainees should at least "be assisted in obtaining access to effective remedies for the vindication of their rights."[78] With regard to Article 5, section 3 of the Convention, the ECtHR points out that "a person subjected to ill-treatment might be incapable of lodging an application asking for a judge to review

[74] Winterwerp v. Netherlands, App. No. 6301/73, Eur. Ct. H.R., Oct. 24, 1979, § 37.

[75] *Id.* at § 37; Rakevich v. Russia, App. No. 58973/00, Eur. Ct. H.R., Oct. 28, 2003, § 26.

[76] *Winterwerp*, *supra* note 74, § 40.

[77] *See* Haas v. Switzerland, App. No. 31322/07, Eur. Ct. H.R., Jan. 20, 2011, § 51.

[78] U.N. Human Rights Committee, International Covenant on Civil and Political Rights, General Comment No. 35, Art. 9, U.N. Doc. CCPR/C/GC/35 (Dec. 16, 2014), http://tbinternet.ohchr.org/_layouts/treatybodyexternal/Download.aspx?symbolno=CCPR%2fC%2fGC%2f35&Lang=en.

their detention; the same might also be true of other vulnerable categories of arrested person, such as the mentally frail…"[79] Still, Article 5, section 3 of the Convention cannot be applied to deprivations of liberty only legitimized by other reasons, such as the deprivation of liberty of vagrants.[80]

2. The Principle of Proportionality

Whereas the deprivation of liberty of persons with infectious diseases is linked to the aim of preventing the spread of the disease, no specific aim is mentioned for the detention of persons of unsound mind, alcoholics or drug addicts, and vagrants. However, in *Guzzardi v. Italy*, the ECtHR held that the requirement for compulsory confinement of "socially maladjusted" persons such as vagrants, mentally ill people, alcoholics, or drug addicts "is not only that they have to be considered as occasionally dangerous for public safety but also that their own interests may necessitate their detention."[81]

Because the length of confinement is not defined (although it may be restricted by national law), it needs to be strictly proportional to the specific circumstances of the individual case. In any case, the detainee must be released as soon as he is not considered dangerous anymore, for example, once he is healed of his infectious disease[82] or because his mental disorder is not of a degree warranting compulsory confinement anymore.[83] While the length of hospitalization in case of persons with infectious diseases seems to be terminated by empirical facts, no equal facts can be found to define the length of confinement of the others. However, the ECtHR has held that the lawfulness of the detention needs to be reviewed "especially as the reasons capable of initially justifying such a detention may cease to exist."[84] Article 5, section 4 of the Convention, therefore, not only provides a right to review the *initial* lawfulness of the detention by an independent judge, but also a *subsequent* judicial review. As the Court has noted, "[t]he very nature of the deprivation of liberty under consideration would appear to require a review of lawfulness to be available at reasonable intervals."[85] This holds true not only for a deprivation of liberty based on a mental disorder, but also for confinement because of vagrancy.[86] Again, the critique itself suggests that there is no further limitation of the "reasonable intervals" other than a period of two years being "excessive."[87] Undeniably, it is of great matter whether the review takes place semiannually, yearly, or every two

[79] McKay v. United Kingdom, [GC], App. No. 543/03, Eur. Ct. H.R., Oct. 3, 2006, § 34.

[80] *See* De Wilde, Ooms and Versyp v. Belgium, App. Nos. 2832/66, 2835/66 and 2899/66, Eur. Ct. H.R., June 18, 1970.

[81] Guzzardi v. Italy, App. No. 7367/76, Eur. Ct. H.R., Nov. 6, 1980, § 98.

[82] Enhorn v. Sweden, App. No. 56529/00, Eur. Ct. H.R., Jan. 25, 2005, § 44.

[83] Winterwerp v. Netherlands, App. No. 6301/73, Eur. Ct. H.R., Oct. 24, 1979, § 39.

[84] X v. United Kingdom, App. No. 7215/75, Eur. Ct. H.R., Nov. 5, 1981, § 58.

[85] *Winterwerp*, *supra* note 83, § 55.

[86] *See* De Wilde, Ooms and Versyp v. Belgium, App. Nos. 2832/66, 2835/66 and 2899/66, Eur. Ct. H.R., June 18, 1970, §§ 82 ff.

[87] *See* Stanev v. Bulgaria [GC], App. No. 36760/06, Eur. Ct. H.R., Jan. 17, 2012, § 156.

years. Therefore, even in case of deprivation of liberty based on an infectious disease, the length of compulsory confinement is not as restricted as it seems.

3. Persons with Infectious Diseases

As mentioned previously, the prevention of the spreading of infectious diseases can only legitimize the deprivation of liberty as long as the person is infectious. The disease itself must be dangerous to the health of the public, meaning that the concerned person may infect an unforeseeable number of other persons with a severe disease. To be sufficient, the form of detention must be the only appropriate way to quarantine the diseased person, for example, if a house arrest is sufficient, the infectious person may not be confined in a hospital (although house arrest can be considered a detention, it is less intense than hospitalization). In some cases, nose, mouth, and finger protection may be sufficient, and when the person is considered trustworthy in applying the measures, a detention may not be proportionate at all, depending on the severity of the disease.

In *Enhorn v. Sweden*, the applicant was infected with HIV, but failed to keep appointments with his medical officer. The appointments seemed to be necessary to prevent the man from having sexual intercourse without using condoms and without informing his sexual partners about his infection. Because of the applicant's lack of cooperation, he was ordered to be kept in compulsory isolation for up to three months, which was subsequently prolonged. The applicant absconded several times, and the orders to prolong his deprivation of liberty were continuously issued every six months totaling almost seven years in isolation.[88] Although an HIV infection was considered dangerous to public health and safety by the Court,[89] the confinement could not be regarded as a last resort since the Swedish government had failed to consider less intense measures. Moreover, with compulsory isolation of the applicant for almost one and a half years in a hospital and orders for confinement in force for almost seven years, the Swedish government had also "failed to strike a fair balance between the need to ensure that the H.I.V. virus did not spread and the applicant's right to liberty."[90]

4. Persons of Unsound Mind

A deprivation of liberty of persons of unsound mind shall not be arbitrary, and is lawful only under certain basic conditions, defined by the ECtHR in various cases.[91] First, to

[88] *See Enhorn v. Sweden*, supra note 82, § 47. [89] *See id.* § 44. [90] *Id.* § 55.

[91] *See* Winterwerp v. Netherlands, App. No. 6301/73, Eur. Ct. H.R., Oct. 24, 1979, §§ 39, 45; Hutchison Reid v. United Kingdom, App. No. 50272/99, Eur. Ct. H.R., Feb. 20, 2003, § 49; Haidn v. Germany, App. No. 6587/04, Eur. Ct. H.R., Jan. 13, 2011, § 78; O.H. v. Germany, App. No. 4646/08, Eur. Ct. H.R., Nov. 24, 2011, §§ 78 ff.; Kronfeldner v. Germany, App. No. 21906/09, Eur. Ct. H.R., Jan. 19, 2012, § 79; Glien v. Germany, App. No. 7345/12, Eur. Ct. H.R., Nov. 28, 2013, § 85; Bergmann v. Germany, App. No. 23279/14, Eur. Ct. H.R., Jan. 7, 2016, § 95 et seq.

avoid arbitrary confinement of persons disobeying the law, the mental disorder must be considered as a "true" mental disorder, shown by objective medical expertise from the very beginning of the detention. Second, to warrant compulsory confinement, the disorder must be of a certain gravity. Third, the length of deprivation is dependent on the persistence of the mental disorder and its severity. However, with respect to the dangerousness of the patient to himself or others, the authorities are allowed to take some time to consider whether the termination of the deprivation can be accountable.

Last, to avoid detention in ordinary prisons, the concerned person must be placed in a hospital, clinic, or other appropriate institution. Placement in a dilapidated social-care institution lacking proper sanitary facilities, heating, activities, and adequate food for the residents also constitutes a breach of Article 5 in conjunction with Article 3 of the Convention (the prohibition of torture).[92] However, the ECtHR sees no breach of the law when the placement in another institution is only temporary, as long as the opposite interests are reasonably balanced.[93]

Article 5, section 1, sub-paragraph (e) of the Convention can also be implicated when a contract or perceived consent concerning the admission of a person to a psychiatric hospital exists. According to the ECtHR, the person's consent is only valid if the person has the intellectual capacity to decide this question. Otherwise, the detention is unlawful.[94]

a. *Dangerousness to Themselves*

In the clinical handling of mentally disordered persons, a change in understanding of the notion of self-determination occurred at the end of the twentieth century. This was due to broad discussion concerning patients' autonomy, informed consent, and integration of disabled persons. In 2008, the United Nations Convention on the Rights of Persons with Disabilities (CRPD) entered into force, reaffirming human rights and fundamental freedoms for all persons with disabilities, including mentally ill persons. Thus, if a mentally disordered person needs clinical treatment such as therapy or medication, it must be taken into account that, in principle, the person has the right to refuse treatment. This right can only be withdrawn for serious reasons concerning the severity of the disorder and lack of the patient's awareness of his pathological condition on the one hand, and the consequences for the patient's health or life on the other. Thus, self-endangering behavior does not always guarantee that deprivation of liberty is lawful. However, in an emergency when the mental condition cannot be analyzed properly, temporary detention to make further examinations may be lawful.[95]

[92] *Stanev v. Bulgaria*, *supra* note 87, §§ 206 f.

[93] Morsink v. Netherlands, App. No. 48865/99, Eur. Ct. H.R., May 11, 2004, §§ 67 ff; Brand v. Netherlands, App. No. 49902/99, Eur. Ct. H.R., May 11, 2004, §§ 64 f; Mocarska v. Poland, App. No. 26917/05, Eur. Ct. H.R., Nov. 6, 2007, § 48; Pankiewicz v. Poland, App. No. 34151/04, Eur. Ct. H.R., Feb. 12, 2008, §§ 44 f.

[94] H.L. v. United Kingdom, App. No. 45508/99, Eur. Ct. H.R., Oct. 5, 2004, § 91 f.; see also David v. Moldova, App. No. 41578/05, Eur. Ct. H.R., Nov. 27, 2007, § 35 (concerning the withdrawal of an agreement to be hospitalized).

[95] *See* Winterwerp v. Netherlands, App. No. 6301/73, Eur. Ct. H.R., Oct. 24, 1979, § 39; X v. United Kingdom, App. No. 7215/75, Eur. Ct. H.R., Nov. 5, 1981, § 41.

b. *Dangerousness to Others*

Posing a threat to the public is more likely to be a lawful reason for detention than dangerousness to oneself. Since the problem of proportionality with regards to "odd" behavior has already been discussed in the introduction, the focus here will shift to aspects concerning mentally ill criminal offenders. The first problem to arise is that mentally ill persons are usually not considered responsible in a legal sense. However, this does not mean that the threat they unintentionally pose to the public must be accepted. The public should not have to tolerate their deviant behavior or the risk they pose to others. Obviously, this would be an inappropriate and unfair distribution of risk. Nevertheless, if coexistence in respect of others' rights is not possible and detention is inevitable, the authorities must provide possible solutions to reduce the time of isolation as much as possible.

As has also been mentioned, to avoid arbitrary confinement of people offending the law, a mental expert must ascertain the mental disorder. Criminal suspects need to be treated according to Article 5, section 1, sub-paragraph (a) or (c) of the Convention. The finding of guilt therefore usually determines the length of detention as prescribed by the law. However, sometimes the line between responsible and non-responsible criminal behavior vanishes. This holds true for all persons regarded as less responsible for mental reasons (including alcoholics and drug addicts), especially those with personality disorders. In case of minor criminal responsibility, an additional measure such as preventive detention in a psychiatric hospital may be added to the finding of guilt, since detainment in ordinary prison is not appropriate to satisfy aims of reintegration. Therefore, despite minor criminal responsibility, the concerned can be confined for an indefinite period of time.

This comes to a head with the terms "psychopathy" or dissocial personality disorder when used to describe persons with extensive and recidivist criminal behavior, which is often considered non-treatable.[96] In *Hutchison Reid v. United Kingdom*, a claim of unlawful detention was brought before the ECtHR with the argument that detention in a hospital is arbitrary when the illness—here, a psychopathic personality disorder—cannot be treated. The Court rejected the argument, stating "Such confinement may be necessary not only where a person needs therapy, medication or other clinical treatment to cure or alleviate his condition, but also where the person needs control and supervision to prevent him, for example, causing harm to himself or other persons."[97] Since persons with severe and recidivist criminal behavior are usually at first charged with penal sentences before they are confined for their personality disorder (that may even be non-treatable), the finding of guilt has either become irrespective of personal guilt or psychiatric confinement irrespective of criminal responsibility. In either case, the switching between penal sentences and indefinite preventive measures is an open gateway for arbitrary confinement.

[96] Although this assumption is not supported by empirical evidence, see Devon L.L. Polaschek, *Adult Criminals with Psychopathy: Common Beliefs About Treatability and Change Have Little Empirical Support*, 23 Current Directions Psychol. Sci. 296 (2014).

[97] Hutchison Reid v. United Kingdom, App. No. 50272/99, Eur. Ct. H.R., Feb. 20, 2003, § 52.

The same situation occurs in cases of sexual offenders who repeatedly abuse children for sexual purposes. Although with pedosexuals, their sexual orientation is not a matter of freedom of choice (which may also be true for persons with a psychopathic personality disorder), they are still held responsible for the harm they cause. In Germany, the discussion about sex offenders after the Belgium Dutroux Case (although Dutroux was not a pedosexual) has provoked some rather hasty revisions of preventive detention in Germany for the purpose of prolonged detention after the penal sentence. Even though the ECtHR has since found that a subsequent extension of the penal sentence for preventative reasons is a breach of Article 5, section 1, sub-paragraph (a) of the Convention,[98] the Court did not find an arbitrary deprivation of liberty when the fully responsible criminal was considered a person of unsound mind after he finished his penal sentence and was subsequently confined in a mental institution.[99]

5. Alcoholics and Drug Addicts

Alcoholics and drug addicts share in principle the previously mentioned problems with reduced liability. However, since criminal drug addicts benefit at least partly from decreasing resentments in Europe since the 1970s, and the misuse of alcohol has always been a rather common phenomenon, these two groups—although considered socially deprived whenever noticeable—are not the focus of discussions about public threats.

When individuals are dangerous to themselves, the possibilities for lawful detention should be quite narrow to avoid a legal collision with the right to respect for private life.[100] However, in some cases of chronic misuse of alcohol, a severe mental disorder may be involved, such as alcoholic dementia, that can lead to incapacity in managing daily routines. In other cases, an acute intoxication can be a reason for forced deprivation of liberty. In this regard, the ECtHR has held that one does not have to be an alcoholic, in the narrow medical sense of the term, to be lawfully detained. The conditions of Article 5, section 1, sub-paragraph (e) of the Convention are already met when the consumption of alcohol poses a threat to others or is a danger to the person concerned.[101] Nonetheless, the consumption of alcohol itself is not sufficient to meet the requirements of sub-paragraph (e).[102]

With respect to dangerousness to others as a consequence of the misuse of alcohol, acute and chronic threats to the public must be treated separately. With acute dangerousness caused by alcohol, a temporary detainment in a sobering-up cell ("drunk tank") is usually sufficient to restore legal order. However, because of the principle of proportionality, it must be ascertained that less intensive measures such as bringing the drunk

[98] *See* M. v. Germany, App. No. 19359/04, Eur. Ct. H.R., Dec. 17, 2009, § 100.

[99] *See* Glien v. Germany, App. No. 7345/12, Eur. Ct. H.R., Nov. 28, 2013, § 87.

[100] *See* European Convention on Human Rights, Art. 8, § 1.

[101] *See* Guzzardi v. Italy, App. No. 7367/76, Eur. Ct. H.R., Nov. 6, 1980, § 98; Witold Litwa v. Poland, App. No. 26629/95, Eur. Ct. H.R., Apr. 4, 2000, §§ 60 f.

[102] *Witold Litwa*, *supra* note 101, § 62.

person to her place of residence or some public-care establishment are not sufficient.[103] With dangerousness to others caused by a chronic misuse of alcohol, similar considerations apply as those for people with unsound minds apply (see Section 4 b).

6. Vagrants

As mentioned in the introduction, the social perception of "vagrants" has undergone some changes. Nowadays, the term is rarely used, but in 1970, the ECtHR encountered a case with three Belgium citizens detained because of vagrancy, but not for criminal reasons. In Belgium, vagrants were even considered so dangerous that preventative measures were applied.[104] According to Article 347 of the Belgian Criminal Code of 1867, "vagrants are persons who have no fixed abode, no means of subsistence and no regular trade or profession."[105] The economic situation of people without housing and regular income, in particular, leads to a sometimes justified prejudice that they "earn" their money not only with begging but with nonviolent crime, such as theft. However, during the twentieh century, the social-economic situation in Europe considerably changed, largely because of industrialization, and many people nowadays benefit from social security systems guaranteeing a minimum living standard. Despite the increasing number of homeless people in many European countries, the reasons for poverty are more differentiated today. Often, psychological factors leading to misuse of alcohol and other drugs are associated with homelessness and circumvent the re-entry into hired labor. Poor living standards, however, do not necessarily lead to discrimination, since the public is more aware of the impact of social problems today than a hundred years ago. Social organizations as well as healthcare professionals offer help and guidance without charge. Being a "vagrant" may sometimes even be a chosen way of living.

Furthermore, views on the type of criminal behavior that must be prevented have changed substantially. Nowadays, the focus is on violent criminal behavior rather than nonviolent behavior. Under this view, a member of a violent gang is more likely to commit severe crimes than a vagrant. Also, terrorism poses a larger threat to the public than vagrancy. Therefore, persons likely to commit crimes, such as suspects linked to the Mafia, cannot be regarded as "vagrants in a wider sense of the term," as the ECtHR points out in *Guzzardi v. Italy*. On the contrary, the Court has held all "exceptions permitted by Article 5 par. 1 (Art. 5–1) call for a narrow interpretation."[106]

Given the shift in public perception of criminal danger from nonviolent to violent offenses, and taking into account that homelessness is no longer regarded as criminal but rather a social problem, vagrancy cannot be regarded as a relevant topic when

[103] *See id.* § 78 et seq.

[104] *See* Sonja Snacken, *Belgien*, in *Kriminalität, Kriminalpolitik, strafrechtliche Sanktionspraxis und Gefangenenraten im europäischen Vergleich* 53, 85 (Frieder Dünkel et al. eds., 2000).

[105] *See* De Wilde, Ooms and Versyp v. Belgium, App. Nos. 2832/66, 2835/66 and 2899/66, Eur. Ct. H.R., June 18, 1970, §§ 33, 68.

[106] Guzzardi v. Italy, App. No. 7367/76, Eur. Ct. H.R., Nov. 6, 1980, § 98.

considering criminal issues. Despite the Belgium case of *De Wilde, Ooms* and *Versyp*, it therefore does not seem proportionate anymore to deprive the liberty of a person only because she has "no fixed abode, no means of subsistence and no regular trade or profession."

References

Council of Europe, Ministry of Foreign Affairs of the Republic of Slovenia, Ministry of Justice of the Republic of Slovenia (ed.), *The Right to Trial Within a Reasonable Time and Short-Term Reform of the European Court of Human Rights: Round Table Organised by the Slovenian Chairmanship of the Committee of Ministers of the Council of Europe*, Ministry of Foreign Affairs, Ministry of Justice Ljubljana (2009), http://www.mzz.gov.si/fileadmin/pageuploads/Zakonodaja_in_dokumenti/knjiznica/bled_proceedings.pdf

European Court of Human Rights, *Guide on Article 5 of the Convention: Right to Liberty and Security* (2014), http://www.echr.coe.int/Documents/Guide_Art_5_ENG.pdf

David Harris et al., *Law of the European Convention on Human Rights* (3d ed. 2014)

Monica Macovei, *The Right to Liberty and Security of the Person: A Guide to the Implementation of Article 5 of the European Convention on Human Rights* (Council of Europe 2002)

Bernadette Rainey et al., *Jacobs, White, and Ovey: The European Convention on Human Rights* (6th ed. 2014)

UN Human Rights Committee, *General Comment No. 35 on Article 9 (Liberty and Security of Person) of the International Covenant on Civil and Political Rights* (2014)

Pre-Trial Detention in the European Union: An Analysis of Minimum Standards in Pre-trial Detention and the Grounds for Regular Review in the Member States of the EU (A.M. van Kalmthout et al. eds., 2009)

Roy Walmsley, *The World Pre-trial/Remand Imprisonment List* (2d ed. 2014)

CHAPTER 24

PRETRIAL AND CIVIL DETENTION OF "DANGEROUS" INDIVIDUALS IN COMMON LAW JURISDICTIONS

BERNADETTE MCSHERRY

I. Introduction

1. Justifications for Pretrial and Civil Detention Schemes

VARIOUS legislative schemes governing "dangerous" individuals have long existed in common law countries.[1] These legislative schemes have been cyclical, falling in and out of favor in response to community concerns about certain groups of individuals and governmental "law and order" policies.[2]

One of the central justifications for such schemes is that removing those considered dangerous from the community is the best way to stop them from harming others.

[1] Bernadette McSherry & Patrick Keyzer, *Sex Offenders and Preventive Detention: Politics, Policy and Practice* ch. 1 (2009); Bernadette McSherry, *Managing Fear: The Law and Ethics of Preventive Detention and Risk Assessment* (2014). For an analysis of the regimes operating in Germany, New Zealand, the United Kingdom, and the United States, see *Preventive Detention: Asking the Fundamental Questions* (Patrick Keyzer ed., 2013).

[2] *See generally* John Pratt, *Governing the Dangerous: Dangerousness, Law and Social Change* (1997); McSherry, *Managing Fear*, *supra* note 1; *Regulating Preventive Justice: Principle, Policy and Paradox* (Tamara Tulich, Rebecca Ananian-Welsh, Simon Bronitt & Sarah Murray eds., 2017); Mark Finnane & Susan Donkin, *Fighting Terror with Law? Some Other Genealogies of Pre-emption*, 2 Int'l J. Crime & Justice 3 (2013).

In this sense, pretrial and civil detention schemes are based on the concept of the prevention of harm. Pretrial detention may thus deprive suspected serious offenders of their liberty not only to ensure they appear before the court, but because they are considered a risk to public safety. Other schemes, such as the detention of those with severe mental health problems, are considered civil rather than criminal in nature because they are not predicated on an offense having been committed. The term "civil detention" may also be used in circumstances where a person has committed a crime and is detained post-sentence not for the purposes of punishment, but because he or she is still considered at high risk of reoffending.

Early criminological theory, as exemplified by Cesare Lombroso's work,[3] focused on the characteristics of potential offenders, locating the danger to the community within the person him- or herself. While the focus may now have shifted to identifying methods of assessing the risk of future harmful behavior, the titles of certain statutes still refer to the idea of the dangerous individual. In England and Wales, programs have been targeted at "dangerous people with severe personality disorder," and in Australia, statutes enabling post-sentence detention include the Dangerous Prisoners (Sexual Offenders) Act 2003 (Qld.) and the Dangerous Sexual Offenders Act 2006 (W.A.).

Sometimes the term "preventive detention" is used to describe the numerous schemes that focus on the deprivation of liberty to prevent harm. Christopher Slobogin points out:

> [P]reventive detention takes place in a number of contexts, sometimes explicitly, sometimes implicitly. Moving from the least intrusive to the most intrusive examples, explicit preventive detention occurs in connection with police stops and frisks; civil commitment; pretrial detention; quarantine; indeterminate sentence and parole decision-making; sexually violent predator statutes; detention of enemy combatants and "terrorists" and administration of the death penalty (when dangerousness is a designated aggravating factor).[4]

Many of these schemes have existed in common law countries for centuries. The term "preventive justice" was first used in the late eighteenth century and linked to laws aimed at preventing future crime by intervening where there exists "a probable suspicion that some crime is intended or likely to happen."[5]

Lucia Zedner has pointed out that "preventive justice, and the measures to which it gives rise, are increasingly widespread and yet remain localized in form and function."[6] This chapter therefore aims to provide a general overview of pretrial and civil detention schemes, rather than attempt to detail the variations that may occur across common law countries.

[3] Cesare Lombroso, *Crime, Its Causes and Remedies* (Henry P. Horton trans., 1911) (first published in Italian 1899).

[4] Christopher Slobogin, *Legal Limitations on the Scope of Preventive Detention*, in *Dangerous People: Policy, Prediction and Practice* 37–47, 37 (Bernadette McSherry & Patrick Keyzer eds., 2011).

[5] William Blackstone, 4 *Commentaries on the Laws of England* 248 (R. Bell 1772).

[6] Lucia Zedner, *Taking the Preventive Justice Project Forward*, in *Regulating Preventive Justice*, *supra* note 2, at xvi.

The next section provides an overview of some of the pretrial and civil detention schemes currently in existence. Some of these schemes are further discussed in Sections II, III, IV, and V.

2. "Pre-Crime," "Pre-Trial," "Post-Crime," and "Post-Sentence" Schemes

The common thread running through pretrial and civil detention schemes is that they are predominantly aimed at community protection. While some civil schemes are aimed at detention for the purposes of treatment, many are aimed at simply removing people from the community because of the perceived risk they pose to others. It may be worthwhile considering these schemes on a continuum from pre-crime to post-sentence detention. Table 1 sets out the types of schemes that will be outlined in this chapter and the people affected by them:

Table 1 Types of pretrial and civil detention schemes

Type of Scheme:	Pre-Crime	Pretrial	Post-Crime (Indefinite Detention at Time of Sentence)	Post-Sentence
Those Affected:	Suspected Terrorists	Suspected Criminals Held on Remand	High-Risk Recidivist Offenders	High-Risk Sex Offenders
	Those with Severe Mental Health Problems and/or Intellectual Disabilities	Those Found Unfit to Plead	Those Found Not Guilty on the Grounds of Mental Impairment	High-Risk Violent Offenders

There are also other civil schemes that enable detention without charge or trial, including the mandatory detention of asylum seekers pending determination of their refugee status, the quarantining of individuals with infectious diseases, the detention for treatment of those with substance dependency, and detention prior to extradition.[7] This chapter focuses on those schemes that involve a risk of future criminal harm.

[7] Ronli Sifris, *An International Human Rights Perspective on Detention Without Charge or Trial*, in *Dangerous People*, *supra* note 4, at 13; Bernadette McSherry & Sarah Lenthall, *Laws to Detain Individuals with Substance Dependency: Breaching Human Rights or Restoring Health?*, 19 J.L. Med. 225–31 (2011).

3. The Rise of Risk Assessment

As well as being justified on the basis of the prevention of harm, most of the schemes discussed in this chapter are dependent on the notion that certain individuals are at high risk of harming others. Risk assessment tools and processes form a core component of certain schemes and mental health professionals are increasingly called upon to identify high-risk offenders primarily in relation to post-crime and post-sentence schemes.

During the 1980s, there was an emphasis on making clinical assessments of dangerousness, which did not provide a medical diagnosis but involved "issues of legal judgment and definition, as well as issues of social policy."[8] Between the mid-1980s until the mid-1990s, the focus of mental health professionals shifted from assessing dangerousness to a focus on statistical or actuarial risk prediction. This shift to risk assessment and risk management has seen the proliferation of instruments aimed at determining where an individual is placed in relation to a range of factors that are thought to be associated with future offending. Michael Davis and James Ogloff describe the development of such instruments as follows:

> [R]esearchers coded a wealth of possible risk factors (e.g. demographic factors, criminal and violence history, psychiatric history, substance abuse history) from correctional and psychiatric files. They subsequently obtained the criminal records of those released and identified who had recidivated violently. Statistical analyses were used to identify those factors that, when combined, most reliably related to violence.[9]

There has been considerable criticism of the use of risk assessment instruments to identify those individuals who are at risk of harming others.[10] However, it appears that "structured professional judgment," which combines the strengths of both actuarial and clinical methods, may in order to develop risk management plans assist in identifying those who are at low, moderate, or high risk of harming others.[11] Whether structured professional judgment should be used to go beyond simply managing risk to supporting pretrial and civil detention schemes, however, raises serious professional ethical issues for mental health professionals.[12]

It is difficult to argue that an offender who has committed a series of serious violent offenses and who has revealed plans to commit fresh offenses should not be subject to some form of supervision, if not detention. There is research suggesting that a small cohort of individuals diagnosed with severe mental illness such as schizophrenia, coupled

[8] H.J. Steadman, *From Dangerousness to Risk Assessment of Community Violence: Taking Stock at the Turn of the Century*, 28 J. Am. Acad. Psychiatry & L. 265–71, 266 (2000).

[9] Michael Davis & James Ogloff, *Risk Assessment*, in *Forensic Psychology and Criminology: An Australian Perspective* 141, 143 (Katarina Fritzon & Paul Wilson eds., 2008).

[10] For an overview of such criticisms, see McSherry, *Managing Fear*, *supra* note 1, at 44–51.

[11] Davis & Ogloff, *Risk Assessment*, *supra* note 9.

[12] For an overview of the ethic of forensic risk assessment, see McSherry, *Managing Fear*, *supra* note 1, at 205–26.

with personality traits that inhibit or prevent their establishing respectful relationships and who are dependent on alcohol or other drugs, pose a greater risk of committing serious offenses than many others.[13] This cohort generally includes young men with a history of disadvantage in childhood, antisocial and violent behavior in adolescence, unemployment, and a disorganized lifestyle.[14] Detention in prison or special facilities has the advantage of removing such individuals from the community, thereby making harm to others in the wider community impossible.

However, as will be explored later in this chapter, the right to liberty is a core human right, and preventive detention schemes run the risk of being overly broad. The limitations of risk assessment need to be acknowledged, rather than being presumed to be highly probative.

4. Outline of Chapter

This chapter will first outline some of the schemes currently in existence in line with the pre-crime, pretrial, post-crime, and post-sentence model set out in Table 1. It will then turn to outlining the criticisms that have been raised on human rights and due process grounds.

II. Pre-crime Schemes

1. Pre-charge Detention of Suspected Terrorists

Following the terrorist attacks on the United States on September 11, 2001, the United States, the United Kingdom, and Australia introduced pre-charge detention schemes for suspected terrorists. These schemes enable individuals to be detained for community protection rather than for the traditional processes of investigation and questioning.[15]

Not all schemes have withstood judicial scrutiny. The preventive detention regime that was introduced in the United Kingdom two months after the September 11 terrorist attacks via the Anti-Terrorism, Crime and Security Act 2001 was repealed by the UK Parliament after it was judicially found to breach the right to liberty. Nine foreign nationals who were detained without charge in Belmarsh prison as suspected international terrorists successfully challenged the provisions that allowed the Home Secretary

[13] Paul E. Mullen, *Schizophrenia and Violence: From Correlations to Preventive Strategies*, 12 Adv. Psychiatric Treat. 239 (2006); Paul E. Mullen, *A Reassessment of the Link Between Mental Disorder and Violent Behavior, and Its Implications for Clinical Practice*, 31 Austl. N.Z. J. Psychiatry 3–11 (2007).

[14] *Id.*

[15] For an overview of preventive detention laws, see Diane Webber, *Preventive Detention of Terror Suspects: A New Legal Framework* (2016).

to detain indefinitely any non-British citizen who was suspected of being a terrorist pending deportation, even if such deportation was prohibited.[16] In lieu of detention in prison, the Terrorism Prevention and Investigation Measures Act 2011 (UK) allows for certain "measures" that serve to restrict a person's liberty. In addition, under Section 41 of the Terrorism Act 2000 (UK), a person may be arrested and detained for up to forty-eight hours without a warrant on the basis of a reasonable suspicion that the person is a terrorist. Detention beyond that time can be extended by a judge for periods that can last up to twenty-eight days from arrest, as laid down in schedule 8 of the Act.

In Australia, the Commonwealth Anti-Terrorism Act (No. 2) 2005 inserted a new Division 105 into the Commonwealth Criminal Code allowing for "preventative detention orders." Detention without charge is permitted for renewable periods of seven days with the maximum time allowable being twenty-eight days.[17] Each Australian state and territory also enables detention without charge of suspected terrorists.[18] These particular provisions have not been the subject of constitutional challenges, but a majority of the High Court of Australia upheld the constitutionality of control orders in *Thomas v. Mowbray*,[19] which implies that these provisions would be upheld "if implemented only when necessary and by proportional means."[20]

In the United States, section 1226a of the Immigration and Nationality Act (as amended by the PATRIOT Act) requires the attorney general to detain a noncitizen (an "alien" in legislative terminology) who is certified as a suspected terrorist for up to six months at a time, pending a decision to remove him or her from the United States.

In addition, under executive orders, suspected terrorists may be subject to preventive detention. On November 13, 2001, President George W. Bush issued a Military Order for the Detention, Treatment and Trial of Certain Non-Citizens in the War against Terrorism, which set up military commissions. There has been a series of court cases testing the boundaries of these powers.[21] In 2009, President Barack Obama temporarily halted military commissions to review their procedures as well as the detention program at Guantanamo Bay in general. Subsequently, the Military Commission Act 2009[22] set out extensive procedural rules for future hearings.[23] The National Defense Authorization Act for Fiscal Year 2017 retains funding for Guantanamo Bay, despite the former Obama administration's attempts to close the detention facility.[24]

[16] A and Others v. Secretary of State for the Home Department [2004] UKHL 56 (U.K.).

[17] *Criminal Code* (Austl.) ss. 105.2, 105.4, 100.1(1), 105.8.

[18] McSherry, *Managing Fear, supra* note 1, Table 4.5, 90–112.

[19] (2007) 233 C.L.R. 307 (Austl.).

[20] Alex Conte, Human Rights in the Prevention and Punishment of Terrorism: Commonwealth Approaches: United Kingdom, Canada, Australia and New Zealand 581 (Springer 2010).

[21] Hamdi v. Rumsfeld, 542 U.S. 507 (2004); Rasul v. Bush, 542 U.S. 466 (2004); Hamdan v. Rumsfeld, 548 U.S. 557 (2006); Boumediene v. Bush, 553 U.S. 723 (2008); For an overview, see McSherry, *Managing Fear, supra* note 1, at 114–16.

[22] (PL 111-84) amending 47A U.S.C.

[23] J.K. Elsea, *The Military Commissions Act of 2009: Overview and Legal Issues* (Washington, DC, Congressional Res. Service 2010).

[24] Office of the Press Secretary of the White House, *Statement by the President on Signing the National Defense Authorization Act for Fiscal Year 2017* (Dec. 23, 2016), https://obamawhitehouse.archives.gov/the-press-office/2016/12/23/statement-president-signing-national-defense-authorization-act-fiscal.

Powers of preventive detention in relation to suspected terrorists have been justified based on the state's duty to provide security for its citizens.[25]

2. Civil Detention of Those with Severe Mental Health Problems and/or Intellectual Disabilities

Civil laws that enable the involuntary detention of individuals with severe mental health problems are widespread across common law jurisdictions. A 2009 study by Elizabeth Fistein and colleagues compares thirty-two such laws.[26]

In general, these laws are couched in terms of treatment, but most contain a criterion of risk of harm to self or others.[27] Some jurisdictions also enable the detention of persons with intellectual disabilities based on a risk of harm to others. For example, in Australia, section 193 of the Disability Act 2006 (Vic.) enables the making of a "supervised treatment order" for a person with an intellectual disability to prevent a significant risk of serious harm to another person. In practice, this means indefinite detention in a special facility.[28] In New Zealand, the Intellectual Disability (Compulsory Care and Rehabilitation) Act 2003 enables indefinite detention of those with intellectual disabilities who have been charged with or convicted of an offense.

The risk of harm criterion in such civil laws has been criticized. Christopher Ryan argues that it is inappropriate to base mental health laws on the risk of harm to others given that those with mental impairments are "by and large, no more dangerous" than other members of society and because of the low base rate of violence among those with mental impairments, asserting it is impossible to predict who will become violent in the future.[29] Similarly, Matthew Large, Christopher Ryan, Olav Nielssen, and Robert Hayes argue that because there are problems associated with predicting the risk of harm to others and there is a tendency of psychiatrists to err on the side of safety, "[t]he dangerousness criterion effectively condones the detention of many mentally ill people who will never become dangerous, so that it might capture the few who will."[30]

Jennifer Skeem, Jillian Peterson, and Eric Silver point out that there is a widely held belief among the public and thus policymakers that "mental illness" causes criminal

[25] Svetlana Tyulkina & George Williams, *Combatting Terrorism in Australia Through Preventative Detention*, in *Regulating Preventive Justice*, *supra* note 2, at 145.

[26] Elizabeth C. Fistein, Anthony J. Holland, Isabel C.H. Clare & Michael J. Gunn, *A Comparison of Mental Health Legislation from Diverse Commonwealth Jurisdictions*, 32 Int'l J. Law Psychiatry 147 (2009).

[27] Bernadette McSherry, *Preventative Justice, Risk of Harm and Mental Health Laws*, in *Regulating Preventive Justice*, *supra* note 2, at 61–74.

[28] Patsie Frawley & Bronwyn Naylor, *Human Rights and People with Disabilities in Closed Environments*, 31 Law in Context 48–83, 53 (2014) [online].

[29] Christopher J. Ryan, *Capacity as a Determinant of Non-consensual Treatment of the Mentally Ill in Australia*, 18 Psychiatry Psychol. & L. 248–62, 248 (2011).

[30] Matthew Large, Christopher Ryan, Olav Nielssen & Robert Hayes, *The Danger of Dangerousness: Why We Must Remove the Dangerousness Criterion from Our Mental Health Acts*, 34 J. Med. Ethics 877, 879 (2008).

behavior.[31] They state that "there is little compelling evidence that (a) mental illness directly causes criminal behavior for this population, or (b) that effective mental health services meaningfully reduce new crimes and new victims."[32] Nevertheless, these civil laws remain closely tied to the notion of risk of harm to others.

III. Pretrial Schemes

1. Remand and Bail

Those accused of certain offenses may be remanded into custody before and during their trial by order of a court. In general, those on remand will be held in special remand facilities. To avoid the impracticalities of all accused persons being detained prior to trial and to uphold the presumption of innocence, accused persons may be released on bail. This practice dates to seventh century England where it "began as an effort to preserve the liberty of Englishmen while ensuring the accused's presence at trial."[33]

In recent years, some common law jurisdictions have tightened bail laws. This has generally been in response to high profile cases where individuals have committed crimes while on bail. For example, in 2015, there was a review of bail laws in New South Wales[34]—which had already been restricted in 2013[35]—following a siege in a café in downtown Sydney, Australia, by a man on bail for numerous sexual assault charges and as an accessory to the murder of his wife. The man executed one hostage and another was killed in the ensuing police rescue.[36] Similarly, in Victoria, Australia, the government is considering recommendations from two reports following a review into its bail system.[37] The review was implemented after six people died and thirty-seven others

[31] Jennifer Skeem, Jillian Petersen & Eric Silver, *Toward Research-Informed Policy for High-Risk Offenders with Severe Mental Illnesses*, in *Dangerous People*, *supra* note 4, at 111.

[32] *Id.* at 113.

[33] Kurt X. Metsmeier, *Preventive Detention: A Comparison of Bail Refusal Practices in the United States, England, Canada and Other Common Law Nations*, 8 Pace Int'l L. Rev. 399–438 (1996).

[34] John Hatzistergos, *Review of the Bail Act 2013* (Sydney, Rpt. for the NSW Premier and Attorney General, June 2015), http://www.justice.nsw.gov.au/Documents/publications-research/jh-review-of-the-bail-act-2013-final-report-june-2015.pdf.

[35] The Bail Act 2013 (N.S.W.) was introduced following a review by the New South Wales Law Commission, *Bail* (Sydney, Report No. 133, Apr. 2012), http://www.lawreform.justice.nsw.gov.au/Documents/Publications/Reports/Report-133.pdf.

[36] State Coroner of New South Wales, *Inquest into the Deaths Arising from the Lindt Café Siege: Findings and Recommendations* (Sydney Coroners Ct. New South Wales, May 2017), http://www.lindtinquest.justice.nsw.gov.au/Documents/findings-and-recommendations.pdf.

[37] Engage Victoria, *Bail Review: The Review into Victoria's Bail System Focused on Legislative and Practical Reforms to Manage Risk and Maximize Community Safety* (Melbourne, Gov't of Victoria, May 8, 2017), https://engage.vic.gov.au/bailreview.

were injured in January 2017 when a man who was out on bail drove his car at speed through a pedestrian mall.[38]

In general, bail may be refused if there is an "unacceptable risk" in relation to endangering public safety[39] or where there are "substantial grounds" for believing that the accused will commit a further offense while on bail.[40] Some jurisdictions including Canada and England have specific presumptions against bail for suspected terrorists.[41]

Nicole Marie Myers points out that, except for England and Wales, common law jurisdictions have seen growth in the numbers of people held in pretrial detention since the year 2000, with Canada and the United States above the international median.[42] England and Wales' remand population may have remained stable partly because there appears to have been an increase in the restrictions on those on bail.[43]

It seems likely that there is a correlation between the emphasis on risk aversion and risk management, on the one hand, and, on the other, the rising rates of prison remand populations and increases in conditions of bail.[44] The New South Wales Law Reform Commission has pointed out that "[t]he use of bail law to prevent a future crime—preventive detention—has always been problematic."[45]

2. Unfitness to Plead

The law on unfitness to plead is based on the premise that individuals should not be put on trial if they are unable to understand the legal process and the charges against them.[46] The common law test of an accused's ability to participate in the criminal trial process is derived from the 1836 English case of *R v. Pritchard*.[47] The "*Pritchard* test," as it is known, requires that the accused must be "of sufficient intellect to comprehend the course of proceedings in the trial so as to make a proper defense, to know that he may challenge any of you to whom he may object and to comprehend the details of the evidence."[48]

[38] Australian Broadcasting Corp., *Bourke Street Attack: Sixth Person Dies Following Car Rampage as Floral Tributes Removed*, ABC News, Jan. 31, 2017, http://www.abc.net.au/news/2017-01-30/sixth-person-dies-following-bourke-street-attack/8225072. A coronial inquest is underway and the trial is expected to take place in 2018.

[39] Bail Act 1977 (Vic.) s. 4(2)(d)(i); Bail Act 2013 (N.S.W.) s. 19.

[40] *See, e.g.*, Bail Act 1976 (England and Wales) sched. 1 s. 2; Criminal Code (Can.) s. 515.

[41] *See, e.g.*, provisions inserted by the Bail Amendment Act 2015 (N.S.W.) and by the Bail Amendment Act (No 2) 2015 (Vic.).

[42] Nicole Marie Myers, *Eroding the Presumption of Innocence: Pre-trial Detention and the Use of Conditional Release on Bail*, 57 Brit. J. Criminology 664, 665 (2017).

[43] Anthea Hucklesby, *Keeping the Lid on the Prison Remand Population: The Experience in England and Wales*, 21 Current Issues Crim. Justice 3 (2009).

[44] Anthea Hucklesby & Rick Sarre, *Bail in Australia, the United Kingdom and Canada: Introduction*, 21 Current Issues Crim. Justice 1–2 (2009).

[45] New South Wales Law Comm'n, *Bail* 154 (Sydney, Report No. 133, Apr. 2012), http://www.lawreform.justice.nsw.gov.au/Documents/Publications/Reports/Report-133.pdf.

[46] Donald Grubin, *Fitness to Plead in England and Wales* 17 (1996).

[47] R v. Pritchard (1836) 7 C. & P. 303 (U.K.). [48] *Id.* at 304.

The test was developed further in *R v. Davies*[49] and *R v. M (John).*[50] To stand trial, an accused must be capable of:

1. Understanding the charges;
2. Deciding whether to plead guilty or not;
3. Exercising the right to challenge jurors;
4. Instructing solicitors and counsel;
5. Following the course of proceedings; and
6. Giving evidence in his or her own defense.[51]

Similar criteria apply in most common law jurisdictions,[52] although the United States Supreme Court's test focuses more heavily on the accused's ability to instruct lawyers.[53] In many jurisdictions the *Pritchard* criteria, or similar tests, have been incorporated into statute.[54]

After a finding is made that an accused is unfit to plead, the charges may be dismissed entirely,[55] or the prosecution case may be tested (albeit in a limited fashion, focusing on the physical elements of the alleged offense) through a "trial of the facts" or a "special hearing."[56] Special hearings vary throughout common law jurisdictions. For example, in most Australian jurisdictions they are conducted "as nearly as possible" to a criminal trial.[57] In some jurisdictions, the requisite standard of proof is lowered significantly.[58]

The important aspect of this process for this chapter is that indefinite detention may follow a finding of unfitness[59] or detention constrained only by a "nominal term."[60] In Western Australia, for example, those found unfit to plead who are given a custodial order are detained "until released by an order of the Governor."[61] This has led to

[49] R v. Davies [1853] Car. & Kir. 328 (U.K.).

[50] R v. M (John) [2003] EWCA Crim 3452 (U.K.).

[51] *Id.* ¶ 20.

[52] For example, see R v. Presser [1958] V.R. 45 at 48 (Austl.).

[53] Dusky v. United States, 362 U.S. 402, 402 (1960); Godinez v. Moran, 509 U.S. 389, 404 (1993); Cooper v. Oklahoma, 517 U.S. 348, 354 (1996).

[54] For example in Australia, see Crimes Act 1900 (A.C.T.) s. 311; Criminal Code 1983 (N. Terr.) s. 43J; Criminal Law Consolidation Act 1935 (S. Austl.) s. 269H; Criminal Justice (Mental Impairment) Act 1999 (Tas.) s. 8; Crimes (Mental Impairment and Unfitness to Be Tried) Act 1997 (Vic.) s. 6; Criminal Law (Mentally Impaired Accused) Act 1996 (W.A.) s. 9.

[55] Criminal Law (Mentally Impaired Accused) Act 1996 (W.A.) s. 24(1); Mental Health Act 2000 (Qld.) s. 283.

[56] For example, see Criminal Procedure (Insanity) Act 1964 (England and Wales) s. 4A.

[57] For example, see Crimes Act 1900 (A.C.T.) s. 315C(a)(ii); Mental Health (Forensic Provisions) Act 1900 (N.S.W.) s. 21(1); Criminal Code 1983 (N. Terr.) s. 43W(1); Criminal Justice (Mental Impairment) Act 1999 (Tas.) s. 16(1); Crimes (Mental Impairment and Unfitness to be Tried) Act 1997 (Vic.) s. 16(1).

[58] Crimes Act 1914 (Cth.) s. 20B(3); Criminal Procedure (Mentally Impaired Persons) Act 2003 (N.Z.) s. 14(3). *See also* Betheli O'Carroll, *Double Standards: Standards of Proof for Persons Found Unfit for Trial*, 22 J.L. & Med. 871 (2015).

[59] Criminal Justice (Mental Impairment) Act 1999 (Tas.) s. 66.

[60] Criminal Code 1983 (N. Terr.) s. 43ZG; Crimes (Mental Impairment and Unfitness to Be Tried) Act 1997 (Vic.) s. 28.

[61] Criminal Law (Mentally Impaired Accused) Act 1996 (W.A.) s. 24(1).

controversial decisions, the most publicized one being in relation to Marlon James Noble, an Indigenous man who was kept in prison for nearly a decade after a finding of unfitness to plead to alleged sexual assaults, despite the alleged victims subsequently informing prosecutors that he had never assaulted them.[62] The United Nations Committee on the Rights of Persons with Disabilities reviewed this matter and found that the "indefinite detention to which [Mr Noble] was subjected amounts to inhuman and degrading treatment."[63]

While unfitness to plead laws are generally justified on the basis that they protect against individuals being punished after a trial which they cannot understand,[64] they can produce adverse outcomes for the individuals concerned.

IV. Post-crime Schemes

1. Indefinite Detention of Recidivist Offenders

Indefinite detention laws have existed in various forms for over a century. Such laws allow the judge to take into account the risk the offender poses to the community when determining the offender's sentence. Courts can generally order an offender to serve an indefinite sentence on its own initiative, or after an application from the prosecution. The appropriateness of an indefinite sentence can be reviewed at various stages.

For example, in Australia, the power to pass an indefinite sentence on offenders who are assessed as posing a danger to society exists in the Northern Territory, Queensland, Tasmania, Victoria, and Western Australia.[65] Some of the provisions specifically refer to violent offenders and sex offenders, while others are broader in their scope. Queensland and South Australia have special indefinite detention schemes for sex offenders, which enable the relevant Attorney-General to apply for an order for continuing detention during the term of imprisonment.[66]

In Canada, section 753 of the Criminal Code enables courts to designate a person as a "dangerous offender," the consequences of which mean "indeterminate detention" in prison unless a sentence of two years or more plus long-term supervision or a regular

[62] Piers Gooding, Bernadette McSherry, Anna Arstein-Kerslake & Louis Andrews, *Unfitness to Stand Trial and the Indefinite Detention of Persons with Cognitive Disabilities in Australia: Human Rights Challenges and Proposals for Change*, 40 Melb. U. L. Rev. 816–65, 818 (2017).

[63] Committee on the Rights of Persons with Disabilities, *Views Adopted by the Committee Under Article 5 of the Optional Protocol, Concerning Communication No. 7/2012*, 16th sess., U.N. Doc. CRPD/C/16/D/7/2012 (Oct. 10, 2016) 17 [8.9].

[64] Arlie Loughnan, *Contemporary Comment: Reforming the Criminal Law on Mental Incapacity*, 25 Current Issues Crim. Justice 703–10, 706 (2013).

[65] Sentencing Act 1995 (N. Terr.) s. 65; Penalties and Sentences Act 1992 (Qld.) s. 163; Sentencing Act 1991 (Vic.) s. 18A; Sentencing Act 1997 (Tas.) s. 19; Sentencing Act 1995 (W.A.) s. 98.

[66] Criminal Law Amendment Act 1945 (Qld.) s. 18; Criminal Law (Sentencing) Act 1988 (S. Austl.) ss. 23(2a), (4).

sentence would adequately protect the public.[67] Dangerous offenders are considered to be those who have committed a serious personal injury offense; who have displayed a pattern of repetitive, persistent aggressive behavior or failure to control sexual impulses; and who present a threat of future harm. The Crown prosecutor presents evidence that the person who has been convicted of sexual assault or other serious personal injury offense is a dangerous offender. Part of this evidence will be assessments of the person by mental health and/or correctional officers and/or individual experts designated by the court.[68]

A similar system exists in England and Wales. The Criminal Justice Act 2003 introduced indeterminate sentences for dangerous offenders whose eligibility for release depends on the level of risk they pose in relation to sexual and violent reoffending. In Scotland, orders for lifelong restriction can be made at the time of sentence.[69] These orders provide for a level of treatment while detained in prison plus supervision in the community post-imprisonment.[70]

Some states and provinces in Australia and Canada, as well as New Zealand, also have discretionary life sentences for serious violent and sexual offenders that may be imposed at the time of sentence, and some states in the United States have automatic life sentences for a third conviction for a serious violent or sexual offense. These varying options for detaining recidivist offenders are available to the sentencing judge at the time of sentence and have differing emphases on treatment and the use of psychiatric facilities.[71]

2. Indefinite Detention of Those Found Not Guilty by Reason of Mental Impairment

Legislative schemes in common law countries concerning individuals found not guilty by reason of mental impairment (some jurisdictions still use the term "insanity") enable the indefinite detention of acquittees on the basis of community protection. For example, in England and Wales, a person must be admitted to a designated hospital if he or she has committed a serious crime.[72] In Canada, a person found not criminally responsible by reason of "mental disorder" generally undergoes a special hearing conducted by a court.[73] The court may order indefinite detention in a hospital after considering the need to protect the public from "dangerous persons."[74]

[67] Criminal Code (Can.) s. 753(4.1).

[68] For an overview of this process, see Public Safety Canada, *The Investigation, Prosecution and Correctional Management of High-Risk Offenders: A National Guide* 14 ff. (Jan. 19, 2016), https://www.publicsafety.gc.ca/cnt/rsrcs/pblctns/2009-pcmg/index-en.aspx.

[69] Criminal Procedure (Scotland) Act 1995 as amended by the Criminal Justice (Scotland) Act 2003.

[70] Innes Fyfe & Yvonne Gailey, *The Scottish Approach to High-Risk Offenders*), in *Dangerous People, supra* note 4, at 201–32.

[71] Lindsay Thomson, *The Role of Forensic Mental Health Services in Managing High-Risk Offenders*, in *Dangerous People, supra* note 4, at 165–81.

[72] Criminal Procedure (Insanity and Unfitness to Plead) Act 1991 (England and Wales) s. 5.

[73] Criminal Code (Can.) s. 672.45.

[74] Criminal Code (Can.) s. 672.54.

The decision to release a person so detained may be made by a minister in England and Wales, New Zealand, and at the Australian Commonwealth level.[75] A review board or tribunal makes the decision in Canada and some Australian jurisdictions;[76] elsewhere in Australia, a court does so.[77]

Community protection plays a significant role in decisions to keep a person detained.[78] Ian Freckelton has studied relevant decisions of the Supreme Court of Victoria and has found that while the Court has varied custodial orders to noncustodial supervision orders, decisions to revoke all supervision are rare.[79] He observes that any downgrading in supervisory status will only occur if there is "substantial and credible reassurance by mental health professionals that the chances of the acquittee offending violently again are remote, very low, slight, insignificant or non-existent."[80]

As with decisions about remand, conservative decision-making on the grounds of community protection appears to be high, particularly if the offense is a serious one.

V. Post-sentence Schemes

1. Post-sentence Detention

In the United States, some twenty states have enacted civil commitment legislation, allowing for "sexually violent predators" to be detained after they have served their sentence.[81] Federal offenders can also be civilly committed if a court determines that they are sexually dangerous. Although this type of civil commitment has been permitted

[75] Criminal Procedure (Insanity) Act 1964 (England and Wales) s. 5A(4); Criminal Procedure (Mentally Impaired Persons) Act 2003 (N.Z.) s. 24 and the Mental Health (Compulsory Assessment and Treatment) Act 2003 (N.Z.); Crimes Act 1914 (Cth.) s. 20BJ.

[76] Criminal Code (Can.) s. 672.81(1.2)(c); Crimes Act 1900 (A.C.T.) s. 323; Mental Health (Forensic Provisions) Act 1900 (N.S.W.) s. 43.

[77] Criminal Justice (Mental Impairment) Act 1999 (Tas.) s. 21; Crimes (Mental Impairment and Unfitness to Be Tried) Act 1997 (Vic.) s. 35.

[78] Victorian Law Reform Comm'n, *Review of the Crimes Mental Impairment and Unfitness to Be Tried) Act 1997* (Melbourne, Final Report No. 28, June 2014) 344, http://www.lawreform.vic.gov.au/sites/default/files/Review_of_the_Crimes_Mental_Impairment_and_Unfitness_to_be_Tried_Act_0.pdf.

[79] Ian Freckelton, *Indefinite Detention in Australia: The Ongoing Risk of Governor's Pleasure Detention*, 21 Psychiatry Pschol. & L. 469 (2014); Ian Freckelton, *The Preventive Detention of Insanity Acquittees: A Case Study from Victoria, Australia*, in *Dangerous People*, *supra* note 4, at 83–96; Ian Freckelton, *Involuntary Detention of Persons Found Not Guilty of Murder by Reason of Mental Impairment or Found Unfit to Stand Trial: A New Jurisprudence from Victoria*, in *Involuntary Detention and Therapeutic Jurisprudence* 383–434 (2002).

[80] Freckelton, *Preventive Detention of Insanity Acquittees*, *supra* note 79, at 89.

[81] Office of the Legislative Auditor Minnesota, *Civil Commitment of Sex Offenders: Evaluation Report* 16 (St. Paul, Mar. 2011), http://www.auditor.leg.state.mn.us/ped/pedrep/ccso.pdf. For an overview of these laws, see John Q. LaFond, *Sexual Offender Commitment Laws in the USA*, in *Dangerous People*, *supra* note 4, at 51–61.

under federal law since 1949, the U.S. Supreme Court upheld its constitutional validity only relatively recently, in 2010 in *United States v. Comstock*.[82]

While the U.S. schemes enable post-sentence detention in special facilities, Australian schemes are unique in enabling post-sentence detention in prison. In 2003, Queensland introduced a new scheme for post-sentence detention in prison and continuing supervision of sex offenders.[83] Western Australia, New South Wales, Victoria, and the Northern Territory followed.[84] The New South Wales legislation was amended by the Crimes (Serious Sex Offenders) Amendment Act 2013 to encompass "high risk sex offenders and high risk violent offenders," but the main features of the scheme remain the same.[85] In 2015, South Australia introduced "continuing detention orders" for high risk offenders.[86] New Zealand considered the Australian example and, after considerable debate,[87] passed the Public Safety (Public Protection Orders) Act 2014. This enables post-sentence continued detention of serious sexual or violent offenders in a secure "residence," which may in fact be located within prison precincts.[88]

In general, Australian post-sentence preventive detention schemes enable an application to be made to a specified court, prior to the offender completing a finite sentence, for an order for continuing detention in prison or for continuing supervision in the community. The court must consider risk assessment testimony from psychiatrists (and/or psychologists) concerning whether the offender poses an unacceptable risk of reoffending. Supervision orders may contain a number of conditions including that the offender must report to and receive visits by certain specified individuals, must obey any curfews relating to leaving his or her residence at certain times, and must not commit an offense or move to a new address without prior written consent.[89] The Dangerous Prisoners (Sexual Offenders) Amendment Act 2007 (Qld) and the Dangerous Sexual Offenders Amendment Act 2012 (WA) introduced provisions enabling the electronic monitoring of sex offenders.[90]

[82] 560 U.S. 126, 130 S. Ct. 1949 (2010). The constitutionality of similar laws by state governments was affirmed earlier in *Kansas v. Hendricks*, 521 U.S. 346 (1997).

[83] Dangerous Prisoners (Sexual Offenders) Act 2003 (Qld.).

[84] Dangerous Sexual Offenders Act 2006 (W.A.); Crimes (High Risk Offenders) Act 2006 (N.S.W.); Serious Sex Offenders (Detention and Supervision) Act 2009 (Vic.); Serious Sex Offenders Act 2013 (N. Terr.).

[85] Crimes (Serious Sex Offenders) Amendment Act 2013 (N.S.W.) sched. 1, ss. 1, 3.

[86] Criminal Law (High Risk Offenders) Act 2015 (S. Austl.).

[87] Colin Gavaghan, Jeanne Snelling & John McMillan, *Better and Better and Better? A Legal and Ethical Analysis of Preventive Detention in New Zealand* (Report for the N.Z. Law Found., Univ. of Otago, Nov. 2014), http://www.otago.ac.nz/law/news/otago083869.pdf.

[88] Public Safety (Public Protection Orders) Act 2014 (N.Z.) s. 114.

[89] Dangerous Prisoners (Sexual Offenders) Act 2003 (Qld.) s. 16; Dangerous Sexual Offenders Act 2006 (W.A.) s. 18; Crimes (High Risk Offenders) Act 2006 (N.S.W.) s. 11; Serious Sex Offenders (Detention and Supervision) Act 2009 (Vic.) ss. 16, 17; Serious Sex Offenders Act 2013 (N. Terr.) ss. 18, 19.

[90] Dangerous Prisoners (Sexual Offenders) Amendment Act 2007 (Qld.) s. 3A, inserting Dangerous Prisoners (Sexual Offenders) Act 2003 (Qld.) s. 16A; Dangerous Sexual Offenders Amendment Act 2012 (W.A.) s. 6 inserting Dangerous Sexual Offenders Act 2006 (W.A.) ss. 19A, 19C.

These post-sentence detention laws, like other preventive detention laws, have been subject to considerable criticism. Some of these criticisms are considered in the next section.

VI. Criticisms of Pretrial and Civil Detention Schemes

1. International Human Rights Law

There is continuing debate about the human rights implications of legislation that authorizes detention on the basis of prevention of harm, particularly in relation to post-sentence imprisonment. Human rights are considered rights inherent to all human beings, regardless of status. The Preamble to the Universal Declaration of Human Rights recognizes the "inherent dignity and inalienable rights of all members of the human family."[91] Human rights are:

> the basic rights that belong to everyone, regardless of age, race, sex, or disability, income or education. They are about treating people fairly and with dignity, and ensuring individual rights are respected.[92]

Relevant to the consideration of the human rights of offenders is Article 9(1) of the International Covenant on Civil and Political Rights, which states that:

> Everyone has the right to liberty and security of person. No one shall be subjected to arbitrary arrest or detention. No one shall be deprived of his [or her] liberty except on such grounds and in accordance with such procedure as are established by law.

However, Article 9(1) indicates that there may be instances where the right to liberty can be subject to reasonable limitations.

The right to liberty and security is also reflected in Article 14 of the United Nations Convention on the Rights of Persons with Disabilities (which applies to individuals with "mental" and "intellectual impairments"[93] as well as physical disabilities), which reiterates the right to liberty and security of the person. In Victoria, section 21 of the Charter of Human Rights and Responsibilities and in the Australian Capital Territory, section 18 of the Human Rights Act 2004 also set out this right.

[91] Universal Declaration of Human Rights, G.A. Res. 217A (III), U.N. Doc. A/810 at 71 (1948).

[92] Michael Brett Young, *From Commitment to Culture: The 2015 Review of the Charter of Human Rights and Responsibilities Act 2006*, at 3 (Melbourne, Victorian Gov't Printer, Sept. 2015).

[93] Art 1.

In 2010, the United Nations Human Rights Committee declared that the Queensland and New South Wales schemes for post-sentence detention of sex offenders breach the prohibition on arbitrary detention under Article 9 of the International Covenant on Civil and Political Rights.[94] Eleven of the thirteen members of the UN Committee agreed that the New South Wales and Queensland schemes enabling post-sentence detention of sex offenders violated the right to liberty.[95] They found that "continued imprisonment or even detention" amounted to a fresh term of imprisonment, which was not permissible in the absence of a criminal conviction. It was viewed as a form of "double punishment." This position aligns with the dissenting decision of Justice Kirby of the High Court of Australia *Fardon v. Attorney-General (Qld.)*[96] in which he observed that:

> punishment is reserved to courts in respect of the crimes that prisoners are proved to have committed. It is not available for crimes that are feared, anticipated or predicted to occur in the future on evidence that is notoriously unreliable and otherwise would be inadmissible and by people who do not have the gift of prophesy.[97]

The Committee on the Rights of Persons with Disabilities has also stated that "[t]he involuntary detention of persons with disabilities based on risk or dangerousness, alleged need of care or treatment or other reasons tied to impairment or health diagnosis is contrary to the right to liberty, and amounts to arbitrary deprivation of liberty."[98]

On September 6, 2011, the Australian government filed a five-page document rejecting the Human Rights Committee's view that there were less restrictive means available to achieve the purposes of the New South Wales and Queensland legislation other than

[94] Human Rights Committee, Views: Communication No. 1629/2007, 98th sess., U.N. Doc. CCPR/C/98/D/1629/2007 (10 May 2010) ("Fardon v. Australia") 8; Human Rights Committee, Views: Communication No. 1635/2007, 98th sess., U.N. Doc. CCPR/C/98/D/1635/2007 (10 May 2010) ("Tillman v. Australia"). On this point, see, e.g., B. McSherry, *Managing Fear, supra* note 1, at ch. 7; Patrick Keyzer, *Preventive Detention: Asking the Fundamental Questions*, in *Preventive Detention: Asking the Fundamental Questions* 1, 5 (Patrick Keyzer ed., 2013); Bernadette McSherry, *Post-sentence Incapacitation of Sex Offenders and the Ethics of Risk Assessment*, in *Incapacitation* 77 (Marijke Malsch & Marius Duker eds., 2012); Ian Freckelton & Patrick Keyzer, *Indefinite Detention of Sex Offenders and Human Rights: The Intervention of the Human Rights Committee of the United Nations*, 17 Psychiatry Psychol. & L. 345 (2010); Patrick Keyzer, *The United Nations Human Rights Committee's Views About the Legitimate Parameters of the Preventive Detention of Serious Sex Offenders*, 34 Crim. L.J. 283 (2010); Patrick Keyzer, *The International Human Rights Parameters for the Preventive Detention of Serious Sex Offenders*, in *Dangerous People, supra* note 4, at 25. International Covenant on Civil and Political Rights, Dec. 16, 1966, S. Treaty Doc. No. 95-20, 6 I.L.M. 368 (1967), 999 U.N.T.S. 171.

[95] Re Fardon v. Australia [2010] Human Rights Committee, Communication No. 1629/2007, U.N. Doc. CCPR/C/98/D/1629/2007 (Apr. 12, 2010); Re Tillman v. Australia [2010] Human Rights Committee, Communication No. 1635/2007, U.N. Doc. CCPR/C/98/D/1635/2007 (Apr. 12, 2010). *See* McSherry, *Managing Fear, supra* note 1, at 180–82 and references therein.

[96] (2004) 223 C.L.R. 575 (Austl.).

[97] (2004) 223 C.L.R. 575 at 647 (Austl.).

[98] Committee on the Rights of Persons with Disabilities, *Guidelines on Article 14 of the Convention on the Rights of Persons with Disabilities: The Right to Liberty and Security of Persons with Disabilities* ¶ 13 (adopted during the Committee's 14th session, Sept. 2015).

detention in prison.[99] Darren O'Donovan and Patrick Keyzer have described these communications and the Australian government's response as providing:

> a stark example of what may be termed normative dissension between an international body and a nation state, illustrating the dynamics of "decoupling," where a state effectively separates its international legal commitments from practical implementation.... [E]ven rich, developed, liberal democracies can pursue a policy of deliberate and persistent non-compliance. Ultimately, access to international justice in this context is meaningless if the parties to international human rights instruments fail to comply.[100]

2. Due Process and Proportionality

In civil hearings, courts, administrative agencies and tribunals are under a duty to comply with the legal requirements of due process, which may also be referred to as procedural fairness or "natural justice."[101] Article 14 of the International Covenant on Civil and Political Rights guarantees the general right to a "fair and public hearing by a competent, independent and impartial tribunal established by law." It then specifies a number of procedural safeguards such as the presumption of innocence.

There is thus a duty on governments to adopt fair procedures that are appropriate and relevant to the circumstances of the particular case. In general, due process in civil hearings is based around two rules:

1. The hearing rule whereby a decision-maker must give the affected person an opportunity to state his or her case; and
2. The bias rule whereby the decision-maker must be impartial and have no personal interest in the matter to be decided.

There have been concerns that some pretrial and civil detention schemes do not comply with due process requirements. In relation to the preventive detention of suspected terrorists, secrecy provisions surrounding such schemes may interfere with the right to a fair trial. In *R v. H*,[102] the House of Lords commented:

[99] Australian Gov't, *Response of the Australian Government to the Views of the Committee in Communication No. 1635/2007 Tillman v. Australia and Communication No. 1629/2007 Fardon v. Australia* 3–4 (Communication to the Human Rights Committee, Sept. 2011). *See* Bernadette McSherry, *Throwing Away the Key: The Ethics of Risk Assessment for Preventive Detention Schemes*, 21 Psychiatry Psychol. & L. 779, 784–85 (2014).

[100] Darren O'Donovan & Patrick Keyzer, *"Visions of a Distant Millennium"? The Effectiveness of the UN Human Rights Petition System*, in *Access to International Justice* (Patrick Keyzer, Vesselin Popovski & Charles Sampford eds., 2014).

[101] Pamela A. O'Connor, Ian R. Freckelton & Peter Sallman, *Policy Manual for Tribunals* ch. 3 (Council of Australasian Tribunals 2006).

[102] [2004] UKHL 3, ¶ [23].

> The problem of reconciling an individual's right to a fair trial with such secrecy as is necessary in a democratic society in the interests of national security or the prevention or investigations of crime is inevitably difficult to resolve in a liberal society governed by the rule of law.

There is also an exception to the disclosure of all information to the accused in matters of public security. This means that on the basis of the "public interest," the accused may not have full access to all the evidence against him or her.[103]

In relation to post-sentence preventive detention schemes, the UN Human Rights Committee has declared that the Queensland and New South Wales schemes for post-sentence detention of sex offenders fail to meet the due process guarantees under Article 14 of the International Covenant on Civil and Political Rights.[104] As outlined above with regard to the UN Committee's finding that the same scheme also breached Article 9, the Australian government has rejected the UN Committee's decision.

Civil detention schemes may also call into play well-established legal principles such as the principles of proportionality and finality in sentencing; the principle that governments should punish criminal conduct, not criminal types; and the principle against double punishment.[105]

Some schemes are of particular concern in relation to the low threshold for proof. For example, in relation to post-sentence detention in Australia, the standard of proof that applies is not the criminal standard of beyond a reasonable doubt, despite the result in many instances being continuing detention in prison. Section 7(2) of the Western Australian Act, for example, requires the Director of Public Prosecutions to adduce "acceptable and cogent evidence" and satisfy the court "to a high degree of probability" that there is an unacceptable risk that "if the person concerned were not subject to a continuing detention order or a supervision order, the person would commit a serious sexual offence."[106] In determining risk, the legislation mandates the court to consider reports from two psychiatrists[107] who have assessed the offender as well as "any other medical, psychiatric, psychological, or other assessment."[108] Hence the focus is on opinion evidence rather than the evidence of witnesses. This means that traditional evidentiary issues in criminal trials such as problems of hearsay can be bypassed.

The New South Wales, Queensland, and Northern Territory laws similarly require "a high degree of probability" that the offender is a serious danger to the community

[103] Jasper v. United Kingdom, App. No. 27052/95, Eur. Ct. H.R., Feb. 16, 2000, § 52.

[104] Human Rights Committee, Views: Communication No. 1629/2007, 98th sess., U.N. Doc. CCPR/C/98/D/1629/2007 (10 May 2010) ("Fardon v. Australia") ¶ 7.4(3); Human Rights Committee, Views: Communication No. 1635/2007, 98th sess., U.N. Doc. CCPR/C/98/D/1635/2007 (10 May 2010) ("Tillman v. Australia"), ¶ 7.4(3).

[105] *See* Bernadette McSherry, *Indefinite and Preventive Detention Legislation: From Caution to an Open Door*, 29(2) Crim. L.J. 94–110 (2005).

[106] Dangerous Sexual Offenders Act 2006 (W.A.) s. 7(1).

[107] Dangerous Sexual Offenders Act 2006 (W.A.) s. 14(2)(a), 37.

[108] Dangerous Sexual Offenders Act 2006 (W.A.) s. 7(3)(b).

based on an unacceptable risk of reoffending.[109] Schedule 1 of the Crimes (Serious Sex Offenders) Amendment Act 2010 (NSW) inserted a new section into the New South Wales Act. This states:

> The Supreme Court is not required to determine that the risk of a person committing a serious sex offence is more likely than not in order to determine that the person poses an unacceptable risk of committing a serious sex offence.[110]

This sets a lower standard of proof than required previously by the Court. Similarly, sections 35(4) and 36(2) of the Serious Sex Offenders (Detention and Supervision) Act 2009 (Vic.) state that "an offender poses an unacceptable risk of committing a relevant offence *even if the likelihood that the offender will commit a relevant offence is less than a likelihood of more likely than not* [emphasis added]." While there is no set standard of proof other than requiring the Supreme Court to be "satisfied" there is an "unacceptable risk" of reoffending,[111] it is clear that the Victorian government intended that evidence of risk be easily proved.[112]

This lowering of the threshold for post-sentence detention raises serious due process concerns. There are also practical considerations for a low standard of proof. John Q. La Fond has pointed out:

> The future is clear: far more sex offenders will be warehoused at exorbitant cost in ever-expanding facilities, growing older and requiring more medical treatment every year.[113]

VII. Conclusion

Schemes premised on removing "dangerous" people from the community have long existed and will continue to exist in common law countries. While there have been challenges to such schemes through international human rights law, domestic courts have upheld the constitutional validity of such schemes. Ultimately, as Mark Finnane and Susan Donkin have pointed out, "the judiciary has been reluctant to impose detention in anticipation of future misconduct but has also been reluctant to interfere with such detention when mandated by statute."[114]

[109] Crimes (High Risk Offenders) Act 2006 (N.S.W.) s. 5B, 5E; Dangerous Prisoners (Sexual Offenders) Act 2003 (Qld.) s. 13(1)–(3)(b), 30(1)–(2)(b); Dangerous Sexual Offenders Act 2006 (W.A.) s. 7(1)–(2)(b); Serious Sex Offenders Act 2013 (N. Terr.) ss. 6, 7(1).

[110] Crimes (Serious Sex Offenders) Act 2006 (N.S.W.) s. 17(3A); now Crimes (High Risk Offenders) Act 2006 (N.S.W.) s. 5B(3).

[111] *See, e.g.*, Serious Sex Offenders (Detention and Supervision) Act 2009 (Vic.) s. 35(1).

[112] As to the need for expert evidence on risk to be "cogent," see Ian R. Coyle, *The Cogency of Risk Assessments*, 18 Psychiatry Psychol. & L., 270–96, 271 & 279–80 (2011).

[113] LaFond, *supra* note 81, at 60.

[114] Mark Finnane & Susan Donkin, *Fighting Terror with Law? Some Other Genealogies of Pre-emption*, 2 Int'l J. Crime, Justice & Social Democracy 3, 12 (2013).

Limitations on and oversight of the use of these schemes are essential because of the possibility that such detention of individuals not for what they have done, but for who they are or for what they might do, becomes an instrument of oppression. While it is unrealistic to believe that a consistent approach across different schemes and jurisdictions can ever be achieved, strict compliance with the rules of due process and proportionality may help ensure that people are not unnecessarily deprived of their liberty. Due process requirements demand that the more serious the consequences of a decision, the higher the standard of proof required. The power of the state compulsorily to detain individuals not for punishment but for the protection of the community must, at the very least, observe due process and rely upon sufficiently cogent evidence.

References

Bernadette McSherry, *Managing Fear: The Law and Ethics of Preventive Detention and Risk Assessment* (2014)

Dangerous People: Policy, Prediction and Practice (Bernadette McSherry & Patrick Keyzer eds., 2011)

Bernadette McSherry & Patrick Keyzer, *Sex Offenders and Preventive Detention: Politics, Policy and Practice* (2009)

John Pratt, *Governing the Dangerous: Dangerousness, Law and Social Change* (1997)

Regulating Preventive Justice: Principle, Policy and Paradox (Tamara Tulich, Rebecca Ananian-Welsh, Simon Bronitt & Sarah Murray eds., 2017)

Diane Webber, *Preventive Detention of Terror Suspects: A New Legal Framework* (2016)

PART V

PREPARATION FOR ADJUDICATION

CHAPTER 25

EVIDENCE DISCOVERY AND DISCLOSURE IN COMMON LAW JURISDICTIONS

DARRYL K. BROWN

I. Introduction

Common law jurisdictions, in accord with their long traditions of adversarial trial process, leave evidence gathering to the parties rather than to judicial or quasi-judicial officials. The adversarial nature of party roles gave rise to the norm that one party should not have to aid an opponent's preparation. That norm retained considerable force in the modern era, despite the rise of professional police forces and prosecution agencies, as well as the demise of private prosecutors, which means state officials dominate evidence gathering in criminal cases. Defendants have some authority—if in practice often a weak capacity—to investigate facts and produce evidence independently. Ordinarily, the judicial role in evidence gathering is minor. Even judicial *access* to evidence collected by the parties is minimal prior to trial, because the adversarial tradition long treated the *trial* as the event at which parties first disclosed their evidence to each other as well as to the court. In earlier eras, mechanisms to uncover evidence outside of trial were limited, especially for defendants. As a consequence, the trial itself could be an important tool for evidence discovery; sometimes *both* parties first heard a witness's account at trial.[1] All schemes of pretrial disclosure, then, are relatively modern shifts away from a tradition in which parties had no duties to disclose evidence prior to trial.

Modern reforms of pretrial disclosure practices, then, occurred against a historical presumption against disclosure. They also occurred in an era in which negotiated guilty

[1] John H. Langbein, *The Origins of the Adversary Criminal Trial* (2003); John H. Langbein, *The Disappearance of the Civil Trial in the United States*, 122 Yale L.J. 522 (2012).

pleas became the predominant process for resolving criminal cases, which has led to the trial becoming an exceptional process.[2] In many jurisdictions, as few as 2 or 3 percent of convictions on serious charges occur through trial judgments; rarely do trials account for more than 10 or 15 percent of convictions.[3] The marginal role of the trial changes the calculus for disclosure rules in adversarial justice systems. If each party is to confront the evidence of its opponent—if evidence is ever to face adversarial scrutiny—then parties will have to disclose evidence prior to—and in lieu of—trial.

In addition, changes in the nature of evidence, and evidence gathering techniques, also undermined the normative viability of nondisclosure. Much expert analysis, for example, simply cannot be confronted effectively at trial without advance notice and preparation. More routinely, effectively challenging witnesses' credibility sometimes requires knowledge of their affiliations, interests, or backgrounds. Finally, pretrial disclosure is generally understood to make both trials and negotiated resolutions more efficient, and (although there has been some dissent on this point) to improve the truth-finding capacity of both procedural routes to criminal judgments.

For these reasons and others, all common law criminal justice systems moved away from their tradition of nondisclosure. But the details of how and the degree to which they have done so vary widely, and disagreement remains on reasons for doing so. Section II of this chapter provides an overview of common law approaches to disclosure obligations. The focus is primarily on the disclosure regimes in England and Wales and in U.S. jurisdictions, which differ sharply on some points, although rules also vary widely among the separate U.S. justice systems. There is some reference to rules in other common law jurisdictions as well, generally to confirm that their disclosure laws are similar to the English scheme. All these jurisdictions started from a shared common law tradition that, at least into the nineteenth century, required virtually no pretrial evidence sharing by the parties. But one now finds sharply different resolutions of a core question for disclosure law: whether the prosecution must share with the defense prior to trial the evidence it would rely on to prove guilt. By contrast, common law jurisdictions share considerable similarities on disclosure rules for other kinds of materials. In the last half century, there has emerged a strong consensus that the government must disclose relevant evidence in its possession that does *not* support the prosecution's case and thus that it would not present at trial—"unused evidence" in English parlance. It is now widely taken as unfair for the prosecution to withhold evidence that could be helpful to the defense.

[2] Plea bargaining has a long history in many places, although it was often an informal and surreptitious practice until recent decades. *See* Mary E. Vogel, *Coercion to Compromise* (2007); George Fisher, *Plea Bargaining's Triumph: A History of Plea Bargaining in America* (2004); Lawrence Friedman & Robert V. Percival, *The Roots of Justice: Crime and Punishment in Alameda County, California, 1870–1910* (1981); Raymond Moley, *The Vanishing Jury*, 2 S. Cal. L. Rev. 97 (1928). For an account of formal *denial* about plea bargaining even when it was routine, *see* John Baldwin & Michael McConville, *Negotiated Justice* (1977).

[3] In U.S. federal courts during 2015–2016, 97.3 percent of convictions came from guilty pleas. In the Crown Courts of England and Wales in 2015–2016, guilty pleas accounted for 89.8 percent of convictions. *See* U.S. Sent'g Comm'n, *Sourcebook for Federal Sentencing Statistics* (2016), fig. C; Crown Prosecution Service, *Annual Report and Resource Accounts 2016–17*, Annex D, at 65, table 7.

In addition, the defense bears greater duties to disclose significant portions of its evidence to the prosecution in advance of trial. For each of these choices, Section II considers the reasons that led jurisdictions to settle on a common rule or follow different paths.

Section III takes a closer look at the rationales and structural choices that adversarial justice systems are required to make in their disclosure schemes. One such choice is how much to empower judges, rather than the parties, to make decisions about disclosure requirements. Policymakers also must choose how to enforce parties' obligations to act against their partisan interest in a system with ingrained adversarial norms and incentives. And the replacement of trials by negotiated guilty pleas in most cases compels the re-evaluation of disclosure rules that are designed in expectation of ("in the shadow of") trial. These choices also require background judgments about which rule option will best serve the epistemic goal of truth-finding, and which best balances epistemic and non-epistemic goals. Rules limiting disclosures to serve the security interests of victims and certain witnesses, for example, implicate both kinds of choices.

II. The Evolution of Pretrial Evidence Disclosure Rules

Disclosure obligations in criminal procedure vary according to the type of evidence, which falls into three broad categories: (1) evidence that the prosecution plans to present at trial to prove the defendant's guilt; (2) evidence in the prosecution's possession that it does not plan to present at trial, either because it favors the defense in some way or because its value is marginal or unknown; and (3) evidence in possession of the defense that it plans to present at trial. In all jurisdictions, requirements to disclose the latter two categories of evidence have expanded considerably over roughly the last half century. However, the story is different with regard to evidence supporting the prosecution's case. Broadly speaking, before the mid-twentieth century, Anglo-American disclosure rules required little in the second and third categories to be disclosed. Now, both parties typically have substantial obligations for such evidence. By contrast, the first category—evidence the prosecution will rely on to prove its case at trial—is the site of perhaps the sharpest differences among disclosure regimes in common law jurisdictions.

1. Prosecution Evidence of Guilt

English and Commonwealth duties regarding prosecution evidence. For well over a century, English courts have recognized a common law duty for prosecutors to disclose, prior to trial, the evidence on which they will rely to prove guilt.[4] In general, the prosecution

[4] Andrew Ashworth & Mike Redmayne, *The Criminal Process* 259 (4th ed. 2010); David Corker & Stephen Parkinson, *Disclosure in Criminal Proceedings* 61–72 (2009); John Sprack, *Emmins on Criminal*

discloses a bundle of witness statements and identifies experts or scientific reports on which it will rely, either when a case is committed to Crown Court or in advance of a magistrate court proceeding for either-way offenses. English courts consider this obligation essential to a fair trial and a requirement of the equality-of-arms principle, having rejected the long-standing argument in the common law world that trial by "surprise" or "ambush" serves the truth-finding enterprise.[5] The same duty for prosecutors to disclose their case in advance of trial or plea now prevails in other Commonwealth jurisdictions as well, including Canada,[6] Australia,[7] and New Zealand.[8]

U.S. duties regarding prosecution evidence. In sharp contrast, U.S. courts and legislatures have never been collectively persuaded to adopt comparable prosecution duties as a matter of common law, constitutional law, procedural rule, or statute.[9] The U.S. Supreme Court has concluded that the federal Constitution—the source of many criminal procedure rules for federal and state courts—provides no basis for ordinary disclosure duties: "there is no general constitutional right to discovery in a criminal case."[10] State courts have been nearly as reluctant to identify disclosure duties in the common law, state constitutions, or their inherent supervisory authority over judicial process.[11] Thus, disclosure duties are products primarily of legislation or formal rule-making processes, which is a key reason that prosecutorial duties vary widely across U.S. jurisdictions. It is

Procedure 122 (9th ed. 2002); Glanville Williams, *The Proof of Guilt: A Study of the English Criminal Trial* 3 (3d ed. 1963); Martin Hannibal & Lisa Mountford, *Criminal Litigation Handbook* 234–35 (2007) (describing prosecution duty to disclose "used material" at an early stage for cases in both Crown and Magistrates courts).

[5] R v. Brown [1994] 1 W.L.R. 1599, at 1606 (prosecution disclosure is a requirement for a fair trial); Crim. P.R. 21.3 (2005) ("advance information"); R (on the Application of the DPP) v. Chorley Justices and Another [2006] EWHC 1795 ("The days of ambushing... are gone."); R v. DPP ex parte Lee [1999] 2 All E.R. 737, [1999] 1 W.L.R. 1950; R v. Ward [1993] 96 Cr. App. R. 1, 51 (advance disclosure of expert evidence essential because "[o]ur law does not tolerate a conviction to be secured by ambush").

[6] *See Public Prosecution Service of Canada Deskbook*, prin. 2.5.2 (2014) (there is "a general duty on the part of the Crown to disclose all material it proposes to use at trial and especially all evidence which may assist the accused even if the Crown does not propose to adduce it."); R v. Wickstead [1997] 1 S.C.R. 307; R v. Stinchcombe [1995] 1 S.C.R. 754, 755 (*Stinchcombe 2*); R v. Stinchcombe [1991] 3 S.C.R. 326, 339 & 343 (*Stinchcombe 1*); Canada Criminal Code, 1985, R.S.C. c. C-46, § 603 ("accused is entitled... to receive... a copy of the evidence...").

[7] Commonwealth DPP, *Statement on Disclosure in Prosecutions Conducted by the Commonwealth* (2017) (Austl.); Commonwealth DPP, *CDPP Summary of State and Territory Disclosure Regimes* (2016); Mallard v. The Queen (2005) 224 C.L.R. 125, [2005] HCA 68 (Austl.); Criminal Procedure Act 1986 (NSW) s 183 (Austl.).

[8] N.Z. L. Comm'n, *Criminal Pre-trial Processes: Justice through Efficiency* 18–20 (2005).

[9] *See* William J. Brennan, *The Criminal Prosecution: Sporting Event or Quest for Truth?*, 1963 Wash. U. L.Q. 279.

[10] Weatherford v. Bursey, 429 U.S. 545, 559 (1977); *see also* Wardius v. Oregon, 412 U.S. 470, 474 (1973) (U.S. Constitution "has little to say regarding the amount of discovery which the parties must be afforded"); Pennsylvania v. Ritchie, 480 U.S. 39, 59–60 (1987) (defendant's right to discovery does not include authority to search through the government's files unsupervised); United States v. Bagley, 473 U.S. 667, 675 (1985) ("prosecutor is not required to deliver his entire file to defense counsel, but only to disclose evidence favorable to the accused that, if suppressed, would deprive the defendant of a fair trial.").

[11] *See* Brennan, *supra* note 9, at 283 (noting in 1963 that only a few state courts had created limited prosecution-disclosure duties).

important to keep in mind that there is no single American model of criminal discovery rules.[12] In particular, the federal rules are not an accurate proxy for the rules in many states, where more than 90 percent of all U.S. criminal prosecutions occur.

In a minority of state justice systems, prosecutors now have very broad disclosure duties comparable to those in Commonwealth jurisdictions. At least six states have adopted such disclosure regimes, sometimes characterized (fairly if imprecisely) as "open file" discovery.[13] (These are the closest U.S. approximations of the comprehensive evidence dossier typical in civil law systems.)[14] By contrast, about fifteen state criminal justice systems continue to operate under rules modeled on the Federal Rules of Criminal Procedure, which likely codify the most limited prosecutorial disclosure regime in the common law world.[15] Under the federal rules, prosecutors still have no duty to disclose their evidence in advance of trial except with regard to a few specific types of evidence such as expert analysis, physical objects, and most prior statements of the defendant. Notably missing from rules in these states and the federal courts are requirements for the prosecution to give advance notice of its nonexpert trial witnesses or to provide an

[12] For a detailed account of differences in discovery rules among U.S. states, *see* Darryl K. Brown, *Discovery in State Criminal Justice*, in *III Reforming Criminal Justice: Bridging the Gap between Scholarship and Reform* 147 (Erik Luna ed., 2017), http://academyforjustice.org/[http://academyforjustice.org/.

[13] Alaska R. Crim. P. 16; Fla. R. Crim. P. 3.220; Minn. R. Crim. P. 9.01–9.05; N.J. Ct. R. 3:13-3, 3:13-4; *Id.* 3:13-3(b)(1)(F) (prosecutor must disclose "any persons whom the prosecutor knows to have relevant evidence or information."); N.C. Gen. Stat. Ann. §§ 15A-902 to 15A-910 (West 2016), also § 15A-903(a)(1)a (West 2016) (prosecutors must share "any other matter or evidence obtained during the investigation of the [alleged] offenses"); Ind. Code Ann. §§ 35-36-2, -4, -11 (West 2012); Ind. Vanderburgh Super. Ct. Crim. R. 2.04 (prosecutors "shall produce to the defense attorney the entire case file, including a list of all evidence held" but defense attorney must keep some witness identifying information confidential).

Five states grant defense attorneys authority to take pretrial witness depositions. *See* Fla. R. Crim. P. 3.220(h)(7); Ind. Code § 35-37-4-3 (2016); Ind. R. Trial Proc. 30; Iowa R. Crim. P 2.13(2); Mo. Sup. Ct. R. Crim. P. 25.12(c), 25.15; Vt. R. Crim. P. 15. Others states allow the defense depositions when a witness refuses to cooperate with a voluntary interview. *See* Ariz. R. Crim. P. 15.3(a). Influential professional organizations endorse broad disclosure requirements. *See ABA Standards for Criminal Justice: Discovery and Trial by Jury* (3d ed. 1996).

[14] *See* Michele Caianiello, *Access to Evidence Dossiers in Civil Law Systems*, chapter 26 in this volume. In civil law systems, judges generally have much more access to the dossier than do their common law counterparts. On the other hand, civil law jurisdictions probably limit access to the dossier only to the defense attorney—barring access by the defendant himself—more than do common law discovery rules. *But see* Ga. Code Ann. §§ 17-16-1 to -10 (prosecution witnesses disclosed to defense attorney but not defendant); Idaho. R. Crim. P. 16(b)(9)(A) (digital media disclosed to defense attorney but not defendant). On the limits of "adversarial" and "inquisitorial" as categorical distinctions, *see* Maximo Langer, *The Long Shadow of the Adversarial and Inquisitorial Categories*, in *Oxford Handbook of Criminal Law* (Markus D. Dubber & Tatjana Hörnle eds., 2014).

[15] Ala. R. Crim. P. 16.1–16.5; Del. Super. Ct. Crim. R. 16; D.C. Super. Ct. Crim. R. 12.1, 12.2, 16; Fed. R. Crim. P. 16; Ga. Code Ann. §§ 17-16-1 to -10 (West 2010); Iowa R. Crim. P. 2.14; Kan. Stat. Ann. §§ 22–3212, 22–3218 to –3220 (West 2015); Ky. R. Crim. P. 7.24; La. Code Crim. Proc. Ann. art. 716–729.6 (West 2016); N.Y. Crim. Proc. Law §§ 240.60–.90, 250.10–.40 (McKinney 2016); R.I. Super. R. Crim. P. 12, 16; S.C. R. Crim. P. 5; S.D. Codified Laws §§ 23a-9-1, 23a-10-1, 23a-13-1 (2016); Tenn. R. Crim. P. 12.1–12.3, 16; Utah R. Crim. P. 15, 16; Va. Sup. Ct. R. 3A:11; Wyo. R. Crim. P. 12.1–12.3, 16. *See generally* Wayne R. LaFave, et al., 5 *Criminal Procedure* § 20.2(b) nn.10, 17, 33–36 (4th ed. 2016).

account of their anticipated testimony.[16] Rules in another seven states are only modestly broader than this narrow model, requiring only that the government give advance notice of trial witnesses' identities.[17]

Rules in the remaining state justice systems—nearly half—fall somewhere between these extremes. The details vary, but in these jurisdictions prosecutors typically must disclose their witnesses' prior statements and criminal records as well as their identity.[18] In sum, then, disclosure requirements for the prosecution in U.S. jurisdictions vary widely but are generally more limited than the long-standing obligations of prosecutors in England, Wales, and elsewhere.

2. Government Evidence That Does Not Favor the Prosecution's Case

There is much more similarity across common law jurisdictions in the development and scope of rules regarding prosecutor's unused evidence—that is, material that prosecutors do not plan to use at trial, either because it favors the defense or because its value is marginal or uncertain. Adhering to the long-standing adversarial norm that neither party has a duty to assist the other, it was not until well into the twentieth century that English, American, and other common law justice systems required the prosecution to turn over evidence in its possession that favored the defense. Over the last several decades, however, all have to some degree required the prosecution to share material that undermines its case, either because it is exculpatory in nature or because it impeaches the credibility of government evidentiary sources.

English common law took the first step in this direction. In 1946, *R v. Bryant and Dickson* recognized, as a fundamental common law right, that the prosecution must make

[16] *See, e.g.*, Fed. R. Crim. P. 16 (disclosure duties); Fed. R. Crim. P. 26.2 (government required to disclose prior statements of its witnesses only after they testify on direct examination at trial); Jencks Act, 18 U.S.C. § 3500 (2016) (same). Some federal courts, however, require pretrial disclosure of witnesses as a matter of local court rules, a standing court order, or court orders in specific cases. *See* Daniel S. McConkie, *Structuring Pre-plea Discovery*, 107 J. Crim. L. & Criminology 1 (2017) (collecting and discussing such local rules and orders). Some state courts may do the same.

[17] Ark. R. Crim. P. 17.1–19.7; Ark. Code Ann. § 16-89-116 (West 2016); Conn. Prac. Book §§ 40–1 to 40–43 (2017); Mass. R. Crim. P. 14; Neb. Rev. Stat. §§ 29–1912 to 29–1927 (2016); Nev. Rev. Stat. §§ 171.1965, 174.233 to 174.235 (2015); Pa. R. Crim. P. 567–573 (witness names disclosed only at discretion of court upon showing by defense); W.Va. R. Crim. P. 12.1, 12.2, 16.

[18] Ariz. R. Crim. P. 15.1–15.9; Cal. Penal Code §§ 1054.1–1054.9 (2016); Colo. R. Crim. P. 16; Haw. R. Penal P. 12.1, 16; Idaho R. Crim. P. 12.1 & 16; Ill. Sup. Ct. R. 412–415; 725 Ill. Comp. Stat. Ann. 5/114-13 (2012); Me. R. Crim. P. 16; Md. R. Crim. P. 4-262, 4-263; Mich. Ct. R. 6.201; Mich. Comp. Laws Ann. §§ 767.40a, 767.94a, 768.20, 768.21, 768.21b, 768.27a (West 2016); Miss. URCCC 9.04–.07; Mo. R. Crim. P. 25; Mont. Code Ann. §§ 46-15-322 to 46-15-329 (West 2015); N.H. R. Super. Ct. 98, 99-a; N.M. Dist. Ct. R. Crim. P. 5–501, 5-502; N.D. R. Crim. P. 12.1, 12.2, 16; Ohio R. Crim. P. 12.1 & 16; Okla. Stat. Ann. tit. 22, § 22–2002 (West 2016); Or. Rev. Stat. §§ 135.815–135.845 (2015); Tex. Code Crim. Proc. Ann. art. 39.14, 39.15 (West 2015); Vt. R. Crim. P. 12.1, 16; Wash. Super. Ct. Crim. R. 4.7; Wis. Stat. Ann. § 971.23 (West 2016).

available to the defendant any witness who can give relevant evidence that might be useful to the defendant. But prosecutors were not required to turn over the *statements*, as well as the identities, of such witnesses until two decades later.[19] At nearly the same time, the U.S. Supreme Court, in *Brady v. Maryland*, held that constitutional due process required state and federal prosecutors to turn over to the defense any exculpatory evidence in its possession. The Court subsequently made clear that this duty applied to information that undermined government witnesses' credibility as well.[20] These developments were part of a broader international trend. Similar disclosure duties were subsequently recognized elsewhere, including in Canada and under the European Convention on Human Rights.[21] Over time, courts and legislatures clarified the government's disclosure duties. Inevitably, the details vary among jurisdictions.

U.S. law. In the United States, subsequent Supreme Court decisions expanded the *Brady* disclosure obligation to include information in the possession of police and other law enforcement agencies, not simply that in prosecutors' files; prosecutors must seek out *all* such evidence possessed by government officials.[22] On the other hand, courts effectively confined the government's constitutional obligation to evidence that meets a standard of "materiality." This has proven problematic. For one, the assessment is made not by judges but by prosecutors, who must carry out the cognitively challenging task of assessing evidentiary value from the defense's point of view, yet without full knowledge of defense evidence and strategy. More awkwardly, "materiality" is defined by standards designed for post-conviction review: evidence is material if its disclosure would be "sufficient to undermine confidence in" a conviction that was achieved in a trial from which it was withheld.[23]

As a matter of constitutional law, U.S. prosecutors are not required to notify either the judge or the defense that it has decided to withhold evidence on the basis that it is not sufficiently material. Some state statutes, however, remove any "materiality" qualification. And like the English standard noted below, some also require notice when information is withheld on grounds that it is privileged or otherwise not discoverable; courts are then authorized to determine whether that nondisclosure is justified.[24] Additionally, statutes in some jurisdictions expand and clarify disclosures in other ways. Some states also require prosecutors to disclose background information about their

[19] R v. Bryant and Dickson [1946] 31 Cr. App. R. 146; Dallison v. Caffrey [1965] 1 Q.B. 348.

[20] Brady v. Maryland, 373 U.S. 83 (1963) (due process requires prosecution disclosure of "evidence favorable to an accused...where the evidence is material either to guilt or to punishment"); Giglio v. United States, 405 U.S. 150, 154 (1972) (*Brady* disclosure applies evidence that tends to impeach the credibility of government witnesses).

[21] *See, e.g.*, R v. Stinchcombe [1991] 3 S.C.R. 326 (Can.); R v. McNeil [2009] 1 S.C.R. 66 (Can.); Jespers v. Belgium App. No. 8403/78, 5 Eur. H.R. Rep. 305, ¶58 (1983) ("equality of arms" requires government to disclose any material that may affect the credibility of a prosecution witness or otherwise assist the defense); Directive 2012/13/EU (right to information in criminal proceedings).

[22] Kyles v. Whitley, 514 U.S. 419, 437–38 (1995) (prosecution duty to find and disclose *Brady/Giglio* material held by police).

[23] United States v. Bagley, 473 U.S. 667, 682 (1985).

[24] *See, e.g.*, Mich. Ct. R. 6.201; Mass. R. Crim. P. 14(a).

witnesses, such as criminal histories, that may be relevant to their credibility. A smaller number demand advance notice about details related to especially worrisome sources such as jailhouse informants.[25]

With regard to prosecutors' unused evidence that is not governed by *Brady* because it is clearly favorable to the defense, disclosure obligations are weaker and more varied.[26] The U.S. Constitution requires only that government officials not destroy such evidence in bad faith, but it imposes no affirmative duty to preserve or disclose evidence of uncertain value (such as untested blood samples recovered from a crime scene). But statutory obligations reach further. Even under the minimalist federal disclosure rules, prosecutors must share documents, objects, and forensic analysis results (but not the identity of persons) that are "material to preparing the defense."[27] More expansive duties apply in several states with robust disclosure statutes. In these jurisdictions, prosecutors must turn over relevant information they do not plan to use at trial, such as the identities of all "persons with knowledge" about the case.[28] Some states also require prosecutors to provide details about law enforcement officials who were involved in gathering evidence, which may be useful in challenging the lawfulness of searches and thus the admissibility of seized evidence.[29]

English law. English disclosure law was transformed in the 1990s, initially with a focus on unused evidence in the government's possession. Beginning with *R v. Ward* in 1993, English courts expanded and clarified the prosecution's disclosure duties under the common law. *Ward* required prosecutors to make available to the defense "all relevant evidence of help to the accused," save for items withheld on public interest grounds with judicial approval.[30] Because of the settled obligation of the prosecution to disclose incriminating evidence, the central concern was evidence on which the government would not rely at trial but that might be useful for the defense. English courts defined such evidence broadly to include anything that is "possibly relevant to an issue in the case," "possibly raise[s] a new issue," or "hold[s] out a real . . . prospect of providing a lead on evidence" relevant to an issue.[31]

This common law scheme was soon superseded by the 1996 Criminal Procedure and Investigation Act (CPIA), which codified broad disclosure duties for the defense and for

[25] Fla. R. Crim. P. 3.220(b)(1)(M)(i)–(v) (requiring disclosure of, inter alia, "the informant witness's prior history of cooperation, in return for any benefit, as known to the prosecutor"); Neb. Rev. Stat. § 29-1912(1)(h)–(k) (2016) (criminal history, law enforcement agreements, and prior prosecution testimony of "jailhouse witness").

[26] Arizona v. Youngblood, 488 U.S. 51 (1988).

[27] Fed. R. Crim. P. 16(a)(1)(E)–(F).

[28] Alaska R. Crim. P. 16(b); Fla. R. Crim. P. 3.220(b); N.J. Ct. R. 3:13-3(c).

[29] *See, e.g.*, Alaska R. Crim. P. 16(b)(6); Fla. R. Crim. P. 3.220(b)(1)(I); Mich. Ct. R. 6.201(B).

[30] R v. Ward [1993] 96 Cr. App. R. 1, [1993] 1 W.L.R. 619; *see also* R v. Davis, Johnson and Rowe [1993] 97 Cr. App. R. 110, [1993] 1 W.L.R. 613 (permitting some prosecution nondisclosures without notifying defense); R v. Brown [1995] 1 Cr. App. R. 191, [1994] 1 W.L.R. 1599, 1606 (adopting a broad definition—developed by Jowitt, J.—on relevance for prosecution disclosure); R v. Keane [1994] 2 All E.R. 478 (whether evidence is "material" turns on "sensible appraisal" of prosecutors).

[31] *Brown*, 1 Cr. App. R. at 199.

the prosecution regarding unused prosecution evidence.[32] In the wake of amendments to the CPIA by the Criminal Justice Act 2003, both sides have extensive though distinct disclosure obligations, and courts are charged with a greater supervisory role. The CPIA definition of relevant evidence that the prosecution must share is narrowed somewhat compared to the earlier common law definition; disclosure is now required for all material that "might reasonably be considered capable of undermining the case... against the accused or of assisting the case for the accused."[33] This narrower definition still encompasses more potential evidence than the U.S. constitutional standard, which applies to "exculpatory" and witness-impeachment evidence but not to relevant evidence that is only "potentially useful" to the defense.[34] Except in rare circumstances, the prosecution should alert the defense to the fact that it has sought judicial approval to withhold otherwise disclosable evidence on public interest grounds. Subsequent rules and guidelines direct police, who gather most evidence, to create detailed schedules documenting disclosed and undisclosed materials, which they pass on to the prosecution. Additionally, police along with prosecutors must ensure evidence and records are retained beyond the disposition of the case.[35] More recently, a judicial protocol directs courts to take a more active role in managing discovery. Judges must approve any prosecution nondisclosures on specific public interest grounds, and should take charge of resolving discovery disputes, rather than leaving those to prosecutors alone or the parties jointly.[36]

3. Defense Disclosure Obligations

Pretrial disclosure duties on the defense are now common in adversarial justice systems. Well into the mid-twentieth century, it was often argued that the privilege against self-incrimination barred any departure from the common law tradition of requiring no pretrial disclosure from the defense. But courts gradually reconceptualized the privilege

[32] Criminal Procedure and Investigation Act 1996. Prosecution obligations in the CPIA were somewhat narrowed from the post-*Ward* common law requirements. *See* Mike Redmayne, *Process Gains and Process Values: The Criminal Procedure and Investigations Act 1996*, 60 Mod. L. Rev. 79, 80, 81–82 (1997).

[33] *Judicial Protocol on Disclosure of Unused Material in Criminal Cases* 5, para. 4 (2013) (quoting CPIA 1996 ss 3 & 7A as amended). *See also* Crown Prosecution Service, *Disclosure Manual* s 10.1 (disclosure duty applies to "any material which may have a bearing on admissibility of any prosecution evidence").

[34] Illinois v. Fisher, 540 U.S. 544, 548 (2004) (only constitutional limit on government handling of non-exculpatory, potentially useful evidence is that it cannot be destroyed in "bad faith").

[35] Ministry of Justice, *CPIA 1996 (section 23(1)) Code of Practice* (2015); Judiciary of England and Wales, *Judicial Protocol on the Disclosure of Unused Material in Criminal Cases* (2013); Attorney General's Office, *Attorney General's Guidelines on Disclosure* (Dec. 2013); CPS, *Disclosure Manual*, ss 5.24–5.28.

[36] *Judicial Protocol*, *supra* note 35, at 17, para. 56; Hannah Quirk, *The Significance of Culture in Criminal Procedure Reform: Why the Revised Disclosure Scheme Cannot Work*, 10 Int'l J. Evid. & Proof 42, 53 (2006) (describing grounds for prosecution nondisclosure).

from one that entitled the defendant not to relinquish incriminating documents or assist the prosecution's preparation in any way to a narrower privilege that merely bars the state from compelling an accused to testify against himself.[37]

U.S. jurisdictions took the first steps on this front: state laws required defendants to give advance notice of alibi defenses as early as the 1920s.[38] All U.S. jurisdictions now require defendants to provide advance notice of certain defenses—alibi, insanity, and often self-defense. And as with the prosecution, the defense must provide some information before trial about any expert witnesses or scientific analysis they will use at trial.[39] Comparable duties were subsequently adopted in most common law jurisdictions. England and Wales imposed similar defense disclosure duties for alibis and expert witnesses in 1967, as did Canada later.[40]

Everywhere these defense disclosure duties are part of "reciprocal" disclosure schemes in which prosecutors are obliged to make comparable disclosures. As a matter of U.S. constitutional law, defense disclosure obligations must be accompanied by equivalent burdens on the prosecution.[41] In many states, defendants now must disclose documents or tangible evidence they intend to use at trial, as well as the identities of their witnesses. A similar reciprocity norm characterizes disclosure laws in England and Wales, although just as prosecution disclosure is broader there than in most U.S. jurisdictions, defense disclosure requirements have expanded in certain respects beyond those in any U.S. justice system. In addition to providing the identities of trial witnesses and of experts they consulted before trial,[42] under the Criminal Justice Act 2003 English defendants must "set[] out the nature of the accused's defence," "indicat[e] the matters of fact on which he takes issue with the prosecution" and explain his reasons for disagreement for each, and indicate "any point of law" and legal authority on which he will rely.[43] For both parties in English and U.S. courts, disclosure duties continue up to the time of trial.[44]

[37] *See* Hannah Quirk, *The Rise and Fall of the Right to Silence* (2017); William J. Stuntz, *Self-Incrimination and Excuse*, 88 Colum. L. Rev. 1227 (1988).

[38] Michigan first had a requirement for notice of alibi and insanity defenses in 1927 Mich. Pub. Acts No. 175, ch.8, § 20, (effective Sept. 5, 1927), now codified at Mich. Comp. Laws §§ 768.20 & 768.20(a) (2016); *see also* Mark A. Esqueda, *Michigan Strives to Balance the Adversarial Process and Seek the Truth with Its New Reciprocal Criminal Discovery Rule*, 74 U. Det. Mercy L. Rev. 317, 329 n.80 (1997).

[39] *See, e.g.*, Fed. R. Crim. P. 16(b).

[40] Criminal Justice Act 1967 (U.K.); *see also* Crown Court (Advance Notice of Expert Evidence) Rules 1987, S.I. No. 716 (L.2) (requiring notice from both parties of experts to be called at trial); Criminal Justice Act 1987 (defense disclosures in serious fraud cases); Criminal Procedure and Investigation Act 1996 (defense duty to set out nature of its defense and reasons it takes issue with prosecution case). R v. Cleghorn [1995] 3 S.C.R. 175 (Can.) (defense requirements to disclose claim of alibi).

[41] Wardius v. Oregon, 412 U.S. 470, 475–76 (1973) ("in the absence of a strong showing of state interest to the contrary, discovery must be a two-way street"); Williams v. Florida, 399 U.S. 78, 81, 83–86, 117 n.17 (1970) (approving defense disclosure requirement that is "carefully hedged with reciprocal duties requiring state disclosure to the defendant").

[42] Criminal Justice Act 2003, pt. 5 ss 32–40.

[43] *Id.* s 33.

[44] For the United States, see Pennsylvania v. Ritchie, 480 U.S. 39, 59–60 (1987) (*Brady* obligation continues throughout proceedings); Fed. R. Crim. P. 16(c). For England and Wales, see CPIA 1996 as amended s 7A.

III. Rationales and Structure of Disclosure Schemes

1. Rationales for Broad Pretrial Disclosure

With this basic picture of common law disclosure policies in place, we now turn to explanations for the broad trends toward greater disclosure duties for the defense and for unused prosecution evidence, and to the reasons for the most notable remaining difference—the reluctance of some U.S. jurisdictions to include evidence supporting the prosecution's case in expansive disclosure schemes.

We already touched on important rationales that have caused all jurisdictions to depart from the tradition of nondisclosure by either party prior to trial. First, broad obligations for parties to share information prior to trial follows from the view that "trial by surprise" hinders more than it helps truth-finding.[45] Conversely, pretrial disclosure in general facilitates rather than impedes accurate judgments. In certain circumstances, surprise undoubtedly can facilitate accurate fact-finding at least with regard to witness testimony, as evidence rules reflect.[46] But the consensus is now that surprise hurts more often than it helps truth-finding, and even the remaining U.S. advocates for limited-disclosure regimes emphasize other concerns, such as witness safety, rather than the accuracy-enhancing advantages of surprise.

This epistemic premise gains support from a second source, the contemporary normative consensus about what constitutes *fair* criminal process. A prosecution practice of never revealing exculpatory evidence to the court or the defense has come to be widely understood as fundamentally unfair and therefore also incompatible with the minister-of-justice role. The same can be said for withholding other kinds of evidence until trial if

[45] At least when they endorse broader disclosure duties for the defense, U.S. judges were persuaded by criticisms that nondisclosure wrongly treated adjudication as a "poker game" or "sporting contest" and hindered the search for truth. *See, e.g.*, Williams v. Florida, 399 U.S. 78, 81–82, 117 n.12 (1970) (citing Brennan, *supra* note 9) ("The adversary system of trial is hardly an end in itself; it is not yet a poker game in which players enjoy an absolute right always to conceal their cards until played."); *id.* at 106 (Burger, C.J., concurring) (praising "an enlarged and truly reciprocal pretrial disclosure of evidence" as a "move away from the 'sporting contest' idea of criminal justice"); Wardius v. Oregon, 412 U.S. 470, 475 (1973):

> The state may not insist that trials be run as a "search for truth" so far as defense witnesses are concerned, while maintaining "poker game" secrecy for its own witnesses. It is fundamentally unfair to require a defendant to divulge the details of the defendant's own case while at the same time subjecting him or her to the hazard of surprise concerning refutation of the very pieces of evidence which he or she disclosed to the state.

[46] Federal Rule of Evidence 613 allows counsel to question a witness about prior statements without first alerting him to independent evidence of such a statement. The rule abolished an earlier common law requirement (long abandoned in England as well) that a witness on cross-examination first be shown his prior statement before being questioned about it. *See* The Queen's Case, 2 Br. & B. 284, 129 Eng. Rep. 976 (1820).

one accepts that surprise trial evidence tends to undermine accurate fact-finding.[47] The pejorative characterization "ambush" implies this notion of unfairness.

Finally, the shift to broad disclosure schemes won wide acceptance because of their reciprocal structure. Both English and American disclosure reforms reflect the idea that prosecution and defense disclosure obligations should be roughly symmetrical and mutual,[48] a structure made possible by reconceiving the privilege against self-incrimination to permit compulsion of most kinds of information short of the defendant's direct testimony rather than a general right not to assist the prosecution.[49] Especially in legislative policy debates, reciprocity has been responsible for justifying greater disclosure from the defense, on the view that this would "level the playing field" in light of prosecution disclosure duties, or that fairness demands greater prosecution disclosure be paired with equivalent defense obligations. Rejecting surprise as an instrument of truth-finding supports this logic. If early disclosure is presumed to improve accuracy, then surprise defense evidence wrongly increases the odds of a "false negative" acquittal. That no longer seems justified as a means for the individual to resist the state.[50]

2. Contrasting Justifications for Prosecution Disclosure Policies

Given the consensus on these points, what explains the biggest difference among common law disclosure regimes—the sharp limits on pretrial disclosure of the prosecution's evidence that prevails in many U.S. jurisdictions but nearly nowhere else? Much of the explanation can be found in disparate calculations on two issues—which kind of disclosure rules maximize the efficiency of criminal process, and how best to manage the risks that could accompany early prosecution disclosure.

a. *Different Routes to Greater Efficiency*

Criminal justice systems worldwide are preoccupied with maximizing the efficiency of the process by which they resolve criminal charges. That concern informs choices about disclosure rules, although it does not lead all jurisdictions to make the same choices. An explicit rationale for English and Canadian rules obliging prosecutors to share their evidence well before trial is to make criminal process more efficient, both by facilitating

[47] *See* Corker & Parkinson, *supra* note 4, at 61–72; Sprack, *supra* note 4, at 122; Brennan, *supra* note 9, at 283, 291.

[48] *See* Quirk, *supra* note 36, at 44 (criticizing the reciprocal premise of CPIA).

[49] U.S. Supreme Court doctrine defines the privilege solely as a protection against "testimonial" statements, not disclosure of physical evidence or trial witnesses. *See* Taylor v. Illinois, 484 U.S. 400 (1988); United States v. Nobles, 422 U.S. 225 (1975); Williams v. Florida, 399 U.S. 78 (1970); Schmerber v. California, 384 U.S. 757 (1966). Comparable understandings prevail in other common law jurisdictions. For an excellent comparative overview, see Quirk, *supra* note 37.

[50] Mike Redmayne, *Disclosure and Its Discontents*, 2004 Crim. L. Rev. 441, 450–51; Jenny McEwan, *Truth, Efficiency, and Cooperation in Modern Criminal Justice*, 66 Current Legal Probs. 203, 209 (2013).

guilty pleas and by clarifying disputed issues for trial. (The same goal motivates England's detailed disclosure requirements for the defense.) Yet paradoxically, the aim to maximize efficiency is part of the U.S. justification for *limited* disclosure duties. What accounts for this difference? The explanation lies in different assumptions about how disclosure rules best contribute to speedier dispositions, and about how to effectively manage risks entailed in broad prosecution disclosure before trial. Both of these lead to a sharp contrast in how disclosure schemes allocate power between parties and judges.

Broad English disclosure policies and narrow American ones start from wholly different foundational inferences about the relationship between disclosure rules and procedural efficiency. U.S. policymakers who opt for limited disclosure assume that early, broad disclosure creates unnecessary burdens that sometimes impede the negotiated dispositions. The assumption is that parties often can reach negotiated resolutions without full disclosure, so requiring early disclosure imposes costs without necessarily leading to more or quicker plea bargains.[51] In contrast, as regards English and Canadian disclosure laws, while recognizing that broad disclosure adds to litigants' workloads, courts and policymakers assume that gains from this practice outweigh the costs because pretrial information-sharing leads to more and quicker plea bargains. For cases that go to trial, disclosure speeds the process by clarifying issues, improving party preparation, and reducing surprise.[52] On this view, disclosure facilitates accuracy as well as efficiency.[53]

b. *Risks of Prosecution Disclosure*

In addition to this difference, restrictive U.S. disclosure policies reflect a greater concern among courts and policymakers about the risks of evidence tampering or witness intimidation that could increase with advance disclosure to criminal defendants. Whether these risks are in fact greater in U.S. jurisdictions than in England, Canada, and elsewhere is impossible to say. The United States has much higher homicide and gun-ownership rates than other developed nations. But that does not necessarily mean that U.S. defendants intimidate witnesses more frequently than their English or Canadian counterparts. And long-standing broad disclosure schemes in large states such as Florida and New Jersey suggest that rule-makers in those jurisdictions find their disclosure policies to work well even in the context of U.S. crime rates. Nonetheless, in federal courts and other U.S. jurisdictions, these concerns continue to be invoked as justifications for not requiring prosecutors to disclose their evidence. And they are convincing enough to help justify patently inefficient rules such as the prosecution's entitlement to

[51] United States v. Ruiz, 536 U.S. 622, 629–31 (2002); *cf.* United States v. Mezzanatto, 513 U.S. 196, 208 (1995) ("precluding waiver can only stifle the market for plea bargains").

[52] *See* R v. Stinchcombe [1991] 3 S.C.R. 326 ¶13 ("comprehensive rules for disclosure... would add to the work-load of some Crown counsel but this would be offset by the time saved" at trial and "by reason of the increase in guilty pleas [or] withdrawal of charges").

[53] Jenny McEwan, *From Adversarialism to Managerialism: Criminal Justice in Transition*, 31 Legal Stud. 519, 532 (2011).

withhold prior statements for its witnesses until they testify at trial, at which point judges must pause the trial to permit defense review of such statements.[54]

c. *Party versus Judicial Control*

The disparate U.S. and English strategies for achieving procedural efficiency and managing risks from prosecution disclosures lead to another distinction in the structure of disclosure regimes. The narrow-disclosure model in the United States puts most of the power over disclosure decisions in the hands of the parties—primarily the *prosecutor*—while the model in England and elsewhere shifts a good bit of that power to the *judge*.

All justice systems recognize the need to keep confidential some sensitive law enforcement information, at least until trial. In addition to specific concerns about witness intimidation or evidence tampering,[55] disclosure can also compromise the viability of government informants, undercover agents, and secret surveillance tactics such as wiretaps. Narrow U.S. disclosure schemes respond to this need for nondisclosure by simply not requiring prosecutors to disclose large categories of information, such as witness identities. That scheme gives prosecutors the power to decide whether to disclose more than the rules require. Many prosecutors often disclose more than the rules demand, but they do so as a matter of discretion and on their own terms.[56] This makes the process more efficient, the theory goes, because it enables prosecutors to save the time and expense of disclosure when the parties can reach a plea agreement without it, and they can avoid the hurdle of judging reviewing decisions to withhold evidence. Proponents of this system also insist that it best protects against risks such as witness intimidation, because prosecutors are in the best position to assess those risks and law enforcement's need for confidentiality. Prosecutors need not provide notice that they have concluded certain material is not exculpatory, or not "material to preparing the defense," or withheld to protect a confidential informant. In most circumstances, defendants have no

[54] Fed. R. Crim. P. 26.2; 18 U.S.C. § 3500 (Jencks Act) (2016). *See also* United States v. Jacobs, 650 F. Supp. 2d 160 (D. Conn. 2009) (when prior statements constitute *Brady* material, district court may require prosecution disclosure before trial rather than during trial in accord with Jencks Act); United States v. Cerna, 633 F. Supp. 2d 1053 (N.D. Cal. 2009) (similar). Some federal trial judges resist this inefficiency by mandating earlier disclosure by means of local rules or standing orders. *See* McConkie, *supra* note 16.

[55] *See* McEwan, *supra* note 53, at 533 (noting "the risks attached to early identification of defence witnesses https://slate.com/culture/2018/09/healthy-chocolate-cake-recipe-no-butter.html ... [who] could be discouraged from cooperating"). It should be noted that the English system is much more concerned with improper influence on witnesses by police and prosecutors than U.S. systems, where the presumption is strong that those officials act properly and risks of improper pressure on witnesses comes overwhelmingly from the defense. Whatever else accounts for this distinction, it is surely linked in part to the stronger English prohibition on prosecutors interviewing and "preparing" witnesses prior to trial. *See* Paul Roberts, *Prosecutors Interviewing Witnesses: A Question of Integrity*, in *The Integrity of Criminal Justice* 163 (Jill Hunter, Paul Roberts et al. eds., 2016).

[56] One criticism of this approach is that prosecutors grant disclosure when it matters least—when the government's evidence is strong, as a means of convincing defendants to plead guilty. But they can withhold their case when it is weakest and thus most in need of adversarial testing. *See* John G. Douglass, *Balancing Hearsay and Criminal Discovery*, 68 Fordham L. Rev. 2097, 2140–41 (2000).

mechanism by which to challenge those decisions, and judges have no authority to review and reverse them.

By contrast, English reforms in recent decades address the same concerns through a different model: they give judges more of this authority over disclosure. (Again, the same is broadly true in other Commonwealth jurisdictions and some U.S. state courts.)[57] For example, judges have the final word over what English law calls "public interest" exceptions to disclosure obligations.[58] (American law more commonly describes these as privileges, or simply as disclosure rule exceptions.) Typically, either prosecutors must get judicial approval to withhold evidence, or they must give notice of nondisclosures, which are then subject to judicial review (perhaps in ex parte hearings). In these ways, judges have much greater authority over what evidence will not be disclosed, and prosecutors have correspondingly less. Proponents of this sort of disclosure regime argue that judges are as capable as prosecutors of assessing risks to witnesses or law enforcement operations. They rightly note that this model ensures that decisions about such risks are not unduly affected by the prosecutor's role as advocate for law enforcement, which could tempt her to withhold advance disclosure of evidence for partisan advantage rather than an objective assessment of the risks that justify nondisclosure.

Related reforms have given English judges greater authority in other aspects of pretrial process as well. Beyond their authority to supervise disclosure, judges have taken on more managerial duties with the explicit aim of improving the efficiency of the adjudication process.[59] This shift has met with notable criticism from English scholars, who express concern that managerialism undercuts the adversarial nature of criminal process and diminishes party control as a safeguard against state power without putting in place adequate alternatives.[60] Critics worry that English judges put a premium on "case management," cost-effectiveness, and speedy dispositions in ways that excessively infringe on adversarial values such as lawyers' priority for clients' interests. Managerial judging nudges criminal procedure from its adversarial roots toward a cooperative, "essentially

[57] *See, e.g.*, Tex. Code Crim. Proc. Ann. art. 39.14(c) (West 2015); Utah R. Crim. P. 16(b)(9)(A)(3), 16(b)(9)(B) (defense can seek review of prosecution's redactions of digital media evidence); Cal. Penal Code § 1054.7 (2016). Federal rules have only modest provisions of this sort. *See* 18 U.S.C. § 3500(c) (2016) (court determines whether prior statements can be withheld on grounds they do "not relate to the subject matter of the testimony of the witness"). On Canadian law, see Murray D. Segal, *Disclosure and Production in Criminal Cases* § 1.5 (2016) ("All relevant information in the possession of the Crown must be disclosed to the defence subject to a reviewable discretion."); R v. Stinchcombe [1991] 3 S.C.R. 326 ¶ 21 ("discretion of Crown counsel is . . . reviewable by the trial judge").

[58] CPIA 1996 ss 14–17, 21; R v. Ward (1993) 96 Cr. App. R. 1, 25; R v. Davis, Johnson and Rowe [1993] 97 Cr. App. R. 110, 112; *see also* Rowe and Davis v. United Kingdom, App. No. 28901/95, Eur. Ct. H.R. [GC], Feb. 16, 2000, ¶¶ 63–65 ("procedure, whereby the prosecution itself attempts to assess the importance of concealed information to the defence and weighs this against the public interest in keeping the information secret, cannot comply with . . . Article 6(1)").

[59] McEwan, *supra* note 53; McEwan, *supra* note 50. The seminar article on managerialism is Judith Resnik, *Managerial Judging*, 96 Harv. L. Rev. 374 (1982).

[60] McEwan, *supra* note 53, at 536 & 544–45. By contrast, civil law systems are fairly characterized as relying on strong judicial managerialism, but checks against incompetence or abuse of power come in the form of multistage, hierarchical review that (in Damaška's description) "audits" the judgment. *See id.* at 520.

bureaucratic" model that lacks a coherent vision about how to balance procedural interests, such as accuracy and fairness, that compete with the goal of efficiency.[61]

Managerial judging has made inroads in U.S. courts as well, although in most jurisdictions it includes little authority over disclosure. But judges set disclosure timetables, facilitate pretrial conferences between parties, and sometimes offer input on plea negotiations.[62] American scholars overall are more positive about managerial judging than their English counterparts.[63] No doubt this is in good part because judges tend to favor more prosecution disclosure and because they lack authority to insist on the detailed defense disclosures about case theory that English law requires.

Similarities in judicial managerialism notwithstanding, the greater party (or prosecutorial) control over disclosure in much of the United States, compared to greater judicial authority in England and elsewhere, is consistent with choices in how to structure other parts of the pretrial process as well.[64] This is especially apparent in the rules and practices that regulate plea bargaining. Sentencing discounts for guilty pleas are explicitly regulated by sentencing guidelines in England and Wales;[65] U.S. jurisdictions have no equivalent constraints on the disparities between sentences after trial versus a guilty plea. This is partly because U.S. constitutional law explicitly endorses prosecutors' unchecked discretion over charging decisions that can create those sentencing disparities.[66] It is also because of the prevalence of mandatory-sentence laws in U.S. jurisdictions, enabling prosecutors to dictate sentencing options by their charging decisions. Both of those features confirm the strong U.S. preference for greater prosecutorial authority and less judicial authority—even for sentencing, a traditionally core judicial function—compared to the justice system in England and Wales. That difference is also apparent in the absence of formal administrative regulation of U.S. prosecutors, compared to the *Code for Crown Prosecutors* in England (which provides English judges some basis for reviewing certain charging decisions).[67] U.S. scholars are mostly critical of the scope

[61] McEwan, *supra* note 53, at 545.

[62] *See* Nancy J. King & Ronald F. Wright, *The Invisible Revolution in Plea Bargaining: Managerial Judging and Judicial Participation in Negotiations*, 95 Tex. L. Rev. 325 (2016) (ten-state study finding that trial judges facilitate plea agreements by requiring early-stage discussions by parties, encouraging greater and earlier disclosure, and responding to proposed plea agreements); *see also* Resnik, *supra* note 59, at 380 (describing similar managerial actions by federal judges in civil cases); Daniel S. McConkie, *The Local Rules Revolution*, 39 Cardozo L. Rev. 59 (2017) (examining federal courts' local rule-making on pretrial discovery).

[63] King & Wright, *supra* note 62.

[64] For example, the emphasis on party responsibility is implicit in disclosure laws that make disclosure obligations contingent on the opposing party's request for information. *See, e.g.*, Fed. R. Crim. P. 16(b); S.C. R. Crim. P. 5; *contrast* Mass. R. Crim. P. 14 (mandatory disclosure duties regardless of party request).

[65] Sentencing Council, *Reduction in Sentence for a Guilty Plea: Definitive Guideline* (2017) (Eng. & Wales).

[66] *See* Bordenkircher v. Hayes, 434 U.S. 357 (1978).

[67] For greater detail on this point, see Darryl K. Brown, *Free Market Criminal Justice: How Democracy and Laissez Faire Undermine the Rule of Law* 91–117 (2016). A classic account of U.S. federal prosecutors' de facto control over adjudication and sentencing is Gerard E. Lynch, *Our Administrative System of Criminal Justice*, 66 Fordham L. Rev. 2117 (1998).

of—and paucity of checks on—U.S. prosecution authority. Consequently, they are inclined to view greater judicial management as a means to moderate that power, and to bolster rather than undermine the best features of adversarial process in the pretrial stage.[68]

IV. Conclusion

Contemporary disclosure schemes in the criminal justice systems of common law countries remain incompletely theorized. Disclosure poses difficult practical trade-offs, such as the form and means of exceptions to disclosure to serve competing interests in witness safety, victim privacy interests,[69] and the efficacy of ongoing law enforcement operations. That challenge is but one example of the competing interests that disclosure laws must accommodate. The structure of disclosure schemes also reflect attempts to balance competing goals of adjudicative accuracy, fundamental fairness, and procedural efficiency. More fundamentally, while the consensus across the common law world (and in civil law jurisdictions as well) has shifted to the view that broad pretrial disclosure *on balance* serves accuracy and fairness better than the limited-disclosure rules of earlier common law eras, it remains true that broad disclosure is not a wholly unmitigated benefit to accurate adjudication. Even if their potency was exaggerated, there were kernels of truth in the traditional arguments that, in specific circumstances, pretrial disclosure of some information can work against accurate fact-finding.

Disclosure laws are also dependent on other features of the criminal justice systems of which they are a part. The case for early disclosure is stronger, for example, when most criminal cases never go to trial. The institutional structure and professional culture of prosecution agencies matters for determining how much authority prosecutors should have over decisions not to disclose. The professional culture and trustworthiness of the defense matters to the efficacy of rules that disclose sensitive information to lawyers that they must keep confidential, perhaps even from their clients.

Outside of certain U.S. jurisdictions, there is wide acceptance in principle for broad, reciprocal disclosure schemes, disagreements about particulars notwithstanding. But even when that consensus is strong among prosecutors, defense lawyers, and judges, there remains an inherent tension between obligations for parties to share information with their opponents and the professional norms and cultures that accompany adversarial

[68] *See, e.g.*, Susan R. Klein, *Enhancing the Judicial Role in Criminal Plea and Sentence Bargaining*, 84 Tex. L. Rev. 2023 (2006).

[69] *See, e.g.*, Ariz. R. Crim. P. 39(b)(8)–(11) (victim's right to refuse an interview or a deposition with defense); Tex. Code Crim. Proc. Ann. art. 39.14(c) (West 2015) (limiting disclosure based on "security and privacy interests of any victim or witness"); Fla. R. Crim. P. 3.220(l) (court can restrict discovery "to protect a witness from harassment, unnecessary inconvenience, or invasion of privacy"); N.C. Gen. Stat. Ann. § 15A-904(a4) (West 2016) (nondisclosure of victim impact statements); Utah R. Crim. P. 16(e) ("reasonable limitations" of "sensitive information" to "protect victims and witnesses from... undue invasion of privacy").

systems of justice. Those norms can undermine compliance. Prosecutors' minister-of-justice norm has not always overcome countervailing tendencies that follow from their role as partisan advocates of charges that they believe are well grounded.[70] Indeed, the demonstrated link between prosecution nondisclosures and wrongful convictions has been an impetus for disclosure reform in both the United Kingdom and the United States.[71] On the other side, some defense attorneys object in principle to assisting the prosecution, which arguably conflicts with the lawyer's duty of undivided loyalty to her client; faced with expanded disclosure obligations, widespread reluctance of English defense attorneys was clear.[72] This inevitable tension between disclosure obligations and adversarial incentives provides the strongest reason for the structure of disclosure schemes that allocate final responsibility for withholding information during the pretrial stage to judges rather than the parties.

Arguments that the dangers arising from disclosure of certain government information can be addressed effectively only by giving prosecutors unfettered discretion about what evidence to withhold are outdated. They now mostly reflect the entrenched preferences (or fears) of prosecutors, who are accustomed to facing minimal disclosure duties. Disclosure schemes in every jurisdiction provide for limits on disclosure to address such circumstances. There is now a considerable track record—across Commonwealth jurisdictions and in a fair number of U.S. state justice systems—of broad prosecutorial disclosure schemes in which exceptions are overseen by judges rather than prosecutors. There is no evidence that judges are less capable than prosecutors of managing these risks. That suggests that the best explanation why many U.S. jurisdictions continue to operate with very limited disclosure duties for prosecutors lies in their political and law-reform processes that empower entrenched preferences of local prosecutors and the inertia of tradition to overcome well-informed policymaking.

References

American Bar Association, *Standards for Criminal Justice: Discovery and Trial by Jury* (3d ed. 1996)

Darryl K. Brown, *Discovery in State Criminal Justice*, in 3 *Reforming Criminal Justice: Bridging the Gap between Scholarship and Reform* 147 (Erik Luna ed., 2017), at http://academyforjustice.org/ (U.S.)

Commonwealth DPP, *Statement on Disclosure in Prosecutions Conducted by the Commonwealth* (2017) (Australia)

[70] *See* Quirk, *supra* note 36; McEwan, *supra* note 53, at 530; R v. Pomfrett [2009] EWCA (Crim) 1471 [4] (noting "countless" appeals on prosecution failures to disclose); United States v. Olsen, 737 F.3d 625, 626 (9th Cir. 2013) (Kozinski, J., dissenting) ("There is an epidemic of *Brady* violations abroad in the land.").

[71] *See* Criminal Cases Review Comm'n, *Annual Report* 2012/13, at 5 & 15, https://www.gov.uk/government/uploads/system/uploads/attachment_data/file/246539/0482.pdf; Brandon L. Garrett, *Convicting the Innocent* 169–70, 209 (2011).

[72] Redmayne, *supra* note 50, at 445; McEwan, *supra* note 53, at 528.

David Corker & Stephen Parkinson, *Disclosure in Criminal Proceedings* (2009) (U.K.)
Brando Matteo Fiori, *Disclosure of Information in Criminal Proceedings: A Comparative Analysis of National and International Criminal Procedural Systems and Human Rights Law* (2015)
Jenny McEwan, *Truth, Efficiency, and Cooperation in Modern Criminal Justice*, 66 Current Legal Probs. 203 (2013)
Cosmas Moisidis, *Criminal Discovery: From Truth to Proof and Back Again* (2008)
Hannah Quirk, *The Rise and Fall of the Right to Silence* (2017)
Murray D. Segal, *Disclosure and Production in Criminal Cases* (2016) (Canada)

CHAPTER 26

ACCESS TO AND LIMITS ON EVIDENCE DOSSIERS IN CIVIL LAW SYSTEMS

MICHELE CAIANIELLO

I. General Framework

Due to their inquisitorial roots, Continental European systems are generally not accustomed to the concept of a phase dedicated to the exchange of information among the parties, as well as to the word "disclosure" itself. Traditionally, in civil law systems, trials are led by the court, not the parties, and therefore there are no preliminary investigations conducted separately by the defense and the prosecutor.

Pretrial inquiries are generally conducted only by the police and supervised by a judicial authority, either the investigating judge, as in the old Napoleonic structure, or the prosecutor, as is more frequent in modern times. Sometimes the system provides for both options, and the selection of the judicial authority required to conduct the investigation is made by the law on the basis of the gravity of the crime. For example, the system may entrust the prosecutor with the duty to run the investigations and supervise police work for minor crimes, while reserving to the investigating judge the burden of performing the same role for the most serious crimes (as in the French system).

This organization of the preliminary phase of criminal proceedings inevitably has consequences for the disclosure phase, which, in the civil law model, takes the form of the right of access to the investigative file. While, in its more ancient form, the preliminary inquiry was secret, and remained secret at the trial phase, in modern times the defense (as well as the victim) is entitled, after a certain point, to consult the case file, where all the information and the evidence collected by the police, the prosecutor, and the investigating judge are assembled. This right of access to the file may occur at the end of the investigation and within a reasonable time before the beginning of the trial. However, when certain decisions during the investigation are taken, the defense can be allowed to consult the investigative file even before the end of the preliminary inquiry. This usually happens, for example, when the court orders pretrial detention or the interception of the defendant's communications.[1]

On the other hand, in certain civil law systems where adversarial reforms have been introduced, the proceedings include a phase dedicated to the exchange of information between the parties. In Italy, for example, which is a civil law system with very significant adversarial features,[2] parties must disclose their strategy before trial, exchanging information about the evidence they plan to require at the trial stage. Italian scholars usually define this phase with the English term "disclosure" (or "discovery"), even if actually the activity conducted by the parties is regulated quite differently from the Anglo-American model. On the whole, however, it remains the case that in civil law systems, no matter how "adversarial" they have become in the last few decades, the right to information assumes the form of a right to access to the file, but it rarely implies a burden for the parties to communicate in advance the strategy they want to pursue in the presentation of their case at trial.

This chapter is divided into four sections. Section I deals with the general aims pursued by the law in regulating the parties' right of access to the file. Section II analyzes several national jurisdictions that are part of the Continental tradition. These are not examined in detail: They are considered in their most significant features, to give a more effective, though general, overview about how access to file works in civil law systems. The aim of the chapter, in other words, is not to describe accurately each national regulation, but rather to give the reader a general overview of how the phase of criminal proceedings concerning the right to information works in the civil law model.

Section III deals with supranational provisions. Continental systems have been strongly influenced by supranational sources, especially by the European Convention on Human Rights (ECHR) and the case law of the European Court on Human Rights (ECtHR). Moreover, in recent years, EU law—particularly the jurisprudence of the Court of Justice of the European Union (CJEU) and certain directives adopted by the EU on the right to information by defendants and by victims—has become a strong factor for change in the criminal procedures of EU Member States. This part of the essay will also discuss disclosure at the International Criminal Court (ICC), since the ICC is sometimes taken as a source of inspiration by scholars of civil law tradition. The ICC can

[1] *See* Giulio Illuminati & Michele Caianiello, *The Investigative Stage of the Criminal Process in Italy*, in *Suspects in Europe: Procedural Rights at the Investigative Stage of the Criminal Process in the European Union* 129, 136–37 (Ed Cape et al. eds., 2007); Michele Caianiello, *Increasing Discretionary Prosecutor's Powers: The Pivotal Role of the Italian Prosecutor in the Pretrial Investigation Phase*, in *Oxford Handbooks Online* (2016), *at* http://www.oxfordhandbooks.com/view/10.1093/oxfordhb/9780199935383.001.0001/oxfordhb-9780199935383-e-122.

[2] *See infra* Section II.4. *See* Ennio Amodio & Eugenio Selvaggi, *An Accusatorial System in a Civil Law Country: The 1988 Italian Code of Criminal Procedure*, 62 Temple L. Rev. 1211, 1211–24 (1989); Giulio Illuminati, *The Accusatorial Process from the Italian Point of View*, 35 N.C. J. Int'l L. & Com. Reg. 297–318 (2010).

be considered a mixed sui generis procedural system, combining elements of common and civil law;[3] therefore, a brief reference to it may be useful to understand how national systems in civil law could evolve on this subject. Finally, Section IV will try to draw some conclusions about how civil law systems have changed in the recent years, what their common features and shortcomings are, and how they could be improved.

With regard to the methodology adopted, this chapter addresses the following four research questions: (1) Who is entitled to the right of access to file? (2) How does access take place? (3) When does access to file take place? (4) What remedies are available when access is illegally denied?

II. Access to the Dossier in Civil Law Countries

1. Introductory Remarks

Most Continental European systems regulate the defense's access to the file differently based on the phase of criminal proceedings. Three critical phases can be outlined here. First, when a measure restricting personal freedom is issued (usually by a judge), the defendant is entitled to consult the investigative file to prepare her defense and challenge her pretrial detention. The second phase concerns the information given before interviewing the defendant during the investigation. These two crucial phases are regulated similarly in most civil law countries because of the common legal framework provided by the European Convention on Human Rights, which all Continental European systems are bound to. However, differences remain in the details of implementation. In particular, the right to consult the file in the above-mentioned phases has to be balanced against the need to protect the effectiveness of the investigation. A premature and excessively broad disclosure might endanger ongoing investigations. This is why, in various ways, national criminal procedure codes permit restrictions of the right to access to the file when this is necessary to protect an ongoing investigation.

The third phase of criminal proceeding during which access to the file is permitted is at the end of the investigation and during the early phases of the trial itself. Here, the right of access must be as broad as possible, since the need to protect ongoing investigations is no longer present.

In none of the Continental systems—with the exception of Italy—does the law regulate disclosure by the defense, usually due to the very limited possibilities given to attorneys to conduct independent investigation.

[3] Megan Fairlie, *The Marriage of Common and Continental Law at the ICTY and Its Progeny, Due Process Deficit*, 4 Int'l Crim. L. Rev. 243, 300–16 (2004).

2. France

a. *Introductory Remarks*

The French system is a traditional civil law system, strongly influenced by the inquisitorial tradition.[4] Currently, though, it is a mixed system, with both inquisitorial and a few accusatorial influences.[5] As in the Continental tradition, law enforcement agencies are obliged to investigate both incriminatory and exculpatory evidence (*à charge et à décharge*).[6] The role of the defense is primarily to challenge the case presented at trial at the end of the investigation phase, though of course at trial the defendant can introduce evidence to prove his or her case.

The rules concerning disclosure are influenced by the way criminal proceedings are shaped. The structure of the proceedings follows the traditional well-known tripartition between *crimes*, the gravest form of criminal offense provided by the system; *délits* (felonies, though less grave than *crimes*); and *contraventions* (misdemeanors). This tripartition gives rise to different forms of the pretrial phase in criminal proceedings.[7] For crimes, the prosecutor is obliged to require the *instruction préparatoire* (the preparatory inquiry), the most formal pretrial phase of French criminal proceedings. Though introduced by a prosecutor's request, the *instruction* is led by an investigating judge (*juge d'instruction*), who takes all relevant decisions. When the offense constitutes a *délit*, the prosecutor is not obliged to involve the investigating judge and can lead the investigation by herself, with the aid of the police. The prosecutor may also opt for a simplified form of investigation, the preliminary inquiry (*enquête preliminaire*), when the case is not complicated.[8] Finally, for less serious crimes (*contraventions*), the pretrial phase always takes the form of a preliminary inquiry, led by police under supervision of the prosecutor.

While the basics of all pretrial investigations are similar (the investigating authority is always obliged to look for both incriminating and exonerating evidence and evidence is assembled in a file that can be used at trial), rules governing the access to the file differ.

[4] *See* Bernard Bouloc, *Procédure pénale* § 65 (24th ed. 2014); Valérie Dervieux, *The French System*, in *European Criminal Procedures* 218 (Mireille Delmas-Marty & J.R. Spencer eds., 2005).

[5] Bouloc, *supra* note 4, at 88; Jean Larguier & Philippe Conte, *Procédure pénale* 480 (24th ed. 2016).

[6] The obligation to investigate both against and in favor of the defense is provided for in Code pénal [C. pén.] [Criminal Code] art. 81 para. 1 for the investigating judge. For the prosecutor, such duty was prescribed expressly in 2016, with an amendment to art. 39–3, para. 3 of the Loi 2016–731 du 3 juin 2016 renforçant la lutte contre le crime organisé, le terrorisme et leur financement, et améliorant l'efficacité et les garanties de la procédure pénale [Law 2016–731 of June 3, 2016 strengthening the fight against organized crime, terrorism and their financing, and improving the efficiency and guarantees of criminal procedure], Journal Officiel de la Republique Française [J.O.] [Official Gazette of France], June 4, 2016.

[7] *Crimes* are adjudicated at trial before the Court of Assizes, a mixed panel of judges and jurors whose creation dates back to the Napoleon 1808 *Code d'instruction criminelle*; *délits* are adjudicated by the *Tribunals correctionelles* (Tribunals of Corrections), ordinarily composed of a panel of three professional judges (though in certain circumstances, since a 2011 reform, lay judges are added to the panel); *Contraventions* are under the jurisdiction either of the *Tribunal de police* (Police Tribunal), constituted by single judges, or of the *Jurisdiction de proximité* (Proximity Jurisdiction), created since 2002 and constituted by retired justices or scholars recruited for a limited period of time. See Bouloc, *supra* note 4, at 558–69.

[8] Bouloc, *supra* note 4, at 506–07; Larguier & Conte, *supra* note 5, at 4615.

During the preparatory inquiry (*instruction preliminaire*), provisions concerning access to the file are more articulated and more sensitive to the rights of the defense; by contrast, fewer safeguards are provided for in a preliminary inquiry (*enquête preliminaire*).[9] Yet the most traditional form of pretrial investigation, the *instruction preliminaire*, takes place in only about five percent of cases.[10] In all other cases, the investigation occurs in a preliminary inquiry. Although some scholars comment that the limited percentage of cases in which the *instruction* operates simply reflects the percentage of cases in which serious felonies are committed, with respect of less serious offenses (*délits* and *contraventions*), this has significant consequences for access to the file. It means that the provisions most articulated and sensitive to the rights of the defense apply in only a very limited number of cases, while for all the others, access to the file is consistently more restricted.

In recent years, provisions concerning access to the file were reformed under the influence of supranational sources, especially decisions of the ECtHR and the directives adopted by the EU to safeguard the defendant's rights in criminal proceedings.[11] While previously, access to information for the defendant could be considered rather limited, the general framework has significantly changed, even if the original inquisitorial footprint remains easily visible, especially during the investigation. The crucial phase in which the right of access to the file needs to be considered is the pretrial phase, because most relevant evidence is collected at that stage (and can, in the absence of a general rule against hearsay, be produced at trial).

b. *Access to the File in Cases of Provisional Arrest* (Garde à Vue)

The *garde à vue* (literally "guard on sight") constitutes a precautionary restriction of the defendant's personal freedom, thanks to which a person suspected of being involved in a crime can be kept at the police or the prosecutor's disposal for a certain period of time (in general, twenty-four hours, which can be extended for a further twenty-four hours by the prosecutor).[12] When such a restriction is imposed,[13] the defendant is entitled to a limited amount of information (Art. 63-1 CPP). The defendant must be informed immediately about his or her placement under *garde à vue*, the nature of the offense the police and prosecutor are investigating, the legal provisions concerning the duration of the restriction (including its extension), and the specific offense of which he or she is suspected. The defendant is entitled to have counsel who, like the defendant, can ask to consult the minutes of the *garde à vue* decision, the medical certificates, and the statements made by the defendant. However, the right of access does not include the right to make copies of

[9] More precisely, the preliminary inquiry is held in any case. Differences come in later, when the prosecutor needs to decide how to prosecute. While for *contraventions* the prosecutor can go directly to trial, for crimes the prosecutor is generally obliged to trigger the instruction. For the *délits*, the prosecutor has discretion to proceed through *instruction* or go directly to trial.

[10] Larguier & Conte, *supra* note 5, at 6079. Most recent data show that *instruction* is selected in merely three percent of cases. However, such a percentage is sufficient to cover the totality of the *crimes*, and the *délits* whose investigation seems complex. For further details, see *Les chiffres clés de la justice 2016*, at http://www.justice.gouv.fr/art_pix/stat_CC%202016.pdf.

[11] *See infra* § 3.2.

[12] Larguier & Conte, *supra* note 5, at 2804.

[13] *See id.* at 2706; Emmanuel Dreyer & Olivier Mouysset, *Procédure pénale* 229 (2016).

the aforementioned acts, but only to review them and take notes. If these formalities are violated, the provisional restriction of the defendant may be declared void. The access to the minutes of the *garde à vue*, the medical certificates, and the statements already given to the police must be granted to the defendant in person, if he or she asks for them and is not represented by counsel.

Originally, access to the file in cases of *garde à vue* was severely limited by law. The French legislature amended in 2016 the provisions of the Code of Criminal Procedure, mostly to implement EU directives adopted to strengthen the rights of the defense across the Union.[14] One could argue, however, that the reform is far from being satisfying. In fact, this basic form of disclosure gives little advantage to the defendant, who in principle is already well aware of his or her previous statements.[15] This change, nonetheless, may be of some help for defense counsel, who acquires direct contact with a crucial piece of evidence collected by the police. In any case, the Constitutional Court (*Conseil constitutional*) declared the reform of the *garde à vue* compatible with the French Constitution,[16] and the Court of Cassation considered the reform compatible with the requirement of Article 6 of the European Convention on Human Rights.[17]

c. *Access to the File after the Beginning of the Prosecution and at Trial*

Before the start of the prosecution, when interrogation of the defendant is ordered by the prosecutor (*interrogatoire de première comparution*—first appearance interrogation), the defendant's counsel can consult the dossier *sur-le-champ* (on the spot), and communicate its content to his or her client.

A much broader and complete disclosure is provided for when the interrogation before the prosecutor or the judge takes place, after prosecution has started and the *instruction* has begun. Here access to the file, according to Article 114 CPP, is rather extensive. Before their interrogation (starting from at least four days before each interrogation date), the defendant and the civil party[18] can access the entire dossier, with a limited exception for acts committed with urgency, a provision that was affirmed as constitutional by the Constitutional Court. Of course, in this phase the dossier may not be

[14] The amendments were adopted with the Loi 2016–731 du 3 juin 2016 renforçant la lutte contre le crime organisé, le terrorisme et leur financement, et améliorant l'efficacité et les garanties de la procédure pénale [Law 2016–731 of June 3, 2016 strengthening the fight against organized crime, terrorism and their fundings, and improving the efficiency and guarantees of criminal procedure], Journal Officiel de la Republique Française [J.O.] [Official Gazette of France], June 4, 2016.

[15] However, awareness is not always granted in the defendant's perspective. See on the matter the critical remarks of Daniel Soulez Larivière, Face aux juges: Ce que tous les honnêtes gens doivent savoir 4–8 (2017).

[16] Conseil constitutionnel [CC] [Constitutional Court] decision No. 2011-191/194/195/196/197QPC, Nov. 18, 2011.

[17] Cour de cassation [Cass.] [Supreme Court] crim., Apr. 9, 2015, Bull. crim., No. 14–87660.

[18] Dreyer & Mouysset, *supra* note 13, at 217–18. It must be outlined that in France, as in most European civil law systems, every person, including legal persons, has a right to take part in criminal proceedings to ask for compensation of damages caused by a crime. The judge, at the end of the trial, may convict the defendant not only because of his or her criminal responsibility, but also to reimburse the civil party for the damages deriving from the crime.

complete yet, because the investigations are still ongoing; however, the defense and the civil party can access all the information gathered so far by the investigating judge or by other law enforcement authorities. After the first appearance of the defendant before the judge, counsel can copy the entire dossier. Restrictions on access to the file may be determined by the judge if this is necessary to protect victims or other defendants, or to preserve the ongoing investigations. However, the parties may appeal such decisions before the President of Chamber of *Instructions* (an organ that hears appeals from decisions of the investigating judge).

Access to the file is not granted directly to the defendant, but only to defense counsel, who can also make copies of the dossier at his or her expense.[19] With the leave of the judge, counsel may then show (or even give a copy of) the file to his or her client—in whole or partially. To this end, counsel must indicate to the judge the list of documents he or she intends to give to the client. This regulation was considered compatible with the ECHR[20] and represents a solution frequently implemented by EU civil law jurisdictions. The judge, in other words, exercises control over the communication of the dossier to the defendant. The counsel's application could be denied if the judge considers that there might be risks of improper influences on the victims, other defendants, their counsel, witnesses, prosecutors, police officers, expert witnesses, or any other persons taking part in the criminal proceedings.[21] A denial by the investigating judge may be appealed by defense counsel to the president of the investigating chamber, whose decision is final. Analogous rules apply to the communication of the dossier to the civil party, which is always intermediated by the counsel (and communicated to the client with the authorization of the investigating judge), and to the defendant in pretrial custody.

It must be noted, lastly, that during the preliminary inquiry, which is secret, the suspect does not have access to the dossier file. However, before any interrogation, the suspect is given a warning with regard to his or her rights (the charges, the date, and the place in which the offense was allegedly committed; the right to leave at any moment the place where the interrogation is conducted;[22] the right to keep silent; the right to an interpreter and to appoint counsel or to have counsel appointed by the court).[23] More generally, the defendant and the civil party may have access to the minutes reporting their previous statements.

At trial, the access to the dossier for all the parties is plain and unrestricted. The illegal denial of appropriate access to the file does not imply an automatic procedural sanction, such as the invalidity (*nullité*) of the hearing. Nullities in the French system are declared by the court only when the procedural violation caused a substantial harm to the claimant.[24] The fact that a dossier, to which the defense or the civil party was given access, was unduly incomplete may not be considered a reason to invalidate the entire proceeding

[19] Frédéric Desportes & Laurence Lazerges-Cousquer, *Traité de Procédure pénale* 379 (3d ed., 2013); Serge Guinchard & Jacques Buisson, *Procédure penale* 386–89 (6th ed. 2010).

[20] Kamasinski v. Austria, App. No. 9783/82, Eur. Ct. H.R., Dec. 19, 1989; Menet v. France, App. No. 39553/02, Eur. Ct. H.R., June 14, 2005.

[21] Larguier & Conte, *supra* note 5, at 7166; Guinchard & Buisson, *supra* note 19, at 386.

[22] However, in such a case the police could decide to issue the *garde à vue*.

[23] Desportes & Lazerges-Cousquer, *supra* note 19, at 1597.

[24] *Id.* at 1319.

or even part of it. More likely, if the judge finds that parties were illegally denied access to relevant information, the judge may opt for further argument on the evidence disclosed in an untimely fashion. This is certainly true for the *instructions* phase: If some piece of evidence is not disclosed to the parties, the Chamber of Instructions may decide to postpone the proceedings, so as to give time to the defense and the civil party to examine the information wrongly withheld, and to prepare for the closing arguments in a subsequent hearing (arts. 197 and 199).[25]

3. Germany

Sharing the same cultural roots, the German rules on access to the file in many ways resemble the French ones, though more emphasis is given to the principle of the equality of arms, which constitutes the basis of the right of access to the file.[26] Restrictions to the right apply only before the trial, that is, during the investigation phase, while afterward the parties have free and full access to the file of the proceeding.

During the investigation phase, the extent of the right to access the file varies depending on whether the accused is kept in pretrial detention. In general terms, when pretrial detention is not at stake, access to the case file can be restricted, to avoid the possibility that the investigation is jeopardized.[27] If the defendant is detained pretrial, the need to ensure an effective defense prevails over that of protecting the investigation. According to ECtHR jurisprudence, the defense must be granted access to all parts of the dossier on which the decision on the pretrial detention order is based.[28] Sensitive evidence may therefore be withheld from the defense, but the judge cannot rely on such evidence to issue or uphold a pretrial detention order against the defendant.

Similarly to the French system, access to the file is granted not to the defendant, but to his or her counsel. Since self-representation is permitted in the German system, this rule has significant consequences on the rights of self-representing defendants. A self-represented defendant will only receive copies or excerpts from the file insofar as this does not interfere with the investigation or is not contrary to the rights of third parties. Due to the potential negative impact on the right of an effective defense and the fairness of the proceeding, this case should possibly become one of mandatory legal representation:

[25] Larguier & Conte, *supra* note 5, at 10001.

[26] Thomas Weigend & Franz Salditt, *The Investigative Stage of the Criminal Process in Germany*, in *Suspects in Europe: Procedural Rights at the Investigative Stage of the Criminal Process in the European Union* 79 (Ed Cape et al. eds., 2007); Dominik Brodowski et al., *Germany*, in *Effective Criminal Defence in Europe* 253 (Ed Cape et al. eds., 2010); Rodolphe Juy-Birmann, *The German System*, in *European Criminal Procedures* 292 (Mireille Delmas-Marty & J.R. Spencer eds., 2005); Jenia I. Turner, *Plea Bargaining and Disclosure in Germany and the United States: Comparative Lessons*, 57 Wm. & Mary L. Rev. 1, 10 (2016).

[27] Strafprozessordnung [StPO] [Criminal Procedure Code] arts. 475, 477.

[28] Lietzow v. Germany, App. No. 24479/94, Eur. Ct. H.R., Feb. 13, 2001; Schöps v. Germany, App. No. 25116/94, Eur. Ct. H.R., Feb. 13, 2001; Garcia Alva v. Germany, App. No. 23541/94, Eur. Ct. H.R., Feb. 13, 2001; *see also* Lamy v. Belgium, App. No. 10444/83, Eur. Ct. H.R., Mar. 30, 1989.

or to put it differently, if limited access to information for the accused who opted for self-representation may undermine an effective defense, the judge could decide to appoint a counsel, despite the contrary will of the accused.[29] As in the French system, access is permitted to the counsel and not to the defendant because counsels are considered more trustworthy given their role as independent organs of the criminal justice system.[30]

Lastly, under German law, the defendant does not have the right to make copies of the file free of charge. However, defense counsel has the right to keep the file for a reasonable time in his or her office, and make copies at his or her expense.

4. Italy: An Example of a Continental System under Change

Despite being part of the civil law and Continental legal tradition, in the last three decades, Italy underwent a vast and radical reform of its criminal process, oriented toward the adversarial model inspired by the Anglo-American tradition. The current Code of Criminal Procedure entered into force on October 24, 1989, thereby replacing the *Rocco* Code of 1930 and bringing some significant changes. An essential feature of the accusatorial model adopted in the Italian system is a strict separation between the investigative phase and the trial. As a consequence, the judge's decision may only be based on the evidence presented at a public trial, granting the right of cross-examination and the equal treatment of the parties.[31]

The 1989 accusatorial Code was introduced to make criminal trials more consistent with the democratic principles of orality, immediacy, and publicity.[32] Some significant changes made by the 1989 reform are the introduction of a double-file system and the abolition of the inquisitorial investigating judge. The primary investigatory responsibility was allocated to the public prosecutor. The evidence and testimony collected during the investigative stage is kept in one dossier. This information is not available to the trial judge, unless it is presented at court, a possibility allowed by the law in very limited cases.[33] The general principle is that information assembled during investigations cannot be used at trial as evidence; accordingly, facts must be proven at trial via oral testimonies formed following the Socratic method of the parties' examination, while the judge remains prevailingly passive.[34] In conclusion, it can be stated that the double dossier system has shifted the responsibility of presenting evidence at trial to the public prosecutor and the defense counsel.

[29] Brodowski et al., *supra* note 26, at 275; Juy-Birmann, *supra* note 26, at 330; Turner, *supra* note 26, at 20.

[30] Brodowski et al., *supra* note 26, at 275; Juy-Birmann, *supra* note 26, at 330; Turner, *supra* note 26, at 19.

[31] Giulio Illuminati, *The Frustrated Turn to Adversarial Procedure in Italy (Italian Criminal Procedure Code of 1988)*, 4 Wash. U. Global Stud. L. Rev. 567 (2005).

[32] *See* Illuminati, *supra* note 2, at 297.

[33] *See* Michele Panzavolta, *Reforms and Counter-reforms in the Italian Struggle for an Accusatorial Criminal Law System*, 30 N.C. J. Int'l. L. & Com. Reg. 578, 585–90 (2005); Michele Caianiello, *The Italian Public Prosecutor: An Inquisitorial Figure in Adversarial Proceedings?*, in *Transnational Perspectives on Prosecutorial Power* 250–67 (Erik Luna & Marianne Wade eds., 2012).

[34] *See* Panzavolta, *supra* note 33, at 586–87.

However, the Continental roots of the system were not completely removed.[35] For example, the prosecutor is obliged to look for both inculpatory and exculpatory evidence during investigations. As in the German system, the principle of "completeness" of the investigations and of the investigative file governs.

As a consequence, on one side, rules governing access to the file maintain an approach similar to the one examined in other civil law countries. On the other, a specific new phase of pretrial disclosure was introduced, with the intent of making the new accusatorial reform effective. To sum up, while one may conclude that the Italian approach follows the traditional civil law path for the most part, it also presents a peculiar phase dedicated to the communication of the evidence among the parties just before the beginning of the trial.

a. *Access to the File in Cases of Precautionary Arrest*

When an arrest takes place, or the judge issues a pretrial custody order, access to the file is broadly granted. In general terms, the defendant has the right to consult the evidence used by the prosecutor against him or her, together with the exculpatory evidence collected by the prosecutor and the police so far (even when such evidence was not presented to the judge who issued the pretrial custody decision).

In other words, just after the serving of a pretrial custody order, the prosecutor is obliged to make available for the defendant and her/his counsel the prosecution's file, containing the evidence presented by the prosecutor to the judge for obtaining a pretrial custody order, as well as the exculpatory evidence collected by police and prosecutors during the investigations. The file must be accessible immediately after the arrest of the defendant. The duty to communicate exculpatory evidence is an ongoing one, which continues to operate for the entire phase of the appeal against the pretrial custody order. Violation of the disclosure duties by the prosecutor may lead to the defendant's release. On one side, the law provides that, within few days after the arrest (five days in case of pretrial custody in jail, or ten days for milder provisional measures limiting personal freedom), the defendant must be interrogated before the judge for the preliminary investigation. The omission of the interrogation leads to the release of the defendant, because under the law, the pretrial custody order loses any legal effect. The jurisprudence of the Supreme Court equated this situation—the omission of the defendant's interrogation after the arrest—with the case in which an interview has been conducted without appropriate disclosure to the defense of the prosecution's file.[36]

Furthermore, when a pretrial custody order is appealed before the tribunal, the prosecutor has analogous disclosure duties toward the defense, and their omission leads to the same consequences (the pretrial custodial judicial measure becomes ineffective and the defendant is released).

When the defendant is interviewed during the investigation without being subject to measures restricting his or her personal freedom, access to the information is far more limited. If the questioning is run by the police, officers may withhold from the defendant both the evidence collected and the charges for which the investigation is being conducted. If the interrogation takes place before the prosecutor, the defendant has the right to

[35] *See id.* at 591–93.

[36] Cass., Sez. Un., 28 June 2005, n. 26798, Vitale, CED no. 231349.

know the facts and the legal qualification of the charges, as well as the evidence against him or her. This latter information may be given by the prosecutor as long as it does not undermine the ongoing investigations. In this phase, thus, there is not an autonomous right of access to the file.[37]

b. *Access to the Dossier after the Beginning of the Prosecution and at Trial*

At the end of the investigation, the prosecutor must notify the defendant and the victims that the investigation is concluded and that they may consult the prosecution's file and copy it. From that point on, access to the file is unlimited for both parties, up until the end of the proceedings.

Violations of discovery duties at the end of the investigation may be sanctioned with the exclusion of the undisclosed evidence. Such a sanction is not as severe as it may appear at first glance. After the end of the investigation, in fact, an intermediate phase takes place before the trial: the preliminary hearing, whose purpose is to establish if the prosecution's case is strong enough to go to trial. At the hearing, the judge may rely on the entire investigative file to adopt his or her decision (there is not a rule against hearsay in this phase), and if he or she considers that the prosecutor has enough evidence to prove the guilt of the defendant at trial, he or she must issue the date of trial.

In this scenario, the prohibition on using undisclosed evidence has more of a symbolic than concrete effect, as it is very difficult, if not impossible, to verify under which criteria the judge of the preliminary hearing considered the case worth bringing to trial. The judge does not provide reasons for the order so as not to bias the judge of the trial, since at trial different rules of evidence apply (above all, the rule against hearsay): As a consequence, however, the lack of judicial reasoning makes it impossible to understand the exact criteria according to which the judge decides to send the case to trial (he or she might have been influenced by evidence that should not have been used according to the law).

The right to copy the file always accompanies the right of access to it, in any phase of the proceedings.

Differently from France and Germany, access to the file in Italy is permitted to the defense, as a whole, without a distinction between the defendant and his or her counsel. However, one must bear in mind that in Italy self-representation is not permitted in criminal cases. Therefore, in practice, it is the defendant's counsel who accesses the file. However, there is no provision regulating the communication between counsel and defendant with regard to the contents of the investigations file. Once the file is copied by the counsel, neither the judge nor the prosecutor can supervise the way in which counsel gives his or her client access to the information collected in the file.

c. *Disclosure*

Ruling on the phase just before the beginning of the trial, the Italian Code of Criminal Procedure provides for a brief exchange of information among the parties inspired by

[37] *See* Michele Caianiello, *Italy*, in *Effective Criminal Defence in Europe* 373 (Ed Cape et al. eds., 2010).

the Anglo-American pretrial disclosure. Each party, including the prosecutor, the defense, and the civil party, is obliged to present a list of witnesses it intends to call to testify at trial. The list must identify every witness, as well as the topics on which the witness will be examined. The omission of this act is sanctioned with the exclusion of the testimony itself. More precisely, the party loses the right to evidence with regard to witnesses not mentioned in the list (unless their existence was discovered only afterward). Nonetheless, the judge reserves the power to call, at the end of the trial, any witness he or she might consider "absolutely necessary" to ascertain the truth. This means that, if a party negligently misses the chance to mention a witness in the pretrial list, it can nonetheless rely on the judge to introduce that evidence (though a higher standard of admissibility is required, because the missing evidence must appear to the judge as absolutely necessary to the final decision).

III. Access to the Dossier in Supranational Systems: Guidelines, Provisions, and Solutions

1. The Guidelines Emerging from the Case Law of the ECtHR

In various decisions in the last three to four decades, the European Court of Human Rights has ruled on the right of access to the file in criminal matters, especially with regard to the position of the accused. The ECtHR's holistic approach, focused on the fairness of the proceedings as a whole, leaves much room for exceptions to the main guidelines and does not imply noteworthy changes for national jurisdictions.

The legal basis for the right of access to the file can be found in Article 6 of the European Convention on Human Rights (ECHR), paragraph 3, sections l*a*–*b*, which provide for the legal regulation of some fundamental defense rights (right to know the nature and cause of the accusation and right to adequate time and facilities to prepare the defense case). Furthermore, a third legal basis may be identified in Article 5 ECHR, providing for the defense right to challenge the deprivation of liberty during pretrial custody.

From these provisions, the ECtHR case law elaborated a right of access to the file, according to which—in principle—the defense must be given access to all the relevant information possessed by the police and the prosecutor or investigating judge. This right is instrumental and represents a crucial aspect of the right of defense, because without a proper disclosure by law enforcement agencies, the defense cannot adequately prepare either its own case or its challenge to the prosecution's case. As such, access to information is also instrumental to ensure the equality of arms in criminal proceedings because, given the disproportion of means between prosecution and defense, no equality would be possible without a thorough disclosure of all collected information. The right must involve both incriminating and exculpatory evidence. This implies that partial disclosure, involving only the evidence on which the prosecutor intends to rely at trial, is not sufficient, as most likely some information relevant for the defense case could be contained in the evidence the prosecutor does not intend to use at trial. Furthermore, a selection of the evidence, done by the prosecutor and given to the defense, is inadequate too, because only the defense is in the proper position to decide what could be favorable to its case. This implies that the defense must be given plain and complete access to the file within an adequate time prior to the beginning of the trial.[38] For example, in the *Öcalan* case, the ECtHR found a breach of the right to a fair trial because the defense was granted access to the file only a few weeks before the start of trial, and the investigations had been very complex and produced an enormous amount of evidence. In particular, the Court sanctioned the prosecution for giving the defendant access to the file only fifteen days before the start of trial.[39]

The same rule should apply when pretrial custody is issued. In that case too, the defense must be allowed full access to the information, because the deprivation of liberty is of such gravity that it deserves to be considered at the same level as the issue of the culpability of the defendant at trial. As a consequence, the defense must be informed of both incriminating and exculpatory evidence.[40]

Finally, complete disclosure duties involve not only evidence in possession of the police and the prosecutor during the investigation phase, but also legal acts presented by the prosecution at any stage of the criminal proceedings.[41] Motions, written legal arguments, appeals, and memoranda must also be showed to the defense in due time. The illegitimate denial of access to such information may lead to the breach of Article 6 ECHR, if in this way, the defense has been denied the opportunity to effectively challenge the prosecution's case.

If ECHR rules concerning disclosure are rather broad, probably broader than the legal provisions of various national jurisdictions, their application in individual cases, as well as the holistic approach to the fair trial principle of the ECtHR, restricts significantly their impact on national practices (and, in the end, has only a limited effect on the administration of the right of access to the file in national practices). The Court's holistic approach to Article 6 ECHR implies that the violation of the right must concretely affect

[38] Brandstetter v. Austria, App. Nos. 11170/84, 12876/87 and 13468/87, Eur. Ct. H.R., Aug. 28, 1991; Nikolova v. Bulgaria [GC], App. No. 31195/96, Eur. Ct. H.R., Mar. 25, 1999; Doorson v. The Netherlands, App. No. 20524/92, Eur. Ct. H.R., Mar. 26, 1996; Paul and Audrey Edwards v. United Kingdom, App. No. 46477/99, Eur. Ct. H.R., Mar. 14, 2002; I.J.L., G.M.R. and A.K.P. v. United Kingdom, App. Nos. 29522/95, 30056/96 and 30574/96, Eur. Ct. H.R., Sept. 19, 2000; Fodale v. Italy, App. No. 70148/01, Eur. Ct. H.R., June 1, 2006; Rowe and Davis v. United Kingdom [GC], App. No. 28901/95, Eur. Ct. H.R., Feb. 16, 2000; Chambaz v. Switzerland, App. No. 11663/04, Eur. Ct. H.R., Apr. 5, 2012.

[39] Öcalan v. Turkey, App. No. 46221/99, Eur. Ct. H.R., May 12, 2005, §§ 30, 36, 138–149.

[40] Fodale v. Italy, App. No. 70148/01, Eur. Ct. H.R., June 1, 2006, §§ 41–42.

[41] Verdu Verdu v. Spain, App. No. 43432/02, Eur. Ct. H.R., Feb. 15, 2007, § 25. *See* Silvia Allegrezza, *La conoscenza degli atti nel processo penale fra ordinamento interno e Convenzione europea*, in *Giurisprudenza europea e processo penale italiano* 143–67 (Antonio Balsamo & Roberto E. Kostoris eds., 2008).

the right to effective defense. In other words, a violation of ECtHR disclosure rules might not be sanctioned by the ECtHR if the judges consider that the defense was not ultimately prejudiced because some remedy was provided to it during the criminal proceedings (for example, at a later stage). Under this perspective, the ECtHR has found that a complete disclosure at the end of the trial, but before the appeals phase, can compensate for the lack of complete access granted before trial.[42] Furthermore, partial disclosure may also go unpunished if the trial verdict was not based substantially on the evidence withheld from the defense. Finally, right of access to the file may be denied when it is necessary to protect ongoing investigations or the private life of third persons involved in criminal proceedings. The limitations recognized by the ECtHR reduce significantly the scope of the right in ECtHR practice. Apart from the cases in which restrictions to information are justified based on the need to protect other legitimate interests, the breach of the right to a fair trial due to a violation of the right of access to the file is not recognized by the Court when the defendant does not prove why and how the illegitimate denial affected his or her case concretely.

2. The Provisions of the European Union on the Right of Access to the File

The EU has developed its own set of rules on access to the file, which are in certain respects different from the rules elaborated by the ECtHR. The Treaty of the EU (one of the fundamental legal sources of the Union) confers to the ECHR, as interpreted by its Court, the nature of EU law. However, nothing prevents the EU from providing for more thorough protection of rights. The ECHR represents the minimum standard for EU legislation, but the EU legislature may develop a higher protection of the rights recognized by the ECHR or acknowledge new rights not protected by the ECHR.

With regard to the matter of access to the file, in the EU it was first developed in legal areas different from criminal law sensu stricto, such as competition law.[43] Subsequently, new provisions were adopted for the administration of criminal proceedings and led some national jurisdictions of the EU to change their legal provisions to implement the new EU laws.

a. *The Right of Access to the File in Directive* 2012/13/*EU on the Right of Information*

In 2012, the EU legislature adopted a new directive with the purpose of enhancing the right of the defense. This directive was part of a plan, the "Stockholm Programme,"

[42] Paul and Audrey Edwards v. United Kingdom, App No. 46477/99, Eur. Ct. H.R., Mar. 14, 2002, §§ 33–39.

[43] Competition law was not defined yet by the ECJ as a matter comparable to criminal law because of its punitive features. However, most scholars consider that this should be the inevitable conclusion, applying the *Engels* criteria to the matter. *See* André Klip, *European Criminal Law: An Integrative Approach* 190–95 (2016).

according to which the Commission intended to strengthen defense rights in criminal proceedings and increase mutual trust and judicial cooperation among EU Member States.[44] Since then, six directives have been adopted to allow a more consistent and effective protection of the defendant's rights across the EU.[45]

Directive 2012/13/EU is dedicated to the right of information for persons involved in criminal proceedings or subject to a European arrest warrant. The main purpose of the directive is to make the persons involved aware of their rights in the undergoing criminal proceeding, or in the proceeding for the surrender, if a European arrest warrant has been issued. According to Article 2, the directive applies "from the time persons are made aware by the competent authorities of a Member State that they are suspected or accused of having committed a criminal offence until the conclusion of the proceedings, which is understood to mean the final determination of the question whether the suspect or accused person has committed the criminal offence, including, where applicable, sentencing and the resolution of any appeal."

The rights the accused or the suspect must be made aware of include: (1) the right of access to a lawyer; (2) any entitlement to free legal aid and the conditions for obtaining such advice; (3) the right to be informed of the accusation, in accordance with Article 6 of the directive; (4) the right to interpretation and translation; and (5) the right to remain silent. The information concerned in the directive must be given in a simple and understandable way (and in writing, when pretrial custody is ordered, or a proceeding for the execution of a European arrest warrant is started).

Among other provisions, Article 7 regulates the right of access to the file ("access to the materials of the case"). According to it:

1. Where a person is arrested and detained at any stage of the criminal proceedings, Member States shall ensure that documents related to the specific case in the possession of the competent authorities which are essential to challenging effectively, in

[44] *Id.* at 260.

[45] Directive 2010/64, of the European Parliament and of the Council of 20 October 2010 on the Right to Interpretation and Translation in Criminal Proceedings, 2010 O.J. (L 180) 1; Directive 2012/13, of the European Parliament and of the Council of 22 May 2012 on the Right to Information in Criminal Proceedings, 2012 O.J. (L 142) 1; Directive 2013/48, of the European Parliament and of the Council of 22 October 2013 on the Right of Access to a Lawyer in Criminal Proceedings and in European Arrest Warrant Proceedings, and on the Right to Have a Third Party Informed upon Deprivation of Liberty and to Communicate with Third Persons and with Consular Authorities while Deprived of Liberty, 2013 O.J. (L 294) 1; Directive 2016/343, of the European Parliament and of the Council of 9 March 2016 on the Strengthening of Certain Aspects of the Presumption of Innocence and of the Right to be Present at the Trial in Criminal Proceedings, 2016 O.J. (L 65) 1; Directive 2016/800, of the European Parliament and of the Council of 11 May 2016 on Procedural Safeguards for Children Who Are Suspects or Accused Persons in Criminal Proceedings, 2016 O.J. (L 132) 1; Directive 2016/1919, of the European Parliament and of the Council of 26 October 2016 on Legal Aid for Suspects and Accused Persons in Criminal Proceedings and for Requested Persons in European Arrest Warrant Proceedings, 2016 O.J. (L 297) 1. In 2012, the EU adopted Directive 2012/29, of the European Parliament and of the Council of 25 October 2012 Establishing Minimum Standards on the Rights, Support and Protection of Victims of Crime, and Replacing Council Framework Decision 2001/220/JHA, 2012 O.J. (L 315) 57.

accordance with national law, the lawfulness of the arrest or detention, are made available to arrested persons or to their lawyers.

2. Member States shall ensure that access is granted at least to all material evidence in the possession of the competent authorities, whether for or against suspects or accused persons, to those persons or their lawyers in order to safeguard the fairness of the proceedings and to prepare the defence.
3. Without prejudice to paragraph 1, access to the materials referred to in paragraph 2 shall be granted in due time to allow the effective exercise of the rights of the defence and at the latest upon submission of the merits of the accusation to the judgment of a court. Where further material evidence comes into the possession of the competent authorities, access shall be granted to it in due time to allow for it to be considered.
4. By way of derogation from paragraphs 2 and 3, provided that this does not prejudice the right to a fair trial, access to certain materials may be refused if such access may lead to a serious threat to the life or the fundamental rights of another person or if such refusal is strictly necessary to safeguard an important public interest, such as in cases where access could prejudice an ongoing investigation or seriously harm the national security of the Member State in which the criminal proceedings are instituted. Member States shall ensure that, in accordance with procedures in national law, a decision to refuse access to certain materials in accordance with this paragraph is taken by a judicial authority or is at least subject to judicial review.
5. Access, as referred to in this Article, shall be provided free of charge.

These provisions do not seem to add significant changes to ECtHR jurisprudence on the matter. They may even be considered less protective of the right of access to the file than ECtHR case law. On the one hand, paragraphs 2 to 5 of Article 7 confirm what the ECtHR has already established in its cases: Access must be full, unconditional, and free of charge. It must encompass both incriminating and exonerating evidence. It may be restricted only for legitimate purposes (which are defined rather clearly in paragraph 4), and only if it is strictly necessary.[46]

The directive, however, remains silent on one crucial aspect, that is, what happens if access is illegally denied. Besides, it seems more restrictive, when compared with the ECtHR jurisprudence, on another extremely important aspect of criminal proceedings, that is, when pretrial custody is at stake.

With regard to the first problem, the directive does not give any indication on how courts should react when the suspect or the accused is illegally deprived of access to the case material. This implies that such a decision is left to national legislatures or national case law. This is not uncommon for EU directives in criminal matters, which typically do not provide for any procedural sanctions for violations of their provisions.

[46] Directive 2014/41, of the European Parliament and of the Council of 3 April 2014 Regarding the European Investigation Order in Criminal Matters, 2014 O.J. (L 130) 1.

With regard to the second critical aspect of proceedings with pretrial custody, the directive seems to be more restrictive than the ECtHR jurisprudence, as according to paragraph 1, the defendant must be given access to the evidence that is "essential" to effectively challenge the lawfulness of the arrest or detention. This does not clearly cover evidence that is collected by police or prosecutor, but is then not used to obtain a pretrial custody order by the judge. Actually, it seems from the wording of the directive that some restrictions on materials considered not relevant by the prosecution could be applied in proceedings concerning arrest or detention. This interpretation is even more plausible considering that, in paragraph 2, the directive imposes the duty to disclose "*all* the material evidence, *whether for or against suspects or accused persons*" (emphasis added). Consequently, when pretrial custody is at stake, some restrictions on the access to evidence could be applied without significant invalidating consequences. This again does not seem consistent with the ECtHR, whose jurisprudence on pretrial detention requires full access to the file, on the same terms as that provided before the beginning of the trial.[47]

b. *The Right of Access to the File in CJEU Jurisprudence*

There is no CJEU case law on the directive on the right to information yet. National laws, as we have seen in Section II, have only slightly changed because of the content of the directives. Essentially Member States kept their systems as they were, apart from some amendments that sometimes improve defense safeguards, but do not undermine the core of domestic regulations. For example, as we have seen, partial and very limited disclosure was introduced in the French system when *garde à vue* is issued.

The CJEU did, however, decide some cases concerning disclosure before the entry into force of the new EU directive on information, in proceedings of a punitive nature, though not criminal sensu stricto. It seems worth examining this jurisprudence briefly as a means of gauging whether some gaps of the directive might be filled.

After all, the right of access to evidence is granted by Article 41 of the Charter of Fundamental Rights of the EU in general terms, involving matters that are external to criminal law. A similar provision was already included in previous versions of the EU Treaties (Article 255 EC), and this allows the conclusion that access to governmental information constitutes a basic principle of the whole EU system. In cases of administrative law with punitive aspects, mainly concerning decisions taken by the European Commission, the ECJ affirmed that the right of access must be granted in due time before the Commission adopts its decision. Access must be plain and unconditional and must include both incriminating and exonerating evidence.[48] It was also observed that belated disclosure of documents in the file could not return the claimant to the situation

[47] *See* Michele Caianiello, *To Sanction (or Not to Sanction) Procedural Flaws at E.U. Level? A Step Forward in the Creation of an E.U. Criminal Process*, 22 Eur. J. Crime, Crim. L. & Crim. Just. 317, 317–29 (2014).

[48] Case C-204/00, Aalborg Portland and Others v. Comm'n, 2004 E.C.R. I-00123; Case T-161/05, Hoechst v. Comm'n, 2009 E.C.R. II-03555; Case T-57/01, Solvay SA v. Comm'n, 2009 E.C.R. II-04621; Case T-66/01, Imperial Chemical Industries v. Comm'n, 2010 E.C.R. II-02631; Case C-407/08 P, Knauf Gips v. Comm'n, 2010 E.C.R. I-06375; Case T-151/07, Kone and Others v. Comm'n, 2011 E.C.R. II-05313; Case T-197/06, FMC v. Comm'n, 2011 E.C.R. II-03179.

he or she would have been in if he or she had been able to rely on these documents in presenting his or her written and oral observations to the Commission.[49]

From this it follows that disclosure must take place in due time before the administrative phase is concluded, to give the interested person the possibility to effectively present observations before the competent authority. The breach of such duties must not go unpunished, and the sanction must restore the defendant to the position he or she would have been in if the violation had not taken place. Finally, disclosure at a later stage, for example, at a judicial stage (in cases when the sanction is imposed at the administrative level, and the person involved is granted the right to appeal before court), does not constitute a sufficient remedy, because the case remains tainted by the previous administrative decision, given without a complete disclosure of the evidence collected.

If we look at the CJEU case law in comparison with Article 7 of Directive 2012/13/EU, we may observe that, in the medium term, some lacunae in national legislation might be addressed through a preliminary ruling by the Court of Justice. To be consistent with its previous decisions, the Court might conclude that some remedies must be granted in case of a violation of the right to information of the defendant, and that access to information must be full, as far as the stage of the proceedings permits it, with respect to disclosure in arrest and detention matters. However, considering that in criminal matters, the CJEU has so far paid extreme caution not to give the Charter an expansive meaning in comparison with other fields of law,[50] such an outcome is far from likely, to say the least.

3. ICC Disclosure Provisions

The proceedings regulated by the International Criminal Court's (ICC) Statute and Rules of Procedure and Evidence represent a mixed system with a largely adversarial structure.[51] There is no investigating judge at the pretrial phase, as the investigations are conducted by the prosecutor. The parties are in charge of introducing evidence at trial and at the pretrial hearing provided to establish if the case of the prosecution is strong enough to merit trial (the *confirmation hearing*). However, some very significant exceptions to the adversarial model lead the system toward a mixed structure, in which one can detect clear and relevant signs of the Continental tradition: There is no jury, and the judges adopt a reasoned judgment, both on the guilt and innocence of the accused and

[49] Case T-57/01, Solvay SA v. Comm'n, 2009 E.C.R. II-04621.

[50] Case C-399/11, Melloni v. Ministerio Fiscal, 2013 Electronic Report of Cases (ECLI:EU:C:2013:107). *See* Christine Janssens, *The Principle of Mutual Recognition in E.U. Law* 209 (2013); Valsamis Mitsilegas, *E.U. Criminal Law After Lisbon: Rights, Trust and the Transformation of Justice in Europe* 1025 (2016); Vanessa Franssen, Melloni *as a Wake-up Call—Setting Limits to Higher National Standards of Fundamental Rights' Protection*, Eur. L. Blog, Mar. 10, 2014, *available at* http://europeanlawblog.eu/2014/03/10/melloni-as-a-wake-up-call-setting-limits-to-higher-national-standards-of-fundamental-rights-protection.

[51] Christoph Safferling, *International Criminal Procedure* 5 (2012); Michele Caianiello, *Disclosure Before the ICC: The Emergence of a New Form of Policies Implementation System in International Criminal Justice?*, 10 Int'l Crim. L. Rev. 23, 23–42 (2010). Kai Ambos, *Treatise on International Criminal Law, Volume III: International Criminal Procedure* 520–47 (2016).

on the potential sanction; judges maintain relevant powers with regard to the definition of the charges, especially at the confirmation hearing, and to evidence. In addition, no clear rules against hearsay are provided, and evidence collected in the pretrial phase of the proceedings may be admitted at trial if it is reliable and if its introduction would not impair the fairness of the proceedings.[52]

Disclosure is regulated mainly in an adversarial manner, leaving the parties with the main responsibility to disclose relevant evidence. The prosecutor has the duty to disclose to the defense all exculpatory evidence, defined as "evidence in the Prosecutor's possession or control which he or she believes shows or tends to show the innocence of the accused, or to mitigate the guilt of the accused, or which may affect the credibility of prosecution evidence."[53] The prosecutor must also give the defense a list of the evidence which he or she intends to produce to support the indictment at least thirty days before the beginning of the confirmation hearing.[54] Any further evidence by the prosecutor must be communicated in advance to the defense not less than fifteen days before the same date of the confirmation hearing.[55] Finally, fifteen days before the confirmation hearing, the defense is also obliged to present its evidence to the Pretrial Chamber.[56] The list of the evidence required by the defense will then be transmitted by the Pretrial Chamber to the prosecutor.[57] The aforementioned provisions are binding, and their violation would lead to the exclusion of the evidence from the hearing.[58]

After the confirmation hearing and before the trial starts, the prosecutor must inform the accused of the names and statements of witnesses he or she intends to present at trial. In addition, the prosecutor must permit the defense to inspect documents, photographs, and any other tangible objects, if this is relevant for the preparation of the defense case.[59] The defense, for its part, is under the obligation to allow the prosecutor access to the documentary evidence in its possession whenever the accused asks to inspect documentary evidence in the hands of the prosecutor.[60] Moreover, the defendant must communicate any specific defense he or she intends to raise at trial. In particular, the defense must disclose to the prosecutor the plan of raising an alibi defense at trial, and all the defenses provided for in Article 31 paragraph 1 of the Statute.[61] In all of these cases, the defendant must communicate the names of witnesses who will be called to testify at trial in support of any affirmative defense.[62] It is worth remembering that the accused is not under any obligation of disclosing statements rendered by those witnesses he or she intends to call at trial on matters concerning his or her legal strategy.

[52] Michele Caianiello, *First Decisions on the Admission of Evidence at ICC Trials: A Blending of Accusatorial and Inquisitorial Models?*, 9 J. Int'l. Crim. Just. 385, 398 (2011); Michele Caianiello, *Law of Evidence at the International Criminal Court: Blending Accusatorial and Inquisitorial Models*, 36 N.C. J. Int'l L. & Com. Reg. 287, 287–318 (2011); Xavier-Jean Keïta, *Disclosure of Evidence in the Law and Practice of the ICC*, 16 Int'l Crim. L. Rev. 1018, 1018–47 (2016).

[53] Rome Statute art. 67 (2). [54] ICC Rules of Procedure and Evidence [RPE] R. 121.

[55] *Id.* [56] *Id.* [57] *See* Caianiello, *supra* note 51, at 27. [58] *See id.*

[59] *See id.* [60] *See id.*

[61] This provision specifically mentions mental disease or defects, intoxication—a state diminishing the capacity to "appreciate the unlawfulness or the nature of the conduct, or the capacity to control the conduct"—self-defense, and duress. *See* Caianiello, *supra* note 51, at 35.

[62] *Id.*

Only the names must be disclosed, while the prior statements of the persons concerned may remain secret.

Finally, as already mentioned, the prosecutor must disclose to the defense any exculpatory evidence. Evidence may be withheld when it is necessary to keep certain information secret or confidential. In a famous case, *Prosecutor v. Lubanga*, the need to keep some information confidential came into conflict with the duty to disclose exculpatory evidence to the defense. The defendant argued that the prosecution had violated its disclosure duties by systematically and broadly relying on confidentiality agreements in collecting information. Such a broad and indiscriminate use of confidentiality agreements, while certainly improving cooperation by states and other bodies with the Office of the Prosecutor, was found to prejudice the right to a fair trial. This led the Pretrial Chamber to suspend the proceedings in June 2008, an order that was reversed only at the beginning of 2009.[63] The Trial Chamber held that the duty to disclose exculpatory evidence is a fundamental prosecutorial duty, which must prevail over the need to ensure cooperation between states and the Office of the Prosecutor. Besides, the duty to communicate exculpatory evidence is an ongoing process, which needs to be fulfilled by the prosecutor at any stage of the proceedings, whenever its Office collects evidence or information that might help the defense.

In conclusion, despite its adversarial structure, the ICC disclosure scheme contains some strong Continental elements. In particular, the prosecution has a duty to investigate both inculpatory and exculpatory evidence and to make the information collected available to the defendant in due time, especially evidence that might help the defense's case. These duties are enforceable with some procedural remedies. However, these remedies do not consist of the automatic exclusion of the undisclosed evidence. In practice, the breach of disclosure duties usually leads to a stay of the proceedings, giving the defense the time to examine the illegally withheld information and to prepare for trial. However, it must be acknowledged that so far no case of disclosure violations has emerged at the appeal stage, where a postponement of the proceedings would not be as useful as it is at trial.

IV. Conclusion

Looking at the civil law tradition in a general perspective, one could argue that access to the file is granted rather liberally when parties are preparing for the adjudication of the case. When the case is sent to trial, and before the trial starts, the parties—and especially the defense—are allowed to have an unlimited access to the file of the proceedings.

[63] Prosecutor v. Thomas Lubanga Dyilo, Case No. ICC-01/04-01/06, Decision on the Consequences of Non-Disclosure of Exculpatory Materials Covered by Article 54(3)(e) Agreements and the Application to Stay the Prosecution of the Accused, Together with Certain Other Issues Raised at the Status Conference on 10 June 2008 (June 13, 2008). *See* William A. Schabas & Carsten Stahn, *Introductory Note: Legal Aspects of the* Lubanga *Case*, 19 Crim. L. F. 431–34 (2008); *see also* Caianiello, *supra* note 51, at 38; Safferling, *supra* note 51, at 602 & n.70.

This might give the impression that disclosure is respected and that basic principles of fairness are effectively implemented, without relevant critical aspects. The prosecutor or the judge has the burden to investigate both exculpatory and inculpatory evidence, and every piece of information collected is made available to the defense (and the victim) when the proceedings arrive at the preliminary stage of the trial. As the analysis has shown, however, the picture is more complicated if one digs beneath the surface. It is true that before trial, actually often just before it, access is generally unlimited for the parties. However, such complete information on the nature and the evidence supporting the case arrives at a rather late stage when, taking into account the features of the civil law tradition, it is often too late to change the course of the proceeding. In other words, disclosure comes too late and often leaves the defense very limited room to influence effectively the outcome of the trial in those systems where inquisitorial features are more significant.

Continental systems are characterized by a lack of rules against hearsay. Therefore, all evidence collected by the police, prosecutor, and judges before the beginning of the trial is assembled in an official file, which can be used without significant limitation at trial to adjudicate the case. The trial is therefore often the place where witnesses confirm what they previously told the police or the prosecutor. For these reasons, the possibility for the defense at trial to undermine the case built up by law enforcement agencies is rather feeble. This is even truer when the defendant is detained pretrial. Pretrial detention orders are reasoned judicial decisions and, as such, part of the official file. As a result, pretrial judicial decisions are likely to influence trial judges' view of the trial's outcome. However, as we have seen, disclosure is not uniformly regulated in the context of pretrial detention, and some systems leave it to the free evaluation of the prosecutor or of the judge of the pretrial phase. The defense is often given a right to appeal restrictions on its right to access the file; however, civil law systems rarely provide for procedural sanctions in cases of violations of this right at the pretrial detention stage.

What emerges therefore is that full access is given only at a time when decisions are (most likely) already made. What could and should be improved is the right of access to the file at an earlier stage, while the investigation is ongoing. Supranational law can be a source of inspiration on this point. From an individual rights perspective, it might be important to make good use of that jurisprudence according to which access to information must be full and must occur in due time to give the parties (that is, mainly the defense) an effective chance to challenge the prosecution's case at trial. When it comes to remedies for violations of the defense's right to access, the ICC experience could also be of help.

The analyses of those jurisdictions presenting some adversarial nuances, in a structure rooted in the civil law tradition, such as Italy, or having a sui generis adversarial model, such as the ICC, raise two other considerations. The first is that, in the field of access to the file, it seems progressively insufficient to make the judge the only authority responsible for the parties' right of access to the file. Put differently, the old inquisitorial tradition according to which all the decisions and the responsibilities should be taken only by the judge today seems at least in part unsatisfactory. A possible development could be represented by a two-step approach: the first step is a process led by the parties, who have much more complete knowledge of what they have gathered during the pretrial phase; the second step places responsibility over disclosure in the hands of the judge, who maintains the responsibility to ensure the fairness of the proceedings and the appropriate balance between prosecution and defense (with due regard to the victims' interests). Under this approach, the parties, as in the ICC, should make the first move, communicating reciprocally the information collected so far before the beginning of the trial. Then the judge should intervene, to grant that the fundamental principles of due process involved by the right of access to the file are respected.

The second consideration is that, no matter how the access to the file phase is shaped, restrictions must never undermine the right of the defense. The defendant in fact must be given full access to any information in due time, before the beginning of the trial. The introduction of adversarial elements in civil law systems, such as Italy, did not change this basic rule. Of course, various forms of witness protection measures can be legitimately adopted. However, the defense must be able to know the identity of the witnesses in adequate time before the testimony is given at trial. In this regard, the practice of Italy and the ICC seems to respect more effectively the right of the defense[64] than the jurisprudence of the ECtHR, according to which, under certain circumstances, anonymous witnesses are admissible.[65]

However, the supranational sources should not be overestimated, for two sets of reasons. On the one hand, supranational institutions are reluctant for political reasons to interfere significantly with national rules and practices when criminal process is at stake, because of the traditional jealousy of states over the administration of criminal justice. This is the reason that in general supranational institutions largely prefer to create a general framework of minimum common standards, rather than to regulate directly and precisely technical procedural aspects of the criminal proceedings. On the other hand, a direct intervention of supranational institutions on the national regulation of procedure is always technically complicated, because in procedure different rules are closely interconnected, and it is unrealistic to amend only certain provisions without dominating the entire procedural field.

If we look forward, the path seems to lead toward two separate, though interrelated, goals: (1) to build up an improved disclosure mechanism when pretrial detention is at stake, including all the evidence on which the prosecution relied in applying for the detention order and any further information that might be exculpatory (since the duty to disclose exculpatory evidence is an ongoing duty that must be continuously respected); and (2) to have full and unlimited access to information at the end of investigation and before the decision is made on sending the case to trial. Despite all the potential variables of every single procedural system, the achievement of such goals does not seem unrealistic, in the long-to-medium term.

[64] *See* Ambos, *supra* note 51, at 543; Keïta, *supra* note 52, at 1026.

[65] The ECtHR declared under limited conditions anonymous witnesses would be admitted, in some pivotal judgments. *See* Balta and Demir v. Turkey, App. No. 48628/12, Eur. Ct. H.R., June 23, 2015; Van Mechelen and Others v. The Netherlands, App. No. 21363/93, 21364/93, 21427/93 and 22056/93, Eur. Ct. H.R., Oct. 30, 1997.

References

Silvia Allegrezza, *La conoscenza degli atti nel processo penale fra ordinamento interno e Convenzione europea*, in *Giurisprudenza europea e processo penale italiano* 143 (Antonio Balsamo & Roberto E. Kostoris eds., 2008)

Kai Ambos, *Treatise on International Criminal Law, Volume III: International Criminal Procedure*) (2016)

Ennio Amodio & Eugenio Selvaggi, *An Accusatorial System in a Civil Law Country: The 1988 Italian Code of Criminal Procedure*, 62 Temple L. Rev. 1211 (1989)

Dominik Brodowski et al., *Germany*, in *Effective Criminal Defence in Europe* 253 (Ed Cape et al. eds., 2010)

Michele Caianiello, *Italy*, in *Effective Criminal Defence in Europe* 373 (Ed Cape et al. eds., 2010)

Michele Caianiello, *Disclosure Before the ICC: The Emergence of a New Form of Policies Implementation System in International Criminal Justice?*, 10 Int'l Crim. L. Rev. 23 (2010)

Michele Caianiello, *First Decisions on the Admission of Evidence at ICC Trials: A Blending of Accusatorial and Inquisitorial Models?*, 9 J. Int'l. Crim. Just. 385 (2011)

Michele Caianiello, *The Italian Public Prosecutor: An Inquisitorial Figure in Adversarial Proceedings?*, in *Transnational Perspectives on Prosecutorial Power* 250 (Erik Luna & Marianne Wade eds., 2012)

Michele Caianiello, *To Sanction (or Not to Sanction) Procedural Flaws at E.U. Level? A Step Forward in the Creation of an E.U. Criminal Process*, 22 Eur. J. Crime, Crim. L. & Crim. Just. 317 (2014)

Valérie Dervieux, *The French System*, in *European Criminal Procedures* 218 (Mireille Delmas-Marty & J.R. Spencer eds., 2005)

Giulio Illuminati, *The Frustrated Turn to Adversarial Procedure in Italy (Italian Criminal Procedure Code of 1988)*, 4 Wash. U. Global Stud. L. Rev. 567 (2005)

Giulio Illuminati, *The Accusatorial Process from the Italian Point of View*, 35 N.C. J. Int'l L. & Com. Reg. 297 (2010)

Giulio Illuminati & Michele Caianiello, *The Investigative Stage of the Criminal Process in Italy*, in *Suspects in Europe: Procedural Rights at the Investigative Stage of the Criminal Process in the European Union* 129 (Ed Cape et al. eds., 2007)

Christine Janssens, *The Principle of Mutual Recognition in E.U. Law* (2013)

Rodolphe Juy-Birmann, *The German System*, in *European Criminal Procedures* 292 (Mireille Delmas-Marty & J.R. Spencer eds., 2005)

Xavier-Jean Keïta, *Disclosure of Evidence in the Law and Practice of the ICC*, 16 Int'l Crim. L. Rev. 1018 (2016)

André Klip, *European Criminal Law: An Integrative Approach* (2016)

Jean Larguier & Philippe Conte, *Procédure pénale* (24th ed. 2016)

Valsamis Mitsilegas, *E.U. Criminal Law After Lisbon: Rights: Trust and the Transformation of Justice in Europe* (2016)

Christoph Safferling, *International Criminal Procedure* (2012)

Larivière Daniel Soulez, *Face aux juges: Ce que tous les honnêtes gens doivent savoir* (2017)

Jenia I. Turner, *Plea Bargaining and Disclosure in Germany and the United States: Comparative Lessons*, 57 Wm. & Mary L. Rev. 1 (2016)

Thomas Weigend & Franz Salditt, *The Investigative Stage of the Criminal Process in Germany*, in *Suspects in Europe: Procedural Rights at the Investigative Stage of the Criminal Process in the European Union* 79 (Ed Cape et al. eds., 2007)

CHAPTER 27

TRANSNATIONAL ACCESS TO EVIDENCE, WITNESSES, AND SUSPECTS

SABINE GLESS

I. Introduction

Criminal proceedings have often been depicted as primarily national affairs, but today investigations often reach beyond state borders. Over the last century, a growing number of frameworks for transnational cooperation have been established to facilitate transnational transfer of evidence. Such international division of tasks in prosecuting crimes is crucial in certain situations if wrongdoers are to be prevented from taking advantage of international borders and the limits of national jurisdiction. However, transnational access to evidence—especially to witnesses and suspects—also raises a number of problems. States must define adequate requirements for cross-border inquiries that give consideration to their own interests as well as individual rights. Investigative findings gleaned within the scope of transnational cooperation are of practical value to domestic law enforcement agencies only if they can be used as evidence. Often specific questions of reliability arise when foreign authorities gather evidence, or the fairness of proceedings is disputed when, for instance, evidence located abroad cannot be accessed by all parties.

Against this backdrop, the following analysis considers whether evidence can be transferred between nation-states without negatively affecting the legitimacy, fairness, and reliability of the fact-finding procedure.

The analysis focuses on basic questions arising from the conflict between the criminal justice systems' genuine interest in comprehensive and reliable fact-finding—a core aspect of the legitimacy of criminal justice globally—and the specific restrictions on fact-finding when evidence is located beyond a state border. Such restrictions protect the various interests of the states or individuals involved if law enforcement authorities pierce international borders.

An outline of the historical roots of transnational access to evidence provides the background of current legal practices (*see infra* Section II). In this chapter the German and U.S. legal frameworks are used as case studies, illustrating pars pro toto the impact of mutual legal assistance in a civil law and a common law jurisdiction (*see infra* Section III). Here as well as when looking at new approaches to transnational access to evidence such as the framework of the European Union (*see infra* Section IV), the emphasis is on safeguards for reliability and fairness of fact-finding. The core argument is that future transnational access to evidence must meet a standard that is functionally equivalent to the standard for evidence obtained in the domestic criminal justice systems (*see infra* Section V).

II. Historical Roots and Current Phenomena

Penal powers and jurisdiction in criminal matters can, in principle, be traced to the Westphalian model of sovereign states, endowed with a monopoly over the use of force in their territory. This understanding of the *ius puniendi* has not only proven favorable for building state power, but also gave rise to procedural codes that, generally, empower authorities to undertake comprehensive fact-finding while bound by certain procedural restrictions at the scene of the crime.[1] While a state can subpoena anyone who may be able to provide information relevant for a criminal case so the evidence can be secured by the authorities, the individual enjoys the guarantees of due process according to the law of the land.[2] The drawback, however, is that this concept leaves states powerless when they need to investigate an alleged crime with evidence located beyond their borders. Unless obligated by treaty, sovereign states are not required to produce documents, witnesses, or suspects for criminal proceedings taking place under another national jurisdiction.[3] If an investigating state were to instigate investigations in a foreign country without giving notice to that country's authorities, it would risk infringing the principle of sovereign equality of states.[4] States prosecuting a transnational case and in need of witness testimony in a neighboring state thus need to follow certain procedures. Similarly, individuals who are approached by foreign authorities with a request to

[1] Sabine Gless, *Bird's-Eye View and Worm's-Eye View: Towards a Defendant-Based Approach in Transnational Criminal Law*, 6 Transnat'l Legal Theory 117 (2015).

[2] *See* Frederick Mark Gedicks, *Originalist Defense of Substantive Due Process: Magna Carta, Higher-Law Constitutionalism, and the Fifth Amendment*, 58 Emory L.J. 585 (2009).

[3] David Whedbee, *The Faint Shadow of the Sixth Amendment: Substantial Imbalance in Evidence-Gathering Capacity Abroad Under the U.S.-P.R.C. Mutual Legal Assistance Agreement in Criminal Matters*, 12 Pac. Rim L. & Pol'y J. 561, 569 (2003).

[4] *See* U.N. Charter, Art. 2, para. 1.

dissolve information that could possibly be used as evidence in a criminal trial abroad may wish to do so, but only if the procedure and conditions are clear.[5]

Although current legal debates address problems of transnational access to evidence, the focus is often on practical problems of fact-finding and issues of legitimacy, reliability, and fairness. It has rarely been debated whether individuals affected by such outreaching state activity receive adequate protection by the law.[6]

1. From a Police Affair to Judicial Proceedings

Until well into the nineteenth century, obtaining information across borders was not perceived as a judicial act but as an intelligence gathering procedure that involved the swapping of information across borders based in principle on *do ut des* (or quid pro quo), when one state "scratched the back" of the other, still lingering in the principle of reciprocity. Prominent examples are provided by spies' activity in Swiss border towns Germans fled to after the failed revolution of 1848 or during political persecution in 1878. Swiss informers reported to German police on involvement in petty crime or political agitation. Police intelligence, prosecution work, and the implications for individual rights were not yet set in strict legal concepts. Even in the Western world, within one jurisdiction, differences were huge: While in England, certain individual rights were secured by the Magna Charta in 1215, it was only during the seventeenth century that the state's police power slowly transformed from an essentially unaccountable government power to a power constrained by, and subject to, the rule of law. The European continent followed suit in the eighteenth and nineteenth centuries with the idea of a *Rechtsstaat* introducing such concepts in Germany. Only during the twentieth and twenty-first centuries did countries gradually establish mutual legal assistance (MLA) in criminal matters on a legal basis, signing and ratifying multilateral mutual legal assistance treaties (MLATs).[7] MLATs, at first, only were formal agreements among states, intended to facilitate law enforcement cooperation, but subsequently, with the adoption of corresponding domestic legislation, extended transnational cooperation to include judicial proceedings.[8]

Finally, proceedings became more formal. Today, for transnational access to evidence, witnesses, or suspects, by way of classic mutual legal assistance, authorities of the

[5] Sabine Gless, *Transnational Cooperation in Criminal Matters and the Guarantee of a Fair Trial: Approaches to a General Principle*, 9 Utrecht L. Rev. 90, 96–97 (2013).

[6] Christopher L. Blakesley & Otto Lagodny, *Finding Harmony Amidst Disagreement over Extradition, Jurisdiction, The Role of Human Rights and Issues of Extraterritoriality Under International Criminal Law*, 24 Vand. J. Transnat'l L. 44–45 (1991); Daniel Schaffner, *Das Individuum im internationalen Rechtshilferecht in Strafsachen—Die dritte Dimension bei schweizerischer Unterstützung fremder Strafverfahren* 2–3 (2013).

[7] Wolfgang Schomburg et al., *Einleitung*, in *Internationale Rechtshilfe in Strafsachen* no. 25 (Wolfgang Schomburg et al. eds., 5th ed. 2011).

[8] Peter Rackow & Cornelius Birr, *Recent Developments in Legal Assistance in Criminal Matters*, 2 Goettingen J. Int'l L. 1087, 1091–93 (2010).

requesting state apply to the competent authorities in the *requested state* by issuing a formal letter (often called a letter rogatory). If the *requested state* agrees to grant assistance, it will in principle obtain the required evidence in accordance with its own procedural rules (*locus regit actum*). Such a course of action not only safeguards sovereign decision-making, but also protects the legal position of individuals who are eventually requested to provide information. Witnesses, suspects, or third persons are subject to coercive measures only according to the laws of the land, albeit subject to modification with regard to MLATs. For instance, among countries that work closely together, such as Member States of the European Union, authorities may apply the law of the country that seeks information ("forum state").[9]

2. Broadening Fact-Finding at the Expense of Reliability and Fairness?

The findings gleaned from transnational cooperation may be of little practical value to domestic law enforcement agencies. If, for instance, witness testimony obtained in Austria is presented before a U.S. federal court that has not been confronted by the defense, chances are high that its evidentiary value will be called into question because the relevant national rules covering the investigative procedure have not been observed in the foreign country. Furthermore, MLATs usually give consideration to protecting state interests. As a result, the execution of a request may be subject to political interests.[10] The United States regularly maintains the right—as a *requested state*—to refrain from cooperation or to restrict the use of certain information as evidence. An exception clause, based on "political offenses" or "human rights," can be drafted into MLATs as a specific basis for denying assistance; this releases a government from any obligation to collaborate with countries that do not share basic values, such as freedom of speech, civil rights, or the separation of powers.[11] The consequence, however, is that material evidence can be withheld from fact-finding. Indeed, there appears to be no accepted threshold as to when information may be withdrawn for the protection of states' interests, since conditions for mutual assistance in criminal matters differ around the globe.

In contrast, individuals wanting access to evidence located abroad find themselves shrouded by legal uncertainty, not least because they are often in fact excluded from using MLATs to obtain evidence in a foreign state. Individuals affected by transnational evidence obtainment—for instance, witnesses who are summoned to give

[9] *See, e.g.*, Art. 4 Convention on Mutual Assistance in Criminal Matters between the Member States of the European Union of 29 May 2000 [E.U.-Convention of 2000], O.J.C 197, 12.07.2000, p. 1.

[10] A reminder of the historical background are reservations of political nature that require among other things an authorization by an appropriate official before a federal judge may issue such an order to execute a request from a foreign authority, see 18 U.S.C. § 3512 para 1.

[11] Whedbee, *supra* note 3, at 563.

testimony—also face ambiguous situations, as it may be unclear which authority asks them to provide information.

Fact-finding based on evidence obtained abroad thus may fall short of domestic standards in different ways. At the same time, it is crucial to use evidence located abroad in order to mitigate the risk of wrongdoers going unpunished. Ultimately, the responsibility to evaluate the reliability and fairness of fact-finding based on evidence gathered abroad falls on domestic courts and other competent national authorities. This begs the question: How is the MLA dilemma solved in individual criminal justice systems?

III. Transnational Access to Evidence

Based on the view that international borders should not offer protection to offenders, virtually all countries have signed MLATs and provided legal rules for transnational access to evidence, witnesses, and suspects.[12] As long as reciprocity is guaranteed, states will grant assistance to one another, irrespective of whether such assistance is underscored by a treaty formalizing such cooperation.[13] Domestic law translates international treaties on transnational access to evidence in procedural rules in the *requesting state* as well as in the *requested state*. Mostly, states will have a specific set of rules governing MLA, but they also rely on general criminal procedure regulation for actually obtaining the evidence, for example, the interrogation of a witness or a suspect in the *requested state* and its evidentiary use in criminal proceedings in the *requesting state*.

From a criminal justice point of view, the laws actually governing access to, and use of, evidence are of particular interest. The following account of German and U.S. laws governing MLA reveals the features of two distinct models for the transnational access to evidence. The models differ because of legal traditions, geopolitical situations, and policy goals. Germany, with its inquisitorial tradition and civil law codification, is a member of various international treaties and agreements (e.g., the Council of Europe, European Union, and the Schengen Agreement) with the nine countries with which it shares a border. The U.S. criminal justice system, based on the adversarial process model and common law tradition, has only two neighboring countries, although it is responsible for four times as many inhabitants. Both countries agree that, for criminal proceedings, discovering the "truth" is a primary goal that can only be achieved with reliable and fair fact-finding. But the methods of achieving that goal differ in each country. During the last decades a number of developments have reduced disparities, especially with continental European countries signing up to a guarantee of a fair trial based on the idea of

[12] *See, e.g.*, Robert Neale Lyman, *Compulsory Process in a Globalized Era: Defendant Access to Mutual Legal Assistance Treaties*, 47 Va. J. Int'l L. 261 (2006).

[13] A terminological distinction between assistance based on MLATs and non-treaty assistance as MLA based on letters rogatory, used in the United States, is not used globally.

equality of arms.[14] Nevertheless, the use of MLA causes different problems in an adversarial system, where two opposing parties investigate the facts and present their story to a neutral court, as opposed to an inquisitorial model, where a government agent (investigating magistrate, court, etc.) is in charge of the fact-finding and must look for exonerating evidence in the same way it looks for incriminating evidence, with little distinction between evidence presented by the defense and prosecution. Practitioners and scholars in both countries are aware that access to evidence abroad is continually growing in importance. At the same time, the MLA is also causing problems, because it is often slow, not always efficient, and creates hurdles if the domestic legal standards in proceedings cannot be enforced abroad.

1. Germany

German law on transnational access to evidence is based on the European blueprint for MLATs: the Council of Europe's Convention on Mutual Assistance in Criminal Matters of April 20, 1959.[15] With this treaty, Germany and its neighboring states (as well as forty other countries) agree to afford each other the widest measure of mutual assistance with a view to gathering evidence, hearing witnesses, experts, suspects, etc. The convention sets out detailed rules for the issuing requests by competent judicial authorities and their execution, which aims to procure or communicate evidence in criminal proceedings. Today, the Convention on Mutual Assistance in Criminal Matters of 1959 also provides a legal basis for facilitated MLA, such as cooperation under the Schengen Convention[16] and various European Union (EU) legal instruments, which will be discussed in Sections IV and V.

Germany has a long tradition of cooperating closely with other countries, including the handling of incoming and outgoing requests with the *Bundesamt für Justiz* or other competent "judicial authorities" (including prosecutors and courts but not defense counsel). It maintains some right to refuse cooperation. The Convention of Mutual Assistance in Criminal Matters from 1959, for instance, stipulates as grounds for refusal of MLA so-called reservations with regard to political offenses, military offenses, or tax offenses. These have been incorporated into the German domestic law, the Act on Assistance in Criminal Matters.[17] The Code of Criminal Procedure provides a subsidiary basis when obtaining evidence for a foreign country, for example, interviewing a witness

[14] *See, e.g.*, Gless, *supra* note 5, at 96–97.

[15] *Entered into force* 12 June 1962, E.T.S. No. 030, https://www.coe.int/en/web/conventions/full-list/conventions/treaty/030.

[16] The *Schengen Acquis* as Referred to in Art. 1(2) of Council Decision 1999/435/EC of 20 May 1999, O.J. L 239, 22.09.2000, p. 19.

[17] Gesetz über die Internationale Rechtshilfe in Strafsachen [Federal Act on International Mutual Assistance in Criminal Matters], *translation at* https://www.gesetze-im-internet.de/englisch_irg/index.html (last visited November 14, 2018).

for proceedings abroad (*locus regit actum*).[18] If the assistance involves taking coercive measures, "dual criminality" is, in principle, required.[19] This means that a witness will only be summoned for an interview if the criminal investigation of the respective offense is not only punishable in the requesting country—for instance, a fraudulent action must not only amount to fraud in the United States, but also in Germany. When it comes to executing a request, Germany, with its inquisitorial setup of authorities looking for incriminating and exonerating evidence, makes no distinction under procedural law as to whether the hearing of a witness is conducted for a foreign authority or in the context of a national criminal investigation.

The inquisitorial tradition also has consequences on outgoing requests. As the authority in charge is obligated to investigate "not only incriminating but also exonerating circumstances," it must make use of MLATs on behalf of the defense.[20] In practice, however, the details of the complex German law for fact-finding, which maintains an inquisitorial approach and combines it with a commitment to "equality of arms," often puts the defense on the back foot: the defense must submit a request to retrieve evidence from abroad to the court, which may decline the request if it can substantiate why it deems the evidence immaterial.[21] German prosecution services may make use of MLATs in their own right.

Germany's detailed laws and huge amount of case law on MLA is representative for continental Europe: With many states close to each other, domestic laws anticipate the need for MLA and clarify standard issues, as does the Swiss Criminal Procedure Code, which explicitly stipulates that the parties have, in general, a right to participate in witness interrogations, but this right may be curtailed when interviews take place abroad.[22] Overall, states in Europe have closed ranks in cross-border prosecution of crimes.

2. United States

Common law jurisdictions have traditionally been more reluctant to get involved in cross-border activity, following the adage that "all crime is local."[23] Before many parts of life became digitized, the actual physical territory on which an act took place or a piece of evidence was located clearly marked jurisdiction. Today, however, the realization

[18] Strafprozessordnung [StPO] [German Code of Criminal Procedure], translation at https://www.gesetze-im-internet.de/englisch_stpo/index.html (last visited November 14, 2018).

[19] Schomburg et al., *supra* note 7, at no. 31.

[20] Sabine Gless, *Sachverhaltsaufklärung durch Auslandszeugen*, in *Festschrift für Ulrich Eisenberg* 499–509 (Henning Ernst Müller et al. eds., 2009).

[21] Strafprozessordnung [StPO] § 244 para. 2 ("in order to establish the truth [the court] shall, *proprio motu*, extend the taking of evidence to all facts and means of proof relevant to the decision"); for the English translation, *see* https://www.gesetze-im-internet.de/englisch_stpo/englisch_stpo.html (last visited July 31, 2017).

[22] Schweizerische Strafprozessordnung [StPO] [Swiss Criminal Procedure Code] Art. 148, translation at https://www.admin.ch/opc/en/classified-compilation/20052319/index.html (last visited November 14, 2018).

[23] Macleod v. Attorney-General (NSW) [1891] AC 455, 458.

that many crimes are transnational has led many countries to introduce forms of international cooperation.[24] The U.S. government has signed more than seventy mutual legal assistance treaties (MLATs). Nevertheless, a certain reservation against cross-border prosecution persists. It is only logical that U.S. federal courts developed an extraterritorial due process doctrine in criminal cases, which requires a sufficient nexus between the defendant and the United States for a case to be brought before its courts.[25] But if cases are heard before a court, MLATs generally provide for access to evidence ("outgoing requests"), as treaty arrangements obligate the competent "judicial authority" to handle "incoming requests."[26] The treaties set international rules for the obligation to execute search warrants and take witness statements. In fact, the U.S. Congress has enacted a variety of measures to assist foreign law enforcement efforts, with the expectation of the United States receiving reciprocal treatment. Incoming requests for MLA are—in contrast to requests for extradition—normally not subject to the condition of dual criminality. The domestic laws governing the taking of evidence, however, offer some procedural protection for witnesses and suspects.[27]

Regarding outgoing requests, if authorities bring cases in which evidence and potential witnesses are located overseas, the prosecution can make use of MLATs, but the defense faces difficulties. The compulsory process clause of the Sixth Amendment—which allows defendants in domestic cases to secure witnesses in their favor through the issuance of a court-ordered subpoena—does not include a right to secure testimony of a witness living in a foreign country.[28]

Here, the adversarial structure of criminal investigations in common law jurisdictions gives an edge to the prosecution, since only government authorities can issue an MLAT-based request, not the defense.[29] This is, however, not an obligatory feature, as the first three MLATs signed by the United States apparently did include provisions granting access to defense counsel.[30]

If only government agents—prosecutors and law enforcement agencies that investigate criminal conduct—have the power to trigger MLA, and the defense does not have access

[24] Virginia M. Kendall & T. Markus Funk, *The Role of Mutual Legal Assistance Treaties in Obtaining Foreign Evidence*, 40(2) Litigation 59 (2014).

[25] *See* Michael Farbiarz, *Extraterritorial Criminal Jurisdiction*, 114 Mich. L. Rev. 507, 512, 516–17 (2016).

[26] Federal Judicial Center, *International Litigation Guide Mutual Legal Assistance Treaties and Letters Rogatory: A Guide for Judges* 4 (2014), https://www.fjc.gov/sites/default/files/2017/MLAT-LR-Guide-Funk-FJC-2014.pdf (last visited November 14, 2018).

[27] For instance, 28 U.S.C. § 1782 can be used to obtain assistance such as the (1) production of government or corporate records or (2) performance of witness interviews. Generally, almost all evidence requiring the use of compulsory process (subpoena or judicial order) may be sought in accordance with U.S. law. The Foreign Evidence Efficiency Act, 18 U.S.C. § 3512, was enacted to help streamline the MLAT process, making it easier for the United States to respond to requests.

[28] U.S. Const. amend. VI ("In all criminal prosecutions, the accused shall enjoy the right . . . to have compulsory process for obtaining witnesses in his favor. . . ."); Lyman, *supra* note 12, at 262.

[29] Michael Abbell, *DOJ Renews Assault on Defendants' Right to Use Treaties to Obtain Evidence from Abroad*, 21 The Champion (1997); L. Song Richardson, *Due Process for the Global Crime Age: A Proposal*, 41 Cornell Int'l L.J. 347–48 (2008).

[30] Kendall & Funk, *supra* note 24.

to evidence located abroad, the defense would be unfairly impaired. Such a grave imbalance in evidence gathering would never be tolerated at the domestic level; it is unclear why it should be tolerated in transnational evidence gathering.[31]

Federal courts have invoked their supervisory powers to order the DOJ to obtain evidence on behalf of defendants through MLAT procedural channels under Rule 15 of the Federal Rules of Criminal Procedure, which allows for a deposition of a witness instead of a witness' oral testimony in exceptional circumstances.[32] Thus today, defendants may petition a court with a "Rule 15" motion to direct the DOJ to request depositions of information in a foreign country,[33] or they can seek evidence from abroad directly through non-treaty-based letters rogatory. Choosing either option, the defendant faces various hurdles in obtaining exculpatory evidence. In fact, depositions of witnesses abroad pursuant to Rule 15 orders may be expressly contrary to MLATs.[34] Courts, however, appear to be quite hesitant to allow defendants' motions to obtain exonerating evidence abroad.[35]

In cases in which requests for assistance are executed successfully, the United States, like all other countries, must ensure that information obtained abroad would also be admitted as evidence at home.[36] For instance, only if the taking of testimony in a foreign country follows the respective federal rules can it be presented before a federal court without further ado. Problems arise when domestic rules of procedure forbid a defendant's lawyer from engaging—or even being present—during the deposition of a witness conducted by a foreign authority. Federal rules aim at mitigating that problem, ensuring, for instance, that whenever a deposition is taken based on a Rule 15 motion, the defendant is not in custody and/or his attorney has the right to be present at the examination.[37] This upholds the "confrontation clause" as a reliability requirement.[38]

3. Safeguarding Accuracy and Fairness of Fact-Finding

The examples of Germany and the United States illustrate that fact-finding by way of MLA, while quite distinct in operation, present similar problems: a quasi-international division of tasks in prosecuting crimes may impair safeguards that ensure accuracy and fairness at the domestic level. This problem is not solved at the international level;

[31] *See, e.g.*, Richardson, *supra* note 29, at 374.

[32] For further information, see *In re Sindona, 450 F. Supp. 672 (S.D.N.Y. 1978) (noting the U.S.-Switzerland MLAT was silent on the rights of "private persons"). *See also* United States v. Filippi, 918 F.2d 244, 246–48 (1st Cir. 1990); United States v. Des Marteau, 162 F.R.D. 364, 372 n.5 (M.D. Fla. 1995); Michael Abbell, *Obtaining Evidence Abroad in Criminal Cases* § 2 no. 5. (2002).

[33] Johnson v. Mammoth Recreations, Inc., 975 F.2d 604, 607 (9th Cir. 1992).

[34] Whedbee, *supra* note 3, at 582–83.

[35] United States v. Mejia, 448 F.3d 436, 444 (D.C. Cir. 2006).

[36] *See, e.g.*, *United States v. Salim, 855 F.2d 944 (2d Cir. 1988).

[37] *See* *18 U.S.C. § 3503 (2002).

[38] United States v. Sines, 761 F.2d 1434, 1441 (1985); United States v. Gifford, 892 F.2d 263, 264 (3d Cir. 1989).

international treaties seem to be indifferent to consequences for reliability of evidence, as they prioritize efficient cooperation. Thus, the question arises whether counterbalancing measures should be adopted at the national level.

a. *A Ubiquitous Problem...*

The capacity to obtain evidence abroad expands the information basis in a criminal trial and thus, in principle, strengthens the overall reliability of a fact-finding procedure. But risks are posed by, for instance, witness testimony that cannot be tested for its accuracy and authenticity because it has been obtained abroad. Indeed, if only the prosecution—and not the defense—can substantiate its story by witness testimony gathered outside the jurisdiction, the fact-finding appears unfair and unreliable. Furthermore, the growing networking of prosecution services based on MLATs and the establishment of close networks, especially in the European Union (e.g., the EU Judicial Network or Eurojust) substantially strengthens the prosecution.[39]

When thinking about possible counterbalances for risks of accuracy and fairness of the fact-finding procedure in a particular criminal justice system, one must identify the real risks for that system. Sticking points are the obligations of judicial authorities put in charge of fact-finding, and thus usually empowered to issue a formal request for evidence obtainment abroad. If these authorities must look for incriminating *and* exonerating evidence, also in foreign jurisdictions, risk is low that MLA will distort fact-finding. If only prosecution services are involved that will not help the defendant to build his story; it may be necessary to see whether courts can be involved in evidence gathering, if evidence is located abroad, and the only means of obtaining it is via a government channel.

MLA fits as a natural part of the investigation in Continental European systems, but it is a more polarizing element in adversarial systems such as in the United States. However, the real world often looks different. In inquisitorial systems, the defense may also find itself in a weak position, as the example of Germany has shown. If the defense must substantiate a request for evidence taking abroad, but a court may decline such a request if it can argue that the evidence is either not material or "unobtainable" for the government using a standard of proof, then, in general, the prosecution is favored.[40] Therefore, the demand for a "transnational due process framework," as proposed by L. Song Richardson for the United States,[41] which would moderate inequality in cases in which evidence must be obtained abroad, appears to have potential for a valid application everywhere. This is because ubiquitously the use of MLA may impair instruments for safeguarding accuracy and fairness of fact-finding on the domestic level, namely, the

[39] Lyman, *supra* note 12, at 278; Ilias Anagnostopoulos, *Criminal Justice Cooperation in the European Union After the First Few "Steps": A Defence View*, 15 ERA Forum 9 (2014).

[40] Strafprozessordnung [StPO] § 244 para. 3 [German Criminal Procedure Code]. For further information, see Gless, *supra* note 20, at 499–509. For a discussion on the obligation to issue a subpoena outside the territorial jurisdiction, see Lyman, *supra* note 12, at 266.

[41] Richardson, *supra* note 29, at 374.

answerability for the chain of custody and the accountability of government agents for evidence gathering in disciplinary proceedings or before a criminal court.

b. ... *and a Ubiquitous Solution: Exclusionary Rules*

Given that a "transnational due process framework" currently seems unrealistic, it is important to point out the last resort commonly available across jurisdictions for cases in which the use of evidence obtained abroad carries the risk of seriously affecting accuracy or fairness: the exclusion of evidence. Exclusionary rules can be found in all criminal justice systems, and in any event, the admission and ultimate use and evaluation of evidence is in the hands of the court or authority deciding the case. Thus, domestic exclusionary rules can be put to use to safeguard the reliability and fairness of transnational collection of evidence.

Today, in both inquisitorial and adversarial models, fact-finding is perceived as reliable and fair only if, at least in theory, the prosecution and defense have equal access to all material evidence and are afforded the opportunity to test it in court. Following these basic ideas, exclusionary rules might be used to omit evidence that could endanger the reliability or fairness of fact-finding. The use of such rules in the United States and Germany, however, indicates that courts are reluctant to utilize them, as they do not want to lose potentially relevant evidence.

For instance, in the United States, if MLATs grant only the prosecution access to evidence located abroad, the defendant could seek on due process grounds the exclusion of evidence obtained abroad by MLAT procedures.[42] And although prosecutors do not have a blanket duty to search for exonerating evidence either domestically or abroad, if they hold information favorable to the defense they are required to share it.[43] This duty accords with the more general obligation of prosecutors to place their interest in gaining convictions secondary to ensuring the reliability and fairness of the criminal trial.[44] Even if courts and prosecutors equalize the parties' access to evidence in these ways, however, other problems of fairness and equal access remain. United States' courts treat unlawful searches and seizures abroad differently from confessions obtained unlawfully abroad. Generally, the Fourth Amendment does not apply to searches and seizures abroad, so U.S. courts do not exclude evidence that was obtained outside U.S. territory by means that would violate U.S. constitutional law if domestic officials had seized it within U.S. borders.[45] By contrast, whether a confession that is coerced abroad (rather

[42] Lyman, *supra* note 12, at 290.

[43] Brady v. Maryland, 373 U.S. 83, 86–87 (1963); *Giglio v. United States, 405 U.S. 150 (1972); Kyles v. Whitley, 514 U.S. 419, 435, 437 (1995).

[44] *See, e.g.*, Berger v. United States, 295 U. S. 78, 88 (1935) ("The [prosecutor] is the representative not of an ordinary party to a controversy, but of a sovereignty... whose interest... in a criminal prosecution is not that it shall win a case, but that justice shall be done").

[45] United States v. Verdugo-Urquidez, 494 U.S. 259 (1990); Mark A. Godsey, *The New Frontier of Constitutional Confession Law—the International Arena: Exploring the Admissibility of Confessions Taken by U.S. Investigators from Non-Americans Abroad*, 91 Geo. L.J. 851, 867–73 (2003).

than simply taken in violation of *Miranda*) would be admissible against a defendant in a U.S. trial is uncertain. Coerced confessions from domestic interrogations are excluded under the due process "involuntary confession rule," but whether the same would be true for a confession coerced abroad is unclear under U.S. law, especially if a foreign official is responsible for the coercion.[46] Evidence transfer raises the questions of evidence reliability, and fairness.

This is also true for Germany, where courts have evaluated the admissibility of unchallenged evidence[47] not with a view to its reliability, but primarily with a view to whether the parties to the German trial had a chance to challenge the evidence or not.[48] If foreign laws, that is, the rules set by the *requested state*, limit the confrontation of incriminating testimony, the evidence may be used, but the curtailment must be taken into consideration when assessing the value of the evidence. This onus, however, has proven to be a weak threshold. The dilemma of wanting to include potentially valuable information, despite the risks for reliability of fact-finding, became obvious in the post 9/11 *Motassadeq* case, in which German courts first admitted, then excluded, and finally partially admitted statements from U.S. intelligence officials to German authorities. The statements took the form of summaries of interrogations of three persons who were suspected of terrorist activities and were then held at unknown locations by U.S. authorities.[49]

IV. New Approaches to Transnational Access to Evidence

States increasingly need to include information located abroad. For certain countries, MLA has grown into a modern international division of tasks in prosecuting crimes, but other countries are still operating under a very traditional cooperation. Both sets of countries struggle with flaws consequential to the origin of MLA, and antiquated ideas of sovereignty and transnational assistance. The logical step forward seems to be to introduce more adequate MLATs. In the light of such considerations the United States and the EU, for instance, signed a MLAT in 2003 (EU-U.S.-MLAT),[50] which entered

[46] Karen Nelson Moore, *Aliens and the Constitution*, 88 NYU L. Rev. 801, 830–33 (2013); Mark A. Godsey, *The New Frontier of Constitutional Confession Law—the International Arena: Exploring the Admissibility of Confessions Taken by U.S. Investigators from Non-Americans Abroad*, 91 Geo. L.J. 851, 852–53 (2003).

[47] For instance, witness testimony obtained abroad, without the possibility of the defense to ask questions or confront the witness.

[48] Bundesgerichtshof [BGH] [Federal Court of Justice], BGHSt 55, 70.

[49] Bundesgerichtshof [BGH] [Federal Court of Justice], BGHSt 51, 144.

[50] Agreement on mutual legal assistance between the European Union and the United States of America [hereinafter EU-US-MLAT], O.J. L 181, 19.07.2003, p. 34.

into force in 2010. This cooperation, a result from a post-9/11 alliance to improve cooperation between EU Member States and the United States, pushes ahead. One prime example of new forms of cooperation is the introduction of so-called Joint Investigation Teams (JITs). Based on case-by-case agreements, authorities put together a team of agents from both countries.[51] JITs enhance efficiencies in gathering evidence without the need for international requests for mutual legal assistance. But the question remains whether such a transnational transfer of evidence can take place without the loss of the legitimacy, fairness, and reliability to the fact-finding procedure.

1. Reforming MLA...

The reform of MLA has been at the heart of various legal acts adopted in the EU framework. Various conventions[52] strive to make MLA more efficient, for instance, by providing a treaty-based foundation for the "spontaneous exchange of information" or for JITs in Europe and the use of evidence collected during their operations.[53] Furthermore, they involve Europol and Eurojust, the EU agencies for criminal justice cooperation in Europe.

Particular convention rules aim to resolve the problem of admissibility of foreign evidence by allowing, for instance, the use of the law of the *requesting state* during evidence collection in another EU Member State. According to the rules governing interrogations of witnesses by videoconference the judicial authority of the requested Member State shall summon the witness to appear according to its law, but "the hearing shall be conducted directly by, or under the direction of, the judicial authority of the requesting Member State in accordance with its own law."[54] The latter concession, however, is restricted to compliance with the fundamental principles of the law of the requested Member State.[55] Thus even modern MLATs still hold on to certain requirements that have been viewed as safeguards for legitimate transnational access to evidence, witnesses, and suspects, namely, the requirement of dual criminality or political offense and humanitarian provisos (*ordre public*).[56] Such limitations of cross-border activity cover sovereignty issues, but also safeguard individual interests—such as legal certainty regarding the exercise of state power. Hence the reforms inside the EU also show the limits of reorganizing traditional cooperation if states still retain conditions for fact-finding.[57]

[51] *See id.* Art. 5 EU-US-MLAT.

[52] Schengen Convention, *supra* note 16; E.U.-Convention of 2000, *supra* note 9, with its additional Protocol, O.J. C 326, 21.11.2001, p. 1.

[53] Nadine Zurkinden, *Joint Investigation Teams: Chancen und Grenzen von gemeinsamen Ermittlungsgruppen in der Schweiz, Europa und den USA* 175–77 (2013).

[54] Arts. 10(4) and (5)(c) E.U. Convention of 2000, *supra* note 9.

[55] *Id.* Art. 10(5)(a) E.U. Convention of 2000.

[56] *See supra* Section II.2 and Section III.1. & 2.

[57] Art. 7 E.U. Convention of 2000, *supra* note 9.

2. ... or Replacing MLA?

A more radical step has been taken in the EU, with Member States partly abandoning the fierce political struggle over a possible shift of the *ius puniendi* from the state level to a supranational level.[58] European institutions and a majority of EU Member States are committed to the political agenda of establishing a European-wide area of freedom, security and justice. Subsequently, different initiatives have been adopted to partly replace MLA with mutual recognition of judicial orders issued by competent authorities of Member States. The legal basis of this restructuring of cross-border cooperation is Article 82 TFEU, which—among other things—foresees the establishment of minimum rules concerning evidence admissibility or concerning the rights of individuals in criminal procedures. The broad legislative mandate thus addresses reliability and fairness. But to spell out the general commitment in detailed legal acts has turned out to be difficult, as different stakeholders have discovered during different legislative procedures.

a. *The European Evidence Order and the European Investigation Order*

After years of intense debate, a framework decision on a European Evidence Order (EEO)[59] was adopted in 2008. It aimed for transnational access to documents, witnesses and suspect statements already taken, based on the principle of mutual recognition. If, for instance, a German court needs witness testimony documented by Polish prosecutors, it will issue an EEO and gain access to it easily and swiftly. Broadly speaking, the EEO wanted to enable competent authorities to reach over borders and to be granted what they need. With consideration to such a radical change in access to evidence, the scope of the EEO had been limited to access to objects, documents, and data already held by judicial authorities in other Member States.

This limitation, however, derailed the initiative. Some Member States feared that the EEO would lead to a further segmentation of cross-border cooperation in a Europe of a *géométrie variable*, that is, a differentiated integration that acknowledges that certain EU Member States may group together to pursue a given goal, while allowing those opposed to hold back. In 2010, seven EU Member States[60] put forward an initiative for a European Investigation Order (EIO). The Directive that introduced the EIO[61] and effectively replaced the EEO was adopted in 2014. Today, when seeking evidence in another EU

[58] *See, e.g.*, the *"Lisbon judgment"* of the Bundesverfassungsgericht [BVerfG] [German Constitutional Court], 2 BvE 2/08, June 30, 2009, paras. 252–255, http://www.bverfg.de/entscheidungen/es20090630_2bve000208en.html (Ger.); Petter Asp, *The Substantive Criminal Law Competence of the EU* 43–69 (2012).

[59] The Framework Decision 2008/978/JHA on the European evidence warrant for the purpose of obtaining objects, documents and data for use in proceedings in criminal matters, O.J. L 350, 30.12.2008, p. 72.

[60] Austria, Belgium, Bulgaria, Estonia, Slovenia, Spain, and Sweden.

[61] Directive 2014/41/EU of the European Parliament and of the Council of April 3, 2014 regarding the European Investigation Order, O.J. L 130, 01.05.2014, p. 1.

Member State, judicial authorities may issue an EIO and—based on the principle of mutual recognition—the competent agency in another state will take the necessary investigative measures. If, for instance, a German prosecutor needs the testimony of a witness living in Paris, she will ask her French counterpart to interrogate the witness and send the minutes.[62] The goal is to make cooperation easier and faster with a request-system that is effectively automated.[63] In contrast to the EEO, however, the EIO does not allow judicial authorities to reach over the border and retrieve evidence.

Prior to the adoption of the EIO, lawyers had campaigned for defense rights to be better protected. In the end, however, the directive provided only very limited extra protection, as it contained very few rules that were weak by nature:[64] It entitles defendants, or lawyers acting on their behalf, to request an EIO to be issued—but only in line with national criminal procedures. In substance, EU law does not strengthen the defendant's position, but maintains the status quo. Nonetheless, EU Member States are required to at least install legal remedies flanking the right to request EIOs, and all persons concerned must be properly informed about these rights.

b. *Mutual Recognition of Evidence?*

Some see the "mutual recognition of evidence" as a logical corollary of a division of tasks in prosecuting crime in Europe. Others point out the risks it poses for fact-finding on the domestic level. The first proposal promoting the idea was put forward by the EU Commission in 2009.[65] The concept derived from the *principle of free movement*, which was developed in the early European Union (then European Community) to establish a single European market; it ensures that products legitimately produced in one EU country are also legal in any other EU country. Similarly, mutual recognition of evidence is based on the assumption that testimonial evidence legally produced in one EU Member State may be used as testimony in any other EU Member State. For example, if Austrian prosecutors interrogated a suspect when his lawyer was present but unable to intervene, the testimony given could be used in a German court even if German law foresees defense participation in its Criminal Procedural Code.[66] But unlike with liquor, beer, or

[62] In fact, the receiving authority can only refuse to execute the order under certain circumstances, for example, if the request is against the country's fundamental principles of law or harms national security interests.

[63] Strict deadlines for gathering the evidence will be applied, Member States have a maximum of thirty days to decide to accept a request. If accepted, there is a ninety-day deadline to conduct the requested investigative measure. Any delay must be reported to the EU country issuing the investigation order.

[64] The issuing authorities must assess the necessity and proportionality of the investigative measure requested.

[65] *Green Paper on Obtaining Evidence In Criminal Matters from One Member State to Another and Securing Its Admissibility*, 11.1.2009, COM [2009] 624.

[66] For further elaboration, see, e.g., Silvia Allegrezza, *Critical Remarks on the Green Paper on Obtaining Evidence in Criminal Matters from One Member State to Another and Securing Its Admissibility*, 9 Zeitschrift für Internationale Strafrechtsdogmatik 569–79 (2010), http://zis-online.com/dat/artikel/2010_9_489.pdf (last visited November 14, 2018).

cheese,[67] the legitimacy gap—arising from reliability and fairness concerns—cannot be bridged by a legal fiction.

Meanwhile, however, the EU's policy agenda for evidence transfer in the so-called European Area of Freedom, Security and Justice appears to have changed. This is apparent, for instance, in the EU Member States' modifications[68] of the EU Commission's Proposal for the establishment of a European Public Prosecutor's Office (EPPO).[69] The European governments have discarded the vision of "one legal space" in favor of a concept of "European Delegated Prosecutors" who will act in their respective domestic jurisdiction and rely on EIO or MLA if evidence is needed from another country.[70] Early projects envisioned more ambitious instruments that set out a standard set of "core" evidence-gathering powers, applicable in transnational cases in all Member States, irrespective of their national rules, transferable throughout the EU as "European evidence."[71]

V. Relapses to Extrajudicial Ways?

The international community has come a long way in the transnational exchange of information—from eighteenth century espionage to a complex system of MLA handled by the judicial authorities. But this development is neither universal nor irrevocable. In many parts of the world, against the backdrop of extrajudicial cross-border cooperation, the rule of law has slowly colored transnational access to evidence in certain countries. But during this development, paralegal instruments have flanked mutual legal assistance in certain situations: The extrajudicial renditions for interrogation purposes[72]

[67] *See* E.C.J. Case 120/78 *Rewe-Zentral AG v. Bundesmonopolverwaltung für Branntwein* (*Cassis de Dijon*) [1979], ECR 649; E.C.J. Case 178/84 *Commission v. Germany* [1987], ECR 1227; E.C.J. Case 286/86 *Ministère Public v. Deserbais* [1988], ECR 4907.

[68] *See* Council doc. 9941/17 of 30 June 2017; Valsamis Mitsilegas, *The European Public Prosecutor's Office Facing National Legal Diversity*, in *The European Public Prosecutor's Office and National Authorities* 11, 21 (Nowak ed., 2016).

[69] Proposal for a Council Regulation on the establishment of the European Public Prosecutor's Office, 17.7.2013, COM [2013] 0534 final, http://eur-lex.europa.eu/legal-content/EN/TXT/?uri=celex:52013PC0534 (last visited Aug. 11, 2017).

[70] For critical assessment, see Ingeborg Zerbes, *Fragmentiertes Strafrecht, Beweiserhebung und Beweisverwertung nach dem Verordnungsentwurf der Europäischen Staatsanwaltschaft*, 10 Zeitschrift für internationale Strafrechtsdogmatik 145, 154 (2015), http://www.zis-online.com/dat/artikel/2015_3_907.pdf (last visited: Aug. 11, 2017).

[71] John Spencer, *The Green Paper on Obtaining Evidence from One Member State to Another and Securing Its Admissibility: The Reaction of One British Lawyer*, 5 Zeitschrift für internationale Strafrechtsdogmatik 602–06 (2010), http://www.zis-online.com/dat/artikel/2010_9_492 (last visited November 14, 2018).

[72] *Cf.* C.o.E. Parliamentary Assembly, Committee on Legal Affairs and Human Rights, (Rapporteur: Dick Marty), Information Memorandum II, AS/Jur (2006) 03 rev, Jan. 22, 2006; C.o.E. Commissioner for Human Rights (Thomas Hammarberg), Memorandum from the Council of Europe Commissioner for Human Rights: Advancing Accountability in Respect of the CIA Black Site in Romania, CommDH (2012) 38, Dec. 18, 2012.

between the United States and European countries and the establishment of "black site" prisons, where inmates were exposed to torture in order to gain information provide prominent recent examples.[73] Such cases, as horrible as they are, appear to be rather uncommon, rogue results.

Of more practical importance—and growing theoretical concern for the framework of transnational access to evidence—are phenomena in MLA, among them the Joint Investigation Teams that in a certain way manage to dismantle the strict and clear procedures of MLA. If, for instance, a JIT member learns about particular information during his deployment and uses it to look for evidence in his jurisdiction, he may never have to explain where he got the lead to start with. In line with this is the expansion of data sharing. Many databases not only serve criminal justice, but also cater to police and border controls and do not provide access to "real evidence" as witness testimony does; they merely provide information that may lead to evidence.

1. Data Sharing in Europe

EU Member States share data in Europol databases, the Schengen Information System (SIS),[74] and various specific databases. By doing so, they have access to information across borders without involving MLA procedures. The SIS, for instance, provides a broad spectrum of alerts on persons and objects. Another data-sharing instrument provides the Member States with the possibility to search each other's national DNA analysis files and automated dactyloscopic identification systems.[75] This search is carried out on a hit/no hit-basis, that is, the national authorities can automatically compare DNA profiles or fingerprints found at a crime scene with profiles held in the databases of other EU Member States. This system considerably speeds up existing procedures, enabling the respective national authority to determine whether information is available within the EU.[76] However, if matching data can be confirmed, the supply of further available data and other information is subject to MLATs.[77]

The fact that states—including those in the broader European area, namely, the Council of Europe—wish to maintain certain limits even with digitalized evidence-transfer in

[73] *See* Al Nashiri v. Poland, App. No. 28761/11, Eur. Ct. H.R., July 24, 2014; Husayn v. Poland, App. No. 7511/13, Eur. Ct. H.R., July 24, 2014, www.un.org/docs/sc/committees/1267/1267mg.htm (last visited November 14, 2018).

[74] Paul de Hert & Serge Gutwirth, *Interoperability of Police Databases Within the EU: An Accountable Political Choice?* 30 (2006).

[75] The Prüm Decision was initially launched to facilitate Schengen cooperation, but—mainly for political reasons—was not incorporated into the EU framework. For further details, see Council Decision 2008/615/JHA on the stepping up of cross-border cooperation, particularly in combating terrorism and cross-border crime, O.J. L 210, 06.08.2008, p. 1.

[76] *See also id.*, Recitals 11, 12.

[77] For access to DNA and dactyloscopic data, see *id.*, arts. 2 and 8.

sight is illustrated by the Cybercrime Convention of 23 November 2001. That Convention grants:

> Trans-border access to stored computer data with consent or where publicly available: A Party may, without the authorization of another Party: (a) access publicly available (open source) stored computer data, regardless of where the data is located geographically; or (b) access or receive, through a computer system in its territory, stored computer data located in another Party, if the Party obtains the lawful and voluntary consent of the person who has the lawful authority to disclose the data to the Party through that computer system.[78]

Thus, in Europe, at present, data sharing is not completely disconnected from MLA. But electronic information traffic has the potential to outgrow MLATs, especially if systems are developed into fully automated data exchanges, that have compatibility and interconnectivity with other IT systems.[79]

2. Trans-Atlantic Data Sharing

One aspect of data sharing between EU and U.S. authorities that may provide leads to evidence[80] is the passenger name record (PNR) data exchange.[81] The EU directive on the use of PNR data for the prevention, detection, investigation, and prosecution of terrorist offenses and serious crime (PNR Directive)[82] obliges EU Member States to establish special entities—passenger information units (PIUs)—responsible for the collection, storage and processing of PNR data and to ensure that air carriers transfer PNR data[83] so that risk assessment can be carried out. The PIUs must report to national law enforcement authorities, Europol, other Member States, or third countries such as the United States.[84] Obviously, such information again constitutes a lead and not hard

[78] Convention on Cybercrime, 23 Nov. 2001, E.T.S. 185, *entered into force* 1 July 2004, Art. 32, http://www.europarl.europa.eu/meetdocs/2014_2019/documents/libe/dv/7_conv_budapest_/7_conv_budapest_en.pdf.

[79] European Comm'n, *Communication from the Commission to the European Parliament and the Council, Stronger and Smarter Information Systems for Borders and Security*, COM [2016] 205 final.

[80] PNR data consists of booking information provided at the time of booking and check-in to air carriers, such as dates of travel, contact details, meal choices, travel agent, means of payment, and baggage information.

[81] Agreement between the United States of America and the European Union on the use and transfer of passenger name records to the United States Department of Homeland Security, O.J. L. 215, 11.08.2012, p. 5.

[82] Directive (E.U.) 2016/681, O.J. L 119, 04.05.2016, p. 132. The Directive applies primarily to extra-EU flights. Member States can however decide to apply it also to intra-EU flights, or to selected intra-EU flights, subject to a notification in this respect to the Commission. Nearly all Member States already announced they will do so in view of the current security situation (*see* Council doc. no. 7829/16 ADD 1). Serious crime is defined by Article 3(9) which further refers to a list of offenses in Annex II of the Directive.

[83] *See id.* Annex I of Directive 2016/681.

[84] *See id.* Art. 6 of Directive 2016/681.

evidence. But the boundaries are unclear. To draw a line between mere leads and hard evidence is increasingly difficult when different tools are combined, as for instance at Europol's European Cybercrime Centre (EC3), where U.S. liaison officers go on cyber patrol with Europeans on JITs and gather information that leads them to hard evidence, while the legal basis is vague. Two bilateral agreements between Europol and the United States allow for the exchange of strategic, technical and operational data. The latter refers to the exchange of information that includes personal data.[85] Furthermore, Europol hosts liaison officers from various law enforcement agencies of the United States, such as the Drug Enforcement Agency, the FBI, and the New York Police Department. As a consequence, U.S. officials are granted access to information in the Europol databases and they are able to use the Europol secure communication network for the exchange of operational and strategic information and intelligence.

3. Data Sharing and Private Business

On top of government databases, authorities are—under certain conditions—granted access to data stored by private enterprises, especially social media and internet enterprises, such as Facebook, Google, or Microsoft. EU-legislation obligated private companies to collect data and make it available for law enforcement purposes. The first important piece of legislation, the so-called "Data Retention Directive,"[86] sought to retain traffic and location data held by telecommunication service providers. If necessary, authorities would have been able to request access to details such as IP addresses and time of use of every email, phone call, and text message, sent or received. In 2014, the European Court of Justice declared the Data Retention Directive invalid since it unjustifiably encroached upon fundamental rights, namely, the respect for private life and the protection of personal data.[87] A potential recast of the data retention directive at the EU level is currently under debate.

In other areas, bilateral agreements arrange for the collection and trans-Atlantic transmission of data, such as from financial messaging. An agreement obligates the Society for Worldwide Interbank Financial Telecommunications (SWIFT)—a cooperative society under Belgian law that provides the most regularly used service communication platform for the worldwide exchange of financial information among financial institutions—to send financial payment messages referring to financial transfers and related data stored in the territory of the European Union to the U.S. Treasury Department.

[85] The agreements are available at the Europol website: https://www.europol.europa.eu/agreements/united-states-of-america (last visited Jul. 31, 2017).

[86] Directive 2006/24/EC of the European Parliament and of the Council of March 15, 2006 on the retention of data generated or processed in connection with the provision of publicly available electronic communications services or of public communications networks and amending Directive 2002/58/EC, O.J. L 105, 13.04.2006, p. 54.

[87] E.C.J., Joined Cases C-293/12 and C-594/12, *Digital Rights Ireland and Seitlinger and Others* [2014].

The agreement adds that the processing of the data in the United States is exclusively for the purpose of the prevention, investigation, detection, or prosecution of terrorism or terrorist financing.[88] The U.S. Treasury Department enters the financial messaging data into the Terrorist Finance Trading Program and analyzes the data. In return, relevant information obtained through that Program is provided to the national police and security authorities of EU Member States, Europol, and Eurojust for law enforcement purposes.[89]

The legal interests and legal protection of the different stakeholders in this area are not yet resolved. The impact on the right to privacy in such data sharing, in particular, has to be clarified.[90] A human right to privacy is acknowledged in Article 12 of the Universal Declaration of Human Rights[91] and codified in Article 17 of the Covenant on Civil and Political Rights.[92] As the individual's legal position is valid across borders, an understanding has emerged since the beginnings of MLA until today: an international division of tasks in prosecuting crimes must not be to the detriment of a defendant or witness.[93] This understanding is threatened by the growing trend toward data sharing.

VI. Conclusion

Transnational access to evidence has grown from a lawless to a rather densely regulated area. In part, this evolution may have been a mere necessity with transnational evidence transfer gaining importance. In part, it pertains to the general development of holding state power accountable, even in international cooperation. While international law has traditionally been perceived as establishing rights and duties for states

[88] *See* Art. 1(a) of the Agreement between the European Union and the United States of America on the processing and transfer of Financial Messaging Data from the European Union to the United States for the purposes of the Terrorist Finance Tracking Program, O.J. L. 195, 22.07.2010, p. 5.

[89] Art. 1(b) of the Agreement, *id.*

[90] *See* Anne Peters, *Surveillance Without Borders? The Unlawfulness of the NSA-Panopticon*, EJIL Talk! Blog of the European Journal of International Law 2013 (01.11), Parts 1 and 2), 1 and 4 November 2013, https://www.ejiltalk.org/surveillance-without-borders-the-unlawfulness-of-the-nsa-panopticon-part-i/ (last visited November 14, 2018).

[91] Universal Declaration of Human Rights, 10 Dec. 1948, U.N.G.A. Res. 217 A (III) (1948).

[92] International Covenant on Civil and Political Rights, 16 Dec. 1966, 999 U.N.T.S. and 1057 U.N.T.S. 407, *entered into force* 23 Mar. 1976 [the provisions of article 41 (Human Rights Committee) entered into force 28 Mar. 1979].

[93] Anne Peters & Sabine Gless, *Verwertungsverbot bei Verletzung der Pflicht zur Belehrung nach Art. 36 WÜK?*, 31 Strafverteidiger 369–377 (2011); Schomburg et al., *supra* note 7, at no. 11, with references to *LaGrand (Germany v. United States of America)* I.C.J. Rep. 2001, 466; International Criminal Tribunal for Rwanda (ICTR), Judgment, *Kayeleli* (ICTR-98-44-A-A), Appeals Chamber, 23.5.2005; *Soering v. The United Kingdom*, App. No. 14038/88, Eur. Ct. H.R, July 7, 1989; Bundesverfassungsgericht [BVerfG] [German Constitutional Court], Decision of 18.6.1997, no 2 BvR 483/95, 2501/95, 2990/95.

only, the legal position of individuals affected by transnational state cooperation is at the core of many debates.[94]

Legal accountability creates a climate favorable for accurate and fair fact-finding, which is a prerequisite for the legitimacy of criminal justice. Since the times of police informers spying on citizens of foreign countries, the terms for transnational access to evidence have changed. Today judicial authorities are in charge. But at the same time, the basic dilemma at the heart of MLA cannot be avoided, namely, that criminal justice systems all strive for comprehensive fact-finding, but cannot enforce the legal standards that bind their search for truth at home. Thus their (own) legal standards tend to be compromised when material evidence can be obtained only with the assistance of foreign state authority.

Although this dilemma plays out differently in domestic judicial systems—as exemplified in this chapter by Germany and the United States, an inquisitorial system and an adversarial system—a common feature seems to be that the defense is disadvantaged by MLA. In certain situations, this may endanger accuracy and fairness of fact-finding. As the public prosecution authorities have driven cross-border cooperation, the interests of defendants have been taken into account only in recent decades.[95]

It seems unclear whether states will take adequate steps to mitigate the flaws of transnational evidence transfer. The need for closer cooperation between states has triggered dynamics that produced ideas for a supranational framework or even a "global" evidence concept.[96] However, instead of addressing basic concerns for reliability and fairness in fact-finding, states may try to evade formal MLA and tend toward an exchange of leads instead of evidence, hoping for fewer legal strings. This seems to be a danger, especially regarding cyber space, where territoriality presents less of an issue and thus traditional concepts may not apply.

Looking ahead the crucial question appears to be whether we will see continued development to closer cooperation over—and juridification of—access to evidence, witnesses, and suspects. If so, the risks to the accuracy and fairness of fact-finding and eventually to the legitimacy of criminal justice could be addressed with a common transnational approach. But perhaps the pendulum will swing back and countries—confronted with worldwide terror networks or cyberattacks, and thus tempted to partake in informal information exchange—will simply revert to fewer legislative hurdles when seeking to prosecute crime across borders.

[94] *See e.g.*, Anne Peters, *Membership in the Global Constitutional Community*, in *The Constitutionalization of International Law* 153, 168–69 (Jan Klabbers et al. eds., 2009).

[95] Malin Thunberg Schunke, *Whose Responsibility? A Study of Transnational Defence Rights and Mutual Recognition of Judicial Decisions Within the EU*, 41–45 (2013).

[96] The idea of a pan-"European" evidence was put forward, for instance, by the E.U.-Commission for fraud prosecution, see Art. 9(2) E.C. Reg. 1073/99: "Reports drawn up on that basis shall constitute admissible evidence in administrative or judicial proceedings of the Member State in which their use proves necessary, in the same way and under the same conditions as administrative reports drawn up by national administrative inspectors. They shall be subject to the same evaluation rules as those applicable to administrative reports drawn up by national administrative inspectors and shall be of identical value to such reports."

References

Sabine Gless, *Transnational Cooperation in Criminal Matters and the Guarantee of a Fair Trial: Approaches to a General Principle*, 9 Utrecht L. Rev. 90 seq. (2013)

Mark A. Godsey, *The New Frontier of Constitutional Confession Law—the International Arena: Exploring the Admissibility of Confessions Taken by U.S. Investigators from Non-Americans Abroad*, 91 Geo. L.J. 851 seq. (2003)

Virginia M. Kendall & T. Markus Funk, *The Role of Mutual Legal Assistance Treaties in Obtaining Foreign Evidence*, 40(2) Litigation 59 seq. (2014)

Robert Neale Lyman, *Compulsory Process in a Globalized Era: Defendant Access to Mutual Legal Assistance Treaties*, 47 Va. J. Int'l L. 261 seq. (2006)

Peter Rackow & Cornelius Birr, *Recent Developments in Legal Assistance in Criminal Matters*, 2 Goettingen J. Int'l L. 1087 seq. (2010)

L. Song Richardson, *Due Process for the Global Crime Age: A Proposal*, 41 Cornell Int'l L.J. 347 seq. (2008)

Wolfgang Schomburg et al., *Einleitung*, in *Internationale Rechtshilfe in Strafsachen* no. 25 (Wolfgang Schomburg et al. eds., 5th ed. 2011)

John Spencer, *The Green Paper on Obtaining Evidence from One Member State to Another and Securing Its Admissibility: The Reaction of One British Lawyer*, 5 Zeitschrift für internationale Strafrechtsdogmatik 602 seq. (2010)

David Whedbee, *The Faint Shadow of the Sixth Amendment: Substantial Imbalance in Evidence-Gathering Capacity Abroad Under the U.S.-P.R.C. Mutual Legal Assistance Agreement in Criminal Matters*, 12 Pac. Rim L. & Pol'y J. 561 seq. (2003)

CHAPTER 28

INTERNATIONAL LAW AND TREATY OBLIGATIONS, MUTUAL LEGAL ASSISTANCE, AND EU INSTRUMENTS

MARTIN BÖSE

I. Introduction: General Framework

International and European law not only establishes standards for domestic criminal proceedings but also provides a legal framework for international cooperation in criminal matters. Due to the territorial boundaries of their investigative and prosecutorial powers, states have a vital interest in international cooperation in criminal matters. This holds especially true for crimes with a transnational dimension (in particular organized crime and terrorism), but it also applies to cases where the need for cooperation does not result from the nature of the crime but from other circumstances (e.g., the suspect has fled to another country). Correspondingly, the relevant provisions of international law form not only part of treaties combatting transnational crime, but also part of bilateral and multilateral agreements establishing a general framework for international cooperation in criminal matters and the new instruments under EU law that are based upon the principle of mutual recognition.

1. Scope and Elements of International Cooperation in Criminal Matters

International cooperation in criminal matters combines elements of criminal process and international relations. On the one hand, international cooperation is traditionally considered a matter of foreign policy, and it is upon each sovereign state to decide whether and to what extent it will enter into cooperation agreements with other states. The external dimension of mutual legal assistance is mirrored in reservations safeguarding sovereign interests of the contracting parties, and also in the institutional and procedural setting (responsibility of the ministry of foreign affairs, diplomatic communication channels), even though the mutual interest in effective cooperation has fostered developments facilitating the transmission of requests (e.g., allowing for direct contact between the competent authorities).[1]

On the other hand, international cooperation in criminal matters is linked to a specific objective, that is, to assist another state in conducting criminal proceedings. In this respect, international cooperation is rooted in the national criminal justice system; this internal dimension is reflected in the application of domestic law of criminal proceedings. Whereas this is self-evident for the requesting state, it seems less obvious for the requested state that does not conduct criminal proceedings on its own but only lends assistance to another state to that end. This difference notwithstanding, the proceedings in the requested state are closely linked to criminal proceedings in the requesting state as they form part of transnational criminal law enforcement. As a consequence, the domestic law of criminal proceedings is—at least in part—applied accordingly to proceedings on mutual legal assistance in the requested state.

The notion of criminal matters is not defined in international law, but it should be construed in a manner that only covers criminal proceedings in the strict sense. This follows e contrario from treaty provisions extending the scope of mutual legal assistance to regulatory offenses subject to the jurisdiction of a criminal court.[2] The cooperation regime applies irrespective of the stage of proceedings (investigation, prosecution, trial, enforcement). International cooperation in criminal matters covers the traditional instruments (e.g., extradition) as well as any form of mutual legal assistance, including transfer of criminal proceedings to another state[3] or transnational gathering of evidence in particular. As the latter is discussed in chapter 32, this chapter will focus on extradition and enforcement of sentences (*infra* Sections II and III).

In any case, international treaties on mutual legal assistance in criminal matters apply to judicial authorities only.[4] In contrast, police cooperation is usually not covered, but is subject to a separate treaty regime.[5] The distinction between judicial cooperation

[1] Second Additional Protocol to the European Convention on mutual assistance in Criminal Matters, Nov. 8, 2001, E.T.S. no. 182, *entered into force* 1 Feb. 2004, Art. 4.

[2] *Id.* Art. 1(3).

[3] U.N. Model Treaty on the Transfer of Proceedings in Criminal Matters, G.A. Res. 45/118 (14 Dec. 1990); European Convention on the Transfer of Proceedings in Criminal Matters, 15 May 1972, E.T.S. no. 73, *entered into force* 30 Mar. 1978.

[4] European Convention on Mutual Assistance in Criminal Matters, 20 Apr. 1959, E.T.S. no. 30, *entered into force* 12 June 1962, Art. 1(1); U.N. Model Treaty on Mutual Assistance in Criminal Matters, G.A. Res. 45/117(14 Dec. 1990), Art. 1(1).

[5] *See, e.g.*, Agreement France—Germany on cooperation of police and customs authorities, 9.Oct. 1997, BGBl. II 1998, p. 2480 (Ger.).

and police cooperation in criminal matters is also reflected in EU law.[6] However, an international treaty may leave it to the contracting parties to determine the domestic authorities that shall be considered as judicial authorities in the framework of mutual legal assistance. Thereby, the scope of judicial cooperation can even be extended to police authorities.[7]

2. International Cooperation in Criminal Matters and Human Rights

International human rights standards, the right to a fair trial in particular,[8] are not only a key issue for each criminal justice system, but also for international cooperation in criminal matters. These standards have to be met irrespective of whether criminal proceedings are conducted with or without assistance of a foreign state. Where states assist each other in criminal law enforcement, the international division of tasks between the requesting and the requested state must not be to the detriment of the defendant.[9] Thus, the functional link between legal assistance granted by the requested state and criminal proceedings in the requesting state calls for an equivalent protection of human rights in the framework of international cooperation in criminal matters.

As a matter of course, the state granting legal assistance has to comply with international human rights standards. Nevertheless, international human rights standards draw a distinction between domestic criminal process on the one hand and mutual legal assistance procedures on the other. For instance, the procedural safeguards for arrest and detention in criminal proceedings (in the requesting state) do not apply to arrest and detention for the purpose of extradition (in the requested state).[10] According to this understanding, it is not a matter for the requested state, but rather is up to the requesting state to assess whether the conditions for pretrial detention are met. Thereby, the international human rights standard refers to the rationale of division of labor that is inherent to international cooperation in criminal matters. The requested state, however,

[6] Art. 82–86 T.F.E.U. (judicial cooperation), Art. 87–89 T.F.E.U. (police cooperation), O.J. C 115/47.

[7] *See, e.g.*, the declarations of Denmark, Finland, and Norway to Article 24 of the European Convention on Mutual Legal Assistance in Criminal Matters, *supra* note 4.

[8] United Nations International Covenant on Civil and Political Rights [I.C.C.P.R.], 19 Dec. 1966, 999 U.N.T.S. 171 and 1057 U.N.T.S. 407, *entered into force* 23 Mar. 1976 (the provisions of article 41 [Human Rights Committee] entered into force 28 Mar. 1979), Art. 14; European Convention for the Protection of Human Rights and Fundamental Freedoms [E.C.H.R.], 4.Nov. 1950, 312 E.T.S. no 5, as amended by Protocol No. 3, E.T.S. 45; Protocol No. 5, E.T.S. 55; Protocol No. 8, E.T.S. 118; and Protocol No. 11, E.T.S. 155; *entered into force* 3 Sept. 1953 (Protocol No. 3 on 21 Sept. 1970, Protocol No. 5 on 20 Dec. 1971, Protocol No. 8 on 1 Jan 1990, Protocol 11 on 11 Jan 1998), Art. 6.

[9] International Criminal Tribunal for Rwanda, Judgment, *Kajelijeli* (ICTR-98-44A-A), Appeals Chamber, 23 May 2005, para. 220.

[10] Art. 5(1)(c), (3) E.C.H.R. [criminal proceedings], Art. 5(1)(f) E.C.H.R. [extradition]; see Quinn v. France, App. No. 18580/91, Eur. Ct. H.R., Mar. 22, 1995, § 53.

may still provide for a higher level of protection (*infra* Section II.1.d on sufficiency of evidence).

Likewise, the scope of fair trial rights is basically limited to domestic criminal proceedings and, as a matter of principle, does not extend to mutual assistance procedures because the latter do not concern the establishment of guilt or innocence.[11] Nevertheless, it is incumbent upon both the requesting and the requested state to ensure that transnational criminal law enforcement does not result in a violation of international human rights standards. Accordingly, the scope of fair trial rights should not be construed too narrowly, but cover transnational criminal proceedings as a whole. This approach is supported by recent jurisprudence of the European Court of Human Rights suggesting that the authorities of the requested state must abide by the right to a fair trial when providing legal assistance.[12] Furthermore, the emergence of fair trial rights in transnational criminal proceedings has been expressly acknowledged in recent EU legislation on procedural rights of the defendant where the scope of these rights covers both domestic criminal proceedings and proceedings for the execution of a European arrest warrant (i.e., extradition proceedings).[13]

Even though it is not upon the requested state to inquire into the criminal justice system of the requesting state (rule of non-inquiry),[14] the international human rights standard does not only bind the requested state when taking the internal measures that are necessary to grant legal assistance (e.g., arrest of the person to be extradited, seizure of the evidence to be transferred to the requesting state). This standard also calls upon the requested state to refuse cooperation that would result in human rights violations by the requesting state. Since the landmark decision in *Soering*, it has been well-established case law of the European Court of Human Rights that the requested state must not extradite a person facing a real risk of exposure to inhuman or degrading treatment or punishment in the requesting state. Thereby, the European Court of Human Rights has established the requested state's indirect responsibility for measures taken by the requesting state, but also implicitly imposed human rights standards on third states that are not party to the Convention.[15] In order to resolve potential conflicts between cooperation duties (e.g., extradition obligations) and human rights standards, international treaties provide for human rights clauses giving priority to the latter (*infra* Section II.2.e.).[16] To that end, a state may also refuse to grant assistance that would prejudice its public order or essential public interests.[17] Even though these *ordre public* reservations mainly aim

[11] Mamatkulov and Askarov v. Turkey [GC], App. Nos. 46827/99 and 46951/99, Eur. Ct. H.R., Feb. 4, 2005, §§ 80, 82.

[12] Stojkovic v. France and Belgium, App. No. 25303/08, Eur. Ct. H.R., Oct. 27, 2011, § 55.

[13] *See, e.g.*, E.U. Directive 2010/64/EU on the right to interpretation and translation in criminal proceedings, O.J. L 280/1, 20.10.2010, Art. 1(1).

[14] Neely v. Henkel, 180 U.S. 109, 122–23 (1901); see also Bundesverfassungsgericht [BVerfG] [Federal Constitutional Court], BVerfGE 109, 38 (61) (Ger.).

[15] Soering v. United Kingdom, App. No. 14038/88, Eur. Ct. H.R., July 7, 1989, §§ 86–88.

[16] U.N. Model Treaty on Extradition, G.A. Res. 45/116 (14 Dec. 1990), Art. 3(f).

[17] Art. 4(a) U.N. Model Treaty on Mutual Assistance in Criminal Matters, *supra* note 4; Art. 2(b) European Convention on Mutual Assistance in Criminal Matters, *supra* note 4.

at protecting state interests,[18] states may also refer to such clauses in order to maintain human rights standards.[19]

International cooperation between EU Member States follows a similar approach. Even though the principle of mutual recognition and its implementation in new cooperation instruments (e.g., the European arrest warrant) establish comprehensive cooperation obligations, they do not relieve the Member States from their obligation to respect human rights. Accordingly, the Court of Justice expressly acknowledged in a recent judgment that a Member State must not execute a European arrest warrant and surrender a person to another Member State if this person would be exposed to a real risk of inhuman or degrading treatment.[20] To some extent, EU legislation expressly provides for a refusal ground referring to the EU Charter of Fundamental Rights.[21] In contrast to the corresponding reservations in international treaties, the refusal ground does not refer to the Member State's national *ordre public* and international human rights standards but only to human rights standards established by EU law (i.e., the "European" *ordre public*).[22] According to the German Constitutional Court, however, the obligation to execute a European arrest warrant is suspended if this would encroach upon the guarantee of human dignity that forms part of the constitutional identity and, thus, is not subject to the primacy of EU law.[23]

3. The Principle of Mutual Recognition and New Cooperation Instruments

In the European Union, the principle of mutual recognition has generated a new generation of cooperation instruments,[24] first and foremost the European arrest warrant.[25] The principle of mutual recognition caused a paradigm shift in cooperation in criminal matters that, as a matter of principle, equated transnational cooperation between Member States to internal cooperation within one and the same state. Thereby, international cooperation within the Union was no longer considered as a matter of external affairs

[18] U.N.O.D.C., Revised Manual on the Model Treaty on Extradition and on the Model Treaty on Mutual Assistance in Criminal Matters, U.N. Doc. E/CN.15/2004/CRP.11 (2004), para. 84; see also the explanatory report to the European Convention on Mutual Assistance in Criminal Matters, p. 4.

[19] Agreement EU—Japan on Mutual Legal Assistance in Criminal Matters, O.J. L 343/1, 11.10.2010, Art. 11(b); U.N. Commentary on the United Nations Convention against Illicit Traffic in Narcotic Drugs and Psychotropic Substances 1988, § 7.50 (United Nations ed. 1998).

[20] C.J.E.U., Joined Cases C-404/15 PPU and C-659/15 PPU *Aranyosi and Căldăraru* [2016], ECLI:EU:C:2016:198, §§ 98, 104.

[21] Directive 2014/41/EU regarding the European Investigation Order in criminal matters, O.J. L 130/1, 3.4. 2014, Art. 11(1)(f).

[22] C.J.E.U., C-399/11 *Melloni* [2013], ECLI:EU:C:2013:107, §§ 63–64.

[23] Bundesverfassungsgericht [BVerfG] [Federal Constitutional Court], BVerfGE 140, 317 (Ger.).

[24] Art. 67(3) and 82(1) T.F.E.U.

[25] Framework Decision 2002/584/JHA on the European arrest warrant and the surrender procedures between Member States [hereinafter FD EAW], O.J. L 190/1, 13.6.2002.

but as part of (transnational) judicial proceedings, which is clearly reflected in terminology that referred to domestic criminal proceedings "warrant" or "order" instead of "request"). The implementation of the mutual recognition principle has enhanced cooperation by procedural measures (direct contact between judicial authorities, standardized procedures, strict time limits, etc.) and a reduction of traditional obstacles that were—at least in part—related to the sovereignty of the requested state (*infra* Section II.2).

On the other hand, the ambit of mutual trust is still rather limited, even in the European Union. The new cooperation instruments still refer to major traditional reservations (e.g., on concurrent jurisdiction and the *ne bis in idem* principle). Thus, mutual recognition does not mean automatic execution of a European arrest warrant, but leaves room for judicial control by the courts of the executing (requested) Member State. This is particularly relevant where international and European human rights standards are at stake; the principle of mutual recognition, however, does not allow for a review that is based upon a national (constitutional) law standard.

The new approach has inspired international treaties providing for similar instruments in other regional cooperation frameworks (MERCOSUR, Nordic cooperation).[26] Despite the parallel terms ("MERCOSUR detention order", "Nordic arrest warrant"), these instruments differ significantly from the corresponding EU measure: due to a lesser extent of integration, the MERCOSUR has adhered to a larger extent to the traditional cooperation regime and maintained major extradition obstacles (e.g., for political and military offenses), whereas Nordic cooperation in criminal matters even goes beyond the implementation of mutual recognition within the EU (e.g., with regard to the double criminality requirement).

II. Extradition

As one of the most important instruments of international cooperation in criminal matters, extradition is the surrender of a person who is sought by the requesting state for criminal prosecution or for the enforcement of a criminal sentence.[27] The term does not cover transfer for any other purpose such as the enforcement of a sentence imposed by the state that transfers the convicted person (*infra* Section III.1) or deportation of illegal residents to their home country. In the European Union, the extradition regime has been replaced by the European arrest warrant. In substance (surrender for prosecution or sentencing), it is still extradition, but the legal and procedural framework has been enhanced significantly.

[26] Convention on surrender on the basis of an offence between the Nordic states [the Nordic arrest warrant], 15 Dec. 2005, Denmark, Finland, Iceland, Norway, and Sweden, *entered into force* 16 Nov. 2012; Agreement on the MERCOSUR Detention Order and Delivery Procedures among MERCOSUR Member and Associated States, 16 Dec. 2010, MERCOSUR/CMC/DEC. no 48/10 (South American states).

[27] Art. 1 U.N. Model Treaty on Extradition, *supra* note 16.

1. Extradition Conditions

As a matter of principle, a sovereign state is free to decide whether or not to extradite a person to another state. However, international law establishes extradition obligations. Such obligations can arise from multilateral and bilateral extradition treaties that define the conditions for and exceptions to the general obligation to extradite a person to the requesting state. The same applies to the obligation to execute a European arrest warrant.

a. *Request*

First, extradition requires a request of the state interested in prosecution or sentencing of the person to be extradited. The request must contain a description of the person wanted for extradition and of the conduct constituting the alleged offense, the text of the relevant criminal offenses, and any other information necessary to decide upon the extradition request; in particular, the requesting state must transmit an arrest warrant (extradition for prosecution) or a judgment (extradition for sentencing).[28] In the European Union, the European arrest warrant serves as a request for extradition.[29]

b. *Double Criminality*

Furthermore, extradition is subject to the condition that the offense for which extradition is requested be a criminal offense according to the domestic law of both the requesting and the requested state (double criminality requirement). This requirement has commonly been derived from the maxim *nullum crimen, nulla poena sine lege* as no person shall be subject to criminal process for a conduct that is not a criminal offense under the law of the requested state. However, extradition—even extradition detention—is not a criminal sentence, but a procedural measure and, thus, does not fall within the scope of the *nulla poena sine lege* principle. The criminal sentence is rather imposed (or has been imposed) according to the criminal law of the requesting state. However, extraditing a person, and thereby assisting the requesting state in exercising its *ius puniendi*, might appear illegitimate if the applicable criminal law of the requesting state fundamentally differs from the criminal justice system of the requested state, in particular where criminal punishment in the requesting state would result in a violation of liberties enshrined in the constitution of the requested state. So, the rationale of the double criminality requirement is to protect the individual from excessive criminal prosecution by the requesting state, but this protection is not absolute. Even where double criminality is lacking, extradition might still be legitimate if the relevant criminal law of the requesting state does not violate human rights.[30] Accordingly, the execution of a European arrest warrant does not require double criminality for thirty-two categories of crime (e.g., terrorism, drug trafficking, money laundering, cybercrime) that are supposed to

[28] *Id.* Art. 5. [29] Art. 8 FD EAW, *supra* note 25.

[30] Otherwise, extradition will be refused on the basis of the *ordre public* clause (*supra* Section I.2, *infra* Section II.2.e).

reflect a common understanding of the EU Member States of what kind of behavior should be considered a criminal offense.[31] Even though these categories are not yet fully harmonized, the Framework Decision is based upon mutual trust that the criminal laws of the Member States are not in breach with fundamental principles and human rights. For similar reasons, the execution of a Nordic arrest warrant does not require double criminality at all.[32]

Scope and content of the double criminality requirement depend upon the underlying rationale. If double criminality is construed as an emanation of the *nulla poena sine lege* principle, the relevant conduct must have been subject to criminal punishment according to the law of the requested state when the crime has been committed; otherwise extradition would violate the prohibition on retroactivity of criminal law provisions.[33] If, in contrast, the double criminality requirement is qualified as safeguard against excessive criminal prosecution, double criminality at the time of surrender is sufficient.[34] A similar controversy is about whether double criminality is only satisfied where all positive and negative (justification, excuse) requirements of criminal liability are met *in concreto* or whether it is sufficient that such conduct is punishable *in abstracto*.[35] In any case, there is a clear tendency toward an interpretation according to which double criminality is examined irrespective of category, denomination, or elements of the relevant criminal offenses in the requesting state and in the requested state.[36]

c. *Extraditable Offenses*

Since extradition seriously interferes with the liberty of the alleged offender, extradition obligations do not apply to petty offenses. As a rule, an extraditable offense must be punishable by imprisonment with a maximum of at least one or two years or by a more severe penalty under the laws of both the requesting and the requested state.[37] International crime control treaties usually determine that the respective crimes shall be deemed as extraditable offenses.[38] Where extradition is requested for the enforcement of a criminal sentence, the duration of the sentence still to be served must be at least four

[31] Art. 2(2) FD EAW, *supra* note 25.

[32] Art. 2(3) Convention on the Nordic arrest warrant, *supra* note 26; see, however, the exception for crimes committed in the executing state, Art. 5(2).

[33] House of Lords, *Regina v. Bow Street Metropolitan Stipendiary Magistrate and others*, ex parte *Pinochet Ugarte (No. 3)*, Mar. 24, 1999, [2000] 1 A.C. 147, 170; see also Inter-American Convention on Extradition, O.A.S.T.S. no. 60, 25 Feb. 1981, Art. 3(1)2.

[34] Bundesverfassungsgericht [BVerfG] [Federal Constitutional Court] (Jemen), BVerfGE 109, 38 (63) (Ger.).

[35] European Committee on Crime Problems [C.D.P.C.]—Committee of Experts on the Operation of European Conventions on Cooperation in Criminal Matters, Note on dual criminality, in concreto or in abstracto, PC-OC (2012) 02 final, 11 May 2012.

[36] Art. 2(2) U.N. Model Treaty on Extradition, *supra* note 16.

[37] *Id.* Art. 2(1); European Convention on Extradition, 13 Dec. 1957, E.T.S. no. 24, Art. 2(1) (one year); Art. 3(1) Inter-American Convention on Extradition, *supra* note 33 (two years).

[38] U.N. Convention against Illicit Traffic in Narcotic Drugs and Psychotropic Substances [U.N.C.I.T.N.D.P.S.], 20. Dec. 1988, 1582 U.NT.S. 95, Art. 6 (2); U.N. Convention against Transnational Organized Crime (U.N.T.O.C.), 15 Nov. 2000, 2225 U.N.T.S. 209, Art. 16(3).

months.[39] If extradition is requested for several separate offenses and only one of them is an extraditable offense, extradition may also be granted with regard to the other offenses ("accessory extradition").[40] In this case, extradition and the related infringement of liberty cannot be considered disproportionate.

The threshold for surrender within the European Union is similar (maximum punishment of one year imprisonment) but refers to the law of the issuing Member State only.[41] As a consequence of the lower threshold and the simplified surrender proceedings, European arrest warrants have also been issued for the prosecution of petty offenses. Therefore, the Member States must pay particular attention to the principle of proportionality when executing a European arrest warrant.[42]

d. *Sufficiency of Evidence*

There is no uniform international standard on whether and to what extent the requested state shall (or may) examine the evidence against the alleged offender before granting extradition. In common law states, the extradition requires that a prima facie case against the requested person be established because otherwise his arrest and surrender for trial in the requesting state would be unfair and illegitimate.[43] In contrast, civil law states are usually satisfied with the arrest warrant that has been issued in and transmitted by the requesting state as the court of the latter has already examined the evidence. Therefore, sufficient evidence to establish a prima facie case against the requested person is not required unless special circumstances call for a review as to whether there are reasonable grounds for prosecution.[44] As a consequence, multilateral and bilateral extradition treaties provide for the transmission of evidence insofar as required by the law of the requested state.[45] Nevertheless, international crime control treaties call upon the contracting parties to simplify such evidentiary requirements in respect of the crimes covered by these treaties.[46]

2. Bars to Extradition

Extradition obligations under international law are subject to various exceptions. Bars to extradition may originate from sovereign interests of the requested state and from

[39] Art. 2(4) U.N. Model Treaty on Extradition, *supra* note 16; Art. 2(3) European Convention on Extradition, *supra* note 37.

[40] Art. 2(1) U.N. Model Treaty on Extradition, *supra* note 16 (four or six months); Art. 2 (1) European Convention on Extradition, *supra* note 37 (four months); Art. 3(3) Inter-American Convention on Extradition, *supra* note 33 (six months).

[41] Art. 2(1) FD EAW, *supra* note 25.

[42] Oberlandesgericht [OLG] [Higher Regional Court] Stuttgart, Neue Juristische Wochenschrift [NJW] 2010, 1617 (Ger.).

[43] Supreme Court of Canada, *United States of America v. Ferras* July 21, 2006 SCC 33, para 19–21, 26.

[44] Bundesverfassungsgericht [BVerfG] [Federal Constitutional Court], BVerfGE 109, 38 (59) (Ger.).

[45] Art. 11(1)(a) Inter-American Convention on Extradition, *supra* note 33; Treaty Canada Germany concerning Extradition, 11 July 1977, BGBl. 1979 II 665, Art. 14(2)(b) (Ger.).

[46] Art. 6 (7) U.N.C.I.T.N.D.P.S., *supra* note 38; Art. 16(8) U.N.T.O.C., *supra* note 38; U.N. Convention against Corruption [U.N.C.A.C.], 31 Oct. 2003, 2349 U.N.T.S. 41, Art. 44(9).

individual rights of the person wanted for extradition. If the corresponding requirements are met, the requested state may refuse extradition (mandatory and optional grounds for refusal).[47] As far as extradition treaties provide for optional refusal grounds, the states may still implement them as they do mandatory extradition bars. This is particularly the case where the ground for refusal is derived from a constitutional guarantee (e.g., the ban on extradition of nationals).

a. *Political, Military, and Fiscal Offenses*

A first group of traditional bars to extradition refers to the category of crimes for which extradition is requested (political, military, and fiscal offenses). These exceptions are based upon reasons of state as the decision on whether or not to surrender is closely linked to the sovereign interests of the requested state. In the European Union, the exceptions for political, military, and fiscal offenses have been abandoned.[48]

The political nature of an offense can result from the purpose and the circumstances of its commission. Since it is up to the requested state to determine whether the crime qualifies as political offense, the exception has a broad scope and may even apply to crimes related to a political offense.[49] Nevertheless, international law has limited the notion of political offense by excluding certain crimes, in particular terrorist offenses, from its scope.[50] The second bar to extradition applies to military offenses that are not offenses under ordinary criminal law (e.g., desertion or insubordination).[51] Unlike the exceptions for political and military offenses, the exception for fiscal offenses is not mandatory, but it allows the contracting parties to agree otherwise.[52] The notion of fiscal offenses covers any offense related to taxes, duties, customs, and exchange, but recent international treaties provide that the exception does not apply to transnational crime.[53]

b. *Double Jeopardy, Concurrent Jurisdiction, and Territoriality*

Further extradition obstacles may arise from the requested state's own interest in prosecution. This is particularly the case if concurrent jurisdiction of the requested state has already triggered criminal proceedings against the alleged offender. Where such

[47] Art. 3 and 4 U.N. Model Treaty on Extradition, *supra* note 16.

[48] Recital (12) and Art. 4(1) FD EAW, *supra* note 25.

[49] Art. 3(1) European Convention on Extradition, *supra* note 37; Art. 4(4) Inter-American Convention on Extradition, *supra* note 33.

[50] European Convention on the Suppression of Terrorism, 27 Jan. 1977, E.T.S. no 90, *entered into force* 4 Aug. 1978, Art. 2; U.N. Convention for the Suppression of Terrorist Bombings, 15 Dec. 1997, 2149 U.N.T.S. 256, *entered into force* 23 May 2001, Art. 11; see also Art. 3(3) European Convention on Extradition, *supra* note 37; Art. 4(4) Inter-American Convention on Extradition, *supra* note 33.

[51] Art. 3(c) U.N. Model Treaty on Extradition, *supra* note 16; Art. 4 European Convention on Extradition, *supra* note 37.

[52] Art. 5 European Convention on Extradition, *supra* note 37.

[53] U.N. Convention for the Suppression of the Financing of Terrorism, 9 Dec. 1999, 2178 U.N.T.S. 197, *entered into force* 10 Apr. 1978, Art. 14; Art. 16(15) U.N.T.O.C., *supra* note 38; Art. 44(6) U.N.C.A.C., *supra* note 46.

proceedings have resulted in a final judgement, the convicted or acquitted person must not be extradited for the same offense (*ne bis in idem*).[54] Moreover, if criminal proceedings in the requested state have been terminated otherwise or if such proceedings have not been instituted at all, some extradition treaties provide for an optional ground for refusal.[55] In this case, the alleged offender does not enjoy absolute protection from further prosecution, but the requested state may refer to the findings of its own investigation that there are no grounds for prosecution. For the very same reasons, the requested state may refuse extradition if the alleged offender is subject to criminal prosecution for the same offense for which extradition is requested (*lis pendens*).[56] States may even rely on this ground for refusal if they initiate criminal proceedings against the requested person after having received the request for extradition.[57] According to some treaty provisions, concurrent jurisdiction provides a ground for refusal irrespective of whether a criminal investigation has been initiated.[58] This reasoning applies in particular where extradition is sought for a crime committed in whole or in part within the requested state's territory (principle of territoriality).[59]

In contrast, jurisdiction of the requesting state is required for any extradition request,[60] but usually not scrutinized in extradition proceedings. However, extraterritorial jurisdiction may give rise to an extradition obstacle if the requested state does not provide for extraterritorial jurisdiction for the kind of offense for which extradition is sought.[61] The reasoning of this exception comes close to the underlying rationale of the double criminality requirement (*supra* Section II.1.b.).

In EU law, the aforementioned exceptions have been maintained in the new extradition regime based upon the European arrest warrant. Due to the transnational dimension of the *ne bis in idem* principle within the Union,[62] the corresponding refusal ground has even been extended to final judgments rendered in a third Member State different from the issuing and the executing state.[63]

[54] Art. 3(d) U.N. Model Treaty on Extradition, *supra* note 16; Art. 9(1) European Convention on Extradition, *supra* note 37; see also Art. 4(1) Inter-American Convention on Extradition, *supra* note 33.

[55] Art. 4(b) U.N. Model Treaty on Extradition, *supra* note 16; Art. 9(2) European Convention on Extradition, *supra* note 37; Art. 4(3) FD EAW, *supra* note 25.

[56] Art. 4(c) U.N. Model Treaty on Extradition, *supra* note 16; Art. 8 European Convention on Extradition, *supra* note 37; Art. 4 (2) FD EAW, *supra* note 25.

[57] Explanatory report to the European Convention on Extradition, p. 8.

[58] Art. 2(3) Inter-American Convention on Extradition, *supra* note 33.

[59] Art. 4(f) U.N. Model Treaty on Extradition, *supra* note 16; Art. 7(1) European Convention on Extradition, *supra* note 37; Art. 4(7) (a) FD EAW, *supra* note 25.

[60] *Cf.* Art. 2(1), (2) Inter-American Convention on Extradition, *supra* note 33.

[61] Art. 4(e) U.N. Model Treaty on Extradition, *supra* note 16; Art. 7(2) European Convention on Extradition, *supra* note 37; see also Extradition Treaty Germany—USA, 20 June 1978, BGBl. II 1980, 647, Art. 1(2) (Ger.); Art. 4(7)(b) FD EAW, *supra* note 25.

[62] Convention Implementing the Schengen Agreement of 14 June 1985 between the Governments of the States of the Benelux Economic Union, the Federal Republic of Germany and the French Republic on the gradual abolition of checks at their common borders (C.I.S.A.), O.J. L 239/19, 19.6. 1990, Art. 54.

[63] Art. 3(2) FD EAW, *supra* note 25.

c. *Nationality*

Multilateral extradition treaties allow the requested state to refuse the extradition of its own nationals.[64] Whereas this ground for refusal is not applied in common law countries, it is widespread among civil law countries and often constitutionally guaranteed.[65] The underlying rationale is to protect nationals from criminal prosecution on the basis of a criminal law that is not at all foreseeable to them and in a foreign criminal justice system where they are confronted with considerable difficulties in effectively exercising their defense rights.[66] The scope of the exception ("nationals") is determined by the law of the requested state; some states have even extended its scope to residents (see also *infra* for EU citizens).[67] Since the bar to extradition may not result in impunity, the requested state shall prosecute the alleged offender on behalf of the requesting state (*aut dedere, aut iudicare*).[68] A compromise balancing the interests of the alleged offender and the public interest in effective transnational law enforcement makes extradition subject to the condition that the offender will be returned to the requested state to serve the sentence imposed as result of the trial in the requesting state.[69]

In its essence, this compromise has been implemented in the European arrest warrant. In principle, the ban on extradition of nationals has been lifted, but nationals of Member States are still protected from serving their sentences abroad as they are not surrendered for the enforcement of a sentence, and surrender for prosecution is subject to the return condition.[70] Nevertheless, the constitutional bans on extradition of nationals are still relevant as they provide guidance for the application of other extradition obstacles to a country's own nationals (e.g., the territoriality principle, *supra* Section II.2.b.). According to the German Constitutional Court, a German citizen must not be surrendered for an offense mainly committed within German territory, but has a constitutional right to stand trial in his home country.[71] Thus, the nationality of the offender is still relevant as a factor establishing the requested state's jurisdiction.

On the other hand, the return guarantee is no longer limited to nationals (citizens); it applies to permanent residents, too.[72] As follows from the principle of non-discrimination

[64] Art. 4(a) U.N. Model Treaty on Extradition, *supra* note 16; Art. 6(1) European Convention on Extradition, *supra* note 37; Art. 7(1) Inter-American Convention on Extradition, *supra* note 33.

[65] *E.g.*, Brazil, Finland, Germany, Italy, Poland.

[66] Bundesverfassungsgericht [BVerfG] [Federal Constitutional Court], BVerfGE 113, 273 (293, 301–302) (Ger.).

[67] Declarations of Denmark, Finland, Iceland, the Netherlands, Norway, Poland (foreigners who have been granted asylum), and Sweden to the Council of Europe Convention on Extradition, Art. 6, http://www.coe.int/en/web/conventions/full-list/-/conventions/treaty/024/declarations?p_auth=uEikxNym (last visited 15 Aug. 2017).

[68] Art. 4(a) U.N. Model Treaty on Extradition, *supra* note 16; Art. 6(2) European Convention on Extradition, *supra* note 37; Art. 8 Inter-American Convention on Extradition, *supra* note 33; see also Art. 6(9) U.N.C.I.T.N.D.P.S., *supra* note 38; Art. 16(10) U.N.T.O.C., *supra* note 38.

[69] Art. 16(11) U.N.T.O.C., *supra* note 38.

[70] Art. 4(6) and Art. 5(3) FD EAW, *supra* note 25.

[71] Bundesverfassungsgericht [BVerfG] [Federal Constitutional Court], BVerfGE 113, 273 (302) (Ger.).

[72] Art. 5(3) FD EAW, *supra* note 25.

on grounds of nationality, Member States must not any more limit the scope of the return guarantee to their own nationals, but have to provide equivalent protection to other EU citizens who have been integrated into the society of the requested Member State.[73] Moreover, the principle of non-discrimination does not only apply to the execution of a European arrest warrant (surrender to another Member State), but also to extradition to third states. Where a EU citizen has moved from his home country to another Member State, the latter must not extradite him to a third state, but must inform the Member State of origin and surrender the alleged offender upon request to this Member State.[74]

d. *Lapse of Time and Immunity from Prosecution*

Since extradition forms part of transnational criminal proceedings, it must not be granted where prosecution is barred in the requesting state (e.g., by lapse of time).[75] As a matter of principle, however, it is not for the requested state to examine whether prosecution is time barred under the law of the requesting state, but this assessment should be made by the requesting state (if necessary, upon request of the requested state).[76] The focus of the requested state is whether prosecution is barred under domestic law. Thereby, the exception follows the same rationale as the double criminality requirement (*supra* Section II.1.b).[77]

Nevertheless, due to the divergence of the laws on immunity from prosecution resulting from lapse of time, the different rules on calculating the expiration of the limitation period and its interruption by procedural measures in particular, the exception has been restricted[78] or even abolished.[79] For instance, the exception may be subject to the condition that the requested state has jurisdiction over the crime for which extradition is requested.[80] Otherwise, the alleged offender cannot expect to benefit from the domestic rules on immunity from prosecution.

Further extradition obstacles originate from other grounds for immunity from prosecution (e.g., amnesty).[81] Like the exception for statutory limitations, the rules

[73] C.J.E.U., C-42/11 *Lopes da Silva Jorge* [2012], ECLI:EU:C:2012:517, § 59, referring to Art. 18 T.F.E.U.

[74] C.J.E.U., C-182/15 *Petruhhin v. Latvijas Republikas Ģenerālprokuratūra*, ECLI:EU:C:2016:630, § 50.

[75] Art. 9 Extradition Treaty Germany—USA, *supra* note 61; see also Art. 4(e) U.N. Model Treaty on Extradition, *supra* note 16; Art. 4(2) Inter-American Convention on Extradition, *supra* note 33; Art. 10 European Convention on Extradition, *supra* note 37.

[76] Explanatory report to the European Convention on Extradition, at 9.

[77] *See also* with regard to the requirement of a complaint made by a party having a legitimate interest in prosecution: Art. 4(6) Inter-American Convention on Extradition, *supra* note 33.

[78] Fourth Additional Protocol to the European Convention on Extradition, Sept. 9, 2012, E.T.S. no 212, *entered into force* 1 June 2014, Art. 1.

[79] Art. 7 Extradition Treaty Canada—Germany, *supra* note 45.

[80] Art. 1(3)(a) Fourth Additional Protocol to the European Convention on Extradition, *supra* note 78; Art. 4(4) FD EAW, *supra* note 25.

[81] Art. 4(e) U.N. Model Treaty on Extradition, *supra* note 16; Art. 4(1) Inter-American Convention on Extradition, *supra* note 33.

on amnesty may be conditioned on concurrent jurisdiction of the requested state.[82] In contrast, other grounds for immunity from prosecution and punishment may originate from the national *ordre public* of the requested state (e.g., extradition of children below the age of criminal responsibility) or even directly from international law (immunity of state representatives) so that they apply irrespective of whether the requested state has jurisdiction over the case.[83]

e. *Non-discrimination and Human Rights*

When deciding upon a request for extradition, the requested state is bound by international human rights standards and, therefore, must not surrender a person to a state where these standards are clearly not met and the requested person faces a real risk of being subject to serious human rights violations (*supra* Section I.2). This general obligation is specified in a number of extradition obstacles aiming at the protection of the requested person against human rights violations in the requesting state.

One extradition obstacle has emerged from the protection of refugees and the prohibition of expulsion and return to a state where the refugee's life or freedom would be threatened on account of her race, religion, nationality, or political opinion.[84] Accordingly, extradition shall not be granted if the requested state has substantial grounds for believing that the request for extradition has been made for the purpose of prosecuting or punishing a person on account of that person's race, religion, nationality, ethnic origin, political opinions, sex, or status (non-discrimination clause).[85] With regard to the European arrest warrant, EU law does not provide for an explicit ground for refusal, but implementing legislation still refers to the general non-discrimination-clause.[86]

Furthermore, obstacles to extradition may arise from the penalty to be imposed and/or enforced in the requesting state. According to several treaties, the requested state may refuse extradition if the requested person faces the risk of being sentenced to death[87] or life imprisonment.[88] In addition, the international *ordre public* bars extradition if the requested person would be subject to torture or inhuman or degrading punishment in the requesting state;[89] under certain circumstances, this might also apply to the death

[82] Second Additional Protocol to the European Convention on Extradition, 17 Mar. 1978, E.T.S. no 98, *entered into force* 5 June 1983, Art. 4; Art. 9 Extradition Treaty Canada—Germany, *supra* note 45; Art. 3(1) FD EAW, *supra* note 25.

[83] Art. 3(3), art. 20 FD EAW, *id.*

[84] U.N. Convention Relating to the Status of Refugees, 28 Apr. 1951, 189 U.N.T.S. 150, *entered into force* 22 Apr. 1954, Art. 33(1).

[85] Art. 3(b) U.N. Model Treaty on Extradition, *supra* note 16; see also Art. 3(2) European Convention on Extradition, *supra* note 37; Art. 4(5) Inter-American Convention on Extradition, *supra* note 33.

[86] *See, e.g.*, Gesetz über die Internationale Rechtshilfe in Strafsachen [IRG] [Act on International Cooperation in Criminal Matters], § 82, referring to § 6(2) (Ger.); see also recital (12) FD EAW, *supra* note 25.

[87] Art. 4(d) U.N. Model Treaty on Extradition, *supra* note 16; Art. 11 European Convention on Extradition, *supra* note 37; Art. 9 Inter-American Convention on Extradition, *supra* note 33.

[88] Art. 9 Inter-American Convention on Extradition, *supra* note 33; see also Footnote to Art. 4(d), U.N. Model Treaty on Extradition, *supra* note 16.

[89] Art. 3(f) U.N. Model Treaty on Extradition, *supra* note 16.

penalty[90] or life imprisonment.[91] These exceptions do not apply if the requesting state gives the assurance that the respective penalty will not be imposed or that, if it is imposed, it will not be enforced.[92] Whereas the death penalty is abolished in all EU Member States and, thus, a corresponding exception does not exist anymore, the execution of a European arrest warrant may be subject to the condition that the law of the issuing state provides for a review of a sentence to life imprisonment or for the application of measures of clemency aiming at non-execution of the penalty.[93] Furthermore, even if not expressly foreseen by EU law, the executing state must refuse surrender if the detention conditions in the issuing state would be such as to expose the requested person to a real risk of inhuman or degrading treatment.[94]

Third, extradition must be refused if the requested person did not or would not receive the minimum guarantees in criminal proceedings, in particular the right to a fair trial.[95] This general principle has been further elaborated in specific refusal grounds related to trials before extraordinary or ad hoc tribunals[96] and trials in absentia.[97] In the latter case, extradition shall be granted if the requesting state gives an assurance considered sufficient to guarantee to the person sought the right to a retrial.[98] In EU law, surrender of persons tried and convicted in absentia is subject to a similar threshold, but the rules are much more detailed; in this regard, Member States have to comply with both the legal framework of the European arrest warrant and the harmonized minimum standard of procedural rights.[99]

f. *Obligations of the Requesting State and the Principle of Specialty*

If the requested state has made the decision to grant extradition and to surrender the alleged offender subject to conditions and the requesting state has accepted these conditions, the requesting state is obliged to comply with these conditions. This applies in particular to assurances given by the requesting state (e.g., with regard to the non-imposition of certain penalties or to the right to a retrial, *supra* Section II.2.e).

[90] Soering v. United Kingdom, App. No. 14038/88, Eur. Ct. H.R., July 7, 1989, § 111 ("death row phenomenon").

[91] Trabelsi v. Belgium, App. No. 140/10, Eur. Ct. H.R., Sept. 4, 2014, §§ 112 ff.

[92] Art. 4(d) U.N. Model Treaty on Extradition, *supra* note 16; Art. 11 European Convention on Extradition, *supra* note 37; Art. 9 Inter-American Convention on Extradition, *supra* note 33.

[93] Art. 5(2) FD EAW, *supra* note 25.

[94] C.J.E.U., Joined Cases C-404/15 PPU and C-659/15 PPU *Aranyosi and Căldăraru* [2016], EU:C:2016:98, §§ 98, 104.

[95] Art. 3(f) U.N. Model Treaty on Extradition, *supra* note 16; see also Soering v. United Kingdom, App. No. 14038/88, Eur. Ct. H.R., July 7, 1989, § 113 ("flagrant denial of justice").

[96] Art. 4(g) U.N. Model Treaty on Extradition, *supra* note 16; Art. 4(3) Inter-American Convention on Extradition, *supra* note 33.

[97] Art. 3(g) U.N. Model Treaty on Extradition, *supra* note 16; Art. 3 Second Additional Protocol to the European Convention on Extradition, *supra* note 82.

[98] Art. 3(g) U.N. Model Treaty on Extradition, *supra* note 16; Art. 3 Second Additional Protocol to the European Convention on Extradition, *supra* note 82.

[99] Art. 4 FD EAW, as amended by Framework Decision 2009/2999/JHA, O.J. L 81/24, 26.2.2009; see also Directive (EU) 2016/343 on the strengthening of certain aspects of the presumption of innocence and of the right to be present at the trial in criminal proceedings, O.J. L 65/1, 26.3.2016.

A further obligation arises from the principle of specialty, which forms part of extradition treaties and customary international law: As extradition is granted with regard to the offense specified in the extradition request, the requesting state must not subject the requested person to criminal proceedings, punishment, or extradition to a third state for any other offense without consent of the requested state.[100] The rule of specialty shall ensure that the alleged offender will be subject to criminal prosecution and punishment only insofar as—according to the assessment by the requested state—the requirements for extradition are met.[101] This rationale does not object to prosecuting the requested person for another offense that is punishable by a maximum penalty not exceeding the maximum penalty for the offense for which extradition has been granted, provided that prosecution and punishment are based on the same facts.[102] If the requesting state intends to prosecute the surrendered person for any other offense, it must apply for the requested state's consent and submit the documents accompanying an extradition request.[103]

Since the principle of specialty originates from the relations between the requesting and the requested state, the U.S. Court of Appeals for the Second Circuit held in *Suarez* that this rule did not confer rights upon the defendant, but only upon the requested state. Therefore, in the absence of protest or objection by that state, the defendant was considered to have no standing to raise a violation of the rule of specialty.[104] This ruling implies a shift of the burden of proof upon the defendant: It is not the consent but the protest of the requested state that must be established. Thereby, the consent requirement is turned upside down, and the defendant is more or less deprived of the protection under the specialty principle. In reaction to the new case law, the German Constitutional Court ruled that extradition would not be granted if the requesting state would not fully comply with the principle of specialty.[105]

Nevertheless, the principle of specialty is not absolute, but subject to exceptions. The specialty rule does not bar criminal proceedings in the requesting state if prosecution is not based upon extradition because the surrendered person has stayed in the requesting state although he had the opportunity to leave, or because he has voluntarily returned to

[100] Art. 14(1) U.N. Model Treaty on Extradition, *supra* note 16; Art. 13(1) Inter-American Convention on Extradition, *supra* note 33; Art. 14(1) European Convention on Extradition, *supra* note 37.

[101] Bundesverfassungsgericht [BVerfG] [Federal Constitutional Court], Neue Zeitschrift für Strafrecht [NStZ] 2017, p. 43, 47 (Ger.).

[102] Footnote to Art. 14(1)(a), U.N. Model Treaty on Extradition, *supra* note 16; Art. 22(3) Extradition Treaty Germany—USA, *supra* note 61; see also Art. 14(3) European Convention on Extradition, *supra* note 37; Art. 22(4) Extradition Treaty Canada—Germany, *supra* note 45: prosecution for any other extraditable offence.

[103] Art. 14(2) U.N. Model Treaty on Extradition, *supra* note 16; Art. 13(1)(c) Inter-American Convention on Extradition, *supra* note 33; Art. 14(1)(a) European Convention on Extradition, *supra* note 37.

[104] *U.S. v. Yesid Rios Suarez* No. 14-2378-cr, June 30, 2015.

[105] Bundesverfassungsgericht [BVerfG] [Federal Constitutional Court], Neue Zeitschrift für Strafrecht [NStZ] 2017, p. 43 (47) (Ger.).

that state after leaving it.[106] Furthermore, the requested person may consent to extradition and expressly renounce his entitlement to the rule of specialty.[107]

In EU law, the principle of specialty is subject to further exceptions. Member States can generally declare a waiver of the rule of specialty.[108] Moreover, the principle of specialty does not bar criminal proceedings if the surrendered person will not be subject to imprisonment or other sentences or measures restricting personal liberty.[109] According to the European Court of Justice, the rule of specialty even allows for criminal proceedings resulting in conviction to imprisonment, and only bars the enforcement of the sentence.[110]

III. Enforcement of Criminal Sentences and Measures

If the accused person has been convicted, the sentence can be enforced by the sentencing state itself (if necessary, subsequent to the extradition) or by another state acting on behalf of the sentencing state. In the latter case, the judgment of the sentencing state is vested with a transnational effect. Thereby, it is closely related to the transnational dimension of the *ne bis in idem* principle that bars further prosecution of the same offense after a final judgment has been delivered.[111]

In principle, the enforcement of foreign judgments is subject to the same conditions and restrictions as extradition. The administering state will not enforce the sentence of another state unless the sentencing state has made a request to that end and the double criminality requirement is met.[112] On the other hand, traditional obstacles to extradition apply accordingly, for example, with regard to political and military offenses, to concurrent jurisdiction and the territoriality principle, to immunity from criminal prosecution, and to the principle of non-discrimination and the *ordre public* reservation.[113] As enforcement cooperation is not related to the pretrial or trial stage but rather to the execution of a final judgment, the exception for lapse of time is only applicable where the sanction imposed can no longer be enforced under the law of the requested

[106] Art. 14(3) U.N. Model Treaty on Extradition, *supra* note 16; Art. 14 (1) (b) European Convention on Extradition, *supra* note 37; see also Art. 13 (1) (b) Inter-American Convention on Extradition, *supra* note 33.

[107] Third Additional Protocol to the European Convention on Extradition, 10 Nov. 2010, E.T.S. no 209, entered into force 1 May 2012, Art. 5(b).

[108] Art. 27(1) FD EAW, *supra* note 25; see, e.g., the declaration of Austria, Council-Doc. 9608/04 9608/04 COPEN 66 EJN 32 EUROJUST 43, 17 May 2004.

[109] Art. 27(2)(b),(c),(d) FD EAW, *supra* note 25.

[110] C.J.E.U., C-388/08 PPU *Leymann and Pustavarov* [2008], ECLI:EU:C:2008:669, § 76.

[111] *Cf.* European Convention on the International Validity of Criminal Judgments, 28 May 1970, E.T.S. no 70, *entered into force* 26 July 1974, Art. 2 ff. (enforcement), Art. 53 ff. (*ne bis in idem*).

[112] *Id.* Art. 3(2), 4(1).

[113] *Id.* Art. 6(a)–(g), (k).

state, that is, the limitation period for criminal prosecution is irrelevant. Furthermore, the enforcement of a sanction may be refused if the sentencing state is able to enforce the sanction by itself or if the requested state is unable to enforce the sentence.[114]

Unlike extradition, the enforcement of foreign judgments is not subject to an exception for the requested state's own nationals. On the contrary, enforcement of foreign judgments requires a link between the convicted person and the administering (requested) state that can be established by the nationality, ordinary residence, or the prospects of social rehabilitation.[115] The underlying rationale of this requirement is that the sentence should not be enforced anywhere but in a state better suited for enforcement than the sentencing state.

1. Transfer of Convicted Persons and Enforcement of Imprisonment Sentences

a. *Conditions and Obstacles*

International treaties on the enforcement of sentences have focused on the transfer of prisoners to their home country.[116] In this respect, enforcement cooperation is not only in the interest of the sentencing state, but even more in the interest of the administering state and its citizens who will be able to serve the sentence in their home country and, thereby, will have a better chance of rehabilitation and reintegration into society. Accordingly, it is not only the sentencing state, but also the administering state that can initiate the transfer by request.[117] Moreover, the sentencing state must inform the convicted person of the treaty framework, and if the convicted person expresses an interest in serving the sentence in his home country, it must inform the administering state accordingly.[118] So, the convicted person may trigger a request but has no right to be transferred to the administering state.

Since transfer to the administering state aims at better rehabilitation and reintegration of the convicted person, transfer is subject to two conditions: The sentenced person must be a national of the administering state and must consent to be transferred to his home country.[119] Consent may not be required if the sentenced person is subject to an expulsion or deportation order by the sentencing state or if the person has fled to the administering state; in the latter case, the convicted person is not transferred, but

[114] *Id.* Art. 6(h), (j), (l). [115] *Id.* Art. 5.

[116] European Convention on the Transfer of Sentenced Persons, 21 Mar. 1983, E.T.S. no 112, *entered into force* 1 July 1985; Inter-American Convention on Serving Criminal Sentences Abroad, 6 Sept. 1993, O.A.S.T.S. no. 76, *entered into force* 4 Dec. 1996.

[117] Art. 2(3) European Convention on the Transfer of Sentenced Persons, *supra* note 116; Art. 5(1) Inter-American Convention on Serving Criminal Sentences Abroad, *supra* note 116.

[118] Art. 4 European Convention on the Transfer of Sentenced Persons, *supra* note 116; Art. 4, 5(1) Inter-American Convention on Serving Criminal Sentences Abroad, *supra* note 116.

[119] Art. 3(1)(a) and (d) European Convention on the Transfer of Sentenced Persons, *supra* note 116; Art. 3(2) and (4) Inter-American Convention on Serving Criminal Sentences Abroad, *supra* note 116.

the administering state will take over the execution of the sentence on request of the sentencing state.[120] Furthermore and in addition to the general rules on enforcement cooperation (final judgment, double criminality), the convicted person must have at least six months of the sentence to serve (minimum threshold).[121]

In EU law, the principle of mutual recognition has brought forth a new instrument for the transnational enforcement of imprisonment sentences.[122] The new system establishes an obligation of the administering (executing) Member State to take over enforcement.[123] At the same time, it is more flexible and does not limit enforcement in the administering state to its own nationals; if the administering state is the home country of the sentenced person, transnational enforcement does not require the consent of that person.[124] Following the same reasoning as the European arrest warrant (Section II.1), traditional obstacles (e.g., for political and military offenses) have been abolished, and the double criminality requirement has been waived for certain categories of serious, transnational crime. Nevertheless, a significant number of traditional obstacles to international enforcement cooperation still apply (e.g., immunity from prosecution, lapse of time, minimum threshold).[125]

b. *Effects*

Transnational enforcement of a sentence implies recognition of the judgment rendered in the sentencing state. As a consequence, the administering state must not prosecute the convicted person for the same offense,[126] but recognizes the sentence that has been imposed in the sentencing state. To that end, the administering state has two options: It can either continue to enforce the foreign sentence, or it can convert the sentence according to domestic law.[127] According to the first model (continued enforcement), the nature and duration of the sentence are binding upon the administering state; the administering state, however, may adapt the sentence insofar as it is incompatible with its domestic law, in particular where the sentence exceeds the maximum penalty prescribed by domestic law.[128] This model is mandatory for mutual recognition of criminal judgments in the EU.[129] If the administering state opts for the second model (conversion of sentence), it imposes a new sentence based upon the facts found in the sentencing state, but meted out according to its own domestic law; however, the sentence must neither be aggravated nor converted to a pecuniary sanction.[130] Since the conversion

[120] Additional Protocol to the European Convention on the Transfer of Sentenced Persons, 18 Dec. 1997, E.T.S. no 167, *entered into force* 1 June 2000, Art. 2, 3.

[121] Art. 3(1)(c) European Convention on the Transfer of Sentenced Persons, *supra* note 116; Art. 3(6) Inter-American Convention on Serving Criminal Sentences Abroad, *supra* note 116.

[122] Framework Decision 2008/909/JHA on the application of the principle of mutual recognition to judgments in criminal matters imposing custodial sentences or measures involving deprivation of liberty for the purpose of their enforcement in the European Union, O.J. L 327/27, 27.11.2008.

[123] *Id.* Art. 8(1). [124] *Id.* Art. 4(1)(c), 6(2). [125] *Id.* Art. 7, 9.

[126] Art. 7(1) Inter-American Convention on Serving Criminal Sentences Abroad, *supra* note 116.

[127] Art. 9 European Convention on the Transfer of Sentenced Persons, *supra* note 116.

[128] *Id.* Art. 10. [129] Art. 8 Framework Decision 2008/909/JHA, *supra* note 122.

[130] Art. 11 European Convention on the Transfer of Sentenced Persons, *supra* note 116.

allows for a significant reduction of the sentence, the convicted person may have a particular interest in being transferred and serving a converted sentence. If the sentencing state has convicted a person on the basis of a confession that has been triggered by assurances of the sentencing state that the offender would be transferred to her home country, the right to fair trial prohibits the sentencing state from not giving its consent to such a transfer because the sentence would be converted.[131]

According to both models, it is not upon the administering state to re-examine the facts on which the conviction has been based. For the same reason, the review of the judgment falls within the exclusive jurisdiction of the sentencing state.[132] The enforcement of the sentence, however, falls within the competence of the administering state and is governed by the law of that state; this applies in particular to decisions on early or conditional release.[133] The administering state may even be competent to grant pardon or amnesty.[134] On the other hand, the enforcement of the sentence is derived from the corresponding interest of the sentencing state. Therefore, the administering state must terminate enforcement if the sentence is no longer enforceable in the sentencing state.[135] Since the sentencing state retains the competence to grant pardon or amnesty, the corresponding decision has the same effect.[136] On the other hand, the sentencing state may no longer enforce the sentence if the administering state has terminated enforcement.[137] Thereby, the convicted person benefits from the enforcement regime that is more favorable to him (principle of favorability).

2. Enforcement of Pecuniary Sanctions and Asset Recovery

Unlike imprisonment sentences, pecuniary sanctions have not been subject to a special treaty regime, but to the general framework of enforcement cooperation.[138] The EU legislator has adopted a mutual recognition instrument for financial penalties (criminal

[131] *See* Buijen v. Germany, App. No. 27804/05, Eur. Ct. H.R., Mar. 9, 2010.

[132] Art. 14 European Convention on the Transfer of Sentenced Persons, *supra* note 116; Art. 8 Inter-American Convention on Serving Criminal Sentences Abroad, *supra* note 116; Art. 19(2) Framework Decision 2008/909/JHA, *supra* note 122.

[133] Art. 9(3) European Convention on the Transfer of Sentenced Persons, *supra* note 116; Art. 7(2) Inter-American Convention on Serving Criminal Sentences Abroad, *supra* note 116; Art. 17(1) Framework Decision 2008/909/JHA, *supra* note 122.

[134] Art. 12 European Convention on the Transfer of Sentenced Persons, *supra* note 116; Art. 19(1) Framework Decision 2008/909/JHA, *supra* note 122.

[135] Art. 9(3) European Convention on the Transfer of Sentenced Persons *supra* note 116; Art. 7(2) Inter-American Convention on Serving Criminal Sentences Abroad, *supra* note 116; Art. 20(2) Framework Decision 2008/909/JHA, *supra* note 122.

[136] Art. 13 European Convention on the Transfer of Sentenced Persons, *supra* note 116; Art. 8 Inter-American Convention on Serving Criminal Sentences Abroad, *supra* note 116; Art. 17(1) Framework Decision 2008/909/JHA, *supra* note 122.

[137] Art. 8(2) European Convention on the Transfer of Sentenced Persons, *supra* note 116.

[138] Art. 2(b) European Convention on the International Validity of Criminal Judgments, *supra* note 111.

fines).[139] Like the European arrest warrant, it significantly facilitates transnational enforcement of fines by reducing traditional obstacles to cooperation; in particular, it exempts certain crimes (e.g., traffic offenses) from the double criminality requirement and makes the exception for lapse of time subject to the condition that the prosecuted offense is subject to the jurisdiction of the executing Member State.[140]

In contrast, confiscation of the proceeds from and instrumentalities of the offense are subject to several multilateral treaties on transnational crime. The corresponding provisions, however, are related to both the cooperation in enforcement of sentences and the general framework of mutual legal assistance since they provide for two different models giving effect to a confiscation order issued by the requesting state. The requested state can either adopt and execute a confiscation order according to its domestic law or recognize and enforce the confiscation order issued by the requesting state.[141] Unlike the second model, the first does not fall within the scope of the cooperation in the enforcement of sentences. Nevertheless, it comes close to a converted sanction (*supra* Section III.1.b) insofar as the requested state is bound by the factual findings on which the conviction and the confiscation order in the requesting state are based.[142] The execution of confiscation orders is closely linked to mutual legal assistance related to investigative and interim measures (identifying and tracing, freezing, and seizure of proceeds and instrumentalities of crime).[143]

In addition to the general conditions for and obstacles to the transnational enforcement of sentences (e.g., double criminality requirement; double jeopardy; lapse of time; exception for political, military, and fiscal offenses; *ordre public* reservation),[144] the bona fide rights of third parties can bar the execution of a confiscation order.[145] Furthermore, the requested state may refuse the execution of non-conviction-based confiscation orders issued by civil courts or administrative authorities.[146] Similar to the corresponding mutual recognition instrument on financial penalties, EU law has reduced the traditional exceptions (double criminality, lapse of time) and widened the scope of application to

[139] Framework Decision 2005/214/JHA on the application of the principle of mutual recognition to financial penalties, O.J. L 76/16, 24.2.2005.

[140] *Id.* Art. 5(1) and (3), Art. 7(2)(c).

[141] Art. 5(4)(a)(i) and (ii) U.N.C.I.T.N.D.P.S., *supra* note 38; Art. 13(1)(a) and (b) U.N.T.O.C., *supra* note 38; Art. 55(1)(a) and (b) U.N.C.A.C., *supra* note 46; European Convention on Laundering, Search, Seizure and Confiscation of the Proceeds from Crime, 8 Nov. 1990, E.T.S. no 141, *entered into force* 1 Sept. 1993, Art. 13(1)(a) and (b).

[142] *Id.* Art. 14(2).

[143] Art. 5(4)(b) U.N.C.I.T.N.D.P.S., *supra* note 38; Art. 13(2) U.N.T.O.C., *supra* note 38; Art. 55(2) U.N.C.A.C., *supra* note 46; Art. 8, 11 European Convention on Laundering, Search, Seizure and Confiscation of the Proceeds from Crime, *supra* note 141.

[144] Art. 18(1) and (4) European Convention on Laundering, Search, Seizure and Confiscation of the Proceeds from Crime, *supra* note 141.

[145] Art. 5(8) U.N.C.I.T.N.D.P.S., *supra* note 38; Art. 13(8) U.N.T.O.C., *supra* note 38.

[146] U.N. Commentary on the United Nations Convention against Illicit Traffic in Narcotic Drugs and Psychotropic Substances 1988, *supra* note 19, § 5.80; see, however, with regard to confiscation orders issued by civil courts, Art. 18(4)(d) European Convention on Laundering, Search, Seizure and Confiscation of the Proceeds from Crime, *supra* note 141.

extended confiscation measures, but still adheres to the majority of enforcement obstacles (e.g., the rights of third parties).[147]

Whereas a request for enforcement usually relieves the sentencing state from its competence to enforce,[148] a confiscation order may be executed by both the requesting and the requested state; however, the total value of the confiscated assets must not exceed the amount of money specified in the confiscation order.[149] Apart from that, the execution of financial sanctions is terminated if further enforcement is barred either in the requesting or the requested state (principle of favorability, *supra* Section III.1.b).[150]

References

Duncan Atkinson, *EU Law in Criminal Practice* (2013)
Neil Boister, *Transnational Criminal Law* (2012)
M. Cherif Bassiouni, *International Extradition: United States Law and Practice* (6th ed. 2014)
John R.W.D. Jones & Rosemary Davidson, *Extradition and Mutual Legal Assistance Handbook* (2d ed. 2011)
André Klip, *European Criminal Law* (3d ed. 2016)
David McClean, *Transnational Organized Crime* (2007)
Clive Nicholls, Clare Montgomery, Julian B. Knowles et al., *Nicholls, Montgomery, and Knowles on the Law of Extradition and Mutual Assistance* (3d ed. 2013)
Steve Peers, *EU Justice and Home Affairs Law, Volume II: Criminal Law, Policing, and Civil Law* (4th ed. 2017)

[147] Framework Decision 2006/783/JHA on the application of the principle of mutual recognition to confiscation orders, O.J. L 328/59, 6.10.2006, Art. 2(d), Art. 6 and Art. 8; see also the Commission proposal for a regulation on mutual recognition of freezing and confiscation orders, 21 Dec. 2016, COM(2016) 819 final.

[148] Art. 11(1) European Convention on the International Validity of Criminal Judgments, *supra* note 111; see also Art. 15(1) Framework Decision 2005/214/EU, *supra* note 139.

[149] Art. 16(1) and (2) European Convention on Laundering, Search, Seizure and Confiscation of the Proceeds from Crime, *supra* note 141; Art. 14(1) and (2) Framework Decision 2006/783/JHA, *supra* note 147.

[150] Art. 9, 11, 12 Framework Decision 2005/214/JHA, *supra* note 139; Art. 12, 13, 15 Framework Decision 2006/783/JHA, *supra* note 147; see also Art. 31(2)(a) European Convention on Laundering, Search, Seizure and Confiscation of the Proceeds from Crime, *supra* note 141.

PART VI

ADJUDICATION: TRIALS AND ALTERNATIVES

CHAPTER 29

CHALLENGES OF TRIAL PROCEDURE REFORM

Is European Union Legislation Part of the Solution or Part of the Problem?

HELMUT SATZGER AND FRANK ZIMMERMANN

I. Introduction

This chapter analyzes the influences of European Union (EU) law that have (or may) become a driving force for trial procedure reforms in Member States' national criminal justice systems. The main factors that will be examined in the following are—to the extent that they have been addressed by EU legislation—the rights of accused persons and victims in trial proceedings. In addition to that, the discussion about the establishment of a European Public Prosecutor's Office will serve as an example for the potential impact of supranational institutions on national trial proceedings. However, the contribution will also draw attention to the well-founded criticism the aforementioned developments face. These concerns may help to identify general challenges that follow from international efforts of trial procedure reform, maybe most prominently the creation of rules determining under which state's jurisdiction a case should fall.

To begin with, it should however be pointed out that the competences of the EU in the field of criminal procedure law are quite limited. This is due to the so-called principle of conferral, which is established by Articles 4(1) and 5(2) of the Treaty on European Union (TEU). The principle provides that "the Union shall act only within the limits of the competences conferred upon it by the Member States in the Treaties" and "[c]ompetences not conferred upon the Union in the Treaties remain with the Member States." In the field of criminal law and procedure, such a conferral has only taken place in a quite limited sense: the EU does not have a genuine competence to adopt supranational criminal law provisions[1] and, thus, no *ius puniendi* of its own. Moreover, a genuine "European code of criminal procedure" does not exist either. Instead, the focus of the European Treaties originally lay on fostering the cooperation in criminal matters between the Member States, that is, the traditionally very cumbersome process of mutual legal assistance. But that form of inter-state cooperation usually takes place before trial (extradition, gathering evidence) or after it (execution of an already imposed sentence or extradition for that purpose). EU law did therefore not have great influence on the trials themselves for a long time.

II. Harmonization of Procedural Rights in the EU

1. Cooperation in Criminal Matters: From Mutual Recognition to Harmonization

In order to strengthen and simplify the cooperation between Member States in criminal matters, the European decision-makers developed the concept of mutual recognition at the Tampere summit in 1999.[2] It was later also enshrined in Article 82(1) of the Treaty on the Functioning of the European Union (TFEU). The recognition approach was inspired by the free circulation of goods in the single European market and basically stipulates that every Member State should recognize and execute a judicial decision by another Member State as if it had been taken by its own authorities.[3] This new mode of cooperation was supposed to make a thorough approximation of the Member States' criminal (procedure) laws—which would have taken a long time and did not seem feasible on the political level—unnecessary.[4] The first legislative act implementing the new principle was the framework decision on the European arrest warrant in 2002.[5] However, it quickly turned out that mutual recognition cannot work without harmonizing the Member States' domestic law. This is because executing foreign decisions presupposes a high level of trust in the other Member States' criminal justice system, which cannot exist without a common minimum of legal standards. For instance, national authorities

[1] An exception may be Consolidated Version of the Treaty on the Functioning of the E.U. Art. 325, Oct. 26, 2012, 2012 O.J. (C 326) 1 [T.F.E.U.], in the area of offenses against the Union's financial interests, but even this is debated. In the affirmative: Helmut Satzger, *International and European Criminal Law* § 6 paras. 24 et seq. (2d ed. 2017); in the negative: Petter Asp, *The Substantive Criminal Law Competence of the EU* 150 et seq. (2012).

[2] *See* conclusions no. 33–37, *available at* http://www.europarl.europa.eu/summits/tam_en.htm (last visited Jan. 21, 2018).

[3] For more details, see Satzger, *supra* note 1, at § 8 paras. 26 et seq.

[4] *See* Libor Klimek, *Mutual Recognition of Judicial Decisions in European Criminal Law* 53 (2017).

[5] Council Framework Decision 2002/584/JHA of 13 June 2002 on the European arrest warrant and the surrender procedures between Member States, 2002 O.J. (L 190) 1.

cannot be expected to surrender a suspect to a Member State where he or she will face proceedings that contradict fundamental rules (often stemming from constitutional law) of the extraditing Member State. Similar concerns will arise when an investigative measure infringes upon fundamental rights under the law of the Member State that shall carry it out. Admittedly, all Member States of the EU have ratified the European Convention on Human Rights (ECHR) and are thus bound by its Article 6, which guarantees suspects in a criminal proceeding the right to a fair trial. But experience shows that the domestic codes of criminal procedure still vary considerably. Therefore, Article 82(2) TFEU today gives the EU the competence to harmonize selected aspects of the Member States' criminal procedure law—but only "[t]o the extent necessary to facilitate mutual recognition."

In the last years, this competence has been increasingly used and the competent European bodies have adopted several directives with minimum rules that aim at strengthening criminal defense rights and victim rights in the EU. The nexus with the principle of mutual recognition shines up in most of these instruments, as they mostly refer to an early stage of criminal proceedings, for example when they oblige Member States to provide certain information to the suspect. But at least some of them also touch heavily upon the trial phase.

2. Rights of Suspects and Accused Persons in the Trial Phase

Ever since the EU institutions started implementing the principle of mutual recognition, their efforts have been criticized for one-sidedly weakening the position of the suspect. With the entry into force of the Lisbon Treaty in 2009, the Council therefore adopted a "roadmap for strengthening procedural rights of suspected or accused persons in criminal proceedings."[6] Subsequently, EU legislation has established minimum rights for suspects and accused persons in a step-by-step-approach. Although this is not the place to assess these instruments in all their detail, a brief overview may help to get a better idea of their potential impact.

a. *The Directive on the Presumption of Innocence and the Right to Be Present*

The most important instrument for the trial phase is probably the directive from 2016 on the presumption of innocence and the right to be present at trial.[7]

Its Article 5 provides that suspects and accused persons shall not be presented as guilty through the use of measures of physical restraint, unless this is necessary in the particular case for security reasons (which obviously includes the security of the suspect) or to prevent the individual concerned from absconding or having contact with third persons.

[6] Resolution of the Council 2009/C 295/01, 2009 O.J. (C 295) 1.

[7] Directive (EU) 2016/343, 2016 O.J. (L 65) 10.

According to Article 6(1), the burden of proof shall lie with the prosecution authority. However, this provision must be interpreted in the light of recital no. 22. It clarifies, *inter alia*, that the provision shall not entirely exclude, but only reasonably limit presumptions of fact or law. That is, of course, a very vague guideline and could largely undermine the apparently clear statement of Article 6(1). But at least the recital requires such presumptions to be rebuttable. This might allow defense lawyers to challenge long-standing jurisprudence, for instance when a person with a certain blood alcohol level (which is not defined in the law) is automatically and without exceptions considered incapable of driving a car safely.[8]

With regard to the standard of proof, Article 6(2) of the directive enshrines the principle of *in dubio pro reo*: "Any doubt as to the question of guilt is to benefit the suspect or accused person, including where the court assesses whether the person concerned should be acquitted." Interestingly, the directive does not repeat the well-known "reasonable doubt" formula, but makes use of the expression "any doubt." However, the second part of the sentence reveals that this is not meant to introduce a stricter standard and does not oblige courts to acquit an accused whenever the slightest doubt as to his or her guilt remains.

Article 7 of the directive implements the paramount maxim of *nemo tenetur se ipsum accusare* by establishing the right of suspects and accused persons to remain silent and not to incriminate themselves. Its paragraph 3 further specifies that this guarantee does not preclude the gathering of evidence whose existence is independent of the individual's will. Pursuant to paragraph 5, a person's silence may not be used as evidence against him or her. However, judicial authorities may take into account cooperative behavior at the stage of sentencing (paragraph 4).

Article 8 of the directive provides that accused persons shall have the right to be present at trial—at least as a matter of principle. However, Member States retain a considerable discretion to conduct proceedings in absentia: it shall suffice that the accused has been informed of the trial and the consequences of his or her nonappearance in due time or that the accused is represented by a lawyer appointed by him/her or the state. Even if these requirements are not fulfilled because it is impossible to locate the accused, a trial in absentia shall be admissible, provided that he or she will have a right to a new trial upon apprehension. Thus, the EU legislator's approach on the matter cannot be regarded as particularly ambitious. What is more, these rules even apply accordingly to accused minors.[9]

b. *Further Harmonization Measures in the Field of Criminal Procedure*

Several other EU directives intended to strengthen the position of suspects or accused persons mainly address the pretrial stage. The right to information in criminal proceedings

[8] The example is inspired by the jurisprudence regarding section 316 of the German criminal code; see Andreas Ernemann, § 316 StGB, in *Strafgesetzbuch Kommentar*, paras 8–10 (Helmut Satzger, Wilhelm Schluckebier & Gunter Widmaier eds., 3d ed. 2016).

[9] Compare article 16(2) of Directive (EU) 2016/800 of 11 May 2016 on procedural safeguards for children who are suspects or accused persons in criminal proceedings, 2016 O.J. (L 132) 1.

(about the alleged offense and the applicable procedural rights),[10] for instance, is crucial to prepare a defense strategy. Thus, the prosecution authority must usually provide such information as soon as criminal proceedings are initiated—or at the latest when the suspect is arrested—and not only when the case is sent to court. Nevertheless, the pertinent directive applies "until the conclusion of the criminal proceedings" and is therefore of relevance also for the trial stage. When the competent authorities find additional evidence during that phase, EU law therefore obliges them to disclose it to the defense early enough to consider it.[11] For obvious reasons also (and *a fortiori*) the right of access to a lawyer[12] and legal aid[13] as well as the right to interpretation and translation[14] apply during the trial phase. Children additionally have the right to be accompanied by their parents during court hearings in which they are accused.[15]

c. *Some Critical Remarks*

Even though the aforementioned legislative efforts to strengthen the rights of suspects and accused persons are, generally speaking, most welcome in order to ensure a certain level of fairness in transnational criminal proceedings within the EU, the following points of criticism have to be brought fourth:

First of all, these EU rights and guarantees often do not go beyond what has already been established by the ECHR and the correspondent jurisprudence of the European Court of Human Rights (ECtHR). As all EU Member States are bound by the ECHR, the question arises what the added value of such instruments actually is. As regards the right to translation and interpretation, for instance, a similar guarantee is to be found in Article 6(3)(e) ECHR. Although the provision only refers to the free assistance of an *interpreter*, the ECtHR held as early as 1978 that this guarantee encompasses the *translation* of "all those documents [...] which it is necessary [...] to understand in order to have the benefit of a fair trial."[16] That the EU directive on the right to translation and interpretation does not go beyond this is illustrated by its Article 3(7). It provides that, instead of a written translation, an oral translation or even an oral summary of an essential (!) case document shall suffice. Against this background, it is probably no exaggeration

[10] Directive 2012/13/EU of 22 May 2012 on the right to information in criminal proceedings, 2012 O.J. (L 142) 1.

[11] Compare the second sentence of article 7(3) of Directive 2012/13, *id.*

[12] Directive 2013/48/EU of 22 October 2013 on the right of access to a lawyer in criminal proceedings and in European arrest warrant proceedings, and on the right to have a third party informed upon deprivation of liberty and to communicate with third persons and with consular authorities while deprived of liberty, 2013 O.J. (L 294) 1.

[13] Directive (EU) 2016/1919 of 26 October 2016 on legal aid for suspects and accused persons in criminal proceedings and for requested persons in European arrest warrant proceedings, 2016 O.J. (L 297) 1.

[14] Directive 2010/64/EU of 20 October 2010 on the right to interpretation and translation in criminal proceedings, 2010 O.J. (L 280) 1.

[15] Article 15 of Directive 2016/800, *supra* note 9.

[16] Luedicke, Belkacem and Koç v. Germany, App. Nos. 6210/73, 6877/75, 7132/75, Eur. Ct. H.R., Nov. 28, 1978, § 48.

to state that the harmonization efforts of the EU do to some extent serve merely symbolic purposes.

A second point of criticism stems from the often rather low level of defense rights guaranteed by the EU instruments, which were briefly presented above. Admittedly, these contain no more than minimum rules, so that every Member State is—in theory—free to go beyond them and provide additional rights for suspects. But the interplay with the concept of mutual recognition should not be neglected: as long as Member State A complies with the EU standard (say on the presumption of innocence), Member State B may be obliged to execute a European arrest warrant or a European investigation order issued in Member State A—irrespective of a more far-reaching understanding of the presumption of innocence in the domestic law of Member State B. This phenomenon can be referred to as a "race to the bottom."[17] To avoid it, the Union must not be too cautious with its efforts and must provide for procedural minimum rights that are more than the "least common denominator" of the various national criminal justice systems.

3. Rights of Victims in the Trial Phase

Although most EU directives aimed at harmonizing the Member States' criminal procedure law focus on the position of the defense, there is also a directive on the position of victims in criminal proceedings.[18] It was preceded by specific rules for victims of selected offenses, namely trafficking in human beings[19] and sexual exploitation of children and child pornography.[20] These provisions can be of great relevance for the criminal trial.

Pursuant to the general rules established by directive 2012/29, victims shall—like suspects and accused persons—have the right to free interpretation and translation of essential case documents (Article 7). However, they shall not only have the possibility to follow the proceedings, but to actively participate. For that purpose, they must be heard and can present evidence (Article 10)—which will normally happen in trial. Where necessary, Member States furthermore have to protect a victim, especially during his or her witness statement in trial (Article 23(3)). To that aim, the national authorities shall ensure that measures are available to avoid visual contact between victims and offenders during the giving of evidence, that the victim can be heard without being present in the courtroom, and that a hearing can take place without the presence of the public.

[17] European Criminal Policy Initiative, *A Manifesto on European Criminal Procedure Law*, 8 Zeitschrift für internationale Strafrechtsdogmatik 430, 444 seq. (2013) (*available at* www.zis-online.com).

[18] Directive 2012/29/EU of 25 October 2012 establishing minimum standards on the rights, support and protection of victims of crime, and replacing Council Framework Decision 2001/220/JHA, 2012 O.J. (L 315) 57.

[19] Directive 2011/36/EU of 5 April 2011 on preventing and combating trafficking in human beings and protecting its victims, and replacing Council Framework Decision 2002/629/JHA, 2002 O.J. (L 101) 1.

[20] Directive 2011/92 of 13 December 2011 on combating the sexual abuse and sexual exploitation of children and child pornography, and replacing Council Framework Decision 2004/68/JHA, 2011 O.J. (L 335) 1.

Generally speaking, witness protection measures are undoubtedly legitimate. But it should also be noted that EU interventions in this field can easily affect the tectonics of a Member State's criminal procedure system. Thus, a certain cautiousness is required. In particular, such efforts risk destroying the balance of criminal proceedings and the equality of arms between prosecution and defense:[21] the more the (alleged) victim is given the possibility to actively participate in criminal proceedings—in particular by presenting evidence—the more the accused is ultimately confronted with another prosecutor, as the (alleged) victim and his or her lawyers step up to this role. Some specific victim guarantees entail further problems for the position of the defense. Most clearly, measures to avoid visual contact with the accused conflict with the latter's right to confront witnesses against him or her (Article 6(3)(d) ECHR). Finally, from a more abstract point of view, it also needs to be emphasized that the legal position of the victim varies considerably in the different Member States. Therefore, EU harmonization instruments in this area can turn out to disturb the coherence of national criminal justice systems. Luckily, the EU legislator has chosen a rather careful approach, in that directive 2012/29 repeatedly points out that measures for the protection of victims shall be without prejudice to the rights of the defense (e.g.: Articles 7(2) and 18). Several times the directive also refers back to national law and thereby avoids friction within the respective Member State's procedural system, for instance, with a view to the right to a decision on compensation in the course of criminal proceedings (Article 16(2)). Nevertheless, this directive shows that criminal procedure law is a very sensitive area and its harmonization requires a very thorough drafting process.

III. European Rules for the Admissibility and Assessment of Evidence

An aspect of criminal procedure law for which European influences might become increasingly important is the admissibility and assessment of evidence. This is traditionally the core of every criminal trial and used to be governed purely by national law. But over the last few years several legislative acts of the EU have begun to address this intricate topic. In this regard, two categories of rules can be distinguished:

1. Evidence Gathered in Breach of EU Law

Some provisions impose (albeit vague) limits on the use of evidence that was gathered in breach of defense rights enshrined in EU directives. To illustrate this, reference can once

[21] European Criminal Policy Initiative, *supra* note 17, at 439.

again be made to Article 7 of the directive on the presumption of innocence.[22] It implements the principle of *nemo tenetur se ipsum accusare* by establishing the accused person's right to remain silent and not to incriminate himself. Article 10(2) of the same directive provides that the assessment of statements obtained in breach of these guarantees must ensure that "the rights of the defense and the fairness of the proceedings are respected." A similar provision applies where a Member State has violated the right of access to a lawyer in criminal proceedings.[23] Comparable rules lack, by contrast, in the two older directives dealing with the right to interpretation and translation and the right to information.

This reveals that EU legislation is not always fully consistent: it does not make a lot of sense to provide for such a remedy when a suspect or accused person is refused access to a lawyer, while the failure to inform him or her about this right does not have the same consequence. From a more optimistic point of view, this example demonstrates the evolution of EU legislation in a field that has not been subject to harmonization until very recently. However, even the two directives that do point to the assessment of evidence as a reaction to the breach of EU minimum rights still leave the Member States a broad margin of discretion. Taking into account that the EU directives—so far—do not at all provide an impressive level of defense rights, this is not satisfactory. Hopefully the Union's evolutionary process in criminal procedure law will continue so that we can see further improvements in the future.

2. Admissibility of Evidence Gathered in Another EU Member State

A second set of rules addresses the admissibility of evidence that was gathered in another Member State. When authorities carry out an investigative measure, they have to follow the law of the state where they act and not the law of the state where the trial will be held. Thus, it may occur that they do not respect procedural rules that are essential for the admissibility of the evidence in the trial state. This problem is almost as old as the idea of European criminal procedure rules itself: already during the European Council in Tampere in 1999 the political leaders of the EU expressed their wish that "evidence lawfully gathered by one Member State's authorities should be admissible before the courts of other Member States."[24] In two green papers from 2001[25] and 2009[26] the European Commission seized the idea. Today Article 82(2)(a) TFEU expressly gives

[22] *Supra* note 7. [23] Directive 2013/48, *supra* note 12, at Art. 12(2).

[24] Conclusion, *supra* note 2, at no. 36.

[25] *Green Paper on Criminal-Law Protection of the Financial Interests of the Community and the Establishment of a European Prosecutor*, at 58 et seq., COM (2001) 715 final (Dec. 11, 2012).

[26] *Green Paper on Obtaining Evidence in Criminal Matters from one Member State to Another and Securing Its Admissibility*, COM (2009) 624 final (Nov. 11, 2009).

the Union a corresponding competence to adopt harmonizing measures. Were this idea to be implemented, it would be mutual recognition in its purest form: every evidence obtained in any EU Member State would have to be recognized (i.e.: admitted) in all other Member States.

Understandable as such tendencies may be at first sight, some critical observations need to be made also in this regard.[27] As mentioned above, the concept of mutual recognition stems from the single market. But evidence in a criminal trial is not a product like beer or sausages. When a criminal court bases a conviction on evidence obtained under legal prerequisites that differ from the ones under its own law, it incorporates a foreign element into the trial. If, for instance, a witness has a right not to testify only in the Member State of trial but not in the Member State where he or she gives evidence, it is clear that the authorities of that second Member State will not inform the witness to these ends. But if the recordings of the statement then become crucial for a conviction in the first Member State, the right not to testify as guaranteed by the legal order of that Member State is ultimately circumvented. Similar concerns arise when the law of the Member State where a witness delivers his or her statement does not require the presence of a defense counsel during a pretrial interrogation. Under the law of that Member State, this may be totally acceptable because the statement would have to be repeated in trial anyway. But if the recorded statement as such is introduced into trial in a different Member State, the defense loses the possibility to confront the witness of the prosecution. Of course one could object that the court in the Member State of trial still can decide not to accept evidence, should it make the proceedings unfair. But European rules on the mutual admissibility of evidence would precisely aim at abolishing or at least limiting this discretion. Since every Member State follows its own concept to establish a fair balance between prosecutorial interests and interests of the defense in criminal proceedings, such exchangeability of evidence could eventually result in a patchwork of procedural systems and prejudice the fairness of the proceedings as a whole.

The so-called *forum regit actum* rule can help to avoid such problems. It means that the authorities of the Member State where an investigative measure needs to be taken shall—at least to the greatest extent possible—gather the evidence not according to their own law, but according to the law of the state where the trial will take place (the forum state).[28] In the above examples, the witness would therefore have to be informed about his or her right not to testify guaranteed only by the law of the trial state, and the defense would be given the opportunity to confront the witness already at the pretrial stage. To some extent, the *forum regit actum* approach therefore implements the idea that also cross-border proceedings should always be conducted in accordance with the law of

[27] *See* Satzger, *supra* note 1, § 8 para. 47; Frank Zimmermann, Sanja Glaser & Andreas Motz, *Mutual Recognition and Its Implications for the Gathering of Evidence in Criminal Proceedings: A Critical Analysis of the Initiative for a European Investigation Order*, 1 Eur. Crim. L. Rev. 56, 71 et seq. (2011); European Criminal Policy Initiative, *supra* note 17, at 434 et seq.; André Klip, *European Criminal Law* 351 (3d ed. 2016).

[28] *See* Satzger, *supra* note 1, § 8 para. 47; Zimmermann, Glaser & Motz, *supra* note 27, at 72; European Criminal Policy Initiative, *supra* note 17, at 435.

only one state (i.e., the forum state).[29] Apart from that, a more far-reaching approximation of the Member States' national procedural rules can further diminish obstacles to the mutual admissibility of evidence. The original idea of obliging national courts to admit evidence simply because it was obtained in another EU Member State, by contrast, would cause new problems rather than solving the old ones.

Therefore, it is to be acknowledged that EU legislation has largely refrained from the seductively easy solution envisaged by the Tampere conclusions. Instead, the directive on the European investigation order, which entered into force in 2014 and establishes rules for the gathering of evidence across borders, enshrines the *forum regit actum* principle.[30] Furthermore, Article 14(7) of said directive states that a Member State issuing an investigation order must ensure respect for the rights of the defense and the fairness of the proceeding when assessing the evidence obtained abroad. At least for the horizontal cooperation of Member States in criminal matters the existing EU legislation should thus largely avoid "patchwork proceedings" and problems regarding the admissibility of evidence gathered abroad in trial. Other challenges connected to mutual recognition, however, remain to be solved (particularly the question as to what extent fundamental rights can be an impediment to cross-border cooperation[31]), but they rather relate to the pretrial stage and extradition than to the admissibility of evidence in a trial.[32] And finally, the admissibility of evidence stemming from another Member State is not only relevant for the horizontal cooperation between Member States, but will also be of concern when supranational institutions such as the (future) European Public Prosecutor's Office get involved in criminal proceedings. In the following part of this contribution, which will be dedicated to this still quite recent development, we shall therefore briefly come back to this aspect.

IV. The European Public Prosecutor's Office and Its Role in the Trial Phase

One of the most significant developments of European criminal law since the adoption of the Treaty of Lisbon is the establishment of the European Public Prosecutor's Office (EPPO). Although the EU is currently facing difficult political times, shaken by far-reaching political developments such as the "Brexit," the "Euro-crisis," and the

[29] *See* Bernd Schünemann, *The Foundations of Transnational Criminal Proceedings*, in *A Programme for European Criminal Justice* 344, 351 (Bernd Schünemann ed., 2006) ("transnational, procedural unity").

[30] Directive 2014/41/EU of 3 April 2014 regarding the European Investigation Order in criminal matters, Art. 9(2) and (4)–(5), 2014 O.J. (L 130) 1.

[31] Compare Tobias Reinbacher & Matthias Wendel, *The* Bundesverfassungsgericht's *European Arrest Warrant II Decision*, 23 Maastricht J. Eur. & Comp. L. 702–13 (2016).

[32] Because Directive 2014/41/EU on the European investigation order, *supra* note 30, Art. 11(1)(f) allows the refusal of the execution of an investigation order that would be incompatible with fundamental rights.

increasing popularity of nationalist movements, the goal to create an EPPO in order to effectively protect the financial interests of the EU has so far continuously been prominent among many Member States and large parts of the European population. Article 86 TFEU provides for a legal basis to create an EPPO, which shall be responsible for investigating, prosecuting, and bringing to judgment offenses against the Union's financial interests. According to Article 86(2)(2) TFEU, the EPPO shall exercise the functions of prosecutor in the competent courts of the participating Member States in relation to such offenses. On the 11th of October 2017, following the approval of the European Parliament, twenty Member States adopted a regulation implementing enhanced cooperation on the establishment of the EPPO pursuant to Article 86 TFEU (EPPO-Regulation).[33] The supporters of the EPPO's creation could not convince all Member States to participate; however, the rather large number of participants promises a wide outreach of the recently created institution. This chapter shall analyze some of the major consequences that the creation of the EPPO will have on the trial phase of criminal proceedings carried out in the participating EU Member States. First, it will explore the question of who will be representing the prosecution in such proceedings, including providing a brief overview of the EPPO's general structure (Section IV.1). Second and closely linked to the first question, we will analyze where a specific case falling in the EPPO's competence will be tried (forum state) and thus which national legal regime shall govern the criminal proceedings and their outcome (Section IV.2). Last, this section will have a closer look on the admissibility of evidence gathered in another EU Member State under the auspices of the EPPO (Section IV.3).

1. The EPPO's General Structure

The institutional structure of the EPPO will have a major influence on the criminal proceedings and particularly the trial phase, as it determines who will be representing the prosecution in an individual case dealing with offenses committed against the EU's financial interests. The idea of granting an "external institution" the position to represent the prosecution in national trials created comprehensible sovereignty concerns among EU Member States, particularly as the field of criminal law has traditionally been considered a *domaine réservé* of national sovereignty. In order to comply with those concerns, the EPPO-Regulation aims for smooth cooperation between national enforcement agencies and the EPPO, which is reflected in the latter's institutional structure. According to its Article 8(2), the EPPO shall be organized at a central and a decentralized level.[34] The central level shall consist of the College, the Permanent Chambers, the European Chief Prosecutor, the Deputy European Chief Prosecutors, the European

[33] Council Regulation (EU) 2017/1939 of 12 October 2017 implementing enhanced cooperation on the establishment of the European Public Prosecutor's Office ("the EPPO"), 2017 O.J. (L 283) 1.

[34] For a more detailed analysis of the EPPO's general structure and a comparison with the Commission's original proposal, see Helmut Satzger & Nicolai von Maltitz, *Wissenswertes zum neugeschaffenen Europäischen Staatsanwalt*, 40 Juristische Ausbildung 153, 155–57 (2018/2).

Prosecutors, and the Administrative Director (Article 8(3) of the EPPO-Regulation). The decentralized level shall consist of European Delegated Prosecutors who shall be located in the participating Member States (Article 8(4) of the EPPO-Regulation). According to 13(1) of the EPPO-Regulation, the Delegated European Prosecutors shall act on behalf of the EPPO in their respective Member States for which they shall have the powers of national prosecutors, particularly including the competence to bring a case to judgment. The European Delegated Prosecutors are nominated by their respective Member States and, upon proposal by the European Chief Prosecutor, appointed by the College (Article 17(1) of the EPPO-Regulation). They shall be active members of the public prosecution service or judiciary of their respective Member State (Article 17(2) of the EPPO-Regulation) and may exercise functions as national prosecutors, to the extent that this does not prevent them from fulfilling their obligations as part of the EPPO (article 13(3) of the EPPO-Regulation). The "double hatted" nature of the European Delegated Prosecutors demonstrates the clear aims for integrating the EPPO with national prosecution services. In view of the EPPO's general structure it seems likely that the work of European Delegated Prosecutors will generally not decisively differ from the work of national prosecutors. Presumably, as long as European Delegated Prosecutors will represent the prosecution, the creation of the EPPO will not per se constitute a paradigm change in national criminal proceedings in this regard. However, the influences of the EPPO's central level on the work of the European Delegated Prosecutors should not be underestimated. European Prosecutors are mandated to supervise the European Delegated Prosecutors' investigations and prosecutions and may in specific cases give them instructions in compliance with applicable national law and the instructions given by the competent Permanent Chamber (article 12(1), (3) of the EPPO-Regulation). Each participating Member State shall nominate three candidates for the position of European Prosecutor, one of whom shall be selected and appointed by the Council, acting by simple majority (article 16(1), (2), (3)). Moreover, the Permanent Chambers shall monitor and direct the European Delegated Prosecutors according to Article 10(2) of the EPPO-Regulation and may, acting through the respective European Prosecutor, give him or her instructions (Article 10(5) of the EPPO-Regulation). According to Article 10(1) of the EPPO-Regulation, the Permanent Chambers shall consist of three members out of the pool of the European Chief Prosecutor and the European Prosecutors. In view of the delicate framework of competences under the umbrella of the EPPO and particularly the different layers of authority attributed to the central and decentralized levels, the consequences of the creation of the EPPO on the trial proceedings cannot be conclusively foreseen. As long as the European Delegated Prosecutors remain in charge of the investigations and prosecutions on the decentralized level, the criminal proceedings may effectively not change a lot due to the involvement of the EPPO. However, the European Prosecutors' and the Permanent Chambers' extensive competences to direct and monitor the Delegated European Prosecutors may also lead to further harmonization of the prosecutorial strategy pursued in trials in which the EPPO is involved, potentially implementing a more integrated "European prosecutorial agenda."

2. The Determination of the Forum State

Closely linked to the issue of who shall be representing the prosecution in cases dealing with crimes against the financial interests of the EU is the question of where, that is, in which participating Member State a certain crime shall be brought to trial. In establishing the EPPO, the EU legislator had to take a stand on this matter because regularly more than one participating Member State will have criminal jurisdiction over an offense affecting the Union's financial interests (so called PIF-offenses[35]). The choice of the competent forum state is of utmost importance for the entire criminal process, as it does not only determine which European Delegated Prosecutor shall be representing the prosecution, but also which procedural and material legal regime will apply. By establishing the EPPO in its current form, the legislator rejected further-reaching ideas of creating a permanent European Criminal Court for the investigation and prosecution of crimes against the financial interests of the EU that could have applied a uniform body of material and procedural law. With the EPPO exercising the functions of prosecutor in the competent courts of the participating Member States, they will generally apply national law, first, with regard to the material offenses to be prosecuted and, second, with regard to the procedural rules governing the criminal proceedings.

a. *Consequences for the Applicable Substantive Law*

In order for such a concept of an EPPO to successfully protect the financial interests of the EU, it became necessary to start harmonizing the substantive law of the Member States. According to Article 22(1) of the EPPO-Regulation, the EPPO shall be mainly competent in respect of criminal offenses provided for in the so-called PIF-Directive,[36] as implemented by national law, irrespective of whether the same criminal conduct could be classified as another type of offense under national law. Generally, the PIF-Directive is intended to establish a certain minimum of criminalization in view of acts harming the financial interests of the EU. At the same time, it forms the basis for the EPPO's material competence, thus, limiting the latter's outreach. If a national criminal offense penalizes more than such conduct covered by the PIF-Directive, the EPPO shall not be competent to represent the prosecution in that regard.[37] Such interpretation of the EPPO-Regulation

[35] French: protection des intérêts financiers = protection of the financial interests.

[36] Directive (EU) 2017/1371 of 5 July 2017 on the fight against fraud to the Union's financial interests by means of criminal law, 2017 O.J. (L 198) 29.

[37] *See also* Dominik Brodowski, *Die Europäische Staatsanwaltschaft—eine Einführung*, 37 *Strafverteidiger* 7 (2017/10).

reduces the risk that the decision of where to investigate and prosecute will be (mis-)used for means of "forum-shopping," that is, selecting a particular forum state to prosecute certain conduct.[38] However, Article 22(3) of the EPPO-Regulation grants the EPPO the additional competence for any other criminal offense that is inextricably linked to criminal conduct covered by the PIF-Directive. As there is no harmonization undertaken with regard to those "ancillary offenses," the decision on the forum state may thus determine whether they will at all be investigated and prosecuted.[39]

Moreover, the PIF-Directive does not comprehensively harmonize the general principles of criminal law to be applied to offenses falling under the competences of the EPPO. Although Member States are obliged to take necessary measures to ensure that inciting, aiding, and abetting, and—limited to certain offenses also—attempt (Article 5 of the PIF-Directive) will be punishable, the material scope of those modes of participation will entirely depend on the national law of the respective forum state.[40] Similarly, the PIF-Directive does not extensively harmonize the criminal sanctions to be imposed on a convicted offender. Again, the PIF-Directive provides for some basic requirements, most importantly that criminal sanctions shall be effective, proportionate, and dissuasive. It does, however, lack a minimum threshold of punishment corresponding to the individual offenses.[41] The decision in which participating Member State the EPPO shall bring an offense to trial will thus determine the exact scope of punishability of the criminal conduct and the sanctions that will be imposed on the accused following a conviction.

b. *Consequences for the Applicable Procedural Law*

The decision on the forum state will not only determine the material, but also the procedural legal regime in criminal proceedings where the EPPO will represent the prosecution. In order to prevent the selection of the forum state from potentially undermining the basic rights of suspects and the accused by means of forum shopping, the EPPO-Regulation assumes and provides for a minimum degree of harmonization with regard to the procedural legal standards of the participating Member States. Its Article 41 thus requests that the activities of the EPPO be carried out in full compliance with the rights of suspects and accused persons enshrined in the EU Charter of Fundamental Rights and determines a number of minimum rights to be respected. Although the implementation of such minimum rights mitigates the consequences of the selection of the forum state, it is undoubtable that the concrete rules governing a criminal trial will always have decisive repercussions on its material outcome.[42] This is implicitly also

[38] On the general danger of "forum shopping" due to differences in substantive law, see Frank Zimmermann, *Choice of Forum and Choice of Law Under the Future Regulation on the Establishment of a European Public Prosecutor's Office*, in *The European Public Prosecutor's Office: Legal and Criminal Policy Perspectives* 156, 157–60 (Petter Asp ed., 83 Skrifter utgivna av Juridiska fakulteten vid Stockholms universiteit, 2015).

[39] Cf. also European Criminal Policy Initiative, *supra* note 17, at 424.

[40] Cf. Zimmermann, *supra* note 38, at 158–59.

[41] *Id.*

[42] European Criminal Policy Initiative, *supra* note 17, at 424.

reflected in Article 41(3) of the EPPO-Regulation, which guarantees the suspect and accused all the procedural rights available under the applicable national law that may exceed the aforementioned minimum standard. Therefore, the decision on the forum state remains of major significance for the process and outcome of the criminal trial.

c. *Choosing the Forum State*

Acknowledging the importance of the choice of the forum state, the EPPO-Regulation aims at establishing a legal regime that guarantees that the decision on where to bring a case to court will be reasonably linked to the case. The Commission's original proposal on the establishment of the EPPO published in July 2013[43] had been largely criticized for potentially leading to arbitrary and coincidental results, as it introduced extensive criteria such as the place where the evidence is located or the habitual residence of the direct victims (Article 27(4)). The latter criterion appeared particularly odd, as all offenses falling under the competence of the EPPO are committed mainly against the financial interests of the EU.[44] Furthermore, the Commission's original proposal did not create a formal hierarchy between the listed criteria, leading to the result that the EPPO would have been granted an excessively wide margin of discretion in choosing the forum state.[45] In contrast, Article 26(4) of the EPPO-Regulation determines that a case shall generally be initiated and investigated by a Delegated European Prosecutor from the participating Member State where the focus of the criminal activity was. A deviation from this rule may only be undertaken where it is duly justified, taking into account three hierarchically listed criteria, that is (1) the place of the suspect's or accused person's habitual residence, (2) his or her nationality, and (3) the place where the main financial damage has occurred. Pursuant to Article 36(3) of the EPPO-Regulation, the same rules apply for the decision on where to bring the case to prosecution. Compared to the Commission's proposal, the final text of the regulation thus creates a more rigorous regime for determining the forum state[46] that corresponds more adequately to the great importance of the issue analyzed in this section.

3. Admissibility of Evidence Gathered in Another Participating EU Member State

The admissibility of evidence gathered outside the forum state will frequently determine the process and outcome of trials falling under the competence of the EPPO. Particularly in transnational cases, the prosecutors of the EPPO, but also the defense will often be dependent on evidential material that is located in other participating EU Member States. Drafting the EPPO-Regulation, the EU legislator could have chosen the strongest

[43] COM (2013) 534 final (July 7, 2013).

[44] European Criminal Policy Initiative, *supra* note 17, at 424.

[45] *Id.*

[46] *See also* Fabio Giuffrida, *Cross-Border Crimes and the European Public Prosecutor's Office*, 11 eucrim 149, 153 (2017).

form of harmonization in this regard by implementing the concept of mutual recognition within the borders of the participating EU Member States. However, the EPPO-Regulation wisely pursues a more differentiated approach; it neither generally precludes nor admits evidence gathered outside of the forum state. Its Article 37(1) guarantees that evidence presented by the prosecutors of the EPPO or the defendant to a court shall not be denied on the mere ground that the evidence was gathered in another participating Member State or in accordance with the law of another participating Member State. Article 37(2) of the EPPO-Regulation assures that the power of the (domestic) trial court to freely assess the evidence shall not be affected.

In addition to this admissibility regime, the EPPO-Regulation adopts an approach based on the *forum regit actum* principle. Article 31(1)(2) of the EPPO-Regulation holds that where a measure needs to be carried out in a participating Member State other than the Member State of the investigating European Delegated Prosecutor, the latter shall decide on the adoption of the measure and assign it to a European Delegated Prosecutor in the Member State where it needs to be taken. According to Article 31(2) of the EPPO-Regulation, the admissibility and adoption of such measures shall generally be governed by the law of the participating Member State of the investigating European Delegated Prosecutor, that is, the forum state.[47] The assigned measures shall be carried out in accordance with the EPPO-Regulation and the law of the Member State of the assisting European Delegated Prosecutor. Formalities and procedures expressly indicated by the investigating European Delegated Prosecutor shall be complied with, unless such formalities and procedures are contrary to the fundamental principles of law of the Member State of the assisting European Delegated Prosecutor (Article 32 of the EPPO-Regulation). With this provision the EPPO-Regulation seeks to ensure that evidence gathered in another participating Member State satisfies the procedural safeguards of the forum state, and it avoids problems regarding the admissibility of such evidence. However, the implementation of this *forum regit actum* principle is only to be welcomed because the EPPO-Regulation provides for detailed rules that clearly determine the forum state from the very outset of the EPPO's investigative activities.[48] If the EPPO's discretion with regard to the decision where to bring a case to court had been more expansive, the implementation of such approach would have created an alarming degree of uncertainty with regard to the applicable legal regime. What is more, it would have created a potential danger of forum shopping by choosing the forum state in view of the (weakest) procedural safeguards regarding the collection of evidence. In fact, the Commission's original proposal would have combined the *locus regit actum* principle with a rule that evidence gathered abroad shall generally be admissible, subject only to a

[47] For a minor exception to this rule in cases of different requirements of judicial authorization for a particular measure under the procedural law of the participating Member States, see Art. 31(3), (4) of the EPPO-Regulation, *supra* note 33.

[48] Cf. D. Helenius, *Admissibility of Evidence and the European Public Prosecutor's Office*, in *The European Public Prosecutor's Office: Legal and Criminal Policy Perspectives* 178, 192–93 (Petter Asp ed., 83 Skrifter utgivna av Juridiska fakulteten vid Stockholms universiteit, 2015).

fundamental rights clause (Article 30).[49] In comparison with that, the final text of the EPPO-Regulation constitutes a major improvement, with a more balanced compromise between the admissibility of evidence on the one hand and the rights of suspected and accused persons on the other.

V. A Project for the Future: Supranational Rules Determining the State of Trial

As illustrated in the preceding section on the EPPO, not only the criminal trial itself is subject to European influences, as the EPPO-Regulation also contains some rules for the preliminary question of where the trial will take place. It is submitted that these are even more important than detailed provisions on selected procedural questions because—as we have seen—this decision determines which procedural and substantive law will apply in toto. Had the regulation remained silent with regard to the choice of the trial state, this would therefore have opened the door for forum shopping. However, overlapping criminal jurisdiction is in no way a particularity of the PIF-offenses, but can occur in many fields because public international law recognizes various principles of jurisdiction.[50] What is more, the EU has made considerable efforts to harmonize national criminal law provisions for the protection of European financial interests. The same cannot be said about all other areas of crime. Thus, the decision where to prosecute is even more important with a view to the applicable substantive law.

In a single area of justice such as the EU with a transnational prohibition of double jeopardy (Article 50 of the Charter of Fundamental Rights of the EU), this situation may lead to a "first come, first serve" mentality—that is, a situation where Member States compete to be the first to finally dispose of a case—and arbitrary results.[51] The efforts of all other Member States are blocked then, no matter how legitimate their interest in prosecution is or whether they are possibly in a better position to adjudicate the case in its entire cross-border dimension. Furthermore (and even without a transnational *ne bis in idem* guarantee), the Member States involved will often seek to coordinate their simultaneous investigations and determine the most appropriate forum for prosecution. Then, again, reasonable criteria for the allocation of the case are needed. To prevent

[49] For an extensive critique of the Commission's original proposal in this regard, see Helenius, *supra* note 48, at 192–202.

[50] For an overview, see Satzger, *supra* note 1, § 4.

[51] *See* the European Commission's *Green Paper on Conflicts of Jurisdiction and the Principle of Ne Bis in Idem in Criminal Proceedings*, at 3, COM (2005) 696 final (Dec. 23, 2005); see also Frank Zimmermann, *Conflicts of Criminal Jurisdiction in the European Union*, 3 Bergen J. Crim. L. & Crim. Just. 1, 2–11 (2015) with many further references.

manipulation, supranational rules should define them as clearly as possible.[52] Thus, it is one of the major challenges for the EU legislator to create European rules for the exercise of criminal jurisdiction and the state where a criminal trial is to be held. Several elaborate proposals have already been made in this regard.[53] And why should something that exists in the area of private law[54] not also be achievable for the criminal law?

VI. Concluding Remarks

This chapter analyzed the influences and challenges of EU law as a driving force for national trial procedure reforms. It outlined the basic principle of mutual recognition and its function as a keystone for EU integration. However, this principle must be complemented by a certain minimum standard of procedural rights for suspected and accused persons. The EU legislator has already taken some harmonizing measures in this regard. The most important one concerning the trial phase is the directive on the presumption of innocence and the right to be present at trial. However, the procedural safeguards implemented by this directive mostly guarantee a standard that does not exceed those rights already enshrined in the ECHR. In light of this fact and in order to effectively prevent a "race to the bottom," the EU legislator should be more determined to implement a minimum standard that does not merely constitute the "least common denominator" of the various criminal justice systems, but an adequate and fair standard for an ever more harmonized "European" criminal procedure.

Moreover, closer analysis of the directive on the position of victims in criminal proceedings demonstrated that any measure taken to harmonize the criminal proceedings (e.g., in favor of victims' participation) must be taken very diligently as not to undermine the coherence of the domestic criminal justice systems.

Concerning the admissibility of evidence, the harmonizing legislation of the EU does unfortunately not yet provide for a full protection of defendants' rights in cases in which evidence was gathered in violation of EU law. As regards evidence collected abroad, however, the EU legislator wisely refrained from implementing a premature mutual admissibility approach. The *forum regit actum* principle, as implemented in the European investigation order and with regard to investigative measures taken by the

[52] European Criminal Policy Initiative, *supra* note 17, at 432.

[53] Recent examples include: Martin Böse, Frank Meyer & Anne Schneider, 2 *Conflicts of Jurisdiction in Criminal Matters in the European Union* 381 et seq. (2014); Arndt Sinn (ed.), *Conflicts of Jurisdiction in Cross-Border Crime Situations* 601 et seq. (2012); Bernd Schünemann (ed.), *A Programme for European Criminal Justice* 258 et seq. (2006); Zimmermann, *supra* note 51, at 15–21.

[54] *See* Regulation (EU) 1215/2012 of 12 December 2012 on jurisdiction and the recognition and enforcement of judgments in civil and commercial matters, 2012 O.J. (L 351) 1 (for the competent civil courts) and (as an example for European rules on the applicable substantive law in civil matters) Regulation (EC) 864/2007 of 11 July 2007 on the law applicable to non-contractual obligations (Rome II), 2007 O.J. (L 199) 40.

(future) EPPO, could help to adequately balance the rights of suspected and accused persons with the admissibility of important evidence.

Moreover, the future EPPO shows how the creation of supranational EU institutions may shape the trial proceedings within EU Member States. With the EPPO exercising the function of prosecutor in the courts of the participating Member States, its legal framework does not only determine who will be representing the prosecution in an individual case, but also the forum state and the applicable substantive and procedural law. Despite the currently challenging political climate within and outside the EU, the establishment of the EPPO could serve as a precursor and stepping stone for further supranational rules determining criminal (trial) proceedings in EU Member States.

References

Petter Asp, *The Substantive Criminal Law Competence of the EU* (2012)

European Criminal Policy Initiative, *A Manifesto on European Criminal Procedure Law*, 8 Zeitschrift für internationale Strafrechtsdogmatik 430 seq. (2013) (*available at* www.zis-online.com)

Fabio Giuffrida, *Cross-Border Crimes and the European Public Prosecutor's Office*, 11 eucrim 149 seq. (2017)

Libor Klimek, *Mutual Recognition of Judicial Decisions in European Criminal Law* (2017)

André Klip, *European Criminal Law* (3d ed. 2016)

Helmut Satzger, *International and European Criminal Law* (2d ed. 2017)

Helmut Satzger & Nicolai von Maltitz, *Wissenswertes zum neugeschaffenen Europäischen Staatsanwalt*, 40 Juristische Ausbildung 153 et seq. (2018)

Bernd Schünemann (ed.), *A Programme for European Criminal Justice* (2006)

Frank Zimmermann, *Choice of Forum and Choice of Law Under the Future Regulation on the Establishment of a European Public Prosecutor's Office*, in *The European Public Prosecutor's Office: Legal and Criminal Policy Perspectives*, 83 Skrifter utgivna av Juridiska fakulteten vid Stockholms universiteit 156 seq. (Petter Asp ed., 2015)

Frank Zimmermann, *Conflicts of Criminal Jurisdiction in the European Union*, 3 Bergen J. Crim. L. & Crim. Just. 1 seq. (2015)

Frank Zimmermann, Sanja Glaser & Andreas Motz, *Mutual Recognition and Its Implications for the Gathering of Evidence in Criminal Proceedings: A Critical Analysis of the Initiative for a European Investigation Order*, 1 Eur. Crim. L. Rev. 56 seq. (2011)

CHAPTER 30

TRIAL PROCEDURES IN RESPONSE TO TERRORISM

NICOLA McGARRITY

I. Introduction

Acts of terrorism are essentially criminal in character. Therefore, in spite of the militarized rhetoric of the "war on terror" that has been prominent in political discourse since the September 11 terrorist attacks, the criminal justice system should be given primacy in preventing and responding to national security threats. This chapter takes as its starting point the principle that no one—regardless of whether he or she has been charged with a terrorism-related or "ordinary" criminal offense—should be deprived of liberty unless there has been a finding of guilt by a court after a criminal trial. While it is a truism that exceptions have been identified and/or abrogations permitted in the interests of community and individual safety, this principle nonetheless reflects the international community's recognition of liberty as a fundamental human right and the significance of the criminal trial as a bulwark against arbitrary state interference with that right.

The protection of individual liberty through this mechanism has been enshrined in both international conventional and customary law as well as in domestic constitutions and human rights instruments. Most notably, the International Covenant on Civil and Political Rights (ICCPR) relevantly provides:

1. Everyone has the right to liberty and security of person. No one shall be subjected to arbitrary arrest or detention. No one shall be deprived of liberty exception on such grounds and in accordance with such procedure as are established by law.

2. Anyone arrested or detained on a criminal charge shall be brought promptly before a judge or other officer authorized by law to exercise judicial power and shall be entitled to trial within a reasonable time or to release.[1]

In the absence of further exposition as to what constitutes a "trial," statements such as that in the ICCPR would be bereft of any meaningful content. That is not, however, the case. This document goes beyond simply mandating a criminal trial to outline its essential institutional characteristics and procedures. It provides that a defendant to a criminal charge must be given a "fair and public hearing" before a "competent, independent and impartial tribunal established by law." These requirements are as much about the public legitimacy of the criminal trial as they are about the rights of the individual. However, the individual is also accorded both procedural and substantive rights, including that he: "be presumed innocent until proven guilty"; "be informed . . . of the nature and cause of the charge"; "[be permitted to] communicate with counsel"; "be tried without undue delay"; "be tried in his presence"; and "not . . . be compelled to testify against himself or confess guilt."

The precise meaning of each of these concepts is controversial to say the least. The purpose of this chapter is not, however, to determine compliance of national legislation with either international or domestic constitutional frameworks. Instead, it sets out one particular lens through which changes to trial procedures in the terrorism context may be conceptualized. Legal scholarship in the counterterrorism context has addressed the extent of executive discretion in considerable detail, especially with regard to the development of the substantive law. For example, the breadth of preparatory terrorism offenses means that it effectively rests with criminal prosecutors to determine what conduct falls within these offenses according to their individual and organizational understandings of dangerousness. What has received less attention is the extent to which executive discretion is also prevalent in the procedural context. This chapter sets out a schema for understanding and tracking the influence of the executive branch of government upon terrorism prosecutions. In light of the uncertainty and flexibility built into the "essential" elements of a criminal trial, it is imperative that we acknowledge that criminal trials are not homogenous and may be conducted in a variety of ways with less and more executive involvement.

To that end, Section II of this chapter will start with an examination of the various fora in which a terrorism trial might be held. At one end of the spectrum are trials conducted before the ordinary criminal courts. At the other are military commissions such as those that were used by the United States for Guantanamo Bay detainees. Section III then moves on to consider the different categories of individuals and entities who might be called upon to decide the question of guilt or innocence. The remainder of the chapter is built upon the recognition that it would be theoretically possible to conduct a fair, independent, and impartial trial regardless of the forum

[1] International Covenant on Civil and Political Rights (New York, 16 Dec. 1966) 999 U.N.T.S. 171 and 1057 U.N.T.S. 407, *entered into force* 23 Mar. 1976.

in which it was conducted and whom the decision-maker was. This is dependent, however, upon the procedures adopted. Section IV will therefore highlight some of the modifications made to criminal trial procedure and examine the consequences of these—whether deliberate or inadvertent—so far as executive control of the trial process is concerned.

II. The Forum

In developing a schema for understanding the nature of the shift in the balance of power from the judiciary to the executive branch of government in terrorism trials, an obvious place to commence is with an analysis of the forum in which such a trial is held. This is important not only in its own right but also because it provides critical background for the remaining sections of this chapter. The forum in which a terrorism trial is held is not simply a matter of accident; it has been chosen by the state in order to achieve a certain purpose and, in furtherance of this, particular rules of procedure have been adopted.

1. Ordinary Civilian Criminal Courts

There is no universal conception of an "ordinary civilian criminal court." The reality is that it would be difficult to find even *two* countries that agree upon the composition and structure of such a court. The most obvious distinction to be drawn is between those countries with an inquisitorial and others with an adversarial model of criminal justice. However, this is only one example of the many ways in which the ordinary criminal courts may differ from one country to another. The heterogeneity of these courts does not render this category meaningless. The essential point is that the ordinary criminal courts are generalist in character and deal with the full range of criminal offenses. The utilization of such courts for terrorism trials therefore reflects an acknowledgment by the state that terrorism is not so exceptional as to necessitate prosecution in a special forum. Instead, the ordinary criminal courts are equally as equipped to deal with terrorism as they are other forms of criminal behavior.

Of course, that having been said, even those countries that utilize the ordinary criminal courts for terrorism trials may nevertheless put in place special rules of procedure to address, for example, the potential disclosure of national security information. The necessity for this step in certain circumstances has been recognized by the Eminent Jurists Panel on Terrorism, Counter-Terrorism and Human Rights (Eminent Jurists Panel). In a 2009 report, the Panel commented that "effective criminal prosecution is an indispensable instrument in the fight against terrorism."[2] Rather than ignoring systemic

[2] Eminent Jurists Panel on Terrorism, Counter-Terrorism and Human Rights, *Assessing Damage, Urging Action* 156 (2009).

problems, it urged that "priority should be accorded to improving the performance of the ordinary criminal justice system, *inter alia* by strengthening judicial independence, increasing the resources of the criminal justice and law enforcement systems, and improving international judicial cooperation."[3]

A number of countries have made limited—or no—changes to the basic structure of their criminal justice system in response to the threat of terrorism. Roach notes that amongst the countries that failed to immediately respond to the September 11 terrorist attacks were "those with tenuous claims to be democracies and those that had been almost universally criticized before 9/11 for their poor human rights records."[4] Such countries may have been unaffected by the threat of terrorism, have lacked the political will to address this threat or, finally, have already had such repressive criminal procedures in place that it was unnecessary to make any modifications to ensure efficient and effective trials. These reasons do not, however, capture all of the jurisdictions that have remained loyal to the ordinary criminal courts. Germany, for example, continues to insist that terrorism trials should be conducted in the ordinary criminal courts and defendants afforded the traditional protections of the criminal justice system. This is particularly striking given that the revelation of a close link between a Hamburg terrorist cell and the planning of the September 11 terrorist attacks in Washington and New York arguably gave Germany an opportunity to overhaul its antiterrorism regime with minimal public outcry. This commitment to the ordinary criminal courts has been maintained even in the face of the reluctance of the domestic courts to prioritize national security over the right to a fair trial. For example, in February 2003, Mounir El Motassedeq was convicted of terrorism offenses relating to his membership of the Hamburg cell.[5] This conviction was quashed by the German Constitutional Court on the ground that the authorities had denied him access to a witness who might have supported his claim to have no knowledge of the plan to weaponize commercial planes. The Constitutional Court ordered a retrial at which Motassedeq was convicted of the membership offense only.

2. Centralization of Terrorism-Related Functions

A variation upon the use of the ordinary criminal courts has been to identify groups of judges within those courts with sole (or primary) responsibility for presiding over terrorism trials. In France, for example, shortly after the dismantling of the State Security Court in the early 1980s, the authorities decided that the ordinary criminal process was inadequate to address the threat of terrorism.[6] The result was the centralization of all terrorism prosecutions with a special section of counterterrorist investigating

[3] *Id.* at 157. [4] Kent Roach, *The 9/11 Effect: Comparative Counter-Terrorism* 77–78 (2011).

[5] For a detailed discussion of this case, see Timo Kost, *Mounir El Motassadeq—A Missed Chance for Weltinnenpolik*?, 8(4) German L.J. 443 (2007).

[6] The exclusive jurisdiction of the Spanish Audiencia Nacional (*Sala de lo Penal*) to try terrorism cases is another example of the centralization of terrorism trials in Spain. For further detail, see Rogelio Alonso &

magistrates in Paris known as the Special Court of Assizes.[7] To this day, serious terrorism trials continue to be heard by a bench of at least three such magistrates rather than the traditional three judges and nine lay jurors. On the one hand, centralization might be seen as a positive development because it allows various participants in the terrorism trial process to develop expertise as well as striking a balance between the traditional protections of the criminal justice system and the need for a special response to address the extraordinary threat of terrorism. The latter was indeed the basis upon which Alain Marsoud, a French parliamentarian and one of the original members of the Special Court, supported the new centralized system. He stated that there must "be a balance between individual liberty on the one hand and the efficiency of the system to protect the public on the other. In an ideal world, I would choose the first, but this is not an ideal world, and when dealing with Islamic extremists we have to be brutal sometimes."[8] However, the basic problem with the centralization of judicial functions is the same as that raised by specialized courts. This will be discussed in more detail in Sections III and IV but, in short, the process is generally accompanied by a loss of true independence and impartiality. The Eminent Jurists Panel commented that "given the constant interaction between investigators and prosecutors specializing in terrorism cases, appearing before the same judges, all involved may gradually come to see themselves as part of the State's counter-terrorism machinery."[9]

In addition to those countries, such as France, which have legislated for a centralized system, others have allowed a de facto centralized system to occur through the regular allocation of terrorism cases to particular judges. In Australia, for example, Bongiorno J (in the Victorian Supreme Court) and Whealy J (in the New South Wales Supreme Court) presided over the bulk of terrorism trials in the decade after the September 11 terrorist attacks. The result in that country has been to achieve many of the same benefits as formal centralization, such as developing expertise and maintaining consistency of decision-making, but without any undermining of judicial independence and impartiality. This has been made possible by two factors. First, an informal system of centralization involves the relevant court—or, more accurately, the chief justice of that court—deciding who to allocate terrorism trials to and thus who should become the expert judge. This contrasts with the situation in France whereby that decision is made by the executive branch of government. Second, the Australian criminal process is based upon the adversarial model whereby judges do not play a role in the gathering of evidence for trial and, furthermore, all factual matters are left for determination by a jury. This means that

Fernando Reinares, *Terrorism, Human Rights and Law Enforcement in Spain*, 17(1) Terrorism & Political Violence 265, 267 (2005).

Maria Angeles Rueda & Miguel Angel Boldova, Spain, in *Comparative Counter-Terrorism Law* 297, 314 (Kent Roach ed., 2015).

7 Frank Foley, *Countering Terrorism in Britain and France: Institutions, Norms and the Shadow of the Past* 193–94 (2013).

8 Quoted in *The Theory and Practice of Islamic Terrorism: An Anthology* 15–16 (Marvin Perry & Howard E. Negrin, eds., 2008).

9 Eminent Jurists Panel on Terrorism, Counter-Terrorism and Human Rights, *supra* note 2, at 142.

there is less need for judges to interact on a regular basis with prosecutors and other state authorities during pretrial proceedings.

3. Specialist Civilian Terrorism Courts

As an alternative to reliance upon the ordinary criminal courts, some countries have established new courts specifically to conduct trials of terrorism offenses and other offenses against the state. Duffy suggests that this has become "a feature of international practice in a surprising number of states."[10] However, in most jurisdictions that have gone down this path, the new judicial bodies have taken the form of national security courts or military tribunals. These will be discussed in Section IV. This discussion here will concentrate upon a more unusual response, namely, the creation of specialist *civilian* courts. This might be described as something of a middle ground between reliance upon the ordinary criminal courts and a militarized response.

Western democratic countries have generally been reticent to establish specialist terrorism courts. This is somewhat surprising given that specialist judicial bodies play a central role in other parts of the terrorism framework. These include the Special Immigration Appeals Commission in the United Kingdom and the Foreign Intelligence Surveillance Court in the United States. However, there is good reason for states to be cautious about the creation of specialist civilian terrorism courts. From a practical perspective, the creation of a parallel judicial system would be both time-consuming and expensive. Thus, it is imperative—as the UN Human Rights Committee has asserted—that it should be "limited to cases where the State party can show that resorting to such trials is necessary and justified by objective and serious reasons, and ... the regular civilian courts are unable to undertake the trials."[11]

Moore suggests that the use of specialist civilian courts has been "linked to a perception ... that the resolution of disputes in a particular area of the law or concerning a particular human activity requires either a particular type of judicial expertise or a particular process of judicial adjudication or both."[12] From the perspective of domestic governments, there would seem to be two key reasons that such a perception may exist in respect of terrorism offenses. Both are grounded in a view that terrorism is so exceptional in its capacity to cause serious damage to property and mass loss of life that prosecutions—and the achievement of convictions—must be prioritized.

The first reason is efficiency. There are significant challenges in prosecuting terrorism offenses due to the complex nature of the overarching legislative regime and the difficulties in gathering sufficient evidence to establish a preparatory offense. As a consequence, defendants may be held on remand for a significant period of time and

[10] Helen Duffy, *The "War on Terror" and the Framework of International Law* 214 (2015).

[11] U.N. Human Rights Committee, General Comment No. 32, *Right to Equality before Courts and Tribunals and to a Fair Trial* (23 Aug. 2007).

[12] Justice Michael Moore, *Federal Court of Australia, The Role of Specialist Courts—An Australian Perspective* LAWASIA J. 139, 141 (2000/2001).

the trial itself will be lengthy. Specialist civilian terrorism courts thus represent a means—especially in countries where terrorism is rife and the courts are under-resourced—for terrorism prosecutions to be fast-tracked without affecting the progression of ordinary criminal trials.

The other reason for the creation of specialist civilian courts for terrorism trials should be treated with a greater degree of skepticism. An editorial in the *Washington Post* from July 27, 2008, argued that

> a specialized national security court would best balance the security needs of the country against the demands of due process.... The president must have the legal flexibility to detain those against whom there is credible, actionable intelligence but not enough evidence to bring charges.[13]

At its core, the assertion is that the exceptional nature of terrorism means that convictions must be achieved at a greater cost to civil liberties than is tolerated for other offenses. The creation of a specialist court would enable traditional criminal justice principles, such as open justice and procedural fairness, to be circumvented.

As noted above, Western democracies, especially those that are constrained by statutory and/or constitutional human rights instruments that protect the right to a fair trial, have generally been resistant to the idea of creating specialist civilian terrorism courts. It is those countries with a flawed record of human rights protection that have tended to go down the path of creating such courts. Whilst Egypt has a long history of using specialist courts to crush political dissent under the guise of addressing the threat of terrorism, such courts became unconstitutional with the adoption of the Constitution of the Arab Republic of Egypt in 2014. Article 97 provides that "no person may be tried except before the ordinary judge and exceptional courts are prohibited." However, just one year after the adoption of the new Constitution, the Egyptian Parliament enacted a Counter-Terrorism Law that established special circuits within the Egyptian criminal courts and courts of first instance.[14] These are presided over by a separate group of so-called ordinary judges. A statement made by the Ministry of Foreign Affairs in 2015 claimed that "[t]his is a more efficient and effective way of dealing with the large caseload of the judiciary."[15] This was followed by an assertion that "[i]n no way does this affect the rights of the accused, their fair trial guarantees or their right to appeal."[16] The nature of the other measures contained within the Counter-Terrorism Law, for example, granting immunity to police officers for the excessive use of force and imposing far-reaching restrictions upon media freedom, suggests that the latter is dubious at best.

[13] Editorial, *Workable Terrorism Trials*, Wash. Post, July 27, 2008, http://www.washingtonpost.com/wp-dyn/content/article/2008/07/26/AR2008072601555.html.

[14] Counter-Terrorism Law (Decree Law No. 94 for the Year 2015), Article 50.

[15] Minister for Foreign Affairs, Arab Republic of Egypt, *Remarks on Egypt's Counter-Terrorism Law*, (Aug. 19, 2015), http://www.mfa.gov.eg/English/Ministry/News/Pages/NewsDetails.aspx?Source=6781921f-3993-444a-859e-ee26ce851de8&newsID=d4b1b0c8-0a48-4209-8512-c957a84e44fe.

[16] *Id.*

4. Military Courts

Where specialist courts have been established, they have frequently been military or quasi-military in character. The Eminent Jurists Panel has identified two sets of circumstances in which such courts have been established. The first is where "pre-existing regimes of martial law, or states of siege, provided for the trial of civilians by military courts."[17] In others, "emergency laws transferred jurisdiction to try certain terrorist or subversive offenses from civilian to military courts."[18] The establishment of military courts to deal with terrorism offenses and other offenses against the state is far from a new phenomenon. For example, the State Security Court was established in France in 1963 to respond to the rise of terrorism in the aftermath of the Algerian war of independence. This quasi-military court presided over terrorism trials until its abolition in 1981.

Most famously, a Military Order issued by the U.S. president in 2001 bestowed power upon military commissions to try noncitizen enemy combatants.[19] This Order relevantly stated:

> (a) To protect the United States and its citizens, and for the effective conduct of military operations and prevention of terrorist attacks, it is necessary for individuals... to be tried for violations of the laws of war and other applicable laws by military tribunals.
>
> (b) Given the danger to the safety of the United States and the nature of international terrorism,... it is not practicable to apply in military commissions under this order the principles of law and the rules of evidence generally recognized in the trial of criminal cases in the United States district courts.

It is understandable why doubts might be expressed about the compatibility of courts staffed by current and former military officers with the requirements of independence and impartiality. However, the language of the Military Order reveals another concern regarding the establishment of military courts. This is that the underlying reason for shifting jurisdiction from the ordinary civilian courts to their military counterparts has been to avoid what are seen as overly unduly onerous procedural safeguards.

In recognition of the problems associated with military courts, the Inter-American Commission on Human Rights cautioned shortly after the September 11 terrorist attacks that these courts should be employed only as a last resort, that is "when no civilian courts exist or where trial by such courts is materially impossible."[20] In Somalia, for example, the establishment, and regular extension of the jurisdiction, of the military courts since the early 1960s has been justified on two bases. These are, first, the vulnerability of the

[17] Eminent Jurists Panel on Terrorism, Counter-Terrorism and Human Rights, *supra* note 2, *at* 34.

[18] *Id.*

[19] Military Order of November 13, 2001, *Detention, Treatment, and Trial of Certain Non-Citizens in the War Against Terrorism*, 66 Fed. Reg. 57,833 (Nov. 16, 2001).

[20] Inter-Am. Comm'n on Human Rights, *Resolution on Terrorism and Human Rights*, 12 Dec. 2001.

ordinary criminal courts to attacks by Al Shabaab terrorists, and, second, the need for special courts to prosecute difficult cases involving members of law enforcement and intelligence agencies.[21] Similarly to the Inter-American Commission, the UN Human Rights Committee has acknowledged that the ICCPR "does not prohibit [military] courts" but "the trying of civilians by such courts should be very exceptional."[22] However, it emphasized that regardless of its character—ordinary, specialist, or military—the court must "genuinely afford the full guarantees stipulated in [A]rticle 14."[23] This is where many military courts have fallen short. For example, Human Rights Watch has expressed concerns regarding both the manner in which people are brought before the Somali military courts—with many caught up in mass security raids—as well as the failure to accord defendants fundamental aspects of the right to a fair trial.[24]

III. The Decision-Maker

We need to acknowledge at the outset the different attitudes toward the decision-making process in civil versus common law systems (albeit that these are becoming increasingly blurred).[25] Civil law systems, historically, did not utilize juries. Instead, decisions as to guilt or innocence were made by a professional judge or panel of judges. This has shifted in the modern era as juries and/or lay judges have been increasingly utilized by civil law countries. By contrast, there is a long tradition in common law legal systems of using juries in a significant share of serious criminal cases.

1. Trial by Judge Alone

To the extent that it is possible to generalize, the trend in the terrorism context has been to either maintain the status quo or to abolish trial by jury. Australia is an example of the former although this is as much a matter of constitutional necessity as it is of political decision-making. The Federal Parliament is constrained by the constitutional requirement that "the trial on indictment of any [federal] offence shall be by jury."[26] This right to trial by jury is so rigorously protected by the courts as a "constitutional guarantee of

[21] Human Rights Watch, *Human Rights Priorities for Somalia's New Government* (May 2017), https://www.hrw.org/news/2017/05/02/human-rights-priorities-somalias-new-government.

[22] U.N. Human Rights Comm., General Comment No. 13, *Equality Before the Courts and the Right to a Fair and Public Hearing by an Independent Court Established by Law* (13 April 1984).

[23] *Id.*

[24] Human Rights Watch, *supra* note 21.

[25] *See* Roderick Munday, *Jury Trial, Continental Style*, 13(2) Legal Studies 204, 204 (1993). *See also* Toby Goldbach & Valerie Hans, *Juries, Lay Judges and Trials*, in *Encyclopaedia of Criminology and Criminal Justice* 2716–27 (Gerben Bruinsma & David Weisburd, eds., 2014).

[26] Commonwealth of Australia Constitution Act 1901 (Cth) s 80.

democratic participation" in the administration of justice that it may not be waived even with the agreement of both parties.[27] This has not, however, prevented intermittent debate that the right should be modified, whether through judicial reinterpretation or constitutional reform.

In the terrorism context, arguments for trial by judge alone have been presented not only on behalf of the state but also by the defense. Central to those arguments is that the prevalence of stereotypes about the nature of terrorism and its relationship to Islam means that a jury of "12 angry men" may not be the best way to achieve a fair trial.[28] It would be preferable to rely upon a professional judge trained in the art of objective decision-making. Such concerns about the ability of laypeople to make an impartial decision are not confined to the Australian context. In *United States v. Goba*, the trial judge commented that:

> [T]he infamous, dastardly and tragic deeds and events of September 11, 2001 have caused a maelstrom of human emotions to be not only released but to also create a human reservoir of strong emotional feelings such as fear, anxiety and hatred as well as a feeling of paranoia in many of the hearts and minds of the inhabitants of this great nation.... They are strong emotions of a negative nature which, if not appropriately checked, cause the ability of one to properly reason to be impeded or to be blinded in applying our basic principles of law.[29]

For the most part, however, the abolition of trial by jury in both common and civil law countries has been driven by state (rather than defense) interests. In Russia, for example, trial by jury was introduced in 1993 as one of the cornerstones of the post-Soviet era. The alien nature of the jury system in this country made it relatively easy in 2008 for Federal Law No. 321-FZ to be passed. This legislation removed the right to trial by jury from people accused of certain offenses, including terrorism and other crimes against the state. As explained by the Head of the Security Committee, the rationale was to prevent unjustified acquittals that had been occurring due to close familial ties in the southern regions of Russia.[30] The inability to secure convictions was also at the core of the decision to suspend jury trial for terrorism offenses in Northern Ireland in the 1970s.[31]

In addition to unjustified acquittals, a further rationale for the adoption of a system of trial by judge alone has been the need to protect national security information from disclosure. Donohue writes that "[w]here national security matters are involved, the government may not want to give ordinary citizens insight into the world of

[27] Alqudsi v. The Queen (2016] HCA 24 (15 June 2016) [140] (Gageler J).

[28] Michael Pelly, *Why Turnball and Accused Terrorist Alqudsi Wanted No Jury at Trial*, The Australian, 24 June 2016, http://www.theaustralian.com.au/business/legal-affairs/why-turnbull-and-accused-terrorist-alqudsi-wanted-no-jury-at-trial/news-story/f6cca64834ob030961da3664d8814516.

[29] United States v. Goba, 220 F. Supp. 2d 182, 184 (W.D.N.Y. 2002).

[30] Anna Gurinskaya, *Trial by Jury in Russia: From the Cornerstone of the Judicial Reform to the Constitutional History Artifact*, 17(1) J. Crim. Justice & Security 62, 70 (2015).

[31] Lord Diplock, *Report of the Commission to consider legal procedures to deal with terrorist activities in Northern Ireland* Cmnd. 5185 (1972). *See also* Laura Donohue, *Terrorism and Trial by Jury: The Vices and Virtues of British and American Criminal Law*, 59 Stan. L. Rev. 1321, 1326 (2007).

intelligence."[32] They may also "be concerned about the potential of jurors providing information to terrorist organizations," especially where deeply divisive political, religious or ethnic violence is present in the jurisdiction.[33]

Of course, the abolition of trial by jury is not a panacea in and of itself. The ideal of judicial decision-making has often been expressed as that of a "tabula rasa" (or blank slate).[34] The reality, however, is that no judge is capable of living up to this. It is inevitable that judges will have preconceptions and opinions about the issues that come before them.[35] What distinguishes judges from ordinary members of the public is their training to bring an open mind to bear upon those issues, that is, to vigorously engage with a range of different perspectives. Even in dealing with relatively banal matters, this is far from an easy task. The problems are, however, magnified in the terrorism context as a result of both the prevalence of stereotypes about terrorism to which judges are not immune to as well as the likelihood that they will be exposed to prejudicial information. Horan and Goodman-Delahunty therefore note that "[j]ury trials have a significant advantage over bench trials, in that jurors are exposed to less inadmissible evidence and pre-trial information than are judges."[36] It is "difficult to imagine anyone, whether juror or judge, being able to deliberately 'forget' relevant information to which they have been exposed."[37]

2. The Jury Selection Process

Even in those jurisdictions that have maintained trial by jury for terrorism offenses, the problems of juror intimidation and bias mentioned previously have not gone unnoticed. They have been addressed through modifications to the traditional process for the selection of jury members. One such modification involves nondisclosure of the identities of members of the jury pool. This limits the potential for intimidation of jurors to undermine the independence of the decision-making process. Another is to allow extensive questioning of potential jurors about their views on particular topics. Such questioning plays a particularly important role in light of the proliferation of stereotypes regarding the close relationship between Islam and terrorism.

In the trial of Mohammed Salameh and his co-accused before the United States District Court, two different approaches were put forward.[38] Defense counsel argued that

[32] Donohue, *supra* note 31, at 1322. [33] *Id.*

[34] Richard Posner, *Not a Suicide Pact: The Constitution in a Time of National Emergency* 26 (2006) ("[a] tabula rasa theory of judging—though proclaimed by many judges ... —is a cognitive impossibility").

[35] Benjamin Cardozo, *The Nature of the Judicial Process* 12–13 (1921) ("We may try to see things as objectively as we please. None the less, we can never see them with any eyes except our own").

[36] Jacqueline Horan & Jane Goodman-Delahunty, *The Legal Landscape in Terrorism Trials*, in *Juries, Science and Popular Culture in the Age of Terror: The Case of the Sydney Bomber* 11, 26 (David Tait & Jane Goodman-Delahunty eds., 2017).

[37] *Id.*

[38] These approaches are discussed in United States v. Salameh, 152 F.3d 88, 120 (2d Cir. 1998).

potential jurors should be given a written questionnaire with seventy-nine questions about their views on "Islam, Muslims and Arabs." Instead, Judge Duffy adopted a three-stage voir dire process. The first stage was to excuse anyone who expressed bias or hesitancy in response to the reading of the charges against the defendants. Next, the judge asked questions aimed at identifying unconscious prejudice against religious, racial, or national groups, for example, "[h]ave you ever moved out of an area because you were disturbed that the area was changing?." Once again, any juror who expressed bias or hesitancy was excused. The final stage involved each juror being questioned individually about pretrial publicity, any trips to the Middle East, their attitudes toward Israel, and whether they had any Muslim friends or colleagues.

Of course, the ability of defense counsel to identify potential jurors who are prejudiced against the defendant is of little utility unless counsel are also able to ensure the prejudiced potential jurors do not form part of the jury. Therefore, in many instances, the courts have seen fit to call a larger pool of potential jurors—sometimes up to several hundred—than would typically be the case, and also to increase the number of challenges available to both the prosecution and the defense.

Importantly, it is not only the defense who benefits from being able to question jurors. In countries where terrorism occurs in the context of a deeply divisive civil war, the reality is that members of the jury are likely to sympathize with one side or the other. For example, guidelines for jury vetting issued by the British government in 1978 allowed the prosecution to force potential jurors to "go to the end of the line" where it believed that they "may be susceptible to improper pressure or may, because of extreme political beliefs be biased against either the prosecution or the defense."[39] This, in combination with the ability to question jurors in detail, offers the prosecution the opportunity to exclude anyone who is predisposed toward the political, religious, or ideological cause that the defendant sought to advance.

3. Undermining the Independence of the Judiciary

The doctrine of the separation of powers exists to protect the independence and impartiality of the judicial process by insulating it from interference by the executive and legislature. It would be unrealistic to expect that these branches will exert no influence. For example, the government is generally responsible for filling vacancies in the courts through the selection of new judges. The transparency of the selection process, the level of accountability of the executive for its decision-making, and the extent to which consultation occurs with interested stakeholders differs from country to country. Regardless, criticisms are often leveled at the selection of judicial officers on the basis that they are motivated by political considerations. The difference in the terrorism context is that the separation of powers has been significantly compromised through modifications to the procedures governing the selection, tenure, and removal of judicial

[39] Donohue, *supra* note 31, at 1333.

officers. This is especially so in those countries where military courts have been established to deal with terrorism offenses.

It is generally the case that judges of military courts must have experience in or detailed knowledge of the armed forces. Similarly, many of the special civilian courts established to deal with terrorism offenses have also required the presence of a military judge. This is not without some justification. A background in the armed forces provides "undoubted competence and experience in the battle against organized crime, including that committed by illegal armed groups."[40] However, it also gives rise to significant concerns about the ability of the courts upon which they sit as judges to make an independent and impartial decision. As the European Court of Human Rights has commented, "[w]hat is at stake is the confidence which the courts in a democratic society must inspire in the public and above all, as far as criminal proceedings are concerned, in the accused."[41] The fundamental issue is that career members of the military are likely to prioritize national security over the defendant's right to a fair trial. Furthermore, as noted by the European Court of Human Rights in *Incal v. Turkey*, the participation of a military judge raises legitimate fears that a court might allow itself to be unduly influenced by considerations that have nothing to do with the facts of the case.[42] It is notable that the Court reached this conclusion notwithstanding the fact that the military judge was sitting on a civilian National Security Court alongside two civilian judges.

This perceived lack of independence is compounded where judges are active duty officers and thus part of the military chain of command. The Centre for the Independence of Judges and Lawyers asserted in a 1995 report that the simple fact is such judges "are not independent."[43] This was reinforced in *Incal v. Turkey*. The Court found that the independence of the military judge was undermined because:

> Firstly, they are servicemen who still belong to the army, which in turn takes its orders from the executive. Secondly, they remain subject to military discipline and assessment reports are compiled on them by the army for that purpose. Decisions pertaining to their appointment are to a great extent taken by the administrative authorities and the army.[44]

The reality, furthermore, is that current or former members of the military may have limited—or even no—knowledge of the traditional criminal justice process and the protections that it offers. This may be because their legal expertise has been gained through the court-martial system or simply because they have no legal experience. For example, the military courts established by Peruvian President Fujimori were comprised of only one legally trained officer with the remaining four members being currently serving officers in the armed forces.[45] Similarly, a U.S. military commission consists of between

[40] Incal v. Turkey, App. No. 22678/93, Eur. Ct. H.R., June 9, 1998, § 70.

[41] *Id.* at § 71. [42] *Id.* at § 72.

[43] Centre for the Independence of Judges and Lawyers, *Attacks on Justice: The Harassment and Persecution of Judges and Lawyers* 254 (1994).

[44] Incal v. Turkey, App. No. 22678/93, Eur. Ct. H.R., June 9, 1998, § 68.

[45] Centre for the Independence of Judges and Lawyers, *Attacks on Justice: The Harassment and Persecution of Judges and Lawyers* 254 (1994).

three and seven current military officers appointed directly by the secretary of defense or his special designee, the Appointing Authority.[46] Only one member of the commission—the presiding officer—is required to be a lawyer. Unlike the court-martial system, whereby a separate judge is appointed by the semi-independent Judge Advocate General's office to rule on legal questions, it is for all members of a military commission to decide questions of both fact and law.

A related issue regarding tenure was raised by the short-lived Australian Military Court. This Court was found by the High Court of Australia to be exercising the judicial power of the Commonwealth in an unconstitutional manner because judges were not given life tenure.[47] Instead, they were appointed for a period of ten years only and their tenure was conditional upon retention in the armed forces. Life tenure was described by Hamilton, one of the Founding Fathers of the U.S. Constitution, as necessary in order to guard against the "encroachments and oppressions of the representative body."[48] Anything less would "be fatal to [the courts'] necessary independence" as a body of judges that held office at the pleasure of the executive and/or legislative would be "unwilling to hazard the displeasure" of these branches of government by making an unpopular decision.[49] This was indeed the situation in Peru during the Fujimori era. The "[m]assive purges of judges and prosecutors sent an unmistakable message that court officers' careers depended on the executive branch."[50] As of January 1995, the Centre for the Independence of Judges and Lawyers estimated that in Peru "60% of all judges now work on a provisional or substitute basis."[51]

IV. Modification of Trial Procedures

1. Open Justice

The holding of trials in public, or open justice, is a central tenet of the criminal justice process. As Lord Justice Gross noted in *Guardian News and Media Ltd v. AB and CD*, this is "both a fundamental principle of the common law and a means of ensuring public confidence in our legal system."[52] The reality, however, is that it is not uncommon for certain portions of terrorism trials to be held in camera.

[46] The following analysis is taken from Serrin Turner & Stephen Schulhofer, *The Secrecy Problem in Terrorism Trials* 56 (2005, Brennan Center for Justice).

[47] Lane v. Morrison (2009) 239 C.L.R. 230. For a discussion of this case, see Andrew Mitchell, *Too Close for Comfort:* Lane v. Morrison *and Its Effect on Australian Military Justice*, 21(5) Pub. L. Rev. 9 (2010).

[48] *The Federalist No. 78*, at 392 (Alexander Hamilton) (Ian Shapiro ed., 2014).

[49] *Id.*

[50] Human Rights Watch, *Report—Peru: Presumption of Guilt, Human Rights Violations and the Faceless Courts in Peru*, 8(5) Hum. Rts. Watch (1996), https://www.hrw.org/reports/1996/Peru.htm.

[51] Centre for the Independence of Judges and Lawyers, *Attacks on Justice: The Harassment and Persecution of Judges and Lawyers—June 1993 to December 1994*, at 252 (1995).

[52] [2015] 1 Cr. App. R. 46, para. 2.

AB and CD—later revealed to be Erol Incedal and Mounir Rarmoul-Bouhadjar—were arrested in October 2013 and charged with preparation for terrorism and collection of information useful to terrorism. In response to an application by the state, the trial judge held that the entirety of the proceedings should occur in closed court with all reports regarding the trial, including the names of the defendants, prohibited from publication.[53] This decision was made on the basis that "there is a significant risk—at the very least, a serious possibility—that the administration of justice would be frustrated were the trial to be conducted in open Court, for what appears to be good reason on the material we have seen, the Crown might be deterred from continuing with the prosecution."[54] The Court of Appeal generally agreed that full compliance with the principle of open justice might frustrate the administration of justice. However, it was guided by the rule that deviations from this principle "must be justified on the facts.... [N]o departure from the principle of open justice must be greater than necessary."[55] The mere reference by the state to "considerations of national security" was not a sufficient justification.[56] The Court of Appeal went on to find that the vast majority of the trial should occur in closed court, with the exception of inter alia the reading of the charges to the jury and the handing down of the verdicts.[57] It was also permissible—so the Court held—for the names of the defendants to be disclosed in public reports regarding the proceedings.[58]

This trial was the subject of significant controversy in the United Kingdom. It was variously described as an "outrageous assault" on the principles of open justice, a "very dangerous precedent," and "inconsistent with the rule of law and democratic accountability."[59] However, in other jurisdictions, closed courts are frequently used in terrorism trials. This especially so in those jurisdictions that rely upon military courts to try terrorism suspects. For example, in 106 of the 274 cases in which the Pakistani military courts have convicted civilians of terrorism offenses, not even the name of the defendant has been disclosed to the public.[60] This has been compounded by an ordinance recently issued by the Pakistani president—which was subsequently codified in legislation—to officially permit military courts to hold in camera trials of terrorism suspects and even to conceal the names of court officials.[61] The high level of secrecy surrounding terrorism trials in Pakistan is not limited to the military courts. As of late 2017, an application was pending before the Islamabad High Court for the trial of Moazzam Ali before the Anti-Terrorism Court to be held in public.[62] The chief commissioner

[53] *Id.* para. 7. [54] *Id.* para. 31. [55] *Id.* para. 2.
[56] *Id.* para. 5. [57] *Id.* para. 16. [58] *Id.* para. 20–21.
[59] Tom Whitehead & David Barrett, *Secret Terror Trial Is "Assault" on British Justice*, The Telegraph, June 4, 2014, http://www.telegraph.co.uk/news/uknews/terrorism-in-the-uk/10876499/Secret-terror-trial-is-assault-on-British-justice.html.
[60] Asad Hashim, *Pakistan to Renew Military Courts for "Terror" Suspects*, Al Jazeera, Mar. 22, 2017, http://www.aljazeera.com/news/2017/03/pakistan-renews-military-courts-terror-suspects-170321143432673.html.
[61] U.S. Dep't of State, *Country Reports on Terrorism 2015—Pakistan*, June 2, 2016, http://www.refworld.org/docid/57518d9713.html.
[62] *Suspect Seeks Trial in Open Court*, The Nation, Apr. 9, 2017, http://nation.com.pk/E-Paper/Lahore/2017-04-09/page-3/detail-1.

of Islamabad has previously ordered that the trial should occur in secret in Alaila Jail Rawalpindi.

It must be acknowledged that the principle of open justice is not—and has never been—absolute. As part of their inherent jurisdiction to control the proceedings before them, the courts are able to close the courtroom in circumstances where they identify a pressing need. Article 14(1) of the ICCPR states:

> The press and the public may be excluded from all or part of a trial for reasons of morals, public order (*ordre public*) or national security in a democratic society, or when the interest of the private lives of the parties so requires, or to the extent strictly necessary in the opinion of the court in special circumstances where publicity would prejudice the interests of justice...

However, it is important that the courts should be open to the public wherever practicable. To ensure that closure only occurs as a last resort, it is critical that the criteria upon which the decision to close is based should be narrowly framed so as to capture only those situations where national security is threatened by disclosure. In other words, the onus should be upon the state to present a compelling justification for the closure of the court in a particular case. These principles may be contrasted with the rules governing proceedings before the U.S. military commissions. The presiding officer may exclude the media, the general public, the defendant, and even his or her legal representative whenever the prosecution seeks to introduce into evidence any "protected information." This includes not only information that is "classified or classifiable" but also that which "concern[s] intelligence and law enforcement sources, methods, or activities" or national security interests.[63]

2. Access to Legal Representation

Integral to the presumption of innocence is the doctrine of equality of arms. This—combined with the burden of proof on the prosecution—exists to ensure that the defendant has an adequate opportunity to present his or her version of the facts. There are few procedural safeguards that are more fundamental than the right of a criminal defendant to immediately access legal representation. As noted by the UN Human Rights Committee, "[t]he availability or absence of legal assistance often determines whether or not a person can access the relevant proceedings or participate them in a meaningful way."[64] Thus, it is critical that a defendant is not barred by legal or practical constraints from obtaining legal assistance. Many domestic and international human rights instruments go a step further by entrenching a right to legal representation "of one's own choosing." Regardless, access to legal representation that satisfies a minimum threshold of competency and is independent from the state is essential in protecting a

[63] Turner & Schulhofer, *supra* note 46, at 61.

[64] U.N. Human Rights Comm., General Comment No. 32, *supra* note 11.

defendant against improper detention. In the antiterrorism context, the reality is that very significant inroads into the right to legal representation have been made.

No one could doubt that it will be necessary in some circumstances to restrict the interaction between a defendant and his or her legal representative in order to protect against the threat of terrorism. As the 2005 conviction of Lynne Stewart in the United States demonstrates, legal representatives are not immune from being co-opted into the overarching apparatus of terrorism. Stewart was found guilty of passing messages between Abdel Rahman, a convicted terrorist and Stewart's client, and an Egyptian militant group.[65]

The issue, therefore, is not that inroads have been made per se into the right to access legal assistance but rather the manner in which this has been done. For the very most part, restrictions upon this right in the counterterrorism context have not had a reasonable and objective basis. Instead, basic rights (such as that to legal representation of one's own choosing and to communicate in private) have too often been restricted because of a generalized fear of the potential for legal representatives to be used to convey information from the defendant to another terrorist or terrorist organization. Even where the identification of a specific risk is required before the right to access legal assistance may be impinged upon, the underlying criteria tend to be overly broad, and the ultimate decision-maker is usually a member of the executive branch. For example, pursuant to an order issued immediately after the September 11 terrorist attacks, the U.S. attorney general may authorize the Bureau of Prisons to monitor lawyer-client relations if "reasonable suspicion exists to believe that a particular inmate may use communications with attorneys or their agents to further or facilitate acts of terrorism."[66]

At one extreme, some countries have refused access to legal representation altogether to terrorism suspects. legislation recently adopted by Tunisia allows the prosecutor to order that a defendant be detained for up to fifteen days without legal representation or access to a judicial officer.[67] However, countries that have historically respected the right to access legal representation have unsurprisingly been reluctant to follow suit. One approach that such countries have taken is to impose restrictions upon access to legal representation during a sometimes-lengthy period of pretrial incommunicado detention. Under French law, for example, people arrested on terrorism charges are not permitted to speak to a lawyer for several days, and, after that, only for thirty minutes.[68] The effectiveness of any advice that the lawyer provides is further limited by the lack of access to the case file and information about the exact charges. Even once access to legal representation has been afforded, the authorities are still permitted to question the suspect in

[65] For a discussion of this case, see Tamar Birckhead, *The Conviction of Lynne Stewart and the Uncertain Future of the Rights to Defend*, 43 Am. Crim. L. Rev. 1 (2006).

[66] Attorney General Order No. 2529-2001, *National Security: Prevention of Acts of Violence and Terrorism*, 28 C.F.R. 500-01 (2001).

[67] Human Rights Watch, *Tunisia: Counterterror Law Endangers Rights: Legislate Safeguards Against Abuse*, July 31, 2015, https://www.hrw.org/news/2015/07/31/tunisia-counterterror-law-endangers-rights.

[68] Human Rights Watch, *In the Name of Security: Counterterrorism Laws Worldwide Since September 11*, 73 (2012).

the lawyer's absence. This not only makes it difficult for the defendant to adopt a coherent defense strategy early in the proceedings but also increases the risk of abuses of power, such as physical mistreatment, while in detention.

Two other common approaches involve restrictions upon the defendant's right to a lawyer of his or her *own choosing*. First, the defendant may be allocated a specific legal representative. For example, under the Spanish Code of Criminal Procedure, individuals suspected of involvement in terrorism may be detained for up to five days before being either released or brought before a judge.[69] A judge may also order that they be held incommunicado. During this period, the suspect does not have the right to a lawyer of his or her own choosing; instead a local Legal Aid lawyer will be assigned. This system has some obvious problems, however, it is nevertheless preferable that an independent organization assign the lawyer rather than the executive branch of government.

In contrast, defendants before the U.S. military commissions are allocated a military lawyer approved by the Department of Defense.[70] The choice is made by the chief defense officer of the Judges Advocate of the U.S. Armed Forces. Although the defendant may choose to be represented by a civilian lawyer as well, the role of the latter at trial is limited by the denial of access to key evidence and exclusion from portions of the proceedings. Similarly, for closed court proceedings before special civil tribunals in the United Kingdom, the attorney general and solicitor general are responsible for appointing a special advocate to represent the subject of the hearing.[71] The defendant may object to the special advocate but only after providing good reason as to why he or she should not act on the defendant's behalf. The UK Select Committee on Constitutional Affairs commented in 2005 that this approach is problematic in that "the Attorney General also acts for the Government which is bringing the case against the appellant."[72] The Select Committee therefore recommended that "an appropriately sized pool of Special Advocates, from which appellants can pick their representation, should be established as soon as practical."[73]

The other common restriction occurs through the imposition of a requirement that the legal representative obtain a security clearance. In theory at least, this offers the defendant more freedom than the "pool" approach put forward by the Select Committee. However, the reality is that before the lawyer may appear at trial, his or her involvement must be approved by the executive. Underpinning this approach is an assumption that the nature of the information presented in a terrorism trial is such that its disclosure to the "wrong" person will be prejudicial to national security. The reality is quite different.

[69] This information is from Judith Sunderland, *Setting an Example?: Counter-terrorism Measures in Spain*, 17(1) Hum. Rts. Watch 1, 29, 31 (2005).

[70] Silvia Borelli, *Terrorism and Human Rights: Treatment of Terrorist Suspects and Limits on International Co-operation*, 16 Leiden J. Int'l L. 803, 816 (2003).

[71] For a discussion of the special advocates regime in the United Kingdom, see Aileen Kavanagh, *Special Advocates, Control Orders and the Right to a Fair Trial*, 73(5) Mod. L. Rev. 836 (2010).

[72] Select Comm. on Constitutional Affairs, U.K. Parliament, *Seventh Report* (2005) para. 69.

[73] *Id.* para. 74.

Many terrorism cases rely upon information that is already in the public domain or is of low sensitivity.

It would be preferable, and indeed consistent with a balancing of the interests of national security against the defendant's right to a fair trial, for the trial judge to decide whether a security clearance is required in light of the evidence to be presented at trial. However, two problems are likely to persist. The probability is that judges will defer to the executive's assessment of whether the nature of the case is such that the disclosure of evidence will prejudice national security.[74] Furthermore, regardless of whether a requirement to obtain a security clearance is enshrined in legislation or left to the discretion of the judge, the potential for executive interference in the trial process remains. As Tamanaha has pointed out in the American context:

> The greatest danger of [a] . . . clearance requirement is that it gives the Department of Justice the ability to control who will work on classified matters for the defense. To eliminate a particularly troublesome opponent, the Justice Department may deny a security clearance to a specific attorney, investigator, or expert witness retained by the defendant, who needs access to classified information to be effective.[75]

3. Presumption of Innocence

Scholars have pointed out that the criminal law is increasingly being utilized to prevent the emergence of future risks.[76] This is especially so in the antiterrorism context where the consequences may include mass loss of life, severe damage to property, and even a destabilizing of the political process. One effect of the criminal law being co-opted as a tool of preemption, for example, through the proliferation of preparatory offenses has been a whittling away of the presumption of innocence. Political leaders have asserted that the adage that it is "better that ten people go free than for one innocent person to be convicted" must be rethought in the terrorism context.[77] There are two primary ways—one substantive and the other procedural—in which this has been done.

In relation to the former, it is now relatively common for antiterrorism legislation to shift at least the *evidential* burden of proving essential elements of an offense onto the defense. The courts have generally been of the view that such provisions do not breach the presumption of innocence.[78] More problematic, however, are offenses where the

[74] For a concrete example of this in the United Kingdom context, see David Dyzenhaus & Murray Hunt, *Deference, Security and Human Rights*, in *Security and Human Rights* 125 (Benjamin Goold & Liora Lazarus eds., 2007).

[75] Brian Tamanaha, *A Critical Review of the Classified Information Procedures Act*, 13 Am. J. Crim. L. 277, 288 (1986).

[76] *See, e.g.*, Lucia Zedner, *Pre-crime and Post-criminology*, 11 Theoretical Criminology 261 (2007); Jude McCulloch & Sharon Pickering, *Pre-crime and Counter-terrorism: Imagining Future Crime in the "War on Terror,"* 49 Brit. J. Criminology 628 (2009).

[77] Elies Van Sliedregt, *A Contemporary Reflection on the Presumption of Innocence*, 80 Revue Internationale de Droit Penale 247 (2009).

[78] *See, e.g.*, Salabiaku v. France, App. No. 10519/83, Eur. Ct. H.R., Oct. 7, 1988.

defendant bears the *legal* burden of proof. For example, the Indian Unlawful Activities (Prevention) Amendment Act 2008, which was enacted in response to the terrorist attacks in Mumbai, states that where arms, explosives, fingerprints, or any other "definitive evidence" is found at a crime scene and is linked to the defendant, the "Court shall presume, unless the contrary is shown, that the accused has committed such offence." This not only represents a reversal of the legal burden of proof but it also has the effect of curtailing the right to silence. The Minister for Home Affairs stated before the Indian Parliament that if evidence points to an accused, "then the accused has a duty to enter the box or let in evidence to say that I am giving contrary evidence."[79]

Related to this, the standard of proof applicable in terrorism trials has on occasion been lowered to that of the balance of probabilities. For example, in 2004, the UK Home Secretary suggested that the burden of proof should be modified to make it easier to convict suspected terrorists.[80] This suggestion was not adopted by the Parliament. Instead, a civil control order regime was introduced to ensure that it was still possible to restrict the liberty of terrorism suspects even where they could not be prosecuted either for reasons of national security or lack of admissible evidence.[81] Although this regime—which has since been repealed—was technically civil in nature, the standard of proof fell short even of the traditional standard of proof required in that context. The Secretary of State need only have "reasonable grounds for suspecting" that the individual is or has been involved in terrorism-related activities.

On its face, the U.S. Military Commissions Act of 2006 has maintained the traditional criminal standard of beyond a reasonable doubt. However, it has, in fact, found an innovative way of circumventing the strictness of this requirement. Only two-thirds of the members of a military commission, or three-quarters where the maximum penalty is imprisonment for ten years or more, are required to vote in favor of a finding of guilt and imposition of a sentence. Given that military commissions may be comprised of as few as three members, the prosecution therefore only has to persuade two people who have been handpicked by the secretary of defense for an individual to be convicted.

The procedural means through which the presumption of innocence has been undermined in the terrorism context is by eroding the right to silence. Article 14(3)(g) of the ICCPR states that everyone is entitled "not to be compelled to testify against himself or to confess guilt." This is integral to the presumption of innocence in that it ensures that it is the prosecution that must prove the guilt of the defendant (as opposed to the defendant having to present a positive case establishing his or her innocence). What the right to silence essentially means is that an individual must not be compelled either before or during trial to answer questions. This is reinforced by the rule that if the defendant chooses to remain silent, his or her silence may not be relied upon as evidence of guilt. It is relatively—and increasingly—common in the civil context for coercive questioning

[79] Indian Parliament, Parliamentary Debates, 17 Dec. 2008.

[80] *Blunkett Anti-Terror Proposals Condemned*, The Guardian, 2 Feb. 2004, https://www.theguardian.com/uk/2004/feb/02/terrorism.september11.

[81] Prevention of Terrorism Act 2005 (U.K.).

powers to be given to administrative bodies charged with, for example, investigating government corruption. However, the right to silence has been vigorously protected by the ordinary criminal courts because it protects against abuses of power by those in authority and ensures the preservation of the basic concepts of justice and fairness.

Western democracies have not—for the very most part—given police, prosecutors, or other government agencies coercive powers of questioning. One of the rare exceptions is the exceptional powers of questioning and detention bestowed upon the Australian Security Intelligence Organisation (ASIO).[82] Under this regime, ASIO may request a judicial warrant authorizing the questioning of a person for up to twenty-four hours where there are "reasonable grounds for believing that [it] will substantially assist the collection of intelligence that is important in relation to a terrorism offence." The coercive nature of these powers is backed up by criminal sanctions for failing to cooperate, as well as the potential for the subject of the warrant to be detained for up to a week. While ASIO is not a law enforcement agency per se, the proliferation of preparatory terrorism offenses means that the functions of intelligence gathering and collection of trial evidence have become blurred.[83] Furthermore, the fact that the legislation only includes a "use"—but not a "derivative use"—immunity means that there is the real possibility that information obtained through ASIO questioning could be used as the basis for a criminal conviction.

Given the engrained nature of the right to silence in the criminal context, the more common approach of Western democracies has been to permit the drawing of adverse inferences at trial from a defendant's decision to remain silent. Such modifications to the right to silence have ostensibly been for the purpose of preventing "ambush" defenses at trial. There may indeed be instances in which a prosecution has failed due to there being insufficient time for the state to prepare its response. However, this seems an inadequate justification for forcing defendants to either disclose all information (including that which is potentially incriminatory) within their knowledge or run the risk of being convicted on the basis of an adverse inference at trial.

4. Procedural Fairness

There are, in essence, two sides to the procedural fairness coin. The first is the right of the defendant to know the case against him or her, and the other is the right to have his or her case heard by the decision-maker.[84] The most problematic way in which a terrorism suspect may be denied procedural fairness is through being tried in absentia, meaning that the trial takes place without the accused being present and often without him or her

[82] Australian Security Intelligence Organisation Act 1979 (Cth) Pt III div. 3.

[83] Kent Roach, *The Eroding Distinction Between Intelligence and Evidence in Terrorism Investigations*, in *Counter-Terrorism and Beyond: The Culture of Law and Justice After 9/11* 48 (Nicola McGarrity, Andrew Lynch & George Williams eds., 2010).

[84] Kanda v. Government of Malaya [1962] AC 322, 337 (Lord Denning).

having advance knowledge of the charges. Not only is this a violation of the defendant's right to a fair trial but it also raises concerns regarding the reliability of a verdict reached after only one party—the state—has had an opportunity to present its case and the lack of legitimacy that the trial is likely to have in the eyes of the public. The right of the defendant to be present at trial is—like many other rights—not absolute. There are some circumstances in which it is appropriate for this right to be abrogated, for example, where the defendant has unequivocally waived his or her right to be present, is a fugitive, or another jurisdiction refuses to extradite him or her. The critical point, however, is that these should be rare exceptions to the general prohibition on trials in absentia. What is concerning in the terrorism context is the increasingly permissible approach to this mode of trial. For example, in Pakistan, the Anti-Terrorism Courts were initially empowered under the Anti-Terrorism Act 1997 to conduct trials in absentia if adequate notice concerning the dates of the trial were published in the media. The decision of the High Court in *Mehram Ali v. Federation of Pakistan* subsequently ordered that the trial procedures before these special courts must be brought into line with that of the ordinary criminal courts.[85] However, this order was circumvented by the creation of a system of military courts that again permitted trial in absentia.[86]

Even where there is a proper justification for a trial in absentia, it is critical that a defendant be able to seek a retrial before the same court. This has been respected—even if reluctantly—by most jurisdictions. For example, in 2000, Abu Qatada—once described as "Osama bin Laden's right-hand man in Europe"—was convicted of terrorism offenses and sentenced in absentia to fifteen years imprisonment by a Jordanian court.[87] Many years later, the United Kingdom agreed to extradite Abu Qatada to Jordan on condition that evidence previously gathered against him in an illegal manner would not be used at a retrial. In September 2014, he was acquitted of all terrorism charges and released. There are, however, some jurisdictions that continue to resist international pressure to afford all defendants—even those implicated in terrorism-related activities—a fair trial. As recently as April 2017, Egypt abolished the entitlement to a retrial for terrorism offenses.[88] No retrial was available even where a representative of the defendant had appeared at the original trial to present a valid reason as to why they were unable to attend.

a. *Right to Know the Case*

This right requires that the defendant be informed of the charges and given an opportunity to view the evidence upon which they are based. While the criminal process has traditionally been weighted in favor of the disclosure of *all* evidence—regardless of whether it is inculpatory or exculpatory—to the defendant, this has never been an

[85] PLD 1998 Supreme Court 1445 (Pak.).

[86] On the complex system of parallel courts in Pakistan, see Section II *supra*.

[87] Lizzie Dearden, *Abu Qatada to Walk Free After Being Cleared of Terrorism Plot Charges by Jordan Court*, The Independent, Sept. 24, 2014.

[88] Amnesty Int'l, *Egypt: New Counter-terrorism Amendments Undermine Fair Trial Standards*, Apr. 1 20, 2017, https://www.amnesty.org.au/egypt-counter-terrorism-moves-undermine-fair-trial/.

absolute rule. This is reflected in the approach taken under the public interest immunity at common law in the United Kingdom. The House of Lords in *R v. Chief Constable of West Midlands*, ex parte *Wiley* stated that:

> Public interest immunity is a ground for refusing to disclose a document which is relevant and material to the determination of issues involved in civil or criminal proceedings. A claim to public interest immunity can only be justified if the public interest in preserving the confidentiality of the document outweighs the public interest in securing justice.[89]

The critical point about this immunity is that if the courts decide against disclosure to the defendant, the relevant evidence may not be relied upon—in any form—at trial. Where the evidence is critical to the prosecution case, this may have the consequence of forcing the prosecution to be withdrawn. If the evidence is exculpatory in nature, the court has the discretion to stay the proceedings on the basis that the defendant is unable to receive a fair trial. It is understandable why the state may be concerned about either of these outcomes in the terrorism context. The reality is that the public interest immunity may result in a person who has engaged in an act of terrorism or committed another terrorism-related offense being released, potentially to commit another offense. Modifications have therefore been made to address some of the perceived problems with the public interest immunity.

There are several ways in which the defendant's right to know the case against him or her has been restricted in the terrorism context. For the most part, these involve giving the defendant only limited access to the supporting evidence. Such limitations represent an attempt by the state to resolve the conflict between protecting sensitive information and ensuring that the defendant is subject to a fair trial. Unfortunately, in most instances the pendulum has swung too far in favor of national security. This has been done in several ways. First, the traditional judicial role under the public interest immunity has been usurped by the executive. For example, in both Italy and Spain, the decision as to whether a document should be classified is left exclusively to the executive branch of government.[90] Any detrimental effects upon procedural fairness are, however, limited by the potential for parliamentary and judicial oversight, as well as the general prohibition upon secret evidence being admitted in criminal proceedings in both Italy and Spain.

Second, even where this function remains with the courts, the scales have been weighted firmly against disclosure. For example, in Australia, the courts are required to give the "greatest weight" to "whether, having regard to the Attorney-General's certificate, there would be a risk of prejudice to national security" as opposed to any "substantial adverse effect on the defendant's right to receive a fair hearing."[91]

[89] [1995] 1 A.C. 274, 280.

[90] This information is taken from Didier Bigo, Sergio Carrera, Nicholas Hernanz & Amandine Scherrer, *National Security and Secret Evidence in Legislation and Before the Courts: Exploring the Challenges* 17–18 (2014).

[91] *See* s 31(8) of the National Security Information (Criminal and Civil Proceedings) Act 2004 (Cth).

Finally, modifications have been made to the manner in which evidence is admitted at trial. In its most extreme form, this involves denying the defense access to evidence. More commonly, however, disclosure has been permitted in a modified form. Again, to use Australia as an example, the courts may admit evidence in the form of either a summary of the information or a statement of facts that the information would, or would be likely to, prove. A similar system was adopted in the United States in the early 1980s under the Classified Information Procedures Act (CIPA) to address the problem of "graymail," that is, threats to release classified information in an attempt to pressure the state to withdraw a prosecution.[92] The key difference between the two systems is that the CIPA requires that the substitute evidence would provide the defendant "with substantially the same ability to make his defense as would disclosure of the specified information." This is consistent with the decision by the European Court of Human Rights that the minimum level of disclosure that must be afforded to the defendant is the "gist" of the allegations against him or her.[93] Such a core of information is necessary in order for the defendant to be able to play a meaningful role in his or her own defense, thus ensuring something akin to an even playing field between the individual and the state. Even in jurisdictions where the judiciary plays a more active role in scrutinizing evidence, such as Israel, the courts continue to insist that the state has an independent duty to disclose the basic allegations to the defendant as well as the full disclosure of evidence to the court.[94]

b. *Right to Be Heard*

This side of the procedural fairness coin mandates that the defendant must be given the opportunity to made submissions to the decision-maker. This obviously has a very close relationship with the discussion in subsection (a). In order for a defendant to be able to make a persuasive case in his or her own defense, that person must be provided with the evidence upon which the charges are based. Furthermore, this evidence should be provided as early as possible. In contrast, Spanish examining magistrates are permitted to seal all or part of the judicial and police undertakings during the investigative phase of proceedings.[95] This includes not only the evidence upon which the prosecution seeks to rely but also the grounds for the defendant being remanded to pretrial detention. Subject to a requirement that the seal must be lifted at least ten days before the end of the investigative phase, secrecy may continue indefinitely. The Spanish Constitutional Court has held that although this system "constitutes a limitation on the right to defense," it "does not imply defenselessness, as it does not prevent the party from fully exercising [this right] as soon as secrecy is lifted having satisfied its purpose."[96]

[92] Tamanaha, *supra* note 75, at 277.

[93] A. and Others v. The United Kingdom, App. No. 3455/05, Eur. Ct. H.R., Feb. 19, 2009.

[94] Sofi v. State of Israel, HCJ 2595/09 (unpublished).

[95] Judith Sunderland, *Setting an Example?: Counter-terrorism Measures in Spain*, 17(1) Hum. Rts. Watch 1, 41 (2005).

[96] Constitutional Court Sentence 176/1988, adopted Oct. 4, 1988, quoted in Sunderland, *supra* note 95, at 45.

Independent agencies have, however, concluded that secrecy "often has a devastating impact on the ability of counsel to secure the release of their client."[97]

The right to be heard may also be impaired by the other examples of modifications to the rules of procedure discussed in this chapter. For example, critical to the right to be heard is access to effective legal representation. This not only means the retention of a lawyer of the defendant's own choosing but also circumstances conducive to the defendant giving full and frank instructions.

Those examples pale into insignificance, however, when compared with the exclusion of the defendant and defense counsel from portions of the trial. As discussed previously, some jurisdictions permit terrorism trials to be conducted in absentia. However, most commonly, exclusion occurs in respect of closed hearings to determine whether the disclosure of particular evidence would prejudice national security and/or the form in which such evidence should be disclosed. In Australia, for example, the trial judge may exclude the defendant and any lawyer without a security clearance from such hearings.[98] The advantages from a fairness perspective of adopting a discretionary approach—as opposed to a blanket legislative requirement—are evidenced by the fact that no Australian trial judge has ever ordered the exclusion of a defendant's legal representative.

Exclusion of the defendant is arguably appropriate. However, the exclusion of the defendant's lawyer goes beyond what is necessary to ensure the protection of national security information. One response to this in the United Kingdom, Canada, and New Zealand has been to allow for the appointment of special advocates.[99] However, there are two main reasons that a special advocates system is a poor substitute for the defendant's right to be heard. First, the role of a special advocate is to represent the defendant's "interests" and not the defendant specifically. Second, an advocate is generally not permitted to communicate with the defendant after being granted access to closed information. This has obvious ramifications for the ability of the special advocate to take instructions from the defendant. Thus, in dissent in *Roberts v. Parole Board*, Lord Steyn commented that "the procedure completely lacks the essential characteristics of a fair hearing... [and] involves a phantom hearing only."[100]

V. Conclusion

While generalizations about domestic legal responses to the threat of terrorism should be made with caution, a common trend in this space has been for the legislature to allow the executive branch of government greater influence upon trials of terrorism suspects.

[97] Sunderland, *supra* note 95, at 45.

[98] National Security Information (Criminal and Civil Proceedings) Act 2004 (Cth) § 29.

[99] For a discussion of the special advocates systems in each of these jurisdictions, see Craig Forcese & Loren Waldman, *Seeking Justice in an Unfair Process: Lessons from Canada, the United Kingdom and New Zealand on the Use of 'Special Advocates' in National Security Proceedings* (2007).

[100] Roberts v. Parole Board [2005] UKHL 45 [93].

In some jurisdictions, this has been done openly and unashamedly through the creation of courts controlled—or even presided over—by the members of the executive. More commonly, however, the focus has been upon modifying what some might describe as the "technicalities" of criminal trial procedure. While it is true that many of these procedures are complex in form and application, dismissing them as technicalities ignores the very substantial role that they play in protecting the fairness of the criminal trial and the impartiality and independence of the decision-maker. It is therefore imperative that scrutiny be brought to bear upon each and every modification—whether to a so-called technicality or otherwise—to determine its necessity in responding to the threat of terrorism. There will undoubtedly be some modifications that satisfy this test. For example, the preemptive nature of terrorism offenses means that intelligence agencies must be allowed to collect evidence for trial. This, in turn, creates a need for increased levels of secrecy with regard to the identity of witnesses and the sources of evidence. Other modifications, however, appear to serve no real purpose other than to increase the conviction rate for suspected terrorists at the cost of the most fundamental precept of the criminal trial, namely, the presumption of innocence.

References

Helen Duffy, *The "War on Terror" and the Framework of International Law* (2d ed. 2015)

Helen Fenwick & Gavin Phillipson, *Covert Derogations and Judicial Deference: Redefining Liberty and Due Process Rights in Counterterrorism Law and Beyond*, 56(4) McGill L.J. 1 (2011)

Helen Fenwick, *Recalibrating ECHR Rights, and the Role of the Human Rights Act Post-9/11: Reasserting International Human Rights Norms in the "War on Terror"?*, 63 Current Legal Probs. 153 (2011)

Conor Gearty, *The Human Rights Act—An Academic Sceptic Changes His Mind but Not His Heart*, 6 Eur. Hum. Rights L. Rev. 582, 586 (2010)

Critical Perspectives on Counter-terrorism 130–49 (Lee Jarvis & Michael Lister eds., 2015)

Eva Nanopoulos, *European Human Rights Law and the Normalisation of the "Closed Material Procedure": Limit or Source?*, 78 Mod. L. Rev. 913 (2015)

Report of the Eminent Jurists Panel on Terrorism, Counter-terrorism and Human Rights, *Assessing Damage, Urging Action* (ICJ 2009)

CHAPTER 31

CRIMINALIZATION AND QUASI-CRIMINALIZATION OF TERRORISM

Emerging Trends and Tensions with Human Rights Law in the UK

HELEN FENWICK

I. Introduction to Criminal Justice Responses to Terrorism

This chapter will focus on two recently emerging trends in counterterrorism against the backdrop of the terrorist attacks in Europe in 2015–2017: the reliance on very broad "precursor" terrorism offenses—the creeping criminalization of terrorism—and the accompanying reliance post-9/11 on quasi-criminal non-trial-based preventive measures. It will explore the interface and overlap between the two sets of measures in the United Kingdom, relating these trends especially to the current counterterrorism and national security context and to resultant tensions with the ECHR rights scheduled in the Human Rights Act 1998 and common law principles. In a 2017 Report on securitization in Europe, Amnesty International identified a "regional trend [in Europe]" of using quasi-criminal executive measures "instead of charging and prosecuting people in the criminal justice system."[1] But it will be argued that although, as far as Europe is concerned, such measures originated in the UK, the UK's enthusiasm for relying on them appears to have diminished recently, while concomitantly its deployment of "precursor" offenses to combat terrorism has increased.

[1] Amnesty Int'l, *Dangerously Disproportionate: The Ever-Expanding National Security State in Europe* 48 (Jan. 17, 2017).

Since 9/11 a range of attacks by Islamic militants have occurred in Europe, including the Madrid bombing in 2004, the London Tube bombing in 2005, the Lee Rigby murder in 2013, the Paris massacre in 2015, the Nice truck attack in 2016, and the Stockholm and Westminster attacks in 2017. A range of terrorist plots have been foiled in the United Kingdom, especially in the years 2012–2017, and the number of arrests and prosecutions for terrorist offenses reached their highest annual rate in 2013–2016. Thus the counterterror response in the UK has been conditioned post-2001 by the threat posed by extremist Islamic groups, the fear of suicide bombing, and the influence on Western supporters of the so-called Caliphate in Syria and Iraq. Fear of multisite attacks, as in Paris in 2015, using machine guns as well as suicide bombs,[2] remains influential, but in some respects concern is even more prevalent as to actions of so-called "lone actors," sometimes inspired rather than directed by members of ISIS or similar groups, using everyday objects such as vehicles or knives to kill or injure persons.

In the UK and Europe generally the emphasis on use of deportation or citizenship-stripping[3] to protect security has diminished in favor of the criminal-justice-based response, combined with the use of liberty-curtailing executive measures, given that many of the attackers were "home-grown." The attacks in January 2015 on *Charlie Hebdo* and at a kosher supermarket, and the Paris terrorist attacks in November 2015, were organized and perpetrated largely by ISIS-supporters, some of whom had fought with ISIS, and almost all of whom were French nationals.[4] The Brussels terrorist strike on March 22, 2016, the deadliest act of terrorism in Belgium's history, was perpetrated by at least three Belgian nationals. The Normandy church attack in July 2016 was perpetrated by French citizens. The perpetrator of the Nice truck attack had a French residency permit. The Westminster attack in March 2017 that also used a vehicle against pedestrians was carried out by a British citizen.

As a result of the form that terrorist attacks have taken, counterterrorist measures adopted post-9/11 and again post-7/7 have tended to be of a proactive (preventive) as opposed to a reactive nature. The proactive tendency has arisen partly because the attacks are usually suicidal, partly because warnings are not given, and partly due to the large number of Islamic suspects judged to be in the UK. These factors mean that the measures taken must have the capacity to allow plots and planning to be disrupted at a very early stage. While the most serious acts of terrorism almost always attract charges under ordinary criminal law,[5] the threat of Islamic terrorism has been met, especially recently, by

[2] Europol warned in January 2016 that ISIS was planning large-scale attacks in European capitals. *See, e.g.*, Kim Willsher & Peter Walker, *Isis Targeting Europe for Paris-Style Attacks, Says EU Police Chief*, The Guardian, Jan. 25, 2016.

[3] *See* Lucia Zedner, *Citizenship Deprivation, Security and Human Rights*, 18 Eur. J. Migration & L. 222 (2016).

[4] *See* Ben Farmer, *Who Is Salah Abdeslam and Who Were the Paris Terrorists? Everything We Know About the Isil Attackers*, The Telegraph, Mar. 18, 2016, http://www.telegraph.co.uk/news/worldnews/europe/france/11996120/Paris-attack-what-we-know-about-the-suspects.html.

[5] *See* David Anderson QC, *The Terrorism Acts in 2012* para. 11.1 (2013) (Independent Reviewer of Terrorism Legislation) [hereinafter 2013 Report].

deployment of proactive offenses. Their purpose is to prevent acts of terrorism, and even to disrupt the radicalization that can lead to such acts.

Such proactive measures have appeared in two forms. First, rather than simply charging persons with terrorist crimes and bringing them to trial, attention has turned also to targeting possible terrorist suspects—persons who may in future commit terrorist acts—and curtailing their liberty via executive measures on the control orders model, in order to prevent terrorist activity before it can occur. The imposition of measures on this model has a quasi-criminal character in that punitive sanctions are imposed (currently on the civil standard) on the basis of signs of engagement in terrorist activity. The attempt has been made to *link* such measures with the criminal process by conceiving of them as investigative measures, in order to provide them with greater legitimacy, but that attempt, as will be discussed, has not been successful. As will be argued, there are a range of drawbacks in relying on such measures: inter alia, they are clearly riskier and raise greater human rights concerns than prosecutions since they are not subject to the normal due process safeguards created by the criminal justice system. Therefore miscarriages of justice may be more likely to occur.

Second, measures have been taken *within* the criminal process in the form of creation of a range of precursor offenses that capture terrorist-linked activity and so also have a capacity to prevent specific terrorist acts before they occur. Such measures may overlap with non-trial-based ones in the sense that the body of evidence required to support imposition of a measure on the control orders model might also support a criminal conviction for a precursor offense.

This chapter evaluates a number of special precursor terrorism offenses and also proactive sanctions applied outside the criminal justice system, and in so doing explores their interaction with human rights,[6] especially those ECHR rights scheduled in the Human Rights Act 1998. A key difference between the current counterterror response and previous ones is that the powers deployed are no longer seen as emergency measures pending a political settlement. Since the response is founded, unsurprisingly, on the view that political negotiation is not possible with groups such as ISIS, the resultant proliferation and normalization of adoption of authoritarian powers, whether in the form of criminal offenses or executive measures, has placed a strain on human rights.

But the relationship between counterterror measures and preserving human rights is a complex one, since the impact of such measures in preserving the human rights of potential victims, as an aspect of preserving security, is a central concern. In the words of the Council of Europe, the efforts of state parties need to be enhanced in "preventing terrorism and its negative effects on the full enjoyment of human rights, in particular the right to life, both by measures to be taken at national level and through international co-operation."[7] Similarly, the UN Security Council recently called on member states to

[6] For a lengthy discussion of such interaction globally, see Helen Duffy, *The "War on Terror" and the Framework of International Law* (2d ed. 2015) esp. 4B2 and part 7.

[7] *See* Council of Europe, *Additional Protocol to the Council of Europe Convention on the Prevention of Terrorism* 12 March 2015, art. 1.

tackle the problem represented by terrorist groups operating in Iraq and Syria. It said that member states should "prevent and suppress the recruiting, organizing, transporting or equipping of individuals who travel to a State other than their State of residence or nationality for the purpose of the perpetration, planning or preparation of, or participation in, terrorist acts or the providing or receiving of terrorist training, and the financing of their travel and of their activities. . . . "[8] As will be argued, the marked tendency to turn attention increasingly to deployment of the precursor offenses, as opposed to the (in certain respects) easier solution of relying extensively on executive measures, is indicative of a maturing response to maintaining human rights while seeking to preserve security in the context of counterterrorism post-9/11.

II. Broad "Precursor" Terrorism Offenses

The severity of certain terrorist attacks in Europe, in particular the Paris attacks in 2015, has not so far been replicated recently in the UK, even taking account of the March 2017 Westminster attack. One reason the UK has not suffered such attacks appears to be that a range of early intervention offenses are available to be used against persons who may be at an early stage of plotting an attack or may be likely to aid in one in future. Not only are a range of such offenses available, but they have been increasingly used successfully recently. Use of such offenses is particularly significant in relation to so-called "home-grown" suspects, because usually they cannot be deported. The UK counterterror effort placed reliance post-9/11 on an array of special "early intervention" or precursor terrorism offenses already in place under a broad counterterror statute—the Terrorism Act 2000 (TA 2000).[9] The range of special precursor offenses in the UK grew in further counterterror statutory provisions, including the Terrorism Act 2006 (TA 2006). Under these precursor offenses, the intention is to reach as far back into pre-action territory as possible in order to criminalize very early manifestations of an intention to engage in terrorist activity, or to encourage or assist others to do so.

1. Special "Precursor" Offenses

A range of "early intervention" or precursor offenses are available that are potentially applicable to those who plot attacks or support terrorist groups in the UK, have supported

[8] U.N. S.C. Res. 2178, ¶ 5 (Nov. 19, 2014); *see also id.* ¶ 10 ("the particular and urgent need to implement this resolution with respect to those foreign terrorist fighters who are associated with ISIL [Islamic State of Iraq and the Levant], ANF [Al-Nusrah Front] and other . . . derivatives of Al-Qaida . . . ").

[9] The Anti-Terrorism Act, SC 2001, ch. 41 in Canada has some similarities since it was based on the UK statute.

or fought with ISIS or similar groups abroad, or provided support for them from within the UK. They include the very broad offense of engaging in any conduct in preparation for terrorism under section 5 Terrorism Act 2006. Under section 5(1), "[a] person commits an offense if, with the intention of (a) committing acts of terrorism, or (b) assisting another to commit such acts, he engages in any conduct in preparation for giving effect to his intention." Under section 5(2), it is "irrelevant for the purposes of sub-section (1) whether the intention and preparations relate to one or more particular acts of terrorism, acts of terrorism of a particular description or acts of terrorism generally." Under section 5(3), the maximum penalty is life imprisonment. This offense overlaps with offenses linked to supporting/membership of proscribed groups in TA 2000,[10] but it obviates the need to show membership in ISIS, al-Qaeda, or a related organization.

Section 5 was obviously intended to be a catch-all offense to enable intervention at a very early stage, before any conduct linked to the actual preparation of a terrorist act has occurred. It is clearly aimed at criminalizing supporters of al-Qaeda or similar groups largely on the basis of that support, but the person in question must have the intention of committing or assisting in the commission of a "terrorist" act,[11] although that need not be a specific act. Hiring a vehicle with the intention of perpetrating a terrorist act would be covered, bearing in mind the use of vehicles to kill or injure pedestrians in the Nice, Berlin,[12] Westminster, and Stockholm attacks.[13] Section 5 could cover conduct preparatory to traveling abroad for terrorist training or to support a terrorist group such as ISIS, or aiding another person in traveling to join such a group, or by sending money to relatives who are fighting with ISIS.

Further very broad offenses are those of encouraging or glorifying terrorism (section 1 TA 2006), included with a view to curbing the inciting or "grooming" of persons, often via the internet and social media, to become involved in terrorism. Sections 59–61 TA 2000 already made it an offense to incite terrorism abroad. The section 1 provision was drafted in the aftermath of the London bombings on July 7. 2005. The offense was intended to apply to figures such as Omar Bakri Muhammad, who had received a great deal of publicity for his reaction to the London bombing. There had been other statements by a number of controversial figures, including Muslim clerics such as Abu Qutada and Abu Hamza al-Masri, about the attacks of September 11, 2001, and attacks on U.S. and UK forces in Iraq. The offenses cover direct encouragement of acts of terrorism (incitement) and the glorification of such acts—a much broader offense.

Statements of indirect encouragement "include every statement which glorifies the commission or preparation (whether in the past, in the future or generally) of such acts or offenses."[14] But this broad provision is qualified in a number of respects by section 1(2), under which a person commits an offense if "he publishes a statement to which this section applies or causes another to publish such a statement on his behalf; and (b) at the time he

[10] Terrorism Act 2000 § 11(1) (covering membership). [11] *Id.* § 1 (defining terrorism).

[12] One of the Berlin truck attack perpetrators was Anis Amri, who was Tunisian and was seeking asylum in Germany.

[13] Nadia Khomami, *Stockholm Attack Suspect Rakhmat Akilov Admits Terrorist Crime*, The Guardian, Apr. 11, 2017.

[14] Terrorism Act 2006 § 1(3).

does so, he intends the statement to be understood as mentioned in sub-section (1) or is reckless as to whether or not it is likely to be so understood."[15] The statements in question include those which "(a) glorifies the commission or preparation (whether in the past, in the future or generally) of such acts or offenses; and (b) is a statement from which those members of the public could reasonably be expected to infer that what is being glorified is being glorified as conduct that should be emulated by them in existing circumstances."[16]

There is a defense of innocent publication where the statement is published electronically, a defense intended to benefit those who run websites on which such statements might be published without their knowledge or consent.[17] Section 2 prohibits the dissemination of a publication that is either (1) likely to be understood as directly or indirectly encouraging terrorism, or (2) includes information that is likely to be understood as being useful in the commission or preparation of an act of terrorism.

Intent or recklessness as to the statement being understood by the audience as mentioned in section 1(2) is required for an offense to be committed. So even if the defendant has no intention of inciting people to support or condone terrorist actions, she could still be committing an offense so long as members of the public might reasonably regard it as direct or indirect encouragement, if she adverted to that possibility.

The array of precursor offenses also includes offenses related to weapons training and of fundraising for terrorism.[18] The offense of using or possessing money or other property for purposes of terrorism[19] is another offense that can readily be used for early intervention purposes. Under it a person commits an offense if he uses or possesses money or other property for the purposes of terrorism or to encourage terrorism, intends that it should be so used, or has reasonable cause to suspect that it may be so used. Section 17 of TA 2000 covers a person becoming concerned in an arrangement as a result of which money or other property is made available or is to be made available to another, and he knows or has reasonable cause to suspect that it will or may be used for the purposes of terrorism. The section 17 offense has been charged in a number of instances in which persons have sent money or property to friends or relatives fighting or supporting ISIS or similar groups in Syria. A range of other offenses have become precursor crimes if they have a "terrorist connection" and are also listed in section 236A Serious Crime Act 2015 (SCA), including section 4 Offences against the Person Act 1861 (soliciting murder) and possession of an explosive under suspicious circumstances, under section 4 Explosive Substances Act 1883.

Section 57 TA 2000 covers possession of articles relevant to terrorism, while section 58 covers possession of records relevant to terrorism. Both sections include defenses of innocent or reasonable possession.[20] The offenses therefore appeared to create a reverse burden of proof so that possession of, for example, a map of a particular city could fall within section 57 unless the defendant could prove that the defense applied. But it was

[15] *Id.* § 1(2). [16] *Id.* § 1(3). [17] *Id.* § 1(6).

[18] See *id.* § 8 (prohibits anyone from being at a place where weapons training is going on, whether in the UK or abroad); Terrorism Act 2000 § 15 (fundraising).

[19] Terrorism Act 2000 § 16. [20] *Id.* §§ 57(2), 58(3).

found in *R v. Zafar*[21] that "a direct connection between the objects possessed and the acts of terrorism" must be proved. Thus, section 57 "should be interpreted as if it reads... he intends it to be used for the purpose..."[22]

Section 38B creates a broad provision of failing to disclose information,[23] making it an offense, subject to an unexplicated defense of reasonable excuse, for *any* person to fail to disclose to a police officer any information that he knows or believes *might* be of material assistance in preventing an act of terrorism or securing the apprehension or conviction of a person involved in such an act.

In terms of the criminalization of terrorism, attention has largely turned since 2006 *not* to continuing to broaden the range of precursor offenses but to extending their impact by widening the territorial reach of these offenses,[24] and to enhancing the severity of penalties. Two separate legislative acts in 2015 increased the maximum sanction for certain terrorism offenses to a life sentence, and for other serious offenses adopted a new sentence made up of a custodial term and a mandatory year of license to ensure that persons are not released early without any consideration of their risk.[25]

2. Deployment of the Offenses against Islamic Terrorism

Some specific examples of prosecutions indicate the type of activity that can be caught by these offenses. In 2012, four men had downloaded computer files containing practical instructions for a terrorist attack, undertaken survival training, and collected funds for terrorist purposes. All four pleaded guilty to charges of engaging in preparation for acts of terrorism.[26] More recently, three others were charged with the same offense and found guilty of assisting a seventeen-year-old jihadi in traveling to Syria from the UK to join ISIS fighters.[27] On return from Syria, another was convicted for preparation of terrorism, attending a terrorist training camp, and receiving weapons training.[28]

The incitement offense, together with the offense of indirect encouragement of terrorism,[29] have been employed on a number of occasions, especially in relation to postings on social media, against those seeking to encourage others to take part in terrorist

21 [2008] EWCA Crim 184.

22 *See also* R v. Samina Malik [2008] EWCA Crim 1450.

23 Section 38B was added by Anti-Terrorism Crime and Security Act 2001 § 117.

24 For example, in the UK, section 81 Serious Crime Act 2015 (SCA) amends section 17 TA 2006 by adding the offenses under sections 5 and 6 to the list of extraterritorial offenses.

25 *See* Criminal Justice and Courts Act 2015, part 1 (increases maximum penalty to life imprisonment for TA 2000 § 54(6)(a) (weapons training) and TA 2006 § 6 (training for terrorism)); SCA 2015 § 3 (adding life sentence eligibility for offenses listed in Criminal Justice Act 2003, Sched. 15B, part 1); SCA Sched. 1 (amending Criminal Justice Act 2003 to add offenses under § 236A ("special custodial sentence")).

26 *See* Terrorism Act 2006 § 5; R v. Zahid Iqbal and Others, Woolwich Crown Ct. (Apr. 18, 2013), http://www.judiciary.gov.uk/media/judgments/2013/rv-iqbal-and-others.

27 BBC News Wales online, Feb. 10, 2016, http://www.bbc.co.uk/news/uk-wales-35482547.

28 *See* R v. Imran Khawaja, Woolwich Crown Ct. (Feb. 6, 2015), https://www.judiciary.gov.uk/judgments/sentencing-remarks-of-mr-justice-jeremy-baker-r-%E2%80%90v%E2%80%90-imran-khawaja/.

29 *See* Terrorism Act 2006 § 1.

acts including murder. For example, the offenses were employed in 2007 as part of a long-term investigation into radicalization of Muslims. A number of persons associated with the extremist Islamic group al-Ghurabaa stood trial on incitement charges. Others praising groups linked to al-Qaeda or ISIS have been found guilty of the glorification offense.[30] Anjem Choudhury was sentenced to five years, six months imprisonment in 2016 for inciting support for ISIS via talks posted on YouTube.[31] When Tareena Shakil returned from Syria she was jailed for four years for her ISIS membership and for two years for encouraging other persons to join ISIS in messages she sent via social media.[32] Ednane Mahmood had traveled to Turkey and used his Twitter account to send messages to people believed to be fighting in Syria; he also sent a friend links to videos and extremist propaganda, with one link taking the recipient to a video that contained footage of a mass execution. Mahmood was convicted in 2015 for preparation of terrorist acts and dissemination of terrorist material.[33] Other ISIS and al-Qaeda supporters were convicted of offenses related to assembling explosives and funding terrorism.[34]

Resort to precursor offenses, rather than to non-trial-based measures (discussed in Section III), has been evident since 2006,[35] but there has been an increase in the last three years in arrests and convictions for precursor-type offenses, often linked to the conflict in Syria and Iraq. There were a total of sixty-nine arrests in the first half of 2014 for a range of such offenses committed by persons who had traveled to Syria or Iraq. Overall during 2014, more than 160 people from the UK were arrested for alleged offenses relating to their activities in Syria.[36]

In 2015–2016 there was a rise in the number of successful prosecutions. In the year ending March 31, 2015, 299 persons had been arrested for terrorism-related offenses, a 31 percent increase on the previous year, and the highest number of arrests since the data collection began in September 2001. Of those charged with terrorism-related offenses, thirty-three were convicted, and at the time of the Report sixty-two were awaiting

[30] For example, in *R v. Alaa Esayed*, the defendant's Twitter and Instagram accounts revealed a large number of messages posted supportive of support for IS in Syria and Iraq and encouraging others. *See "Twitter Terrorist" Alaa Esayed Jailed for Tweets*, BBC News, June 11, 2015, http://www.bbc.co.uk/news/uk-england-london-33097609.

[31] *See* May Bulmer & Caroline Mortimer, *Anjem Choudary: Radical Cleric Sentenced to Five Years for Supporting Isis*, The Independent, Sept. 6, 2016, http://www.independent.co.uk/news/uk/crime/anjem-choudary-sentenced-five-years-isis-daesh-a7228211.html.

[32] *British Woman Tareena Shakil Guilty of Joining IS*, BBC News, Jan. 29, 2016.

[33] Terrorism Act 2006 §§ 2, 5; *see* BBC News Online Dec. 11, 2015, http://www.bbc.co.uk/news/uk-england-lancashire-35069746.

[34] David Anderson QC, *The Terrorism Acts in 2015* para. 9.23 (Dec. 2016) [hereinafter 2016 Report] (life sentences for two ISIS supporters for assembling explosives to be used for terrorism); *Two Men Convicted of Involvement in Funding Syrian Extremists*, The Guardian, Dec. 23, 2016 (two found guilty of sending money to a Syrian group linked to al-Qaeda).

[35] Home Office, *Statistics on Terrorism Arrests and Outcomes Great Britain September 11, 2001 to March 31, 2008* (04/09, Home Office, London, 2009).

[36] *See* Home Office, *The Government Response to the Annual Report on the Operation of the Terrorism Acts in 2013* (Cm 9032, Mar. 2015).

prosecution.[37] According to a Home Office counterterrorism report, in 2015 law enforcement and security and intelligence agencies disrupted six terrorist plots to attack Great Britain.[38] Of the 280 people arrested in 2015, 83 were charged with a terrorism-related offense, and 13 with other offenses; 40 were charged with terrorism-related offenses and have already been prosecuted; 38 of these have been convicted. "The commonest charge in 2015 was once again for preparation of terrorist acts under TA 2006 section 5, which was charged 19 times as a principal offense."[39]

Andrew Parker, Head of MI5, stated in late 2016 that twelve jihadi terror plots had been foiled by the security services in the past three years since June 2013.[40] The Home Office (2016) "Operation of police powers under the Terrorism Act 2000,"[41] found that there were 280 terrorism related arrests in Great Britain in 2015. Fifty-six trials for terrorism-related offenses were completed in 2015 as against thirty-eight in 2014 and forty-four in 2013.[42] David Anderson, the former independent reviewer of terrorism legislation, notes that Norwegian Defense Research "identifie[d] 16 plots planned or launched in 2015, the highest figure of the century so far, with 2016 occupying second place even after only eight months of the year."[43]

3. Relationship with the Human Rights Act

Given that such special offenses rely on a minimal mens rea or actus reus, and at times on reversed burdens of proof, they place special pressure on the criminal process as protected in the UK under European Convention on Human Rights Article 6 and common law principles. Two offenses in particular stand out in terms of widening the net of criminal liability significantly by reference to a minimal actus reus—sections 1 and 5 TA 2006.

The section 5 offense requires intention, but the actus reus is exceptionally broad. The addition of "acts of terrorism generally" brings this offense closer to "thought-crime,"[44] but this "pre-crime" offense can be justified due to the magnitude of the harm it is intended

[37] Home Office, *Operation of Police Powers under the Terrorism Act 2000 and Subsequent Legislation*, § 3 (Sept. 10, 2015).

[38] Home Office, *CONTEST—The United Kingdom's Strategy for Countering Terrorism: Annual Report for 2015* para. 2.6 (July 2016).

[39] Anderson, 2016 Report, *supra* note 34, para. 9.3.

[40] Paul Johnson & Ewen MacAskill, *"There Will Be Terrorist Attacks in Britain," Says MI5 Chief*, The Guardian, Nov. 1, 2016 (interview with Andrew Parker, head of MI5).

[41] Home Office, *Operation of Police Powers Under the Terrorism Act 2000* (Mar. 2016) (quarterly update to December 2015).

[42] Anderson, 2016 Report, *supra* note 34, para. 9.5. For example, on April 15, 2016, counterterror police in the West Midlands arrested five people on suspicion of preparing terrorist acts following an investigation that involved Belgian and French authorities.

[43] *Id.* at 9–10 (reporting figures from the National Consortium for the Study of Terrorism and Responses to Terrorism [START] country reports on terrorism 2015, June 2016, annex of statistical information).

[44] *See* Stuart Macdonald *Prosecuting Suspected Terrorists: Precursor Crimes, Intercept Evidence and the Priority of Security*, in *Critical Perspectives on Counter-Terrorism* 130–49 (Lee Jarvis & Michael Lister eds., 2015).

to prevent, including multisite attacks similar to those in Paris in November 2015. Lord Carlile, then government reviewer of terrorism legislation, supported introduction of this offense, allowing for very early intervention in preparatory activity, on the basis that "there is clear evidence that such an offense would provide for some cases a way of dealing with suspects more acceptable in perceptual terms than control orders. It is better that sanctions should follow conviction of crime rather than mere administrative decisions."[45] This is clearly laudable in principle, especially as the control orders/TPIMs scheme, discussed later on in the chapter is overbroad in human rights terms but under-inclusive in security terms since the orders do not at the moment include detention. But as the widest offense introduced so far in the counterterrorist scheme, section 5 again relies heavily on executive discretion in deploying it and on judicial determination to interpret the offense cautiously. David Anderson has found on this point: "the responsible exercise of its powers by the CPS, coupled with the resourcefulness of counsel and the courts... have combined to produce a workable code...."[46]

Doubts may readily be raised as to the compatibility of the broad glorification offense under section 1 TA 2006 with ECHR Article 10 (the right to freedom of expression), under the existing Strasbourg case law. Obviously that would depend on whether the restrictions created as to *indirect* incitement to commit violent terrorist offenses are, under Article 10(2), defined with sufficient precision to satisfy the requirements of legal certainty, necessary and proportionate to the legitimate aims of national security, public safety, the prevention of crime, and protection of the rights of others. In terms of imprecision of the new offense, the Joint Committee on Human Rights has found "[t]he legal certainty concern is that terms such as glorification, praise and celebration are too vague to form part of a criminal offense which can be committed by speaking."[47] The Committee has found that no "bright line" distinction can be drawn between glorifying and explaining in this context.[48]

It can also be argued that the offense is overbroad. The offense relies on the very broad definition of "terrorism" in section 1 TA 2000, which covers the use or threat, "for the purpose of advancing a political, religious or ideological cause," of action anywhere in the world "designed to influence a government or to intimidate the public or a section of the public," which involves serious damage to property. The section 1 TA 2006 offense makes it criminal to vocalize support for armed opposition to regimes viewed by the speaker and by others in the international community as tyrannous and illegitimate. Since "terrorist" acts are defined so broadly under section 1 TA 2006, it is not necessary that the acts glorified could threaten life. The glorification offense includes, on its face, the glorification of threats to damage property abroad in furtherance of the cause of a

[45] Report on the Operation in 2005 of the Terrorism Act 2006, para. 33.

[46] Anderson, 2013 Report, *supra* note 5, para. 11.6.

[47] Joint Comm. on Human Rights, Report on the Prevention of Terrorism Bill (2005-6) HL Paper 75-1, HC 561-1, para. 28.

[48] *Id.* para. 28 ("the content of comments and remarks will have to be carefully analyzed in each case,... and there will be enormous scope for disagreement between reasonable people as to whether a particular comment is merely an explanation or... amounts to encouragement, praise or glorification.").

group fighting to establish a democratic regime in an oppressive state, since that action is covered by section 1 TA. It also includes the "glorification" of "acts of terrorism" in the past. It is reasonably clear, however, that although the offense covers such speech, it was not intended for use against those speaking to condone or defend actions of groups operating only abroad, such as the PMOI in Iran who are "terrorists" within section 1 TA but could probably be regarded as "freedom fighters." But obviously it hands a very broad discretion to the executive as to its application.

The question of the compatibility of the offense with Article 10 was considered in 2012 in *R v. Ahmed Faraz.*[49] The defendant, referred to in the press as "the terrorists' favourite bookseller," successfully challenged seven convictions for disseminating "terrorist publications" (books and DVDs) under section 2 TA 2006. But the convictions were successfully challenged only on the ground that prejudicial material had gone before the jury. The defendant had argued in relation to freedom of expression that, in dealing with publications expressing "political or religious ideas," it should not be possible to convict someone who was merely *reckless* as to whether the publication was likely to encourage terrorism. Actual intent should be required. He also argued that publication of a "legitimate expression of a political or religious view" should not be an offense. His arguments did not reflect the position under Article 10, as the Court of Appeal found the mere fact that a publication reflected a religious view would not mean that a conviction in respect of it could not be justified under Article 10(2) (or at common law) if it also encouraged terrorist acts. The Court also considered that the directions given by the judge in respect of the offense were compatible with Article 10.

The offense under section 38B TA 2000 relating to disclosure of information also raises Article 10 concerns. Journalists are among the groups of ordinary citizens potentially affected by the duties of disclosure of information, and the offense may be curbing journalistic investigation into the activities of a very wide range of groups, since journalists are unlikely to be prepared to incur the risk of a lengthy prison sentence. The offenses also potentially place journalists investigating, or in some way associated with, the activities of certain groups, such as the Kurdish PKK or TAK, in a very difficult position, especially where they have contacts within the group. It would appear almost impossible for journalists to investigate in such circumstances without risk of incurring a five-year sentence. The provision requiring the surrender of information might mean that the identity of sources could not be protected. But it is clear that the two offenses may be deterring investigative journalism in relation to certain groups, which would have the counterproductive effect of helping to keep the activities of the more secretive groups out of the public eye.

These provisions may accord insufficient recognition to the role of the media in investigating matters of public interest and informing the public. Strasbourg gives preeminence to the role of the press in a democracy, so restrictions placed on the press in performing this vital role have been subjected to the strictest scrutiny.[50] Charging a journalist

[49] [2012] EWCA Crim 2820.

[50] *See* Goodwin v. The United Kingdom, App. No. 17488/90, Eur. Ct. H.R., Mar. 27, 1996.

with these offenses would clearly, therefore, amount to an interference with the Article 10 guarantee requiring the domestic court to scrutinize closely the need for the interference.

4. Conclusions

Recently, more effective use of intelligence-led policing in the UK and data sharing between European partners appears to be enabling arrests of suspects under precursor offenses at an early stage in planning strikes or aiding in supporting terrorist-relating activity, whether abroad or in the UK. Until the Westminster attack in March 2017, there had only been two terrorist-related deaths in the UK in the last decade: the deaths in 2013 of Lee Rigby and of Mohammed Saleem in the West Midlands. Further, the risk posed by ISIS or al-Qaeda-sympathizers in the UK, including "foreign terrorist fighters,"[51] has largely been addressed by placing reliance on this array of offenses. Anderson found (writing before the 2017 Westminster attack): "The absence of recent fatal incidents in the U.K. reflects well on the security and intelligence agencies, on counter-terrorism policing, and on a criminal justice system which has shown itself equal to the task of prosecuting terrorists."[52]

III. The Interface between Criminal and Civil (Preventive) Justice

The immense and unprecedented scope of special precursor offenses has been viewed since 2001 by successive governments as not fully adequate to address the terrorist threat post-9/11. A key change in antiterrorist policy post-9/11 can be described as a trend toward relying on intelligence-based proactive executive measures to prevent rather than respond to terrorist attacks. The criminal offenses discussed have therefore run alongside a range of preventive, non-trial-based, liberty-invading measures that have been more controversial, since they interfere with the liberty of suspects before any offenses have been committed, or where it appears difficult to prove that they have been committed. But the enthusiasm for relying partly on such measures has tended to diminish over the last ten years, while reliance on the precursor offenses appears to have increased.

In the UK, such measures have taken the form of control orders and Terrorism Prevention and Investigation Measures (TPIMs), under the 2011 Act of that name

[51] It is thought that UK foreign terrorist fighters—persons who have fought with ISIS abroad and returned to the UK or are likely to return—number around 850, of whom around half have already returned. *See* Anderson, 2016 Report, *supra* note 34, at 10.

[52] *Id.* para. 2.8.

(amended in 2015) allowing inter alia for overnight house arrest and forced relocation.[53] Such measures resemble criminal offenses, since there must be grounds for considering that the suspect has engaged in terrorist-related activity, and the obligations that can be applied, while intended to be preventive, are likely to be viewed by the subject as punitive. They rely on a process of court review akin to a trial but do not require proof to the reasonable doubt standard, and the proceedings can rely on secret evidence; thus, they tend to create greater tensions with human rights law than trial-based offenses do.

1. The Control Orders Model

Liberty-invading non-trial-based measures, in particular executive detention, have at various times been resorted to by democracies as part of their counterterror strategies, but in general the most repressive measures have not been used post–World War 2[54] against their own citizens. In the United States, the notorious creation of "legal black holes" via executive detention in CIA offshore "dark sites" occurred only in respect of noncitizens, while in the UK control orders emerged under the Prevention of Terrorism Act 2005 (PTA) as a response to the failed attempt at reconciliation between reliance on detention without trial for noncitizens and human rights law[55] via use of a derogation.[56] The control orders represented the determination to continue to rely on non-trial-based measures falling short of imprisonment but were applicable alike to suspect nationals and non-nationals. Derogating control orders were also introduced, but they were never deployed in practice, so since the non-derogating version alone was relied on, reconciliation with human rights law had to occur by other means. The orders were designed to approach or possibly overstep the parameters of human rights law. In effect, they relied, in relation to their early iteration as "heavy-touch" orders,[57] on reinterpretations requiring a minimizing recalibration of relevant ECHR rights that exploited gaps and ambiguities, and in effect redefined rights more weakly or implied new exceptions.[58] The repressive

[53] Other states have similar measures. Canada has relied on Security Certificates governed by the Immigration and Refugee Protection Act 2005, which only applies to non-nationals and allows for detention and deportation. Under the Act, the federal government can issue a certificate naming a permanent resident or any other non-citizen perceived to be a threat to national security, suspected of violating human rights, or of membership within organized crime. Certain states in Europe are have introduced or are about to introduce similar measures, including France.

[54] For example, during World War II in the United States, 62 percent of those interned were U.S. citizens. *See* War Relocation Auth., *Semi-Annual Report of the War Relocation Authority, for the Period January 1 to June 30, 1946* (1946). The use of internment during the Troubles in Northern Ireland provides an exception to this trend.

[55] A and Others v. Secretary of State for the Home Dept. (2004) UKHL 56.

[56] Under Article 15, from Article 5 ECHR, and under Article 4 from Article 9 ICCPR.

[57] *See, e.g.*, the order at issue in Secretary of State for the Home Dept. v. JJ [2007] 3 W.L.R. 642.

[58] A 2009 report on global terrorism identified this trend in the UK and other countries in the face of terrorism. *See* Eminent Jurists Panel on Terrorism, Counter-Terrorism and Human Rights, *Assessing Damage, Urging Action* (2009); *id.* at 91 (finding this trend was most overtly expressed by the UK Home Secretary).

nature of the early control orders—which included eighteen hours house detention a day, sometimes combined with forced relocation—indicated implicit reliance on a minimal notion of "deprivation of liberty" under Article 5.[59] The courts were also impliedly required to reinterpret and minimize the fair trial right under Article 6 in reviewing the orders.

But in response recalibration of the *orders* also occurred: the modifications imposing, as Gearty puts it, a "civil libertarian dilution" on the scheme[60] brought it into closer compliance with both Articles 5 and 6 ECHR, meaning that it became in various respects less repressive.[61] But although the courts' response to the control orders scheme meant that it had to be modified to achieve greater ECHR-compatibility, albeit this time without rejecting it wholesale,[62] the courts also partially acquiesced in the notion of finding that the ECHR could accommodate the scheme by accepting somewhat attenuated versions of Article 5 and 6. A scheme in 2005 compatible with the ECHR only on the basis of presupposing a narrow interpretation of those Articles, was transmuted into a modified version by 2011 that came closer to achieving compatibility. However, since significant interferences with liberty[63] without trial had been accepted by the courts as compatible with Article 5, such interferences could then be viewed as having received a judicial imprimatur. The same can be said of the acceptance—once gisting, or providing a summary of the evidence, was in place—that relying on closed material proceedings to impose the orders was compatible with Article 6.

2. Introducing More Article 5-Compliant TPIMs

The attempt to reconcile control orders with human rights law via recalibrations of rights, which may have contributed to underuse of the orders,[64] was also deemed to have

[59] *See* Helen Fenwick, *Recalibrating ECHR Rights, and the Role of the Human Rights Act Post-9/11: Reasserting International Human Rights Norms in the "War on Terror"?*, 63 Current Legal Probs. 153 (2011).

[60] Conor Gearty, *The Human Rights Act—An Academic Sceptic Changes His Mind but Not His Heart*, 6 Eur. Hum. Rights L. Rev. 582, 586 (2010).

[61] In particular, it was found that eighteen hours house detention a day, combined with other restrictions, would breach Article 5 ECHR, so shorter periods had to be imposed deemed not to create a deprivation of liberty. *See* Secretary of State for the Home Dept. v. JJ [2007] 3 W.L.R. 642; Secretary of State for the Home Dept. v. B and C [2010] 1 W.L.R. 1542. It was also found under Article 6 that in reviewing the imposition of the control order, the gist of the case against the controlee had to be disclosed to him in the proceedings. *See* A and Others v. The United Kingdom [GC], App. No. 3455/05, Eur. Ct. H.R., Feb. 19, 2009, applied to domestic law via section 2 HRA under Article 6(1) in Secretary of State for the Home Dept. v. AF (No 3) [2009] 3 W.L.R. 74.

[62] *See* Secretary of State for the Home Dept. v. AP [2010] 3 W.L.R. 51.

[63] They included some acceptance of up to sixteen hours a day house detention; *see JJ* [2007] 3 W.L.R. 642 [105]. That could be combined with forced relocation where no special features particularly "destructive of family life" arose; *see AP* [2011] 3 W.L.R. 53 paras. 19–24.

[64] *See* David Anderson QC, *Control Orders in 2011* 4–5 (Mar. 2012) [hereinafter 2012 Report] (by the end of 2011, nine control orders were in force and fifty-two persons had been subjected to them between 2005 and 2011).

failed by the Coalition government in 2011, which decided to abandon them on civil liberties grounds while retaining a version of the control orders *model* in more Article 5-compliant TPIMs under the Terrorism Prevention and Investigation Measures Act 2011 (TPIMA).[65] The continued use of such measures had received the support of the Home Office Counter-Terrorism Review,[66] the independent reviewer of terrorist legislation[67] and, in effect, the courts.[68] The rise post-2005 in "home-grown" terrorism, relying more on strikes on soft targets such as restaurants by "self-starters,"[69] meant that the search for effective executive measures against nationals remained a concern, as the threat from foreign nationals decreased due to the sustained use of deportation.[70]

The design of TPIMA clearly took lessons from the ECHR-based control orders litigation. Under the non-derogating control orders regime any obligations that the Secretary of State considered necessary for the purpose of preventing or restricting involvement in terrorism-related activity (TRA) could be imposed,[71] with the implied requirement that they did not breach the ECHR, in particular Article 5.[72] But under TPIMA the obligations are specified and also more limited; they are clearly designed to ensure that Article 5 is very unlikely to be breached, taking account of the control orders case law. The lengthier house detention requirements under control orders were relaxed, becoming only an "overnight residence requirement,"[73] and the relocation provisions were dropped under the original iteration of TPIMs. TPIM orders provide for a range of more limited restrictions relating to movement (including electronic tagging),[74]

[65] Following the model of Part 4 ACTSA preventive detention, control orders could be imposed by the Home Secretary, but with court review, on the basis of reasonable suspicion; that model was also used for TPIMs, except that the standard of proof was initially that of "reasonable belief." *See* TPIMA §§ 3(2), (6)(b), (6)(c).

[66] Home Office, *Review of Counter-Terrorism and Security Powers* (Cm. 8004, 2011).

[67] *See* Anderson, 2012 Report, *supra* note 64, para. 6.2 ("the control order came to occupy a small but important niche in the counter-terrorism armoury, useful and indeed necessary.").

[68] The courts did not declare the control orders scheme *in general* incompatible with certain ECHR rights, in particular Articles 5 and 6.

[69] As occurred in Paris in November 2015. *See* Home Affairs Comm., *Counter-Terrorism: Seventeenth Report of Session 2013–14*, (Apr. 30 2014) [hereinafter Counter-Terrorism Report]; Home Office, *CONTEST—The United Kingdom's Strategy for Countering Terrorism Annual Report 2012* 8 (2013) and *CONTEST—The United Kingdom's Strategy for Countering Terrorism Annual Report 2013* 15 (2014). *See also* Alejandro Beutel, *Radicalization and Home-Grown Terrorism in Western Muslim Communities* (Minaret of Freedom Institute, Aug. 30, 2007); Marc Sageman, *Leaderless Jihad* (2008).

[70] Detention or stringent bail conditions can be imposed if deportation can be seen as imminent since the exception under Article 5(1)(f) ECHR is viewed as applicable. *See* R. (on the application of Hardial Singh) v. Governor of Durham Prison [1984] W.L.R. 704. *See also* Anderson, 2012 Report, *supra* note 64, at 4 ("At the start of the control order regime in 2005, all controlled persons were foreign nationals. By the end in 2011, all were British citizens.").

[71] The obligations listed in the PTA were, formally speaking, illustrative only (PTA § 1(3)), although in practice they were relied on.

[72] Certain orders were quashed on the basis that they were in fact derogating orders that the Home Secretary had had no power to make. In particular, see Secretary of State for the Home Dept. v. JJ [2007] 3 W.L.R. 642.

[73] TPIMA Sched. 1 para. 1.

[74] *Id.* Sched. 1 para. 12.

communication, and property.[75] A TPIM also has far less impact on liberty long-term since it can only be imposed for a two-year maximum period.[76] In contrast to the previous control order regime, no TPIM has been quashed by the courts.[77]

But a lack of confidence in the efficacy of TPIMs in a crisis manifested itself in section 26 TPIMA, which introduces enhanced TPIMs, allowing for reliance on heavier touch TPIMs similar to the early control orders, if it is urgent to do so when Parliament is in recess.[78]

3. Bringing TPIMs Closer to Control Orders

TPIMs, like control orders, were underused,[79] leading to the criticism that they were too ineffective to deploy.[80] Their lack of use and their perceived inefficacy led to the recommendation that they needed strengthening,[81] which occurred under the Counter-Terrorism and Security Act 2015 Part 2 (CTSA). In terms of repressiveness, the new

[75] Travel abroad is prevented without permission of the Secretary of State; *id.* Sched. 1 para. 2. The restrictions cover reporting to the police, *id.* Sched.1 para. 10; the placing of restrictions on transfers of property and requirements to disclose details of property, *id.* Sched.1 para. 6; seeking prior permission from the Secretary of State before meeting or communicating with "specified persons or specified descriptions of persons," *id.* Sched. 1 para. 8(2)(a); a requirement not to carry out specified work or studies, *id.* Sched. 1 para. 9.

[76] TPIMA §§ 5(1),(2), 13(7). A fresh TPIM can then be imposed if a reasonable belief can be shown that "new" terrorism-related activity has occurred after the imposition of the first notice. *Id.* §§ 3(2), (6)(b), (6)(c).

[77] Mr B Wallace (Minister for Security) Oct. 26, 2016, Col. 4, Third Delegated Legislation Committee.

[78] Section 26(1) provides that the Secretary of State "may make a temporary enhanced TPIM order [while Parliament is in recess]" if he/she "considers that it is necessary to do so by reason of urgency." An order made under section 26 is made on the same basis and provides for certain of the same obligations as an order that could be made under the ETPIM Bill. *See infra* note 92. No temporary ETPIMs have yet been introduced under section 26.

[79] Their use was "[w]ithering on the vine as a counter-terrorism tool of practical utility." Joint Comm. on Human Rights, *Post-Legislative Scrutiny: Terrorism Prevention and Investigation Act 2011* 5 (10th Rpt. of Session 2013–2014, HL 113 HC 1014, Jan. 2014).

[80] Two TPIM subjects absconded in 2012 and 2013. *See* Nicholas Watt, *Cameron and Clegg Seek Agreement in Anti-terror Talks*, The Guardian, Sept. 1, 2014 (quoting Yvette Cooper, then Shadow Home Secretary, "There are currently no TPIMs in use because the experts have warned that the police and the security services do not believe they are effective enough to be worth using..."), http://www.theguardian.com/uk-news/2014/sep/01/cameron-clegg-anti-terror-talks-british-born-jihadis-syria-iraq; Home Affairs Comm., *Counter-Terrorism Report, supra* note 69, para. 109 (found that TPIMs need to be strengthened to prevent absconding). *See* HC Deb Vol. 585, Cols 24–6, Sept. 1, 2014. *See also* Cooper, "The truth is that TPIMs have not worked. TPIMs simply do not contain enough powers to be useful for the agencies or the police, or to be worth the extra effort involved." (Dec. 2, 2014: Column 221, second reading Counter-terrorism and Security Bill, 2015 HC). Only three TPIMs were still in force by August 31, 2015. *See* Home Office, *HM Government Transparency Report: Disruptive and Investigatory Powers* 22 (Cm 9151, 2015).

[81] Reinstatement of relocation had been recommended in 2014 by David Anderson QC, *Terrorism Prevention and Investigation Measures in 2013*, at 57 (Mar. 2014) (recommendation 4) [hereinafter 2014 Report].

iteration of TPIMs resembles control orders somewhat more closely. In particular, the forced relocation obligation previously available under control orders was reinstated by CTSA in somewhat modified form.[82] This is clearly the most dramatic change to TPIMs, but CTSA also amended TPIMA to impose a new travel measure, allowing travel to be restricted outside the area where the TPIM subject lives;[83] new prohibitions relating to access to firearms and explosives were also included.[84] CTSA also significantly increased the penalties for breaching the TPIMs limits on travel abroad.[85] In the impact assessment that accompanied that Act, the government anticipated that these changes to the TPIM regime would lead to a significant increase in the use of TPIMs,[86] which has not so far materialized.

However, lessons had been learned from the interaction between the control orders regime and human rights law: safeguards under TPIMA were also improved by CTSA. Thus, TPIMA now allows a wider range of TPIMs restrictions to be deployed, but only so long as proof of involvement in terrorism-related activity to the civil standard is available.[87] The definition of such activity was also somewhat narrowed.[88] The 2015 changes also did not reintroduce the longer periods of house arrest available under control orders, nor did they extend the time period during a TPIM.

In 2016 the government reaffirmed its commitment to relying on TPIMs and sought to renew TPIMA until 2021.[89] Initially, the CTSA had no impact on usage of TPIMs; only two TPIMs were in force early in 2016, and then only one.[90] But in mid-2016 a modest revival of their use occurred,[91] which may be linked to the current threat from ISIS-supporters considered previously. If in the future a returnee from Syria succeeds in mounting a terrorist attack in the UK, or if some other ISIS or al-Qaeda-inspired crisis arises, enhanced TPIMs provided for in the ETPIM Bill 2012 might be introduced

[82] TPIMA Sched. 1 sub-paragraph 3A (amended by CTSA 2015, pt. 2 § 16).

[83] *Id.* Sched. 1 para. 2(2).

[84] *Id.* Sched. 1 para. 6A. To facilitate deradicalization, suspects can also be required to meet with specified persons; *id.* Sched. 1 para. 10A(1).

[85] The penalty was increased from five to ten years. *See* TPIMA section 23(3A). If the measure is breached by leaving the UK, amendment under CTSA section 17 disallows reliance on a "reasonable excuse" for doing so. TPIMA section 23(1A).

[86] *See* Home Office, *Counter-terrorism and Security Bill Impact Assessment* 7 (No: HO0146, Nov. 2014) (estimating five to fifteen new TPIMs would be imposed).

[87] The 2015 Act increased the safeguards against the wrongful imposition of a TPIM, to an extent, by raising the standard of proof for such imposition to the civil standard (section 20(1) of CTSA amending section 3(1) TPIMA).

[88] The definition in TPIMA section 4(1) was narrowed by CTSA section 20(2).

[89] *See* Home Office, *Memo to the Home Affairs Committee, Post-legislative Scrutiny of the Terrorism Prevention and Investigation Measures Act 2011* para. 26 (Cm 9348, Oct. 2016) ("In the five years since the Act received Royal Assent, TPIM notices have been and remain a crucial component of the Government's national security response").

[90] *See Only One TPIM Terror Control Order is in Place in Britain amid "Severe" Threat Level*, The Telegraph, July 28, 2016; EB v. Secretary of State for the Home Dept. [2016] EWHC 137 (Admin).

[91] *See* Home Office, *Memo*, *supra* note 89, para. 37 (in the period June 1, 2016 to August 31, 2016, six notices came into force—five for British citizens).

quickly to meet the emergency.[92] The design of the ETPIM Bill indicated that some lessons, in human rights terms, had been learned from the control orders saga. In providing for enhanced restrictions similar to those available via control orders, including forced relocation and longer periods of house arrest[93] combined with extending the controlled period,[94] it also added the somewhat greater safeguard of a higher standard of proof.[95] But arguably the key lesson learned manifested itself in the determination over the last five years not to introduce ETPIMs (Enhanced Terrorism Prevention and Investigation Measures). After the Westminster terror attack in March 2017, the prime minister did not advert to this possibility, or to any ratcheting up of the counterterror response.

4. Reconciliation with the ECHR?

The wide executive discretion created by the PTA, especially in relation to imposing lengthy periods of house detention of up to eighteen hours a day under early control orders, which led to findings that the measures imposed by *individual* control orders breached Article 5,[96] is partially replicated by the re-strengthened TPIMs regime (and would be more so by the ETPIM Bill).[97] But it is assumed, unless a derogation is sought, that that case law will be relied upon if ETPIMs are introduced to ensure that obligations imposed under ETPIMs stay just within the boundaries of the ECHR rights.

Since the package of measures now available under a TPIM includes forcible relocation, specific TPIMs are now somewhat more likely to be found to breach Article 5. The UK Supreme Court has found that the imposition of fourteen hours daily house detention, combined with forced relocation, can create a deprivation of liberty[98] where an unusually high degree of social isolation is created.[99] But that has not subsequently been taken

[92] *See* Home Office, *Draft Enhanced Terrorism Prevention and Investigation Measures Bill* (Cm. 8166, 2011); Draft Enhanced Terrorism Prevention and Investigation Measures Bill, First Report, HL 70, HC 495 (Nov. 27, 2012); *see also id.* para. 3 (bill can be introduced in response to "exceptional circumstances" that "cannot be managed by any other means"). Parliamentary scrutiny was already provided by the ETPIM Bill Joint Committee.

[93] ETPIM Bill, *supra* note 92, at Sched. 1. A limit on the length of house detention is not specified.

[94] Clause 2(6)(c). A suspect subject to a TPIM could be transferred to an ETPIM without necessarily showing "new" TRA, for another two years.

[95] Imposition of an ETPIM was based on a higher standard of proof (the civil standard) than for a TPIM prior to 2015; *see* ETPIM Bill, *supra* note 92, at cl. 2(1).

[96] *See* discussion in Section III, *supra.*

[97] Lord Plant has pointed out that while "the schemes may be compatible, the question is whether the individual combination of measures imposed on suspects [could] create a deprivation of liberty." HL Deb vol. 744, col. GC349, 23 April 2013.

[98] Secretary of State for the Home Dept. v. AP [2010] 3 W.L.R. 51. The Court relied on the holistic deprivation concept from *Guzzardi v. Italy*, App. No. 7367/76, Eur. Ct. H.R., Nov. 6, 1980, in coming to this conclusion.

[99] Lord Brown found that a control order with a sixteen-hour curfew and a fortiori one of fourteen hours, would not be struck down as involving a deprivation of liberty, unless the other conditions imposed were "unusually destructive of the life the controlee might otherwise have been living." *AP* [2010]

to mean that specific relocations would necessarily infringe Article 5, barring special circumstances,[100] while under Article 8 the relocation obligation has been found to be a necessary and proportionate measure to protect the public.[101] Since TPIMs do not allow for more than about ten hours overnight curfew, as opposed to fourteen hours, the imposition of relocation is less likely, looking at the combination of restrictions, to create a breach of Article 5.[102] Further, the CTSA amendment to TPIMA—specifying 200 miles as the limit on relocating a person compulsorily away from their residence where they may have family or friends—appears to represent an attempt, albeit of a somewhat limited nature, to meet the Article 5-based concern as to social isolation. But the possibility of finding a breach of Article 5 due to the impact on a particular suspect of a more repressive range of measures *in combination* under a newly strengthened TPIM cannot be ruled out. Other TPIM restrictions have been found to create ECHR breaches; the restrictions on electronic communications affecting the children of a TPIM-subject have been found to breach Article 8,[103] and the wearing of an electronic tag breaches Article 3 due to its impact on the applicant's fragile mental state.[104]

Article 6 concerns also remain. The extensive literature on closed material procedure and special advocates has criticized the level of due process maintained in control order/ TPIM proceedings[105] via the Civil Procedure Rules Part 76.[106] Disclosure of the gist of the case against him to the TPIM subject is mandatory, and in that respect differentiation between allegations against a suspected terrorist and the case for the Secretary of State in opposition to an abuse of process application, cannot be created.[107] The Secretary of State must "elect between a modicum of disclosure and withdrawing from reliance on

3 W.L.R. 51, para. 4. On the specific facts, the forced relocation of AP was found to satisfy the "unusually destructive of normal life" test.

[100] In BM v. Secretary of State for the Home Dept. [2011] EWHC 1969 (Admin), the High Court upheld the Secretary of State's decision to require BM to live in a city outside London. The Court considered that the relocation did amount to a serious infringement of his Article 8 rights, but the Court found that any such infringement was both necessary and proportionate.

[101] For example, that was found to be the case under Article 8(2) in CD v. Secretary of State for the Home Dept. [2011] EWHC 1273 (Admin). David Anderson notes that the courts have refused to uphold a relocation obligation "in only four of the 23 cases in which it was imposed." Anderson, 2014 Report, *supra* note 81, at para. 6.20.

[102] *See supra* discussion in Section III.

[103] DD v. Secretary of State for the Home Dept. [2015] All E.R. (D) 53 (Jul).

[104] *Id.*

[105] *See* Eva Nanopoulos, *European Human Rights Law and the Normalisation of the "Closed Material Procedure": Limit or Source?*, 78 Mod. L. Rev. 913 (2015); Helen Fenwick & Gavin Phillipson, *Covert Derogations and Judicial Deference: Redefining Liberty and Due Process Rights in Counterterrorism Law and Beyond*, 56(4) McGill L.J. 863 (2011).

[106] Rule 76.22. The Special Advocate may only communicate with the relevant party before closed material is served upon him, save with permission of the court. *See* Rules 76.2, 76.28(2). The Justice and Security Act 2013 makes provision for closed material proceedings (CMP) in PT II, § 6, which covers TPIM hearings.

[107] Mohamed and CFF v. Secretary of State for the Home Dept. [2014] EWCA Civ 559; [2014] 1 W.L.R. 4240, para. 16.

wholly undisclosed material,"[108] but the question of the *degree* of disclosure required to the suspect has not been fully resolved.[109]

The effects therefore of use of strengthened TPIMs mean that once again provisions that come close to overstepping the parameters set by ECHR rights form part of the package of counterterror measures. However, the drawbacks, discussed in Section IV, of relying on TPIMs as proactive measures, rather than on precursor offenses, appears to be influencing recent counterterror policy.

IV. Relying on "Precursor" Offenses as Opposed to Non-Trial-Based Measures

Walker found in 2009 that "what happened between 2001 and 2005 appeared to be a swing away from prosecution... [towards executive measures]. The London bombings of July 7, 2005, aggravated this hostility to criminal justice...." He found that that trend was fading by 2009, but that there are drawbacks to relying on counterterror criminal prosecutions, including "the appearance of judges being co-opted into the work of the executive, resulting in damage to their reputation. The danger is that minority communities, upon whom the anti-legislation unevenly impacts, will feel distrust leading to lessening cooperation."[110] It is argued here that the trend toward criminal prosecution has not only continued after 2009 but has strengthened more recently, and that, despite the concerns articulated previously as to the strain placed on the criminal justice system by the nature of "precursor" offenses, it is one that should be strongly welcomed.

TPIMs shadow the criminal process, and overlap with it in the sense that some persons subjected to a TPIM could probably have been prosecuted under one or more of the special precursor terrorism offenses instead. Clearly, it is in certain respects less burdensome for the executive to impose a TPIM than to charge a person with an offense. Proof of involvement in a specific offense is not needed to the reasonable doubt standard, only proof to the civil standard of involvement in terrorism-related activity. The activity alleged may not overlap clearly with an existing offense, despite the breadth of the precursor offenses. The precursor offenses require proof of mens rea, but imposition of a TPIM does not; in effect TPIMs are concerned only with an actus reus of involvement in terrorism-related activity. Security material need not be produced in the form of evidence in a criminal trial, but only—in the open material—in the form of a gist in a civil action; most of the material on which suspicion rests can remain closed.

[108] [2014] 1 W.L.R. 4240, para. 17 (following Secretary of State for the Home Dept. v. AF [2009] UKHL 28, [2010] 2 A.C. 269).

[109] *See* AT v. Secretary of State for the Home Dept. [2012] EWCA Civ 42 (finding insufficient disclosure had occurred to satisfy Article 6).

[110] Clive Walker, *Prosecuting Terrorism: The Old Bailey versus Belmarsh*, 79 Amicus Curiae 21, 21–22 (2009).

On the other hand, it is argued that in terms of maintaining the legitimacy and credibility of the use of state power against terrorism, there are greater advantages in using the criminal process system, as opposed to measures on the control orders model. It has greater transparency than reliance on the imposition of TPIMs by the executive with subsequent court review, which includes use of closed material and closed proceedings, since a criminal trial will occur in default of a guilty plea, which will normally comply with common law and Article 6-based notions of open justice. Proceedings in camera and restrictions on reporting or disclosing evidence on grounds of national security remain exceptional, although they are permitted. The Court of Appeal in *Guardian News and Media Ltd v. R & Erol Incedal*[111] confirmed not only that trials can be held in private on national security grounds, but that reporting restrictions surrounding the trial can be maintained after its conclusion.[112] The case of *Yam* concerned the question, in relation to ECHR rights, of maintaining secrecy regarding the use of in camera proceedings after the trial was over. The claim before the UK Supreme Court in *R (on the application of Yam) v. Central Criminal Court*[113] concerned an application to the Strasbourg Court in which the appellant sought to be permitted, in his response to the government's resistance to his claim, to disclose and refer to contents of evidence given at his trial in camera partly on grounds of national security. The limited issue before the Supreme Court was whether the English courts have any discretionary power to refuse to permit the appellant to do this at the application stage of the proceedings before the European Court of Human Rights. This decision was of potential relevance to the recent acceptance in criminal trials that part or all of the proceedings can be held in camera on national security grounds. In such trials disclosure of sensitive material might be sought in relation to the effective exercise of the right of individual petition under Article 34 ECHR; this decision made it clear that at the complaint stage sensitive material need not be disclosed.

Reporting restrictions under inter alia section 4(2) Contempt of Court Act 1981 may be ordered in relation to terrorist trials, for example where a judge considers that reporting should be postponed to avoid prejudicing a future, linked trial. In *Attorney General v. Random House Group Ltd*,[114] the court took the unusual step of determining that an injunction should be maintained, under section 2(2) of the 1981 Act, preventing a book that had some relevance to the trial from continuing to be sold. The basis was that if the book remained available the very sensitive trial for terrorism that was underway (and was already a retrial) could be seriously impeded via jury challenges, possibly causing it to be abandoned.

[111] [2016] EWCA Crim 11. *See* Canada, R v. Ahmad [2011] 1 S.C.R. 110. *See also* R v. Khyam [2008] EWCA Crim 1612 (in which parts of the judgment were redacted).

[112] Reporting restrictions had been imposed under section 4(2) and 11 of the Contempt of Court Act 1981. The Central Criminal Court judge had ordered that the trial should be held entirely in camera. The Court of Appeal upheld the order to hold the trial in private, but made an order allowing accredited journalists to attend the trial, but which also prohibited them from reporting what they had seen and heard. The journalists' appeal after the conclusion of the trial for the restrictions to be lifted, failed.

[113] [2015] UKSC 76.

[114] [2009] EWHC 1727.

Nonetheless, despite such incursions into the principle of open justice, that principle is maintained in a criminal trial to a far greater extent than in a TPIM proceeding due to the need to disclose only a gist of the closed material to the suspect. Also, obviously closed material cannot be reported on by journalists. The demands of fairness in terms of legal representation are met in a minimal fashion in such a proceeding compared to a criminal trial since a Special Advocate is appointed to represent the suspect, but he/she cannot communicate with the suspect after seeing the closed material, apart from that conveyed in the gist.[115] The danger that the integrity of the judiciary is being undermined by participation in TPIM proceedings, given their minimal compliance with Article 6, and common law due process standards, is axiomatically greater than in respect of criminal trials, since those standards are higher.

The requirement to prove mens rea in a criminal trial means that the personal responsibility of the defendant is demonstrated publicly, whereas lack of such a requirement in imposition of a TPIM could give the impression that a particular minority group is being unfairly targeted. The lack of a need to prove guilt beyond reasonable doubt to impose a TPIM could also contribute to that impression, and could also mean that some TPIMs are wrongfully imposed. The claim that they have been wrongfully imposed, even if false, may be accorded credibility by the claim that if the person had been guilty of an offense he would have been charged instead. A criminal trial, conviction, and imprisonment also contributes more strongly to an appearance of state credibility in terms of ensuring security, given that TPIMs do not control a suspect's movements at all times, and TPIM subjects have absconded.[116]

V. Conclusions

There is arguably a mismatch between the current underuse of TPIMs, despite their 2016 revival, and findings in 2015–2017 as to the risk posed by the number of British citizens who present a threat of carrying out terrorist acts.[117] It is notable that TPIMs are being relied on only to a minor extent, even in their newly strengthened form,[118] in the face of current estimates of the threat of terrorist attacks in the UK.

[115] Lord Steyn found in *R v. Roberts* that "the special advocate procedure undermines the very essence of elementary justice." [2005] UKHL 45, para. 88. The procedure has improved since 2005, but nevertheless does not maintain high due process standards.

[116] *See* sources cited *supra* note 80.

[117] *See* sources cited Johnson & MacAskill, *supra* note 40 (Andrew Parker interview), and David Anderson, *A Question of Trust: Report of the Investigatory Powers Review*, para. 3.15 (June 2015); *see also* Home Affairs Comm., *8th Report—Radicalisation: The Counter-Narrative* 3, 9 (HC 135 25, Aug. 2016), which partly relies on Anderson's Report and noted that terrorism-related arrests in the UK were 35 percent higher in 2015 than in 2010. The terrorist threat was summarized in Home Office, *CONTEST Report 2015*, *supra* note 38, para. 1.4 (noting about 850 persons who had traveled to Syria and Iraq, of whom half had returned).

[118] *See supra* notes 82–85 (discussing CTSA 2015).

Nevertheless, far from relying extensively on newly strengthened TPIMs or introducing ETPIMs, the risk posed by ISIS or al-Qaeda sympathizers in the UK has largely been addressed by placing reliance on the array of "early intervention" or precursor terrorism offenses discussed.[119] Further, the notion that deployment of TPIMs is linked to triggering the criminal process has largely been abandoned. TPIMs were intended to provide a more effective route to prosecution than control orders—hence the use of the term "investigation" in their designation. But they have failed to do so,[120] except indirectly and unintentionally in the sense that their perceived inefficacy as part of the counterterror infrastructure may have encouraged use of precursor terrorist offenses instead.

Taking the criminal process route to counterterrorism not only has greater benefits in security terms since a TPIM subject might abscond, it also has greater legitimacy than increasing the reliance on TPIMs (or ETPIMs, or a new variation of control orders). The difficulty of seeking to reconcile use of executive measures with human rights law, illustrated by the control orders saga, is not as acute in relation to reliance on criminal offenses, although precursor offenses do give rise to certain human rights concerns. Nor is the danger of a miscarriage of justice as high, given that the offense must be proved beyond reasonable doubt. While the integrity of the criminal process could be damaged, due to the widening of the criminal law net to include very early stage activities linked to terrorism, such concerns, and those as to reversed burdens of proof, pale in significance compared to the easily satisfied requirements needed to impose a TPIM. Although obviously the consequences of TPIM imposition in terms of the impact on the suspect fall well short of imprisonment.

It is argued that the decisions of successive governments post-2005 not to seek a derogation or to maintain or introduce the most repressive measures on this model ("heavy-touch" or derogating control orders or ETPIMs) have demonstrated a serious engagement with human rights law, partly attributable to the impact of the Human Rights Act. The refusal to rely on those more repressive measures, combined with restrained use of control orders/TPIMs, and a currently increasing reliance on prosecutions for "precursor" offenses, demonstrates that lessons have been learned over time by the executive as well as by judges about striking the balance between individual interests and the societal concern to combat terrorism in the sixteen years since 9/11. The previous discussion has sought to demonstrate that measures on the control orders model have undergone a process of human rights tempering since they were first introduced in 2005. Nevertheless, they remain fundamentally problematic as punitive sanctions imposed without trial. The increased preference for deploying the criminal process, as opposed to executive measures with such sanctions, indicates that a more mature and practiced expertise is in use in assessing the aims and nature of the counterterror

[119] Blackbourne and Walker find that TPIMs "continue to be enforced only to a meagre extent compared to criminalisation." Jessie Blackbourne & Clive Walker, *Interdiction and Indoctrination: The Counter-terrorism and Security Act 2015*, 79 Mod. L. Rev. 840, 842 (2016).

[120] *See* David Anderson, 2014 Report, *supra* note 81, paras. 6.3, 6.4; Helen Fenwick, *Redefining the Role of TPIMs in Combatting "Home-Grown" Terrorism Within the Widening Counter-terror Framework*, 2015 (1) Eur. Hum. Rights L. Rev. 41.

response, despite the increase in terrorist activity in Europe in 2015–2017 and the worst terrorist attack in the UK since 7/7, in 2017. It is concluded that in devising and deploying early intervention counterterror measures, a closer focus than in 2001 is currently apparent on creating a human-rights-compliant balance between rights and security, bearing in mind that terrorist activity is damaging to the enjoyment of rights.

References

Helen Duffy, *The "War on Terror" and the Framework of International Law* (2d ed. 2015)

Helen Fenwick & Gavin Phillipson, *Covert Derogations and Judicial Deference: Redefining Liberty and Due Process Rights in Counterterrorism Law and Beyond*, 56(4) McGill L.J. 1 (2011)

Helen Fenwick, *Recalibrating ECHR Rights, and the Role of the Human Rights Act Post-9/11: Reasserting International Human Rights Norms in the "War on Terror"?*, 63 Current Legal Probs. 153 (2011)

Conor Gearty, *The Human Rights Act—An Academic Sceptic Changes His Mind but Not His Heart*, 6 Eur. Hum. Rights L. Rev. 582, 586 (2010)

Critical Perspectives on Counter-Terrorism 130–49 (Lee Jarvis & Michael Lister eds., 2015)

Eva Nanopoulos, *European Human Rights Law and the Normalisation of the "Closed Material Procedure": Limit or Source?*, 78 Mod. L. Rev. 913 (2015)

Report of the Eminent Jurists Panel on Terrorism, Counter-Terrorism and Human Rights, *Assessing Damage, Urging Action* (ICJ 2009)

CHAPTER 32

COMPARING PLEA BARGAINING AND ABBREVIATED TRIAL PROCEDURES

GWLADYS GILLIÉRON

I. Introduction

Confronted with an ever-growing caseload, criminal justice systems have progressively introduced alternatives to contested trials for legal disputes, such as plea bargaining and penal order proceedings. These various procedures have a common feature in that they allow for a resolution of the case based upon the consent of the parties. Today, alternatives to criminal trials play such an important role that only a small minority of cases goes through the regular criminal process. In the United States, the phenomenon of negotiated justice is well established, with most criminal cases resolved via plea bargaining. In Europe, many criminal justice systems have been adopting abbreviated trial proceedings during the last two decades. Besides the use of penal orders, various forms of bargaining have emerged. Although alternative proceedings are an efficient way to reduce the workload of courts, their use remains controversial. In light of the growing importance of consensual criminal procedures across jurisdictions, this contribution considers the following questions: Why do such procedures exist? To what extent do abbreviated trial procedures in civil law systems differ from plea bargaining in the U.S. system? What are the problems inherent in consensual criminal procedures, and are there any solutions? What future direction should such procedures take?

II. The Emergence of Consensual Criminal Procedures

Criminal justice systems are confronted with growing caseload numbers. As a consequence, it is not possible to give every defendant a trial. Methods must be found to reserve full trials for complex cases and serious offenses, and treat strong cases, typically minor offenses, differently. In this context, consensual criminal procedures are a simple way of rationalizing criminal procedures, since their aim is to eliminate the usual time-consuming trial hearing. The court is able to dispose of a case quickly and will therefore conserve scarce resources. The trend toward avoiding the expense of full criminal trials has even been encouraged by international organizations such as the Council of Europe. Recommendation No. R (87) 18 of the Committee of Ministers of the Council of Europe, adopted September 17, 1987, considered negotiated justice a possible way to simplify criminal justice, and therefore invited states, wherever constitutional and legal traditions allowed it, to introduce simplified proceedings such as "guilty pleas."

In the following sections, U.S. plea bargaining is compared with plea-bargaining-type procedures and penal orders in Continental Europe. Since Continental Europe is made up of many countries, each of which has its own criminal justice system, it is not possible to include them all in this contribution. For illustration purposes, Switzerland, Germany, and France are considered. Although the three civil law systems surveyed have their common roots in the inquisitorial system, their approaches to plea bargaining and penal orders remain distinct.

1. Plea Bargaining in the U.S. Criminal Justice System

A plea bargain is "a negotiated agreement between a prosecutor and a criminal defendant whereby the defendant pleads guilty or no contest to a lesser offense or to one of multiple charges in exchange for some concession by the prosecutor, usually a more lenient sentence or a dismissal of the other charges."[1] All crimes, even the most serious ones such as homicide, can be subject to plea bargaining.

The emergence of plea bargaining in the U.S. system may be situated in the nineteenth century, when "the rise of adversary procedure and the law of evidence injected vast complexity into jury trial and made it unworkable as a routine dispositive procedure."[2] In fact, "the guilty plea system emerged to displace jury trials when professionals, police and lawyers, entered the fray and set the system right, i.e., with due regard to notions of cost efficiency and justice."[3] Furthermore, the rise of plea bargaining may also be linked

[1] *Black's Law Dictionary* 1963 (Bryan A. Garner ed., 10th ed. 2014).

[2] John H. Langbein, *Understanding the Short History of Plea Bargaining*, 13 L. & Soc'y Rev. 261 (1979).

[3] Mike McConville & Chester L Mirsky, *Jury Trials and Plea Bargaining* 327 (2005).

to "changing ideas of punishment and sentencing, as well as expansion of the criminal law."[4] Finally, the development of plea bargaining may also have been facilitated by the adversarial system of justice. This system relies heavily on advocacy by each party with a passive judge acting as an umpire. Thus, the judge cannot go beyond what the parties present to her. Under these circumstances, it does make sense not to conduct a full trial if the defendant admits his guilt.

At the federal level, plea bargaining is regulated in Rule 11 of the Federal Rules of Criminal Procedure. In addition, the U.S. Attorneys' Manual provides for general guidelines. At the state level, different legal statutes and rules govern the practice. Prosecutors' offices often adopt general guidelines with respect to handling plea bargaining. Despite the different sources of regulation, the process is essentially the same.

A plea bargain can take several forms.[5] Usually, a distinction is made between charge bargaining, sentence bargaining, and fact bargaining. In a charge bargain, the prosecutor offers to dismiss certain charges or to amend the crimes that a defendant has been charged with to a lesser offense that carries a lesser penalty. The decision to modify the charges remains entirely in the prosecutor's discretion. In sentence bargaining, the prosecutor agrees to make a favorable sentence recommendation to the court. However, even when there is an agreement between the prosecution and defense, there still may be some uncertainties for the defendant since the sentence bargain must be approved by the judge. Only in those jurisdictions where judges are allowed to participate in plea discussions will the parties be sure of the outcome of a guilty plea as there has been a preapproval by the judge.[6] Most U.S. jurisdictions limit the extent of judicial involvement in plea negotiations, however, and at the federal level, the rules prohibit judges from being a party to plea discussions. The main reason for this is the potential for coercion of defendants if the judge is involved.[7] Fact bargaining occurs when prosecutors and defendants bargain over what circumstances of an event should be stipulated as true by the parties and presented to the court. A special feature of the U.S. criminal justice system is that a defendant can plead guilty while at the same time actively professing innocence (*Alford* plea).[8] Most state and federal courts have further concluded that, as part of a plea agreement, a defendant may explicitly waive the right to appeal.[9]

A guilty plea is subject to court approval. A judge will accept the plea if he is convinced that the defendant is making a voluntary and knowing waiver of her trial rights.

[4] Lynn M. Mather, *Comments of the History of Plea Bargaining*, 13 L. & Soc'y Rev. 281 (1979).

[5] On the forms of plea bargaining, see Wayne R. LaFave et al., *Criminal Procedure* § 21.1(a) (4th ed. 2015).

[6] On the considerable variation among jurisdictions as to the legal position on judicial involvement in plea negotiations, see *id.* § 21.3(d).

[7] *See infra* Section I.2.a.iii discussing the German criminal justice system, which involves judges in the negotiations.

[8] North Carolina v. Alford, 400 U.S. 25 (1970).

[9] Marc L. Miller & Ronald Wright, *Criminal Procedures: Cases, Statutes, and Executive Materials* 1115–16 (3d ed. 2007).

In addition, the judge must ascertain that there is a factual basis to support the charges to which the defendant pleads guilty. The use of threats and promises intended to deprive the defendant of her freedom of choice constitutes a denial of procedural fairness. However, in light of the U.S. Supreme Court case law, it is difficult to define under which circumstances promises and threats are considered coercive. The threat of additional charges made during plea negotiations is not considered to be a denial of due process but is legitimate to induce a plea.[10] Furthermore, the prosecutor's offer of a more lenient sentence does not constitute coercion. Along the same lines, courts have held that the guilty plea is not necessarily involuntary even if a defendant pleads guilty to avoid a possible death sentence after trial.[11]

Defendants have no constitutional right to a plea bargain, or even to plead guilty. It is up to the prosecutor to decide whether to initiate or agree to enter plea negotiations. Equal protection requirements are the only constitutional limits on prosecutorial discretion in this regard.[12] The defendant has the right to counsel during the guilty plea process but can waive it.[13] Defendants also have a constitutional right to a competent lawyer's advice when deciding whether to accept a plea agreement.[14]

The criminal justice system recognizes the responsibility to the victim in plea negotiations. In fact, under many victims' rights statutes, victims have the right to have input in the plea bargaining process. Victims may confer with the prosecutor or may be heard at the plea hearing before the judge. The rejection of a plea agreement by the victim is not binding upon the court.[15]

In the U.S. criminal justice system, the overwhelming majority of criminal charges are disposed of by plea bargaining. About 95 percent of felony convictions and at least as many misdemeanor convictions are the product of guilty pleas.[16]

2. Abbreviated Trial Procedures in Civil Law Systems

Criminal justice systems in civil law countries have also been adopting alternative proceedings to the standard trial in the last few decades to relieve heavy caseloads. There is great institutional variety. In addition to penal orders, elements of bargaining have emerged, and several countries use some form of accelerated proceedings. Below, Section II.2.a discusses plea bargaining in civil law systems and, before considering Switzerland, Germany, and France in greater depth, it explains why plea bargaining was

[10] Bordenkircher v. Hayes, 434 U.S. 357 (1978).

[11] *See, e.g.*, Brady v. United States, 397 U.S. 472 (1970); Parker v. North Carolina, 397 U.S. 790 (1970); North Carolina v. Alford, 400 U.S. 25 (1970).

[12] Joseph F. Lawless, *Prosecutorial Misconduct: Law, Procedure, Forms* § 6:06, n.55 (4th ed. 2008).

[13] Iowa v. Tovar, 541 U.S. 77 (2004).

[14] Missouri v. Frye, 132 S. Ct. 1399 (2012); Lafler v. Cooper, 132 S. Ct. 1376 (2012).

[15] On the role of victims in plea bargaining, see LaFave et al., *supra* note 5, § 21.3(f).

[16] *Innocents Who Plead Guilty*, National Registry of Exonerations (Nov. 24, 2015), *at* http://www.law.umich.edu/special/exoneration/Documents/NRE.Guilty.Plea.Article1.pdf.

rather unlikely to emerge in civil law systems. Section II.2.b presents the various forms of penal order proceedings.

a. *Plea Bargaining*

I. OBSTACLES TO THE INTRODUCTION OF PLEA BARGAINING IN CIVIL LAW SYSTEMS

Civil law systems are characterized by inquisitorial features. In inquisitorially rooted procedures, the court not only has an adjudicative role but also plays an active role in collecting the evidence and determining guilt. Therefore, judges actively seek the truth. Under these circumstances, the role of Continental judges does not allow a guilty plea by the defendant to remove the judicial power to investigate the facts of the case and to decide on the guilt of the defendant. In addition, in an inquisitorial system the investigation is led by officials of the state (i.e., a prosecutor or investigating magistrate) in order to determine the truth. The prosecutor is obliged to investigate in an objective and neutral way and must therefore take into account both the incriminating and the exculpatory circumstances. Like the judge, he is obliged to determine the facts and is not a party to the case but a neutral justice official. Finally, in inquisitorial systems there is ordinarily a requirement of compulsory prosecution (such as in Switzerland and Germany), which means that all cases must go to trial whenever there is sufficient evidence to justify a conviction.[17] Hence, prosecutors do not have discretion as to which cases they want to try. From all this follows that there are fundamental tensions between the inquisitorial foundations and the notion of negotiation, making it highly unlikely that an inquisitorial system would ever adopt adversarial procedures such as plea bargaining.

II. SWISS PLEA BARGAINING: ABBREVIATED PROCEEDINGS

The possibility of ending a case by way of abbreviated proceedings (*abgekürztes Verfahren*) nationwide was introduced in Switzerland in January 2011, when the first Swiss Code of Criminal Procedure (CH-CCP)[18] became legally effective and replaced the twenty-six cantonal criminal procedure codes. Prior to the introduction of the CH-CCP, there was no informal negotiation practice. Only three out of twenty-six cantons had previously implemented such an alternative procedure between 1999 and 2003. The abbreviated proceedings in the CH-CCP are regulated in only five articles.[19] Swiss case law on abbreviated proceedings is quite scarce due to the limited possibility of appeal and the novelty of the procedure. This rather rudimentary regulation favors different approaches

[17] However, with the growth of mass crimes, this principle has been tempered more and more with elements of discretion. For less serious crimes, the German prosecutor, for instance, has the power to drop the charge due to a lack of public interest or to dismiss the case in exchange for a payment or other positive activity furnished by the suspect.

[18] Schweizerische Strafprozessordnung [StPO/CH-CCP] [Swiss Code of Criminal Procedure] Oct. 5, 2007, SR 312, *translation at* https://www.admin.ch/opc/en/classified-compilation/20052319/index.html.

[19] CH-CCP arts. 358–362.

to this proceeding across cantons and the emergence of different challenges. The following discussion describes the abbreviated proceedings and briefly addresses some of these controversial points.

The abbreviated proceedings allow the prosecutor to make a deal with the defendant provided that the defendant agrees to plead guilty and that the prosecution requests the imposition of a prison sentence not exceeding five years (article 358 CH-CCP). The assistance by a lawyer is mandatory and results from the principle of equality of arms (article 130 lit. e CH-CCP). The abbreviated proceedings are used to handle serious and less serious felonies and misdemeanors that cannot be dealt with by penal order.[20] Sentence bargaining and charge bargaining are both possible.[21] Unlike in the United States, fact bargaining is prohibited.[22] According to the current practice of the Federal Supreme Court, a confession may lead to a reduction of one-fifth to one-third of the foreseen penalty.[23] In the abbreviated proceedings, a further reduction is possible if additional reasons to mitigate responsibility exist, such as sincere repentance and confession of other crimes. The opinion of the victim is considered, and the victim can veto the use of abbreviated proceedings (article 360 paras. 2–5 CH-CCP).[24]

The abbreviated proceedings are initiated by the defendant submitting an application to the prosecution in which he accepts liability for those circumstances that are essential to the legal evaluation of the case and the civil claims (article 358 para. 1 CH-CCP). This application can be made at any point before charges are filed. To protect against coercion by the prosecutor, only the defendant is allowed to submit an application.[25] However, the prosecutor is entitled to inform a defendant about this alternative.[26] The prosecutor evaluates the application and decides whether the case is to be conducted by way of abbreviated proceedings. In making her decision she has full discretion and does not have a duty to provide reasons. The accused has no legal remedies against the decision (article 359 para. 1 CH-CCP). Defendants retain the right to resubmit an application.[27]

The law does not prescribe the format of the negotiations. Should they be conducted in writing or orally, but with an obligation to keep records, or without any particular form? The prevailing legal doctrine, as well as the Federal Penal Court of Switzerland, are of the opinion that negotiations must be documented,[28] although in practice it is not uncommon that negotiations are conducted orally after a hearing or by phone between

[20] Georges Greiner & Irma Jaggi, in *Basler Kommentar, Schweizerische Strafprozessordnung, Jugendstrafprozessordnung*, art. 358 Margin No. 112 (M.A. Niggli et al. eds., 2d ed. 2014).

[21] *Id.* Vorbemerkungen zu Art. 358–362, Margin Nos. 26–29.

[22] Irma Jaggi, *Die strafprozessuale Absprache vor den Schranken des Gerichts—Rolle und Einfluss des Gerichts im abgekürzten Verfahren* 22–23 (2016).

[23] Entscheidungen des Schweizerischen Bundesgerichts [BGE] 121 IV 202, 205–06 (Decision of the Federal Supreme Court of 25 Sept. 1995).

[24] On the victim's position in the abbreviated proceedings, see Greiner & Jaggi, *supra* note 20, art. 360, Margin Nos. 24–33.

[25] *Id.* art. 358, Margin No.1.

[26] *Id.* Margin No. 3.

[27] *Id.* art. 359, Margin No. 3.

[28] Stéphane Grodecki, *Expériences pratiques de la procédure simplifiée*, Forumpoenale 45, 50–51 (2016); Decision of the Federal Criminal Court dated 2 October 2013 (PC 2013.34).

lawyers and prosecutors. Informal discussions have also occurred prior to the submission of an application by the defendant.

Successful negotiations are closed by an indictment that the prosecution transmits together with the files to the court of first instance (article 360 para. 4 CH-CCP). On the other hand, if negotiations fail, the prosecution will conduct ordinary proceedings, and declarations provided by the defendant with respect to the abbreviated proceedings cannot be used as evidence (article 360 para. 5 and article 362 para. 4 CH-CCP per analogiam).

The court cannot reject abbreviated proceedings based on the criminal offense the defendant is accused of or based on its preference to conduct ordinary proceedings in certain situations.[29] The examination of the court is limited to ascertaining that the defendant's rights have been respected and that the confession is credible. Party pleadings usually do not take place. The duty of the court is to determine whether the use of abbreviated proceedings is lawful and appropriate, whether the charge corresponds to the conclusions of the main hearing[30] and to the files, and whether the sanctions requested are reasonable (article 362 para. 1 CH-CCP).

Legal criteria for the evaluation of appropriateness are missing, so that it is up to the courts to develop such criteria. Courts have not yet developed clear criteria. However, it seems reasonable to take into account legal equality. A judgment that would significantly deviate from judgments pronounced in similar cases in ordinary proceedings should be deemed inappropriate.[31] Practical experience shows that the sanctions requested have generally been approved by the courts, although they may have often been considered to be only nearly proportionate to the defendant's guilt.[32]

If the court concludes that the requirements for a judgment by way of abbreviated proceedings are fulfilled, it converts the indictment into a judgment (article 362 para. 2 CH-CCP). The defendant may only appeal on the basis that he did not accept the indictment or that the judgment does not correspond to the indictment (article 362 para. 5 CH-CCP). The extent to which a petition for revision remains possible is a matter of debate. While the Federal Council in its message to the Parliament of December 21, 2005, on the unification of criminal procedure excludes such a possibility,[33] some legal scholars argue that the use of this legal remedy should remain possible to correct wrongful convictions caused by false confessions.[34] Recently, the court of justice in the canton of Geneva agreed with the latter position.[35]

[29] Greiner & Jaggi, *supra* note 20, art. 362, Margin No. 8a.

[30] At the main hearing the court questions the defendant to establish whether he accepts the circumstances of the case on which the charge is based, and whether this assertion corresponds to the facts as set out in the files. CH-CCP Art. 361 para. 2.

[31] Greiner & Jaggi, *supra* note 20, art. 362, Margin Nos. 6–8.

[32] Jaggi, *supra* note 22, at 184–85.

[33] Bundesrat, Botschaft zur Vereinheitlichung des Strafprozessrechts vom 21. Dezember 2005, at 1281 (2006).

[34] *See, e.g.*, André Kuhn, *La procédure pénale suisse selon le CPP unifié*, 128 Zeitschrift für Schweizerisches Recht 125, 169–70 (2009).

[35] Decision of the Court of Justice of the Canton of Geneva, May 30, 2015 (AARP/168/2015).

If the court comes to the conclusion that the requirements for abbreviated proceedings are not fulfilled, the prosecution will proceed by ordinary proceedings. The court's decision on this point cannot be challenged (article 362 para. 3 CH-CCP). While declarations provided by the defendant with respect to the abbreviated proceedings cannot be used, confessions given prior to the application to the prosecution to conduct the case by way of abbreviated proceedings can still be. A matter of debate concerns whether the same or another prosecutor than the one having conducted the abbreviated proceedings should be entrusted with the ordinary proceedings. In order to guarantee that the content of negotiations and the confession have no influence in further investigations, the majority of legal scholars argue that the case should be assigned to another prosecutor and that the judges in the ordinary proceedings should not be the same as the ones in the abbreviated proceedings.[36] However, the Federal Penal Court of Switzerland has decided that instead of rejecting the indictment resulting from the abbreviated proceedings, with the consent of the parties, it is open to the court to amend the indictment as well as the legal qualification of the act, with the consequence that the same prosecutor will remain involved in the case and the same judge(s) will decide upon the case.[37] The cantonal court of Zurich has decided in the same way.[38]

Abbreviated proceedings were originally introduced for reducing the workload in the area of economic crimes.[39] However, the experience so far shows that this alternative is mainly used for drug, property, sexual, and road traffic offenses.[40] Nationwide statistical data are not available, so it is not possible to estimate how frequently abbreviated proceedings are used at the national level.

When looking at different cantons, various trends can be identified. In the canton of Basel-City, abbreviated proceedings are rarely used. Applications to the prosecution for the case to be conducted by way of abbreviated proceedings decreased from fifteen to eight between 2011 and 2014. The applications were rejected by the prosecutor in about half of the cases.[41] The reasons included insufficient confessions, failure to achieve an agreement concerning the sentence, or a late submission of application that was made shortly before charges were brought before the court. Agreements concerned mainly sentence bargaining. The court has always confirmed the indictments.[42]

On the contrary, in cantons such as Zurich, St. Gallen, Bern, and Geneva, the application of abbreviated proceedings is steadily growing. In the canton of Geneva, for instance, the number of abbreviated proceedings increased from 119 to 180 between 2012 and 2014. However, when comparing the number of indictments in ordinary

[36] Greiner & Jaggi, *supra* note 20, art. 362, Margin Nos. 37–41.

[37] Decision of the Federal Criminal Court dated 27 May 2015 (PC 2015.8), 4.1; *see also* Bundesrat, *supra* note 33, at 1297.

[38] Judgment of the Cantonal Court of the Canton of Zurich dated 23 January 2015.

[39] Bundesrat, *supra* note 33, at 1295.

[40] Gwladys Gilliéron, *Public Prosecutors in the United States and Europe. A Comparative Analysis with Special Focus on Switzerland, France, and Germany* 242–43 (2014); Grodecki, *supra* note 28, at 48.

[41] Internal statistics of the Public Prosecutor's Office of the canton Basel-City.

[42] *Id.*

proceedings with those in abbreviated proceedings in the same canton, those in the latter still play a minor role with about 13 percent of all criminal cases closed with an indictment in 2014.[43] The canton of Zurich shows similar numbers.[44] In the canton of St. Gallen and Bern, if we make the same comparison, we see that abbreviated proceedings are used more frequently, with 23 percent and 25 percent of all criminal cases closed with an indictment, respectively.[45] The most frequently pronounced sentence in abbreviated proceedings in the canton of Geneva is a prison sentence with complete or partial probation.[46] At the federal level, the use of this alternative reached 45 percent of the cases closed with an indictment in 2013 and continuously decreased to 17.5 percent in 2016.[47]

III. GERMAN PLEA BARGAINING: AGREEMENTS

Germany was once known as a "land without plea bargaining."[48] This assumption belongs to the past. Plea bargaining in Germany has been common practice since the 1980s. On May 28, 2009, the German Federal Parliament passed a law amending the German Code of Criminal Procedure (D-CCP)[49] to regulate plea bargaining, and with this the legislation ratified a practice that had developed informally more than two decades before. The German Federal Constitutional Court ruled on March 19, 2013, that the provisions on plea agreements are compatible with the German Constitution (*Grundgesetz* or "Basic Law").[50]

The law indicates that discussions about the status of the proceedings are allowed at every stage of the proceedings.[51] The central provision is article 257c D-CCP. It regulates the agreement among the court, the prosecution, and the defendant. The involvement of counsel is only mandatory if there is a case for necessary defense.[52] The verdict of guilt, as well as measures of rehabilitation and security, may not be part of a negotiated

[43] Grodecki, *supra* note 28, at 48.

[44] Nils Stohner, *Abgekürzte Rechtsstaatlichkeit—Überlegungen zum abgekürzten Verfahren gemäss Art. 358–362 StPO*, Forumpoenale 168, 169 (2015).

[45] *Id.* at 169; Thomas Hansjakob, *Zahlen und Fakten zum Strafbefehlsverfahren*, Forumpoenale 160, 163 (2014).

[46] Grodecki, *supra* note 28, at 49.

[47] *See* the Annual Reports of the Office of the Attorney General of Switzerland on its activities for the attention of the supervisory authority, http://www.bundesanwaltschaft.ch/dokumentation/00024/index.html?lang=en.

[48] John H. Langbein, *Land Without Plea Bargaining: How the Germans Do It*, 78 Mich. L. Rev. 204 (1979).

[49] Deutsche Strafprozessordnung [StPO/D-CCP][Code of Criminal Procedure], *translation at* https://www.gesetze-im-internet.de/englisch_stpo/index.html.

[50] Bundesverfassungsgericht [BVerfG] [Federal Constitutional Court] Mar. 19, 2013, Case No. 2 BVR 2628/10.

[51] *See* D-CCP Arts. 160b, 202a, 212, 257b.

[52] Mandatory defense arises when the main hearing at first instance is held at the Higher Regional Court or at the Regional Court, the accused is charged with a felony, the proceedings may result in an order prohibiting the pursuit of an occupation, proceedings for preventive detention are conducted, or remand detention is executed against an accused, among others. D-CCP Art. 140.

agreement. In addition, the legislation prohibits any bargains that include a waiver of the right to appeal the verdict or the sentence. The agreement may only concern the legal consequences that may be imposed in a judgment, other procedural measures related to trial proceedings, and procedural acts of the parties.[53] As in ordinary proceedings, dismissals for reasons of prosecutorial efficiency (articles 154 and 154a D-CCP) can also be considered in agreements.[54] Hence, in practice, negotiations have been found to concern both the sentence and, at times, the charges.[55] Fact bargaining seems to occur rarely, if at all.[56]

A confession forms an integral part of any negotiated agreement in Germany, and it is commonly rewarded with a sentence reduction between 25 and 33 percent of the foreseen penalty.[57] Prior to the Constitutional Court Decision of March 19, 2013, the hearing of evidence was not absolutely necessary in order to check the accuracy of a confession. Research by Altenhain and colleagues conducted in 2012 (in which 190 judges, 68 prosecutors, and 76 defense lawyers were surveyed in North Rhine-Westphalia) showed that 28 percent of the judges admitted to verifying the credibility of the confession only from time to time or rarely.[58] Furthermore, in most cases the control was limited to comparing whether the confession corresponds to the facts and charges as set out in the files.[59] Since the trial court in plea bargaining proceedings is not relieved from its obligation to find the objective truth, the Constitutional Court Decision of March 19, 2013, requires the examination of the confession during the main trial and the hearing of additional evidence to prove the credibility of the confession. For instance, this can occur by examining the investigative file to determine if it contains independent evidence corroborating the confession or by questioning the leading investigator as a witness.[60]

In contrast to the other systems considered in this contribution, German law gives the court an important role in the negotiations. Judges in Germany may initiate negotiations and indicate the maximum and minimum sentence they would impose as part of the bargain.[61] The parties have the right to comment on the proposed sentencing range. The defendant and the prosecutor have to agree to the court's proposal in order to conclude the agreement (article 257c subs. 3 D-CCP).[62]

[53] Dirk Saurer & Sebastian Münkel, *Absprachen im Strafprozess* 102–04, Margin Nos. 249–254 (2d ed. 2014).

[54] *Id.* at 103 Margin No. 253.

[55] Karsten Altenhain et al., *Die Praxis der Absprachen in Strafverfahren* 77–80 (2013).

[56] Jenia I. Turner, *Judicial Participation in Plea Negotiations: A Comparative View*, 54 Am. J. Comp. L. 199, 229 (2006).

[57] Altenhain et al., *supra* note 55, at 116.

[58] *Id.* at 99. From the point of view of defense lawyers and prosecutors, judges were even more negligent in this matter.

[59] *Id.* at 100. [60] Saurer & Münkel, *supra* note 53, at 146–48, Margin Nos. 330–335.

[61] *Id.* at 133–36, Margin Nos. 314–318.

[62] On the participation of the parties to the proceedings, see *id.* at 106–07, Margin Nos. 259–261.

The court may ultimately reject a bargain it helped negotiate if legal or factually important circumstances have been overlooked or have arisen after the agreement was concluded, and if the court is of the opinion that for this reason the predicted sentence is no longer proportionate to guilt. The court may also reject the agreement when later conduct by the accused contradicts the basis on which the court made its sentence prediction (article 257c subs. 4 D-CCP).[63] The aim of this provision is twofold. It highlights the fact that the court has an independent duty to investigate the truth and that the court must impose a sentence proportionate to guilt. If the court rejects a bargain because it cannot sentence according to its initial sentence prognosis, the defendant's confession may not be used as evidence against him in subsequent proceedings. However, since the same judges who have heard the excluded confession would be the ones conducting the subsequent trial, the practical effect of this rule is more than questionable. In fact, it will be very difficult for the court to disregard a confession after it had previously accepted it, which it can only do if it is convinced, according to the concept of substantive truth, that the admission of guilt was genuine. Under such circumstances, the court is prejudiced by the previous confession and thus a change of the judges should occur.

All negotiations before and during trial have to be announced during the main trial hearing and read into the record (article 243 subs. 4 D-CCP). The recording of all negotiations and agreements serves transparency and ensures that arrangements can be reviewed by an appeals court.[64] However, despite this rule and the principle of public trial, the details of agreements still remain hidden. Only the essential content of the negotiated agreement has to be presented in open court, while negotiations do not have to be carried out in public. In addition, research by Altenhain and colleagues in 2012—before the Constitutional Court issued its decision—shows that more than 60 percent of the surveyed judges admitted to making a deal without recording it.[65] Whether this practice has changed in light of the 2013 decision remains an open question.

It is not possible to give statistical information on the number of cases resolved through agreements since this is usually included in the total number of cases brought before the court. If informal negotiations take place prior to the main hearing, it is possible that the case will either be dismissed[66] or be dealt with by penal order. Empirical research conducted in Germany since the 1990s shows that agreements occur most often in economic, environment, and drug-related crimes.[67]

[63] *Id.* at 108–10, Margin Nos. 262–271.

[64] *Id.* at 111–12, Margin Nos. 275–276.

[65] Altenhain et al., *supra* note 55, at 151.

[66] Cases can be dismissed by unconditional dismissals (e.g., lack of public interest; dismissal for reasons of prosectorial efficiency) or conditional dismissals according to article 153a D-CCP (e.g., perform a specific service in order to make reparations for damage caused by the offense; pay a sum of money to a non-profit-making institution or to the Treasury).

[67] Kiyomi v. Frankenberg, *Grundlagen Konsensual Konfliktlösungsprozesse— eine empirische Analyse von Konsensbildungsprozessen in abgesprochenen Wirtschaftsstrafverfahren* 49 (2013) (PhD dissertation, Albert-Ludwigs University, Freiburg i. Br.).

IV. FRENCH PLEA BARGAINING: PLEA NEGOTIATIONS

Plea negotiations (*Comparution sur reconnaissance préalable de culpabilité/plaider coupable* or CRPC) were introduced in France in 2004. As enshrined in articles 495-7 to 495-16 of the French Criminal Code of Procedure (F-CCP),[68] this type of procedure is available to defendants charged with an offense carrying a prison sentence of up to ten years (*délits*) who have consented to the procedure and have admitted their guilt. The French guilty plea procedure cannot be used for certain offenses, such as those that, by nature, imply an adversarial debate (i.e., involuntary homicide[69]) and those whose procedure is defined by a special law (i.e., media and political offenses). In addition, the most serious offenses (*crimes*), such as murder or rape, cannot be dealt with by plea negotiations. When proceeding through the CRPC procedure, the prosecutor can propose to the defendant a prison sentence not exceeding one year (article 495-8 F-CCP). Although not expressly mentioned in the law, CRPC is applicable in cases with clear and simple factual circumstances and thus in cases that would be ready for trial.[70]

The guilty plea procedure may be initiated by the prosecutor, the defendant, or his lawyer (article 495-7 F-CCP). The assistance of a lawyer is mandatory in this proceeding.[71] After a brief discussion between the offender, his lawyer, and the prosecutor about the facts of the case, in which the prosecutor asks the defendant to confirm that he has committed the offense, the prosecutor will propose a sentence she considers the most appropriate according to the gravity of the offense and the offender's personal and professional situation.[72] The defendant is free to accept or refuse the proposed sentence. The defendant may also be granted a reflection period of ten days before communicating a decision (article 495-8 F-CCP).[73] It is important to mention that the French guilty plea procedure is not really a plea bargain as known under U.S. law since negotiations are not conducted on either the nature or category of the alleged offense or on the sentence proposed by the public prosecutor.[74]

If the defendant accepts the proposed penalty, his case is brought to the court. During the public hearing, where the presence of the prosecutor is not mandatory, the judge verifies that the charges and the prosecution's case are factually and legally correct and that they match with the defendant's confession (article 495-9 F-CCP). Furthermore, the judge checks the appropriateness of the sentence proposed by the prosecutor

[68] Code de procédure pénale [C. Pr. Pén./F-CCP][Criminal Procedure Code], *translation at* https://www.legifrance.gouv.fr/Traductions/Liste-des-traductions-Legifrance.

[69] In France, adversarial debate is required for certain offenses of greater gravity. *See* Ministère de la Justice, *Circulaire CRIM 2004–12 E8 du 2 septembre 2004 relative à la présentation des dispositions de la loi n° 2004–204 du 9 mars 2004 portant adaptation de la justice aux évolutions de la criminalité relatives à la procédure de comparution sur reconnaissance préalable de culpabilité*, at 7.

[70] *Id.* § 1.2.2.2.

[71] Serge Guinchard & Jacques Buisson, *Procédure pénale*, Margin No. 1577 (7th ed. 2011).

[72] *Id.* Margin No. 1575.

[73] *Id.* Margin No. 1579.

[74] Ministère de la Justice, *supra* note 69, at § 2.2.3.

(article 495-11 F-CCP).[75] If the judge disagrees with the evaluation of the prosecutor, she can neither impose nor propose a new sentence that she believes to be appropriate, but has to send the case to be tried before the court (article 495-12 F-CCP).[76] Where the victim of the offense is known, he is invited to appear before the court at the same time as the defendant, and is accompanied, where appropriate, by his lawyer, in order to constitute himself as a civil party and to request damages for any harm done against him (article 495-13 F-CCP).[77] Although the victim can object to a plea agreement at the approval hearing, his refusal is not binding upon the court.[78] If the judge approves the guilty plea, the approval has the effect of a guilty verdict (article 495-11 F-CCP). It may be subject to appeal by the convicted person, the civil party, and the prosecutor (articles 495-11 and 495-13 F-CCP).[79]

If either the defendant or the court refuses to accept the prosecutor's proposal, the case will be tried by ordinary proceedings (article 495-12 F-CCP). At trial, neither the defendant nor the prosecutor may make use of any statements made or documents given over the course of the guilty plea procedure (article 495-14 F-CCP).[80]

Since its introduction in 2004, the use of this alternative is steadily increasing. While in 2007, 9.3 percent of the cases brought before the *tribunal correctionel*[81] ended with a guilty plea, in 2015, more than 12 percent of the cases were resolved this way.[82]

b. *Penal Orders*

For the adjudication of criminal cases, continental European prosecutors may apply for a penal order. The penal order constitutes an offer to the parties for an out-of-court settlement of the criminal case or a proposed judgment. The penal order is a simplified procedure in writing that allows conviction without a trial and where the sanction imposed is typically a fine. As will be described below, depending on jurisdiction, this alternative may vary in terms of possible sanctions, the gravity of offenses, and the authority issuing the decision.

This alternative is used when the investigation has clearly established the facts the defendant is accused of or when the defendant has acknowledged his guilt. It is usually reserved for minor crimes. However, in Switzerland, the most serious crimes such as murder may theoretically be handled in this way since there is no restriction concerning the gravity of offenses. The scope of application is instead limited by the length of the prison sentence that can be imposed, which is six months (article 352 CH-CCP). In the French penal order, only a fine may be imposed (articles 495-1 and 525 F-CCP), while in the German penal order, a prison sentence of up to one year combined with

[75] Guinchard & Buisson, *supra* note 71, Margin Nos. 1580–1582; 1585.

[76] *Id.* Margin No. 1584; Babacar Niang, *Le Plaider Coupable en France et aux Etats-Unis au Regard des Principes Directeurs du Procès Pénal* 107, Margin No. 99 (2014).

[77] Guinchard & Buisson, *supra* note 71, Margin No. 1583.

[78] Niang, *supra* note 76, at 452.

[79] Guinchard & Buisson, *supra* note 71, Margin No. 1586.

[80] *Id.* Margin Nos. 1587–1589.

[81] *Tribunal correctionel* is the court of first instance that decides criminal cases classified as *délits*.

[82] *See* Ministry of Justice, Key Figures of Justice, *available at* http://www.justice.gouv.fr/statistiques-10054/chiffres-cles-de-la-justice-10303.

probation may be pronounced (article 407 D-CCP). When the imposition of a prison sentence by penal order is considered in Germany, which happens in less than 1 percent of the cases,[83] the defendant has to be represented by defense counsel (article 408b D-CCP), while such an obligation is missing in Switzerland.[84] In all jurisdictions studied, penal orders are usually applied in cases of traffic offenses, minor thefts, and possession of drugs.[85]

In the German and French criminal procedures, although the court is involved in the final stage to impose a sanction, the prosecutor plays a crucial role. In both jurisdictions, it is the prosecutor who does the preparatory work and formulates a written recommendation to the judge by using a standard form. Since the court only rarely refuses to follow the prosecutor's advice, the prosecutor's decision effectively adjudicates the case.[86] In the Swiss legal system, the court is not involved in the decision to issue a penal order. It is the prosecutor who has the sole responsibility to impose a sanction (article 352 para 1 CH-CCP).

Despite these differences, all penal order proceedings have in common that the decision is usually taken without a prior hearing of the defendant. This decision may then be appealed by the defendant within a certain deadline that varies between ten days in Switzerland (article 354 CH-CCP), fourteen days in Germany (article 410 D-CCP), and forty-five days in France (article 495-3 F-CCP). In this case, the defendant is given a public hearing. If the objection is not lodged in time, the penal order becomes final and has the same effect as a judgment following a main hearing.

In Switzerland over 90 percent of the cases that may in principle be brought before court are dealt with by penal order.[87] By contrast, German prosecutors resolve approximately 25 percent[88] and French prosecutors 12 percent[89] of the trial-ready cases in this way.

[83] Statistisches Bundesamt, *Staatsanwaltschaften* § 2.2.1.1 (2016).

[84] Article 130 CH-CCP enumerates the situations in which the appointment of a defense lawyer is mandatory.

[85] Gwladys Gilliéron, *The Risks of Summary Proceedings, Plea Bargains, and Penal Orders in Producing Wrongful Convictions in the US and Europe*, in *Wrongful Convictions and Miscarriages of Justice: Causes and Remedies in North American and European Criminal Justice Systems* 237, 239 (Ronald C. Huff & Martin Killias eds., 2013).

[86] Jörg-Martin Jehle, *The Function of Public Prosecution Within the Criminal Justice System: Aim, Approach and Outcome of a European Comparative Study*, in *Coping with Overloaded Criminal Justice Systems: The Rise of Prosecutorial Power Across Europe* 3, 23 (Jörg-Martin Jehle & Marianne Wade eds., 2006).

[87] Doris Hutzler, *Ausgleich struktureller Garantiedefizite im Strafbefehlsverfahren. Eine Analyse der zürcherischen, schweizerischen und deutschen Regelungen, unter besonderer Berücksichtigung der Geständnisfunktion* 125 (2010).

[88] Gilliéron, *supra* note 40, at 280; Franz Riklin, *Strafbefehlsverfahren—Effizienz auf Kosten der Rechtsstaatlichkeit?* 152 Zeitschrift des bernischen Juristenvereins 475, 491 (2016); *see also* Statistisches Bundesamt, *supra* note 83, § 2.2.1.1 (including only ordinary crimes that may in principle be brought before court).

[89] *See* Ministry of Justice, Key Figures of Justice, *available at* http://www.justice.gouv.fr/statistiques-10054/chiffres-cles-de-la-justice-10303.

Penal order proceedings may infringe several rights guaranteed by Article 6 of the European Convention on Human Rights (ECHR). Article 6 of the ECHR contains the right to a fair trial. This provision guarantees among others the right to a public hearing in the determination of any criminal charge by an independent and impartial court. As described above, penal orders are usually issued without a hearing of the defendant. In addition, when the prosecutor in Switzerland issues the penal order, the prosecutor does not enjoy judicial independence or impartiality. However, under the European Court of Human Rights (ECtHR) case law, this does not necessarily mean that the Convention is breached. In fact, as long as domestic law provides for the possibility to have all aspects of the decision reviewed by a judicial institution, which does comply with the conditions set out in Article 6, penal order proceedings do not violate the Convention.[90] Criminal justice systems that have a penal order proceeding give the defendant the possibility to raise an objection and ask for a full trial. The right to be heard and all other procedural rights guaranteed by the ECHR are subsequently respected. When no opposition is made, it is assumed that the defendant waives the procedural guarantees of the ECHR. Such a waiver is valid as long as it is clear and unequivocal, which presupposes that the defendant makes his decision with the full knowledge of the legal and factual situation of the case.[91] However, several factors raise doubts as to whether such waivers can be seen as effective: the frequent lack of information about the case by the defendant, and the difficulties that many defendants have in understanding a text of some legal complexity.[92] Furthermore, cases decided by the ECtHR concerned only minor offenses punished with a fine and not with imprisonment. In light of the provisions regulating the penal order proceedings in Switzerland, it is uncertain whether the ECtHR would still decide a case concerning penal orders in the same way.

Pursuant to Article 6 of the ECHR, judgments have to be pronounced publicly. The ECtHR interprets this as either oral pronouncement of judgments, or depositing the judgments in a publicly accessible registry.[93] The public availability of judgments aims at building public confidence in the administration of justice. In contrast to the right of an independent and impartial judge or tribunal, the defendant cannot waive the public pronouncement of the judgment as this right belongs to the public. To comply with this provision, in the Swiss criminal justice system, penal orders are to be open for public inspection (article 69 para 2 CH-CCP). However, the different implementations of this ruling may hinder the effective exercise of this right. In some cantons, the access to penal orders is possible for seven days, in others it is possible for thirty days. In some cantons, public access to penal orders is possible during the period of appeal, while in others, this occurs only after the decision has become final.[94]

[90] Belilos v. Switzerland, App. No. 10328/83, Eur. Ct. H.R., Apr. 29, 1988, §§ 69–73.

[91] Deweer v. Belgium, App. No. 6903/75, Eur. Ct. H.R., Feb. 27, 1980, § 49.

[92] Gilliéron, *supra* note 85, at 241; Riklin, *supra* note 88, at 493.

[93] Pretto and Others v. Italy, App. No. 7984/77, Eur. Ct. H.R., Dec. 8, 1983, §§ 25 f.; BGE 124 IV 234, 240 (Decision of the Federal Supreme Court of 18 May 1998).

[94] Riklin, *supra* note 88, at 494.

III. Plea Bargaining and Abbreviated Trial Procedures: Similarities and Differences

Table 32.1 provides a comparative overview of U.S. plea bargaining and abbreviated trial procedures in civil law systems, including plea-bargaining-type procedures and penal orders.

Caseload pressures have pushed many civil-law criminal justice systems to develop alternatives to full trials. In this context, they have looked to U.S. plea bargaining as a possible model. However, they generally have not implemented plea bargaining to the same extent. Instead each legal system has adapted the practice to meet its own needs and values. This section summarizes the common and different features of the plea bargaining practice in the law systems under review. In addition, it addresses differences between plea bargaining and penal order proceedings.

All plea bargaining procedures have in common that defendants must confess their guilt. The reduction of the penalty granted after an admission of guilt differs between jurisdictions. In Switzerland, the admission of guilt is commonly rewarded with one-fifth to one-third reduction of the foreseen penalty. In case of sincere repentance, a further reduction is possible. In Germany, a confession may lead to a reduction of one-fourth to one-third of the expected sentence. In U.S. federal courts, the sentence after a guilty plea may lead to the same reduction.[95] However, a recent study reveals that "federal defendants convicted at trial receive sentences that are sixty-four percent longer than similar defendants who plead guilty, excluding the effects of charge and fact bargaining."[96]

With the exception of France, where plea bargaining is only available to defendants charged with misdemeanors and low-level felonies (i.e., offenses with a ten-year maximum statutory sentence), in the other law systems considered, all offenses may be handled through this alternative. In some criminal justice systems, the maximum penalty that may be imposed by the prosecutor is defined by law. This is the case in Switzerland, where the prosecutor can request a prison sentence of no more than five years. In France, this sentence is limited to one year.

As a result of the equality of the arms and in order to protect the defendant from coercion, representation by counsel is mandatory in almost all justice systems. However, in the United States, the defendant may waive his right to counsel. The waiver must be intelligent and competent in order to be valid.[97] In Germany, counsel is only mandatory if there is a case for necessary defense. In the majority of the jurisdictions studied,

[95] Andrew Chongseh Kim, *Underestimating the Trial Penalty: An Empirical Analysis of the Federal Trial Penalty and Critique of the Abrams Study*, 84 Miss. L.J. 1195, 1200 (2015).

[96] *Id.* at 1202.

[97] On this right, see LaFave et al., *supra* note 5, at § 21.3 (a), 826–28.

Table 32.1 Overview over plea bargaining, plea bargaining-type procedures, and penal orders in the United States, Switzerland, Germany, and France

Law System	Eligible Crimes	Constraints on punishment in cases resolved through special procedures	Representation by counsel
Plea Bargaining and Plea-Bargaining-Type Procedures			
United States	All	None	Right to effective assistance of counsel (Sixth Amendment); waiver of right to counsel is possible
Switzerland	All	Up to five years prison sentence	Mandatory
Germany	All	None	Mandatory if there is a case for necessary defense[98]
France	*Délits* (Offenses with a ten-year maximum statutory sentence); Excluded for certain offenses[99]	Up to one year prison sentence for negotiated judgments	Mandatory
Penal Order			
Switzerland	All	Up to six months prison sentence	Not mandatory
Germany	Misdemeanors[100]	Up to one year suspended prison sentence	Mandatory in case of prison sentence
France	*Contraventions*[101] and certain *délits*[102]	Only fines	Not mandatory

[98] Mandatory defense arises when the main hearing at first instance is held at the Higher Regional Court or at the Regional Court, the accused is charged with a felony, the proceedings may result in an order prohibiting the pursuit of an occupation, proceedings for preventive detention are conducted, or remand detention is executed against an accused, among others. D-CCP Art. 140.

[99] Certain voluntary and involuntary offenses against the person and against sexual integrity if they are punished with a prison sentence of more than five years; cases of press offenses, political offenses, involuntary homicide offenses. F-CCP Art. 495–7.

[100] Felonies (*Verbrechen*) in Germany are punishable by a minimum of one year imprisonment, misdemeanors (*Vergehen*) by less.

[101] Contraventions in France are punishable by a fine.

[102] The *délits* listed under article 495 F-CCP can be dealt with by penal order and include for instance thefts and road traffic offenses.

informal negotiations take place only between the prosecutor and the defense attorney. Germany is thus an exception, since judges are usually involved.

Negotiations in Switzerland and Germany may concern the charges, the sentence, or both. Mandatory prosecution in these systems limits prosecutorial charging discretion since prosecutors are expected to charge defendants with those offenses that match the action alleged. Unlike in the United States, fact bargaining in Switzerland and Germany is basically prohibited. For France, it is important to emphasize that the procedure of the guilty plea is in reality an accelerated procedure, since negotiations are neither conducted on the nature or category of the alleged offense nor on the sentence proposed by the public prosecutor. The European models of plea bargaining reject the idea of defendants pleading guilty while at the same time contesting their guilt, while in the United States, *Alford* pleas are accepted.

The involvement of the victim in plea bargaining procedures differs from one jurisdiction to the other. In the Swiss criminal justice system, the refusal by the victim of the negotiated agreement prevents the use of this alternative, and the prosecution is obliged to conduct ordinary proceedings. In Germany, the court can consult the victim as a joint plaintiff before an agreement is reached, whereby the victim's opinion is not binding upon the court.[103] In France and the United States, the situation is similar. The victim can object to a plea agreement at the approval hearing in France and the plea hearing in the United States. However, the victim's refusal of the agreement is not binding.

Generally, although legal remedies remain available in plea bargaining procedures, some legal systems restrict their scope of application. In Switzerland, an appeal is only possible on the basis that the defendant or the private claimant did not accept the indictment or that the judgment did not correspond to the indictment. A defendant may not file a petition for revision based on new evidence, since an evidentiary hearing has not been conducted. While in the European legal systems surveyed, a negotiated waiver of the right to file an appeal is prohibited, in the United States, most state and federal courts have concluded that a defendant may explicitly waive the right to appeal as part of the agreement.

The penal order that is used in many European legal systems has been commonly referred to as the continental form of plea bargaining.[104] However, penal order proceedings differ in many ways from plea bargaining. Penal order proceedings are usually reserved for minor crimes. In such a procedure, the subordination of the defendant still exists in the sense that the prosecution and the accused do not stand on an equal footing. The defendant need never appear in court. The case is exclusively evaluated by the prosecutor. Unlike in plea bargaining, representation by counsel is usually not mandatory. The prosecutor mostly makes his decision without hearing the defendant, so the defendant usually does not participate in the preliminary proceedings. She may only accept or refuse the decision by raising an objection with the court or prosecution

[103] Meyer-Gossner, *Strafprozessordnung, Gerichtsverfassungsgesetz, Nebengesetze und ergänzende Bestimmungen* (*Beck'scher Kurzkommentar StPO*) Section 257c, Margin No. 24 (54th ed. 2011).

[104] John H. Langbein, *Controlling Prosecutorial Discretion in Germany*, 41 U. Chi. L. Rev. 439 (1974).

depending on jurisdiction. A bargain between the prosecution and defendant does not take place. Finally, the defendant does not risk a harsher punishment by going to trial. Since a penal order can only be issued for an offense that is in line with established facts, overcharging is not possible to the same extent as it is in the United States. Thus, civil law systems restrict the risk of innocent defendants accepting a penal order to avoid a worse outcome in case of a full trial.[105] Studies confirm that judges in Germany do not impose more severe punishments on those who reject penal orders and ask for a full trial.[106]

IV. Risk of Wrongful Convictions

1. Plea Bargaining

A main advantage of plea bargaining is that it significantly shortens the trial. However, independently of the law system in which plea bargaining is implemented, there is a risk that the court will not verify the factual basis for the defendant's admission of guilt with the same diligence as it would in an ordinary proceeding. There may be a danger that plea bargaining leads to a worse outcome for the defendant than a full trial if the defense attorney and the prosecutor make an incorrect assessment of the facts established earlier in the proceedings.

This section compares the risk of wrongful convictions in the U.S. criminal justice system to those in civil law systems, considering mainly some theoretical aspects. Empirical research on this subject, especially in civil law systems, hardly exists.

a. *Plea Bargaining in the United States*

The risk of innocent people pleading guilty has preoccupied many scholars.[107] Critics argue that coercion in plea bargaining is a major problem, especially for the poor, who cannot afford lawyers and must rely on overworked public defenders to represent them. This alternative may be misused by overzealous prosecutors who prioritize winning over seeing justice done. Thus, there is a serious risk that prosecutors force defendants to waive their rights to jury trial by threatening them with ever-greater sanctions if they refuse to plead guilty and instead ask for a jury trial. In this context, the risk that innocent persons might plead guilty is obvious. The actual doctrine of the Supreme Court and the possibility of *Alford* pleas offers only little protection for defendants.[108]

[105] Martin Killias, *Wrongful Convictions in Switzerland—The Experience of a Continental Law Country*, in *Wrongful Conviction: International Perspectives on Miscarriages of Justice* 139, 143 (Ronald C. Huff & Martin Killias eds., 2008).

[106] William L.F. Festiner, *Plea Contracts in West Germany*, 13 Law & Soc'y Rev. 309, 314–15 (1979).

[107] Lucian E. Dervan, *Bargained Justice: Plea-Bargaining's Innocence Problem and the* Brady *Safety-Valve*, 2012 Utah L. Rev. 51, 82.

[108] On the actual doctrine of the U.S. Supreme Court and *Alford* plea, see supra Section II.1 and notes 10–11.

The National Registry of Exonerations founded in 2012 provides detailed information about every known exoneration in the United States since 1989.[109] As of November 2015, 15 percent of known exonerees pleaded guilty. Forty-four innocent murder defendants agreed to a plea bargain to avoid the death penalty. Nearly all manslaughter guilty plea exonerations started as murder cases and were plea bargained down to manslaughter. Finally, the more the prosecutors were willing to sweeten the deal in homicide cases, the higher the proportion of innocent defendants who pleaded guilty.[110]

The proportion of guilty pleas among the exonerees in the Registry seems to indicate that innocent defendants tend to elect trials over pleas. For various reasons this does not reflect the whole reality. With the exception of twenty-eight misdemeanors, the Registry contains only serious cases. This represents a highly atypical group, since misdemeanors make up at least 80 percent of criminal convictions.[111] In addition, innocent defendants who plead guilty have difficulties in convincing others of their innocence. Furthermore, the pathway to exoneration is extremely time-consuming. Therefore, it is likely that those wrongfully convicted to long sentences will have an interest in proving their innocence, while the others would rather put the injustice behind them and accept their convictions. It may fairly be assumed that wrongful convictions after plea bargain occur to a higher extent than the Registry would suggest. Although it is not possible to give exact data about the number of wrongful convictions in plea bargaining, the Registry confirms the concerns expressed by legal scholars.

b. *Plea-Bargaining-Type Procedures in Civil Law Systems*

Plea-bargaining-type procedures in civil law systems face many of the same concerns as U.S. plea bargaining. Some legal scholars argue that there might be a risk of increased wrongful convictions since the defendant might admit his guilt to avoid the uncertainties of trial outcomes.[112] Furthermore, the prosecutor might accuse the defendant of a more serious crime or of an additional crime in order to induce a plea to the proper crime. Another concern is that this alternative proceeding might prejudice socially weaker defendants since a state-appointed lawyer does not necessarily defend them with the same diligence as a lawyer of their choice would.[113] In France, because this alternative is applicable for

[109] National Registry of Exonerations, a project of the Newkirk Center for Science & Society at University of California Irvine, the University of Michigan Law School and Michigan State University College of Law, *available at* http://www.law.umich.edu/special/exoneration/Pages/about.aspx (last visited May 7, 2017).

[110] Six percent of exonerated homicide defendants who pleaded guilty were sentenced to life with parole, 10 percent of exonerated homicide defendants who pleaded guilty were sentenced to lesser terms of imprisonment for murder, and 49 percent of exonerated homicide defendants who pleaded guilty were sentenced for manslaughter. For detailed results, see *Innocents Who Plead Guilty, supra* note 16.

[111] National Registry of Exonerations, Why So Few Misdemeanor Exonerations?, *available at* https://www.law.umich.edu/special/exoneration/Pages/misdosoct2015.aspx (last visited Sept. 19, 2017).

[112] *See, e.g.*, Daniel Jositsch & Patrick Bischoff, *Das abgekürzte Verfahren gemäss Art. 365–369 des Entwurfs zu einer Schweizerischen Strafprozessordnung*, in *Festschrift für Franz Ricklin*, 429, 435 (M.A. Niggli et al. eds., 2007); Kuhn, *supra* note 34, at 167.

[113] Georges Greiner, *Schuld ohne Sühne? Am Beispiel des "plea bargaining" nach neuer StPO*, Forumpoenale 234, 236 (2009).

offenses that carry a prison sentence of up to ten years and enables the prosecutor to impose a sentence of no more than one year imprisonment, the pressure on the defendant to confess may be problematic. In Switzerland, since the introduction in 2011 of the abbreviated proceedings, no empirical studies have been conducted to verify whether the concerns expressed by legal scholars are justified and whether this alternate proceeding contributes to more wrongful convictions than ordinary proceedings. The situation is similar in France. Although the French guilty plea was introduced in 2004, empirical research evaluating this procedure is still missing.

The peculiarities of the German plea bargaining, where the judge is usually involved in negotiations, has the advantage of involving a neutral party in the bargaining process. At the same time, this requirement raises certain additional concerns about judicial bias and coercion. Critics argue that pleas are not supervised carefully enough by judges and that a dominant judge might coerce a defendant into entering a guilty plea.[114] In order to make sentence bargaining more attractive, the judge might inform the defendant during informal negotiations that the sentence imposed after a trial would be much higher than the sentence in the case of a confession. To minimize the potential risk of a disproportionate negotiated sentence, the Federal Supreme Court has held that sentences must neither be too lenient as a result of plea bargaining, nor too harsh where plea negotiations have failed.[115] In addition, to reduce this risk of coercion, the Federal Supreme Court has held that the defendant cannot be pressured to enter a plea bargain through threats of a higher sentence or through unlawful promises.[116] Although procedural rules guarantee that the judge is obliged to announce in open court the content of the agreement, it may be assumed that potentially unlawful promises or threats that might influence the defendant to accept the bargain will not be presented. Hence, this rule is not an efficient safeguard against judicial coercion.[117] The most recent survey on plea bargaining conducted in 2012 in Germany found that more than half of the surveyed defense lawyers had one client that they believed had made a false confession to get away with a more lenient sentence.[118]

2. Penal Orders

When proceedings are simplified in a way that gives the prosecutor wide power and restricts the rights of defendants, this can lead to more convictions of innocent people. Four factors inherent in penal order proceedings may increase the risk of wrongful convictions: (1) negligent investigation, (2) the authority issuing the decision, (3) the form and time limit to contest the charges, and (4) the defendant's background or behavior (e.g., indifference, ignorance of the law, and fear of an unfavorable outcome, such as the costs of a contested hearing).

[114] Turner, *supra* note 56, at 232. [115] For an overview of decisions, see *id.* at 217 n.86.
[116] *Id.* at 232. [117] *Id.* at 232–33. [118] Altenhain et al., *supra* note 55, at 134.

From the criminal justice systems considered in this contribution, recent research on wrongful convictions has only been conducted in Switzerland. The Swiss research analyzed all successful petitions of revision in Switzerland between 1995 and 2004 and found that penal order proceedings were more vulnerable to error compared to ordinary proceedings.[119] Over the considered time period, from a total of 236 admitted petitions of revision, 159 concerned penal orders.[120] Although this number is not out of proportion when considering the number of penal orders issued, it is highly probable that in this area, there are many more wrongful convictions than those discovered by the research, since it can be assumed that a high percentage of convicted persons waive their right to file an objection and prefer to pay a fine.[121]

The results of the research suggest that wrongful convictions of factually innocent persons after a trial play a relatively minor role. In the majority of cases, when a defendant's petition of revision was successful, the legal error concerned the sentence and not the verdict; frequently, the sentence imposed by the court was too high because the court had failed to recognize a reduced criminal responsibility due to some mental problems of the defendant.[122] In contrast, the research revealed that successful petitions for revision in penal order cases mainly concerned factually innocent defendants. Wrongful identification and poorly conducted investigation by the police and the prosecution were the leading factors contributing to wrongful convictions.[123]

V. Prospects for Reform

1. Plea Bargaining in the United States and in Civil Law Systems

In the U.S. criminal justice system, plea deals are the common way to handle criminal cases. However, this practice remains controversial. As discussed previously, critics argue that coercion is a major concern.

Different solutions may be envisaged to reduce coercion and the risk of wrongful convictions. Professor Laura Appleman proposes the introduction of citizens into the process by convening a plea jury.[124] Members of the plea jury would consider the terms

[119] Martin Killias et al., *Erreurs judiciaires en Suisse de 1995 à 2004: Rapport au Fonds National Suisse de la Recherche Scientifique* (2007).

[120] *Id.* at 22.

[121] Killias, *supra* note 105, at 150–51; Gwladys Gilliéron, *Strafbefehlsverfahren und plea bargaining als Quelle von Fehlurteilen* 102, 135 (2010).

[122] Killias et al., *supra* note 119, at 39; Gwladys Gilliéron, *Wrongful Convictions in Switzerland: A Problem of Summary Proceedings*, 80 U. Cin. L. Rev. 1145, 1159–60 (2012).

[123] Killias et al., *supra* note 119, at 4, 42; Gilliéron, *supra* note 122, at 1160–61. For a detailed discussion, see Gilliéron, *supra* note 121, at 101–46.

[124] Laura Appleman, *Defending the Jury: Crime, Community, and the Constitution* 124–58 (2015).

of each plea deal brought before the court and then decide whether it is fair. A plea jury would allow the community to provide a check on prosecutors. Other solutions inspired by foreign legal systems might include limiting the practice to less serious crimes, offering a lower sentencing discount for confessing to an offense, and permitting full access to the prosecutor's files.[125]

In the European criminal justice systems surveyed, plea bargaining is not nearly as frequently used as in the United States. Although the risk of wrongful convictions certainly exists, this issue is only rarely addressed by scholars. In this field, research remains to be done. However, as compared to the United States, overall, the practice in Europe is less coercive. It is not possible for defendants to plead guilty while at the same time asserting their innocence, and judges are still oriented toward truth-seeking. In inquisitorial justice systems, the prosecutor is obliged to investigate in an objective way, taking into account exculpatory and inculpatory evidence with equal care. Fuller investigation of the facts has the advantage that prosecutors will be less likely to charge innocent persons and that they will be less likely to propose enormous sentence reductions to defendants who have committed serious offenses.

2. Penal Orders

The modalities and the scope of application of penal orders differ between the criminal justice systems studied. Common features are that the prosecutor is not obliged to hear the defendant prior to the decision and that there is no court hearing. Given the limited procedural guarantees, this procedure should be reserved for minor offenses. However, in the Swiss criminal justice system, prosecutors can impose a custodial sentence of up to six months imprisonment. In addition, the law does not require the defendant to be represented by a lawyer when a custodial sanction is a possibility. Since penal order proceedings may produce wrongful convictions, this Swiss rule must be criticized. European criminal justice systems should refrain from the tendency to extend penal order proceedings to more serious crimes. They should insert rules that best respect the defendant's legal rights such as a compulsory hearing when the prosecutor intends to impose a custodial sanction.

VI. Conclusions

Criminal trials have traditionally been the normative procedure for determining criminal charges. In modern criminal justice systems, criminal convictions are overwhelmingly the result of plea bargaining or abbreviated procedures. Prosecutors in

[125] Gilliéron, *supra* note 40, at 336–37; Jenia I. Turner, *Plea Bargaining and Disclosure in Germany and the United States: Comparative Lessons*, 57 Wm. & Mary L. Rev. 1549 (2016).

these proceedings play the central role. In fact, their decisions are to a large extent adjudicatory. This is particularly true for the Swiss penal order, where prosecutors have the power to impose a prison sentence of up to six months without approval of the court. It is up to the defendant to raise an objection and ask for a full trial. Although plea bargaining proceedings still require a decision by the court, the main hearing in these procedures provides restriction on prosecutorial power of a much lesser degree than in the ordinary proceedings. In civil law systems, instead of conducting an evidentiary proceeding at the principal hearing, the examination of the court will be limited to ascertaining that the rights conferred to the defendant have been respected and that the confession of the accused is credible. Thus, the assessment of the defendant's responsibility is in reality made within the office of the prosecutor.

The accumulation of too much power in the hands of prosecutors without effective control mechanisms over their activity may increase the risk of abuse and with it the risk of wrongful convictions. Although the risk of wrongful convictions in plea bargaining has preoccupied many scholars in the United States, this issue has mainly been discussed on a theoretical basis. In civil law systems, this problem is rarely addressed by scholars. The lack of empirical research, especially in civil law systems, makes it difficult to identify the strengths and weaknesses of alternatives to trials.

Caseload pressure and the call for greater efficiency in criminal justice systems do not predict a decrease of the prosecutor's power. However, legislators must find a way to effectively control the prosecutor's activity in order to prevent abuse of power. Evaluation of alternative proceedings and looking at other criminal justice systems to see how they deal with similar problems can help legislators in this difficult task.

References

Gwladys Gilliéron, *Public Prosecutors in the United States and Europe. A Comparative Analysis with Special Focus on Switzerland, France, and Germany* (2014)

Gwladys Gilliéron, *The Risks of Summary Proceedings, Plea Bargains, and Penal Orders in Producing Wrongful Convictions in the US and Europe*, in *Wrongful Convictions and Miscarriages of Justice: Causes and Remedies in North American and European Criminal Justice Systems* (Ronald C. Huff & Martin Killias eds., 2013)

Irma Jaggi, *Die strafprozessuale Absprache vor den Schranken des Gerichts—Rolle und Einfluss des Gerichts im abgekürzten Verfahren* (2016)

Susanne Kobor, *Bargaining in the Criminal Justice Systems of the United States and Germany: A Matter of Justice and Administrative Efficiency Within Legal, Cultural Context* (2008)

Victoria Kopec, *Plaider Coupable et vérité juridique en France et aux États-Unis. Le Droit et la morale entre raison et passion* (2011)

The Prosecutor in Transnational Perspective (Erik Luna & Marianne Wade eds., 2012)

Babacar Niang, *Le "plaider coupable" en France et aux États-Unis au regard des principes directeurs du procès pénal* (2014)

Julia Peters, *Urteilsabsprachen im Strafprozess. Die deutsche Regelung im Vergleich mit Entwicklungen in England & Wales, Frankreich und Polen* (2011)

Jean Pradel, *Le plaider coupable, confrontation des droits américain, italien et français*, in *Revue internationale de droit comparé* 57 (2005)
Christoph Safferling & Elisa Hoven, Special Issue Editors, *Special Issue—Plea Bargains in Germany*, 15 German L.J. (2014)
Dirk Sauer & Sebastian Münkel, *Absprachen im Strafprozess* (C.F. Müller 2d ed. 2014)
Jenia I. Turner, *Plea Bargaining Across Borders* (2009)

CHAPTER 33

PLEA BARGAINING UNDER THE COMMON LAW

MARY VOGEL

I. Introduction

Among the most paradoxical features of Anglo-American criminal law is the practice of plea bargaining. Our popular image of justice under the common law is that of a jury trial. Yet, in actual fact, a very different process produces most convictions—plea bargaining, a practice whereby a defendant enters a plea of guilty in anticipation of leniency from a prosecutor or judge.[1] This tendency to reward those claiming to be guilty, and who thus are undeserving, aroused much early controversy. Debate now centers on the fairness and voluntariness of the practice, and the quality of "justice" done. Yet despite the intense disagreement that plea bargaining evokes—even in the United States, where it flourishes—an astonishing amount remains unknown, including much about its origins, causes, consequences, and dynamics.[2] One sign of this is that

[1] Thus defined, it does not require that each individual defendant receive a benefit as a result of her or his plea. It is only necessary that those pleading guilty be accorded leniency with sufficient regularity to inspire hope of it on the part of any given defendant. The question of how much of a discount is won, or conversely the penalty for going to trial, still remains. *See* Candace McCoy, *Plea Bargaining as Coercion: The Trial Penalty and Plea Bargaining Reform*, 50 Crim. L.Q. 67 (2005). The "bargain" may be explicit or tacit. The question of how to determine the extent of a discount in the latter case where customary norms are silently at work and terms are unstated has led many studies to understate the frequency of the practice.

[2] For significant overviews the then-extant literature on plea bargaining, *see* Malcolm Feeley, *Perspectives on Plea Bargaining*, 13 L. & Soc'y Rev. 199 (1979); Bruce P. Smith, *Plea Bargaining and the Eclipse of the Jury*, 1 Ann. Rev. L. & Social Sci. 131 (2005). One of the biggest problems has been how to operationalize bargaining practice in order to study it. A methodological approach for operationalizing and analyzing patterns of bargaining is presented in Mary E. Vogel, *Coercion to Compromise: Plea Bargaining, the Courts and the Making of Political Authority* (2007).

support for bargaining is often based on rationales that are challenged by empirical evidence. Uncertainty has made it hard to determine whether plea bargaining should be welcomed, reformed, or even eliminated if one knew how to do so.[3] Mass incarceration and widespread cynicism about criminal justice also suggest something gone awry. Nearly all agree that the nature, logic, and consequences of this controversial practice need to be clarified. If, as Holmes suggested, "law is what the courts do," it is crucial indeed that we do so. This chapter explores what we know today.

This work aims to do several things. It focuses primarily on plea bargaining in the United States and England with brief comparisons to Canada, Australia, and New Zealand, although plea bargaining operates in some form in most of the countries of the British Commonwealth such as India, Pakistan, and South Africa. In what follows, we explore, first, the nature, frequency and patterns of variation of Anglo-American plea bargaining today. The next section examines key goals of criminal justice and controversies about plea bargaining's ability to foster them. The controversies point to outcomes this work explores empirically. Constitutionality, particularly in the U.S. context, asks if plea bargaining is consistent with autonomy, fairness, and efficiency. Next, we problematize competing accounts of how plea bargaining developed by delving into its causes. We will see that reasons it began have faded with time and been supplanted by arrangements with different dynamics. Finally, we analyze the consequences of plea bargaining for the nature of "justice" meted out.

II. Pervasiveness and Patterns of Variation

1. U.S. Plea Bargaining

Across the countries of the common law, plea bargaining has emerged as the dominant mode of disposing of criminal cases. Plea bargaining has had a checkered history in the United States. It existed there as early as the 1830s and 1840s, although it was not formally acknowledged by the American courts until later in the century.[4] Once established in the United States, plea bargaining met with a mixed reception. Initially, it spread to encompass the majority of convictions in Boston's Municipal Court and, by 1845 it appeared in New York's mid-tier courts and in Essex County, Massachusetts.[5] By the

[3] Michael Gorr, *The Morality of Plea Bargaining*, 26 Social Theory & Practice 129 (2000).

[4] *See* Vogel, *supra* note 2; Mary E. Vogel, *The Social Origins of Plea Bargaining: Conflict and the Law in the Emergence of Plea Bargaining, 1830–1860*, 33 L. & Soc'y Rev. 161 (1999); Mike McConville & Chester L. Mirsky, *Jury Trials and Plea Bargaining: A True History* (2005); Lawrence M. Friedman, *Crime and Punishment in American History* (1993). One heavily contested account suggests a slightly earlier start to American plea bargaining in Essex County, Massachusetts, in the late 1700s. George Fisher, *Plea Bargaining's Triumph* (2003). *See* discussion of Fisher's argument *infra* Section V.2.

[5] McConville & Mirsky, *supra* note 4; Fisher, *supra* note 4.

early 1900s, we see reform commissions in New York expressing explicit concern about the practice.[6] The few court cases that addressed the guilty plea and its negotiation during the late nineteenth century tended mainly to challenge it.[7] While initially a practice in which, at least in U.S. courts, judges played a key role, plea bargaining ultimately became one in which prosecutors played a leading part.[8] Other common law countries vary in that regard. After a period of increased respectability during the mid-1900s, the late 1960s and early 1970s saw a renewal of earlier opposition to bargained pleas.[9] Criticism peaked in America in 1973 with a proposal from the National Advisory Commission on Criminal Justice Standards and Goals that plea bargaining be abolished by 1978—one not adopted because it was unclear both how to accomplish it and what its results would be.

In the United States, by the 1920s bargained guilty pleas were the most frequent route to case disposition for felonies.[10] The practice grew steadily in subsequent decades.[11] Today, plea bargaining is estimated to account for the disposition of 90 percent or more of all criminal cases.[12]

Guilty plea rates vary by type of offense. The more serious the charge, the less likely, generally, a defendant is to plead guilty.[13] Trial rates are lower for drug offenses and burglaries, for example, than for rape and murder—although for every type of crime a majority of convictions are achieved by guilty pleas rather than trial. Overall guilty pleas accounted for 97.4 percent of all federal criminal convictions in 2012. The acquittal rate

[6] N.Y. State Crime Commission, *Report to the Commission of the Sub-Committee on Statistics* (1927).

[7] *See, e.g.*, Commonwealth v. Battis, 1 Mass. 94 (1804); Edwards v. People, 39 Mich. 760 (1878); People v. Lepper, 51 Mich. 196, 16 N.W. 377 (1883); Saunders v. State, 10 Tex. Crim. 336 (1881); Meyers v. State, 115 Ind. 554, 18 N.E. 42 (1888); Mounts v. Commonwealth, 89 Ky. 274, 12 S.W. 311 (1889); Cornelison v. Commonwealth, 84 Ky. 583, 2 S.W. 235 (1886); Wolfe v. State, 102 Ark. 295, 144 S.W. 208 (1912); Pope v. State, 56 Fla. 81, 47 So. 487 (1908); and People v. Bonheim, 307 Ill. 316, 138 N.E. 627 (1923).

[8] Fisher, *supra* note 4.

[9] A. Davis, *Sentences for Sale: A New Look at Plea Bargaining in England and America*, 1971 Crim. L. Rev. 150, 218.

[10] Albert W. Alschuler, *Plea Bargaining and Its History*, 13 L. & Soc'y Rev. 211, 215 (1979).

[11] For earlier estimates, *see, e.g.*, Brady v. United States, 397 U.S. 742, 752 n.10 (1970); Harry Kalven & Hans Zeisel, *The American Jury* (1966) (guilty plea rates ranging from 89 percent for auto theft to 34 percent for murder); Donald J. Newman, *Conviction: The Determination of Guilt or Innocence Without Trial* 3 (1966) (estimating in 1966 that "roughly 90% of all [American] criminal convictions . . . [were] by pleas of guilty"); Herbert S. Miller, *Plea Bargaining in the United States* (1978) (estimating slightly lower figure); Mona Lynch, *Hard Bargains* (2016); Abraham S. Blumberg, *Criminal Justice* (1976); Arthur Rossett & Donald Cressey, *Justice by Consent: Plea Bargaining in the American Courthouse* (1976).

[12] *See* Mark Motivans, Bureau of Justice Statistics, DOJ, NCJ 248470, *Federal Justice Statistics 2012—Statistical Tables* 17 tbl.4.2 (2015). In U.S. federal courts in 2007–2011, guilty plea rates increased from 95.8 to 96.9 percent of all convictions; the percentage of convictions following trial declined from 4.2 to 3.1 percent. U.S. Sentencing Commission, *2011 Sourcebook of Federal Sentencing Statistics* fig.C, https://perma.cc/V8K2-AA86. For data on U.S. state courts, *see* Brian A. Reaves, Bureau of Justice Statistics, DOJ, NCJ 243777, *Defendants in Large Urban Counties, 2009—Statistical Tables* 22, 24 tbl.21 (2013) (in state courts in the seventy-five largest counties, reporting guilty plea rates for major crimes and summarizing: "nearly all convictions were the result of a guilty plea rather than a trial").

[13] James E. Bond, *Plea Bargaining and Guilty Pleas* (1975).

in felony trials in federal courts the same year was a mere 0.5 percent; the rate of dismissals was only slightly higher at 6.2 percent.[14]

All the foregoing American research infers plea bargaining's frequency primarily from guilty pleas. But a few studies have examined the process of negotiation directly. In the 1960s, Vetri interviewed 205 prosecutors and found wide variation: 13.6 percent of offices never bargained, while 5 percent bargained in nine out of ten cases. Nearly a third indicated they bargained—more or less explicitly—a majority of their guilty pleas.[15] But studying explicit bargaining underestimates its frequency because it overlooks tacitly anticipated leniency—known as "implicit bargaining." When explicit negotiations decrease, implicit forms may compensate. It is also not uncommon in some jurisdictions, notably U.S. federal courts, for the defense and prosecution to negotiate before charges are filed, and about which charges will be filed—a practice that can be hard to document or study.[16] "Charge bargaining" is explicitly permitted after initial charges are filed as well. Negotiation over this discretionary decision is possible (and tempting) because prosecutors often have the option to pursue a case under several different statutes—each carrying very different penalties.[17]

With judicial acceptance of plea bargaining in the United States has come somewhat greater regulation. When negotiated in federal court, bargains must accord with Rule 11 of the Federal Rules of Criminal Procedure, which provides that the prosecution and defense "may discuss and reach a plea agreement" pursuant to which the prosecution will:

> (a) not bring, or will move to dismiss, other charges; (b) recommend a particular sentence or sentencing range is appropriate...; or (c) agree that a specific sentence or sentencing range is the appropriate disposition of the case, or that a particular provision of the Sentencing Guidelines... does or does not apply.[18]

Note that the second kind of agreement may have no precise analog in many other common law countries, where tradition prohibits prosecutors from arguing for a specific sentence (as opposed to summing up for the court the law and facts relevant to a defendant's sentence). An agreement on the federal prosecutor's sentencing recommendation does not bind the judge, but an agreement on a specific sentence or range is binding once the judge accepts the plea agreement. Among the most common bases for judges to reduce federal sentences below the recommended guideline range is the prosecutor's

[14] *See* Motivans, *supra* note 12; Reaves, *supra* note 12.

[15] Dominick R. Vetri, *Guilty Plea Bargaining: Compromises by Prosecutors to Secure Guilty Pleas*, 112 U. Pa. L. Rev. 864, 897–99 (1964).

[16] *See* G. Nicholas Herman, *Plea Bargaining* 131–35 (2012).

[17] *See* Irby v. United States, 390 F. 2nd 423, 429 (D.C. Cir. 1976) (Bazelon J., dissenting) ("[O]ften it takes nothing more than a fertile imagination to spin several crimes out of a single transaction."); Herman, *supra* note 16, at 129.

[18] Fed. R. Crim. Pro. 11(c). The U.S. Supreme Court in *United States v. Booker*, 543 U.S. 220 (2005), struck down the mandatory nature of the federal sentencing guidelines—previously in effect since 1987—converting them into advisory, but still influential, guidelines. Post-*Booker*, district courts still must take the guidelines into account but have greater authority to depart from the narrow sentencing ranges recommended by the guidelines.

confirmation that the defendant provided "substantial assistance" to law enforcement, typically by providing information against other defendants, so that topic is likely to be a one of active negotiation.[19] Plea agreements must be in writing and can be accepted or rejected by the court, but federal judges are prohibited from participating in plea discussions.[20] Nonetheless, Rule 11 increased judicial scrutiny of plea agreements; rules in many states now authorize some judicial involvement in bargaining, at least to give English-style sentence indications or provide an advance notice of whether an agreement would likely be approved.[21] Pleas bargained in state courts are often less formal and well-documented. For all guilty pleas, the judges "address the defendant personally" to assure a guilty plea's voluntariness and "determine that there is a factual basis for the plea."[22]

Finally, we should note that both U.S. and English criminal justice systems employ distinct kinds of agreements closely analogous to negotiated guilty pleas. Immunity agreements provide potential defendants with an assurance of non-prosecution in exchange for especially valuable assistance to law enforcement through testimony ("Queen's evidence" in the UK), information disclosures, or other means.[23] And both countries now employ non-prosecution agreements (often in corporate crime cases), pursuant to which defendants, without acknowledging guilt, agree to certain terms—civil fine or restitution payments, ongoing reporting requirements, regulatory compliance, internal corporate reforms, etc.—in exchange for an assurance of non-prosecution.[24] Additionally, in both countries civil forfeiture agreements are sometimes components of negotiated resolutions, especially in drug trafficking or organized-crime cases.[25]

2. Plea Bargaining in England and Wales

In England, by contrast, less is known, and the earliest years of plea bargaining are still being explored. As recently as the 1990s, the very existence of "plea bargaining" was explicitly denied, particularly by Downing Street. Due largely to official denials, the

[19] *See U.S. Sentencing Guidelines Manual* §§ 5K1.1 & 5K3.1; Herman, *supra* note 16, at 131–36.

[20] Fed. R. Crim. Pro. 11(c). *But see* William McDonald, *Plea Bargaining* (U.S. Gov't Printing Office: 1985) (reporting that whether written agreements were signed varied widely across U.S. localities).

[21] *See* Nancy J. King & Ronald F. Wright, *The Invisible Revolution in Plea Bargaining: Managerial. Judging and Judicial Participation in Negotiations*, 95 Tex. L. Rev. 325 (2016) (study of state judges' roles in plea bargaining); Samuel Walker, *Taming the System: The Control of Discretion in Criminal Justice, 1950–1990*, at 106 (1993).

[22] Fed. R. Crim. Pro. 11(b); *see also* Walker, *supra* note 21, at 105–06 (1993) (discussing Rule 11 and noting U.S. judges reject only 2 percent of proffered guilty pleas); Herman, *supra* note 16, at 1–4 & 100–10 (describing components of plea bargains).

[23] *See* Serious Organised Crime and Police Act 2005 ss 71–73 (U.K.); 18 U.S.C. §§ 6002–6003 (2016).

[24] *See* Brandon L. Garrett, *International Corporate Prosecutions*, in this volume (describing deferred- and non-prosecution agreements with corporate defendants in the United States and UK); Colin King & Nick Lord, *Negotiated Justice and Corporate Crime: The Legitimacy of Civil Recovery Orders and Deferred Prosecution Agreements* (2018); U.S. Dep't of Justice, *U.S. Attorneys' Manual* § 9-27.220 (prosecutors may decline to file criminal charges when effective non-criminal options exist).

[25] *See* Herman, *supra* note 16, at 194–95. On prosecution policy, *see U.S. Attorneys' Manual* §§ 9-113.100 to -113.106; Crown Prosecution Service, *Proceeds of Crime—Legal Guidance* (2018) (Engl. & Wales).

historical development of English bargaining is only slowly coming to light.[26] Nonetheless, it is clear that "trial bargaining" has been occurring for some time.[27] In that practice, judges were marginalized while prosecuting and defending barristers took center stage and negotiated informally. Under the *Turner* rules, judges were formally barred from offering a sentence indication as to the discount on offer for a guilty plea.[28] Sanders and Young suggested that nevertheless consultations, often by indirection, were more common than many believe.[29] This more tacit sentence bargaining coexisted by the 1990s with more explicit, if informal, "cup of tea"-style negotiation between prosecuting and defending barristers. Charge bargains and "fact" bargains increased as well.

Plea bargaining is now pervasive in English practice and widely acknowledged among solicitors, barristers, and scholars.[30] Most convictions in England are produced by a guilty plea and, of those, a majority are bargained.[31] If still somewhat less widespread than in the United States, recent developments, such as *Goodyear*'s abandonment of the *Turner* rules, have opened the way for wider acceptance of the practice. One motivation was the waste of resources from so-called "crack'd trials"—bargains negotiated on the eve of trial (perhaps because barristers who argue an English case come onstage only shortly before trial). As recently as 2004, 22.5 percent of total Crown Court cases were resolved at this late stage.[32]

English plea bargaining long remained less technically developed than U.S. practice, especially that in the federal courts, at least partly due to official denials that it occurred. However, that is changing. Finally, in 1991, the Criminal Justice Act officially recommended leniency for those pleading guilty. In 1994, the Criminal Justice and Public Order Act affirmed the principle that defendants pleading guilty should generally receive a lighter sentence than those convicted at trial. This principle was reaffirmed by the Criminal Justice Act of 2003, which took things a bit farther.[33] In 2004, the Sentencing Guidelines Council issued the first definitive guideline requiring judges to grant a sentence reduction of up to one-third less than the post-trial sentence when a guilty plea is entered.[34] In 2005, *Goodyear* completed England's formal acceptance of

[26] *See* Mary E. Vogel, *Plea Bargaining and Democratic Politics: Legal Discretion and Elite Power in the Great Ages of English Reform* (forthcoming).

[27] John Baldwin & Mike McConville, *Negotiated Justice* (1977).

[28] R v. Turner [1970] 2 Q.B. 321.

[29] Richard Young & Andrew Sanders, *Plea Bargaining and the Next Criminal Justice Bill*, 144 New L.J. 1200 (1994) ("In practice, both defence counsel and judges have abused their right to meet in private... by engaging in sentence bargaining on a wide scale.").

[30] Andrew Sanders & Richard Young, *Criminal Justice* (2010); Danielle Alge, *Pressures to Plea Guilty or Playing the System?: An Exploration of the Causes of Cracked Trials* (2008).

[31] In the Crown Courts of England and Wales in 2009–2012, about 73 percent of charged defendants pled guilty and 91 percent of convictions occurred through guilty pleas. Crown Prosecution Service, *Annual Report and Accounts 2011–12*, at 85 tbl.7 (2012), https://perma.cc/GL6GAKCL. Of the 26.5 percent of charged defendants who did not plead guilty, approximately 13–14 percent went to trial (where 7–8 percent were convicted); the remainder were dismissed or received a judicial acquittal. *Id.*

[32] *Pleas Please Me*, *The Economist*, Sept. 23, 2004.

[33] Criminal Justice Act of 2003 s 144(1).

[34] For the current guidelines, *see* Sentencing Council, *Reduction in Sentence for a Guilty Plea: Definitive Guideline* 5 (2017) (England & Wales) ("The maximum level of reduction in sentence for a guilty plea is one-third"); *see also* the Coroners and Justice Act 2009 s 125(1) ("every court must... follow any sentencing guidelines which are relevant").

plea bargaining by abandoning the *Turner* prohibition on judicial sentence indications and authorizing Crown Court judges to indicate the type (e.g., fine, custody, probation) and magnitude of a sentence on offer should a guilty plea be entered.[35] (Two years earlier, the Criminal Justice Act 2003 authorized an indication of type and magnitude of sentence in the Magistrate's Court.) Plea negotiation received a final boost from the Serious Organised Crime and Police Act of 2005. It extended the power of the Crown Prosecution Service to secure cooperation of minor criminal figures by using strategies that were time honored in England and also authorized under the U.S. Racketeer Influenced and Corrupt Organizations Act of 1970, which permitted immunity in exchange for testimony against codefendants.[36]

Despite long-standing restrictions, the tendency of guilty pleas to elicit leniency in England has historically been well known by judges, lawyers, and, to some extent, defendants alike. This helps illuminates the prevalence of guilty pleas in England's Crown Courts since the early to mid-1800s,[37] and why in recent years more than 70 percent of defendants charged in Crown Court plead guilty (and the rate is nearly as high in Magistrates' Courts).[38] While this guilty plea rate is high, it pales alongside U.S. guilty plea rates of approximately 95 percent today. Whether as cause or effect of the lower guilty plea rate is a matter of some debate, but note that the English acquittal rate of 22 percent in Crown Court contrasts markedly with the aforementioned much lower American felony acquittal rate.

3. Plea Bargaining in Commonwealth Countries

Plea bargaining in some form is widespread in other common law countries as well, although many avoid that term.[39] Data on rates of plea bargaining are scarce in many places, but it is clear that a large majority of convictions are achieved through guilty pleas in Canada and Australia, for example.[40] New Zealand criminal justice likewise

[35] R v. Goodyear [2006] 1 Cr. App. R. (S) 23 (authorizing judges to provide defendants with advance indication of the sentence to follow a plea; any such indication is discretionary with the judge but binding if made).

[36] 18 U.S.C. §§ 1961–1968 (2016).

[37] *See* Vogel, *supra* note 26 (forthcoming).

[38] *See* CPS, *Annual Report*, *supra* note 31, at 86 tbl. 7 (Crown Courts); *id.* 83 tbl. 3 (67.6–68.4 percent guilty pleas in Magistrates' Courts in 2009–2012).

[39] *See generally*, Peter Marcus, et al., *A Comparative Look at Plea Bargaining in Australia, Canada, England, New Zealand and the United States*, 57 Wm. & Mary L. Rev. 1147 (2016).

[40] On Canada, *see* R v. Burlingham [1995] 2 S.C.R. 206, 208 (Can.) (recognizing plea bargaining as an "integral element of the Canadian criminal process"); Marcus et al., *supra* note 39, at 1168 (estimating "a strong majority of criminal prosecutions are resolved by pleas"). In Australia, a leading High Court decision recognizing plea bargaining is GAS v. The Queen (2004) 217 C.L.R. 198, 210–211. *See also* Arie Freiberg, *Non-adversarial Approaches to Criminal Justice*, 17 J. Judicial Admin. 205, 206–07 (2007) (noting guilty plea rates in various Australian courts of 73–95 percent); For data on guilty pleas and plea bargaining in Victoria, *see* Asher Flynn & Kate Fitz-Gibbon, *Bargaining with Defensive Homicide: Examining Victoria's Secretive Plea Bargaining System Post-law Reform*, 35 Melb. U. L. Rev. 905, 912 (2011). On Australia generally, *see* Sharon Roache Anleu & Kathy Mack, *Intersections between In-Court Procedures and the Production of Guilty Pleas*, 10 Australian & New Zealand J. Criminology 1375 (2009).

takes advantage of negotiated guilty pleas. The practice was folded into a broader procedural framework by 2011 legislation, which, among other things, permits judges to facilitate the process through sentence indications.[41] Practice in these Commonwealth jurisdictions broadly share two features with the English system that distinguishes them from U.S. jurisdictions. As previously noted, often prosecutors do not make as adversarial sentencing recommendations (although it can be a fine line between that practice and speaking to relevant facts and sentencing law), and so the parties do not negotiate actively over such recommendations. Judges generally retain greater sentencing discretion than in many U.S. jurisdictions (though often subject to sentencing guidelines), and consequently judicial sentencing indications are generally more important to the plea bargaining process.[42]

One result of this growth of guilty pleas has been very high conviction rates. Beginning in the last decades of the twentieth century, this surge of convictions began to produce an exploding prison population with the introduction of mandatory sentencing laws, which prescribed standardized sentences based on seriousness of a crime and criminal history with adjustments up and down based on a specific series of factors. By the 1990s, "three strikes" provisions in many jurisdictions mandated life imprisonment for a third offense. These policies, together with tougher drug laws, helped to boost both frequency of incarceration and length of sentences, contributing to the exploding prison population in the United States and England since the late 1980s.[43] These practices help explain why rates of imprisonment failed to decrease once crime began to drop in the late 1990s.

III. Critiques of Plea Bargaining

Plea bargaining has been criticized on a number of grounds. The criticisms include: (1) erosion of adversarialism, (2) unconstitutionality, (3) frequency of false convictions, (4) sentencing inequities and irrationalities, (5) administrative shortcomings, (6) reduced deterrence, and (7) diminished rehabilitative capacity. These criticisms have been countered by supporters of the practice. While proponents mainly laud plea bargaining for its efficiencies, critical debate extends beyond expedience.[44] It asks what costs and distortions justice can tolerate.

[41] Criminal Procedure Act 2011 (N.Z.).

[42] *Id.* pt. 1, ss 60, 62 (N.Z.); Marcus et al., *supra* note 39; Arie Freiberg, *Australia: Exercising Discretion in Sentencing Policy and Practice*, 22 Fed. Sent. Rptr. 204, 204 (2010) (sentence indications in Australia).

[43] National Research Council, *The Growth of Incarceration in the United States: Exploring the Causes and Consequences* (2014).

[44] For a fuller overview of these debates, *see* Richard L. Lippke, *The Ethics of Plea Bargaining* (2011); *see also* William J. Stuntz, *Plea Bargaining and Criminal Law's Disappearing Shadow*, 117 Harv. L. Rev. 2548 (2004); Stephen J. Schulhofer, *Plea Bargaining as Disaster*, 101 Yale L.J. 1978 (1992); Moise Berger, *The Case against Plea Bargaining*, 62 A.B.A. J. 621 (1976).

A first critique argues that bargaining erodes adversarialism by fostering cooperation. Others counter that an adversarial approach is ill-suited to produce impartial decisions or even unbiased portrayal of case facts.[45] They argue that bargaining may thus foster a better model. This challenges the institutional bases of adjudication generally and so is tabled for now.[46]

Constitutional challenges contend that bargaining may be coercive and that it may exert a "chilling effect" on a U.S. defendant's Fifth and Sixth Amendment rights against self-incrimination and to a fair trial.[47] For the United Kingdom, plea bargains must satisfy the right to a fair trial under the European Convention on Human Rights.[48] Courts have accepted views of bargaining's advocates that a guilty plea is voluntary, informed and, with assistance by competent counsel, noncoercive. Lately, this claim is bolstered by a view of bargains as contracts that remove a defendant, by agreement, from legal provisions that would usually apply.[49]

The next three criticisms raise issues of fairness, equity, and efficiency. One risk is unfairness in the form of a false conviction. Here critics ask if offers of leniency or penalties following trial exert such strong influence that defendants may plead guilty even when innocent or, at least, do so when a trial acquittal is likely. If the largest discounts are offered in weakest cases, and evidence is usually weakest against the wrongly accused, then innocent defendants may face greatest pressure to plead. Supporters of bargaining respond that defendants should be able to address the risk of wrongful trial convictions through bargaining; one who was falsely accused and then convicted at trial would be sentenced more severely than one who bargained. Thus, they suggest, potential loss is limited and costs and stresses of trial are bypassed. Supporters of bargaining also argue that plea bargaining reduces the risk that the guilty inadvertently walk free. Critics counter that where judges and law enforcement perceive injustice, they may increase dismissals or screen cases for prosecution more closely.

Critics next argue that plea bargaining aggravates sentencing inequities. Legal philosophers and constitutional or human rights law call for proportionality in sentencing.[50] Critics argue that bargaining distorts proportionality by introducing sentencing factors

[45] Jerome Frank, *The "Fight" Theory versus the "Truth" Theory*, in *Courts on Trial: Myth and Reality in American Justice* 80–102 (1949).

[46] Robert A. Kagan, *Adversarial Legalism: The American Way of Law* (2003).

[47] *See, e.g.*, McCoy, *supra* note 1.

[48] On the ECHR and plea bargaining, *see* Jenia Iontcheva Turner & Thomas Weigend, *Negotiated Justice*, in *International Criminal Procedure: Principles and Rules* 1376, 1398–99 (Goran Sluiter et al. eds., 2013).

[49] On bargaining as contract, *see, e.g.*, Frank H. Easterbrook, *Plea Bargaining as Compromise*, 101 Yale L.J. 1968 (1992).

[50] *See, e.g.*, Andrew Von Hirsch & Andrew Ashworth, *Proportionate Sentencing: Exploring the Principles* (2005); Ewing v. California, 538 U.S. 11 (2003) (summarizing the U.S. Supreme Court's weak proportionality doctrine under the cruel and unusual punishment clause); R v. Smith, [1987] 1 S.C.R. 1045 (Can.) (striking down sentence as unconstitutionally disproportionate). For recent decisions defining ECHR Art. 3 limits on sentencing disproportionality, *see* Öcalan v. Turkey, App. No. 24069/03, Eur. Ct. H.R., Mar. 18, 2014; Vinter and Others v. the United Kingdom [GC], App. No. 66069/09, Eur. Ct H.R., July 9, 2013; Rrapo v. Albania, App. No. 58555/10, Eur. Ct. H.R., Sept. 25, 2012.

other than seriousness, boosting prosecutorial power at the expense of the judge,[51] and allowing experienced recidivists to negotiate unduly lenient sentences.[52] They query whether unfettered ability to forfeit trial may yield discriminatory sentencing. Those who favor bargaining retort that the practice allows individualized sentencing, offsets overly harsh sentencing, and enables rewards to remorseful and cooperating defendants.

Critics further contend plea bargaining ushers in administrative shortcomings and ultimately had little effect on case backlogs. They also counter that other means, such as the "bench trial" or more intensive "prosecutorial screening" procedures, can facilitate efficiency in criminal process equally well with much less undue pressure on defendants.[53] Defenders of the practice insist that bargaining alleviates crowding, speeds cases to disposition, and avoids the costs of trial.

Two final criticisms focus on whether bargaining adversely affects deterrence and rehabilitation. These last two challenges raise the question of what criminal justice goals we prioritize—a question that must be settled before plea bargaining's effects on them can be fully estimated. Thus, we reserve these two issues for consideration elsewhere.

Our assessment of the persuasiveness of these critiques turns on an analysis of bargaining's consequences. We ask, first, does bargaining breach constitutional guarantees? Second, does it convict unfairly? Third, does plea bargaining nurture inequity? Fourth, does plea bargaining improve administrative efficiency? We turn now to probe its basic constitutionality. Since assessing impacts of the practice is aided by knowing why plea bargaining occurs, we examine what is known about bargaining's causes. We conclude by exploring bargaining's consequences for fairness in conviction, equity in disposition and sentencing, and administrative efficiency.

IV. Constitutionality and Human Rights

During the late twentieth and early twenty-first centuries, the U.S. Supreme Court and the English Court of Appeals gradually but explicitly approved plea bargaining. Prior to the 1970s, the U.S. Supreme Court avoided general findings on plea bargaining and, instead, reviewed challenges on a case-by-case basis. During the 1950s and 1960s, the

[51] By enhancing prosecutorial discretion, critics argue, bargaining may foster discrimination since it precludes most avenues of appeal or review.

[52] Alge, *supra* note 30.

[53] *See* Ronald Wright & Marc Miller, *The Screening/Bargaining Tradeoff*, 55 Stan. L. Rev. 29 (2002); Stephen J. Schulhofer, *Is Plea Bargaining Inevitable?* 97 Harv. L. Rev. 1037 (1984) (in Philadelphia, only 25 percent of convictions stem from guilty pleas); *see also* Donald McIntyre & David Lippman, *Prosecutors and Early Disposition of Felony Cases*, 56 A.B.A.J. 1154, 1157 (1970) (80 percent of criminal cases in Baltimore resolved by bench trials); D. Newman *Conviction: The Determination of Guilt or Innocence Without Trial* (1966).

Court showed tolerance—mainly by sidelining the issue of plea bargaining. However, beginning about 1970, the U.S. Supreme Court decided a series of direct challenges to bargaining's practices. It consistently affirmed the constitutionality of the core practices of plea bargains, including pleading guilty in order to avoid a harsher penalty after a trial conviction.

In 1970 in *Parker v. North Carolina*, the U.S. Supreme Court authorized a form of trial penalty when it held that "an otherwise valid plea is not involuntary because [it is] induced by the defendant's desire to limit the maximum...penalty to less than that authorized if there is a jury trial."[54] The same year in *North Carolina v. Alford*,[55] the Court similarly held that a guilty plea for a life sentence when the trial alternative is the death penalty is not unconstitutionally coercive. The justices reasoned that the fact the defendant "would not have pleaded guilty except for the opportunity to limit the possible penalty [of death] does not...demonstrate that the plea was not a free and rational choice."[56] This decision revealed the Court's presumption that the defendant consistently reaps a benefit for pleading guilty in such a situation and that this does not contravene voluntariness. Also in 1970, in *McMann v. Richardson* the Court considered the validity of a plea bargain when induced through defendant's mistaken belief that the prosecution could use his allegedly coerced confession as trial evidence. The Court held that the guilty plea, based on an implicit bargain, was valid if the defendant had "sufficient awareness of the relevant circumstances and likely consequences."[57] In these decisions and subsequent ones, the Court cited advantages accruing to defendants who bargain while acknowledging that "the decision to plead guilty before the evidence is in frequently involves the making of difficult judgments."[58]

In 1971, the U.S. Supreme Court in *Santobello v. New York* used the term "plea bargain" for the first time in a majority opinion and affirmed the practice to be legitimate.[59] *Santobello* held that a bargained guilty plea is invalid if its terms are breached by a prosecutor. Writing for the majority, Chief Justice Burger embraced plea bargaining: "disposition of charges after plea discussions is not only an essential part of the [judicial] process but highly desirable."[60] The Court underscored the state's interest in speedy case disposition, which it presumed plea bargaining to advance. This presumption periodically would recur.

Two decisions in 1978 affirmed the use of so-called trial penalties in plea bargaining. In *Bordenkircher v. Hayes*,[61] the Court held that the fact a prosecutor adds charges in order to greatly enhance a post-trial sentence after a defendant refuses to plead guilty does not violate due process. Justice Stewart asserted that, in the negotiation between prosecution and defense, both "arguably possess relatively equal bargaining power." This explicit presumption of equality of arms, in Stewart's view, justifies why, as long

[54] 397 U.S. 790, 795 (1970), citing Brady v. United States, 397 U.S. 742 (1970).

[55] 400 U.S. 25 (1970).

[56] 400 U.S. at 31. *Alford* also held that a court can accept a guilty plea and enter a valid judgment of conviction even if the defendant merely consents to conviction and does not admit his factual guilt.

[57] 397 U.S. 759, 766 (1970). [58] 397 U.S. at 769. [59] 404 U.S. 257, 260 (1971).

[60] 404 U.S. at 261. [61] 434 U.S. 357 (1978).

as the defendant is free to reject an offer, "there is no . . . element of punishment or retaliation."[62] *Corbitt v. New Jersey* involved a challenge to a homicide statute that mandated life in prison for defendants convicted at trial but authorized a lesser sentence for those who entered a plea of *nolo contendere*.[63] The Court held that the sentencing distinction did not unconstitutionally burden the defendant's decision to go to trial, noting "that not every burden on the exercise of a constitutional right, and not every pressure or encouragement to waive such a right, is invalid. Specifically, there is no per se rule against encouraging guilty pleas. We have squarely held that a State may encourage a guilty plea by offering substantial benefits in return for the plea . . . [including] a lesser penalty than that required to be imposed after a guilty verdict by a jury."[64]

Throughout these decisions, two themes stand out. First, the U.S. Supreme Court emphasizes a compelling state interest in efficient case resolution and the Court believes that plea bargaining is critical to that interest. Second, the Court views plea bargaining as a voluntary and noncoercive practice in which equality of arms exists between defendant and the State. Third, the Court conceives of plea bargaining as closely analogous to private contract negotiations, which leads it to incorporate private contract norms into the constitutional law of plea bargaining and to describe plea bargaining as a market-like process. "[P]lea bargains are essentially contracts,"[65] and by definition are characterized by "mutuality of advantage" and are "mutually beneficial."[66] Judicial regulation for "fairness" might "stifle the market for plea bargains."[67]

Finally, against these developments, two recent U.S. Supreme Court decisions have modestly strengthened defendants' ability to confront the state in a bargaining-dominated justice system. *Lafler v. Cooper* and *Missouri v. Frye* hold that defendants' right to competent legal representation includes the right to be informed by their lawyer of any plea bargain offers and to receive competent legal advice about the choice between a trial and a guilty plea.[68]

Given the many presumptions in the Court decisions about how plea bargaining operates, we should ask how the system works and what are its consequences. We shall see that the Court's presumptions thus far find little support in existing research literature.

[62] 434 U.S. at 362–63. *See also* United States v. Goodwin, 457 U.S. 368 (1982) (holding that it was not unconstitutionally vindictive for a prosecutor to add charges for trial after plea negotiations broke down).

[63] 439 U.S. 212 (1978).

[64] 439 U.S. at 218–20. *United States v. Jackson*, 390 U.S. 570 (1968), can be distinguished from *Corbitt*; in *Jackson*, the death penalty could be imposed only at trial.

[65] Puckett v. United States, 556 U.S. 129, 137 (2009). The Court cites treatises on private contract law to support its constitutional law decisions on plea bargaining. *See, e.g.*, Mabry v. Johnson, 467 U.S. 504, 507–09 (1984) and United States v. Hyde, 520 U.S. 670, 677–78 (1997).

[66] *Corbitt*, 439 U.S. at 222.

[67] United States v. Mezzanatto, 513 U.S. 196, 208 (1995). For an extended discussion of private market and contract themes in this body of law, *see* Darryl K. Brown, *Free Market Criminal Justice* 91–118 (2016).

[68] Missouri v. Frye, 566 U.S. 134 (2012); Lafler v. Cooper, 566 U.S. 156 (2012).

V. Causes of Plea Bargaining in England and America

Despite the prominence of plea bargaining, much about its causes is still largely unknown. We consider now existing research on its causes, which was produced by scholars in the post–World War II years who told a then-astonishing story: the jury trial was disappearing, replaced by plea bargaining. Earliest sociolegal scholars advanced four competing explanations for the emergence of plea bargaining.

1. Early Sociolegal Models

Rationality. From the standpoint of a "rational" model of organizations, which includes the law and economics approach of "bargaining in the shadow of trial," plea bargaining occurs because it moves beyond a zero-sum interaction to produce cooperation that cuts cost, time, and effort to boost efficiency. It suggests parties forecast an expected trial outcome, discount it by the probability of acquittal, and offer a proportional discount. The problem is that, on this model, bargaining would always have yielded savings. Yet historically, plea bargaining has not always existed. Thus efficiency alone cannot explain the practice.

Bureaucracy. A second approach analyzes criminal justice as a bureaucracy. It was described variously as a "natural" or "functional system" or in terms of institutional "bounded rationality" or "bureaucratic politics." For functionalists, adaptive organizations utilize available incentives and sanctions in ways suited to build collective purpose, produce behavior needed to achieve their goals, and survive. Despite formalized roles, however, incentives and sanctions often fail to achieve desired actions because officials are also motivated to pursue their own agendas. For example, Feeley contends that plea bargaining signals a dysfunctional trial process. But functional accounts of this type have been contested by "bounded rationality" and "power politics" theorizing.

For the bounded rationality theorists, members of organizations also receive inducements (e.g., money, prestige) to work on the group's behalf. The image here is of loosely coupled actors operating on imperfect information, planning incrementally and "satisficing" by developing routines and "rules of thumb" to guide action. Once more, side payments do not always suffice because members' own goals (e.g., leisure) may diverge. Models of "bureaucratic politics" focus on incentives inherent in institutional structures, effectiveness of coalition formation, and financial inducements from pay structures. These studies include some work from a conflict perspective. Baldwin and McConville's landmark study of English plea bargaining, which raised the incentives posed by lawyers' agendas, workload, and fee structure, lies in this tradition.[69]

[69] Baldwin & McConville, *supra* note 27.

These two groups of studies explain more richly than functionalism the tensions between individuals and the group. As causal arguments, most bureaucratic models struggle with the fact that historically plea bargaining arose well before the courts developed into large-scale institutions at the close of the nineteenth century. However, studies such as Baldwin and McConville's have much to say about the forces shaping bargaining's dynamics.

Complexity. Feeley argues, following Langbein, that growing procedural complexity in the trial process opened the way for plea negotiations as the trial ultimately collapsed under its own weight.[70] Langbein had earlier argued that complexity made the trial unworkable.[71] However, Feeley intermixes arguments about factors *causing* plea bargaining initially with influences that *shaped* it over time. Feeley initially sought to use increased complexity to explain the origin of plea bargaining during the late nineteenth century. Yet subsequent historical studies have shown that plea bargaining had already arisen in Boston and New York by the 1830s and 1840s—well before the years Feeley targets. During the early to mid-nineteenth century, trials in America's lower courts were relatively simple. Procedural complexity may have reshaped bargaining during the late 1800s or 1900s but it founders as an account for plea bargaining's beginnings.

Workgroups. Finally, Eisenstein and Jacob have proposed a workgroup model and argue that courtroom personnel develop informal norms and procedures for handling caseloads cooperatively,[72] due to their self-interest and mutual dependence. Schulhofer, an influential critic of plea bargaining, has challenged the inevitability of such cooperation, pointing to use of bench trials in half of all cases in Philadelphia.[73] Again history offers a stern test. Workgroup incentives to cooperate existed and could, by their logic, have precipitated bargaining anytime anywhere but did not. Workgroups in themselves, then, are not enough to explain the rise of plea bargaining.

2. Historical Accounts of the Origins of Plea Bargaining

Historical research, which argues that plea bargaining arose as a matter of historical contingency when circumstances combined to produce legal change, led to a sea change in our understanding by pushing backward in time the point at which we know the practice first to have occurred. These historical studies appeared in two waves. The first focused primarily on internal dynamics within the courtroom. The second explores changes in courtroom practice but highlights the interplay of law and society, or "contextuality," in shaping them.

70 Malcolm Feeley, *The Process Is the Punishment* (1979).

71 John Langbein, *Torture and Plea Bargaining*, 46 U. Chi. L. Rev. 3 (1978); *see also* the discussion of Langbein, *infra* at notes 71–72.

72 Herbert Jacob, *Justice in America: Courts, Lawyers, and the Judicial Process* (1978); James Eisenstein & Herbert Jacob, *Felony Justice: An Organizational Analysis of Criminal Courts* (1977).

73 *See* Schulhofer, *supra* note 53.

a. *Professionalization and/or Complexity: The First Wave*

In the early 1980s, a series of articles concluded that plea bargaining dated back to the late nineteenth century, and probably not before. All suggested causes of plea bargaining that centered, in one way or another, on the "professionalization" and growing complexity of criminal justice. They highlighted establishment of the police, prosecutors, and judges as full-time, salaried, expert professionals and the development of complex rules of criminal procedure, especially on evidence, to guide ever more rationalized trials. They explored the inner workings of the courts.

Some authors linked the rise of plea bargaining to an expanding role of the public prosecutor and prosecutorial discretion. Others intimated that the practice stemmed from establishment of a professional police force that spawned cooperation or, perhaps, from the old corrupt police practice of compounding a felony—an earlier form of negotiation. A third line of thinking pointed to the growing role of lawyers, mushrooming complexity of criminal trial procedure, and rules of evidence, all of which were said to increase the burden of an adversarial trial. A corollary thesis pointed to growing caseload pressure for the prosecutor. Still a fourth line of thought depicted plea bargaining as a modernized form of the traditional compensation known as "satisfaction" paid to a victim by the accused.[74] Finally, some contended that, as the burden of decision-making shifted from the courtroom and juries to lawyers and other professionals, plea bargaining developed as part of a rationalization and professionalization of criminal justice.

Despite the importance of this work, many of these "professionalization" or "complexity" studies encountered serious obstacles of the sort common to pioneering works. Some proponents of the "professionalization" and/or "complexity" arguments tended not to systematically examine the dockets of one or more locales to test their hypotheses.

On historical grounds, these early "professionalization" arguments on the cause of plea bargaining ran into historiographical limitations. For example, the office of the prosecutor in New York substantially predated what we now know to be the initial rise of guilty pleas there during the 1840s and 1850s, which undermines the idea that professional prosecutors were a cause of bargaining. The "compounding" of felonies (paying victims not to prosecute), mentioned by Alschuler[75] and by Friedman, is also a weak candidate; that practice harked back to precolonial England, predated the establishment of a professional police force in America, and was practiced primarily by police detectives descended from the old constabulary that had operated for more than a century before the 1830s and 1840s.[76] The establishment of a professional police force as a potential cause is interesting, since such a force began in London a decade before one appeared in America. However, no evidence yet exists that the police in England were involved

[74] On "satisfaction," see discussion of Allen Steinberg's work, *infra* at note 83.

[75] Albert W. Alschuler, *Plea Bargaining and Its History*, 13 L. & Soc'y Rev. 211 (1979).

[76] Leon Radzinowicz, *A History of English Criminal Law* 313–18 (1956). Similarly, the tradition of offenders paying "satisfaction" to victims to settle a case preexisted plea bargaining by many decades; some contend it is descended from the seventh-century Anglo-Saxon practice of accepting "blood money" to forego vengeance; *see* Oscar Handlin & Mary Flug Handlin, *Commonwealth: A Study of the Role of Government in the American Economy: Massachusetts, 1774–1862* (1969).

at that point in bargaining. More important, the police were established in the United States in 1839, which is several years after plea bargaining had begun.

Similarly, while procedural complexity appears to have increased in the late nineteenth century, plea bargaining operated in the American courts decades earlier. In England, procedural complexity blossomed during the late eighteenth century, but, as records of the Old Bailey show, it was accompanied by a modest dip in guilty pleas to both initial and reduced charges. Relatedly, caseload pressure, Fisher's corollary candidate as a cause of bargaining, had been a complaint about American courts since colonial days, so that it, too, long predated bargaining.

Finally, plea bargaining substantially predates the rationalization of work when courts became large, bureaucratic institutions in the late nineteenth century. On grounds of proximity, necessity, and sufficiency, these arguments all encountered empirical problems. Yet, despite their flaws, these "professionalization" accounts of the rise of plea bargaining contribute importantly to our sense of forces transforming plea bargaining. More research is needed to fully grasp the impact of the police.

Let us turn now to the "professionalization" and trial or procedural "complexity" studies that are empirically embedded in the records of a jurisdiction. Langbein's account of plea bargaining arises from his innovative work on the origins of the adversarial criminal trial in England based on cases from London's Old Bailey and pamphlet accounts of trials. Langbein depicts the rise of adversarialism as produced by a change from lawyer-free to lawyer-dominated proceedings. Defendants traditionally were denied counsel in English felony cases. Early trials provided an "altercation" between the defendant, offering unsworn testimony, and a private prosecutor, usually the victim. By the 1730s, Langbein shows that judges began allowing defendant's counsel to cross-examine accusing witnesses. Those lawyers "captured" budding adversarialism and crowded out the accused. By the dawn of the nineteenth century, trials changed from a chance for the accused to tell their story into a place for the defense to contest the prosecution's case. With this transformation, Langbein argues, the complexity of criminal procedure and the intricacy of rules of evidence grew. Similar changes also appeared in America later. For Langbein the expanding role of lawyers and mounting complexity of criminal procedure, especially rules of evidence, "ultimately destroyed the system . . . [by] render[ing] trials [virtually] unworkable as [a] routine dispositive [process] for . . . serious crime."[77] This complexity, along with proliferation of lawyers, created, he argues, strong pressure to negotiate guilty pleas. In Langbein's words, "when trials were short and rapid, the Crown had no incentive to engage in exchange, and thus the defendant had no bargaining chips." Moreover, "[t]rial judges [initially] actively discouraged criminal defendants from tendering guilty pleas."[78] This important work raises two questions. First, if lawyer-dominated proceedings and complexity sparked guilty pleas in England after 1780, how can this be reconciled with a dip in guilty pleas during the 1770s and 1780s at the Old Bailey? Perhaps John Langbein implies that it takes some time for the effects of

[77] John Langbein, *Understanding the Short History of Plea Bargaining*, 13 L. & Soc'y Rev. 261, 265 (1979).

[78] John Langbein, *The Origins of the Adversary Criminal Trial* 19 (2003).

evidentiary complexity to be realized. Second, how can one explain the early appearance of plea bargaining in Boston's lower court by the 1830s (as shown by Ferdinand and Vogel), where proceedings were brief and expeditious?

Like Langbein, Friedman and Percival emphasize a growing role for lawyers. They also point to rationalization of the law, professionalization of police, and increasing use of scientific evidence as primary causal factors inducing plea bargaining by making trials more burdensome.[79] In their study of a California county, Friedman and Percival situate the birth of plea bargaining almost a hundred years later than Langbein, although they point to similar causal factors. They dispute Langbein's claim of earlier complexity in America, possibly because they study lower courts. Friedman later summarized, "trials were short, most defendants had no lawyer and had to cobble together... their own defence, and there was not much quibbling about niceties of evidence."[80] Yet viewing U.S. criminal justice from its "colonial past to the end of the twentieth century," he observed, professionalization "is surely one of the master trends of the... period."[81] Here one must note that American professionalization is primarily a late nineteenth century phenomenon, making it an unlikely cause given that bargaining already operated earlier in the antebellum years. To his credit, Friedman was agnostic on whether plea bargaining occurred earlier, asserting only that it "certainly existed in the late nineteenth century, and perhaps even earlier."[82]

Feeley likewise points to an expanded role for lawyers and the growing complexity of criminal process as causes of plea bargaining based on his study of the courts of New Haven, Connecticut, and later on the Old Bailey in London. Perhaps because he initially examined a lower court outside a major city, Feeley likens nineteenth century American trials to those of eighteenth-century England. "Defendants were not represented by counsel; they did not confront hostile witnesses... [meaningfully]; they rarely challenged evidence or offered defenses of any kind," and trials were conducted quickly, often at the pace of several per day.[83] Countering claims that resource limits and crowding produced plea bargaining, Feeley argues that the reality is just the opposite—increased resources, growing involvement of lawyers, and complexity of cases produced American plea bargaining.[84] He claims that adversarialism increased as complexity grew after mid-century and so concurs with Langbein and Friedman that bargaining arose as a result of the burdens of growing complexity in late nineteenth century America. Here, Feeley encountered problems of historical sequencing too due to the earlier rise of American bargaining.

Almost twenty years later, Feeley launched a new argument that plea bargaining began in England in the 1780s, and he attributes its rise there to several causal factors: the rise of the public prosecutor, more complex offenses, growing procedural complexity,

[79] Lawrence M. Friedman & Robert V. Percival, *The Roots of Justice: Crime and Punishment in Alameda County, California, 1870–1910* (1981).

[80] Friedman, *supra* note 4, at 237–38. [81] *Id.* at 67. [82] *Id.* at 251.

[83] Malcolm Feeley, *Plea Bargaining and the Structure of the Criminal Process*, 7 Justice Sys. J. 338, 345 (1982).

[84] *Id.* at 342.

and the rise of court professionals, especially lawyers, including defense attorneys.[85] Yet while defense attorneys first appear in felony cases in England around 1740 and procedural complexity subsequently grows, there is as yet no sign of a start of guilty-plea-based bargaining there decades later, or evidence of a high rate of guilty pleas at all. Data from the Old Bailey for the decade 1780-89 shows a rate of 0.22 percent for guilty pleas to an initial charge, 4.82 percent for guilty pleas to a reduced charge, and 5 percent for the combination of the two. The rate for guilty pleas to initial charge is higher for literally every other decade of the century. The rate for 1760-69 of guilty pleas to a lesser charge was 5.19 for 1760-69 and 4.35 percent for 1750-59; both were periods before complexity increased. The combined rate were higher for 1700-19 as well.[86] Thus, guilty pleas actually dropped slightly during the late eighteenth century—challenging the claim that complexity sparked an increase.

Ferdinand and Fisher focus on the growing role of the prosecutor. Ferdinand argues that plea bargaining begins in Boston's lower court during the 1830s. He finds guilty plea rates rising from 5.2 percent in 1832 to 19 percent in 1838 and climbing thereafter.[87] Ferdinand examines regulatory and vice cases and claims bargaining begins there. Analysis of concessions is limited. Ferdinand claims the expanding prosecutorial power and discretion generates bargaining—though micro-dynamics are unspecified. Clarification of the roles of the court clerk, police officials, and the public prosecutor who appears in the lower court in the 1840s (in serious cases) would add strength. The logic of regulatory cases in the Anglo-American courts—which aim to threaten prosecution to prompt remediation—calls for attention.

Fisher too points to prosecutorial power, along with heavy caseload and rigid/mandatory sentencing, as the causes of plea bargaining. He studies regulatory and murder cases in mid-tier courts 1789–1910 in Massachusetts.[88] Fisher describes plea bargaining as the "reaction of two chemical ingredients"—existence of a public prosecutor and prosecutorial power to bargain conferred by mandatory sentencing.[89] Caseload pressure motivates. He contends the earliest bargaining began in the late eighteenth century (for regulatory crimes), disappeared in the early nineteenth, and reappeared in the 1840s (for both regulatory and murder offenses).[90] Bargaining began, he argues, over charges, and later over sentences. The sample is 4,142 cases, but only 122 cases occurred between 1789 and 1809.[91] Fisher bases his argument on evidence that forty-four of sixty-six cases between 1789 and 1809 ended in a "plea."[92] "Plea," for Fisher, has an unexpected meaning—not guilty pleas but pleas of *nolo contendere*.[93] "Guilty plea," he states, refers to cases where "the record reveals no compensating concession."[94] Fisher tells us that, until the 1830s, all "clear bargains" in liquor cases involved pleas of *nolo contendere*.[95]

[85] Malcolm Feeley, *Legal Complexity and the Transformation of the Criminal Process: The Origins of Plea Bargaining*, 31 Israel L. Rev. 183 (1997).

[86] Mary Vogel, *Plea Negotiation in the Age of Reform: Origins in 19th and Early 20th Century England* (forthcoming 2019).

[87] Theodore N. Ferdinand, *Boston's Lower Criminal Courts, 1840–1859* (1992). For a fuller critique of the data and analysis, *see* Vogel, *supra* note 2.

[88] Fisher, *supra* note 4. [89] *Id.* at 36. [90] *Id.* at 33. [91] *Id.* at 234.

[92] *Id.* at 22 & 249. [93] *Id.* at 249 n.23. [94] *Id.* at 22. [95] *Id.* at 249.

The work has little to say about guilty pleas until the 1840s. Analysis of concessions is limited.[96] Tonry has argued that prosecutors and mandatory sentencing have coexisted historically without sparking plea bargaining; he argues that defendants contest cases more vigorously.[97] Heumann shows that new prosecutors must be "socialized" to bargain.[98] Fisher, like Vogel, envisions a transformation of plea bargaining to a more bureaucratic process by the end of the nineteenth century.[99] At this point, his argument about the role of the prosecutor—as it does for professionalization and complexity theorists—becomes useful.

b. *"Contextual" Arguments on Interpenetration of Law and Politics: Second Wave*

By the 1990s, the early historical studies were being countered, in some respects, by a second wave of work. These accounts, all embedded in local records, emphasized the contingent influence of political and social context on the courts. The new series of historical studies start with a presumption of the embeddedness of the courts in society. They show plea bargaining to emerge earlier in America than do the "professionalization" and "complexity" studies.

Roots in Private Prosecution. Steinberg first pushed back in time the point at which plea bargaining began to Philadelphia in the 1870s, arguing the practice arose out of private prosecution whereby complainants advanced their own cases and sometimes granted leniency through "satisfaction."[100] Steinberg argues that, as the American state developed after the Civil War, we see a transition of the prosecution function to a fully public one. At this point, he argues, the concessionary approach was incorporated within an increasingly public prosecutorial regime.[101] As we know, other work has now found plea bargaining operating earlier in the nineteenth century—including my own work and that of McConville and Mirsky, discussed next. Philadelphia's courts, however, have always been unique and Steinberg's important work may be unearthing a distinctive path of development there.

3. Political Stabilization, Social Ordering, and Legitimation of Authority

My work shows that plea bargaining emerged in Boston during the 1830s.[102] This is the earliest instance of the practice known so far to exist. It appeared amidst the crime,

[96] *Id.* at 54. Thus Fisher essentially revives the account of nolo contendere pleas in 1890s Massachusetts in Oscar & Mary Handlin, *Commonwealth* (1947).

[97] Michael Tonry, *Mandatory Penalties*, in 16 *Crime and Justice* 250 (Michael Tonry ed., 1992).

[98] Milton Heumann, *Plea Bargaining: The Experiences of Prosecutors, Judges, and Defense Attorneys* 26 (1978).

[99] Vogel, *supra* note 2.

[100] Alan Steinberg, *The Transformation of American Criminal Justice: Philadelphia, 1800–1880*, at 46, 64 (1989).

[101] *Id.* at 185–200, 252–56.

[102] Vogel, *supra* note 2.

violence, and stirrings of popular politics of the Age of Jackson, a politically crucial time when the United States made the transition from republic to democracy. We statistically analyzed the complete docket of the Boston Municipal Court at ten-year intervals from 1830 to 1890 to explore the effect of guilty pleas on type and magnitude of sentencing imposed. The study reveals how plea bargaining, and the courts more generally, became part of an innovative institutional framework of governmentality in post-Revolutionary America and a foundation for a regime for the normalization of conduct. Its aim was a productive workforce, responsible citizens, and a people committed to ethical living.[103]

By the 1830s, Boston was a national hub of legal innovation from which new ideas and practices spread by diffusion to other cities. Plea bargaining was one such advance. An urban elite, "Brahmins," seeking to sustain its besieged power, as democratic populism surged, played a key part in reforging order. It was their response to rampant crisis and risk, coupled with efforts to consolidate order, legitimacy of institutions of self-rule, and their own position that led them to create new legal forms. Plea bargaining appears to have had its American origin in a modestly counterrevolutionary phase of elite reaction to transformative change—a dynamic that appears to have had its counterpart in England at this same time.[104] During the 1830s and 1840s, crime, rioting, and unrest were pervasive. Industrialization proceeded apace and growing cities drew migrants from the countryside who created a vibrant and volatile urban life. Officials sensed risk to property, order, and prosperity. Disorder and violence abounded. Religious beliefs, long a wellspring of cohesion and consensus, weakened.

Because self-rule was still new and little in the way of local governance was yet set in place, there arose a perceived threat to property, to the social order, and to elite power embedded in that way of life. Concern was rife as to whether the new republic would survive. City officials were well-aware of rioting in England with the political potential it held. By the mid-1830s, extension of the franchise added electoral challenge. Efforts to reconsolidate control elicited new state responses. To re-establish social control without fanning resentment, leaders turned to the ideology of a rule of law as a rationale for compliance, and to the discretionary capacities of the courts.

The courts stepped forward to play a key role. To reconsolidate order, city leaders began incremental initiatives at reform. They approached social control not coercively but in ways that reinforced their party's claim to represent the popular will. Judicial decision-making and court practice took on a policy focus as economic and cultural elites turned there as a new venue for pursuing their agendas.[105] During the "formative era" judges re-envisioned law in terms of its policy implications beyond the case at hand. Judges reimagined themselves as agents of "popular sovereignty."

Given the nascent state of local political institutions, the courts stepped forward to shape relations of citizens to the state, promote political stability, and bolster public regard for institutions of self-rule. Reaching back into the traditions of the common law,

[103] Mary E. Vogel, *Between Markets and Hierarchies*, 22 King's College L.J. 335 (2011).
[104] Vogel, *supra* note 86.
[105] See Morton Horwitz, *The Transformation of American Law* (1987).

the courts embraced time-honored mechanisms of episodic, or intermittent, leniency and reworked them for a new context of popular politics.[106] What was distinctive about these mechanisms was that to receive leniency, one needed the testimony of character witnesses.[107] Thus, its receipt was contingent on one's embeddedness in the web of social relationships of community and everyday life.[108] By drawing witnesses from the ranks of household and community governance, traditional hierarchies were reinforced. Proceedings were broadly educative and formative of a new political subject.[109] During the 1830s and 1840s, judges recrafted elements of discretionary leniency into a new legal practice of plea bargaining. While closing cases in a hotly demanded reform, it retained for the courts substantial control over sentencing. Judges took practices such as the pardon and moved them up before a judgment—lending leniency a more contractual quality.[110] Simpler, less costly, and almost always conditionless, guilty plea bargains quickly surpassed pleas of *nolo contendere* in volume. Plea bargains came to prominence initially in criminal cases—especially larceny and assault.

Plea bargaining emerged as a significant innovation during the 1830s; by 1840 the practice of granting leniency where a guilty plea had been entered was well established.[111] The practice reflected incremental improvisation by an elite attempting to bolster the order crucial to robust market functioning, economic development, and their own besieged political fortunes. Plea bargaining was accepted by old and new elites because of the ongoing control it gave them, through sentencing discretion, over policy implementation. Defendants, largely lower class persons in the lower court, acceded to the practice because it held out a sense of recurring leniency, the appearance of control over one's fate through negotiation, and elimination of burdensome state oversight of defendants' lives through the practice of keeping cases "open" on file.

Plea bargaining also held gains for judges and eventually for prosecutors and defense attorneys, which helps to explain its acceptance by courts. For judges, plea bargaining offered a rejoinder to the failed codification movement that had sought to restrict their discretion; it offered a new, more conciliatory, customary means of retaining discretion and a predictable, familiar menu of penalties, which, in contrast to common law, were knowable in advance. It also had the capacity to deter. For prosecutors, bargaining afforded latitude in high profile cases; the high conviction rate afforded by plea bargains became much valued. For defense attorneys, criminal cases were not highly lucrative, so they lost little in fees by expeditious bargaining. And bargaining expanded their discretion too.

[106] *See* Vogel, *supra* note 2; Vogel, *supra* note 4.

[107] Nicola Lacey, *The Resurgence of Character*, in *Philosophical Foundations of Criminal Law* (R.A. Duff & Stuart Green eds., 2011).

[108] Mark Granovetter, *Economic Action and Social Structure: The Problem of Embeddedness*, 91 Am. J. Sociology 481 (1985).

[109] Vogel, *supra* note 103.

[110] W. F. Kuntz, *Criminal Sentencing in Three Nineteenth Century Cities: A Social History of Punishment in New York, Boston and Philadelphia, 1830–1855* (1988).

[111] *See* Vogel, *supra* note 2; Vogel, *supra* note 4.

What occurred was a sort of "triage" or social sorting. In relying on character witnesses, employment records, and family ties, the courts attempted to identify for leniency those accused who were hardworking family people who had simply made a misstep in a generally worthy life. These could be reclaimed as productive labor and virtuous citizens. They were distinguished from transients and "ne'er-do-wells" who were sentenced to custody. Those granted leniency were often released under the watchful eye of their intercessors in a nascent community-based approach to justice.

4. Politicization of the Courts through Tammany Patronage at Mid-Nineteenth Century

Finally, McConville and Mirsky locate the rise of plea bargaining in New York to the 1840s. They argue plea bargaining emerged amidst a transformation of criminal justice in the New York City Court of General Sessions during early to mid-nineteenth century. McConville and Mirsky state: "Although a small percentage of...guilty pleas...[occurred] earlier..., the...dramatic transformation to guilty pleas occurred...only after mid-century."[112] They depict guilty plea rates ranging from zero to 10 percent between 1810 and 1845 with a jump to over 40 percent by 1850, which is sustained, with increases, thereafter.[113] During this period, McConville and Mirsky note, "there was a dramatic shift in trial outcomes...through a reduction in the proportion of top count convictions, an increase in the proportion of uncharged lesser included-offence convictions and an increase in acquittals on the top counts."[114]

The authors point to a vibrant lawyering culture in New York, which, in the early nineteenth century celebrated the jury trial. In New York at mid-century, this trial suddenly gave way to plea bargaining. McConville and Mirsky argue that "[a]fter mid-century, significant changes in the socio-political character of New York City occurred whereby...population [growth,]...reorganization of city government, expanded suffrage and the emergence of professional politicians linked to the Tammany Society...inaugurated an era of [politicization and] 'ward heeling'...." The authors suggest that "the proliferation of non-trial dispositions occurred during a process of professional degradation" and politicization of the courts.[115]

According to McConville and Mirsky, one "result of politicization appears to have been that the prosecution's...[position was weakened] because of the inherent unreliability of a pre-trial process that involved...Tombs' lawyers and elected Police Justices." They also point to problems at trial and tell us: "Moreover, the District Attorney became an operative of Tammany Hall patronage whose constituents were...[often] subject to prosecution...[and] resulted in the District Attorney exercising favour" on their behalf. Finally, they note: "Similarly, in those cases that were prosecuted,...judges..., now

[112] MConville & Mirsky, *supra* note 4, at 194. [113] *Id.* at 200. [114] *Id.* at 202.
[115] *Id.* at 219.

nominated and vetted by Tammany loyalists, engaged in criminal misdeeds favouring defendants with political connections."[116]

McConville and Mirsky argue that "the idea that the transformation to guilty pleas... [was] is an aspect of 'history as progress' brought forth by the rise of professionalism is troubling because evidence abounds that the shift... occurred... abruptly and was not... an evolutionary process... [that related to an increase in]... [capable] lawyers." Their work also rebuts what they term "the functionalist argument" that crowding in the courts produced plea bargaining. They state that "[t]hroughout the entire period, 1800–1865, delay was not a factor and cases moved expeditiously, taking little more than a month from initial appearance before the magistrate to final disposition."[117] In a challenge to Fisher, McConville and Mirsky conclude: "Indeed, our data demonstrate that there was little relationship between caseload and guilty plea rate."[118] They find growing diversity among court personnel by mid-century that leads them, after mid-century, to downplay responsiveness to elite concerns.

In both their repudiation of the caseload pressure hypothesis and their emphasis on the appearance of plea bargaining by mid-nineteenth century, the import of political economy, and the growing influence of patronage politics in patterns of case disposition and/or sentencing after mid-century, McConville and Mirsky's work shares common ground with my own study of the origins of plea bargaining in Boston. Yet, their work differs in pointing to a significant rise of guilty pleas in New York only after the mid-nineteenth century. Both their work and mine see a role for patronage politics—though later in Boston and never as fully corrupt as in New York. While they differ on the role of elites and key dynamics, they are mutually broadly confirmatory.[119]

VI. Consequences

This chapter now brings together, for the first time, the results of research over the last fifty years on the consequences of plea bargaining. Perhaps because of the rocky theoretical terrain, much of the empirical research on consequences of contemporary bargaining tends to be a bit thinly conceptualized. In addition, critical analysis is limited and methodological quality is uneven. We return to those outcomes to which the critiques of plea bargaining directed us: false convictions, wrongful acquittals/dismissals, equity in sentencing, and administrative efficiency.

[116] *Id.* at 219–20. [117] *Id.* at 284–85. [118] *Id.* at 221.

[119] British literature on the origins of plea bargaining has been slower to develop than studies of U.S. jurisdictions. For examples, *see* Baldwin & McConville, *supra* note 27 (focused primarily on twentieth century practices); Vogel, *supra* note 86 (examining guilty pleas in Quarter Sessions and Assizes in late eighteenth and nineteenth century England and identifying surges of guilty pleas in English courts in the 1690s and early 1800s).

1. False Convictions and Wrongful Acquittals/Dismissals

One crucial concern is plea bargaining's effect on courts' capacity, relative to trial, to distinguish innocent from guilty persons and to convict the guilty. To some extent, these objectives exist in tension. Minimizing false convictions involves a commitment to "due process." Maximizing convictions of the guilty prioritizes "crime control." For reasons we will see, compared to trials plea bargaining appears to produce fewer errors in the form of acquittals (though not necessarily dismissals) of the guilty and more in the form of false convictions.[120] What emerges is a practice that is rightly a cause for concern. It appears plea bargaining is most prone to falsely convict where guilty plea rates are high and mandatory sentencing is in effect.

a. *False Convictions*

An equitable court should acquit the innocent while convicting the guilty. Where inequity exists, innocents may disproportionately be falsely convicted. To the extent plea bargaining convicts those acquittable at trial, it boosts unfairness. Only two empirical studies address bargaining's effect on false conviction. They are, however, strong ones. Two others present literature-based conceptual analyses. The studies are exclusively American; British work has focused more on the decision to plead guilty and its impact on sentencing. The empirical studies show that plea bargaining increases rates of false conviction. Best estimates say between 35 and 69 percent of defendants convicted through plea bargains would have won at trial. Although limited methodologically, these studies support concern about amplified false convictions.

In the 1970s, Finkelstein studied guilty plea practices in federal courts to test the assumption in some U. S. Supreme Court decisions that defendants convicted through plea bargains would have lost at trial.[121] He computed "implicit rates of non-conviction" and concluded the assumption is unfounded. Instead, he argued that "more than two-thirds of 'marginal' plea bargain defendants (i.e., defendants pleading guilty above the share who would have been convicted if all went to trial) would have been acquitted or dismissed... [had they] contest[ed] their cases."[122] He found a correlation between "implicit rates of non-conviction" and guilty plea rates. Finkelstein argued that, while the U.S. Supreme Court's presumption that a defendant would have lost at trial may be valid for *strong* cases, prosecutors also bargain (perhaps more often) over weak ones. He concluded the assumption is especially problematic in weak cases—precisely most

[120] Numerous confirmed wrongful convictions in the United States have occurred through negotiated guilty pleas. *See* Brandon L. Garrett, *Convicting the Innocent: Where Criminal Prosecutions Go Wrong* (2011) (examining 250 DNA-based exonerations).

[121] Michael O. Finkelstein, *A Statistical Analysis of Guilty Plea Practices in the Federal Courts*, 89 Harv. L. Rev. 293 (1975).

[122] *Id.* at 293. His method, in brief, is as follows: If a 10 percent increase in guilty pleas leads to no change in the percent of non-convictions, it suggests all those pleading guilty would have been convicted at trial. However, if a 10 percent increase in guilty pleas leads to a 5 percent decrease in non-convictions, then 5 percent more defendants are being convicted than would have been at trial.

likely to involve innocent defendants. Methodologically, the study, though strong, raises a few issues that we cannot consider here, although Finkelstein acknowledged and tried to address them.

Rhodes also estimated the probability that defendants who plead guilty would have been convicted at trial, using data on 845 cases.[123] He estimated likely acquittals at rates nearly equal those for defendants actually tried. To control for differences between cases tried and those resolved by guilty pleas, Rhodes specified a model in which probability of conviction is a function of the defendant's age, arrest on same day as crime, availability of physical evidence, number of charges, arrest at scene of the offense, number of lay witnesses, defendant's release on personal recognizance, third party release, corroboration that a crime was committed, and presence of exculpatory evidence. The effect of each variable on the probability of conviction was then estimated by using a Probit model and data for defendants convicted at trial.[124]

Rhodes found that 34 percent of defendants pleading guilty to assault would have been acquitted compared to the 65 percent of those at trial, for robbery 84 percent compared to 78 percent tried, for larceny 69 percent compared to 66 percent tried, and for burglary 68 percent compared to 69 percent tried. Rhodes concludes that, but for guilty pleas, the conviction rate would be substantially reduced. Rhodes's study, while thought-provoking, must be viewed cautiously for reasons arising from its methodology; the estimating equation, for example, leaves out variables such as race, employment record, and prior convictions.

Building on growing evidence by the 1990s of plea bargaining's tendency to increase false convictions, Scott and Stuntz argue that the practice's inability to detect innocent defendants is not an inherent drawback but results from a flawed bargaining structure. Imagining plea bargaining as a contract, they assert the problem lies in structural impediments to efficient negotiation. They explore the potential for duress, unconscionability due to information deficits or unequal power of the parties, poor judgment or other inability of defendants to discern their "true" interests, and cognitive biases. Other hurdles are information deficits, which make it harder for innocent defendants to identify themselves, stem from the costs of getting information, barriers to testing for or signaling information about innocence, and heterogeneity of defendants that preclude reliance on shared norms instead of signaling. Thus, they problematize the presumptions about voluntariness underpinning U.S. Supreme Court decisions. The solution, they argue, is real. It requires regulating bargaining rather than abolition.[125]

Specifically, Scott and Stuntz contend that it would be better to boost the ability of the bargaining process to detect innocence directly. The difficulty, they argue, is that

[123] William M. Rhodes, *Plea Bargaining: Who Gains? Who Loses?* (report for Law Enforcement Assistance Administration; Institute of Law and Social Research, Washington, DC, 1978). Of the 845 cases drawn from the Prosecutorial Management Information System, 234 were assaults, 174 were robberies, 268 were larcenies, and 169 were burglaries.

[124] Estimated coefficients were then applied to comparable data for those pleading guilty to compute their predicted probabilities of conviction if tried. *Id.*

[125] Robert E. Scott & William J. Stuntz, *Plea Bargaining as Contract*, 101 Yale L.J. 1909, 1934 (1992).

innocence claims are hard to test and the trial process to do so is costly. Scott and Stuntz recommend "second best solutions"—improving the defendants' "welfare by ensuring that cases 'sixty percent...' likely to be convicted at trial are 'priced' differently from cases 'ninety percent....' likely to be" so disposed of. They note that "current law inexplicably... [encourages] prosecutors to treat close cases the same as clear ones."[126] Scott and Stuntz suggest new rules governing both fixing and enforceability of sentences. Their argument, however, overlooks the fact that, by facilitating more lenient sentences for weak cases, this may increase chances of false conviction.

A final study by Wright offers a "trial distortion theory" positing that plea bargaining is dysfunctional when pleas distort outcomes expected at trial. Such distortion is not always problematic—for example, when falling acquittals and/or dismissals result from improved screening or better-prepared prosecutors.[127] Reduced acquittals, however, may signal that the prosecution or defense is striking agreements too cheaply or that judicial penalties for trial are too high. Wright shows that "the federal system... [since the 1980s features] increasingly severe sentences... [even as] adoption of federal sentencing guidelines...enhance[s] prosecutorial and judicial power to reward [defendants'] cooperation." Wright points out that districts using these techniques heavily "produced both higher guilty plea rates and lower acquittal rates." He concludes that the substantial differentials in sentencing on offer "convinced more defendants to abandon worthwhile defenses."[128] By producing those surplus convictions, plea bargaining increases false convictions.

b. *Acquittal/Dismissal of the Guilty*

Negotiated guilty pleas by definition achieve convictions. But they are often induced by dismissal of one or more charges. If plea bargaining increases non-convictions of the guilty beyond the rate we would see at trial, this introduces injustice. But studies suggest that plea bargaining may reduce dismissals: where bargaining is prohibited and officials cannot temper unduly harsh sanctions, judges dismiss more cases.[129] Plea bargaining, by providing a way to moderate sanctions, may inhibit that.

In a landmark study, Newman concludes that dismissal of charges, despite evidence to convict at trial, is not uncommon. Usually, he argues, this occurs where "punishment... appears... useless [or] unduly harsh."[130] Rhodes affirms that dismissals are often entered for defendants who could be convicted at trial.[131] Because plea bargaining tempers sanctions and substitutes for full acquittal or dismissal, equity may be enhanced by convicting some guilty. Newman concurs that bargaining reduces dismissals—especially of defendants "known" to be guilty—with minimal increase in false convictions.

[126] *Id.* at 1952.

[127] Ronald F. Wright, *Trial Distortion and the End of Innocence in Federal Criminal Justice*, 154 U. Pa. L. Rev. 79, 83 (2005).

[128] *Id.* at 85–86.

[129] Tonry, *Mandatory Penalties*, *supra* note 97.

[130] Donald J. Newman, *Conviction: The Determination of Guilt or Innocence without Trial* xv (1966).

[131] Rhodes, *supra* note 123.

Two other studies similarly suggest plea bargaining reduces dismissals of the guilty; both show that when explicit bargaining is restricted, dismissal rates rise.[132] Therefore, we find that, besides reducing acquittals, plea bargaining also decreases dismissals by offering graduated penalties. In both ways, the practice convicts more criminal offenders including more of the guilty.

2. Equity in Sentencing

One of plea bargaining's most controversial features is the differential it generates between sentences that follow guilty pleas and trial convictions. If the differential is too great, voluntariness of the plea may be undermined.

It is widely held that, for equity, sentencing severity should be gauged relative to the seriousness of a crime. When plea bargaining offers leniency, it distorts both rehabilitative and retributive rationales for punishment. Overall, the evidence from previous research suggests that defendants who plead guilty generally receive lighter sentences. However, the results of these studies are surprisingly mixed. Further, little is known about the conditions for implementing concessions.

Several studies from the 1960s and 1970s found that defendants pleading guilty are actually treated more leniently than at trial. Using data from California, Greenwood and coauthors found evidence that guilty pleas elicit sentencing concessions.[133] Blumberg found in a metropolitan court that "the defendant who... [is] convicted after trial receives... less generous treatment than one who... negotiate[s]."[134] Miller et al. similarly concluded from researching twenty county courts that "evidence of differential sentencing... exists in many jurisdictions."[135] Newman reported that "judges in all three states [studied]... show greater leniency... to the defendant who pleads guilty than... [one] who demands a jury trial." Newman notes, however, that concessions may be "more apparent than real" since they can be nullified by post-conviction decisions.[136]

132 Thomas Church, Jr., *Plea Bargains, Concessions and the Courts: An Analysis of a Quasi-experiment*, 10 L. & Soc'y Rev. 377 (1976); Note, *The Elimination of Plea Bargaining in Black Hawk County: A Case Study*, 60 Iowa L. Rev. 1053 (1975).

133 Peter W. Greenwood et al., *Prosecution of Adult Felony Defendants in Los Angeles County: A Policy Perspective* (Rand Corp. 1973) (study controlled for type of crime but not other factors, including prior convictions and offense seriousness).

134 Abraham S. Blumberg, *Criminal Justice* 31 (1967).

135 Herbert S. Miller et al., *Plea Bargaining in the United States* 41 (Institute of Law and Criminal Procedure, Georgetown University Law Center, for Law Enforcement Assistance Administration 1978). Methodologically, these studies tend to link data and conclusions informally through the author's judgment rather than an explicit analytic scheme.

136 Donald J. Newman, *Conviction: The Determination of Guilt or Innocence without Trial* 61, 98 (1966); *see also* Dominick R. Vetri, *Guilty Plea Bargaining: Compromises by Prosecutors to Secure Guilty Pleas*, 112 U. Pa. L. Rev. 864 (1964) (finding 55 percent of prosecutors believed reductions were regularly granted for guilty pleas, and more felt such reductions are justified). *But see* H.J. Shin, *Do Lesser Pleas Pay: Accommodations in the Sentencing and Parole Processes*, 1 J. Crim. Justice 27 (1973) (finding concessions granted by prosecutors may subsequently be revoked by parole boards).

Two studies from this era reached more mixed conclusions. Rhodes found that for assault, larceny, and burglary, defendants who pled guilty received sentences comparable to those tried. For robbery, however, pleading guilty elicited noticeable concessions.[137] The findings run contrary to the belief that plea bargaining universally produces leniency and highlight the importance of looking for variability across offenses. Alschuler's informal survey of prosecutors also yielded mixed findings on differential sentencing, reflecting controversy among prosecutors about whether and how sentencing leniency occurs. Regarding charge bargaining, Alschuler reported that some prosecutors felt "reduction in level of a charge, like a reduction in number of [counts], rarely affects the defendant's sentence," although "others dispute this contention."[138] The sole arguments that sentence reductions do not occur as a result of plea bargains come from a pair of 1970s studies of court operations. Jacob concluded that "[plea bargains] do not... produce more lenien[cy] when one controls for the type of case... handled."[139] Jacob's earlier research with Eisenstein on courts in Baltimore, Detroit, and Chicago found defendants received comparable sentences at trial to those pleading guilty,[140] although their regression analysis raises questions about the validity of their findings.[141]

By contrast, more than three decades later, Eisenstein with other coauthors found clear evidence of an average 15 percent "trial penalty" in U.S. federal courts.[142] This finding is consistent with other recent studies; Albonetti found comparable trial penalties in a study of federal drug trafficking crimes.[143] A notable recent study by Kim, however, took issue with the methodology of earlier work and concluded instead that, properly assessed, federal defendants incur a sentence on average 64 percent longer if they are convicted at trial.[144] As for U.S. state court systems, King's recent study of trial versus guilty-plea sentences in five states with sentencing guidelines found that differentials

[137] Rhodes, *supra* note 123. Note, however, that the proportion of variance explained (R^2) by Rhodes's estimating equation is low; the study did not test statistical significance.

[138] Albert W. Alschuler, *The Prosecutor's Role in Plea Bargaining*, 36 U. Chi. L. Rev. 50, 97 (1968).

[139] Herbert Jacob, *Justice in America: Courts, Lawyers, and the Judicial Process* 191 (1978).

[140] James Eisenstein, & Herbert Jacob, *Felony Justice: An Organizational Analysis of Criminal Courts* (1977).

[141] Specifically, Eisenstein and Jacob dismissed the impact of guilty pleas due to the small additional variance explained by the disposition mode variable in their stepwise regression. This study design holds two particular hazards. One is that multicollinearity between disposition mode and the variables previously selected by the stepwise regression may have biased the results. The second is that there may be too little variance in the mode-of-disposition variable, due to the frequency of guilty pleas, to generate statistical evidence of a relationship even if one exists.

[142] Jeffery T. Ulmer, James Eisenstein & Brian D. Johnson, *Trial Penalties in Federal Sentencing: Extra-Guidelines Factors and District Variation*, 27 Just. Q. 560, 575 (2010).

[143] Celesta A. Albonetti, *Sentencing Under the Federal Sentencing Guidelines: Effects of Defendant Characteristics, Guilty Pleas, and Departures on Sentence Outcomes for Drug Offenses, 1991–1992*, 31 Law & Soc'y Rev. 789, 805 tbl.2 (1997) (trial penalties of 6 to 14 percent for both black and white defendants).

[144] Andrew Chongseh Kim, *Underestimating the Trial Penalty: An Empirical Analysis of the Federal Trial Penalty and Critique of the Abrams Study*, 84 Miss. L.J. 1195 (2015).

varied widely among offenses but that there was clear evidence that guilty pleas led to sentence discounts for a large majority of crimes.[145]

Beyond sentencing reductions, Nardulli and coauthors in the 1980s examined effects of bargaining on sentencing *consistency*—that is, whether bargaining leads to greater variability in penalties. They contended that plea bargaining produces marked consistency in sentencing patterns and pointed to a "high level of consistency... in... measures of sentence clusters" and "uniform treatment of plea cases is also fairly consistent across various classes of defendants." The data, they concluded, suggest a coherent "bureaucratic justice" in which felony courts provide justice "premised not on strict adherence to due process ideals, or committed to the refined, individualized treatment of individuals... but rather one premised on strict adherence to a bureaucratic routine [and]... pragmatic concerns." This is, however, "consistent with the existence of a trial tariff which punishes defendants who request 'unreasonable' trials."[146] In the same era, Miethe also observed consistency in plea bargaining sentencing when he examined bargaining under mandatory sentencing rules. He found that uniformity from mandatory sentencing was not eroded by socioeconomic or other disparities due to plea bargaining, and concluded that "social differentiation [between persons receiving harsh or lenient sentences]... did not... [change] appreciably after implementing [determinate sentencing] guidelines."[147] Routinized bargaining, then, may produce predictable outcomes. It may also yield no greater socioeconomic disparity than trial, although English scholarship shows that members of ethnic minorities may be less likely to "bargain" at all because of distrust of the system.[148]

In sum, several clear themes surface. Despite public concern that its leniency favors the guilty, plea bargaining also appears to assure that more guilty persons are convicted than at trial. Both acquittals and dismissals decline. Perhaps the greatest drawback of this practice is its propensity to convict the innocent, especially where bargaining is widespread and includes the weakest cases. As to whether leniency is actually received by those who negotiate, the evidence remains somewhat divided. The preponderance of findings suggests that bargaining usually does yield concessions. To the extent that defendants make decisions based on a calculation of costs and benefits, it is reasonable to think they are influenced by the leniency on offer.[149]

145 Nancy J. King et al., *When Process Affects Punishment: Differences in Sentences after Guilty Plea, Bench Trial, and Jury Trial in Five Guidelines States*, 105 Colum. L. Rev 959, 973–975 (2005) (assessing sentences in five states for a variety of offenses and finding that, for most, there is strong evidence of more severe sentences after trial than after a guilty plea).

146 Peter F. Nardulli et al., *Criminal Courts and Bureaucratic Justice*, 76 J. Crim. L. & Criminology 1103, 1129–30 (1985). The study does not consider that mitigating and aggravating factors may be muted.

147 Terance D. Miethe, *Charging and Plea Bargaining Practices Under Determinate Sentencing: An Investigation of the Hydraulic Displacement of Discretion*, 78 J. Criminal L. & Criminology 155, 171–173 (1987).

148 *See* Sanders & Young, *supra* note 30; Roger Hood, *Race and Sentencing* (1992).

149 Research from England explicitly reveals such a calculus at work. *See* Sanders & Young, *supra* note 30; Carol Hedderman & David Moxon, *Magistrates' Court or Crown Court? Mode of Trial Decisions and Sentencing* (Home Office Research Study, 1992) (finds 66 percent of guilty pleas are driven by expectation of discount).

3. Administrative Efficiency

Proponents of plea bargaining, including the U.S. Supreme Court, argue it promotes administrative efficiency and conserves court resources. Some argue this creates a "compelling" state interest in bargaining and that caseload pressure induces bargaining. Studies have produced mixed evidence for these claims.

Berger studied effects of a 1971 prohibition on plea bargaining for three serious crimes in Maricopa County, Arizona. He saw no increase in trials, although his analysis was relatively casual. For example, he concluded that the bargaining ban "did not cause a rise in number of trials" and that guilty plea rates remained about 70 percent.[150] But that does not tell us whether fewer cases were charged, more were dismissed, or tacit bargaining continued despite the formal ban.

Another study examined effects (during two months) of eliminating plea bargaining for felonies in an Iowa county. Elimination of bargaining was, here, accompanied by four other supportive actions.[151] In that case, abolishing plea bargaining "increased efficiency" when coupled with other reforms, such as new laws permitting immunity for witnesses who testify for the state and an alternative to prosecution through deferred judgments and supervised release.[152] Cases filed declined 23 percent, dismissals decreased 50 percent, verdicts of guilty were reached in 50 percent more cases, and trials increased by only one single case.

A third study that also looked at consequences on caseloads in one county of banning charge bargaining for drug-sale cases yielded markedly different findings. Based on interviews with twenty-three prosecutors, judges, and defense attorneys, Church concluded that after charge bargaining stopped, the trial rate "soared" and cases resolved by guilty pleas "fell considerably," although guilty pleas still produced 75 percent of convictions.[153] From this Church inferred that implicit bargaining emerged (possibly tacit sentence bargains), prosecutors sought more dismissals, and trials increased for judges who were unlikely to engage in tacit sentence bargains. Church concluded that the elimination of *all* bargaining "would be accompanied by a... considerable increase in the number of trials."[154]

Schulhofer argued that bargaining is driven neither by caseload pressure nor courthouse workgroup cooperation. Based on observing the efficient operation of the bench

[150] Moise Berger, *The Case against Plea Bargaining*, 62 A.B.A. J. 621, 623 (1976).

[151] The four concomitant changes included: (1) enactment of a deferred judgment statute whereby a defendant might plead guilty to an offense and, without conviction, be placed on probation; (2) increased police/prosecutor cooperation beginning in 1973; (3) additional funds to supervise deferred judgment releases; and (4) passage of a statute enabling a prosecutor to offer witnesses immunity in return for their testimony.

[152] Note, *The Elimination of Plea Bargaining in Black Hawk County*, *supra* note 132; King & Lord, *supra* note 24.

[153] Church, *supra* note 132, at 383 (1976). *Compare* Robert A. Weninger, *The Abolition of Plea Bargaining: A Case Study of El Paso County, Texas*, 35 UCLA L. Rev. 265 (1987) (finding the trial rate doubled and delay in case processing increased during the two years following a plea bargaining ban).

[154] Church, *supra* note 132, at 399.

trial system used to resolve 49 percent of cases at the Philadelphia courts, he made the case that plea bargaining is pervasive not because it is necessary but because it serves a popular but problematic conception of justice. Schulhofer insisted that "competitive norm[s] may strongly affect behavior" within organizations as in markets. He argued that expeditious trials, aggressive prosecutorial policies, a strong public defender's office, and professional norms that disfavor quick compromises preserve the adversarial process and reduce bargaining.[155]

In sum, while evidence is mixed on bargaining's administrative consequences, overall the work counsels skepticism about the assumption that bargaining fosters efficiency. Research suggests a more complex interplay among bargaining, caseloads, professional culture, and other factors.

VII. Conclusion

The U.S. Supreme Court has shifted from an essentially tolerant stance toward plea bargaining to one of explicit support in recent years. However, many of its decisions rest on assumptions about equity, voluntariness, and administrative efficiency, which are challenged by critics and empirical evidence. The Court continues to set a high bar for recognizing coercion and to maintain that large trial penalties, as well as vastly differential resources available to prosecution and defense, have no effect on voluntariness or fairness. Yet confirmed cases of innocent persons who falsely plead guilty challenge that stance. Overall, England has been much more attuned to minimizing coercion in plea bargaining, notably by limiting discounts in the Sentencing Guidelines that can be offered in exchange for guilty pleas.

Research on plea bargaining provides some notable findings even though much remains to be learned. The preponderance of the evidence supports a fairly robust conclusion that bargained pleas do, often, induce more lenient sentences. However, in the presence of mandatory sentencing, the overall impact is to generate higher rates of conviction and longer sentences. Research reflects consensus that plea bargaining reduces the likelihood that guilty defendants will go free, because compared to a system with many more trials, fewer offenders avoid conviction due to dismissals or acquittals on technicalities. Available evidence about effects on administrative efficiency, while mixed, does not support even speculative conclusions that plea bargaining expedites case flow and eases caseload pressure. Emerging work on the origins of plea bargaining challenges arguments that the practice arose as a response to crowding in the courts. New work suggests that in England guilty pleas surged briefly during the 1690s and then continually from the early 1800s onward, although we await the story of its origins.

[155] Schulhofer, *supra* note 53, at 1096, 1099. An earlier study of California courts also found robust adversarial norms in bench trials and other settings. *See* Lynn M. Mather, *Plea Bargaining or Trial? The Process of Criminal Case Disposition* (1979).

Original causes of U.S. plea bargaining appear to have been political, arising during the Jacksonian era's transition to broad democracy in the 1830s and 1840s. Particularly in America, plea bargaining, together with mandatory sentencing, has played an important role in the carceral turn that produced mass incarceration since the 1990s.

References

John Baldwin & Mike McConville, *Negotiated Justice* (1977)
G. Nicholas Herman, *Plea Bargaining* (2012)
John Langbein, *The Origins of the Adversary Criminal Trial* (2003)
Richard L. Lippke, *The Ethics of Plea Bargaining* (2011)
Mike McConville & Chester L. Mirsky, *Jury Trials and Plea Bargaining: A True History* (2005)
Mary E. Vogel, *Coercion to Compromise: Plea Bargaining, the Courts and the Making of Political Authority* (2007)

CHAPTER 34

FORENSIC SCIENCE EVIDENCE, ADVERSARIAL CRIMINAL PROCEEDINGS, AND MAINSTREAM SCIENTIFIC "ADVICE"

GARY EDMOND

I. Introduction

This chapter offers an overview of adversarial responses to forensic science evidence. The focus is contemporary, with particular attention directed to the aftermath of recent reviews by peak scientific organizations, along with the implications of notorious mistakes identified through innocence projects, criminal cases review commissions, public inquiries, and appeals. Following a brief introduction to the main rules and procedures regulating the admission and use of expert opinion evidence in adversarial criminal proceedings, along with an overview of findings and recommendations of the scientific reviews, the chapter will consider legal engagement with forensic science evidence and related scientific advice. Recent scientific reviews concluded that many forensic science procedures, including those routinely relied upon in criminal investigations and prosecutions throughout the common law world, have never been formally evaluated and so are not known to be reliable. These strands will then be brought together to suggest that lawyers and judges have not developed an endogenous awareness of the depth and range of problems with the forensic sciences, the kinds of information required to evaluate such evidence, and what these might mean for our understanding of conventional legal practice in accusatorial proceedings; particularly the efficacy of traditional adversarial trial mechanisms, the fairness of proceedings, and the rectitude of legal decision-making.

Conventionally, legal reliance on forensic science and medicine evidence is associated with the rise of scientific or rational policing and criminal justice processes. The reception of non-legal (i.e., exogenous) expertise within legal processes of fact-finding predates the Enlightenment,[1] though formal development and rationalization occurred during the Enlightenment and was consolidated in the nineteenth century throughout the common law world.[2] Forensic medicine became a regular feature of serious criminal proceedings during the nineteenth century[3] and the forensic sciences assumed significance from around the turn of the twentieth century, following legal recognition of fingerprint evidence.[4] The forensic sciences (and forensic medicine) expanded in the first half of the twentieth century as crime scene, fingerprint, handwriting, firearm, hair, shoe, footwear, tire, and fiber analyses were refined and institutionalized in specialized bureaus, frequently under the control of law enforcement.[5]

This chapter endeavors to problematize the implicit orderliness and taken-for-granted evidentiary value of some of these historical (i.e., pre-DNA) forensic *sciences* and the legal assumptions and practices that developed symbiotically alongside them. The word "sciences" is italicized because many of our contemporary forensic sciences were originally "rough heuristics to aid criminal investigations and were not grounded in ... scientific research."[6] Many procedures, including some still in use, were developed and refined through investigations and non-systematic experiments by investigators (few of whom were trained scientists) working in police laboratories.[7] Surprisingly few procedures have been formally evaluated using orthodox experimental designs.[8] Nevertheless, opinions derived from these procedures (and occasional case-related experiments) have informed investigations, charge decisions, and pleas, and were routinely admitted and relied upon in criminal prosecutions. Revealingly, reliance on forensic science evidence in plea bargains and trials seems to have consolidated emerging practices and even conferred legitimacy on nascent "fields."[9]

In this historical sketch, it is important to note that notwithstanding the use and adaption of techniques from chemistry, as early as the nineteenth century, it was only during attempts to stabilize DNA profiling evidence more than a century later that *non*-forensic scientists began to take a sustained interest in the forensic sciences. More than

[1] Buckley v. Rice Thomas (1554) 1 Plowden 118.

[2] Conspicuously Folkes v. Chadd (1782) 3 Doug KB 157.

[3] *Legal Medicine in History* (Michael Clark and Catherine Crawford eds., 1994); Ian Burney, *Bodies of Evidence: Medicine and the Politics of the English Inquest, 1830–1926* (2000).

[4] Simon A. Cole, *Suspect Identities: A History of Fingerprinting and Criminal Identification* (2001).

[5] David A. Harris, *Failed Evidence: Why Law Enforcement Resists Science* (2012).

[6] National Research Council, *Strengthening Forensic Science in the United States: A Path Forward* 32–35 (2009), http://www.nap.edu/catalog.php?record_id=12589 [hereinafter NRC Report].

[7] I use the terms "forensic scientist" and "forensic practitioner" interchangeably, although a significant proportion of forensic *scientists* do not possess formal scientific qualifications. *See also* Jennifer L. Mnookin et al., *The Need for a Research Culture in the Forensic Sciences*, 58 UCLA L. Rev. 725 (2011).

[8] That is, through rigorous processes of formal validation.

[9] These were not necessarily linked to accurate outcomes, and often followed confessions and convictions where the identity of the actual offender was uncertain.

any other factor—though in conjunction with high profile wrongful convictions (some predating innocence projects), the appearance of scholarly critiques and a few prominent mistakes—DNA profiling and controversies over its legal application cast an unprecedented scientific light on the traditional forensic sciences.[10] For the first time, from about the mid-1990s, the traditional forensic sciences began to be critically contrasted with procedures that had been formally validated and conclusions that were expressed in statistically sophisticated terms.[11]

Generations of prosecutors and judges have acted as though—and sometimes insisted that—adversarial proceedings and procedural mechanisms such as cross-examination afforded adequate scrutiny of expert evidence adduced by the state in criminal proceedings.[12] Indeed, so successful was legal recognition, and sociolegal legitimation, that there were remarkably few challenges to forensic science evidence, especially the underlying methods and conclusions, during the course of the twentieth century. While the credibility of individual forensic practitioners was occasionally engaged and their conspicuous exaggeration questioned, techniques such as fingerprint, firearm, tool mark, microscopic hair, and bite mark comparisons were widely accepted as reliable and perhaps even infallible methods of identifying (and excluding) offenders through the ability to link a trace to a person or object. Legal recognition and reliance upon knowledge claims that were untested and sometimes inconsistent with mainstream scientific methods constitute a conspicuous backdrop to the discussion in this chapter. Indeed, the way in which investigators, investigative agencies, forensic practitioners, prosecutors, courts, and defense counsel have, through their evidentiary assumptions, procedures, and practices, *together* constructed and represented conventional forensic sciences as epistemologically robust and implicitly scientific might be understood as a pathological form of sociolegal co-production.[13]

While the emergence of the forensic sciences cannot be understood without sensitivity to mobilization beyond courtrooms—the role of institutionalization and professional organizations, the politicization of law and order, responses to terrorism, media interest in crime and the forensic sciences, technological advances, in conjunction with a large number of (apparently) successful investigations and prosecutions—the focus of this essay is restricted to the courts.[14] It endeavors to explain how commitment to conventional legal practices—to the party presentation of evidence, the myopic concern with individual cases, the privileging of procedures and trial safeguards, along with pervasive professional beliefs about the critical-skeptical abilities of lawyers (and judges)—seems to have blinded trial and appellate judges to pervasive epistemic problems with a great

[10] For an account of the most prominent error by U.S. fingerprint examiners, see Office of the Inspector General, *A Review of the FBI's Handling of the Brandon Mayfield Case* (2006).

[11] Jay Aronson, *Genetic Witness: Science, Law, and Controversy in the Making of DNA Profiling* (2007).

[12] Peter J. Neufeld, *The (Near) Irrelevance of* Daubert *to Criminal Justice and Some Suggestions for Reform*, 95 Am. J. Pub. Health S107 (2005).

[13] Compare *States of Knowledge: The Co-Production of Science and the Social Order* (Sheila Jasanoff ed., 2004).

[14] Christopher Lawless, *Forensic Science: A Sociological Introduction* (2016).

deal of forensic science evidence adduced by the state. Even in the wake of authoritative independent reviews—by peak scientific organizations, unprecedented in terms of the skeptical tone directed toward legal performances—courts struggle to appreciate that legal practices, the abilities of legal personnel, and the way evidence is presented, (sometimes) challenged, and evaluated, are very often displaced from, and even inconsistent with, mainstream scientific and technical practices and commitments. This conclusion might encourage us to reflect upon the value of collective legal experience, the way courts and investigative agencies understand their own practices and engage with exogenous (i.e., non-legal) forms of knowledge and advice, as well as the lack of empirical evidence about the performance of legal procedures (including safeguards) and personnel.

II. "*Laissez faire*": Accommodating the State's Forensic Evidence

Admissibility standards and procedures regulating expert opinion evidence are not uniform across the various jurisdictions that make up the common law world. There are, as we shall see through a restricted survey, a variety of different approaches applied in criminal proceedings in the United States, Canada, England and Wales, Australia, and New Zealand. Notwithstanding these formal differences, one of the revealing features of legal practice across all of these jurisdictions is the remarkable consistency in admissibility outcomes. Put simply, few judges operating in the adversarial tradition exclude forensic science evidence.

Forensic science evidence is typically generated during some kind of investigation. Where deemed significant, it is integrated into the investigation (or case), charge decision, plea negotiation, and/or prosecution. Most cases remain unsolved, are dropped, or are resolved through a plea. Accusations, as such, are contested in only a tiny proportion of cases. Where cases include the products of forensic science this evidence is rarely (seriously) contested. Even when contested, forensic science evidence is not necessarily disclosed, presented, or qualified in ways that would be satisfying to those with methodological, statistical, or psychological sophistication. These issues will re-emerge in the ensuing discussion. This section provides an introduction to some of the more prominent admissibility and procedural rules regulating the admission of forensic science evidence in accusatorial proceedings.

Before the U.S. Supreme Court imposed a reliability threshold in the mid-1990s, no common law jurisdiction had required *reliability*—in the sense of trustworthiness—as a condition for the admission of expert opinion evidence.[15] In criminal proceedings,

[15] In this essay, "reliability" is used as a synonym for trustworthiness whereas "scientific reliability" refers to repeatability, reproducibility, and accuracy. *See* Pres. Council of Advisors on Sci. & Tech., *Forensic Science in Criminal Courts: Ensuring Scientific Validity of Feature-Comparison Methods* 47 (2016), https://obamawhitehouse.archives.gov/administration/eop/ostp/pcast/docsreports [hereinafter PCAST Report].

questions about the reliability of expert opinion evidence were considered (and in many cases remain) issues of weight for the trier of fact.[16] Before *Daubert v. Merrell Dow Pharmaceuticals*, rules regulating the admissibility of expert opinion evidence in criminal proceedings had not changed significantly for decades, even centuries.[17] Evidence obtained through the institutionalized forensic sciences, including early DNA profiling, was almost always deemed admissible in the decades before reliability entered admissibility jurisprudence.

Before the reliability "revolution" popularly associated with *Daubert*, the admission of expert opinion in most common law jurisdictions required the party proffering the evidence to identify the relevant "field" of expertise and locate the proposed witness in that field on the basis of training, study, or experience.[18] Such requirements were sometimes supplemented with concerns about the evidence being "necessary" (e.g., Canada) or capable of "assisting the trier of fact" (e.g., England and Wales).[19] Some courts asked judges to consider the probative value and risk of unfair prejudice as part of the exception for expert opinion (e.g., Canada). Other courts treated that as a discrete consideration once the admissibility of the opinion had been resolved (e.g., the United States, Australia, New Zealand, England and Wales).

Few courts applied these rules in ways that led to the exclusion of forensic science evidence adduced by the state.[20] Indeed, most of the modern formulations and criteria were formalized after the traditional forensic sciences—such as latent fingerprint, firearm, handwriting, and many other types of comparison, as well as blood spatter, arson, and accident investigation—had gained access to the courts and been institutionalized by law enforcement.[21] Occasionally, following defense objection, courts expressed interest in the admissibility of a new procedure or a novel use of an existing technology, though this was rarely an obstacle to admission. Writing for the English Court of Appeal in a case involving the admissibility of opinions about the identity of a robber captured by a security camera, Steyn LJ explained that: "It would be entirely wrong to deny to the law of evidence the advantages to be gained from new techniques and *new advances in science*."[22]

[16] There are some exceptions. Challenges to DNA profiling evidence, where there often has been experimental research, or awareness of the need for such research, have tended to focus on empirical evidence. *See, e.g.*, United States v. Yee, 134 F.R.D. 161 (N.D. Ohio 1991); People v. Castro, 545 N.Y.S.2d 985 (N.Y. Sup. Ct. 1989); R v. Karger [2001] SASC 64 (S. Austl.).

[17] Tal Golan, *Laws of Men and Laws of Nature* (2004).

[18] The terms "training," "study," and "experience" are frequently equated with expertise. Contrast Kristy Martire & Gary Edmond, *Re-thinking Expert Evidence*, 41 Melbourne U. L. Rev. 967 (2017).

[19] R v. Mohan [1994] 2 S.C.R. 9 and R v. Turner [1975] Q.B. 834.

[20] Conspicuous exceptions are some types of polygraph and early DNA profiling evidence.

[21] Clark v. Ryan [1960] 103 C.L.R. 486; R v. Mohan [1994] 2 S.C.R. 9 and R v. Turner [1975] Q.B. 834; and Daubert v. Merrell Dow Pharms., 509 U.S. 579 (1993).

[22] *Clarke* [1995] 2 Cr. App. R. 425 at 429–30 (emphasis added). *See also* R v. Dallagher [2003] 1 Cr. App. R. 195 at [27]. The quote implies that the techniques are steeped in science, even though this did not form part of any admissibility test in England and Wales and was not part of the record in *Clarke*.

The strictest admissibility criterion, at least in theory, appeared in some U.S. courts.[23] It directed attention to the "general acceptance" of the procedure. In response to a precursor to the modern polygraph—adduced by the defense and excluded—an American federal judge explained that:

> while the courts will go a long way in admitting experimental testimony deduced from a well recognized scientific principle or discovery, the thing from which the deduction is made must be sufficiently established to have gained general acceptance in the particular field in which it belongs.[24]

In practice, questions about the levels of acceptance and precisely what needed to be accepted and by whom, were addressed by the witness(es), often based on their impressions and hearsay. Courts in several jurisdictions (e.g., England) considered "general acceptance" too demanding, as it prevented courts from accessing the most modern insights. Where "general acceptance" was applied in criminal proceedings it was usually satisfied by witnesses appealing to a parochial "field"—such as the community of fingerprint examiners, isolated from the scientific mainstream—insisting that fingerprint comparison was "accepted."[25] Once a procedure or type of expertise was legally recognized, that decision often provided a resource or precedent available to experts, lawyers, and judges across jurisdictions—whatever their particular admissibility standards. In some cases (e.g., bite mark comparison) constraints imposed on first appearances were not always imposed in subsequent prosecutions—a kind of *admissibility creep*.[26]

Accommodating approaches toward forensic science evidence appeared set to change in the 1990s when the U.S. Supreme Court imposed a reliability standard on opinions based on "scientific, technical, and other specialized knowledge"—a phrase drawn from Federal Rule of Evidence 702—in *Daubert*.[27] Considering the admissibility of scientific (and medical) evidence in mass tort litigation, a majority insisted that "scientific knowledge" required reliability (and validity):

> in order to qualify as "scientific knowledge," an inference or assertion must be derived by the scientific method. Proposed testimony must be supported by appropriate validation—i.e., "good grounds," based on what is known. In short, the requirement that an expert's testimony pertain to "scientific knowledge" establishes a standard of evidentiary reliability.[28]

[23] General acceptance is often presented as the dominant twentieth century admissibility standard in the United States, though there is some controversy over the breadth of *Frye's* influence before an apparent resurgence in the 1980s.

[24] Frye v. United States, 293 F. 1013 (D.C. Cir. 1923).

[25] Paul Giannelli, *The Admissibility of Novel Scientific Evidence:* Frye v. United States, *a Half-Century Later*, 80 Colum. L. Rev. 1197 (1980).

[26] Michael J. Saks et al., *Forensic Bitemark Identification: Weak Foundations, Exaggerated Claims*, 3 J.L. & Biosci. 1 (2016).

[27] Commentators were initially divided as to whether *Daubert* represented a liberalization of tightening of admissibility standards.

[28] Daubert v. Merrell Dow Pharms., 509 U.S. 579, 590 (1993).

Daubert introduced criteria designed to help a trial judge determine whether scientific evidence was sufficiently reliable for admission.[29]

> Ordinarily, a key question to be answered in determining whether a theory or technique is scientific knowledge that will assist the trier of fact will be whether it can be (and has been) tested.... Another pertinent consideration is whether the theory or technique has been subjected to peer review and publication.... Additionally, in the case of a particular scientific technique, the court ordinarily should consider the known or potential rate of error... and the existence and maintenance of standards controlling the technique's operation.... Finally, "general acceptance" can yet have a bearing on the inquiry.[30]

These criteria were presented as a resource, to be used flexibly, in admissibility "gatekeeping."

Daubert was extended by the Court in *Kumho Tire v. Carmichael*.[31] *Kumho* was concerned with the admissibility of opinion based on "technical, and other specialized knowledge"—the residual part of the phrase from Rule 702. The *Kumho* decision reiterated the need for trial judges to focus on reliability-sensitive criteria.

> [A]s a matter of language, the Rule applies its reliability standard to all "scientific," "technical," or "other specialized" matters within its scope.... The trial judge's effort to assure that the specialized testimony is reliable and relevant can help the jury evaluate that foreign experience, whether the testimony reflects scientific, technical, or other specialized knowledge.[32]

Rule 702 was revised in 2000 (and 2011) in order to explicitly incorporate the Supreme Court's interest in reliability. It now requires that "testimony is the product of reliable principles and methods" and that "the expert has reliably applied the principles and methods to the facts of the case." The expansion in *Kumho* served as a potential constraint on forensic practitioners who began to represent themselves as technicians, rather than scientists, in order to circumvent the perceived rigor of the *Daubert* criteria.

Daubert and *Kumho*—and *Joiner*, which defined the standard of review for admissibility under Rule 702—were all *civil* appeals. This is revealing. In the decade when DNA profiling was rapidly expanding, and starting to expose both wrongful convictions and incongruities in the way other forensic sciences operated, the U.S. judiciary appears to have been more apprehensive about the threat posed by so-called "junk science" in civil proceedings.[33] Judicial anxiety, and the need for rigorous gatekeeping, because of the threat posed by questionable expert opinion evidence adduced by plaintiffs in implicitly unmeritorious class actions, was not extended to criminal justice practice.[34] When

[29] *Daubert* applied to federal litigation though many state courts adopted it.

[30] *Daubert*, 509 U.S. at 593.

[31] Kumho Tire v. Carmichael, 526 U.S. 137 (1999).

[32] *Id.* at 589–90.

[33] *See* Norman Foster & Peter Huber, *Judging Science: Scientific Knowledge and the Federal Courts* (1997).

[34] Michael Risinger, *Navigating Expert Reliability: Are Criminal Standards of Certainty Being Left on the Dock?*, 64 Albany L. Rev. 99 (2000); Edward Cheng & Albert Yoon, *Does* Frye *or* Daubert *Matter? A Study of Scientific Admissibility Standards*, 91 Va. L. Rev. 471 (2005).

confronted with *Daubert* (i.e., reliability) challenges in criminal proceedings, U.S. judges demonstrated a reluctance to apply the criteria to exclude the state's evidence. Where the evidence relied upon a traditionally admissible form of evidence (i.e., deemed admissible in the years before *Daubert*), most courts used long-standing practice and precedent to effectively "grandfather" the evidence.[35] Overwhelmingly, the interest in reliability and vigorous gatekeeping was reserved for civil proceedings. American judges maintain confidence in the value of forensic science evidence produced by the state and in the abilities of juries in *criminal* proceedings.

Within a decade of *Daubert* the Supreme Court of Canada superimposed a reliability threshold on the Canadian common law, drawing explicitly on the *Daubert* criteria.[36] Notwithstanding the Supreme Court's concern with the reliability of forensic science evidence, indexed to a series of high profile wrongful convictions, intermediate appellate courts (and therefore trial judges as well) have experienced difficulties excluding speculative opinion evidence or rigorously applying meaningful criteria to expert opinion evidence proffered by the state, particularly in cases where the *Daubert* criteria were not considered an appropriate fit.[37]

Across the Atlantic, courts had referred to "reliability"—specifically "the ordinary tests of relevance and reliability"—as part of the English common law for several decades.[38] Significantly, those admissibility "tests" did not require trial judges to consider the trustworthiness, let alone validity or scientific reliability, of contested forensic science evidence.

> [S]o long as the field is sufficiently well-established to pass the ordinary tests of relevance and reliability, then no enhanced test of admissibility should be applied, but the weight of the evidence should be established by the same adversarial forensic techniques applicable elsewhere.[39]

In England, "reliability" is satisfied by the opinion of an individual from a field that is legally recognized and appears to offer assistance to the trier of fact: "[t]here is, however, no enhanced test of admissibility for such evidence."[40] As in the United States, "adversarial . . . techniques" are said to provide appropriate means of assessing proffers of expertise.

[35] Simon A. Cole, *Grandfathering Evidence: Fingerprint Admissibility Rulings from* Jennings *to* Llera Plaza *and Back Again*, 41 Am. Crim. L. Rev. 1189 (2004).

[36] R v. DD [2000] 2 S.C.R. 275; R v. J-LJ [2000] 2 S.C.R. 600; R v. Trochym, [2007] 1 S.C.R. 239; Re Truscott, 2007 ONCA 575; R v. Abbey 2009 ONCA 624 at paras. [62]–[70]; Stephen Goudge, *Inquiry into Pediatric Forensic Pathology in Ontario* (2008).

[37] *See, e.g.*, R v. Abbey 2009 ONCA 624 and R v. Aitken, 2012 BCCA 134. *See* Gary Edmond & Kent Roach, *A Contextual Approach to the Admissibility of the State's Forensic Science and Medical Evidence*, 61 U. Toronto L.J. 343 (2011).

[38] Curiously, drawn from the South Australian decision in *Bonython* [1984] 38 SASR 45.

[39] R v. Dallagher [2003] 1 Cr. App. R. 12, [29].

[40] R v. Reed [2010] 1 Cr. App. R. 23, [111]. *See also* R v. Turner [1975] Q.B. 834, 841.

This approach has not been without its critics. Following a review, the Law Commission of England and Wales characterized prevailing admissibility practice as excessively liberal:

> ... we explained that the common law approach to the admissibility of expert opinion evidence is one of laissez-faire, with such evidence being admitted without sufficient regard to whether or not it is sufficiently reliable to be considered by a jury.[41]

In response, the Law Commission drafted legislation incorporating a formal reliability standard; informed by *Daubert* and the revision to the U.S. Federal Rules of Evidence in 2000. Following the global financial crisis in 2007–2008, the conservative government invoked the need for restraint as the primary rationale for declining to enact the Commission's statutory admissibility standard.

Australia's two largest jurisdictions (New South Wales and Victoria) have explicitly rejected the need for judges to consider reliability when determining the admissibility of opinions based on "specialised knowledge" under section 79 of the Uniform Evidence Law (UEL).[42] Whereas the U.S. Supreme Court interpreted the word "knowledge" from Rule 702 to require reliability (and validity for scientific evidence), Australian courts have been unwilling to read "an extraneous idea such as 'reliability'" into the requirement for "knowledge" in their evidence statutes.[43]

Beyond formal admissibility rules, several adversarial jurisdictions have adapted civil procedural rules or developed new criminal procedures with the aim of improving the quality and transparency of expert opinion evidence.[44] Procedural rules, and codes of conduct for expert witnesses, remind the expert that they owe a primary duty to the court and ought to act impartially. They also prescribe what should be included in expert reports along with other pretrial obligations. In some jurisdictions procedural reforms have assumed significance because of difficulties encountered reforming admissibility standards.[45]

Courts in England and Wales and Victoria (in Australia) have recently introduced procedural rules specifically oriented to criminal proceedings and emerging concerns about the reliability of some forensic science and medicine evidence.[46] Like the reliability-indexed admissibility standards following *Daubert*, the new procedural rules have yet to

[41] Law Commission of England and Wales, *Expert Evidence in Criminal Proceedings in England and Wales* [1.8], [1.17], [1.27], [3.3] (2011).

[42] Most Australian jurisdictions are governed by evidence statutes based on the *Uniform Evidence Law*. See Australian Law Reform Comm'n, *Uniform Evidence Law Report* (ALRC Report 102, 2005). The relevant provision in the UEL was adapted from the original version of FRE 702.

[43] R v. Tang [2006] NSWCCA 167, [137]; Tuite v. The Queen [2015] VSCA 148.

[44] Wood v. The Queen [2012] 84 NSWLR 581, 618.

[45] Historically, procedural rules, particularly those governing expert conduct and the form and content of reports, were developed for civil proceedings and subsequently extended to criminal proceedings. *See* The "*Ikarian Reefer*" (1993) 20 FSR 563, 565–566; R v. Harris, Rock, Cherry & Faulder [2005] EWCA Crim 1980, [271]ff; R v. Bowman [2006] EWCA Crim 417, [174]ff.

[46] *See* Criminal Procedure Rules, Part 19 (England) and Practice Note: Expert Evidence in Criminal Trials (Victoria).

exert discernible influence on practice. In Australia, for example, a significant proportion of the expert reports produced by the state do not comply with the terms of procedural rules—specifically practice notes and codes of conduct (for expert witnesses).[47] Remarkably few expert reports prepared by the state (or for the state) refer to validation studies, limitations and error rates, the reasons for the particular expressions (whether "match" or identification to a "reasonable degree of ballistic certainty"), human factors and bias, controversies in the "field," or recent critical reviews—discussed in Section III. Opinions based on specialized knowledge are not typically presented in a form that explains what was done, enables the defense to make informed decisions, enables the trial judge to determine whether admissibility rules are satisfied, facilitates independent review, or facilitates evaluation by the trier of fact.[48] These oversights, when raised (by the defense), tend to be treated as issues of weight—for the tribunal of fact. Procedural rules and codes for expert evidence are not rules of admissibility per se, and only serious breaches might lead to discretionary exclusion.

In addition to rules regulating the admission and form of expert evidence, most adversarial jurisdictions have developed discretionary rules and/or maintain an inherent ability for the court to exclude otherwise admissible (expert) evidence where the probative value is outweighed by (unfair) prejudice to the accused or the interests of justice require it.[49] When confronted with admissibility challenges, these "discretionary" rules are very rarely successfully employed to exclude otherwise admissible expert opinion evidence.[50] In Australia, for example, trial judges are formally prevented from considering the reliability of the evidence or the credibility of the witness when gauging the probative value of evidence as part of the balancing exercise (UEL section 137). Such proscriptions emasculate protections. Where forensic science evidence is assumed to be reliable, many of the risks of unfair prejudice to the accused tend, by definition, to evaporate in the eyes of the judges who assume the evidence is reliable.

A recent review of admissibility decision-making in four adversarial jurisdictions (namely Australia, Canada, England and Wales, and the United States) concluded that notwithstanding differences in jurisdictional rules and procedures there were few discernible differences in admissibility outcomes.[51] Regardless of whether the jurisdiction maintained a formal reliability standard or some formulation insensitive to reliability, the same types of forensic science evidence were, by and large, routinely admitted in all of these jurisdictions.[52] For the reasons developed in Section III, the validity

[47] Gary Edmond, Kristy Martire & Mehera San Roque, *Expert Reports and the Forensic Sciences*, 40 UNSW L.J. 590 (2017).

[48] *See HG v. R* [1999] HCA 2, [39].

[49] For an overview, see Haddara v. The Queen [2014] VSCA 100.

[50] In Canada, this tends to form part of the common law admissibility test from *Mohan*: in U.S. federal and many state courts on the basis of FRE 403 or its equivalent, in England PACE § 78, in Australia §§ 135 and 137 of the UEL and Christie v. R [1914] AC 545 (at common law), and in New Zealand § 8 of the Evidence Act 2006.

[51] Gary Edmond et al., *Admissibility Compared: The Reception of Incriminating Expert (i.e., Forensic Science) Evidence in Four Adversarial Jurisdictions*, 3 U. Den. Crim. L. Rev. 31 (2013).

[52] *Id.*

and reliability of forensic science evidence is unlikely to be a persuasive explanation for uniformity in admissibility outcomes.

When confronted with admissibility challenges, trial judges rarely exclude forensic science evidence adduced by prosecutors. With the exception of DNA evidence, where judges are sometimes presented with scientific research and engage with it, when determining the admissibility of forensic science evidence judges rarely consider the kinds of factors recommended by independent scientists (to some extent embodied in the *Daubert* criteria)—discussed in Section III. In all jurisdictions, including those with formal reliability standards and case law referring to the need for validation, judges have tended to place emphasis on factors that tend to provide inferior insights. Drawing on institutional traditions, and to some extent admissibility rules and jurisprudence, trial and appellate courts place considerable store in what might be described as *legal heuristics*: the training and experience of the forensic practitioner, the practitioner's confidence and demeanor, previous appearances by the individual practitioner, the practitioner's ability to withstand cross-examination, previous legal recognition of the field or procedure (perhaps in another jurisdiction), the standing of the forensic practitioner's institution, the apparent plausibility of the procedure and opinion, and the overall strength of the case. In some jurisdictions, weak and speculative forms of opinion evidence are admitted because courts insist that judicial instructions and warnings will ameliorate the risk of misunderstanding or misuse. With the state's forensic practitioners and prosecutors taking advantage of very accommodating admissibility regimes, the value of trial safeguards and the sophistication of judges and juries assume considerable importance.

One conspicuous departure from the receptive responses to forensic science evidence adduced by prosecutors is the asymmetric treatment of expert evidence adduced by those accused of criminal acts. Some common law judges have demonstrated a willingness to hold defense expert witnesses to standards not always required of those called by the state. Such asymmetrical responses might be considered contrary to principle. If courts really are committed to the presumption of innocence, "equality of arms," the rational evaluation of evidence, and not convicting the innocent, then they should be open to receiving critical insights adduced by the defense. Reception of critical perspectives—particularly those focused on methods, the strength of conclusions, and error—would be as important as secondary objectives such as trial efficiency. Occasionally, judges prevent scientists (and others who are not forensic practitioners but nonetheless informed) from questioning the value of "abstract" methodological criticisms; see Section V.

Daubert has been influential in bringing reliability to the attention of lawyers, judges, and forensic scientists, but it has not stimulated a revolution, not even a quiet revolution, in criminal proceedings. *Daubert* may have made its main contribution beyond the courts. Forensic practitioners appear to be far more concerned about *Daubert* and their ability to satisfy the various criteria than most judges and prosecutors. *Daubert*, the introduction of formal reliability standards, and changes to procedural rules, all have considerable potential. At this stage, however, apart from the occasional decision excluding or qualifying—often temporarily—the use of forensic science evidence, admissibility rules have not been read and applied in ways that require the institutions responsible for producing and presenting forensic science evidence to make significant changes to the way evidence is collected, analyzed, presented, and evaluated. Whatever the jurisdictional standard, common law courts typically consider forensic science evidence adduced by the state as sufficiently reliable for use in criminal proceedings.

III. Independent Reviews and Emerging Problems

From the late 1980s commentators, mainly in the United States, began to openly question specific types of forensic science evidence along with the individuals responsible for producing it. By the mid-to-late 1990s among attentive audiences, problems with forensic science evidence were no longer conceived as occasional mistakes, the work of bad apples, or the result of inadequate training and organizational problems in some institutions responsible for forensic science evidence.[53] Rather, legal commentators began to look at institutional and structural issues, in the process recognizing that some procedures and even entire fields lacked scientific foundations or operated in ways that were inconsistent with, or insensitive to, mainstream scientific methods and advice.

Aside from a focus on notorious mistakes (e.g., the Birmingham Six in England and those exonerated through innocence projects) American scholars began to challenge whole "fields." Criticisms of handwriting comparison were quickly applied to latent fingerprints, toolmark and ballistics, bite marks, and arson investigation, as well as the way early DNA profiling evidence was prepared and presented.[54] Slowly, observers and commentators began to sense that many of the problems with the traditional (i.e., pre-DNA) forensic sciences were endemic. Growing awareness of problems, and their breadth, led to increasingly strident criticisms.[55] These suggestions were strenuously resisted by the institutionalized forensic sciences (e.g., the FBI), relevant government agencies (e.g., the U.S. Department of Justice), forensic practitioners' professional organizations (e.g., the International Association of Identification), and prosecutors. However, it was a mistaken fingerprint attribution—in the aftermath of the Madrid train bombing in 2004, leading to the wrongful arrest and detention of a U.S. citizen (Mayfield)—that led the U.S. Congress to intervene by funding the National Academies

[53] Brandon L. Garrett, *Convicting the Innocent: Where Criminal Prosecutions Go Wrong* (2011).

[54] Prominent examples include D. Michael Risinger, Mark P. Denbeaux & Michael J. Saks, *Exorcism of Ignorance as a Proxy for Rational Knowledge: The Lesson of Handwriting "Expertise,"* 137 U. Pa. L. Rev. 731, 731–35 (1989); Cole, *supra* note 4; Adina Schwartz, *A Systemic Challenge to the Reliability and Admissibility of Firearms and Toolmark Identification*, 6 Colum. Sci. & Tech. L. Rev. 2 (2004).

[55] Michael J. Saks & Jonathan J. Koehler, *The Coming Paradigm Shift in Forensic Identification Science*, 309 SCI. 892, 892–95 (2005).

to establish a National Research Council (NRC) committee to undertake an independent review of the forensic sciences.

The NRC's *Strengthening Forensic Science in the United States: A Path Forward* report in 2009 was the culmination of an extensive review involving submissions and formal hearings.[56] For the first time a non-aligned, unquestionably authoritative institution undertook an assessment of the state of the forensic sciences based upon a review of the available research and by comparing practices in the forensic sciences with mainstream scientific methods and expectations.[57] The report was censorious. It emphasized the need for empirical research: "validation studies must be performed."[58] It insisted on measuring and reporting error, as well as directing attention to human factors such as cognitive bias. The report also recommended removing the forensic sciences from the control of law enforcement, along with sweeping changes to the education and training of forensic practitioners.

The NRC report provided a remarkably disparaging assessment of the existing research base for many forensic sciences. The forensic comparison methods, in particular, prompted perhaps the most notorious conclusion in the report.

> With the exception of nuclear DNA analysis, however, no forensic method has been rigorously shown to have the capacity to consistently, and with a high degree of certainty, demonstrate a connection between evidence and a specific individual or source.[59]

This was, after all, aimed directly at comparisons of latent fingerprints, toolmarks, ballistics, bite marks, hair and fibers, shoe, foot and tire prints, voices, and images of persons and objects, as well as blood spatter and so on. That is, many of the most prominent procedures used in criminal investigation and prosecution.

The NRC report emboldened critical commentators and cast them, for the first time, from the margins into the mainstream. The NRC's assessment was quickly endorsed in subsequent inquiries and reports. In Scotland, Justice Campbell undertook a lengthy inquiry (*The Fingerprint Inquiry*) in response to a mistaken fingerprint attribution in a serious criminal investigation. Simultaneously, a review of human factors in latent fingerprint comparison (co-sponsored by the U.S. National Institute of Standards and Technology (NIST) and the Department of Justice) placed unprecedented emphasis on interpretation and other risks to examiner cognition.[60] These detailed reports, focused exclusively on latent fingerprint comparison, were consistent with the concerns expressed by the NRC. These later reports not only reiterated concerns about the fingerprint "methodology" but insisted that fingerprint examiners should not equate a "match"

[56] NRC Report, *supra* note 6.

[57] A review of the forensic sciences by the Department of Justice, just a decade earlier, had been much less critical. *See* National Institute of Justice & Department of Justice, *Forensic Sciences: Review of Status and Needs* (1999).

[58] NRC Report, *supra* note 6, at 113. [59] *Id.* at 7–8.

[60] Lord Anthony Campbell, *The Fingerprint Inquiry Report* (2011) [hereinafter Fingerprint Report]; National Institute of Standards and Technology, *Latent Print Examination and Human Factors: Improving the Practice Through a Systems Approach* (2012) [hereinafter NIST Report].

with the identification of a specific person (i.e., individualization) or opine that their procedures are free from error.[61] The NIST report recommended that:

> Because empirical evidence and statistical reasoning do not support a source attribution to the exclusion of all other individuals in the world, latent print examiners should not report or testify, directly or by implication, to a source attribution to the exclusion of all others in the world.[62]

The Fingerprint Inquiry report recommended that examiners discontinue some of their long-standing practices and associated claims. For example, "[e]xaminers should discontinue reporting conclusions on identification or exclusion with a claim to 100% certainty or on any other basis suggesting that fingerprint evidence is infallible."[63]

The NRC report also recommended establishing a large, well-funded national institute to begin to address ubiquitous problems across the domain. A more modest National Commission on Forensic Science was established under the auspices of NIST and the Justice Department in 2013 "to enhance the practice and improve the reliability of forensic science."[64] The activities of the Commission, through its various committees, are ongoing.

Most recently, in 2016, the U.S. President's Council of Advisors on Science and Technology (PCAST), reported on developments in the aftermath of the NRC report. PCAST's review was the first conducted exclusively by scientists, engineers, and statisticians (i.e., no forensic practitioners or lawyers). The Council produced another highly critical assessment, stridently reiterating the importance of validation. The PCAST report explained that:

> Scientific validity and reliability require that a method has been subjected to empirical testing, under conditions appropriate to its intended use, that provides valid estimates of how often the method reaches an incorrect conclusion.[65]

According to the President's Council, "[f]oundational validity is a *sine qua non*, which can only be shown through empirical studies."[66] "Nothing can substitute for it."[67] To put this another way, the PCAST report explained:

> Without appropriate estimates of accuracy, an examiner's statement that two samples are similar—or even indistinguishable—is scientifically meaningless: it has no probative value, and considerable potential for prejudicial impact. Nothing—not

[61] NRC Report, *supra* note 6, at 142, 184 ("... fingerprint identification experts should exhibit a greater degree of epistemological humility. Claims of 'absolute' and 'positive' identification should be replaced by more modest claims about the meaning and significance of a 'match.'"), quoting Jennifer Mnookin, *The Validity of Latent Fingerprint Identification: Confessions of a Fingerprinting Moderate*, 7 L. Prob. & Risk 127 (2008).

[62] NIST Report, *supra* note 60, at 72 (Recommendation 3.7), 77.

[63] Fingerprint Report, *supra* note 60, Recommendation 3.

[64] National Commission on Forensic Science, https://www.justice.gov/ncfs (last visited Feb. 20, 2017).

[65] PCAST Report, *supra* note 15, at 143. [66] *Id.* at 66 & 147. [67] *Id.* at 6.

> training, personal experience professional practices—can substitute for adequate empirical demonstration of accuracy.[68]

PCAST undertook a review of the publicly available research supporting seven prominent forensic comparison methods, namely "(1) DNA analysis of single-source and simple-mixture samples, (2) DNA analysis of complex-mixture samples, (3) bitemarks, (4) latent fingerprints, (5) firearms identification, and (6) footwear analysis" as well as microscopic hair comparison.[69] The Council concluded that only two of the seven—simple DNA analysis and latent fingerprint comparison—were foundationally valid. The assessment of basic DNA profiling was hardly surprising. The review of the other comparison methods was more revealing.

The first ever validation studies for fingerprint comparisons had been undertaken following—and in response to—the NRC report. The results confirmed that trained latent fingerprint examiners possessed demonstrable expertise, but simultaneously revealed that fingerprint examiners do not perform at the level customarily suggested in reports and testimony. Experiments confirmed that highly trained and experienced fingerprint examiners make errors. PCAST considered that fingerprint examiners and their institutions had not responded appropriately to the results of the emerging studies. According to PCAST, it was incumbent upon the state to disclose information about the known rate of false positives.

> PCAST finds that latent fingerprint analysis is a foundationally valid subjective methodology—albeit with a false positive rate that is substantial and is likely to be higher than expected by many jurors based on longstanding claims about the infallibility of fingerprint analysis. The false-positive rate could be as high as 1 error in 306 cases based on the FBI study and 1 error in 18 cases based on a study by another crime laboratory. In reporting results of latent-fingerprint examination, it is important to state the false-positive rates based on properly designed validation studies.[70]

Failure to disclose this information threatens rational evaluation and is likely to lead to overvaluation (threatening rectitude and introducing risks of unfair prejudice). For PCAST the two available fingerprint studies—one of which was compromised by not having been reviewed and published—provided the only credible basis for making claims about the probative value of latent fingerprint evidence.

The other five comparison methods were, by contrast, found to lack validity. To be clear, that does not mean they are unreliable, but rather that their scientific reliability (i.e., repeatability, reproducibility, and accuracy) is unknown and yet to be demonstrated. This finding—following the NRC's assessment—might be considered alarming. Particularly in the case of microscopic hair and bite mark comparisons, where PCAST recommended against continuing research and investment. The forensic comparison methods reviewed by PCAST may not be representative of other procedures, although

[68] *Id.* at 46 & 143.　[69] *Id.* at 7 & 27–29.

[70] *Id.* at 9–10; *see also id.* at 87–104; NRC Report, *supra* note 6, at 136–45; NIST Report, *supra* note 60; Fingerprint Report, *supra* note 60.

many—most conspicuously those that predate DNA profiling—are yet to be rigorously evaluated. Interestingly, some emerging forensic sciences have not been particularly attentive to the NRC and PCAST reports. Consider the use of covert voice recordings and CCTV images for identification purposes (particularly face and gait comparison), the analysis of computers and other devices (so-called digital forensics), and the application of new statistical methods and algorithms to the increasing volume of collected and stored electronic information (i.e., big data).[71]

Because of the strength and austerity of its conclusions, the PCAST report generated some resistance. Responses, though, have not been concerned with, and have not disputed, the need for research and the primacy of validation. Instead, they have focused on whether the validation studies for complex DNA samples are adequate and how to calculate and express error and opinions.[72] In the weeks before Donald Trump assumed office, PCAST emphatically rejected concerns raised by forensic scientists and their organizations. For members of the President's Council, the use of procedures and the way opinions are expressed must be governed by publicly available scientific evidence. Those claiming special abilities, or high levels of performance, must support those claims with methodologically rigorous studies.

The mainstream scientific response to the forensic sciences, particularly the traditional feature comparison methods, sits very awkwardly when contrasted with the very accommodating approach of courts in adversarial jurisdictions. Relatively few judges and even fewer juries seem to have been exposed to the kinds of concerns expressed authoritatively by the NRC and PCAST. The inability of forensic scientists, lawyers, and judges to identify, let alone appreciate and credibly explore, problems with many areas of forensic science led to exasperation. This is evident in the NRC report:

> In a number of forensic science disciplines, forensic science professionals have yet to establish either the validity of their approach or the accuracy of their conclusions, and the courts have been utterly ineffective in addressing this problem. For a variety of reasons—including the rules governing the admissibility of forensic evidence, the applicable standards governing appellate review of trial court decisions, the limitations of the adversary process, and the common lack of scientific expertise among judges and lawyers who must try to comprehend and evaluate forensic evidence—the legal system is ill-equipped to correct the problems of the forensic science community.[73]

Lack of engagement with mainstream scientific perspectives might be comprehensible if courts were already conversant with limitations because of the effectiveness of trial practices, particularly trial safeguards, or through other forms of exposure to independent

[71] Erin Murphy, *The Mismatch Between Twenty-First-Century Forensic Evidence and Our Antiquated Criminal Justice System*, 87 S. Cal. L. Rev. 633 (2014).

[72] Following requests for further information, PCAST dismissed the comments of critiques. The Justice Department withdrew its concerns when specific evidence was requested.

[73] NRC Report, *supra* note 6, at 53.

scientific advice. Unfortunately, three decades of critical commentary, beginning with scholarly criticisms in the late 1980s and culminating in authoritative consensus reports prepared by prestigious scientific organizations (such as the NRC and PCAST), appear to have exerted remarkably limited influence on legal practice in most adversarial jurisdictions.

IV. Engagement with the Reports and Relevant Scientific Research

One of the most curious and, for attentive observers, frustrating dimensions of the recent appearance of a range of authoritative reviews is the lack of legal engagement and "uptake."[74] This lack of engagement applies to both lawyers and judges; although in common law jurisdictions the parties are responsible for locating and adducing evidence relevant to their case. Appellate courts conceive of trial judges as constrained and implicitly passive; remote from the investigation and prevented from undertaking their own inquiries or adducing evidence. The lack of systematic engagement with relevant and authoritative scientific research and advice has meant that judicial responses to proffers of forensic science are heavily reliant on traditional legal heuristics and the parties' resources, abilities, and interests. Consequently, forensic science evidence is frequently evaluated by nontechnical audiences, in conditions where challenges, to the extent that they occur, tend not to be scientifically informed. Legal decision-makers—lawyers, judges, and juries—are habitually making decisions deprived of important, and arguably essential, information. Most challenges focus on the demeanor and credibility of individual forensic practitioners, perhaps the continuity of samples and contamination, and other issues of less import than whether, how well, and in what conditions the underlying procedure works.

1. Authoritative Reports in U.S. Litigation

In jurisdictions where lawyers have sought to introduce the findings and recommendations from authoritative reports, courts have not been especially receptive. U.S. judges and prosecutors have developed a range of strategies to inoculate against the impact of critical perspectives and their potentially disruptive implications, even where the reports are directly applicable to local practices and admissibility standards.[75] Strategies include placing weight on legal traditions of admission and reliance. For example, "[w]e are not

[74] There are some exceptions; see the engagement with medical evidence following controversy in R v. Harris, Rock, Cherry & Faulder [2005] EWCA Crim 1980, [2006] 1 Cr. App. R. 5.

[75] *See* Simon A. Cole & Gary Edmond, *Science Without Precedent: The Impact of the National Research Council Report on the Admissibility and Use of Forensic Science Evidence*, 4 Brit. J. Am. Stud. 585 (2015).

prepared to throw out decades of precedent based on a single report."[76] Courts have characterized the reports as non-legal documents, thereby blunting their potential application even in jurisdictions requiring validity and reliability for admission. The fact that the reports were written by scientists rather than forensic practitioners has been used to discount criticisms: "The relevant scientific fingerprint community does not consider the NRC report a learned treatise."[77] Current practices are sometimes excused because recommendations are characterized as aspirational or a counsel of perfection. Occasionally, the fact that forensic science providers are in the process of reform is used as a warrant for the reception of evidence produced using traditional procedures—the very procedures subject to criticism. Several courts have required forensic practitioners to modify the language used to express their opinions. Superficially attractive, and apparently consistent with mainstream scientific advice, this example illustrates how such impositions might not be based on (or responsive to) scientific research and may not constitute an improvement in accuracy or assist with comprehension.

> However, because of the limitations on the reliability of firearms identification evidence discussed above, [the witness] will not be permitted to testify that his methodology allows him to reach this conclusion as a matter of scientific certainty. [He] also will not be allowed to testify that he can conclude that there is a match to the exclusion, either practical or absolute of all other guns. He may only testify that, in his opinion, the bullet came from the suspect rifle to within a reasonable degree of certainty in the firearms examination field.[78]

2. Authoritative Reports beyond the United States

Outside the United States, the various reports have been almost invisible to lawyers and courts engaged in the regulation and evaluation of proffers of forensic science and medical evidence. Whereas foreign judgments—from jurisdictions with different admissibility standards—are occasionally used to support admissibility decisions, foreign reports with direct application to forensic science evidence—that transcend jurisdictional boundaries—have encountered qualified engagement.[79] Where the defense challenged

[76] North Carolina v. Leonard, 726 S.E.2d 647 (N.C. 2013). *See also* Illinois v. Morris, 997 N.E.2d 847, 871 (Ill. 2013); United States v. Rose, 672 F. Supp. 2d 723, 725 (D. Md. 2009); Jones v. United States, 27 A.3d 1130, 1137–38 (D.C. 2011).

[77] Gee v. United States, 54 A.3d 1249, 1262–63, 1266 (D.C. 2012). "Learned treatise" has a particular exception to the hearsay rule in Fed. R. Evid. 803(18).

[78] United States v. Taylor, 663 F. Supp. 2d 1170, 1180 (D.N.M. 2009). *See also* United States v. Sebbern, 2012 WL 5989813 (E.D.N.Y. 2012); Melcher v. Holland, 2014 WL 31359, 13 (N.D. Cal. 2014); United States v. Willock, 696 F. Supp. 2d 536, 546 (D. Md. 2010). Contrast National Commission on Forensic Science, *Testimony Using the Term "Reasonable Scientific Certainty"* (2013).

[79] *See, e.g.*, the use in R v. Otway, [2011] EWCA Crim 3 (Eng.) and in R v. Aitken, 2012 BCCA 134 (Can.). England does not have a formal reliability standard whereas the Supreme Court of Canada had insisted upon the need to attend to reliability, particularly (though not exclusively) where the procedure was novel.

forensic gait comparison, proffered by a clinical podiatrist, an English appellate court reviewing admission focused on the individual witnesses and the specifics of the case.[80] The evidence of a defense witness, seeking to invoke the NRC report, specifically in response to the absence of any validation, was discounted because he was not a podiatrist (offering a contrary interpretation of the gait) and because English case law had previously excused the failure to validate and the absence of a database (of face and body features) when considering the admissibility of interpretations of persons in CCTV images.[81] The English court placed emphasis on the podiatrist's opinion and the facts of the case—as if that orientation somehow circumvented the methodological oversights and consequential ignorance.

In *R v. Bornyk*, a Canadian retrial based entirely on a single latent fingerprint recovered from a burglary, the trial judge (sitting alone) received detailed argument around the NRC and PCAST reports and some of the studies cited therein.[82] The trial judge nevertheless convicted the accused because, notwithstanding a range of serious methodological problems—including suggestion, non-blind review. and the form of conclusion adopted by the fingerprint examiner (i.e., individualization)—the defense did not identify an actual error. Methodological problems, in conjunction with nondisclosure of limitations by the state, were insufficient to raise reasonable doubt in a fingerprint-only prosecution.

Only two courts in Australia have cited the NRC report. One was a passing reference; the other, by the Victorian Court of Appeal, referred to the NRC report and problems with forensic science evidence when considering the relationship between "reliability" and probative value in the admission of forensic science evidence according to section 137 of the Uniform Evidence Law. Recognizing the need for reliability and validity, in *Tuite v. The Queen*, the Court concluded that new algorithms designed for analyzing complex DNA samples were valid and scientifically reliable—a conclusion inconsistent with PCAST's assessment. The Court of Appeal's interest in reliability and validity appears to have been inadvertently overruled by Australia's highest court, which recently insisted that trial judges must not consider reliability when gauging probative value.[83]

Surprisingly few lawyers have raised the various publicly available reports.[84] Where defense lawyers have endeavored to mount challenges to the scientific foundations of particular procedures—particularly in the United States—courts have expressed a preference for hearing from (experienced) forensic practitioners rather than from scientists and other scholarly commentators familiar with validation and the implications of its absence. With the exception of DNA profiling evidence, lawyers and courts in all jurisdictions have generally been more interested in the opinions of forensic

[80] *See* Gary Edmond & Emma Cunliffe, *Cinderella Story: The Social Production of a Forensic "Science,"* 106 J. Crim. L. & Criminology 219 (2017). *See also* The Royal Society (UK), *Forensic Gait Analysis: A Primer for the Courts* (2017).

[81] R v. Otway, [2011] EWCA Crim 3, [18].

[82] R v. Bornyk, 2015 BCCA 28. Discussed in Gary Edmond, David Hamer & Emma Cunliffe, *A Little Ignorance Is a Dangerous Thing: Engaging with Exogenous Knowledge Not Adduced by the Parties*, 25 Griffith L. Rev. 383 (2016).

[83] IMM v. The Queen [2016] HCA 14.

[84] *See e.g.*, JP v. DPP [2015] NSWSC 1669.

practitioners, and in some cases whether a rebuttal expert (dis)agrees about the specific interpretation or an actual error has been identified, than with the scientific foundations of the procedure or the frequency with which errors occur.

Revealingly, it has been forensic practitioners and police who seem to have been most responsive, once independent scientific organizations lent their weight to what was initially an academic critique. Scientists, along with some forensic scientists and their institutions, have begun to engage in fundamental research. The United States established a commission to facilitate and supervise the response to the NRC report.[85] In the UK, the government in 2008 created the position of Forensic Science Regulator to advise on the provision of forensic science services (by public and commercial providers), a role that has assumed considerable significance following the closure of the Forensic Science Service in 2012.

V. Unshaken Confidence in the Trial and Trial Safeguards

> Vigorous cross-examination, presentation of contrary evidence, and careful instruction on the burden of proof are the traditional and appropriate means of attacking shaky but admissible evidence.[86]

Liberal approaches to the admission of forensic science evidence continue, in large part, because of the confidence in adversarial procedures and trial safeguards. This confidence is pervasive, though perhaps most conspicuous in the United States. The epigraph above is from the majority decision in *Daubert*—a case ushering a new reliability standard for the admission of expert opinion evidence.

One way to think about the effectiveness of traditional adversarial trial mechanisms and safeguards (along with the value of "legal experience" and the "collective experience of judges") is to consider legal familiarity with mainstream scientific perspectives and the way scientific advice has been accommodated within admissibility jurisprudence, procedural rules, and practice. Without contending that responses to forensic science evidence have been entirely uniform, there is, even in jurisdictions with formal reliability standards, very little evidence of lawyers and judges appreciating the evidentiary implications of recent reports and their recommendations. Notwithstanding preeminent scientists (from a broad array of disciplinary backgrounds) insisting that in the absence of validation forensic science procedures should not be used, or used very cautiously with modest conclusions, lawyers and judges have tended to trivialize or ignore such concerns. They frequently rehearse legal faith in the implicit effectiveness of

[85] The commission's charter was allowed to expire under the Trump administration, although a range of scientific committees persist under the auspices of the National Institute of Standards and Technology.

[86] Daubert v. Merrell Dow Pharms., 509 U.S. 579, 595 (1993). *See also* Melendez-Diaz v. Massachusetts, 557 U.S. 305, 129 S. Ct. 2527 (2009).

adversarialism and its safeguards, or refer to "problems" in rather abstract terms—as if limitations and error rates do not apply to specific case-based applications where actual error is not identified. A handful of senior judges and courts have expressed concerns about problems, including the U.S. Supreme Court, Supreme Court of Canada, the Victorian Court of Appeal, and the Chief Justice of England and Wales.[87] But few decisions have resulted in more exclusionary orientations (or the exclusion of much evidence), and relatively few decisions formally address validation (with the conspicuous exception of challenges to DNA evidence), limitations, uncertainty, error, proficiency, or human factors.

This is an important, and perhaps profound, observation because it seems to suggest that an awareness of serious methodological problems did not emerge through endogenous legal practice or (collective) legal experience. By and large, most of the limitations were identified from without, by those conversant with scientific research methods and statistics. Valorized procedures and trial safeguards have not exerted much apparent influence on legal consciousness or legal practices. Notwithstanding the considerable scope for lawyers to adduce evidence and question witnesses, there seem to be remarkably few signs of legal sensitivity to the depth or breadth of epistemic problems with many forensic sciences. Courts continue to perceive problems with expert opinion evidence in terms of bias and partisanship, witnesses trespassing beyond the boundaries of (legally constructed) "fields," the danger of the trier of fact deferring to the witness (the so-called white-coat effect), and distortions introduced by media (from shows such as *CSI*).

For attentive audiences conversant with both conventional legal practice and scientific reports, it is difficult to comprehend legal indifference to mainstream scientific recommendations and advice. The concern is not that most people convicted in cases where forensic science is relied upon, whether through plea or at trial, are not guilty, although the role of mistaken or misleading forensic science evidence in wrongful convictions is hardly a trivial issue. Rather, the problem is that the value or weight of much forensic science evidence is simply unknown and, along with its limitations, this is not systematically disclosed and explained to decision-makers. To varying degrees a large number of trials may have been (and continue to be) substantially unfair because abilities and opinions were misrepresented—almost always in ways that advantaged the prosecution.[88] Forensic practitioners often testify in evocative terms—such as "one and the same," "identified to," "no meaningful differences" and "to a reasonable degree

[87] Conspicuously: Harry T. Edwards, *Solving the Problems That Plague the Forensic Science Community*, 50 Jurimetrics J. 5, 7 (2009); Ian Binnie, *Wrongful Convictions and the Magical Aura of Science in the Courtroom*, 10 Judicial Rev. 141 (2011); Lord Thomas, Chief Justice of England, *Expert Evidence and the Future of Forensic Science in Criminal Trials* (Criminal Bar Association Kalisher Lecture, 14 Oct. 2014); Lord Leveson, *Expert Evidence in Criminal Courts—The Problem* (Lecture to the Forensic Science Society, UK, Nov. 2010); Nancy Gertner, *Commentary on "The Need for a Research Culture in the Forensic Sciences,"* 58 UCLA L. Rev. 789 (2011).

[88] The exception is probabilistic DNA evidence informed by population statistics, but these results do not include indicative error rates. *See* Jay J. Koehler, *Proficiency Tests to Estimate Error Rates in the Forensic Sciences*, 12 L. Prob. & Risk 89 (2012).

of ballistic certainty"—that are highly suggestive though often lacking scientific warrant.[89] Relatively few practitioners proactively draw attention to limitations or acknowledge the ever-present risk of error. Most imply or suggest that such dangers are remote (even hypothetical) or prevented by the use of processes (e.g., non-blind verification) that have not been evaluated and so are not known to be effective.[90]

In the absence of information about validation, scientific reliability, limitations, error rates, and management of human factors, decision-makers are not in a position to rationally evaluate the evidence. They are, in effect, compelled to rely on legal heuristics—really secondary criteria and epiphenomena. These sources of information may not be without value, but they do not—individually or in combination—address or supplant the need for validation. They do not indicate whether a procedure works, how well it works, in what conditions, or whether the particular practitioner is proficient.

Trial safeguards are unlikely to adequately identify and convey limitations where the kinds of issues raised by the NRC and PCAST reports and by *Daubert* are not disclosed or identified.[91] Cross-examination may not be very effective where the examiner or the audience is not conversant with relevant issues—such as the primacy of validation relative to experience. Cross-examination would seem to have limited utility identifying actual errors where they might have been the result of unconscious cognitive processes such as suggestion. Judicial instructions, directions, and warnings are incapable of exposing and explaining problems or assisting with the weighing of evidence if fundamental issues are not understood or clearly explained. Defense witnesses, offering methodological criticisms by way of rebuttal, may make criminal proceedings appear fair(er), but they are unlikely to correct or balance the positive evidence proffered by experienced state-employed investigators—regardless of whether that evidence is accurate or mistaken. Rebuttal experts are unlikely to exert balancing effects even when testifying about serious dangers notorious among mainstream scientists and even when the opposed opinion is exaggerated or mistaken.[92] Defense access to expert witnesses and expert advice is becoming less common as the number of cases proceeding to trial decreases and the resources provided to the defense are more closely scrutinized.[93] And as we have seen, judges seem to expect the defense to identify actual errors rather than require information about the validity and scientific reliability of procedures, indicative error rates, and the proficiency of individuals.[94]

[89] NRC Report, *supra* note 6, at 185–86; PCAST Report, *supra* note 15, at 29–30; National Commission, *supra* note 64.

[90] PCAST Report, *supra* note 15, at 3. *See also* Kaye Ballantyne et al., *Peer Review in Forensic Science*, 277 Forensic Sci. Int'l 66 (2017).

[91] Dawn McQuiston-Surrett & Michael J. Saks, *Communicating Opinion Evidence in the Forensic Identification Sciences: Accuracy and Impact*, 59 Hastings L.J. 1159 (2008).

[92] Discussed with other issues in Gary Edmond & Mehera San Roque, *The Cool Crucible: Forensic Science and the Frailty of the Criminal Trial*, 24 Current Issues Crim. Just. 51 (2012).

[93] Contrast Ake v. Oklahoma, 470 U.S. 68 (1985).

[94] David Faigman, John Monahan & Chris Slobogin, *Group to Individual (G2i) Inference in Scientific Expert Testimony*, 81 U. Chi. L. Rev. 417 (2014).

Courts store great confidence in the trial providing the decision-maker (whether jury or judge) with the means of evaluating the evidence and determining guilt or innocence. Again, in terms of assessing the actual effectiveness of trial mechanisms and safeguards, the fact that information said to be foundational, by both the NRC and PCAST, is not disclosed and may not be discussed or even available, suggests that legal decision-making is often far from optimal. It is unlikely that trial safeguards and appeals are very effective where lawyers act in ignorance or do not have the resources or technical abilities to understand or meaningfully contest forensic science evidence. Judges and juries cannot evaluate scientific, medical, and technical evidence deprived of essential information. Moreover, trial judges are not positioned to provide assistance to juries when they are insufficiently attentive to the very information or insights that would enable a decision-maker to rationally evaluate procedures and derivative opinions.

The NRC and the Law Commission of England and Wales do not share the widespread faith in the effectiveness of trial mechanisms and legal personnel. The Law Commission expressed doubts about the ability of trial safeguards to consistently identify, let alone repair, problems with insufficiently reliable forensic science evidence.

> Cross-examination, the adduction of contrary expert evidence and judicial guidance at the end of the trial are currently assumed to provide sufficient safeguards in relation to expert evidence... However,.... it is doubtful whether these are valid assumptions.[95]

The NRC report went further:

> The bottom line is simple: In a number of forensic science disciplines, forensic science professionals have yet to establish either the validity of their approach or the accuracy of their conclusions, and the courts have been utterly ineffective in addressing this problem. For a variety of reasons—including the rules governing the admissibility of forensic evidence, the applicable standards governing appellate review of trial court decisions, the limitations of the adversary process, and the common lack of scientific expertise among judges and lawyers who must try to comprehend and evaluate forensic evidence—the legal system is ill-equipped to correct the problems of the forensic science community. In short, judicial review, by itself, is not the answer.[96]

Criticizing the courts without recognizing diachronic shifts in criminal justice policies, procedures, and funding might seem unfair. The gradual decline in resources, particularly for the defense, may have contributed to problems. However, shrinking budgets and changing approaches to law and order do not explain the very restricted legal engagement with mainstream scientific advice. Diminution in the resources available to the defense does mean, however, that those accused of criminal acts are increasingly reliant upon forensic science evidence produced by the state being valid and reliable. The ability to seriously challenge forensic science evidence is in most cases little more than a theoretical possibility unlikely to manifest in practice. Relatively few cases proceed to

[95] Law Commission, *supra* note 41, at 1.20 & 1.24.

[96] NRC Report, *supra* note 6, at 53. *See also* Neufeld, *supra* note 12, at S110.

trial. Ironically, it is not the possibility of error that is remote but the ability to effectively contest forensic science evidence that may not be scientifically supported. This difficulty is compounded by the reticence of trial and appellate courts to appreciate or credibly engage with concerns expressed by attentive independent scientists. Defendants are increasingly dependent upon forensic scientists, prosecutors, and judges in conditions where the frailties of forensic science evidence are not routinely disclosed and may not be recognized.

VI. The Myth of the "Gate" and the Problem of Legal Learning

Controversially, this chapter questions whether there are meaningful standards regulating the admission of forensic science evidence. Most types of opinion evidence adduced by the state are routinely admitted in criminal proceedings. Alongside this accommodating response to the forensic sciences, courts have been cautious, even reluctant to engage with, authoritative scientific advice. Recent reviews and reports by peak scientific and technical organizations have placed emphasis on the need for procedures to be formally evaluated—most conspicuously validated. Scientific concern with validation and reliability is, as we have seen, inconsistent with contemporary practice in most adversarial jurisdictions, including those with formal reliability standards. Authoritative interventions also cast doubts on the value of traditional legal assumptions and practices pertaining to expertise. Common law courts seem to have encountered difficulty engaging with exogenous perspectives, and explaining why legal practice does not or need not align with a chorus of mainstream scientific advice. Liberal admissibility practices shift issues of reliability from determinations by trial judges to issues for the jury to resolve during the course of adversarial proceedings. In the vast majority of the cases resolved in criminal justice systems, whether through plea and charge negotiations or trial, potential limitations and errors associated with forensic science procedures may never be disclosed to, and therefore considered by, defendants, the lawyers representing them, and those deciding guilt or innocence.

Our courts have been complicit in the rise of forensic science procedures that are not systemically grounded in scientific research. The traditional forensic sciences operated largely (though not entirely) by police and other investigators, treated admission and/or conviction as adequate forms of support. Admission was characterized as a de facto form of legitimation, even validation. This is a category mistake. It is highly undesirable because it misconceives the very serious constraints on "testing" in legal settings. Legal institutions and proceedings are not substitutes for formal evaluation of procedures and proficiency. Criminal proceedings almost never provide conditions where the correct answers are known. Moreover, convictions do not provide evidence of validity or insight into levels of accuracy and error. Defense challenges, where they occur, are usually superficial and ad hominem. This reality is at odds with pervasive and entrenched judicial commitments.

In the absence of persuasive reasons for not following consensual mainstream scientific advice, courts should adopt *and* apply admissibility standards that focus directly on validity and scientific reliability (or scientifically robust alternatives in those instances where these are not appropriate). These standards should be applied to new types of procedures and retrospectively to techniques that have never had to justify their admission and use in terms of validity, scientific reliability, error rates, and so forth. Prosecutors should be reluctant to rely upon untested or inadequately tested procedures and the opinions of forensic practitioners who, however experienced, have never had to demonstrate their proficiency with validated procedures.

The threat posed by forensic science evidence persists as does the legacy of pathological legal co-production. Weak admissibility standards, detached from appropriate indicia of reliability, threaten rectitude of decisions, fairness, and legal legitimacy.

References

Jay Aronson, *Genetic Witness: Science, Law, and Controversy in the Making of DNA Profiling* (2007)

Ian Burney, *Bodies of Evidence: Medicine and the Politics of the English Inquest, 1830–1926* (2000)

Simon A. Cole, *Suspect Identities: A History of Fingerprinting and Criminal Identification* (2001)

Gary Edmond & Emma Cunliffe, *Cinderella Story: The Social Production of a Forensic "Science,"* 106 J. Crim. L. & Criminology 219 (2017)

David A. Harris, *Failed Evidence: Why Law Enforcement Resists Science* (2012)

Law Commission of England and Wales, *Expert Evidence in Criminal Proceedings in England and Wales* (2011)

Legal Medicine in History (Michael Clark & Catherine Crawford eds., 1994)

Kristy Martire & Gary Edmond, *Re-thinking Expert Evidence*, 41 Melbourne U. L. Rev. 967 (2017)

Jennifer L. Mnookin et al., *The Need for a Research Culture in the Forensic Sciences*, 58 UCLA L. Rev. 725 (2011)

Erin E. Murphy, *Inside the Cell: The Dark Side of Forensic DNA* (2015)

National Research Council, *Strengthening Forensic Science in the United States: A Path Forward* (2009)

President's Council of Advisors on Science & Technology, *Forensic Science in Criminal Courts: Ensuring Scientific Validity of Feature-Comparison Methods* (2016)

CHAPTER 35

BEYOND COMMON LAW EVIDENCE

Reimagining, and Reinvigorating, Evidence Law as Forensic Science

JOHN JACKSON AND PAUL ROBERTS

> I suppose there never was a more slapdash, disjointed and inconsequent body of rules than that which we call the Law of Evidence. Founded apparently on the proposition that all jurymen are deaf to reason, that all witnesses are presumptively liars and that all documents are presumptively forgeries, it has been added to, subtracted from and tinkered with for two centuries until it has become less of a structure than a pile of builder's debris.
>
> C. P. Harvey, *The Advocate's Devil* (1958)

I. Introduction

C.P. Harvey's mid-twentieth century depiction of "the Law of Evidence"[1] expresses a familiar refrain in legal scholarship and policy argument, and more generally in jurisprudential thinking stretching back at least to Bentham. According to this view, rules of evidence in the common law world are the haphazard and irrational product of a historical legacy owing more to practical institutional imperatives, adversarial strategy, and happenstance than rational planning.[2] The common law's artifice is then contrasted

[1] When capitalized as a proper noun, "the Law of Evidence" (and its cognates "Evidence," "Evidence law," etc.) refer to the disciplinary specialism, as presented in textbooks and taught in universities, rather than simply describing the law applicable to evidence.

[2] Sir Rupert Cross famously averred (as recalled by William Twining, *Rethinking Evidence* 1 (2d ed. 2006)) that he was working for the day when his subject would be abolished. Seventy-five years earlier, Thayer declared that "our law of evidence is a piece of illogical, but by no means irrational, patchwork,

unfavorably with Continental European models of trial procedure, predicated on a more overtly and self-consciously rational system of "free proof." Yet such cartoonish comparisons are inevitably superficial and potentially misleading. Continental legal procedures embraced "free proof" as an emphatic rejection of formalistic Roman-canon classifications of evidence types and mechanistic quantifications of probative value, to which the common law tradition was never strongly committed. To this day, a prominent characteristic of the jury system that has shaped the contours of common law evidence rules[3] is the freedom of lay fact-finders to return verdicts based on ordinary common sense reasoning, formulated in secret and with limited opportunity for meaningful appellate scrutiny of jury fact-finding.[4] Conversely, to describe civil law systems as comprehensively governed by a principle of "free proof" is also an increasingly inadequate caricature. Partly under the harmonizing influence of European fair trial rights and Article 6 of the European Convention on Human Rights (ECHR), contemporary Continental procedural systems place a variety of constraints on the admissibility and uses of certain types of evidence similar, in many respects, to evidentiary devices and doctrines familiar to common lawyers.[5]

The most truly distinctive feature of common law approaches to evidence and proof is the very idea of a discrete and unified Law of Evidence, disaggregated from procedural regulation more generally but pertaining—at least in its key principles, doctrines, and assumptions, and as a first approximation subject to contextual adaptations—to fact-finding in all types of legal adjudicative process. Over the past two-and-a-half centuries, treatise writers and English courts have developed the Law of Evidence as a discrete body of law and practice, separated from the study of substantive law and as a subset of legal process focused on evidentiary considerations at trial—especially questions of admissibility. While civil law jurisdictions have seemingly had little use for such a doctrinal taxonomy,[6] the disciplinary specialism of Evidence is well entrenched within the common law world, albeit far from uncontroversial in its format, scope, or ambitions; as

not at all to be admired, nor easily to be found intelligible . . . that submits too often to a mistaken application of its precedents, that is often shortsighted and ill-instructed, and that needs to be taken in hand by the jurist": James B. Thayer, *The Present and Future of the Law of Evidence*, 12 Harv. L. Rev. 71, 72 (1898).

[3] To say that the jury trial has *shaped* evidentiary doctrine is not the extravagant claim, propounded by Thayer and repeated many times since, that the jury trial begat common law evidence. *See further*, Mirjan R. Damaška, *The Jury and the Law of Evidence: Real and Imagined Interconnections*, 5 L. Prob. & Risk 255 (2007); Frederick Schauer, *On the Supposed Jury-Dependence of Evidence Law*, 155 U. Pa. L. Rev. (2006).

[4] *See* John D. Jackson, *Unbecoming Jurors and Unreasoned Verdicts: Realising Integrity in the Jury Room*, in *The Integrity of Criminal Process* (Jill Hunter, Paul Roberts, Simon N.M. Young & David Dixon eds., 2016); Paul Roberts, *Does Article 6 of the European Convention on Human Rights Require Reasoned Verdicts in Criminal Trials?*, 11 Hum. Rts. L. Rev. 213 (2011).

[5] John D. Jackson & Sarah J. Summers, *The Internationalisation of Criminal Evidence* (2012); Stefan Trechsel with Sarah Summers, *Human Rights in Criminal Proceedings* (2005); Sarah J. Summers, *Fair Trials: The European Procedural Tradition and the European Court of Human Rights* (2007).

[6] *See, e.g.*, Johannes F. Nijboer, *Common Law Tradition in Evidence Scholarship Observed from a Continental Perspective*, 41 Am. J. Comp. L. 299 (1993).

Harvey's broadside colorfully illustrates. Jeremy Bentham began an abolitionist crusade in the early nineteenth century with his advocacy for a "natural" system of proof to replace the common law's rigid and "artificial" technicalities.[7] His overarching, "anti-nomian" principle was that all relevant evidence should be admitted in trials and assessed according to its individualized merits, not on the basis of any preconceived classification or metric. Many of the particular evidentiary rules and doctrines that attracted Bentham's withering criticism have since either disappeared entirely or declined in importance, partly owing to the force of the Benthamite critique and its impetus to institutional reform;[8] but also as a consequence of the gradual erosion of the traditional institutional environment in which common law rules of evidence have flourished.[9] In an influential contribution to the debate, Mirjan Damaška identified concentrated trial proceedings, adversary procedure, and trial by jury as three major pillars of the Law of Evidence. As all three pillars have tottered and crumbled in recent decades, Damaška suggests, common law Evidence has been cast adrift from its secure institutional moorings.

Viewed from another perspective, however, the "Law of Evidence," far from being marooned and rudderless, is as buoyant as ever. Bentham's reforming zeal was propelled by a consequentialist utilitarian philosophy that has never been fully accepted by the legal establishment (or by law reformers and society more broadly). Neither his "natural" system of proof nor his "anti-nomian" insistence on unfettered contextual appraisal of evidence have garnered widespread support as fundamental principles for the design of common law systems of adjudication. A major barrier to Benthamite or any other form of instrumentalism is the law's emphasis on intrinsic procedural rights, grounded in neo-Kantian or more broadly deontological values, which have only increased in prominence in an era of heightened sensitivity to human rights protection. Although they are undeniably a source of recurrent controversy, individual rights have supplied enduring rationales for many characteristically common law rules of evidence, notwithstanding broader procedural shifts and realignments over time. Evidentiary doctrines such as compulsory process, legal professional privilege, the exclusion of unlawfully obtained evidence, and the right of silence have been elevated to the status of constitutional guarantees in many common law (as well as in civilian) jurisdictions.[10] To be sure, the vitality of evidentiary doctrine is largely confined to criminal adjudication, whereas the status of evidence law in civil proceedings has been in sharp decline for some time in

[7] *See* William Twining, *Theories of Evidence: Bentham and Wigmore* ch. 2 (1985); Gerald J. Postema, *The Principle of Utility and the Law of Procedure: Bentham's Theory of Adjudication*, 11 Ga. L. Rev. 1393 (1977).

[8] *See* Ian Dennis, *Reconstructing the Law of Criminal Evidence*, 42 Current Legal Probs. 21, 26 (1989); Twining, *supra* note 2, at 170–71.

[9] Mirjan Damaška, *Evidence Law Adrift* (1997).

[10] *See* Paul Roberts, *Excluding Evidence as Protecting Constitutional or Human Rights?*, in *Principles and Values in Criminal Law and Criminal Justice* (Lucia Zedner & Julian V. Roberts eds., 2012); John D. Jackson, *Adrift but Still Clinging to the Wreckage*, 49 Hastings L.J. 369, 377 (1998).

most, but apparently not all,[11] common law jurisdictions. While this trend suggests an argument—which one of us has previously elaborated[12]—for disaggregating the Law of Evidence into its civil and criminal components and aligning these topics more closely with their respective procedural and institutional contexts, the majority of influential textbooks, in England and Wales and across the common law world, still continue to treat the Law of Evidence as a single, unified subject. Moreover, the doctrinal substance of Evidence Law appears to expand inexorably with each successive edition summarizing the seemingly inexhaustible supply of new legislation, case law, informal sources, and secondary literature. *Cross & Tapper on Evidence*, arguably the most authoritative and widely cited scholarly text on English Evidence Law, is now in its twelfth edition and stretches to 735 pages. Evidence textbooks in Australia, Canada, the United States, and elsewhere boast comparable heft. If the star of common law Evidence is truly waning, it must still be in its red giant phase with no signs of contracting to a white dwarf anytime soon.

It is not our aim, in this chapter, to join the ranks of those calling (rather simplistically, we fear) for the abolition of the rules of evidence, nor do we disparage "Evidence" as a subject eminently worthy of study in the law school curriculum. But we do take issue with the dominant conception of the Law of Evidence that has informed—and we would say, constrained—legal pedagogy, judicial reasoning, and law reform for the last century or more. This "common law model" of the Law of Evidence, we suggest, adopts a strikingly narrow doctrinal focus, which marginalizes (if it does not ignore altogether) the dynamic processes through which evidence is collected, organized, presented, tested, and evaluated in legal proceedings. The common law model, in keeping with the vast majority of doctrinal teaching and scholarship, is fixated on appellate court pronouncements but seldom addresses first instance trials. It also pays too little attention to the character and techniques of inferential reasoning in juridical evidence and proof, and—in short—has not responded adequately to William Twining's cogent and patiently reiterated arguments for "taking facts seriously."[13] Another notable deficiency of the common law model of the Law of Evidence is that it is insufficiently attentive to the normative priorities of particular types of adjudication, implicitly—and sometimes expressly—falling back on the default assumption that accurate fact-finding is the ultimate value and justification of all procedural norms. None of these arguments is especially novel, taken in isolation, but previous iterations have appeared piecemeal over multiple generations and in increasingly fragmented specialized literatures, such that their force has been dissipated and their message has gone unheeded by what ought

[11] *Cf.* Samuel Gross, *Law in the Backwaters: A Comment on M. Damaška's* Evidence Law Adrift, 49 Hastings L.J. 369, 369–70 (1998) (commenting that if a nineteenth century lawyer were transported to contemporary San Francisco to litigate a civil case, he would find evidence law and trial practice—but not pretrial procedure—reasonably familiar).

[12] Paul Roberts, *Rethinking the Law of Evidence*, 55 Current Legal Probs. 297 (2002).

[13] William Twining, *Taking Facts Seriously*, in *Essays on Legal Education* (Neil Gold ed., 1982) & reprinted as Twining, *Rethinking Evidence* ch. 2 (2d ed. 2006); William Twining, *Taking Facts Seriously—Again*, in *Innovations in Evidence and Proof* 65 (Paul Roberts & Mike Redmayne eds., 2007).

to have been their primary audiences. In some respects, the wisdom of former ages has been lost to contemporary jurisprudence, legal practice, and law reform.

This chapter attempts to recover and weave together disparate strands of criticism to argue for a comprehensive "reimagining" of Evidence law, a new organizing principle that stretches beyond conventional common law concepts, topics, and taxonomies; beyond common law jurisdictions; and, mindful that international courts now routinely grapple with novel and difficult questions of evidence and proof, beyond domestic law. Evidence law, on our conception, should take its proper place within a broader conception of forensic science, understood in a manner closer to its original, etymological meaning, as the science of legal analysis, argumentation, and inferential reasoning. But before we spell out more of what this disciplinary reimagining might entail, it will be helpful to explain more fully what we mean by the orthodox "common law model" of the Law of Evidence and to diagnose its debilitating ailments.

II. The Orthodox Common Law Model of Evidence Law

In his groundbreaking work on the intellectual history of Anglo-American Evidence scholarship, Twining identified four principal architects of an explicit general theory of the "Law of Evidence" in the common law tradition. Gilbert, Bentham, Stephen, and Thayer all shared very similar assumptions about the nature and ends of adjudication (rectitude of decision premised on accurate fact-finding) and the processes of judicial proof. Twining memorably characterized these shared tenets as the "rationalist tradition."[14] Bentham stands out from the others in that his theory was explicitly "censorial" and adopted the stance of the external critic, while the other three were "rationalizers and systematizers who advanced creative interpretations of common law doctrine"[15] with a juristic sensibility. All of them could be sharp-tongued critics on occasion, but only Bentham was an iconoclast.

Gilbert's pioneering treatise on the Law of Evidence, published in 1754,[16] presented a hierarchy of evidence types formulated around an organizing "best evidence" principle. Somewhat reminiscent of the Roman-canon idea of prescribed predefined evidential weights, Gilbert's typology of evidence was an oven-ready target for Bentham's "antinomian" roasting. Bentham ridiculed the notion that any such rank ordering could be logically sustained. The intuition that certain categories of evidence are more reliable or have greater probative value than others nonetheless appealed to subsequent textbook

[14] Twining, *supra* note 2, ch. 3. *See also* C.J.W. Allen, *The Law of Evidence in Victorian England* (1997); John H. Langbein, *Historical Foundations of the Law of Evidence: A View from the Ryder Sources*, 96 Colum. L. Rev. 1168 (1996); Stephan Landsman, *From Gilbert to Bentham: The Reconceptualization of Evidence Theory*, 36 Wayne L. Rev. 1149 (1990).

[15] Twining *supra* note 2, at 203.

[16] Jeffrey Gilbert, *The Law of Evidence* (1754).

writers who were concerned with cataloging existing evidentiary rules. Gilbert's best evidence principle influenced expositions of the law of evidence throughout the nineteenth century, and it still has its supporters even today, long after it is any longer plausible to subsume all Evidence Law under a single controlling notion of "best evidence."[17] The difficulty has always been, however, that individual writers advance very different interpretations of the best evidence principle, some seeing it in a more expansive light as allowing "inferior" evidence to be received when no other "better" evidence is available, while others considered it to be a hard-and-fast rule of exclusion rejecting "inferior" evidence *tout court*, even when it is the best that can be had in the circumstances.

Cutting through the din and distraction of Bentham's attack on Gilbert, Stephen set about systematizing the law of evidence under a different rubric, that of relevancy. His explicitly stated objective was to carve out a distinctive Law of Evidence, differentiated from other branches of the law with which it had become entangled in previous treatises.[18] Thus, for Stephen, topics such as pleadings and presumptions, which are concerned with processes of proof rather than evidence sensu stricto, should be reassigned to their respective branches of substantive law. Notoriously, Stephen himself stretched the concept of "relevance" beyond its serviceable limits, confusing relevance per se and the canons of inductive logic with institutional tests of legal *admissibility*.[19] The turn-of-century American scholar James Bradley Thayer subsequently took up the idea of relevancy as a guiding principle and developed it in a way that still dominates orthodox thinking in the common law world (and has been enshrined doctrinally, for example, in the U.S. Federal Rules of Evidence).

Rather than conceptualizing relevance or its predecessor, "best evidence," as positive guides to fact-finding in adjudication, Thayer adopted Bentham's negative conception of the *law* of evidence as a set of precepts constraining the trier of fact's ordinary, "common sense" reasoning processes. As Thayer grandly put it, "the law has no mandamus to the logical faculty."[20] In other words, legal writ cannot compel or rewrite inferential logic or human psychology. The enduring Thayerite model of the Law of Evidence rests on two strikingly simple, complementary principles: (1) nothing is to be received that is not logically probative of some matter requiring proof, and (2) everything that is probative should be received unless excluded by some rule or principle of law.[21] The first principle engages questions of relevance and materiality, and while questions of materiality are largely settled by the applicable substantive law, relevancy, as Thayer taught succeeding generations of scholars and practitioners, is essentially a matter of logic and common

[17] Dale Nance, *The Best Evidence Principle*, 13 Iowa L. Rev. 227 (1988). In modern times, a "best evidence" approach has been advocated in relation to hearsay reform: see Lord Justice Auld, *Review of the Criminal Courts of England and Wales* ch. 11 (2001); discussed in John R. Spencer, *Hearsay Evidence in Criminal Proceedings* 31–32 (2d ed. 2013).

[18] James Fitzjames Stephen, *A Digest of the Law of Evidence* x (1876).

[19] Twining, *supra* note 2, at 90–91.

[20] James Bradley Thayer, *A Preliminary Treatise on Evidence at the Common Law* 314 (1898).

[21] *Id.* at 265, 530.

sense, not legal directives. Thayer's twin guiding principles in effect separate the law of admissibility, whose function is to determine "as among probative matters... what classes of things shall not be received,"[22] from the reasoning processes of the trier of fact. Relevancy is conceptualized as the province of logic. The law's supplementary task is to filter out suspect, faulty, or objectionable, but ex hypothesi relevant, information from the fact-finding process. It is this predominantly "exclusionary" conception of the Law of Evidence that has dominated Anglo-American scholarship and practice to this day, and that can fairly be characterized as the fulcrum of the orthodox "common law model" of Evidence.

Thayer never managed to work up his influential "preliminary" treatise into the planned comprehensive account of the law of evidence, and it was left to others to complete his project of disciplinary renewal. Evidentiary concepts, including the core triumvirate of relevance, materiality, and admissibility, were further developed and refined over the course of the twentieth century by numerous textbook writers, scholars, and judges working in—and working out—the common law tradition. Thayer's own account of evidentiary principles of exclusion was sketchy. Toward the end of the *Preliminary Treatise* four exclusionary principles were identified, which still today account for major areas of common law doctrine: insufficient probative value, hearsay, opinion, and character.[23] But these are evidently general, underspecified criteria, and the basic Thayerite conception has been repeatedly glossed and expanded upon over the course of a century or more in which common law Evidence has grown and transformed into the subject we recognize today.[24]

From a U.S. perspective, the most significant glossator is undoubtedly Thayer's own pupil, John Henry Wigmore. Indeed, in actually producing the comprehensive treatise on Evidence law that Thayer only envisaged, Wigmore arguably eclipsed his teacher in both achievement and reputation. Until the game-changing introduction of the Federal Rules of Evidence in 1975, Wigmore's monumental *Treatise on the Anglo-American System of Evidence in Trials at Common Law* (aka "Wigmore") was amongst the most authoritative and widely cited works of legal scholarship ever written. One of Wigmore's conceptual innovations was a suggested dichotomy between "rules of extrinsic policy" and "rules of auxiliary probative policy." The former type of exclusionary rule imposes constraints on the pursuit of factual rectitude (e.g., the various testimonial privileges that allow witnesses to suppress certain kinds of information), while the latter type of rule is designed to promote rectitude of outcome by excluding evidence that might otherwise (so it is thought) unduly prejudice, mislead, or confuse a jury.[25] Wigmore accepted that certain procedural issues are properly within the domain of the Law of Evidence, because they are intimately related to evidential matters. They include familiar topics such as the burden of proof and presumptions, the functional division of labor

[22] *Id.* at 264.

[23] Eleanor Swift, *One Hundred Years of Evidence Law Reform: Thayer's Triumph*, 88 Cal. L. Rev. 2437, 2452 (2000).

[24] Twining, *supra* note 2, at 206–10.

[25] Denis Galligan, *More Scepticism About Scepticism*, 8 Oxford J. Legal Stud. 249 (1988).

between judges making admissibility determinations and jury fact-finding, and substitutes for proof (e.g., judicial notice and formal admissions) on which no evidence can, or need be, presented.[26] Other textbook writers have adopted Wigmore's conventions. *Cross & Tapper on Evidence*, for example, devotes separate chapters to matters not requiring proof, burdens of proof, the functions of the judge and jury, witnesses, and the course of evidence, before going on to expound the detailed exclusionary rules that populate the greater part of the treatise. Other works stress the importance of procedural context to a proper understanding of evidentiary doctrine.[27]

An original and long-running controversy in common law evidentiary theory concerns the extent to which trial judges may properly innovate in the development or application of exclusionary rules. Debates on the legitimate scope of judicial discretion in evidentiary rulings were reflected throughout the twentieth century in contrasting views on whether, and if so how, the rules of evidence should be codified. Thayer himself recognized the importance of judicial discretion, which he believed should be broadened and buttressed by an appropriately deferential standard of appellate review. This view has achieved greater traction over time. The Federal Rules of Evidence (FRE)—and mutatis mutandis their numerous state counterparts—replicate Thayer's two fundamental propositions: that no irrelevant evidence shall be admitted and that all relevant evidence shall be received unless excluded by "the United States Constitution, a federal statute, these rules, or other rules prescribed by the Supreme Court pursuant to statutory authority."[28] The FRE in large part codify preexisting common law precedents, but also grant judges significant new discretionary powers. Notably, Rule 403 permits judges to exclude evidence if its probative value is substantially outweighed by the danger of unfair prejudice, confusion of the issues, or misleading the jury, or by considerations of undue delay, waste of time, or needless presentation of evidence. Commentators have discerned a "powerful trend" toward expanding judicial discretion in serial Rules amendments, Supreme Court interpretative jurisprudence, and trial court decisions since the FRE were first implemented in 1975.[29]

One could plausibly tell a similar story about the trajectory of doctrinal developments in procedural law in the United Kingdom and Ireland over the last several decades. For example, the major hearsay reform introduced in England and Wales by the Criminal Justice Act 2003 includes an overriding inclusionary discretion for probative hearsay;[30] an innovation that the English courts steadfastly refused to create at common law,[31] even after apex courts in other Commonwealth jurisdictions had already conceded the argument.[32] In fact, the Criminal Justice Act 2003 is riddled with judicial discretions, both inclusionary

[26] John H. Wigmore, *A Treatise on the System of Evidence in Trial at Common Law* (Peter Tillers rev., 1983) § 3.

[27] Paul Roberts & Adrian Zuckerman, *Criminal Evidence* ch. 2 (2d ed. 2010).

[28] Fed. R. Evid. 402.

[29] Swift, *supra* note 23, at 2441.

[30] Criminal Justice Act 2003, s. 114(1)(d) (Eng. & Wales).

[31] Myers v. DPP [1965] A.C. 1001 (H.L.).

[32] *See* P.B. Carter, *Hearsay: Whither and Whether?*, 109 L.Q. Rev. 573 (1993); A.A.S. Zuckerman, *LCCP No 138 on Hearsay (1): The Futility of Hearsay* [1996] Crim. L. Rev. 4.

and exclusionary. However, one must not get carried away with reductive generalizations or overstate the case. Some modern criminal evidence legislation narrows, rather than expands, judicial discretion—for example, in relation to the cross-examination of complainants on their previous sexual history.[33] Likewise, legislative interpretation by the Court of Appeal sometimes emphatically endorses trial judges' prerogative to use their own judgment in applying general evidentiary rules to the unique facts of the instant case,[34] but then at other times reverts to a much more directive style, instructing trial judges that they must follow prescribed reasoning procedures and conform with clear precedents.[35] In broader institutional terms, while fairly systematic reforms of hearsay, bad character and special measures for vulnerable or intimidated witnesses might be viewed as a collection of "mini-codifications," there is no foreseeable prospect of comprehensive Evidence legislation akin to the FRE, or the more recent Australian Uniform Evidence Acts,[36] for England and Wales.

III. Orthodoxy Deconstructed

Twining's account of the orthodox model of common law Evidence, on which Section II heavily leans, was intended primarily as an exercise in descriptive intellectual history rather than any kind of normative blueprint for institutional design. Much as Twining presents himself as a Benthamist rather than a Benthamite,[37] the orthodox model is a heuristic rather than a program. In implicitly, if not explicitly, confining the Law of Evidence to questions of admissibility at trial, the common law model is arbitrarily narrow in its focus; and this arbitrariness is the source of puzzlement and obscurity in the exposition and application of evidentiary doctrines. Without careful analytical scrutiny, moreover, it too often produces confusion and error.

While a Thayerite paring down of the scope of the Law of Evidence might be welcomed as "inspired ground-clearing,"[38] the orthodox model is difficult to defend in terms of robust disciplinary boundaries differentiating that which is specifically *evidentiary*

[33] Youth Justice and Criminal Evidence Act 1999, s. 41 (Eng. & Wales).

[34] *See, e.g.*, R v. Renda [2006] 1 W.L.R. 2948, [2005] EWCA Crim 2826, [3] (Sir Igor Judge P warning counsel that "the trial judge's 'feel' for the case is usually the critical ingredient of the decision at first instance which this court lacks. Context therefore is vital. The creation and subsequent citation from a vast body of so-called 'authority', in reality representing no more than observations on a fact-specific decision of the judge in the Crown Court, is unnecessary and may well be counter-productive").

[35] *See, e.g.*, R v. Turpin [2006] EWCA Crim 2273, [26] (directions on standard of proof in self-defense); and R v. Farooqi [2014] 1 Cr. App. R. 8, [2013] EWCA Crim 1649, [151] (warning of the "particular dangers in departing from the wording approved" for directing juries on majority verdicts).

[36] *See* Andrew Ligertwood & Gary Edmond, *Australian Evidence* (6th ed. 2017); Ian Dennis, *Codification and Reform of Evidence Law in Australia* [1996] Crim. L. Rev. 477.

[37] William Twining, *Hot Air in the Redwoods, A Sequel to the Wind in the Willows*, 86 Mich. L. Rev. 1523, 1536–37 (1988).

[38] Twining, *supra* note 2, at 204.

from broader aspects of substantive and procedural law.[39] Evidence and procedure mesh together in adjudicative proof processes, as Wigmore rightly insisted. Textbook writers in the common law tradition conventionally include burdens and presumptions as central topics within the Law of Evidence. In recognition of the inherently probabilistic and defeasible nature of all empirical inference, requiring fact-finders to render their verdicts under conditions of irremediable uncertainty, a law of evidence must also specify decisional standards of proof that exclude not only mathematical certainty but also the kinds of epistemic worry that preoccupied Descartes and the classical sceptics.[40] If jurors start getting sidetracked into debating whether they are brains in vats or prisoners of *The Matrix*,[41] the entire business of the administration of justice would be in danger of grinding to a halt! Textbooks such as *Cross & Tapper on Evidence*, which play a significant practical role in demarcating and sustaining disciplinary boundaries, also contain chapters on the examination of witnesses and "the course of evidence." Some of the rules related to these topics govern the admissibility of evidence, but other doctrines regulate procedural matters such as memory refreshing,[42] the scope of questioning in cross-examination, and "hostile" witnesses.[43] Technical rules of narrative and collateral-finality are a blended mixture of strictly evidentiary and procedural elements.[44] The orthodox common law model of the Law of Evidence pragmatically incorporates facets of trial procedure that are not easily severable from admissibility doctrines, but it has done so in a selective and rather haphazard fashion. If we agree, for example, that rules governing witness examination at trial are a proper subject matter for the Law of Evidence, why should the rules for conducting pretrial interviews with witnesses not equally be brought within the disciplinary domain of Evidence law?[45] And what about police interviews with suspects, and allied topics such as access to custodial legal advice and the nature and content of that advice when it is given?[46] It is not easy to make good sense of rules regulating the admissibility of confessions, or on drawing adverse inferences from silence, without paying attention to the way in which police interviews with suspects operate. Similar methodological points can be made in relation to the production of

[39] *See also Theoretical Foundations of Criminal Trial Procedure* (Paul Roberts ed., 2014); Paul Roberts, *Groundwork for a Jurisprudence of Criminal Procedure*, in *Philosophical Foundations of Criminal Law* 379, 382 (R.A. Duff & S.P. Green eds., 2011).

[40] Mike Redmayne, *The Structure of Evidence Law*, 26 Oxford J. Legal Stud. 805 (2006).

[41] *Cf. Philosophers Explore* The Matrix (Christopher Grau ed., 2005).

[42] Originally at common law, now see Criminal Justice Act 2003, s. 139.

[43] Still regulated by Criminal Procedure Act 1865, s. 3.

[44] Roberts & Zuckerman, *supra* note 27, ch.8.

[45] *See further*, Paul Roberts, *Prosecutors Interviewing Witnesses: A Question of Integrity*, in *The Integrity of Criminal Process* (Jill Hunter et al. eds., 2016); Paul Roberts & Candida Saunders, *Introducing Pre-Trial Witness Interviews—A Flexible New Fixture in the Crown Prosecutor's Toolkit* [2008] Crim. L. Rev. 831.

[46] *See further*, John D. Jackson, *Responses to* Salduz: *Procedural Tradition, Change and the Need for Effective Defense*, 79 Mod. L. Rev. 987 (2016); Pascoe Pleasence, Vicky Kemp & Nigel J. Balmer, *The Justice Lottery? Police Station Advice 25 Years on from PACE 1984* [2011] Crim. L. Rev. 3; Layla Skinns, *The Right to Legal Advice in the Police Station: Past, Present and Future* [2011] Crim. L. Rev. 19; John Baldwin, *Police Interview Techniques: Establishing Truth or Proof?*, 33 Brit. J. Crim. 325 (1993); David Dixon, *Integrity, Interrogation and Criminal Injustice*, in *The Integrity of Criminal Process* (Jill Hunter et al. eds., 2016).

forensic science evidence in criminal investigations and through pretrial interactions with police and lawyers and their implications for legal doctrines regulating the admissibility of expert witness testimony at trial.[47] Rules determining how pertinent information and artifacts are to be identified, collected, organized, presented, and evaluated are no less plausibly "rules of evidence" than rules of procedure, yet such rules and their associated practices are marginalized and largely ignored under the orthodox model.[48] The truth is that it is very difficult to draw hard-and-fast distinctions between evidence and procedure, or between trial and pretrial processes, that are either intellectually defensible or practically useful—or even, increasingly, doctrinally sound.

Drawing on the Realist tradition of Llewellyn and Pound, Twining has long criticized the "court-centredness" of the orthodox model, whereby the bulk of Anglo-American legal scholarship on evidence has preoccupied itself with events in the courtroom and treated the contested jury trial as paradigmatic.[49] There is now a burgeoning and highly informative sociolegal literature on pretrial and post-trial processes, including quite extensive specialist sub-genres on topics such as miscarriages of justice and victims' rights. This material, which goes hand in hand with procedural reforms regulating criminal investigations, prosecutions, pretrial, and post-conviction processes, may be taught in courses on criminal process or constitutional law but tends to remain beyond the pale of Evidence Law teaching. Part of the reason is that much criminal justice scholarship is generated by criminologists, sociologists, and behavioral scientists who have little knowledge or interest in the more technical aspects of evidentiary doctrines, or in their jurisprudential foundations. It is also right to say that Evidence teaching and textbooks are bound to respect pragmatic constraints of time, length, expertise, and attention span, lest the subject should become too bloated, diffuse, and unruly to be taught in a tractable fashion or studied coherently. Nonetheless, there is a balance to be struck here, and there is precious little indication that the orthodox model of the Law of Evidence has ever seriously considered this balance, let alone struck it effectively. Systematic neglect of investigative and pretrial processes in common law Evidence teaching and scholarship fosters compartmentalized thinking, whereby the pretrial processes through which judicial evidence is constructed are screened off from the classification and evaluation of evidence at trial. One is left not only with an impoverished conception of adjudicative processes, but also with an incomplete grasp of admissibility doctrines—supposedly the orthodox common law model's forte.

The common lawyers' penchant for distilling out a "pure" Law of Evidence from a dynamic process of adjudication may have contributed to the discipline's reputation for sterile doctrinalism. Focusing overwhelmingly on what counts as "evidence" in law disregards much of the information that fact-finders actually use in reaching their verdicts, including their own visual impressions of trial proceedings, suggestions by counsel in submissions and argument, and the trial judge's directions and summing-up (in England and Wales, summarizing the key facts and evidence as well as the

[47] Paul Roberts, *Science in the Criminal Process*, 14 Oxford J. Legal Stud. 469 (1994).

[48] Jackson & Summers, *supra* note 5, at 2.

[49] Twining, *supra* note 2, at 170.

applicable law),[50] not to mention the vast amounts of "common sense" information, preconceptions, and practical heuristics that fact-finders bring with them into the courtroom. Reducing the Law of Evidence to rules of admissibility narrows the analytical focus to a fixed point in trial proceedings when determinations of admissibility are made. Concomitantly, it encourages an "atomistic" approach to thinking about evidence, which is to be assessed piece by piece for its compliance with admissibility tests, rather than being modeled holistically as one piece in a complex, three-dimensional and interactive jigsaw representing a dynamic process of proof.

These criticisms feed off, and into, Twining's long-running campaign for "taking facts seriously" in legal education.[51] Although Thayer is rightly credited with refounding the modern Law of Evidence on a logical conception of relevance, purged of scholastic sophistry, a weakness of the Thayerite legacy, as Twining himself recognized,[52] is that it has fostered precisely that reductive conflation of Evidence law with admissibility doctrines that we have been criticizing. If fact-finding is a matter of logic and common sense, what more is there for *the law* to say about it? Having pinpointed the priority of inferential reasoning about facts as a logical precursor to the application of legal tests of admissibility, the orthodox model almost invites one to skip straight to the knotty doctrinal problems that have enthralled and frustrated generations of scholars and students. Relevance is enthroned only to be ignored. Thayer, indeed, did not regard fact-finding as part of the Law of Evidence, since the law "does not re-enact, nor does it displace, the main rules which govern human thought," and that are all "taken for granted" as presuppositions.[53] But here one should tread very carefully. Even were it true (though it is not) that the doctrinal law of evidence is limited to exclusionary rules, it does not follow that judges and legal practitioners applying the rules, or scholars researching and criticizing the rules, or students learning the rules, can safely confine themselves to doctrinal arguments and materials. There is absolutely no equivalence, in other words, between the collection of exclusionary rules qualifying relevancy on the Thayerite model and the disciplinary domain of the Law of Evidence. This conflation, to the extent that it has ever truly characterized common law thinking, is fallacious.

In reality, relevancy and legal doctrine frequently cannot be separated in such a tidy, dogmatic fashion, because some of the most prominent rules of evidence exclude inferences or presuppositions traditionally viewed as problematic rather than turning on typologies of inadmissible evidence. The very definition of "hearsay" in the hearsay prohibition, perhaps the most prototypical of all the traditional common law exclusions, turns on the purpose for which any out-of-court statement is adduced. "Hearsay-ness" at common law is a property of the inferential uses of information in litigation as much as it concerns the defective pedigree of any statement tendered in evidence (made out of

[50] Now see *The Crown Court Compendium—Part I: Jury and Trial Management and Summing Up* (2017); and for (common law) comparative context, see Paul Marcus, *Judges Talking to Jurors in Criminal Cases: Why US Judges Do It So Differently from Just About Everyone Else*, 30 Ariz. J. Int'l. & Comp. L. 1 (2013).

[51] *See supra* note 13.

[52] Twining, *supra* note 2, at 210–18.

[53] Thayer, *supra* note 20, at 527.

court, not on oath, untested by direct cross-examination, etc.). According to another iconic common law doctrine (which has been enshrined in the FRE, but is controversial in English criminal jurisprudence)[54] evidence of the accused's bad character may not be adduced as direct proof of criminal propensity but *may* still be admissible in support of "non-prejudicial" inferences, such as proof of identity or guilty knowledge or in rebuttal of an alibi.[55] Whatever the true logic, status, or merits of the common law's traditional distaste for propensity evidence, it is an unassailable methodological truth that sensible critical discussion of the admissibility of bad character evidence cannot even begin without paying close attention to the inferential logic of common sense factual reasoning.[56] A third example (and many more could be enumerated) concerns the common law's traditional ban on drawing adverse inferences from the accused's pretrial silence or decision not to testify in his own defense at trial. Bentham was entirely justified in arguing that people naturally equate silence with guilt,[57] thinking that "there is no smoke without fire" and assuming that an innocent defendant would jump at the chance of asserting his innocence in the courtroom. But *contra* Bentham, it is precisely because these common-sense assumptions might well not hold in the artificial and pressurized context of criminal proceedings that common law juries have traditionally been instructed *not* to infer guilt from mere silence.[58] Since 1995, English law has permitted juries to draw adverse inferences from silence,[59] but only in ways that actually reinforce the argument we are making here about the scope and structural properties of Evidence law. When the possibility of an adverse inference is triggered, trial judges are obliged to give detailed and often complex[60] directions spelling out both (1) the essential preconditions for drawing any such inference, and (2) the precise scope of the permissible inference if the jury chooses to draw one. In these and countless other instances, admissibility is predicated on proper analysis of the logic of inferential reasoning.

[54] *Cf.* Paul Roberts, *Redmayne's Character and Criminal Jurisprudence*, 79 Mod. L. Rev. 706, 721–22 (2016).

[55] Makin v. Attorney-General for New South Wales [1894] A.C. 57 (P.C.).

[56] For fuller elucidation, see Mike Redmayne, *Character in the Criminal Trial* (2015).

[57] "[I]nnocence never takes advantage of it," he declared, "innocence claims the right of speaking, as guilt invokes the privilege of silence": Jeremy Bentham, *Treatise on Judicial Evidence* 241 (M. Dumont ed., 1825). For discussion, see Michael A. Menlowe, *Bentham, Self-Incrimination and the Law of Evidence*, 104 L.Q. Rev. 286 (1988).

[58] For one strikingly counterintuitive development of this thought, see Daniel J. Seidmann & Alex Stein, *The Right to Silence Helps the Innocent: A Game-Theoretic Analysis of the Fifth Amendment Privilege*, 114 Harv. L. Rev. 431 (2000); Alex Stein, *The Right to Silence Helps the Innocent: A Response to Critics*, 30 Cardozo L. Rev. 1115 (2008).

[59] Criminal Justice and Public Order Act 1994, ss. 34–38.

[60] Sometimes tortuously complex, to the point where it might be wondered whether the effort is truly worth the forensic advantage. For critical discussion, see Hannah Quirk, *Twenty Years On, The Right of Silence and Legal Advice: The Spiralling Costs of Unfair Exchange*, 64 N. Ir. Legal Q. 465 (2013); Mike Redmayne, *English Warnings*, 30 Cardozo L. Rev. 1047 (2008); Roger Leng, *Silence Pre-trial, Reasonable Expectations and the Normative Distortion of Fact-Finding*, 5 Int'l. J. Evid. & Proof 240 (2001); Di Birch, *Suffering in Silence: A Cost-Benefit Analysis of Section 34 of the Criminal Justice and Public Order Act 1994* [1999] Crim. L. Rev. 769.

Evidentiary doctrines such as these have been characterized as rules of "use," in that they exclude a particular *use* rather than a designated category of evidence.[61] An alternative generic designation, proposed by Roberts and Zuckerman, is "forensic reasoning rules."[62] Whatever one's preferred terminology, the upshot is that when a party wishes to adduce evidence, there are not two discrete stages of proving, first, that the evidence is relevant to a material fact and then, second, that such evidence is not rendered inadmissible by a categorical exclusionary rule. Instead, there is only one continuous process of demonstrating to the trial judge that the evidence is relevant to the material facts for a legally permissible inference, for example that it demonstrates the speaker's knowledge or simply that a statement was made irrespective of its truth (so the evidence is not hearsay);[63] or that evidence of the accused's extraneous misconduct reveals an unusual or otherwise distinctive pattern of offending (and is therefore not pure propensity evidence);[64] or that the accused is now relying on a fact that she ought reasonably to have mentioned when questioned by the police in the course of the investigation, thus permitting the inference that her defense is a late fabrication (but not the simplistic equation of silence with guilt).[65]

Artificial separation between inferential reasoning about facts and a doctrinal "law of evidence" becomes even harder to sustain the more that rigid exclusionary rules give way to flexible standards, guidelines, or balancing tests. "Rules versus discretion" is an eternal jurisprudential story, and the Law of Evidence has its own lengthy chapter. We have already noted the broad trend in recent decades across the common law world toward greater reliance on judicial discretion in the application of evidentiary standards. Such determinations necessarily require trial judges to consider the logic of inference and make assessments of probative force in the routine process of ruling on disputed claims of admissibility. At the same time, the modern shift away from categorical exclusionary rules toward a more pro-admissibility philosophy, which is certainly a discernible trend in recent British legislation, reinforces the practical and doctrinal significance of forensic reasoning rules. Juries are now routinely being exposed to evidence that in previous decades would have been regarded as too risky, misleading, or prejudicial to be admitted into the trial. This policy preference, which is sometimes expressly advocated on the basis of trusting juries,[66] places an enhanced premium on limiting instructions to

[61] *See* Philip McNamara, *The Canons of Evidence—Rules of Exclusion or Rules of Use?*, Adelaide L. Rev. 341 (1986); Mike Redmayne, *Analysing Evidence Case Law*, in Roberts & Redmayne, *supra* note 13, at 119.

[62] Roberts, *supra* note 12, at 321. *See also* Roberts & Zuckerman, *supra* note 27, at 676–84.

[63] R v. Twist [2011] 2 Cr. App. R. 17, [2011] EWCA Crim 1143; Ratten v. R [1972] A.C. 378, 387 (P.C.) *per* Lord Wilberforce: "A question of hearsay only arises when the words are spoken 'testimonially,' i.e., as establishing some fact narrated by the words."

[64] *See, e.g.*, R v. Chopra [2007] 1 Cr. App. R. 16, [2006] EWCA Crim 2133; D.P.P. v. Boardman [1975] A.C. 421 (H.L.); R v. Straffen [1952] 2 Q.B. 911 (C.C.A.).

[65] R v. Webber [2004] 1 W.L.R. 404, [2004] UKHL 1; Condron v. The United Kingdom, App. No. 35718/97, Eur. Ct. H.R., May 2, 2000.

[66] *See, e.g.*, R v. H [1995] 2 W.L.R. 737, 750 (H.L.) (Lord Griffiths asserting that, "with better educated and more literate juries the value of those old restrictive rules of evidence is being re-evaluated and many are being discarded or modified... This seems to me to be a wholly desirable development of law.

use the evidence in an appropriate way, and burdens trial judges with additional responsibilities to give helpful directions that insulate fact-finders against faulty inferential reasoning and steer them away from hasty or otherwise unwarranted factual conclusions. While formal corroboration requirements have declined in many common law jurisdictions, judicial directions are now required, in England and Wales, in relation to various types of "suspect" or dubiously reliable evidence, whether that be "fleeting glance" eyewitness identifications[67] (the infirmities of which have been thoroughly researched and demonstrated by social psychologists over many decades),[68] alleged jail-cell confessions[69] or other evidence from witnesses who may have their own self-serving agenda (so-called *Beck* warnings),[70] or certain types of problematic expert testimony.[71] In relation to such matters as the accused's proven lies (*Lucas* directions),[72] evidence of good[73] or bad character,[74] the probative value of DNA match probabilities,[75] and—as previously mentioned—the accused's pretrial silence or reliance on the privilege against self-incrimination at trial, judges must elucidate in some detail legally acceptable schemas of inferential reasoning for the benefit of the jury and warn jurors away from impermissible inferences. Juries remain the ultimate fact-finder, but their freedom of decision is constrained by legally mandated norms of epistemic rationality. Indeed, judicial directions on the burden and standard of proof, which have long been accepted as part of the orthodox Evidence law canon and which have undergone significant development in England and Wales in recent years,[76] are prototypical forensic reasoning rules.

As it becomes ever more difficult in litigation practice to disentangle evidence law from factual reasoning, so the impetus toward "taking facts seriously" becomes not just a desirable optional extra but a necessary foundation of the trial lawyer's education.

The basic reason why criminal cases are heard by juries rather than by a judge alone is that our society prefers to trust the collective judgment of 12 men and women drawn from different backgrounds to decide the facts of the case rather than accept the view of a single professional judge").

[67] R v. Turnbull [1977] Q.B. 224 (C.A.).

[68] *See, e.g.*, Dan Simon, *In Doubt: The Psychology of the Criminal Justice Process* ch. 3 (2012); Tim Valentine, *Forensic Facial Identification*, in *Witness Testimony* (Anthony Heaton-Armstrong et al. eds., 2006); Richard A. Wise, Clifford S. Fishman & Martin A. Safer, *How to Analyze the Accuracy of Eyewitness Testimony in a Criminal Case*, 42 Conn. L. Rev. 435 (2009).

[69] R v. Stone [2005] EWCA Crim 105; Pringle v. R (P.C. Jam.) Appeal 17/2002 (17 Jan. 2003), W.L. 116971.

[70] R v. Beck [1982] 1 W.L.R. 461 (C.A.); R v. Spencer [1987] A.C. 128 (H.L.).

[71] *See, e.g.*, R v. Flynn and St John [2008] 2 Cr. App. R. 20, [2008] EWCA Crim 970; R v. Luttrell [2004] 2 Cr. App. R. 31; [2004] EWCA Crim 1344.

[72] R v. Lucas [1981] Q.B. 720 (C.A.); R v. Goodway (1994) 98 Cr. App. R. 11 (C.A.).

[73] R v. Vye [1993] 1 W.L.R. 471 (C.A.); R v. Hunter [2015] 1 W.L.R. 5367, [2015] EWCA Crim 631.

[74] *See, e.g.*, R v. Campbell (Kenneth) [2007] 1 W.L.R. 2798, [2007] EWCA Crim 1472; R v. Edwards [2006] 1 Cr. App. R. 3, [2005] EWCA Crim 1813, [3].

[75] R v. Doheny and Adams [1997] 1 Cr. App. R. 369 (CA). *See also* R v. Thomas [2011] EWCA Crim 1295; R v. Broughton [2010] EWCA Crim 549.

[76] *See, e.g.*, R v. Blackford [2009] EWCA Crim 1684; R v. Majid [2009] EWCA Crim 2563; R v. Smith (Rocky) [2009] EWCA Crim 2461.

Twining's original argument emphasized that so much of what lawyers do in practice involves investigating, collecting, organizing, presenting, and arguing about facts that the Law of Evidence ought to be reconceptualized more holistically and contextually as Evidence, Proof, and Fact-Finding.[77] However, appealing to the practical realities of litigation can cut both ways in terms of staking out the province of the Law of Evidence as an academic subject. The case for integrating fact analysis into the mainstream Evidence curriculum is not necessarily advanced by talking up skills training for legal practitioners, especially in the British context where sharp institutional divisions have been maintained between the "academic" and "vocational" stages of legal education.[78] Indeed, it may have been interpreted as *reinforcing* the Thayerite dichotomy implying that fact analysis is one thing, "academic" Evidence law quite another. This represents a serious misapprehension of the *intellectual* significance of recent shifts in doctrine and practice. As doctrinal procedural (including evidentiary) law becomes increasingly and self-evidently more *about* fact analysis and inferential reasoning, it becomes all the more imperative to equip law students with the methodological tools for making sense of facts not only or even mainly as preparation for legal practice but as integral to understanding and applying evidence law as a scholarly enterprise.

Over-concentration on rules of admissibility and failure to engage with the logic of inferential reasoning are broad criticisms that can fairly be laid at the door of the orthodox common law model of Evidence. A third, discrete but cumulative, line of criticism challenges the implicit unity of this model, whereby rules of evidence are imagined to apply in an undifferentiated manner to both civil and criminal proceedings. Even if a unified model may have been plausible in the past, it gives a very misleading picture of what evidence law comprises in many jurisdictions today. While the fiction of a single, unified "Law of Evidence" is still the common law's default setting and is routinely presupposed and discussed without a second critical thought, the reality for English law, as one of us remarked many years ago, is that the disciplinary vista we confront today is at least four-fifths criminal evidence "with a rump presence on the civil side centred on legal professional privilege and 'public policy'."[79] The argument for disaggregation of the civil and criminal components of a unified Law of Evidence does not rest merely on the desirability of more realistically reflecting existing legal doctrine and practice. Even in jurisdictions, such as U.S. states, where the rules still apply more generically to civil as well as criminal proceedings, there is an argument to be made for disaggregation on the ground that the respective aims and values of civil process and criminal justice are markedly different, such that basic juridical conceptions and taxonomies should underscore, rather than obscure, these distinctive normative underpinnings. If criminal procedure, in particular, is a practical extension of political morality, it should follow

[77] Twining, *supra* note 2, ch. 2.

[78] But this long-standing arrangement is currently under active reconsideration: *see* Solicitors Regulation Authority, *Training for Tomorrow: Assessing Competence* (SRA, Dec. 7, 2015), www.sra.org.uk/sra/consultations/t4t-assessing-competence.page (last visited July 19, 2017).

[79] Roberts, *supra* note 12, at 318–19.

that evidentiary doctrines within criminal procedure should be explicitly linked to these deeper, explanatory and justificatory, philosophical rationales.[80]

Of course, it is not plausible to suggest that rules of evidence apply equally to civil and criminal proceedings without *any* distinction, supplement, or modification whatever, and the orthodox common law model is entirely comfortable in acknowledging some important differences. It is accepted within the standard common law conception, for example, that divergent standards of proof apply in civil and criminal cases. This differentiation is typically rationalized in terms of accommodating the asymmetrical costs imposed by errors in different kinds of adjudication. In civil proceedings, the parties are in a position of (notional) equality, and there is no reason why claimants, as a class, should systematically shoulder greater risks of adjudicative error than defendants. A standard of proof "on the balance of probabilities" thus distributes risks of error equally across all litigants.[81] But the presumption of litigant equality does not hold in criminal proceedings, where one "party" is the state and the censure for serious wrongdoing communicated by a guilty verdict and the grave consequences that may attend such a verdict motivate the need for strenuous institutional efforts to avoid wrongful convictions.[82] Thus, in criminal adjudication, but not in civil proceedings, we find a steeply asymmetrical burden and standard of proof requiring the prosecutor to prove the state's case to a very high degree of epistemic confidence conventionally articulated in common law systems as "proof beyond reasonable doubt."[83] This much is elementary received wisdom. Yet the significance of distinctive procedural philosophies is underplayed in the orthodox model by characterizing the difference only in terms of variations in the standard of proof. The constitutional doctrine of the presumption of innocence, which is also recognized in human rights law,[84] is an altogether more powerful concept for describing the need for an especially demanding standard of proof in criminal cases, but Evidence scholars in the common law tradition have seemingly been reluctant to develop

[80] *See further*, Paul Roberts ed., *Theoretical Foundations of Criminal Trial Procedure* (2014); Hock Lai Ho, *A Philosophy of Evidence Law: Justice in the Search for Truth* (2008); Antony Duff, Lindsay Farmer, Sandra Marshall & Victor Tadros, *The Trial on Trial, Volume 3: Towards a Normative Theory of the Criminal Trial* (2007).

[81] Mike Redmayne, *Standards of Proof in Civil Litigation*, 62 Mod. L. Rev. 167 (1999).

[82] Paul Roberts, *Taking the Burden of Proof Seriously* [1995] Crim. L. Rev. 783; Paul Roberts, *Double Jeopardy Law Reform: A Criminal Justice Commentary*, 65 Mod. L. Rev. 393 (2002); Ronald Dworkin, *Principle, Policy, Procedure*, in *Crime, Proof and Punishment* (C.F.H. Tapper ed., 1981). One important implication of this analysis is that criminal verdicts require appropriately rigorous epistemic warrant; *cf.* Craig R. Callen, *Human Deliberation in Fact-finding and Human Rights in the Law of Evidence*, in *Criminal Evidence and Human Rights* (Paul Roberts & Jill Hunter eds., 2012).

[83] Though in England and Wales, the test is now one of "being sure" of guilt before convicting: *see The Crown Court Compendium—Part I: Jury and Trial Management and Summing Up* 5–8 (Feb. 2017), www.judiciary.gov.uk/publications/crown-court-bench-book-directing-the-jury-2/ (last visited July 20, 2017); R v. Majid [2009] EWCA Crim 2563. Generally, see Roberts & Zuckerman, *supra* note 27, ch. 6.

[84] Hock Lai Ho, *The Presumption of Innocence as a Human Right*, in Roberts & Hunter, *supra* note 82; Paul Roberts, *Criminal Procedure, the Presumption of Innocence and Judicial Reasoning Under the Human Rights Act*, in *Judicial Reasoning Under the UK Human Rights Act* (Helen Fenwick, Gavin Phillipson & Roger Masterman eds., 2007).

sophisticated normative conceptions of "presuming innocence" as a principle of legitimate government. Habituated to thinking in terms of generic evidentiary concepts, they have predictably stuck to the more prosaic, doctrinal notions of burdens and standards of proof.[85] The orthodox model also plays down the normative significance of other rules that have elsewhere been expressed in constitutional terms. Rules governing the admissibility of confessions and the right of silence, for example, have traditionally been treated as exceptions to the hearsay rule, with silence categorized as part of the law on "informal admissions" rather than being linked, conceptually and normatively, to the privilege against self-incrimination.[86]

Allied to this reluctance to ground the rules of criminal evidence in constitutional and human rights protection has been an attachment in the orthodox model to the presumption that the general principles of relevance and probative weight and the rules governing the admissibility of evidence should be the same in every context and apply symmetrically in criminal cases to both prosecution and defense. In practice, judges whose intuitions belie such formalistic approaches to equality of treatment may apply different thresholds of admissibility.[87] In other cases, courts have insisted on formal equality and parity of treatment in admissibility determinations even in the teeth of palpable injustice to the accused. While it is impossible to quantify how often such results are actually produced—and clear instances, it is fair to say, are rare birds in the case law[88]—the diffuse cultural power of the idea that evidentiary rules must apply "equally" to "the parties" tends to diminish the importance of individual rights within the criminal justice system and preempt proper consideration of the possibility that rules of evidence may need to be applied asymmetrically to mitigate unacceptable risks of wrongful conviction or to uphold procedural integrity.[89] It is at least worthy of further consideration, for example, whether greater judicial latitude ought to be afforded to novel scientific evidence adduced by the defense, if only because scientific evidence too shaky to contribute to a criminal conviction, and therefore inadmissible for the prosecution, might still be capable of raising a reasonable doubt justifying an acquittal.[90] Likewise, one might argue that the hearsay rule should apply more strictly to prosecution evidence because it

[85] *See further*, Paul Roberts, *Loss of Innocence in Common Law Presumptions*, 8 Crim. L. & Phil. 317 (2014). But now cf. Richard L. Lippke, *Taming the Presumption of Innocence* (2016).

[86] Compare, e.g., Andrew L.-T. Choo, *The Privilege Against Self-Incrimination and Criminal Justice* (2013); with Peter Mirfield, *Silence, Confessions and Improperly Obtained Evidence* (1997). See also Roberts & Zuckerman, *supra* note 27, ch. 13.

[87] D. Michael Risinger, *Baserates, the Presumption of Guilt, Admissibility Rulings, and Erroneous Conviction*, 4 Mich. St. L. Rev. 1051, 1060 (2003).

[88] One notorious illustration is Sparks v. R [1964] A.C. 965 (P.C.), critically discussed by Andrew L.-T. Choo, *Hearsay and Confrontation in Criminal Trials* 66 (1996) (commenting that, "if there was ever a case in which defence hearsay evidence should clearly have been admitted, *Sparks* was that case").

[89] For elucidation, see Paul Roberts et al., *Introduction: Re-examining Criminal Process Through the Lens of Integrity*, in *The Integrity of Criminal Process* (Jill Hunter et al. eds., 2016).

[90] *Cf.* Adam Jackson, Gethin Rees & Natalie Wortley, *Sleep Disorders/Sexsomnia: The Role of the Expert and the External/Internal Dichotomy*, in *Mental Condition Defences and the Criminal Justice System* 236 (Ben Livings et al. eds., 2015).

is vital that evidence supporting a conviction should be tested by cross-examination whereas the imperative of placing all potentially exculpatory material before the fact-finder argues, in some instances, for relaxation of the hearsay prohibition in favor of the accused.[91] One rationale for recognizing a freestanding right to confrontation is precisely that exceptions to the hearsay rule are now so numerous and obliging that the rule is unable to protect defendants sufficiently.[92]

These are just two of many possible illustrations, and all of them raise difficult issues of doctrinal principle and legal policy that we do not purport to settle here. Arguments for asymmetrical applications of particular rules of evidence need to be examined carefully and judged on their individualized merits. Our argument in this section is structural and methodological. Its descriptive claim is that the orthodox common law model's pre-commitment to generic concepts and formal symmetry ("equality between the parties") in the application of evidence law has a tendency to foreclose other possibilities for better theorizing and enhanced procedural justice. For example, the traditional common lawyer's concepts of burden and standard of proof might be better conceptualized, from the perspective of a fundamentally asymmetrical criminal procedure, in terms of the presumption of innocence. Conversely, having rejected the false unity of a procedurally undifferentiated Law of Evidence, we should no longer think it strange or per se objectionable that any rule of criminal procedure or evidence is formulated, or applied in practice, in a way that treats the accused differently from the public prosecutor.

IV. Methodological Leverage through Reimagination

Although the common law model of Evidence has been preeminent and widely influential for many decades, it has not gone without challenge or intermittent calls for radical reconstruction or systematic rethinking.[93] While Twining's long-standing advocacy for "taking facts seriously" may have achieved only limited impact on mainstream Evidence

[91] *Cf.* Terese Henning & Jill Hunter, *Finessing the Fair Trial for Complainants and the Accused: Mansions of Justice or Castles in the Air?*, in *Criminal Evidence and Human Rights* (Paul Roberts & Jill Hunter eds., 2012).

[92] For UK-orientated discussion, see Ian Dennis, *The Right to Confront Witnesses: Meanings, Myths and Human Rights* [2010] Crim. L. Rev. 255; Mike Redmayne, *Confronting Confrontation*, in *Criminal Evidence and Human Rights* (Paul Roberts & Jill Hunter eds., 2012); William E. O'Brian Jr., *The Right of Confrontation: U.S. and European Perspectives*, 121 L.Q. Rev. 481 (2005).

[93] From a UK perspective, see, e.g., Dennis, *supra* note 8; Roberts, *supra* note 12; John D. Jackson, *Analysing the New Evidence Scholarship: Towards a New Conception of the Law of Evidence*, 16 Oxford J. Legal Stud. 309 (1996). *See also* Alex Stein, *Foundations of Evidence Law* (2005); Larry Laudan, *Truth, Error, and Criminal Law: An Essay in Legal Epistemology* (2006); Ronald J. Allen, *Laudan, Stein, and the Limits of Theorizing About Juridical Proof*, 29 Law & Phil. 195 (2010).

scholarship and teaching, it coincided with a revival of academic interest in the discipline coalescing around what came to be known as "the New Evidence Scholarship." Meanwhile, far beyond the traditional disciplinary domain of Evidence doctrine, developments in comparative and international legal theory and practice indicative of a growing cosmopolitanism have opened up exciting new horizons for Evidence scholarship.

1. The New Evidence Scholarship

The term "New Evidence Scholarship," as originally coined by U.S. legal scholars in the 1970s, is not entirely transparent or unproblematic. Taken literally, it might simply be equated with all that is relatively "new" in theoretical or doctrinal work on evidence law. On a more expansive reading, however, the term could embrace all of the many varied strands of multidisciplinary interest in the subject of "evidence," which, aside from doctrinal analysis, could include procedural scholarship, sociological or sociolegal studies of legal institutions and processes, the logic of inference, intelligence analysis and "information science," discourse analysis (including structuralism, deconstruction, semiotics, rhetoric, narrative, and phenomenological approaches), psychological research, scientific and technical developments including forensic science, computer applications and expert systems, and historical inquiries relating to all of the above.[94] In Evidence Law professors' circles, the term "New Evidence Scholarship" has, somewhat less ambitiously, tended to be equated with a more specifically American interest in the study of the science of proof, in which formal logic, mathematics, and probability theory feature prominently.[95]

In many respects, this "interdisciplinary turn"[96] was a journey back to the future. Wigmore, who had emphatically *not* drawn the lesson from Thayer's teachings that lawyers could afford to ignore the logic of inferential reasoning, had advocated studying the logic of proof as an indispensable precursor to instruction in the doctrinal law of evidence. Wigmore's 1913 primer on *The Principles of Judicial Proof*[97] was intended to be complementary to his doctrinal *Treatise*, but although it achieved its third edition in 1937, *The Principles* (rebranded as *The Science of Judicial Proof* for its final edition) was largely neglected—whereas the *Treatise* thrived.[98] One might almost consider it ironic testament to the seductiveness of the common law model that Wigmore was effectively co-opted into propagating the Thayerite conflation of evidence law with rules of

[94] Twining, *supra* note 2, at 246.

[95] *See* Richard O. Lempert, *The New Evidence Scholarship: Analyzing the Process of Proof*, 66 B. U. L. Rev. 439 (1986); Roger C. Park, *Evidence Scholarship, Old and New*, 75 Minn. L. Rev. 849 (1991).

[96] Roger C. Park & Michael J. Saks, *Evidence Scholarship Reconsidered: Results of the Interdisciplinary Turn*, 47 B.C. L. Rev. 1 (2006).

[97] John H. Wigmore, *The Principles of Judicial Proof as Given by Logic, Psychology and General Experience and Illustrated in Judicial Trials* (1913).

[98] *See* Peter Tillers & David Schum, *Charting New Territory in Judicial Proof: Beyond Wigmore*, 9 Cardozo L. Rev. 907 (1988); Twining, *supra* note 2, ch. 3.

admissibility, in direct contradiction of his express and unwavering pedagogical position. It was not until the late 1960s, when scholars began debating the application of probability theory to legal adjudication—triggered, it would seem, by a botched attempt to apply statistical reasoning to assess the weight of evidence in the Californian case of *People* v. *Collins*[99]—that a recognizably "new" strand of evidence scholarship enters onto the scene. The increasing prevalence of statistical evidence and probabilistic reasoning in criminal investigations, prosecutions, and trials, not least in the form of technologically sophisticated forensic science evidence such as DNA profiling, lent the New Evidence Scholarship a salience and pressing significance beyond the parochial confines of U.S. law journals. It was rapidly becoming apparent that all of the professionals involved in criminal adjudication should be able to understand and deal with probability and statistics appropriately.[100] Recurring instances of appalling miscarriages of justice partly attributable to erroneous inferential reasoning, including mishandling of probability and statistics,[101] became plain for all to see.

From the earliest days of the New Evidence Scholarship, advocacy of probabilistic reasoning in legal adjudication has been met with vigorous opposition reasserting orthodox evidentiary values and perspectives.[102] Irrespective of how skeptical, or otherwise, one might be about the application of formal tools of probability theory to legal disputes, however, there can be little doubt that this discussion has broadened the conceptualization of evidence and proof beyond the traditional parameters of the orthodox model. While, in particular, applications of Bayes theorem in legal contexts have possibly generated more overheated dispute than broader illumination,[103] the "likelihood ratio" is indubitably a useful heuristic for thinking about the strength of evidence, and it may have important practical applications besides.[104]

[99] 68 Cal. 2d 319 (1968).

[100] *See* Colin Aitken, Paul Roberts & Graham Jackson, *Fundamentals of Probability and Statistical Evidence in Criminal Proceedings*, RSS Practitioner Guide No. 1 (2010), http://www.rss.org.uk/statsandlaw (last visited September 15, 2018); C.G.G. Aitken & F. Taroni, *Fundamentals of Statistical Evidence—A Primer for Legal Professionals*, 12 Int'l. J. Evid. & Proof 181 (2008). The argument for statistical literacy is not recent: *see* David H. Kaye, *Thinking Like a Statistician: The Report of the American Statistical Association Committee on Training in Statistics in Selected Professions*, 34 J. Legal Ed. 97 (1984).

[101] *See, e.g.*, R v. Cannings [2004] 1 W.L.R. 2607, [2004] EWCA Crim 1; R v. Sally Clark [2003] EWCA Crim 1020. For critical discussion, see Deborah Tuerkheimer, *Flawed Convictions: "Shaken Baby Syndrome" and the Inertia of Injustice* (2014); Emma Cunliffe, *Murder, Medicine and Motherhood* (2011); Paul Roberts, *Fue el Bebé Sacudido? Preuba, Pericia y Epistemologia Juridica en el Proceso Penal Inglés*, in *Estandares de prueba y prueba cientifica* (Carmen Vázquez ed., 2013); Mike Redmayne, *Expert Evidence and Criminal Justice* (2001); Robert Matthews, *Why No One Understands Probability*, Fin. Times, Jan. 9, 2004.

[102] *See* in particular, Laurence H. Tribe, *Trial by Mathematics: Precision and Ritual in the Legal Process*, 84 Harv. L. Rev. 1329 (1971). For an updated restatement of skeptical doubts, see Ronald J. Allen & Michael Pardo, *The Problematic Value of Mathematical Models of Evidence*, 36 J. Legal Stud. 107 (2007).

[103] For entry points into a vast literature, see Paul Roberts ed., *Expert Evidence and Scientific Proof in Criminal Trials* (2014), Part III; Ronald J. Allen & Mike Redmayne eds., *Bayesianism and Juridical Proof*, 1(5) Int'l. J. Evid. & Proof 243 (1997); Ron Allen & Paul Roberts eds., *Special Issue on the Reference Class Problem*, 11(4) Int'l. J. Evid. & Proof 253 (2007).

[104] *See, e.g.*, Graham Jackson, Colin Aitken & Paul Roberts, *Case Assessment and Interpretation of Expert Evidence*, RSS Practitioner Guide No. 4 (2014); Alex Biedermann & Joëlle Vuille, *Digital Evidence, "Absence" of Data and Ambiguous Patterns of Reasoning*, 16 Digital Invest. S86 (2016); European Network

The likelihood ratio (LR) is a comparative measure of the weight of evidence.[105] It encapsulates the essential insight that evidence is only evidence *for* some proposition, hypothesis, argument, or case *relative to* some other, competing proposition(s), hypothes(e)s, argument(s), or case(s). For example, finding the accused's fingerprint at the victim's flat might support the prosecution's argument that the accused is responsible for a burglary; but it might equally, or more strongly, support the accused's explanation that he used to be the victim's tenant. Conversely, the probability of finding particular evidence or traces in the light of the prosecution's allegations might be very small; but this is nonetheless still relevant evidence for the prosecution if the probability of the evidence in light of the defense case is *even smaller*. LRs can thus be used to interrogate and clarify certain counterintuitive properties of evidence, and to increase precision where conventional language sometimes leads us astray (as with misleading formulations such as "the evidence is consistent with the accused having burgled the premises," which does not logically exclude a much higher probability that "the evidence is consistent with the accused *not* having burgled the premises"). Vigorous debate surrounds the merits and risks of employing Bayes theorem or LRs in the trial process, but the theoretical usefulness of these probabilistic concepts has been demonstrated in studies reconsidering particular exclusionary rules, such as the traditional common law prohibition on evidence of the accused's extraneous misconduct ("bad character," "the propensity rule," etc.), or reassessing the probative value of certain types of evidence.[106] Formalizations of evidential weight also open up the possibility of exploiting the computational power of microcomputers, through analytical tools such as Bayesian Networks.[107] These computerized models enable us to explore dynamic inferential networks, and to identify phenomena such as hidden conditional interdependencies between ostensibly unrelated facts, at a speed and level of complexity that the unaided human mind cannot begin to match.

Critics of Bayesianism and other probabilistic formalizations of evidence and proof have proposed alternative, more naturalistic models of forensic reasoning employing schemas and stories to fill in logical gaps and to interpret the meaning of evidence.[108]

of Forensic Science Institutes, *ENFSI Guideline for Evaluative Reporting in Forensic Science* (v. 3.0, Mar. 8, 2015), www.enfsi.eu/news/enfsi-guideline-evaluative-reporting-forensic-science (last visited September 15, 2018).

105 For accessible and reliable explanations, see Ian Evett, *The Logical Foundations of Forensic Science: Towards Reliable Knowledge*, 370 Phil. Trans. Royal Soc'y B 20140263 (2015); Charles E. Berger & Klaas Slooten, *The LR Does Not Exist*, 56 Sci. & Just. 388 (2016); Bernard Robertson & G.A. Vignaux, *Probability—The Logic of the Law*, 13 Oxford J. Legal Stud. 457 (1993); David A. Schum, *The Evidential Foundations of Probabilistic Reasoning* (1994).

106 *See, e.g.*, Richard D. Friedman, *Character Impeachment Evidence: Psycho-Bayesian [!?] Analysis and a Proposed Overhaul*, 38 UCLA L. Rev. 637 (1991); Redmayne, *supra* note 56, at 35–41. *See generally*, Richard O. Lempert, *Modeling Relevance*, 75 Mich. L. Rev. 1021 (1977).

107 Franco Taroni et al., *Bayesian Networks for Probabilistic Inference and Decision Analysis in Forensic Science* (2d ed. 2014).

108 Pioneering contributions include Nancy Pennington & Richard Hastie, *A Cognitive Theory of Jury Decision Making: The Story Model*, 13 Cardozo L. Rev. 519 (1991); Ronald J. Allen, *Factual Ambiguity and a Theory of Evidence*, 88 Nw. U.L. Rev. 606 (1994); Willem A. Wagenaar, Peter J. van Koppen & Hans F.M. Crombag, *Anchored Narratives* (1993).

Again, it is hard to deny that these contextual, more holistic conceptualizations enrich our understanding of the inferential dynamics of adjudicative processes and serve as necessary correctives to the atomistic tendencies of the orthodox common law model.[109] Atomistic approaches to forensic fact-finding chime with a focus on admissibility determinations, whereby the probative value of individual pieces of information may be assessed discretely and largely in abstraction from the case as a whole.[110] However, final verdicts rest on holistic assessments of the entirety of the evidence in the case, not on disaggregated evaluations of particular pieces of evidence; albeit that common law juries return enigmatic general verdicts with no requirement, or procedural opportunity, to explain how their factual conclusions were reached.[111] Holistic approaches also seem more realistic, and potentially useful as a source of reasoning strategies, tools, and protocols, in relation to police investigations and prosecutorial case-building in the earlier phases of criminal proceedings. This work of "case construction"[112] is propelled by narrative scripts, professional cultural expectations, "common sense" generalizations, imaginative conjectures, and abductive reasoning in the generation and testing of explanatory hypotheses.[113] Only incidentally or in special contexts (such as in the generation of certain kinds of forensic science evidence) do investigators and prosecutors utilize quasi-deductive reasoning or probabilistic formalizations characteristic of "atomistic" evidentiary analysis.

By redirecting some of the research focus from rules to facts, the New Evidence Scholarship shed fresh light on legal fact-finding processes and extended the intellectual domain and conceptual resources of the traditional common law model. It might be viewed as the precursor, and part instigator, of a more comprehensive "interdisciplinary turn" in Evidence scholarship in recent years, which has questioned and tested many of the prevailing assumptions underlying evidentiary doctrine and inspired notable procedural reform (though the experimental findings of laboratory-based psychology and cognitive science require careful interpretation and demonstrable ecological validity before they can safely be extrapolated to real-world settings).[114] The New Evidence Scholarship has, however, tended to regard accurate fact-finding as the self-evident ambition of legal adjudication, and has largely overlooked the significance of other,

[109] *See further*, Michael S. Pardo, *Juridical Proof, Evidence, and Pragmatic Meaning: Toward Evidentiary Holism*, 95 Nw. U. L. Rev. 399 (2000); John D. Jackson, *Towards a Dialectic Theory of Proof*, 154 J. Royal Stat. Soc'y 107 (1991).

[110] *See* Mirjan R. Damaška, *Atomistic and Holistic Evaluation of Evidence: A Comparative View*, in *Comparative and Private International Law* (David S. Clark ed., 1991). *Cf.* Ronald J. Allen, *Rationality, Algorithms and Judicial Proof: A Preliminary Inquiry*, 1 Int'l J. Evid. Proof 254 (1997).

[111] Jackson, *supra* note 4.

[112] *See* classic sociolegal studies such as Doreen J. McBarnet, *Conviction* (1981); and Mike McConville, Andrews Sanders & Roger Leng, *The Case for the Prosecution* (1991).

[113] *See further*, William Twining, *Narrative and Generalizations in Argumentation About Questions of Fact*, 40 S. Tex. L. Rev 351 (1999); David A. Schum, *Species of Abductive Reasoning in Fact Investigation in Law*, 22 Cardozo L. Rev. 1645 (2001); Michael S. Pardo & Ronald J. Allen, *Juridical Proof and the Best Explanation*, 27 Law & Phil. 223 (2008).

[114] *Cf.* Roderick Bagshaw, *Behavioural Science Data in Evidence Teaching and Scholarship*, in P. Roberts & M. Redmayne, *supra* note 13, at 219; Richard O. Lempert, *The Economic Analysis of Evidence Law: Common Sense on Stilts*, 87 Va. L. Rev. 1619, 1709 (2001).

non-epistemic values and goals in legal proceedings.[115] Perhaps this is partly attributable to the continuing dominance of the FRE in U.S. teaching and scholarship, grounded—as we have seen—in the Thayerite epistemic assumptions of the orthodox common law model. From broader comparative vantage points, scholars working outside the United States have noted the progressive contraction of civil evidence and its de facto absorption within an expanded disciplinary conception of civil procedure.[116] The field of Evidence law has consequently largely been ceded to *criminal* evidence, inviting more sustained reflection on the distinctive procedural context of criminal adjudication and the broader values and priorities of the criminal justice system.[117] Evidence scholars in the United Kingdom and across the Commonwealth have confronted issues of fairness, (human) rights, and legitimacy much more directly than most of their American counterparts.[118] Although much of this scholarship to date can fairly be characterized as remaining anchored within the traditional doctrinal paradigm, it is by no means hostile toward or methodologically incompatible with the interdisciplinary approaches pioneered by the New Evidence Scholars. Indeed, part of the reason for this enduring doctrinalism may be disarmingly prosaic. Evidence scholars in the United Kingdom, Ireland, Canada, New Zealand, South Africa, and elsewhere have in recent decades been stretched to capacity in trying to comprehend, assimilate, and rationalize a ceaseless barrage of legislation, law reform reports, constitutional directives, and an ever-burgeoning case law constantly reforming the local landscape of criminal procedure and evidence. Working up close and almost in crisis-management mode, there is little time or opportunity for stepping back to survey tectonic shifts in the disciplinary landscape.

2. A New Cosmopolitanism

It is a striking feature of contemporary legislative and other institutional developments in criminal procedure law in many common law jurisdictions that there is a great deal of cross-border traffic, policy transfer, and doctrinal borrowing, markedly more than has been commonplace for at least a century. Admittedly, the common law itself is an English export. Back in the nineteenth century colonial administrators saw to it that English models of evidence and procedural law were implemented across the British Empire, and prior to that—of course—the American colonists had already transported

[115] *See also* Michael L. Seigel, *A Pragmatic Critique of Modern Evidence Scholarship*, 88 Nw. U. L. Rev. 995 (1994); Ronald J. Allen, *Truth and Its Rivals*, 49 Hastings L.J. 309, 310 (1998).

[116] *See* Adrian Zuckerman, *Zuckerman on Civil Procedure: Principles of Practice* (3d ed. 2013).

[117] John D. Jackson, *Modern Trends in Evidence Scholarship: Is All Rosy in the Garden?*, 21 Quinn. L. Rev. 893, 901 (2003).

[118] *See, e.g.*, Roberts & Zuckerman, *supra* note 27; Hunter et al., *supra* note 4; Roberts & Hunter, *supra* note 82; Andrew L.-T. Choo, *Abuse of Process and Judicial Stays of Criminal Proceedings* (2d ed. 2008); Andrew Ashworth, *Human Rights, Serious Crime and Criminal Procedure* (2002); Dennis, *supra* note 8; Adrian Zuckerman, *Miscarriage of Justice and Judicial Responsibility* [1991] Crim. L. Rev. 492.

Blackstone to the New World.[119] But for the greater part of the twentieth century, cross-jurisdictional commerce in common law evidence has generally been limited to occasional citation of foreign authority on difficult points such as the scope of hearsay exceptions. In recent decades, however, we have witnessed an unprecedented intensification of transnational judicial and policymaking activity, propelled by "globalization" in its various forms (economic, political, cultural, technological, etc.) and characterized by somewhat competing pressures toward convergence *and* hybridity in institutional models and practices. This new cosmopolitanism, which one of us detected nearly twenty years ago,[120] has made deep and lasting impressions on common law Evidence, in England and Wales and in many other parts of the legal Anglosphere. One significant cosmopolitan trend is the international victims' rights movement and associated policies aimed at alleviating the plight of complainants, which have been cashed out procedurally in terms of new "special measures" for vulnerable or intimidated witnesses.[121] These developments have required major adjustments to traditional common law doctrines regulating the admissibility of hearsay, confrontation rights, and the scope of cross-examination, especially regarding witnesses' credibility. Another general area of transnational policy transfer and cosmopolitan judicial "conversations" relates to the procedural fallout from the post 9/11 "war on terror" and globalized security policies, which have influenced undercover policing practices and their evidentiary regulation, the law of confessions, applications to withhold information on grounds of "public interest immunity," and the innovation of "special advocates" to represent the accused's interests in ex parte closed hearings.[122] Arguably the most emblematic and consequential driver of cross-fertilization in contemporary common law Evidence, however, has been the impact of a global human rights framework and its rapidly expanding corpus of interpretative jurisprudence, through which apex national ("supreme" or "constitutional") courts and international tribunals are fashioning something approaching a "common law of human rights,"[123] which is reshaping the contours of domestic legal proceedings.

The impact of human rights law at the domestic level plainly varies according to local politics, culture, and myriad institutional factors. Human rights law has been a major

[119] *See* Michael Hoeflich, *American Blackstones*, in *Blackstone and His Commentaries* (Wilfrid Prest ed., 2014).

[120] Roberts, *supra* note 12.

[121] *See* Laura Hoyano, *Reforming the Adversarial Trial for Vulnerable Witnesses and Defendants* [2015] Crim. L. Rev. 107; Emily Henderson, *All the Proper Protections: The Court of Appeal Re-writes the Rules for the Cross-Examination of Vulnerable Witnesses* [2014] Crim. L. Rev. 93; Laura Hoyano & Caroline Keenan, *Child Abuse: Law and Policy Across Boundaries* (2007); Louise Ellison, *The Adversarial Process and the Vulnerable Witness* (2001).

[122] *See* John Jackson, *Justice, Security and the Right to a Fair Trial: Is the Use of Secret Evidence Ever Fair?* [2013] Public Law 720; John Ip, *The Rise and Spread of the Special Advocate* [2008] Public Law 717.

[123] Roberts & Hunter, *supra* note 82; Michael Kirby, *Domestic Courts and International Human Rights Law: The On-going Judicial Conversation*, 6 Utrecht L. Rev. 168 (2010); Jeremy Waldron, *Foreign Law and the Modern* Ius Gentium, 119 Harv. L. Rev. 129 (2005); Christopher McCrudden, *A Common Law of Human Rights? Transnational Judicial Conversations on Constitutional Rights*, 20 Oxford J. Legal Stud. 499 (2000).

influence on criminal procedure reform in South Africa, Hong Kong, and the Republic of Ireland, for example,[124] but the finer details of its institutional impact and specific doctrinal formations are always mediated by each jurisdiction's own unique political history and procedural traditions (e.g., a peaceful transition to a constitutional democracy, ceding a colonial possession to its original owner, or a successful war of independence). The United States remains something of an outlier in the common law world in its doctrinal resistance to global human rights law. This aloofness is doubtless attributable both to the precocious constitutionalization of some aspects of U.S. criminal procedure and evidence through the Bill of Rights, which established an indigenous scheme of suspects' and defendants' rights before equivalent rights protection had gained much recognition in other common law systems,[125] as well as to the politics of American exceptionalism, amongst other factors. The Human Rights Act 1998, which came into force in 2000, has had a major impact on all the legal systems of the UK, including England and Wales. English courts, practitioners, scholars, and law teachers have since been grappling with the Strasbourg European Court of Human Rights' (ECtHR) approach to interpreting the Convention, most particularly—in the context of the present discussion—the scope and meaning of the right to a "fair trial" under Article 6 of the ECHR. The Human Rights Act effectively imported into English law a range of new, or newly reconfigured, ECHR concepts such as "equality of arms," the right to "adversarial procedure," the presumption of innocence, the privilege against self-incrimination, and the right to cross-examination, none of which is precisely congruent with traditional common law understandings. On one level, this might be regarded as empowering English courts to innovate, employing human rights doctrines and arguments as leverage against intransigent common law traditions that might otherwise resist needed reform. It should be stressed that the primary responsibility for upholding human rights protection under the Convention system rests with *domestic* courts and institutions, with the Strasbourg Court operating by way of corrective to national efforts as a last-resort "back-stop" in the adjudication of individual claims and guarantor of jurisprudential consistency across the forty-seven states parties to the Convention. Nonetheless, the UK's legal jurisdictions are also now, in their turn, subject to supranational review of traditional common law evidentiary doctrines and procedural frameworks for compatibility with the ECHR. This arrangement has been the source of some tension and discomfort for common law courts, which are not accustomed to being told how to interpret domestic criminal law statutes by international judges, the great majority of whom have been schooled in the civilian legal tradition and may have only a tenuous grasp of common law concepts and evidentiary practice.[126]

[124] Roberts & Hunter eds., *supra* note 82.

[125] Akhil Reed Amar, *The Constitution and Criminal Procedure: First Principles* (1997); Joshua Dressler & Alan C. Michaels, *Understanding Criminal Procedure* (vol. I 6th ed. 2013; vol. II 4th ed. 2014).

[126] Note that the ECHR is sponsored by the Council of Europe, which is a self-standing international organization entirely separate from the European Union. Thus, Brexit—when and if it happens—will have no direct bearing on the European Convention system of human rights protection. How widely this nuance is perceived, amongst British parliamentarians or the public at large, remains to be seen.

The Strasbourg Court is at pains to emphasize that a state's policy choices regarding particular criminal procedure models, institutional frameworks, admissibility doctrines, and adjudicative mechanisms are in principle beyond the scope of ECHR supervision, which is limited to ensuring compliance with the fundamental rights enumerated in the Convention. In ECHR terminology, the forty-seven states parties to the Convention are afforded a wide "margin of appreciation" (local discretion) in determining how, in practice, the requirements of Article 6 should be met.[127] Thus, the Convention system tolerates, and possibly even encourages, procedural pluralism within a relatively loose framework of fundamental rights. One of the Strasbourg Court's favorite mantras is that "the admissibility of evidence is primarily a matter for regulation by national law and as a general rule it is for the national courts to assess the evidence before them."[128] Thus, "[i]t is not the role of the Court to determine, as a matter of principle, whether particular types of evidence—for example, unlawfully obtained evidence -may be admissible or, indeed, whether the applicant was guilty or not. The question which must be answered is whether the proceedings as a whole, including the way in which the evidence was obtained, were fair."[129] In fact, such protestations of jurisdictional restraint cannot be taken at face value. There is, to be sure, no indication that the ECtHR has grand ambitions for harmonizing European criminal procedures, nor indeed does it have the institutional authority or competence to promote systematic convergence even if had the appetite. But this does not prevent Strasbourg from weighing in on what common lawyers would regard as evidentiary questions whenever it discerns that domestic processes for generating, testing, or evaluating evidence improperly impinge on fair trial rights. Nor does the Strasbourg Court shy away from making suggestions for normative procedural reform, even though its rulings are technically confined to adjudicating alleged human rights violations in the instant case.

One recent judicial flashpoint concerned the question whether triers of fact could legitimately base a conviction on untested out-of-court statements by witnesses who did not appear at trial, where such evidence constituted the "sole or decisive" evidence against the accused. Previous Strasbourg jurisprudence appeared to say that a trial conducted on this footing was inherently unfair, implicitly imposing a corroboration requirement for unconfronted hearsay, even where the declarant was deceased or otherwise permanently unavailable.[130] The UK Supreme Court in *Horncastle*[131] took strong exception to this interpretation of Article 6, as both intellectually unsustainable and incompatible with English statute law. A temporary standoff was in the end resolved by the Grand Chamber of the ECtHR propounding a somewhat more flexible reading of

[127] *See, e.g.*, Taxquet v. Belgium, App. No. 926/05, Eur. Ct. H.R., Nov. 16, 2010, § 83.

[128] *See, e.g.*, Teixeira de Castro v. Portugal, App. No. 25829/94, Eur. Ct. H.R., June 9, 1998, § 34; Schenk v. Switzerland, App. No. 10862/84, Eur. Ct. H.R., July 12, 1988, § 40.

[129] Khan v. The United Kingdom, App. No. 35394/97, Eur. Ct. H.R., May 12, 2000, § 34.

[130] Al-Khawaja and Tahery v. The United Kingdom, App. Nos. 26766/05 and 22228/06, Eur. Ct. H.R., Jan. 20, 2009; Lucà v. Italy, App. No. 33354/96, Eur. Ct. H.R., Feb. 27, 2001.

[131] R v. Horncastle [2010] 2 A.C. 373, [2009] UKSC 14.

the "sole or decisive" test in *Al-Khawaja*,[132] which allowed both sides to claim victory, of sorts, and depart the field with honor intact.[133] Although in this particular instance institutional harmony was restored through respectful "dialogue" between domestic and international judiciaries, the "*Al-Khawaja* saga" nicely illustrates the tension between rival jurisprudential approaches to regulating evidence and proof in criminal trials. In contrast to the common law's characteristically atomistic admissibility determinations (deferring holistic evaluation of evidence to the jury), the ECtHR considers whether reliance on particular kinds of evidence might have impacted unfairly on the proceedings as a whole, taking account of any countervailing measures to ameliorate the accused's evidential predicament. Unfamiliar as this broad-brush approach may be to common lawyers, it nevertheless opens the door to reimagining different ways in which evidence might be regulated in adjudicative processes. Indeed, one might tentatively draw parallels between the "forensic reasoning rules" increasingly prevalent in common law jurisdictions and the ECtHR's efforts to structure "free proof" in the civilian tradition.[134] In both instances, one might discern the development of a human-rights-based framework of evidentiary norms owing little, if anything, to rules of admissibility on the traditional common law model.

If cosmopolitan human rights jurisprudence is forcing (some) common lawyers to set their sights beyond the horizons of common law orthodoxy, another impetus—and opportunity—for reimagining traditional evidentiary processes arises from the astonishing proliferation over the last thirty years of international courts and tribunals established to try individuals for international crimes beyond domestic law.[135] International human rights law has played a central role in grounding the legitimacy of international criminal adjudication.[136] In particular, the fair trial standards articulated by Article 14 of the International Covenant on Civil and Political Rights have been incorporated into the procedural frameworks of all the UN-sponsored international criminal tribunals, as well as into the Statute of the permanent International Criminal Court (ICC).[137] In some ways more challenging than securing global agreement on these broadly worded fair trial standards, however, is the task of formulating detailed rules of criminal procedure and evidence that are both fit for institutional purposes and normatively acceptable to

[132] Al-Khawaja and Tahery v. The United Kingdom, App. Nos. 26766/05 and 22228/06, Eur. Ct. H.R., Dec. 15, 2011.

[133] For critical discussion, see Mike Redmayne, *Hearsay and Human Rights*: Al-Khawaja *in the Grand Chamber*, 75 Mod. L. Rev. 865 (2012); Laura Hoyano *What Is Balanced on the Scales of Justice? In Search of the Essence of the Right to a Fair Trial* [2014] Crim. L. Rev. 4; John Jackson & Sarah Summers, *Confrontation with Strasbourg: UK and Swiss Approaches to Criminal Evidence* [2013] Crim. L. Rev. 114.

[134] A recent illustration is Schatschaschwili v. Germany, App. No. 9154/10, Eur. Ct. H.R., Dec. 15, 2015.

[135] Generally, see Robert Cryer et al., *An Introduction to International Criminal Law and Procedure* (3d ed. 2014); Gary Jonathan Bass, *Stay the Hand of Vengeance: The Politics of War Crimes Tribunals* (2000).

[136] Salvatore Zappalà, *Human Rights in International Criminal Proceedings* (2003); Christoph J.M. Safferling, *Towards an International Criminal Procedure* (2001).

[137] *See* Yvonne McDermott, *Fairness in International Criminal Trials* (2016); Kai Ambos, *Treatise on International Criminal Law, Volume III: International Criminal Procedure* 57–98 (2016).

the international community as a whole. It is therefore not surprising that the tribunals have borrowed freely from domestic procedural traditions to produce hybrid, "sui generis" models that are neither "adversarial" nor "inquisitorial" in the conventional sense in which comparative lawyers use these terms.[138] Domestic law theories, concepts, and procedures are not, without imaginative adaptation, conducive to the project of constructing rules of procedure and evidence capable of doing justice to the peculiar context of international criminal adjudication.[139] Procedural solutions of the "one size fits all" variety are unlikely to be appropriate or successful across a diverse range of institutional environments, demanding flexibility and suitable contextual adjustments to meet "local" exigencies (always assuming compliance with fundamental fair trial standards). What appears to be evolving, even within the unitary institutional structure of the ICC, is a plethora of different practices that, from a theoretical perspective, might be regarded as "experiments" in procedural pluralism, hybridity[140] and convergence.[141] Researchers are thereby presented with new opportunities for re-examining the comparative strengths and weaknesses of different procedural and evidentiary mechanisms projected onto the international plane.[142] This is not just a question of which mechanisms are best suited to promote truth-finding, extending the epistemic preoccupations of common law scholarship's Thayerite legacy. It also invites exploration of how adjudicative processes contribute to the complex variety of—sometimes centrifugal, if not directly conflicting—objectives and normative values that are routinely claimed for international criminal justice.[143]

International criminal adjudication should be regarded as a valuable resource for Evidence scholars, in terms of *both* its epistemological practices and controversial normative foundations.[144] Indeed, one might discern a nascent "new evidence scholarship"

[138] *See, e.g.*, Kai Ambos, *International Criminal Procedure: "Adversarial," "Inquisitorial" or "Mixed"?*, 3 Int'l. Crim. L. Rev. 1 (2003); Alphons Orie, *Accusatorial v. Inquisitorial Approach in International Criminal Proceedings Prior to the Establishment of the ICC and in the Proceedings Before the ICC*, in *The Rome Statute of the International Criminal Court: A Commentary, Volume 2* (Antonio Cassese, Paola Gaeta & John R.W.D. Jones eds., 2002); Daryl Mundis, *From "Common Law" Towards "Civil Law": The Evolution of the ICTY Rules of Procedure and Evidence*, 14 Leiden J. Int'l. L. 287 (2001).

[139] John D. Jackson & Yassin M. Brunger, *Witness Preparation in the ICC: An Opportunity for Principled Pragmatism*, 13 J. Int'l. Crim. J. 601 (2015).

[140] Mireille Delmas-Marty, *Reflections on the "Hybridisation" of Criminal Procedure*, in *Crime, Procedure and Evidence in a Comparative and International Context* (John Jackson, Maximo Langer & Peter Tillers eds., 2008).

[141] John D. Jackson & Yassin M. Brunger, *Fragmentation and Harmonisation in the Development of Evidentiary Practices in International Criminal Tribunals*, in *Pluralism in International Criminal Law* (Elies van Sliedregt & Sergey Vasiliev eds., 2014); Diane Marie Amann, *Harmonic Convergence? Constitutional Criminal Procedure in an International Context*, 75 Ind. L.J. 809 (2000).

[142] Paul Roberts, *Comparative Law for International Criminal Justice*, in *Comparative Law: A Handbook* 339, 354 (Esin Örücü & David Nelken eds., 2007).

[143] *See* Mirjan R. Damaška, *What Is the Point of International Criminal Justice?*, 83 Chi.-Kent L. Rev. 329 (2008); Mark A. Drumbl, *Atrocity, Punishment, and International Law* (2007); Paul Roberts, *Restoration and Retribution in International Criminal Justice: An Exploratory Analysis*, in *Restorative Justice and Criminal Justice* (Andrew von Hirsch et al. eds., 2003).

[144] Paul Roberts, *Why International Criminal Evidence?*, in Roberts & Redmayne, *supra* note 13, at 347.

in international criminal law (ICL) developing along a similar trajectory to the original, domestic law iterations described in this chapter.[145] Early ICL works focused on rules of admissibility and charted a process of liberalization in the general direction of "free proof"— not without resistance.[146] Nancy Combs' *Fact-Finding without Facts* then marked a significant turn toward critical examination of evidence evaluation and processes of proof in international criminal trials.[147] The next logical step was to review methods, tools, and heuristics for analyzing evidence in domestic legal processes and to consider their potential application to the international context. Thus, the cutting edge of evidentiary scholarship in ICL has begun to explore practical applications of tools such as Bayesian networks,[148] which harness computing power in assessing the probative value of evidence, and graphical models of inference (such as modified Wigmore Charts)[149] that attempt to provide vivid, synoptic visualizations of the inferential logic of forensic reasoning. These are just two examples of a range of formalizations and techniques discussed in the information science literature that may be employed as litigation support aids or as analytical devices to improve the quality of legal argumentation and analysis of evidence. Modified Wigmorean analysis has been advocated as an effective approach to identifying crucial phases in complex arguments about evidence and subjecting them to detailed critical scrutiny, either to build up the strength of one's own evidential position or to attack an opponent's contentions: a technique styled "going for the jugular" by Anderson, Schum and Twining.[150] In several illuminating case studies of evidence and proof before the International Criminal Tribunal for the Former Yugoslavia, Yvonne McDermott has employed the chart method to pinpoint gaps in the prosecution's case against the accused and to support the Appeals Chamber's factual findings in relation to command responsibility.[151] As well as contributing to ongoing debates in ICL, these exploratory studies add ballast and diversity to an expanding, if somewhat diffuse and disorganized, interdisciplinary literature on evidence and proof.

[145] *See* Yvonne McDermott, *Strengthening the Evaluation of Evidence in International Criminal Trials*, 17 Int'l. Crim. L. Rev. 1, 3 (2017); Paul Roberts, *The Priority of Procedure and the Neglect of Evidence and Proof*, 13 J. Int'l. Crim. J. 479 (2015).

[146] Peter Murphy, *No Free Lunch, No Free Proof: The Indiscriminate Admission of Evidence Is a Serious Flaw in International Criminal Trials*, 8 J. Int'l. Crim. J. 539 (2010).

[147] Nancy Combs, *Fact-Finding Without Facts* (2010). But for earlier intimations, see, e.g., Lawrence Douglas, *The Memory of Judgment: Making Law and History in the Trials of the Holocaust* (2001); Kenneth Mann, *Hearsay Evidence in War Crimes Trials*, in *War Crimes in International Law* (Yoram Dinstein & Mala Tabory eds., 1996); Telford Taylor, *The Anatomy of the Nuremberg Trial* (1993).

[148] Yvonne McDermott & Colin Aitken, *Analysis of Evidence in International Criminal Trials Using Bayesian Belief Networks*, 16 L. Prob. & Risk 111 (2017).

[149] Yvonne McDermott, *Inferential Reasoning and Proof in International Criminal Trials*, 13 J. Int'l. Crim. J. 507 (2015). *See generally*, Paul Roberts & Colin Aitken, *The Logic of Forensic Proof: Inferential Reasoning in Criminal Evidence and Forensic Science*, RSS Practitioner Guide No. 3 (2014), www.rss.org.uk/statsandlaw (last visited September 15, 2018); Terrence Anderson, David Schum & William Twining, *Analysis of Evidence* (2d ed. 2005).

[150] Anderson, Schum & Twining, *supra* note 149, at 124.

[151] McDermott, *supra* note 149.

V. Conclusion: Toward an Interdisciplinary Forensic Science

This chapter has made the case for extending evidentiary scholarship and teaching "beyond common law." Many of the arguments have been made previously, including by us, but the common law's traditional model of the Law of Evidence has proved remarkably resilient and, in its disciplinary orientation and basic concepts, resistant to change. Various pragmatic explanations might be conjectured, ranging from the avalanche of legislative reform and case law precedents that have kept Evidence scholars and teachers gainfully employed for many decades (and has sometimes threatened to smother us with its suffocating bulk), to the natural tendency toward institutional stasis and reproduction of existing pedagogical practice through sheer force of habit. But it is also the case that significant institutional developments have occurred at a rapid pace in recent times, and may be already in the process of rendering traditional concepts and approaches obsolescent before the textbook writers have had a chance to take stock. Meanwhile, many useful resources for disciplinary renewal languish in siloed literatures apparently invisible ("open access" and electronic databases notwithstanding) to mainstream Evidence scholarship. Reimagining Evidence law is partly an exercise in bringing together fragmentary strands of argument and disparate intellectual resources and joining up the dots. Periodic rethinking should be regarded as part and parcel of keeping any disciplinary specialism relevant and vital.

The orthodox common law model of the Law of Evidence, rooted in a Thayerite conception of relevancy and focused predominantly on exclusionary rules, has always been a partial (i.e., perspectival *and* incomplete) reconstruction of institutional practice. Legal treatises *constitute* disciplinary specialisms, through programmatic selection and classification, as much as they simply catalogue legislative and judicial output. From the early 1970s onward, the New Evidence Scholarship broke free of the doctrinalism of previous decades, reinventing or rediscovering the broader epistemic agendas of the earliest architects of the common law evidentiary tradition, prominently including Gilbert and Bentham. Focusing on epistemological considerations provides intellectual grounding for a unified Law of Evidence on the traditional common law model, but it does not treat admissibility as the only, or even as the most important, institutional question. Legal epistemology concerns itself with analysis of evidence, inferential reasoning, and processes of proof, and is mirrored in litigation practice by the proliferation of forensic reasoning rules, which either supplement admissibility doctrines or, in some instances, have effectively replaced them. In those common law systems in which there has been a pronounced divergence between civil and criminal procedure, however, the traditional common law model of a unified Law of Evidence increasingly seems out of touch with reality. Standard Evidence textbooks delineate a mythical abstraction. The distance between civil and criminal procedure is growing even wider in jurisdictions, such as those of the UK and Ireland, where human rights law is materially shaping adjudicative processes. The advent of international criminal adjudication is a further cosmopolitan ingredient in modern Evidence scholarship, calling for sustained reflection on the normative values and objectives of particular types of legal proceedings and their further implications for evidence law and practice in particular contexts. While an epistemological orientation will emphasize generic aspects of evidentiary processes, more careful attention to institutional context tends toward particularism and disaggregation. Equality of treatment between the parties may be a reasonable default assumption for civil litigation, for example, but criminal proceedings are predicated on a principled asymmetry systematically favoring the accused. Justice is *not* procedural equality in criminal adjudication.

The pedagogical and disciplinary implications of our argument are doubtless conditioned by local institutional factors. In the United States, the FRE have institutionalized an essentially Thayerite model of Evidence law; and this must naturally be a significant consideration for law teachers and textbook writers. England and Wales operates under no such constraint, and indeed to focus exclusively on criminal evidence (or alternatively, on civil procedure and Evidence) is really only to acknowledge contemporary doctrinal reality. Irrespective of local jurisdictional variations, however, we have stressed that choices in the ways in which procedural law is conceptualized and structured are not merely questions of abstract theory. Alternative characterizations of Evidence law's purposes and fundamental principles have predictable repercussions for the way in which detailed evidentiary doctrines are taught and understood (or misunderstood), in the classroom and in the courtroom. In short, choice of conception, taxonomy, and basic concepts *matters*. A clear methodological implication of this argument is that such choices should be made intelligently, for articulated good reasons, and kept under review to ensure they remain appropriate in light of prevailing institutional and social conditions. Reproducing the orthodox common law model simply because common lawyers have always thought and talked about evidence law in this fashion is not intellectually respectable, on this view, nor does it promote exemplary legal practice or intelligent policymaking.

Reconceptualizing evidence law as part of an interdisciplinary "forensic science," as this chapter advocates, thus entails integrating epistemologies of evidence and proof with serious engagement with the normative foundations of legal adjudication. Forensic science, in the pertinent sense, connects doctrinal precepts to the logic of factual inference, and structures inferential reasoning according to the principles and values of particular adjudicative processes. Legal doctrine, factual inference, and normative principles are interconnected and mutually conditioning. Approaches to evidence law that single out only one of these dimensions, or which stress some institutional features to the detriment or exclusion of others, are inevitably lopsided and question-begging. Forensic science is a comprehensive approach to juridical evidence and proof. Like any disciplinary domain of similar magnitude, it anticipates collective endeavor with sensible, pragmatic divisions of labor, partly predicated on existing distributions of methodological expertise. Nobody can know it all, or do it all. Lawyers will need to call on a range of specialists, in psychology, cognitive science, economics, philosophy, computing, statistics, and so forth, to augment their core jurisprudential knowledge and practical wisdom.[152]

There is one further programmatic benefit to be derived from translating Evidence scholarship into "forensic science," and this concerns *forensic science evidence*, the "forensic science" of popular imagination. It is a frequently rehearsed commonplace, long anticipated by astute commentators,[153] that forensic science and other forms of expert testimony have become increasingly influential in modern litigation. Science looms large in twenty-first century law, as it does in twenty-first century society and modern life. If the day has not yet arrived when the paradigmatic form of judicial evidence is a scientific report rather than the traditional image of the lay witness testifying under oath, it might not be too far distant. Yet the common law model of Evidence marginalizes the entire topic of experts under the oblique rubric of "opinion evidence." It is high time that expert evidence assumed a more central position in jurisprudential thinking about evidence and proof. Particularly in the context of criminal adjudication, where forensic science presents distinctive institutional challenges and has lately been going through a period of soul-searching and methodological renewal,[154] legal scholars and practitioners have much to learn, and some important things to teach, about the epistemic credentials and normative limitations of expert witness testimony for the proper administration of justice.

References

Terrence Anderson, David Schum & William Twining, *Analysis of Evidence* (2d ed. 2005)
Mirjan Damaška, *Evidence Law Adrift* (1997)
Evidence, Inference and Enquiry (Philip Dawid, William Twining & Mimi Vasilaki eds., 2011)
Ian Dennis, *The Law of Evidence* (6th ed. 2017)
John D. Jackson & Sarah J. Summers, *The Internationalisation of Criminal Evidence* (2012)
Theoretical Foundations of Criminal Trial Procedure (Paul Roberts ed., 2014)
Expert Evidence and Scientific Proof in Criminal Trials (Paul Roberts ed., 2014)
Criminal Evidence and Human Rights (Paul Roberts & Jill Hunter eds., 2012)
Innovations in Evidence and Proof (Paul Roberts & Mike Redmayne eds., 2007)

[152] To similar effect, see *Evidence, Inference and Enquiry* (Philip Dawid, William Twining & Mimi Vasilaki eds., 2011); William Twining, *Evidence as a Multi-disciplinary Subject*, 2 L. Prob. & Risk 91 (2003); Paul Roberts, *The New Interdisciplinary Forensic Science*, 43 J.L. Soc'y 647 (2016).

[153] A century before Damaška, *supra* note 9, at 143, identified "the creeping scientization of factual inquiry" as a threat to traditional common law models of adjudication, Holmes prophesized that "the black-letter man may be the man of the present, but the man of the future is the man of statistics and the master of economics": Oliver Wendell Holmes, *The Path of Law*, 10 Harv. L. Rev. 457, 469 (1897).

[154] *See further*, Paul Roberts, *Making Forensic Science Fit for Justice*, 49 Austl. J. Forensic Sci. 502 (2017); Paul Roberts, *Forensic Science and Criminal Justice*, in *Criminal Justice* (Anthea Hucklesby & Azrini Wahidin eds., 2013); *Expert Evidence and Scientific Proof in Criminal Trials* (Paul Roberts ed., 2014).

Paul Roberts & Colin Aitken, *The Logic of Forensic Proof: Inferential Reasoning in Criminal Evidence and Forensic Science*, RSS Practitioner Guide No. 3 (2014), www.rss.org.uk/statsandlaw

Paul Roberts & Adrian Zuckerman, *Criminal Evidence* (2d ed. 2010)

Colin Tapper, *Cross and Tapper on Evidence* (12th ed. 2010)

William Twining, *Rethinking Evidence* (2d ed. 2006)

CHAPTER 36

EXCLUSION OF WRONGFULLY OBTAINED EVIDENCE

A Comparative Analysis

HO HOCK LAI*

I. Introduction

Two events must occur for the issue of excluding wrongfully obtained evidence to arise before a trial court. The first is the wrongful procurement of evidence.[1] Typically, the procurer is the police.[2] When the police look for evidence, a major purpose is to supply the prosecutor (or, in some jurisdictions, the investigating judge) with evidence of potential use in securing a criminal conviction. The second preceding event is the step taken by the relevant official (prosecutor or investigating judge) to adduce the evidence at the trial or, in civil law systems, to include the evidence in the dossier for the trial court.

To exclude wrongfully obtained evidence is, in one sense, to prevent the prosecution from adducing it to discharge its burden of proof. In another sense, it is about the trial court being barred from relying on the evidence in determining the guilt of the accused person and, where reasons are required, in justifying its finding of guilt. Rules that compel or permit the exclusion of wrongfully obtained evidence are sometimes called "exclusionary rules." In some civil law systems, exclusion is achieved by way of the

* I thank Jenia I. Turner for her valuable comments and Ho Yijie for his research assistance.

[1] The procurement may be wrongful in the sense of being unlawful or in breach of extralegal standards of conduct. *See infra* Section III.4.

[2] In the nontypical context where the evidence was obtained by persons acting in a private capacity, see David R.A. Caruso, *Public Policy and Private Illegality in the Pursuit of Evidence*, 21 Int'l. J. Evid. & Proof 87 (2017).

procedural concept of nullity.[3] For example, if a search was conducted unlawfully, the judicial chamber has the power to declare it null and void, and the evidence gathered from the nullified search is then excluded from the investigation dossier.[4]

Section II discusses three lines of objections relating to wrongfully obtained evidence. As we will see, they have prompted different rationales and theories for exclusion. Section III explores the different approaches that have been taken to wrongfully obtained evidence. An analysis of legal forms and techniques will be followed by a discussion of the major factors that have been treated as relevant in deciding on exclusion.

II. Objections, Rationales, and Theories

It aids analysis of the topic to separate three lines of objection. Each of them is directed at a different institutional actor. The first objection is to the manner in which the police have obtained the evidence; the second is to the use of the evidence by the prosecution to prove its case against the accused, or to the inclusion of the evidence in the trial dossier; and the third is to the trial court's reliance on the evidence in finding the accused guilty as charged or, where the provision of reasons is required, in supporting that finding. Different theories or rationales for the exclusion of wrongfully obtained evidence have clustered around these three lines of objection. It is usual to find more than one theory or rationale at work in shaping the law.

1. Exclusion Grounded in Objections to Police Misconduct in Procuring the Evidence

In the standard case, the evidence in question was obtained wrongfully by the police. The problem of admitting or relying on such evidence at a criminal trial is connected to the prior problem of the police misconduct in obtaining it. At one level, the connection is plain to see: the court would not be facing the issue of exclusion had the police not acquired the evidence wrongfully. The relationship between the two problems has, in addition, a purposive dimension. A major aim of criminal investigation is to secure evidence that is capable of standing up in court as proof of guilt. What makes the police conduct wrongful is, in part, that it was directed at getting evidence for use at a criminal trial; the conduct may otherwise be lawful. For example, the law may allow the compulsory

[3] *See* Stephen C. Thaman, *Balancing Truth Against Human Rights: A Theory of Modern Exclusionary Rules*, in *Exclusionary Rules in Comparative Law* 403, 410–12 (Stephen C. Thaman ed., 2013).

[4] Dimitrios Giannoulopoulos, *The Exclusion of Improperly Obtained Evidence in Greece: Putting Constitutional Rights First*, 11 Intl. J. Evid. & Proof 181, 190 (2007).

acquisition of information from a person in the course of a purely administrative investigation but not allow it if it was for the purpose of supporting a criminal prosecution.[5]

While the two problems are related, they are separable. First, one can arise without the other. The problem of police misconduct in evidence gathering can easily exist independently of any question of relying on wrongfully obtained evidence in the determination of guilt. For example, an unlawful search may not yield any evidence, and even if it does yield evidence, it may not end up before the court, or the accused may decide to plead guilty, thus forgoing a trial. In all these situations, there is no occasion for a trial judge to exclude wrongfully obtained evidence.

Second, the permissibility of the method used by the police in obtaining evidence and the permissibility of reliance on the evidence by the court are different issues. Wrongfully obtained evidence is not always excluded. Further, even where the police have an excuse for obtaining evidence in a wrongful way, and even where it is proper to employ wrongfully obtained evidence for investigative or other non-judicial purposes, it may be objectionable to allow use of the evidence in the legal determination of guilt. In *A v. Secretary of State for the Home Department (No 2)*,[6] which concerns the admissibility of evidence allegedly obtained from third parties by torture at the hands of foreign agents, the House of Lords of the United Kingdom stressed that the executive and the judiciary have different functions and responsibilities. While the executive may be entitled or even bound in some circumstances to rely on wrongfully obtained evidence in making operational decisions, it is quite another thing to use the evidence in legal proceedings.

Third, there are many ways of addressing the problem of police misconduct in gathering evidence that do not involve exclusion of the evidence, and the effectiveness of exclusionary rules in dealing with the problem is questionable. The direct way of handling a particular instance of police misconduct is to institute disciplinary or criminal action against the errant officer. Prophylactic measures targeted at the police as a profession include providing better training and clearer investigative rules. Personal remedies may also be obtained by instituting collateral proceedings. In some legal systems, these include financial compensation by the state as a public law remedy to the person whose right had been violated by the police in the course of seeking evidence.[7] Another possibility is the award of damages under tort law in an action brought by the person against the police.[8]

These ways of addressing the police misconduct occur outside of the criminal proceeding for which the evidence was procured. Responses to the wrongdoing can also occur in the criminal proceeding itself. Some jurisdictions are open to treating the

[5] *See Human Rights and Criminal Justice* 617 (Ben Emerson et al. eds., 3d ed., 2012).

[6] [2006] 2 A.C. 221.

[7] Such a remedy is available, for example, in the United States (Bivens v. Six Unknown Named Agents of Federal Bureau of Narcotics, 403 U.S. 388 (1971)) and in New Zealand (Simpson v. Attorney-General [Baigent's Case] [1994] 3 N.Z.L.R. 667).

[8] For a defense of this remedy in the United States, see Akhil Reed Amar, *The Constitution and Criminal Procedure: First Principles* 31–45 (1997); Christopher Slobogin, *Why Liberals Should Chuck the Exclusionary Rule*, 1999 U. Ill. L. Rev. 363 (1999).

police misconduct as a mitigating factor in sentencing[9] or, in especially egregious cases, even as a ground for putting a stop to (by granting a stay of) the prosecution.[10] One theory defends exclusion as another form of remedy—and as the most appropriate remedy[11]—for the violation of rights committed by the police in securing the evidence.[12] Where the evidence sought to be used against the accused person has been obtained in serious transgression of his or her rights, the most effective remedy for the transgression is to prevent the evidence from being so used. This puts the accused in the position he or she would have been in had his or her right not been infringed. Since it is the violation of the accused's rights and not the police wrongdoing of itself that justifies exclusion, the theory cannot explain, for example, why evidence obtained by torturing a third party should be excluded. In this situation, it was the victim's—and not the accused person's—fundamental right not to be tortured that was breached. One implication of this theory is that the accused would lack standing to call for exclusion if it was someone else's legal right that had been infringed. This standing requirement exists in several jurisdictions, including the United States and Germany.[13]

The remedial theory is rights-based, and backward-looking, and defends exclusion as a direct response to the specific wrong committed by the police in getting the evidence. An alternative theory is policy-based, and forward-looking, and justifies exclusion in terms of its impact on future police behavior. On this theory, exclusion of wrongfully obtained evidence is analyzed, as it is most prominently in the United States, as a matter of public policy that works indirectly to address malpractices in criminal investigation. The hope is that the exclusion would help to shape police behavior by deterring similar misconduct in the future or by educating the police on the importance of complying with the law. On this rationale, the effect and purpose of exclusion coincide. But, conceptually, the two are distinct. In many other jurisdictions, deterrence is not the (primary) purpose of exclusion. (Other possible rationales are explored below in Sections II 2–3.) Where the adopted rationale is other than deterrence, the exclusionary rule may still have a deterrent effect on the police. But that is beside the point. Even where the purpose of the rule is to deter police misconduct, the problem addressed by the

[9] *See* Criminal Procedure Code of the Netherlands § 359a; Matthias J. Borgers & Lonneke Stevens, *The Netherlands: Statutory Balancing a Choice of Remedies*, in *Exclusionary Rules in Comparative Law* 183, 190 (Stephen C. Thaman ed., 2013). For a proposal to move in a similar direction in the United States, see Guido Calabresi, *The Exclusionary Rule*, 26 Harv. J.L. & Pub. Pol'y 111 (2003).

[10] *See* Criminal Procedure Code of the Netherlands §359a.

[11] In New Zealand, the availability of monetary compensation and sentence reduction is generally irrelevant in deciding whether to exclude evidence obtained in breach of the Bill of Rights Act: R v. Shaheed [2002] 2 N.Z.L.R. 377, 386, 421.

[12] *See* Andrew Ashworth, *Excluding Evidence as Protecting Rights*, [1977] Crim. L. Rev. 723; William A. Schroeder, *Restoring the Status Quo Ante: The Fourth Amendment Exclusionary Rule as a Compensatory Device*, 51 Geo. Wash. L. Rev. 633 (1983); Jerry E. Norton, *The Exclusionary Rule Reconsidered: Restoring the Status Quo Ante*, 33 Wake Forest L. Rev. 261 (1998).

[13] On the German position, see Sabine Gless, *Germany: Balancing Truth Against Protected Constitutional Interests*, in *Exclusionary Rules in Comparative Law* 113, 122 (Stephen C. Thaman ed., 2013). The position is different in Greece. There "the exclusionary rule applies even in cases where evidence has been obtained through a violation of the right to privacy of a person other than the defendant." Giannoulopoulos, *supra* note 4, at 197.

exclusion of evidence is, strictly speaking, still conceptually different from the problem of police misconduct. In allowing the evidence to be used, the court risks sending a wrong signal to the police (that is, of legitimizing or giving judicial approval to their method of obtaining evidence) whereas exclusion would impress upon them the futility of such endeavors (by eliminating the incentive for engaging in similar evidence-gathering operations in the future). Hence, even if exclusion is for the sake of deterrence, the problem of allowing wrongfully obtained evidence to be used at the trial is the problem of signaling and incentivization, and not simply the problem of police misconduct.

The deterrence rationale raises a host of questions and rests on a number of assumptions. To deter the police from breaking rules on evidence gathering, they must know what the rules are. It is questionable whether they do possess adequate knowledge.[14] Exclusion will have little signaling and disincentivization impact if there is no communication channel that keeps the police in the loop every time the court rejects the evidence that they have collected. The deterrence rationale also supposes that the police care or have reason to care sufficiently about exclusion. This will not be so if the culture is such that they perceive their job as done once an arrest is made and investigation closes and their job performance is evaluated by the clearance rate. Even supposing that the police care about exclusion, if they believe that their misconduct will probably not be discovered, they will not be deterred by the threat of exclusion. The motivation for collecting evidence is not always to support a criminal prosecution. Much of police work is about maintaining order without resorting to formal law enforcement. When the police in collecting evidence are not seeking it for use at a trial, the fear of exclusion by the court will not be playing on their mind.[15] Empirical studies on the deterrent effect of exclusionary rules in deterring police misconduct are inconclusive.[16]

2. Exclusion Grounded in Objections to the Prosecution Using Wrongfully Obtained Evidence to Discharge Its Burden of Proof

In an adversarial trial, to exclude evidence wrongfully obtained by the police is to prevent the prosecution, as a party to the dispute, from presenting it as a means of discharging

[14] Inadequate knowledge was reported in a study conducted in the United States: William C. Heffernan & Richard W. Lovely, *Evaluating the Fourth Amendment Exclusionary Rule: The Problem of Police Compliance with the Law*, 24 U. Mich. J.L. Reform 311, 356 (1991).

[15] Dallin H. Oaks, *Studying the Exclusionary Rule in Search and Seizure*, 37 U. Chi. L. Rev. 665, 720 (1970).

[16] The best-known empirical study is probably Oaks, *id.* Although this study is often cited as casting doubt on the deterrent value of the exclusionary rule in the United States, Oaks himself was careful to acknowledge its limitations. *Id.* at 716: "In view of the complexity of the inquiry, it presently appears to be impossible to design any test or group of tests that would give a reliable measure of the overall deterrent effect of the exclusionary rule on law enforcement behavior." On the impact of this article, and for references to other empirical studies, see Albert W. Alschuler, *Studying the Exclusionary Rule: An Empirical Classic*, 75 U. Chi. L. Rev. 1365 (2008).

its burden of proof. Where the trial is by jury, exclusion will keep the fact-finder wholly ignorant of the evidence. Exclusion works differently in an inquisitorial setting; there, it is essentially about the trial court not discussing the evidence at the trial and not taking it into account in the reasons that it has to give for the verdict.

In some jurisdictions that are based on or influenced by civil law, there appears to be a notion of exclusion by the prosecutor. This seems to refer to the prosecutor removing the evidence from the dossier prepared for the trial judge or leaving the evidence aside in deciding how or whether to proceed with the case.[17] In practical terms, the position is not much different in common law systems. There, the prosecutor can similarly choose to leave the wrongfully obtained evidence aside in making prosecutorial decisions and, if the case proceeds to trial, choose not to present the evidence at the trial.[18] The common law, however, does not speak of exclusion by the prosecutor, at least not when "exclusion" is used as a technical term. The power of exclusion lies with the court, and whether wrongfully obtained evidence may be adduced is a question of law for the trial judge to decide.

Two other differences between common law and civil law legal systems bear on the present topic. First, in common law legal systems, the functions of the police department and the prosecution office tend to be clearly demarcated and these institutions operate with a degree of independence from each another. The same cannot be said of civil law jurisdictions where criminal investigations are normally led by a prosecutor or an examining magistrate. Second, in an adversarial setting, the prosecution is a party to a proceeding that is often characterized as a contest, and, in this contest, it carries the general burden of proving the charge that it has brought against the accused. Exclusion of evidence is an action taken by the trial judge, whose role is popularly depicted as that of an "umpire," to prevent the prosecution from presenting the evidence as proof. An inquisitorial trial is structured differently. In Germany, for instance, witnesses are, with rare exceptions, called by the court on its own initiative and evidence given at the trial is considered as "the court's evidence"; as such, the view is taken that "excluding a piece of evidence would not be depriving the offending party of 'its' evidence but would interfere with the court's effort to obtain a complete picture of the relevant facts."[19]

[17] *See, e.g.*, Giulio Illuminati, *Italy: Statutory Nullities and Non-usability*, in *Exclusionary Rules in Comparative Law* 235, 239 (Stephen C. Thaman ed., 2013); Chinese Criminal Procedure Law 2012, art. 54 (English translation available from the website of the Office of the High Commissioner, United Nations Human Rights: http://tbinternet.ohchr.org/_layouts/treatybodyexternal/Download.aspx?symbolno=INT%2fCAT%2fADR%2fCHN%2f20050&Lang=en); Swiss Criminal Procedure Code art. 141(5) (English translation available from the website of the Swiss government: https://www.admin.ch/opc/en/classified-compilation/20052319/index.html).

[18] *See* Russell M. Gold, *Beyond the Judicial Fourth Amendment: The Prosecutor's Role*, 47 U.C. Davis L. Rev. 1591 (2014) (arguing that prosecutors in the United States have a constitutional and ethical responsibility to refrain from using evidence obtained in breach of the Fourth Amendment regardless of judicial admissibility).

[19] Thomas Weigend, *Throw It All Out? Judicial Discretion in Dealing with Procedural Faults*, in *Discretionary Criminal Justice in a Comparative Context* 185, 189 (Michele Caianiello & Jacqueline S. Hodgson eds., 2015).

Resistance to exclusion from an adversarial perspective stresses two related factors. First, it is the duty of the prosecution office to prosecute those who are believed to have committed crimes. Second, in systems that maintain clear lines of functional demarcation, the police act independently and as a separate entity from the prosecution. The exclusion of evidence proffered by the prosecution hampers the prosecution in discharging its burden of proof and in carrying out its public duty to prosecute crimes. Why should the execution of this public duty be thwarted by the misconduct of the police? On the "fragmentary" conception of government attacked by Schrock and Welsh,[20] and on the "separation thesis" criticized by Ashworth,[21] the misconduct of the police, acting as a separate and distinct entity in procuring the evidence, ought not to prejudice the prosecution whose hands are, so to speak, clean.

Various theories have been offered to justify barring the prosecution from proffering wrongfully obtained evidence. One theory invokes the principle that the state should not profit from its own wrongdoing.[22] In the situation where evidence has been obtained through a wrongful act of an agent of the state (namely, the police), to allow the state (through the prosecution) to use the evidence against the accused is to allow the state to derive an unfair advantage over the accused in their adversarial contest. A different theory rests on the claim that the prosecutor's (or the state's) moral standing to call for criminal condemnation of the accused is undermined by the unlawful conduct employed in securing the means by which it seeks to condemn the accused.[23]

Both theories face the already mentioned difficulty raised in the fragmentation or separation thesis. Insofar as the police had acted independently in wrongfully procuring the evidence, the prosecution would arguably not be benefitting from *its* own wrong in using the evidence at the trial. For the same reason that the prosecution was not involved in the wrongdoing, the police misconduct would not undermine the prosecution's moral standing to seek a criminal conviction. One way of meeting this criticism is to find complicity by the prosecution in choosing to use the evidence as legal proof. Another is to reject the fragmentation or separation thesis by denying the separate agency of the police and prosecution; we should view them, instead, as members of the single collective agent that is the state.[24] If the police and the prosecutor are members of the same collective agent, the wrong of one qua member of the collective agent is attributable to the other qua member of the same collective agent. In short, while different hands are at work, there is but one actor.

[20] Thomas S. Schrock & Robert C. Welsch, *Up from* Calandra: *The Exclusionary Rule as a Constitutional Requirement*, 59 Minn. L. Rev. 251 (1974); *see also* Ruth W. Grant, *The Exclusionary Rule and the Meaning of Separation of Powers*, 14 Harv. J.L. & Pub. Pol'y 173 (1991).

[21] Andrew Ashworth, *Exploring the Integrity Principle in Evidence and Procedure*, in *Essays for Colin Tapper* 107 (Peter Mirfield & Roger Smith eds., 2003).

[22] *See, e.g.*, Peter Chau, *Excluding Integrity? Revising Non-consequentialist Justifications for Excluding Improperly Obtained Evidence in Criminal Trials*, in *The Integrity of Criminal Process: From Theory into Practice* 267 (Jill Hunter et al. eds., 2016); Antony Duff et al., *The Trial on Trial: Towards a Normative Theory of the Criminal Trial* 107–08 (2007).

[23] *See, e.g.*, Duff et al., *supra* note 22, at 109.

[24] *See* Ho Hock Lai, *The Criminal Trial, the Rule of Law and the Exclusion of Unlawfully Obtained Evidence*, 10 Crim. L. & Phil. 109 (2016).

3. Exclusion Grounded in Objections to the Court Relying on Wrongfully Obtained Evidence in Reaching or Justifying a Conviction

A third group of theories focuses on objections to the trial court relying on wrongfully obtained evidence in determining or justifying a finding of guilt. If, on the arguments explored in Section II.2, it is objectionable for the prosecution to use the wrongfully obtained evidence at the trial, it would be objectionable for the court to allow the prosecution to do so by admitting the evidence. This merely brings us back to the arguments just considered. But there is more to be said. The court's reliance on the evidence in finding the accused guilty, or in justifying that finding, may be problematic in its own right.

a. *Reliability*

Notwithstanding the oft-made, and occasionally exaggerated, claim that there is greater respect for material truth in the civilian tradition than at common law, a widely accepted aim of a trial, be it an inquisitorial or adversarial one, is to ascertain the truth in the charge brought against the accused person. Given the relevance of wrongfully obtained evidence, its exclusion would, prima facie, run counter to this aim. This is a major source of pressure *against* exclusion.

However, reliability concerns may also be a source of pressure *for* exclusion. Evidence may be unreliable because of how it was obtained. Use of unreliable evidence increases the risk of error in fact-finding. Exclusion would serve the truth-seeking purpose of a trial. Unreliability of evidence is the criterion employed in exclusionary rules such as Article 69(7) of the Statute of the International Criminal Court. But the exclusion of wrongfully obtained evidence on this ground faces theoretical and practical difficulties. It has been noted in relation to confessions that unreliability is a matter that, theoretically, should "go to the weight and not to the admissibility of the evidence,"[25] and, at the practical front, there are difficulties in devising "a clear, administratively feasible means of evaluating the trustworthiness of specific confessions."[26]

Other exclusionary rules focus instead on the reliability of the method used in obtaining the evidence. Certain methods of obtaining evidence carry a significantly high risk of producing unreliable evidence. Where evidence is excluded under these rules, it is because the evidence was obtained by an unreliable method and not because the evidence is unreliable. For instance, a provision in the Indian Evidence Act requires the exclusion of a confession if its making was "caused by any inducement, threat or promise."[27] In applying this exclusionary rule, the court has to consider if any of these three forms of pressure was exerted on the accused person in getting him or her to confess; the court does not undertake an assessment of the reliability of the confession itself. A method of

[25] Ibrahim v. R [1914] A.C. 599, 610; A v. Secretary of State for the Home Department (No. 2), *supra* note 6, at 287.

[26] Welsh S. White, *What Is an Involuntary Confession Now?*, 50 Rutgers L. Rev. 2001, 2028 (1998).

[27] Indian Evidence Act § 24.

obtaining a confession is unreliable insofar as it generates a significant risk of falsity in confessions procured by that method. The method is unreliable even if its use on a particular occasion produces a true confession. To draw an analogy, speeding is a dangerous way to drive as it increases the risk of an accident occurring. This proposition holds up even if a driver managed to avoid causing any accident while speeding on a particular occasion. Similarly, that a confession obtained by an unreliable method happens to be true does not establish that the method is therefore reliable. Sometimes, the test for exclusion is the unreliability of the method and not unreliability of the evidence.[28]

Tensions between the interest in admitting reliable relevant evidence and the value of exclusion come to the fore where the wrongfully obtained evidence leads to the discovery of other evidence. The latter is often called "derivative evidence" or described metaphorically as "fruit of the poisonous tree,"[29] and its reliability is usually not in doubt. At common law, the derivative evidence is generally admissible.[30] This reflects the priority given to the interests in uncovering guilt and crime control. In other jurisdictions, such as the United States, the exclusionary rule extends, with exceptions, to derivative evidence.[31] This serves the interest of deterrence. There is even less reason for the police to engage in wrongful procurement of evidence if they do not stand to benefit even indirectly from such acts.

Another situation where tension exists is where facts are subsequently discovered that establish the reliability of a wrongfully obtained statement. If reliability of evidence is the crucial consideration, the initial ground for excluding the wrongfully obtained statement dissipates with the new discovery. In Singapore, the statement now becomes admissible.[32] The position is different under English common law, under which the statement would generally remain inadmissible.[33] This is because while "the inherent unreliability of involuntary statements is one of the reasons for holding them to be inadmissible there are other compelling reasons also."[34] As noted earlier, the law is normally underpinned by multiple rationales. We now turn to these other compelling reasons.

b. *Integrity*

Many theories of exclusion invoke the values of "integrity" and "legitimacy." These two terms are used interchangeably in the literature. The two concepts will be delineated in order to isolate, and facilitate the systematic exposition of, the different arguments that

[28] On this distinction in England, see Ian Dennis, *The Law of Evidence* 238–39 (6th ed. 2017), and in the United States, see Yale Kamisar, *What Is an "Involuntary" Confession? Some Comments on Inbau and Reid's* Criminal Interrogation and Confessions, 17 Rutgers L. Rev. 728, 753 (1963); White, *supra* note 26; Eve Brensike Primus, *The Future of Confession Law: Toward Rules for the Voluntariness Test*, 114 Mich. L. Rev. 1 (2015).

[29] For a comparative study, see Kerri Mellifont, *Fruit of the Poisonous Tree: Evidence Derived from Illegally or Improperly Obtained Evidence* (2010).

[30] R v. Warickshall (1783) 1 Leach 263.

[31] Silverthorne Lumber Co. v. United States 251 U.S. 385 (1920).

[32] Criminal Procedure Code, Cap. 68, 2012 rev. ed., §258(6)(c) (Sing.).

[33] Lam Chi-ming v. The Queen [1991] 2 A.C. 212.

[34] A v. Secretary of State for the Home Department (No. 2), *supra* note 6, at 249; Lam Chi-ming v. The Queen, *supra* note 33, at 220.

come under their labels. Legitimacy will be treated, as it is in social and political theory, as a concept that is associated with claims of authority. Legitimacy-based arguments for exclusion will be addressed in the next section. This section considers integrity as a value underpinning exclusionary rules.[35] There are two prominent conceptions of integrity in this area of the law.

On one conception, integrity is about abiding by principles and being steadfast in recognizing rights as trumps. It is the duty of the court to vindicate the legal rights of individuals in their dealings with the state.[36] This duty is especially grave where the rights are constitutional or fundamental in nature. Judicial integrity reinforces the remedial theory of exclusion discussed earlier.[37] There is an abdication of judicial duty in the failure to exclude wrongfully obtained evidence where exclusion is the only or most meaningful way of vindicating the right that has been breached.

A different argument conceives of integrity as moral coherence.[38] It emphasizes the nature of the criminal law as a censuring institution. A criminal conviction blames and condemns a wrongdoer for the wrong that the person has done. To expand on the collective agency analysis mentioned previously, the court, in convicting a person, is acting as one component of the collective agent that is the criminal justice machinery of the state. This is sometimes described as integrity as integration. Exclusion upholds the value of integrity understood as normative coherence in the operations of the criminal justice system considered as an integrated whole. There is a lack of normative coherence when the state itself violates the law in its attempt to enforce the law; in the first, the state violates the law through the agency of the police in obtaining evidence, and in the second, the state attempts to enforce the law through the agency of the court in seeking a criminal conviction.

c. *Legitimacy*

Another group of arguments focuses on the concept of legitimacy. The court in seeking to achieve the internal aim of finding the truth is subject to side-constraints based on values external to the trial. Such side-constraints are necessary if the court or, more broadly, the administration of justice or, even more broadly, the government is to have legitimacy in the sense of drawing (and being deserving of) public confidence and respect. This was a driving force in the development of exclusionary rules by the U.S. Supreme Court before the ascendancy of the deterrence rationale. To preserve

[35] *See generally* Ashworth, *supra* note 21. For an example of an exclusionary rule that turns on the concept of integrity, see Rome Statute of the International Criminal Court art. 69(7).

[36] Under Article 40 of the Constitution of Ireland, the "State guarantees. . . . [b]y its laws to defend and vindicate the personal rights of the citizen." The Irish courts have founded the exclusionary rule on this constitutional guarantee. *See, e.g.*, D.P.P. v. J.C. [2015] I.E.S.C. 31 at [4.18] (Judgment of Clarke J.); *see also* Tony Ward & Clare Leon, *Excluding Evidence (or Staying Proceedings) to Vindicate Rights in Irish and English Law*, 35 Legal Stud. 571 (2015).

[37] *See supra* Section II.1.

[38] *See, e.g.*, Duff et al., *supra* note 22, ch. 8; Paul Roberts & Adrian Zuckerman, *Criminal Evidence* 157–60 (2004); Ho Hock Lai, *State Entrapment*, 31 Legal Stud. 71, 88–91 (2011) (applying the same type of argument to entrapment).

judicial legitimacy, and to avoid being tainted by the executive's dirty hands, the court has to renounce and disassociate itself from the police illegality by refusing to accept and act on the product of the illegality.[39] A similar approach is taken, albeit from a broader perspective, under Section 24(2) of the Canadian Charter of Rights and Freedoms. Exclusion under this provision turns on whether admission of evidence obtained in breach of the Charter "would bring the administration of justice into disrepute." This is determined objectively from the viewpoint of a reasonable and informed person. The focus is on social policy considerations pertaining to the damage that might prospectively be done, in the long term, to the legitimacy of the justice system if the court were seen as condoning the illegal practices of the police.[40] Even more broadly, legitimacy is also an attribute of the government. As will be discussed later, the introduction of exclusionary rules in China was, on one account, prompted by the interest of the Communist Party in preventing erosion of its authority.[41]

But legitimacy is a double-edged sword. Just as legitimacy of the criminal process would be eroded if "the court as a dispenser of justice ... is seen to condone illegality," it would also be undermined if "the public perceives that factually guilty people are getting away with serious crimes because of a trivial breach of legislation."[42] Hence, the Canadian approach treats society's interest in the adjudication of cases on their merits as a relevant countervailing consideration. Exclusion of the prosecution's evidence is seen as being detrimental to the social interest in having an effective law enforcement system. This is controvertible. Exclusion may produce a net positive gain for law enforcement over the long term. Schulhofer, Tyler, and Huq argue, in the context of Fourth Amendment violations in the United States, that "judicial tolerance for [such] violations will generate disrespect for authority, chill voluntary compliance, and discourage law-abiding citizens from offering the cooperation that makes it possible to apprehend and convict other offenders in future cases."[43]

Thus far, the discussion has been on the legitimacy of institutions. We may also speak of the legitimacy of a verdict. Some have argued that the purpose of a trial is not simply to get to the truth but to legitimize the verdict. On this account, legitimacy is an internal aim, not merely an external value, of the trial process. The legitimacy of the verdict has a positive and a normative meaning. Briefly, a verdict is legitimate in the positive sense if it is to gain general acceptance by the public, and it is legitimate in the normative sense if

[39] *See* Robert M. Bloom, *Judicial Integrity: A Call for Its Re-emergence in the Adjudication of Criminal Cases*, 84 J. Crim. L. & Criminology 462 (1993); Robert M. Bloom & David H. Fentin, *A More Majestic Conception: The Importance of Judicial Integrity in Preserving the Exclusionary Rule*, 13 U. Pa. J. Const. L. 47 (2010); Fred Gilbert Bennett, *Judicial Integrity and Judicial Review: An Argument for Expanding the Scope of the Exclusionary Rule*, 20 UCLA L. Rev. 1129 (1973).

[40] *See, e.g.*, R v. Grant, 2009 S.C.C. 32; R v. Harrison, 2009 S.C.C. 34.

[41] *See infra* Section II.3.d.

[42] S.M. Summit Holdings Ltd. v. P.P. [1997] 3 S.L.R. 922 at [48] (High Court of Singapore). This point is stressed by Adrian A.S. Zuckerman in advocating a balancing approach: *Illegally-Obtained Evidence—Discretion as a Guardian of Legitimacy*, 40 Current Legal Probs. 55 (1987).

[43] Stephen J. Schulhofer et al., *American Policing at a Crossroads: Unsustainable Policies and the Procedural Justice Alternative*, 101 J. Crim. L. & Criminology 335, 364 (2011).

it is worthy of such acceptance.[44] On a wholly positive reading, legitimacy is a matter of public opinion, rightly or wrongly held. Courts have tended to emphasize the normative dimension of the concept.[45]

A verdict that is the product of an unfair trial lacks legitimacy. The concepts of "fairness" and "reliability" are intertwined. Just as we can say that it is unfair (or unjust) to convict a person who is innocent, we can also say that it is unfair (or unjust) to reach a guilty verdict on evidence that is unreliable. Where the evidence is unreliable, it is incapable of giving us sufficient assurance that the accused person is in fact guilty. Reliance on evidence that is unreliable by virtue of its wrongful provenance would undermine the fairness of a trial and, thence, the legitimacy of the verdict. This is to interpret the concept of a fair trial in terms of reliability. English courts predominantly take this interpretation of fairness when applying the exclusionary discretion in Section 78(1) of the Police and Criminal Evidence Act 1984.[46] However, if the fair trial rationale is to be independent of the reliability rationale, it cannot be driven only by the concern about reliability.

The right to a fair trial is contained in Article 6(1) of the European Convention of Human Rights (ECHR). It is well-established that the reception of evidence obtained in breach of certain rights protected under the ECHR may render the trial unfair. In making this determination, the European Court of Human Rights (ECtHR) will assess the fairness of the proceedings considered as a whole and engage in a balancing of relevant and competing considerations. One relevant factor is "whether the circumstances in which [the evidence] was obtained... cast doubts on its reliability or accuracy."[47] But other factors must also be weighed in the overall assessment. They include, for example, whether the rights of the defense have been respected and the opportunities afforded the accused to challenge the authenticity of the evidence and oppose its use or admissibility.[48] What is clear from the Strasbourg jurisprudence is that fairness means more than reliability. What is lacking is a clear explanation of how the admission of unlawfully obtained evidence can render the trial unfair.[49]

d. *Rule of law*

In addition to finding the truth and ensuring the legitimacy of a criminal conviction, another purpose of the trial is arguably to uphold the rule of law by ensuring the legality

[44] *See generally* Ho Hock Lai, *A Philosophy of Evidence Law—Justice in the Search for Truth* 57–61 (2008); Ian Dennis, *The Law of Evidence* 52–63 (6th ed. 2017).

[45] *See, e.g.*, R v. Grant, *supra* note 40, at [68], [84] (Can.); P.J. Schwikkard & S.E. van der Merwe, *South Africa*, in *Criminal Procedure: A Worldwide Study* 471, 488 (Craig Bradley ed., 2007) (S. Afr.).

[46] *See, e.g.*, Andrew L.-T. Choo, *England and Wales: Fair Trial Analysis and the Presumed Admissibility of Physical Evidence, in Exclusionary Rules in Comparative Law* 331 (Stephen C. Thaman ed., 2013); D. Ormerod & D. Birch, *The Evolution of the Discretionary Exclusion of Evidence*, [2004] Crim. L. Rev. 767.

[47] Gäfgen v. Germany [GC], App. No. 22978/05, Eur. Ct. H.R., June 1, 2011.

[48] *Id.*

[49] *See* John D. Jackson & Sarah J. Summers, *The Internationalisation of Criminal Evidence—Beyond the Common Law and Civil Law Traditions* 184 (2012).

of the executive enforcement of criminal law. Across the world, countries on the path to democracy, with the experience of authoritarian oppression still in vivid memory, have adopted exclusionary rules as a symbol of political progress. The exclusionary rules are adopted, at least in part, because they embody "the idea of restraining government power and promoting the rule of law."[50] How does the exclusion of evidence uphold the rule of law? Some of the theories previously canvassed provide quick answers: the exclusion of evidence upholds the rule of law by deterring the police from breaking the law or by vindicating the rights of citizens guaranteed by the law.

On another theory, the rule of law rationale runs more deeply. A central idea of the rule of law is that the government should be subject to and accountable under the law. One way of achieving this is to have separation of powers under a system of checks and balances. The criminal trial is an important feature of this system; it is where the executive branch is held to account on its bid to enforce the criminal law by way of a conviction and sentence. The court's role is to scrutinize the legality of this bid. On a narrow view, the scrutiny must remain focused on whether the prosecution has discharged the burden of establishing that the accused is guilty as charged. On a more "majestic" view,[51] the court's duty to ensure that the executive's bid for a conviction is in accordance with law also includes the responsibility to prevent it from getting a conviction through its own unlawful conduct. An upshot of this is that it must prevent the executive from using evidence that it had acquired unlawfully to support a criminal prosecution.[52]

This rule-of-law rationale differs from the legitimacy-based arguments considered earlier. Even an authoritarian regime, by virtue of its self-interest in possessing legitimacy, has a place for exclusionary rules. Such rules can serve not just to constrain government power but also to concentrate and strengthen governmental control. In China, concerns about political stability have grown out of widespread adverse reactions to miscarriages of justice caused by evidence (mostly false confessions) that had been obtained wrongfully by the police. Public anger aroused by such cases poses the risk of social unrest and erosion of state authority. The central government has found it necessary to introduce exclusionary rules through a series of reforms and to vocally promote a tougher stance in the enforcement of those rules. These measures are aimed at appeasing public disquiet, stemming the abuses of police power, and correcting failures in governance at the local level. They are an attempt by the central government to preserve and exert political power through "rule by law."[53]

[50] Jenia Iontcheva Turner, *The Exclusionary Rule as a Symbol of the Rule of Law*, 67 SMU L. Rev. 821 (2014).

[51] Herring v. United States, 129 S. Ct. 695, 707 (2009) (Ginsburg, J., dissenting).

[52] *See, e.g.*, Ho Hock Lai, *The Criminal Trial, the Rule of Law and the Exclusion of Unlawfully Obtained Evidence*, 10 Crim. L. & Phil. 109 (2016); Schrock & Welsch, *supra* note 20; Grant, *supra* note 20.

[53] Margaret K. Lewis, *Controlling Abuse to Maintain Control: The Exclusionary Rule in China*, 43 NYU J. Int'l L. & Politics 629 (2011). On exclusion under Chinese law, see generally Zhiyuan Guo, *Exclusion of Illegally Obtained Confessions in China: An Empirical Perspective*, 21 Int'l. J. Evid. & Proof 30 (2017); Kuo-hsing Hsieh, *The Exclusionary Rule of Evidence—Comparative Analysis and Proposals for Reform* Part II (2014).

III. Legal Approaches to the Exclusion of Wrongfully Obtained Evidence

We now turn to the legal mechanisms by which wrongfully obtained evidence is excluded (Sections III 1–2) and the competing considerations that have been acknowledged as having a bearing on the decision to exclude (Sections III 3–4).

1. Determinacy of Application

An exclusionary rule is at its most determinate where the necessary and sufficient conditions that must be met to trigger it are stated in a manner that is clear and specific and the applicability of the rule on the facts in individual cases permits of only one possible answer. Such an approach to exclusion may be described as "categorical" or "automatic." (These two descriptions are not terms of art. "Categorical" or "automatic" can also refer to another feature, discussed later, about the operation of an exclusionary rule.) The determinacy of an exclusionary rule is a matter of degree. It may be weakened in one or more of the three ways described in this section. Where it is weakened in one or more of these ways, the judge is often said, accurately or not, to have discretion. The concept of discretion is a slippery one. Generally speaking, discretion involves a choice between different interpretations or applications of the law. The choice is to be made not on personal whim but in the exercise of a judgment that is expected to be capable of reasoned and principled defense.

First, many conditions for applying an exclusionary rule are stated broadly. Exclusion may turn on whether admission of the wrongfully obtained evidence would undermine the "fairness of the proceedings," bring "the administration of justice into disrepute," or damage "the integrity of the proceedings." The abstract concepts contained in these conditions ("fairness," "justice," "disrepute," "integrity," and so forth) permit different possible interpretations, the choice between which is left open by the rule. It is true that many other narrower (and seemingly factual) terms also permit different interpretations. What counts as a "search" for the purposes of the Fourth Amendment exclusionary rule, or a "custodial interrogation" that triggers the *Miranda* requirement of a warning of rights? Answers to these questions can also be highly contentious. But "fairness" and "justice" are thinner concepts—telling us less of what we should be looking for in applying them—than "search" and "custodial interrogation." The thinner the concept used in an exclusionary rule, the greater the tendency to describe the rule as discretionary.

Second, the concepts, interpreted in the abstract, have to be applied to the facts of individual cases. Guidance is sometimes provided, "without limiting the matters that the court may take into account," by setting out a non-exhaustive list of relevant factors.[54] Other rules simply instruct the court to consider "all the circumstances."[55] The judge is left to his or her own devices in identifying the relevant circumstances.

Third, the application of many exclusionary rules require a balancing of factors. Under Scottish law, the court has to weigh the interest of the citizen to be protected from wrongful invasion of his liberties against the interest "to secure that evidence bearing upon the commission of the crime and necessary to enable justice to be done shall not be withheld."[56] In Australia, Section 138(1) of the uniform evidence legislation directs the judge to weigh the desirability of admitting wrongfully obtained evidence against the undesirability of doing so. The balancing approach is taken not only in applying an exclusionary rule as in these examples: it can also come into play in developing exceptions to the rule. In the United States, exceptions to the rule excluding evidence obtained in breach of the Fourth Amendment protection against unreasonable search and seizure have been created by balancing the costs of exclusion against the benefits of deterring similar violations.[57] In all of these instances, the judge has to work out ways of determining, in the case at hand, the relative importance of the competing considerations and how a compromise or resolution is to be reached.

In general, predictability in the application of an exclusionary rule increases with its determinacy. The less determinate the rule, the less likely that there is a uniquely correct answer to its application. And given the existence of a range of acceptable positions that can be taken, the less likely it is that an appeal from the first instance application of the rule will succeed. But this does not mean, as use of the term "discretion" might wrongly imply, that the accused person has no legal *right* to exclusion. Indeed, his or her right to exclusion under non-determinate rules such as Article 35(5) of the South African Constitution and Article 6 of the ECHR are of a constitutional or fundamental nature.

2. Wrongful Provenance of Evidence as the Direct and Indirect Ground for Exclusion

Evidence is sometimes excluded simply by virtue of its wrongful provenance. In some jurisdictions, that the evidence was gathered in an unlawful search, without more, compels its exclusion (unless an exception to the rule applies). Evidence obtained by

[54] *See, e.g.*, New Zealand Evidence Act 2006, §30(3); Australian Uniform Evidence Legislation §138(3). The latter legislation refers to the model Statute on evidence proposed by the Australian Law Reform Commission in 1987 that has been adopted with minor modifications and variations in a number of Australian states and in the Capital Territory.

[55] *See, e.g.*, Canadian Charter of Rights and Freedoms §24; Police and Criminal Evidence Act 1984, §78 (Eng. & Wales).

[56] Lawrie v. Muir, 1950 J.C. 19. For a critique, see Findlay Stark & Fiona Leverick, *Scotland: A Plea for Consistency*, in *Exclusionary Rules in Comparative Law* 69 (Stephen C. Thaman ed., 2013).

[57] *See* Wesley MacNeil Oliver, *Toward a Better Categorical Balance of Costs and Benefits of the Exclusionary Rule*, 9 Buffalo Crim. L. Rev. 201 (2005).

torture is widely treated as inadmissible simply because it has been obtained in that unlawful manner. Where a rule requires evidence to be excluded by the very fact of its wrongful provenance, as it does in these examples, there is nothing else to consider. Wrongfulness straightforwardly entails exclusion, without room for further consideration save for the possibility of an exception to the rule applying. This approach to exclusion has also attracted the label "categorical" or "automatic." An exclusionary rule that is "categorical" or "automatic" in this sense is quite different from one that is "categorical" or "automatic" in the sense of being highly determinate. For instance, the rule that excludes evidence extracted by torture is "categorical" or "automatic" in the present sense but it is not "categorical" or "automatic" in the sense of being highly determinate; the concept of "torture" is amenable to different interpretations, and whether a form of ill treatment amounts to "torture" (a legal term that is distinct from "inhuman or degrading") calls for a contestable evaluation of a highly charged standard.

The wrongfulness of the means by which the evidence was gathered does not always lead directly to exclusion. In the examples we have encountered, exclusion depends on the adverse impact that admitting the evidence would have on the fairness of the trial, repute of the administration of justice, or integrity of the proceedings.

3. Interest in Convicting the Guilty

Many factors have been treated as relevant to the decision to exclude wrongfully obtained evidence.[58] There are two main sets of considerations. The first set bears on what the Canadian Supreme Court has called the "interest in ensuring that those who transgress the law are brought to trial and dealt with according to the law."[59] How greatly this interest calls for admission of relevant but unlawfully procured evidence has been treated as depending on factors such as: (1) the degree to which the evidence is probative of guilt, (2) the availability of other evidence to support the prosecution's case, and (3) the severity of the alleged crime. These three factors are not free from controversies. First, caution is sounded against putting too much store on probative value of the evidence as this might "foster the quite erroneous view that if such evidence be but damning enough that will of itself suffice to atone for the illegality involved in procuring it."[60] Similar caution has been sounded against the second factor. Giving decisive weight to the importance of the evidence to the prosecution's case and the nonavailability of other evidence would result in exclusion only when it matters least to the prosecution.[61]

[58] *See* Petra Viebig, *Illicitly Obtained Evidence at the International Criminal Court* 163–86 (2016); Christopher Slobogin, *A Comparative Perspective on the Exclusionary Rule in Search and Seizure Cases*, in *Comparative Criminal Procedure* 280, 293–99 (Jacqueline E. Ross & Stephen C. Thaman eds., 2016). A list of relevant factors is set out in New Zealand Evidence Act 2006, §30(3) and the Australian Uniform Evidence Legislation §138(3).

[59] R v. Grant, *supra* note 40, at [79].

[60] Bunning v. Cross (1978) 141 C.L.R. 54, 79 (Australian High Court).

[61] As Slobogin, *supra* note 58, at 292, puts it, "this factor, if taken seriously, suggests that clean judicial hands are a concern only when they cost the system nothing."

The third factor cuts both ways. It is not just the interest in convicting the guilty that increases with the seriousness of the alleged crime; the gravity of the condemnation in and harm following a conviction likewise increases. As Mirfield has pointed out, "the more serious are the consequences of conviction for the accused, the more punctilious should be the authorities in observing the various rights and privileges granted by law to the suspect."[62]

4. Gravity of the Wrong Committed in Obtaining the Evidence

The second set of considerations relates to the nature of the wrong committed in obtaining the evidence and the circumstances in which the act was done. A stronger approach is generally taken when the wrong is more serious. At one end lie methods of procurement that are ethically wrongful but fall short of being unlawful. In Singapore, it seems that this can of itself give no cause for exclusion in criminal cases.[63] In Australia and New Zealand, on the other hand, the court is explicitly empowered to exclude evidence not only when it was obtained unlawfully but also when it was acquired "unfairly"[64] or "improperly."[65] Where evidence was acquired unlawfully, the unlawfulness in question may occasion greater or lesser concern. The illegality committed in collecting evidence differs in gravity. It may be of a technical nature. There is reluctance to exclude evidence, with the potential consequence of letting a criminal go free, on a mere technicality.[66] Under Article 141(3) of the Swiss Criminal Procedure Code, evidence remains admissible even though it "has been obtained in violation of administrative regulations."[67]

In some legal systems, evidence obtained in breach of constitutional or fundamental rights is subject to a special exclusionary rule that is explicitly provided for in the constitution or bill or rights.[68] But there is not always a constitutional right to exclusion of evidence obtained unconstitutionally. The exclusion of evidence obtained in breach of the Fourth Amendment to the U.S. Constitution "is a judicially created remedy designed to safeguard Fourth Amendment rights generally through its deterrent effect, rather than a personal constitutional right of the party aggrieved."[69]

62 Peter Mirfield, *Silence, Confessions and Improperly Obtained Evidence* 364 (1997); *see also* Ashworth, *supra* note 21, at 120.

63 *See* Wong Keng Leong Rayney v. Law Society of Singapore, [2007] 4 S.L.R. 377 at [27] (Singapore Court of Appeal). A different position is taken by the Australian High Court: Ridgeway v. R., (1995) 184 C.L.R. 19, 36.

64 New Zealand Evidence Act 2006, §30(5)(c).

65 Australian Uniform Evidence Legislation §138(1).

66 A reluctance that Cardozo, J., famously expressed in People v. Defore, 242 N.Y. 13, 21 (N.Y. 1926): "The criminal is to go free because the constable has blundered."

67 Swiss Criminal Procedure Code art. 141(3).

68 *See, e.g.*, Canadian Charter of Rights and Freedoms. § 24(2); S. Afr. Const. art. 35(5); Gr. Const. art. 19(3).

69 United States v. Calandra, 414 U.S. 338, 348 (1974).

Even where a special exclusionary rule is not explicitly provided, the courts have been known to develop—and it has been argued that they should apply[70]—a stricter test for evidence obtained in breach of constitutional or fundamental rights than for evidence obtained in other unlawful ways. In Ireland, evidence obtained in "deliberate and conscious" (non-inadvertent) violation of the constitution is strictly inadmissible save in extraordinary excusing circumstances.[71] Exclusion is discretionary for other types of illegally obtained evidence. Although there are recent indications of readiness to take a similar approach to evidence obtained in deliberate and conscious breach of non-constitutional legal rights, it is at the same time acknowledged that "a court might well more readily find fault beyond inadvertence in relation to a breach of constitutional rights [as compared to other] legal rights."[72]

Not all breaches of constitutional or fundamental rights are treated alike. For example, while the ECtHR treats evidence procured in breach of the right against torture in Article 3 of the ECHR as automatically or categorically inadmissible, it adopts a weaker, balancing approach toward evidence obtained in violation of the right to privacy in Article 8.[73]

The seriousness of the wrong committed in procuring evidence is not only a matter of the status of the norm that has been breached. It is also a matter of the degree to which the protected interest of the accused person was affected.[74] "Plucking a hair from the suspect's head" is far less intrusive of privacy than "a body cavity or strip search."[75] Also going to the seriousness of the wrong are the motive of the police officer in transgressing the law and the blameworthiness of his or her conduct.[76] A breach committed mala fide is a more troubling display of excess or abuse of power, and calls more pressingly for deterrence and judicial renunciation and disavowal, than a breach committed in good faith.[77] The exclusionary pressure is also greater where the breach is not an isolated incident but part of a systemic problem.[78] Excuses for committing the wrong may be present. In New Zealand, it matters "whether there was any urgency in obtaining the

[70] See Ashworth, *supra* note 21, at 109–110; Thaman, *supra* note 3.

[71] This exclusionary rule does not apply if the police did not know they were acting in breach of the constitution and their action was not reckless or grossly negligent: D.P.P. v. J.C. [2015] I.E.S.C. 31 departing from the earlier leading cases of *People (A.G.) v. O'Brien* [1965] I.R. 142 and *People (D.P.P.) v. Kenny* [1990] 2 I.R. 110. For a commentary, see Yvonne Marie Daly, *Overruling the Protectionist Exclusionary Rule: D.P.P. v. J.C.*, 19 Int'l. J. Evid. & Proof 270 (2015).

[72] D.P.P. v. J.C. [2015] IESC 31 at [6.3] of the judgment of Clarke J. A similar two-tier approach was taken in New Zealand until it was abandoned by the Court of Appeal in *R v. Shaheed* [2002] 2 N.Z.L.R. 377.

[73] *See* Andrew Ashworth, *The Exclusion of Evidence Obtained by Violating a Fundamental Right: Pragmatism Before Principle in the Strasbourg Jurisprudence*, in *Criminal Evidence and Human Rights—Reimagining Common Law Procedural Traditions* 145 (Paul Roberts & Jill Hunter eds., 2012).

[74] This is one line of inquiry in applying the Charter exclusionary rule in Canada. *See* R v. Grant, *supra* note 40, at [125]. It is also listed as a relevant factor in New Zealand Evidence Act 2006, § 30(3)(a).

[75] R v. Grant, *supra* note 40, at [103].

[76] *Id.* at [124].

[77] *See, e.g.*, United States v. Leon, 468 U.S. 897 (1984) (good faith exception to the Fourth Amendment exclusionary rule).

[78] R v. Grant, *supra* note 40, at [75]; People v. O'Brien [1965] I.R. 142, 160 (Supreme Court of Ireland).

improperly obtained evidence"[79] and "whether the impropriety was necessary to avoid apprehended physical danger to the Police or others."[80] Conversely, that the police could have obtained the evidence through alternative and lawful means has been treated as a factor supporting exclusion.[81]

IV. Conclusion

The exclusion of wrongfully obtained evidence may be aimed at deterring similar police misconduct or educating the police on the importance of abiding by the law, or it may be a remedy that vindicates the right that the police had breached. It may be unfair to allow the prosecution to use the evidence or such use may morally compromise the standing to blame the accused. On another set of theories, wrongfully obtained evidence is rightly excluded where it is at odds with our interests in the reliability of the trial process or with different conceptions of integrity and legitimacy. Last, exclusionary rules symbolize and are means of upholding the rule of law. Legal approaches to wrongfully obtained evidence vary. Exclusionary rules differ in determinacy and in the test adopted for exclusion. On some tests, the wrongful manner in which the evidence was acquired is sufficient to trigger its exclusion; on other tests, exclusion turns what the effect would be of allowing the wrongfully evidence to be used at the trial. A common approach is to require a balancing of competing considerations. These considerations include the importance of the evidence in ascertaining the truth of the criminal charge and the gravity of the wrong committed by the police in acquiring the evidence.

References

Tracey Maclin, *The Supreme Court and the Fourth Amendment's Exclusionary Rule* (2013)
Peter Mirfield, *Silence, Confessions and Improperly Obtained Evidence* (1997)
Steven R. Schlesinger, *Exclusionary Injustice: The Problem of Illegally Obtained Evidence* (1977)
Stephen J. Schulhofer, *More Essential than Ever: The Fourth Amendment in the Twenty-First Century* (2012)
Stephen C. Thaman ed., *Exclusionary Rules in Comparative Law* (2013)
James J. Tomkovicz, *Constitutional Exclusion: The Rules, Rights, and Remedies That Strike the Balance Between Freedom and Order* (2011)
Petra Viebig, *Illicitly Obtained Evidence at the International Criminal Court* (2016)

79 New Zealand Evidence Act 2006, § 30(3)(h).
80 *Id.* § 30(3)(g).
81 *Id.* § 30(3)(e); Australian Uniform Evidence Legislation, § 138(3)(h).

CHAPTER 37

RIGHTS AND METHODS TO CHALLENGE EVIDENCE AND WITNESSES IN CIVIL LAW JURISDICTIONS

LORENA BACHMAIER

I. Introduction

WHILE many Continental European legal systems and other non-European legal orders that might be labeled "civil law systems" share certain common evidentiary rules and principles, there is no "civil law" system of evidence.[1] Rules of evidence, including rules concerning admissibility and the grounds for challenging evidence, are very diverse across civil law jurisdictions, as each system is influenced by the context of criminal proceedings, the role of criminal procedure, and the extent to which criminal procedure follows an adversarial or inquisitorial model.[2] Indeed, if viewed close up, the civil law and common law traditions of evidence have disappeared to become a "set of country or even locality-specific practices."[3]

[1] This work is mainly focused on the Continental European legal systems, although other non-European countries could be included within the "civil law" tradition, such as many of the Latin-American legal systems and the Japanese legal system.

[2] On the dichotomy between adversarial and inquisitorial systems and the features of accusatorial criminal proceedings, see generally *Proceso penal y sistemas acusatorios* (Lorena Bachmaier ed. 2008).

[3] Richard Lempert, *Anglo-American and Continental Systems: Marsupials and Mammals of the Law*, in *Crime, Procedure and Evidence in a Comparative and International Context: Essays in Honour of Professor Mirjan Damaška* 411 (John D. Jackson et al. eds., 2008).

Despite this variety, there are certain features of the rules of evidence that are identified with the Continental European procedure as opposed to common law proceedings, although such classification inevitably entails a certain degree of simplification.[4] Although Continental European criminal justice systems have for a long time now moved away from regarding the search for the truth as an absolute tenet of procedure,[5] the goal of matching the judgment to a historical factum is still important in most Continental European systems.

The traditional understanding that in European civil law systems, criminal procedure is predominantly an instrument for implementing policy and protecting the public interest, rather than primarily a mechanism used for dispute resolution, affects how evidence is gathered, presented, and challenged. The admissibility of evidence depends largely on the institutional environment, the importance a legal system attaches to the principles of the criminal process, and the role the judge plays in the procedural battle. A system where the judge enjoys more trust will accept greater judicial discretion in deciding on the admissibility of evidence than those systems where the passive role of the judge is considered necessary for preserving impartiality.

Historical constraints also influence how the admissibility of evidence is handled.[6] Systems that have opted for a strict accusatorial model in an effort to overcome the abuses of the inquisitorial model will have a stronger stance with regard to the right to confrontation and the production of evidence at the public hearing. In fact, those systems where the oral concentrated trial has been given absolute preeminence in the adjudicating process will tend to deprive of evidentiary value any out-of-court statements, including those made during the pretrial stage.

In purely adversarial systems, the competitive mode of examining evidence in court and the control by the parties of the facts to be presented also lead to a different way of challenging evidence than in civil law systems,[7] where the objective inquiry undertaken by the public prosecution (with or without the direction of an investigating judge) will also determine the approach to evidentiary challenges. Official evidence gathering by a neutral authority is expected to be less partisan than the presentation of evidence by each of the parties seeking to prove *its* case. In a procedure where each party strives to make its own case, cross-examination plays a much more relevant role in challenging

[4] In addressing such a broad topic of evidence law in civil law systems, a generalization is unavoidable. As I will focus on distinguishing features and more visible differences, I am subject to the critiques by Mirjan Damaška against the "folklore" in the analysis of procedural models. *See* Mirjan Damaška, *The Faces of Justice and State Authority: A Comparative Approach to Legal Process* 5 (1986).

[5] At least since the famous work of Ernst Beling, *Die Beweisverbote als Grenzen der Wahrheitsforschung im Strafprozess* (1903), where the author already elaborated a theory of exclusionary rules of evidence based on the protection of due process and fundamental rights. Nevertheless, certain exclusionary rules were earlier recognized in Canon law. *See* Frank R. Herrmann, *The Establishment of a Rule Against Hearsay in Romano-Canonical Procedure*, 36 Va. J. Int'l L. 1 (1995).

[6] On the features of the historical adversarial and inquisitorial models of evidence, see the comprehensive study of Emmanouil Billis, *Die Rolle des Richters im adversatorischen und im inquistorischen Beweisverfahren* 62 ff. (2015).

[7] Mirjan Damaška, *Evidence Law Adrift* 75–87 (1997).

the reliability and credibility of witnesses than in systems where a comprehensive investigation is carried out by a neutral body, not to advance its own case, but rather to investigate the facts and come close to the historical truth.

Just as there is no uniform approach to the rules on admissibility of evidence in domestic civil law traditions, there are also no common rules set out by the European Court of Human Rights (ECtHR). The Court has widely applied the doctrine of the margin of appreciation in this regard[8] and largely left questions of admissibility to Member States.[9]

Within the European Union, as part of the establishment of a single Area of Freedom, Security and Justice, and fostering the international judicial cooperation in criminal matters, it was considered that common rules on admissibility of evidence should be promoted. This is why Article 86.2 of the Lisbon Treaty gives the EU legislator competence in this field:

> To the extent necessary to facilitate mutual recognition of judgments and judicial decisions and police and judicial cooperation in criminal matters having a cross-border dimension, the European Parliament and the Council may, by means of directives adopted in accordance with the ordinary legislative procedure, establish minimum rules. Such rules shall take into account the differences between the legal traditions and systems of the Member States.

They shall concern:

(a) mutual admissibility of evidence between Member States....

Scholars have long debated whether it would be desirable to harmonize rules on admissibility of evidence within the EU, but up to now, due to the lack of consensus, there has not been much progress at the legislative level.

This contribution seeks to address the main grounds for challenging the admissibility of evidence, the methods to do it, and the consequences those challenges can have in civil law systems, insofar as common features can be discerned. This should allow us to better understand the interplay of the rules of evidence and the aims of the proceedings and to identify new trends and approaches that might be interesting when comparing civil law and common law traditions and their possible convergence.

To that end, I will start with an overview of the principles set out by the ECtHR on admissibility of evidence as it provides the overall framework all European countries have to follow. Next, I will address exclusionary rules of evidence and the admissibility of the out-of-court witness testimonies in civil law systems in Europe. A comprehensive approach to rules of evidence would exceed the scope of this study; therefore, I do not

[8] *See* Yuraka Arai-Takahashi, *The Margin of Appreciation Doctrine and the Principle of Proportionality in the Jurisprudence of the ECHR* 60 ff. (2002). On the justification and concept of the margin of appreciation beyond a technique for adjudication, but justified in deference, see, in relation with the ECHR, Andrew Legg, *The Margin of Appreciation in International Human Rights Law* 27–31 (2012).

[9] For a compilation of the leading cases of the ECtHR in this field, see Jeremy McBride, *Human Rights and Criminal Procedure: The Case Law of the European Court of Human Rights* 205 ff. (2009).

address details on particular issues related to the integrity and authenticity of certain pieces of evidence (e.g., biological samples, the chain of custody, or the process for ensuring the integrity of electronic evidence). Likewise, a comprehensive comparative analysis is beyond the scope of the chapter, although reference to particular regulations of certain states will be made when appropriate.[10]

The chapter will show that although methods for excluding evidence and for questioning witnesses still differ greatly, a convergence between common law and civil law systems is occurring, particularly with regards to the grounds for challenging the evidence. This may be explained perhaps by the openness of the Continental European systems toward adversarial influences and the adoption of cross-examination of witnesses as an essential right of the defendant. However, I argue that some features of the "inquisitorial" system of questioning witnesses could perhaps be considered as useful in common law systems to supplement the party-driven cross-examination and reach a more truthful narrative of the facts.

II. Admissibility of Evidence—The European Court of Human Rights' Approach

The jurisprudence of the ECtHR does not prohibit the use of unlawfully obtained evidence as a matter of principle. The Court has repeatedly stated that it is normally for the national courts to decide on the admissibility of evidence. However, the way the evidence was obtained and the role that the evidence played at trial is examined by the Court in the context of ascertaining whether the trial, as a whole, was fair.

When it comes to evidence obtained through a violation of certain non-derogable rights of the European Convention of Human Rights (for example, evidence obtained through torture), however, the stance of the Court has been clear: No evidence obtained by means of oppression, entrapment, or coercion should be admitted. As the Court explained in *Jalloh v. Germany*:

> Incriminating evidence—whether in the form of a confession or real evidence—obtained as a result of acts of violence or brutality or other forms of treatment which can be characterised as torture—should never be relied on as proof of the victim's

[10] For a comprehensive comparative study, see *Exclusionary Rules in Comparative Law* (Stephen C. Thaman ed. 2013) [hereinafter *Exclusionary Rules in Comparative Law*], and in particular, within that volume, the excellent study by Stephen C. Thaman, *Balancing Truth Against Human Rights: A Theory of Modern Exclusionary Rules* 403–46; *see also* Network of Independent Experts on Fundamental Rights, *Opinion on the Status of Illegally Obtained Evidence in Criminal Procedures in the Member States of the European Union*, of 30 November 2003, *available at* http://ec.europa.eu/justice/fundamental-rights/files/cfr_cdf_opinion3_2003_en.pdf.

> guilt, irrespective of its probative value. Any other conclusion would only serve to legitimate indirectly the sort of morally reprehensible conduct which the authors of Article 3 of the Convention sought to proscribe. . . .[11]

Evidence obtained under torture is therefore clearly inadmissible. As for the admissibility of evidence obtained in violation of Article 3 of the European Convention of Human Rights (ECHR), that is, through conduct that does not amount to torture, but constitutes inhuman or degrading treatment, the Court has not been as clear. In *Jalloh*, the Court says that "it cannot be excluded . . ." that evidence obtained "by intentional acts of ill-treatment not amounting to torture" can render the trial unfair.[12] By using this expression, the Court does not clearly say that every violation of Article 3 will affect the fairness of the trial.[13] In deciding whether the right to a fair trial has been infringed, the public interest in prosecuting a serious crime could be balanced against the gravity of the violation of Article 3 ECHR.[14] In *Jalloh*, the Court considered that the public interest (given the small amount of drugs the drug dealer was carrying) was insufficient to justify the illegal and degrading treatment in the gathering of the evidence. Admissibility of the evidence in that case would violate the right to a fair trial under Article 6 ECHR.

In a later case, *Gäfgen v Germany*,[15] the Court again took the balancing approach and weighed the competing interests at stake instead of strongly condemning the gathering of evidence through ill-treatment. The Court noted that such evidence could violate the fairness of the proceedings—and thus be inadmissible—but this would depend on the severity of the ill-treatment, the seriousness of the offense charged, and the effect of the evidence on the outcome of the trial. In sum, violation of Article 3 ECHR would lead to a violation of Article 6 only if the illegally obtained evidence affected the outcome of the proceedings.

With regard to evidence obtained in violation of the right against self-incrimination, the Court has not followed the same line.[16] In some judgments, the Court has stated explicitly that the public interest does not justify the violation of the right against self-incrimination and has held that evidence obtained in violation of the right is inadmissible. On other occasions, however, the Court has opted to invoke the public interest in deciding whether evidence obtained in violation of the right against self-incrimination rendered the trial unfair. In *Saunders v. United Kingdom*, the Court held that answers obtained through compulsion of the defendant should be excluded.[17] Later, in *Teixeira de Castro v. Portugal*, the Court remained firm in declaring that evidence obtained through police entrapment was inadmissible, regardless of the gravity of the offense or the public

[11] Jalloh v. Germany, App. No. 54810/00, Eur. Ct. H.R., July 11, 2007, § 105.

[12] *Id.* § 106.

[13] *See* Andrew Ashworth, *The Exclusion of Evidence Obtained by Violating a Fundamental Right: Pragmatism Before Principle in the Strasbourg Jurisprudence*, in *Criminal Evidence and Human Rights: Reimagining Common Law Procedural Traditions* 154 (Paul Roberts & Jill Hunter eds., 2012).

[14] *Jalloh*, *supra* note 11, § 106.

[15] Grand Chamber Judgment, Gäfgen v. Germany, App. No. 22978/05, Eur. Ct. H.R., June 1, 2011, § 178; *see also* Ashworth, *supra* note 13, at 156.

[16] Ashworth, *supra* note 13.

[17] Saunders v. United Kingdom, App. No. 19187/91, Eur. Ct. H.R., Dec. 17, 1996.

interest in prosecuting drug crimes.[18] According to these judgments, courts should not apply a balancing test in deciding the admissibility of evidence obtained in violation of the right against self-incrimination.[19] However, in *Bykov v. Russia*,[20] the Court held that a confession obtained through a secret recording by an undercover agent did not violate the right to a fair trial, taking into account the degree of compulsion (no coercion was found) and the fact that the recorded conversation played only a limited role in the "complex of evidence assessed by the court." [21]

When it comes to evidence obtained in violation of other rights—in particular the right to privacy under Article 8 ECHR—the Court has generally left its admissibility to the regulation of national law.[22] In *P.G. and J.H. v. United Kingdom*,[23] the Court explained:

> It is not the role of the Court to determine, as a matter of principle, whether particular types of evidence—for example, unlawfully obtained evidence—may be admissible or, indeed, whether the applicant was guilty or not. The question that must be answered is whether the proceedings as a whole, including the way in which the evidence was obtained, were fair. This involves an examination of the alleged "unlawfulness" in question and, where violation of another Convention right is concerned, the nature of the violation found.[24]

The ECtHR has adopted the position that the use of illegally obtained evidence does not necessarily render the proceedings unfair.[25] Therefore, whether the right to a fair trial under Article 6(1) ECHR is violated by the use of illegally obtained evidence will usually depend on the different circumstances present at the case: whether the evidence could be contradicted in trial, whether the defendant had the possibility to challenge the authenticity of the evidence, whether it was the only evidence on which the conviction

[18] Teixeira de Castro v. Portugal, App. No. 44/1997/828/1034, Eur. Ct. H.R., June 8, 1998.

[19] Nevertheless, in *O'Halloran and Francis v. United Kingdom*, App. Nos. 15809/02 and 25624/02, Eur. Ct. H.R., June 29, 2007, the Court decided that being sanctioned for not identifying the driver of a vehicle in a road offense case is compatible with the privilege against self-incrimination. In this case, the Court, taking note of all circumstances and the low level of compulsion involved, considered that the "very essence" of the right against self-incrimination had not been destroyed. This sanction, which amounts to a legalized coercion, is viewed as compatible with human rights principles. *See* Ashworth, *supra* note 13, at 151.

[20] Bykov v. Russia, App. No. 4378/02, Eur. Ct. H.R., Mar. 10, 2009.

[21] *Id.*, § 104.

[22] Hümmer v. Germany, App. No. 29881/07, Eur. Ct. H.R., July 19, 2012; *see also* Karen Reid, *A Practitioner's Guide to the ECHR* 119 ff. (3d ed. 2008). For a more detailed approach, see Stefano Maffei, *The Right to Confrontation in Europe: Absent, Anonymous and Vulnerable Witnesses* 80 ff. (2012).

[23] P.G. and J.H. v. United Kingdom, App. No. 44787/98, Eur. Ct. H.R., Sept. 25, 2001.

[24] *Id.* § 76; Allan v. United Kingdom, App. No. 48539/99, Eur. Ct. H.R., Nov. 5, 2002, § 42.

[25] *See, e.g.*, Schenk v. Switzerland, App. No. 10862/84, Eur. Ct. H.R., July 12, 1988; Khan v. United Kingdom, App. No. 35394/97, Eur. Ct. H.R., May 12, 2000. *Schenk* related to a violation of domestic law in the gathering of evidence. *Khan* is the first case where the Court addressed the question of whether evidence obtained in violation of a right recognized under the Convention nevertheless could be used in a criminal trial, without this entailing a violation of Article 6(1) ECHR.

was based, and the way in which the evidence was gathered.[26] The seriousness of the offense and the weight attached to the evidence are also circumstances to be taken into account.

This position of the Court has been controversial, and some judges and scholars have argued that a trial cannot be described as fair where evidence obtained in breach of a fundamental right guaranteed under the Convention has been admitted, especially when the infringement relates to one of the "core and absolute rights," such as Article 3 ECHR. According to Judge Tulkens, "in concluding that there has been no violation of Article 6, the Court renders Article 8 completely ineffective."[27]

In judging the admissibility of evidence obtained in violation of Article 8 ECHR, the Court has followed the so-called "separation thesis": the infringement of each of the rights is addressed separately. Different from most national constitutional courts, in relying on the "separation thesis," the ECtHR has failed to find a violation of Article 6 when there has been a breach of Article 8 ECHR. In other words, the consequences of the infringement of the right to privacy in obtaining the evidence do not extend to the fairness of the proceedings. The two breaches are to be assessed separately, and one does not necessarily affect the other.[28]

Regarding the production of evidence, in assessing whether the proceedings as a whole were fair, respect for defense rights requires that in principle all evidence must be produced in the presence of the accused at a public hearing where it can be challenged in an adversarial procedure.[29] And the rights of the defense will in principle be irreparably prejudiced when incriminating statements made during police interrogation without access to a lawyer are used for a conviction.[30]

This requires, as a rule, the presence of the adverse witnesses at trial, so that the defense can question them and comment on their evidence.[31] Although this is the general rule, the Court has allowed exceptions to the right to confront the witness at the public hearing: As long as there was an opportunity to cross-examine the witness before trial, and the defendant had the assistance of lawyer, the evidence is admissible at trial without the need for additional confrontation even if the pretrial witness examination did not take place before a judicial authority.[32] If the right to cross-examine

[26] For example, if it had also caused a violation of the right against self-incrimination or it was obtained by way of provoking to commit an offense. *See* Teixeira de Castro v. Portugal, App. No. 25829/94, Eur. Ct. H.R., June 9, 1998.

[27] P.G. and J.H. v. United Kingdom, App. No. 44787/98, Eur. Ct. H.R., Sept. 25, 2001 (Tulkens, J., dissenting).

[28] However, the application of the separation thesis by the ECtHR is not consistent, as pointed out by Ashworth, *supra* note 13, at 157.

[29] Barberá and Others v. Spain, App. No. 10588/10589/10590/83, Eur. Ct. H.R., Dec. 6, 1988; Bricmont v. Belgium, App. No. 10857/84, Eur. Ct. H.R., July 7, 1989, Kostovski v. The Netherlands, App. No. 11454/85, Eur. Ct. H.R., Nov. 20, 1989.

[30] Salduz v. Turkey, App. No. 36391/02, Eur. Ct. H.R., Nov. 27, 2008.

[31] *See* Kamasinski v. Austria, App. No. 9783/82, Eur. Ct. H.R., Dec. 19, 1989.

[32] *See, e.g.*, Asch v. Austria, App. No. 12398/86, Eur. Ct. H.R., Apr. 26, 1991; Lüdi v. Switzerland, App. No. 12433/86, Eur. Ct. H.R., June 15, 1992; Gani v. Spain, App. No. 61800/08, Eur. Ct. H.R., Feb. 19, 2013.

the witness could not be granted, the Court has only very exceptionally admitted such statements as evidence, usually in cases of vulnerable witnesses (victims) and if there were counterbalancing elements to conclude that the fairness of the proceedings have been respected.[33]

It is difficult to identify the rules on the admissibility of witness evidence without cross-examination, as the Court does not examine Article 6(3)(d) ECHR separately, but jointly with the right to a fair trial (Article 6(1) ECHR).[34] Because the Court assesses the overall fairness of the proceedings, it has not clarified the elements for the admissibility of a witness statement without cross-examination.[35] Only by taking a look at the precise facts of several cases decided by the ECtHR is it possible to draw some conclusions on general principles regarding the right to cross-examine witnesses and its exceptions.

The general rule is that evidence obtained without the opportunity for the defense to cross-examine the witness is inadmissible. However, the ECtHR has on occasion allowed such evidence to be taken into account as long as it is not the sole and decisive evidence for the conviction or there are other counterbalancing elements, the non appearance of the witness is justified, and the trial court shows that it had made reasonable efforts to ensure the presence of the witness at trial. In *Al-Khawaja and Tahery v. United Kingdom*, a case concerning an indecent assault by a physician against a patient, one of the two victims in the case (Al-Khawaja) had died before the trial and, in the absence of other direct evidence, her statement was read to the jury.[36] The defense was able to cross-examine other witnesses, who testified what the deceased victim had told them about the incident shortly after it occurred; the second victim also testified as to a similar indecent assault by the doctor, and there was no evidence that the two victims had colluded in their allegations; and as the trial concluded, the judge reminded the jury that they had not seen the deceased victim give evidence or be cross-examined.[37] The defendant was subsequently convicted by a unanimous jury.[38] The Grand Chamber held in this case (contrary to the prior judgment of the Chamber) that "viewing the fairness of the proceedings as a whole [...] notwithstanding the difficulties caused to the defence [...] there were sufficient counterbalancing factors to conclude that the admission in evidence of the victim's statement did not result in a breach of Article 6.1 read in conjunction with Article 6 (3) (d) of the Convention."[39]

[33] S.N. v. Sweden, App. No. 34209/96, Eur. Ct. H.R., July 2, 2002; Al-Khawaja and Tahery v. United Kingdom, App. No. 26766/05 and 22228/06, Eur. Ct. H.R., Dec. 15, 2011.

[34] *See, e.g.*, Salduz v. Turkey, App. No. 36391, Eur. Ct. H.R., Nov. 27, 2008; Al-Khawaja and Tahery v. United Kingdom, App. Nos. 26766/05 and 22228/06, Eur. Ct. H.R., Dec. 15, 2011, § 142; T. v. United Kingdom, App. No. 24724/94, Eur. Ct. H.R., Dec. 16, 1999, § 83; Stanford v. United Kingdom, App. No. 16757/90, Eur. Ct. H.R., Feb. 23, 1994, § 26.

[35] *See* Lorena Bachmaier, *Transnational Criminal Proceedings, Witness Evidence and Confrontation: Lessons from the ECtHR's Case Law*, 9 Utrecht L. Rev. 126–48 (2013).

[36] Al-Khawaja and Tahery v. United Kingdom, App. Nos. 26766/05 and 22228/06, Eur. Ct. H.R., Dec. 15, 2011.

[37] *Id.* §§ 156 ff. [38] *Id.* § 19. [39] *Id.* § 158.

The Court also does not always exclude the use of pretrial statements when the witness who is present at trial refuses to testify. For the Court, the fact that the witness exercises his right not to testify does not preclude the possibility to use his pretrial statements as evidence, as long as such evidence is not sole and decisive.[40] The Court has not laid down any guidelines on this issue, but refers to the domestic rules on the admissibility of evidence.

In *S.N. v Sweden*, the conviction was based solely on the statement of a witness who could not be cross-examined at trial. The witness was a minor and was the alleged victim of a sexual offense by the defendant. He was questioned by the police twice without the presence of counsel, and the first statement was videotaped, while the second was audiotaped.[41] The Court noted that the videotape of the first police interview was shown during the trial and appeal hearings, and the second interview was read out before the trial court.[42] The videotape was again played before the Court of Appeals. The Court stated that Article 6(3)(d) ECHR does not require that questions be put directly to the witness by the accused or defense counsel. The circumstances of the case were considered sufficient to enable the applicant to challenge the victim's statements and his credibility in the course of the criminal proceedings.[43]

In brief, the ECtHR gives broad leeway to the states to decide on the admissibility of evidence, as long as (with a few exceptions) the right to cross-examine witnesses is safeguarded. In general, within the European landscape, national rules of criminal procedure are more protective of the rights of the accused than is required by the Court when interpreting Article 6(1) ECHR. Regarding the moment or method to challenge the inadmissible evidence, the ECtHR does not set out any guidelines or principles, leaving this also to domestic regulation. Yet in certain circumstances, the court's refusal to admit or gather evidence may render the proceedings unfair and therefore rise to a violation of Article 6.

III. Challenging Evidence in Civil Law Countries

1. Unreliable Evidence

Common law systems exclude certain relevant evidence (for example, bad character evidence) because it may mislead or prejudice the fact-finder. By contrast, civil law does not provide for the exclusion of evidence on the grounds that the evidence might be erroneously assessed by the fact-finder, have a misleading effect, or unfairly predispose

[40] Sievert v. Germany, App. No. 29881/97, Eur. Ct. H.R., July 19, 2012.

[41] S.N. v. Sweden, App. No. 34209/96, Eur. Ct. H.R., July 2, 2002, §§ 10, 13.

[42] *Id.* § 52. [43] *Id.*

the fact-finder toward an outcome.[44] Criminal defendants generally may not challenge evidence on the basis that it could cause an unfair bias against them.

In contrast to common law systems, Continental European systems do not always exclude unreliable evidence. Instead, they admit it and leave it to the assessment of the professional judge, who is trusted to weigh its reliability. The different approach is said to be based on the differences in fact-finders; in common law systems, there is a greater concern that jurors might be unduly prejudiced by unreliable evidence. If this is the commonly accepted explanation for the exclusion of unreliable evidence,[45] it is also suggested that such exclusionary rule would be explained as a means to control lawyers and not only the jury.[46] In favor of the latter approach, it could be argued that, if the exclusion is based on the protection of laypersons from being unduly influenced by unreliable evidence, it should be questioned if such inadmissibility rule should continue to apply, when most of the trials are not held with a jury and do not even reach the trial stage.

Certainly the fact that the collection of evidence in adversarial systems is left in the hands of the parties and that their approach to the procedure is partisan impacts the scope of the exclusionary rules of evidence. In a system where the information reaches the fact-finder in the form of two one-sided accounts, and it is for the parties to decide which evidence to collect, present, or dispute, it is logical that the exclusionary rules of evidence are broader than in civil law systems, which are based on a comprehensive collection of the evidence.[47] This quasi-unilateral process of evidence gathering, as long as the public prosecutor who conducts it is truly neutral and autonomous, will lead to fewer challenges to the evidence. Although the trials in civil law countries are formally structured in an adversarial fashion, they are still to a large extent a stage for testing the veracity of the evidence that was collected in an objective and methodical fashion at the investigative stage. Accordingly, the challenges to such evidence tend to focus more on the legality of the collection and less on the content of the evidence as such.

There is another factor in the very structure of the process that has a major influence on the rules of evidence, and this is the lack of a requirement in common law systems that juries provide reasons for their verdicts. The strict requirement of a reasoned judgment in civil law systems, in some countries enshrined in the constitution, works as a mechanism to legitimize judicial power. As all judgments have to be reasoned, and the

[44] Rule 403 of the U.S. Federal Rules of Evidence provides for the possible exclusion of evidence when the prejudicial nature of the evidence outweighs its probative value. There is no equivalent in civil law systems.

[45] Numerous empirical studies question this reasoning, however, and show that jurors are quite capable of discounting hearsay testimony. *See* Hock Lai Ho, *A Philosophy of Evidence: Justice in the Search of Truth* 234 (2008).

[46] Maffei, *supra* note 22, at 123 (quoting Dale A. Nance, *The Best Evidence Principle*, 73 Iowa L.R. 229 (1988)) (noting that due to the "strongly partisan role that counsel play in the selection and presentation of evidence before the court," exclusionary rules of evidence play a role in deterring certain conduct of lawyers).

[47] *Id.* at 117.

reasoning extends to the assessment of the evidence, the control over the admissibility of the evidence can also be carried out ex post, when writing the judgment. The admissibility test is often done at a later stage than in common law jury trials, and the reasoning of the lower court allows appellate courts to see what use has been made of inadmissible evidence.

By contrast, in an Anglo-American jury proceeding, the absence of a reasoned judgment means that the exclusion of evidence must necessarily be carried out in advance and not at the moment of issuing the judgment. This factor, and not only the protection of the jury against undue influences by unreliable or illegally obtained evidence, determines the time and method of excluding inadmissible evidence: It has to occur beforehand, because the general verdict does not allow appellate courts to check whether the exclusionary rule has been applied correctly.

Finally, in civil law systems, the recording of all the pretrial measures in the dossier makes it difficult to exclude completely any unreliable evidence from the fact-finder.

For all these reasons, common law systems exclude unreliable evidence, while exclusion for lack of reliability is almost unknown in civil law systems, where the inner conviction of the judge can be based on any kind of evidence, as long as it has been legally obtained.

The best example in this regard is hearsay. Hearsay evidence is considered unreliable, and thus common law systems consider it presumptively inadmissible.[48] However, numerous exceptions allow the use of hearsay, when such evidence is necessary and exhibits circumstantial guarantees of reliability. Civil law systems have also identified the risks of derivative evidence and exhibit a preference for primary evidence over derivative evidence. However, the response is different. Instead of excluding derivative evidence, its impact is mitigated by giving it less probative value and requiring corroboration.

At present, there is a curious paradox: while in certain common law systems, such as England and Wales, hearsay evidence can be exceptionally admitted and given full evidentiary value without cross-examination if considered reliable, in civil law countries, where it is legally not excluded, it cannot be used as the sole and decisive evidence, because that would undermine the right to cross-examination as generally defined by the ECtHR (the *Al-Khawaja* judgment representing an exception to the rule).[49]

At the end, although the exclusion of hearsay has always been mentioned as one of the major differences in challenging relevant evidence, in practice, the many exceptions to hearsay in common law systems, together with the limited probative value assigned to hearsay in civil law countries, seems to show a major convergence in this area.

[48] On hearsay in England and Wales and the impact of the reform of the Judicial Act of 2003, see generally John R. Spencer, *Hearsay Evidence in Criminal Proceedings* 75 ff. (2014).

[49] Mike Redmayne, *Confronting Confrontation*, in *Criminal Evidence and Human Rights: Reimagining Common Law Procedural Traditions* 303–07 (Paul Roberts & Jill Hunter eds. 2012).

2. Irrelevant or Unnecessary Evidence

In civil law systems, the admissibility of the evidence can be limited by the judge on the basis of relevance and need. Refusal of evidence proposed or requested (*Beweisanträge*) can occur in cases where such evidence is not necessary, because the facts are considered sufficiently proven by other means, when the evidence is considered irrelevant to adjudicating contested facts, or when the facts are publicly known or otherwise sufficiently known by the court. This is the case under Article 244 of the German Criminal Procedure Code and Article 139 of the Swiss Criminal Procedure Code. In Italy, the trial court, which can issue subpoenas for witnesses and expert witnesses, can also exclude some of the witnesses proposed by the parties if it considers that they are not necessary (*manifestamente sovrabbondanti* or manifestly redundant). In these circumstances, courts refuse to admit evidence on the grounds of efficiency, in order to provide a speedier adjudication of the case. The German Criminal Procedure Code expressly contemplates that a court may refuse to admit evidence when it finds that the request for the evidence seeks to delay the proceedings.[50]

Article 659 of the Spanish Code of Criminal Procedure states that the judge will admit all relevant evidence proposed by the parties. But in deciding on the admissibility of evidence, the trial court must balance any conflicting interests. Specifically, it must take into account the right of defense, the relevance of the evidence proposed, and the right to a process without undue delays.

Relevance has a twofold meaning: (1) the functional, related to the formal requirements necessary for the use of the evidence; and (2) the material, related to the potential effect on the outcome of the proceedings. The first requires a connection between the evidence and the facts of the case; relevance is the relationship between the proposed evidence and the subject of the trial that constitutes *thema decidendi*. In the second meaning, relevance "exists when the non-performance of such evidence, due to its connection to the facts to which the conviction or acquittal is tied could alter the judgment in favour of the proponent." If the omission of the proposed item of evidence could not have influenced the verdict or the sentence, such evidence can be excluded.[51]

Despite the logic behind excluding irrelevant evidence, in Continental European criminal proceedings, judges tend to admit useless or unnecessary evidence rather than refusing evidence proposed by the parties. This is explained by the assumption that it is better to err on the side of admitting more evidence, which is not likely to cause much harm, than to refuse evidence that the parties might consider crucial for their arguments. Excluding evidence may entail a breach of the right to a fair process, while admitting irrelevant evidence usually will not. The relevance test is therefore

[50] Klaus Roxin & Bernd Schünemann, *Strafverfahrensrecht* 381 (28th ed. 2014). The test for excluding evidence upon this reason (*Verschleppungsabsicht*) has been elaborated by the courts and affects only evidence that for the court appears not to be relevant. In general, exclusion upon this ground is to be used very cautiously.

[51] Supreme Court Judgment STS 3508/2004, May 21, 2004.

applied quite leniently, except in those cases where admitting irrelevant evidence would have a clear impact on the right to a trial without undue delay or would be unreasonably costly.

With respect to witness evidence, while there are very few substantive exclusionary rules in civil law systems (that are based on the content of the questions and answers), the infringement of procedural rules can lead to the nullity of the evidence. If the infringement is expressly sanctioned with the nullity in the law, the evidence should be excluded from the pretrial file. Otherwise it will remain in the file, and the court will consider whether such evidence should be used in grounding the judgment.

3. Illegally Obtained Evidence

There is a broad consensus that evidence obtained with torture or inhuman or degrading treatment (Article 3 ECHR) cannot be admitted as evidence. The prohibition of torture is treated as absolute and requires the exclusion of the evidence gathered against such prohibition. However, there is not a uniform pattern across civil law systems when it comes to the admissibility of evidence obtained in violation of other fundamental rights. Some countries provide for a categorical general exclusionary rule for evidence obtained in violation of fundamental or constitutional rights; others rely on nullities when statutory provisions have been infringed in gathering evidence. Spain[52] and Greece[53] fall in the first group, where evidence obtained directly or indirectly in violation of fundamental rights and liberties shall have no effect.

However, in other European civil law countries, evidence obtained in violation of fundamental rights will not be automatically excluded, but will be evaluated according to a balancing test (e.g., the Netherlands,[54] or Denmark[55]). In undertaking such an assessment, courts consider different factors, such as: the seriousness of the infringement committed in the collection of the evidence, the gravity of the crime, the impact such violation may have on the reliability of the evidence or the importance of that evidence for discovering the facts and establishing the guilt of the accused, and the question of whether the use of such evidence would violate the fairness of the proceedings as a whole.[56]

[52] *See* Lorena Bachmaier, *Spain: The Constitutional Court's Move from Categorical Exclusion to Limited Balancing*, in *Exclusionary Rules in Comparative Law, supra* note 10, at 209–34.

[53] *See* Greek Code of Criminal Procedure art. 171.1(d); *see also* Georgios Triantafyllou, *Greece: From Statutory Nullities to a Categorical Statutory Exclusionary Rule*, in *Exclusionary Rules in Comparative Law, supra* note 10, at 261–86.

[54] In the Dutch system, Article 359(a)(2) of the Code of Criminal Procedure provides for a balancing test for breaches committed during the pretrial investigation. In deciding on the exclusion of evidence, the following elements are to be taken into account: "the interest that the breached rule serves, the gravity of the breach and the harm that it causes."

[55] *See* Lars Bo Langsted et al., *Criminal Law in Denmark* 164 (2011).

[56] *See* Stephen C. Thaman, *Balancing Truth Against Human Rights: A Theory of Modern Exclusionary Rules*, in *Exclusionary Rules in Comparative Law supra* note 10, at 403–44.

In general, it is accepted that categorical exclusionary rules should be limited to situations where fundamental rights are violated,[57] and many civil law systems have moved toward a balancing test. The Belgian practice is paradigmatic in this sense, where the illegally obtained evidence is rarely excluded, unless it is shown to be unreliable or incompatible with the fairness of the proceedings.[58]

4. The Process for Challenging the Admissibility of Evidence

Common law proceedings provide for the enforcement of exclusionary rules of evidence at pretrial hearings, so that the adjudicating body (mainly the jury) would not be prejudiced by the excluded evidence. In contrast, Continental European systems traditionally have had no problems in allowing the trial court to see the tainted evidence, considering that the professional judge, knowing the rules of evidence, could differentiate which evidence should or should not be taken into account when rendering the judgment. This is one of the reasons that might explain why most Continental European systems treat exclusionary rules of evidence as a prohibition on evaluating the evidence. On the other hand, the unitary structure of the adjudicating body in civil law systems (where the same body decides on the facts and on the sentencing) makes it more difficult to separate the decision on admissibility from the assessment of the evidence. Therefore, the moment for challenging illegally obtained evidence is at trial, something that has raised numerous debates.

In many countries, the decision on the admissibility of evidence is taken by the trial court when setting the case for trial. The court receives from the parties the names of witnesses and experts to be summoned to appear at trial. The court's decision is based mainly on relevance, as historically the legality of the evidence was presumed. The investigating phase had been under control of the public prosecutor or the investigating judge, and both were specifically tasked with the protection of the lawfulness of the proceedings; accordingly, the only check to be carried out by the trial court was for relevance.

On the other hand, in many cases, it is quite difficult to render a decision on the admissibility of the evidence without reviewing the evidence as a whole. A motion to suppress illegally obtained evidence requires hearing witnesses and reviewing many facts, which might already come close to the effort and time it would take for the trial itself. This approach can be seen as inefficient and in some cases may run counter to the procedural strategy of the parties, as they will, in practice, have to present some of their arguments on the merits ahead of the trial.

[57] *Id.* at 416.

[58] *See* Joachim Meese, *The Use of Illegally Obtained Evidence in Belgium: A 'Status Questionis,'* 10 Digital Evid. & Electronic Signature L. Rev. 63, 65 (2013).

These efficiency considerations and the fact that exclusionary rules in civil law countries were underdeveloped until recently might explain why the post-Napoleonic criminal procedure codes in Continental Europe generally do not provide for the possibility of challenging the admissibility of evidence before trial. Even today, as a rule, if the evidence proposed by the parties passes the relevance test, it is admitted at trial. This situation has remained unchanged in several Continental European criminal proceedings, and has led to the unsatisfactory situation that if any of the parties objects at trial to the lawfulness of evidence that has already been admitted, there is no way to entirely exclude such evidence from the proceedings. Even if it is not introduced at trial, it will be in the written file that has been handed over to the trial court (except, for example, in Italy, where there are separate files for the prosecution and for the trial).[59] In most countries, judges will simply be prohibited from considering illegally obtained evidence in their judgment. As a rule, there is no pretrial hearing foreseen for deciding on the exclusion of illegally obtained evidence.

Such a system has unsurprisingly given rise to criticism that it fails to prevent the adjudicating body from seeing pieces of evidence that are inadmissible. For example, the Spanish Criminal Procedure Code does not provide for a specific hearing to challenge and assess the legality of the evidence-gathering methods. Likewise, the German Criminal Procedure Code provides for an extensive list of prohibitions on assessing illegally obtained evidence (*Beweisverwertungsverbote*), which apply strictly,[60] but only at the moment of the assessment; there is not a preliminary hearing for filtering out the illegally obtained evidence from the proceedings entirely (although there are rules prohibiting the gathering of certain evidence, *Beweiserhebungsverbote*).

But the fact that such a hearing is not expressly foreseen should not justify ineffective protection of fundamental rights. In Spain, for example, there is no case law holding that illegally obtained evidence cannot be challenged at the pretrial stage or that the only remedy for such illegality is that the court is simply prohibited from assessing the evidence; some courts have even favored excluding the illegally obtained evidence from trial. But so far no legal provision has been introduced to prevent illegally obtained evidence from being produced at trial.[61]

In brief, the prohibition on considering illegally obtained evidence acts as the last filter, but there are strong reasons to exclude illegally obtained evidence from the

[59] As a rule, illegally obtained evidence is to be excluded from the trial file (*fascicolo per il dibattimento*), according to Articles 191 and 431 of the Italian Code of Criminal Procedure.

[60] *See generally* Claus Roxin & Bernd Schünemann, *Strafverfahrensrecht* 169 ff. (28th ed. 2014) and the extensive literature cited there. The evidence that does not fall under a legal prohibition of assessment shall be excluded following a balancing test taking into account all the competing interests. The application of this *Abwägungsprozess* must be done on a case-by-case basis, which has been the subject of debate. *See* Kai Ambos & Oscar J. Guerrero, *Las prohibiciones probatorias* 64 ff. (2009).

[61] Scholars have argued that evidence obtained through a breach of fundamental rights should be excluded at the pretrial stage in order to restore, as much as possible, the effectiveness of the fundamental right violated. *See* José M. Asencio Mellado, *La exclusión de la prueba ilícita en la fase de instrucción como expresión de garantía de los derechos fundamentales*, 8009 La Ley (Jan. 25, 2013).

process beforehand and not allow it to reach the adjudicating body.[62] In systems where the same judge who adjudicates the case also decides on the admissibility of the evidence, "the taint from the forbidden but persuasive information cannot be avoided: it always affects the decision maker's thinking."[63] A person cannot forget what he or she has heard or seen, even when he or she is very aware that such elements cannot be used as the basis for a verdict. The tainted evidence will have contributed to the judge's appreciation of the facts and can influence the judge regarding the guilt or innocence of the accused. It is difficult for a judge to act against her own inner conviction and render a decision she considers not to match the facts. The judgment will follow the narrative that is true for the judge, even if it avoids referring to the illegally obtained evidence. Only in cases where such evidence is the sole basis for the judgment will the exclusionary rules of evidence have to be enforced strictly. Where there is lawfully obtained corroborating evidence, it is almost impossible to determine what evidence really led to the final outcome.

Obviously in order to enforce the exclusionary rule adequately and to deprive it from any effect on the "inner conviction" of the judges, the exclusion of illegal evidence should occur before trial and the evidence should then be removed from the case file that reaches the trial court. This approach has been initiated by the Italian system. Article 191 of the Italian Criminal Procedure Code applies a strict exclusionary rule for illegally obtained evidence by rendering the illegally obtained evidence inadmissible and also non-usable.[64] It provides for mechanisms to ensure that illegally obtained evidence will not reach the trial. The illegally obtained evidence can be challenged at any moment of the proceedings. If challenged and found inadmissible during the pretrial stage, the evidence will not be included in the file that will be handed to the trial judge.

Making the illegally obtained evidence disappear from the trial file is an important step forward toward the effective implementation of exclusionary rules of evidence and the protection of the fundamental rights in the criminal procedure. However, most Continental European systems still accept the notion that it is sufficient that the illegally obtained evidence is kept out of the reasoning of the judgment. Given the reality that judges do not entirely disregard the evidence in the file before them, even when such evidence is deemed unlawfully obtained, this approach to exclusion does not appear to be very effective.

Finally, the system of excluding the illegally obtained evidence before trial provides more certainty for the parties as to their expectations toward the outcome of the trial. This has a clear effect on the greater willingness to enter into plea agreements as the parties will know beforehand which evidence will not reach the adjudicating body.

[62] The Spanish Constitutional Court has declared that it is necessary that the illegal evidence be excluded before the case is set for trial, thus before the accusatory plea is filed (STC 184/2003, of 23 October 2003 and 149/2001, of 27 June 2001).

[63] Damaška, *supra* note 7, at 47.

[64] *See* Giulio Illuminati, *Italy: Statutory Nullities and Non-usability*, in *Exclusionary Rules in Comparative Law supra* note 10, at 235, 237–59.

5. Cross-Examination of Witnesses

a. *The Method of Cross-Examining Witnesses*

The way in which the witnesses are cross-examined in civil law countries is quite different than in common law jurisdictions. The general approach in civil law systems is that the witnesses are not limited in their answers to the questions put by the parties. Instead, the witness's examination usually starts with a free account of the facts by the witness. Only after that will the parties be able to question the witness, challenge the accuracy of the recollection, and try to cast doubts upon the reliability and credibility of the witness. This system appears to combine the advantages of the two systems: the traditional Anglo-American cross-examination by the parties as to precise issues, with the complete account of the facts typical in Continental European systems.[65]

Spontaneous and fluent recollection of the facts is what is sought in a Continental European criminal trial, and to underpin the reliability of the testimony, previous contacts with the witness by one of the parties in order to prepare the questions and answers are seen as highly suspicious.

While the examination of the witness in a common law courtroom is carried out under continuous interruptions by objections of the opposing lawyer (on the basis of hearsay, leading questions, relevance, and other exclusionary rules), this is not the case in Continental European criminal proceedings. Several factors account for this: first, there are not as many exclusionary rules in Continental European systems; second, it is assumed that the control over the adequacy of the questions is done by the trial judge, who will ensure that the questions comply with rules of procedure and evidence and are relevant to the case. In any event, as most of the exclusionary rules in Continental European systems apply at the trial stage, there are no effective evidentiary sanctions that can be imposed for the use of leading questions or opinions expressed by a witness. Here again, the Continental European system relies on the assumption that a professional judge is able to disregard any evidence that is to be excluded, even if he has heard it during the trial.[66]

Traditionally, in common law criminal proceedings, questions related to bad character were to be excluded, as those questions were considered prejudicial against the defendant. While these were usually excluded in Anglo-American proceedings, in civil law jurisdictions, such questions about the previous behavior of the defendant were admissible.[67] However, since the English Criminal Justice Act of 2003 (Part 11.1) has abolished the common law rules governing admissibility of evidence of bad character in criminal proceedings (Section 99),[68] this is no longer seen as a point of difference between common law and civil law rules of evidence.

[65] In the same sense, arguing for such a combination of types of testimony and witness examination, which can be viewed as complementary, see also Billis, *supra* note 6, at 377–78.

[66] *See* Maffei, *supra* note 22, at 183.

[67] *See* John R. Spencer, *Evidence of Bad Character* 7–11 (3d ed. 2016).

[68] For an empirical study on the incidence of bad character evidence on prejudice, see Mike Redmayne, *Bad Character in Criminal Trial* 51–63 (2015) (concluding that there is no evidence that it will affect negatively the juror's assessment of the facts).

In Continental European systems, the professional judge is expected to differentiate facts from the morals and past conduct of the defendant.[69] The role of a judge is not that of a gatekeeper who protects the jury from possible prejudices; instead, the system relies on the capabilities of the professional and experienced judges to disregard those items of evidence that are not reliable or trustworthy. This is the theory behind the different approach in Continental European criminal proceedings, although it is hard to say if the judges are really able to refrain in reaching a verdict from relying on the information heard.

Continental European systems have also abolished the oath for witnesses testifying in front of the court, but the witness is warned by the court about his obligation to tell the truth and about the consequences of criminal liability for false testimony.[70] The witness is also informed about the right not to testify against certain relatives and to preserve professional confidentiality. The scope of such testimonial privileges differs greatly among the Continental European criminal justice systems.

b. *The Role of the Trial Court*

Traditionally in Continental European criminal proceedings, the questioning of witnesses was primarily a function for the judge, as part of her duty to find out the facts and discover the truth. Only after questioning by the judge were the parties allowed to ask questions, highlight contradictions, or require more precise explanations of factual recollections. The cross-examination by the parties was therefore not seen as important as in purely adversarial systems. The move toward more adversarial proceedings in most Continental European systems has reinforced the role of the parties in the cross-examination of witnesses and in parallel has reduced the role of the judge, who today tends in several civil law countries to adopt more of a role of a spectator rather than an inquisitor.

So far there is no uniform approach along the different European systems, and the level of intervention by the judge in the questioning is still debated, ranging from those who consider that any questioning affects negatively the perception of the judge's impartiality to those who consider that the questions of the judge are necessary in order to provide for a complete and accurate comprehension of the facts.[71]

In Continental European systems, as criminal procedure is not primarily conceived as a mechanism of dispute resolution, but rather as an instrument for truth-seeking and

[69] This explains the traditional principle of freedom of proof, or *liberté de la preuve*, recognized expressly in the French Criminal Code of Procedure, art. 427 ("Hors les cas où la loi en dispose autrement, les infractions peuvent être établies par tout mode de preuve et le juge décide d'après son intime conviction. Le juge ne peut fonder sa décision que sur des preuves qui lui sont apportées au cours des débats et contradictoirement discutées devant lui.").

[70] Criminal codes in Europe often provide for the offense of false testimony even when the witness did not testify under oath.

[71] Joan Picó i Junoy, *Reflexiones en torno a la cuestionada iniciativa probatoria del juzgador penal*, Justicia 1–1996, 158–59; José Antonio Díaz Cabiale, *Principios de aportación de parte y acusatorio: la imparcialidad del juez*, 199, 420 (1996); Lorena Bachmaier Winter, *Imparcialidad y prueba en el proceso penal—reflexiones sobre la iniciativa probatoria del juez*, 4 Rev. Bras. de Direito Processual Penal, 501–32 (2018).

dispensing justice through the state, active questioning by the judge is not viewed automatically as a sign of bias toward one of the parties or as an unlawful interference in the dispute. It is widely accepted as a means of helping the fact-finder reach a more accurate decision about the criminal responsibility of the accused.

There is of course the risk that the judge's active intervention in questioning a witness may negatively affect the perception of the judge's impartiality, particularly if the questions are overtly directed toward establishing the guilt of the defendant or they resemble an inquisitorial interrogation. This is why, for example, in Spain, certain decisions have held that if the trial court is too inquisitorial or heavy-handed in questioning the witnesses, this violates the accusatorial principle. In a case where the judge had put seventy-eight questions to the witness, the Supreme Court considered that the judge had gone far beyond complementing the cross-examination or seeking clarification of the answers of the witness, but had adopted the role of an interrogator.[72]

However, in Germany such interrogating practices are not seen as negative, as it is assumed that the role of the judge in finding the truth requires such an objective inquiry.

Conversely, in Italy, where criminal procedure was reformed along adversarial lines, the Code of Criminal Procedure has not eliminated the judge's authority to pose questions to the witnesses. The Code has, however, tried to ensure that the role of the judge remains secondary to that of the parties, in two ways: (1) by establishing that only after the parties have carried out the cross-examination can the judge question the witnesses,[73] and (2) by excluding the possibility that the trial judge would be familiar with the pretrial investigation file in advance of the trial. Thus, while not entirely passive, the judge is not biased by the previous access to the file, and this fosters a more objective approach to the evidence produced at trial.

In summary, consistent with the traditional inquisitorial model in which the judge was the protagonist of collecting the testimony, in most Continental European systems today, judges are still allowed to put the questions they consider useful for the discovery of the truth or for their own understanding of the facts. However, due mainly to the influence of the common law systems and their understanding of adversarialism, the trend is toward a more passive role for trial judges, giving a prominent role to the parties in questioning the witness, even in the face of some reluctance by judges to accept a passive position. And as has been seen in Spain, unduly intensive questioning by the court can eventually lead to the infringement of the accusatorial principle. Finally, it has to be pointed out that the intervention of the judge in questioning witnesses has a very different impact in a system where the witnesses are not witnesses "for the parties,"

[72] *See* Supreme Court Judgment 922/2016, of 10 March 2016, where the Criminal Chamber of the Spanish Supreme Court said that the impartiality of the judge is not affected when he makes a reasonable and moderate use of the possibilities to introduce questions in the cross-examination of witnesses in order to obtain clarifications of their testimonies. In considering if the trial court has overstepped its powers, the court must take the following elements into account: the complexity of the case and the nature and the form of the questions put by the judge.

[73] Italian Code of Criminal Procedure art. 506.

but for the case: the possible perception of bias by the judge when questioning a witness is diluted in a system where witnesses are not linked to any of the parties.

c. *Confrontation and Out-of-Court Witness Statements*

When it comes to the exclusion of out-of-court pretrial statements, the rules regarding the scope and grounds for exclusionary rules in civil law systems are neither uniform, nor completely clear. While some common law systems directly opt for a very strict approach toward any kind of out-of-court statements to be introduced at trial,[74] most Continental European systems consider that pretrial statements should be known by the court in order to adjudicate with more accuracy.

In general, all systems adhere to the principle that evidence is to be produced in a public hearing allowing the defendant to confront the witnesses and cross-examine them. Direct contact with the sources of evidence is deemed necessary for a better assessment of the evidence. It is beyond debate that testimony rendered at trial, directly before the fact-finder and with full respect of confrontation rights, helps the fact-finder better assess the reliability and credibility of the witness. What continues to be discussed is the scope of the confrontation right. In other words, how strictly is the right to confront witnesses to be interpreted, and what exceptions to it can be accepted for a better assessment of the facts? Two main issues are to be addressed here: (1) the admissibility of out-of-court witness statements when the witness is unavailable, and (2) the use of out-of-court statements to impeach a witness testifying in court, when there are inconsistent statements.

Consider the example of the Swiss Criminal Procedure Code, enacted in 2011. It does not establish as an absolute rule that the witness shall be cross-examined at the public trial, but rather regulates this as just one possibility. The general rule is that a witness statement taken during the pretrial stage (not necessarily in front of a judge; it can be before the police or the public prosecutor), with the opportunity for the defense to cross-examine the witness, is later admissible as evidence at trial, regardless of the availability of the witness. The judgment can be based upon evidence produced either during the pretrial stage or during the trial. The court has access to the pretrial file before the commencement of the trial, and if it considers that the live testimony of the witness is not needed, the pretrial statements have evidentiary value. Only if the witness statement is the sole and decisive evidence must additional safeguards be observed—in that instance, confrontation must also occur at trial. In other words, it is enough that the witness be cross-examined at some point, but there is broad leeway as to the moment and the method: Neither personal appearance, nor live examination is required, and out-of-court statements are admissible regardless of the availability of the witness at trial.[75]

[74] Especially in the United States, where since the Supreme Court judgment in *Crawford v. Washington*, 541 U.S. 36 (2004), the confrontation clause of the Sixth Amendment to the U.S. Constitution is to be interpreted in a very strict way: No testimonial statement against the accused will be admissible unless the accused has had the opportunity to be confronted with and cross-examine the witness.

[75] Ariane Kaufmann, *Das Unmittelbarkeitsprinzip und die Folgen seiner Einschränkung in der Schweizerischen Strafprozessordnung* 256 ff. (2013); Franz Riklin, *Das Unmittelbarkeitsprinzip im schweizerischen Strafverfahrensrecht*, 126-1 ZSTW 173–84 (2014).

While this approach has been accepted by the ECtHR as long as the fairness of procedure is respected, the Strasbourg Court has never gone so far as admitting as a rule that the witness evidence is not given in the public hearing. The Swiss Code has thus turned the exception into the rule, undermining the role of the public hearing and the general rule that evidence should be produced in the trial.

In the Spanish criminal justice system, the oral trial is considered the core stage of the proceedings, and all pretrial acts are only aimed at preparing the trial and not to produce evidence.[76] This is a general principle that was set out in the original Code of Criminal Procedure of 1882 and has been repeatedly underlined by the Supreme Court and the Constitutional Court: The pretrial investigatory acts serve to determine if there is sufficient evidence to proceed to trial.[77] The function of the pretrial investigative acts is not to establish in a definitive way the facts for adjudicating the case, "but to prepare the trial, to provide the prosecution and the defense with the necessary elements to make their own case in an adversarial debate before the trial court."[78] This is the understanding of the "accusatorial" principle in Spain, where the oral presentation of the evidence is granted constitutional protection under Article 120.2 of the Spanish Constitution, which states that "[p]roceedings shall be predominantly oral, especially in criminal cases."

Despite the general rule that pretrial statements are not evidence, the numerous exceptions to this principle and the fact that those testimonies are included in the file available to the trial court,[79] tend in practice to reduce the value of confrontation rights. The law provides for exceptions when a witness in unavailable at trial and when the pretrial statement can be used to impeach a witness whose statement in court contradicts the testimony made previously in front of the police, the public prosecutor, or the investigating judge.

In those cases where the witness will not be available at trial (due to illness, age, or other circumstances), or it will be very difficult to ensure her attendance (e.g., because she is living abroad or does not have a known place of residence), a preliminary hearing will be held in order to "secure" the evidence.[80] At this hearing, evidence is taken following the same safeguards as are used at trial: in the presence of the parties and giving the defense the opportunity to cross-examine the witness. This hearing must be video-recorded to be played later at trial if the witness is in fact unavailable at the time of trial.[81] The admissibility of this out-of-court statement, as long as it is kept as an exceptional measure, complies with the right to cross-examination, and allows the parties to discuss the credibility of the witness before the trial court, poses no further constitutional problems.

[76] Spanish Code of Criminal Procedure art. 741.

[77] Spanish Supreme Court Judgment 644/2001, July 20, 2001.

[78] Spanish Constitutional Court Judgment 138/1988, July 7, 1988; STC 217/1989, Dec. 21, 1989.

[79] They are included even as "documentary evidence." *See* Spanish Code of Criminal Procedure art. 726.

[80] On the advanced practice of the evidence, albeit in front of the investigating judge, see José M. Asencio Mellado, *Prueba prohibida y prueba preconstituida* 171 ff. (1989).

[81] Spanish Code of Criminal Procedure art. 730.

The pretrial statement can also be read out or shown in video format at the trial if the live statement contradicts an earlier statement made by the witness. According to Article 714 of the Spanish Code of Criminal Procedure, when the pretrial witness statement contradicts a previous statement made by the witness, any party can request the reading of the pretrial statement at trial. The law permits the trial judge to give greater weight to the pretrial statements, even if those were made in front of the police and without cross-examination; the possibility of discussing the statement in court is considered sufficient to accept the evidentiary value of such pretrial statements.[82] French law approaches the probative value of prior statements in a very a similar way, as French courts also have full access to the file and can confront a witness at any time with previously made statements that contradict those made at trial.[83] Although the ECtHR has accepted this practice,[84] such a broad acceptance of inconsistent out-of-court statements as evidence is problematic, insofar as the out-of-court statements are introduced into the trial (through the file) and are assessed there.

Italy follows a different model, under which out-of-court statements are not made available to the trial court and can be introduced by the parties only to impeach the credibility of a witness who testifies at trial. If a witness makes use of a privilege not to testify, those previous testimonies cannot be read out or used as evidence.[85] This approach is also followed in Germany, where the *Zeugnisverweigerungsrecht* prevents the introduction of out-of-court statements of a witness who invokes a privilege and refuses to testify at trial.

In brief, civil law systems provide a number of exceptions to the right to confront witnesses, as long as the opportunity to cross-examine the witnesses has been afforded to the defense at some point in the process.[86]

6. Concluding Remarks

Like their common law counterparts, civil law systems regard derivative and unreliable evidence as presenting a danger to the accurate assessment of the facts. But in civil law systems, the method of dealing with such evidence is different. Courts do not exclude the evidence from the proceedings entirely, but rather take into account its derivative nature and potential unreliability when weighing its probative value.

With respect to evidence obtained in violation of fundamental rights, civil and common law systems are converging and adopting similar exclusionary rules based on the

[82] Spanish Constitutional Court Judgments 155/2002, July 22, 2002; 82/1988, Apr. 28, 1988; and 51/1990, Mar. 26, 1990.

[83] *See* Jocelyne Leblois-Happe, *Das Unmittelbarkeitsprinzip im französischen Strafverfahrensrecht*, 126-1 ZStW 185–193, 189 (2014).

[84] *See Camilleri v. Malta*, Appl. No. 51760/99, 16 Mar. 2000. For a critique of the Spanish approach, see also Asencio Mellado, *supra* note 80, at 193–94.

[85] Italian Code of Criminal Procedure art. 500.3.

[86] Along the same lines, see Richard D. Friedman, *The Confrontation Right Across Systemic Divide*, *in* Jackson et al., *supra* note 3, at 261, 270–71.

protection of fundamental rights. Despite these similarities, structural and functional factors provide for a different impact of inadmissible evidence in civil and common law proceedings. This is largely due to the different method of challenging the evidence. Two factors are to be highlighted here. First, while in common law proceedings, it is for the defense and prosecutor to challenge the admissibility of evidence, in civil law countries, the more neutral role played by the prosecutor and the investigating judge at the pretrial stage results in a presumption of legality of the evidence obtained officially. Because public prosecutors and investigating judges are strictly bound by the law, and one of their main duties is to ensure that the investigation complies with the law and procedural rules, it is assumed that they act correctly.[87] Nevertheless, as in practice legal provisions might have been infringed, a defense attorney's role at trial is to question the legality, reliability and relevance of the evidence produced by the prosecutor and seek to exclude its admissibility.

Second, in many civil law countries, exclusionary rules are implemented by prohibiting the consideration of the tainted evidence (or giving it lesser weight) and not by excluding it from the case file that reaches the trial court. Accordingly, the trial court has contact with evidence that is inadmissible. This method of enforcing exclusionary rules is not ideal, but it has a lesser negative impact in civil law systems than it would have in common law systems. This is because in civil law systems, the trial court is required to provide reasons for its judgment, which reduces the risk that the judgment will be influenced by the tainted evidence.

With respect to hearsay evidence, the differences between civil law and common law systems are vanishing, and despite a theoretical divergent approach, both systems seem to be close in their approaches. While common law systems (other than the United States) have introduced important exceptions to the inadmissibility of hearsay evidence, civil law systems have adopted measures to counterbalance the lesser reliability of hearsay by requiring corroboration.

Finally, when it comes to cross-examination, the methods used to question witnesses still differ starkly. In common law systems, the discovery of the truth relies mainly on the ability of the lawyers to make the witness say what the lawyers deem beneficial for their own case. In civil law systems, the nonpartisan role of the public prosecutor, together with the thorough official (and impartial) investigation of the facts and the possibility of the court to supplement the witness testimony, should lead to a more thorough and objective probing of the facts. While cross-examination is an essential mechanism to establish the facts and to check the credibility of the witnesses, it is worth asking why a party-driven interrogation has to exclude a comprehensive account of the facts by the witness or the possibility of introducing complementary questions or clarifications by the trial judge. At this point, it is clear that the civil law tradition has adopted cross-examination for improving fact-finding within the criminal trial, while the common law tradition has not been open to civil law influences in this area.

[87] In the same sense for the Belgian public prosecutor's department, which is presumed to act accordingly to the law, see Meese, *supra* note 58, at 64.

Regardless of whether criminal procedure is seen as a mechanism of dispute resolution or as a tool for enforcing a criminal policy of the state, the outcome should be based upon facts. Combining certain adversarial and inquisitorial ways of presenting and producing the evidence, without infringing the impartiality of the court, might be best for fulfilling the aims of the criminal proceedings.

The few aspects addressed here show that there is a visible convergence of common law and civil law systems when it comes to the grounds for challenging evidence. Yet both legal traditions are still far apart in the way they handle the exclusionary rules of evidence. Mirjan Damaška's comment thus still rings true: "[T]here is no gainsaying that a great deal of information, inadmissible under common law evidentiary rules, reaches the continental adjudicators."[88] However, as long as such information does not negatively affect the fairness of the trial and its probative value is limited, the right balance between the efficiency of the criminal proceedings and the protection of fundamental rights might not be harmed.

References

Proceso penal y sistemas acusatorios (Lorena Bachmaier ed., 2008)

Emmanouil Billis, *Die Rolle des Richters im adversatorischen und im inquistorischen Beweisverfahren* (2015)

Mirjan Damaška, *Evidence Law Adrift* (1997)

The Oxford Handbook of Criminal Law (Markus D. Dubber & Tatjana Hörnle eds., 2014)

Law of the European Convention on Human Rights (David J. Harris et al. eds., 3d ed. 2009)

Crime, Procedure and Evidence in a Comparative and International Context: Essays in Honour of Professor Mirjan Damaška (John D. Jackson et al. eds., 2008)

Stefano Maffei, *The Right to Confrontation in Europe: Absent, Anonymous and Vulnerable Witnesses* (2012)

The Oxford Handbook of Comparative Law (Matthias Reimann & Reinhard Zimmermann eds., 2006)

Criminal Evidence and Human Rights: Reimagining Common Law Procedural Traditions (Paul Roberts & Jill Hunter eds., 2012)

Claus Roxin & Bernd Schünemann, *Strafverfahrensrecht* (29th ed. 2017)

John R. Spencer, *Hearsay Evidence in Criminal Proceedings* (2014)

Exclusionary Rules in Comparative Law (Stephen C. Thaman ed., 2013)

Stefan Trechsel, *Human Rights in Criminal Proceedings* (2005)

[88] Mirjan Damaška, *Evidentiary Barriers to Conviction and Two Models of Criminal Procedure*, 121 U. Penn. L. Rev. 506–89, 511 (1973).

CHAPTER 38

THE CONFRONTATION RIGHT

RICHARD D. FRIEDMAN

I. Introduction

The right of a criminal defendant to be confronted with the witnesses against him[1] has perhaps the oldest roots of any right in the criminal law. It has been a central aspect of the common law system of criminal jurisprudence for half a millennium, and of other systems before that. It is explicitly expressed and protected in the Sixth Amendment to the United States Constitution. In recent decades, it has also gained a significant foothold in the civil law world under the European Convention on Human Rights. And yet the right has often been misunderstood, and perhaps in large part for that reason, it has sometimes been treated cavalierly by judicial systems.

The basic idea behind the confrontation right is very simple: Any rational system of adjudication depends in large part on the testimony of witnesses. It is therefore essential that the system prescribe the method by which witnesses may give their testimony. Most systems, for example, insist that the witness first take an oath, or make an affirmation that has much the same effect. This procedure provides some assurance that the witness understands the solemnity of the occasion and the potential consequences of her conduct. This understanding is fortified by recognition that lying in these circumstances carries severe adverse consequences for the witness; in older days, the common belief was that damnation would follow,[2] but today the more widespread perception is that the witness is exposing herself to a perjury prosecution. Another condition on which some systems have insisted is that the witness testify face to face with the party against whom

[1] This essay will use a convention that, when speaking in general terms, it will refer to defendants as masculine and to witnesses as feminine.

[2] *See generally* Helen Silving, *The Oath: I*, 68 Yale L.J. 1329 (1959).

the evidence is presented, especially if that party is an accused—or put another way, that the witness confront the accused.[3]

Note that other methods of giving testimony are possible. For example, an adjudicative system might require that witnesses give their testimony in writing. This was the prevailing system for a time in ancient Greece.[4] In some settings, modern systems rely on affidavits, which are a written form of testimony, confirmed by oath or affirmation. Or an adjudicative system might require that the witness give her testimony orally to an official, in a proceeding closed to parties to the litigation. This method has characterized some Continental systems. Systems adhering to the confrontation right reject such other methods and instead insist that the witness give her testimony openly, face to face with the adverse party—and, in the modern day, not only under oath but subject to adverse questioning by that party.

Note also that this right is a procedural one, not merely one assessing the quality of evidence and rejecting evidence that might be deemed to hurt more than help the search for truth. That is, it is a right to insist that adverse testimony be given under certain prescribed procedures. The distinction is an important one because procedural rights tend to have a categorical nature rather than being subject to a cost-benefit analysis in each case. In this sense, the confrontation right is similar to, for example, the right to counsel. A court does not ask whether it is worthwhile in the given case, weighing the expense and possible delay that counsel might create against the potential improvement in the quality of the proceeding, that the accused be represented by counsel; rather, the accused simply has the right to counsel, because this is the procedure by which the system operates. Similarly, presenting the witnesses face to face with the accused when they give their testimony, and requiring that they be under oath or affirmation and subject to questioning on behalf of the accused, is the way an adjudicative system may operate. If so, there is no need for an assessment of costs and benefits in the particular case.

Though the confrontation right is itself a procedural rather than an evidentiary one, a system adhering to it will likely need to rely on a rule excluding secondary evidence of testimony. Suppose that a witness testifies out of court, not subject to confrontation, but the substance of the testimony is relayed to trial and presented to the trier of fact. Perhaps,

[3] The wording chosen here—the witness confronts the accused, and the accused has a right *to be confronted with* the witness—is very purposeful. The accused has a right to insist that the prosecutorial authority bring the adverse witnesses in front of him; the accused does not have to present the witnesses. In some settings, the distinction is very significant. *See, e.g.*, Melendez-Diaz v. Massachusetts, 557 U.S. 305, 324–25 (2009) (holding that "the Confrontation Clause [of the Sixth Amendment to the United States Constitution] imposes a burden on the prosecution to present its witnesses, not on the defendant to bring those adverse witnesses into court"; the prosecution may not present its evidence via affidavit and leave it to the witness to subpoena the affiant if he chooses).

[4] 5 Demosthenes, *Private Orations* 46:6, at 247–49 (A.T. Murray trans., 1939; Loeb Classical Library) (oration attributed to Apollodaurus: "The laws . . . ordain that . . . [a witness's] testimony must be committed to writing in order that it may not be possible to subtract anything from what is written, or to add anything to it."); Aristotle, *The Athenian Constitution* 53:4, at 145 (H. Rackham trans., 1942; Loeb Classical Library) ("The litigants are not permitted to put in laws or challenges or evidence other than those passed on by the Arbitrator, that have been put into the deed-boxes.").

for example, an in-court witness testifies (under oath and subject to confrontation and cross-examination) to what the primary witness said. If that evidence is allowed, then the confrontation right is substantially undermined, because the adjudicative system has endorsed a method by which a witness can testify in effect by speaking to another person and relying on that other person to pass her statement on to the trier of fact. In the common law system, the evidentiary doctrines preventing such evasion of the confrontation right have often been treated under the rubric of the rule against hearsay. But that rule is very broad, characterized by a jumble of exceptions, and often perplexing, both in operation and in underlying rationale. Furthermore, development of the rule against hearsay since about 1800 appears to have obscured the confrontation right until recently. The relatively recent development of a confrontation right under the European Convention on Human Rights, which primarily governs systems that do not have a hearsay rule, is a welcome and interesting advance.

Though the confrontation right is, or should be recognized to be, categorical in nature, it can be waived or forfeited. Waiver occurs rather readily, if the accused does not object to the presentation of testimony not taken subject to confrontation. Suppose, for example, a prosecutor wishes to introduce results of a forensic laboratory test; a report of that test should ordinarily be considered a testimonial statement by the analyst who prepared the report. The accused may nevertheless decide that there is no advantage to him in insisting that the analyst come to trial as a live witness; if the prosecution wishes to save money by presenting just the report, and the accused has no plausible basis for impeaching it, he may be satisfied that the evidence will be presented in a rather undramatic fashion.

Forfeiture of the right is generally thought to require wrongful conduct on the part of the accused that predictably caused (and, in one view, was designed to cause) the witness to be unavailable. In that circumstance, it may be inequitable if the court were to exclude testimony on the ground that the accused had no opportunity for confrontation; it was, after all, the accused's own wrongful conduct that caused that lack of opportunity. Conduct leading to forfeiture includes murdering the witness, intimidating her, or otherwise preventing her from coming to court.

The confrontation right, of course, comes with costs, in time, money, ordeal, and often in the loss of valuable evidence. It is therefore not surprising that most jurisdictions have not enforced the right with consistent rigor.

That is unfortunate. Despite its costs, the confrontation right is a central protection of a satisfactory criminal justice system; indeed, it may be said to create a genuine, open criminal trial. Section II of this chapter will develop this point, discussing the nature of the confrontation right, the purposes it serves, and its costs. Section III will discuss the history of the right. Section IV will discuss an array of issues that may arise in any jurisdiction (or in some cases, any common law jurisdiction). It will use as a touchstone the current status of the right in the United States, where it is best developed and explicitly protected by constitutional text, and where the conception of the right, bringing it closer to its historical roots, has dramatically changed in recent years. And Section V will discuss the status of the right in Europe.

II. Nature, Purposes, and Costs

What we today think of as the confrontation right has two distinct aspects, which usually exist together, but need not do so. First is what we may call the right of confrontation proper—the right of an accused to insist that adverse witnesses be brought face to face with him to give their testimony. Second is the right of cross-examination—the right of the accused to pose adverse questions to the witness, testifying under penalty of perjury.[5] This second aspect of the right may be considered part of a broader right to impeach an adverse witness—that is, to show reasons that the witness's testimony may not be credible.

John Henry Wigmore, the great American evidence scholar of the first half of the twentieth century, belittled the first of these aspects. The accused, he says, demands confrontation "not for the idle purpose of gazing upon the witness, or of being gazed upon by him, but for the purpose of cross-examination."[6] Ironically, as the next section will show, the right of confrontation proper developed long before the right of cross-examination. And it still serves important purposes.

Requiring a witness to testify face to face with the accused serves much the same purpose as the oath, and for many witnesses perhaps in a more meaningful way: It focuses the attention of the witness on the solemnity of the occasion, making it more likely that she will realize that her testimony may have serious adverse consequences for the particular person in whose presence she is testifying. As the United States Supreme Court has noted, "[t]he phrase still persists, 'Look me in the eye and say that.' "[7] Professor Sherman Clark has elaborated:

> We have decided that if one is willing to play [the witness's] central, crucial role in taking a man's liberty, one ought also to be willing to look him in the eye and literally stand behind his accusation. More to the point, and recognizing the strong sense in which rules of criminal procedure are a form not only of self-regulation but also self-definition, we have decided that we want to be the kind of people who stand face to face with those we would accuse.[8]

The right of confrontation proper therefore may be considered a basic requirement for the fundamental fairness of the system. It also helps ensure an open, transparent system

[5] In the early seventeenth century, treason defendants in England clearly had the right to demand that prosecution witnesses testify face to face, but they did not have a right to cross-examine. By contrast, in the old equity practice, parties had the right to pose adverse questions to the witness, in writing, but not the right to demand that the witness testify face to face. And in some settings, a modern-day court may allow an accused to cross-examine orally, through an attorney, without requiring the witness to come face to face with him. *E.g.*, Maryland v. Craig, 497 U.S. 836 (1990).

[6] 5 John Henry Wigmore, *Evidence* § 1395, at 150 (Chadbourn rev. 1974), *quoted in* Davis v. Alaska, 415 U.S. 308, 316 (1974), *and in* Coy v. Iowa, 487 U.S. 1012, 1029 (1988) (Blackmun, J., dissenting).

[7] *Coy*, 487 U.S. at 1018.

[8] Sherman J. Clark, *An Accuser-Obligation Approach to the Confrontation Clause*, 81 Neb. L. Rev. 1258, 1261 (2003).

of justice: There is no doubt what the witness's testimony is, and the chance that the testimony is the product of intimidation, or even torture (a very plausible possibility in earlier times) is eliminated.

As for cross-examination, Wigmore called it "beyond any doubt the greatest legal engine ever invented for the discovery of truth."[9] Though the statement may be hyperbolic, it certainly at least contains an element of truth. A witness's testimony may, for one or more of several reasons, be less probative than it first appears. Perhaps the witness had a poor opportunity to observe the events or conditions on which she reports, or she has poor powers of perception in general. Perhaps she has a poor memory of those events or conditions, or a poor memory in general. Perhaps some factor biases her, deflecting her from a sense of obligation in the particular case to tell the truth, or she may have little regard in general for the value of truth-telling. And perhaps she uses words, and in particular the words of her testimony, in a way that could mislead the trier of fact as to her intended meaning. If a witness were able to testify without being subjected to probing questions designed to reveal such flaws in her testimony, those flaws would more likely go unnoticed by the trier of fact. What is more, without the prospect of probing questions, the witness might feel free to be looser with her testimony; knowledge that she will be examined closely, and not by a friendly interrogator, is a powerful incentive to be careful and accurate. Questioning by a neutral interrogator, such as the judge presiding over the trial, may have considerable benefit. But the judge is unlikely to have the incentive to prepare and press searching lines of examination. No alternative procedure is likely to reveal flaws in the testimony as thoroughly as is cross-examination, and no alternative procedure is likely to assure the accused that the testimony has been thoroughly tested. But the right to impeach the witness need not be limited to cross-examination; for example, the testimony of other witnesses may demonstrate that a critical accusatory witness has a bias against the accused.

Of course, both aspects of the confrontation right come with costs as well. Most pervasive are costs in money and time: It may be expensive and time-consuming for a witness to appear at trial (or at another testimonial event attended by the accused); cross-examination, and responses to it, are likely to consume a great deal of time, both in preparation and in court. Insisting on the confrontation right also sometimes causes the outright loss of evidence, most obviously because a witness may become unavailable, by death or otherwise, before she testifies subject to cross-examination.

Both aspects of confrontation—coming face to face with the accused and having to endure cross-examination and other forms of impeachment—also increase the personal ordeal of testifying. In some cases, even the prospect of confrontation may intimidate a witness from testifying at all, though her testimony would be truthful if she gave it; this possibility is of special concern when the witness is a vulnerable one who is the victim of the crime charged. If the witness does testify, intimidation may cause her to fail to do so fully or convincingly.

[9] Wigmore, *supra* note 6, § 1367, at 32.

Further, the confrontation right gives defendants, or their supporters, an incentive to prevent witnesses from testifying subject to confrontation, if they believe they can do so without detection. Measures of prevention might include intimidation, keeping the witness out of the way, or murder. And because of that possibility, it may be necessary for the prosecution to take unusual measures to protect a vulnerable witness, both before and after the testimony.

The costs are therefore considerable. Ultimately, though, the confrontation right is justified by its role in helping to create a just and free society. One of the primary needs for such a society is to ensure that the punitive powers of the state are, and are perceived to be, exercised fairly and openly, in such a way as to minimize the chance of wrongful conviction and to give the accused ample opportunity to challenge the evidence against him.

III. History

The principle that a witness testifying against an accused person must do so face to face with the accused is apparent as early as the time of the ancient Hebrews.[10] The ancient Romans similarly insisted on the practice.[11] Medieval adjudicative systems, by contrast, searched by means such as the ordeal for indications of the judgment of God, but when these systems lost the support of the Catholic Church in 1215, the necessity of relying on witnesses was restored. Continental systems took the testimony of witnesses behind closed doors, though the accused was sometimes allowed to pose written questions.[12] The English, by contrast, took testimony in the open, in the presence of the accused, and for centuries English jurists celebrated this confrontational style of testimony as one of the great glories of their system.[13]

This is not to say that the English always adhered to their own principles; in particular, the practice was inconsistent in politically contentious treason trials. But Parliament repeatedly and explicitly insisted that, even in this setting, the witnesses be brought face to face. By the middle of the seventeenth century, courts carefully protected the right in this context as in others. At first, they did not allow the accused to pose questions directly to the witness, but that right soon became established as well.[14]

The confrontation right naturally traveled to America with the English colonists, and perceived violations of it by the Crown during the tensions that led to revolution became one of the colonies' complaints. The earliest state constitutions, adopted shortly after

[10] Deuteronomy 17:6 and 19:15–18 strongly suggest the necessity of face-to-face testimony. The requirement is made explicit in the Dead Sea Scrolls, which provided, in effect, for a deposition to preserve testimony by bringing the witness in the presence of the accused. Richard D. Friedman, *Confrontation: The Search for Basic Principles*, 86 Geo. L.J. 1011, 1023 n.64 (1998).

[11] Acts 25:16.

[12] Richard D. Friedman & Bridget McCormack, *Dial-In Testimony*, 150 U. Pa. L. Rev. 1171, 1202–03 (2002).

[13] *Id.* at 1203–04.

[14] Friedman, *supra* note 10, at 1024 & n. 74.

independence, all protected the right—some speaking of confrontation and others using the time-honored "face to face" formula. And when the new nation adopted a Bill of Rights in 1791, it included, in the Sixth Amendment to the Constitution, protection of the right of an accused "to be confronted with the witnesses against him."[15]

Around the same time, however, a broader and more pliable doctrine took form in common law jurisprudence. This was the rule against hearsay, which is not limited to testimonial statements but covers *any* out-of-court statement that a party seeks to offer to prove the truth of an assertion it makes. It appears that the rule grew because of the increasing presence in civil litigation of lawyers, who articulated the disadvantages of being unable to cross-examine the maker of any out-of-court statement used adversely to them—and indeed, they were able to extend the principle even more broadly to those whose out-of-court conduct was offered to prove the truth of a belief apparently reflected by the conduct, even if the conduct did not articulate that belief.[16]

The rule against hearsay soon dominated discourse; courts excluded a statement on the ground that it was hearsay without speaking about bringing a witness face to face with the adverse party. But a blanket exclusion of all hearsay would be excessive, and so the rule has always been subject to an array of exceptions. As a result of these developments, the rationale behind the hearsay rule appeared nebulous. Courts began to treat the rule as a nuisance to be avoided when possible. The essential core behind the rule, the ancient confrontation right, became occluded.

A spur to change occurred in 1965, when the U.S. Supreme Court held that the Sixth Amendment confrontation clause binds state as well as federal courts. It thus became essential to determine just what the clause prohibits. (A federal court could reach any result contemplated by the clause by speaking of hearsay rather than of confrontation, but the clause only authorizes the Supreme Court to constrain state courts when there has been a violation of the confrontation right.) After fifteen years, the Court attempted in 1980 to articulate a general test.[17] It regarded the clause as a substantive protection against unreliable evidence, operating largely as a constitutionalization of the law of hearsay.

This approach, lacking any historical foundation or clear constraint and failing to articulate a principle worthy of respect, provided paltry protection of the confrontation right. At last, in 2004, the Court rediscovered the long-standing meaning of the right. In *Crawford v. Washington*,[18] the Court recognized that the clause creates not a substantive limitation on evidence that a court might deem to be unreliable, but rather a substantive procedural right that states the conditions under which a witness against an accused must give testimony—face to face, subject to cross-examination, and, if reasonably possible, at trial. *Crawford* was a transformational decision; it left unanswered, and even unposed, many important operational questions, some of which will be addressed in Section IV.

[15] Friedman & McCormack, *supra* note 12, at 1206–08.
[16] *Wright v. Tatham*, 5 Cl. & F. 670, 7 E.R. 559, 47 Rev. Rep. 136 (H.L. 1838).
[17] Ohio v. Roberts, 448 U.S. 56 (1980). [18] 541 U.S. 36 (2004).

Even before *Crawford*, some non-adversarial systems, unburdened by the obscurity created by the rule against hearsay, began articulating a right of confrontation as a fundamental guarantee of criminal procedure.[19] Ironically, then, though for centuries England was the cradle of the right, and had scorned Continental systems for failure to recognize it, its nature has been so obscured by the rule against hearsay[20] that in recent years it has been compelled to adhere to the right by a court sitting on the European Continent.[21]

IV. Issues Arising under the Confrontation Right: The Case of the United States

This section focuses on the right as it stands in the United States, but it identifies issues that may be significant in any system, or in some cases, in any common law system.

1. The Basic Structure of the Right

Under *Crawford* and its progeny, the confrontation right applies to a statement that is testimonial in nature. That is not an adventitious choice of term. Testifying is the action of a witness.[22] (In many languages, the words for "testify" or "testimony" and for "witness" have the same root.) The purpose of the confrontation right is to ensure that witnesses testify face to face with the accused at trial, or if necessary at some other formal testimonial event.

Notice the negative implication: If a statement is *not* testimonial in nature, then the confrontation right does not apply.[23] The right is thus not nearly as broad as the rule against hearsay, which applies in general (but subject to many exemptions) to all out-of-court statements offered to prove the truth of what they assert. The right concerns only the procedure by which witnesses give their testimony.

[19] *E.g.*, Kostovski v. The Netherlands, App. No. 11454/85, Eur. Ct. H.R., Nov. 20, 1989; Delta v. France, App. No. 11444/85, Eur. Ct. H.R., Dec. 19, 1990.

[20] English courts do not speak of a confrontation right; they speak of the rule against hearsay, which continues to be very broad but subject to numerous exceptions and further undercut by statute. *E.g.*, Criminal Justice Act 2003, §§ 116(2)(a)–(d) (broad exemptions for statements made by persons who cannot be easily made trial witnesses).

[21] *See, e.g.*, William E. O'Brian Jr., *Confrontation: The Defiance of the English Courts*, 15 Int'l J. Evid. & Proof 93 (2011).

[22] *See Crawford*, 541 U.S. at 51 (noting that the confrontation clause "applies to 'witnesses' against the accused—in other words, those who 'bear testimony.' 1 N. Webster, An American Dictionary of the English Language (1828).").

[23] Davis v. Washington, 547 U.S. 813, 823–24 (2006).

If an out-of-court statement is testimonial, then (for the moment assuming that the accused has not waived or forfeited the right, and putting aside the possibility of exceptions to the right) it cannot be used against the accused to prove the truth of what the statement says unless the accused has had, or will have, an adequate opportunity for confrontation, which includes cross-examination.[24] Moreover, that right must occur at trial, unless the witness has become unavailable, by death or otherwise; in that case, evidence of the prior testimonial statement may be admitted.

In other words, the confrontation right contains an absolute rule (subject again to the same caveats) and a rule of preference. The absolute rule is that the testimony of witnesses may not be presented against an accused unless the accused will have had an adequate opportunity for confrontation, including cross-examination. The rule of preference is that unless the witness is deemed unavailable to testify at trial, the opportunity for confrontation must occur at trial; only if the witness is then unavailable may her prior testimonial statement be introduced for the truth of what it asserts.

This, of course, leaves open the central question of what should be considered a testimonial statement. The *Crawford* case did not attempt to resolve the matter. It did offer illustrations—such as "[a]n accuser who makes a formal accusation to government officers"[25]—and cited possible definitions, but it did not adopt one.

Under the most satisfactory of the definitions *Crawford* considered, testimonial statements are those made under circumstances that "would lead an objective witness reasonably to believe that the statement would be available for use at a later trial."[26] The Court appeared to come close to adopting that definition in *Melendez-Diaz v. Massachusetts*, when, in rendering what it regarded as a "rather straightforward application" of *Crawford* to hold that a forensic laboratory report was testimonial, it regarded as sufficient that the analyst who authored the report clearly understood its anticipated evidentiary use.[27] But the Court has not consistently held to this approach.

2. Fresh Accusations

Crawford involved a statement by an observer of a knifing. She made the statement to the police, at a station house, "in response to structured police questioning" and under

[24] Melendez-Diaz v. Massachusetts, 557 U.S. 305, 309 (2009) ("A witness's testimony against a defendant is... inadmissible unless the witness appears at trial or, if the witness is unavailable, the defendant had a prior opportunity for cross-examination."). Note that the right applies only if the statement is presented to prove the truth of what it asserts; though the confrontation right has not been satisfied, it may be introduced for another purpose. The classic case is *Tennessee v. Street*, 471 U.S. 409 (1985). There, the accused contended that he had been coerced into repeating the substance of a confession given by a confederate. The prosecution was allowed to present the confederate's confession—not to prove the truth of the factual assertions made in it but to show that it was in fact substantially different from the accused's.

[25] 541 U.S. at 51.

[26] *Id.* at 52 (quoting Brief for National Association of Criminal Defense Lawyers).

[27] 557 U.S. 305, 309–12 (2009).

conditions of considerable formality, some hours later. In this context, the Supreme Court held, the statement was in response to a law-enforcement interrogation, and so testimonial "under any conceivable definition."[28] Subsequent cases involving accusations made closer to the time of the incident and under less formal conditions tested the bounds of the category of testimonial statements.

A pair of cases heard in tandem by the Court both concerned accusations of domestic violence made to the authorities shortly after the fact by women who did not ultimately testify at trial. The Court declared:

> Statements are nontestimonial when made in the course of police interrogation under circumstances objectively indicating that the primary purpose of the interrogation is to enable police assistance to meet an ongoing emergency. They are testimonial when the circumstances objectively indicate that there is no such ongoing emergency, and that the primary purpose of the interrogation is to establish or prove past events potentially relevant to later criminal prosecution.[29]

One might, of course, question (as one justice did) whether it is practical or even theoretically coherent, when the statement is made in the course of an emergency, to determine that one purpose or another is the primary one (assuming for purposes of argument that only one purpose can be primary, a matter that has not been resolved). Consider the facts of one of the two cases, *Davis v. Washington*. There, the accusations were made, as part of an emergency call, while the accused was not at large, but apparently still in the presence of the caller herself, who was in an obvious state of imminent distress. By a 9-0 vote, the Court concluded that at least the caller's first statements were not testimonial. Certainly the statement was made in significant part for assistance in resolving the emergency. But was it not made as well in expectation that it would cause legal consequences to be imposed on the alleged assailant? The fact that early on in the conversation the operator asked for the full name—including middle name[30]—of the suspect lends force to this view. So does the fact that, at the end of the call, the operator dispatched officers *to find the accused*,[31] not to go first to the caller to protect her.

By contrast, in the companion case, *Hammon v. Indiana*, the Court held by an 8-1 vote that the accusation was testimonial, and it indicated that it did not regard the issue as particularly close. There, after police responded to an emergency call, the woman made the statement to one officer in her living room while another officer held her husband, the accused, at bay in another room. The Court recognized that the interrogation lacked certain features in *Crawford* that helped demonstrate the testimonial nature of the statements there—that the questioning occurred in the station house, that it was tape-recorded, and that the speaker had been given formal warnings—but it declined to prescribe an independent condition that only statements bearing certain earmarks of

28 541 U.S. at 53 n.4.

29 Davis v. Washington, 547 U.S. 813, 822 (2006).

30 *Id.* at 817–18.

31 *Id.* at 818.

formality would be considered testimonial. The statements in *Hammon* were "formal enough" to be deemed testimonial because "[o]bjectively viewed, the primary, if not indeed the sole, purpose of the interrogation was to investigate a possible crime." The statements were "an obvious substitute for live testimony" because they did "precisely *what a witness does* on direct examination."[32]

The Court further expanded on the emergency idea in *Michigan v. Bryant*.[33] In that case, it appeared that, after being mortally wounded by gunshot, the victim drove himself several blocks to a parking lot. There, he made statements to various police officers identifying the assailant. None of the officers made any attempt to find the assailant immediately or to protect themselves or the victim, who died several hours later. Nevertheless, a majority of the Court concluded that the victim's statements were not testimonial. The majority thought the condition of the victim was of significance, because it shed light on whether he was capable of having "any purpose at all" in responding to the officers' questions (though many victims seem, even in extremis, to have a well-developed purpose to identify their assailants) and also on the officers' purpose in conducting the questioning. (Justice Scalia, the author of *Crawford* and *Davis*, pointed out in dissent that the proper perspective to take in assessing the testimonial quality of the statement is that of the speaker, the purported witness, not that of a questioner, if there is one.) The majority also thought that the fact that the assault was by firearm bore on the emergency question—even though there was no immediate attempt to find the shooter. It also suggested that there might be factors other than emergency that might lead a court to conclude that the "primary purpose" of the exchange was to prove facts for future prosecution.

Bryant indicates that the law governing fresh accusations is in an unfortunate state. The "primary purpose" test is unhelpful, and it tends to cause focus on the questioner, when there is one, rather than on the purported witness. It is too easy for a court to identify a purpose of a conversation other than proof of facts for prosecution and characterize that purpose as primary. It would be better if courts spoke in terms of the reasonable anticipation of the speaker (the purported witness), taking into account that any purpose of an interrogator, if apparent to the speaker, may be significant in assessing the reasonable anticipation of a person in the speaker's position. If such a reasonable anticipation is that the statement would likely be used in prosecution, the statement should be deemed testimonial.

In *Bryant*, it is difficult avoid the conclusion that the victim must have known that his statement would in all probability be used to prosecute the person he had identified as the shooter. If, in context, it would nevertheless be an unappealing result to prevent the trier of fact from learning of the accusation, that is presumably because if the accused did in fact kill his victim, he should not be able to complain about the absence of confrontation—which his wrongdoing had caused. This suggests that the shooter may have forfeited the right, a matter that is discussed in Section IV.4.

[32] *Id.* at 829–30. [33] 562 U.S. 344 (2011).

Bryant suggests that the law governing fresh accusations is in a dissatisfactory state. The "primary purpose" test does not correspond to the nature of the confrontation right and cannot provide clear guidance. The critical question should be whether a reasonable person in the position of the speaker would anticipate prosecutorial use.

3. Forensic Laboratory Reports

Forensic laboratory reports provide another situation in which the question of whether a statement is testimonial frequently arises. Before *Crawford*, it had become a common practice in many states for the prosecution to introduce such a report rather than presenting the live testimony of the analyst who prepared it. But in *Melendez-Diaz*, the Supreme Court, by a 5–4 vote, held that certificates attesting that analyzed substances contained cocaine were testimonial; it was clear that the analysts who prepared the reports were aware of the evidentiary use to which they would be put.

The *Melendez-Diaz* majority swept aside a slew of objections to its holding—that the statements in the report were not accusatory, that the analysts were not conventional or ordinary witnesses of the type traditionally associated with the confrontation right, that the reports did not recount historical events but rather presented the results of "neutral, scientific testing," that the reports were akin to the types of business records traditionally admitted, that the accused in each case could have called the analyst as his own witness had he so chosen, and that requiring the attendance of the analysts would be unduly costly. As to this last objection, and some of the others, the Court regarded it as not only insufficient in principle but as factually dubious. And indeed, some states had long managed perfectly well even while protecting the right of the accused to demand that the prosecution bring the lab analyst in as a live witness. The fact is that in most contexts—but not all—the accused has no desire for the lab analyst to testify live against him and is willing to allow the admission of the less dramatically potent report. The dissenters may well have thought that it is a worthless exercise to require lab analysts to come to court from time to time to answer, under oath, adverse questions posed on behalf of the accused persons whom their reports might condemn to punishment. But that idea should have been dispelled long ago by the recurrence of scandals that have besmirched some forensic laboratories. Moreover, the *Melendez-Diaz* Court made clear that a state can ease the burden by adopting a simple "notice and demand" statute. Under these statutes, if the prosecutor gives timely notice of intent to offer a written laboratory report, the accused must, if he wishes the author to testify live, make a timely demand to that effect or be deemed to have waived the confrontation right.

The four *Melendez-Diaz* dissenters did not give up, however.[34] In *Bullcoming v. New Mexico*,[35] they sought to limit the scope and effect of the doctrine. There, the analyst

[34] Indeed, almost immediately after the *Melendez-Diaz* decision, they made what appears to have been an abortive attempt to take advantage of a change of membership on the Court to secure reversal of one of its holdings. The attempt, if that is what it was, did not succeed. Briscoe v. Virginia, 130 S. Ct. 1316 (2010).

[35] 564 U.S. 247 (2011).

who prepared the report in question had been placed on administrative leave and did not testify at trial. In his place, the state presented another analyst from the same laboratory who had not observed the testing that underlay the report. The four *Melendez-Diaz* dissenters thought that was satisfactory—but five justices did not.

Subsequently, however, in *Williams v. Illinois*,[36] the bloc of four, while outvoted on virtually every principle it attempted to establish, was able to find a fifth vote for the result it sought. This was a "cold hit" DNA rape case. That is, at the time a swab (presumably containing the perpetrator's DNA) was taken from the victim, the authorities had not yet identified a suspect. The swab was sent to an out-of-state laboratory, which sent back a report asserting that male DNA with a given profile stated in the report had been found on the swab. Search of a database of DNA profiles identified the accused, Williams, who was then charged with the crime. At trial, no one from the out-of-state lab testified at trial. Indeed, the report itself was never formally presented in evidence; rather, the state presented an in-court witness who testified that, in her opinion, the profile matched that of the accused.[37] The four *Melendez-Diaz* dissenters concluded that there was no violation of the confrontation right; they did not believe the laboratory's report was presented for the truth of what it asserted, and they did not regard it as testimonial.

Five justices rejected the first of these contentions, which was based on the perception that the report was used only as the basis for the opinion of the in-court witness; the only proof of the DNA profile found on the crime-scene swab, an essential predicate for the in-court witness's opinion, was from the report made by the out-of-state laboratory.[38] And the four-justice bloc based their conclusion that the report was not testimonial in large part on the contention that the report was not directed at a "targeted individual."[39] The other five justices also rejected this contention, which seems to have no basis in the history or rationale of the confrontation right; there is much testimony, such as a description of the crime scene or of the crime itself, that is clearly subject to the confrontation right but that might be made before any targeted suspect is identified. But Justice Thomas—who had been the sole dissenter in *Hammon v. Indiana*, on the ground that

[36] 567 U.S. 50 (2012).

[37] The state did present a witness who had analyzed the sample containing the accused's known DNA profile.

[38] The predicate for the in-court witness's statement was that a competent forensic analyst had accurately generated a profile of DNA found on the crime-scene swab. The evidence may have been presented under an alternative theory that would have obviated the problem; the prosecution could have declined to rely on the accuracy of the lab but simply pointed to the remarkable coincidence that the lab had reported a series of numbers that happened to match the DNA of a person who lived near the crime scene and was a plausible suspect. It was extremely improbable that the lab would come up with a profile matching the accused's in any way other than by accurately testing his DNA—either by concocting a profile, or by mistakenly analyzing someone else's DNA, or by accurately analyzing the DNA of another person who happened to have the same DNA profile as the suspect (a remote possibility because it is highly unlikely, unless the suspect has an identical twin, that there is such a person). Given this extreme improbability, the inference becomes strong, even without relying on the accuracy of the lab, that in fact the lab analyzed the accused's DNA.

[39] 567 U.S. at 84.

the statement there was insufficiently formal to be testimonial—reached a similar conclusion here about the lab report because, although it was signed by two analysts and clearly contemplated evidentiary use, it was not formally certified. That made a majority of the Court for the proposition that the report was not testimonial, though there was no opinion for the Court, because Justice Thomas rejected the reasoning of the other four in the majority and no other justice joined in his idiosyncratic view.

Indeed, that view seems to turn matters on their head. It provides an incentive for states to encourage the production of, and to allow admissibility of, reports that are plainly produced in contemplation of prosecutorial use but that lack certification or some other measure of extreme formality. And it mistakes the significance of formality. A statement is not rendered non-testimonial by the absence of formalities. Rather, some formalities—notably the oath and, if they can be considered formalities, confrontation and cross-examination—are necessary to make testimony *acceptable*. In the Court's most recent case, Justice Thomas spoke of solemnity rather than formality; that may get closer to the mark if one recognizes that solemnity is not a matter of the mood with which one makes a statement but rather a measure of the speaker's recognition of the gravity of the consequences that might follow from prosecutorial use of her statement.

In the meantime, the 4–1–4 split in *Williams* has created a good deal of confusion, which is likely to persist until the Court once again turns to the realm of forensic lab reports.

4. Waiver and Forfeiture

Although the confrontation right is categorical in nature, the accused can waive or forfeit it. Waiver may be explicit or implicit. The accused waives the right simply by not making a timely objection to evidence that might violate it—and under a valid "notice and demand" statute, the objection may have to be made before trial.

The accused may forfeit the confrontation right when he engages in serious misconduct that foreseeably renders the witness unavailable to testify at trial. In that circumstance, it seems inappropriate to allow the accused to object on grounds of lack of confrontation to secondary evidence of the witness's testimony; after all, it was the witness's misconduct that caused the unavailability. The most common types of such misconduct are intimidating the witness and murdering her; in some cases, the accused may by force or trickery keep the witness from coming to court. It is also sufficient if the accused acquiesced in the wrongful conduct that caused the witness's unavailability.[40]

A forfeiture contention requires proof that satisfies the court in a side proceeding that the accused did in fact engage or acquiesce in the alleged misconduct and that it did

[40] *Cf.* Fed. R. Evid. 804(b)(6) ("a party that wrongfully caused—or acquiesced in wrongfully causing—the declarant's unavailability as a witness"). Note the far more lenient approach taken in England and Wales: fear on the part of the witness is enough to excuse her from testifying at trial, without any need of showing that the accused played a role in creating that fear. Criminal Justice Act 2003, §§ 116(2)(e), 116(3).

indeed prevent the witness from testifying. This can be a difficult matter. Furthermore, a court carefully applying forfeiture doctrine should ask whether, even assuming the defendant engaged in the conduct and it led to the witness's unavailability, the prosecution could have taken measures to mitigate the problem. For example, if the witness is intimidated, the prosecution might take steps to protect her—before, during, and after her testimony.[41] And even if the accused mortally wounded the witness, there may be a period in which it would be feasible, and not inhumane, for the prosecution to take the witness's deposition subject to confrontation.[42]

A special problem arises when the conduct that allegedly caused the witness to be unavailable is the same as the conduct with which the accused is charged. Consider the facts of *Giles v. California*.[43] Giles's former girlfriend, Avie, made a statement to police describing an assault by Giles. Three weeks later, he shot Avie to death. He claimed self-defense. The prosecution sought to introduce evidence of the prior statement. Giles objected; the statement was testimonial under *Hammon v. Indiana*, and he had not had an opportunity to cross-examine Avie. But, said the prosecution, that was because Giles killed Avie. And that, of course, is the very conduct with which Giles was charged.

The identity of issues should not in itself be considered a problem. The same issue has become material to the case for two different reasons—determining whether Giles committed the crime charged and whether he forfeited the confrontation right—but that is neither unusual[44] nor a logical conundrum; the issue can be decided separately for each purpose. Indeed, if there is a jury, as in most American criminal trials, it will decide if the accused is guilty of the crime, but beforehand, the judge will decide, after a side proceeding and perhaps on a different evidentiary base, whether the accused has forfeited the confrontation right.

In *Giles*, however, the Supreme Court imposed another limitation on forfeiture doctrine: It is not sufficient for forfeiture that the misconduct have caused the unavailability of the witness and that this result was foreseeable; the misconduct must have been *intended* for that purpose.[45] Thus, even if the trial judge, in determining the forfeiture question, were to find that Giles had murdered Avie, there could be no forfeiture, no

[41] *See, e.g.*, Richard Devine, *Targeting High Risk Domestic Violence Cases: The Cook County, Chicago, Experience*, 34 APR Prosecutor 30 (Mar./Apr. 2000) (describing Target Abuse Call, which achieves goals of holding offenders accountable, with a 90 percent conviction rate, and ensuring safety of victims, approximately 80 percent of whom participate in prosecution).

[42] *See, e.g.*, R v. Forbes, Holt 599, 171 E.R. 354 (1812). Indeed, this consideration may explain the traditional hearsay exception for dying declarations; that exception only applies if the speaker appeared to be on the verge of death. The justification usually given for the exception is the dubious idea that the imminence of death guarantees reliability of the statement. A more plausible justification is that the traditional law reflects the confrontation right as qualified by the forfeiture doctrine, which in turn is limited by the prosecution's responsibility of mitigation—and that the necessity to mitigate by taking a victim's deposition subject to confrontation ends when death is imminent.

[43] 554 U.S. 353 (2008).

[44] For example, a defendant may be accused of a conspiracy crime, and the admissibility of a statement by another person may depend on showing that she and the defendant were members of the same conspiracy. *See, e.g.*, Fed. R. Evid. 801(d)(1)(E).

[45] 554 U.S. at 359–60; *see also* Fed. R. Evid. 804(b)(6) ("... and did so intending that result").

matter how abhorrent his reasons may have been, unless the evidentiary consequences of killing her were part of his thinking.

The *Giles* Court justified the result in part on equitable grounds, but it is difficult to see the equity in allowing a murderer to complain about his inability to cross-examine a witness when he himself rendered the witness unavailable by murdering her, and to succeed in the complaint because he was motivated to kill by unacceptable reasons other than desire to prevent live testimony.

Because the *Giles* rule yields unappealing results, a predictable consequence was that it would lead courts to compensate by adopting an unduly narrow conception of what statements are testimonial. And indeed, this appears to have come about in *Michigan v. Bryant*, discussed in Section IV.2, in which, because of *Giles*, a ruling of forfeiture was not available, and the Court permitted admissibility by taking a restrictive view of what is testimonial.

5. Children

Particularly vexing problems are presented when prosecutors offer the observations of children. This problem has become more salient in recent decades, as prosecutions for child abuse have become more common.

Evidence of the statement of a child may be highly probative evidence of a crime. Often, indeed, the statement describes, and is critical proof of, a crime of abuse imposed upon the child herself. But testifying at trial, especially in the presence of the person she is accusing, may be a particularly difficult ordeal for a young child, at least in the short term. The child's reaction, either in anticipation or in the event, may be to refuse to speak or otherwise to become incommunicative.

Nevertheless, the defendant's rights must be respected. It is a most unsatisfactory result for an accused to be subjected to criminal punishment, possibly very severe, and not have any opportunity to pose questions to the person whose statement is principally responsible for his conviction. Furthermore, prosecutors, recognizing that the live testimony of the child will likely have a powerful impact on the jury, often want the child to testify at trial. Sometimes, adequate preparation will mitigate the problem; if, for example, the prosecutor acclimates the child to the courtroom, lets her sit where she will be during trial, and shows her where the accused will be, the child may better able to testify face to face with the accused.

But when the child cannot, or will not, testify at trial, or at a pretrial proceeding subject to cross-examination and confrontation, courts may face a difficult choice. The situations may be broken down into two separate categories, depending on whether the witness appears willing and able to testify at trial under modified conditions. Further, the child's age and stage of development, and the audience of the statement, are factors that may critically affect analysis,

In the first category, the child is willing to testify at trial, but the prosecution seeks to modify the usual conditions of testimony. In a pre-*Crawford* case, *Maryland v. Craig*,[46] the

[46] 497 U.S. 836 (1990).

Supreme Court held that upon a sufficient showing of likely trauma to the child—there a girl six years old—the defendant's confrontation right must give way in part, and the child may testify out of the presence of the accused and the jury, so long as they can observe the testimony, including the witness's demeanor, by video transmission and the accused can communicate electronically with counsel. The *Craig* decision, reflecting an open-textured weighing of costs and benefits, is totally incongruous with the later decision in *Crawford*, but the Supreme Court has not shown any disposition to revisit the matter. In some cases, trial courts take seriously the burden of making a case-specific determination of whether the child is likely to suffer trauma from testifying in front of the accused; in others they reach that conclusion more perfunctorily.

In the second category of situations, when the child is determined to be completely unable to testify at trial, the court must determine whether the confrontation right precludes prosecution use of her earlier statement. If the child is very young, the court is unlikely to conclude that the statement was testimonial. Indeed, in *Ohio v. Clark*,[47] the only post-*Crawford* case in which the Supreme Court has considered the confrontation clause implications of statements by children, the Court indicated that it would be very unlikely that a statement by a very young child would ever be considered testimonial.[48]

One can go further, in a sense: A sound view is that below some threshold of age or cognitive development a child is incapable of being a witness altogether for purposes of the confrontation right. Very young children do not have the capacity to realize the solemn potential consequences of their statements—that their statements might cause others to change their view of reality and therefore to impose punishment on an accused person.[49] Arguably, they also are not at a stage of moral development at which it is appropriate to impose on them the burden and ordeal of being a witness.[50] On this view, thinking of very young children as witnesses under the framework used for adults is altogether inappropriate. (Views might vary as to what age or stage of development might be considered very young for these purposes.)

But to say that a very young child should not be considered a witness for purposes of the confrontation right does not mean that the accused should be left bereft of rights altogether. It still must be recognized that the child's statement may be critical evidence used to condemn the accused, and it appears to violate fundamental norms of fairness (expressed in the U.S. Constitution by the due process clauses of the Fifth and Fourteenth Amendments) to allow the accused to be convicted by virtue of the child's statement without having had an opportunity, if one can be reasonably afforded, to pose questions to the child in some manner. But such questioning should not be considered a testimonial event, and it need not be conducted by an attorney. Rather, the examination should be conducted, under an approved protocol, by a qualified expert; the child, in this view, is not a witness, but she is still a source of important evidence, and the examination is

[47] 135 S. Ct. 2173 (2015). [48] *Id.* at 2182.

[49] This is not inconsistent with the fact, known to parents of multiple children, that a very young child may come to understand that pointing a finger in blame to a sibling may cause the pointer to avoid punishment. That is a learned behavior of association, which does not require the complex understanding that one's statement may alter another person's understanding of reality.

[50] Clark, *supra* note 8.

not cross-examination, but rather expert examination of that source, who happens to be a very young human.[51]

Older children, who are fully able to appreciate the gravity of their statements, should be treated in the same manner as adults and thus subject to confrontation when their statements are fairly characterized as testimonial.

One other recurrent issue, which affects adults as well, arises with particular frequency with respect to children. After a suspected incident of abuse, the child may be examined by medical and social service personnel. Prosecutors will argue that the primary purpose of such an examination is care and treatment of the child, and that therefore any statements made by the child during the course of the examination should not be considered testimonial. But if the child is of sufficient maturity to realize that her statements will in all likelihood be passed on to police or prosecutorial authorities, and therefore used in legal proceedings against the alleged perpetrator, such statements should be deemed testimonial. Indeed, treating them otherwise gives the authorities a perverse incentive to stand back and allow medical and social service personnel to conduct whatever inquiry may be appropriate for law enforcement as well as other purposes, with everybody involved knowing full well that the child's statements will be used in an attempt to convict the accused person.

6. Remote Confrontation

As discussed in Section IV.5, the Supreme Court has provided that in some circumstances a child may testify from outside the courtroom, and outside the presence of the jury, with her testimony shown in the courtroom by electronic video transmission. The temptation arises to use the same technique when it is difficult or impossible to bring the witness to the courthouse. This can occur, for example, when a witness is very ill, or beyond the reach of the jurisdiction to compel her live appearance, or when an expert lives and works at a great distance from the court.

The accused might consent to have the testimony given remotely. And in some circumstances, though it is not possible for the witness to be brought to court, it is possible for the accused and counsel to be brought to the witness, where a deposition might be taken; given the unavailability of the witness at trial, the deposition would be admissible under traditional principles.

If we put these possibilities aside, we see that analysis of a procedure for remote testimony must take into account the two basic aspects of the confrontation right—the right to have witnesses brought face to face and the right to pose adverse questions. The former, as discussed in the historical section, has older roots, and if one gives it force then testimony given outside the physical presence of the accused raises a serious issue. Even before *Crawford*, the Supreme Court reflected this view. In 2002, it declined, by a

[51] This view is fully elaborated in Richard D. Friedman & Stephen J. Ceci, *The Child Quasi Witness*, 82 U. Chi. L. Rev. 89 (2015).

7–2 vote, to pass on to Congress (as it usually does with proposals emerging from the complex federal rule-making process) a proposal that, in some exigent circumstances and under prescribed conditions, would allow testimony to be taken away from court and outside the presence of the jury, but presented in the courtroom by contemporaneous two-way electronic-video transmission. "Virtual confrontation might be sufficient to protect virtual constitutional rights," wrote Justice Scalia, explaining his agreement with the decision. "I doubt whether it is sufficient to protect real ones."[52] Under a less categorical rule, the question would depend on whether the effects of confrontation are substantially diminished by the fact that the accused is visible to the witness only on screen rather than being immediately present. This is a subject on which, at present, there is little empirical basis for a firm conclusion.[53]

If the system puts little or no weight on the witness being brought face to face with the accused, and emphasizes only the right of adverse examination, it will naturally be more receptive to remote testimony given outside the presence of the accused. Even if so, assuming that the questioning counsel, as well as the accused, is not in the same room as the witness, there remains an open question whether the separation is likely to make adverse examination substantially less effective.

In any event, if remote testimony is to be allowed, a court should ensure that the quality of the transmission is sufficiently good, without noticeable lags, to prevent any gratuitous impairment of the ability of the cross-examiner to press the witness. And it should also ensure that each of the participants in the trial has a clear view of what is happening in the other room.

7. The Extent of Constitutionally Protected Impeachment

Now suppose that the witness does testify face to face with the accused, as the confrontation right demands. The right is not yet satisfied: The accused has a right to cross-examine the witness, and more broadly to impeach her. But plainly the accused's right must be limited; he cannot demand an answer to any question he pleases. And by nature, those limits must be dependent on the facts of the particular case. (This aspect of the right therefore stands in contrast with the categorical right to demand that an adverse witness be brought face to face.) Some guideposts may be stated, however.

On the one hand, the accused has no right to use confrontation as an opportunity for no or insubstantial reason, to harass the witness, to prolong the trial, or to create a distraction. And in some circumstances, if the accused poses a question to a witness and the witness fails to answer it, that is all the accused can demand.[54]

52 Amendments to Rule 26(b) of the Federal Rules of Criminal Procedure (April 29, 2002) (statement of Scalia, J.), 207 F.R.D. 89, 94.

53 *See* Richard D. Friedman, *Remote Testimony*, 35 U. Mich. J.L. Ref. 695 (2002).

54 In some circumstances, failure to answer fully may help the accused by suggesting that the witness is evasive and has not been telling the truth. But if a prior statement of the witness has been admitted and

On the other hand, the accused should be given a full opportunity to explore all potential sources of weakness in the witness's testimony. He should have some opportunity to reveal defects in the witness's general testimonial capacities—the abilities to perceive, remember, and communicate, and inclination to tell the truth. And especially, he should have ample opportunity to reveal defective operation of those capacities in the particular case.

Of particular importance is bias, which may be considered a factor relating to the particular case or parties that, whatever the witness's general character for truthfulness, may tend to dissuade her from telling the truth with respect to a given matter in the circumstances of the case being tried. The importance of allowing the accused to reveal bias is so important that *in some settings* it demands that other policies be overridden. These may include, for example, a rule against disclosure of a juvenile's prior disciplinary record[55] and the ordinarily strong policy against disclosure, in a rape case, of the complainant's sexual inclinations and prior sexual history.[56]

V. The Confrontation Right in Europe

In recent decades, many adjudicative systems outside the common law world have adopted a form of the confrontation right.[57] Most important is Article 6(3)(d) of the European Convention on Human Rights, which guarantees a criminal defendant the right "to examine or have examined witnesses against him...."[58] (Article 14, § 3(e), of the International Covenant on Civil and Political Rights is virtually identical.) Construction of this right has for the most part been unburdened by the presence of a rule against hearsay, because most of the systems to which the Convention applies have no such rule.

As with the confrontation clause of the U.S. Constitution, Article 6(3)(d) raises the question of who shall be considered witnesses. It has been clearly established that this is a term that has an "autonomous meaning" for purposes of the Convention—national courts cannot limit the coverage of the Convention—and that witnesses do not include only those who testify in court. Despite some loose language by the European Court on Human Rights that might suggest that anybody who makes a statement that is before the court and potentially used in fact-finding may be a witness, there seems to be an

the witness fails to confirm its substance, the natural conclusion may be that the witness believes her prior statement to be accurate but has since been intimidated.

[55] Davis v. Alaska, 415 U.S. 308 (1974).

[56] Lewis v. Wilkinson, 307 F.3d 413 (6th Cir. 2002) (holding that the confrontation right was violated by excluding portion of complainant's diary that could reasonably be read to imply that complainant fabricated rape charge for personal reasons).

[57] Stefano Maffei, *The Right to Confrontation in Europe: Absent, Anonymous and Vulnerable Witnesses* 9 (2d ed. 2009).

[58] The same provision also guarantees the right "to obtain the attendance and examination of witnesses on his behalf under the same conditions as witnesses against him."

underlying standard that, as in the United States, only statements testimonial in nature should invoke the right.[59] Statements made to investigating authorities are likely to make one be considered a witness, but other statements may have this effect as well.[60] The right is ordinarily exercised at trial, but the European Court has at least suggested that, if it is exercised at an earlier time, there may be no need for the witness to testify live at trial.[61] The right is one to put questions—ordinarily through counsel, but a system may provide that the defense has only the right to suggest questions for the judge to put.[62] The Convention has not been held to provide a right to have the witnesses brought face to face.[63]

The right to have witnesses examined is treated as part of a broader right to a fair trial under Article 6(1), and the European Court is sometimes quite lenient if it believes that, overall, the trial was fair. This passage from *Doorson v. The Netherlands* is characteristic:

> 80. Despite the Court of Appeal's efforts it was impossible to secure R.'s attendance at the hearing. In the circumstances it was open to the Court of Appeal to have regard to the statement obtained by the police, especially since it could consider that statement to be corroborated by other evidence before it. . . . Accordingly, no unfairness can be found in this respect. . . .

The Court is also tolerant at times of anonymous evidence, though the result appears to depend on a case-specific weighing of all the circumstances.[64] The Court is receptive to special procedures in the case of child witnesses, and there appears to be a greater tendency in Europe than in the United States to apply such procedures as well with respect to adult complainants in sexual offense cases.[65]

[59] Maffei, *supra* note 57, at 85 (asserting that the practice of the European Court on Human Rights "fully aligns—albeit not explicitly—with the definition of *testimonial statements* developed in the U.S. after *Crawford*"). Maffei cites *Atánasov v. Macedonia (No. 2)*, App. No. 41188/06, Eur. Ct. H.R., Apr. 19, 2011, in which the domestic court had improperly relied on an accusatory letter, evidently written to the authorities.

[60] Maffei, *supra* note 57, at 84–85.

[61] Stefan Trechsel, *Human Rights in Criminal Proceedings* 307–08 (2005).

[62] *Id.* at 310–11.

[63] *See* Doorson v. The Netherlands, App. No. 20524/92, Eur. Ct. H.R., Mar. 26, 1996, § 25.

[64] Trechsel, *supra* note 61, at 315–18; Maffei, *supra* note 57, at 55–60.

[65] One analysis suggests that, in addition to protecting child witnesses from trauma, considerations that persuade a court in the United States that video testimony is justified include the need to combat international drug smuggling and to protect the national security, the health of a seriously ill witness, or a witness who has been intimidated (though note that in that case the forfeiture doctrine should apply). Jessica Smith, *Remote Testimony and Related Procedures Impacting a Criminal Defendant's Confrontation Rights*, University of California School of Government, Administration of Justice Bulletin No. 2013/02, at 10–11 (Feb. 2013). Although numerous commentators have advocated allowing such remote testimony in the case of adult rape complainants, e.g., *Allowing Adult Sexual Assault Victims to Testify at Trial via Live Video Technology*, National Crime Victim Law Institute, Violence Against Women Bulletin (Sept. 2011), it appears that so far very few courts have actually done so. *See R.T. v. Maria O.*, 56 Misc.3d 820, 53 N.Y.S. 3d 889 (Family Ct., Bronx Cty. 2017) (reviewing case law and highlighting *People v. Burton*, 556 N.W.2d 201 (Mich. App. 1996), a case involving a mentally infirm witness).

VI. Conclusion

Crawford and the development of an extensive body of law under Article 6(3)(d) to protect the right of an accused to question adverse witnesses have both been important and favorable developments. Over the long run, less categorical approaches such as that of the European Court may break down more quickly. The accused's right comes up against the interest in allowing a court to consider all highly probative evidence, and the temptation to favor the latter will often be difficult to resist unless the right is articulated in sturdy, categorical terms.

References

Sherman J. Clark, *An Accuser-Obligation Approach to the Confrontation Clause*, 81 Neb. L. Rev. 1258 1261 (2003)

Richard D. Friedman, *Confrontation: The Search for Basic Principles*, 86 Geo. L.J. 1011 (1998)

Richard D. Friedman, *Remote Testimony*, 35 U. Mich. J.L. Ref. 695 (2002)

Richard D. Friedman & Stephen J. Ceci, *The Child Quasi Witness*, 82 U. Chi. L. Rev. 89 (2015)

Richard D. Friedman & Bridget McCormack, *Dial-In Testimony*, 150 U. Pa. L. Rev. 1171 (2002)

Stefano Maffei, *The Right to Confrontation in Europe: Absent, Anonymous and Vulnerable Witnesses* (2d ed. 2009)

Jessica Smith, *Remote Testimony and Related Procedures Impacting a Criminal Defendant's Confrontation Rights*, University of California School of Government, Administration of Justice Bulletin No. 2013/02 (Feb. 2013)

Stefan Trechsel, *Human Rights in Criminal Proceedings* (2005)

CHAPTER 39

COMPARATIVE ASSESSMENT OF SENTENCING LAWS, PRACTICES, AND TRENDS

TATJANA HÖRNLE

I. Introduction

Criminal courts have to make decisions about the type and quantity of punishment. In contemporary legal systems, common sanctions are imprisonment or non-custodial sentences such as loss of assets or income (fines) and community service.[1] Judges sometimes claim that a natural sense of justice and their intuition leads them to the sentence that fits both the offense and the offender. However, legal systems under the rule of law require interpersonal rules regarding how to proceed at every stage of criminal proceedings including sentencing. The first part of this chapter covers theoretical foundations. Sentencing presupposes deliberations about punishment as a response to past wrongdoing or as a means to prevent future crimes. Desert-based sentencing requires criteria on how to assess the seriousness of crimes (Section II.). In the second part, I will sketch the framework for sentencing and sentencing procedures in different legal systems (Section III.). In the last section, the focus is on the overall sentence severity or punitiveness of legal systems (Section IV).

[1] I will not deal with the specific problems of sanctions that target offenders' bodies such as the death penalty (*see* for its prevalence Amnesty International, *Global Report: Death Sentences and Executions 2016*, at 4–10 (2017)) and corporal punishment (*see* Rudolph Peters, *Crime and Punishment in Islamic Law. Theory and Practice from the Sixteenth to the Twenty-First Century* (2005)).

II. Sentencing Theories

1. Single-Rationale Models, Mixed Models, Hybrid Models

Sentencing theory can be based on a single rationale (either desert or prevention) or combine different rationales in mixed models or hybrid models. *Single-rationale models* develop a uniform sentencing purpose for *all types* of offenses and offenders. Under a desert-based single-rationale model, wrongdoing and guilt must be evaluated and sanctions chosen accordingly—without taking other considerations into account. Under a prevention-based single-rationale model, decision-makers should, for instance, consider the most promising intervention to rehabilitate the offender, without spending much time on evaluating the seriousness of the offense.

Alternatives to single-rationale models are *mixed models*. One possibility would be to assign different rationales to different types of crime. For instance, deterrence could be the single rationale for the sentencing of tax crimes or all white-collar crimes, desert for crimes against persons. Or it might be left to judges to follow their preferences and beliefs, with the effect that, for the criminal justice system as a whole, the sentencing structure would be described as mixed, or, more precisely, eclectic.

The third category consists of *hybrid models* that combine desert and prevention in the justification of sentences.[2] Most modern legal systems apply some version of a hybrid model. The basic assumption is that desert should be a central or anchoring criterion, however, other sentencing rationales can be taken into account, too. One version of hybrid models argues that desert sets both upper and lower limits: criminal punishment must neither be too lenient nor too severe with regard to the seriousness of the offense. This is a widespread approach both in sentencing theory[3] and among courts. The German Federal Court of Justice labels it hybrid theory *Spielraumtheorie* (margin theory).[4] Other types of hybrid models emphasize upper limits drawn by desert but either dispense with lower limits or opt for an asymmetric approach that accords more importance to the upper limits.[5] This allows preventive reasoning (for instance, that the offender has made good progress toward rehabilitation) to justify sentences that would be too lenient from a desert perspective. A third approach argues that desert should be the determining principle, unless it causes an intolerable level of crime and the utilitarian calculus does not cause intolerable injustice.[6]

[2] *See* Richard Frase, *Just Sentencing: Principles and Procedures for a Workable System* 81–120 (2012).

[3] *See* Norval Morris, *Desert as a Limiting Principle*, in *Principled Sentencing: Readings on Theory & Policy* 180 (Andrew von Hirsch & Andrew Ashworth eds., 2d ed. 1998).

[4] Tatjana Hörnle, *Moderate and Non-arbitrary Sentencing without Guideline: The German Experience*, 76 Law & Contemp. Probs. 189, 194 (2013).

[5] Frase, *supra* note 2, at 25–31.

[6] Paul Robinson, *Hybrid Principles for the Distribution of Criminal Sanctions*, 82 Nw. Univ. L. Rev. 19, 39 (1987).

2. Prevention-Based Sentencing

a. *Rehabilitation*

The attraction of the rehabilitative ideal lies in its combination of public policy considerations and humanitarian claims. Rehabilitation was a popular notion from the nineteenth century until the mid-twentieth century, for instance in the American prison system.[7] In the second half of the twentieth century, criticism was raised on normative and empirical grounds.[8] Looking solely at offenders' personal deficiencies rather than at their criminal acts clashes with intuitions of justice. Empirical studies have weakened beliefs in the malleability of adult human beings through criminal punishment.[9] Skepticism about an inflated rehabilitative ideal does, however, not necessarily mean to abandon *all* considerations regarding offenders' future lives. Even a single-rationale desert-based approach leaves some leeway if two different types of sanctions, for example a heavy fine or community service, are comparable in their severity. And desert-based sentencing does, of course, not preclude admission to treatment programs after the duration of imprisonment or another sanction that has been determined according to offense seriousness. If the underlying sentence theory is a hybrid version that combines desert and prevention, courts may choose a somewhat longer custodial sentence for the completion of a treatment program (within the margins of desert) or opt for the lower sentence range if the risk of recidivism is low. Hybrid models that acknowledge upper but not lower desert-based limits open even more space to treat individual offenders mildly. Whether this is a good reason to adopt such a hybrid model depends on a normative choice. Minimizing human suffering and reducing costs are benefits, but if justice is seen as the most important value in the criminal justice system, it is not recommendable to give substantial privileges to the small group of offenders who are socially well adjusted.

b. *Incapacitation*

Incapacitation means to imprison offenders or to create other physical restraints. Even from the perspective of consequentialist thinking, this approach has limits. Restraining *all* offenders for long periods of time would be too expensive and a waste of resources because some will not reoffend anyway. Additionally, obvious justice concerns must be raised against serious restrictions of liberty even after minor offenses. Incapacitation could only be one element *within* a mixed sentencing model that

[7] Edgardo Rotman, *The Failure of Reform: United States 1865–1965*, in *The Oxford History of the Prison: The Practice of Punishment in Western Society* 151 (Norval Morris & David Rothman eds., 1998).

[8] *See* Andrew von Hirsch, *Doing Justice* (1976); Francis Allen, *The Decline of the Rehabilitative Ideal: Penal Policy and Social Purpose* (1981).

[9] *See* Douglas Lipton et al., *The Effectiveness of Correctional Treatment* (1975); Stephen Brody, *The Effectiveness of Sentencing: A Review of the Literature*, in *Offenders or Citizens?: Readings in Rehabilitation* 148 (Philip Priestley & Maurice Vanstone eds., 2011); for a more optimistic assessment, see Francis Cullen, *Rehabilitation: Beyond Nothing Works*, in *Crime and Justice in America, 1975–2025*, 42 *Crime and Justice* 299 (Michael Tonry ed., 2013).

applies different rationales to different offenders. Selective incapacitation strategies have been discussed for offenders with a particularly high risk of serious future crimes[10]—others would be sentenced according to a proportionate sentencing-scheme, perhaps with an emphasis on noncustodial sentences. Mixed sentencing theories that include selective incapacitation presuppose that it is possible to identify a subgroup of high-risk offenders. Despite improvements in risk assessment techniques, it is not possible to avoid errors.[11] Under a regime of selective incapacitation, it is hardly avoidable that some offenders will be subjected to long-term restraints who would have terminated their criminal career earlier. The false-positives problem gives us good reasons not to include selective incapacitation in a standard sentencing model for a wide variety of criminal offenses.

These reservations can, however, be set aside in *extreme cases*: if personality disorders create a propensity to continue with highly aggressive crimes such as killings or brutal sexual offenses. Long-term confinement of such persons can meet the requirements of desert, for instance, if a serial murderer is sentenced to life imprisonment. For other cases, selective incapacitation beyond desert can be defensible if the harm to be expected from future offending is very serious and if there are clear indications of dangerousness. Legal systems allow selective incapacitation in different schemes, see for instance Sexually Violent Predator laws in the United States[12] or mandatory life imprisonment or an extended sentence for dangerous offenders in England.[13] In Germany, preventive detention of indeterminate, potentially life-long duration, is a (not frequently applied) "measure" that can be added to criminal punishment.[14] The best way to organize measures of preventive detention is as a system segregated from criminal punishment.[15]

c. *Deterrence*

Within a general justification theory of criminal law and criminal justice systems, deterrence must play a role. Criminal prohibitions and the institutions enforcing them aim to deter citizens from engaging in certain kinds of behavior. Our topic is, however, neither punishment theory nor policing but sentencing. In this context, the crucial question is whether deterrence should figure as a single-rationale or one component in mixed or

[10] *See* Peter W. Greenwood & Allan Abrahamse, *Selective Incapacitation* (1982).

[11] Christopher Slobogin, *Risk Assessment*, in *The Oxford Handbook of Sentencing and Corrections* 196, 198 (Joan Petersilia & Kevin Reitz eds., 2012).

[12] *See* Charles Patrick Ewing, *Justice Perverted: Sex Offense Law, Psychology, and Public Policy* ch. 1 (2011); Eric Janus, *Preventive Detention of Sex Offenders: The American Experience Versus International Human Rights Norms*, 31 Behav. Sci. & L. 328 (2013).

[13] Sect. 224a, 225, 226a Criminal Justice Act 2003.

[14] § 66 Strafgesetzbuch [German Criminal Code] (*Sicherungsverwahrung*). In 2015, German courts ordered detention in forty-seven cases (Statistisches Bundesamt, Rechtspflege—Strafverfolgung 2015, Fachserie 10, Reihe 3, at 341 (2017)). For the Netherlands: Jan de Keijser, *Never Mind the Pain, It's a Measure! Justifying Measures as Part of the Dutch Bifurcated System of Sanctions*, in *Retributivism Has a Past—Has It a Future?* 188 (Michael Tonry ed., 2011); for the Danish and Norwegian *forvaring* Tapio Lappi-Seppälä, *Nordic Sentencing*, in *Sentencing Policies and Practices in Western Countries: Comparative and Cross-National Perspectives*, 45 *Crime and Justice*, 17, 47–48 (Michael Tonry ed., 2016).

[15] Paul Robinson, *Distributive Principles of Criminal Law: Who Should be Punished How Much?* 130–33 (2008).

hybrid models. The general public and also judges[16] often assume that higher sentences have deterrent effects. A more fine-grained analysis does, however, not support the simple conclusion that deterrence should be a sentencing aim. One could expect significant deterrent effects if every offense, even trivial ones, would be sanctioned with long-term imprisonment. For obvious reasons, this would not be a recommendable strategy, not even from a strictly consequentialist point of view, because costs would explode. With regard to smaller shifts in sentence severity, it is difficult to come up with evidence for marginal deterrence.[17] Judges who explain a moderate increase of punishments with alleged deterrent benefits often make an unsubstantiated claim.

3. Desert-Based Sentencing

a. *Underlying Theories of Punishment*

Different punishment theories converge into a desert-based approach to sentencing. The backward-looking notion of desert can be developed as a matter of intrinsic justice,[18] or as a means to vindicate victims' rights,[19] or in other versions of expressive punishment theories.[20] According to expressive theories, the crucial feature of punishment is censure. As the censuring message is not expressed verbally, but conveyed implicitly *through* the criminal sanction, it is necessarily quantified censure. Punishment expresses not only that the offender has acted wrongfully and is blamed for it, but also *how much* wrong he has done and *how much* blame is appropriate.

Theories that are summarized with the term "positive general prevention" in Germany[21] and "empirical desert" in the United States[22] come to similar conclusions regarding sentencing. They assume that sanctions are necessary because otherwise

[16] Andrew Ashworth, *Sentencing and Criminal Justice* 107–108 (6th ed. 2015) for the English judiciary.

[17] *See* for empirical research Robinson, *supra* note 15, ch. 3 & 4; Travis Pratt et al., *The Empirical Status of Deterrence Theory: A Meta-Analysis*, in *Taking Stock: The Status of Criminological Theory* 367 (Francis Cullen et al. eds., 3d ed. 2011); Daniel Nagin, *Deterrence in the Twenty-First Century*, in *Crime and Justice in America, 1975–2025*, 42 *Crime and Justice* 199 (Michael Tonry ed., 2013); Anthony Bottoms & Andrew von Hirsch, *The Crime-Preventive Impact of Penal Sanctions*, in *The Oxford Handbook of Empirical Legal Research* 96 (Peter Cane & Herbert Kritzer eds., 2010).

[18] *See* for instance Michael Moore, *Placing Blame* Part 1 (1997); Arthur Ripstein, *Force and Freedom: Kant's Legal and Political Philosophy* ch. 10 (2009).

[19] Tatjana Hörnle, *The Role of Victim Rights in Punishment Theory*, in *Penal Censure. Engagements Within and Beyond Desert Theory*, ch. 13 (Antje du Bois-Pedain & Anthony Bottoms eds., 2019).

[20] Joel Feinberg, *The Expressive Function of Punishment*, reprinted in *Why Punish? How Much? A Reader on Punishment* 111 (Michael Tonry ed., 2011); Andrew von Hirsch, *Censure and Sanctions* ch. 2 (1993); R.A. Duff, *Punishment, Communication, and Community* (2001); Christopher Bennett, *The Apology Ritual. A Philosophical Theory of Punishment* (2008).

[21] Markus D. Dubber, *Theories of Crime and Punishment in German Criminal Law*, 53 Am. J. Comp. L. 679, 699–703 (2005); Claus Roxin, *Prevention, Censure and Responsibility: The Recent Debate on the Purposes of Punishment*, in *Liberal Criminal Theory. Essays for Andreas von Hirsch* 23, 28–29 (A.P. Simester et al. eds., 2014).

[22] Paul Robinson, *Intuitions of Justice and the Utility of Desert* ch. 8 (2013).

citizens who are aware of others' delinquent behavior would lose trust in the validity of social and legal norms, and crime rates would rise. Citizens should perceive sentences as just sentences, which means that sentences should be proportionate to the offense.[23]

b. *Evaluating Offense Seriousness*

What is the appropriate method to evaluate offense seriousness? Two competing approaches exist: normative theorizing or measurement of public perceptions. The second approach relies on surveys that ask participants to read descriptions of crimes and to rank them according to their perception of seriousness. Respondents tend to come to similar results,[24] but despite this, surveys could not replace normative sentencing theory. The range of possible crimes is too wide. Surveys cannot cover the panoply of circumstances, culpability, and consequences in all imaginable combinations. In order to approach comprehensiveness, one would need to present not hundreds but many thousands, perhaps millions, of narratives to participants—an impossible task. And the more nuanced and comprehensive descriptions of crimes become, the more one has to expect divergent rankings. Developing criteria for ranking the seriousness of offenses remains a central task for sentencing theory.

Assessing offenses requires a number of normative judgments that are not only complex but also controversial.[25] This concession does not make sentencing theory futile. The aim is a more modest one: to get beyond the traditional judicial approach of "simply knowing the right sentence." Intuitive judgments that jump from an unspecified sentiment regarding seriousness to a numerical sentence should be replaced with a more structured approach. In order to evaluate the seriousness of offenses in a systematic way, the first step should analyze the objective features of the wrong done, divided into two subcategories: outcome-related wrong and other objective elements. Further steps take subjective elements of wrongdoing (in English terminology: mens rea) and graduations of offenders' guilt into account.

c. *Outcomes*

With regard to offenses against persons, outcomes can be described by focusing on the violation of the victim's right to nonintervention[26] and the concrete harm. The first step should consist in assessing the relative importance of the legally protected right (such as the right to life, right to property, or sexual autonomy). Contemporary societies tend to have high esteem for the personal sphere of individuals. Crimes against bodily integrity, sexual autonomy, and dignity are taken seriously, while replaceable goods of moderate

[23] Ulfrid Neumann, *The "Deserved" Punishment*, in *Liberal Criminal Theory. Essays for Andreas von Hirsch* 67, 76 (A.P. Simester et al. eds., 2014); Robinson, *supra* note 22.

[24] *See* Thorsten Sellin & Marvin Wolfgang, *The Measurement of Delinquency* (1964), and for replication studies Charles F. Wellford & Michael Wiatrowski, *On the Measurement of Delinquency*, 66 J. Crim. L. & Criminology 175 (1975); Robinson, *supra* note 22, ch. 2.

[25] *See* Jesper Ryberg, *The Ethics of Proportionate Punishment. A Critical Investigation* (2004).

[26] Tatjana Hörnle, *"Rights of Others" in Criminalisation Theory*, in *Liberal Criminal Theory. Essays for Andreas von Hirsch* 169 (A.P. Simester et al. eds., 2014).

value have become less important. Invasions of privacy can increase wrongdoing: burglary, for instance, should be ranked more serious than simple theft of an equally valuable item. The second step examines the size of the harm done through the particular incident. Harm could be assessed from two different perspectives: the subjective perception of the individual victim or a third person's assessment. In legal systems that emphasize equality in sentencing, the individual victim's subjective assessment cannot be decisive.[27] The crucial question rather should be how this kind of outcome *typically* diminishes a person's well-being and resources.[28]

For crimes against collective interests (bribery, tax offenses, counterfeiting money, environmental pollution, etc.), rankings *within* the same offense category should not be too difficult. To compare cases of tax evasions, for instance, the amount of money and repeated behavior versus singular incident could be decisive. It is more difficult to compare crimes against collective interests with crimes against persons. A possible solution could be to switch from impact on victims to offenders' gains. If the gain through tax evasion corresponds to the gain made by theft of a wallet, they can be compared.[29] The alternative is to eschew the notion that crimes against persons and crimes against collective interests must be ranked on the same seriousness scale. Rather than assuming one unified entity called "the criminal law," one can acknowledge two distinct subsystems: one protecting the rights of individuals, the other serving regulatory interests. On this understanding, the notion of proportionality between crime seriousness and sanction severity should apply *within* each subsystem without requiring cross-comparisons.

d. *Other Elements of Objective Wrongdoing*

After assessing rights violations and harms, sentencers need to consider whether other features of the act and the relationship between offender and victim modify seriousness upward or downward. The description of a right's violation as an attack (rather than endangerment) increases seriousness.[30] If no harm occurred, because an attempt was unsuccessful or because the offense description requires only the creation of a risk, a crucial point will be how close the offender came to causing harm. Other aggravating factors can be the violation of special duties toward the victim (such as abuse of trust), duties toward the public (for instance, if the offender acted as a state official), or interferences with the victim's liberty or dignity that are not covered by the offense description. Wrongdoing can also be mitigated due to factors in the relationship between victim and offender that preceded the act, for example, if the victim provoked the offender through wrongful behavior.[31]

[27] Martin Wasik, *Crime Seriousness and the Offender/Victim Relationship in Sentencing*, in *Fundamentals of Sentencing Theory*: Essays in Honour of Andrew von Hirsch 103, 105–06 (Andrew Ashworth & Martin Wasik eds., 1998).

[28] Andrew von Hirsch & Nils Jareborg, *Gauging Criminal Harm: A Living-Standard Analysis*, 11 Oxford J. Legal Studies 1 (1991).

[29] Ashworth, *supra* note 16, at 119.

[30] R.A. Duff, *Answering for* Crime: Responsibility and Liability in the Criminal Law ch. 7 (2009).

[31] Andrew von Hirsch & Nils Jareborg, *Provocation and Culpability*, in *Responsibility, Character and the Emotions* 241 (Ferdinand Schoeman ed., 1987).

e. *Subjective Elements*

Modern legal systems require for all or most criminal offenses[32] that the offender acted with a certain mental attitude such as intention, recklessness, conditional intent (*bedingter Vorsatz*), or negligence. There is no general consensus about how variations of mental attitudes should influence sentencing. Criminal laws, courts, and participants in surveys rate similar acts with similar outcomes significantly more serious if they are committed intentionally rather than negligently.[33] Other constellations are more complicated. Should *all* possible differences in mental attitudes impact assessments of offense seriousness? It has been argued that careful planning is more culpable than impulsive acts,[34] but this view could be challenged: premeditation does not necessarily demonstrate more disrespect for the law and the victims, at least not if the planning process has included doubts and hesitations. Another point of disagreement is the relevance of intention versus knowledge or direct and oblique intention.[35] Some argue that intention is at the top of the scale of culpability.[36] However, if one compares the intention that X should happen with knowledge that X will happen, it is not evident that the mental attitude *as such* must influence the seriousness of the offense. Yet another debate concerns unforeseen consequences after an intentional breach of the law. Participants in surveys tend to factor unforeseen consequences in.[37] Theorists argue that legal judgments should only trace individuals' choices and thus oppose higher sentences in such cases,[38] but this is a too narrow view on liability. To exclude strange twists of fate, it is necessary but also sufficient that consequences were foreseeable, not that the individual offender paid attention to this possibility.

Another topic for discussion is the role of motives. It is widely assumed that sentencing decisions should assess motives.[39] During the last decades, criminal laws have introduced higher punishments if crimes are driven by hostility toward minority groups (hate crimes).[40] The relevance of motives for sentencing deserves, however, critical scrutiny. The counter-thesis is that legal judgments should be narrower than moral judgments and focus on the impact of actions rather than on offenders' inner selves. For

[32] Some legal systems include strict liability offenses (*see* A.P. Simester et al., *Simester and Sullivan's Criminal Law: Theory and Doctrine* ch. 6 (6th ed. 2016)). Others, such as German law, always require subjective liability, see §§ 15, 18 Strafgesetzbuch [German Criminal Code].

[33] *See* for assessments in surveys Leslie Sebba, *Is Mens Rea a Component of Perceived Offense Seriousness?*, 71 J. Crim. L. & Criminology 124 (1980).

[34] Ashworth, *supra* note 16, at 157.

[35] *See* Itzhak Kugler, *Direct and Oblique Intention in the Criminal Law: An Inquiry into Degrees of Blameworthiness* (2002).

[36] Michael Moore, *Intention as a Marker of Moral Culpability and Legal Punishability*, in *Philosophical Foundations of Criminal Law* 179, 184 (R.A. Duff & Stuart P. Green eds., 2011).

[37] Sebba, *supra* note 33, at 134.

[38] Ashworth, *supra* note 16, at 133.

[39] George Fletcher, *Basic Concepts of Criminal Law* 124–25 (1998); Douglas Husak, *The Philosophy of Criminal Law. Selected Essays* 53 (2010).

[40] *See* for the United States Phyllis Gerstenfeld, *Hate Crimes: Causes, Controls, and Controversies* 27–34 (4th ed. 2018); for English law Ashworth, *supra* note 16, at 168; for German law § 46 II Strafgesetzbuch [German Criminal Code].

sentencing, the crucial question should be if the offender expressed hostility through the crime or its attendant circumstances while it is questionable whether hidden motives enhance legal blameworthiness. Offenders' diminished guilt (or, to use another term, reduced culpability) may become relevant, too. Conditions that almost, but not completely, fulfill the requirements for an excuse can mitigate the sentence.[41]

f. *Prior Convictions*

It is common practice to treat prior convictions as an aggravating factor.[42] In some legal systems, for instance in the United States, the additional punishment for recidivism can be higher than the sentence for the offense as such.[43] But can recidivist premiums be justified within desert-based assessments? Desert theorists have developed arguments why a lack of prior convictions might be a *mitigating* factor. The progressive loss of mitigation models argues that offenders should receive sentence discounts for their first lapses, as a matter of limited tolerance for human fallibility.[44] A more circumscribed approach allows mitigation only once, for the very first conviction, and only if the offense is of relatively low seriousness.[45] Mitigation models presuppose not only lack of prior convictions but also lack of prior offenses—in real life, the offender might have committed numerous criminal acts before the first formal response. Another desert-based concept justifies recidivist premiums by pointing to offenders' duties. Persons with prior convictions might have a more substantial duty to obey the law than persons with a clean record, and the violation of this duty might constitute an additional wrong.[46] The crucial question is how such a duty could be justified. The general duty to obey the law cannot be quantified—it is the same duty for everyone. A more specific obligation might arise after a criminal conviction, in the form of a duty to rearrange one's life in ways that help to avoid future offending,[47] but this invites the question how to deal with offenders who had made some efforts but failed nevertheless.

In the context of hybrid models, recidivist premiums can be justified beyond desert, with preventive reasoning. One possible argument of this sort points to individual

[41] Martin Wasik, *Excuses at the Sentencing Stage*, Crim. L. Rev. 450 (1983).

[42] *See* for the weight assigned to prior convictions in different countries Julian Roberts, *The Role of Criminal Record in the Sentencing Process*, in 22 *Crime and Justice* 303 (Michael Tonry ed., 1997); Mirko Bagaric, *The Punishment Should Fit the Crime—Not the Prior Convictions of the Person That Committed the Crime: An Argument for Less Impact Being Accorded to Previous Convictions in Sentencing*, 51 San Diego L. Rev. 343 (2014).

[43] *See* for a critique of these practices Michael Tonry, *Equality and Human Dignity*, in *Sentencing Policies and Practices in Western Countries: Comparative and Cross-National Perspectives*, in 45 Crime and Justice 459, 482–488 (Michael Tonry ed., 2016).

[44] Andrew von Hirsch, *Past or Future Crimes: Deservedness and Dangerousness in the Sentencing of Criminals* 81–91 (1986); Andrew von Hirsch, *Proportionality and the Progressive Loss of Mitigation*, in *Previous Convictions at Sentencing* 1 (Julian Roberts & Andrew von Hirsch eds., 2010).

[45] Julian Roberts, *First-Offender Sentencing Discounts*, in *Previous Convictions at Sentencing* 17, 31–33 (Julian Roberts & Andrew von Hirsch eds., 2010).

[46] Youngjae Lee, *Repeat Offenders and the Question of Desert*, in *Previous Convictions at Sentencing* 49 (Julian Roberts & Andrew von Hirsch eds., 2010).

[47] *Id.* at 59–66.

deterrence, with the argument that sentences must be increased to finally impress this individual. The expectation that this might work is, however, not realistic: the more experiences offenders have with correctional institutions, the less likely it seems that yet another exposure to the same procedures will influence their behavior. Another argument could rely on the notion of positive general prevention: if offenders continue to commit crimes that are, seen in an isolated way, moderately serious or even trifling, such as persistent trespassing or minor thefts, a *moderate* recidivist premium can be justified because prohibitory norms need to be reconfirmed with more vigor if they are disregarded repeatedly. If the crimes harm victims in very serious ways, incapacitation of repeat offenders might be considered. In general, however, hybrid theories allow only moderate sentence enhancements for preventive purposes.[48] The logic of incapacitation can be best realized with a separate track beyond criminal punishment.[49]

4. Sentencing without Certainty about the Question of Guilt?

Despite considerable differences between legal systems, a widely shared basic assumption is that decisions about sentencing presuppose a decision about guilt. Courts or juries must find defendants guilty beyond reasonable doubt before considering sentences. Some criminal scholars challenge this assumption and argue against "all or nothing"-sentencing. According to this view, decision-making could be probabilistic and the severity of the punishment correlated with the probability of guilt. The promise is to enhance deterrence.[50] Such proposals clash with the idea that only those found guilty may be punished as a matter of fundamental justice and human dignity.

III. Sentencing Procedures

1. Who Decides?

a. *Sole Responsibility versus Mixed Responsibility*

Who decides on sentencing rules and outcomes in individual cases? The choice is between four types of decision-makers (legislatures, sentencing commissions, sentencing judges, and agencies that decide about parole) and between sole-responsibility versus mixed-responsibility models. Conceivably, *sole responsibility* for sentencing decisions could be given to legislatures, sentencing commissions, judges, or parole boards. For instance, criminal laws could determine sentences, without leaving discretionary choices

[48] Frase, *supra* note 2, at 48–50. [49] *See* supra Section II.b.

[50] *See* Talia Fisher, *Conviction Without Conviction*, 96 Minnesota L. Rev. 833 (2011); Doron Teichmann, *Convincing with Reasonable Doubt: An Evidentiary Theory of Criminal Law*, 93 Notre Dame L. Rev. 757 (2017).

to judges, or judges could be given unlimited sentencing power without any prescribed upper or lower limits, or, in indeterminate sentencing schemes, post-conviction parole decisions could regulate the duration of imprisonment.

Contemporary legal systems tend to avoid sole-responsibility solutions. Leaving sentencing to the unfettered choices of judges or parole boards would increase unwarranted sentence disparity, and this option would not be compatible with the (in some countries constitutional)[51] idea that citizens must be informed of what they have to expect if they offend. The opposite approach that shifts responsibility exclusively to legislatures or sentencing commissions necessarily sacrifices the notion of proportionality. It is impossible to describe degrees of offense seriousness ex ante, in abstract laws, in a way that would cover *every* particular offense. Adapting sentences to criminal incidents requires post-crime judgments.

The dominant model today is *mixed responsibility*. Mixed-responsibility schemes typically divide the task of sentencing between legislatures and sentencing commissions on the one hand and judges on the other hand. In many systems, not only in Europe, but also in some U.S. states,[52] reliance on parole release means passing part of the responsibility for the amount of punishment to parole courts or parole boards. Crucial questions nowadays ask *who* is responsible for pre-structuring sentencing decisions (legislatures or sentencing commissions), and *how much* remaining discretion should mixed-responsibility approaches leave to judges or those who decide about parole.

b. *Pre-Structuring Sentencing: Legislatures or Commissions?*

Why do some countries, but not others, assign the task to pre-structure sentencing to independent or semi-independent bodies (sentencing commissions or councils)? A common reconstruction of the U.S. movement toward sentencing commissions[53] emphasizes the dissatisfaction with the system of indeterminate sentencing: crashing disappointment as a reaction to overconfidence in the rehabilitative ideal.[54] In countries without a similar tradition of indeterminate sentencing, there never was much public debate about deep-seated problems and thus no desire for fundamental reforms. But even in countries that previously relied on indeterminate sentencing and held strong optimism with regard to rehabilitation such as the Scandinavian countries, penal reforms do not necessarily result in the installment of sentencing commissions.[55]

Preferences for either commissions or legislature can be read as differences between legal cultures. Public tasks in general and criminal justice in particular can be approached by emphasizing formalistic issues that are seen as important for legitimacy,

[51] *See* Art. 103 II Grundgesetz [German Basic Law], principle of legality. The German Federal Constitutional Court argues that not only convictions but also sentences must be foreseeable: Entscheidungen des Bundesverfassungsgerichts (BVerfGE) 105, 135, 153 (2002).

[52] Kevin Reitz, *The "Traditional" Indeterminate Sentencing Model*, in *The Oxford Handbook of Sentencing and Corrections* 270 (Joan Petersilia & Kevin Reitz eds., 2012).

[53] Robert Weisberg, *The Sentencing Commission Model, 1970s to Present*, in *The Oxford Handbook of Sentencing and Corrections* 299 (Joan Petersilia & Kevin Reitz eds., 2012).

[54] Reitz, *supra* note 52, at 289.

[55] *See* Lappi-Seppälä, *supra* note 14, at 22, 49–50.

or in a more technocratic and outcome-oriented fashion. The Anglo-American approach tends to value expertise and efficiency, while the Continental European tradition deem legitimacy provided by Parliament as important. The German constitutional term *Gesetzesvorbehalt* refers to the idea that restrictions on individuals' liberty must be supported by parliamentary laws.[56] This does not mean that criminal laws necessarily provide a fine-meshed structure for sentencing. But a preference for a legalistic rather than a consequentialist foundation of criminal justice[57] explains unwillingness to transfer power to sentencing commissions.

c. *Leeway Left to Judges and Parole Boards*

In contemporary legal systems, either the legislature (through provisions in criminal statutes) or sentencing commissions (through sentencing guidelines) establish limits for judges' exercise of discretion. This leads to the question how wide or narrow the remaining leeway is. In the United States, the idea behind the Federal Sentencing Guidelines was to considerably restrict discretion, which included initially the mandatory nature of the Guidelines. The U.S. Supreme Court has since declared them advisory,[58] with the effect of increased disparity[59] and inconsistent practices of appellate courts regarding some very harsh mandatory minimums in the U.S. Sentencing guidelines.[60] In the states that form the United States, many jurisdictions have sentencing guidelines, too.[61] Some of these allow the judiciary more leeway.[62] Another way to increase influence on sentencing outcomes are laws that proscribe mandatory minimums for certain crimes or offenders. Such laws apply in the United States to drug crimes, crimes with firearms, and repeat offenders (see for instance "three strikes laws").[63] These laws often require sentences that are disproportionately harsh with regard to the wrong done and in comparison to sentences for other crimes.[64]

In England and Wales, guidelines structure sentencing for an increasing number of offenses.[65] The English guidelines take a different approach than the U.S. guidelines.

[56] *See, e.g.*, Entscheidungen des Bundesverfassungsgerichts (BVerfGE) 47, 46, 78 (1977).

[57] Mirjan Damaška, *The Faces of Justice and State Authority: A Comparative Approach to the Legal Process* 21 (1986).

[58] United States v. Booker, 543 U.S. 220 (2005).

[59] Ryan W. Scott, *Inter-judge Sentencing Disparity After Booker: A First Look*, 63 Stanford L. Rev. 1 (2010).

[60] *See* Carol Steiker, *Lessons from Two Failures: Sentencing for Cocaine and Child Pornography Under the Federal Sentencing Guidelines in the United States*, 76 Law & Contemp. Probs. 27 (2013).

[61] Listed on the homepage of the National Association of Sentencing Commissions (NASC).

[62] *See* for the more flexible guidelines in Washington State Kate Stith, *Principles, Pragmatism, and Politics: The Evolution of Washington State's Sentencing Guidelines*, 76 Law & Contemp. Probs. 105 (2013) and in Minnesota Kevin Reitz, *Comparing Sentencing Guidelines*, in *Sentencing Guidelines. Exploring the English Model* 182 (Andrew Ashworth & Julian Roberts eds., 2013).

[63] Jeremy Travis et al., *The Growth of Incarceration in the United States: Exploring Causes and Consequences* 83–85 (2014).

[64] *Id.* at 85–89.

[65] *See* the homepage of the Sentencing Council, https://www.sentencingcouncil.org.uk/. For the history of the English guidelines and the constitutional position of the Sentencing Council, see Andrew Ashworth & Julian Roberts, *The Origins and Nature of the Sentencing Guidelines in England*

They do not specify a range of sentences in sentencing grids, but prescribe a sequence of evaluative steps that judges ought to follow.[66] The basic idea is to screen the case for harm-related and culpability-related circumstances and sort those in categories of seriousness to which a numerical starting point is assigned (for instance, years, months, or weeks). Beginning with this starting point, judges move the sentence upward or downward, going through a checklist of aggravating and mitigating factors and other circumstances such as guilty pleas or dangerousness. As the English guidelines do not prescribe how these additional factors should be weighed, courts still have leeway to exercise discretion.[67]

In Continental Europe and in other countries, for instance Canada,[68] but also in about half of the U.S. states,[69] sentencing commissions and sentencing guidelines have not taken hold and trial judges enjoy a wide scope of discretion.[70] In some legal systems, there are no or few mandatory minimums.[71] In Germany, the law stipulates sentence ranges,[72] but for misdemeanors the minimum often is the most minimal fine,[73] and more severe minimums for standard cases of felonies are counterbalanced by clauses for exceptional cases with a lower minimum.[74] The German Criminal Code does not give much guidance on how judges should proceed when choosing sentences within the wide legal ranges.[75]

From a comparative perspective, the question arises why some legal systems make serious attempts to curtail judges' discretion while in others no principled objections are raised against sentencing dominated by the judiciary. An explanation can be found if

and Wales, in *Sentencing Guidelines. Exploring the English Model* 1 (Andrew Ashworth & Julian Roberts eds., 2013); Ashworth, *supra* note 16, at 58–64.

66 Julian Roberts, *Sentencing Guidelines in England and Wales: Recent Developments and Emerging Issues*, 76 Law & Contemp. Probs. 1, 5 (2013).

67 Mandeep Khami, *A "Decision Science" Perspective on the Old and New Format Guidelines*, in *Sentencing Guidelines. Exploring the English Model* 165, 180–81 (Andrew Ashworth & Julian V. Roberts eds., 2013).

68 Anthony Doob & Cheryl Webster, *Canadian Sentencing Policy in the Twenty-First Century*, in 45 *Sentencing Policies and Practices in Western Countries: Comparative and Cross-National Perspectives*, 45 *Crime and Justice* 359, 369 (Michael Tonry ed., 2016).

69 Reitz, *supra* note 52, at 274–76. *See* for a list of U.S. states with sentencing commissions *supra* note 61.

70 *See* for France Jacqueline Hodgson & Laurène Soubise, *Understanding the Sentencing Process in France*, in *Sentencing Policies and Practices in Western Countries: Comparative and Cross-National Perspectives*, 45 *Crime and Justice* 221, 224, 242 (Michael Tonry ed., 2016); and for Belgium Veerle Scheirs et al., *Belgian Sentencing as a Bifurcated Practice?*, *id.* at 267, 281.

71 *See* for the abolition of minimum sentences in France Hodgson & Soubise, *supra* note 70, at 242; for the introduction of some mandatory minimums in Canada Doob & Webster, *supra* note 68, at 374, 382.

72 An exception is murder (§ 211 Strafgesetzbuch [German Criminal Code]: life-long imprisonment).

73 Simple theft or bodily assault can be punished with any sanction between a minimal fine and five years imprisonment: §§ 242, 223 Strafgesetzbuch [German Criminal Code].

74 For instance, the regular minimum for rape is two years imprisonment and for armed robbery five years, the reduced minimum six months (rape) and one year (armed robbery), see §§ 177, 250 Strafgesetzbuch [German Criminal Code].

75 Hörnle, *supra* note 4, at 192–93; Wolfgang Frisch, *From Disparity in Sentencing Towards Sentencing Equality: The German Experience*, 28 Crim. L. Forum 437, 449–50 (2017).

one analyzes the general role of the judiciary. If, as in the United States, judges obtain their office through public elections and if they are seen as individuals who are open to political influences,[76] this promotes both inequality in sentencing outcomes and desires to restrict the scope of judicial discretion. In contrast, judges in Germany in many ways resemble other civil servants in Continental European states. They enter the profession at a young age, chosen according to their grades in state exams that are specifically designed to select judges, and they become part of a large bureaucracy. Such career paths tend to advance uniformity and neutrality and to suppress individuality.[77] A professional image of the judiciary also means that no need is seen for commissions to enhance expertise und uniformity.

Differences between legal systems can also be found with regard to parole decisions. First, there is the question: Who makes post-conviction decisions—administrative bodies or courts? In some U.S. states, parole boards still carry substantial responsibility for the length of imprisonment.[78] Other legal systems, such as Germany, assign this responsibility to courts,[79] obviously based on the assumption that judicial decisions convey a higher degree of legitimacy than administrative choices. Second, opinions are divided on whether parole should be an option at all. In many countries, parole is granted regularly (see Section IV.1.), while in the United States the "truth in sentencing"-movement has led to the abolishment of parole in some (but not all) states that have introduced sentencing guidelines.[80]

d. *Influence of Prosecutors*

To what degree do prosecutors affect sentencing? To answer this question, indirect and direct influences should be distinguished. In all legal systems, prosecutors exercise *indirect* influence on sentencing through their prior screening decisions, charges, and fact bargaining.[81] Decisions to discontinue a case, to drop some charges, or to charge the defendant with an offense that carries a lesser or higher punishment, have a bearing on the outcome of the proceedings. To say that these influences are indirect is not to say that they are unimportant. Prosecutorial choices matter for individual defendants *and* they influence overall punitiveness.[82] Observers of the situation in the United States ascribe the increase in imprisonment rates over the last decade primarily to prosecutors'

[76] Michael Tonry, *Differences in National Sentencing Systems and the Differences They Make*, in *Sentencing Policies and Practices in Western Countries: Comparative and Cross-National Perspectives*, 45 *Crime and Justice* 1, 3 (Michael Tonry ed., 2016).

[77] *See* for the professionalization of judges in hierarchical systems Damaška, *supra* note 57, at 18–19; Hörnle, *supra* note 4, at 206–09.

[78] Reitz, *supra* note 52, at 49.

[79] *See* § 454 Strafprozessordnung [German Code of Criminal Procedure].

[80] Reitz, *supra* note 52, at 273–74.

[81] Ronald Wright, *Charging and Plea Bargaining as Forms of Sentencing Discretion*, in *The Oxford Handbook of Sentencing and Corrections* 247 (Joan Petersilia & Kevin Reitz eds., 2012).

[82] Marie Gottschalk, *Bring It On: The Future of Penal Reform, the Carceral State, and American Politics*, 12 Ohio State J. Crim. L. 559, 573–79 (2015).

choices to charge defendants with felonies rather than with misdemeanors.[83] The scope of prosecutorial power (and also expectations regarding assertiveness within the profession) differ between systems. In France and in Germany, the power of prosecutors is more limited than in the United States. They may drop minor charges, and this option is used frequently,[84] but there is neither a strong commitment to get high sentences[85] nor much leeway to control outcomes with regard to serious crimes. For serious cases, prosecution is mandatory, and prosecutors cannot decide how facts will be classified legally.[86]

Another question is how prosecutors can shape sentencing in more direct ways. An obvious gateway is sentence bargaining.[87] In the United States, the introduction of sentencing guidelines has not effectively restricted the bargaining power of prosecutors.[88] Since 2009, German law formally acknowledges the possibility of negotiations about sentence outcomes, but these negotiations take place within the court, not in an isolated way with the prosecutor, and they do not involve a formal plea of guilt, but require judges' conviction of the defendant's guilt.[89] In trials without prior consultations and agreements, prosecutors can exercise some influence on sentencing outcome, too, if their final statements in trials include a sentencing proposal.[90] Courts are not bound by these proposals, but the setting of an anchoring point is likely to influence the decisions of judges,[91] and often the actual sentence is coming close to the prosecutor's proposal.[92] For this reason, equality in sentencing can be increased if, within a bureaucratic system of prosecution, the head of the organization issues directives concerning sentence proposals.[93]

[83] John Pfaff, *Locked In: The True Causes of Mass Incarceration and How to Achieve Real Reform* (2017). *See* for the influence of prosecutors and interactions between judges and prosecutors Byungbae Kim et al., *Federal Sentencing as a Complex Collaborative Process: Judges, Prosecutors, Judge-Prosecutor Dyads, and Disparity in Sentencing*, 53 Criminology 597 (2015).

[84] *See* §§ 153, 153a, 154 Strafprozessordnung [German Code of Criminal Procedure]; Thomas Weigend, *No News Is Good News: Criminal Sentencing in Germany since 2000*, in *Sentencing Policies and Practices in Western Countries: Comparative and Cross-National Perspectives*, 45 *Crime and Justice* 83, 84–85, 98 (Michael Tonry ed., 2016); for France Hodgson & Soubise, *supra* note 70, at 228–229.

[85] *See* for the importance of professional cultures and the legal framework that enables them Shawn Boyne, *German Prosecutors and the Rechtsstaat*, in *Prosecutors and Democracy: A Cross-National Study* 138 (Máximo Langer & David Alan Sklansky eds., 2017); Hodgson & Soubise, *supra* note 70, at 243.

[86] § 265 Strafprozessordnung [German Code of Criminal Procedure]; see Weigend, *supra* note 84, at 84–85.

[87] Wright, *supra* note 81, at 251.

[88] Ilene Nagel & Stephen J. Schulhofer, *A Tale of Three Cities: An Empirical Study of Charging and Bargaining Practices under the Federal Sentencing Guidelines*, 66 S. Cal. L. Rev. 501 (1992).

[89] § 157c Strafprozessordnung [German Code of Criminal Procedure]. *See also Special Issue: Plea Bargains in Germany*, 15 German L.J. 1–106 (2014).

[90] *See* for France Hodgson & Soubise, *supra* note 70, at 228, 243; for Germany Weigend, *supra* note 84, at 86; for the Nordic countries Lappi-Seppälä, *supra* note 14, at 40.

[91] Birte Englich & Thomas Mussweiler, *Sentencing Under Uncertainty: Anchoring Effects in the Courtroom*, 31 J. Applied Social Psychol. 1535 (2001).

[92] Hodgson & Soubise, *supra* note 70, at 243; Weigend, *supra* note 84, at 86–87.

[93] *See* Frisch, *supra* note 75, at 461–63.

e. *Appellate Courts and Constitutional Review*

Appellate sentence review exists in many countries, but not in all. For instance, only some states within the United States have effective appellate reviews.[94] In other legal systems, supreme courts give some guidance to lower courts.[95] A closer analysis, however, reveals that these efforts could be improved.[96] Appellate courts will typically declare that a range of sentences is acceptable rather than striving for more fine-tuned sentencing principles. Appellate judges have understandable reasons to refrain from a detailed review of trial courts' decisions—otherwise, they would be overrun by appeals. Legal systems have developed strategies to restrict appeals that challenge sentencing. Trial judges' scope of discretion can be protected by releasing them from giving reasons for their sentencing decisions.[97] The goal to keep sentencing appeals within reasonable limits is probably the reason the German Federal Court of Justice sticks to the notoriously vague notion of *Spielraumtheorie* (margin theory).[98]

Sentences might also be challenged on constitutional grounds. In the United States, the Eighth Amendment (prohibiting cruel and unusual punishment) can be evoked. The U.S. Supreme Court argues that the Eighth Amendment includes the notion of proportionality,[99] but with regard to outcomes, this has been characterized as "largely meaningless as a constraint."[100] The majority of the U.S. Supreme Court has, for instance, not objected to life sentences for drug possession or theft.[101] The German Federal Constitutional Court acknowledges the principle of guilt (*Schuldprinzip*), deduced from the right to dignity and the right to autonomy (Article 1 I, Article 2 I German Basic Law), and demands that punishment must be proportionate to the seriousness of the offense and the offender's guilt.[102] The Court relied on the principle of human dignity to declare life imprisonment without parole unconstitutional.[103] This does, however, not mean that the German Constitutional Court routinely devotes time to scrutinizing sentencing decisions. The principle of guilt appears in decisions about the constitutionality of laws rather than in complaints about individual criminal sentences.

[94] Tonry, *supra* note 43, at 479.

[95] Lappi-Seppälä, *supra* note 14, at 50, for the Nordic countries, and for Germany Frisch, *supra* note 75, at 471–72.

[96] Hörnle, *supra* note 4, at 193–94; Frisch, *supra* note 75, at 473–74.

[97] Hodgson & Soubise, *supra* note 70, at 235.

[98] Hörnle, *supra* note 4, at 194.

[99] *Weems v. United States*, 217 U.S. 349, 367 (1910); *Graham v. Florida*, 560 U.S. 48, 59 (2010).

[100] Youngjae Lee, *The Constitutional Right Against Excessive Punishment*, 91 Va, L. Rev. 677, 681 (2005).

[101] *Harmelin v. Michigan*, 501 U.S. 957 (1991); *Ewing v. California*, 538 U.S. 11 (2003). In *Graham v. Florida*, 560 U.S. 48 (2010) and *Miller v. Alabama*, 567 U.S. 460 (2012), the Supreme Court reversed convictions to life imprisonment without parole, however, the crucial factor was the offenders' juvenile status.

[102] *See* for instance Entscheidungen des Bundesverfassungsgerichts (BVerfGE) 110, 1, 13 (2004); 120, 224, 254 (2008); 133, 168, 198 (2013).

[103] Entscheidungen des Bundesverfassungsgerichts (BVerfGE) 45, 187 (1977).

2. Sentencing Procedures

a. *Bifurcated Trials versus Single Verdicts*

Criminal trials can be organized in two stages: first, proceedings that end with conviction, followed by sentencing hearings. The alternative is a uniform trial with a single verdict that convicts the defendant *and* imposes a sentence. The bifurcated procedure is common in jurisdictions that rely on juries to decide about guilt in trials for felonies. The decision about conviction is left to juries while professional judges decide on sentences.[104] In systems with only professional judges or mixed tribunals with both professional and lay judges, the court will deliberate and decide on conviction and sentence at the same point in time.[105]

b. *Victim Statements*

Should victims be heard in sentencing procedures? In many English-speaking countries, such as Britain, the United States, Canada, and Australia, victims are entitled to make personal statements or impact statements.[106] Other legal systems, such as Germany, do not have formalized procedures, but leave it to the discretion of judges whether hearing the victim is seen as necessary. Victim statements fulfill two different functions. They can introduce facts by describing the degree of immediate and more remote harms, that is, negative consequences for victims later in their lives. Victim statements can also have an expressive side: to be heard and to be visible in the trial. Immediate harms must be taken into account to compare the seriousness of crimes.[107] These comparisons should primarily be based on the typical negative impact for persons' lives,[108] but enhanced sensitivity can augment harm,[109] for instance, if the victim's age or fragility leads to more serious bodily injuries. The relevance of remoter harms deserves more scrutiny. The weight of offenders' contributions to later negative developments in victims' lives will often be diluted by other factors. The main worries about victim statements are that they might evoke intense and inappropriate emotions[110] and exert subconscious influence on judges. However, it is in general a part of the professional role of judges to

[104] *See* Richard Frase, *Sentencing and Comparative Law Theory*, in *Crime, Procedure and Evidence in a Comparative and International Context. Essays in Honour of Professor Mirjan Damaška* 351, 353 (John Jackson et al. eds., 2008).

[105] *See* for Germany Weigend, *supra* note 84, at 87.

[106] Carolyn Hoyle, *Victims, the Criminal Process, and Restorative Justice*, in *The Oxford Handbook of Criminology* 398, 412–13 (Mike Maguire et al. eds., 5th ed. 2012).

[107] Wasik, *supra* note 27.

[108] *See* von Hirsch & Jareborg, *supra* note 28; Andreas von Hirsch, *Deserved Criminal Sentences* 64–67 (2017).

[109] *See* Anthony Bottoms, *The "Duty to Understand": What Consequences for Victim Participation?*, in *Hearing the Victim. Adversarial Justice, Crime Victims and the State* 17, 30–37 (Anthony Bottoms & Julian Roberts eds., 2010).

[110] Susan Bandes, *Empathy, Narrative, and Victim Impact Statements*, 63 Univ. Chi. L. Rev. 361 (1996).

filter out relevant facts without paying too much attention to strong emotional currents in courtrooms.[111]

c. *Standards of Proof and Explanations*

In some legal systems, sentencing lacks procedural formality compared to the proceedings before convictions.[112] U.S. jurisdictions do not generally require "proof beyond reasonable doubt" for sentencing facts;[113] they allow aggravating the punishment for offenses that were not even part of the conviction,[114] and judges are not required to give reasons for the sentence.[115] More formalized legal systems, such as Germany, do not officially lower requirements for sentencing compared to conviction, but there might be some discrepancies between the law in the books and the law in practice. If standards of proof were taken seriously, it would, for example, not be sufficient to rely on defendants' self-reports about their income in day-fine systems. In routine criminal proceedings, it is hardly possible to collect comprehensive evidence for every sentencing detail. Judges tend to react to the requirement under German law that judgments must explain the sentence[116] in a rhetorical way that is not very helpful in understanding their actual considerations.

IV. Comparing Overall Sentence Severity

1. Differences between Countries

Sentencing theory does not tell us much about the severity of sentences. Ranking the seriousness of crimes on an ordinal scale is one thing. The other crucial step is to assign numerical values to crimes. Even if customs are similar regarding the assessment of offense seriousness and preventive reasoning, outcomes can be very different due to disparate overall levels of sentence severity.[117] Comparisons of systems' punitiveness often

[111] Julian Roberts & Edna Erez, *Communication in Sentencing: The Expressive Function of Victim Impact Statements*, in *Hearing the Victim. Adversarial Justice, Crime Victims and the State* 232, 247–48 (Anthony Bottoms & Julian Roberts eds., 2010).

[112] *See* Nancy King, *Procedure at Sentencing*, in *The Oxford Handbook of Sentencing and Corrections* 317 (Joan Petersilia & Kevin Reitz eds., 2012).

[113] Kevin Reitz, *Proof of Aggravating and Mitigating Facts at Sentencing*, in *Mitigation and Aggravation at Sentencing* 228, 232–35 (Julian Roberts ed., 2011); King, *supra* note 112, at 320.

[114] Reitz, *supra* note 113, at 237–40.

[115] King, *supra* note 112, at 321.

[116] § 267 III Strafprozessordnung [German Criminal Code of Procedure].

[117] *See* for the difference between ordinal proportionality and cardinal magnitude of punishment scales von Hirsch, *supra* note 108, at 55–62.

make use of imprisonment rates (the number of prisoners per 100.000 population). Within Europe, in 2016, the Scandinavian countries, Switzerland, Germany, and Italy still had relatively low imprisonment rates (between 55 and 90 per 100,000), while in Eastern European countries such as Poland and the Baltic states the rates lied between 180 and 250.[118] In the United States, numbers are considerably higher: the imprisonment rate for offenders sentenced to more than one year was 450 in 2016.[119] The substantial gap between the United States and other countries is often cited as an indicator for radically different levels of punitiveness,[120] but three caveats are necessary regarding such conclusions. First, one has to keep in mind that higher imprisonment rates do not necessarily prove harshness in sentencing—they might also reflect higher numbers of convicted offenders and/or a higher percentage of serious crimes and/or successful criminal investigations.[121] Second, looking at larger units such as states can hide important local differences. For instance, there are remarkable differences *between* U.S. states.[122] Third, general statements about overall punitiveness might become blurry if attention turns to details. It might be the case that sentences for specific crimes or groups of offenders are rather severe while other features are less punitive.[123]

In what way do sentencing decisions contribute to differences in a legal system's overall punitiveness? One factor are preferences for certain sanction types. If fines are a frequently chosen option, this can considerably moderate punitiveness (provided that many convicted persons pay these fines).[124] In many European criminal justice systems, fines are the most frequently used punishment.[125] In Germany, more than 80 percent of all punishments are fines (regulatory offenses, *Ordnungswidrigkeiten*, and traffic

[118] Council of Europe Annual Penal Statistics: SPACE I-2016, p. 37; *available at* http://wp.unil.ch/space/files/2018/03/SPACE-I-2016-Final-Report-180315.pdf.

[119] Bureau of Justice Statistics, *Prisoners in 2016*, table 6, *available at* https://www.bjs.gov/content/pub/pdf/p16.pdf. The overall number, *including* offenders sentenced to imprisonment of one year or less, must be higher.

[120] *See*, for instance, Peter Ennis, *Incarceration Nation. How the United States Became the Most Punitive Democracy in the World* 2–5 (2016); Michael Tonry, *Sentencing Fragments. Penal Reform in America, 1975–2025*, at 10–12 (2015).

[121] David Nelken, *Comparative Criminal Justice: Making Sense of Difference* 61–63 (2010); John van Kesteren, *Public Attitudes and Sentencing Policies Across the World*, 15 Eur. J. Crim. Policy Research 25, 41 (2009).

[122] *See* Bureau of Justice Statistics, *supra* note 119, at tbl. 6.

[123] David Nelken, *When Is a Society Non-Punitive? The Italian Case*, in *The New Punitiveness. Trends, Theories, Perspectives* 218, 222 (John Pratt et al. eds., 2005).

[124] Sentencing offenders to fines does not always circumvent imprisonment—in the case of nonpayment, prison can be the backup sanction.

[125] *See* for England and Wales Julian Roberts & Andrew Ashworth, *The Evolution of Sentencing Policy and Practice in England and Wales, 2003–2015*, in *Sentencing Policies and Practices in Western Countries: Comparative and Cross-National Perspectives*, 45 *Crime and Justice* 307, 315 (Michael Tonry ed., 2016); for Belgium Scheirs et al., *supra* note 70, at 284. In Finland, Denmark and Sweden, between 50 percent and 70 percent of sanctions are fines (while in Norway, fines are seldom used); see Lappi-Seppälä, *supra* note 14, at 56.

offenses excluded),[126] in France and Italy a somewhat smaller proportion of sentences are fines.[127]

The length of prison sentences is another important factor that shapes a system's punitiveness. Andrew Ashworth points out that English sentencing can be clearly distinguished from practices in other European countries by the greater length of sentences.[128] But there are also differences between Continental European legal systems regarding long-term imprisonment.[129] In Germany, only a tiny fraction (less than 2 percent) of all prison sentences exceed five years.[130] If one compares legal sentence ranges for violent and sexual offenses in the German Criminal Code with starting points in the English sentencing guidelines for the same offense types, similar outcomes could be expected—starting points in the English Guidelines tend to be somewhere in the middle of the sentence range in the German Criminal Code. However, in countries with low imprisonment rates, judges do *not* pick sentences from the middle part of the allowed range but use the lower quarter or lower third.[131]

Other important factors that influence overall punitiveness are the percentages of conditional versus unconditional prison sentences and the option to release prisoners on probation after serving parts of the sentence. In Germany, 70 percent of all prison sentences are suspended,[132] and probation is possible after half of the sentence (first time offenders) or two-thirds have been served. In Belgium, release on probation is possible after only one-third of the sentence has been served.[133]

2. Factors behind Different Levels of Punitiveness

What are factors *behind* systems' preferences for milder punishments (large percentage of fines and suspended sentences, low anchoring points) or more severe sentencing patterns (large percentage of unsuspended prison sentences, high anchoring points, long sentences)? Explanations can be found in different fields. Complaints about increased

[126] *See* Weigend, *supra* note 84, at 95; Statistisches Bundesamt, *supra* note 14, at 92.

[127] Hodgson & Soubise, *supra* note 70, at 232. In Italy, even for misdemeanors, fines are chosen only in about 50 percent of all cases, *see* Alessandro Corda, *Sentencing and Penal Policies in Italy* 1985–20, in *Sentencing Policies and Practices in Western Countries: Comparative and Cross-National Perspectives*, 45 *Crime and Justice* 107, 144 (Michael Tonry ed., 2016).

[128] Ashworth, *supra* note 16, at 325–26.

[129] In France, the percentage of prison sentences of more than five years still is higher; *see* Direction de l'Administration Pénitentiaire, *Séries Statistiques des Personnes Placées Sous Main de Justice, 1980–2014*, Tableau 24, *available at* http://www.justice.gouv.fr/art_pix/ppsmj_2014.PDF.

[130] Statistisches Bundesamt, *supra* note 14, at 160–61 (even if traffic offenses are excluded, the percentage of long prison sentences does not exceed 2 percent).

[131] *See* Lappi-Seppälä, *supra* note 14, at 51; for Germany Bert Götting, *Gesetzliche Strafrahmen und Strafzumessungspraxis* (1997); for Italy Corda, *supra* note 127, at 136.

[132] Statistisches Bundesamt, *supra* note 14, at 93. *See also* for German sentencing Stefan Harrendorf, *Sentencing Thresholds in German Criminal Law and Practice*, 28 Crim. L. Forum 501, 519–30 (2017).

[133] Scheirs et al., *supra* note 70, at 287.

punitiveness often focus on social psychology (fear of crime, moral panics) and politics (populist political movements that exploit voters' emotions).[134] James Whitman points to deeper historical roots that explain why European countries tend to show more respect and mildness toward offenders than the United States.[135] Michael Tonry distinguishes between a Substantive Justice Model that emphasizes fair treatment and human dignity and a Democratic Accountability Model based on the assumption that sentences should reflect public attitudes and emotions.[136]

Why are criminal justice systems more or less insulated against political movements and public pressures? One explanatory factor is the legal framework for sentencing. It is easier to exert political influence in a systematic way and within a short period of time if sentencing is pre-structured by guidelines or detailed laws. Political shifts can be implemented in a direct way through changes in these guidelines or laws. Influencing the judiciary tends to be more difficult.[137] How difficult depends on the organization and self-concept of the judiciary. Sentencing patterns will be stable over rather long periods of time if judges see themselves as part of a collective, as part of the judiciary as a bureaucratic system, rather than as individuals. A crucial factor is the self-concept that prevails within the judiciary and is reproduced in law schools.[138] Sentencing will be well insulated against punitive currents in the media and politics if the Substantive Justice Model and a sense of civic responsibility are cornerstones of the professional self-concept.[139] If sentencing is structured through guidelines, it is also easier for judges not to feel personally responsible for harsh punishments while loose regulations promote the perception of being morally responsible for outcomes.[140]

Explaining punitiveness with arguments from social psychology, political sciences, history, and sociology of organizations does not yet give a comprehensive picture. The relatively low levels of punitiveness in Western Europe cannot be unraveled without reference to the cultural, social, and economic background in the second half of the twentieth century. Social welfare programs that ameliorate poverty and inequality can contribute to lower crime rates.[141] The social shape of societies is also likely to influence sentence severity independently of crime rates.[142] The Substantive Justice Model was successful in Europe under favorable conditions: prosperity combined with a high

[134] *See* Anthony Bottoms, *The Philosophy and Politics of Punishment and Sentencing*, in *The Politics of Sentencing Reform* 17 (C.M.V. Clarkson & Rodney Morgan eds., 1995); Michael Tonry, *Thinking About Crime. Sense and Sensibility in American Penal Culture* (2004); Bruce Western, *Punishment and Inequality in America* ch. 3 (2006); for Italy Corda, *supra* note 127, at 161.

[135] James Whitman, *Harsh Justice. Criminal Punishment and the Widening Divide Between America and Europe* (2003).

[136] Tonry, *supra* note 76, at 8–12.

[137] *See* for Canada Doob, *supra* note 68, at 409.

[138] Hörnle, *supra* note 4, at 206–10.

[139] *See also* Frase, *supra* note 104, at 365–66; for the vision of "civic responsibility toward society at large" see Corda, *supra* note 127, at 113.

[140] Antje du Bois-Pedain, *In Defence of Substantial Sentencing Discretion*, 28 Crim. L. Forum 391, 423–27 (2017).

[141] Gottschalk, *supra* note 82, at 597.

[142] *See* Michael Cavadino & James Dignan, *Penal Systems: A Comparative Approach* (2006).

degree of social and cultural homogeneity and mutual trust developed under these conditions. For instance, ample use of fines and probation presupposes that defendants typically are persons who have something to lose and who accept suspended sentences as punishment rather than as "getting away for free."

3. Prospects for the Future

Within the United States, in the twenty-first century politicians from different backgrounds are beginning to explore ways of decreasing prison populations.[143] This move is not necessarily bolstered by an increasing commitment to a Substantive Justice Model. The simple fact that very high imprisonment rates put a heavy strain on public budgets is an important argument in itself. Criminal law theorists argue for the replacement of moralistic approaches to punishment with a sober political analysis regarding how to distribute limited budgets on *all* the tasks states have to fulfill.[144] Proposals are made how to decrease punitiveness by using modifications in sentencing provisions and organizational changes.[145] It remains to be seen what the impact of these efforts will be.

In European countries, punitiveness is likely to increase as societies move in the direction of the United States[146] and egalitarian visions of citizenship get weaker. Affluent European societies that emphasize fairness and human dignity attract large numbers of migrants, which also entails growing numbers of persons without legal residential status, regular income, and sociocultural bonds with the domestic population. These developments might influence overall sentence severity in several ways. Fines and suspended sentences that today make up the bulk of all criminal punishments do not make sense for defendants who have neither income nor a long-term perspective for their lives. Increasing social problems and racial intolerance promote feelings of alienation and frustration both in the domestic population and migrant groups, which weakens social cohesion and social trust.[147] The positive element in European countries consists in a judiciary that is conservative in the sense of preserving traditional levels of low sentence severity and is slow to respond to shifting moods. In the long run, however, social fragmentation might increase overall sentence severity.

[143] Gottschalk, *supra* note 82, at 568–70; Tonry, *supra* note 120, at 6–10; Elizabeth Pelletier et al., *Assessing the Impact of Georgia's Sentencing Reforms* (2017).

[144] Vincent Chiao, *Mass Incarceration and the Theory of Punishment*, 11 Crim. L. & Philosophy 431 (2017).

[145] Tonry, *supra* note 120, at ch. 6.

[146] *See* for broader explanations for mass incarceration in the United States Jonathan Simon, *Mass Incarceration: From Social Policy to Social Problem*, in *The Oxford Handbook of Sentencing and Corrections* 23 (Joan Petersilia & Kevin Reitz eds., 2012).

[147] *See* for the role of social trust Tapio Lappi-Seppälä, *Explaining Imprisonment in Europe*, 8 Eur. J. Criminology 303, 312–13 (2011).

References

Andrew Ashworth, *Sentencing and Criminal Justice* (6th ed. 2015)

Andrew Ashworth & Julian V. Roberts, eds., *Sentencing Guidelines. Exploring the English Model* (2013)

Richard Frase, *Just Sentencing: Principles and Procedures for a Workable System* (2012)

Joan Petersilia & Kevin Reitz, eds., *The Oxford Handbook of Sentencing and Corrections* (2012)

Julian Roberts, ed., *Mitigation and Aggravation at Sentencing* (2011)

Julian Roberts & Andrew von Hirsch, eds., *Previous Convictions at Sentencing. Theoretical and Applied Perspectives* (2010)

Paul Robinson, *Distributive Principles of Criminal Law* (2008)

Jesper Ryberg, *The Ethics of Proportionate Punishment. A Critical Investigation* (2004)

Gerhard Schäfer, Günther Sander & Gerhard van Gemmeren, *Praxis der Strafzumessung* (6th ed. 2017)

Michael Tonry, ed., *Sentencing Policies and Practices in Western Countries: Comparative and Cross-National Perspectives* (2016)

Michael Tonry, *Sentencing Fragments* (2016)

Andrew von Hirsch, *Doing Justice* (1976)

Andrew von Hirsch, *Past or Future Crimes* (1987)

Andrew von Hirsch & Andrew Ashworth, *Proportionate Sentencing. Exploring the Principles* (2005)

CHAPTER 40

RESTORATIVE JUSTICE AS AN ALTERNATIVE TO PENAL SANCTIONS

ELISAVET SYMEONIDOU-KASTANIDOU

I. Introduction

In recent years, efforts have been made to find alternatives to penal sanctions, and especially to custodial sentences, due to the problems of overloaded prisons faced by many countries, but also because these sanctions pose serious obstacles to the reintegration of perpetrators. In this context, community sanctions and measures have been promoted, including restorative justice.

Of course, restorative justice does not establish an alternative only to penal sanctions but also to prosecution and criminal proceedings. More than that, it constitutes an alternative proposal for an integrated policy to confront criminality. Specifically, restorative justice aims at resolving the conflict between offenders and victims by redressing the harm within a voluntary and organized process, based on the interaction of the affected parties—the offender, the victim, and, where appropriate, members of the community—through the help of an impartial third party. This approach is grounded on the fundamental principle that responses to criminal behavior should not be purely punitive, but should aspire to healing harms and restoring relations as well as to making offenders responsible for their acts.[1]

Consensual models for conflict resolution have of course been implemented since antiquity and continue to be used in less-developed communities in Africa, Latin America,

[1] Vasso Artinopoulou, *Restorative Justice: The Challenge of Modern Legal Systems* 18 seq. (2010) (in Greek); Joanna Shapland et al., *Situating Restorative Justice Within Criminal Justice*, 10 Theoretical Criminology 505, 506 (2006).

and Asia.[2] In modern states, however, restorative justice programs have been developed only since the 1960s. Initially they were established in North America, where they were used to deal with juvenile delinquency and criminal acts of lesser gravity in the framework of the family or the neighborhood. In the 1970s, they were expanded to Europe, and their use has been incorporated in the rhetoric of the movements for the participation of the general public in the criminal justice system. Since then, and especially since the mid-1990s, restorative justice has developed rapidly in both theory and practice.

At the same time, however, many reservations have been expressed with regard to the conformity of restorative justice with the existing criminal justice system, and especially its compliance with the fundamental right to a fair trial and the principle of legality in prosecution. Its effectiveness is also disputed. Moreover, the development of restorative justice in many states is rather limited, despite the fact that international and European institutions have promoted it, setting specific quality standards to ensure that its implementation is consistent with the basic principles of existing legal systems and the fundamental rights of persons involved.

Against this backdrop, this chapter aims to identify the underlying causes for which, despite support, restorative justice does not seem to gain the position it deserves, even in countries with significantly overloaded criminal justice systems. More specifically, Section II presents restorative justice as developed in practice, while Section III describes its advantages but also the problems of its implementation. Next, Section IV refers to the support offered by international and European institutions, the quality standards set by them, and the influence of their interventions on national legal orders. The chapter ends with conclusions and proposals for initiatives to promote restorative justice in practice.

II. Restorative Justice in Practice

1. Basic Schemes

Restorative justice has developed in two basic schemes:

a. *The First Scheme*

The first scheme arose not through legislation but mainly in practice. Restorative justice procedures emerged "in the shadow of the law" without formal structures,[3] implemented on an ad hoc basis at the discretion of services and agencies. This approach can be found in countries with a common law tradition such as the United States or the

[2] Ivo Aertsen et al., *Rebuilding Community Connections—Mediation and Restorative Justice in Europe* 11 seq. (2004).

[3] Theo Gavrielides, *Restorative Justice in the United Kingdom*, in *Restorative Justice in Criminal Matters: Comparative Research in 11 European Countries* 269 (Angelika Pitsela & Elisavet Symeonidou-Kastanidou eds., 2013) [hereafter *Restorative Justice in Criminal Matters*].

United Kingdom, and also in countries that are deeply influenced by this tradition, such as the Netherlands. Further examples include the *sulha* peacemaking process in the Middle East and community-based mediation programs in Guatemala.[4]

The absence of specific provisions allowed the wide development of restorative justice practices through adaptability. Over time, some regulation of restorative justice processes has been developed in individual states, but this does not necessarily take the form of a formal law. Frequently, mediation practice is directed by agency policies or ministerial circulars, and more often by the practice standards of mediation organizations.

b. *The Second Scheme*

The second scheme was introduced by specific legislation. Restorative justice measures are either integrated into criminal law and procedure codes or in separate statutory provisions, and they typically provide procedural and organizational directions for judicial authorities and guidance for practice. This is mostly the case in countries based on the civil law tradition.

However, even in these countries, restorative justice processes have often developed experimentally prior to the introduction of specific law provisions. In Finland, for example, mediation can be traced back to 1982, when an experimental program was implemented in one municipality. In the 1990s, experimental mediation programs expanded to nine more municipalities using various organizational models and relying on volunteers without any state supervision. The legal framework was first introduced in 1997, and the current mediation system entered into force in 2006 following 2005 legislation.[5] The story is similar in Denmark, where after several years of local experimental implementation, the code on victim-offender mediation came into force in 2010.[6]

2. Models of Restorative Justice Processes

Restorative justice processes have taken many forms. The main models are the following:[7]

a. *Village or Tribal Justice Forums*

These are customary procedures in which a community collectively tries to resolve disputes or criminal charges between some of its members. Forums of this sort are well established in developing nations, especially in rural areas. For example, in the Democratic Republic of Congo, due to the absence of courts, community members

[4] *Handbook on Restorative Justice Programmes* 51 (U.N. Office on Drugs and Crime ed., 2006), *available at* www.unodc.org/pdf/criminal_justice/06-56290.

[5] *See* Pirjo Laitinen & Mirva Lohiniva-Kerkelä, *Restorative Justice in Finland*, in *Restorative Justice in Criminal Matters, supra* note 3, at 63 seq.

[6] Anette Storgaard, *Restorative Justice in Denmark*, in *Restorative Justice in Criminal Matters, supra* note 3, at 45 seq.

[7] Explanatory Memorandum to the Council of Europe, Recommendation of the Comm. of Ministers R(99) 19 (Sept. 15, 1999).

generally turn to local chiefs and elders to settle disputes and render judgments even in cases of serious criminal conduct.

b. *Reparation Negotiation*

These processes are employed in some jurisdictions for the limited purpose of determining the amount of restitution an offender will pay to a victim. Typically courts initiate these negotiations and then order payment of the agreed-upon amount. Sometimes a mediation meeting between parties may take place, but usually the procedure involves separate negotiations with each party, which are fairly simple and brief. Reparation negotiation processes are not concerned with reconciliation between the parties, but only with arranging material reparation.

c. *Community and Family Group Conferences*

These aim to produce comprehensive agreements that address sanctions and future obligations as well as reparation or restitution. These conferences, developed in Australia and New Zealand, rely on facilitators and bring together victims and offenders, along with police or public officials, offenders' relatives, and other community support persons, including supporters for the victim. Any agreement must satisfy the victims and be designed to keep the offender from future wrongdoing.

d. *Circle Sentencing*

Circle sentencing, which is used in Canadian aboriginal communities, involves a similarly broad range of participants—a judge, defense attorney, prosecutor, and police, as well as the victim and the offender, along with their families and community members. All sit in a circle, so that they face one another. Participants strive to reach consensus about how best to settle conflicts and sanction the offender. Broad representation in the process ensures that interests of the victim, community, and offender are taken into account. Ordinarily, sentencing circles occur as part of the criminal justice process to inform the sentencing decision, and usually only in cases in which the offenders have pled guilty.

e. *Victim-Offender Mediation*

This is perhaps the most familiar model of restorative justice. The parties meet in the presence of an appointed mediator, who sometimes is a volunteer. In direct mediation, both parties are present. But if a victim declines to meet the offender, the process can be indirect, with the mediator meeting separately with each party. Ideally and as much as is feasible, the outcome of a mediation process includes reparation and compensation for victims. Mediation might take place at any point in the criminal proceedings. Sometimes it is part of a diversion program or accompanies a police caution, but mediation can also accompany an ordinary prosecution, be included in a sentencing order, and even occur after sentencing. In some places mediated settlements affect court decisions about plea agreements or dismissal of criminal charges as well as sentencing orders.

3. Crimes to Which Restorative Justice Processes May Be Applied

The type or gravity of the crimes to which restorative justice processes may be applied is not the same in all countries. In many countries, there are no restrictions regarding this issue. This is the case in common law countries such as the United States, Canada, and the United Kingdom, but also in many countries of the Continental law tradition such as Denmark, Finland, and Poland.

Still, in some countries, restorative justice processes are regarded as appropriate only for certain kinds of criminal offenses, that is, offenses of lesser gravity or offenses against property interests. In Hungary, for example, only crimes for which a custodial sentence of no more than five years is provided may be dealt with through restorative justice procedure.[8] In Greece, a punishment may not be imposed when the perpetrator has repaired the harm caused by theft, embezzlement, fraud, or other offenses against property interests and the victims declare that they have no other claims.[9] However, similar victims' declarations are not significant for the rest of the crimes. An exception is made only for family violence, for which the institution of mediation has been formally introduced.[10] Still, even for these crimes, mediation is provided only for misdemeanors and not for felonies.

In any case, it is noteworthy that even in countries where restorative justice processes are permitted only for certain types of offenses, there is a broad consensus that the field of juvenile justice is a more appropriate area for restorative justice both in law and in practice.[11]

4. Internal Coherence of Provisions on Restorative Justice

Some countries—such as Finland, Hungary, or Denmark—have developed a general, overall, and coherent scheme on restorative justice for all crimes to which restorative justice processes may be applied. More specifically in Hungary, mediation, accompanied by diversion, was introduced in the Code of Criminal Procedure in 2007 for all criminal offenses against persons, traffic violations, or criminal offenses against property with a maximum punishment of five years' imprisonment.[12] The same rules and

[8] Ilona Görgényi & Judit Jacsó, *Restorative Justice Strategy in Hungary*, in *Restorative Justice in Criminal Matters*, *supra* note 3, at 125, 131.

[9] Art. 284, 406A of Poinikos Kodikas [Criminal Code] (in Greek).

[10] Law 3500/2006 gia tin antimetopisi tis endooikogeneiakis vias [on the confrontation of family violence] (in Greek).

[11] Angelika Pitsela et al., *Towards a New European Perspective for Restorative Justice in Criminal Matters. Comparative Analysis and Proposals*, in *Restorative Justice in Criminal Matters*, *supra* note 3, at 311, 318.

[12] Görgényi & Jacsó, *supra* note 8.

procedures exist for all these crimes. In Denmark, according to the nationwide program on mediation, implemented according to the 2010 Code on victim-offender mediation, all penal cases are examined by the police for referral to mediation.[13]

In other countries, however, restorative justice processes are fragmented in separate, incoherent provisions, a fact that reflects legislators' skepticism towards them. In these countries, restorative justice is neither organically incorporated into the official criminal justice system nor efficiently supported by reliable institutions and restorative justice services. In Greece, for example, while victim-offender mediation is provided as an educational measure imposed by a judicial decision in case of juvenile offenders since 2003,[14] there are no legislative provisions regarding its implementation. At the same time, Law 3500/2006,[15] which has formally introduced the institution of mediation in cases of family violence, contains analytical rules on the relevant procedure, but its implementation is not supported by sufficiently reliable institutions or services.

5. Rules and Procedures

Restorative justice programs vary considerably in their primary objectives, level of formality, relation to the criminal justice system, and extent of party involvement.[16]

Many programs do not involve arbitration. Others involve an element of arbitration, while yet other programs essentially constitute a process of arbitration. The same variety exists as regards the involvement of legal counsel. Some programs do not provide legal assistance, whereas in others, legal assistance of victims and offenders is considered a key issue.

Likewise, involvement of criminal justice professionals such as prosecutors varies. In some countries, justice professionals are not obliged to inform victims and offenders about the possibility to refer a case to restorative justice; in others they are legally bound to do so. On the other hand, after referring a case to mediation, justice professionals usually do not intervene in the conciliation procedure. But this is not the case in circle sentencing, where officials carry out their ordinary duties—prosecutors announce or recommend charges, judges may clarify what a statute requires—and then participate actively in the circle, thus having the possibility to influence the process.

Great differences exist regarding the parties responsible for the operation of restorative justice programs. Many programs are operated by public sector bodies, such as the police or the courts, as, for example, in Belgium.[17] Public programs usually rely on professional facilitators. Elsewhere, many programs are administered by nonprofit organizations, which are more likely to use trained volunteers. Moreover, in many cases there are no strict regulations on the qualifications and the training of facilitators or the relevant procedure.

[13] Storgaard, *supra* note 6.

[14] Art. 122 of Poinikos Kodikas [Criminal Code] (in Greek).

[15] *Supra* note 10.

[16] *See Handbook on Restorative Justice Programmes*, *supra* note 4, at 15 seq.

[17] Aertsen, *supra* note 2, at 51.

Last but not least, restorative justice processes in some jurisdictions are required by law to have an ethical commission, which usually serves two purposes. First it provides a procedure for all persons involved to lodge complaints, and additionally it develops ethical guidelines for practitioners. Still, many countries do not provide for such a commission.

6. Stages of Criminal Proceedings Where Restorative Justice Processes May Be Applied

In general, a restorative justice process can be initiated at four main levels within a criminal justice system: : (1) the police level, prior to charging, (2) the prosecution level, during the period between charging and trial, (3) the court level, during the pretrial or sentencing stages, or (4) the correctional level, after conviction, either in lieu of incarceration, during incarceration, or after custodial release.

However, recourse to restorative justice is not possible at all these stages in all countries. In Denmark, for example, a restorative justice process may be initiated only at the police level. Cases are referred to restorative justice by the police, and the process is facilitated by the local police or private institutions. In Bulgaria, initiation of restorative justice processes is allowed at the prosecution level only for juveniles, but at the court and correctional level for adult and juvenile offenders. In Finland, restorative justice processes may commence only at the police and prosecution level, while in the Netherlands, the United Kingdom, or Poland, they may take place at all levels.[18]

The same variety exists with regard to simultaneous criminal proceedings. In some countries, restorative justice processes are used as alternatives to the criminal justice system. This is the case, for example, in the United Kingdom or Greece for restorative justice programs at the police level. In other countries, however, such as Turkey, Denmark, or the Netherlands, the initiation of restorative justice processes does not preclude the simultaneous continuation of formal criminal proceedings.[19]

III. Advantages and Problems of Restorative Justice

1. The Advantages of Restorative Justice

Reasons for the shift to restorative justice in recent years are many. Overburdened criminal justice systems, delays in criminal cases, and citizens' consequent disappointment

[18] Pitsela, *supra* note 11, at 321 seq. [19] *Id.* at 324.

and frustration are certainly among the most important reasons. As noted by the UN Economic and Social Council (ECOSOC), "while a significant number of minor offenses jeopardize citizens' security and comfort, traditional criminal justice mechanisms do not always provide an appropriate and timely response to those phenomena, whether from the perspective of the victim or in terms of adequate and appropriate penalties."[20] Thus, the referral of a case to restorative justice aims to reduce the time within which the dispute can be resolved as well as the burden on courts. Moreover, restorative justice, as an alternative to traditional criminal proceedings and sentencing, has potential to reduce custodial sentences and to help address the problem of overcrowded prisons, which would decrease prison costs as well.[21]

Still, these are not the only or even the most significant reasons for this turn to restorative justice. Restorative justice is an integrated model for responding to criminal behavior. Contrary to traditional justice systems that mainly focus on punishing the offender, "restorative justice is considered as an evolving response to crime that respects the dignity and equality of all persons involved, builds understanding, and promotes social harmony through the healing of victims, offenders and communities."[22]

More specifically, restorative justice aims to benefit victims.[23] It provides them with an opportunity to participate actively in the whole process, to express their feelings, and to receive a personal apology and explanation from the offender. Often these practices reduce victims' anger and fear and thereby assist in emotional healing. Furthermore, victims are better able to negotiate a form of reparation that best suits their needs.

Conciliation with the victim also helps to sensitize the offenders to the harm they caused to victims. In addition, through restorative justice proceedings they can play a direct role in resolving the conflict and determining the form reparation will take, which in turn can assist in rehabilitation and integration back into the community.

Last but not least, by enlisting victims and offenders to participate directly and by relying on programs run by community-based agencies, restorative justice can tie the criminal justice system more closely to the larger community. That can improve both public understanding of crime and support for victims. And in as much it helps to reintegrate offenders, this kind of community involvement has the potential to support crime prevention more generally.[24]

[20] ECOSOC Res. 1999/26 (July 28, 1999), *available at* www.un.org/documents/ecosoc/docs/1999/e1999-inf2-add2.pdf.

[21] Explanatory Memorandum, *supra* note 7.

[22] ECOSOC Res. 2002/12 (July 24, 2002), *available at* www.un.org/en/ecosoc/docs/2002/resolution%20 2002-12.pdf.

[23] Directive 2012/29/EU establishing minimum standards on the rights, support and protection of victims of crime, and replacing Council Framework Decision 2001/220/JH, recital 46, 2012 O.J. (L 315) 57.

[24] As regards the complex relationship between restorative justice and crime prevention, see Restorative Justice and Crime Prevention: *Presenting a Theoretical Exploration, an Empirical Analysis and the Policy Perspective* (Final report of the European Project on Restorative Justice and Crime Prevention 2010), *available at* www.euforumrj.org/assets/upload/Restorative_Justice_and_Crime_Prevention_Final_report.pdf.

Restorative justice is therefore not, or at least not only, promoted as a last resort to address serious problems of traditional criminal justice, but as an *alternative for preventing and confronting crime that is significantly better for all parties involved*—offenders, victims, and society. Especially for certain categories of criminal behavior, such as domestic violence, juvenile delinquency or low gravity criminality, many scholars and practitioners consider restorative justice to be clearly advantageous.

Admittedly, these advantages of restorative justice are not always easily verifiable in practice. However, a number of studies confirm its effectiveness. Only a few examples will be mentioned.

A meta-analysis of thirty-two restorative justice programs conducted in 2001 by the Canadian Department of Justice concluded that adding restorative justice programs to the traditional criminal justice system enhanced victim satisfaction and encouraged more offenders to take responsibility for their actions and repair some of the harm they caused through restitution. Moreover, it found a very close relationship between restorative justice and reduced recidivism by those who choose to participate.[25] Other research found that victims who participated in restorative justice processes benefit across a wide range of outcomes including post-traumatic stress, while as regards offenders, substantial reductions in repeat offending for both violence and property crime was found.[26]

Other research that specifically explored victims' satisfaction with restorative justice processes also came to positive conclusions, noting that most victims interviewed were satisfied with their experiences, including the offer of mediation, the communication process, and its outcome.[27]

Many studies that focus on the potential of restorative justice to reduce recidivism are also encouraging. One study conducted under the European Forum for Restorative Justice in 2015[28] concluded that victim-offender mediation and conferencing have the potential to influence desistence, because they help offenders to understand the actual consequences of their behavior and the seriousness of the damage caused and ultimately to change their attitude towards crime. The potential of restorative justice to initiate changes for juveniles and young offenders was particularly clear. A statistical analysis confirmed that offenders who participated in restorative justice programs committed significantly fewer offenses (measured by reconvictions) in the subsequent two years

[25] Jeff Latimer et al., *The Effectiveness of Restorative Justice Practices: A Meta-analysis, Report Prepared for the Department of Justice Canada* (2001), *available at* www.justice.gc.ca/eng/rp-pr/csj-sjc/jsp-sjp/rp01_1-dr01_1/rp01_1.pdf.

[26] Lawrence W. Sherman & Heather Strang, *Restorative Justice: The Evidence* (2007), *available at* www.iirp.edu/pdf/RJ_full_report.pdf.

[27] Victims and Restorative Justice: An Empirical Study of the Needs, Experience and Position of the Victim Within Restorative Justice Practices. Country Reports 139 seq. (Daniela Bolívar et al. eds., 2015), *available at* www.euforumrj.org/wp-content/uploads/2015/05/report_victimsandRJ-2.pdf.

[28] Katrien Lauwaert, *Conclusions*, in *Desistance and Restorative Justice Mechanisms for Desisting from Crime within Restorative Justice Practices* 180 seq. (Katrien Lauwaert & Ivo Aertsen eds., 2015), *available at* www.euforumrj.org/wp-content/uploads/2015/11/Research-report-desistance-and-RJ-total-doc-24-11-final.pdf.

than offenders who did not participate in such programs.[29] Other research concludes that restorative justice procedures are associated with a reduction in recidivism for perpetrators of certain categories of crimes, especially crimes of lesser gravity,[30] while research conducted over a three-year observation period in Austria suggests that reoffending rates are positively affected by completed mediation. In the case of first-time offenders, reoffending among the sample was less than half that of the control group; among previously convicted offenders, the proportion was about two-thirds.[31] The results of the implementation of restorative justice programs in prison have also been regarded as positive, provided that the meetings are carefully prepared and the procedure is monitored by highly experienced mediators working in prisons.[32]

Concerning the acceptance of restorative justice by the general public, findings of several studies have shown that knowledge of and familiarity with victim-offender mediation or conferencing clearly enhances public acceptance.[33] Moreover, researchers have pointed out that the attitude of the general public is not as punitive as is often believed or claimed by policymakers or the judiciary,[34] while other studies have found that prosecutors can have more punitive attitudes than the general public.[35]

Finally, in terms of alleviating burdens on traditional criminal justice institutions, some states have reported very positive results. In Slovenia, for example, mediation has reduced the workload in the criminal justice system with 837 fewer trials in 2000, that is, the equivalent of the workload of five judges in a first-instance court. In this way, mediation frees up resources to be deployed to other cases.[36]

2. Problems of Implementation

Despite its advantages, the implementation of restorative justice procedures has significant obstacles. Two main categories are (1) organizational and operational obstacles, and (2) ideological or conceptual obstacles.

[29] Joanna Shapland et al., *Does Restorative Justice Affect Reconviction? The Fourth Report from the Evaluation of Three Schemes* (Ministry of Justice Research Series 10/08, June 2008), p. 66, *available at* www.ncjrs.gov/app/abstractdb/AbstractDBDetails.aspx?id=246606.

[30] James Bonta et al., *Restorative Justice and Recidivism: Promises Made Promises Kept?*, in *Handbook for Restorative Justice: A Global Perspective* 116 (Dennis Sullivan & Larry Tifft eds., 2006).

[31] David Miers, *An International Review of Restorative Justice* 11 (Crime Reduction Research Series Paper 10 2001), *available at* orca.cf.ac.uk/id/eprint/44560.

[32] Arthur Hartmann et al., *Prison Mediation in Germany*, in *Responsibility-Taking, Relationship-Building and Restoration in Prisons* 205 seq. (Tünde Barabás et al. eds., 2012).

[33] Borbala Fellegi, *Meeting the Challenges of Introducing Victim-Offender Mediation in Central and Eastern European Countries* 4 (Final Report of AGIS project JAI/2003/AGIS/088, 2005), *available at* euforumrj.org/assets/upload/FinalAGIS2publication.pdf.

[34] Elmar G.M. Weitekamp, *Research on Victim-Offender Mediation: Findings and Needs for the Future*, in *Victim-Offender Mediation in Europe: Making Restorative Justice Work* 99 seq. (European Forum for Victim-Offender-Mediation ed., 2000).

[35] Klaus Sessar, *Wiedergutmachen oder strafen: Einstellungen in der Bevölkerung und in der Justiz: ein Forschungsbericht* (1992).

[36] Alenka Meznar, *Victim Offender Mediation in Slovenia*, 3 Newsletter of the European Forum for Restorative Justice 1–3 (2002).

Without doubt, there are some notable differences between countries concerning these obstacles, especially between those countries where restorative justice programs were implemented many years ago through a general scheme and those where they have been introduced through a fragmented, incoherent, or reluctant approach into the criminal justice system. However, it seems that similar problems and obstacles exist in most countries and that they differ only in the intensity and the extent.

a. *Organizational and Operational Obstacles*

I. THE ABSENCE OF LEGISLATION

Restorative justice procedures often originate informally in local communities or trial courts and rely on customs and norms. Nonetheless, legal regulation is critical, particularly in the context of criminal prosecutions, where the state must ensure rights and procedural safeguards for defendants and victims.[37] This is especially important in countries where prosecution is based on the principle of legality, because their criminal justice authorities have little discretion over whether or how to proceed with criminal cases.[38] Even in countries where the principle of legality in prosecution does not exist or at least not in an absolute way, as for example, in the United Kingdom, the lack of sufficiently clear legislation is regarded to be an obstacle to the expansion of restorative justice programs,[39] mainly because there is great insecurity regarding their quality and the protection of the parties' fundamental rights.

Therefore, the lack of clear legislation constitutes a serious obstacle to implementing restorative justice programs. As research has shown, this legislation should not only cover the way that a case is referred to restorative justice but also the procedure itself, at least in its basic elements, as well as the way that the agreements arising from it are implemented.[40]

II. INSUFFICIENCY OF RESOURCES AND INSTITUTIONS

The emphasis in restorative justice processes is not on the punishment but on seeking reconciliation between the offender and the victim, and, when possible, the community. This aim requires time, financial resources, well-educated and trained facilitators, specialized implementation bodies, sufficient availability of programs, and a central advisory authority to coordinate and promote relevant procedures. Achieving all this requires reliable evaluation mechanisms and central databanks on restorative justice programs and their (measurable) results.

All this can be guaranteed only by the state, local administration, or strong private bodies, the support of which may not always be forthcoming. On the contrary, as shown

[37] *See* Kathleen Daly, *Revising the Relationship Between Retributive and Restorative Justice*, in *Restorative Justice: Philosophy to Practice* 34 (Heather Strang & John Braithwaite eds., 2000); Antony Duff, *Restorative Punishment and Punitive Restoration*, in *Restorative Justice and the Law* 97 (Lode Walgrave ed., 2002).

[38] Guy Masters, *What Happens when Restorative Justice Is Encouraged, Enabled and/or Guided by Legislation*, in *Critical Issues in Restorative Justice* 227 (Howard Zehr & Barb Toews eds., 2004).

[39] Gavrielides, *supra* note 3, at 278.

[40] *See* Pitsela et al., *supra* note 11 at 368.

in recent research,[41] insufficient human and financial recourses constitutes a major obstacle even in countries with a long tradition of restorative justice procedures such as the United Kingdom.

III. DIFFERENCES BETWEEN NATIONAL LEGAL FRAMES

Last but not least, the differences between national legal frameworks pose additional barriers to the adoption of restorative justice processes, because an agreement within a restorative justice process in one state might not be binding in another state where such process is not provided for the specific crime. Just as confidence in the decision of a foreign court presupposes mutual trust in the judicial system of the foreign country, confidence in foreign restorative justice agreements presupposes mutual trust in the restorative justice system of the other country, especially if the *ne bis in idem* principle comes into play. This is a key issue for the offender and the victim when they decide whether to resort to restorative justice processes.

b. *Ideological and Conceptual Obstacles*

I. SKEPTICISM ON BEHALF OF CRIMINAL JUSTICE PRACTITIONERS

Skepticism and concern on behalf of criminal justice practitioners seem to constitute another very serious obstacle to further implementation of restorative justice.[42] In many countries, police services, public prosecutors, and occasionally even judges are neither always fully informed of restorative processes nor aware of their potential advantages. Moreover, even if they are informed, they do not seem favorable toward these processes because of the assumption that restorative justice might be considered "unjust" or "unequal" for the criminal cases and the persons involved, or that it does not give priority to the presumption of innocence or the principles of equality or proportionality. In many cases, these concerns are also confirmed by dangerous amateurism in the implementation of restorative justice programs, largely due to the lack of binding legislation for implementing and evaluating these programs. That was the case for a program used in Canberra, where all the stakeholders agreed that it would be a good idea for a young offender to wear a T-shirt stating "I'm a thief."[43]

The same reluctance to refer cases to restorative justice procedures can also be observed in lawyers who seem to be more interested in a long trial than in restoring peace between the offender and the victim.[44]

II. LACK OF PUBLIC AWARENESS AND LIMITS OF SOCIAL ACCEPTANCE

In most countries, criminal justice is considered the sole responsibility of the state. For this reason, although mediation is easily accepted in civil cases, public opinion is not as

[41] *Id.* at 369. [42] *Id.* at 370.

[43] John Braithwaite, *Setting Standards for Restorative Justice*, 42 Brit. J. Criminology 565 (2002).

[44] Barbara Stańdo-Kawecka, *Restorative Justice in Poland—Limitations and Prospects for Development*, in *Restorative Justice in Criminal Matters: Towards a New European Perspective* 319 (Angelika Pitsela & Elisavet Symeonidou-Kastanidou eds., 2013).

ready to accept restorative criminal proceedings. This attitude is particularly intense when there is an increase in crime, which in turn results in a growing demand for strict crime management and marginalization of the perpetrator by imprisonment.

In addition, the public is often not even aware of the possibility of referring a case to restorative justice procedures. At the same time, even if it is informed, problems often arise from the impromptu implementation of restorative justice programs, the lack of legislation that would guarantee the rights of the parties, and the uncertainty as to the fulfillment of the commitments resulting from a possible agreement. All these constitute factors that prevent the establishment of trust in these programs.

3. Legal Reservations

Restorative justice has been subject to specific reservations and objections regarding its incorporation in the existing legal system.[45]

It was argued in particular that restorative justice is not consistent with the content of Article 14 of the UN International Covenant on Civil and Political Rights, Article 6 of the European Convention of Human Rights, and Articles 47 and 48 of the Charter of Fundamental Rights of the European Union, all of which provide for a right to a fair trial to help guarantee the rule of law. First, restorative justice is criticized for violating the "right to a court," because it replaces the court with nonjudicial bodies. Critics also argue that it violates other basic rights inferred from the fair trial principle, specifically the rights to legal counsel, an impartial judge, a public trial, the presumption of innocence, silence, and proceedings of reasonable length.

However, it should first be noted that according to the European Court of Human Rights (ECtHR) case law "the right to a court, which is a constituent element of the right to a fair trial, is no more absolute in criminal than in civil matters" and it could be "subject to implied limitations," as for example in case of a decision not to prosecute or an order for discontinuance of the proceedings.[46] Moreover, the "right to a court" could be waived by the parties both in civil matters, notably through arbitration clauses in contracts, and in criminal matters by means, inter alia, of "fines paid by way of composition." The ECtHR has judged that this waiver, "which has undeniable advantages for the individual concerned as well as for the administration of justice, does not in principle offend against the Convention." It is crucial that the parties give their free and informed

[45] *See* relevantly Stergios Alexiadis, *The Restorative Justice: An Alternative to the Confrontation of the "Criminal Phenomenon"*, in *Honorary Volume for I. Manoledakis, II* 1008 seq. (Maria Kaiafa-Gbandi ed., 2007) (in Greek); Bruce Archibald, *Restorative Justice and the Rule of Law: Rethinking Due Process Through a Relational Theory of Rights* (2013), *available at* papers.ssrn.com/sol3/papers.cfm?abstract_id=2395224; Julien Lhuillier, *The Quality of Penal Mediation in Europe*, CEPEJ-GT-MED(2007)8, *available at* www.antoniocasella.eu/restorative/Lhuillier_22aug2007.pdf; Allison Morris, *Critiquing the Critics: A Brief Response to Critics of Restorative Justice*, 42 Brit. J. Criminology 596 seq. (2002).

[46] Deweer v. Belgium, App. No. 6903/75, Eur. Ct. H.R., Feb. 27, 1980, § 49; Le Compte, Van Leuven & De Meyere v. Belgium, App. No. 6878/75, 7238/75, Eur. Ct. H.R., June 23, 1981, § 25; both *available at* www.echr.coe.int.

consent to waive the guarantees provided by the court explicitly or tacitly,[47] but in any case unequivocally.[48]

Admittedly, the fact that the ECtHR permits voluntary waiver of the guarantees provided by a court does not mean that it also permits the waiver of the rest of the aforementioned fundamental rights ensured through the principle of a fair trial. Still, restorative justice does not preclude these rights if safeguards for its implementation are provided. This is the case when restorative justice complements rather than replaces traditional judicial procedure, impartiality of the facilitator is guaranteed, both the victim and the offender have access to a lawyer, and their dignity is fully respected. Fundamental rights are also assured by the participants' option to withdraw their consensus at any time before the end of the procedure, at which point the case is transferred to the court. Likewise, there is no violation when participation in the restorative justice process is not regarded as an acceptance of guilt and when a reasonable length of proceedings is guaranteed, taking into account the purposes of repairing damage and restoring human relations. Last, it is also important that the final decision is not imposed by third parties (e.g., judges), but is agreed by the parties themselves. There remains of course the right to the "publicity" of procedure, which some models of restorative justice, such as victim-offender mediation, may not ensure. However, if there are specific interests that justify an exception to the rule of publicity, even a trial may not be public. This is inevitably the case in mediation, where the discussions between the two parties are based on trust and confidentiality. Consequently, restorative justice does not breach the principle of a fair trial if those safeguards are met.

It has also been argued that restorative justice is incompatible with legal systems where the principle of legality in prosecution (mandatory prosecution) is enshrined, because in such systems the diversion of judicial proceedings is unacceptable.

However, the principle of legality in prosecution is not a supranational principle, and therefore, even when it is recognized as a general principle in a state, exceptions may be made in specific cases. In most systems where the principle of legality applies, many exceptions have already been adopted for various reasons, such as the protection of the victim or a better functioning of the criminal justice system. Moreover, the principle of legality is not really violated if judicial proceedings are not diverted but rather complemented.

Finally, reservations have also been expressed regarding the effective protection of the public interest. Critics argue that the state's claim for respect of fundamental social values is ignored through restorative justice procedures, and the crime is ultimately handled as a private affair for which only the will of the offender and the victim are crucial.

[47] Kwiatkowska v. Italy, App. No. 52868/99, Eur. Ct. H.R., Nov 30, 2000, *available at* www.echr.coe.int.

[48] Håkansson & Sturesson v. Sweden, App. No. 11855/85, Eur. Ct. H.R., Feb. 21, 1990, § 66, *available at* www.echr.coe.int.

Nevertheless, by integrating restorative justice processes in a legal system, criminal justice is not transformed into a private affair. This is because, as already noted, bringing a case to a court is always an option both for the victim and the offender, and more importantly because restorative justice processes apply only in cases where the state has acknowledged that the public interest is not prejudiced. On the other hand, protection of the public interest does not always presuppose a trial in a criminal court or a custodial sentence. For this reason, many crimes are prosecuted only if the victim submits a complaint, while in the last few years there is a significant increase in rules that permit the abstention from prosecution when it is considered that the public interest—specifically the public interest in the effective operation of the criminal justice mechanism or in the restoration of disrupted social peace—is better served that way.

IV. Intervention of International and European Institutions to Promote Restorative Justice

1. The Positive Attitude of International and European Institutions toward Restorative Justice

Since the mid-1970s, and especially since the end of the twentieth century, international and European institutions are paying more and more attention to the development of restorative justice, with direct reference to its advantages, its forms, principles, and values.

The United Nations firmly has supported restorative justice for more than forty years as a key means to improve the administration of criminal justice. This positive attitude was expressed in the conclusions of the UN Fifth Congress on Crime Prevention and the Treatment of Offenders (Geneva, 1975), which proposed the introduction of social control institutions such as community councils, family courts, neighborhood committees, and councils for conciliation as effective policies for the prevention of crime. This favorable attitude was confirmed in later texts. The 1985 UN Declaration on "Basic Principles of Justice for Victims of Crime and Abuse of Power" urges member states to consider using informal mechanisms for the resolution of disputes, including mediation, arbitration, and customary justice for the benefit of the victims,[49] and the 2000 Vienna Declaration on "Crime and Justice: Meeting the Challenges of the Twenty-First Century" calls on member states not only to "consider" but to "develop" restorative justice policies

[49] U.N. Doc. A/RES/40/34 (Nov. 29, 1985), *available at* www.un.org/documents/ga/res/40/a40r034.htm.

and programs.[50] One year earlier, ECOSOC urged member states to formulate policies for mediation and restorative justice.[51] The same Commission, after the General Assembly had endorsed the Vienna Declaration, adopted the "Basic Principles on the Use of Restorative Justice Programs in Criminal Matters," which offered definitions and specific rules for operating restorative justice programs and encouraged formulation of national strategies to develop restorative justice.[52] This support continued even more intensely in the 2005 Bangkok Declaration,[53] the 2010 Salvador Declaration[54] and the 2015 Doha Declaration,[55] all of which promote restorative justice primarily as an alternative to custodial sentences.

In the same vein, the Council of Europe has promoted restorative justice since the 1980s in a series of recommendations that, although referring to different subjects, all tend to support adoption of restorative justice initiatives. The recommendations promote mainly mediation, initially as an essential component for building a modern criminal policy.[56] But subsequent statements also recommend it as a means for improving the functioning of the criminal justice system and particularly for reducing the number of cases in criminal courts,[57] decreasing the number of prisoners,[58] and deescalating the cost of prison systems.[59] At the same time, mediation is promoted as a means to protect the rights of the victims, who can actively participate in the process and achieve satisfaction of their claims,[60] and as an effective means for treatment of offenders that substantially facilitates social inclusion and prevents stigmatization through a custodial

[50] U.N. Doc. A/RES/55/59 (Jan. 17, 2001), *available at* www.unodc.org/documents/commissions/CCPCJ/Crime_Resolutions/2000-2009/2000/General_Assembly/A-RES-55-59.pdf.

[51] ECOSOC Res. 1999/26, *supra* note 20.

[52] ECOSOC Res. 2002/12, *supra* note 22.

[53] *Synergies and Responses: Strategic Alliances in Crime Prevention and Criminal Justice* (U.N. Doc. A/RES/60/177 Mar. 20, 2006), *available at* undocs.org/A/RES/60/177.

[54] Comprehensive Strategies for Global Challenges: Crime Prevention and Criminal Justice Systems and Their Development in a Changing World (U.N. Doc. A/RES/65/230 Apr. 1, 2011), *available at* documents-dds-ny.un.org/doc/UNDOC/GEN/N10/526/34/PDF/N1052634.pdf?OpenElement.

[55] Integrating Crime Prevention and Criminal Justice into the Wider United Nations Agenda to Address Social and Economic Challenges and to Promote the Rule of Law at the National and International Levels, and Public Participation, *available at* www.unodc.org/documents/congress//Declaration/V1504151_English.pdf.

[56] Rec(83)7 on the participation of the public in crime policy, and Rec(92)17 concerning consistency in sentencing, *available at* www.coe.int/en/web/cdpc/resolutions-recommendations.

[57] Rec(86)12 concerning measures to prevent and reduce the excessive workload in the courts, *available at* www.coe.int/t/dghl/cooperation/cepej/textes/ListeRecRes_en.asp; Rec(87)18 concerning the simplification of Criminal Justice, and Rec(95)12 on the management of Criminal Justice, *available at* www.coe.int/en/web/cdpc/resolutions-recommendations.

[58] Rec(99)22 concerning prison overcrowding and prison population inflation *available at* www.coe.int/en/web/cdpc/resolutions-recommendations.

[59] CM/Rec(2017)3 on community sanctions and measures, *available at* search.coe.int/cm/Pages/result_ details.aspx?ObjectID=0900001680700a5a.

[60] Rec(85)11 on the position of the victim in the framework of criminal law and procedure, and Rec(87)21 on assistance to victims and the prevention of victimization, replaced by Rec(2006)8 on assistance to crime victim, *available at* www.coe.int/en/web/cdpc/resolutions-recommendations.

sentence.[61] There are also recommendations that stress the role of mediation in tackling juvenile delinquency[62] as well as domestic violence,[63] and as the best way to resolve disputes with and among prisoners.[64]

The European Union's attitude toward restorative justice is also positive. In particular, Framework Decision 2001/220/JHA on the standing of victims in criminal proceedings[65] was the first EU instrument that called upon Member States to promote mediation in criminal matters for offenses they consider appropriate for this sort of measure. In a more decisive way, Directive 2012/29/EU establishing minimum standards on the rights, support, and protection of victims of crime,[66] which replaced the 2001 Framework Decision, asserted that restorative justice programs such as mediation, family group conferencing, and sentencing circles can be of great benefit to the victim,[67] and urged Member States to "facilitate the referral of cases, as appropriate to restorative justice services, including through the establishment of procedures or guidelines on the conditions for such referral."[68]

Admittedly, as noted in the Directorate General Justice guidance for Directive 2012/29/EU,[69] Member States are not obliged to introduce restorative justice processes in their law. The Court of Justice for the European Union has also stressed that a state may introduce restorative justice processes for certain crimes without being obliged to extend them to other crimes, even if they are of comparable gravity.[70] Nevertheless, Member States are encouraged to adopt these procedures in the interest of victims, ensuring that there will be no secondary victimization and that any harm caused by the crime will be repaired.

2. Quality Standards for Restorative Justice Programs

The support of international and European institutions for restorative justice has not been given unconditionally. The interest of these institutions not only to promote

[61] Rec(99)19 concerning mediation in penal matters, *available at* www.coe.int/en/web/cdpc/resolutions-recommendations, which is one of the most important instruments on the implementation of restorative justice in Europe.

[62] Rec(87)20 on social reactions to juvenile delinquency, Rec(2003)20 concerning new ways of dealing with juvenile delinquency and the role of juvenile justice, CM/Rec(2008)11 on the European rules for juvenile offenders subject to sanctions or measures, *available at* www.coe.int/en/web/cdpc/resolutions-recommendations.

[63] Rec(98)1 on family mediation, *available at* www.coe.int/t/dghl/cooperation/cepej/textes/ListeRecRes _en.asp.

[64] Rec(2006)2 on the European prison rules, *available at* www.coe.int/en/web/cdpc/resolutions-recommendations.

[65] 2001 O.J. (L 82) 1.

[66] 2012 O.J. (L 315) 57.

[67] *Id.* preamble, para. 46.

[68] *Id.* article 12.

[69] European Commission, *DG Justice Guidance Document related to the Transposition and Implementation of Directive 2012/29/EU* 32 (Ref. Ares(2013)3763804–19.12.2013).

[70] CJEU, Case C-205/09, Eredics, 2010 E.C.R. I-10231 and Joined Cases C-483/09 and C-1/10, Gueye and Sanchez, 2011 E.C.R. I-08263.

participatory justice but also to ensure the protection of fundamental rights and interests of victims and offenders is already evident from the first texts. To ensure that restorative justice processes do not violate these rights, both the UN and the Council of Europe, while inviting Member States to consider the advantages of restorative justice and introduce it in their legal systems, adopted a set of rules defining the minimum quality requirements for restorative justice processes. These rules are included in the 2002 ECOSOC Resolution regarding the Basic Principles on the Use of Restorative Justice Programs in Criminal Matters and in the Council of Europe Recommendation No.R(99)19.[71]

Both texts acknowledge basic rights for victims and offenders, specifically rights: (1) to consult with legal counsel; (2) to be fully informed (in a language they understand) about their rights, the nature of the process, and the possible consequences of their decision; (3) not to participate if they do not want to at the beginning or at any stage of the proceedings; and for minors (4) to the assistance of a parent or guardian.

The basic safeguards are also similar in both texts and can be described as follows:

a. Participation is not evidence of guilt.
b. Agreements should be voluntary and reasonable.
c. Discussions in restorative processes that are not conducted in public should be confidential.
d. Judicial supervision, where appropriate, should be ensured.
e. Failure to reach an agreement should not be used against the offender in subsequent criminal justice proceedings.
f. No increased punishment for failure to implement an agreement should be allowed.

Both UN and Council of Europe texts stress the importance of legislation that provides guidelines and standards to regulate administration of restorative justice programs, while taking into account that these programs should be regulated only to the extent that it is strictly necessary. More precisely, the UN *Handbook* recommends that guidelines cover the criteria for referring cases to restorative justice processes; how cases are handled in such processes; the qualifications, training, and assessment of facilitators; and how programs are administered.[72]

Moreover, it is noteworthy that specific principles for implementing restorative justice programs have been acknowledged in both texts. These can be summarized as follows:

a. Recourse to restorative justice programs should be ensured at all stages of criminal proceedings.
b. Restorative processes should be used only where there is sufficient evidence to charge the offender.

[71] *See* U.N. Office on Drugs and Crime, *supra* note 4; Explanatory Memorandum to the Recommendation No. (99) 19, *supra* note 7.

[72] *Handbook*, *supra* note 4, at 35.

c. The victim and the offender should normally agree on the basic facts of a case as the basis for their participation in a restorative process. This does not mean that the accused should accept guilt, which would infringe the principle of the presumption of innocence. It is sufficient that they admit some responsibility for what has happened.
d. The acceptance of facts or even "confession of guilt" by the accused, in the context of restorative justice, should not be used as evidence in subsequent criminal proceedings.
e. Disparities leading to power imbalances, as well as the safety of parties and cultural differences among them, should be taken into consideration in referring a case to, and in conducting, a restorative process.
f. Facilitators should be independent and perform their duties in an impartial manner, with due respect for the dignity of the parties. In that capacity, facilitators should ensure that the parties act with respect toward each other.[73]

Finally, there are also some very important stipulations solely found in the Council of Europe Recommendation, which, as noted, refers only to mediation and not to all forms of restorative justice. The Recommendation emphasizes that:

a. Mediation should be generally available. This, as stated in the *Explanatory Memorandum*, implies that mediation should be officially recognized as an alternative or complement to traditional criminal proceedings. It should normally have funding from a public budget (state and/or municipality) and face some kind of public accountability.
b. A decision to refer a criminal case to mediation should be accompanied by a reasonable time limit within which the competent criminal justice authorities should be informed of the state of the mediation procedure.
c. Discharges based on mediated agreements should have the same status as judicial decisions or judgments and should preclude prosecution in respect of the same facts (*ne bis in idem*).

3. The Influence of the Interventions of International and European Institutions on National Legal Orders

As research shows, the intervention of international and European institutions has definitely contributed to further implementing restorative justice practices in many states.[74]

[73] *See* Explanatory Memorandum, *supra* note 7, at 5–7; *Handbook*, supra note 4, at 35–38.

[74] *See* indicatively for the EU Member States Emanuela Biffi et al., *IVOR Report: Implementing Victim-Oriented Reform of the Criminal Justice System in the European Union* 135 seq. (2016), *available at* www.apav.pt/ivor/images/ivor/PDFs/IVOR-Repot-WebVersion.pdf.

However, although it has been more than fifteen years since these regulations have been put into place, in many countries there are still significant deviations from them that limit and degrade the importance of restorative justice. These deviations are also observed in European countries where the rules have already been introduced by the Council of Europe since 1999, while the European Union has been clearly promoting restorative justice since 2001 with binding texts for Member States.

In particular, in many countries, as already noted, no specific legislation on restorative justice exists that would cover all criminal acts, and for this reason many programs are still being implemented experimentally. Consequently, the importance of restorative justice is limited and its relationship to the existing criminal justice system remains undefined. In these countries, adherence to basic principles and quality standards cannot always be guaranteed, especially if there are no evaluating mechanisms.

On the other hand, in many countries where a legal framework on restorative justice has been introduced, the possibility of a restorative procedure is not provided for all crimes, as recommended by international and European institutions, but only for specific types of criminal acts. Moreover, even when such a possibility is provided for some crimes, criminal authorities are not always obliged to inform victims and perpetrators about its existence, which obviously undermines its importance. It is also noteworthy that in many cases, although legislation providing recourse to restorative justice is in place—for example, in Greece for juvenile delinquency—no regulations have been adopted for implementing relevant programs. Consequently, existing legislation cannot be applied.

Additionally, even in countries where a legal framework on restorative justice exists, the possibility of recourse to restorative processes is not provided at all stages of criminal procedure, despite the guidelines by international and European institutions. Moreover, the existence of a sufficient legal framework for restorative justice does not automatically imply that services are available and/or competent in the given state.[75] Limited accessibility to restorative justice remains one of the main obstacles to its further development in Europe.[76]

All these deviations from the international and European rules on restorative justice are to a great extent due to states' reluctance to recognize the importance of restorative justice processes. The basic reason for this attitude seems to be ideological and is linked to the centralized exercise of power in many modern states, where state mechanism appears uniform and compact and criminal justice administration constitutes only a part of this mechanism, essentially depicting the way the state operates. In this context, community intervention in criminal justice seems to "limit" the state power and at the same time to certify its inability to fulfill one of its major tasks, which is preventing and addressing crime. That is why restorative justice is much easier to develop in countries

[75] *Id.* at 135.

[76] Brunilda Pali (for the European Forum for Restorative Justice), Briefing Paper about the Regulation of Restorative Justice in the Directive 2012/29/EU, p. 20 (2016), *available at* www.euforumrj.org/wp-content/uploads/2017/03/EFRJ-Briefing-Paper-RJ-in-the-Victims-Directive.pdf.

with a tradition of public participation in the exercise of power, than in countries where such a tradition does not exist.

It is worth mentioning that even in countries where there are many problems of overburdened courts and overcrowded prisons, it seems to be easier to adopt measures that are strictly controlled by the state rather than institutions that are beyond its control. It seems for example easier to adopt plea bargaining than to adopt measures that would help the rationalization of the criminal justice system, such as decriminalization and reduction of sanctions, and especially measures that would introduce a new ideology in preventing and addressing crime, as is the case with restorative justice.

Of course, the lack of resources in many states must not be underestimated. Even though investment in restorative justice may produce long-term benefits in terms of preventing crime, restricting recidivism, improving imprisonment conditions, and reducing the cost of criminal justice, it should not be overlooked that usually long-term planning takes place in states that do not have to face immediate pressing financial problems.

V. Conclusions and Proposals

To summarize, there is strong evidence that restorative justice can serve as a tool for conflict management, for reducing reoffending, and for repairing harm, offering at the same time an alternative to the overloaded official criminal justice system. For these reasons, the UN, the Council of Europe and the European Union have promoted its introduction in the legal systems of their Member States. Despite this, restorative justice has not developed in the desired way in all countries, and therefore further initiatives should be undertaken.[77]

In this context, taking into account the skepticism of many states toward institutions of participatory democracy, expressed in the area of criminal justice through restorative justice, the role of international and European institutions appears to be of particular importance. Even when these institutions do not have the authority to establish binding rules, they may very well direct Member States to integrate restorative justice processes into their criminal justice systems through their evaluation mechanisms. When, for example, a state is repeatedly convicted for insulting human dignity in prisons, UN control mechanisms may point out the need to adopt restorative justice processes to address the problem. Additionally, international and European institutions may establish central evaluating mechanisms for the existing restorative justice programs as well as databases for the cases resolved and the procedure adopted.

[77] *See* European Commission for the Efficiency of Justice (CEPEJ), *Guidelines for a Better Implementation of Existing Recommendations Concerning Mediation in Penal Matters* (2007)13, *available at* wcd.coe.int/ViewDoc.jsp?p=&id=1223865&Site=&direct=true; Lhuillier, *supra* note 45; Pitsela et al., *supra* note 11, at 372 seq.

At a national level, a first major intervention is of course the formation of *a clear legal framework* that will effectively connect restorative justice processes with the official criminal justice system, so that the referral to these processes would be essentially "automated." In this context, it is crucial that referral to restorative justice be possible for all crimes, and at all stages of the criminal justice procedure, irrespective of the fact that the consequences of a successful outcome may not be the same in all cases. Specific provisions for every model of restorative justice processes as well as for juveniles' offenses should be encouraged. It is also crucial to establish the responsibility of all legal professionals, including judges, prosecutors, police, and lawyers, to advise both victims and offenders on restorative justice opportunities, including the potential benefits and risks.

Moreover, it is important to ensure the *quality* of restorative justice processes in fostering both the citizens' and the judicial authorities' confidence in them. This is not only important for the parties involved and primarily for the victim, but it is also essential for the acceptance of their results in other countries according to the *ne bis in idem* principle, when this principle is valid between these countries, as it is the case between EU Member States.[78] For this reason, it has been proposed[79] that the European Union should introduce a Directive on restorative justice, through which the key aspects of its processes, common training standards for facilitators, a code of ethics for the participants, and common evaluation mechanisms could be determined in a binding way in accordance with the texts adopted by international and European institutions. This European legislative framework is an increasingly important matter, especially since the Court of Justice of the European Communities has ruled that the termination of criminal proceedings by an authority required to play a part in the administration of criminal justice in one EU Member State, without the involvement of a court, entails under certain conditions the application of the *ne bis in idem* rule in the other Member States.[80]

Additionally, *the actual implementation of legal provisions* is essential. Therefore, states should promote restorative justice by financial and other forms of support, such as by organizing services responsible for the implementation of restorative justice programs, formulating the conditions of participation in these programs, setting up workable restorative justice schemes at all stages of the criminal justice procedure, and creating trustworthy evaluation mechanisms. Particular emphasis should be placed on improving the education and practical training of facilitators, for which states should care in the same way that they care for the training of judges and prosecutors. Facilitators should, as a minimum, be aware of the basic principles and aims of restorative justice, its relationship to criminal justice, the legal framework of restorative justice, and the techniques of communicating and working with victims, offenders, and others engaged in restorative justice processes. Securing their independence and impartiality is of utmost importance.

[78] *See* Article 50 of the EU Charter of Fundamental Rights, which, by virtue of the first subparagraph of Article 6(1) of the Treaty on European Union, has the same legal value as the Treaties (2010 O.J. (C 83) 1).

[79] Pitsela et al., *supra* note 11, at 381 seq.

[80] CJCE (11.2.2003), Cases C-187/01 and C-385/01, Gözütok and Brügge, 2003 E.C.R. I-01345.

The establishment of an advisory commission responsible for receiving complaints by persons who participated in a restorative justice process, as well as for investigating and addressing complaints, is also crucial for the acceptance and legitimacy of the restorative justice process.

Last but not least, much work has to be done on national strategies aiming at the development and further expansion of restorative justice among the competent justice and social authorities, as well as among public and local communities. Judges, prosecutors, and other criminal justice authorities including the police must be offered adequate training and be fully informed about existing restorative justice processes, about their obligation to inform victims and offenders on the possibility of recourse to these processes, and about their advantages and risks. Lawyers should also be motivated to promote the referral to restorative justice processes. For this reason, it is important that basic knowledge about restorative justice be included in the curricula of law schools. Codes of conduct for lawyers should also include an obligation for them to take steps to provide relevant information and, where appropriate, suggest the use of restorative justice processes to their clients. Finally, states, with the support of existing restorative justice services, should develop appropriate strategies—online, with information campaigns at schools and universities, articles, conferences, seminars, or advisory centers—to raise awareness of the benefits of restorative justice among the general public.

References

Ivo Aertsen *et al.*, *Rebuilding Community Connections: Mediation and Restorative Justice in Europe*, Council of Europe Publishing, Strasbourg (2004)

Vasso Artinopoulou, *Restorative Justice: The Challenge of Modern Legal Systems*, Nomiki Bibliothiki, Athens (2010)

Tünde Barabás et al. eds., *Responsibility-Taking, Relationship-Building and Restoration in Prisons, Mediation and Restorative Justice in Prison Settings*, National Institute of Criminology, Budapest (2012)

John Braithwaite, *Restorative Justice & Responsive Regulation*, Oxford University Press, New York (2002)

James Dignan, *Understanding Victims and Restorative Justice*, Open University Press, New York (2005)

Susan Herman, *Parallel Justice for Victims of Crime*, National Center for Victims of Crime, Washington DC (2010)

Gerry Johnstone, *Restorative Justice: Ideas, Values, Debates*, Routledge, London, New York (2d ed. 2011)

David Miers & Jolien Willemsens eds., *Mapping Restorative Justice: Developments in 25 European Countries*, European Forum for Victim-Offender Mediation and restorative justice, Leuven (2004)

Angelika Pitsela & Elisavet Symeonidou-Kastanidou eds., *Restorative Justice in Criminal Matters: Comparative Research in 11 European Countries*, Sakkoulas Publications, Athens, Thessaloniki, (2013)

Klaus Sessar, *Wiedergutmachen oder strafen: Einstellungen in der Bevölkerung und in der Justiz: ein Forschungsbericht*, Centaurus—Verlagsgesellschaft, Pfaffenweiler (1992)

Joanna Shapland et al., *Situating Restorative Justice Within Criminal Justice*, 10 Theoretical Criminology 505 (2006)

Heather Strang, *Repair or Revenge: Victims And Restorative Justice*, Oxford University Press, New York (2002)

Dennis Sullivan & Larry Tifft eds., *Handbook for Restorative Justice: A Global Perspective*, Routledge, London, New York (2008)

Daniel Van Ness & Karen Strong, *Restoring Justice*, Routledge, London, New York (5th ed. 2014)

Howard Zehr, *Changing Lenses: Restorative Justice for Our Times, Herald Press, Harrisonburg, Virginia, Kitchener, Ontario* (25th ann. ed. 2015)

Howard Zehr & Barb Toews eds., *Critical Issues in Restorative Justice*, Criminal Justice Press and Willan Publishing, Monsey, New York, Cullompton, Devon, UK (2004)

PART VII

APPEALS AND POST-CONVICTION REVIEW

CHAPTER 41

APPEAL AND CASSATION IN CONTINENTAL EUROPEAN CRIMINAL JUSTICE SYSTEMS

Guarantees of Factual Accuracy, or Vehicles for Administrative Control?

STEPHEN C. THAMAN

I. Introduction

The number of innocents exonerated in the United States keeps rising,[1] and there is increasing evidence of a significant number of grave miscarriages of justice in Europe.[2] These cases, based on either false or utterly insufficient evidence, nearly all made it through post-conviction review without being discovered and rectified. In two of my previous publications, I dealt with the weaknesses of evidence law, and in Europe, the inadequacy of judgment reasons, in preventing convictions of the innocent for grave crimes they did not commit.[3]

[1] The use of DNA analysis has exonerated 350 people. Innocence Project, *at* https://www.innocenceproject.org (last visited July 21, 2017); 159 innocent people have been exonerated after having been sentenced to death since 1976. Death Penalty Information Center, Facts About the Death Penalty, *available at* https://deathpenaltyinfo.org/documents/FactSheet.pdf (last visited July 21, 2017).

[2] *See* Thomas Darnstädt, *Der Richter und sein Opfer* (2013) (discussing notorious cases in Germany). Cf. Stephen C. Thaman, *Reanchoring Evidence Law to Formal Rules: A Step Toward Protecting the Innocent from Conviction for Capital Crimes?*, in *Visions of Justice: Liber Amicorum Mirjan Damaška* 383, 384–435 (Bruce Ackerman et al. eds., 2016) [hereinafter Thaman, *Reanchoring Evidence Law*] (discussing wrongful convictions in the Netherlands and elsewhere).

[3] Stephen C. Thaman, *Ensuring the Factual Reliability of Criminal Convictions: Reasoned Judgments or a Return to Formal Rules of Evidence?*, in *Comparative Criminal Procedure* 75, 75–114 (Jacqueline E. Ross

In this chapter, I will train my focus on the two main procedural vehicles for challenging criminal judgments rendered by European trial courts, appeal and cassation. I will describe their historical and procedural particularities, and investigate the extent to which they actually serve as guarantees of factual accuracy in criminal judgments or function more as vehicles for hierarchical control by the high courts over the work of lower courts. I will concentrate on the five countries with which I am most familiar, France, Germany, Italy, Russia and Spain, and make frequent reference to their codes of criminal procedure.[4]

When I speak of "appeal," I use the term in the way it is conventionally used in civil law systems,[5] where it refers, classically, to a true second factual instance, a fresh retrial of the case in its entirety, independent of any need to allege error in the first instance. It looks something like the trial de novo, found in some U.S. states.[6] The appeals court traditionally issued a new judgment replacing that of the lower trial court.

When I speak of "cassation," I refer to what was traditionally a limited remedy used to allege legal, not factual, errors committed in the trial court. The court of cassation would decide based solely on the written record of the first instance trial, a procedure not unlike a U.S. appeal.[7] The cassational court traditionally "broke"[8] or reversed the first instance judgment and remanded the case to the lower level jurisdiction, which then corrected the error or conducted a new trial.

Whereas criminal judgments in the United States become final and sentences may be imposed immediately upon the court pronouncing judgment following a guilty verdict or plea, on the European continent, both "appeal" and "cassation" were traditionally remedies to be invoked before a criminal judgment became final and punishments could be imposed. In Europe, there is no "presumptively final first instance decision."[9] The importance of the judgment in the initial trial is undercut by the "quality control" exercised by higher judges at the higher instances.[10]

The classic remedy in Europe for attacking the factual inadequacy of a final judgment (which has proceeded through an appeal and/or cassation), is "review," also called a reopening of the case based on the discovery of new facts. Although review was

& Stephen C. Thaman eds., 2016) [hereinafter Thaman, *Ensuring the Factual Reliability*]; Thaman, *Reanchoring Evidence Law*, *supra* note 2, at 383–409.

[4] For France, the *Code de Procédure Pénale* (C. pr. pén.); for Germany, the *Strafprozessordnung* (StPO), for Italy, the *Codice di Procedura Penale* (C.p.p.); for Russia, the *Ugolovno-protsessual'nyy kodeks* (U.P.K.), and for Spain, the *Ley de Enjuiciamiento Criminal* (L.E. Crim.). All citations translated by me. *See* References for full citations.

[5] The procedure is called *appel* in France, *appello* in Italy, *apelación* in Spain, *apelliatsiia* in Russia, and *Berufung* in Germany.

[6] For instance, in Massachusetts, trial is by a single judge for some lesser offenses, but the defendant has an automatic right to a trial by jury if she is not content with the results of the first trial. *See* Ludwig v. Massachusetts, 427 U.S. 618, 619–22 (1976).

[7] Called *cassation* in France, *cassazione* in Italy, *casación* in Spain, *kassatsiia* in Russia. In Germany, the remedy is called *Revision*.

[8] Derived from the French *casser*, which means "to break."

[9] Mirjan R. Damaška, *The Faces of Justice and State Authority* 48–49 (1986).

[10] *Id.*

conceived primarily as a remedy for righting wrongful convictions,[11] it has not had much success in this respect.[12] Due to space considerations, I will not be able to go into further detail regarding the theory and practice of this classic, but underused and largely ineffective procedure.

A brief review of structural and philosophical differences between Continental European (civil law) and common law systems will aid in understanding how appeal and cassation have developed from their classical forms, and assessing how they function today.

II. The Hierarchical Model of Civil Law Criminal Procedure

In the civil law system, one talks of instances, levels of collection, and review of evidence, from the lowest rungs of the court system to the high cassational courts.[13] The common law originally recognized only one instance, the presentation of mainly oral evidence before a lay jury, which returned an oral verdict that immediately went into force. The jury, representing the community, possessed inherent authority and legitimacy, and its word had the force of law. The common law "did not embrace avenues of appeal."[14] Although the United States finally allowed appeals of guilty judgments in the late nineteenth century, jury acquittals are still final and may not be appealed by prosecutor or victim.

Recently, England and Wales has allowed motions to reopen acquittals based on the discovery of new evidence.[15] Acquittals of the French *cour d'assises*, once a pure jury, but since 1941 a mixed court, where professional and lay judges deliberate together, used to be final, as in the United States, but may now be appealed to an expanded mixed court, the *cour d'assises d'appel*. Otherwise, acquittals may be challenged by the prosecutor and sometimes the victim in virtually all European systems through appeal and/or cassation.

The complex hierarchy of courts in Europe, from single judge courts, sometimes called peace courts, to collegial courts composed of professional and lay judges (mixed courts) such as the German *Schöffengericht*, three-judge panels, jury courts, or even special antiterrorism courts, on to post-conviction appeals, cassational and review courts, well reflects Mirjan Damaska's hierarchical model of "professional officials,

[11] *See* C. pr. pén. (Fr.) § 622; C.p.p. (It.) § 631; L.E. Crim. (Spain) § 954(1)(d).

[12] Jörg Kinzig, *Rechtsvergleichender Querschnitt*, in 1 *Rechtsmittel im Strafrecht. Eine internationale vergleichende Untersuchung zur Rechtswirklichkeit und Effizienz von Rechtsmitteln* 553, 573 (Monica Becker & Jörg Kinzig eds., 2000) [hereinafter *Rechtsmittel im Strafrecht*].

[13] In Russia, one has even invented a noun to render its importance: *instantsiannost* (or "instance-ness"). A.V. Kudravtseva & V.P. Smirnov, *Appelatsionnoe proizvodstvo v ugolovnom protsesse Rossii* 26 (2013).

[14] Damaška, *supra* note 9, at 60.

[15] Criminal Justice Act 2003, c. 44, § 76.

vertically organized, and deciding according to rules," as opposed to the common law tradition of "nonprofessional decisionmakers, organized into a single level of authority, deciding on community standards," his coordinate model.[16]

The establishment of mechanisms of review by higher judges of the decisions of lower judges was important in the destruction of feudal court structures on the European continent and the consolidation of the nation-state, especially in France.[17] The invention of the printing press was also instrumental to this new written, file-based system, which was not so much concerned with due process, as with ensuring "continuity and accuracy in decisionmaking" and supporting "regulatory review of subordinate officials."[18]

In her recent study of France's new requirement that its *cour d'assises* give reasons for its judgments, Mathilde Cohen made the following assertion about the ECtHR's decision[19] that triggered the reform: "[w]hile the European court's rhetoric may suggest that a human right for defendants to understand their conviction and sentence is in the making, in reality, that right can also be analyzed as a mechanism to monitor judges and administer the courts in line with the civil law tradition of a tightly monitored judiciary."[20]

In the inquisitorial system, the first and perhaps the most important "instance" was the secret preliminary investigation by a magistrate, which resulted in the assemblage of written reports of investigative measures into a dossier. After all, the magistrate questioned the witnesses and the defendant, in most cases very soon after the alleged crime, when their memories were surely fresher than months or even years later during the first instance trial.

However, even after European civil law countries largely moved to a "mixed" system with an oral trial after the French Revolution, and have, since the 1970s, begun replacing the investigating magistrate with the prosecutor as the chief investigative official, Anglo-American critics still find European trials to be primarily a review of the accuracy of the findings collected in the dossier.[21] The file continues to be the "bulwark of the hierarchical process" and "if the evidentiary significance of the file is totally and effectively denied, the hierarchical process is no more."[22] The German trial judge, for instance, still reads the investigative file and the prosecutor's conclusions of guilt before the first instance trial begins, leading to a *Schulterschluß* or "embrace" between judge and prosecutor

[16] Damaška, *supra* note 9, at 17.

[17] Richard Vogler, *A World View of Criminal Justice* 31–32 (2005).

[18] *Id.* at 20.

[19] *See* Taxquet v. Belgium [GC], App. No. 926/05, Eur. Ct. H.R., Nov. 16, 2010.

[20] Mathilde Cohen, *The French Case for Requiring Juries to Give Reasons: Safeguarding Defendants or Guarding the Judges?*, in *Comparative Criminal Procedure*, *supra* note 3, at 434.

[21] Damaška, *supra* note 9, at 192. From my viewing of Spanish trials before juries and professional panels, from 1996 to 2014, the first question asked of a witness by the prosecutor, or judge, is very often: "do you confirm the statement you made at the preliminary investigation?"

[22] *Id.* at 50. As I have written in relation to the former Soviet system: "The raw material of the Soviet inquisitorial assembly line of predetermined justice was the dossier, which each official inspected, added value to, and stamped for quality as it passed to the next stage of production." Stephen C. Thaman, *The Two Faces of Justice in the Post-Soviet Legal Sphere: Adversarial Procedure, Jury Trial, Plea Bargaining, and the Inquisitorial Legacy*, in *Crime, Procedure and Evidence in Comparative and International Context: Essays in Honour of Professor Mirjan Damaška* 99, 100–01 (John Jackson et al. eds., 2008).

that many believe undermines the presumption of innocence and leads to a prejudging of the facts in favor of guilt.[23] I do not share the inherent trust placed by Continental lawyers in the evidence assembled in the secret preliminary investigation, traditionally in the absence of defense counsel, whether it be confessions of the defendant, identifications, or witness statements, and believe it should be treated with care, or even excluded from evidence as having been "police-created."[24]

Despite the tendency of the file-based system to undermine the presumption of innocence, as well as the oral and immediate nature of the trial, the file or dossier does provide a receptacle of the evidence and the procedural acts that can be crucial in determining the accuracy of decisions of appellate, but especially cassational, courts, as they traditionally relied exclusively on written records of trial and pretrial courts.

Cassation, the classic form of post-conviction remedy, which hearkens back to sixteenth century France, was originally a political means for assuring the application of royal legislation. As the institution developed, unification of jurisprudence and with it, political unity, became its main function.[25] The unification of jurisprudence is still perhaps the chief function of courts of cassation, but it will not be the focus of this chapter.

The French court of cassation was more of a legislative organ at the outset with no capacity to decide facts, and only became integrated into the judiciary in 1804.[26] Until recently, courts of cassation always accepted the fact-finding of the lower courts, and at most could overturn a judgment if the trial court made a mistake of law in determining that the facts it found to be true constituted a particular criminal offense.[27]

Appeal, a remedy of more recent origin than cassation, was originally not available to challenge judgments in serious felony cases, which often were rendered by jury courts until they were largely abolished or converted into mixed courts in the first half of the twentieth century. It was available only to challenge judgments emanating from lower, often single-judge courts, which processed lesser crimes.[28] The new judgment issued by the appeals court could then be reviewed for legal errors in cassation.

Article 2 of Protocol 7 of the European Convention of Human Rights (ECHR) was added in 1984 to provide, in pertinent part, for the following:

> 1. Everyone convicted of a criminal offence by a tribunal shall have the right to have his conviction or sentence reviewed by a higher tribunal (…)

[23] *See* Thaman, *Ensuring the Factual Reliability*, *supra* note 3, at 86–89 (citing the work of Bernd Schünemann).

[24] Thaman, *Reanchoring Evidence Law*, *supra* note 2, at 402–03.

[25] Roger Merle & André Vitu, 2 *Traité de droit criminel* 843 (4th ed. 1979).

[26] Andrés Martínez Arrieta, *El Recurso de Casación y de Revisión Penal* 15 (2d. ed. 2013).

[27] Thaman, *Ensuring the Factual Reliability*, *supra* note 3, at 90.

[28] This was true in the 1864 Code of Criminal Procedure of the Russian Empire. Kudravtseva & Smirnov, *supra* note 13, at 11–12. It was also true in the 1877 German StPO. Monika Becker, *Das deutsche Rechtsmittelsystem*, in 2 *Rechtsmittel im Strafrecht: Eine internationale vergleichende Untersuchung zur Rechtswirklichkeit und Effizienz von Rechtsmitteln* 1, 6–8 (Monica Becker & Jörg Kinzig eds., 2000). The "Exposition of Reasons" accompanying the 1882 L.E. Crim. stated: "a second instance (i.e. appeal) is repugnant to the concept of an oral and public trial." Martínez Arrieta, *supra* note 26, at 31.

2. This right may be subject to exceptions in regard to offences of a minor character, as prescribed by law, or in cases in which the person concerned was tried in the first instance by the highest tribunal or was convicted following an appeal against acquittal.

As can be seen from the ECHR text, no precision exists as to whether this "review by a higher tribunal" may be satisfied by appeal only, or also by cassation. What is clear is that it only applies to appeals of convictions.

III. Appeal

1. Introduction

While nearly all the countries on the European continent have a second-instance appeal procedure, it is today seldom a genuine "new" trial, as would be the case if a conviction were reversed in cassation and remanded to the first instance for a new trial. Although an appeals trial addresses both the facts and the law, as does any first instance trial, today the procedure often looks more like a broader form of cassation. Appeal, according to some, has become more an instance for control of first instance decisions, the classic role of cassation, than a new trial on the merits.[29]

Generally speaking, the more "appeal" stays close to the original form of an actual new trial before a new judge, the more it applies only to judgments of the lower courts involving lesser offenses. The more the remedy looks like a cassational review of the first instance trial, the more it tends to apply across the board, even to more serious felonies.

2. When Is Appeal Available to Challenge a First Instance Judgment?

One of the original justifications for limiting appeals to judgments from low level courts was that the quality of trial in entry level single-judge courts is considered to be inferior to that in the higher level courts. The judges are often younger members of the judicial bureaucracy who lack the experience needed to carefully evaluate evidence and render error-free justice. These courts have heavy caseloads, which sometimes leads to rapid and sloppy trials. Cases may be tried within a short time of arrest, making it difficult for defense and prosecution to adequately prepare their cases.[30] It is further a problem that some jurisdictions do not provide for appointed counsel for low-level crimes.[31]

[29] Ercole Aprile, *Appello,ricorso per cassazione e revisione* 165–66 (2013).

[30] Kinzig, *supra* note 12, at 622–23.

[31] Becker, *supra* note 28, at 5, 16.

Logically, then, the "appeal" would be to a higher, more qualified judge or panel of judges, with a less-crowded docket, and capable of reasoning and deliberating in a more comprehensive manner.[32] Often, appeals of judgments of single-judge courts indeed go to three-judge panels, as is the case in Germany. Sometimes the judgment of a mixed court in the first instance is appealed to a similarly constituted mixed court at a higher level.[33] These setups make sense, if one adheres to the position that judgments of lay courts should not be set aside by panels of professional judges.[34] In France, decisions of the *cour d'assises* in the first instance, which is composed of six lay assessors and three professional judges, may be appealed to a *cour d'assises d'appel* composed of three professional judges and nine lay assessors, which will theoretically provide for greater powers of fact-finding and deliberation. In Norway, the judgment of a mixed court in the first instance could traditionally be appealed to a jury composed of ten lay jurors and three professional judges.[35]

In most countries, if the first instance judgment results in no punishment other than a fine, or a fine under a specified amount, no appeal lies.[36] The ECtHR, in interpreting the right to appeal under section 2(2) of Protocol 7 ECHR, pays no attention to whether the legislator has labeled an offense as a criminal infraction, misdemeanor, or administrative violation, but rather to whether the appellant was sentenced to a significant period of deprivation of liberty, in deciding whether a right to appeal must be guaranteed.[37]

Many European countries have simplified, consensual procedures, involving guilty pleas or stipulations, or acceptance of a written prosecutorial punishment recommendation (penal orders). A defendant who has accepted such a resolution of her case may be denied the right to appeal.[38] The ECtHR, in interpreting section 2 of Protocol 7 ECHR, has also put limits on a state's ability to limit appeal from consensual procedures.[39]

Appeal is still not a remedy applicable to judgments from the upper-level courts that try serious felonies in Germany and Spain. This has led to criticism that those convicted of the most serious crimes have fewer remedies than those charged with petty offenses.[40]

[32] *See* Perfecto Andrés Ibáñez, *Los Hechos en la Sentencia Penal* 109 (2005).

[33] This is true in Germany. Becker, *supra* note 28, at 32–33. In Italy, appeals from the *corte d'assise*, composed of six lay assessors and two professional judges, go to a *corte d'assise d'appello*, with a similar constitution.

[34] Alberto Alonso Rimo, *Spanien*, in *Rechtsmittel im Strafrecht*, *supra* note 12, at 419, 439.

[35] It appears, however, that the Norwegian parliament in 2017 voted to replace this appeals jury with a mixed court. *Norway to Drop Jury System on Appeal*, News in English, Jan. 20, 2017, *at* http://www.newsinenglish.no/2017/01/20/norway-to-drop-jury-system-on-appeal.

[36] Kinzig, *supra* note 12, at 598–99.

[37] Stanchev v. Bulgaria, App. No. 8682/02, Eur. Ct. H.R., Oct. 1, 2009, §§ 46 ff.

[38] Stephen C. Thaman, *A Typology of Consensual Criminal Procedures*, in *World Plea Bargaining* 297, 339–42, 347–50, 370–71 (Stephen C. Thaman ed., 2010).

[39] Rostovtsev v. Ukraine, App. No. 2728/16, Eur. Ct. H.R., July 25, 2017, §§ 32–38 (defendant admitted facts but sought to appeal court's legal qualification thereof).

[40] Hans-Heiner Kühne, *Strafprozessrecht: eine systematische Darstellung des deutschen und europäischen Strafverfahrensrechts* 668 (9th ed. 2015).

Jury judgments for murder may be "appealed" in Russia and Spain, but, as we shall see, these "appeals" are not trials de novo, but cassation-like procedures aimed at reviewing the lower court's decision.

3. Appeal to the Detriment of the Defendant

If only the defendant appeals a conviction, she is protected from receiving a graver penalty. But if the public or private prosecutor appeals, the protection against *reformatiu in peius*,[41] which is not recognized by the ECHR,[42] is set aside. Acquittals may be replaced by convictions, and lesser punishments may be replaced by higher ones.[43] The public prosecutor will typically meet a defense appeal solely for the purpose of canceling the protection of *reformatiu en peiu*.[44]

In Italy, in 2006, a law amending the Italian Code of Criminal Procedure to explicitly require proof beyond a reasonable doubt included a prohibition against appealing an acquittal in the absence of decisive supervening evidence of guilt. The Italian Constitutional Court, however, held that the prohibition of appeals of acquittals violated the constitutional principle of equality of arms, by putting the prosecutor in a worse position than the defense, and thus making the collective members of the public unable to defend their rights through its representative.[45]

4. The Appellate Trial

French and German appeals, when first introduced in the nineteenth century, triggered an automatic right to a new trial on the merits.[46] This classic form of appeal, in which the appeals court rehears the first instance evidence and takes new evidence, if necessary, before issuing its own new judgment, is rapidly disappearing.[47] The strongest contemporary version is perhaps in Germany, where appellants have an automatic right to a new trial in all but minor cases where the punishment does not exceed a certain level of fine.[48]

In most systems today, would-be appellants must articulate reasons for exercising the remedy, and courts may dismiss an appeal without a hearing if the reasons are inadequate. The decisions of courts of appeal are becoming thereby increasingly "cassational" in that they review the judgment of the first instance court for errors (factual and legal)

[41] Prohibition on worsening the situation of someone who appeals a judgment.
[42] Stefan Trechsel, *Human Rights in Criminal Procedure* 362 (2005).
[43] *Cf.* C. pr. pén. (Fr.) § 380–3, 515; StPO (Ger.) § 331(1); C.p.p. (It.) § 597(2-3); U.P.K. (Russ.) § 389.24.
[44] Becker & Kinzig, *supra* note 12, at 202.
[45] *See* Dec. No. 26, 2007, Italian Constitutional Court. *See* discussion in Antonino Fallone, *Appello dell'assoluzione, motivazione rafforzata, principio dell'oltre ogni ragionevole dubbio, rinnovazione dibattimentale; la giurisprudenza italiana e della corte di Strasburgo*, in *Cassazione penale No.* 2, at 821–22 (2015).
[46] Becker, *supra* note 28, at 4.
[47] Kinzig, *supra* note 12, at 593–94.
[48] StPO (Ger.) § 313.

before admitting the case for trial.[49] The so-called appeal of Spanish jury judgments to an intermediate court of justice only lies if the appellant can articulate one of several statutory grounds, thus making it indistinguishable from Spanish cassation.

With this blurring of the lines between appeal and cassation, the way has been opened to combine them into one unified procedural remedy. This step has been taken in Russia, which since 2013 considers an "appeal" to be a remedy against a non-final judgment and "cassation" to be an extraordinary remedy to attack judgments that have already become final. In this new system, the statutory grounds that must be alleged on "appeal" and "cassation" are virtually identical.[50]

Most codes stipulate that appellate trials shall follow the rules of first instance trials, except where the code makes specific exceptions.[51] One standard exception is that a member of the court opens the trial by presenting a summary of the evidence presented and the judgment rendered in the first instance court.[52] When the convicted defendant appeals, which is overwhelmingly the case, the defense presents its case first, followed by the prosecutor and/or victim.[53] If an appeal is really a new trial on the charges in the accusatory pleading, the prosecutor should still have the burden of proof and present its case first. Placing the burden of proof on the convicted defendant puts us again more in the ambit of cassational control of lower court judgments, rather than that of a classic appeal.

As the appeals trial is, in theory, a new trial on the merits, the defendant should be present, unless her presence is waived. This means that an imprisoned defendant must be produced in court. Presence by video link is permitted in some countries[54] and has been upheld as not violating the right of confrontation guaranteed by Article 6(3)(c) ECHR.[55]

The ECtHR has conceded, however, that the rules of evidence on appeal need not be as strict as in first instance trials and that the presence of the defendant and even the requirement of a public hearing can be dispensed with in the interests of procedural economy. In deciding whether failure to bring an incarcerated defendant before the court violates the right to a fair trial under Article 6(1) ECHR, it looks at the following factors: (1) whether the jurisdiction of the appeals court extends to both legal and factual issues, and the court is empowered to consider additional arguments which had not been examined in the first-instance; (2) the seriousness of the charges against the applicant; and (3) the severity of the possible sentence.[56] The ECtHR has found a violation of Article 6(1) ECHR when an appellate court, which is being asked to aggravate

[49] Kinzig, *supra* note 12, at 595.

[50] Kudravtseva & Smirnov, *supra* note 13, at 5.

[51] *Cf.* C. pr. pén. (Fr.) § 512; StPO (Ger.) § 332; C.p.p. (It.) § 598; U.P.K. (Russ.) § 389.13(1).

[52] Anne-Solène Heurtin, *Frankreich*, in *Rechtsmittel im Strafrecht*, *supra* note 12, at 43, 57; Stefania Carnevale & Renzo Orlandi, *Italien*, in *Rechtsmittel im Strafrecht*, *supra* note 12, at 85, 123.

[53] *Cf.* C. pr. pén. (Fr.) § 380–1, 513; L.E. Crim. (Spain) §§ 791(2), 846bis e.

[54] U.P.K. (Russ.) § 389.12(1)–(2).

[55] Viola v. Italy, App. No. 45106/04, Eur. Ct. H.R., Oct. 5, 2006, §§ 64–67.

[56] Rozhkov v. Russia, App. No. 11469/05, Eur. Ct. H.R., Oct. 31, 2013, § 20.

the sentence given the defendant at the first instance, refuses to bring the defendant before the court to be personally heard.[57]

Unlike cassational courts, appeals courts were originally expected to rehear the evidence, reassess it, and reach a new judgment. Most appeals legislation provides for the recalling of first instance witnesses, and the calling of new witnesses. Despite these powers, appeals courts today either only rehear first instance witnesses when their testimony is called into question or, more often, fail to hear either the trial witnesses or take new evidence.[58]

In practice, appeals courts base their rulings prima facie on the transcripts of the testimony taken in the first instance, unless that testimony is contested by one of the parties.[59] Transcripts of testimony taken in the first instance are freely admissible in appeals court trials, despite the fact that many codes have a strict requirement that evidence be taken orally in the presence of the fact-finders and subject to cross-examination.[60] Parties may also stipulate to have the decision of the appellate court based on the record of the first instance trial.[61]

Even when a party moves to have testimony retaken, many codes give the appeals court discretion to deny the motion if it believes the repetition of the testimony will not be helpful.[62] This has led to a situation where in France, Italy, and Spain, the typical appeals trial includes neither a retaking of evidence adduced in the first instance nor the taking of new evidence.[63] The appeals court will thus have limited knowledge of the evidence placed before the first instance court.[64]

In Spain and Russia, the appeals courts are, like cassational courts, bound to the findings of fact made by the first instance court. In Spain, a re-evaluation may only occur if it does not violate the principles of orality and immediacy, for instance, if it only involves the interpretation of documents rather than witness testimony.[65] In Russia, a reevaluation is only possible if the witnesses are recalled, or the trial testimony is read out in the appeals trial.[66]

It appears that European appellate courts are, in a sense, allergic to immediacy. They would rather conduct a paper review of the quality of the first instance trial than be irritated by closeness to the sources of the facts that they must evaluate, that is, the first instance witnesses. The ECtHR, however, has found violations of the right to a fair trial and to confrontation when a defendant convicted for a serious felony

[57] Zahirovic v. Croatia, App. No. 58590/11, Eur. Ct. H.R., Apr. 25, 2013, §§ 57, 62–64.

[58] Becker & Kinzig, *supra* note 12, at 202.

[59] For Russia, see Kudravtseva & Smirnov, *supra* note 13, at 71.

[60] The principles of orality, immediacy, and confrontation. This is the case in Italy. Carnevale & Orlandi, *supra* note 52, at 87.

[61] StPO (Ger.) § 325; U.P.K. (Russ.) § 389.13(7).

[62] StPO (Ger.) § 323(2); C.p.p. (It.) § 603(1); U.P.K. (Russ.) § 389.13(5); L.E. Crim. (Spain) § 791(1).

[63] Kinzig, *supra* note 12, at 610. [64] Aprile, *supra* note 29, at 165–66.

[65] Luis Gómez Amigo, *Los motivos de la apelación contra sentencias del Tribunal del Jurado. Estudio de jurisprudencia*, in *Actualidad Penal No. 21* at 423, 426–27 (1999).

[66] Kudravtsev & Smirnov, *supra* note 13, at 100.

demands an acquittal on appeal, claiming the testimony of the complaining witnesses was false, and the appeals court upholds the conviction in camera without hearing the testimony of either the appellant or the complaining witnesses who testified in the first instance court.[67]

The ECtHR has also consistently held that an appeals court may not issue a new judgment of guilt, after an acquittal in the first instance, without hearing the defendant or any of the witnesses heard in the first instance.[68] For example, an Italian court of appeal entered a guilty judgment following a first instance acquittal, without questioning the witnesses whom the first instance court had found not credible. By reading the written record of the trial, the appeals court found itself able to resurrect the credibility of the witnesses enough to find proof beyond a reasonable doubt. The ECtHR found a violation, reiterating that courts that pronounce on guilt or innocence must normally "hear the witnesses in person and evaluate their credibility."[69] The united penal chamber of the Italian Court of Cassation has since adopted this ECtHR jurisprudence.[70]

The Spanish Constitutional Court has also come to a similar decision, finding a violation of the right to a fair trial and the presumption of innocence in a case where the appeals court drew inferences of guilt from the same circumstantial evidence that the first instance court had ruled did not support such an inference.[71]

In France, the court of appeals may hear new evidence.[72] In some countries, however, it is admissible only if the presiding judge deems it absolutely necessary for deciding the case properly.[73] At times, a party moving to introduce new evidence must show why such evidence was not available at the first instance.[74] One reason for limiting the admission of new evidence on appeal is a fear that parties will "sandbag" by withholding evidence in the first instance in order to use it to prevail in the more important second instance.[75]

In Italy, the failure to introduce new evidence not available at the time of the first instance trial could constitute grounds for cassation, whereas rehearing the trial witnesses is discretionary.[76] While "supplementary evidence" is admissible in the new Russian appeals trial, there is a dispute as to whether this refers only to evidence that

[67] R.H. v. Finland, App. No. 34165/05, Eur. Ct. H.R., June 2, 2009, §§ 34 ff.; Lajos Kiss v. Hungary, App. No. 26958/04, Eur. Ct. H.R., Sept. 29, 2009, §§ 25 ff.

[68] Constantinescu v. Romania, App. No. 28871/95, Eur. Ct. H.R., June 27, 2000, §§ 58–61; Destrehem v. France, App. No. 56651/00, Eur. Ct. H.R., May 18, 2004, § 45; Manolachi v. Romania, App. No. 36605/04, Eur. Ct. H.R., Mar. 5, 2013, §§ 19, 48–52.

[69] Lorefice v. Italy, App. No. 63446/13, Eur. Ct. H.R., June 29, 2017, §§ 27–28, 36–47.

[70] C. Cass. (Sez. un.) 27620/16 of 16 July 2016 (Case of Dagupta).

[71] STC 88, 2013 (Apr. 11, 2013), B.O.E. No. 112, May 10, 2013. The ECtHR found a violation on similar grounds in *Almenara Alvarez v. Spain*, App. No. 50224/07, Eur. Ct. H.R., Oct. 25, 2011, §§ 44–50.

[72] Jean Pradel, *Procédure Pénale* 740–41 (9th ed. 1997).

[73] StPO (Ger.) § 323(3); C.p.p. (It.) § 603(2); U.P.K. (Russ.) § 389.13(6); L.E. Crim. (Spain) § 790(3).

[74] U.P.K. (Russ.) §389.6(1.1). *Cf.* Kinzig, *supra* note 12, at 612.

[75] Kudravtseva & Smirnov, *supra* note 13, at 67.

[76] C.p.p. (It.) § 606(1)(d). *See* Aprile, *supra* note 29, at 225–38.

need not undergo adversarial testing, such as documents, physical evidence, etc., or whether it includes evidence not available in the first instance.[77]

No new evidence is admissible in "appeals" of Spanish jury judgments,[78] another indication that one is really dealing with disguised cassation.

5. The Appellate Decision

The court of appeals traditionally pronounced its own judgment, as would any first instance court, and this is still the case in some countries.[79] Today, with the gradual change to a "weak appeal" with cassation-like characteristics and reliance on the file and secondhand material, rather than on oral testimony, there are more and more instances where the appeals court remands to the trial court, rather than itself issuing a new judgment.

In many countries, the appeals court will only decide a case itself if it can "purge" or correct errors discovered in the decision of the first instance, but it will remand to the lower court if this is not possible or if the lower court errors are grounds for an absolute reversal, sometimes called an "absolute nullity."[80]

After the Italian Constitutional Court overturned the prohibition on appeals of acquittals, the Court of Cassation returned to its previous approach, which required the reasoning of an appellate conviction following a first instance acquittal to be a "more persuasive" and "better reasoned" interpretation of the same evidence introduced in the first instance. Otherwise, the appellate judgment would be "unsuitable to eliminate reasonable doubt as to the guilt of the accused."[81]

In other courts, however, there is an increasing consensus that the appellate court should remand overturned acquittals to the first instance for retrial.[82]

6. Appeals in Practice

In many countries, appeal rates are fairly low. A study of appeals in Germany in 1995 revealed that the remedy is used in only about 5 percent of cases.[83] Most appeals, of course, are by the defense of convictions, as acquittals in the first instance are a rare occurrence.[84] A study some years ago also found that only about 4 percent of French

[77] Kudravtseva & Smirnov, *supra* note 13, at 92–94.

[78] Alonso Rimo, *supra* note 34, at 447.

[79] *Cf.* C. pr. pén. (Fr.) §§ 516–20; StPO (Ger.) § 328(1).

[80] U.P.K. ((Russ.) § 389.22(1)–(1.1). For Spain, see Alonso Rimo, *supra* note 34, at 448.

[81] Fallone, *supra* note 45, at 823–24; Aprile, *supra* note 29, at 242.

[82] *See* L.E. Crim (Spain) § 792(2); Kudravtseva & Smirnov, *supra* note 13, at 60–61.

[83] Becker & Kinzig, *supra* note 12, at 206.

[84] Around 3 percent in Germany, but less than 1 percent in Russia. An outlier is Spain, where as of 1998, both juries and professional courts acquitted at a rate of 19 percent. Thaman, *Ensuring the Factual Reliability*, *supra* note 3, at 85–86.

convictions out of the police and correctional courts (excluding penal orders) are appealed, and 12 percent of these ended in acquittal.[85] An exception can be found in Spain, where 80 percent of convicted persons appeal and are at least partially successful in around 20 percent of cases.[86]

Although over 50 percent of German appeals were at least in part successful,[87] the appeals court acquitted in only around 3 percent of cases.[88] Similarly, in Italy, although about 53.8 percent of appeals in the period 1989–1995 ended in some modification, only 1.6 percent ended in an acquittal.[89]

Although prosecutors appeal much less frequently than defendants,[90] they are much more successful, especially when they appeal acquittals. One reason for appealing acquittals is to avoid state responsibility for damages to the acquitted person.[91] Around 60 percent of acquittals in Spain are appealed by the private prosecutor, but only around 15 percent by the public prosecutor.[92] It is also remarkable that in France, according to statistics compiled in 2008, the *cour d'assises d'appel*, composed of nine lay judges and three professional judges, overturns 57 percent of all acquittals appealed by the public prosecutor.[93]

IV. Cassation

1. Introduction

Much as appeal is becoming more like cassation in countries such as Russia, Spain, and Italy,[94] cassational courts now act more like appeals courts, most importantly, by engaging in a review of the factual findings of the first instance court, something that was strictly prohibited in classical cassation.

Appeal is called an "ordinary" remedy, in that there were traditionally few obstacles to a defendant's right to a retrial of the facts. Cassation, on the other hand, is often called an "extraordinary" remedy, in that one must allege specific statutory grounds before a hearing will be granted. Cassation remedies are typically available before a

[85] Richard S. Frase. *France*, in *Criminal Procedure: A Worldwide Study* 143, 179 (Craig M. Bradley ed., 1999).

[86] Kinzig, *supra* note 12, at 653.

[87] Becker, *supra* note 28, at 48.

[88] Monika Becker & Martin Lugan, *Die Aktenanalyse*, in *Rechtsmittel im Strafrecht*, *supra* note 12, at 69,156.

[89] Carnevale & Orlandi, *supra* note 52, at 139.

[90] Ninety-five percent of appeals in Spain are filed by the defense and private prosecutor, and only 5 percent by the public prosecutor. Alonso Rimo, *supra* note 34, at 458.

[91] Monika Becker & Anna Luczak, *Interviews mit Praktikern*, in *Rechtsmittel im Strafrecht*, *supra* note 12, at 176, 177.

[92] Alonso Rimo, *supra* note 34, at 456.

[93] Cohen, *supra* note 20, at 442.

[94] Kinzig, *supra* note 12, at 592–93.

judgment becomes final, except in Russia, where its new version of cassation is now a remedy to reopen final judgments.[95]

Judgments of the lowest courts must normally first be appealed to the next highest court, and then, in cases of alleged errors of law, review may be sought in cassation, normally in the Supreme Court or Court of Cassation. Decisions of high-level felony trial courts, as has been noted, can often only be attacked in cassation.[96] The courts of cassation often sit in panels of three[97] to five judges.[98]

Acquittals, with few exceptions,[99] may also be challenged in cassation by the public or private prosecutor.

Germany allows a party who wants only to challenge a violation of the law to skip the appeal stage and go directly to the cassational court, a procedure called *Sprungrevision*.[100] The same is true in Italy, where the procedure is called "immediate cassation."[101] It is not possible to leapfrog over appeal to the cassational court in France and Spain.[102]

2. The Record upon which Courts of Cassation Base Their Decisions

Since cassational courts usually do not take testimony, the procedure relies predominantly on records from the first instance trial. Appellate courts in the United States have a full verbatim transcript of the trial available for them in conducting their cassation-like review. If a claim of insufficiency of evidence is made, the court has the possibility of assessing the totality of the evidence. This is not, however, the case in most civil law countries. In Russia and Germany, the only record of the case is a summary of the evidence created by the clerk of the court with little or no input of the parties. Although audio recordings are theoretically available in France,[103] Spain, and elsewhere, they are seldom used by the higher courts.[104] Even when recordings exist, the Spanish Supreme Court refuses to use them for assessing the credibility of witnesses.[105] Efforts to require a verbatim record of trials have continually been defeated in Germany and are opposed by the courts.[106]

95 U.P.K. (Russ.) § 389.35.

96 *Cf.* StPO (Ger.) § 333; L.E. Crim. (Spain) § 848 (in nonjury cases).

97 C. pr. pén. (Fr.) § 567-1-1.

98 The criminal panel of the Spanish Supreme Court sits with three judges, in normal cases, but five if the punishment could exceed twelve years. Alonso Rimo, *supra* note 34, at 436.

99 Acquittals in the *cour d'assises d'appel* in France are final.

100 StPO (Ger.) § 335.

101 Carnevale & Orlandi, *supra* note 52, at 106.

102 Kinzig, *supra* note 12, at 590.

103 C. pr. pén. (Fr.) § 308.

104 Thaman, *Ensuring the Factual Reliability*, *supra* note 3, at 92.

105 Miguel Carmona Ruano, *Recursos contra sentencias. Revisión del hecho probado*, in *La Ley del Jurado: Problemas de Aplicación Práctica* 827, 846 (Luis Aguiar de Luque & Luciano Varela Castro eds., 2004).

106 Thaman, *Ensuring the Factual Reliability*, *supra* note 3, at 92.

In reality, many cassational courts decide their cases based on the written judgment of the court of first instance, and nothing else. This is the case in Germany, Spain, and Italy.[107] With the multiple levels of review in hierarchical civil law systems, "information must be simplified, generalized, deprived of its particularity for the decision of the superior level of the hierarchy."[108] In this process, trial judges will often carefully describe facts, circumstantial evidence, and statements that fit in with their conclusions, but will sometimes omit controversial and doubtful points.[109] Possible erroneous interpretations, twisting of facts, or conscious falsifications are very difficult then to uncover.[110] One must thus distinguish between the cassational court's judgment of the facts and its "judgment of the judgment."[111]

3. General Grounds for Cassation

Four general grounds for cassation can be found in most codes: (1) structural errors dealing with the trial court's jurisdiction and makeup, etc.,[112] (2) failure to properly apply the substantive penal law to the facts found true by the first instance court,[113] (3) failure to properly apply procedural rules that give rise to a nullity,[114] and (4) missing or inadequate judgment reasons.[115]

Besides the general grounds of cassation, Spain's Code of Criminal Procedure section 852 allows petitioners in cassation to simply claim the violation of a constitutional right. Typically an allegation of a violation of the presumption of innocence, or a denial of trial "with all the guarantees" serves as a "juridical funnel" to get the case to the Supreme Court.[116]

4. Inadequate Judgment Reasons as a Ground of Cassation

Since 1846, when the great German jurist Savigny suggested that judges should be bound in their evaluation of the facts by the "laws of thought, experience and human knowledge," European doctrine began recognizing a ground of cassation based in the lack of logic, clarity, or scientific acceptability of the judgment reasons.[117]

[107] *Id.* In Italy, cassation based on faulty reasons is limited to the text of the judgment, so as to prevent the Court of Cassation from entering into a re-evaluation of the evidence. Aprile, *supra* note 29, at 263.

[108] Damaška, *supra* note 9, at 20.

[109] Andreas Geipel, *Handbuch der Beweiswürdigung* 40 (2008).

[110] *Id.*

[111] Andrés Ibáñez, *supra* note 32, at 92 (citing Luigi Ferrajoli).

[112] C.p.p. (It.) § 606(1)(a)(2).

[113] C.p.p. (It.) § 606(1)(b)(3); U.P.K. (Russ.) § 401.15(1); L.E. Crim. (Spain) § 849(1)(a).

[114] C.p.p. (It.) § 606(c); StPO (Ger.) § 337; U.P.K. (Russ.) § 401.15(1); L.E. Crim. (Spain) § 849(1)(a).

[115] *See infra* Section IV.4.

[116] José Bonet Navarro, *Presunción de inocencia a favor del actual recurso de casación*, in *La Ley Penal No. 64*, at 31, 49 (2009).

[117] Thaman, *Ensuring the Factual Reliability*, *supra* note 3, at 82.

The codes and/or case law in many countries expressly require judgments to adhere to the rules of "logic, science and common sense," or similar incantations.[118] In Spain, the cassational petitioner must point to the insufficiency or the lack of rationality in the factual reasons, or a violation of the maxims of experience or reason.[119] The codes sometimes speak in terms of the contradictoriness, or lack of clarity of the judgment reasons, or the lack of reasons as to why certain facts were proved and others not, as a ground for cassation.[120]

In Italian and Spanish doctrine, the "subjective" decision of the first instance court that certain facts constituting guilt were proved, or not proved beyond a reasonable doubt, is untouchable in cassation. But the objective rationality of this decision, that is, whether it was carried out in conformity with principles of logic and rationality, is a question of law open to review in cassation.[121]

Since a true appeal in the form of a second trial on the facts is not available in Spain from judgments in the provincial courts that handle serious felonies, the Spanish Supreme Court has declared that it has "interpreted the cassational ground of presumption of innocence in the broadest possible way, so that it practically achieves the possibilities of evidentiary review which are typical for an 'appeal' without the repetition of the trial. . . ."[122] In other words: "penal cassation should fulfill, in our procedural system, among other goals, that of constituting this double penal instance."[123]

In Germany, one of the main causes for reversals of judgments by the courts of cassation is the inadequate rendition or description of the facts in the judgment reasons, or *Darstellungsrüge*. In the words of the German Supreme Court: "[T]he judgment reasons must reveal that the trier of fact took account of all circumstances which influenced its decision and included them in its considerations. The cassational court can only review the decision if the testimony of the incriminating witness is reproduced and discussed, in order for it to judge the development of the testimony and its consistency."[124]

The stubborn refusal of Germany to require a verbatim record of trials makes it all the more important for the judgment reasons to restate the facts that were crucial to the judge's decision. In France, as well, if the judgment reasons are "insufficient to allow the court to exercise its control and recognize if the law has been violated," cassation will ensue.[125] It is not a question of what happened in reality, but whether the facts contained in the judgment are an adequate basis for the conclusion drawn by the judge.[126] What

[118] C.p.p. (It.) § 607(1)(e) ("manifest lack of logic").

[119] L.E. Crim. (Spain) §§ 790(2), 846 bis c(e).

[120] C.p.p. (It.) § 607(1)(e); U.P.K. (Russ.) § 389.16; L.E. Crim. (Spain) §§ 849(1)–(2), 851, 846 bis c(a).

[121] Fallone, *supra* note 445at 829–33. In Spain, providing irrational judgment reasons is deemed to violate the presumption of innocence. Stephen C. Thaman, *Should Juries Give Reasons for Their Verdicts? The Spanish Experience and the Implications of the European Court of Human Rights Decision in* Taxquet v. Belgium, 86 Chi.-Kent. L. Rev. 613, 643–45 (2011).

[122] STS 2047/2002, *cited in* Carmona Ruano, *supra* note 105, at 835.

[123] *Id.* at 836 (citing STS 106/1988).

[124] BGH 5 StR 63/12, StV 2013, 7 (Mar. 14, 2012).

[125] C. pr. pén. (Fr.) § 593 ¶1.

[126] Detlef Burhoff & Peter Kotz, *Handbuch für die strafrechtlichen Rechtsmittel und Rechtsbehelfe* 731 (2013).

goes on is a "mediated" checking of the facts through their portrayal in the judgment reasons. One should distinguish between the evaluation of the evidence and the "justification of the evaluation of the evidence."[127]

5. Overturning Acquittals in Cassation due to Inadequate Reasons

I have written extensively on how the Russian Supreme Court, acting as a court of cassation prior to the introduction of the new unified appeals system, overturned around 50 percent of all acquittals emanating from the new jury courts, often basing its decisions on specious or even trivial alleged violations that were not even pleaded by the prosecution, while reversing far fewer convictions.[128]

We have already seen how prosecutors tend to use their appeal powers to overturn acquittals, and the same is true in cassation. In Russia, a judgment of acquittal must include, inter alia, the "reasons for acquitting the defendant and the evidence supporting them" and "the reasons why the judge rejected the evidence presented by the prosecution."[129]

The Spanish courts have struggled with the question of whether acquittal judgments need be as exhaustively reasoned as are judgments of guilt.[130] The Spanish Constitutional Court, in a decision in 2004, maintained that reasons for convictions had to be "more rigorous" than those for acquittals, because of the presumption of innocence, but it stressed than an acquittal based on a mere expression of doubt was insufficient. Because of the constitutional prohibition of arbitrary judgments, the jury must explain *why* it acquitted. A strong dissent, however, found that the requirement of reasons for jury acquittals violates the presumption of innocence.[131]

The ECtHR, however, recently found a violation of Article 6(1) ECHR where the Spanish Supreme Court not only referred to evidence in the investigative dossier not admitted at the trial in which the defendant was acquitted, but found guilty mens rea based on the same facts that did not convince the first instance court beyond a reasonable doubt. The ECtHR held that a cassational court, if it wishes to replace an acquittal with a conviction, may not reinterpret the facts without hearing the witnesses and the defendant.[132] Here the Supreme Court really thought it was sitting as a court of appeal!

In Germany, which has no juries, the Supreme Court at times appears to require trial courts that issue an acquittal to explain in the reasons why the defendant's rendition of events was true. In one case, it held that the trier of fact may not simply find a reasonable

[127] Kühne, *supra* note 40, at 677–78.

[128] For example, in 2004, it reversed 45.8 percent of all jury acquittals, and 3.9 percent of jury convictions. Thaman, *supra* note 22, at 115–16.

[129] U.P.K. (Russ.) § 305. [130] *See* Thaman, *supra* note 121, at 655–60.

[131] *Id.* at 656–59 (discussing STC 169/2004).

[132] Serrano Contreras v. Spain, App. No. 49138/08, Eur. Ct. H.R., Mar. 20, 2012, §§ 36–42.

doubt based on uncontradicted exculpatory testimony of the accused.[133] In a 2010 case, the court overturned the acquittal of a woman for having inflicted injuries on her son, even though it acknowledged that the "reasons given by the trial court were sufficient on their face," because the trial court did not look into the "history and personality of the defendant" for evidence supporting the prosecution's version of events. In other words, according to the German Supreme Court, the trial court should have used its inquisitorial powers to probe the character of the defendant in search of a motive for guilt, a seeming violation of the presumption of innocence.[134]

6. Selective Filtering of Cases

A petitioner in cassation must clearly plead a statutory ground to get her case heard in cassation.[135] In Germany, the petitioner must lay out all of the evidence upon which it bases its claims so that the cassational judges need not look at the record.[136] The Supreme Court can reject the cassation petition without a hearing if it decides, unanimously, that the judgment has no legal or factual errors.[137]

These preliminary decisions to reject cassation petitions often go unpublished. The German Supreme Court receives from 3,000 to 3,500 cassation petitions each year, but issued reasoned judgments in only around 6.6 percent of them in the 1990s.[138] In Italy, in the period from 1989 to 1995, the Court of Cassation rejected around 48.5 percent of all appeals without issuing a reasoned judgment.[139] In France, in 2013, the criminal panel of the Court of Cassation summarily rejected, without an opinion, 68.4 percent of all appeals in cassation.[140]

A study of cassation cases in Germany in the 1990s showed that there is little information about the facts or the reasons for the Supreme Court's summary rejection of cassation petitions. Only in 20 percent of the cases was there a mention of the facts. Eighty-seven percent of all defense cassations were dismissed in this manner as "clearly unsubstantiated" in standardized and formulaic rulings,[141] a reason the procedure is nicknamed the "cassation guillotine."[142]

For example, in the case of Horst Arnold, a teacher with no criminal record who was wrongfully convicted of rape based on the utterly fantastic uncorroborated testimony of a fellow teacher, the German Supreme Court laconically stated that the "review of the judgment...reveals no legal errors to the detriment of the defendant." It then ordered

[133] BGH, 1 StR 600/10, NStZ 5 (2011), 302–03, *cited in* Thaman, *Ensuring the Factual Reliability*, *supra* note 3, at 98–99.

[134] *Id.* at 99 (discussing BGH 4 Str 22/10, 10 NStZ 2010, 529).

[135] C. pr. pén. (Fr.) §§ 605–06; StPO (Ger.) § 344; C.p.p. (It.) § 591; L.E. Crim. (Spain) § 858.

[136] Christoph Knauer, *Vom Wesen und Zweck der Revision*, 1 Neue Zeitschrift für Strafrecht 1, 4–5 (2016).

[137] StPO (Ger.) § 349(2). For similar provisions, see C.p.p. (It.) § 610(1), U.P.K. (Russ.) §§ 401.5, 401.8.

[138] Thaman, *Ensuring the Factual Reliability*, *supra* note 3, at 91–92.

[139] *Id.*

[140] *Id.*

[141] Becker, *supra* note 28, at 42–43.

[142] Kühne, *supra* note 40, at 684–85.

the innocent man to pay all costs of the trial, including those of the perjurous complaining witness.[143]

7. The Cassational Hearing

No witnesses or new evidence are adduced in a typical hearing in the cassational court. In Germany, it has been said that "the essence of cassation is in the categorical exclusion of fact-finding from cassational review."[144]

In Russia, this traditional approach was found in the Russian code of criminal procedure of 1864, but was modified by the Bolsheviks in 1917, and a "mixed" form was introduced, opening up the possibility of introducing new evidence, and calling witnesses that testified in the first instance. Russian cassation, since the changes in 2013, has maintained this "mixed" form that allows review of both the law and the facts.[145]

Despite the appeals court's clear authority to adduce new evidence or recall first instance witnesses, the Russian Supreme Court has interpreted the new law so as to prohibit the cassational court from questioning witnesses or ordering new expert testimony, limiting it to evaluating written documentary evidence taken in the first instance.[146]

In most civil law countries, if a case makes it past the "guillotine" of preliminary dismissal, the actual hearing is usually held in public session.[147] There is also no automatic right of the defendant to be present. In some jurisdictions, the defendant, if out of custody, may attend the cassation hearing but not if he or she is in custody.[148] In Russia, however, an incarcerated defendant may take part in the hearing through video link.[149]

8. The Decision in Cassation

How a case will come out in cassation, in Germany, depends to a large extent on the personality of the reporting judge. Although decisions are supposed to be reached by five judges, Supreme Court judge Thomas Fischer has written that the reporting judge is usually the only judge to read the file, and it is usually his or her personality that determines the outcome of the appeal.[150]

In Italy, if a defendant is convicted in both the first and appellate instances, so-called "double conformity," this fact has the same value as the verdict of the jury in the United States and will seldom be overturned. In cases of "double deformity," where

[143] Thaman, *Ensuring the Factual Reliability*, *supra* note 3, at 92.
[144] Knauer, *supra* note 136, at 2 (citing Meyer & Goßner-Schmidt).
[145] Kudravtseva & Smirnov, *supra* note 13, at 14–15, 105–06. [146] *Id.* at 14–15.
[147] C. pr. pén. (Fr.) § 602; C.p.p. (It.) § 614. [148] StPO (Ger.) § 350(2).
[149] U.P.K. (Russ.) § 401.13(2). [150] Thaman, *Ensuring the Factual Reliability*, *supra* note 3, at 93.

a conviction in first instance is followed by an acquittal on appeal, the petition will not be rejected prima facie as being without merit.[151]

The cassational court normally "breaks," or reverses, the judgment of the trial court and remands the case to the first instance for a new trial or new decision.[152] It is often said that the reason the court of cassation cannot itself decide the case is that it is not a competent fact-finder, not having had the evidence presented to it in an immediate and oral fashion and thus not being able to assess the credibility of the witnesses.[153]

Nonetheless, cassational courts today often decide the case as if they were courts of appeal, without remand. This can be done to the benefit of the defendant, if the case should have never been charged, on grounds of insufficiency of evidence or double jeopardy.[154] In Spain, the cassational court may decide without remand if no new evidence needs to be taken.[155] In Germany, this is possible if there is only a substantive legal error, such as an erroneous application of the penal law to the facts proved, or only the punishment needs to be adjusted.[156]

The general rule is that the cassational court may not go beyond the issues pleaded by the parties in their petitions and responses.[157] There are, however, exceptions in which cassational court judges wield administrative power not constrained by adversary or accusatory principles.

One example is Russia, where the Supreme Court, much like in Soviet times, may decide an appeal or cassation petition on any issue it wishes, even if not pleaded by the parties.[158] In several countries, judges may act *sua sponte* to rule on absolute nullities even if not pleaded by the parties.[159]

9. Cassation in Practice

We already know that most cassation petitions are dismissed without a hearing. In France in 1996, only 7.5 percent of cassation petitions were successful.[160] In Germany in 2009, the Supreme Court rendered a full judgment in only 5.6 percent of cassation cases[161] and the defense was successful in well under 10 percent of its petitions.[162] In Italy, only around 0.5 percent of cassation petitions led to a change in the judgment.[163] Defendants in Germany who have confessed, or have a bad criminal record, have virtually no chance of prevailing, and one finds superficial, or "lean" justice, where one would least expect it:

[151] Francesco Mauro Iacoviello, *Lo standard probatorio dell'al di là di ogni ragionevole dubbio e il suo controllo in cassazione*, in *Cassazione penale* 3869, 3879 (2006).

[152] C. pr. pén. (Fr.) §§ 609–10; StPO (Ger.) § 354(2); C.p.p. (It.) § 623; U.P.K. (Russ) § 401.14.

[153] Kinzig, *supra* note 12, at 647.

[154] C.p.p. (It.) §§ 620–21. For France, see Heurtin, *supra* note 52, at 75–76.

[155] Becker & Kinzig, *supra* note 12, at 203–04. [156] StPO (Ger.) § 354(1).

[157] *Cf.* C.p.p. (It.) § 609. [158] U.P.K. (Russ.) § 401.16(1).

[159] As to Italy, Carnevale & Orlandi, *supra* note 52, at 132–33. As to France, Heurtin, *supra* note 52, at 72.

[160] *Id.* at 79. [161] Knauer, *supra* note 136, at 6.

[162] Kühne, *supra* note 40, at 693. [163] Carnevale & Orlandi, *supra* note 52, at 140–41.

in grave cases with high punishments.[164] These statistics confirm my view that the most serious cases, involving murder and sexual assault, are the most likely to end up in miscarriages of justice.[165]

The public prosecutor files cassation petitions much less frequently than the defense, but is successful at a much higher rate, around 25 percent of the time in Germany.[166] If the Prosecutor General in Germany files a petition in cassation, however, the success rate is around 67 percent, and some panels of the Supreme Court rubber-stamp petitions of certain federal prosecutors 100 percent of the time.[167]

V. Conclusion: Control of Fact-Finding, but to What Purpose?

Can appeal and cassation, in their current forms, serve to uncover and correct miscarriages of justice in serious cases based on erroneous fact-finding in the first instance? Although appeals courts have the tools to re-examine questionable evidence, these tools are either used exclusively in retrying minor cases coming out of the lower courts, or have been abandoned altogether as appeals courts become more cassational and prefer examining the paper residue of the lower courts, rather than the live evidentiary sources.

There have been successes. The Superior Court of Justice of Andalucia, sitting as a jury "appeals" court, and the Spanish Supreme Court, sitting as court of cassation, both threw out the wrongful conviction of Dolores Vasquez for killing the daughter of her lesbian lover, due to the inadequacy of the jury's reasons for deducing guilt from the shoddiest of circumstantial evidence.[168]

The marathon murder case against Amanda Knox and her Italian boyfriend for killing an English student, Meredith Kercher, is at most a mixed bag. Convicted in the first instance *corte d'assise* of murder based on flimsy circumstantial evidence, they were acquitted by a *corte d'assise d'appello*, which actually heard new expert testimony that undermined the credibility of the original evidence. But then the Court of Cassation reversed the acquittal, ignoring the new expert testimony, and another *corte d'assise d'appello* convicted, without hearing any live evidence. The Court of Cassation, on its

164 Becker, *supra* note 28, at 43–45. In such serious cases, defense lawyers call the procedure the "cassation lottery," reflecting one's microscopic chances of winning. Knauer, *supra* note 136, at 2–3. On the substantial number of wrongful convictions occurring in cases with confessions in the United States, but also in the Netherlands and Germany, see Thaman, *Reanchoring Evidence Law*, *supra* note 2, at 201–02.

165 *Id.* at 384–85. One reason is the social pressure on police and prosecutors to find the perpetrators of such heinous crimes, leading to arrests of the "usual suspects" and use of suspect forms of proof. *Id.*

166 Kinzig, *supra* note 12, at 654.

167 Becker, *supra* note 28, at 44.

168 *See* Thaman, *supra* note 121, at 639–43.

second time around, dismissed without remand based on the overall shoddiness of the investigation and evidence.[169]

Although it may be easy to overturn wrongful convictions based on a jury's inadequate reasons, the opposite is the case when the reasons are crafted by a professional judge. Most European judges profess that, in a close case, they can draft cassation-proof reasons justifying either a conviction or an acquittal.[170] Indeed, the French presiding judge in the *cour d'assises* will often draft reasons justifying both guilt and acquittal before she knows how the court will vote.[171]

Acquittals seem to get enhanced scrutiny on appeal and cassation in Europe. There are few of them to begin with, but prosecutors (and victims) challenge a large number, and with higher success rates than those of defendants challenging convictions. Although the ECtHR has tried to place limits on appeals courts convicting following an acquittal without even hearing any testimony, the fact is that many acquittals in serious cases are overturned in just such a way in cassation, based on inadequate reasons.

Due to their preference for reviewing the (mostly incomplete) records of lower court trials and/or the highly mediated and teleologically crafted judgments that issue therefrom, rather than getting close to the facts through re-examining witnesses or reading verbatim transcripts, both courts of appeal and cassation have opted to function as control organs that administratively vet the work of lower court judges, rather than truth-finders. Whether this is due to a daunting caseload, which makes it impossible for them to give justice to each case, or to a preference for written procedure, which has a long history in Europe, is unclear.

References

Ercole Aprile, *Appello, ricorso per cassazione e revisione* (2013)

Rechtsmittel im Strafrecht. Eine internationale vergleichende Untersuchung zur Rechtswirklichkeit und Effizienz von Rechtsmitteln (Monica Becker & Jörg Kinzig eds., 2000)

Detlef Burhoff & Peter Kotz, *Handbuch für die strafrechtlichen Rechtsmittel und Rechtsbehelfe* (2013)

A.V. Kudravtseva & V.P. Smirnov, *Appelatsionnoe proizvodstvo v ugolovnom protsesse Rossii* (2013)

Andrés Martínez Arrieta, *El Recurso de Casación y de Revisión Penal* (2d ed. 2013)

Stephen C. Thaman, *Ensuring the Factual Reliability of Criminal Convictions: Reasoned Judgments or a Return to Formal Rules of Evidence?* in *Comparative Criminal Procedure* 75–114 (Jacqueline E. Ross & Stephen C. Thaman eds., 2016)

Stephen C. Thaman, *Reanchoring Evidence Law to Formal Rules: A Step Toward Protecting the Innocent from Conviction for Capital Crimes?*, in *Visions of Justice. Liber amicorum Mirjan Damaška* 383–409 (Bruce Ackerman et al. eds., 2016)

[169] *See* Thaman, *Ensuring the Factual Reliability*, *supra* note 3, at 102–04.

[170] Thaman, *Reanchoring Evidence Law*, *supra* note 2, at 394.

[171] Cohen, *supra* note 20, at 435–36.

Codes

Code de Procédure Pénale. Title 1, and Book 1, introduced by Law No. 57–1426, of 31 December 1957; Books 2–5, introduced by Ordonnance No. 58–1296 of 23 December 1958. Available at; https://www.legifrance.gouv.fr

Codice di Procedura Penale. Decree of the President of the Republic 22-9-1988, no. 447. *Available at* http://www.altalex.com/index.php?idnot=2031

Ley de Enjuiciamiento Criminal, Royal Decree of 14 September 1882. BOE, no. 260, 17 September 1882. *Available at* http://www.boe.es/buscar/act.php?id=BOE-A-1882-6036&tn=2

Die Strafprozessordnung, 1 February 1877 (RGBl. 253; BGBl III 312–2 in the version of 7 April 1987). *Available at* www.juris.de

Ugolovno-protsessual'nyy kodeks Rossiyskoy Federatsii. Passed by State Duma 22 November 2001; Ratified by the Federation Council. 5 December 2001. Signed by the President of the RF on 18 December 2001 (No. 174-F3). *Available at* www.consultant.ru

CHAPTER 42

EXCEPTIONAL PROCEDURES TO CORRECT MISCARRIAGES OF JUSTICE IN COMMON LAW SYSTEMS

KENT ROACH*

I. Introduction

THIS chapter will examine exceptional procedures to correct miscarriages of justice. Exceptional procedures will be defined to include what are essentially second or subsequent appeals or extraordinary forms of collateral review after the ordinary appellate or collateral review process has been exhausted. This is a particularly interesting topic in the criminal process because no consensus has emerged even in the rather restricted confines of the common law world about: (1) the optimal procedure or institutions that should be used, or (2) the appropriate substantive grounds for granting relief to correct miscarriages of justice.

The first and most studied exceptional procedure is the Criminal Cases Review Commission (CCRC). It has been operating for England, Wales, and Northern Ireland since 1997. Many have advocated that other common law jurisdictions should follow the CCRC model, often suggesting that it will be proactive and bring inquisitorial elements into adversarial common law systems.

Although the CCRC has been a success in terms of referring over 600 convictions and sentences back to the appeals court, with about 66 percent of them being overturned, it also rejects over 95 percent of applications to it. Not surprisingly, it has engendered

* I thank Jackie Hodgson and Juliet Horne as well as the editors for helpful comments on an earlier draft and acknowledge the financial support of the Pierre E. Trudeau Foundation.

controversy concerning how proactive it actually has been, with respect to both investigating individual cases and addressing systemic issues.

One interesting modification of the CCRC idea is North Carolina's Innocence Inquiry Commission (NCIIC). This commission, created in 2006, as well as the U.S. Supreme Court's 2009 recognition of original habeas corpus as a means clearly to establish a person's innocence,[1] reflects the focus in the United States on factual innocence, something that is not required with respect to the CCRC or other exceptional procedures in the common law world. The focus on factual innocence is an example of American exceptionalism related to the punitive nature of its legal and political culture, though some in the UK argue the CCRC is not concerned enough with factual innocence.[2]

Other models that will be examined in this chapter include a Scottish commission similar to the CCRC, the creation of a second right of appeal based on "fresh and compelling evidence" in two Australian states, and Canada's 2002 reform of a system that allows the political executive to grant relief on applications for mercy and clemency.

The profound lack of consensus about the proper procedure and the proper substantive grounds for exceptional procedures to correct miscarriages of justices may help explain why most common law jurisdictions have yet to create new institutions and procedures to correct miscarriages of justice, and still rely on the political executive to order new appeals.

The focus on new institutions and procedures in this chapter should not obscure the conservatism of many common law countries, including most American and Australian states, in devising new approaches to correcting wrongful convictions, despite increased recognition of the reality and prevalence of wrongful convictions.[3] This conservatism also extends to those jurisdictions that have created new exceptional procedures, because appeals courts in the UK apply the same standards for appellate review of cases referred by the commissions that they would in any other appeal from a conviction.

The study of exceptional procedures to correct miscarriages of justice demands a systems approach that is attentive to both the manner in which a convicted person can access the exceptional procedure and the links between the exceptional procedures and the way courts review convictions that are referred to them as a result of the exceptional procedure.

The lack of consensus about exceptional procedures facilitates discussion of how the criminal process ought to respond to exceptional demands to reopen convictions and the implications in terms of values and incentives for the procedural and substantive choices that are made. In short, we are in an era of experimentation and innovation that demands comparative analysis.

[1] *In re* Davis, 557 U.S. 952 (2009).

[2] *The Criminal Cases Review Commission: Hope for the Innocent?* (Michael Naughton ed., 2010); Michael Naughton, *The Innocent and the Criminal Justice System* (2013).

[3] A report on the first 1,600 wrongful convictions in the United States revealed that 1,240 of these cases were dismissals by courts, often with the consent of prosecutors, 112 cases involved pardons by the governor or other representatives of the political executive, and only 49 involved explicit findings of innocence. Nat'l Registry of Exonerations, *The First 1600 Exonerations* 2–3 (2015).

II. The Criminal Cases Review Commission for England and Wales

The logical starting point is to examine the oldest, most influential, most discussed, and most controversial of exceptional procedures used in the common law world to correct miscarriages of justice. In 1995, England and Wales created an independent agency, the Criminal Cases Review Commission (CCRC), to examine claims of miscarriages of justice.

1. Origins

The origins of the CCRC reveal much about the politics behind the creation of exceptional mechanisms to correct miscarriages of justice. From 1989 to 1992, the Home Secretary referred twenty-eight cases involving forty-nine people to the Court of Appeal including the famous Guildford Four, Birmingham Six, and Maguire Seven cases involving wrongful convictions and cases involving police misconduct by the West Midlands Serious Crime Squad.[4] The Court of Appeal had itself been created in 1907 in response to public controversies over two miscarriages of justice.[5]

Exceptional procedures to correct miscarriages of justice often arise from well-publicized wrongful convictions. This suggests a possible cycle of criminal justice reform driven by well-publicized and sympathetic cases. In examining the publicity campaigns that led to these wrongful convictions eventually, after repeated requests, being overturned, Richard Nobles and David Schiff suggest that "[w]hen the meta-narrative of crisis has passed, deference towards the legal system's construction of criminal justice (the only workable basis for appeals) once again becomes acceptable."[6] This may well be true both with respect to the 1907 creation of the Court of Appeal and the 1995 creation of the CCRC.

The CCRC emerged from proposals both by the civil society group JUSTICE[7] and two royal commissions that an independent and more proactive body replace the ability of the executive in the form of the Home Secretary to decide whether he or she "thought fit"[8] to refer convictions back to the Court of Appeal for a second appeal. The Runciman Commission concluded that the Home Secretary's role as part of the political executive

[4] Report of the Royal Commission on Criminal Justice Cm 2263, at 181 (1993).

[5] Richard Nobles & David Schiff, *Understanding Miscarriages of Justice* chs. 3 & 4 (2000).

[6] *Id.* at 169.

[7] Justice Society & George Waller, *Miscarriages of Justice* 5.23 (1989) (contemplating a body not consisting "solely of lawyers" that would "be able to operate along inquisitorial lines, examining the petitioner, his lawyer, the police and the prosecution" and that would be in a better position than the Home Secretary or the appeals court "to get at the truth of the matter."). On the background, see David Kyle, *Correcting Miscarriages of Justice: The Role of the Criminal Cases Review Commission*, 52 Drake L. Rev. 657 (2004).

[8] Criminal Appeal Act 1968, c. 19, § 17.

in the cabinet responsible for criminal justice and policing was "incompatible with the constitutional separation of powers as between the courts and the executive."[9] It called for a proactive body that would "have access to specialist advisors, such as forensic scientists, as necessary." The new body would also draw attention "to general features of the criminal justice system that it had found unsatisfactory in the course of its work" and make "recommendations for changes that it thinks fit."[10] The Runciman Commission perceptively did not view the CCRC in isolation and recommended that the Court of Appeal be more receptive to accepting new evidence and reversing convictions in case of serious doubt.[11]

2. Composition

The *Criminal Appeal Act, 1995* provided for the creation of the CCRC consisting of eleven people, one-third of whom would be lawyers with ten years of experience and two-thirds with knowledge or experience with criminal justice. Thus the CCRC was intended to have a lay component from the start, representing some dissatisfaction with the existing system. Two-thirds of those on the CCRC are to be criminal justice specialists, but the emphasis was on expertise rather than on ensuring that particular stakeholders in the criminal justice system, such as police, prosecutors, or defense lawyers, were represented.

In addition to its appointed commissioners, the CCRC relies heavily on a full-time staff of case review managers. The CCRC received a 30 percent cut in its budget between 2009/2010 and 2014/2015. This translated into an annual budget of just over 5 million pounds and reductions of case review managers from forty-two to thirty-four at a time when applications increased significantly. This has increased delays in processing applications.[12] The independence and performance of review commissions can be affected by budget cuts. The alternative, however, is to rely on even less transparent budgeting processes within the political executive or on private funding, legal aid, or pro bono legal services, as do systems that require convicted persons to initiate second appeals or collateral review proceedings in the courts.

3. Powers

The CCRC has powers to obtain new expert reports[13] and to appoint investigating officers to obtain new evidence.[14] These are important powers that allow the CCRC to obtain new evidence that is often critical to reversing convictions. At the same time,

[9] Royal Commission on Criminal Justice, *supra* note 4, at 182.

[10] *Id.* at 185. [11] *Id.* at 173.

[12] Criminal Cases Review Commission, House of Commons Justice Comm., *Twelfth Report of Session 2014–15*, HC 850, ¶ 31.

[13] *Id.* ¶ 21. [14] *Id.* ¶ 19.

their use should not be overestimated. Elks reports that in the first ten years of its operation, the CCRC appointed thirty-three investigating officers, eighteen of whom were from an outside force. These cases resulted in sixteen referrals to the courts.[15] Thus the image of the CCRC as actively reinvestigating cases is only true in a small minority of the thousands of applications that it processes.

From its creation in 1995 to 2016, the CCRC only had powers to obtain relevant documents from public but not private bodies.[16] Although the CCRC experienced some problems of delay and noncompliance, it used these powers to obtain relevant documents from police, prosecutors, courts, public providers of forensic science, and criminal injury compensation boards.[17] In 2016, however, a private members bill was passed that gave the CCRC additional powers to obtain documents with court assistance from private bodies, such as private sector providers of forensic evidence.[18] This brings the CCRC's powers into line with those possessed by similar commissions in Scotland and North Carolina as well as with the broad investigative powers available under the Canadian ministerial review process.

4. Applications

From the start of its operations in April 1997 to July 31, 2018, the CCRC decided 23,177 applications, for an average of over 1,000 applications a year. The number of applications made to the CCRC per year increased 70 percent between 2009/2010 and 2012/2013 to 1,625[19] as a result of the introduction of an easy-to-read application and increased outreach. In 2017/2018, it received 1, 439 applications. At present, the CCRC seems to be the most accessible of all the exceptional procedures examined in this chapter.

The accessibility of the CCRC comes, however, with a price. The CCRC has rejected about 97 percent of all the applications it received, often at a preliminary stage and frequently on the basis that no appeal has been taken. Decisions to reject an application may be made by only one Commissioner. Applicants are invited to respond within a month in writing to a provisional letter rejecting their application. The CCRC is prohibited by statutory provisions on confidentiality from making public its reasons for such decisions.[20] This lack of transparency may be justified for privacy reasons, but it makes it difficult to evaluate much of the CCRC's work.

There has been no systematic study of the perceptions of those who have their applications rejected, though some innocence projects have reported that some applicants view the CCRC's rejection of their applications as "reinforcement of the prosecution's

[15] Laurie Elks, *Righting Miscarriages of Justice? Ten Years of the Criminal Cases Review Commission* 22 (2008).

[16] Criminal Appeal Act 1995, c. 35, § 17.

[17] Elks, *supra* note 15, at 20.

[18] Criminal Cases Review Commission (Information) Act 2016, c. 17.

[19] Criminal Cases Review Commission, *supra* note 12, ¶ 31.

[20] Criminal Appeal Act 1995, c. 35, §§ 23, 24.

case."[21] In 2015/2016, there were sixty-three complaints made against the CCRC and twenty-one applications for judicial review of dismissals, one of which was successful.[22] This suggests that at least some of the applicants to the CCRC are quite dissatisfied with their treatment.

A doctoral study found 26 of 404 decisions not to refer to be "troubling," before ultimately concluding that in each of the 26 decisions that researcher would have applied the real possibility test in the same way and not referred the cases. This is a start, but more research into the vast majority of applications that the CCRC rejects is required with a view to evaluating those cases in terms of whether they achieve procedural and substantive justice for the rejected applicants.[23]

The minority of cases that the CCRC refers to the court are much more transparent and easier to study than the vast majority of its rejected applications. This asymmetry in the treatment of rejected and successful applications to the CCRC mimics other criminal justice processes where only a small minority of cases sees the sunlight of adversarial trial. Despite frequent rhetoric about the CCRC being "proactive" and "inquisitorial," it suffers from a similar lack of transparency as the rest of common law criminal justice systems that resolve the vast majority of cases without trial.

One finding that emerges from the comparative study in this chapter is that increased access in the form of increased applications seems to be related to higher rejection rates. Conversely, more onerous application processes seem to attract cases more likely to be corrected by the courts. To be sure, this is not an argument against increased access. It may increase public confidence and provide a form of procedural justice to applicants even if their application is not successful. Nevertheless, more research needs to be done on the reactions and perceptions of rejected applicants. Lack of access to the CCRC's reasons for rejecting applications and privacy concerns are barriers to this important research. In the absence of such research, it should not be assumed that increased access is an unqualified good.

5. Referrals to the Court

In common with all the nonjudicial exceptional procedures examined in this chapter, the CCRC does not have the power to reverse a conviction. Throughout the common law world, there is a reluctance to allow even an independent executive body to reverse a conviction. In common law countries both with written and unwritten constitutions, it is believed to be necessary to refer suspect convictions first entered by judges and juries back to the courts for consideration of whether the conviction should be overturned. In this sense, executive exceptional procedures supplement, but do not replace or usurp

[21] Andrew Green, *Challenging the Refusal to Investigate Evidence Neglected by Trial Lawyers*, in *The Criminal Cases Review Commission: Hope for the Innocent?*, *supra* note 2, at 57.

[22] Criminal Cases Review Commission, *Annual Report and Accounts 2015/2016*, at 30–31 (2016).

[23] Stephen Heaton, *A Critical Evaluation of the Utility of Using Innocence as a Criterion in the Post Conviction Process* 273 (2013), *cited in* Criminal Cases Review Commission, *supra* note 12, ¶ 19.

judicial responsibility for the ultimate correction of miscarriages of justice. This is an important point that those who only focus on the exceptional referral procedures such as the CCRC ignore at their peril. In short, executive exceptional procedures are closely tied to judicial procedures for correction of wrongful convictions.

Under Section 13 of the *Criminal Appeal Act, 1995*, the CCRC has the power to refer a case back to the Court of Appeal if there is a "real possibility" that the conviction or sentence would not be upheld on appeal. The courts have interpreted this test as requiring "more than an outside chance or bare possibility" but less "than a probability or a likelihood or a racing certainty."[24] As will be seen, this is a lower standard on paper than some of the standards used by other commissions and processes in the common law world. Nevertheless, it has still attracted criticism and controversy.

The CCRC is directed to consider new evidence or arguments not previously made, but this requirement "shall not prevent the making of a reference if it appears to the Commission that there are exceptional circumstances which justify making it."[25] The CCRC has a power but not a duty to refer cases to the appellate court. Former commissioners have commented that this discretion would be used not to refer cases on technical grounds that would not benefit the applicant or the administration of justice.[26] Amendments made in 2003 restrict appeals on referral by the CCRC to grounds identified by the CCRC or otherwise allowed by the Court of Appeal.[27]

From the start of its work in 1997 to July 31, 2018, the CCRC has referred 652 cases, with 433 appeals being allowed and 196 dismissed.[28] This translated into a "success" rate of 66 percent, though it should be noted that the CCRC is not a party to an appeal in the Court of Appeal, much less an advocate. As Professor Hodgson noted in her testimony to the Parliamentary committee, one would expect a lower success rate if the real possibility test requires something less than probability.[29]

There are, however, limits to a purely quantitative approach, especially with respect to the small numbers in play. The Court of Appeal has on a number of occasions criticized the CCRC for making specific referrals. Both the CCRC and the SCCRC are more aggressive than the North Carolina Commission or Canada's Minister of Justice in making referrals that courts (or prosecutors) subsequently do not accept as justification for overturning a conviction.

Decisions made by the CCRC to refer cases are tied to section 2 of the *Criminal Appeal Act, 1995*, which provides as the exclusive ground for allowing appeals that the Court of Appeal "shall allow an appeal against conviction if they think that the conviction is unsafe." Although the CCRC has rejected the contention that it simply makes

[24] R. v. Criminal Cases Review Comm'n ex parte Pearson [1999] EWCA (Admin) 452.

[25] Criminal Appeal Act 1995, c. 35, § 13(2).

[26] Elks, *supra* note 15, at 19-20; Peter Duff, *Straddling Two Worlds: Reflections of a Retired Criminal Cases Review Commissioner*, 72 Mod. L. Rev. 693 (2009).

[27] Criminal Justice Act 2003, c. 44, § 315.

[28] Criminal Cases Review Commission, Case Statistics, *at* http://www.ccrc.gov.uk/case-statistics/ (last visited Sept. 15, 2018).

[29] Criminal Cases Review Commission, *supra* note 12, ¶ 18.

predictions about what cases the Court of Appeal will overturn as unsafe, it is undeniable that the two standards are intimately connected, thus revealing how the CCRC is simply one actor in the wider system of appeals.

The 1993 Runciman Commission that recommended the creation of the CCRC was widely criticized for its focus on factual guilt and its hostility to due process. It nevertheless demonstrated a consistent concern about innocence by recommending that the Court of Appeal be more willing to consider new evidence and more aggressive in quashing convictions in cases of "serious doubt."[30] No such statutory reforms were made. The Court of Appeal has generally been unwilling to apply a more searching standard based on "lurking doubt" in reviewing convictions.[31] Laurie Elks, a former and long-serving member of the CCRC has stressed that the CCRC, like the Court of Appeal, has assumed that it "should be extremely hesitant to substitute its own judgment of the facts for the verdict of the jury, which has had the benefit of seeing and hearing the witnesses give evidence."[32] The Court of Appeal has also not always been consistent or generous in its approach to allowing fresh evidence. The CCRC has borne the brunt of the criticism from disappointed applicants, but as Michael Zander, a member of the Runciman Commission has pointed out, such criticisms "could perhaps with more justice be directed at the Court of Appeal."[33] Appellate courts may remain more conservative and less controllable even when the legislature creates new referral mechanisms in response to crises caused by well-publicized wrongful convictions.

The convictions referred by the CCRC back to the courts include less serious offenses than are dealt with under exceptional procedures in North America. Even its more serious homicide cases frequently involve claims based on changes of law, modern standards of fairness, diminished responsibility, misconduct of investigators, and the unreliability of witnesses.[34] Most of these cases do not relate to factual innocence. The CCRC has consistently maintained that it is concerned with the safety of the conviction and not the freestanding question of innocence.

A 2015 Parliamentary committee concluded that while some of the criticism of the CCRC's caution in administering the real possibility test was warranted, the Law Commission should also study a possible expansion of the grounds for the Court of Appeal to overturn convictions from safety to serious doubt, notwithstanding the traditional deference of the appeals court toward jury verdicts.[35] The development of new referral mechanisms such as the CCRC may highlight problems surrounding the high

[30] Royal Commission on Criminal Justice, *supra* note 4, at 173. This recommendation was in part based on the English Court of Appeal's willingness for a time to reverse convictions based on a "lurking doubt." R. v. Cooper [1969] 1 Q.B. 267, 271. Courts in Australia and Canada have both resisted such a standard and it is rarely used in England. *See* Bibi Sangha et al., *Forensic Investigations and Miscarriages of Justice* chs. 3–5 (2010).

[31] R. v. Pope [2012] EWCA (Crim) 2241.

[32] Elks, *supra* note 15, at 15.

[33] Michael Zander, *Foreword* to *The Criminal Cases Review Commission: Hope for the Innocent?*, *supra* note 2, at xviii.

[34] Elks, *supra* note 15, at 186–90.

[35] Criminal Cases Review Commission, *supra* note 12, ¶¶ 27–28.

value that appellate courts in the common law world attach to the finality of convictions and jury verdicts.

6. Systemic Reform

The Runciman Commission contemplated that the CCRC would be well placed to make reform proposals that could help prevent future miscarriages of justice. The CCRC, however, has generally not performed this role. This may reflect its lack of resources or a more fundamental tension between its quasi-judicial duties to investigate and refer cases and to make policy change proposals.[36]

None of the commissions examined in this chapter have focused on systemic reform or made concrete proposals to prevent wrongful convictions. Indeed, there is some support for the idea that the commissions benefit from having a reputation for impartiality and not acting as advocates either for applicants or for the cause of systemic reform to reduce wrongful convictions.[37] At the same time, however, there is still a need for systemic reform. Professors Nobles and Schiff have suggested that the CCRC may only be getting at the tip of the iceberg of wrongful convictions even if one assumes that miscarriages of justice only happen in 3.5 percent of all serious cases.[38] This raises the question of the optimal balance between error correction in individual cases and systemic reform to reduce the risk of future error.[39] The CCRC and other commissions stress error correction over systemic reform.

The 2015 Parliamentary committee recommended that the CCRC become more engaged with other criminal justice system actors about lessons learned from miscarriages of justice and steps that could be taken to avoid them in the future.[40] The CCRC's response in this regard has largely been restricted to observing that it has allowed academics access to its work. This is laudable, but not a replacement for the CCRC conducting its own research to increase knowledge about miscarriages of justice. Again this raises the question of the degree to which the CCRC's reticence to become involved with systemic issues[41] reflects its limited resources or the degree to which it sees such involvement as in tension with its quasi-judicial role in deciding which applications should be referred back to the appeals court.

[36] Kent Roach, *The Role of Innocence Commissions: Error Discovery, Systemic Reform or Both?*, 85 Chi.-Kent L. Rev. 89 (2010).

[37] Robert P. Mosteller, *N.C. Innocence Inquiry Commission's First Decade: Impressive Success and Lessons Learned*, 94 N.C. L. Rev. 1725 (2016).

[38] Richard Nobles & David Schiff, *After Ten Years: An Investment in Justice?*, *in The Criminal Cases Review Commission: Hope for the Innocent?*, *supra* note 2, at 153.

[39] This issue is discussed in Roach, *supra* note 36.

[40] Criminal Cases Review Commission, *supra* note 12.

[41] The SCCRC is more active in undertaking corporate research and has conducted research on controversial subjects such as equality and the effect of legal representation.

III. The Scottish Criminal Cases Review Commission

1. Origins

The Scottish Criminal Cases Review Commission (SCCRC) was created in 1999. The impetus was not that Scotland had numerous high-profile wrongful convictions, but rather that it made little sense for the political executive to continue deciding petitions to reopen cases for Scotland when it no longer did for the rest of the United Kingdom after the creation of the CCRC.[42]

2. Composition

Like the CCRC, the SCCRC is designed to ensure some lay representation with one-third of its members being lawyers with at least ten years of experience and two-thirds of its members having experience with the criminal justice system.[43] At present, the Commission has seven members, a chief executive, a head of corporate services, a head of case work, two senior legal officers, and six legal officers.[44] Like the CCRC, the SCCRC has experienced budget and staff reduction over the recent years while the number of applications made to it has increased.

3. Powers

From the start, the SCCRC has had broad powers to summon relevant information from public and private bodies;[45] to undertake inquiries and obtain statements, opinions, or reports;[46] and to require reluctant persons to provide information through a judicial process.[47] In response to investigations stemming from its investigation of the Lockerbie terrorism case, the SCCRC was given powers in 2010 relating to obtaining assistance abroad.[48] It has referred cases to the courts even in the absence of an application,[49] illustrating some of the values of a self-initiation and an inquisitorial approach.

A former Commissioner, Peter Duff, has stated that the commission's role is not to advocate for applicants but to act as an independent and inquisitorial seeker after the

[42] Lisa Griffin, *International Perspectives on Correcting Wrongful Convictions: The Scottish Criminal Case Review Commission*, 21 Wm. & Mary Bill Rts. J. 1153, 1158 (2013).

[43] Criminal Procedure (Scotland) Act 1995, c. 46, § 194A.

[44] Scottish Criminal Cases Review Commission, *Annual Report 2017–2018*, at 8, 49.

[45] Criminal Procedure (Scotland) Act 1995, c. 46, § 194I.

[46] *Id.* § 194F. [47] *Id.* § 194H. [48] *Id.* § 194IA.

[49] Johnston v. H.M. Advocate [2006] H.C.J.A.C. 30 (Scot.).

truth. He also sees the commission as an entity that "negotiates the tensions between the 'legal system' inhabited by the appeals courts and the 'lay world', of media, politics and public discourse."[50] He comments that in none of the referrals that he participated in was he absolutely certain that the applicant was innocent.[51]

4. Applications

From the start of its work on April 1, 1999, to March 31, 2018, the SCCRC made decisions on 2,445 applications, including 1,207 applications that were decided after full review. Like the CCRC, people can apply for review of both convictions and sentences, including in less serious criminal cases. This broad mandate has produced a broader range of cases being referred back to the courts than is typically the case in North America or Australia, where the focus is on murder cases. The SCCRC has also seen an increase in applications, with 160 applications being received in 2017/2018.[52]

5. Referrals to the Court

The SCCRC may refer cases to the appeals court if it concludes: "a) that a miscarriage of justice may have occurred; and b) that it is in the interest of justice that a reference should be made."[53] At first glance, this seems like a broader ground for referral than the CCRC, but all convictions in Scotland, even on regular appeals, can only be overturned on miscarriage of justice grounds.

The SCCRC, like the CCRC, has discretion not to refer cases even where purely legal grounds may exist. Peter Duff has revealed that lay members of the commission have been more opposed than the lawyers on the committee to referring cases based on "legal technicalities" and when the factual guilt of the applicant seems clear.[54] This raises interesting issues about whether increased lay representation on these commissions would lead them to focus more on factual innocence and guilt. In any event, the exercise of the discretion not to refer is not very transparent.

The referral standard used by the SCCRC ensures that, like the CCRC, it is influenced and must have regard to the practices of the appellate court. It tried in one situation to refer a case on the basis of a lurking doubt, but the conviction was affirmed by the appeals court.[55] As in England, the degree to which the commission is dependent on the appeals court is a matter of controversy, with disappointed campaigners more likely to claim that the commission is dependent on or subservient to the court and criminal justice insiders more likely to see that the commission can at times push the courts to act

[50] Duff, *supra* note 26, at 694. [51] *Id.* at 704, 721.

[52] Scottish Criminal Cases Review Commission, Case Statistics, *at* http://www.sccrc.co.uk/case-statistics (last visited Sept. 15, 2018).

[53] Criminal Procedure (Scotland) Act 1995, c. 46, § 194C. [54] Duff, *supra* note 26, at 704.

[55] Harper v. H.M. Advocate [2005] H.C.J.A.C. 23 [33].

more creatively and independently.[56] Such controversies for both commissions seem intractable. The commissions can apply more generous standards than the courts, but if the appeals courts resist, the applicants will be disappointed, and the public may lose confidence in a system that seems to produce two official verdicts on whether there has been a miscarriage of justice. The root of the problem is the standard used by appeals courts, but they may be reluctant to soften their traditional emphasis on finality.

It is not only the appeals court that has affirmed finality. In 2010, the *Criminal Procedure (Scotland) Act* was amended to require the SCCRC to have "regard to the need for finality and certainty in the determination of criminal proceedings" when deciding whether it was in the interest of justice to refer a case.[57] This concern was reinforced by giving the appeals court the power to reject and not hear a referral on the grounds that the appeal was not in the interests of justice. In making this determination, the appeals court also "must have regard to the need for finality and certainty in the determination of criminal proceedings."[58] This legislative reaffirmation of the importance of finality may have been a political reaction to the SCCRC's referral of the conviction of one of the men convicted of the Lockerbie bombing after an extensive and costly investigation. The appeal was abandoned after Mr. Al Megrahi was released on compassionate grounds in 2009. In any event, the 2010 amendments were extraordinary. None of the other commissions examined in this chapter operate under such mandatory directions with respect to finality. Moreover, once the CCRC or the NCIIC make a referral, the appeals court must consider the case on the merits and, unlike the Scottish courts, does not have the ability to refuse to hear a referral. Fortunately for the integrity of the system, the 2010 changes do not seem to have affected the commission's referral rates and have now been repealed by the *Criminal Justice (Scotland) Act, 2016*. They do, however, underline that these new institutions are fragile both to political and judicial interventions that place emphasis on the finality of convictions. They also suggest that new commissions may understandably seek where possible not to provoke legislative or judicial resistance.[59]

[56] Stephanie Roberts & Lynne Weathered, *Assisting the Factually Innocent: The Contradictions and Compatibility of Innocence Projects and the Criminal Cases Review Commission*, 29 Oxford J. Legal Stud. 43, 58 (2009); James Chalmers & Fiona Leverick, *The Scottish Criminal Cases Review Commission and Its Referrals to the Appeal Court: The First 10 Years*, 8 Crim. L. Rev. 608 (2010).

[57] Criminal Procedure (Scotland) Act 1995, c. 46, § 194C(2), as amended by Criminal Procedure Act (Scotland), 2010 but repealed by Criminal Justice (Scotland) Act 2016, (A.S.P. 1) § 96.

[58] *Id.* § 194DA(2).

[59] Some family members of the Lockerbie victims filed another application to refer Al Megrahi's conviction but the SCCRC cautiously referred the question of whether they had sufficient standing to the courts, which held that they did not. Scottish Criminal Cases Review Comm'n v. Swire [2015] H.C.J.A.C. 76. The Commission made a subsequent and controversial decision that it was not in the interests of justice to refer the case given it had not been given access to Al Megrahi's abandoned appeal material. Scottish Criminal Cases Review Commission, *News Release: Application on behalf of Mr. Abdelbaset Ali Mohmed Al Megrahi* (Nov. 5, 2015). Al Megrahi has filed another petition, and the SCCRC announced in May 2018 it would be subject to a full review. SCCRC, News Release, May 3, 2018,

From 1999 to March 31, 2018, the SCCRC referred 133 cases of its 2,445 completed applications. This represents a referral rate of 5.4 percent, slightly higher than the CCRC's referral rate of 3 percent. The SCCRC, unlike the CCRC, usefully distinguishes between conviction and sentence appeals. Of the seventy-six conviction appeals, thirty-seven have been allowed by the appeals court as miscarriages of justice, but thirty-eight have been disallowed, with one appeal pending. This is a much lower success rate than the CCRC's 66 percent success rate on referral appeals on both conviction and sentence. Caution is in order in dealing with relatively small data sets, but this evidence supports the idea that the SCCRC is more aggressive than the CCRC in making referrals but that the Scottish appeal court is more inclined to reject appeals on referrals.[60] In any event, it affirms the need to examine the commission and the appeals court as an integrated system.

6. Systemic Reform

The SCCRC has been more active than the CCRC on systemic issues by commissioning and publishing research on a range of systemic topics, including the higher correlation between legal representation of applicants and referrals back to the court.[61] Similar research findings have been made with respect to the CCRC, albeit not in research published by the CCRC.[62] These research findings should put to rest any facile conclusions that either commission functions simply as an inquisitorial institution that can dispense with adversarial legal representation. One problem, however, is that correlation is not causation, and it is difficult to separate the degree to which stronger cases attract or are strengthened by legal representation.

The SCCRC, like the CCRC, does not appear to have made recommendations about criminal justice reform to better prevent miscarriages of justice. As with the CCRC, this could be attributed to resource restraints and/or an unwillingness to depart from its quasi-judicial role in deciding individual applications.

at https://irp-cdn.multiscreensite.com/8f56052e/files/uploaded/3%20May%202018%20-%20SCCRC%20News%20Release%20-%20Application%20on%20behalf%20of%20Mr%20Abdelbaset%20Ali%20Mohmed%20Al%20Megrahi_09FvY8PRUGg8N2Fr2ArQ.pdf (last visited Sept. 15, 2018).

[60] Research conducted on the tenth anniversary of the SCCRC demonstrates that eighteen of thirty conviction referrals had resulted in convictions being overturned. Chalmers & Leverick, *supra* note 56, at 616. This analysis concludes that the appeals court, while receptive to grounds of appeal relating to misdirection, failures to disclose, and new evidence, was more hostile to referrals suggesting that defense counsel had not provided sufficient representation, judicial or jury misconduct conduct, and lurking doubt. *Id.* at 616–18.

[61] Scottish Criminal Cases Review Commission, *The Impact of Legal Representation on Applications to the Scottish Criminal Cases Review Commission* (2010); Fiona Govan, Scottish Criminal Cases Review Commission, *Research & Development—The Impact of Legal Representation on Applications to the Commission—01/01/2010–31/12/2015* (2017), *both available at* http://www.sccrc.org.uk/research.

[62] Jacqueline Hodgson & Juliet Horne, *The Extent and Impact of Legal Representation on Applications to the Criminal Cases Review Commission (CCRC)* (2009), *available at* https://papers.ssrn.com/sol3/papers.cfm?abstract_id=1483721.

IV. North Carolina Innocence Inquiry Commission

1. Origins

Despite calls by numerous Canadian public inquiries to create an independent body like the CCRC, the first North American jurisdiction to create such a body was North Carolina. In August 2006, the North Carolina legislature created the North Carolina Innocence Inquiry Commission (NCIIC).

The impetus for this reform was the recommendation of a voluntary thirty-person commission called the North Carolina Actual Innocence Commission (NCAIC). It was formed in 2002 with broad representation of different parts of the justice system. After a presentation by David Kyle, a CCRC commissioner, in June 2004, the NCAIC developed its own draft legislation for a North Carolinian version of the CCRC. In a successful attempt to gain public support, however, it departed from the CCRC model by limiting the commission to serious cases where actual innocence could be established by clear and convincing evidence. It also opted for more transparency than either of the UK commissions by requiring public hearings before the new commission could refer a conviction back to the courts. Much of the draft legislation prepared by the NCAIC was enacted by the North Carolina legislature in 2006. The result was to create the first commission in North America with powers to direct convictions back to the courts.[63]

2. Composition

By statute, the NCIIC must include a superior court judge, a prosecutor, a defense attorney, a victim advocate, and a sheriff, thus ensuring a broad representation of criminal justice personnel and stakeholders. The appointments also include a person who is not an attorney or employed by the judiciary and two others, thus ensuring some lay representation.[64] Reflecting the U.S. tradition of judicial ownership of the issue of wrongful convictions, the appointments are made by the chief judges of North Carolina's trial and appeals courts and not by the government, as is the case with the UK commissions. All of the members of the Commission, including the lay members, volunteer their time, though their expenses are paid.

Like the CCRC, the NCIIC faces budget challenges. It has been able to supplement its budget of just over $557,000 through federal funding tied to DNA cases. This and its

[63] Christine C. Mumma, *The North Carolina Innocence Inquiry Commission: Catching Cases That Fall Through the Cracks*, in *Wrongful Conviction and Criminal Justice Reform: Making Justice* 249, 255 (Marvin Zalman & Julia Carrano eds., 2014).

[64] N.C. Gen. Stat. § 15A-1463 (2015).

factual innocence mandate may help explain the prevalence of DNA cases in its exonerations. The NCIIC has an executive and deputy executive director, two legal counsel, one staff member financed through DNA specific grants, one legal investigator, and one case coordinator.[65]

3. Powers

The NCIIC has broad powers of investigation. It can issue process to compel the attendance of witnesses and the production of oaths. It can even grant immunity to witnesses who claim the protection against self-incrimination under the Fifth Amendment so as to compel their testimony.[66] The state has a duty to preserve all relevant files and to turn over material for DNA and other forensic testing once the commission provides notice of an inquiry.[67] The NCIIC can also appoint a special prosecutor to represent the state's case if there is credible evidence of prosecutorial misconduct in the case.[68] The focus is on obtaining "some credible, verifiable evidence of innocence that has not previously been presented at trial or considered at a hearing granted through post-conviction relief" and regardless of whether the evidence could have been obtained with due diligence at trial as required in other procedures.[69] In a recent review of its first decade, Robert Mosteller has stressed the NCIIC's use of inquisitorial powers and suggested that many of its exonerations would not have occurred had the applicants, poor and in some cases mentally challenged people, been left to their own resources.[70]

The NCIIC is obliged to inform victims and co-accused of any formal inquiry it commences. Unlike the CCRC and the SCCRC, it is protected from judicial review by a provision that its decisions and the decisions of a three-judge panel are final and not subject to review.[71] A petition to the NCIIC, however, does not preclude other forms of relief by the petitioner. Some of the cases investigated by the NCIIC have been resolved through other motions, such as the Motion for Appropriate Relief available under North Carolina law.[72]

4. Applications

From its creation in 2006, the NCIIC was limited to applications made by living persons convicted of felonies. A 2016 law has restricted its mandate further by requiring that applicants have been convicted of homicide, robbery, sexual offenses, or other serious felonies and requiring them to waive procedural rights, including those relating to

[65] N.C. Innocence Inquiry Commission, Staff, *at* http://www.innocencecommission-nc.gov/staff.html.

[66] N.C. Gen. Stat. §§ 15A-1467(d), 1468(a.1) (2015).

[67] *Id.* § 15A-1471.

[68] *Id.* § 15A-1469(a.1).

[69] *Id.* § 15A-1460(1).

[70] Mosteller, *supra* note 37, at 1743.

[71] N.C. Gen. Stat. § 15A-1470 (2015).

[72] *Id.* §§ 15A-1411 to 1422 (2015).

self-incrimination and right to counsel, before the NCIIIC will do any DNA testing or even interview the applicant.[73]

Despite these high hurdles and the fact that the state has a population of fewer than 10 million (albeit with a prison population of about 40,000), the NCIIC has received about 200 applications a year. From the start of its work in 2007 to June 30, 2018, the NCIIC has decided 2,360 applications and received over 2,432 applications.

The NCIIC can discontinue an investigation where the applicant fails to cooperate, for example, by failing to waive confidentiality or procedural rights, as is required to proceed. This has only been a reason for dismissal of an application in about 1 percent of cases. The leading reasons for dismissals of applications are: no new evidence, in 28 percent of cases; not claiming factual innocence, in 19 percent of cases; and "no way to prove," in 17 percent of cases.[74]

Rules promulgated by the NCIIC prohibit applicants or their counsel from commenting in the media about a case under investigation without the permission of the Executive Director of the Commission.[75] As with the other commissions, the NCIIC's reasons for rejecting applications are not public. This reflects similar concerns about the confidentiality of information submitted by rejected applicants, but also limits the transparency of the commission's work.

5. Referrals to the Court

The NCIIC is limited by statute to "claims of factual innocence," which are defined as "complete innocence of any criminal responsibility for the felony for which the person was convicted and for any other reduced level of criminal responsibility relating to the crime, and for which there is some credible, verifiable evidence of innocence that has not previously been presented at trial or considered at a hearing granted through postconviction relief."[76] This requires fresh evidence and precludes claims based on unfairness in the investigative or trial processes or defenses that would reduce the level of criminal responsibility.

Unlike the UK commissions, the NCIIC can only refer cases back to the court after a formal and public hearing before all eight members of the commission. It has only held twelve such hearings out of 1985 completed applications. This is a rate of 0.6 percent, a rate that is even lower than the CCRC's 4 percent referral rate to the Court of Appeal. Once the Executive Director of the NCIIC has found that a hearing before the

[73] N.C. Innocence Inquiry Commission, *2016 Annual Report* (2017), *at* http://www.innocencecommission-nc.gov/Forms/pdf/gar/2016%20Annual%20Report%20(Submitted%20in%202017).pdf.

[74] N.C. Innocence Inquiry Commission, Case Statistics, *at* http://innocencecommission-nc.gov/about/ (last visited Sept. 15, 2018).

[75] N.C. Innocence Inquiry Commission, The North Carolina Innocence Inquiry Commission Rules and Procedures Art. 3(c), *at* http://www.innocencecommission-nc.gov/Forms/pdf/statutes%20and%20rules/NCIIC-Rules-and-Procedures-Updated-9.2.2016.pdf.

[76] N.C. Gen. Stat. § 15A-1460 (2015).

full commission is warranted, then not surprisingly, the case for actual innocence is quite strong. The NCIIC has found that there was insufficient evidence to merit a referral back to the courts in only two cases, one being the first case it considered and the other being a case where all eight persons on the commission would have to agree to a referral because the accused had pled guilty.[77] In cases not involving guilty pleas, only a vote of five of eight of the commissioners is required to refer a case back to the court.[78] By requiring public hearings, the NCIIC is more transparent than the other commissions about its referrals.

The appeals that are conducted in those cases that the NCIIC refers are unique proceedings different from ordinary appeals. In these proceedings, three judges without previous involvement in the case have to be unanimously satisfied that the "convicted person has proven by clear and convincing evidence that the convicted person is innocent of the charge."[79] This departs from the approach used in England, Scotland, and Canada, which allows courts to apply the regular standards on appeal once a commission or the political executive has referred a case back to the court.

In only one case has the three-judge panel concluded that the high clear and convincing proof of innocence standard had not been discharged by the accused. The process has resulted in ten people being exonerated and found factually innocent. Although many of the exonerations involve DNA and other forms of forensic evidence, not all do. The commission played an important role in investigating a case where a mentally disabled man had made a false confession and was shown `to the satisfaction of the prosecutor not to have participated in the crime.[80]

Many of the other exonerations have depended on the NCIIC's broad powers to obtain relevant material and compel people to testify, including in one case a four-day search of state premises to discover relevant evidence.[81] There is a trend in recent cases for prosecutors to agree with the defense at the three-judge panel hearing that the conviction should be overturned, generally in cases that involve the discovery of new DNA evidence.[82]

Judges who have declared people innocent in these cases have praised the NCIIC as "perhaps one of the best changes in the judicial system of North Carolina in the last 100 years."[83] At the same time, the procedure is much more demanding than the UK commissions in being limited to proof of factual innocence in the most serious cases.

[77] Although the NCIIC did not refer the case because it was not unanimous, the three men in the case who have pled guilty were subsequently exonerated through a motion for appropriate relief that in some respects is even more demanding than the NCIIC process because it requires that new evidence not have been obtainable by due diligence. On this case, see Mosteller, *supra* note 37.

[78] N.C. Gen. Stat. § 15A-1460, 1468 (2015). [79] *Id.* §15A-1469(h).

[80] Mosteller, *supra* note 37, at 1814. [81] *Id.* at 1839.

[82] This occurred in the cases of the DNA exonerations of Henry Lee McCollum and Leon Brown (2014), Joseph Sledge (2015), Edward Charles McInnis (2015), Knolly Brown Jr, (2016), and the false confession exoneration of William Womble (2014). *See* N.C. Innocence Inquiry Commission, Cases, *at* http://www.innocencecommission-nc.gov/cases.html (last visited Sept. 15, 2018).

[83] Mumma, *supra* note 63, at 264. Mosteller has similarly stressed that the NCIIC has earned a reputation as a neutral objective state agency with broad investigative powers that can reinvestigate meritorious claims of innocence and present such evidence in a public setting. Mosteller, *supra* note 37.

6. Systemic Reform

The NCIIC was created as a part of a bipartisan and widely representative systemic reform process initiated by the North Carolina Actual Innocence Commission that also resulted in other systemic reforms designed to reduce wrongful convictions. Like the other commissions examined in this chapter, however, its focus is on error correction and not on championing or researching issues of systemic reform.

V. Other Exceptional American Procedures Tied to Innocence

The demanding North Carolina standard of proving innocence on clear and convincing evidence to three judges, though very different from the more generous standards used by the UK commissions, has some analogues in other American exceptional procedures.

The use of habeas corpus as a means of collateral attack of convictions in American state and federal courts is notoriously complex, and a full discussion is beyond the scope of the chapter. Habeas corpus review has traditionally focused on legal and constitutional error. It has not been tied to innocence or factual reviews of the verdict, but courts and legislatures have imposed innocence requirements often as a means of restricting habeas corpus review.

In 1993, the U.S. Supreme Court stated that the burden on a habeas corpus applicant to demonstrate innocence (in addition to a violation of constitutional rights) must be "extraordinarily high…because of the very disruptive effect that entertaining claims of factual innocence would have on the need for finality in capital cases, and the enormous burden that having to retry cases on stale evidence would place on the States."[84] That case also stressed that habeas corpus was not the only possible remedy and that convicted persons, including those on death row, could seek clemency or pardons from the political executive.

The U.S. Supreme Court has distinguished threshold innocence claims tied to restrictions on the availability of habeas corpus from freestanding innocence claims.[85] Threshold innocence claims are demanding and influenced by many factors particular to the American system, including the deference of federal courts to state processes, congressional restrictions on the availability of habeas corpus,[86] and concerns about opening floodgates in a high-volume criminal justice system. They are also influenced

[84] Herrara v. Collins, 506 U.S. 390 (1993). [85] House v. Bell, 547 U.S. 518 (1996).

[86] Antiterrorism and Effective Death Penalty Act of 1996, Pub. L. No. 104–132, 110 Stat. 1217–1226 presumes that facts as found by state courts are correct and requires a habeas petitioner to "establish by clear and convincing evidence that but for constitutional error, no reasonable fact-finder would have found the applicant guilty of the underlying offense" in addition to violation of clear federal law. *See* 28 U.S.C. 2254 (1996).

by concerns about the finality of criminal verdicts and deference to the jury found in all common law systems.

In the 2009 Troy Davis case, the U.S. Supreme Court exercised its original habeas corpus jurisdiction for the first time in fifty years to recognize a freestanding innocence claim. The Supreme Court did not decide the case on the merits, but rather remanded the case to a district court to give Mr. Davis an opportunity to demonstrate that evidence "that could not have been obtained at the trial clearly establishes petitioner's innocence."[87] The district court denied relief, stressing that a "federal court simply cannot interpose itself and set aside the jury verdict in this case absent a truly persuasive showing of innocence. To act contrarily would wreck [sic] complete havoc on the criminal justice system."[88] It concluded that there was no clear and convincing evidence that no reasonable juror would have convicted in light of new evidence that nine of the eleven witnesses who had identified Mr. Davis as the killer of a police officer had recanted their testimony, with one of the remaining witnesses being identified by many as the real killer. The Supreme Court denied three other requests for review of the district court's denial of relief.[89] Troy Davis was executed on September 21, 2011.

Both the North Carolina and original habeas corpus exceptional procedures place higher hurdles on applicants than all the other exceptional procedures examined in this chapter. Other American states also have special procedures, often tied to DNA and other forms of new scientific evidence, which require strong evidence of innocence.[90] All of these developments suggest that a focus on factual innocence promoted by American Innocence Projects and DNA exonerations can produce more demanding standards for exceptional reversals of criminal convictions, compared to concerns about miscarriages of justice and the safety of convictions found in the rest of the common law world.[91] This raises concerns about the possible migration of an

[87] *In re* Davis, 557 U.S. 952, 952 (2009). On the case, see Joshua M. Lott, *The End of Innocence? Federal Habeas Corpus Law After* In re Davis, 27 Ga. St. U. L. Rev. 443 (2011).

[88] *In re* Davis, No. CV409-130, 2010 U.S. Dist. LEXIS 87340, at *214 (S.D. Ga. Aug. 24, 2010).

[89] Davis v. Humphrey, 563 U.S. 901 (2011) (dismissing appeal from Georgia District Court, denying petition for writ of habeas corpus, and denying a common law writ of certiorari); Davis v. Humphrey, 563 U.S. 904, (2011) (denying petition for writ of certiorari to Eleventh Circuit); *In re* Davis, 563 U.S. 903 (2011) (denying petition for writ of habeas corpus). On the role of innocence in federal habeas review, see Keith A. Findley, *Defining Innocence*, 74 Alb. L. Rev. 1157 (2011) and Robert J. Smith, *Recalibrating Constitutional Innocence Protection*, 87 Wash. L. Rev. 139 (2012).

[90] In 2013, the Texas legislature with overwhelming majorities enacted a new law providing habeas corpus relief that allows new scientific evidence not available with reasonable diligence to be considered at trial. S.B. 344, 2013 Leg., 83rd Reg. Sess. (Tex. 2013) (adding Art. 11.073 to the Texas Code of Criminal Procedure). This followed from the recommendation of a commission created after Timothy Cole, an Army veteran and university student, was posthumously exonerated of rape on the basis of new DNA evidence and after he died in prison. For a survey of other state requirements, suggesting that some are even more onerous than the "clear and convincing evidence that no reasonable juror would convict" standard used with respect to original habeas corpus in federal court, see Paige Kaneb, *Innocence Presumed: A New Analysis of Innocence as a Constitutional Claim*, 50 Cal. W. L. Rev 220, 220–24 (2014).

[91] Kent Roach, *More Procedure and Concern About Innocence but Less Justice? Remedies for Wrongful Convictions in the United States and Canada*, in *Wrongful Convictions and Miscarriages of Justice: Causes*

American focus on proof of innocence to these other common law jurisdictions.[92] At the same time, the success of the NCIIC and the Innocence Projects in producing exonerations based on the demanding factual innocence model is undeniable. It is a significant achievement given the United States's punitive environment and continued use of the death penalty.

VI. The Canadian Reformed Ministerial Application

1. Origins

Canada, like most common law countries, has relied upon petitions to the political executive as the mechanism for exceptional corrections of miscarriages of justice. Canada's first Criminal Code enacted in 1892 provided that the Minister of Justice, an elected cabinet official, could on "any application for the mercy of the Crown" by a person convicted of an indictable offense direct a new trial if "after such inquiry as he thinks proper," the Minister "entertains a doubt whether such person ought to have been convicted."[93] Under subsequent amendments to the Code, the Minister's discretion was made even less structured by removing references to the doubt standard. The Minister was also given the option of directing a new appeal or requesting an appeals court to answer a specific question in relation to the mercy application.

The Minister of Justice's unstructured discretion became problematic after the Minister referred David Milgaard's wrongful conviction, but only after the accused's mother met with the Prime Minister after the Minister of Justice had denied her son's previous petition. This irregular process highlighted a lack of transparency in the petition process. A subsequent inquiry even failed to find out on what basis the first ministerial application was denied and the second application was granted.[94] The administrative practice was changed in 1994 to regularize the ministerial review process.[95] These changes were

and Remedies in North American and European Criminal Justice Systems (C. Ronald Huff & Martin Killias eds., 2013).

[92] For arguments that a focus on innocence can disadvantage women and racialized groups such as Indigenous persons, see Debra Parkes & Emma Cunliffe, *Women and Wrongful Convictions: Concepts and Challenges*, 11 Int'l J.L. Context 219 (2015); Kent Roach, *The Wrongful Conviction of Indigenous People in Australia and Canada*, 17 Flinders L.J. 203 (2015).

[93] Criminal Code, S.C. 1892, c. 29, s. 748.

[94] Edward P. MacCallum, Government of Saskatchewan, *1 Report of the Commission of Inquiry into the Wrongful Conviction of David Milgaard* 361–62 (2008).

[95] The administrative practice introduced by Minister of Justice Alan Rock in 1994 became the basis for the 2002 legislative reforms and continuing practice. Both require the applicant to establish a reasonable basis that a miscarriage of justice likely occurred, and indicate that an application is not a further appeal but rather an extraordinary remedy that will often be supported by new matters of significance

codified in 2002 legislation.[96] These reforms, however, disappointed many who had hoped that the government would create a Canadian version of the CCRC, as recommended by numerous public inquiries into wrongful convictions.

2. Composition

As part of the 2002 changes, a Criminal Conviction Review Group was created as a separate entity within the Department of Justice and a special advisor, a retired judge, was appointed to provide independent advice.[97] The federal Minister of Justice still makes decisions about whether to order a new trial or appeal.

3. Powers

The 2002 reforms gave the Minister of Justice broad powers under the Inquiries Act to compel the production of relevant documents. It also allows these powers to be delegated to lawyers, retired judges, or others with similar background and experience.[98] These powers have been used to allow those independent of the Department of Justice to conduct investigations, though the ultimate decision on whether to refer a case remains that of the Minister of Justice. When an investigative report is prepared, the applicant has access to that report and a year to prepare additional information for the Minister to consider.

Ministerial investigations of petitions frequently take years to resolve as they involve both investigation by the Minister or his or her delegate and submission of material by applicants. A number of Canadian courts have creatively granted petitioners bail pending a ministerial decision in cases involving a strong prima facie case of a miscarriage of justice.[99] These decisions have placed an important and creative judicial gloss on the statutory procedures for petitioners who remain in custody.

Ministerial decisions can also be subject to judicial review. Courts have required the Minister to apply correct judicial tests regarding the admission of fresh evidence.

not previously considered by the courts. Since 1994, the Minister of Justice has used a four-stage process based on: (1) a preliminary assessment to determine if a miscarriage of justice could have occurred, (2) an investigation if the application goes beyond the first threshold, (3) the preparation of an investigative summary that is disclosed to the applicant for comments, and (4) a decision by the Minister of Justice based on the recommendation of the Criminal Conviction Review group, the applicant's submission, and applicant and the investigative summary. *Id.* at 361–63.

[96] Criminal Law Amendment Act, S.C. 2002, c.13, s. 71.

[97] Narissa Somji, *A Comparative Study of the Post-conviction Review Process in Canada and the United Kingdom*, 58 Crim. L.Q. 137, 162–65 (2012).

[98] Criminal Code, S.C. 1892, c. 29, s. 696.2 as amended by Criminal Law Amendment Act, 2001, S.C. 2002, c.13.

[99] R. v. Phillion [2003] O.J. No. 3422; R. v. Driskell [2004] M.B.Q.B. 3; R. v. Unger [2005] M.B.Q.B. 238; Ostrowski v. The Queen [2009] M.B.Q.B. 327; R. v. Assoun [2014] N.S.S.C. 419.

Although the Minister of Justice is not required to follow the advice of independent persons to whom the Minister delegates his or her investigative powers, he or she cannot err in the "assessment of important material facts," in part because "the Minister did not interview the witnesses or read the volumes of documents assembled in the investigation."[100]

4. Applications

Perhaps reflecting disappointment among innocence campaigners at the government's refusal to create a Canadian version of the CCRC, the number of applications to the Minister of Justice under the reformed system has been low. From November 2002, when the new provisions took effect, to March 31, 2017, the Minister of Justice decided ninety-one applications.

Another factor explaining the low number of applications is that courts, including the Supreme Court of Canada, have been receptive to creative attempts to avoid the petition process. For example, in cases where criminal convictions were subject to a first appeal, but new evidence was subsequently discovered, the Supreme Court has allowed appeals out of time and remanded the cases back to the Court of Appeal to consider the new evidence.[101]

5. Referrals to the Court

Under the 2002 reforms, the Minister of Justice may refer a case to an appeals court or direct a new trial if he or she is "satisfied that there is a reasonable basis to conclude that a miscarriage of justice likely occurred."[102] This seems to impose a higher standard closer to probability than the English real possibility test. It also seems to contemplate a discretion not to refer cases that otherwise satisfy the standard. It also gives the Minister an option that the other commissions examined in this chapter do not have: ordering a new trial where the prosecution would have to establish guilt beyond a reasonable doubt. This discretionary option is, however, rarely exercised.

The 2002 provisions direct the Minister of Justice to consider "new matters of significance" and state that the application of ministerial review "is not intended to serve as a further appeal and any remedy available on such an application is an extraordinary remedy."[103] This represents a legislative affirmation of the importance of finality.

[100] Ross v. Canada [2014] F.C. 338 [57]. For a case recognizing that the Minister of Justice could be held civilly liable for acting in bad faith or with serious recklessness on an application for ministerial review, see Hinse v. Canada (Attorney General), 2015 S.C.C. 35.

[101] *See, e.g.*, R. v. Marquardt [2009] S.C.C.A. 7; *see also* Kent Roach, *Comparative Reflections on Miscarriages of Justice in Australia and Canada* 17 Flinders L.J. 381, 424–25 (2015).

[102] Criminal Code, R.S.C., 1985, c. C-34, s. 696.3, as amended by Criminal Law Amendment Act, 2001, S.C. 2002, c.13, s 71.

[103] *Id.* § 696.4.

In practice, both applications and referrals to the Canadian Minister of Justice are exceptional. Since 2002, the Minister has made decisions on ninety-one applications, referring sixteen of these cases back to the courts. This is a considerably higher referral rate (18 percent) than the CCRC, suggesting that the more onerous Canadian process tends to attract more applications with merit compared to the CCRC. In addition, there is evidence that the Minister of Justice has been more risk averse than the UK commissions in making referrals because almost all of the cases that the Canadian ministers have sent back to the courts have resulted in courts overturning convictions or prosecutors deciding not to proceed with a new trial.[104]

6. Systemic Reform

The Criminal Conviction Review Group issues annual reports that provide information on the review process, but do not generally discuss systemic reforms. At the same time, groups of senior prosecutors in Canada have prepared two editions of an extensive report dealing with systemic recommendations to prevent miscarriages of justice. Most of the material for these valuable reports comes not from data prepared by those who administer the exceptional section 696.1 procedure, but from public inquiries that provinces had appointed at their discretion to examine notorious wrongful convictions. It is these public inquiries, often conducted by sitting and retired judges, and not the ministerial review process that have contributed to systemic reform. Moreover, all of the provincial public inquiries into wrongful convictions have recommended as a systemic reform that the Minister of Justice's role in overturning convictions be replaced with that of an independent executive body patterned after the CCRC.[105]

VII. Australia

1. Origins

Those who have exhausted appeals in Australia can petition Ministers of Justice to refer convictions back to appeals courts. In contrast to Canada, these petitions are made at the state level, which is usually directly implicated in the alleged miscarriages of justice. In Canada, the federal Minister of Justice is responsible for only a minority of all criminal prosecutions. Also, unlike in Canada, Australian courts have refused to

[104] Kent Roach, *An Independent Commission to Review Claims of Wrongful Convictions: Lessons from North Carolina?*, 58 Crim. L.Q. 283, 290 (2012) (but noting that some of these dispositions favorable to the applicant were achieved by prosecutorial decisions).

[105] Kent Roach, *Wrongful Convictions in Canada*, 80 U. Cin. L. Rev. 1465, 1494–1501 (2012).

review ministerial decisions on the grounds that they are discretionary and do not involve legal rights.[106]

Some Australian states have exceptional procedures that allow an appellate court to convene a judicial inquiry if "it appears that there is doubt or question as to the convicted person's guilt."[107] Such provisions place responsibility on the judiciary as opposed to the executive to decide whether exceptional procedures are warranted to correct miscarriages of justice. Such procedures have the potential to inject inquisitorial elements into the adversarial system, though some inquiries have been conducted in a contested adversarial manner, and many contend that a permanent CCRC would be preferable.

A bill was introduced by an independent member of the South Australian legislature in 2010 to create a CCRC. A legislative committee heard testimony about the inadequacy and lack of transparency of the petition procedure. It recommended the creation of a forensic science review panel and the creation of a second statutory right of appeal instead of the creation of a CCRC. South Australia introduced in 2013 such legislation allowing second and subsequent appeals in the interests of justice on the basis of fresh and compelling evidence. Tasmania enacted similar legislation in 2015.[108] In both cases, attorneys general conceded that the petition procedure lacked transparency.[109] The bills had bipartisan support in part because they were patterned on previous legislation designed to abrogate double jeopardy and allow new prosecutions to correct "wrongful acquittals" when fresh and compelling new evidence is discovered about an acquitted person's guilt.

2. Composition

Because Australia has opted not to create a new commission to consider claims of wrongful convictions, powers to consider second or subsequent appeals in Southern Australia and Tasmania, powers to initiate inquiries as part of the appeal process and powers to consider fresh evidence are exercised by regularly constituted courts of appeal in the states.

[106] Von Einem v. Griffin (1998) 72 S.A.S.R. 110 [156] ("It would be inappropriate for this Court to review an unfettered discretion of the executive for the purpose of compelling the executive to bring a matter before the Court."). For persuasive criticism of this case, see Bibi Sangha & Robert N. Moles, *Miscarriages of Justice: Criminal Appeals and the Rule of Law in Australia* 116–21 (2015). For a Canadian decision recognizing that ministerial decisions on petitions even before the 2002 reforms were subject to limited judicial review for bad faith, see Hinse v. Canada (Attorney General) [2015] S.C.C. 35.

[107] Crimes (Appeal and Review) Act 2001, s. 79 (N.S.W.).

[108] Statutes Amendment (Appeals) Act 2013 (adding § 353A to Criminal Law Consolidation Act 1935 (S.A.)); Criminal Code Amendment (Second or Subsequent Appeal for Fresh and Compelling Evidence) Act 2015.

[109] Bibi Sangha, *The Statutory Right to Second or Subsequent Criminal Trial Appeals in South Australia and Tasmania*, 17 Flinders L.J. 471, 486 (2015).

3. Powers

The new right for second and subsequent appeals in South Australia and Tasmania requires a petitioner to obtain leave for the appeal on the basis of "fresh and compelling" evidence, with "fresh" being defined as evidence that was not and could not with due diligence have been produced at trial, and "compelling" being defined as reliable, substantial evidence that is "highly probative in the context of the issues in dispute at the trial of the offence."[110] The requirement of fresh and compelling evidence is more restrictive than the requirements governing the commissions or the Canadian process. This reflects the fact that the second appeals are based on provisions that abrogate double jeopardy, and also that they involve direct access to appeals courts as opposed to an executive process.

Australian courts have indicated that even if there is fresh and compelling evidence, they still have discretion to decline leave to appeal as not in the interests of justice.[111] In some ways this is similar to the discretion that the CCRC and the SCCRC have not to refer a case, or the power that Scottish courts previously had to refuse in the interests of justice to hear a case on referral from the SCCRC. In all these cases, the discretion might be used in cases where the accused's guilt is overwhelming despite there being compelling new evidence about a particular aspect of the case. This suggests that factual guilt or innocence may play a role even in systems that do not recognize them as a formal substantive ground.

If the court grants leave for the second or subsequent appeal, it can allow the appeal if it concludes that there has been a "substantial miscarriage of justice." This is somewhat different than the ordinary grounds of appeal in Australia, which are based on "miscarriages of justice," "unreasonable verdicts," or errors of law. It requires that there be a "significant possibility that the jury, acting reasonably, would have acquitted the appellant had the fresh evidence been before it at trial" in light of all the evidence.[112] As in North Carolina, a different standard for allowing appeals is applied when the exceptional mechanism is employed. This differs from the situation in the UK and Canada, where once a case is referred, the ordinary grounds of appeal apply. Bibi Sangha and Robert Moles have argued that these differences between first and subsequent appeals may be in tension with the rule of law, including international law. At the same time, they also conclude that the subsequent appeal provisions are a "substantial advance over appeal rights" in other Australian states, as well as in the UK and Canada.[113]

[110] Criminal Law Consolidation Act 1935, ss. 353A(1), (3) (S.A.).

[111] The Australian High Court has suggested that this discretion not to consider fresh and compelling evidence could be exercised in cases where "the applicant has made a public confession of guilt" but not simply on the basis that the conviction is "long standing." Van Beelen v. The Queen [2017] HCA 48 at [30]; *see also* R. v. Keogh (No 2) [2014] S.A.S.C.F.C. 136 [115]; R. v. Bromley [2018] SASC 41 [386].

[112] Van Beelen v. The Queen [2017] HCA 48 at [22-23] [32]; *see also* Bibi Sangha et al., *Forensic Investigations and Miscarriages of Justice* 134–38 (2010).

[113] Sangha & Moles, *supra* note 106, at 13.

As Justice Michael Kirby has explained, the objective of these new rights of appeal was "to replace the petition to the Executive Government (with its lack of transparency) by a process initiated for the prisoner before the Independent Judicial Branch of Government."[114] This means that unlike in other exceptional procedures discussed in this chapter, no new institution or division of the executive was created. Instead, the onus was placed on private parties to convince the court that they had fresh and compelling evidence and that they have suffered a substantial miscarriage of justice.

4. Applications

The experience with these new rights of appeal is limited, in part because they were only recently adopted and in part because of the considerable onus they place on convicted persons to produce fresh and compelling evidence. So far, two convictions have been overturned in South Australia, with two other applications being denied. The use of second appeals will depend on the private initiative of applicants who will have an explicit burden of producing fresh and compelling new evidence.

5. Referrals to the Court

In both South Australian cases of a successful second appeal, the appeals court accepted that new evidence was fresh and compelling evidence and that, in light of it, there was a substantial miscarriage of justice. In one case, the court held that disclosure violations at the original trial helped reveal that the new forensic evidence was fresh and compelling.[115] The appeals court ordered new trials in both cases, but they were not held and the cases are accepted as wrongful convictions.[116] At the same time, two subsequent applications have been denied.[117] Such a 50 percent success rate is consistent with a hypothesis that systems that place more barriers on applicants will tend to have higher reversal or success rates than systems such as the CCRC that minimize access barriers. At the same time, this should not be taken as a criticism of eased access. Indeed, there are concerns that the new rights of appeal place too much of a burden on the convicted person. In particular, a strong case can be made for a proactive audit of cases in South

[114] *Id.* at ix. [115] R. v. Drummond (No 2) [2015] S.A.S.C.F.C. 82.

[116] R. v. Keogh (No 2) [2014] S.A.S.C.F.C. 136.

[117] Van Beelen v. The Queen [2017] HCA 48 at [22–23] [32] (holding that while new forensic pathology evidence was fresh and compelling, it did not indicate that the conviction would be a substantial miscarriage of justice in light of all the evidence); R. v. Bromley [2018] SASC 41 at [386–388] (holding that fresh forensic pathology evidence and fresh evidence relating to an eyewitness was not compelling and in the alternative created no substantial miscarriage of justice in light of all the evidence including new evidence offered by the prosecution about the applicant's propensity to commit similar crimes. *Id.* [507–509].

Australia, especially those involving forensic evidence, as indeed was recommended in 2010 by the legislative committee that recommended the new right of appeal.[118]

6. Systemic Reform

It remains to be seen whether other Australian states will follow South Australia and Tasmania in creating second and subsequent appeals or whether other systemic reforms such as the creation of a CCRC will occur. As in the United States, state jurisdiction over criminal law has allowed experimentation with reforms in some but not all states. In contrast, exclusive federal jurisdiction over criminal law and procedure in Canada means that exceptional procedure reform can only take place at the federal level.

The focus under either the new second appeal procedures or those in other Australian states that allow courts to order inquiries into disputed matters has firmly been on error correction in individual cases as opposed to achieving systemic reforms to reduce miscarriages of justice in future cases. Australia suffers from a comparative lack of systemic reform mechanisms such as the Canadian public inquiries.

VIII. Conclusion

Most Australian and American states continue to rely on unfettered executive discretion on applications for mercy or clemency as their exceptional means to correct miscarriages of justice. The durability of this approach reflects the conservatism of the legal system and the great emphasis that it accords to the finality of guilty verdicts even in the face of much greater acceptance in the DNA era of the reality of wrongful convictions.

The conservatism of the criminal justice system persists even in those states that have adopted new exceptional procedures because the appellate courts in the UK, Scotland, and Canada continue to apply the same standards for reversing convictions in cases referred back to the courts from the exceptional procedures as are used in regular first appeals from criminal convictions. This means that these exceptional procedures should be viewed as part of a system that includes the appellate courts. In North Carolina and in South Australia and Tasmania, appellate courts apply different, but more onerous standards in considering cases that are referred to them or initiated by exceptional procedures. The North Carolina courts apply a *de jure* standard of factual innocence at this point, while the Australian courts, in rejecting some second appeals, have come close to applying a *de facto* factual innocence requirement when they have concluded that even fresh and compelling new evidence does not warrant overturning a conviction.

[118] Robert Moles, *Institutional Reform in the Context of Criminal Appeals in South Australia*, 17 Flinders L.J. 331 (2015).

Much of the criticism directed at the CCRC with respect to particular referrals might equally be directed at the Court of Appeal in its application of standards of new evidence and with respect to the safety of convictions. Both the 1993 Royal Commission that proposed the CCRC and the 2015 Parliamentary committee that recommended it be retained correctly recognized the need to expand the Court of Appeal's grounds for allowing appeals and receiving new evidence. At the same time, comparative study should temper some of the criticisms of the UK commissions as captives of their appellate courts. The UK commissions have been more aggressive in referring cases than their North American counterparts, as measured by referrals that resulted in the courts sustaining the original conviction.

Despite significant conservatism with respect to grounds of appeals, we are in an exciting era of procedural and substantive experimentation with respect to exceptional mechanisms. With some notable detractors,[119] many in the common law world advocate in favor of a CCRC-type institution. Still, there are many important and contested design issues in creating new institutions. They include whether, as in North Carolina, the mandate should be limited to factual innocence[120] or should reflect the ordinary or other grounds of appeal. Other issues are the appropriate mix of inquisitorial powers and adversarial safeguards, the degree to which independent legal representation of applicants should be encouraged, and whether such an institution should have the responsibility for making systemic recommendations to prevent wrongful convictions or just focus on error correction. Any serious discussion of new and exceptional mechanisms also leads one back to discussing the role of appellate courts and the appropriate weight that should be given to the finality of convictions.

The most accessible exceptional new procedure is the CCRC in England. It now entertains about 1,400 applications a year under its simplified application process. At the same time, the CCRC's accessibility is accompanied by a 97 percent rejection rate of its applications. The only comparable rejection rate is that of the NCIIC, which is related to its much more limited factual innocence mandate. More needs to be known about rejected applications, just as more needs to be known about the majority of criminal cases that are resolved without trial. Some rejected applicants, often those represented by volunteer innocence projects, have been quite critical of the CCRC.

There may be a trade-off between the increased accessibility seen in the CCRC and higher rejection rates. Another consequence of the increased accessibility of the CCRC is that its cases are not dominated by murder and other serious criminal convictions, as is the case with North American and Australian exceptional procedures. More work needs to be done on how factors and procedures used to correct miscarriages of justice

[119] For arguments that the old petition procedure should be revived and free pardons awarded in cases of factual innocence, see Naughton, *supra* note 2.

[120] David Hamer, *Wrongful Convictions, Appeals and the Finality Principle: The Need for a Criminal Cases Review Commission*, 37 U.N.S.W. L.J. 270 (2014) (recommending CCRC but limited to factual innocence); Sangha et al., *supra* note 30 (recommending CCRC on a broader miscarriage of justice grounds).

in the most serious cases may also apply in less serious cases, and the UK commissions have examined less serious cases more than the other exceptional procedures examined in this chapter.

Applicants to the CCRC and the SCCRC who have their own lawyers are more likely to be successful in having their cases referred back to the courts than applicants who are not represented. Such correlations between legal representation and successful applications do not establish causation, but they should temper simplistic reform rhetoric that celebrate and promote institutions such as the CCRC on the basis that they are proactive and inquisitorial.

The minimal Canadian reforms to the ministerial petition process attract far fewer applications than the UK commissions or even the more restrictive innocence-based North Carolina commission. The South Australia subsequent appeal right is quite new, but it seems that relatively few people will be able to take advantage of it by producing fresh and compelling evidence. Even if they do, their appeals may be rejected on the grounds that it is not in the interests of justice to consider the new evidence or that the new evidence does not reveal a substantial miscarriage of justice producing a significant possibility that the jury would not have convicted. Legal representation of those who seek a second appeal seems to be a necessity. Many of those who championed a second appeal in Australia acknowledge that the creation of an Australian CCRC and systemic reforms especially in the area of forensic science are still necessary. More generally, exceptional procedures can reveal cases that are symptoms of larger systemic problems that facilitate miscarriages of justice.

The lower use of Canadian and South Australian exceptional procedures by those who have been convicted is probably a product of the greater burdens they place on applications than the commission process. The Canadian experience may also reflect a lack of trust or confidence in a process that relies on an elected Minister of Justice to make the ultimate decision whether to refer a case, even if assisted by those with more independence from the government.

The Canadian system is comparatively slow, perhaps because it combines inquisitorial investigations with time to allow the accused party both to develop the file and respond to the Minister's investigation. This may achieve more procedural justice than less adversarial approaches, but its combination of inquisitorial and adversarial approaches results in slower processing of cases than in other systems examined in this chapter, with the possible exception of South Australian systems of second appeals, which rely completely on the adversarial system.

All of the commissions have focused on error correction and processing individual cases in a quasi-judicial manner as opposed to research or advocacy for systemic reform to decrease miscarriages of justice in the future. The North Carolina commission, because it deliberately represents a wide variety of criminal justice stakeholders including prosecutors, sheriffs, and victim advocates, might be a potent advocate, were it so inclined. Given limited budgets, as well as concerns about appearing impartial, however, it is perhaps understandable why the commissions have not advocated for systemic reform. Although none of the commissions have become advocates, they hold data that could help inform systemic reform. The SCCRC seems particularly active in not only encouraging, but also conducting its own research.

There is evidence of American exceptionalism because only the NCIIC and the American original habeas corpus require clear and convincing proof of factual innocence. All other common law jurisdictions employ broader and more flexible concepts of miscarriages of justice or unsafe or unreasonable convictions. The migration of the CCRC idea to North Carolina has produced a commission that is only concerned with factual innocence, that is restricted to serious crimes, and that represents prosecutors, sheriffs, and victims of crime in an attempt to sustain some of the bipartisan political support enjoyed by the American innocence movement. This may represent the limits of possible reforms in the punitive and partisan American environment. Nevertheless, such an approach could have regressive effects if transferred uncritically to other common law countries.

References

Peter Duff, *Straddling Two Worlds: Reflections of a Retired Criminal Cases Review Commissioner*, 72 Mod. L. Rev. 693 (2009)

Laurie Elks, *Righting Miscarriages of Justice? Ten Years of the Criminal Cases Review Commission* (2008)

David Hamer, *Wrongful Convictions, Appeals and the Finality Principle: The Need for a Criminal Cases Review Commission*, 37 U.N.S.W. L.J. 270 (2014)

Robert P. Mosteller, *N.C. Innocence Inquiry Commission's First Decade: Impressive Success and Lessons Learned*, 94 N.C. L. Rev. 1725 (2016)

The Criminal Cases Review Commission: Hope for the Innocent? (Michael Naughton ed., (2010))

Kent Roach, *The Role of Innocence Commissions: Error Discovery, Systemic Reform or Both?*, 85 Chi.-Kent L. Rev. 89 (2010)

Stephanie Roberts & Lynne Weathered, *Assisting the Factually Innocent: The Contradictions and Compatibility of Innocence Projects and the Criminal Cases Review Commission*, 29 Oxford J. Legal Stud. 43 (2009)

Bibi Sangha, *The Statutory Right to Second or Subsequent Criminal Trial Appeals in South Australia and Tasmania*, 17 Flinders L.J. 471 (2015)

Narissa Somji, *A Comparative Study of the Post-conviction Review Process in Canada and the United Kingdom*, 58 Crim. L.Q. 137 (2012)

PART VIII

PROCEDURE IN INTERNATIONAL TRIBUNALS

CHAPTER 43

PLURALISM IN INTERNATIONAL CRIMINAL PROCEDURE

JENIA I. TURNER*

I. Introduction

OVER the last two decades, international criminal procedure has become a recognized body of law, with textbooks, treatises, and law review articles discussing its rules and principles and theorizing its goals and methods.[1] The term refers to the procedures used at the international criminal courts and tribunals created to address some of the most serious offenses, such as genocide, crimes against humanity, and war crimes. Some of these courts are fully international, such as the International Criminal Tribunal for the former Yugoslavia (ICTY), the International Criminal Tribunal for Rwanda

* I thank Nicola Hines and Brooke Olsen for excellent research assistance and the SMU Law Faculty Excellence Fund for supporting the research for this chapter.

[1] *See, e.g.*, Kai Ambos, *Treatise on International Criminal Law: Volume III, International Criminal Procedure* (2016); *International Criminal Law Practitioner Library: Volume III, International Criminal Procedure* (Gideon Boas et al. eds., 2011); Karim Khan et al., *Archbold International Criminal Courts: Practice, Procedure, and Evidence* (2014); *International Criminal Procedure: The Interface of Civil Law and Common Law Legal Systems* (Linda Carter & Fausto Pocar eds., 2013); Christoph Safferling, *International Criminal Procedure* (2012); Christine Schuon, *International Criminal Procedure: A Clash of Legal Cultures* (2010); *International Criminal Procedure: Principles and Rules* (Göran Sluiter et al. eds., 2013); *International Criminal Procedure: Towards a Coherent Body of Law* (Goran Sluiter & Sergey Vasiliev eds., 2009); Frédéric Mégret, *Beyond Fairness: Understanding the Determinants of International Criminal Procedure*, 14 UCLA J. Int'l L. & Foreign Aff. 37 (2009); Mirjan Damaška, *Reflections on Fairness in International Criminal Justice*, 10 J. Int'l Crim. Just. 611 (2012); Gregory S. Gordon, *Toward an International Criminal Procedure: Due Process Aspirations and Limitations*, 45 Colum. J. Transnat'l L. 635 (2007); Jens David Ohlin, *A Meta-theory of International Criminal Procedure: Vindicating the Rule of Law*, 14 UCLA J. Int'l L. & Foreign Aff. 77 (2009); Colin Warbrick, *International Criminal Courts and Fair Trial*, 3 J. Armed Conflict L. 45 (1998).

(ICTR), and the permanent International Criminal Court (ICC). Others are "hybrid courts," featuring a mix of domestic and international personnel, laws, and practices. They include the Special Court for Sierra Leone (SCSL), the East Timor Special Panels for Serious Crimes, the Bosnia and Herzegovina War Crimes Chamber, the Extraordinary Chambers in the Courts of Cambodia (ECCC), and the Special Tribunal for Lebanon (STL). More hybrid courts are being created and proposed today, even as the appetite for international institutions is declining.[2]

Even as international criminal courts have proliferated and international criminal procedure has attained recognition as an independent corpus of law, foundational questions about the field remain. Can the diverse procedures used by these institutions be treated as part of a single, coherent system? Is international criminal procedure a blend of domestic traditions or a sui generis body of law, reflecting the special goals and needs of international criminal trials? What goals does it pursue, and how does it balance competing objectives?

Section II of the chapter traces the development of modern international criminal procedure, first at the ad hoc tribunals for the former Yugoslavia and Rwanda and then at hybrid courts and the International Criminal Court.[3] Section III discusses the ambitious and at times conflicting goals that international criminal procedure is said to pursue. These include goals commonly associated with domestic trials—providing a fair trial, establishing the truth, and enforcing the criminal law effectively. But some commentators believe that international courts—and by extension, the process these courts rely upon—also pursue broader, political goals, such as promoting the rule of law, fostering peace and reconciliation, creating a historical record as a means to educate future generations, and providing a sense of closure for injured individuals and communities. The international community has failed to agree on a clear ranking of these various objectives, however, and debates persist about which goal should take precedence when different goals are in tension. As Section IV documents, the disagreement about priorities helps explain much of the diversity we see in international criminal procedures, both across different courts and within the same court.

[2] *See*, e.g., Agreement between the Government of the Republic of Senegal and the African Union on the creation of the Extraordinary African Chambers in the Senegalese Courts (in French) (creating the Extraordinary African Chambers to try international crimes committed in Chad from 7 June 1982 to 1 December 1990); Agreement between the United Nations and the State of Guatemala to Establish the International Commission against Impunity in Guatemala (establishing a special prosecutor's office within the Guatemalan justice system to prosecute human rights violations by security forces); Agreement on the Resolution of the Conflict in the Republic of South Sudan, Addis Ababa, Ethiopia, August 17, 2015, ch. V (proposing a Hybrid Court for South Sudan); Patryk I. Labuda, The Road Ahead—Building Momentum for Justice in the Central African Republic, https://justiceinconflict.org/2017/06/07/the-road-ahead-building-momentum-for-justice-in-the-central-african-republic%E2%80%A8/(discussing Special Criminal Court for CAR).

[3] Although the International Military Tribunals for Nuremberg and the Far East (Tokyo) can be seen as the first examples of courts using "international criminal procedure," the procedural rules used at the tribunals were not as fully developed as modern rules and are therefore not examined here.

Accordingly, international criminal procedure is currently not a coherent legal system, but is rather best described as the product of a decentralized "network" or "community" of courts.[4] Section V argues that the international legal community should embrace the pluralist character of international criminal procedure and learn from the dialogue and "labs of experimentation" it encourages. The diversity of procedures can help international criminal courts arrive at solutions that address more effectively the unique political, practical, and forensic challenges of dispensing international criminal justice. Over time, the circulation of information and personnel around the different international criminal courts and tribunals can help spread procedural practices from one court to the next and bring some level of coherence to the enterprise.[5] But at least in the foreseeable future, such piecemeal efforts to bring greater uniformity to international criminal procedure are likely to run up against the desires of the creators of different international courts to establish and maintain court-specific procedural frameworks that reflect the political priorities and legal traditions of the populations affected.

While pluralism across courts may be inevitable and, in many ways, desirable, procedural pluralism within the same court raises legitimate concerns about notice, predictability, and equal treatment. Section V therefore argues that international criminal courts must respond to these concerns and that they can do so through clearer rules and appellate jurisprudence that promotes procedural coherence. Predictability and equal treatment within the same legal institution are critical elements of fair trials and the rule of law and indispensable to the legitimacy of the international criminal justice system.

II. Development of International Criminal Procedure

In the aftermath of atrocities committed during ethnic conflicts in the former Yugoslavia and Rwanda in the 1990s, the UN Security Council established the International Criminal Tribunals for the former Yugoslavia (ICTY) and for Rwanda (ICTR) to address international crimes arising out of these conflicts. The tribunals had jurisdiction over genocide, crimes against humanity, and war crimes. They were the first international courts since the post-World War II Nuremberg and Tokyo Tribunals to address such crimes.

[4] Elies van Sliedregt & Sergey Vasiliev, *Pluralism: A New Framework for International Criminal Justice*, in *Pluralism in International Criminal Law* 3, 13 (Elies van Sliedregt & Sergey Vasiliev eds., 2014); William W. Burke-White, *A Community of Courts: Toward a System of International Criminal Law Enforcement*, 24 Mich. J. Int'l L. 1, 3 (2002).

[5] Burke-White, *supra* note 4, at 4; Elena Baylis, *Tribunal-Hopping with the Post-Conflict Justice Junkies*, 10 Oregon Rev. Int'l L. 361 (2008).

The procedural law that the tribunals applied included their founding statutes, their rules of procedure and evidence, and standard international law sources such as treaties and custom. Because international criminal law and procedure were not well developed when the ICTY and ICTR began their work, the tribunals had to fashion and interpret rules of procedure with reference to domestic laws and practices. Both the common law and civil law traditions influenced the development of criminal procedure at the tribunals. At the outset, the common law, or adversarial, approach predominated,[6] but over time, tribunal procedure became more inquisitorial and influenced by civil law principles, as part of an effort to expedite proceedings.[7]

Soon after the ICTY and ICTR began their proceedings, in 1998, state delegations from around the world negotiated and signed the Rome Treaty establishing the International Criminal Court (ICC). Like the ICTY and ICTR before it, the ICC adjudicates some of the most serious international crimes, including war crimes, crimes against humanity, and genocide (and possibly in the near future, the crime of aggression). On matters of procedure, the ICC applies its own statute and rules of procedure and evidence, as well as treaties and "principles and rules of international law."[8] It must interpret the norms drawn from these sources of law in a manner "consistent with internationally recognized human rights."[9]

Reflecting the greater diversity of their drafters, ICC procedural rules are more closely aligned with the inquisitorial approach than were the rules of the ad hoc tribunals. ICC judges have the authority to exercise significant control over the proceedings by directing the presentation of evidence[10] and overseeing charging decisions of prosecutors.[11]

[6] Daryl A. Mundis, *From "Common Law" Towards "Civil Law": The Evolution of the ICTY Rules of Procedure and Evidence*, 14 Leiden J. Int'l L. 367, 368 (2001).

[7] *See, e.g.*, Kai Ambos, *International Criminal Procedure: "Adversarial," "Inquisitorial" or Mixed?*, 3 Int'l Crim. L. Rev. 1, 18–19 (2003); Claus Kress, *The Procedural Law of the International Criminal Court in Outline: Anatomy of a Unique Compromise*, 1 J. Int'l Crim. Just. 603, 612 (2003). Other commentators have argued that rather than becoming more inquisitorial, the ICTY became more "managerial," changing its procedures to promote efficiency rather than to facilitate a more thorough objective inquiry into the facts. *See, e.g.*, Maximo Langer, *The Rise of Managerial Judging in International Criminal Law*, 53 Am. J. Comp. L. 835, 835–36 (2004).

[8] Rome Statute art. 21(1). The Regulations of the Court, adopted by ICC judges, are a subsidiary source of procedural law. ICC Regulations of the Court Reg. 1.

[9] Rome Statute art. 21(3).

[10] *Id.* art. 69(3) (providing that judges can request the submission of evidence that they consider "necessary for the determination of the truth."); *id.* art 64(8)(b) (authorizing judges to "give directions for the conduct of the proceedings").

[11] *See, e.g.*, *id.* art. 61 (providing for an adversarial hearing on the basis of which the "Pre-Trial Chamber shall . . . determine whether there is sufficient evidence to establish substantial grounds to believe that the person committed each of the crimes charged"); *id.* art. 56 (3) (giving Pre-Trial Chambers the authority to take special investigative measures in certain limited circumstances, even if the prosecutor has not sought such measures, where "the Pre-Trial Chamber considers that such measures are required to preserve evidence that it deems would be essential for the defense at trial"); Prosecutor v. Lubanga, Case No. ICC-01/04-01/06, Judgment on the Appeals of Mr Lubanga Dyilo and the Prosecutor Against the Decision of Trial Chamber I of 14 July 2009 Entitled "Decision Giving Notice to the Parties and Participants that the Legal Characterisation of the Facts may be Subject to Change in Accordance with Regulation 55(2) of the Regulations of the Court," ¶¶ 77, 93 (Dec. 8, 2009) (noting that judges can, after

Victims can also actively participate in the proceedings in their own capacity, from pre-trial to appeal.[12] Furthermore, ICC prosecutors have obligations to not only disclose, but also collect exonerating and incriminating evidence.[13] These and other related features bring ICC procedure closer in line with the inquisitorial model.

When it comes to hybrid tribunals, procedure is influenced in part by the ICTY, ICTR, and ICC models and in part by the legal system within which the hybrid tribunal is located. The Special Court for Sierra Leone heavily borrowed from ICTR rules and remained largely adversarial, consistent with the modern legal tradition of Sierra Leone.[14] By contrast, the procedures of the Extraordinary Chambers in the Courts of Cambodia (ECCC) and the Special Tribunal for Lebanon (STL) have more inquisitorial features, such as investigative judges (ECCC), victim participation (ECCC and STL), and trials in absentia (STL).[15] Once again, this reflected the intention of the drafters to make the procedures of these tribunals consistent with the procedures of the country where the crimes were committed and whose population was the target audience of the tribunals.[16]

III. Guiding Values and Objectives

International criminal procedure follows a number of goals that are similar to those of domestic criminal procedure—establishing the truth, enforcing criminal laws effectively, and ensuring fairness in the process. But just as different domestic courts place different weights on each of these values, so do different international criminal courts. Furthermore, international criminal courts may pursue additional, more ambitious goals, such as establishing a historical record about the crimes, promoting peace and

giving notice to the parties, change the legal characterization of the facts, although the Trial Chamber may not exceed the facts and circumstances described in the charges confirmed by the Pre-Trial Chamber).

[12] *See infra* Section IV.B. [13] Rome Statute art. 54(1)(a).

[14] Antonio Cassese, Report on the Special Court for Sierra Leone 21 (2006), *at* http://www.rscsl.org/Documents/Cassese%20Report.pdf.

[15] Law on the Establishment of Extraordinary Chambers in the Courts of Cambodia for the Prosecution of Crimes Committed during the period of Democratic Kampuchea, 10 August 2001, with inclusion of Amendments as promulgated on 27 October 2004 art. 23 [hereinafter ECCC Statute]; Extraordinary Chambers in the Courts of Cambodia, Internal Rules, Rev. 9, R. 23 (2015); Statute of the Special Tribunal of Lebanon arts. 17, 22 [hereinafter STL Statute]; Special Tribunal of Lebanon Rules of Procedure and Evidence, Rev. 9, R. 86, 87 (2017).

[16] *See, e.g.*, STL Statute art. 28(2) (noting that in drafting STL rules, STL judges should "be guided, as appropriate, by the Lebanese Code of Criminal Procedure, as well as by other reference materials reflecting the highest standards of international criminal procedure, with a view to ensuring a fair and expeditious trial."). *See generally* Nancy Combs, *Seeking Inconsistency: Advancing Pluralism in International Criminal Sentencing*, 41 Yale J. Int'l L. 1, 17–18 (2016) (discussing the different substantive and procedural laws and different mandates of the main international and hybrid tribunals).

reconciliation, and modeling respect for human rights. These more ambitious goals may at times conflict with the narrower, adjudicative goals of the process, and courts differ in how they resolve the tension.

1. Truth-Seeking

The duty to seek the truth is a primary goal of the process at all international criminal courts, as it is for domestic courts.[17] Dedication to truth-seeking means at the very least that international courts should use investigative and trial procedures that produce reliable evidence.[18] Some courts and commentators have gone beyond the focus on reliability, however, and have interpreted the duty to seek the truth to mean also that courts must contribute to the establishment of an accurate historical record about the underlying conflict.[19]

This broad interpretation of the court's duty to seek the truth has been controversial. Trials face obstacles in producing reliable history, given judges' lack of historical training, the parties' disincentives to produce an objective record, and the limitations imposed by formal evidentiary rules.[20] In addition, the focus on producing a complete historical record may conflict with the court's primary task of determining individual culpability.[21] An approach aimed at building a historical record may focus on issues such as mass complicity and foreign involvement, but this may prejudice the court's decision with respect to the specific charges leveled against the defendant.[22] It may also interfere with the defendant's right to be tried without undue delay.[23]

Even when courts adopt the narrower conception of truth-seeking, they confront a host of practical challenges unique to the international level. The first such challenge is the heavy dependence of international criminal courts on the cooperation of national authorities in investigating crimes and apprehending suspects. National authorities are

[17] *See, e.g.*, Prosecutor v. Ngudjolo, Case No. ICC-01/04-02/12 A, Judgment on the Prosecutor's Appeal Against the Decision of Trial Chamber II Entitled "Judgment Pursuant to Article 74 of the Statute," ¶ 256 (Feb. 27, 2015) ("The establishment of the truth is one of the principal objectives of the Statute, to which the Trial Chamber must actively contribute.").

[18] Richard L. Lippke, *Fundamental Values of Criminal Procedure*, in this volume.

[19] *See, e.g.*, Prosecutor v. Nikolić, Case No. IT-02-60/1-S, Sentencing Judgement, ¶ 60 (Int'l Crim. Trib. for the Former Yugoslavia Dec. 2, 2003); Stuart Ford, *A Social Psychology Model of the Perceived Legitimacy of International Criminal Courts: Implications for the Success of Transitional Justice Mechanisms*, 45 Vand. J. Transnat'l L. 405, 472–75 (2012).

[20] Mirjan Damaška, *What Is the Point of International Criminal Justice?*, 83 Chi.-Kent. L. Rev. 329, 333, 337–38 (2008).

[21] Mark J. Osiel, *Ever Again: Legal Remembrance of Administrative Massacre*, 144 U. Pa. L. Rev. 463, 524 (1995); Damaška, *supra* note 20, at 333, 337–38.

[22] *Developments in the Law—The Promises of International Prosecution*, 114 Harv. L. Rev. 1957, 1973 (2001); Allison Marston Danner & Jenny S. Martinez, *Guilty Associations: Joint Criminal Enterprise, Command Responsibility, and the Development of International Criminal Law*, 93 Calif. L. Rev. 75, 95 (2005).

[23] Jenia I. Turner, *Defense Perspectives on Law and Politics in International Criminal Trials*, 48 Va. J. Int'l L. 529, 541 (2008).

frequently unwilling or unable to provide such cooperation, and in some cases, may deliberately interfere with the investigations.[24]

Another major hindrance is the difficulty of ensuring the safety of witnesses, particularly when international prosecutors are investigating crimes in areas of continued conflict or instability.[25] Security concerns may also extend to the investigators themselves, whether they work for the prosecution or the defense. More so than domestic courts, international criminal courts must further contend with national security and other confidentiality concerns with respect to sources they rely upon. This affects the ability of prosecutors to present evidence and comply with their disclosure obligations to the defense.

More broadly, the ability of international criminal courts to uncover the truth is hampered by language and cultural barriers for the fact-finders, who come from various countries, typically different from the countries in which the crimes occurred. The long time lapse between the commission of the crimes and the international prosecutions presents additional evidentiary challenges for international courts, as memories fade, witnesses disappear or die, and evidence is destroyed.[26] Furthermore, mass atrocities frequently occur in developing nations, and investigators in these countries have traditionally been less able to rely on "audio, video, or cellular evidence" or even on written records.[27] As a result, international criminal proceedings have had to rely heavily on eyewitness testimony, which is frequently unreliable in the context of ordinary domestic crimes, but is even more so in the context of mass atrocities, where the events witnessed are traumatic and often occurred in the distant past.[28] Scholars have documented widespread inconsistencies in testimony at various international criminal courts.[29]

Finally, the massive evidentiary base of international crimes adds to the difficulty of determining individual responsibility. The crimes alleged are often widespread and committed with the assistance of complex organizations or state organs. Disentangling responsibility in the relevant political or military hierarchies is a daunting task for international courts. Just the trial of Slobodan Milošević, for example, which ended prematurely because of the defendant's death, involved 466 days of hearings, 295 witnesses, 5,000 exhibits, and a transcript of over 49,000 pages.[30] The enormity of the

[24] *E.g.*, Nancy Combs, *Deconstructing the Epistemic Challenges to Mass Atrocity Prosecutions*, 75 Wash. & Lee L. Rev. 223, 252–53 (2018).

[25] *Id.* at 247.

[26] *Id.* at 249–51.

[27] *Id.* at 234. As cell phones become more ubiquitous throughout the world, however, digital evidence is likely to become more commonly available even in international prosecutions. *See, e.g.*, Alex Whiting, *The ICC's New Libya Case: Extraterritorial Evidence for an Extraterritorial Court*, *Just Security Blog*, Aug. 23, 2017, *available at* https://www.justsecurity.org/44383/iccs-libya-case-extraterritorial-evidence-extraterritorial-court.

[28] Combs, *supra* note 24, at 238, 264–67.

[29] Nancy Amoury Combs, *Testimonial Deficiencies and Evidentiary Uncertainties in International Criminal Trials*, 14 UCLA J. Int'l L. Foreign Aff. 235 (2009); Alexander Zahar, *The Problem of False Testimony at the International Criminal Tribunal for Rwanda*, in 25 *Annotated Leading Cases of International Criminal Tribunals: International Criminal Tribunal for Rwanda* 2006–2007, at 509 (André Klip & Göran Sluiter eds., 2010).

[30] Damaška, *supra* note 20, at 341.

evidentiary base complicates charging, disclosure, and evidence presentation choices, and calls on the prosecution to make compromises in the process, such as relying on overly expansive modes of liability and on insider witnesses who may not be fully credible.[31]

Because of the massive evidentiary challenges facing international prosecutors, the search for truth can seem too costly. Accordingly, like certain of their domestic counterparts, international tribunals have occasionally restrained their truth-seeking ambitions for the sake of efficiency.[32] At other times, international criminal courts have subordinated truth-seeking to attain other important goals, such as the protection of individual rights.[33] In short, while truth-seeking remains a primary goal of international criminal process, it frequently must be balanced against competing goals such as effectiveness, efficiency, and the protection of human rights.

2. Ensuring the Effective and Expeditious Enforcement of International Criminal Law

International criminal courts seek the truth not only for its own sake, but also to advance their broader goal of repressing international crime. As the preamble to the Rome Statute affirms, the international community has an essential interest that "the most serious crimes of concern to the international community as a whole must not go unpunished" and that effective prosecution at the national and international level would "put an end to impunity for the perpetrators of these crimes and thus... contribute to the prevention of such crimes."[34] To accomplish this goal, international criminal procedure must effectively and efficiently "screen suspects, determine guilt, and secure appropriate dispositions of persons convicted of crime."[35]

In addition to helping secure the enforcement of international criminal law, efficient procedure is regarded as an important goal of its own. Expeditiousness is a component of the accused's right to a fair trial that guards against an unreasonably long detention of innocent individuals and minimizes the social, emotional, and economic burdens on defendants facing public accusation.[36] Expeditiousness is also beneficial to victims, witnesses, and the relevant national and international communities:

[31] Combs, *supra* note 24, at 261.

[32] *See, e.g.*, Jenia Iontcheva Turner, *Plea Bargaining and International Criminal Justice*, 48 McGeorge L. Rev. 219 (2017).

[33] Courts have done so, for example, when they have excluded relevant and reliable evidence to remedy violations of individual rights. *See, e.g.*, Prosecutor v. Katanga, Case No. ICC-01/04-01/07, Decision on the Prosecutor's Bar Table Motions, ¶¶ 57, 60, 62–63 (Dec. 17, 2010).

[34] Rome Statute pmbl.

[35] Herbert L. Packer, *Two Models of the Criminal Process*, 113 U. Pa. L. Rev. 1, 9 (1964).

[36] *Cf.* Barker v. Wingo, 407 U.S. 514, 526–27 (1972).

> It ensures [victims] of receiving justice and of going on through a healing process quickly. For witnesses, it relieves them as soon as possible of the anxiety of having to appear in court to give evidence. Unreasonable delay in commencing or finalizing a trial may also diminish public interest and public support for, and cooperation with the Court.[37]

As Section III.1 discussed, enormous practical challenges hinder the ability of prosecutors to investigate international crimes effectively and expeditiously and of judges to adjudicate those crimes. In a world of unlimited resources, international criminal courts might be able to make up for many of the evidentiary difficulties by hiring more investigators, prosecutors, and translators, and paying more for witness protection. Yet this is far from the reality of international court operations. Instead of steady financial support, international courts typically encounter pressure to cut costs. Investigators, prosecutors, defense attorneys, and judges end up having to handle exceedingly complex cases faced simultaneously with serious practical challenges and with insufficient funding.

Furthermore, political support is also not always forthcoming for international trials, even in situations where the international community, through the UN Security Council, establishes these courts or refers situations to them. As a result, when national authorities balk at arrest warrants and cooperation requests, international criminal courts generally remain powerless to respond effectively.[38]

In short, even as truth-seeking, effectiveness, and efficiency remain central goals of the international criminal process, courts have had to contend with serious practical and political challenges in pursuing those goals. Courts have responded in part by adapting their procedures to meet these challenges. For example, the ICTY and ICTR introduced a host of managerial reforms to expedite proceedings—limiting indictments, relying more heavily on written evidence and plea bargaining, and restricting interlocutory appeals. The ICC has also recently begun experimenting with measures aimed at expediting the process, including greater judicial control over investigations, charging,[39] disclosure, and evidence presentation.[40] These reforms show how practical

[37] Prosecutor v. Katanga, Case No. ICC-01/04-01/07, Judgment on the Appeal of Mr Katanga Against the Decision of Trial Chamber II of 20 November 2009 Entitled "Decision on the Motion of the Defence for Germain Katanga for a Declaration on Unlawful Detention and Stay of Proceedings," ¶ 46 (July 12, 2010).

[38] *See, e.g.*, Prosecutor v. Al Bashir, Case No. ICC-02/05-01/09, Decision Under Article 87(7) of the Rome Statute on the Non-Compliance by South Africa with the Request by the Court for the Arrest and Surrender of Omar Al-Bashir, ¶ 138 (July 6, 2017).

[39] *See, e.g.*, Prosecutor v. Mbarushimana, Case No. ICC-01/04-01/10, Judgment on the Appeal of the Prosecutor Against the Decision of the Pre-Trial Chamber I of 16 December 2011 Entitled "Decision on the Confirmation of Charges," ¶ 44 (May 30, 2012) (encouraging prosecutors to have investigations largely completed before the confirmation of charges hearing).

[40] *See, e.g.*, Statement by Judge Sang-Hyun Song, President of the ICC, Remarks to the Assembly of States Parties 9th Session, Dec. 6, 2010, at 3, *at* https://asp.icc-cpi.int/iccdocs/asp_docs/ASP9/Statements/ICC-ASP9-statements-SangHyunSong-ENG.pdf (noting that the requirement of in-depth analysis charts of the evidence by the prosecution has enhanced the efficiency of the proceedings); Prosecutor v.

difficulties are pushing the criminal process to adapt and rebalance international courts' commitments to, on the one hand, defense rights and truth-seeking, and on the other, efficiency.

3. Respecting Human Rights and the Right to a Fair Trial

International criminal courts do not simply focus on adjudicating crimes efficiently—they aim to do so while respecting human rights and due process.[41] Even as international courts vary in their procedural orientations—more inquisitorial or more adversarial—they are universally committed to following international standards of due process and human rights. The Rome Statute for the ICC is explicit about this commitment and provides that "the application and interpretation of law pursuant to this article must be consistent with internationally recognized human rights."[42] The STL Statute likewise requires that rules of procedure be guided by, inter alia, "reference materials reflecting the highest standards of international criminal procedure."[43] Even though not all international criminal courts have an express statutory requirement to observe human rights, they all have provisions guaranteeing the right to a fair trial and other fundamental defense rights, and judicial decisions have repeatedly emphasized the courts' commitment to respecting human rights.[44] This shared commitment promotes coherence in international criminal procedure.

Yet human rights principles relating to fair criminal trials remain quite vague in many respects and allow for multiple interpretations.[45] For example, while the principle of fair trial has been interpreted to require that evidence favorable to the defendant be disclosed to him before trial, human rights law does not regulate critical details, such as the timing and scope of disclosure. Nor does human rights law specify how courts are to resolve conflicts between the right to exculpatory evidence and the international community's interests in effective investigations, witness protection, and the protection of national security information. Unsurprisingly, in this area and many others,

Gombo, Case No. ICC-01/05-01/08, Decision on the Disclosure of Evidence by the Defence, ¶¶ 9–10 (Dec. 5, 2008) (requiring the prosecution to submit an in-depth analysis chart); Prosecutor v. Gbagbo, Case No. ICC-02/11-01/11, Decision Establishing a Disclosure System and a Calendar for Disclosure (Jan. 24, 2012) (setting a disclosure timeline); *see also* Megan Fairlie, *The Abiding Problem of Witness Statements in International Criminal Trials*, 50 N.Y.U. J. Int'l L. & Pol. 75 128-30 (2018) (noting several recent decisions by Chambers to prosecutors to rely more heavily on written witness statements rather than oral testimony).

[41] Mégret, *supra* note 1, at 49. [42] Rome Statute art. 21(3). [43] STL Statute art. 28(2).

[44] *E.g.*, Statute of the International Tribunal for the Prosecution for Serious Violations of International Humanitarian Law Committed in the Territory of the Former Yugoslavia Since 1991 art. 20(1), May 25, 1993, U.N. Doc. S/RES/827 (1993); Statute of the International Criminal Tribunal for Rwanda art. 19(1), Nov. 8, 1994, U.N. Doc. S/RES/955; Prosecutor v. Kordić, Case No. IT-95-14/2-A, Judgement, ¶ 242 (Int'l Crim. Trib. for the Former Yugoslavia Dec. 17, 2004).

[45] *See, e.g.*, Mégret, *supra* note 1, at 53–55.

international criminal tribunals have found that human rights can support a range of procedures, affirming that human rights "provide a mere skeleton of what is required."[46]

In addition to being vague and open-ended, human rights law is ambivalent in its demands on the criminal process because it attempts to mediate between defendants' rights and victims' rights. Victims' rights are seen as an inextricable component of human rights law, which in turn is a key component of international criminal law and procedure.[47] Because international crimes are typically state-sponsored, under international law, victims have the right to a remedy for the breach of their fundamental human rights by state agents. The right to a remedy has been used by some to argue for reinterpreting the notion of a fair trial in international criminal proceedings to include victims and not just defendants.[48] Restorative justice advocates have argued further that giving victims a voice in the criminal process should be an independent objective of international courts as a means of promoting peace and reconciliation in conflict-torn areas.[49]

The dual commitment to procedural fairness and victims' rights is reflected in the statutes and rules of procedure of international criminal courts. Provisions on fair trial expressly reference the interests of victims alongside the rights of the accused; even though the latter are supposed to be prioritized, the need to consider the interests of victims reflects a level of ambivalence in international criminal procedure.[50] Some opinions have gone beyond an emphasis on victims' rights and have suggested that prosecutors, too, can claim a right to a fair trial.[51] And as Section IV.B describes in greater detail, courts such as the ICC and ECCC give victims extensive participation rights in the proceedings.

An emphasis on victims' rights at trial, while commendable in many ways, has raised concerns about its effects on defendants' right to a fair trial. Does the commitment to victims' rights—particularly when accompanied by direct victim participation in the proceedings, put pressure on judges to lower standards of proof?[52] Does "[t]he idea that

[46] Warbrick, *supra* note 1, at 50; *see also* Mégret, *supra* note 1, at 58.

[47] *See, e.g.*, Mégret, *supra* note 1, at 57. [48] *Id.*

[49] *See, e.g.*, Roy S. Lee, *The International Criminal Court: Elements of Crimes and Rules of Procedure and Evidence*, at lxiv (2001) (noting that the ICC has been transformed into a "court administering restorative justice" that would provide reparations to victims and give victims the opportunity to participate in the proceedings); Gilbert Bitti & Hakan Friman, *Participation of Victims in the Proceedings*, in *The International Criminal Court: Elements of Crimes and Rules of Procedure and Evidence* 456, 457 (Roy S. Lee ed., 2001) (linking victim participation to the restorative justice aims of the court); Tom Dannenbaum, *The International Criminal Court, Article 79, and Transitional Justice: The Case for an Independent Trust Fund for Victims*, 28 Wis. Int'l L.J. 234, 238 (2010) (noting that victim detachment from international criminal proceedings at the ICTR is seen by some as undermining that court's efforts to bring lasting peace and reconciliation to the region); *see also* Sara Kendall & Sarah Nouwen, *Representational Practices at the International Criminal Court: The Gap Between Juridified and Abstract Victimhood*, 76 Law & Contemp. Probs. 235, 239–41 (2013) (noting that some NGOs have made the link between victim-oriented justice and peace).

[50] *See, e.g.*, Rome Statute art. 64(2) (requiring judges to "ensure that a trial is fair and expeditious and is conducted with full respect for the rights of the accused and due regard for the protection of victims and witnesses").

[51] Yvonne McDermott, *Fairness in International Criminal Law* 109–16 (2016).

[52] Damaška, *supra* note 20, at 334.

an acquittal could be justified on grounds of procedural impropriety, even if serious, become[] well-nigh preposterous"?[53] However each international court resolves the tension between victims' rights and the rights of the accused, what is clear is that human rights law leaves a broad margin of discretion in this regard.

4. Promoting the Rule of Law

Beyond respecting human rights in their own proceedings, international criminal courts are often expected to serve as procedural models for domestic justice systems. Under this view, international courts ought to spread to national justice systems a "human rights culture."[54] They must lead by example and set the highest standards for the fairness of trials.[55] Some scholars have argued that it is the central mission of international criminal courts to exemplify respect for the rule of law to countries where international crimes have occurred, which are frequently struggling to re-establish the rule of law after the end of violent conflicts or authoritarian regimes.[56]

Yet the ability and desirability for international criminal courts to model a commitment to the highest norms of procedural fairness remains debatable. Recognizing the serious political and practical challenges facing the ICC, some have argued that it is sufficient for the ICC to be "fair enough" rather than attempting to set the highest standards of fairness.[57] International courts lack the state machinery that helps domestic courts effectively enforce criminal law. In this environment, adding procedural requirements that are overly demanding may entirely thwart international prosecutions and undermine the broader commitment to provide justice and accountability for international crimes. Rather than providing a pristine model of fair trial, international criminal procedure may compel us to "re-interrogat[e] the tradition of due process in light of the particular exigencies of international criminal justice."[58]

IV. Pluralism in International Criminal Procedure: Two Examples

As the previous brief discussion highlighted, international criminal procedure pursues multiple, and at times competing, goals. Disagreement persists both on how best to align procedures with these goals and how to balance the different objectives when they

53 *Id.* at 334; *see also* Darryl Robinson, *The Identity Crisis of International Criminal Law*, 21 Leiden J. Int'l L. 925, 930–31 (2008).

54 Damaška, *supra* note 1, at 614.

55 McDermott, *supra* note 51; Ohlin, *supra* note 1, at 82–83, 103.

56 Ohlin, *supra* note 1, at 82–83.

57 Mégret, *supra* note 1, at 60; Warbrick, *supra* note 1, at 54; Damaška, *supra* note 1, at 615.

58 Mégret, *supra* note 1, at 76.

come into conflict with one another.[59] Even if consensus about the ranking of the several goals could be accomplished, opinions would continue to vary on the best means of accomplishing the same goals.

Dissension about the goals and methods of international criminal trials has led to inconsistent rules and case law on procedural matters. This section discusses two examples of procedures that have received divergent interpretation and implementation within and across international criminal courts, at least in part because of disagreement among judges—or the drafters of the procedures—about the ranking of different objectives or the best means of accomplishing these objectives.

1. Judicial Management of the Proceedings

The involvement of judges in managing international criminal proceedings has varied significantly, both across and within different courts. Some of the variation can be attributed to the diverse legal backgrounds of the individual judges—judges from the adversarial tradition have tended to act consistently with the tradition of the passive referee while those from the inquisitorial tradition have been more likely to play a pro-active role.[60] At the ICTY and ICTR, judges' legal education and experience influenced the style of judicial management of the proceedings and decision-making on a host of procedural matters:

> Judges coming from civil law countries tend[ed] to be more active during the testimonial process and [we]re more willing to pose questions to witnesses than their common law colleagues [we]re. Similarly, there [wa]s variance in the ICTY judges' exercise of their case-management duties in the pre-trial process and degrees of judicial activity in streamlining cases before they [went] to trial. "Procedural pluralism" [wa]s not limited to specific areas but extend[ed] virtually to all essential procedural or evidentiary matters, including questioning of witnesses, admission of documents, treatment of hearsay, setting and enforcing time limits for the presentation of cases, and admission of expert evidence proposed by the parties.[61]

Variation with respect to judicial management of the proceedings has also occurred across courts, as a function of different formal rules reflecting different priorities. The following sections discuss examples of both inter-court and intra-court variation on this question.

[59] As Mirjan Damaška has argued:

Managing tensions among the goals, and dealing with the courts' limitations in attaining some of them, would be greatly facilitated if a set of priorities existed based on an understanding of the relative weights of competing goals. Acceptable terms of trade-offs among the contenders could then be identified, and greater coherence established in decision making. Procedural means also could be designed to facilitate the realization of what is agreed upon as most important to the mission of international criminal courts. Yet no clear set of priorities has emerged so far from the operation of international criminal courts.

Damaška, *supra* note 20, at 339.

[60] Van Sliedregt & Vasiliev, *supra* note 4, at 27.

[61] *Id.* at 27–28.

a. *Inter-Court Variation*

At the ICTY and ICTR, the rules initially assigned a relatively passive role to the judges—the parties were in charge of investigating and presenting the evidence, and prosecutors had significant charging discretion. But as the tribunals came under pressure to expedite proceedings, the heavily party-driven framework was faulted for producing lengthy, overly complex, and costly trials. To address these problems, the judges amended the rules to provide themselves with greater managerial powers, to encourage guilty pleas, to limit interlocutory appeals, and to allow more extensive reliance on written evidence. This change reflected a new emphasis on efficiency and a somewhat lesser concern for establishing a detailed historical record;[62] according to some, it also reflected a lesser concern for ensuring the highest standards of procedural fairness.[63]

A somewhat different model of judicial authority has emerged at the ICC. As a compromise between delegates from inquisitorial and adversarial traditions, the rules give judges significant authority to shape the proceedings. Judges can hold status conferences to set filing schedules, discuss questions about disclosure, regulate the evidence to be presented, direct the manner in which the evidence is presented, and set time limits on arguments.[64] Although the rules do not require it, some chambers have also demanded that parties disclose evidence directly to the court in order to enable judges to establish the truth.[65] Reflecting inquisitorial influences, judges can also change the legal characterization of the facts (that is, amend the charges pursued by the prosecutor) and reject admissions of guilt if the "interests of justice" require a fuller airing of the facts.[66] At the pretrial stage, judges must approve any decision of the prosecutor to open an investigation on her own initiative,[67] and they conduct probing confirmation of charges hearings to test the sufficiency of the evidence supporting the prosecutor's charges.[68] In certain defined situations early in the investigations, pretrial judges may also independently take measures to preserve evidence that they consider "essential for the defense at trial," even if the prosecutor disagrees that such measures are necessary.[69] In all these ways, ICC judges exercise broad oversight of prosecutorial actions, in many ways more significantly than did judges at the ICTY and ICTR.[70]

It is too early to know what the effects of judicial managerialism at the ICC have been. A recent survey of defense attorneys found that such "managerialism" has generally not

[62] Langer, *supra* note 7, at 836.

[63] Prosecutor v. Milošević, Case No. IT-02-54-AR73.4, Dissenting Opinion of Judge Hunt, ¶¶ 20–22 (Int'l Crim. Trib. for the Former Yugoslavia Oct. 21, 2003); Geert-Jan Alexander Knoops, *The Dichotomy Between Judicial Economy and Equality of Arms Within International and Internationalized Criminal Trials: A Defense Perspective*, 28 Fordham Int'l L.J. 1566, 1589 (2005).

[64] ICC Rules of Procedure and Evidence R. 121; ICC Regulations of the Court 2004, ICC-BD/01-01-04, reg 54.

[65] Prosecutor v. Gombo, Case No. ICC-01/05-01/08, Decision on the Evidence Disclosure System and Setting a Timetable for Disclosure Between the Parties, ¶¶ 8–25 (July 31, 2008).

[66] ICC Regulations of the Court 2004, ICC-BD/01-01-04, reg. 54; Rome Statute art. 65(4).

[67] Rome Statute art. 15(3). [68] *Id.* art. 61. [69] *Id.* art. 56(3).

[70] Hanna Kuczynska, *The Accusation Model Before the International Criminal Court: Study of Convergence of Criminal Justice Systems* 123–25 (2015).

infringed defense rights and has in fact at times helped the defense by reining in the prosecution in its investigative, disclosure, and charging decisions.[71] But as the ICC comes under increasing pressure to do more with fewer resources, what began as a more inquisitorial system may morph into the heavily managerial style of judging that prevailed in the later days of the ICTY. Instead of promoting deeper inquiry into the facts, managerial judging may be used to expedite the proceedings at the expense of procedural fairness and the search for truth.[72]

The ECCC has so far been the most inquisitorial of international criminal courts when it comes to the question of judicial authority. In addition to entrusting the investigation to investigative judges, the ECCC rules assign a very active role to judges at trial.[73] Critically, ECCC rules enable judges to perform that role more effectively by providing them with the dossier compiled by the investigative judges at the pretrial stage.[74] As Vasiliev explains, at the ECCC:

> There are no distinct partisan cases but a single "case of the truth", which comprises the evidence amassed in the dossier and supplemented by any proof proposed by the parties and admitted by the court.... The examination at trial is dominated and tightly controlled by the Trial Chamber, with parties playing second fiddle. Questions may only be posed to the accused, witnesses, experts, and civil parties with the permission of the President.[75]

Despite rules entrusting judges with broad authority to streamline proceedings, the ECCC process has remained remarkably slow. The languid pace cannot be attributed to the procedural setup, however, as a number of financial, institutional, political, and case-specific factors combined to delay the proceedings; it is quite likely that the proceedings would have been even slower under a more adversarial process.[76] And whatever effects ECCC procedural rules may have had on the pace of the proceedings, they have arguably succeeded in advancing other central goals of the court: to uncover the truth through detailed and impartial judge-led investigations and evidence presentation and to engage victims in the process as part of a broader effort at promoting national reconciliation.[77]

[71] Jenia Iontcheva Turner, *Defense Perspectives on Fairness and Efficiency at the International Criminal Court*, in *Oxford Handbook on International Criminal Law* (Kevin Jon Heller et al. eds.) (forthcoming 2018), *available at* https://papers.ssrn.com/sol3/papers.cfm?abstract_id=2940483.

[72] Knoops, *supra* note 63; Natacha Fauveau-Ivanovic, *Quelle réalité pour les droits de la défense au sein de la Cour pénale internationale?* 5 Revue des droits de l'homme 2, 7 (2014).

[73] Jessica Peake, *A Spectrum of International Criminal Procedure: Shifting Patterns of Power Distribution in International Criminal Courts and Tribunals*, 26 Pace Int'l L. Rev. 182, 224–25, 226–30 (2014).

[74] *Id.* at 230–31.

[75] Sergey Vasiliev, *The Trial Process at the ECCC: The Rise and Fall of the Inquisitorial Paradigm in International Criminal Law*, in *The Extraordinary Chambers in the Courts of Cambodia: Assessing Their Contribution to International Criminal Law* 389, 396 (Simon Meisenberg & Ignaz Stegmiller eds., 2016).

[76] *See id.* at 423, 430–31.

[77] *See id.* at 428, 430; Jeudy Oeung, *Expectations, Challenges and Opportunities of the ECCC*, in *The Extraordinary Chambers in the Courts of Cambodia: Assessing Their Contribution to International Criminal Law* 103, 107–12 (Simon Meisenberg & Ignaz Stegmiller eds., 2016).

b. *Intra-Court Variation*

ICC chambers have repeatedly taken different approaches to the role of the judge in overseeing prosecutorial charging decisions, managing the proceedings, and regulating the evidence to be admitted. For example, initially, ICC Trial Chambers decided that they would, contrary to case law and practice at the ICTY and ICTR, ban the party-led preparation of witnesses for testimony.[78] The new approach reflected not any significant difference in the formal rules at the tribunals and the ICC,[79] but rather two distinct procedural orientations. At the ICC, where a more inquisitorial approach prevails, witnesses were seen as "belonging" to the court, not to either party; accordingly, their preparation by a party to the proceedings was seen as inappropriate.[80] Along the same lines, ICC judges believed that preparation may distort witnesses' testimony, whereas an unprepared witness is more likely to be spontaneous and authentic.[81] Ultimately, the ICC's approach was grounded in a more inquisitorial approach to judicial authority, which rests on the belief that to establish the truth, judges must gather and examine evidence independently and not rely exclusively on the parties for this task.

More recently, however, two ICC chambers have charted a new path and have permitted the parties to prepare their witnesses.[82] They have reasoned that witness preparation helps expedite the process, without undermining the search for truth, as judges can adequately assess the credibility of witnesses even if those witnesses have been thoroughly prepared by one of the parties. Particularly in cases of great complexity, spanning a broad time period and involving numerous exhibits, the chambers concluded that "witness preparation will enable the calling party to engage with the witness in order to define the most effective way to discover the truth during trial."[83] A different weighing of the values at stake, as well as a different view of the relationship between witness preparation and truth-seeking, led to a new approach within the same court.

[78] Prosecutor v. Gombo, Case No. ICC- 01/05-01/08, Decision on the Unified Protocol on the Practices Used to Prepare and Familiarise Witnesses for Giving Testimony at Trial, ¶ 34 (Nov. 18, 2010); Prosecutor v. Katanga, Case No. ICC-01/04-01/07, Decision on a Number of Procedural Issues Raised by the Registry, ¶ 18 (May 14, 2009); Prosecutor v. Lubanga, Case No. ICC-01/04-01/06, Decision Regarding the Practices Used to Prepare and Familiarise Witnesses for Giving Testimony at Trial, ¶ 57 (Nov. 30, 2007) [hereinafter *Lubanga* Trial Chamber I Decision on Witness Preparation].

[79] *See, e.g.*, John D. Jackson & Yassin M. Brunger, *Witness Preparation in the ICC*, 13 J. Int'l Crim. Just. 601, 604 (2015).

[80] *See Lubanga* Trial Chamber I Decision on Witness Preparation, ¶ 34; Prosecutor v. Lubanga, Case No. ICC-01/04-01/06, Decision on the Practices of Witness Familiarisation and Witness Proofing, ¶ 36 (Nov. 8, 2006) (noting the inquisitorial approach on this issue and ultimately agreeing with it).

[81] *Lubanga* Trial Chamber 1 Decision on Witness Preparation, ¶¶ 51–52.

[82] Prosecutor v. Muthaura, Case No. ICC-01/09-02/11, Decision on Witness Preparation, ¶¶ 52–54 (Jan. 2, 2013) [hereinafter *Muthaura* Decision on Witness Preparation]; Prosecutor v. Ntaganda, Case No. ICC-01/04-02/06, Decision on Witness Preparation, ¶ 16 (June 16, 2015) [hereinafter *Ntaganda* Decision on Witness Preparation].

[83] *Ntaganda* Decision on Witness Preparation, ¶ 18; *Muthaura* Decision on Witness Preparation, ¶ 35 ("A witness who testifies in an incomplete, confused and ill-structured way because of a lack of preparation is of limited assistance to the Chamber's truth finding function.").

Witness preparation is not the only area where ICC chambers have taken diverging approaches to managing the proceedings. Divergence can also be found in judicial decisions on disclosure requirements,[84] the standard of proof for confirming charges,[85] limitations on cumulative charges,[86] and requirements for prosecutors to complete investigations before the confirmation hearing.[87] This has led to concerns among some defense attorneys about their ability to represent clients effectively, in light of the unpredictability in the court's procedures.[88]

2. Victim Participation

International criminal courts have also taken contrasting approaches to the involvement of victims in the proceedings. While courts influenced by the adversarial tradition have largely relegated victims to the role of witnesses, the ICC and the ECCC, reflecting inquisitorial orientations, have incorporated robust victim participation in their procedures. The move toward more extensive victim participation has also been supported by advocates of restorative justice. They have argued that allowing victims to tell their stories helps provide closure and promote healing and reconciliation, and should therefore be a priority objective of international criminal courts.[89] Critics of extensive victim participation, on the other hand, have argued that it is too costly and that it endangers the

[84] Some chambers have held that prosecutors must disclose "the bulk" of exculpatory evidence before confirmation, whereas others have required that "the totality" of exculpatory evidence be disclosed before the confirmation of charges hearing. *Compare* Prosecutor v. Lubanga, Case No. ICC-01/04-01/06, Decision on the Final System of Disclosure and the Establishment of a Timetable, ¶¶ 124–133, (May 15, 2006), *with* Prosecutor v. Ruto, Case No. ICC-01/09-01/11, Decision Setting the Regime for Evidence Disclosure and Other Related Matters, ¶ 6 (Apr. 6, 2011).

[85] *See, e.g.*, Prosecutor v. Lubanga, Case No. ICC-01/04-01/06, Decision on the Confirmation of Charges, ¶¶ 37–39 (Jan. 29, 2007) (requiring "compelling" evidence and "concrete and tangible proof"); Triestino Mariniello, *Questioning the Standard of Proof: The Purpose of the ICC Confirmation of Charges Procedure*, 13 J. Int'l Crim. Just. 579, 580, 589, 595–96 (2015); Ignaz Stegmiller, *Confirmation of Charges*, in *The Law and Practice of the International Criminal Court* 897 (Carsten Stahn ed., 2015).

[86] Kuczynska, *supra* note 70, at 135–36 (discussing inconsistent approaches to cumulative charging at the ICC).

[87] On the requirement that the prosecution be "trial ready" at confirmation, see, for example, Prosecutor v. Mbarushimana, Case No. ICC-01/04-01/10, Judgment on the Appeal of the Prosecutor Against the Decision of Pre-Trial Chamber I of 16 December 2011 Entitled "Decision on the Confirmation of Charges," ¶ 44 (May 30, 2012); *see also* Prosecutor v. Muthaura, Case No. ICC-01/09-02/11, Decision Requesting Observations on the "Prosecution's Request to Amend the Final Updated Document Containing the Charges Pursuant to Article 61(9) of the Statute," ¶ 9 (Jan. 29, 2013); Prosecutor v. Gbagbo, Case No. ICC-02/11-01/11, Decision Adjourning the Hearing on the Confirmation of Charges Pursuant to Article 61(7)(c)(i) of the Rome Statute, ¶ 25 (June 3, 2013).

[88] Turner, *supra* note 71, at *22 n.144.

[89] *E.g.*, Sigall Horovitz, *The Role of Victims*, in *International Criminal Procedure* 166, 174–75 (Linda Carter & Fausto Pocar eds., 2013); Dannenbaum, *supra* note 49, at 238–41; Jenia Iontcheva Turner, *Decision on Civil Party Participation in Provisional Detention Appeals, Case No. 002/19-09-2007-Eccc/ocij (PTC01), Extraordinary Chambers in the Courts of Cambodia*, 103 Am. J. Int'l L. 116, 120–21 (2009); *see also* Kendall & Nouwen, *supra* note 49, at 239–41.

defendant's right to a fair trial. As with judicial management of the proceedings, we find both inter-court and intra-court variation in the approaches to victim participation.

a. *Inter-Court Variation*

Reflecting the influences of certain key continental European traditions, as well as restorative justice concerns, the Rome Statute of the ICC allows victims to participate in the proceedings at all stages, from pretrial to appeals.[90] Victims are entitled to legal representatives to represent their views adequately. The victims' legal representatives can question witnesses, review and file briefs and motions, and present evidence. The ICC proceedings also include a reparations stage, where victims can participate with a view to receiving reparations for the injuries they have suffered as a result of the defendant's conduct.[91]

The ECCC includes a similarly comprehensive scheme of victim participation as part of which victims, through their legal representatives, can take part at all major stages of the proceedings and are designated as "civil parties."[92] The ECCC procedure is expressly modeled on domestic Cambodian law on "civil parties," which in turn is patterned on French criminal procedure. Under this model, victims can become parties to criminal cases and participate actively at the pretrial and trial stage by examining evidence, requesting investigative action, and making written submissions. The victim participation scheme is in important respects broader than that of the ICC because it does not require victims to make a special showing that their personal interest is affected before taking part in a specific stage of the proceeding.[93]

While the victim participation schemes at the ICC and ECCC have been hailed by many as the fulfillment of the human rights ideal of providing closure and fuller reparation to victims, they have also been increasingly criticized for their expense, impracticability, and burden on defense rights.[94] The victims' application process at the ICC has been particularly cumbersome, and the participation at both the pretrial and trial stages has significantly delayed the proceedings and imposed logistical and financial burdens on the court and on the parties. Victim participation has also been criticized for pitting the defense against multiple accusers and requiring under-resourced defense counsel to

[90] Rome Statute art. 68(3) ("Where the personal interests of the victims are affected, the Court shall permit their views and concerns to be presented and considered at stages of the proceedings determined to be appropriate by the Court and in a manner which is not prejudicial to or inconsistent with the rights of the accused and a fair and impartial trial. Such views and concerns may be presented by the legal representatives of the victims where the Court considers it appropriate, in accordance with the Rules of Procedure and Evidence.").

[91] Rome Statute art. 75.

[92] *See, e.g.*, Turner, *supra* note 89.

[93] *E.g.*, Co-Prosecutors v. Nuon Chea, Case No. 002/19-09-2007-ECCC/OCIJ (PTC01), Decision on Civil Party Participation in Provisional Detention Appeals, ¶ 49 (Mar. 20, 2008).

[94] Christine Van den Wyngaert, *Victims Before International Criminal Courts: Some Views and Concerns of an ICC Trial Judge*, 44 Case W. Res. J. Int'l L. 475, 481 (2011); Sergey Vasiliev, *Victim Participation Revisited—What the ICC Is Learning About Itself*, in *The Law and Practice of the International Criminal Court* 1133, 1138–43 (Carsten Stahn ed., 2015).

expend time reviewing victim applications and responding to victim submissions.[95] At this point, critiques of victim participation are so widespread that, as one commentator concluded, "alarmed accounts outweigh by far the more positive and hopeful ones."[96]

Whether anticipating some of the difficulties with extensive victim participation or simply following the adversarial blueprint on this issue, the first modern international tribunals, the ICTY, ICTR, and SCSL, took a more limited view of victim participation. Victims participated as witnesses for the prosecution and could present statements to the court at sentencing. This approach was criticized for failing to consider victims' concerns and to promote national reconciliation, but it was consistent with the adversarial tradition and helped advance efficiency and protect defense interests.

Whatever one's views on the advantages and disadvantages of the different approaches, the experimentation with a range of victim participation schemes across different courts provides a useful reference point for the ICC and for fledgling hybrid courts as they decide how to design—or reform—rules on victim involvement.

b. *Intra-Court Variation*

Judicial decisions within the same court have also offered diverging interpretations of the scope and mechanics of victim participation. At the ICC, chambers have experimented with different approaches to victim applications and the mode of victim participation at trial, which has "reinforced . . . cross-chamber pluralism."[97]

On the question of victim applications to participate in the proceedings, for example, some chambers have encouraged or required a collective or partly collective approach to an application while others have favored a more individualized process, allowing victims to express their distinct harms and interests more fully.[98] Likewise, judicial decisions have differed on whether relatives of deceased victims can apply to participate in the proceedings. Some chambers have read the term "natural persons" in Rule 85(a) narrowly to exclude deceased persons. Others have looked to international human rights law, which takes a broader view of the group of people entitled to compensation for human rights abuses, and have interpreted the term "natural persons" to mean that, if a victim has died as a result of a crime charged at the ICC, then his or her family members have the right to participate in the criminal proceedings before the ICC.[99]

Chambers have also disagreed on the scope of victim involvement at trial. While uniformly allowing victims to present and challenge evidence,[100] some ICC chambers have also permitted oral submissions by the victims themselves as a way of permitting the presentation of the victims' "views and concerns" to the court.[101]

This intra-court pluralism on victim participation can be attributed in large part to the novelty of the ICC victim participation regime and the ambiguity of the

[95] Van den Wyngaert, *supra* note 94, at 488, 493; Vasiliev, *supra* note 94, at 1172.

[96] Vasiliev, *supra* note 94, at 1139. [97] *Id.* at 1153. [98] *See id.* at 1153–59.

[99] Héctor Olásolo & Alejandro Kiss, *The Role of Victims in Criminal Proceedings Before the International Criminal Court*, 81 Int'l Rev. Penal L. 125, 128–30 (2016).

[100] Vasiliev, *supra* note 94, at 1169, 1173–74. [101] *Id.* at 1168.

governing law.[102] But another reason chambers have split on these issues is that conflicting values underlie the different sides of victim participation debates. On the one hand, the sheer numbers of victim applicants, combined with a complex, individualized application process and a broad pretrial and trial participation scheme, have significantly strained the capacity of the ICC. The unwieldy victim participation practice has also raised questions about the burdens on the defense to respond to victim applications and victim interventions during trial and pretrial. Concerns about efficiency and about the defendant's right to a fair trial therefore weigh in favor of restricting victim participation. On the other hand, a more individualized victim application process and more extensive victim involvement at trial are consistent with the emphasis on victims' rights and restorative justice, which motivated the drafting of the Rome Statute provisions on victim participation. This explains why, even as the ICC moves away from a full-blown emphasis on restorative justice and becomes more pragmatic in its approach to victim participation,[103] intra-court divergence on the issue persists, leading to incoherence and unpredictability in ICC procedural law.

V. The Promise and Challenge of Pluralism in International Criminal Procedure

While some observers may have hoped that the creation of a permanent international criminal court would bring coherence to international criminal procedure, this has not occurred. Pluralism of procedural approaches persists both within and across international criminal courts, and the creation of new hybrid courts to pursue international criminal justice is only likely to expand procedural diversity.[104]

This diversity of procedural approaches might be regarded as an example of the broader phenomenon of fragmentation of law within international institutions. But the use of the term "fragmentation" seems inapt in this context. As van Sliedregt and Vasiliev observe, international criminal procedure did not begin as a coherent system of law that slowly disintegrated over time, as a result of inconsistent interpretations of the same rules.[105] Rather, international criminal procedure has been built up incrementally in self-contained legal regimes at the several international courts.[106] These courts are governed by independent statutes and rules of procedure and pursue different mandates. Their procedures are intentionally designed to develop on separate tracks, and there is

[102] *See* Rome Statute arts. 68(3), 69(3); ICC Rules of Procedure and Evidence R. 85, 89, 91(3).
[103] Vasiliev, *supra* note 93, at 1196.
[104] Beth van Schaack, *The Building Blocks of Hybrid Justice*, 44 Denv. J. Int'l L. & Pol'y 101, 104 (2016).
[105] Van Sliedregt & Vasiliev, *supra* note 4, at 16. [106] *Id.*

no overarching legal instrument on procedure that binds all of them. As discussed earlier, human rights law provides only the bare bones of common principles for international criminal procedure.

One might still expect to see convergence in international criminal procedure over time, if the courts aimed to accomplish similar objectives, or if, as one scholar puts it, "the central project of international criminal courts [were] to build a normative community."[107] Yet an underlying agreement on the goals of international criminal process does not appear to be forthcoming. The international community continues to pursue multiple goals and to disagree on the ranking of different goals. The creators of international criminal courts also turn to a range of procedures to accomplish the same goals, as debates about the superiority of adversarial versus inquisitorial procedures continue. Neither the states creating international courts, nor the judges on the courts, appear to be trying to build common procedural norms across international criminal institutions.

If pluralism in international criminal procedure is here to stay, is this a cause for concern? To answer this question, we must distinguish between procedural diversity within the same court and diversity across courts. Lack of coherent procedural approaches is more problematic in the former than in the latter. In fact, variance of approaches across courts is beneficial for international criminal procedure, for two principal reasons.

First, diversity allows international courts to calibrate their procedures to reflect the priorities of their primary local or regional audiences. While the international community remains an important audience for all courts adjudicating international crimes, at least ad hoc and hybrid courts created to address crimes on a particular territory primarily aim to address the national and regional communities most directly affected by the courts' work.[108] Indeed, this is expressly recognized by the courts' founding documents. The ICTY aimed (among else) to advance peace and reconciliation in the former Yugoslavia, the ICTR did the same in Rwanda, the ECCC in Cambodia, and so forth. Adjusting the procedural approach of each court to match the priorities of the primary target audience could help strengthen the court's local political legitimacy and therefore its ability to accomplish its goals.

Likewise, procedures can be adjusted somewhat to address specific practical challenges that each war crimes court is likely to encounter with respect to the cases it adjudicates. For example, if a court is likely to operate in a setting of ongoing conflict or an environment of broad witness intimidation, it may be particularly important for that court to provide for a range of witness protection measures.[109] Such a court may be more open to arguments in favor of video testimony or greater reliance on documentary evidence.[110] It may also be more open to arguments for trials in absentia,

[107] Margaret deGuzman, *Harsh Justice for International Crimes*, 39 Yale J. Int'l L. 1, 27 (2016).
[108] *See, e.g.*, Combs, *supra* note 16, at 21, 27–28.
[109] *See, e.g.*, Rules of Procedure and Evidence Before the Kosovo Specialist Chambers R. 80.
[110] *See id.* R. 80, 100.

particularly if such procedures are available in the domestic legal regime of the relevant national jurisdiction.[111]

Second, even if one posited that over time, international criminal courts should work toward developing a coherent system of international criminal procedure, permitting the flourishing of diverse procedural approaches may still be beneficial. Different courts can serve as "labs of experimentation" for procedural rules in international criminal cases. As Anthony Colangelo has argued in the context of international law more broadly, "fragmentation may be a necessary and important growing pain that attends the international legal system's maturation."[112] Even if international criminal courts begin with different procedural aims and rules, over time, as judges cite to decisions from other international courts and as international criminal law professionals move from one court to the next, procedures might incrementally evolve toward a shared understanding of "best practices."[113]

At the same time, a legal regime that encourages the flourishing of diverse procedural approaches to identical issues invites the criticism that it undermines certainty, notice, and equality of treatment. This critique is less poignant when different courts, bound by their own independent legal instruments, develop contrasting criminal procedures. As long as all courts abide by the minimal threshold set by international human rights law (within the broad margin of appreciation that they receive under that body of law), inconsistent procedural approaches appear legitimate and, as noted earlier, even beneficial.

But when inconsistent approaches occur within the same court, which is supposed to follow the same statute and rules of procedure, concerns about predictability and equal treatment are well grounded. In the examples discussed in Section IV, we see variation not just from one court to the next, but also within the same court.

Some scholars have argued that intra-court pluralism is legitimate when a court's governing statute and rules contain open-ended provisions that permit the testing of different evidentiary and procedural approaches. In this view, as long as such procedural experimentation is "properly managed and procedural uncertainty is minimized by consultations and detailed guidance handed down by the Chamber," it can be valuable.[114] It could help the court tailor its process "to [its] epistemic needs . . ., as well as to forensic challenges posed by the situation on the ground and the nature of witnesses."[115]

While some procedural experimentation may be necessary as part of the "growing pains" of a new international criminal court and the need to adjust to unexpected practical challenges, it is important for each court to work toward a coherent interpretation of its own rules. Basic notions of justice and fairness require that, within the

[111] STL Statute art. 22. *See generally* IBA International Criminal Court and International Criminal Law Programme, Report on the "Experts' Roundtable on Trials in Absentia in International Criminal Justice" (2016).

[112] Anthony J. Colangelo, *A Systems Theory of Fragmentation and Harmonization*, 49 N.Y.U. J. Int'l L. & Pol. 1, 7 (2016).

[113] *See* Baylis, *supra* note 5, at 377–82; Combs, *supra* note 16, at 20.

[114] Van Sliedregt & Vasiliev, *supra* note 4, at 29.

[115] *Id.*

same jurisdiction, like cases be treated alike, and that the parties have a reasonable expectation of which rules would apply to their case.[116] This is particularly important in criminal cases, where notice about the applicable law is a bedrock principle and where the right to a fair trial encompasses the right to "adequate time and facilities for the preparation of the defence."[117] Procedural inconsistency hampers the ability of the parties to predict the rules that the court will follow and to prepare and present their case accordingly. Not surprisingly, in a recent survey of ICC defense attorneys, several respondents identified procedural consistency as one of top three procedural reforms they would encourage the court to adopt.[118]

To reduce unwelcome procedural unpredictability, commentators have encouraged international criminal judges to adopt practice manuals and have called on appeals chambers to harmonize the law on key procedural issues.[119] Appeals chambers have a critical role to play in this regard, as they can quickly remedy inconsistent procedural decisions among lower chambers by issuing an authoritative interpretation of the relevant rules and statutory provisions.[120] To do so, ICC judges must become more open to interlocutory appeals, which allow for a speedy correction of procedural mistakes even if the mistakes may not prejudice the outcome of the case.

Currently, for an interlocutory appeal to reach the Appeals Chamber at the ICC, the lower chamber whose decision is being challenged must grant leave to appeal to the moving party.[121] The rules on interlocutory appeals are similar at other international criminal courts, although the ICTY and ICTR have interpreted these rules in a permissive fashion that encourages review of interlocutory matters.[122] At the ICC, interlocutory appeals have been granted quite rarely, leaving many procedural conflicts unresolved for long periods of time.[123] To promote procedural coherence, it would help to relax somewhat the standards for leave to file an interlocutory appeal and to place the decision of whether to accept an interlocutory appeal with the Appeals

[116] Colangelo, *supra* note 111, at 23.

[117] Rome Statute art. 67(1)(b).

[118] Turner, *supra* note 71, at *32.

[119] *Id.* at *32–33; Guénaël Mettraux et al., Expert Initiative Report on Promoting Effectiveness at the International Criminal Court 34, 209–10 (2014).

[120] *See* International Bar Association, Enhancing Efficiency and Effectiveness of ICC Proceedings: A Work in Progress 21 (2011).

[121] Rome Statute art. 82(1)(d) (providing that a party may appeal a "decision that involves an issue that would significantly affect the fair and expeditious conduct of the proceedings or the outcome of the trial, and for which, in the opinion of the Pre-Trial or Trial Chamber, an immediate resolution by the Appeals Chamber may materially advance the proceedings").

[122] ICTY Rules of Procedure and Evidence R. 72, 73; ICTR Rules of Procedure and Evidence R. 72, 73; SCSL Rules of Procedure and Evidence R. 72; ECCC Internal Rules R. 74, 75; War Crimes Research Office, Interlocutory Appellate Review of Early Decisions by the International Criminal Court 53–61 (2008).

[123] A recent study found that out of 458 issues on which the defense sought leave to appeal, Chambers granted leave for only 51 issues, yielding an average grant rate of 11.13%. Out of ninety issues for which the prosecution requested leave to appeal, Chambers granted leave on thirty-four issues, yielding an average grant rate of 37.78%. Turner, *supra* note 71, at *26–27; *see also* War Crimes Research Office, Expediting Proceedings at the International Criminal Court 12 (2011) ("although the Appeals Chamber regularly takes multiple months to rule on an interlocutory appeal, the resulting judgment is often brief and provides little guidance to the parties and lower chambers of the Court").

Chamber itself, rather than with the chamber whose decision is being impugned.[124] Even where revising the rules of interlocutory appeals may be difficult to accomplish—as procedural amendments are at the ICC—pretrial and trial chambers can easily relax the way they interpret the standards for interlocutory appeals (perhaps at the direction of a practice manual). Such steps would help advance procedural coherence and equal treatment of the parties in international criminal courts.

VI. Conclusion

International criminal procedure is likely to remain a pluralist enterprise for the foreseeable future, as the international community continues to disagree on the values and goals that the process should pursue and the means that can best accomplish these goals. While experimentation with different procedures at different courts can be useful and informative, such experimentation should be discouraged within the same court, even if the court's rules permit it. Procedural coherence is a basic element of the rule of law and is a minimum requirement for a fair and legitimate international criminal process. For that reason, lower chambers within the same court should attempt to promote coherence by adopting practice manuals to guide judges and the parties, and rules on interlocutory appeals should be amended to allow appeals chambers to resolve procedural variation in lower chamber rulings more quickly and effectively.

References

Kai Ambos, *International Criminal Procedure: "Adversarial", "Inquisitorial" or Mixed?*, 3 Int'l Crim. L. Rev. 1 (2003)

Kai Ambos, *Treatise on International Criminal Law: Volume III, International Criminal Procedure* (2016)

Elena Baylis, *Tribunal-Hopping with the Post-Conflict Justice Junkies*, 10 Oregon Rev. Int'l L. 361 (2008)

William W. Burke-White, *A Community of Courts: Toward a System of International Criminal Law Enforcement*, 24 Mich. J. Int'l L. 1 (2002)

International Criminal Procedure: The Interface of Civil Law and Common Law Legal Systems (Linda Carter & Fausto Pocar eds., 2013)

Nancy Combs, *Seeking Inconsistency: Advancing Pluralism in International Criminal Sentencing*, 41 Yale J. Int'l L. 1 (2016)

Mirjan Damaška, *Reflections on Fairness in International Criminal Justice*, 10 J. Int'l Crim. Just. 611 (2012)

Gregory S. Gordon, *Toward an International Criminal Procedure: Due Process Aspirations and Limitations*, 45 Colum. J. Transnat'l L. 635 (2007)

[124] This was the original framework for interlocutory appeals at the ad hoc tribunals, and it was seen as critical to establishing guiding case law on procedural matters at these tribunals. War Crimes Research Office, *supra* note 121, at 47–49.

Karim Khan et al., *Archbold International Criminal Courts: Practice, Procedure, and Evidence* (2014)
Claus Kress, *The Procedural Law of the International Criminal Court in Outline: Anatomy of a Unique Compromise*, 1 J. Int'l Crim. Just. 603 (2003)
Maximo Langer, *The Rise of Managerial Judging in International Criminal Law*, 53 Am. J. Comp. L. 835 (2004)
Yvonne McDermott, *Fairness in International Criminal Law* (2016)
Frédéric Mégret, *Beyond Fairness: Understanding the Determinants of International Criminal Procedure*, 14 UCLA J. Int'l L. & Foreign Aff. 37 (2009)
Daryl A. Mundis, *From "Common Law" Towards "Civil Law": The Evolution of the ICTY Rules of Procedure and Evidence*, 14 Leiden J. Int'l L. 367 (2001)
Jens David Ohlin, *A Meta-Theory of International Criminal Procedure: Vindicating the Rule of Law*, 14 UCLA J. Int'l L. & Foreign Aff. 77 (2009)
Christoph Safferling, *International Criminal Procedure* (2012)
International Criminal Procedure: Principles and Rules (Göran Sluiter et al. eds., 2013)
Pluralism in International Criminal Law (Elies van Sliedregt & Sergey Vasiliev eds. 2014)
Sergey Vasiliev, *The Trial Process at the ECCC: The Rise and Fall of the Inquisitorial Paradigm in International Criminal Law*, in *The Extraordinary Chambers in the Courts of Cambodia: Assessing Their Contribution to International Criminal Law* 389 (Simon Meisenberg & Ignaz Stegmiller eds., 2016)
Colin Warbrick, *International Criminal Courts and Fair Trial*, 3 J. Armed Conflict L. 45 (1998)

Index

Note: Tables are indicated by an italic *t* following the page number.